THE ANATOMY

OF THE

DOMESTIC ANIMALS

THE ANATOMY

OF THE

DOMESTIC ANIMALS

BY

SEPTIMUS SISSON, S.B., V.S., D.V.Sc.

LATE PROFESSOR OF COMPARATIVE ANATOMY IN THE OHIO STATE UNIVERSITY, COLUMBUS, OHIO
MEMBER OF THE AMERICAN ASSOCIATION OF ANATOMISTS
FELLOW OF THE AMERICAN ASSOCIATION FOR THE ADVANCEMENT OF SCIENCE

REVISED BY

JAMES DANIELS GROSSMAN, G.PH., D.V.M.

PROFESSOR OF VETERINARY ANATOMY IN THE COLLEGE OF VETERINARY MEDICINE,
THE OHIO STATE UNIVERSITY, COLUMBUS, OHIO

WITH 736 ILLUSTRATIONS
MANY IN COLOR

FOURTH EDITION, REVISED

PHILADELPHIA AND LONDON

W. B. SAUNDERS COMPANY

1953

MADE IN U. S. A.

PRESS OF

W. B. SAUNDERS COMPANY

PHILADELPHIA

LIBRARY OF CONGRESS CATALOG CARD NUMBER: 52-11367

To My Wife

LILLIE CARR GROSSMAN

in grateful recognition
for the inspiration and
assistance so graciously given

SEPTIMUS SISSON, D.V.Sc., S.B., V.S.

Septimus Sisson, Professor of Comparative Anatomy in the College of Veterinary Medicine, The Ohio State University, son of George and Mary (Arnott) Sisson, was born October 2, 1865, at Gateshead, England. He came to America in 1882. Dr. Sisson received the certificate of V.S. in 1891 from the Ontario Veterinary College, Toronto, Canada; the degree S.B. in 1898 from the University of Chicago; and in 1921 the University of Toronto conferred upon him the degree of D.V.Sc. During 1905 and 1906 he was a student in Anatomy in Berlin and Zurich.

He was united in marriage October 5, 1892, to Katherine Oldham of Manhattan, Kansas, who resides at Long Beach, California.

Dr. Sisson was demonstrator of Anatomy in the Ontario Veterinary College, 1891 to 1899; Associate Professor of Veterinary Science and Zoology, Kansas State Agricultural College, 1899, and Professor of Zoology, 1900. In 1901 he came to The Ohio State University as Associate Professor of Veterinary Medicine, which title he held until 1903, when he was made Professor of Comparative Anatomy.

His published work consists of a translation: The Horse; A Pictorial Guide to its Anatomy, from the Anatomie der Tiere für Künstler by Ellenberger-Baum; Text-book of Veterinary Anatomy, The Anatomy of the Domestic Animals, Report of The Committee on Revision of Veterinary Anatomical Nomenclature, a Veterinary Dissection Guide, and many articles to the technical journals. The thoroughness and accuracy of his works place them above all other works in English.

He was the originator of the intravascular injection of formalin or other hardening fluid whereby the natural form and topography of the soft organs of the chief domestic animals could be determined, using it first at Kansas State Agricultural College, 1899, on small animals and at The Ohio State University, 1901, on large animals.

He was a fellow of the American Association for the Advancement of Science; a member of the American Association of Anatomists; the American Veterinary Medical Association; the American Association of University Professors; member and past-president of the Ohio State Veterinary Medical Association; and the Society of Sigma Xi. He was a member of Kinsman Lodge of F. and A.M., Columbus, Ohio. He was commissioned Lieutenant Colonel in the Veterinary Reserve Corps of the U.S. Army in January, 1924.

Dr. Sisson was modest and retiring, but held the highest ideals for his chosen profession. He read extensively, liked travel, enjoyed only the best music, and was an expert photographer. Dr. Sisson was a good teacher and a most enthusiastic worker in anatomical research. His well-trained analytical mind and unusual skill in technical manipulation enabled him to delve into the unknown with a thoroughness and accuracy attained by few research workers in the field of anatomy.

In Dr. Sisson's death at Berkeley, California, July 24, 1924, the Veterinary Profession, the University and the nation suffered a profound loss.

PREFACE TO THE FOURTH EDITION

In considering the revision of The Anatomy of the Domestic Animals it is necessary to keep in mind that it is a text to be used by persons not specially schooled in applying anatomy in the medical field, and also that the terminology and text material are very important items. The terminology must be standard and uniform, with good basis for its selection. The text material must be of plain facts simply and briefly stated, that they may be easily built into the thinking process of the student. The terminology is that which is published by the American Veterinary Medical Association, "Nomina Anatomica Veterinaria." The familiar landmarks of The Anatomy of the Domestic Animals by Dr. Septimus Sisson known to generations of veterinary students and veterinarians have not been changed in this edition.

The change in the placing of descriptive terms and the rearrangement of the osteology of the horse was done that the student might be able to make a more efficient use of the text early in his study of anatomy.

Many new figures have been added: diagrams and photographs of dissections and sections, to illustrate some new points of view that have been developed by research to meet the needs of the various fields of the profession.

Dr. Robert Getty, of the Iowa State College, assisted in preparing many of the figures and his work is greatly appreciated.

The author is indebted to Dr. H. M. Amstutz, M.D., Lancaster, Ohio for use of some references and figures from his unpublished work, and to Dr. W. D. Pounden, D.V.M., Ph.D. of the Ohio Agricultural Experiment Station for figures and references.

The author wishes to acknowledge the assistance of his colleague Dr. Charles D. Diesem, and the inspiration and counsel from his associates Drs. W. F. Guard, C. R. Cole and W. L. Ingalls.

The W. B. Saunders Company deserve great credit for the high degree of excellence attained in the publication of this text.

JAMES DANIELS GROSSMAN

Ohio State University
Columbus, Ohio
January, 1953

CONTENTS

ANGIOLOGY

NEUROLOGY—THE NERVOUS SYSTEM

ÆSTHESIOLOGY

THE CHICKEN

THE ANATOMY OF THE DOMESTIC ANIMALS

INTRODUCTION

Anatomy is the branch of biological science which deals with the form and structure of organisms. It is therefore in close correlation with physiology, which treats of the functions of the body.

Etymologically the word "anatomy" signifies the cutting apart or disassociating of parts of the body. In the earlier phases of its development anatomy was necessarily a purely descriptive science, based on such observations as were possible with the unaided eye and simple dissecting instruments—the scalpel, forceps, and the like. At this time, therefore, the term adequately expressed the nature of the subject. But as the scope of the science extended and the body of anatomical knowledge grew, subdivisions became necessary and new terms were introduced to designate special fields and methods of work. With the introduction of the microscope and its accessories it became possible to study the finer details of structure and minute organisms hitherto unknown, and this field of inquiry rapidly developed into the science of **microscopic anatomy** or **histology** as conventionally distinguished from **macroscopic** or **gross anatomy**. In the same way the study of the changes which organisms undergo during their development soon attained sufficient importance to be regarded on practical grounds as a separate branch known as **embryology.** This term is usually limited in its application to the earlier phases of development during which the tissues and organs are formed. The term **ontogeny** is used to designate the entire development of the individual. The ancestral history or **phylogeny** of the species is constituted by the evolutionary changes which it has undergone as disclosed by the geological record.

Comparative anatomy is the description and comparison of the structure of animals, and forms the basis for their classification. By this means—including extinct forms in the scope of inquiry—it has been possible to show the genetic relationship of various groups of animals and to elucidate the significance of many facts of structure which are otherwise quite obscure. The deductions concerning the general laws of form and structure derived from comparative anatomical studies constitute the science of **morphology** or **philosophical anatomy.** The morphologist, however, deals only with such anatomical data as are necessary to form a basis for his generalizations. The anatomical knowledge required in the practice of medicine and surgery is evidently of a different character and must include many details which are of no particular interest to the morphologist.

Special anatomy is the description of the structure of a single type or species, *e. g.,* anthropotomy, hippotomy.

Veterinary anatomy is the branch which deals with the form and structure of the principal domesticated animals. It is usually pursued with regard to professional requirements, and is therefore largely descriptive in character. As a matter of convenience, the horse is generally selected as the type to be studied in detail and to form a basis for comparison of the more essential differential characters in the other animals.

Two chief methods of study are employed—the **systematic** and the **topographic.** In the former the body is regarded as consisting of systems of organs or apparatus which are similar in origin and structure and are associated in the performance of certain functions. The divisions of **systematic anatomy** are:

1. Osteology (Osteologia), the description of the Skeleton
2. Arthrology (Arthrologia), the description of the Joints
3. Myology (Myologia), the description of the Muscles and accessory structures
4. Splanchnology (Splanchnologia), the description of the Viscera. This includes the following subdivisions:

    (1) Digestive System (Apparatus digestorius)
    (2) Respiratory System (Apparatus respiratorius)
    (3) Urogenital System (Apparatus urogenitalis)
        (a) Urinary Organs (Organa uropoetica)
        (b) Genital Organs (Organa genitalia)

5. Angiology, the description of the Organs of Circulation
6. Neurology, the description of the Nervous System
7. Æsthesiology, the description of the Sense Organs and Common Integument

The term **topographic anatomy** designates the methods by which the relative positions of the various parts of the body are accurately determined. It presupposes a fair working knowledge of systematic anatomy. The consideration of anatomical facts in their relation to Surgery, Physical Diagnosis, and other practical branches is termed **applied anatomy.**

Topographic Terms.—In order to indicate precisely the position and direction of parts of the body, certain descriptive terms are employed, and must be understood at the outset. In the explanation of these terms it is assumed here that they apply to a quadruped such as the horse in the ordinary standing position. The surface directed toward the plane of support (the ground) is termed **ventral** (or inferior), and the opposite surface is **dorsal** (or superior); the relations of parts in this direction are named accordingly. The longitudinal **median plane** divides the body into similar halves. A structure or surface which is nearer than another to the median plane is **medial** (or internal) to it, and an object or surface which is further than another from the median plane is **lateral** (or external) to it. Planes parallel to the median plane are **sagittal.** **Transverse** or **segmental** planes cut the long axis of the body perpendicular to the median plane, or an organ or limb at right angles to its long axis. A **frontal** plane is perpendicular to the median and transverse planes. The term is also used with reference to parts of the limbs or various organs in a similar sense. The head end of the body is termed **anterior** or **cranial**; and the tail end **posterior** or **caudal**; relations of structures with regard to the longitudinal axis of the body are designated accordingly. With respect to parts of the head, the corresponding terms are **oral** and **aboral.** Certain terms are used in a special sense as applied to the limbs. **Proximal** and **distal** express relative distances of parts from the long axis of the body. The anterior face of the distal part of the thoracic limb is termed **dorsal,** and the opposite face **volar.** In the corresponding part of the pelvic limb the terms are **dorsal** and **plantar** respectively. In the same regions **radial** and **ulnar** (thoracic limb), **tibial** and **fibular** (pelvic limb) may be used to designate that side of the extremity on which the corresponding bone is situated; they are therefore equivalent, respectively, to medial and lateral in the animals with which we are concerned. The terms **superficial** (superficialis) and **deep** (profundus) are useful to indicate relative distances from the surface of the body.

It is evidently advantageous to employ terms which are as far as possible independent of the position of the body in space and capable of general application, e. g., dorsal, ventral, proximal, etc. It is also desirable that the terms internal and external be reserved to indicate relations of depth in cavities or organs, and medial and lateral to designate relations to the median plane. Such terms are coming into more extensive use in human and veterinary anatomy, but the older nomenclature is very firmly established and cannot well be discarded at once and entirely. To facilitate the transition, a table of the older and more recent terms is given below; the recent terms are in the first column and the older equivalents in the second.

A. Relating to Head, Neck, and Trunk:

Dorsalis.....................................Superior
Ventralis....................................Inferior
Medialis....................................Internal
Lateralis....................................External
Cranialis }
Oralis   } ....Anterior
Caudalis }
Aboralis } ....Posterior

B. Relating to Limbs:

Proximalis...................................Superior
Distalis.....................................Inferior
Dorsalis.....................................Anterior
Volaris   }
Plantaris } ....Posterior
Radialis   }
Tibialis   } ....Internal
Ulnaris   }
Fibularis } ....External

DESCRIPTIVE TERMS

The surfaces of the bones present a great variety of eminences and depressions, as well as perforations. The prominences and cavities may be articular, or non-articular, furnishing attachment to muscles, tendons, ligaments, or fascia. A number of descriptive terms are used to designate these features, and the following are some of those in general use:

Process (Processus) is a general term for a prominence.

A **tuberosity** (Tuber, Tuberositas) is a large, rounded non-articular projection; a **tubercle** (Tuberculum) is a smaller one.

The term **trochanter** is applied to a few non-articular prominences, e. g., the trochanters of the femur.

A **spine** (Spina) or **spinous process** (Processus spinosus) is a pointed projection.

A **crest** (Crista) is a sharp ridge.

A **line** (Linea) is a very small ridge.

A **head** (Caput) is a rounded articular enlargement at the end of a bone; it may be joined to the shaft by a constricted part, the **neck** (Collum).

A **condyle** (Condylus) is an articular eminence which is somewhat cylindrical; a non-articular projection in connection with a condyle may be termed an **epicondyle** (Epicondylus).

A **trochlea** is a pulley-like articular mass.

A **glenoid cavity** (Cavitas glenoidalis) is a shallow articular depression, and a **cotyloid cavity** or **acetabulum** is a deeper one.

The term **facet** is commonly applied to articular surfaces of small extent, especially when they are not strongly concave or convex.

The terms **fossa, fovea, groove** or **sulcus,** and **impression** are applied to various forms of depressions.

A **foramen** is a perforation for the transmission of vessels, nerves, etc.

A **sinus** is an air-cavity within a bone or bones; it is lined with mucous membrane and communicates with the exterior.

Other terms, such as **canal, fissure, notch,** etc., require no explanation.[1]

---

[1] As might be expected from the history of anatomy, a good many of these terms are more or less interchangeable; furthermore, a given skeletal feature may differ greatly in various species.

OSTEOLOGY

THE SKELETON

The term **skeleton** is applied to the framework of hard structures which supports and protects the soft tissues of animals. In the descriptive anatomy of the higher animals it is usually restricted to the bones and cartilages, although the ligaments which bind these together might well be included.

In zoölogy the term is used in a much more comprehensive sense, and includes all the harder supporting and protecting structures. When the latter are situated externally, they form an **exoskeleton,** derived from the ectoderm. Examples of this are the shells and chitinous coverings of many invertebrates, the scales of fishes, the shields of turtles, and the feathers, hair, and hoofs of the higher vertebrates. The **endoskeleton** (with which we have to deal at present) is embedded in the soft tissues. It is derived from the mesoderm, with the exception of the notochord or primitive axial skeleton, which is of entodermal origin.

The skeleton may be divided primarily into three parts: (1) axial; (2) appendicular; (3) splanchnic.

The **axial skeleton** comprises the vertebral column, ribs, sternum, and skull.

The **appendicular skeleton** includes the bones of the limbs.

The **splanchnic** or **visceral skeleton** consists of certain bones developed in the substance of some of the viscera or soft organs, e. g., the os penis of the dog and the os cordis of the ox.

The **number** of the bones of the skeleton of an animal varies with age, owing to the fusion during growth of skeletal elements which are separate in the fœtus or the young subject. Even in adults of the same species numerical variations occur, e. g., the tarsus of the horse may consist of six or seven bones, and the carpus of seven or eight; in all the domestic mammals the number of coccygeal vertebræ varies considerably.

The bones are commonly divided into four **classes** according to their shape and function.[1]

(1) **Long bones** (Ossa longa) are typically of elongated cylindrical form with enlarged **extremities.** They occur in the limbs, where they act as supporting columns and as levers. The cylindrical part, termed the **shaft** or **body** (Corpus), is tubular, and incloses the **medullary cavity,** which contains the medulla or marrow.

(2) **Flat bones** (Ossa plana) are expanded in two directions. They furnish sufficient area for the attachment of muscles and afford protection to the organs which they cover.

(3) **Short bones** (Ossa brevia), such as those of the carpus and tarsus, present somewhat similar dimensions in length, breadth, and thickness. Their chief function appears to be that of diffusing concussion. Sesamoid bones, which are developed in the capsules of some joints or in tendons, may be included in this group. They diminish friction or change the direction of tendons.

(4) **Irregular bones** (Ossa irregularia). This group would include bones of irregular shape, such as the vertebræ and the bones of the cranial base; they are median and unpaired. Their functions are various and not so clearly specialized as those of the preceding classes.

[1] This classification is not entirely satisfactory; some bones, e. g., the ribs, are not clearly provided for, and others might be variously placed.

STRUCTURE OF BONES.[1]

Bones consist chiefly of **bone tissue,** but considered as organs they present also an enveloping membrane, termed the **periosteum, endosteum, marrow, vessels,** and **nerves.**

The architecture of bone can be studied best by means of longitudinal and transverse sections of specimens which have been macerated so as to remove most of the organic matter. These show that the bone consists of an external shell of dense **compact substance,** within which is the more loosely arranged **spongy substance.** In typical long bones the shaft is hollowed to form the **medullary cavity** (Cavum medullare).

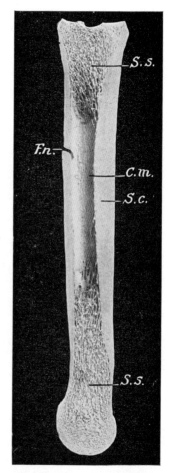

The **compact substance** (Substantia compacta) differs greatly in thickness in various situations, in conformity with the stresses and strains to which the bone is subjected. In the long bones it is thickest in or near the middle part of the shaft and thins out toward the extremities. On the latter the layer is very thin, and is especially dense and smooth on joint surfaces. Circumscribed thickenings are found at points which are subject to special pressure or traction.

The **spongy substance** (Substantia spongiosa) consists of delicate bony plates and spicules which run in various directions and intercross. These are definitely arranged with regard to mechanical requirements, so that systems of pressure and tension plates can be recognized, in conformity with the lines of pressure and the pull of tendons and ligaments respectively. The intervals between the plates are occupied by marrow, and are termed **marrow spaces** (Cellulæ medullares). The spongy substance forms the bulk of short bones and of the extremities of long bones; in the latter it is not confined to the ends, but extends a variable distance along the shaft also. Some bones contain air-spaces within the compact substance instead of spongy bone and marrow, and hence are called **pneumatic bones** (Ossa pneumatica). These cavities are termed **sinuses,** and are lined with mucous membrane; they communicate indirectly with the external air. In certain situations the two compact layers of flat bones are not separated by spongy bone, but fuse with each other; in some cases of this kind the bone is so thin as to be translucent, or may undergo absorption, producing an actual deficiency.

FIG. 1.—SAGITTAL SECTION OF LARGE METATARSAL BONE OF HORSE (RIGHT).

S.c., Compact substance; *S.s.,* spongy substance; *C.m.,* medullary cavity; *F.n.,* nutrient foramen. Note the greater thickness of the compact substance of the anterior part of the shaft.

The flat bones of the cranial vault and sides are composed of an outer layer of ordinary compact substance, the **lamina externa,** an inner layer of very dense bone, the **lamina interna** or **tabula vitrea,** and between these a variable amount of spongy bone, here termed **diploë.**

The **periosteum** is the membrane which invests the outer surface of bone, except where it is covered with cartilage. It consists of an outer protective fibrous

[1] Only the gross structure is discussed here. For the microscopic structure reference is to be made to histological works.

layer, and an inner cellular osteogenic layer. During active growth the osteogenic layer is well developed, but later it becomes much reduced. The fibrous layer varies much in thickness, being in general thickest in exposed situations. The adhesion of the periosteum to the bone also differs greatly in various places; it is usually very thin and easily detached where it is thickly covered with muscular tissue which has little or no attachment. The degree of vascularity conforms to the activity of the periosteum.

The **endosteum** is a thin fibrous membrane which lines the medullary cavity and the larger Haversian canals.

The **marrow** (Medulla ossium) occupies the interstices of the spongy bone and the medullary cavity of the long bones. There are two varieties in the adult— red and yellow. In the young subject there is only **red marrow** (Medulla ossium rubra), but later this is replaced in the medullary cavity by **yellow marrow** (Medulla ossium flava). The red marrow contains several types of characteristic cells and is a blood-forming substance, while the yellow is practically ordinary adipose tissue.[1]

Vessels and Nerves.—It is customary to recognize two sets of **arteries**—the **periosteal** and the **medullary.** The former ramify in the periosteum and give off

FIG. 2.—CROSS-SECTION OF PROXIMAL THIRD OF SHAFT OF RIGHT HUMERUS OF HORSE.

FIG. 3.—CROSS-SECTION OF DISTAL THIRD OF SHAFT OF LEFT HUMERUS OF HORSE.

Section passes through nutrient foramen and canal.

innumerable small branches which enter minute openings (Volkmann's canals) on the surface and reach the Haversian canals of the compact substance. Other branches enter the extremities of the long bones and supply the spongy bone and marrow in them. In the case of the larger bones—and especially the long bones— the large **nutrient** or **medullary artery** (Arteria nutricia) enters at the so-called **nutrient foramen** (Foramen nutricium), passes in a canal (Canalis nutricius) through the compact substance, and ramifies in the marrow; its branches anastomose with the central branches of the periosteal set. The larger **veins** of the spongy bone do not, as a rule, accompany the arteries, but emerge chiefly near the articular surfaces. Within the bone they are destitute of valves. The **lymph-vessels** exist as perivascular channels in the periosteum and the Haversian canals of the compact substance. They also form a fine subperiosteal network, from which the larger vessels proceed, usually in company with veins. Lymph-spaces exist at the periphery of the marrow.

The **nerves** appear to be distributed chiefly to the blood-vessels. Special nerve-endings (Vater-Pacini corpuscles) in the periosteum are to be regarded as sensory, and probably are concerned in mediating the muscle sense (kinesthesia).

[1] Since yellow marrow is formed by regressive changes in red marrow, including fatty infiltration and degeneration of the characteristic cells, we find transitional forms or stages in the process. In aged or badly nourished subjects the marrow may undergo gelatinous degeneration, resulting in the formation of gelatinous marrow.

DEVELOPMENT AND GROWTH OF BONE

The primitive embryonal skeleton consists of cartilage and fibrous tissue, in which the bones develop. The process is termed **ossification or osteogenesis,** and is effected essentially by bone-producing cells, called **osteoblasts.** It is customary, therefore, to designate as **membrane bones** those which are developed in fibrous tissue, and as **cartilage bones** those which are preformed in cartilage. The principal membrane bones are those of the roof and sides of the cranium and most of the bones of the face. The cartilage bones comprise, therefore, most of the skeleton. Correspondingly we distinguish **intramembranous** and **endochondral ossification.**

In **intramembranous ossification** the process begins at a definite **center of ossification** (Punctum ossificationis), where the osteoblasts surround themselves with a deposit of bone. The process extends from this center to the periphery of the future bone, thus producing a network of bony trabeculæ. The trabeculæ rapidly thicken and coalesce, forming a bony plate which is separated from the adjacent bones by persistent fibrous tissue. The superficial part of the original

Fig. 4.—Right Femur of Young Pig, Posterior View.

The bone at this age is divided by the epiphyseal cartilages (*E. c.*) into a shaft (*S.*), proximal (*E. p.*), and distal extremity (*E.d.*). The proximal extremity consists of two parts, head (*H.*), and trochanter major (*T.m.*), which have separate centers of ossification.

tissue becomes periosteum, and on the deep face of this successive layers of periosteal bone are formed by osteoblasts until the bone attains its definitive thickness. Increase in circumference takes place by ossification in the surrounding fibrous tissue, which continues to grow until the bone has reached its definitive size.

In **endochondral ossification** the process is fundamentally the same, but not quite so simple. Osteoblasts emigrate from the deep face of the perichondrium or primitive periosteum into the cartilage and cause calcification of the matrix or ground-substance of the latter. Vessels extend into the calcifying area, the cartilage cells shrink and disappear, forming primary marrow cavities which are occupied by processes of the osteogenic tissue. There is thus formed a sort of scaffolding of calcareous trabeculæ on which the bone is constructed by the osteoblasts. At the same time perichondral bone is formed by the osteoblasts of the primitive periosteum. The calcified cartilage is broken down and absorbed through the agency of large cells called **osteoclasts,** and is replaced by bone deposited by the osteoblasts. The osteoclasts also cause absorption of the primitive bone, producing the marrow cavities; thus in the case of the long bones the primitive central spongy bone is largely absorbed to form the medullary cavity of the shaft, and persists chiefly in the extremities. Destruction of the central part and formation of subperiosteal bone continue until the shaft of the bone has completed its growth.

A typical long bone is developed from three primary centers of ossification, one, which appears first, for the **diaphysis** or shaft and one for each **epiphysis** or extremity. Many bones have secondary centers from which processes or apophyses develop.

The foregoing outline accounts for the growth of bones except in regard to length. Increase in length may be explained briefly as follows: Provision for continued ossification at either end of the diaphysis is made by a layer of actively growing cartilage—the **epiphyseal cartilage**—which intervenes between the diaphysis and the epiphysis. It is evident that so long as this cartilage persists and grows, new bone may continue to be formed at its expense, and increase of length is possible. When the epiphyseal cartilage ceases to grow, it undergoes ossification, the bone is consolidated, and no further increase in length is possible. This fusion takes place at fairly definite periods in the various bones, and it is of value to know the usual times at which it occurs in the larger bones of the limbs at least. In the case of membrane bones, increase in circumference is provided for by the ossification and new formation of the surrounding fibrous tissue.

After the bones have reached their full size, the periosteum becomes relatively reduced and inactive so far as its osteogenic layer is concerned; the bone-forming function may be stimulated by various causes, as is well seen in the healing of fractures and the occurrence of bony enlargements.

Profound changes occur in the skeleton after birth, and during the period of growth the bones are much more plastic than might be supposed. In the new-born foal, for example, it is evident that the metacarpal and metatarsal bones are relatively long and the scapula and humerus short; also that in general the shafts of the long bones are slender in comparison with the extremities. The various prominences are much less pronounced than in the adult, and most of the minor surface markings are absent, so that the bones have a relatively smooth appearance. The period of growth may be regarded as terminating with the union of the extremities and shafts of the long bones and the fusion of the parts of other bones. During adult life the skeletal changes proceed more slowly; they comprise accentuation of the larger prominences and depressions and the appearance of smaller ones. These secondary markings are chiefly correlated with the attachments of muscles, tendons, and ligaments, or are produced by pressure exerted by various structures on the bones. Later in life ossification invades more or less extensively the cartilages and the attachments of tendons and ligaments. Senile changes in the bones, consisting of decrease of the organic matter and rarefaction of the bone tissue, render them brittle and liable to fracture.

CHEMICAL COMPOSITION OF BONE

Dried bone consists of **organic** and **inorganic** matter in the ratio of 1 : 2 approximately. The animal matter gives toughness and elasticity, the mineral matter hardness, to the bone tissue. Removal of the organic matter by heat does not change the general form of a bone, but reduces the weight by about one-third, and makes it very fragile. Conversely, decalcification, while not affecting the form and size of the bone, renders it soft and pliable. The organic matter (ossein) when boiled yields gelatin. The following table represents the composition in 100 parts of ox bone of average quality:

Gelatin	33.30
Phosphate of lime	57.35
Carbonate of lime	3.85
Phosphate of magnesia	2.05
Carbonate and chlorid of sodium	3.45
	100.00

PHYSICAL PROPERTIES OF BONE

Fresh dead bone has a yellowish-white color; when macerated or boiled and bleached, it is white. The specific gravity of fresh compact bone is about 1.9. It is very hard and resistant to pressure. Its compressive strength is about 20,000 pounds per square inch, and its tensile strength averages 15,000 pounds per square inch—considerably higher than white oak.

THE SKELETON OF THE HORSE

General statements, of comparative nature, regarding the bones will be included at the beginning of the descriptive material for each group of bones of the horse.

The skeleton of the horse consists of 205 bones, as shown in the following table:

Vertebral column	54
Ribs	36
Sternum	1
Skull (including auditory ossicles)	34
Thoracic limbs	40
Pelvic limbs	40
	205

In this enumeration the average number of coccygeal vertebræ is taken to be 18, the temporal and os coxæ are not divided into parts, the usual number of carpal and tarsal elements is taken, and the sesamoids are included.

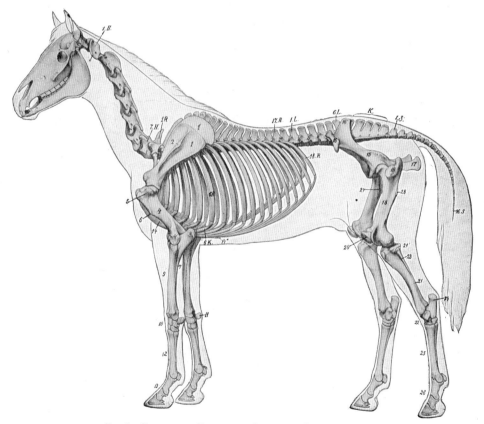

Fig. 5.—Skeleton of Horse, with Outline of Contour of Body.

1.H., Atlas; *7.H.*, seventh cervical vertebra; *1.R.*, first thoracic vertebra; *17.R.*, seventeenth thoracic vertebra; *1.L.*, first lumbar vertebra; *6.L.*, sixth lumbar vertebra; *K*, sacrum; *1.S.*, first coccygeal vertebra; *16.S.*, sixteenth coccygeal vertebra; *6.R.*, sixth rib; *6.K.*, costal cartilage; *18.R.*, last rib; 1, scapula; 1′, cartilage of scapula; 2, spine of scapula; 4, humerus; 4′, lateral epicondyle of humerus: 5, lateral tuberosity of humerus; 6, deltoid tuberosity; 7, shaft of ulna; 8, olecranon; 9, radius; 10, carpus; 11, accessory carpal bone; 12, metacarpus; 13, phalanges; 14, sternum; 14″, xiphoid cartilage; 15, ilium; 16, 16′, angles of ilium; 17, ischium; 18, femur (shaft); 19, trochanter major; 20, patella; 21, tibia (shaft); 21′, lateral condyle of tibia; 22, tarsus; 23, fibula; 24, tuber calcis; 25, metatarsus; 26, phalanges; 27, trochanter minor of femur; 28, trochanter tertius of femur. The patella is placed much too low. (After Ellenberger-Baum, Anat. für Künstler.)

THE VERTEBRAL COLUMN

The **vertebral column** (Columna vertebralis) is the fundamental part of the skeleton. It consists of a chain of median, unpaired, irregular bones which extends from the skull to the end of the tail. In the adult certain vertebræ have become fused to form a single bony mass with which the pelvic girdle articulates. Vertebræ so fused are termed **fixed** (or "false") **vertebræ** (Vertebræ immobiles), as distinguished from the **movable** (or "true") **vertebræ** (Vertebræ mobiles).

The column is subdivided for description into **five regions,** which are named according to the part of the body in which the vertebræ are situated. Thus the vertebræ are designated as **cervical, thoracic, lumbar, sacral, coccygeal** (Vertebræ cervicales, thoracales, lumbales, sacrales, coccygeæ). The number of vertebræ in a given species is fairly constant in each region except the last, so that the **vertebral formula** may be expressed (for the horse, for example) as follows:

$$C_7 T_{18} L_6 S_5 Cy_{15\text{-}21}.$$

The vertebræ in a given region have characters by which they may be distinguished from those of other regions, and individual vertebræ have special characters which are more or less clearly recognizable. All typical vertebræ have a common plan of structure, which must first be understood. The parts of which a vertebra consists are the **body,** the **arch,** and the **processes.**

The **body** (Corpus vertebræ) is the more or less cylindrical mass on which the other parts are constructed. The anterior and posterior extremities of the body are attached to the adjacent vertebræ by intervertebral fibro-cartilages, and are usually convex and concave respectively. The dorsal surface is flattened and enters into the formation of the vertebral canal, while the ventral aspect is rounded laterally, and is in relation to various muscles and viscera. In the thoracic region the body presents two pairs of facets (Foveæ costales) at the extremities for articulation with part of the heads of two pairs of ribs.

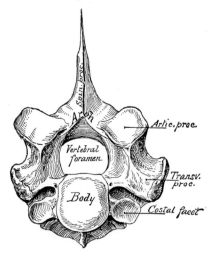

Fig. 6.—First Thoracic Vertebra of Horse.
To illustrate plan of structure of vertebræ.

The **arch** (Arcus vertebræ) is constructed on the dorsal aspect of the body. It consists originally of two lateral halves, each of which is considered to consist of a pedicle and a lamina. The pedicle (Radix arcus vertebræ) forms the lateral part of the arch, and is cut into in front and behind by the **vertebral notches** (Incisura vertebralis, caudalis). The notches of two adjacent vertebræ form **intervertebral foramina** (Foramina intervertebralia) for the passage of the spinal nerves and vessels; in some vertebræ, however, there are complete foramina instead of notches. The laminæ are plates which complete the arch dorsally, uniting with each other medially at the root of the spinous process.

The body and the arch form a bony ring which incloses the **vertebral foramen** (Foramen vertebrale); the series of vertebral rings, together with the ligaments which unite them, inclose the **vertebral canal** (Canalis vertebralis), which contains the spinal cord and its coverings and vessels.

The **articular processes**, two **anterior** and two **posterior** (Processus articulares craniales, caudales), project from the borders of the arch. They present articular surfaces adapted to those of adjacent vertebræ, and the remaining surface is roughened for muscular and ligamentous attachment.

The **spinous process** or spine (Processus spinosus) is single, and projects dorsally from the middle of the arch. It varies greatly in form, size, and direction in different vertebræ. It furnishes attachment to muscles and ligaments.

The **transverse processes** (Processus transversi) are two in number and project laterally from the sides of the arch or from the junction of the arch and body. In the thoracic region each has a facet for articulation with the tubercle of a rib (Fovea costalis transversalis). They also give attachment to muscles and ligaments.

Some vertebræ have also a **ventral spine** or a **hæmal arch.**

Mammillary processes (Processus mamillares) are found in most animals on the posterior thoracic and anterior lumbar vertebræ, between the transverse and anterior articular processes or on the latter.

Accessory processes (Processus accessorii), when present, are situated between the transverse and posterior articular processes.

Development.—The vertebræ are developed by ossification in the cartilage which surrounds the notochord and forms the sides of the neural canal. There are **three primary centers** of ossification, one for the body and one for each side of the arch. **Secondary centers** appear later for the summit of the spinous process (except in the cervical region), the extremities of the transverse processes, and the thin epiphyseal plates at the extremities of the body. The three primary centers and the thin epiphyseal plates constitute the usual five centers of development for all typical vertebræ.

Sometimes there are at first two centers for the body, which soon fuse. The process of ossification extends from the lateral centers to form, not only the corresponding part of the arch, but also the processes and a part of the body next to the root of the arch (Radix arcus). In the horse and ox the body and arch are fused at birth or unite very soon after, but the epiphyses do not fuse till growth is complete. In the pig, sheep, and dog the body and arch are united at birth by cartilage (neurocentral synchondrosis), but fuse in the first few months.

The vertebral formula of the horse is $C_7T_{18}L_6S_5Cy_{15-21}$.

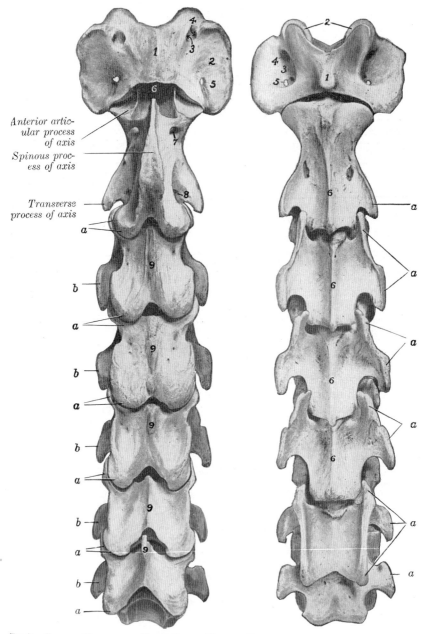

FIG. 7.—CERVICAL VERTEBRÆ OF HORSE; DORSAL VIEW.

a, Articular processes; *b*, transverse processes; *1*, dorsal arch of atlas; *2*, wing of atlas; *3*, intervertebral foramen of atlas; *4*, alar foramen of atlas; *5*, foramen transversarium of atlas; *6*, dens of axis; *7*, intervertebral foramen of axis; *8*, foramen transversarium of axis; *9*, spinous processes.

FIG. 8.—CERVICAL VERTEBRÆ OF HORSE; VENTRAL VIEW.

a, Transverse processes; *1*, ventral tubercle of atlas; *2*, anterior articular cavities of atlas; *3*, fossa atlantis; *4*, alar foramen; *5*, foramen transversarium; *6*, ventral spines.

THE CERVICAL VERTEBRÆ

The cervical vertebræ (Vertebræ cervicales) are seven in number.

The first and second cervical vertebræ are highly modified in conformity with the special functions of support and movements of the head. The sixth and seventh present special characters, but do not differ greatly from the type. With the exception of the first, they are quadrangular, massive, and longer than the vertebræ of other regions; they decrease in length from the second to the last. The **third, fourth,** and **fifth** have the following characters:

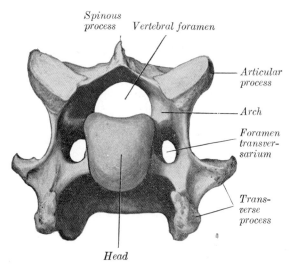

FIG. 9.—SIXTH CERVICAL VERTEBRA OF HORSE; ANTERIOR VIEW.

The **body** is long as compared with those of other vertebræ. The **ventral surface** presents a median **ventral spine,** which becomes more prominent as it is traced backward, and is tuberculate at its posterior end; it separates two concave areas. The **dorsal surface** has a flat central area which is narrow in the middle of the vertebræ, and wide at either end; it gives attachment to the dorsal longitudinal ligament. On either side of this area there is a groove which lodges the longitudinal spinal vein. These lateral grooves are connected about the middle of the surface by a transverse furrow, in which there are several foramina through which veins emerge from the spongy substance of the body. The **anterior extremity** or head (Caput vertebræ) has an oval articular surface which faces forward and downward; it is strongly convex, and wider above than below. The **posterior extremity** is larger and has a nearly circular cotyloid cavity (Fossa vertebræ).

The **arch** is large and strong. It is perforated on either side by a foramen which communicates with the foramen transversarium. The vertebral notches are large.

The **articular processes** are large. Their articular surfaces are extensive, oval in outline, and slightly concave; the anterior ones are directed dorso-medially; the posterior, ventro-laterally. The remaining surface is mainly roughened for ligamentous and muscular attachment. A crest connects

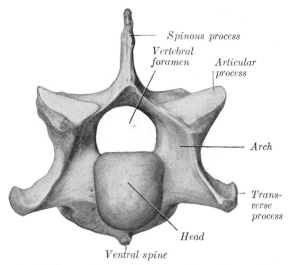

FIG. 10.—SEVENTH CERVICAL VERTEBRA OF HORSE; ANTERIOR VIEW.

the articular processes of the same side on the fourth and fifth; on the third it does not reach the anterior process.

The **transverse processes** are large and plate-like. Each arises by two roots, one from the arch and one from the body; between these is the **foramen transversarium,** through which the vertebral vessels and a nerve pass. The aggregate of these foramina constitutes the **canalis transversarius.** The process divides laterally into anterior and posterior branches, which are thickened and rough for muscular attachment.

The **spinous process** has the form of a low crest (Crista spinosa), which widens behind, and is connected by ridges with the posterior articular processes.

The **sixth** cervical vertebra has the following distinctive features: It is shorter and wider than the fifth. The **arch** is large, especially posteriorly. The **posterior articular processes** are shorter, thicker, and further apart; each is connected with the corresponding anterior one by a thick ridge. The **spinous process** is less rudimentary; it is half an inch or more (ca. 1.5 cm.) in height. The **transverse processes** have three branches; the third part is a thick, almost sagittal plate, which forms with its fellow and the body a wide ventral groove; the other branches correspond to those of the typical vertebræ, but are short and thicker. The **foramen transversarium** is large; below its posterior end there is a fossa. The **ventral spine** is small and is less prominent posteriorly. The third branch of the transverse process and the fossa are sometimes absent or reduced on one side.

The **seventh** cervical vertebra is readily distinguished by the following characters: It is **shorter** and **wider** than the others. The **body** is flattened dorso-ventrally and wide, especially behind; here it has a **facet** on each side for articulation with part of the head of the first rib. The **arch** and its **notches** are large. The **anterior articular processes** are wider and longer than the posterior pair. The **spinous process** is an inch or more (ca. 3 cm.) in height. The **transverse process** is undivided, and has no foramen transversarium. The ventral crest is replaced by a pair of tubercles. In some specimens a large foramen transversarium is present on one side or (rarely) on both sides.

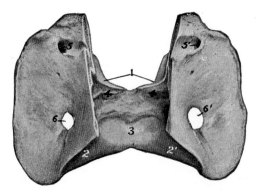

FIG. 11.—ATLAS OF HORSE, DORSAL VIEW AFTER REMOVAL OF DORSAL ARCH.

1, Anterior articular cavities; *2, 2',* posterior articular surfaces; *3,* articular surface of ventral arch for dens of axis; *4,* transverse ridge; *5, 5',* alar foramina; *6, 6',* foramina transversaria.

THE ATLAS

This vertebra is decidedly atypical in form and structure. The body and spinous process are absent. It has the form of a strong ring, from which two curved plates, the **wings,** project laterally. The ring incloses a very large vertebral foramen, and consists of two **lateral masses** connected by **dorsal** and **ventral arches.**

The **lateral masses** (Massæ laterales) present two deep oval **anterior articular cavities** (Foveæ articulares craniales) which receive the occipital condyles; they are separated by a wide notch above and a narrow one below. The lateral margin is also notched, and a triangular non-articular depression cuts into the medial part of each cavity. The **posterior articular surfaces** (Facies articulares caudales) are somewhat saddle-shaped; they are confluent on the ventral arch, but are widely separated dorsally, and do not conform in shape to the corresponding surfaces of the axis.

The **dorsal arch** (Arcus dorsalis) presents a median **dorsal tubercle** (Tuberculum dorsale) and is concave ventrally. It is perforated on either side near its anterior margin by the **intervertebral foramen** (Foramen invertebrale). The **anterior border** is deeply notched, and the **posterior border** is thin and concave.

The **ventral arch** (Arcus ventralis) is thicker, narrower, and less curved than the dorsal. On its lower surface is the **ventral tubercle** (Tuberculum ventrale), into which the terminal tendon of the longus colli muscle is inserted. The upper face has posteriorly a transversely concave articular surface, the **fovea dentis,** on which the dens or odontoid process of the axis rests. In front of this is a transverse rough excavation and a ridge for the attachment of the ligamentum dentis.

The **wings** (Alæ atlantis) are modified transverse processes. They are extensive curved plates which project ventro-laterally and backward from the lateral masses. The dorsal surface is concave. Between the ventral aspect of the wing and the lateral mass is a cavity, the **fossa atlantis**; in this there is a foramen which opens into the vertebral canal. The **border** is thick and rough; its position can be recognized in the living animal. Two foramina perforate each wing. The anterior one, the **foramen alare,** is connected with the intervertebral foramen by a short groove. The posterior one is the **foramen transversarium.**

Development.—The atlas ossifies from **four centers,** two for the ventral arch, and one on either side for each lateral mass, wing, and half of the dorsal arch. At birth the bone consists of three pieces—the ventral arch and two lateral parts, which are separated by a layer of cartilage in the dorsal median line and by two ventro-lateral layers. These parts are usually fused at about six months.

THE AXIS

The **axis** (Axis s. Epistropheus) is the longest of the vertebræ, and is characterized by the presence of the dens or odontoid process, which projects from the anterior part of the body.

The anterior extremity of the **body** presents centrally the **dens** or odontoid

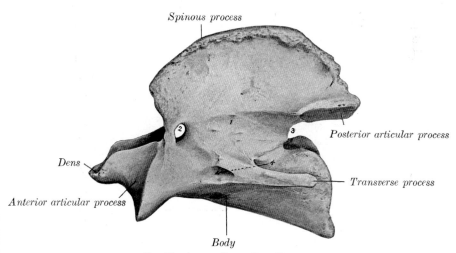

Fig. 12.—Axis of Horse, Left View.

1, Arch; *2,* intervertebral foramen; *3,* notch; *4,* foramen transversarium.

process (Dens axis); this has a convex articular surface ventrally for articulation with the ventral arch of the atlas, and two rough depressions for the attachment of the ligamentum dentis dorsally. Flanking this on either side are the modified **anterior articular processes,** which have saddle-shaped articular surfaces confluent ventrally with that of the dens. The posterior extremity has the usual cavity. The ventral spine resembles that of the typical vertebræ.

The **arch** presents in the young subject a notch on each side of its anterior border; this is converted into a foramen by a ligament which ossifies later. A groove which extends downward and backward from the foramen indicates the position of the ventral branch of the second cervical nerve. The posterior border has the usual notches.

The **posterior articular processes** are typical.

The **transverse processes** are small, single, and project backward. The **foramen transversarium** is small.

The **spinous process** is very large and strong. Its free border is rough, thickens posteriorly, and is continued to the articular processes by two ridges. The lateral surfaces are concave and rough for muscular attachment.

Development.—The axis has **six** or **seven centers** of ossification. In addition to the usual five, one or two appear for the dens, which is regarded as the displaced body of the atlas. A nucleus behind the dens, which remains distinct to three or four years of age, is considered to be the head of the axis.

THE THORACIC VERTEBRÆ

The thoracic vertebræ (Vertebræ thoracales) are usually eighteen in number in the horse, but there are sometimes nineteen, rarely seventeen. As regional characters we note the surfaces for articulation with the ribs and the length and form of the spinous processes. Those in the middle of the series are the most typical and present the following features:

The **bodies** are short and constricted in the middle. The ends are expanded and have articular surfaces which are not strongly curved; the anterior surface is convex, the posterior concave. On the upper part of each side are anterior and posterior **costal facets** (Fovea costalis cranialis, caudalis), which, with those of adjacent vertebræ and the intervening fibrocartilages, form sockets for the heads of the ribs.

The **arches** are small. Their posterior notches are relatively large and are often converted into foramina.

The **articular processes** are small. The anterior processes are in fact represented only by two oval facets on the anterior part of the arch which face almost directly upward.

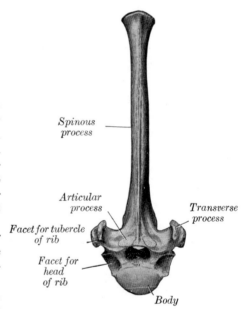

FIG. 13.—SEVENTH THORACIC VERTEBRA OF HORSE, ANTERIOR VIEW.

The posterior processes spring from the base of the spinous process; their facets face almost directly downward.

The **transverse processes** are short, thick, and tuberous at the free end. Each has a **facet** (Fovea transversaria) for articulation with the tubercle of the rib which has the same serial number.

The **spinous process** is large, narrow, and slopes upward and backward. The anterior border is thin, the posterior wider and furrowed. The summit is expanded and rough.

The **first thoracic vertebra** has the following specific characters: The **body** is wide and flattened dorso-ventrally. In front it has a head like the cervical verte-

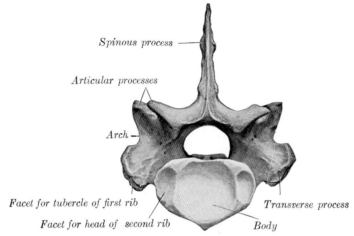

FIG. 14.—FIRST THORACIC VERTEBRA OF HORSE, POSTERIOR VIEW.

bræ, and behind a cavity somewhat deeper than any other thoracic vertebra. **Two large costal facets** are found on either side, and a well-marked spine ventrally.

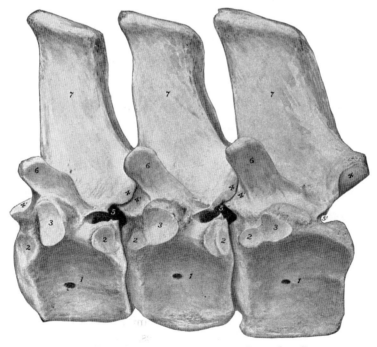

FIG. 15.—LAST THREE THORACIC VERTEBRÆ OF HORSE, LEFT VIEW.
1, Body; *2, 2*, facets for head of rib; *3*, facet for tubercle of rib; *4, 4'*, articular processes; *5*, intervertebral foramen; *6*, mammillary process; *7*, spinous process.

The **arch** is large and strong, and has large notches. The **articular processes** are much larger than those of other thoracic vertebræ, and resemble a good deal those of the seventh cervical. The **transverse processes** are short and thick, and each has on its ventral aspect a large concave facet for articulation with the tubercle of the first rib. The **spinous process** is curved backward and tapers to a point. Its length is usually about three or four inches (ca. 8 to 10 cm.). This vertebra may be mistaken at first glance for the last cervical, but is promptly identified by the three costal facets on each side and the length of the spine.

The **last thoracic vertebra** is distinguished by the absence of the posterior pair of costal facets, and the confluence of the anterior pair with those on the transverse processes.

The serial position of others may be determined at least approximately by the following data: (1) The bodies gradually diminish in length and width to the middle of the region and then increase slightly. Their costal facets become smaller and less concave from first to last. The ventral crest is distinct on three or four vertebræ at either end of the region. (2) The transverse processes diminish in size and are placed lower down as they are traced backward. Their costal facets become smaller and lower in position; on the last (and sometimes on its predecessor also) it fuses with the costal facet of the body. The upper non-articular part of the process gradually becomes more sharply defined, and in the last four or five forms a distinct **mammillary process.** (3) The spinous processes increase in length to the third and fourth, and then gradually diminish to the fifteenth, beyond which they have about the same length. The backward inclination is most pronounced in the second, the sixteenth is vertical, and the last two are directed a little forward. The longest spines (*i. e.*, those of the withers) are the thickest and have expanded summits which remain more or less cartilaginous; the others are more plate-like, and are surmounted by a thick lip. The second spine is more than twice as large as the first. The summits of the fourth and fifth usually form the highest point of the withers.

Development.—There are **six** or **seven centers** of ossification, three for the body, two for the arch, and one for the spinous process; some of the latter have an additional center for the summit.

The occurrence of a nineteenth rib-bearing vertebra is not at all uncommon. In such cases there may be only five typical lumbar vertebræ.

THE LUMBAR VERTEBRÆ

The lumbar vertebræ (Vertebræ lumbales) are usually six in number in the horse. They are characterized by the size and form of their transverse processes.

The **bodies** of the first three are semi-elliptical on cross-section, and present a distinct ventral crest. From the fourth backward they become wider and flatter and the ventral crest subsides.

The **arches** of the first three are about equal in size and similar to that of the last thoracic; behind this they increase in breadth and height. The posterior notches are much deeper than the anterior ones.

The **anterior articular processes** are fused with the mammillary processes, and present dorsally concave surfaces for articulation with the posterior pair of the preceding vertebra. The **posterior articular processes** project distinctly from the arch at the base of the spinous process, and have ventrally convex articular surfaces, which fit into the concave surfaces of the anterior pair of the next vertebra.

The **transverse processes** are elongated plates, flattened dorso-ventrally, which project outward and may incline slightly upward or downward; their length increases to the third or fourth, and then diminishes to the last. The first one or two usually curve somewhat backward, the last two decidedly forward. Those of the fifth have an oval concave facet on the medial part of the posterior border for articulation with the sixth process; the latter has a corresponding convex facet on the anterior border, and a larger concave surface on the posterior border for articulation with the wing of the sacrum. Sometimes the fifth process has a small surface for articulation with the fourth. The medial part of the sixth process is thick, the lateral part thinner, narrower, and curved forward. The medial part of the fifth is also somewhat thickened. Medial to the articular surfaces the edges of the transverse processes are cut into by notches, which form foramina by apposition with each other and the sacrum.

The **spinous processes** resemble those of the last two thoracic vertebræ.

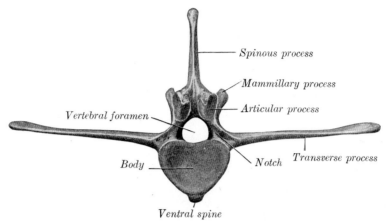

Spinous process

Mammillary process

Articular process

Vertebral foramen

Body

Notch

Transverse process

Ventral spine

Fig. 16.—Second Lumbar Vertebra of Horse; Posterior View.

They are usually about equal in height, but minor differences are common, and the width diminishes in the last three.

Development.—This is similar to that of the thoracic vertebræ. The extremities of the transverse processes remain cartilaginous for some time after ossification is otherwise complete.

The transverse processes of this region are considered equivalent to the proper transverse process + the costal element; hence the distinctive term processus costarius is used to designate

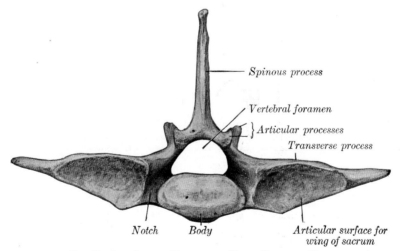

Spinous process

Vertebral foramen

}*Articular processes*

Transverse process

Notch   *Body*

Articular surface for wing of sacrum

Fig. 17.—Last Lumbar Vertebra of Horse; Posterior View.

the costal homologue. The occurrence of a rib in connection with the transverse process of the first lumbar vertebra is common. In other cases there is a costiform prolongation of the process. Reduction of the number to five has been observed frequently, and may or may not be compensated by an additional thoracic vertebra. Very few cases are recorded of seven lumbar vertebræ—especially with the normal thoracic number. An anomalous vertebra with mixed thoracic and lumbar characters sometimes occurs at the junction of the two regions.

THE SACRUM

The **sacrum** (Os sacrum) is formed by the fusion of five vertebræ, and is conveniently described as a single bone. It is triangular in form and is wedged in between the ilia, with which it articulates very firmly on each side. Its long axis is gently curved and slightly oblique, so that the posterior end is a little higher than the anterior. It presents two surfaces, two borders, a base, and an apex.

The **dorsal surface** (Facies dorsalis) presents centrally the five sacral spines (Processus spinosi), which are directed upward and backward, and have (with the exception of the first) tuberous summits which are sometimes bifid.

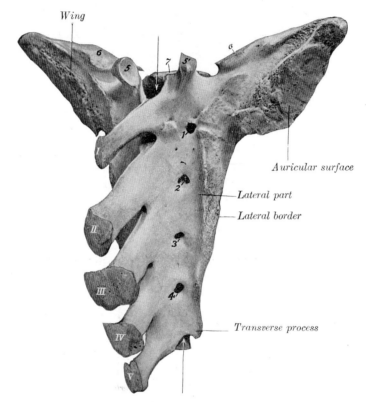

FIG. 18.—SACRUM OF HORSE; DORSO-LATERAL VIEW.

I–V, Spinous processes; *1–4*, dorsal sacral foramina; *5, 5'*, articular processes; *6*, surfaces of wings for articulation with transverse processes of last lumbar vertebra; *7*, body of first sacral vertebra. Arrows point into sacral canal.

The first spine is relatively thin and narrow, and is not so high as the sacral angle of the ilium. The second is stouter and is commonly the longest and highest, and the length and height diminish to the last. The bases of the spines are often fused in old subjects.

On either side of the spines there is a groove, in which are the four **dorsal sacral foramina** (Foramina sacralia dorsalia); the dorsal branches of the sacral nerves emerge through them.

The **pelvic surface** (Facies pelvina) is concave in its length, wide in front, narrow behind. The curvature is variable and is more pronounced in the mare than in the stallion. It is marked by four more or less distinct **transverse lines** (Lineæ transversæ), which indicate the demarcation of the bodies of the vertebræ. At the ends of these lines are the **ventral sacral foramina** (Foramina sacralia ventralia), which are larger than the dorsal series and diminish in size from first to last; they transmit the ventral divisions of the sacral nerves.

The dorsal and ventral foramina communicate with the sacral canal and are together equivalent to the usual intervertebral foramina.

The **lateral borders** are rough, thick in front, thin behind.

The **base** (Basis ossis sacri) is directed forward, and is relatively very wide. It presents centrally the **body** of the first sacral segment, which is wide transversely, flattened dorso-ventrally, and has a rounded surface which articulates with the last lumbar vertebra through the medium of an intervertebral fibro-cartilage. The ventral margin projects slightly, forming the **promontory** (Promontorium). On

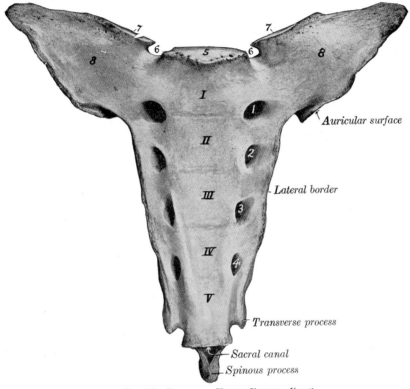

Fig. 19.—Sacrum of Horse; Ventral View.

I–V, Bodies of original five vertebræ, marked off by transverse lines; *1–4*, ventral sacral foramina; *5*, articular surface of body of first vertebra; *6, 6*, notches; *7, 7*, surfaces of wings for articulation with transverse processes of last lumbar vertebra; *8, 8*, wings.

either side of the body there is a smooth notch, which, with one on the last lumbar vertebra, forms a large foramen for the passage of the ventral branch of the last lumbar nerve. Above the body is the entrance to the sacral canal, flanked by a pair of **articular processes,** which project upward and forward from the arch, and have concave surfaces medially for articulation with those of the last lumbar vertebra. Lateral to each of these is a smooth notch which is converted into a foramen by apposition with the last lumbar vertebra. The lateral parts of the base, the **alæ** or **wings** (Alæ sacrales), are strong prismatic masses with pointed ends. Each has in front a large, oval, slightly convex surface for articulation with the transverse process of the last lumbar vertebra. Posteriorly there is an elongated oval area which faces dorso-laterally; this is the **auricular surface** (Facies auricularis), which articulates with the ilium; it is slightly concave in its length, and somewhat rough and irregular. The rest of the dorsal surface of the wing is roughened for ligamentous attachment, while the ventral surface is smooth.

The **apex** (Apex ossis sacri) is the posterior aspect of the last sacral vertebra and is quite small. It presents the elliptical flattened surface of the body, above which is the triangular posterior opening of the sacral canal, surmounted by the last sacral spine. There is a pair of narrow notches between the arch and body, above which rudiments of articular processes may occur.

The name **sacral canal** (Canalis sacralis) is applied to that part of the vertebral canal which traverses the sacrum. Its anterior part is large and has the form of a triangle with the angles rounded off; its width is nearly twice its height. Traced backward it is seen to diminish in size rapidly, and the posterior opening is small and triangular.

The term **lateral part** (Pars lateralis) designates the portion lateral to the foramina, which results from the fusion of the transverse processes.

Development.—The several sacral vertebræ ossify in the typical manner. Separate centers for costal elements in the lateral parts have not yet been found in the domesticated animals. Fusion begins in front, and is usually not complete till adult age. The lateral parts unite before the bodies. It is rather curious that the epiphyseal plates of adjacent segments unite with each other before they fuse with the main portion of the bodies. It is not rare to find fusion of some of the bodies incomplete even in adult subjects.

THE COCCYGEAL VERTEBRÆ

The coccygeal vertebræ (Vertebræ coccygeæ) vary considerably in number, but eighteen may be taken as an average. From first to last they become reduced in size and, with the exception of a few at the beginning of the series, consist of

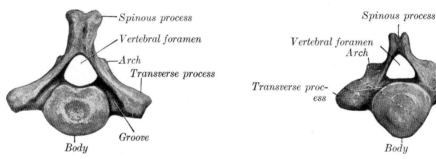

FIG. 20.—FIRST COCCYGEAL VERTEBRA OF HORSE; POSTERIOR VIEW.

FIG. 21.—SECOND COCCYGEAL VERTEBRA OF HORSE; POSTERIOR VIEW.

Leader to arch points to rudimentary articular process.

bodies only. The first three have bodies which are somewhat flattened dorsoventrally, constricted in the middle, and have at the ends convex, elliptical, articular surfaces. The ventral surface has a median groove (Sulcus vasculosus) for the coccygeal artery. The arch is small and triangular; it is formed of two flat plates which are prolonged to form a short spinous process with a thickened and often double summit. The anterior notches are absent. Functional articular processes are not present, but small rudiments of the anterior pair commonly occur. The transverse processes are relatively large plates which project horizontally outward. Further back the arch becomes incomplete dorsally, and soon disappears; the transverse processes gradually fade out, and the vertebræ are reduced to cylindrical rods of diminishing size. The last one has a pointed end.

Variations.—The number is said by good observers to vary between fourteen and twenty-one. In old age the first is often fused with the sacrum, and sometimes with the second. The arch of the third may be open.

THE VERTEBRAL COLUMN AS A WHOLE

In the mid-dorsal line is the series of **spinous processes,** which are low ridges in the cervical region with the exception of the second and seventh, reach their maximum height at the fourth and fifth thoracic vertebræ, and diminish to the fifteenth or sixteenth thoracic. Behind this they are about equal in height as far as the last lumbar and first sacral, which are somewhat lower. The second sacral spine is about as high as the middle lumbar; behind this they diminish rather rapidly in height and fade out about the third coccygeal. Their **inclination** backward is most decided at the second thoracic and diminishes from the sixth or seventh to the sixteenth thoracic, which is vertical and is termed the **anticlinal** or **diaphragmatic vertebra.** Behind this they are inclined a little forward until the sacrum is reached; here there is an abrupt change to the backward inclination, so that a considerable interspinous angle is formed.

On either side of the spinous processes is a vertebral groove which contains the deep muscles of the spine. The floor of the groove is formed by the arches and articular processes. It is wide in the neck and narrows progressively in the back.

Viewed from the side, the column presents a series of **curves.** When the head and neck are in the ordinary neutral position, the anterior part of the cervical spine forms a gentle curve, concave ventrally. The posterior cervical and first thoracic vertebræ form a more pronounced curve in the opposite direction. At the junction of the cervical and thoracic regions there is a marked change of direction, forming a ventral projection or angle. At the second thoracic vertebra a gentle curve, concave ventrally, begins. This is continued to the lumbo-sacral junction, where there is a change of direction, and hence a promontory. The sacrum has a variable, but never very pronounced, ventral concave curvature, which is continued in a much accentuated form in the coccygeal region. It should be noted that a line through the summits of the spines does not correspond to these curves formed by the bodies.

The **vertebral canal** corresponds in its curvature to that of the bodies. Its **caliber** varies greatly at different points. The greatest diameter is in the atlas, where it contains the dens of the axis in addition to the spinal cord, and provision must be made for extensive movement. It is very much smaller in the axis. It widens considerably at the junction of the cervical and thoracic regions to accommodate the cervical enlargement of the spinal cord. Beyond this it diminishes, and is smaller in the middle of the back than at any preceding point; this is correlated with the small size of the spinal cord and the very limited movement of the spine here. Beyond the middle of the lumbar region it again enlarges considerably to contain the lumbar enlargement of the spinal cord. The caliber diminishes very rapidly from the second sacral segment backward, and the canal ceases to be complete at the fourth coccygeal vertebra.

The transverse and vertical diameters of the vertebral canal at various points are given in the annexed table. The measurements were made on a horse of medium size; they represent the maximum width and height in the middle of the vertebra and are expressed in centimeters.

Vertebra	C1	C2	C4	C7	T10	L3	L6	S1	S5
Transverse..................	5.2	2.6	2.6	3.5	2.3	2.4	4.0	4.0	1.8
Vertical..................	4.2	2.5	2.1	2.5	1.7	1.8	2.5	2.1	1.5

The **articular processes** are very large and wide apart in the neck, greatly reduced and much closer together in the back, larger and interlocking in the lumbar region.

The **transverse processes** are large and outstanding in the neck, where they form the lateral boundary of a ventral groove occupied by the longus colli muscle. In the back they are short and stout, and are characterized by the facets for the tubercles of the ribs. On the first thoracic vertebra this facet is large, deeply concave, and situated almost directly outward from the cavity for the head of the rib; traced backward it becomes smaller and flatter, and gradually comes to lie behind the cavity for the head of the rib, with which it is fused on the last and often also on the next to the last thoracic vertebra. The processes in the lumbar region have a characteristic elongated plate-like form. In the sacral region they are fused to form the wings and lateral parts of the sacrum. In the coccygeal region they are at first of considerable size relatively, but undergo rapid reduction, and disappear at the fifth or sixth vertebra.

The cavities for the heads of the ribs diminish progressively in size and depth from first to last.

The **mammillary processes** are usually distinct on the fourteenth to the seventeenth thoracic vertebræ. In front of these they blend with the transverse, behind with the anterior articular, processes.

The length of the vertebral column (including the intervertebral fibro-cartilages) in a horse of medium size is about nine feet (ca. 2.7 meters). The relative lengths of the various regions appear to vary most in the neck and back. The following average lengths of the several regions were obtained by measurement of several subjects: Cervical, 70 cm.; thoracic, 86 cm.; lumbar, 34 cm.; sacral, 20 cm.; coccygeal, 60 cm. The percentage values are approximately 26, 32, 12.5, 7.5, 22.

THE RIBS

The ribs (Costæ) are elongated, curved bones which form the skeleton of the lateral thoracic walls. They are arranged serially in pairs which correspond in number to the thoracic vertebræ. There are usually eighteen pairs of ribs in the horse, but a nineteenth rib on one side or both is not uncommon. Each articulates dorsally with two vertebræ and is continued ventrally by a costal cartilage. Those which articulate with the sternum by means of their cartilages (eight pairs) are termed **sternal** ribs (Costæ sternales); the remainder are **asternal** ribs (Costæ asternales). Ribs at the end of the series which have their ventral ends free and not attached to an adjacent cartilage are named **floating** ribs (Costæ fluctuantes). The intervals between the ribs are termed **intercostal spaces** (Spatia intercostalia).

Ribs from different parts of the series vary greatly in length, curvature, and other characters. We will, therefore, first consider as a type a rib from the middle of the series, and afterwards note the chief serial differences.

A typical rib (the term is employed here, as is usual in descriptive anatomy, to designate only the bony part of the rib (Os costale); morphologically it includes the cartilaginous part also) consists of a shaft and two extremities. The **shaft** (Corpus costæ) is band-like and varies in length, breadth, and curvature in different ribs. The curvature is not uniform, but is accentuated at a certain point, termed the angle of the rib (Angulus costæ) which is most pronounced in the dorsal third and marked by a rough ridge (a distinct angle can scarcely be said to exist in the bone), and the ventral part is twisted and inclined inward, so that when a rib is laid with its lateral surface on the table, the sternal end is raised. The **lateral surface** (Facies lateralis) is convex in its length and also transversely; its anterior part is, however, grooved longitudinally. The **medial surface** (Facies medialis) is smooth, concave in its length, rounded from side to side; the **costal groove** (Sulcus costæ), situated posteriorly, is very distinct above and fades out about the middle; it contains the **intercostal vein.** The **anterior** and **posterior borders** (Margo cranialis, caudalis) are thin and sharp on some ribs, rounded on others.

The **vertebral extremity** (Extremitas vertebralis) consists of the head, neck and tubercle. The **head** (Capitulum costæ) is the actual end of the rib, and is rounded and somewhat enlarged. It presents two convex facets (Facies articularis capitulæ costæ), anterior and posterior, for articulation with the bodies of two adjacent thoracic vertebræ and the intervertebral fibro-cartilage; these surfaces are separated by a groove (Sulcus capitulæ) for the attachment of the conjugal ligament. The **neck** (Collum costæ) joins the head to the shaft and is roughened

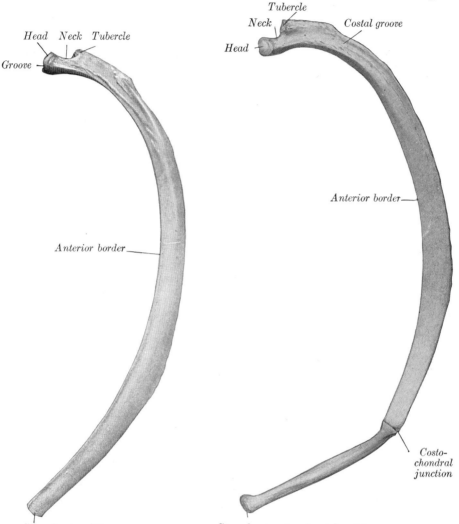

FIG. 22.—LEFT EIGHTH RIB OF HORSE; LATERAL VIEW.

FIG. 23.—RIGHT EIGHTH RIB AND COSTAL CARTILAGE OF HORSE; MEDIAL VIEW.

above and in front. It varies in length and diameter. Its lateral surface is rough, its medial smooth. The **tubercle** (Tuberculum costæ) projects backward at the junction of the neck and shaft; it has a facet (Facies articularis tuberculi costæ) for articulation with the transverse process of the posterior vertebra of the two with which the head articulates. The tubercle gradually approaches the head in the posterior ribs, and eventually fuses with it.

The **sternal extremity** (Extremitas sternalis) is commonly slightly enlarged and is roughened at the junction with the costal cartilage.

The **first rib** is easily distinguished. It is the shortest and the shaft widens greatly toward the sternal end. At the lower part of the anterior border there is a smooth impression where the brachial vessels curve around it; above this there is commonly a small tubercle (Tuberculum scaleni) which indicates the lower limit of the origin of the scalenus muscle. The costal groove is absent. The head is large and has two facets of unequal extent, which meet at an acute angle in front; the smaller one faces forward and articulates with the last cervical vertebra; the larger one is directed medially and articulates with the first thoracic vertebra. The neck is thick and very short. The tubercle is larger than that of any other rib and has an extensive articular surface which is convex in its length. The sternal end is larger than that of any other rib; it is thick and very wide, and is turned a little forward.

The **last rib** is the most slender and regularly curved. It is usually but little longer than the second. The facet on the tubercle is confluent with that of the head. (This feature, however, is common on the seventeenth also, and may occur on the sixteenth.)

The serial position of the other ribs may be determined approximately by the following considerations: The **length** increases from the first to the tenth and eleventh and then diminishes. The **width** increases somewhat to the sixth and then diminishes.

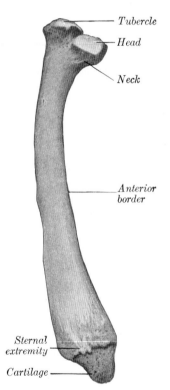

The **anterior border** is thin and sharp from the second to the eighth, and behind this becomes thick and rounded. The groove of the lateral surface is distinct on the fourth to the eighth inclusive. The **curvature** increases in degree rapidly from the second to the seventh, remains about the same to the sixteenth, and then decreases very noticeably. In regard to dorso-ventral **direction,** the first rib inclines a little forward, the second is about vertical, while behind this they slope backward in increasing degree, so that a transverse plane tangent to the ventral ends of the last pair cuts the third lumbar vertebra. The **head** and **tubercle** diminish in size from first to last. Their relative positions change, in that the tubercle of the first rib is almost directly lateral to the head, while further back it gradually comes to lie behind it. The **neck** is longest on the longest ribs, and is absent on the last two or three. A **costo-transverse foramen** (Foramen costo-transversarium) is formed between the neck and the transverse process.

Development.—The ribs ossify in cartilage from **three centers,** one each for the shaft (and sternal end), head, and tubercle; the third center is absent in some of the posterior ribs.

Fig. 24.—Left First Rib of Horse; Medial View.

Variations—A nineteenth rib on one side or both is not at all rare. It is usually imperfectly developed and quite variable. In many cases it is a mere strip of cartilage connected by fibrous tissue with the first lumbar transverse process; in other cases it is well developed, and may be fused with the process; in others again it is connected with a vertebra which may be thoracic or lumbar or ambiguous in character. It is often floating, but may be attached to the eighteenth costal cartilage. Reduction in number is less frequent. In rare cases the first rib is imperfectly developed and does not reach to the sternum. Partial fusion of adjacent ribs and other anomalies occur.

THE COSTAL CARTILAGES

The costal cartilages (Cartilagines costales) are bars of hyaline cartilage which continue the ribs. Those of sternal ribs articulate with the sternum, while those of asternal ribs overlap and are attached to each other by elastic tissue to form the costal arch (Arcus costarum). The cartilages of floating ribs are not attached to those adjacent.

The first costal cartilage is an inch or more (2.5 to 3 cm.) in length. The dorsal end is very wide and thick. The sternal end is small. The two articulate with each other as well as with the sternum. The cartilages of the other sternal ribs increase progressively in length and become more rounded. The sternal end is enlarged and has an elliptical convex facet for articulation with the sternum. The cartilages of the asternal ribs are long, slender and pointed, they overlap and are attached to each other by elastic tissue, forming the costal arch (Arcus costarum). The ninth is very firmly attached to the eighth; it and the next two are the longest, and behind this they diminish progressively in size. Except in the case of the first, the cartilage does not continue the direction of the rib, but forms with the latter an angle which is open in front, and increases from second to last. More or less extensive ossification is to be regarded as a normal occurrence, especially in the cartilages of the sternal ribs.

THE STERNUM

The **sternum** (or breast-bone) is a median segmental bone which completes the skeleton of the thorax ventrally, and articulates with the cartilages of the sternal ribs laterally. It consists of six to eight bony segments (Sternebræ) connected by intervening cartilage in the young subject. Its form varies with that of the thorax in general and with the development of the clavicles in animals in which these bones are present. Its anterior extremity, the **manubrium sterni** or **presternum,** is specially affected by the latter factor, being broad and strong when the clavicles are well developed and articulate with it (as in man), relatively small and laterally compressed when they are absent (as in the horse) or rudimentary (as in the dog). The cartilages of the first pair of ribs articulate with it. The **body** or **mesosternum** (Corpus sterni) presents laterally, at the junction of the segments, concave facets (Incisuræ costales) for articulation with the cartilages of the sternal ribs. The posterior extremity or **metasternum** presents the **xiphoid cartilage** (Processus xiphoideus) thin and wide, as in the horse and ox, or narrow and short, as in the dog.

The sternum of the horse is shaped somewhat like a canoe; it is compressed laterally, except in its posterior part, which is flattened dorso-ventrally. It is curved and inclined obliquely so that the posterior end is about six to eight inches (15 to 20 cm.) lower than the anterior.

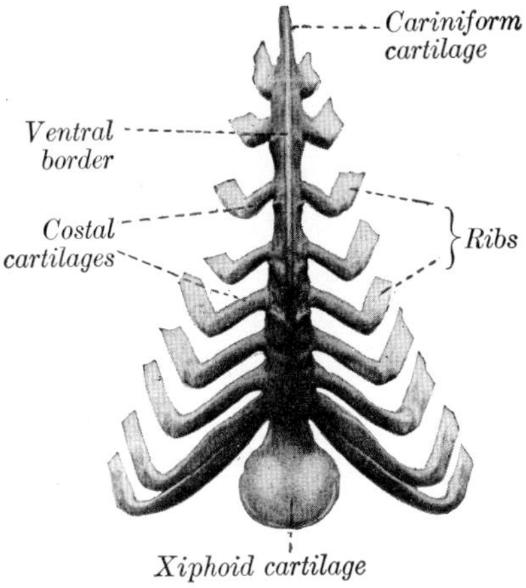

The **dorsal surface** (Facies dorsalis) has the form of a very narrow isosceles triangle with the apex in front. It is concave longitudinally, flattened transversely.

The **lateral surfaces** (Facies laterales) are convex above, slightly concave below, and diminish in extent behind. Each presents on its upper part seven **costal cavities** (Foveæ costales), with which the sternal ends of the second to the eighth costal cartilages inclusive articulate. These cavities are situated in series at the intersternebral junctions. The first four are elliptical in outline with the long diameter vertical, and are separated by considerable regular intervals. The others are progressively smaller, more circular, and closer together. The area below these cavities gives attachment to the pectoral muscles.

Cariniform cartilage

Ventral border

Costal cartilages

Ribs

Xiphoid cartilage

Fig. 25.—Sternum and Costal Cartilages of Horse; Ventral View. (After Ellenberger-Baum, Anat. f. Künstler.)

The **dorso-lateral** borders separate the dorsal and lateral surfaces. They give attachment to the lateral branches of the sternal ligament.

The **ventral border** forms the prominent keel-like **crest** of the sternum (Crista sterni) which may be felt in the living animal; it fades out behind.

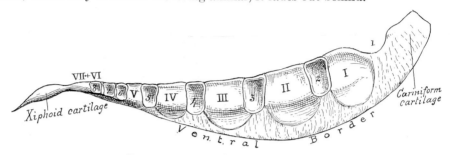

FIG. 26.—STERNUM OF HORSE; LATERAL VIEW
The sternebræ are designated by Roman numerals and the costal facets by ordinary figures.

The **anterior extremity** or **manubrium sterni** can be distinctly felt in the central furrow of the breast. It consists largely of a laterally compressed cartilaginous prolongation, commonly called the **cariniform cartilage.** Its lateral surfaces are flat and furnish attachment to muscles of the breast and neck. The ventral border is rounded, and is continued backward on the body of the bone. The dorsal border is concave and has an articular cavity for the first pair of costal cartilages.

The **posterior extremity** is formed by the **xiphoid cartilage** (Processus xiphoideus). This is a thin plate, connected in front with the last bony segment by a relatively thick, narrow neck, and expanding in nearly circular form behind and laterally. Its dorsal surface is concave, and gives attachment to the diaphragm. The ventral surface is convex and furnishes attachment to the transversus abdominis and the linea alba. The free margin is very thin.

Development.—The cartilaginous sternum is formed by the fusion medially of two lateral bars which unite the ventral ends of the first eight or nine costal cartilages, and is primitively unsegmented. The manubrium ossifies from a single center, but the centers for the other segments appear to be primitively paired. The sternum never becomes completely ossified. At birth the sternum of the horse consists of seven bony segments, termed sternebræ, which are united by intersternebral cartilages. The last two sternebrae fuse in the second month, but the others do not usually unite completely even in old age. The sternebræ consist of very vascular spongy bone covered by a very thin layer of compact substance. The adult sternum thus consists to a very considerable extent of persisting cartilage, viz., the intersternebral cartilages, the ventral keel, and the extremities; in old age these undergo partial ossification.

THE THORAX

The skeleton of the thorax comprises the thoracic vertebræ dorsally, the ribs and costal cartilages laterally, and the sternum ventrally. The **thoracic cavity** (Cavum thoracis) resembles in shape an irregular truncated cone; it is compressed laterally, especially in front, and the dorsal wall or roof is much longer than the ventral wall or floor. The **anterior aperture** or inlet (Apertura thoracis cranialis) is bounded by the first thoracic vertebra dorsally, the first pair of ribs and costal cartilages laterally, and the manubrium sterni ventrally. The **posterior aperture** (Apertura thoracis caudalis) is bounded by the last thoracic vertebra, the last pair of ribs, the costal arches, and the anterior part of the xiphoid cartilage.

It may be noted here that the diaphragm (which forms the partition between the thoracic and abdominal cavities) does not follow the costal arches in its posterior attachment, so that the posterior ribs enter also into the formation of the abdominal wall.

The bony thorax of the horse is remarkably compressed laterally in its anterior part, but widens greatly behind. The **anterior aperture** (Apertura thoracis cranialis) is oval and very narrow below; in a horse of medium size its great-width is about 4 inches (10 cm.), and its height 7 to 8 inches (ca. 18–20 cm.). The **ventral wall** or floor is about 16 inches (40 cm.) long, and the **dorsal wall** or roof about 38 to 40 inches (95–100 cm.) long. The height at the last segment of the sternum is about 18 inches (ca. 45 cm.)—more than twice that of the anterior aperture; this is due to the obliquity and divergence of the roof and floor. The greatest width of the posterior aperture is about 20 to 24 inches (50–60 cm.). The intercostal spaces (measured in their middles) average a little more than an inch (ca. 3 cm.) in width. The first is narrow and they widen to the fourth or fifth. Further back they gradually diminish to the last two or three, where they again increase.

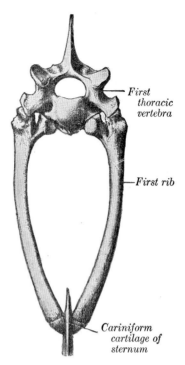

FIG. 27.—ANTERIOR APERTURE OF THORAX OF HORSE. (After Schmaltz, Atlas d. Anat. d. Pferdes.)

THE SKULL

The term skull is usually understood to include all of the bones of the head. The head consists of the cranium and the face, and it is therefore convenient to divide the bones into cranial and facial groups.

The **cranial bones** (Ossa cranii) inclose the brain with its membranes and vessels and the essential organs of hearing. They concur with the facial bones in forming the orbital and nasal cavities, in which the peripheral organs of sight and of smell are situated.

The **facial bones** (Ossa faciei) form the skeleton of the oral and nasal cavities, and also support the pharynx, the larynx, and the root of the tongue.

Most of the bones of the skull are flat bones, developed in membrane; those of the cranial base may be classed as irregular, and are developed in cartilage. Only two form permanent movable joints with other parts of the skull. The mandible (or lower jaw-bone) forms diarthrodial joints with the temporal bones, and the hyoid bone is attached to the latter by bars of cartilage. The other bones form immovable joints, most of which disappear with age.

(A) BONES OF THE CRANIUM

The bones of the cranium (Ossa cranii) are the occipital, sphenoid, ethmoid, interparietal, parietal, frontal, and temporal. The first three are single, the others paired.

THE OCCIPITAL BONE

The **occipital bone** (Os occipitale) is situated at the posterior part of the cranium, of which it forms the posterior wall and part of the ventral wall or base.

Its lower part is perforated centrally by a large, almost circular opening, the **foramen magnum** (Foramen occipitale magnum), at which the cranial cavity and vertebral canal join. The foramen is bounded laterally and dorsally by the **lateral parts** of the bone, and ventrally by the **basilar part**. Above the lateral parts—but not entering into the formation of the foramen magnum—is the **squamous part.**

The **lateral parts** (Partes laterales) bear the **occipital condyles** (Condyli occipitales), which articulate with the atlas. The condyles are obliquely placed, wide apart dorsally, and separated ventrally by a small interval (Incisura intercondyloidea). The articular surface is curved so sharply in the dorso-ventral

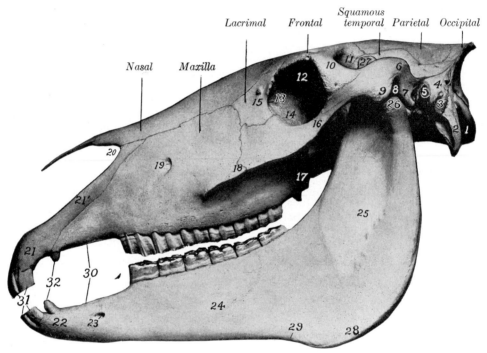

FIG. 28.—SKULL OF HORSE; LEFT VIEW.

1, Occipital condyle; *2*, paramastoid process; *3*, mastoid process; *4*, posterior process of squamous temporal bone; *5*, external acoustic process; *6*, zygomatic process of temporal bone; *7*, postglenoid process; *8*, glenoid cavity of squamous temporal bone; *9*, condyle of same; *10*, supraorbital process of frontal bone; *11*, temporal part of frontal bone; *12*, orbital part of frontal bone; *13*, fossa sacci lacrimalis; *14*, orbital surface of lacrimal bone; *15*, lacrimal tubercle; *16*, zygomatic process of malar bone; *17*, maxillary tuberosity; *18*, facial crest; *19*, infraorbital foramen; *20*, naso-maxillary notch; *21*, body of premaxilla; *21'*, nasal process of same; *22*, body of mandible; *23*, mental foramen; *24*, *25*, horizontal and vertical parts of ramus of mandible; *26*, condyle of mandible; *27*, coronoid process of mandible; *28*, angle of mandible; *29*, vascular impression; *30*, interalveolar margin; *31*, incisor teeth; *32*, canine teeth.

direction as to form a blunt ridge. The cranial surface is concave and smooth. Lateral to the condyle is the **paramastoid process** (Processus paramastoideus), a strong plate of bone which projects downward and backward; its lateral surface is convex and roughened for muscular attachment; its medial surface is concave from end to end. Between the root of this process and the condyle is a smooth depression, the **condyloid fossa** (Fossa condyloidea ventralis); in this is the **hypoglossal foramen** (Foramen hypoglossi), which transmits the nerve of like name.

The **basilar part** (Pars basilaris) is a strong, somewhat prismatic bar, which extends forward from the ventral margin of the foramen magnum. It is wide and flattened behind, narrower and thicker in front. The ventral surface is rounded. The cranial surface is concave and smooth; its posterior part supports the medulla oblongata, and its anterior part has a shallow cavity on which the pons rests. The lateral borders are thin and sharp, and form the medial margin of the **foramen lacerum.** The anterior end has, in the young subject, a semicircular, flat, pitted surface which is attached to the body of the sphenoid bone by a layer of cartilage; in the adult there is complete fusion. On the ventral aspect of the junction are the **basilar tubercles** (Tubercula basilaria) for the attachment of the ventral straight muscles of the head (Fig. 50).

The **squamous part** (Squama occipitalis)[1] is the somewhat quadrilateral mass

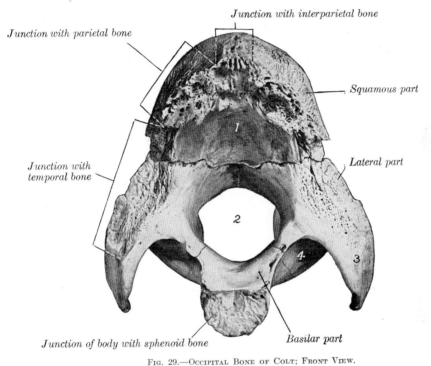

Junction with interparietal bone

Junction with parietal bone

Squamous part

Junction with temporal bone

Lateral part

Junction of body with sphenoid bone

Basilar part

Fig. 29.—Occipital Bone of Colt; Front View.

1, Depression of squamous part for cerebellum; *2*, foramen magnum; *3*, paramastoid process; *4*, condyloid fossa.

situated dorsal to the lateral parts, from which it remains distinct till the second year. The **external surface** is crossed by a very prominent ridge, the **nuchal crest** (Crista nuchalis); the middle part of this is thick, transverse in direction, and forms the highest point of the skull when the head is in the ordinary position; laterally it becomes thinner and runs downward and forward to join the temporal crest.[2] The crest divides the surface into two very unequal parts; the small dorsal area (Planum parietale) presents a median ridge which is the posterior part of the **external parietal crest** (Crista sagittalis externa); the large area ventral to the crest (Planum nuchale) has a central eminence, the **external occipital protuberance,** on which the funicular part of the ligamentum nuchæ is attached. The **internal surface** is con-

[1] Also known as the supraoccipital.

[2] The nuchal crest of this description is equivalent to the external occipital protuberance and superior nuchal line of man; it has been commonly termed the occipital crest, but is not the equivalent of that feature of the human skull. A curved line a little lower down, which is continued on the paramastoid process, represents the inferior nuchal line of man.

cave and presents a deep central depression and two shallower lateral ones which adapt it to the surface of the cerebellum.

The **parietal border** (Margo parietalis) is united by suture with the parietal and interparietal. The **mastoid border** (Margo mastoideus) joins the petro-mastoid part of the temporal bone. The basilar part is connected by cartilage (in the young subject) with the body of the sphenoid. The condyles articulate with the atlas.

Development.—The occipital bone ossifies in cartilage from four centers, and consists at birth of four pieces as described above. The lateral parts unite with

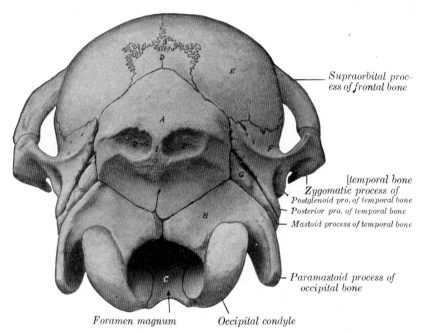

Fig. 30.—Cranium of New-born Foal; Posterior View.

A, B, C, Squamous, lateral, and basilar parts of occipital bone; D, interparietal bone; E, parietal bone; F, squamous temporal bone; G, petro-mastoid part of temporal bone; 1, external occipital protuberance; 2, 2, depressions in which complexus tendons are attached; 3, sutural (preinterparietal?) bone.

the basilar part at three to four months, and with the squamous part in the second year, when the bone is consolidated.

The parieto-occipital suture and the spheno-occipital synchondrosis are obliterated about the fifth year usually. The occipito-mastoid suture partially ossifies in old subjects.

The Sphenoid Bone

The **sphenoid bone** (Os sphenoidale) is situated in the base of the cranium, its central part lying in front of the basilar part of the occipital. It consists of the body, two pairs of wings, and two pterygoid processes (Figs. 31, 33, 48, 50, 51, 53, 54).

The **body** (Corpus) is situated medially; it is cylindrical, but flattened dorso-ventrally, and wider in front than behind. Its **ventral surface** (Facies externa) is convex in the transverse direction, and its anterior part is concealed to a large extent by the vomer and pterygoid bones. The **cerebral surface** (Facies cerebralis) presents the following features: (1) In front there is a raised, flattened part (Jugum sphenoidale) which is partially subdivided by a median elevation into two slightly concave lateral areas; this part has a posterior, thin, free margin (Limbus sphenoidalis), which overlies the entrance to the optic canals. The median ridge is termed the **ethmoidal spine,** since it fits into a notch of the cribriform plate of the ethmoid bone and joins the crista galli. (2) Just behind this and at a lower level is a smooth transverse depression, the **optic groove** (Sulcus chiasmatis), on which the optic chiasma rests. (3) From each end of this groove the **optic canal** (Canalis opticus) passes forward and outward and opens in the orbit at the **optic foramen.** (4) Further back there is a central depression, the **hypophyseal** or **pituitary fossa** (Fossa hypophyseos), which lodges the hypophysis cerebri or pituitary body. The **anterior end** is expanded, and joins the ethmoid and palatine bones; it is excavated to form the **sphenoidal sinuses.** These cavities extend back as far as the optic groove, and are usually continuous in front with the cavities in the vertical parts of the palate bones;[1] they are separated by a complete septum which is not always median. The **posterior end** is flat and is joined to the basilar part of the occipital; at the line of junction there is dorsally a slight transverse elevation, the **spheno-occipital crest** (Crista spheno-occipitalis) and ventrally are the **basilar tubercles.**

The **orbital wings** (Alæ orbitales) curve dorso-laterally from the sides of the body of the presphenoid. Their **cerebral surface** is concave, and is marked by **digital impressions** (Impressiones digitatæ) for the gyri of the cerebrum. The **lateral surface** is convex and is largely concealed by the overlapping temporal wing and the squamous temporal and frontal bones; a narrow part of it (Facies orbitalis) is uncovered on the medial wall of the orbital cavity at the sphenoidal notch of the frontal bone. The **dorsal border** unites with the frontal bone at the spheno-frontal suture. The **anterior border** joins the ethmoid at the spheno-ethmoidal suture; at its lower part it concurs with the ethmoid and frontal in the formation of the **ethmoidal foramen** (Foramen ethmoidale). The **posterior border** is overlapped by the temporal wing and the squamous temporal. The **root** of the wing is perforated by the

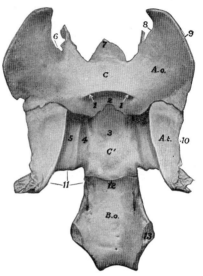

Fig. 31.—Sphenoid Bone and Basilar Part of Occipital Bone of New-born Foal; Dorsal View.

C, Body of presphenoid; *C′,* body of postsphenoid; *B.o.,* basilar part of occipital bone; *A.o.,* orbital wing of sphenoid bone; *A.t.,* temporal wing of sphenoid bone; 1, 1, optic foramina; 2, optic groove; 3, hypophyseal fossa; 4, 5, grooves; 6, ethmoidal notch; 7, ethmoidal spine; 8, junction with cribriform plate of ethmoid bone; 9, junction with frontal bone; 10, junction with squamous temporal bone; 11, margin of foramen lacerum anterius; 12, spheno-occipital crest; 13, junction of basilar part of occipital bone with lateral part.

optic foramen (Foramen opticum). Immediately below and behind the latter (*i. e.,* beneath the root) is the **foramen orbitale.** Below this, and separated from it usually by a thin and often incomplete plate, is a larger opening, the **foramen rotundum,** which is bounded externally by the root of the pterygoid process.

The **temporal wings** (Alæ temporales) extend outward and somewhat upward from the body of the postsphenoid; they are smaller than the orbital wings and

---

[1] The cavity so formed may be termed the sphenopalatine sinus. The sphenoidal sinus may be a separate cavity which communicates only with the ventral ethmoidal meatuses; this arrangement exists in about a third of the cases according to Paulli.

are irregularly quadrilateral in outline. The **temporal surface** (Facies temporalis) enters into the formation of the infratemporal fossa, and bears the pterygoid process on its anterior part; at the junction with the body there is a small groove which leads forward to the pterygoid canal. The **cerebral surface** (Facies cerebralis) presents, at the junction with the body, two longitudinal **grooves** (Sulci nervorum). The lateral groove is the larger, and leads forward to the foramen rotundum; it contains the maxillary nerve. The medial groove conducts to the foramen orbitale, and contains the cavernous sinus of the dura mater. The outer groove is bounded laterally by a thin overhanging crest, on which is a small groove for the trochlear nerve. The remainder of the surface is concave and supports the pyriform lobe of the brain. The **dorsal border** joins the squamous temporal at the spheno-squamous suture. The **anterior border** joins the orbital wing above; below this it is free and forms the **pterygoid crest** (Crista pterygoidea). The crest is continued on the pterygoid process; on or under its upper part there is usually a small opening, the **trochlear foramen** (Foramen trochleare). Just behind the crest is the **foramen alare parvum,** through which the anterior deep temporal artery emerges from the alar canal of the pterygoid process. The **posterior border** forms the anterior boundary of the foramen lacerum; it presents **three notches,** which are, from within outward, the carotid, oval, and spinous (Incisura carotica, ovalis, spinosa). The angle of junction of the dorsal and posterior borders articulates with the parietal bone.

The **pterygoid processes** (Processus pterygoidei) arise from the temporal wings and the body. They project downward and forward, and curve outward at the lower part. The root is perforated by the **alar canal** (Canalis alaris), which transmits the internal maxillary artery. From this canal a branch leads upward and forward to open at the foramen alare parvum. The **lateral surface** is concave, and is marked by lines for muscular attachment. The **medial surface** is convex; it is largely concealed by the overlapping palatine and pterygoid bones.

The **pterygoid canal** (Canalis pterygoideus) continues the groove noted on the ventral surface of the temporal wing at its junction with the body. It extends forward and upward between the root of the pterygoid process, the presphenoid, and the pterygoid bone, and opens in the posterior part of the pterygo-palatine fossa. It transmits the nerve of the pterygoid canal.

Development.—The sphenoid is ossified in cartilage, and consists in early life of two distinct parts, the presphenoid and postsphenoid. The former develops from two centers, one in each wing; the latter has three centers, one for the body and one for each wing. The pterygoid processes ossify from the centers of the temporal wings. In the new-born foal the unossified dorsal part of the orbital wing fits into a hiatus of the frontal bone; in some cases it comes to the surface through a defect in the frontal bone at the place where the horn process is situated in animals which have frontal horns.

THE ETHMOID BONE

The **ethmoid bone** (Os ethmoidale) lies in front of the body and orbital wings of the sphenoid. It projects forward between the orbital parts of the frontal bones and enters into the formation of the cranial, nasal, and paranasal cavities.[1] It consists of four parts—the cribriform plate, two lateral masses, and the perpendicular plate (Figs. 32, 33, 44, 53, 54, 58).

The **cribriform plate** (Lamina cribrosa) is a sieve-like partition between the cranial and nasal cavities. Its margin joins the orbital wings of the sphenoid

---

[1] On account of its deep situation and the fact that it cannot be separated from its surroundings, the ethmoid must be studied by means of appropriate sagittal and transverse sections of the skull.

laterally, the body of the sphenoid ventrally, and the cranial plate of the frontal bones dorsally. Its **cerebral surface** is divided into two parts by a median ridge, the **ethmoidal crest** (Crista ethmoidalis), which may be regarded as the intracranial projection of the perpendicular plate. Each half forms a deep oval cavity, the **ethmoidal fossa,** which lodges the olfactory bulb. The plate is perforated by numerous small foramina for the passage of the olfactory nerve filaments, and on either side is the much larger **ethmoidal foramen.** The **nasal surface** is convex, and has the lateral masses attached to it.

Each **lateral mass** or **labyrinth** (Labyrinthus ethmoidalis) is conical in shape and its base is attached to the cribriform plate. It projects forward into the posterior part of the nasal cavity. The **medial surface** is separated by a narrow

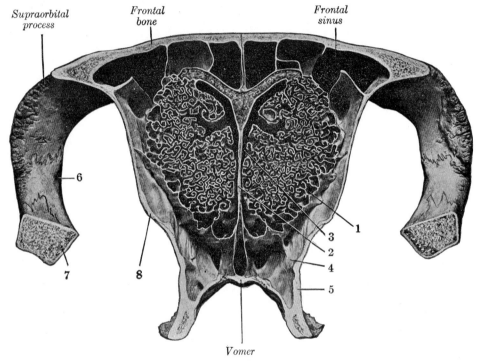

Supraorbital process   *Frontal bone*   *Frontal sinus*

Vomer

FIG. 32.—CROSS-SECTION OF CRANIUM OF HORSE. THE SECTION PASSES THROUGH THE MIDDLE OF THE ORBITS AND IS VIEWED FROM IN FRONT.

1, Lateral mass of ethmoid bone; 2, perpendicular plate of same; 3, common nasal meatus; 4, sphenopalatine sinus; 5, perpendicular part of palatine bone; 6, zygomatic process of temporal bone; 7, zygomatic arch; 8, orbital part of frontal bone.

space from the perpendicular plate. The **lateral surface** is convex and faces chiefly into the frontal and maxillary sinuses, but is attached behind to the inner wall of the orbital cavity; it is covered by a very thin layer of bone, the **lamina lateralis.** The mass consists of a large number of delicate, scroll-like plates of bone, termed **ethmo-turbinates.** These are attached to the lamina lateralis, and are separated by narrow intervals termed **ethmoidal meatuses,** which communicate with the nasal cavity. In the fresh state the ethmo-turbinates are covered with mucous membrane. The lateral mass is a very complex structure, the arrangement of which may be understood by examination of cross-sections. Each mass consists of six turbinates which extend almost to the perpendicular plate and are termed **endoturbinates.** These diminish in size from above downward; the largest is attached to the nasal bone, and is hence usually called the dorsal or nasal turbinate; the second is much smaller, and is very commonly termed the great ethmoid cell. The cavity enclosed by this communicates laterally with the maxillary sinus, but not directly with the nasal cavity. Between the endoturbinates are twenty-one small **ectoturbinates,** and all are beset with secondary and tertiary coiled lamellæ.

The **perpendicular plate** (Lamina perpendicularis) is median, and forms the posterior part of the septum nasi. Its **lateral surfaces** are nearly plane, but are marked below by some grooves and ridges; they are covered by the nasal mucous membrane. The **anterior border** is irregular and is continuous with the septal cartilage. The **posterior border** projects into the cranial cavity as the ethmoidal

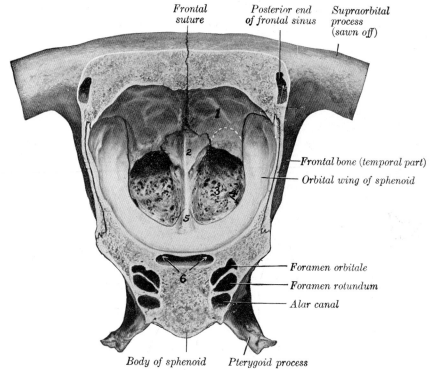

Frontal suture — Posterior end of frontal sinus — Supraorbital process (sawn off)

Frontal bone (temporal part)
Orbital wing of sphenoid

Foramen orbitale
Foramen rotundum
Alar canal

Body of sphenoid   Pterygoid process

Fig. 33.—Cross-section of Cranium of Horse. The Section is Cut Just in Front of the Temporal Condyle and Is Viewed from Behind.

1, Internal plate of frontal bone; 2, ethmoidal crest; 3, cribriform plate; 4, ethmoidal foramen; 5, ethmoidal spine of sphenoid bone; 6, optic canals. Dotted line below 1 indicates limit of concealed part of ethmoidal fossa.

crest. The **dorsal border** joins the frontal bones at their line of junction. The **ventral border** is received into the groove of the vomer.

Development.—The ethmoid develops in cartilage from five centers, two for each lateral mass, and one for the perpendicular plate; from the latter ossification extends into the cribriform plate. At birth the perpendicular and cribriform plates are cartilaginous. By the time ossification is complete the ethmoid has united with surrounding bones to such an extent that it cannot be separated intact for study.

THE INTERPARIETAL BONE

This bone (Os interparietale) is centrally placed between the squamous part of the occipital and the parietal bones. It is usually described as a single bone, although it ossifies from two chief lateral centers, and is often distinctly paired in skulls of young foals (Figs. 30, 34, 47, 52, 54).

The external, **parietal surface** (Facies parietalis) is quadrilateral and is flat and smooth in the very young foal; later it presents the parietal crest medially. The internal, **cerebral surface** (Facies cerebralis) presents the **internal occipital protuberance,** a three-sided process which projects downward and forward into the cranial cavity between the cerebral hemispheres and the cerebellum; it has three concave surfaces and three sharp borders. The lateral borders form part of the tentorium osseum and the anterior one gives attachment to the falx cerebri. Behind the base of the protuberance there is a transverse groove for the sinus communicans of the dura mater. The **posterior border** is thick; it joins the squamous part of the occipital bone. The **lateral** and **anterior borders** are united with the parietal bones.

Development.—The interparietal ossifies in membrane from two chief lateral centers. It fuses first with the parietals, somewhat later with the occipital, but the period at which this union takes place is quite variable.

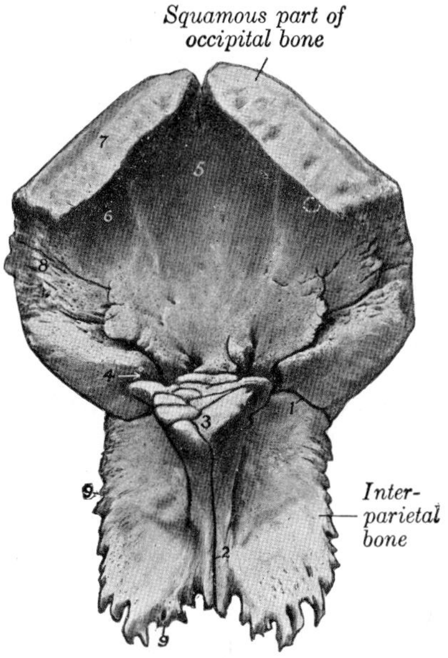

THE PARIETAL BONES

The two **parietal bones** (Ossa parietalia) form the greater part of the roof of the cranium; they unite in the median line, forming the **parietal suture.** Each is quadrilateral in outline and has two surfaces and four borders (Figs. 28, 30, 35, 36, 47, 52, 54).

The external, **parietal surface** (Facies parietalis) is convex, and is marked by a more or less prominent curved line, the **external parietal crest;** this is median in its posterior part, and is continuous with the crest of like name on the interparietal and occipital; in front it curves outward and is continuous with the frontal crest. The surface lateral to the crest (Planum temporale) enters into the formation of the temporal fossa, and is roughened for the attachment of the temporal muscle.

The internal, **cerebral surface** (Facies cerebralis) is concave. It presents numerous **digital impressions** (Impressiones digitatæ) which correspond to the gyri, and **ridges** (Juga cerebralia) which correspond to the

FIG. 34.—INTERPARIETAL AND SQUAMOUS PART OF OCCIPITAL BONE OF NEW-BORN FOAL; VENTRAL VIEW.

1, Junction of interparietal with squamous part of occipital bone; 2, interparietal suture; 3, internal occipital protuberance; 4, transverse groove for sinus; 5, depression for vermis cerebelli; 6, depression for hemisphere of cerebellum; 7, junction of squamous part with lateral part of occipital bone; 8, junction of occipital with petro-mastoid; 9, 9, junction of interparietal with parietal.

sulci, of the cerebrum. There are also furrows (Sulci vasculosi) for the meningeal arteries. Along the medial border there is a **sagittal groove** (Sulcus sagittalis) for the dorsal longitudinal sinus.

The **anterior border** joins the frontal bone at the **parieto-frontal suture** (Sutura parieto-frontalis).

The **posterior border** meets the occipital bone at the **parieto-occipital suture.** Below this junction it curves inward and concurs with the temporal bone in the formation of the **temporal canal** (Meatus temporalis). A **transverse groove** (Sulcus transversus) connects this canal with the sagittal sulcus.

The **medial border** is thick and serrated. It joins its fellow in great part at the **parietal suture,** but (in the young subject) meets the interparietal at its posterior part. The line of junction of the two parietal bones is marked internally by the **internal parietal crest** (Crista parietalis interna).

The **lateral border** is beveled and is overlapped by the squamous temporal

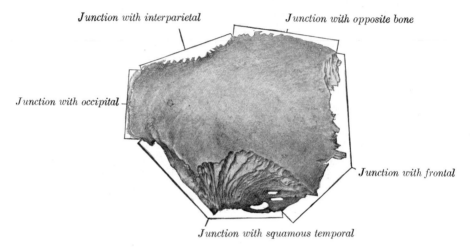

Junction with interparietal   *Junction with opposite bone*

Junction with occipital

Junction with frontal

Junction with squamous temporal

FIG. 35.—RIGHT PARIETAL BONE OF NEW-BORN FOAL; DORSO-LATERAL VIEW.

bone, forming the **squamous suture** (Sutura squamosa). The postero-lateral angle joins the posterior angle of the temporal wing of the sphenoid.

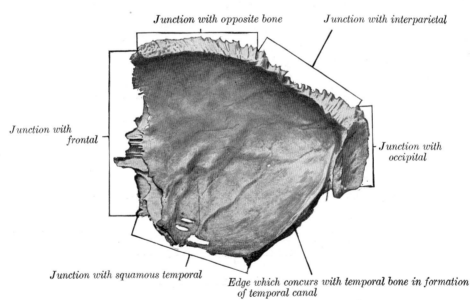

Junction with opposite bone   *Junction with interparietal*

Junction with frontal

Junction with occipital

Junction with squamous temporal

Edge which concurs with temporal bone in formation of temporal canal

FIG. 36.—RIGHT PARIETAL BONE OF NEW-BORN FOAL; CEREBRAL SURFACE.

Arrow indicates transverse groove.

Development.—Each parietal bone ossifies in membrane from a single center. In the young foal the central part of the bone is more convex than in the adult and forms a prominence similar to the pronounced tuber parietale of the young child; the external parietal crest is not present, and the external surface is smooth. The parietal suture is usually closed at four years, the parieto-occipital at five years, and the squamous at twelve to fifteen years.

THE FRONTAL BONES

The **frontal bones** (Ossa frontalia) are situated on the limits of the cranium and face, between the parietals behind and the nasal bones in front. Each is irregularly quadrilateral, and consists of naso-frontal, orbital, and temporal parts (Figs. 28, 32, 33, 37, 44, 47, 48, 52, 54, 58).

The **naso-frontal part** (Pars naso-frontalis) forms the basis of the forehead. Its **external** or **frontal surface** (Facies frontalis) is nearly flat, and is smooth and subcutaneous; it is separated from the temporal part by the **external frontal crest** (Crista frontalis externa). At the junction with the orbital part the **supraorbital** or **zygomatic process** (Proc. zygomaticus) curves outward and downward to join the zygomatic arch. The process partially separates the orbit from the temporal fossa; its root is perforated by the **supraorbital foramen** (Foramen supraorbitale), or presents instead a notch on its anterior border; its upper surface is convex, while the orbital surface is concave and smooth, forming a shallow fossa for the lacrimal

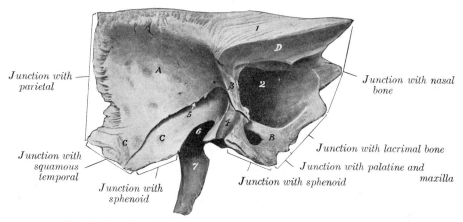

FIG. 37.—LEFT FRONTAL BONE OF NEW-BORN FOAL; VENTRO-MEDIAL VIEW.

A, Cerebral surface; *B*, orbital part; *C, C*, temporal part; *D*, nasal surface; 1, surface of junction with opposite bone; 2, frontal sinus; 3, ridge to which cribriform plate of ethmoid bone is attached; 4, groove for ethmoidal artery; 5, fissure into which orbital wing of sphenoid bone fits; 6, sphenoidal notch; 7, supraorbital process.

gland (Fossa glandulæ lacrimalis). The **internal surface** enters into the formation of the cranial and nasal cavities. The two plates of the bone separate and diverge in front, and thus inclose a large air-space which is part of the **frontal sinus**. The internal plate curves downward and forward and joins the cribriform plate of the ethmoid. Beyond this it inclines upward and joins the external plate at the naso-frontal suture. The **cerebral surface** presents digital impressions for the cerebral gyri. The **nasal surface** is longitudinally grooved. The external plate extends forward and joins the nasal and lacrimal bones.

The **orbital part** (Pars orbitalis) forms the major part of the medial wall of the orbital cavity. It is separated from the naso-frontal part by a prominent ridge which is part of the orbital margin. Its **orbital surface** (Facies orbitalis) is concave and smooth, and presents superiorly a small depression (Fovea trochlearis), which is bridged by a small bar of cartilage, around which the superior oblique muscle of the eye is reflected. The lower border concurs with the orbital wing of the sphenoid in the formation of the ethmoidal foramen. The **nasal surface** faces into the frontal sinus and is to a small extent united with the lateral mass of the ethmoid.

The **temporal part** (Pars temporalis) is separated from the orbital part by the deep **sphenoid notch** (Incisura sphenoidalis), which is closed by the orbital wing of the sphenoid. Its **lateral surface** forms part of the inner wall of the temporal fossa. The **medial surface** is largely covered by the orbital wing of the sphenoid but part of it faces into the cranial cavity and presents digital impressions.

The principal connections of the frontal bone are as follows: (1) The medial border joins its fellow at the **frontal suture.** (2) The anterior border meets the nasal and lacrimal at the **naso-frontal** and **fronto-lacrimal sutures.** (3) Laterally it forms the **spheno-frontal suture** with the orbital wing of the sphenoid, and also joins the palatine bone and maxilla at the **fronto-palatine** and **fronto-maxillary sutures.** (4) Posteriorly it meets the parietal at the **parieto-frontal suture,** and articulates below this with the squamous temporal at the **squamous suture.** (5) The extremity of the supraorbital process unites with the zygomatic process of the temporal bone.

Development.—Each ossifies in membrane from one center which appears in the root of the supraorbital process. In the new-born foal there is a slit between the cranial plate and the orbital and temporal plates which receives the unossified dorsal part of the orbital wing of the sphenoid.

THE TEMPORAL BONES

The **temporal bone** (Os temporale) forms the greater part of the lateral wall of the cranium. It is situated between the occipital behind, the parietal dorsally, the frontal in front, and the sphenoid ventrally. It consists in the horse of two distinct parts, **squamous** and **petrous** (Figs. 28, 38, 41, 47, 48, 50, 54).

1. The **squamous temporal bone** (Squama temporalis) is a shell-like plate which has two surfaces and four borders.

The **cerebral surface** (Facies cerebralis) is concave and is largely overlapped by the surrounding bones, but its central part is free and presents digital impressions and vascular grooves.

The **temporal surface** (Facies temporalis) is convex, and enters into the formation of the temporal fossa. From its ventral part there springs the **zygomatic process** (Processus zygomaticus), which forms the lateral boundary of the temporal fossa. The process is at first directed outward, and is wide and flattened dorso-ventrally. It then turns forward, becomes narrower, and is twisted so that its surfaces are medial and lateral. Its anterior end is pointed and joins the zygomatic process of the malar bone, with which it forms the **zygomatic arch** (Arcus zygomaticus). The narrow anterior part has a convex lateral surface and a concave medial one. Its dorsal border has a rough area for articulation with the supra-orbital process of the frontal. Its ventral border is wide and rough. The wide posterior part presents on its ventral face a surface for articulation with the condyle of the mandible. This surface consists of a transversely elongated **condyle** (Condylus temporalis), behind which is the **glenoid cavity.** The fossa is limited behind by the **postglenoid process** (Processus postglenoidalis), the anterior surface of which is articular. Behind this process there is a fossa, in which is the **postglenoid foramen** (F. postglenoidale), the external opening of the temporal canal. The dorsal surface is concave and forms the lateral boundary of the temporal fossa. The dorsal border is sinuous and is continuous behind with the temporal crest.

The **posterior process** (Processus aboralis) springs from the posterior part of the squama. Its lateral surface bears the temporal crest, which forms here the lateral limit of the temporal fossa. The medial surface forms the outer boundary of the temporal canal, and is elsewhere applied to the petrous portion. It divides into two branches, upper and lower; the upper branch unites with the occipital bone, while the lower one curves downward behind the external acoustic process and overlaps the mastoid process.

The **dorsal border** of the squamous temporal articulates with the parietal, forming the **squamous suture**. The **ventral border** joins the temporal wing of the sphenoid at the **spheno-squamous suture**. The **anterior border** unites with the frontal bone at the **squamo-frontal suture**, and the **posterior** with the occipital and petrous temporal bones.

2. The **petrous temporal bone** (Os petrosum) is placed between the occipital

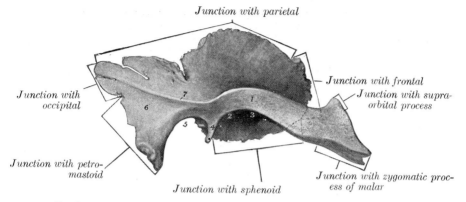

FIG. 38.—RIGHT SQUAMOUS TEMPORAL BONE OF NEW-BORN FOAL; LATERAL VIEW.
1, Zygomatic process; 2, glenoid cavity; 3, condyle; 4, postglenoid process; 5, notch; 6, posterior process; 7, temporal crest.

behind and the parietal in front, and is largely overlapped by the squamous temporal. It has the form of a four-sided pyramid, the base of which is ventral.

The **lateral surface** is mainly concealed by the squamous temporal, but two features are visible. A short tube of bone, the **external acoustic process** (Processus acusticus externus), protrudes from the lowest part through the notch of the squa-

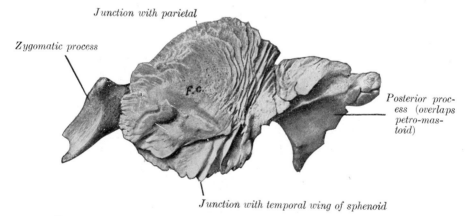

FIG. 39.—RIGHT SQUAMOUS TEMPORAL BONE OF NEW-BORN FOAL; MEDIAL VIEW.
F.c., Cerebral surface.

mous temporal. The process is directed outward, upward, and a little forward. It gives attachment to the annular cartilage of the ear. Its lumen, the **external acoustic meatus** (Meatus acusticus externus), conducts to the cavity of the middle ear (tympanum) in the dry skull, but is separated from it by the tympanic membrane in the natural state. The **mastoid process** (Processus mastoideus) projects ventrally in the interval between the posterior process of the squamous temporal and the root of the paramastoid process of the occipital bone. It is crossed by a groove which leads to the **mastoid foramen** (Foramen mastoideum), from which a canal extends forward to the temporal canal.

The **medial surface** faces into the cerebellar fossa of the cranium. It is concave and smooth, but irregular. In its ventral part is the entrance to a short canal, the **internal acoustic meatus** (Meatus acusticus internus), which transmits the facial and acoustic nerves.

The entrance to the meatus is termed the porus acusticus internus. The fundus of the meatus is divided by a crest into two fossæ. In the superior one is the origin of the **facial canal,** which curves through the bone and opens externally at the stylo-mastoid foramen; it transmits the facial (seventh cranial) nerve. The inferior fossa presents small foramina for the passage of fibers of the acoustic (eighth cranial) nerve.

Behind the meatus and near the posterior margin of the surface is the slit-like external opening of the aquæductus vestibuli (Apertura externa aquæductus ves-

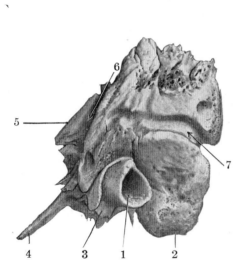

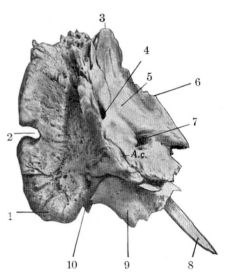

Fig. 40.—Left Petrous Temporal Bone of Horse; Lateral View.

1, External acoustic meatus; 2, mastoid process; 3, hyoid process; 4, muscular process; 5, petrosal crest; 6, groove which concurs in formation of temporal canal; 7, groove for posterior meningeal artery.

Fig. 41.—Left Petrous Temporal Bone of Horse; Postero-medial View.

1, Mastoid process; 2, notch which concurs with occipital bone in formation of mastoid foramen; 3, apex; 4, opening of aquæductus vestibuli; 5, medial surface; 6, petrosal crest; 7, internal acoustic meatus; 8, muscular process; 9, bulla tympanica; 10, stylo-mastoid foramen; A.c., opening of aquæductus cochleæ.

tibuli), covered by a scale of bone. Below this there is a narrow fissure, the orifice of the aquæductus cochleæ (Apertura externa aquæductus cochleæ).

The **anterior surface** looks upward and forward. The greater part articulates with the parietal bone, but a small medial part faces into the cerebral fossa of the cranium. A sharp border, the **petrosal crest** (Crista petrosa), separates this surface from the medial one.

The **posterior surface** is slightly concave and is attached to the lateral part of the occipital bone.

The **base** forms the lateral boundary of the foramen lacerum. It is very irregular and presents a number of important features. The **hyoid process** (Processus hyoideus) is a short rod which projects downward and forward below the base of the external acoustic process, inclosed in a bony tube; it is connected by a bar of cartilage with the hyoid bone. The **stylo-mastoid foramen** (F. stylomastoideum) is situated between the hyoid process and the mastoid process; it is the external opening of the facial canal, through which the facial nerve emerges. The **bulla tympanica** is a considerable eminence situated centrally; it is thin walled and incloses a cavity which is part of the tympanum. The **muscular process** (Processus muscularis) is a sharp spine which projects downward and forward from the anterior part of the base; it gives origin to the tensor and levator palati muscles. Lateral to the root of the preceding is the small **petrotympanic fissure** (Fissura petrotympanica) for the passage of the chorda tympani nerve. The osseous **auditory or Eustachian tube** (Tuba auditiva ossea) is a semicanal at the medial side of the root of the muscular process; it leads to the tympanum. At the medial side of the preceding is the slit-like orifice of the petrosal canal, which communicates with the facial canal.

The **apex** projects upward and backward between the squamous temporal and the occipital bone.

Development.—The squamous temporal develops in membrane. The petrous temporal may be regarded as consisting of petro-mastoid and tympanic parts. The latter includes the external acoustic process, the bulla tympanica, and the muscular process; it is developed in membrane. The petro-mastoid is developed in the cartilaginous ear capsule. Its petrous part consists of very dense bone which contains the labyrinth or internal ear and forms the medial wall of the tympanum.

The auditory ossicles and the interior of the petrous temporal bone are described in the section on the organ of hearing.

The **temporal canal** (Meatus temporalis) is a continuation of the transverse groove noted previously at the base of the internal occipital protuberance. It is directed downward, forward, and somewhat outward, and opens externally in front of the root of the acoustic process. It is bounded by the squamous temporal laterally, the petrous behind, and the parietal in front and medially. Several foramina open from it into the temporal fossa. It contains a large vein (Vena cerebralis dorsalis), the continuation of the transverse sinus of the dura mater.

The **foramen lacerum** (**basis cranii**) is a large, irregular opening in the cranial base, bounded medially by the basilar part of the occipital bone, laterally by the petrous temporal, and in front by the temporal wing of the sphenoid. It consists of a large anterior part (Foramen lacerum anterius), and a narrow posterior part (Foramen lacerum posterius). It transmits the internal carotid artery, the middle meningeal artery, the mandibular, glosso-pharyngeal, vagus, and accessory nerves, and the ventral cerebral vein.

In the fresh state the foramen is occupied by a dense fibrous membrane which is perforated by apertures for the various structures transmitted. Thus there are three openings in front for the internal carotid artery, the mandibular nerve, and the middle meningeal artery respectively; these are named (from within outward) the foramen caroticum, ovale, spinosum.

(B) BONES OF THE FACE

The bones of the face (Ossa faciei) are the maxilla, premaxilla, palatine, pterygoid, nasal, lacrimal, malar, dorsal turbinate, ventral turbinate, vomer, mandible, and hyoid. The last three are single, the others paired.

THE MAXILLÆ

The **maxillæ** are the principal bones of the upper jaw and carry the upper cheek teeth. They are situated on the lateral aspect of the face, and articulate with almost all of the facial bones and the frontal and temporal also. For description each may be divided into a body and two processes.

The **body** (Corpus maxillæ) presents two surfaces, two borders, and two extremities. The **lateral surface** (Facies lateralis) is somewhat concave in front and convex behind. In the young horse the anterior part of the surface decidedly convex over the embedded parts of the premolar teeth. As the latter are extruded the surface flattens and becomes concave in old subjects. The form of the underlying teeth may be indicated by ridges (Juga alveolaria), and sometimes in young horses there may be defects in the bone over the teeth. On its posterior part there is a horizontal ridge, the **facial crest** (Crista facialis); in a skull of medium size its anterior end is about an inch and a half (3 to 4 cm.) above the third or fourth cheek tooth, and it is continued behind on the malar bone. About two inches (5 cm.) above and a little in front of the anterior end of the crest is the **infraorbital foramen** (Foramen infraorbitale); this is the external opening of the infraorbital canal.

The **medial** or **nasal surface** (Facies nasalis) is concave dorso-ventrally; it forms the greater part of the lateral wall of the nasal cavity. Its upper part is crossed obliquely forward and downward by the shallow **lacrimal groove** (Sulcus lacrimalis), which contains the naso-lacrimal duct; in the adult the posterior part of the groove is converted into a canal, which is continuous with that on the inner surface of the lacrimal bone. Below the groove is the **ventral turbinate crest** (Crista turbinata ventralis), to which the ventral turbinate bone is attached. Lower down and parallel with the turbinate crest is the **palatine process,** which

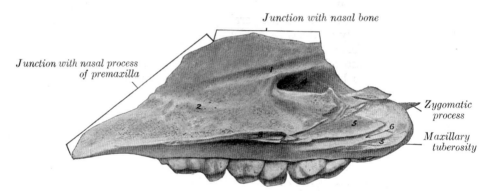

FIG. 42.—RIGHT MAXILLA OF NEW-BORN FOAL; MEDIAL VIEW.

1, Lacrimal groove; 2, ventral turbinate crest; 3, palatine process; 4, maxillary sinus; 5, 5, area of articulation with palatine bone; 6, groove which concurs with one on the palatine bone to form the palatine canal.

projects horizontally like a shelf. Behind this the surface is rough for articulation with the palatine bone; this area is crossed by a groove which concurs with one on the palatine bone in the formation of the **palatine canal** (Canalis palatinus). The posterior part of the bone is excavated to form part of the maxillary sinus.

The **dorsal border** is irregular and scaly. Its anterior part is grooved and its posterior part beveled for articulation with the nasal process of the premaxilla and the nasal and lacrimal bones.

The **ventral** or **alveolar border** (Processus alveolaris) is in its greater part thick, and presents six large cavities, the **dental alveoli,** for the cheek teeth. The alveoli are separated by transverse **interalveolar septa.** There is often a small alveolus for the first premolar ("wolf tooth") close to the first large one. At the bottom of the alveoli there are small openings (Foramina alveolaria) for the passage of vessels and nerves. Further forward the border is narrow and forms part of the **interalveolar** or **interdental space** (Margo interalveolaris). Behind the last alveolus is a rough area, the **alveolar tuberosity** (Tuber alveolare).

The **anterior extremity** is pointed. It joins the premaxilla, and forms with it the alveolus for the canine tooth.

The **posterior extremity** forms a rounded prominence, the **maxillary tuberosity** (Tuber maxillare). Medial to the tuberosity is a deep recess (Recessus maxillaris), in which are three foramina. The upper one, the **maxillary foramen** (Foramen maxillare), leads into the infraorbital canal. The lower one, the **posterior palatine foramen** (Foramen palatinum aborale), is the entrance to the palatine canal. The **sphenopalatine foramen** (Foramen sphenopalatinum) perforates the medial wall of the recess and opens into the nasal cavity.

The **zygomatic process** (Processus zygomaticus) projects backward, dorso-lateral to the tuberosity; it is overlapped by the corresponding part of the malar and also joins the zygomatic process of the temporal bone. A small curved plate (Processus temporalis) extends medially from it and joins the frontal and palatine bones, forming part of the floor of the orbit.

The **palatine process** (Processus palatinus) projects like a shelf from the lower part of the medial surface of the body and forms the greater part of the basis of the hard palate. Its **nasal surface** is smooth and is concave transversely; on its anterior part, close to the medial border, there is a shallow groove in which the vomero-nasal organ is situated. The **palatine surface** is slightly concave from side to side, and presents along its lateral part the **palatine groove** (Sulcus palatinus); this is continuous at the **anterior palatine foramen** (Foramen palatinum orale) with the palatine canal, and contains the palatine vessels and nerve. In old subjects there are sometimes impressions corresponding with the ridges and veins of the palate. The **medial border** unites with its fellow to form the **median palatine suture;** its nasal aspect bears the **nasal crest** (Crista nasalis), which forms, with that of the opposite process, a groove for the vomer. The **posterior border** unites with the horizontal part of the palatine bone at the **transverse palatine suture.** Variable **accessory palatine foramina** perforate the process.

The **infraorbital canal** (Canalis infraorbitalis) extends almost horizontally from the maxillary foramen to the infraorbital foramen. It is placed at the upper edge of the inner plate of the maxilla, and traverses the maxillary sinus. Near the infraorbital foramen it gives off a small canal (Canalis alveolaris incisivus) which lies above the roots of the premolars and extends also into the premaxilla, carrying vessels and nerves to the teeth there.

Development.—The maxilla ossifies in membrane ventral and lateral to the cartilaginous nasal capsule. It has one chief center and a supplementary one in the region of the deciduous canine tooth (Martin).

THE PREMAXILLÆ

The **premaxillæ** (Ossa incisiva) form the anterior part of the upper jaw and carry the incisor teeth. Each consists of a body, a nasal process, and a palatine process (Figs. 28, 43, 44, 47).

The **body** (Corpus) is the thick anterior part which carries the incisor teeth. Its **labial surface** (Facies labialis) is convex and smooth, and is related to the upper lip. The **palatine surface** (Facies palatina) is concave and usually presents a foramen a little behind its middle. The **medial surface** (Facies medialis) is rough, and joins the opposite bone; it is marked by a curved groove, which forms, with that on the opposed surface, the **foramen incisivum.** The **alveolar border** (Limbus alveolaris) separates the palatine and labial surfaces; it is curved and thick where it presents three deep alveoli for the incisor teeth; behind the third alveolus it is thin and free, forming part of the **interalveolar space.**

The **nasal process** (Processus nasalis) projects backward and upward from the body, forming here the lateral wall of the nasal cavity. The two **surfaces, facial** and **nasal,** are smooth and rounded. The **dorsal border** is free, thick, and smooth; it concurs with the free margin of the nasal bone in forming the **naso-maxillary notch** (Incisura nasomaxillaris). The **ventral border** is dentated and joins the maxilla; at its anterior end it forms with the latter the alvelous for the permanent canine tooth.[1] The **posterior extremity** fits into the interval between the nasal bone and the maxilla.

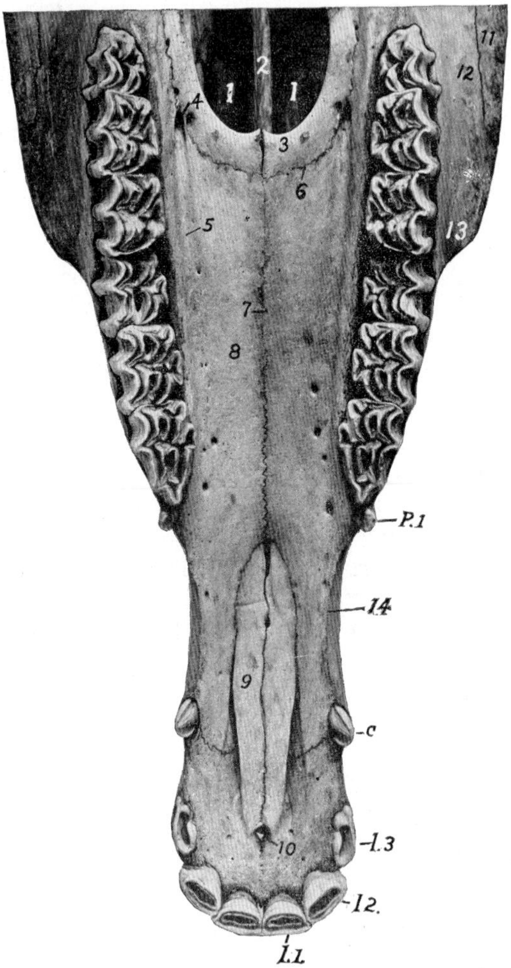

The **palatine process** (Processus palatinus) is a thin plate which forms the anterior part of the basis of the hard palate. Its **nasal surface** (Facies nasalis) has a longitudinal ridge which forms with that of the other side a groove for the septal cartilage; lateral to the ridge there is a groove for the vomero-nasal organ. The **palatine surface** (Facies palatina) is flat. The **medial border** is serrated and meets its fellow at the median palatine suture. The **lateral border** is separated from the maxilla and the nasal process by the **palatine fissure** (Fissura palatina). The **posterior extremity** fits into the interval between the vomer and the palatine process of the maxilla.

Development.—The premaxilla ossifies from a single center. Fusion of the two bones is complete at the end of the third or the beginning of the fourth year.

Fig. 43.—Upper Jaw of Horse About Four and a Half Years Old; Ventral View.

1, 1, Choanæ or posterior nares; 2, vomer; 3, horizontal part of palatine bone; 4, anterior palatine foramen; 5, palatine groove; 6, transverse palatine suture; 7, median palatine suture; 8, palatine process of maxilla; 9, palatine process of premaxilla; 10, foramen incisivum; 11, malar bone; 12, maxilla; 13, anterior end of facial crest; 14, interalveolar space; *I. 1–3*, incisor teeth; *C*, canine tooth; *P.1*, first premolar or "wolf" tooth. The opening lateral to 9 is the palatine fissure.

THE PALATINE BONES

The **palatine bones** (Ossa palatina) are situated on either side of the choanæ or posterior nares, and form the posterior part of the hard palate. Each is twisted so as to form a horizontal and a perpendicular part (Figs. 43, 44, 48, 50).

The **horizontal part** (Pars horizontalis) is a narrow plate which forms the posterior part of the hard palate. It presents smooth **nasal** and **palatine surfaces** (Facies nasalis, palatina). The **medial border** meets its fellow at the median palatine suture, on the nasal aspect of which is the **nasal crest.** The **anterior border** joins the palatine process of the maxilla at the transverse palatine suture, and forms with it the **anterior palatine foramen** (Foramen palatinum anterius). The **posterior border** is concave and free; it gives attachment to the aponeurosis of the soft palate.

---

[1] The alveolus for the temporary canine tooth is commonly formed in the maxilla alone.

The **perpendicular part** (Pars perpendicularis) is more extensive and forms most of the lateral wall of the choanæ or posterior nares. The **nasal surface** (Facies nasalis) is in the greater part of its extent concave and smooth, but presents a narrow rough area to which the pterygoid bone is attached. Below this the bone curves outward, forming the **pterygoid process**. The **maxillary surface** (Facies maxillaris) presents three areas for consideration. The largest articulates with the maxilla; it is rough and is crossed by a groove which concurs with one on the maxilla in the formation of the **palatine canal**. Behind this is a smooth part which assists in forming the **pterygopalatine fossa** (Fossa pterygopalatina). The rough area below this is overlapped by the pterygoid process of the sphenoid bone. The **dorsal border** is perforated by the **sphenopalatine foramen**. Behind the foramen the two plates of the bone separate to inclose part of the **sphenopalatine sinus**. The inner plate curves medially to articulate with the vomer. The outer plate joins the maxilla and frontal and the orbital wing of the sphenoid; it may join the lacrimal bone also.

Development.—The palatine bone ossifies in membrane from a single center.

THE PTERYGOID BONES

The **pterygoid bones** (Ossa pterygoidea) are narrow, thin, bent plates, situated on either side of the posterior nares (Figs. 44, 48, 50, 51). Each has two surfaces and two extremities. The **medial surface** is smooth, and forms part of the wall of the posterior nares. The **lateral surface** articulates with the palatine, vomer, and sphenoid, concurring with the last in the formation of the **pterygoid canal**. The **ventral extremity** is free, turned slightly outward, and forms the **hamulus pterygoideus**; this is grooved externally and forms a pulley around which the tendon of the tensor palati muscle is reflected.

Development.—The pterygoid ossifies in membrane from a single center.

THE NASAL BONES

The **nasal bones** (Ossa nasalia) are situated in front of the frontal bones and form the greater part of the roof of the nasal cavity. They have an elongated triangular outline, wide behind, pointed in front. Each presents two surfaces, two borders, and two extremities (Figs. 28, 44, 47, 57, 58).

The **facial surface** is smooth and is convex transversely; the profile contour is usually slightly wavy, with a depression about its middle and a variably prominent area in front.

The **nasal surface** is smooth and concave from side to side. About in its middle it presents the **dorsal turbinate crest** (Crista turbinata dorsalis), which is parallel with the medial border, and has the dorsal turbinate bone attached to it. Most of this surface faces into the nasal cavity, but its posterior part, lateral to the turbinate crest, enters into the formation of the frontal sinus; the latter area is marked off by an oblique ridge which corresponds to the septum between the anterior and posterior parts of the dorsal turbinate bone.

The **medial border** is straight, and meets the opposite bone at the **nasal suture**.

The **lateral border** is irregular. Its anterior third is free and concurs with the nasal process of the premaxilla in forming the **naso-maxillary notch** (Incisura naso-maxillaris). Behind this it joins the end of the nasal process, the maxilla, and the lacrimal, forming the **naso-maxillary** and **naso-lacrimal sutures**.

The greater part of the edge is beveled and fits into a groove on the upper border of the nasal process, the maxilla, and the lacrimal bone.

The **posterior extremity** or base is beveled and overlaps the frontal bone, forming the **naso-frontal suture**.

The **anterior extremity** or apex is pointed and thin.

Development.—Each nasal bone ossifies in membrane from a single center. The nasal suture does not close completely even in old age. In some cases the two plates separate to inclose a small air-space (nasal sinus) in the posterior part.

THE LACRIMAL BONES

The **lacrimal bones** (Ossa lacrimalia) are situated at the anterior part of the orbit, and extend forward on the face to the posterior border of the maxilla. Each presents three surfaces and a circumference (Figs. 28, 47, 48, 57, 58).

The lateral face is clearly divided into orbital and facial parts by the orbital margin. The **orbital surface** (Facies orbitalis) is triangular in outline, smooth and concave; it forms part of the medial and front wall of the orbit. Near the orbital margin it presents a funnel-like **fossa** (Fossa sacci lacrimalis), which is the entrance to the lacrimal canal; the fossa is occupied by the lacrimal sac, which is the dilated origin of the naso-lacrimal duct. Behind this is a depression in which the inferior oblique muscle of the eye takes origin. The **facial surface** (Facies facialis) is more extensive, and has the form of an irregular pentagon. It is slightly convex and smooth in the foal, flattened in the adult. It usually bears the small **lacrimal tubercle**, which is situated nearly an inch (ca. 2 cm.) from the orbital margin. The **orbital margin** (Margo orbitalis) is concave, rough above, smooth below.

The **nasal surface** (Facies nasalis) faces into the frontal and maxillary sinuses. It is concave and very irregular, and is crossed almost horizontally by the **osseous lacrimal canal** (Canalis lacrimalis osseus).

The **circumference** articulates dorsally with the frontal and nasal bones, ventrally with the malar and maxilla, in front with the maxilla, and behind with the frontal. The various sutures so formed are designated by combinations of the names of the bones.

Development.—Each ossifies in membrane from a single center.

THE MALAR BONES

The **malar** or **zygomatic bones** (Ossa zygomatica) are placed between the lacrimal above and the maxilla below and in front. Each is irregularly triangular in outline and presents three surfaces, three borders, and a process (Figs. 28, 47–50).

The **facial surface** (Facies facialis) is smooth, slightly convex, wide in front, and narrow behind. At its lower part it presents the **facial crest,** which is continuous in front with the similar ridge on the maxilla and behind with the zygomatic process of the temporal; the crest is rough below, where the masseter muscle is attached to it.

The **orbital surface** is much smaller than the facial surface, from which it is separated by the concave **orbital margin** (Margo orbitalis). It is concave and smooth, and forms part of the lower and front wall of the orbit.

The **nasal surface** is concave and faces into the maxillary sinus. In the young foal a considerable part of it articulates with the maxilla.

The **dorsal border** articulates with the lacrimal chiefly, but to a small extent behind with the maxilla also.

The **ventral** and **anterior borders** articulate with the maxilla.

The posterior extremity is formed by the **zygomatic process,** which is beveled above and is overlapped by the zygomatic process of the temporal bone.

Development.—Each ossifies in membrane from one or two centers.

THE TURBINATE BONES

These (Ossa turbinata) are delicate, scroll-like bones, four in number, which are attached to the lateral walls of the nasal cavity. They project into the cavity and greatly diminish its extent. Each is composed of a very thin lamina, cribriform in many places, and covered on both sides with mucous membrane in the fresh state. They are arranged in two pairs, dorsal and ventral.

The **dorsal turbinate bone** (Os turbinatum dorsale)[1] is somewhat cylindrical in form, but is flattened from side to side and tapers at each end. It is attached to the turbinate crest of the nasal bone and the nasal plate of the frontal bone. The anterior part is rolled like a scroll one and a half times, thus inclosing a cavity which communicates with the middle meatus nasi. The arrangement is best seen on a cross-section (Fig. 55). The posterior part is curved and its ventral border is attached to the lateral nasal wall, thus helping to inclose a large space which is part of the frontal sinus (Fig. 56). This cavity is separated from that of the scroll-like part by a transverse septum. The **medial surface** is flattened, and is separated from the septum nasi by a narrow interval, the **common nasal meatus** (M. nasi communis). Another narrow passage, the **dorsal nasal meatus** (M. nasi dorsalis), separates the dorsal surface from the roof of the nasal cavity. The space between the ventral surface and the ventral turbinate is the **middle nasal meatus** (M.

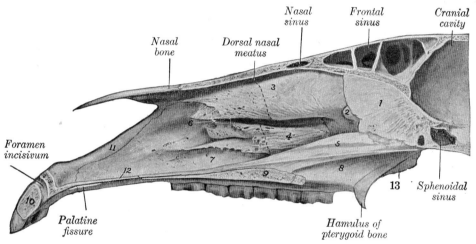

Fig. 44.—Part of Sagittal Section of Skull of Horse.

1, Perpendicular plate of ethmoid bone; 2, great ethmo-turbinate; 3, dorsal turbinate; 4, ventral turbinate; 5, vomer; 6, middle nasal meatus; **7,** ventral nasal meatus; 8, perpendicular part of palatine bone; 9, palatine process of maxilla; 10, body of premaxilla; **11,** nasal process of premaxilla; 12, palatine process of premaxilla; 13, pterygoid process of palatine bone. Dotted lines indicate septa.

nasi medius). The anterior extremity is prolonged toward the nostril by two small bars of cartilage. The posterior extremity is small, and joins the cribriform plate and lateral mass of the ethmoid.

The **ventral turbinate bone** (Os turbinatum ventrale) is shorter and smaller than the upper one. It is attached to the ventral turbinate crest, and consists, like the upper one, of an anterior coiled and a posterior curved portion.

To express briefly the mode of coiling of the two bones of the same side we may say that they are rolled toward the septum and each other. The cavity of the middle part of the dorsal turbinate is divided into several parts by bony plates. The middle part of the ventral turbinate contains a large bulla. These features are seen when the medial part of the bone is removed (Fig. 450a).

The ventral and posterior borders of the posterior part are attached to the maxilla, thus helping to inclose a cavity which is part of the maxillary sinus. The lower surface is separated from the floor of the nasal cavity by the **ventral nasal**

[1] This bone is really a greatly developed first ethmoturbinate (vide p. 51).

meatus (M. nasi ventralis), which is much larger than the other nasal passages. The anterior extremity is prolonged toward the nostril by a curved bar of cartilage.

Development.—Each ossifies in cartilage from a single center.

THE VOMER

The **vomer** is a median bone, which assists in forming the ventral part of the septum nasi. It is composed of a thin lamina which is bent (except in its posterior part) so as to form a narrow groove (Sulcus vomeris), in which the lower part of the perpendicular plate of the ethmoid bone and the septal cartilage are received. The **lateral surfaces,** right and left, are highest near the posterior end and diminish gradually to the anterior end; they are slightly convex dorso-ventrally, and are covered by the nasal mucous membrane during life. The **ventral border** is thin and free in its posterior third, and divides the choanæ or posterior nares medially; in the remainder of its extent it is wider and is attached to the nasal crest. The **anterior extremity** lies above the ends of the palatine processes of the premaxillæ. The **posterior extremity** consists of two **wings** (Alæ vomeris) which extend outward below the body of the presphenoid; posteriorly they form a notch (Incisura vomeris), and laterally join the palatine and pterygoid bones (Fig. 50).

Development.—The vomer is primitively double, and ossifies from a center on either side in the membrane covering the cartilaginous septum nasi; the two laminæ then fuse below and form a groove.

THE MANDIBLE

The **mandible** (Mandibula), or lower jaw bone, is the largest bone of the face. The two halves of which it consists at birth unite during the second or third month, and it is usually described as a single bone. It carries the lower teeth, and articulates by its condyles with the squamous temporal on either side. It consists of a body and two rami (Figs. 28, 45, 51, 59).

The **body** (Corpus mandibulæ) is the thick anterior part which bears the incisor teeth. It presents two surfaces and a border. The **lingual surface** (Facies lingualis) is smooth and slightly concave; during life it is covered by mucous membrane, and the tip of the tongue overlies it. The **mental surface** (Facies mentalis) is convex and is related to the lower lip. It is marked by a median furrow which indicates the position of the primitive symphysis mandibulæ. The curved **alveolar border** (Limbus alveolaris) presents six **alveoli** for the incisor teeth, and a little further back two alveoli for the canine teeth in the male; in the mare the latter are usually absent or small.

The **rami** (Rami mandibulæ) extend backward from the body and diverge to inclose the **mandibular space** (Spatium mandibulare). Each ramus is bent so as to consist of a horizontal part (Pars molaris) which bears the lower cheek teeth, and a vertical part (Pars articularis) which is expanded and furnishes attachment to powerful muscles; the term **angle** is applied to the most prominent part of the curve. The ramus presents two surfaces, two borders, and two extremities. The **lateral surface** is smooth and slightly convex from edge to edge on the horizontal part; at the junction with the body it presents the **mental foramen** (Foramen mentale), which is the external opening of the mandibular canal. On the vertical part it is somewhat concave and presents a number of rough lines for the attachment of the masseter muscle. The **medial surface** of the horizontal part is smooth, and presents a shallow longitudinal depression in its middle; above this there is often a faint **mylo-hyoid line** (Linea mylohyoidea) for the attachment of the muscle of like name. At the lower part of the junction with the body there is a small fossa for the attachment of the genio-hyoid and genio-glossus muscles. On the vertical part the surface is concave, and is marked in its lower and posterior part by rough lines for the attachment of the medial pterygoid muscle. In front of its middle is the **mandibular foramen** (Foramen mandibulare), which is the posterior orifice of the **mandibular canal** (Canalis mandibulæ). The canal curves downward and passes forward below the cheek teeth, opening externally at the mental foramen; it is continued into the body of the bone as a small canal (Canalis alveolaris incisivus), which carries the vessels and nerves to the incisor teeth. The **dorsal** or **alveolar border** (Limbus alveolaris) forms anteriorly part of the **interalveolar space;** here it is thin. Behind this it is thick and is excavated by six **alveoli** for the lower cheek teeth. Behind the last alveolus it curves sharply upward and is narrow and rough. In the young foal there is commonly a small alveolus for the vestige of the first premolar ("wolf tooth") close to the first large one. The **ventral border** of the horizontal part is nearly straight; it is thick and rounded in the young horse, becoming narrower and sharp in old subjects. At its pos-

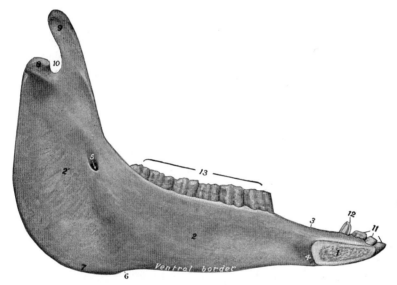

FIG. 45.—LEFT HALF OF MANDIBLE OF HORSE; MEDIAL VIEW.

1, Body of mandible (median section); 2, 2', horizontal and vertical parts of ramus; 3, interalveolar border; 4, depression for attachment of genio-hyoideus muscle; 5, mandibular foramen; 6, vascular impression; 7, angle; 8, condyle; 9, coronoid process; 10, mandibular notch; 11, incisor teeth; 12, canine tooth; 13, cheek teeth.

terior part there is a smooth impression (Incisura vasorum) where the facial vessels and parotid duct turn round the bone. Behind this point the border curves sharply upward, forming the **angle of the mandible** (Angulus mandibulæ); this part is thick and has two roughened lips, separated by a considerable intermediate space; near the condyle it becomes narrower. The **anterior extremity** joins the body. The **articular extremity** comprises the **coronoid process** in front and the **condyle** behind, the two being separated by the **mandibular notch** (Incisura mandibulæ), through which the nerve to the masseter muscle passes. The **coronoid process** (Processus coronoideus) is thin transversely and curved slightly medially and backward. It projects upward in the temporal fossa and furnishes insertion to the temporal muscle. The **condyle** of the mandible (Condylus mandibulæ) lies at a much lower level than the end of the coronoid process. It is elongated transversely and articulates with the squamous temporal through the medium of an articular disc. The part below the condyle is usually termed the **neck** of the mandible (Collum mandibulæ); on its antero-medial part is a depression, the **fovea** pterygoidea, in which the lateral pterygoid muscle is attached. The middle of the vertical part of the ramus consists to a large extent of a single plate of compact substance which may be so thin in places as to be translucent.

Development.—The mandible develops from two chief centers in the connective tissue which overlies the paired Meckel's cartilages. At birth it consists of two symmetrical halves which meet at the median **symphysis mandibulæ.** Fusion usually occurs in the second or third month.

Age Changes.—These are associated largely with the growth, and later with the reduction, of the teeth. In the young horse, in which the teeth are long and are in great part embedded in the bone, the body is thick and strongly curved, and the horizontal part of the ramus is also thick. Later, as the teeth are extruded from the bone, the body becomes flattened and narrower, and the horizontal part of the ramus is thinner, especially in its lower part. In the old subject the angle, the vascular impression in front of it, and the lines for the attachment of tendinous layers of the masseter and pterygoid muscles are more pronounced.

THE HYOID BONE

The **hyoid bone** (Os hyoideum) is situated chiefly between the vertical parts of the rami of the mandible, but its upper part extends somewhat further back. It is attached to the petrous temporal bones by rods of cartilage, and supports the root of the tongue, the pharynx, and the larynx. It consists of a body, a lingual process, and three pairs of cornua.

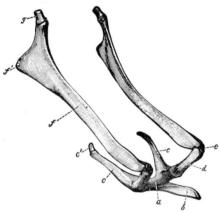

The **body** or **basihyoid** (Corpus ossis hyoidei) is a short transverse bar, compressed dorso-ventrally. The dorsal surface is concave and smooth in its middle, and presents at each end a convex facet or tubercle for articulation with the small cornu. The ventral surface is flattened and is slightly roughened for muscular attachment. The anterior border carries medially the lingual process. The posterior border is concave and smooth in its middle, and carries on either side the thyroid cornu. The body, the lingual process, and the thyroid cornua are fused and may be compared to a spur or a fork with a very short handle.

FIG. 46.—HYOID BONE OF HORSE, VIEWED FROM THE SIDE AND SOMEWHAT FROM IN FRONT.

a, Body; *b*, lingual process; *c*, thyroid cornu; *c'*, cartilage of *c; d*, small cornu; *e*, middle cornu; *f*, great cornu; *f'*, muscular angle of great cornu; *g*, cartilage of great cornu. (Ellenberger-Baum, Anat. d. Haustiere.)

The **lingual process** (Processus lingualis) projects forward medially from the body, and is embedded in the root of the tongue during life. It is compressed laterally and has a blunt-pointed free end. The lateral surfaces are slightly concave. The dorsal border is thin and irregular, and the ventral border is thick and rough.

The **thyroid cornua** or **thyrohyoids** (Cornua thyreoidea)[1] extend backward and upward from the lateral parts of the body. They are compressed laterally (except at their junction with the body), and the posterior end has a short cartilaginous prolongation which is connected with the anterior cornu of the thyroid cartilage of the larynx.

The **small cornua** or **keratohyoids** (Cornua minora) are short rods which are directed upward and forward from either end of the body. Each is somewhat constricted in its middle part and has slightly enlarged ends. The ventral end has

---

[1] These correspond to the great cornua of man.

a small concave facet which articulates with the body. The dorsal end articulates with the great cornu, or with the middle cornu when present.

The **great cornua** or **stylohyoids** are much the largest parts of the bone. They are directed dorsally and backward, and are connected above with the base of the petrous temporal bones. Each is a thin plate, seven or eight inches (ca. 18 to 20 cm.) long, which is slightly curved in its length, so that the lateral surface is concave and the medial surface is convex; both are smooth. The borders are thin. The dorsal extremity is large and forms two angles; the articular angle is connected by a rod of cartilage with the hyoid process of the petrous temporal bone; the muscular angle is somewhat thickened and rough for muscular attachment. The ventral extremity is small, and articulates with the small or the middle cornu.

The **middle cornua** or **epihyoids** are small, wedge-shaped pieces or nodules interposed between the small and great cornua. They are usually transitory, and unite with the great cornua in the adult.

Development.—The hyoid ossifies in the cartilages of the second and third visceral arches. Each part has a separate center, except the lingual process, which ossifies by extension from the body. In the foal there is a separate nucleus at each end of the body which intervenes between the latter and the thyroid cornu; it articulates with the small cornu. The anterior part of the lingual process may be a separate piece.

THE SKULL AS A WHOLE

The skull of the horse has, as a whole, the form of a long, four-sided pyramid, the base of which is posterior. It is convenient, however, to exclude the mandible and hyoid from present consideration. The division between the cranium (Cranium cerebrale) and the face (Cranium viscerale) may be indicated approximately by a transverse plane through the anterior margins of the orbits.

The **dorsal** or **frontal surface** (Norma frontalis) (Fig. 47) is formed by the squamous part of the occipital, interparietal, parietal, frontal, nasal, and premaxillary bones. It may be divided into parietal, frontal, nasal, and premaxillary regions. The **parietal region** extends from the nuchal crest to the parieto-frontal suture. It is marked medially by the **external parietal crest,** which bifurcates in front, the branches becoming continuous with the **frontal crests.** The latter curve outward on either side to the root of the supraorbital process. The **frontal region** is the widest part of the surface, and is smooth and almost flat. It is bounded in front by the naso-frontal suture. On either side of it is the root of the **supraorbital process,** pierced by the **supraorbital foramen.** The **nasal region** is convex from side to side, wide behind, narrow in front. Its profile is in some cases nearly straight; in others it is undulating, with a variably marked depression about its middle and at the anterior end. The **premaxillary region** presents the **osseous nasal aperture** (Apertura nasalis ossea) and the **foramen incisivum.**

The **lateral surface** (Norma lateralis) (Fig. 28) may be divided into cranial, orbital, and preorbital or maxillary regions.

The **cranial region** presents the temporal fossa, the zygomatic arch, and the outer part of the petrous temporal bone. The **temporal fossa** is bound medially by the parietal and frontal crests, laterally by the temporal crest and the zygomatic arch, and behind by the nuchal crest. Its upper and middle parts are rough for the attachment of the temporal muscle. In its lower posterior part are several **foramina** which communicate with the temporal canal. The fossa is continuous in front with the orbital cavity. The **zygomatic arch** is formed by the zygomatic processes of the temporal, malar, and maxilla. Its ventral face presents the **condyle** and **glenoid cavity** for articulation with the lower jaw, through the medium of the articular disc. Behind the glenoid cavity is the **postglenoid process,** and

behind this the **temporal canal** opens.   The **external acoustic process** projects
outward through a deep notch in the ventral margin of the squamous temporal
below the temporal crest.   A little further back is the **mastoid process,** which is
crossed in its upper part by a groove for the posterior meningeal artery (Fig. 40).

The **orbital region** comprises the orbit and the pterygo-palatine fossa.   The

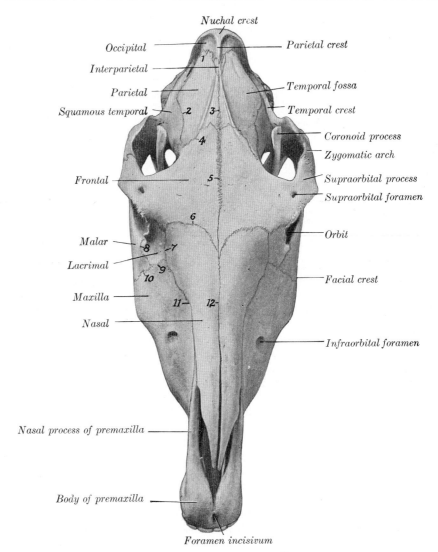

FIG. 47.—SKULL OF HORSE; DORSAL VIEW.

1, Parieto-occipital suture; 2, squamous suture; 3, parietal suture; 4, parieto-frontal suture; 5, frontal suture;
6, naso-frontal suture; 7, naso-lacrimal suture; 8, lacrimo-malar suture; 9, lacrimo-maxillary suture; 10, maxillo-
malar suture; 11, naso-maxillary suture; 12, nasal suture.

orbit is a cavity which incloses the eyeball, with the muscles, vessels, and nerves
associated with it.   It is directly continuous behind with the temporal fossa.
The **axis** of the orbit (Axis orbitæ), taken from the optic foramen to the middle of
the inlet, is directed forward, outward, and slightly upward.   The **medial wall**
(Paries medialis) is complete and extensive.   It is concave and smooth, and is
formed by the frontal and lacrimal and the orbital wing of the sphenoid.   In its

extreme anterior part is the fossa for the lacrimal sac. Behind this there is a small depression in which the inferior oblique muscle of the eye arises; here the plate which separates the orbit from the maxillary sinus is very thin. The **dorsal wall** (Paries dorsalis) is formed by the frontal and to a small extent by the lacrimal bone. It presents the supraorbital foramen, which perforates the root of the supraorbital process. The **ventral wall** (Paries ventralis) is very incomplete, and is formed by the malar, the zygomatic process of the temporal, and to a small extent by the maxilla. The **lateral wall** (Paries lateralis) is the supraorbital process. At the extreme posterior part is the **orbital group of foramina.** Four are situated in front of the pterygoid crest. Of these, the uppermost is the **ethmoidal foramen,** which trans-

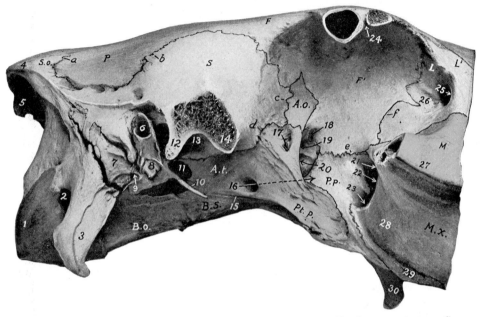

FIG. 48.—CRANIAL AND ORBITAL REGIONS OF SKULL OF HORSE; LATERAL VIEW. THE ZYGOMATIC ARCH AND SUPRA-ORBITAL PROCESS HAVE BEEN SAWN OFF.

S.o., Squamous part of occipital; *P,* parietal; *S,* squamous temporal; *B.o.,* basilar part of occipital; *B.s.,* body of sphenoid; *A.t.,* temporal wing of sphenoid; *A.o.,* orbital wing of sphenoid; *Pt.p.,* pterygoid process of sphenoid; *P.p.,* perpendicular part of palate bone; *F, F′,* facial and orbital parts of frontal bone; *L, L′,* orbital and facial parts of lacrimal bone; *M,* facial part of malar bone; *M.x.,* maxilla; *a,* parieto-occipital suture; *b,* squamous suture; *c, d,* spheno-squamous suture; *e,* fronto-palatine suture; *f,* fronto-lacrimal suture. 1, Occipital condyle; 2, condyloid fossa; 3, paramastoid process; 4, nuchal crest; 5, external occipital protuberance; 6, external acoustic meatus; 7, mastoid process; 8, hyoid process; 9, stylomastoid foramen; 10, muscular process; 11, foramen lacerum; 12, postglenoid process; 13, glenoid cavity; 14, temporal condyle; 15, pterygoid groove; 16, alar canal of pterygoid process indicated by arrow; 17, alar foramen; 18, ethmoidal foramen; 19, optic foramen; 20, foramen orbitale; 21, maxillary foramen; 22, sphenopalatine foramen; 23, posterior palatine foramen; 24, supraorbital foramen (opened); 25, fossa for lacrimal sac; 26, depression for origin of obliquus oculi inferior; 27, facial crest; 28, maxillary tuberosity; 29, alveolar tuberosity; 30, hamulus of pterygoid bone.

mits the ethmoidal vessels and nerve. The **optic foramen** is situated a little lower and further back; it transmits the optic nerve. Just below the optic is the **foramen orbitale,** which transmits the ophthalmic, oculomotor, abducens, and often the trochlear nerve; commonly there is a very small **trochlear foramen** in the crest for the last-named nerve. The **foramen rotundum** is below the foramen orbitale, from which it is separated by a thin plate; it transmits the maxillary nerve. The **alar canal** opens in common with the foramen rotundum, and the anterior opening of the pterygoid canal is also found here. The **foramen alare parvum** is just behind the pterygoid crest and on a level with the foramen orbitale. It is the upper opening of a canal which leads from the alar canal, and through it the anterior deep temporal artery emerges. The **inlet** of the orbital cavity (Aditus orbitæ) is circumscribed by a complete bony ring, which is nearly circular. Its infraorbital margin (Margo infraorbitalis) is smooth and rounded; the supraorbital margin (Margo supraorbitalis) is rough and irregularly notched. During life the cavity is completed by the periorbita, a conical fibrous membrane, the apex of which is attached around the optic foramen. Ventral to the orbital cavity is the **pterygopalatine fossa.** Its wall is formed by the pterygoid process, the perpendicular part of the palate bone, and the tuber maxillare. Its deep anterior recess contains three foramina. The upper one, the **maxillary foramen,** is the entrance to the in-

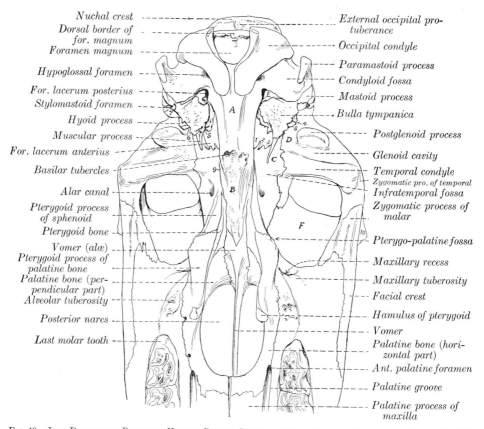

FIG. 49.—LINE DRAWING OF POSTERIOR HALF OF BASE OF SKULL OF HORSE, WITHOUT MANDIBLE. (Key to Fig. 50.)

A, Basilar part of occipital; *B*, body of sphenoid; *C*, temporal wing of sphenoid; *D*, squamous temporal bone; *E*, petrous temporal bone; *F*, orbital part of frontal bone. *1*, Incisura carotica; *2*, incisura ovalis; *3*, incisura spinosa; *4*, external orifice of temporal canal; *5*, osseous auditory or Eustachian tube; *6*, petro-tympanic fissure; *7*, external acoustic process; *8*, hyoid process; *9*, pterygoid groove; *10*, supraorbital process.

fraorbital canal, which transmits the infraorbital nerve and vessels. The **sphenopalatine foramen** perforates the medial wall of the recess and transmits vessels and nerves of like name to the nasal cavity. The lower foramen, the **posterior palatine,** transmits the palatine artery and nerve to the palatine canal. The upper part of the fossa is smooth, and is crossed by the internal maxillary artery and the maxillary nerve. The lower part is chiefly roughened for the attachment of the lateral pterygoid muscle, but is crossed in front by a smooth groove in which the palatine vein lies. In its extreme posterior part is the small opening of the pterygoid canal.

The **preorbital** or **maxillary** region is formed chiefly by the maxilla, but also by the premaxilla and the facial parts of the lacrimal and malar bones. Its contour is approximately triangular, the base being posterior. It offers two principal features. The **facial crest** extends forward from the ventral margin of the orbit, and ends abruptly at a point about an inch and a quarter (ca. 3 to 3.5 cm.) above the

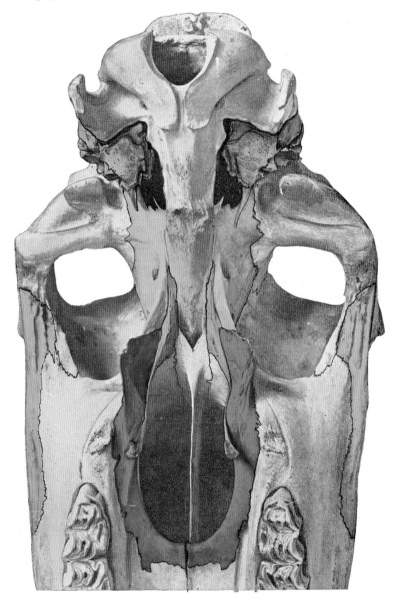

Fig. 50.—Ventral Surface of Skull of Horse, Posterior Half Without Mandible. The skull is inclined slightly. Perpendicular part of palatine bone not in red. (Notation on key Fig. 49.)

third or fourth cheek tooth;[1] its ventral aspect is rough for the attachment of the masseter muscle. The **infraorbital foramen** is situated in a transverse plane about an inch (ca. 2 to 3 cm.) in front of the end of the crest and about two inches (5 cm.)

[1] This relation varies with age. In the new-born foal the posterior part of the second tooth, in the young horse the posterior part of the third tooth, in the older subject the fourth, lies below the end of the crest usually.

above it. The foramen opens forward, and through it the infraorbital artery and nerve emerge. The surface over the premolar teeth varies greatly with age, in conformity with the size of the embedded parts of the teeth. In the young horse the surface here is strongly convex, the outer plate of bone is thin and even defective sometimes in places, and the form of the teeth is indicated by eminences (Juga alveolaria). In the old animal the surface is concave on account of the extrusion of the teeth from the bone. The downward curve of the premaxilla is pronounced in the young subject, very slight in the aged. In some skulls there is a distinct depression a short distance in front of the orbit; here the levator labii superioris proprius arises.

The **ventral** or **basal surface** (Norma basalis), exclusive of the mandible, consists of cranial, choanal, and palatine regions.

The **cranial region** (Basis cranii externa) extends forward to the vomer and pterygoid processes (Fig. 50). At its posterior end is the **foramen magnum,** flanked by the **occipital condyles.** Lateral to these is the **condyloid fossa,** in which is the **hypoglossal foramen,** which transmits the hypoglossal nerve and the condyloid vein. Further outward are the **paramastoid processes** (Processus jugulares) of the occipital bone. Extending forward centrally is a prismatic bar, formed by the basilar part of the occipital and the body of the sphenoid bone; at the junction of these parts are tubercles for the attachment of the ventral straight muscles of the head. On either side of the basilar part of the occipital bone is the **foramen lacerum** (basis cranii), bounded laterally by the base of the petrous temporal bone. In front of these the region becomes very wide on account of the lateral extension of the **zygomatic processes,** which present ventrally the **condyle** and **glenoid cavity** for articulation with the mandible. Beyond this the process turns forward and joins the zygomatic process of the malar, completing the zygomatic arch and the surface for the attachment of the masseter muscle. On either side of the body of the sphenoid is the **infratemporal fossa,** formed by the temporal wing and the root of the pterygoid process of the sphenoid bone. It is bounded in front by the pterygoid crest, which separates it from the orbit and the pterygo-palatine fossa. In it is the **alar canal,** which transmits the internal maxillary artery. A little lower is the entrance to the **pterygoid canal.**

The **choanal region** presents the pharyngeal orifice of the nasal cavity. This is elliptical and is divided in its depth medially by the vomer into two **choanæ** or **posterior nares.** It is bounded in front and laterally by the palate and pterygoid bones, behind by the vomer. It is flanked by the hamular process of the pterygoid bone. The plane of the opening is nearly horizontal, and the length is about twice the width.

The **palatine region** comprises a little more than half of the entire length of the base of the skull (Fig. 43). The **hard palate** (Palatum durum) is concave from side to side, and in its length also in the anterior part. It is formed by the palatine processes of the premaxillæ and maxillæ, and the horizontal parts of the palatine bones. It is circumscribed in front and laterally by the alveolar parts of the maxilla and premaxilla. The **interalveolar space** (Margo interalveolaris) is that part of the arch in which alveoli are not present. Behind the last alveolus is the **alveolar tuberosity,** and medial to this is a groove for the palatine vein. In the middle line is the **median palatine suture** (Sutura palatina mediana). In the line of the suture, a little behind the central incisors, is the **foramen incisivum,** through which the palato-labial artery passes. On either side, parallel with the alveolar part of the maxilla, is the **palatine groove** (Sulcus palatinus), which contains the palatine vessels and nerve. It is continuous at the anterior palatine foramen with the palatine canal, which is situated between the maxilla and the palatine bone. The **palatine fissure** is the narrow interval along the lateral margin of the palatine process of the premaxilla; it is closed in the fresh state by a process of the cartilage of the septum nasi. Scattered along each side of the palate are several accessory foramina. The **transverse palatine suture** (Sutura palatina transversa) is about half an inch from the posterior border. The latter is opposite to the fifth cheek tooth in the adult, and is concave and free.

The **nuchal** or **occipital surface** (Norma occipitalis) is formed by the occipital

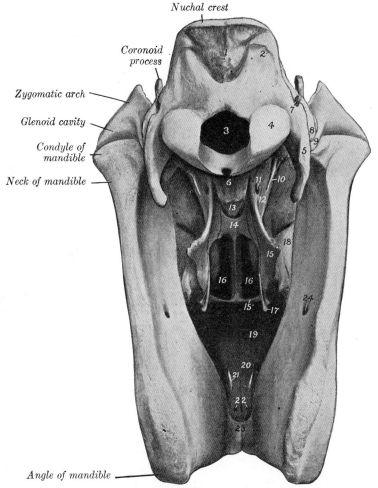

FIG. 51.—SKULL OF HORSE; POSTERIOR VIEW. THE HYOID BONE HAS BEEN REMOVED.

1, External occipital protuberance; 2, curved line; 3, foramen magnum; 4, occipital condyle; 5, paramastoid process; 6, basilar part of occipital; 7, mastoid foramen; 8, mastoid process; 9, postglenoid process; 10, muscular process of petrous temporal; 11, alar canal; 12, pterygoid process of sphenoid; 13, body of sphenoid; 14, vomer; 15, 15', perpendicular and horizontal parts of palatine bone; 16, 16, posterior nares or choanæ; 17, hamulus of pterygoid bone; 18, maxillary tuberosity; 19, palatine process of maxilla; 20, palatine process of premaxilla; 21, palatine fissure; 22, accessory palatine foramina; 23, body of mandible; 24, mandibular foramen.

bone. It is trapezoidal in outline, wider below than above, concave dorso-ventrally, convex transversely. It is separated from the dorsal surface by the **nuchal crest.** Below the crest are two rough areas for the attachment of the complexus muscles. A little lower is a central eminence, the **external occipital protuberance,** on which the ligamentum nuchæ is attached. At the lowest part centrally is the **foramen magnum.** This is bounded laterally by the **occipital condyle,** lateral to which is the **paramastoid process.**

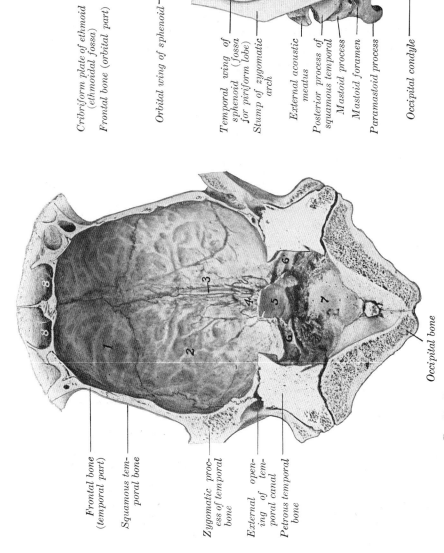

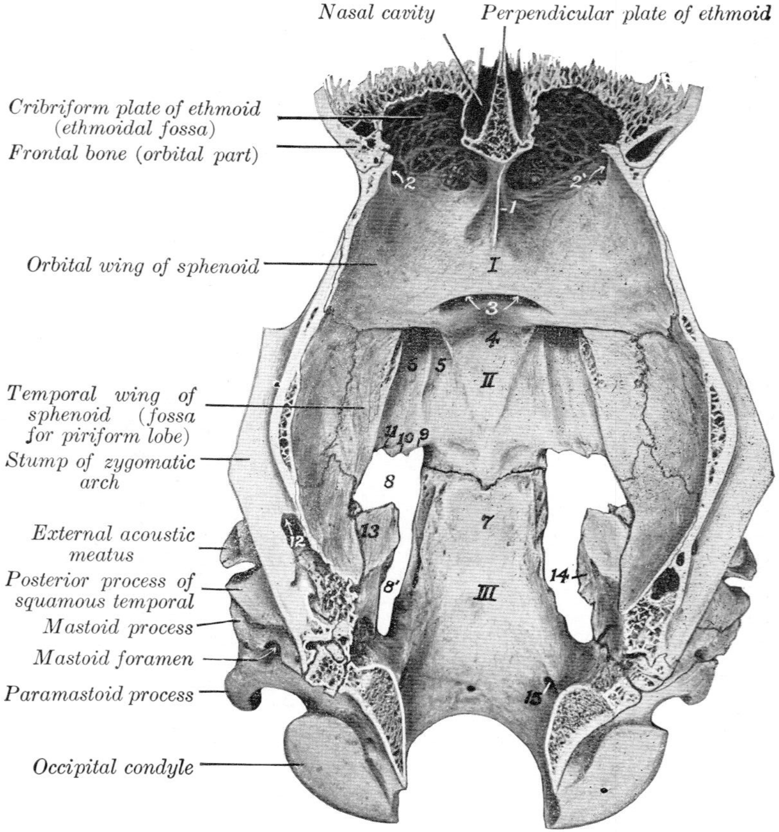

Fig. 53.—Floor of Cranium of Horse.

I, II, III, Anterior, middle, and posterior fossæ of cranium; 1, ethmoidal crest; 2, 2', ethmoidal foramina; 3, optic foramina; 4, hypophyseal or pituitary fossa; 5, groove for cavernous sinus; 6, groove for maxillary nerve; 7, basilar part of occipital bone; 8, 8', foramen lacerum; 9, 10, 11, carotid, oval, and spinous notches of temporal wing of sphenoid; 12, temporal canal; 13, petrous temporal bone; 14, internal acoustic meatus; 15, hypoglossal foramen.

Labels (Fig. 53): Perpendicular plate of ethmoid; Nasal cavity; Cribriform plate of ethmoid (ethmoidal fossa); Frontal bone (orbital part); Orbital wing of sphenoid; Temporal wing of sphenoid (fossa for piriform lobe); Stump of zygomatic arch; External acoustic meatus; Posterior process of squamous temporal; Mastoid process; Mastoid foramen; Paramastoid process; Occipital condyle.

Fig. 52.—Roof of Cranium of Horse.

1, Frontal bone (internal plate); 2, parietal bone; 3, internal parietal crest; 4, interparietal bone; 5, internal occipital protuberance; 6, 6', grooves for transverse sinuses; 7, depression for vermis cerebelli; 8, 8', frontal sinuses.

Labels (Fig. 52): Frontal bone (temporal part); Squamous temporal bone; Zygomatic process of temporal bone; External opening of temporal canal; Petrous temporal bone; Occipital bone.

The **apex** of the skull is formed by the bodies of the premaxillæ and mandible, carrying the incisor teeth.

THE CRANIAL CAVITY

This cavity (Cavum cranii) incloses the brain, with its membranes and vessels. It is relatively small and is ovoid in shape.

The **dorsal wall** or **roof** (Calvaria) (Fig. 52) is formed by the supraoccipital, interparietal, parietal, and frontal bones. In the middle line is the **internal parietal crest,** which joins the ethmoidal crest in front, and furnishes attachment to the falx cerebri. Posteriorly the crest is continued by the sharp anterior margin of the

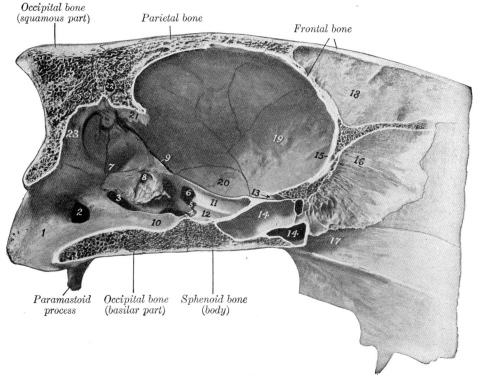

FIG. 54.—SAGITTAL SECTION OF CRANIUM OF HORSE.

1, Lateral wall of foramen magnum; 2, hypoglossal foramen; 3, foramen lacerum posterius; 4, 5 6, carotid, oval, and spinous notches; 7, floccular fossa; 8, internal acoustic meatus; 9, petrosal crest; 10, pons (Fossa pontis) depression; below 12 is the hypophyseal fossa; 11, groove for maxillary nerve; 12, groove for cavernous sinus; 13, optic foramen; 14, 14, sphenoidal sinus; 15, ethmoidal crest; 16, perpendicular plate of ethmoid bone; 17, vomer; 18, septum between frontal sinuses; 19, orbital wing of sphenoid; 20, temporal wing of sphenoid; 21, internal occipital protuberance; 22, canalis transversus; 23, depression for vermis cerebelli.

internal occipital protuberance, which projects downward and forward into the cavity, and gives attachment to the tentorium cerebelli by its sharp lateral edges. Behind this the roof is grooved centrally for the middle lobe or vermis of the cerebellum. **Transverse grooves** pass from the base of the protuberance to the **temporal canals.** The anterior part of the roof is hollowed by the frontal sinus. The occipital part is very thick and strong.

The **lateral wall** (Fig. 54) is formed chiefly by the temporal and frontal bones and the orbital wing of the sphenoid. It is crossed obliquely by the **petrosal crest,** which concurs with the margin of the parietal bone and the internal occipital protuberance in dividing the cavity into cerebral and cerebellar compartments. Behind the crest is a depression for the hemisphere of the cerebellum. Behind this are the internal acoustic meatus and the openings of the aquæductus vestibuli and aquæ-ductus cochleæ.

The roof and lateral walls are marked by digital impressions and vascular grooves.

The **ventral wall** or **floor** (Basis cranii interna) (Fig. 53) may be regarded as forming three fossæ. The **anterior fossa** (Fossa cranii oralis) supports the frontal and olfactory parts of the cerebrum. It is formed chiefly by the presphenoid, and lies at a higher level than the middle fossa. In front the fossa is divided medially by the **ethmoidal crest,** lateral to which are the deep **ethmoidal fossæ** for the olfactory bulbs. The **ethmoidal foramen** perforates the cranial wall at the outer side of these fossæ. Further back the central part of the surface is slightly elevated, and is flanked by shallow depressions which support the olfactory tracts. Posteriorly is a bony shelf which covers the entrance to the **optic canals;** the edge of this shelf and the posterior borders of the orbital wings of the sphenoid may be taken as the line of demarcation between the anterior and middle fossæ. The **middle fossa** (Fossa cranii media) is the widest part of the cavity. It extends backward to the spheno-occipital and petrosal crests, thus corresponding to the postsphenoid. In its middle is the hypophyseal fossa in which the hypophysis cerebri lies. On either side are two grooves: the medial one transmits the cavernous sinus and the ophthalmic, third, and sixth nerves to the foramen orbitale; the lateral one leads to the foramen rotundum, and lodges the maxillary nerve. Lateral to the grooves is a depression for the piriform lobe of the cerebrum. The **posterior fossa** (Fossa cranii posterior) corresponds to the basilar part of the occipital bone. It contains the medulla oblongata, pons, and cerebellum. In front is a median depression (Fossa pontis) for the pons. The surface behind this (Fossa medullæ oblongatæ) is concave transversely and slopes gently downward to the foramen magnum; it supports the medulla oblongata. On either side are the **foramen lacerum** and the **hypoglossal foramen.**

The **anterior** or **nasal wall** (Fig. 33) is formed by the cribriform plate of the ethmoid, which separates the cranium from the nasal cavity. It is perforated by numerous foramina for the passage of the olfactory nerve-bundles.

THE NASAL CAVITY

The **nasal cavity** (Cavum nasi) is a longitudinal passage which extends through the upper part of the face. It is divided into right and left halves by a median **septum nasi.** The **lateral walls** are formed by the maxilla, premaxilla, the per-pendicular part of the palatine, and the turbinate and ethmoid bones in part. This wall is crossed obliquely by the **lacrimal canal** and **groove** for the **naso-lacrimal duct,** and its posterior part is perforated by the **sphenopalatine foramen.** The **dorsal wall** or **roof** is formed by the frontal and nasal bones, which form a median prominence at their junction. It is concave from side to side, and nearly straight longitudinally, except in the posterior part, where it curves downward. The **ven-tral wall** or **floor** is formed by the palatine processes of the premaxillæ and max-illæ, and the horizontal parts of the palate bones. It is wider but considerably shorter than the roof. It is concave transversely, and nearly horizontal from before backward, except in the posterior third, where there is a slight declivity. The anterior part presents a median groove for the cartilage of the septum, and a furrow for the vomero-nasal organ (of Jacobson) on either side. Posteriorly there is a median elevation, the **nasal crest,** to which the vomer is attached. Lateral to the palatine process of the premaxilla is the **palatine fissure.** The **septum nasi osseum** is formed by the perpendicular plate of the ethmoid behind and the vomer below (Fig. 44). In the fresh state it is completed by the **cartilage of the septum nasi** (Fig. 328).

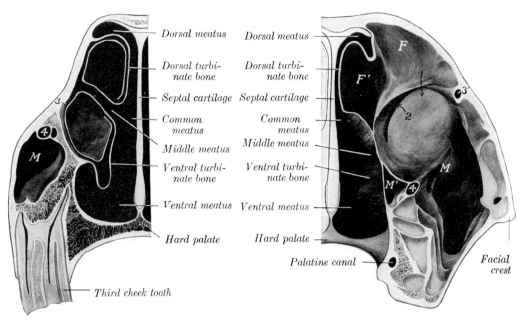

FIG. 55.—PART OF CROSS-SECTION OF NASAL REGION OF SKULL OF HORSE. SECTION IS CUT ABOUT 2 CM. IN FRONT OF FACIAL CREST AND VIEWED FROM IN FRONT.

FIG. 56.—PART OF CROSS-SECTION OF SKULL OF HORSE. SECTION IS CUT JUST IN FRONT OF MEDIAL CANTHUS AND VIEWED FROM BEHIND.

M, Maxillary sinus and M', its turbinate part; F, frontal sinus, and F', its turbinate part; 1, fronto-maxillary opening; 2, naso-maxillary fissure; 3, lacrimal groove; 3', lacrimal canal; 4, infraorbital canal.

The turbinate bones divide each half of the nasal cavity into three **meatus nasi**. The **dorsal meatus** (Meatus nasi dorsalis) is a narrow passage between the roof and the dorsal turbinate bone. It ends at the cribriform plate of the ethmoid.

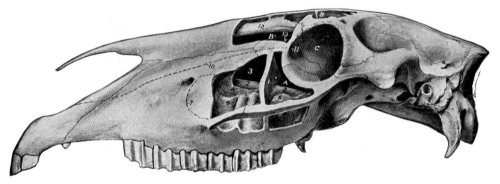

FIG. 57.—SKULL OF YOUNG HORSE; LATERAL VIEW, WITH SINUSES OPENED UP.

A', A, Anterior and posterior compartments of maxillary sinus; B, B', frontal and turbinate parts of frontal sinus; C, orbit; 1, septum between compartments of maxillary sinus; 2, 2, infraorbital canal; 3, turbinate part of maxillary sinus; 4, 5, 6, last three cheek teeth (covered by thin plate of bone); 7, anterior limit of maxillary sinus in older subject; 8, infraorbital foramen; 9, anterior end of facial crest; 10, course of naso-lacrimal duct; 11, fossa for lacrimal sac; 12, dorsal turbinate bone; 13, fronto-maxillary opening.

The **middle meatus** (Meatus nasi medius) is the space between the two turbinate bones. In its posterior part is the very narrow opening into the maxillary sinus. The **ventral meatus** (Meatus nasi ventralis) is the channel along the floor which is overhung by the ventral turbinate bone; it is much the largest and is the direct path between the nostrils and posterior nares.

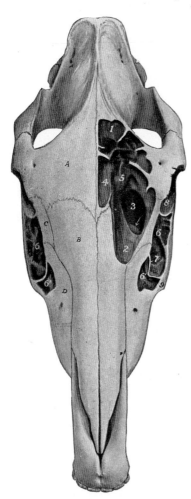

FIG. 58.—SKULL OF YOUNG HORSE; DORSAL VIEW, WITH SINUSES OPENED UP.

1, 2, Ends of frontal sinus; 3, fronto-maxillary opening; 4, dorsal turbinate bone; 5, lateral mass of ethmoid bone; 6, 6′, two compartments of maxillary sinus; 7, septum between 6 and 6′; 8, orbit; 9, anterior end of facial crest; A, frontal bone; B, nasal bone; C, lacrimal bone; D, maxilla. Note difference in position and form of septum in maxillary sinus as compared with preceding figure.

The osseous nasal aperture (Apertura nasi ossea) is bounded by the nasal bones and the premaxillæ.

The posterior extremity or fundus is separated from the cranial cavity by the cribriform plate of the ethmoid, and is largely occupied by the lateral masses of that bone.

THE PARANASAL SINUSES

Connected directly or indirectly with the nasal cavity, of which they are diverticula, are four pairs of air-sinuses (Sinus paranasales), viz., maxillary, frontal, sphenopalatine, and ethmoidal.

The **maxillary sinus** (Sinus maxillaris) is the largest. Its lateral wall is formed by the maxilla, the lacrimal, and the malar. It is bounded medially by the maxilla, the ventral turbinate, and the lateral mass of the ethmoid bone. It extends backward to a transverse plane in front of the root of the supraorbital process, and its anterior limit is indicated approximately by a line drawn from the anterior end of the facial crest to the infraorbital foramen. Its dorsal boundary corresponds to a line drawn backward from the infraorbital foramen parallel to the facial crest. The ventral wall or floor is formed by the alveolar part of the maxilla; it is very irregular and is crossed by bony plates running in various directions. The last three cheek teeth project up into the cavity to an extent which varies with age; they are covered by a thin plate of bone. The cavity is divided into anterior and posterior parts by an oblique **septum** (Septum sinus maxillaris). The lateral margin of the septum is commonly about two inches (ca. 5 cm.) from the anterior end of the facial crest; from here it is directed inward, backward, and upward. The upper part of the septum (formed by the posterior end of the ventral turbinate bone) is very delicate and usually cribriform.

The position and shape of the septum are very variable. It is often further forward—in some cases even as far forward as the anterior end of the facial crest. Exceptionally it is much nearer the orbit than is stated above. In the recent state, i. e., when covered by the mucous membrane on both surfaces, it is nearly always complete, but in very exceptional cases there is an opening of variable size in the upper part. In the mule the septum may be partial or entirely absent.

The **anterior compartment** (often called the inferior maxillary sinus) is partially divided by the infraorbital canal into a lateral maxillary part and a medial smaller turbinate part. The latter communicates with the middle meatus by a very narrow slit situated at its highest part. The **posterior compartment** (often called the superior maxillary sinus) is also crossed by the infraorbital canal, over which it opens freely into the sphenopalatine sinus. It communicates dorsally with the frontal sinus through the large oval **fronto-maxillary opening,** situated at the level of the osseous lacrimal canal and the corresponding part of the medial wall of the orbit; the orifice is commonly about one and a half to two inches (ca. 4 to 5 cm.) long and an inch or more (2 to 3 cm.) wide. Just in front of this, and covered by a thin plate, is the narrow **naso-maxillary opening** (Ostium maxillare), by which the sinus opens into the posterior part of the middle meatus.

The foregoing statements refer to the arrangement in the average adult animal. In the foal the cavity (with the exception of its turbinate part) is largely occupied by the developing teeth. In horses five to six years of age the maxillary part of the sinus is filled up to a large degree by the embedded parts of the teeth. As the teeth are extruded to compensate the wear, more and more of the cavity becomes free, until in old age only the short roots project up in the floor, covered by a layer of bone. Other facts in this connection will be given in the description of the teeth. In exceptional cases the posterior part of the ventral turbinate is smaller than usual and leaves a considerable interval, through which the maxillary sinus communicates with the nasal cavity. The fronto-maxillary opening is very variable in size.

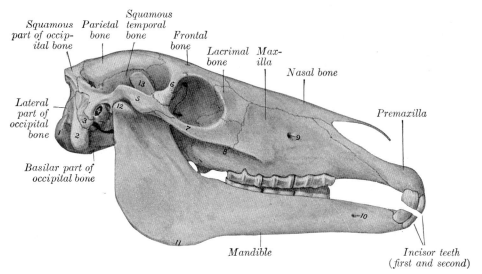

FIG. 59.—SKULL OF FOAL ABOUT TWO MONTHS OLD.

This figure illustrates differential features of skull of young foal as compared with that of adult animal shown in Fig. 28. 1, Occipital condyle; 2, paramastoid process; 3, mastoid process; 4, external acoustic meatus; 5, zygomatic process of temporal bone; 6, supraorbital process of frontal bone; 7, zygomatic process of malar bone; 8, facial crest; 9, infraorbital foramen; 10, mental foramen; 11, angle of mandible; 12, condyle of mandible; 13, coronoid process of mandible.

The **frontal** or **fronto-turbinate sinus** (Sinus frontalis) consists of frontal and turbinate parts. The **frontal part** is bounded chiefly by the two plates of the frontal bone, but its floor is formed in part by the lateral mass of the ethmoid. It extends forward to a plane through the anterior margins of the orbits, backward to one through the temporal condyles, and outward into the root of the supraorbital process. It is separated from the sinus of the opposite side by a complete **septum** (Septum sinuum frontalium). It is partially subdivided by a number of bony plates. The **turbinate part** is situated in the posterior part of the dorsal turbinate bone, roofed in by the nasal and lacrimal bones. It extends forward to a transverse plane about half-way between the anterior margin of the orbit and the infraorbital foramen. It is in free communication behind with the frontal part over the lateral mass of the ethmoid. It is separated from the nasal cavity by the thin turbinate plate. The frontal and maxillary sinuses communicate through the large opening described above.

The **sphenopalatine sinus** (Sinus sphenopalatinus) consists of two parts which usually communicate under the lateral mass of the ethmoid. The sphenoidal (posterior) part is excavated in the body of the presphenoid. The palatine (anterior) part is between the two plates of the perpendicular part of the palatine bone, under the lateral mass of the ethmoid; it communicates freely with the maxillary sinus. The septum between the right and left sinuses is not usually median in the sphenoidal part. In about one-third of the cases (according to Paulli) the sphenoidal and palatine parts are separated by a transverse septum, and the sphenoidal part then communicates only with the ventral ethmoidal meatuses.

The term **ethmoidal sinus** is often applied to the cavity of the largest ethmoturbinate. It communicates with the maxillary sinus through an opening in the lateral lamina.

THE BONES OF THE THORACIC LIMB

The thoracic limb (Extremitas thoracalis) consists of four chief segments, viz., the shoulder girdle, the arm, the forearm, and the manus.

The **shoulder girdle** (Cingulum extremitatis thoracalis), when fully developed, consists of three bones—the **scapula** (or shoulder-blade), the **coracoid,** and the **clavicle** (or collar-bone). In the domesticated mammals only the scapula, a large, flat bone, is well developed, and the small coracoid element has fused with it, while the clavicle is either absent or is a small rudiment embedded in the brachiocephalicus muscle. There is therefore no articulation of the shoulder with the axial skeleton.

The shoulder girdle is fully developed in birds and the lower mammals (monotremata). In the higher mammals the coracoid is reduced to the coracoid process of the scapula, and the development of the clavicle is in conformity with the function of the limb. Thus in typical quadrupeds, such as the horse and ox, in which the forelimbs are used only for support and locomotion, the clavicle is absent. Other animals which use these limbs for grasping, burrowing, climbing, etc. (*e.g.*, man, apes, moles), have well-developed clavicles which connect the scapula with the sternum.

The **arm** (Brachium) contains a single long bone, the **humerus** (or arm bone).

In the **forearm** (Antibrachium) are two bones, the **radius** and **ulna.** These vary in relative size and mobility. In the horse and ox the two bones are fused, and the distal part of the limb is fixed in the position of pronation. The radius is placed in front and supports the weight. The ulna is well developed only in its proximal part, which forms a lever for the extensor muscles of the elbow. In the pig the ulna is the larger and longer of the two bones, but is closely attached to the back of the radius. In the dog the ulna is also well developed and a small amount of movement is possible between the two bones.

The **manus,**[1] the homologue of the hand in man, consists of three subdivisions, viz., the **carpus, metacarpus,** and **digit** or **digits.**

The **carpus,** popularly termed the "knee" in animals, and homologous with the wrist of man, contains a group of short bones, the **ossa carpi.**[2] These are typi-

---

[1] It is unfortunate that there is no popular name for this part of the limb. The term "forefoot" is sometimes applied to it, but this leads to confusion, since the word "foot" has long been used in a different sense.

[2] The term "knee" as applied to this region is unfortunate, but the usage is very firmly established and there is no other popular name.

cally eight in number and are arranged in two transverse rows—a proximal or anti-brachial, and a distal or metacarpal. The bones of the proximal row, named from the radial to the ulnar side (*i. e.*, from within outward), are the **radial, intermediate, ulnar,** and **accessory** carpal bones. The bones of the distal row are designated numerically, in the same direction, as **first, second, third,** and **fourth** carpal bones.

This nomenclature, introduced by Gegenbaur, and now used largely by comparative anatomists, seems decidedly preferable to the variety of terms borrowed from human anatomy and based on the form of the bones in man. The following table of synonyms in common use is appended for comparison. The Latin terms and abbreviated notations are given in parentheses. The central carpal bone (Os carpi centrale) is omitted, since it is not a separate element in the animals under consideration here.

```
Radial (Os carpi radiale, Cr)..................................Scaphoid
Intermediate (Os carpi intermedium, Ci).....................Semilunar
Ulnar (Os carpi ulnare, Cu)..................................Cuneiform
Accessory (Os carpi accessorium, Ca).........................Pisiform
First carpal (Os carpale primum, C1).........................Trapezium
Second carpal (Os carpale secundum, C2).....................Trapezoid
Third carpal (Os carpale tertium, C3).......................Os magnum
Fourth carpal (Os carpale quartum, C4)......................Unciform
```

The **metacarpus** contains typically five **metacarpal bones** (Ossa metacarpalia I–V), one for each digit; they are long bones and are designated numerically from the radial to the ulnar side (*i. e.*, from within outward). This arrangement occurs in the dog, although the first metacarpal is much smaller than the others, and the second and fifth are somewhat reduced. Further reduction has taken place in the other animals, resulting in the perissodactyl and artiodactyl forms. In the horse the first and fifth metacarpals are absent, the third is the large supporting metacarpal bone and carries the single digit, while the second and fourth are much reduced. In artiodactyls (*e. g.*, ox, sheep, pig) the third and fourth are the chief metacarpals and carry the well developed digits; they are fused in the ox and sheep. The others are variously reduced or absent, as noted in the special descriptions to follow.

The fossil remains of the ancestors of the existing Equidæ illustrate in a most complete manner the reduction which has occurred in this respect. The earliest known ancestor of the horse, Eohippus of the Lower Eocene, had four well developed metacarpal bones, each of which carried a digit; the first metacarpal bone was small. Intermediate forms show the gradual evolution of the race from this primitive animal, which was about the size of the domestic cat. There is reason to believe that earlier forms had five digits.

The **digits** (Digiti manus) are homologous with the fingers of man, and are typically five in number. They are designated numerically from the radial to the ulnar side, in correspondence with the metacarpus. The full number is present in the dog. In the ox and pig the third and fourth are well developed and support the weight, while the second and fifth are reduced. The existing horse has a single digit, the third of his pentadactyl ancestors. The skeleton of each fully developed digit consists of three **phalanges** and certain **sesamoid bones.** The **first phalanx** (Phalanx prima) articulates with the corresponding metacarpal bone above and with the **second phalanx** (Phalanx secunda) below. The **third phalanx** (Phalanx tertia) is inclosed in the hoof or claw, and is modified to conform to the latter. The **sesamoid bones** (Ossa sesamoidea) are developed along the course of tendons or in the joint capsules at points where there is increased pressure. Two **proximal sesamoids** (Ossa sesamoidea phalangis primæ) occur at the flexor side of the metacarpo-phalangeal joint and form a pulley for the flexor tendon. The **distal sesamoid** (Os sesamoideum phalangis tertiæ) is similarly placed between the deep flexor tendon and the joint between the second and third phalanx; it is absent in the dog, which has a small sesamoid on the extensor side of the metacarpo-phalangeal joint, and often at the proximal interphalangeal joint also.

Numerous cases are recorded of the occurrence of supernumerary digits (hyperdactylism) in the horse and other animals. In some pigs, on the other hand, the two chief digits are fused, and the condition (syndactylism) appears to be inherited.

THE SCAPULA

The **scapula** is a flat bone which is situated on the anterior part of the lateral wall of the thorax; its long axis extends obliquely from the fourth thoracic spine to the sternal end of the first rib. It is curved slightly and slopes outward in adaptation to the form of the thoracic wall. It is triangular in outline, and has two surfaces, three borders, and three angles.

The **lateral surface** (Facies lateralis) is divided into two fossæ by the **spine of the scapula** (Spina scapulæ), which extends from the vertebral border to the neck of the bone, where it subsides. The free edge of the spine is thick, rough, and in great part subcutaneous. A little above its middle there is a variable prominence, the **tuber spinæ,** to which the trapezius muscle is attached. The **supraspinous fossa** (Fossa supraspinata) is situated in front of the spine, and the **infraspinous fossa** (Fossa infraspinata) behind it. The former is much the smaller of the two; it is smooth and is occupied by the supraspinatus muscle. The infraspinous fossa lodges the infraspinatus muscle; it is wide and smooth in its upper part, narrower below, where it is marked by several rough lines for muscular attachment; near the neck is the **nutrient foramen,** and a little lower is a **vascular groove.**

The **costal surface** (Facies costalis) is hollowed in its length by the **subscapular fossa** (Fossa subscapularis); this occupies nearly the whole of the lower part of the surface, but is pointed above and separates two rough triangular areas, **facies serrata,** to which the serratus ventralis muscle is attached. In the lower third there is a **vascular groove** with several branches.

The **anterior border** (Margo cranialis) is convex and rough above, concave and smooth below.

The **posterior border** (Margo caudalis) is slightly concave. It is thick and rough in its upper third, thin in its middle, and thickens again below.

The **vertebral border** (Margo vertebralis) carries the **scapular cartilage** (Cartilago scapulæ). In the young subject this edge of the bone is thick, and is pitted by impressions into which the cartilage fits. The cartilage is the unossified part of the fœtal scapula. Its lower edge fits the depressions and elevations of the bone. It thins out toward the free edge, which is convex and lies alongside of the vertebral spines. In front it continues the line of the bone, but behind it forms a rounded projection. The lower part of the cartilage undergoes more or less ossification, so that the vertebral border of the bone in old subjects is thin, irregular, and porous.

The **anterior** or cervical **angle** (Angulus cranialis) is at the junction of the

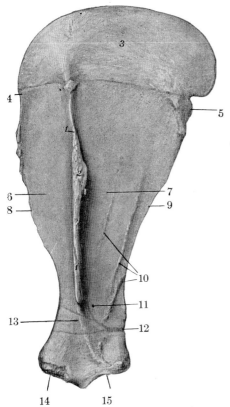

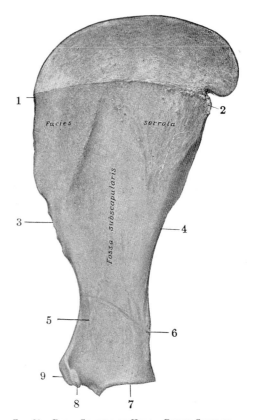

FIG. 60.—LEFT SCAPULA OF HORSE; LATERAL SURFACE,

1, Spine; 2, tuber spinæ; 3, cartilage; 4, anterior angle; 5, posterior angle; 6, supraspinous fossa; 7, infraspinous fossa; 8, anterior border; 9, posterior border; 10, muscular lines; 11, nutrient foramen; 12, vascular groove; 13, neck; 14, tuber scapulæ; 15, glenoid cavity.

FIG. 61.—RIGHT SCAPULA OF HORSE; COSTAL SURFACE.

1, Anterior angle; 2, posterior angle; 3, anterior border; 4, posterior border; 5, neck; 6, vascular groove; 7, glenoid cavity; 8, coracoid process; 9, tuber scapulæ.

anterior and vertebral borders and lies opposite to the second thoracic spine. It is relatively thin and is about a right angle.

The **posterior** or dorsal **angle** (Angulus caudalis) is thick and rough; it is opposite to the vertebral end of the seventh rib, and its position can be determined readily in the living animal.

The **glenoid** or articular **angle** (Angulus glenoidalis) is joined to the body of the bone by the **neck of the scapula** (Collum scapulæ). It is enlarged, especially in the sagittal direction. It bears the **glenoid cavity** (Cavitas glenoidalis) for articulation with the head of the humerus. The cavity is oval in outline, and its margin is cut into in front by the **glenoid notch** (Incisura glenoidalis), and is rounded off laterally; just above its postero-lateral part is a tubercle to which a tendon of the teres minor is attached. The **tuber scapulæ**[1] is the large rough prominence in front, to which the tendon of origin

[1] Formerly termed the bicipital tuberosity.

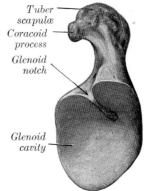

FIG. 62.—GLENOID ANGLE OF LEFT SCAPULA OF HORSE; END VIEW.

of the biceps brachii is attached; projecting from its medial side is the small **coracoid process** (Processus coracoideus), from which the coraco-brachialis muscle arises.

Development.—The scapula has four centers of ossification, viz., one each for the body of the bone, the tuber scapulæ and coracoid process, the anterior part of the glenoid cavity, and the tuber spinæ. The last ossifies after birth and fuses with the spine about the third year. The tuber scapulæ and coracoid process fuse with the body of the bone about the end of the first year.

In old subjects the spongy substance disappears at the middle part of the fossæ, so that the bone consists here of a thin layer of compact substance. Considerable ossification of the cartilage is usual, the borders become much rougher, the muscular lines are more pronounced, and a medullary cavity may appear in the neck. Much variation occurs in dimensions and slope. The average ratio between the length and breadth (scapular index) is about 1 : 0.5, but in many cases the base is relatively wider. The inclination on a horizontal plane varies from 60 to 70 degrees. Exceptionally the coracoid process reaches a length of an inch or more (2½ to 3 cm.), and the chief nutrient foramen may be on the posterior border or in the subscapular fossa.

THE HUMERUS

The **humerus** is a long bone which extends from the shoulder above, where it articulates with the scapula, to the elbow below and behind, where it articulates with the radius and ulna. It is directed obliquely downward and backward, forming an angle of about 55 degrees with a horizontal plane. It consists of a shaft and two extremities.

The **shaft** (Corpus humeri) is irregularly cylindrical and has a twisted appearance. It may be regarded as having four surfaces. The **lateral surface** (Facies lateralis) is smooth and is spirally curved, forming the **musculo-spiral groove** (Sulcus musculi brachialis), which contains the brachialis muscle; the groove is continuous with the posterior surface above and winds around toward the front below. The **medial surface** (Facies medialis) is nearly straight in its length, rounded from side to side, and blends with the anterior and posterior surfaces. Just above its middle is the **teres tuberosity** (Tuberositas teres), to which the tendon of the latissimus dorsi and teres major muscles is attached. The **nutrient foramen** is in the distal third of this surface. The **anterior surface** (Facies cranialis) is triangular, wide and smooth above, narrow and roughened below. It is separated from the lateral surface by a distinct border, the **crest** of the humerus (Crista humeri), which bears above its middle the **deltoid tuberosity** (Tuberositas deltoidea). From the latter a rough line curves upward and backward to the lateral surface of the neck, and gives origin to the lateral head of the triceps muscle. Below the tuberosity the border inclines forward, becomes less salient, and ends at the coronoid fossa. The **posterior surface** (Facies caudalis) is rounded from side to side and smooth.

The **proximal extremity** (Extremitas proximalis) consists of the head, neck, two tuberosities, and the intertuberal groove. The **head** (Caput humeri) presents an almost circular convex articular surface, which is about twice as extensive as the glenoid cavity of the scapula, with which it articulates. In front of the head is a fossa, in which are several foramina. The **neck** (Collum humeri) is well defined behind, but is practically absent elsewhere.[1] The **lateral tuberosity** (Tuberositas lateralis) is placed antero-laterally, and consists of two parts: the anterior part forms the lateral boundary of the intertuberal or bicipital groove and gives attachment to the lateral branch of the supraspinatus muscle; the posterior part gives attachment to the short insertion of the infraspinatus, while its outer surface is coated with cartilage, over which the chief tendon of the same muscle passes to be

---

[1] This is the so-called "surgical neck" (Collum chirurgicum). The "anatomical neck" (Collum anatomicum) is, however, indicated by the shallow depression which separates the head from the tuberosities, and gives attachment to the joint capsule.

inserted into a triangular rough area below the anterior part. The **medial tuberosity** (Tuberositas medialis) is less salient, and consists of anterior and posterior parts; the anterior part forms the medial boundary of the intertuberal groove, and furnishes insertion to the medial branch of the supraspinatus above, and the posterior deep pectoral muscle below; the posterior part gives attachment to the subscapularis muscle. The **intertuberal** or **bicipital groove** (Sulcus intertuberalis)[1] is situated in front; it is bounded by the anterior parts of the tuberosities, and is subdivided by an intermediate ridge. The groove is covered in the fresh state by

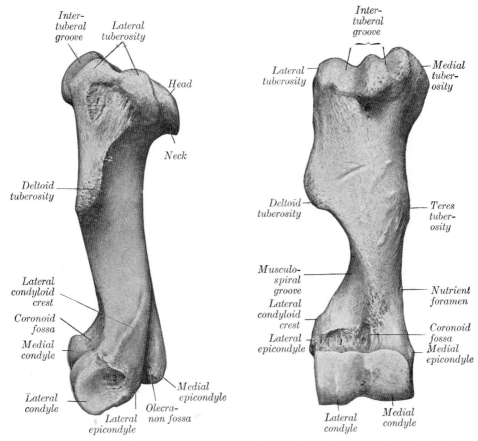

FIG. 63.—LEFT HUMERUS OF HORSE; LATERAL VIEW.

1, Rough area to which tendon of infraspinatus is attached; 2, curved line; 3, depression for attachment of lateral ligament.

FIG. 64.—RIGHT HUMERUS OF HORSE; FRONT VIEW.

1, Rough area for attachment of extensor carpi radialis and extensor digitalis communis; 2, synovial fossa.

cartilage, and lodges the tendon of origin of the biceps brachii muscle. Just below the intermediate ridge is a small fossa in which several foramina open.

The **distal extremity** has an oblique surface for articulation with the radius and ulna, which consists of two condyles of very unequal size, separated by a ridge. The **medial condyle** (Condylus medialis) is much the larger, and is crossed by a sagittal groove, on the anterior part of which there is usually a synovial fossa. Posteriorly the groove extends upward considerably above the rest of the articular surface and reaches the olecranon fossa, and this part articulates with the semilunar

[1] The name "intertuberal" is designative of the position of the groove, while the term "bicipital" has reference to its occupation by the tendon of the biceps brachii. The term "sulcus intertubercularis" is also in common use.

notch of the ulna. The **lateral condyle** (Condylus lateralis) is much smaller and is placed somewhat lower and further back, giving the extremity an oblique appearance; it is marked by a wide shallow groove. The **coronoid fossa** (Fossa coronoidea) is situated in front, above the groove on the medial condyle; it furnishes origin to part of the extensor carpi, and lateral to it is a rough depression from which the common digital extensor arises. Behind and above the condyles are two thick ridges, the epicondyles. The **medial epicondyle** (Epicondylus medialis) is the more salient; it furnishes origin to flexor muscles of the carpus and digit, and bears a tubercle for the attachment of the medial ligament of the elbow joint. The **lateral epicondyle** (Epicondylus lateralis) bears laterally the **condyloid crest** (Crista condyloidea), which forms here the outer boundary of the musculo-spiral groove, and gives origin to the extensor carpi radialis. Below this is a rough excavation in which the lateral ligament is attached. The distal border of the epicondyle gives attachment to the ulnaris lateralis. Between the epicondyles is the deep **olecranon fossa** (Fossa olecrani), into which the processus anconæus projects.

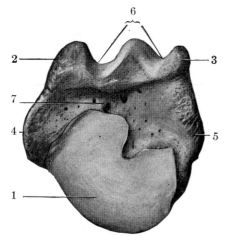

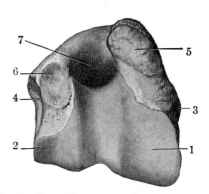

Fig. 65.—Proximal Extremity of Left Humerus of Horse; End View.

1, Head; 2, 3, anterior parts of lateral and medial tuberosities; 4, 5, posterior parts of lateral and medial tuberosities; 6, intertuberal groove; 7, fossa.

Fig. 66.—Distal Extremity of Left Humerus of Horse; End View.

1, Medial condyle; 2, lateral condyle; 3, part of medial epicondyle to which medial ligament is attached; 4, depression in which lateral ligament is attached; 5, 6, areas of attachment of flexor and extensor muscles of carpus and digit; 7, olecranon fossa.

Development.—The humerus ossifies from six centers, viz., three primary centers for the shaft and extremities, and three secondary centers for the lateral tuberosity, the deltoid tuberosity, and the medial epicondyle respectively. The proximal end fuses with the shaft at about three and one-half years, the distal at about one and a half years of age.

THE RADIUS

The **radius** is much the larger of the two bones of the forearm in the horse. It extends in a vertical direction from the elbow, where it articulates with the humerus, to the carpus. It is gently curved, the convexity being dorsal. It consists of a shaft and two extremities.

The **shaft** (Corpus radii) is curved in its length, somewhat flattened from before backward, and widened at its ends. It presents for description two surfaces and two borders. The **dorsal surface** (Facies dorsalis) is smooth, slightly convex in its length, and rounded from side to side. The **volar surface** (Facies volaris) is correspondingly concave in its length and is flattened in the transverse direction. At its proximal part there is a smooth shallow groove, which concurs with the ulna in the formation of the **interosseous space** of the forearm (Spatium interosseum antibrachii); the nutrient foramen is in the lower part of this groove. Below this there is in the young subject a narrow, rough, triangular area to which the ulna is

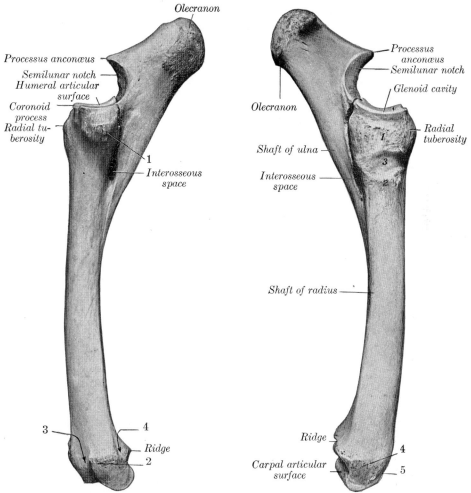

FIG. 67.—LEFT RADIUS AND ULNA OF HORSE; LATERAL VIEW.

1, Tuberosity for attachment of lateral ligament of elbow joint, and common and lateral extensor muscles; 2, tuberosity for attachment of lateral ligament of carpal joint; 3, groove for common extensor tendon; 4, groove for lateral extensor tendon.

FIG. 68.—LEFT RADIUS AND ULNA OF HORSE; MEDIAL VIEW.

1, Tuberosity for attachment of short part of medial ligament of elbow; 2, prominence for long part of same; 3, groove for end of brachialis muscle; 4, tuberosity for attachment of medial ligament of carpal joint; 5, oblique groove for tendon of extensor carpi obliquus.

attached by an interosseous ligament; in the adult the two bones are fused here. A variable rough elevation distal to the middle and close to the medial border gives attachment to the radial check ligament. The **medial border** (Margo medialis) is slightly concave in its length and is largely subcutaneous; at its proximal end there is a smooth area on which the tendon of insertion of the brachialis muscle lies, and a small rough area just below gives attachment to that muscle and the long medial ligament of the elbow-joint. The **lateral border** (Margo lateralis) is more strongly curved, but presents no special features.

The **proximal extremity** or **head** (Extremitas proximalis radii) is flattened from before backward and wide transversely. It presents the **humeral articular surface** (Facies articularis humeralis) which corresponds to that of the distal end of the humerus; it is crossed by a sagittal ridge, which has a synovial fossa on its posterior part, and ends in front at a prominent lip, the **coronoid process** (Processus coronoideus). Just below the posterior border, and separated by a depression, there are two concave **facets** (Facies articularis ulnaris) for articulation with the ulna, and between these and the interosseous space is a quadrilateral rough area at which the two bones are united by an interosseous ligament. At the medial side of the dorsal surface is the **radial tuberosity** (Tuberositas radii), into which the biceps tendon is inserted. The **medial tuberosity** (Tuberositas proximalis medialis) is continuous with the preceding eminence, and gives attachment to the short part of the medial ligament of the elbow-joint. The **lateral tuberosity** (Tuberositas proximalis lateralis) is more salient; it gives attachment to the lateral ligament and to the common and lateral extensor muscles of the digit.

The **distal extremity** is also compressed from before backward. It presents the **carpal articular surface** (Facies articularis carpea), which consists of three parts. The medial facet is the largest, is quadrilateral, concavo-convex from before backward, and articulates with the radial carpal bone; the intermediate one is somewhat similar in form but smaller, and articulates with the intermediate carpal bone; the lateral facet is smaller, is convex, and articulates below with the ulnar carpal and behind with the accessory carpal. The dorsal surface presents three **grooves,** separated by ridges. The middle one is vertical and gives passage to the tendon of the extensor carpi radialis; the lateral one is similar and contains the tendon of the common digital extensor; the medial one is small and oblique and lodges the tendon of the extensor carpi obliquus. The volar aspect is crossed by a rough ridge, below which are three depressions. On each side is a tuberosity (Tuberculum ligamenti) to which the collateral ligament is attached; the lateral one is marked by a small vertical groove for the passage of the lateral extensor tendon.

Development.—The radius ossifies from four centers, viz., one each for the shaft, the two extremities, and the lateral part of the distal end; the last is morphologically the distal end of the ulna which has fused with the radius, and the line of fusion is often indicated by a distinct groove on the carpal articular surface. The proximal extremity unites with the shaft at about one and a half years, the distal end at about three and a half years usually.

THE ULNA

The **ulna** of the horse is a reduced long bone situated behind the radius, with which it is partially fused in the adult.

The **shaft** (Corpus ulnæ) is three-sided and tapers to a point distally. The **dorsal surface** (Facies dorsalis) is applied to the volar surface of the radius, and below the interosseous space the two bones are fused in the adult. The surface which enters into the formation of the space is smooth and usually presents a small nutrient foramen, directed upward. Above the space it is rough and is attached to the radius by an interosseous ligament which is usually permanent. The **medial surface** (Facies medialis) is smooth and slightly concave. The **lateral surface** (Facies lateralis) is flattened. The **medial** and **lateral borders** (Margo medialis, lateralis) are thin and sharp, except at the interosseous space. The **volar border** (Margo volaris) is slightly concave in its length and is rounded. The distal end is pointed and is usually a little below the middle of the radius. It is commonly continued by a fibrous cord to the distal tuberosity of the radius, but this band may be replaced in part or entirely by bone.

The **proximal extremity** (Extremitas proximalis) is the major part of the bone. It projects upward and somewhat backward behind the distal end of the humerus, and forms a lever arm for the extensor muscles of the elbow. The **medial surface** is concave and smooth. The **lateral surface** is convex and is roughened above. The **dorsal border** bears on its middle a pointed projection, the **processus anconæus** or "beak," which overhangs the **semilunar notch** (Incisura semilunaris). The latter is triangular in outline, concave from above downward, convex transversely, and articulates with the humerus; in its lower part there is an extensive synovial fossa. Just below the notch are two convex **facets** which articulate with those on the volar aspect of the proximal end of the radius. The **volar border** is nearly straight, and is thick and rounded. The free end or summit is a rough tuberosity, the **ole-cranon**, which gives attachment to the triceps brachii and other muscles.

The primitive **distal extremity** has, as previously stated, fused with the radius.

Development.—The ulna ossifies from three centers, of which one is for the main part of the bone, one for the olecranon, and one for the distal end. The cartilaginous embryonic ulna extends the entire length of the forearm. The distal part of the shaft is usually reduced to a small fibrous band or may disappear entirely; in some cases a variable remnant of it ossifies. The distal ex-

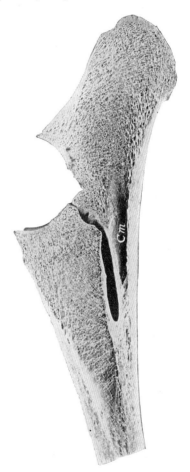

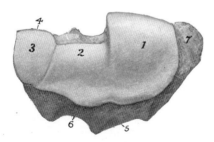

FIG. 69.—DISTAL END OF LEFT RADIUS AND ULNA OF HORSE; END VIEW.

1, 2, 3, 4, Facets which articulate with radial, intermediate, ulnar, and accessory carpal bones respectively; 5, groove for tendon of extensor carpi radialis; 6, groove for tendon of common digital extensor; 7, tuberosity for attachment of medial ligament of carpal joint.

FIG. 70.—SAGITTAL SECTION OF UPPER PART OF RADIUS AND ULNA OF HORSE.

Cm, Medullary cavity of ulna.

tremity fuses before birth with the radius. The olecranon unites with the rest of the bone at about three and a half years. A medullary cavity appears to occur constantly in the adult—contrary to the statements of some authors.

THE CARPAL BONES

The carpal skeleton consists of seven or eight **carpal bones** (Ossa carpi) arranged in two rows, proximal or antibrachial and distal or metacarpal. The (abbreviated) names and relative positions of the bones of the left carpus are indicated below:

		Proximal Row:			
Medial	Radial	Intermediate	Ulnar	Accessory	Lateral
		Distal Row:			
	First	Second	Third	Fourth	

THE RADIAL CARPAL BONE

The **radial carpal** bone (Os carpi radiale) is the largest bone of the proximal row; it is somewhat compressed transversely, and is clearly six-sided. The **proximal surface** is convex in front, concave behind, and articulates with the medial facet on the distal end of the radius. The **distal surface** is also convex in front and concave behind; it articulates with the second and third carpal bones. The **lateral surface** bears upper and lower facets on its anterior part for articulation with the intermediate; between and behind these it is excavated and rough. The **dorsal surface** is rough and slightly convex. The **medial surface** and the **volar surface** are rough and tuberculate.

THE INTERMEDIATE CARPAL BONE

The **intermediate carpal** bone (Os carpi intermedium) is somewhat wedge-shaped, wider in front than behind. The **proximal surface** is saddle-shaped, and articulates with the middle facet on the distal end of the radius. The **distal surface** is smaller, convex in front, concave behind, and articulates with the third and fourth carpal bones. The **medial surface** has upper and lower facets for articulation with the radial carpal, and between these it is excavated and rough. The **lateral surface** is similar to the preceding and articulates with the ulnar carpal. The **dorsal surface** is rough and slightly convex. The **volar surface** bears a tuberosity on its lower part.

THE ULNAR CARPAL BONE

The **ulnar carpal** bone (Os carpi ulnare) is the smallest and most irregular bone of the proximal row. The **proximal surface** is concave and fits the lower part of the lateral facet on the distal end of the radius. The **distal surface** is oblique and undulating for articulation with the fourth carpal bone. The **medial surface** has upper and lower facets for articulation with the intermediate. The **dorsal** and **lateral surfaces** are continuous, convex, and rough. The **volar surface** is oblique, and bears a concave facet for articulation with the accessory carpal bone; below this is a tubercle.

THE ACCESSORY CARPAL BONE

The **accessory carpal** bone (Os carpi accessorium) is situated behind the ulnar carpal bone and the lateral part of the distal end of the radius. It is discoid and presents for description two surfaces and a circumference. The **medial surface** is concave and forms the lateral wall of the carpal groove. The **lateral surface** is convex and rough; a smooth groove for a tendon crosses its anterior part obliquely downward and slightly forward. The **dorsal border** bears two facets; the proximal one is concave and articulates with the back of the lateral facet on the distal end of the radius; the distal one is convex and articulates with the ulnar carpal bone. The remainder of the circumference is rounded and rough.

The accessory does not directly bear weight, and may be regarded as a sesamoid bone interposed in the course of the tendons of the middle and lateral flexors of the carpus, which it enables to act at a mechanical advantage. The posterior border furnishes attachment to the transverse carpal ligament, which completes the carpal canal for the flexors of the digit.

THE FIRST CARPAL BONE

The **first carpal** bone (Os carpale primum) is a small inconstant bone, commonly about the size and shape of a pea, which is embedded in the distal part of the medial ligament of the carpus, behind the second carpal bone. It appears to be absent on both sides in about half of the cases; in a good many subjects it is present on one side only. In size it varies from a minute nodule to a discoid or cylindrical mass 12–15 mm. in length. In exceptional cases it articulates with both the second carpal and the second metacarpal bone, in other cases with the former only, but in the majority of specimens no articular facet is present.

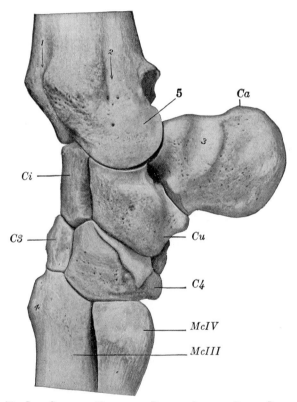

Fig. 71.—Left Carpus of Horse, with Parts of Adjacent Bones; Lateral View.

Ci, Intermediate carpal; Cu, ulnar carpal; Ca, accessory carpal; C3, third carpal; C4, fourth carpal; **McIII**, McIV, metacarpal bones; 1, groove for common extensor tendon; 2, groove for lateral extensor tendon; 3, groove for long tendon of ulnaris lateralis; 4, metacarpal tuberosity; 5, original distal end of ulna, which is fused with the radius and regarded as part of the latter.

THE SECOND CARPAL BONE

The **second carpal** bone (Os carpale secundum) is the smallest constant bone of the distal row, and is irregularly hemispherical in shape. The **proximal surface** is a convex facet, which is continued upon the **volar surface** and articulates with the radial carpal. The **lateral surface** faces obliquely outward and forward, and bears three facets for articulation with the third carpal bone. The **dorsal** and **medial surfaces** are continuous and bear a tuberosity to which the collateral ligament is attached. The **distal surface** is articular and consists of a large flattened facet for the second or inner metacarpal bone, and a small one for the third or large metacarpal bone. Some specimens have a small facet on the lower part of the volar surface which articulates with the first carpal bone.

THE THIRD CARPAL BONE

The **third carpal** bone (Os carpale tertium) is much the largest bone of the

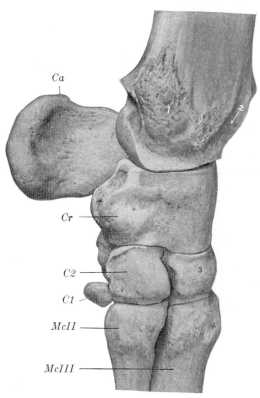

Ca

Cr

C2

C1

McII

McIII

FIG. 72.—LEFT CARPUS OF HORSE, WITH PARTS OF ADJACENT BONES; MEDIAL VIEW.

Cr, Radial carpal; *Ca*, accessory carpal; *C1*, first carpal; *C2*, second carpal; *McII*, *McIII*, metacarpal bones; 1, tuberosity of radius for attachment of medial ligament of carpus; 2, groove for tendon of extensor carpi obliquus; 3, third carpal; 4, metacarpal tuberosity.

distal row, forming more than two-thirds of the width of the latter. It is flattened from above downward, and is twice as wide in front as behind. The **proximal surface** consists of two facets separated by an antero-posterior ridge; the medial facet is concave and articulates with the radial carpal; the lateral facet— for the intermediate carpal—is concave in front and convex behind, where it encroaches on the volar surface. The **distal surface** is slightly undulating, and articulates almost entirely with the third or large metacarpal bone, but it usually bears a small oblique facet at its medial side for the second metacarpal, and there is commonly a non-articular depression laterally. The **medial surface** faces backward and inward, and bears three facets for articulation with the second carpal, between which it is excavated and rough. The **lateral surface** has three facets for articulation with the fourth carpal, and is depressed and rough in its middle. The **dorsal surface** is convex and is crossed by a rough transverse ridge. The **volar surface** is relatively small, and is rounded; its upper part is encroached upon by the proximal articular surface, below which it is rough.

THE FOURTH CARPAL BONE

The **fourth carpal** bone (Os carpale quartum) is somewhat wedge-shaped, and is readily distinguished from the second by its greater size and its volar tubercle. The **proximal surface** articulates with the intermediate and ulnar; it is convex and curves outward, backward, and downward, encroaching on the lateral and volar surfaces. The **distal surface** bears two medial facets for the third or large metacarpal and a lateral one for the fourth or lateral metacarpal bone. The **medial surface** has three facets for articulation with the third carpal, between which it is excavated and rough. The **dorsal surface** is convex and rough. The **lateral sur-**

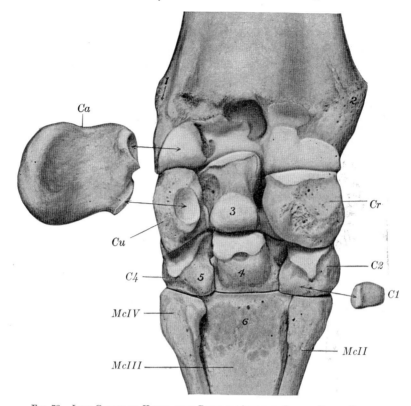

FIG. 73.—LEFT CARPUS OF HORSE, WITH PARTS OF ADJACENT BONES; VOLAR VIEW.

The accessory and first carpal bones have been moved out of their natural position and their articular connections indicated by arrows. *Cr*, Radial carpal; 3, intermediate carpal; *Cu*, ulnar carpal; *Ca*, accessory carpal; *C1*, first carpal; *C2*, second carpal; 4, third carpal; *C4*, fourth carpal; 1, groove for lateral extensor tendon; 2, tuberosity of radius for medial ligament of carpal joint; 5, volar tubercle of fourth carpal; 6, rough area on large metacarpal bone for attachment of suspensory ligament.

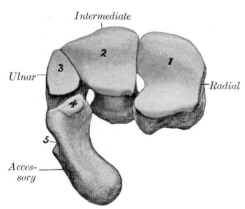

FIG. 74.—PROXIMAL ROW OF LEFT CARPUS OF HORSE;
PROXIMAL VIEW.

1–4, Articular facets corresponding with those on Fig. 69;
5, groove for tendon of ulnaris lateralis.

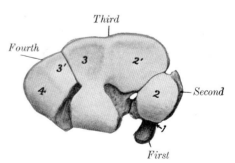

FIG. 75.—DISTAL ROW OF LEFT CARPUS OF HORSE:
PROXIMAL VIEW.

1, Articulation of first carpal with second; 2, 2', facets for radial; 3, 3', facets for intermediate; 4. facet for ulnar.

face is small, being encroached upon by the proximal articular surface.   The **volar surface** bears a tubercle on its distal part.[1]

THE CARPUS AS A WHOLE

The bones of the carpus, exclusive of the accessory, form an irregular quadrangular mass, the width of which is about twice the height or the dorso-volar diameter. The **dorsal surface** is convex from side to side, depressed along the line of junction of the two rows, and prominent below.   The **volar surface** is in general slightly

convex, but very irregular.   It forms with the accessory carpal the **carpal groove** (Sulcus carpi), which in the recent state is rendered smooth by the volar ligament; it is converted into the **carpal canal** (Canalis carpi) for the flexor tendons by the transverse carpal ligament, which stretches across from the accessory bone to the medial side.   The **proximal surface** is widest medially and is elevated in front, concave behind; it is entirely articular and adapted to the carpal articular surface of the radius.   The **distal surface** is also articular and is irregularly faceted in adaptation to the surfaces of the metacarpal bones; each of the distal bones usually articulates with two metacarpal bones, but sometimes the third rests on the third metacarpal only. The **medial** and **lateral surfaces** are both irregular and rough, the former being the wider.   With the exception of the accessory, ulnar, and second, each bone articulates with two bones of the other row.

Development.—Each ossifies from a single center.

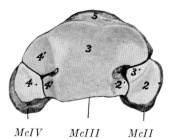

McIV   McIII   McII

Fig. 76.—Right Metacarpal Bones of Horse; Volar View.

1, Nutrient foramen of large (third) metacarpal bone; 2, 3, 4, proximal extremities; 5, surface for attachment of suspensory ligament; 6, sagittal ridge of distal end of large metacarpal bone; 7, 7′, distal ends of small (second and fourth) metacarpal bones.

Fig. 77.—Proximal Extremities of Left Metacarpal Bones of Horse; End View.

2, 2′, Facets for second carpal bone; 3, 3′, facets for third carpal bone; 4, 4′, facets for fourth carpal bone; 5, metacarpal tuberosity.

THE METACARPAL BONES

Three **metacarpal bones** (Ossa metacarpalia) are present in the horse.   Of these, only one, the third or large metacarpal bone, is fully developed and carries a digit; the other two, the second and fourth, are much reduced, and are commonly called the small metacarpal or "splint" bones.

THE THIRD OR LARGE METACARPAL BONE

This (Os metacarpale tertium) is a very strong long bone, which is situated vertically between the carpus and the first phalanx.   It consists of a shaft and two extremities.

---

[1] This bone is probably equivalent to the fourth and fifth carpals of forms in which five carpal elements are present in the distal row.

The **shaft** (Corpus) is semicylindrical, and presents two surfaces and two borders. The **dorsal surface** is smooth, convex from side to side, and nearly straight in its length. The **volar surface** is somewhat convex from side to side and, with the small bones, forms a wide groove which lodges the suspensory ligament. On either side of its proximal two-thirds it is roughened for the attachment of the small metacarpal bones. The **nutrient foramen** occurs at the junction of the proximal and middle thirds. The distal part is wider and flattened. The **borders,** lateral and medial, are rounded.

The **proximal extremity** (Extremitas proximalis) bears an undulating articular surface adapted to the distal row of carpal bones. The greater part supports the third carpal bone; the oblique lateral part, separated from the preceding by a ridge, articulates with the fourth, and a small facet for the second is usually found at the medio-volar angle. On either side is a notch separating two small facets which articulate with the proximal ends of the small metacarpal bones. Toward the medial side of the dorsal surface is the **metacarpal tuberosity,** into which the extensor carpi radialis is inserted. The volar surface is roughened for the attachment of the suspensory ligament.

The **distal extremity** (Extremitas distalis) presents an articular surface for the first phalanx and the proximal sesamoid bones, which is composed of two condyles, separated by a sagittal ridge; the medial condyle is slightly the larger. On either side is a small fossa, surmounted by a tubercle, for the attachment of the collateral ligaments of the fetlock joint.

The large metacarpal is one of the strongest bones in the skeleton. The compact substance is specially thick in front and medially. The medullary cavity extends further toward the ends than in most of the long bones of the horse and there is little spongy substance.

THE SMALL METACARPAL BONES

These, numerically the second and fourth metacarpal bones (Ossa metacarpalia secundum et quartum), are situated on either side of the volar surface of the large metacarpal bone, and form the sides of the metacarpal groove. Each consists of a shaft and two extremities.

The **shaft** (Corpus) is three-sided and tapers to the distal end. It is variably curved, convex toward the middle line of the limb. The **attached surface** is flattened and is rough, except in its lower part; it is attached to the large metacarpal bone by an interosseous ligament, except near the distal end. The **dorsal or abaxial surface** is smooth and rounded from side to side above, grooved below. The **volar** or **axial surface** is smooth and concave from edge to edge, except below, where it forms a rounded edge.

The **proximal extremity** (Extremitas proximalis) is relatively large. In the case of the medial bone it usually bears two facets above which support the second and third carpal bones, while the lateral bone has here a single facet for articulation with the fourth carpal bone. Each has also two facets for articulation with the large metacarpal, and is elsewhere roughened for the attachment of ligaments and muscles. The medial bone may present a small facet behind for the first carpal bone.

The **distal extremity** (Extremitas distalis) is usually a small nodule, which projects to a variable extent in different subjects, and is easily felt in the living animal. It is situated two-thirds to three-fourths of the way down the region.

The small metacarpal bones vary much in length, thickness, and curvature. In the majority of cases the medial bone is the longer; in other subjects the lateral one is the longer or there is no material difference. Sometimes the curvature is very pronounced, so that the distal end causes a decided projection. The distal end is very variable in size and may be a mere point; in other cases, especially in large draft horses, it may present a prolongation which is regarded as the vestige of the digital skeleton.

Development.—The large metacarpal bone ossifies from three centers. The proximal extremity unites with the shaft before birth, the distal extremity toward the middle of the second year. The small metacarpal bones ossify from two centers, one of which is for the proximal extremity. Their distal ends are cartilaginous at birth. Fusion of the middle part of the shaft with the large metacarpal bone is common.

THE PHALANGES

THE FIRST PHALANX

The **first phalanx** (Phalanx prima) is a long bone, and is situated between the large metacarpal bone and the second phalanx. It is directed obliquely downward and forward, forming an angle of about 55 degrees with the horizontal plane in well-formed limbs. It consists of a shaft and two extremities.

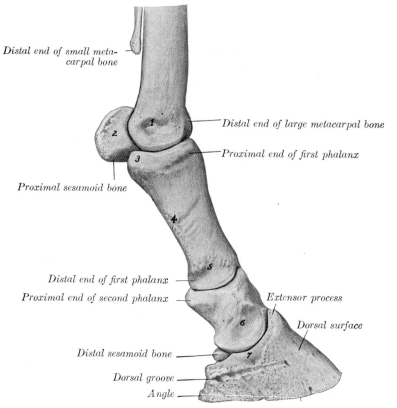

FIG. 78.—SKELETON OF DIGIT AND DISTAL PART OF METACARPUS OF HORSE; LATERAL VIEW.
1–7, Eminences and depression for attachment of ligaments. Cartilage of third phalanx is removed.

The **shaft** (Corpus) is wider and much thicker above than below, and presents two surfaces and two borders. The **dorsal surface** is convex from side to side and smooth. The **volar surface** is flattened, and bears a triangular rough area, bounded by ridges which begin at the proximal tuberosities and converge distally; this area furnishes attachment to the distal sesamoidean ligaments. The **borders, medial** and **lateral,** are rounded and have a rough area or a tubercle on their middle parts.

The **proximal extremity** (Extremitas proximalis) is relatively large. It bears an articular surface adapted to the distal end of the large metacarpal bone, consisting of two glenoid cavities separated by a sagittal groove; the medial cavity is a little larger than the lateral one. On each side is a buttress-like tuberosity for ligamentous attachment. The dorsal surface has a slight elevation for the attachment of the extensor tendons.

The **distal extremity** (Extremitas distalis) is smaller, especially in its dorsovolar diameter. It presents a trochlea for articulation with the second phalanx, consisting of a shallow sagittal groove separating two condyles; the medial con-

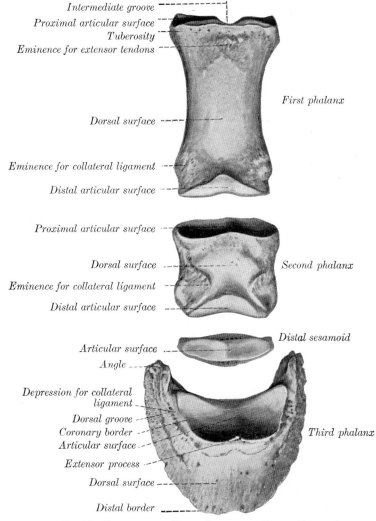

Intermediate groove
Proximal articular surface
Tuberosity
Eminence for extensor tendons

First phalanx

Dorsal surface

Eminence for collateral ligament
Distal articular surface

Proximal articular surface

Dorsal surface
Second phalanx
Eminence for collateral ligament
Distal articular surface

Distal sesamoid
Articular surface
Angle
Depression for collateral
    ligament
Dorsal groove
Coronary border
Articular surface
Third phalanx
Extensor process
Dorsal surface

Distal border

FIG. 79.—PHALANGES AND DISTAL SESAMOID OF HORSE; DORSAL ASPECT.

dyle is a little the larger, and the two are separated posteriorly by a notch. On either side, just above the margin of the articular surface, is a depression surmounted by a tubercle, to both of which the collateral ligament is attached. Behind the tubercle is a distinct mark to which the superficial flexor tendon is attached.

Development.—The first phalanx ossifies from three centers. The distal end unites with the shaft before birth, the proximal end at about one year of age.

The first phalanx contains a small medullary cavity below the middle of the shaft. It may be remarked that the bone is twisted slightly; when placed volar surface down on the table, it touches the latter by three points only, the proximal tuberosities and the medial condyle.

THE SECOND PHALANX

The **second phalanx** (Phalanx secunda) is situated between the first and third phalanges, its direction corresponding to that of the first phalanx. It is flattened from before backward, and its width is greater than its height. It may be described as possessing four surfaces.

The **proximal surface** presents two glenoid cavities separated by a low ridge, and articulates with the first phalanx. The middle of the dorsal border is elevated and roughened in front for the attachment of the common extensor tendon. The volar border is thick and overhanging; in the fresh state its middle part is covered with cartilage, over which the deep flexor tendon passes. On either side there is an eminence, to which the collateral ligament and the superficial flexor tendon are attached.

The **distal surface** is trochlear, and articulates with the third phalanx and distal sesamoid bone. It resembles somewhat the trochlea of the first phalanx, but is more extensive and encroaches more on the dorsal and volar surfaces.

The **dorsal surface** is convex from side to side and smooth in its middle; on each side of its distal part is a rough depression, surmounted by a tuberosity, to both of which ligaments are attached.

The **volar surface** is smooth and flattened. The borders which separate the dorsal and volar surfaces are concave from above downward, rounded from before backward.

Development.—The second phalanx ossifies like the first, but the proximal end unites with the shaft two or three months earlier.

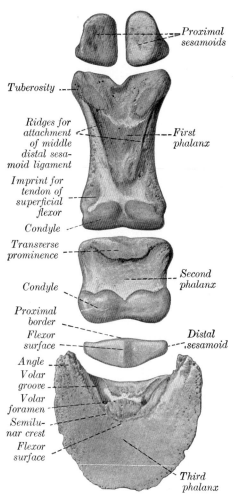

Labels on figure:
Proximal sesamoids
Tuberosity
Ridges for attachment of middle distal sesamoid ligament
Imprint for tendon of superficial flexor
Condyle
Transverse prominence
Condyle
Proximal border
Flexor surface
Angle
Volar groove
Volar foramen
Semilunar crest
Flexor surface
First phalanx
Second phalanx
Distal sesamoid
Third phalanx

FIG. 80.—DIGITAL BONES OF FORE LIMB OF HORSE; VOLAR ASPECT.

THE THIRD PHALANX

The **third phalanx** (Phalanx tertia) is entirely inclosed by the hoof, to which it conforms in a general way. It presents for examination three surfaces, three borders, and two angles.

The **articular surface** (Facies articularis) faces upward and backward, and is chiefly adapted to the distal surface of the second phalanx, but a narrow, flattened area along the volar border articulates with the distal sesamoid. The **proximal** or **coronary border** bears a central eminence, the **extensor process** (Processus extensorius), to which the common extensor tendon is attached. On either side is a depression for the attachment of the collateral ligament.

The **dorsal** or wall **surface** (Facies dorsalis) slopes downward and forward. The angle of inclination on the ground plane is about 45 to 50 degrees in front.

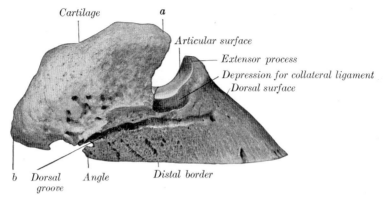

Cartilage   *a*

Articular surface

Extensor process

Depression for collateral ligament

Dorsal surface

b   Dorsal   *Angle*   *Distal border*
groove

FIG. 81.—THIRD PHALANX OF HORSE; LATERAL VIEW.

a, b, Anterior and posterior extremities of cartilage.

Laterally the height diminishes, and the slope becomes steeper, especially on the medial side. From side to side the curvature is almost semicircular. The surface is rough and porous, somewhat resembling pumice stone. It is perforated by numerous foramina of various sizes, a series of larger ones (Foramina marginalia) being on or near the distal border. On each side the **dorsal groove** (Sulcus dorsalis) passes forward from the angle and ends at one of the larger foramina. In the fresh state this surface is covered by the corium of the wall of the hoof. The **distal border** is thin, sharp, and irregularly notched; there is commonly a wider notch in front.

The **volar surface** (Facies volaris) is arched, and divided into two unequal parts by a curved rough line, the **semilunar crest** (Crista semilunaris). The larger area in front of the crest is crescent-shaped, concave, and comparatively smooth; it corresponds to the sole of the hoof, and may be termed the **sole surface.** The part behind the crest is much smaller, and is semilunar; it is related to the deep flexor tendon, and is hence called the **flexor surface** (Facies flexoria).[1] It presents a central prominent rough area, on either side of which is the **volar foramen**

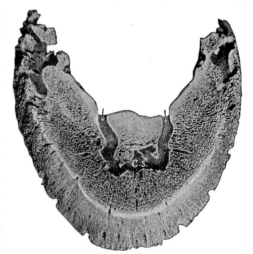

FIG. 82.—SECTION OF THIRD PHALANX OF HORSE.

Section is cut approximately parallel with volar surface and opens up the semilunar canal (*C.s.*). Volar foramina indicated by arrows.

(Foramen volare), to which the **volar groove** (Sulcus volaris) conducts from the angle. The foramina lead into the **semilunar canal** (Canalis semilunaris) within the bone, from which small canals lead to some of the foramina of the dorsal surface. The deep flexor tendon is inserted into the semilunar crest and the central

[1] This may be regarded as the true volar surface.

rough area behind it. The volar grooves and foramina transmit the terminations of the digital arteries into the semilunar canal, where they meet and form a terminal arch, from which branches pass through canals in the bone and emerge through the foramina on the dorsal surface.

The **angles** (Anguli) are prismatic masses which project backward on either side; the medial one is usually the shorter. Each is divided into upper and lower parts by a notch, or is perforated by a foramen or canal which leads to the dorsal groove. The proximal border carries the cartilage.

The **cartilages** of the third phalanx (Cartilagines phalangis tertiæ) are rhomboid curved plates which surmount the angles on either side. They are relatively large and extend above the margin of the hoof sufficiently to be palpable (Fig. 710). The abaxial surface is convex, the axial concave. The proximal border is sinuous and thin; the distal is thicker and is in part attached to the angle. The anterior end is attached by ligament to the side of the second phalanx. The posterior end curves toward its fellow at the heel, and is perforated by numerous foramina for the passage of veins.

The size and form of the angles vary much in different specimens. In the newborn foal the lower part of the angle is a small, pointed projection. Later the process of ossification invades the lower part of the cartilage to a varying extent. In some cases the greater part of the cartilage is ossified—a condition commonly termed "sidebone." In the young subject the cartilage is hyaline, but later it changes to the fibrous type.

Development.—The ossification of the third phalanx is peculiar. While the proximal articular part is still cartilaginous, a perichondrial cap of bone is formed in relation to the hoof. Later the process extends into the upper part.

Structure.—The interior of this bone is channeled by numerous canals for vessels, most of which radiate from the semilunar canal to the dorsal surface; these are not canals for nutrient vessels of the bone, but transmit arteries to the corium of the hoof. Thick layers of compact substance are found at the articular and flexor surfaces and the extensor process, i. e., at the points of greatest pressure and traction.

Fig. 83.—Phalanges of New-born Foal; Dorsal View.

Cartilages of third phalanx removed.

Fig. 84.—Phalanges and Distal Sesamoid of New-born Foal; Volar View.

Cartilages of third phalanx removed.

The Sesamoid Bones

The two **proximal sesamoids** (Ossa sesamoidea phalangis primæ) are situated behind the distal end of the large metacarpal bone, and are closely attached to the first phalanx by strong ligaments. Each has the form of a three-sided pyramid. The **articular surface** (Facies articularis) conforms to the corresponding part of the distal end of the large metacarpal bone. The **flexor surface** (Facies flexoria) is flattened and oblique; in the fresh state it is covered by a layer of cartilage which also fills the interval between the opposed borders of the two bones, and forms a smooth groove for the deep flexor tendon. The **abaxial surface** is concave, and gives attachment to part of the suspensory ligament: it is separated from the flexor surface by a rough everted border. The **base** is distal, and furnishes attachment to the distal sesamoidean ligaments. The **apex** is proximal and is rounded.

The **distal sesamoid** or **navicular bone** (Os sesamoideum phalangis tertiæ) is shuttle-shaped, and is situated behind the junction of the second and third phalanges. Its long axis is transverse, and it possesses two surfaces, two borders, and two extremities. The **articular surface** (Facies articularis) faces upward and forward; it consists of a central eminence, flanked by concave areas, and articulates with the distal end of the second phalanx. The **flexor** or **tendon surface** (Facies flexoria) is directed downward and backward. It resembles the articular surface in form, but is more extensive and not so smooth. In the fresh state it is coated with cartilage and the deep flexor tendon plays over it. The **proximal border** (Margo proximalis) is wide and grooved in its middle, narrower and rounded on either side. The **distal border** (Margo distalis) bears in front a narrow facet for articulation with the third phalanx. Behind this is a groove, which contains a number of relatively large foramina, and is bounded behind by a prominent edge. The **extremities** are blunt-pointed.

Development.—Each ossifies from a single center.

THE BONES OF THE PELVIC LIMB

The pelvic limb (Extremitas pelvina), like the thoracic, consists of four segments, viz., the pelvic girdle, thigh, leg, and the pes; the last is subdivided into tarsus, metatarsus, and digits.

The **pelvic girdle** (Cingulum extremitatis pelvinæ) consists of the **os coxæ** (or hip bone), which joins its fellow of the opposite side ventrally at the symphysis pelvis, and articulates very firmly with the scarum dorsally. The two coxal bones, together with the sacrum and the first three or more coccygeal vertebræ, constitute the bony pelvis. The os coxæ consists originally of three flat bones, the **ilium, ischium,** and **pubis,** which meet at the acetabulum, a large cotyloid cavity with which the head of the femur articulates. These three parts are fused before growth is complete, but are considered separately for convenience of description. The **ilium** (Os ilium) is situated in the lateral wall of the pelvis; the **pubis** (Os pubis) is in the anterior part, and the **ischium** (Os ischii) in the posterior part of the ventral wall.

The **thigh** (Femur), like the arm, contains a single long bone, the **femur** (or thigh bone) (Os femoris).[1] This articulates with the acetabulum above and the tibia and patella below.

The skeleton of the **leg** (Crus) comprises three bones (Ossa cruris), viz., the **tibia, fibula,** and **patella.** The **tibia** is a large, prismatic long bone which supports the weight, and articulates distally with the tibial tarsal bone. The **fibula** is situated along the lateral border of the tibia, from which it is separated by the **interosseous space** of the leg. It is much more slender than the tibia and does not articulate with the femur. In the pig and dog it has a complete shaft and two extremities, but in the horse and ox it is much reduced and otherwise modified. The **patella** (or "knee-cap") is a short bone which articulates with the trochlea of the distal end of the femur; it is to be regarded as a large sesamoid bone intercalated in the tendon of the quadriceps femoris muscle.

---

[1] The word femur denotes the thigh, but has long been applied to the thigh bone.

The **pes,**[1] the homologue of the foot of man, consists of three subdivisions, viz., the **tarsus, metatarsus,** and **digit** or **digits.**

The **tarsus** (or "hock") contains a group of short bones, the **ossa tarsi,** numbering five to seven in the different animals. The proximal or crural row consists of two bones, the **tibial** and **fibular tarsals;** the former is situated at the tibial (medial) side, and has a trochlea for articulation with the distal end of the tibia; the latter, situated at the fibular (lateral) side, has a process, the **tuber calcis,** which projects upward and backward and constitutes a lever for the muscles which extend the hock joint. The distal or metatarsal row consists of four bones when seven tarsal elements are present, as in the pig and dog. They are best designated numerically as **first tarsal, second tarsal,** etc. The **central tarsal** is interposed between the rows.

The preceding terms are anglicized abbreviations of those introduced by Gegenbaur into comparative anatomy. The Latin names and synonyms are given in the following table:

Tibial (Os tarsi tibiale, Tt.)...................Astragalus or Talus
Fibular (Os tarsi fibulare, Tf.)................Calcaneus or Os calcis
Central (Os tarsi centrale, Tc.)................Scaphoid or Navicular
First Tarsal (Os tarsale primum, T1)...........First or internal cuneiform
Second Tarsal (Os tarsale secundum, T2).......Second or middle cuneiform
Third Tarsal (Os tarsale tertium, T3)..........Third or external cuneiform
Fourth Tarsal (Os tarsale quartum, T4).........Cuboid

The **metatarsal** and **digital bones** resemble in general those of the corresponding regions of the thoracic limb; the differential features will be noted in the special descriptions.

OS COXÆ

The **os coxæ** or hip bone is the largest of the flat bones. It consists primarily of three parts, the **ilium, ischium,** and **pubis,** which meet to form the **acetabulum,** a large cotyloid cavity which articulates with the head of the femur. These parts are fused at about one year of age, but it is convenient to describe them separately.[2]

THE ILIUM

The **ilium** (Os ilii) is the largest of the three parts. It is irregularly triangular and presents two surfaces, three borders, and three angles.

The wide part of the bone is the **wing** (Ala ossis ilii). Its **gluteal surface** (Facies glutæa) faces dorso-laterally and backward. It is wide and concave in front, narrower and convex behind. The wide part is crossed by the curved **gluteal line** (Linea glutæa), which extends from the middle of the medial border toward the tubar coxæ. This surface gives attachment to the middle and deep gluteal muscles.

The **pelvic surface** (Facies pelvina) faces in the opposite direction; it is convex, and consists of two distinct parts. The medial triangular part (Pars articularis) is roughened for ligamentous attachment, and bears an irregular facet, the **auricular surface** (Facies auricularis), for articulation with the sacrum. The lateral quadrilateral part (Pars iliaca) is, in general, smooth. It is crossed by the **ilio-pectineal line** (Linea iliopectinea), which begins below the auricular surface and is continued

---

[1] There is no popular equivalent for this term with reference to animals.

[2] The proper terms, strictly speaking, for these bones are os ilii, os ischii, and os pubis, but the names given above are sanctioned by common usage.

on the shaft of the bone to join the anterior border of the pubis. The line is interrupted by furrows for the iliaco-femoral vessels, and below these it bears the **psoas tubercle** (Tuberculum psoadicum), which gives attachment to the psoas minor muscle. The iliacus muscle is attached to the surface lateral to the ilio-pectineal line.

The **anterior border** or **crest** (Crista iliaca) is concave, thick, and rough.

The **medial border** (Margo medialis) is deeply concave. Its middle part forms the **greater sciatic notch** (Incisura ischiadica major) and it is continuous behind with the **ischiatic spine.**

The **lateral border** (Margo lateralis) is concave and in great part rough. Its anterior part is crossed by grooves for the ilio-lumbar vessels, which are continued

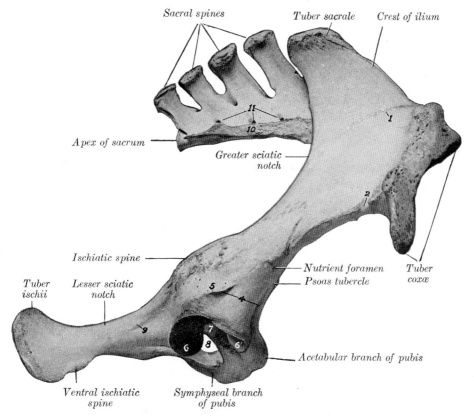

Fig. 85.—Right Os Coxæ and Sacrum of Horse; Right Lateral View.

1, Gluteal line; 2, impression of ilio-lumbar artery; 3, impression of iliaco-femoral artery; 4, depressions for attachments of tendons of origin of rectus femoris; 5, crest to which lateral tendon of rectus femoris and capsularis are attached; 6, 6', articular surface of acetabulum (facies lunata); 7, acetabular fossa; 8, obturator foramen; 9, line for attachment of gemellus muscle; 10, lateral border of sacrum; 11, dorsal sacral foramina.

on the pelvic surface. The **nutrient foramen** is usually situated on or near the posterior part of this border.

The medial angle is termed the **tuber sacrale;** it curves upward and a little backward opposite to the first sacral spine, and forms here the highest point of the skeleton. It is somewhat thickened and rough.

The lateral angle, **tuber coxæ,** forms the basis of the point of the hip. It is a large quadrangular mass, narrow in its middle, and enlarged at either end, where it bears a pair of tuberosities. It is roughened for muscular attachment.

The **acetabular angle** (Angulus acetabularis) meets the other two bones at the acetabulum, of which it forms about two-fifths. Its prominent dorsal border forms

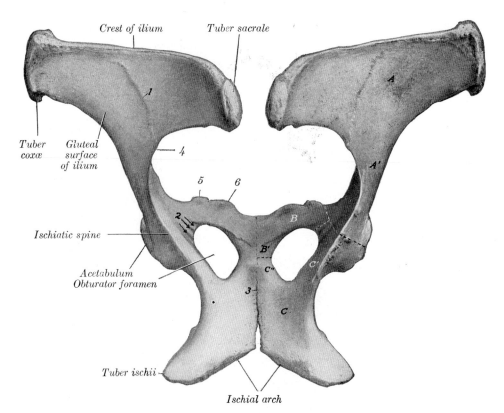

Crest of ilium   *Tuber sacrale*

Tuber coxæ   *Gluteal surface of ilium*

Ischiatic spine

Acetabulum Obturator foramen

Tuber ischii

Ischial arch

FIG. 86.—Ossa Coxarum of Horse; Dorsal View.

A, Wing; *A'*, shaft of ilium; *B*, acetabular, *B'*, symphyseal branch of pubis; *C*, body, *C'*, acetabular branch (or shaft), *C''*, symphyseal branch, of ischium; 1, gluteal line; 2, grooves for obturator nerve and vessels; 3, symphysis pelvis; 4, greater sciatic notch; 5, ilio-pectineal eminence; 6, pubic tubercle. Dotted lines indicate primitive separation of three bones.

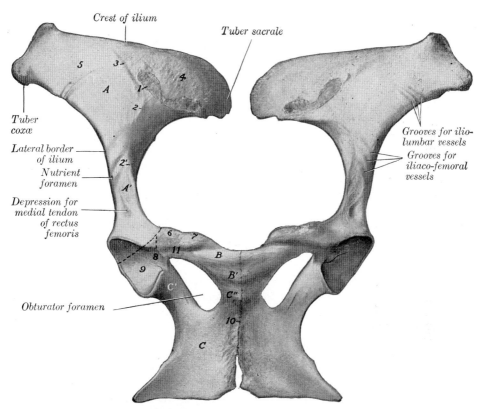

FIG. 87.—OSSA COXARUM OF MARE; VENTRAL VIEW.

A, Wing, *A'*, shaft of ilium; *B*, acetabular branch, *B'*, symphyseal branch, of pubis; *C*, body, *C'*, acetabular branch (shaft), *C''*, symphyseal branch, of ischium; 1, auricular surface; 2, ilio-pectineal line; 2', psoas tubercle; 3, arcuate line; 4, articular part, 5, iliac part, of pelvic surface of ilium; 6, ilio-pectineal eminence; 7, pubic tubercle; 8, acetabular fossa; 9, articular surface of acetabulum (facies lunata); 10, symphysis pelvis; 11, pubic groove. Dotted lines indicate primitive division of os coxæ.

part of the **ischiatic spine** (Spina ischiadica), which is roughened laterally, smooth medially. Two depressions above and in front of the acetabulum give attachment to the tendons of origin of the rectus femoris muscle. This angle is connected with the wing or wide part of the bone by a constricted part, termed the **shaft** (Corpus ossis ilium). The latter is of three-sided, prismatic form. Its lateral surface is convex and rough, and gives attachment to the deep gluteus muscle. Its pelvic surface is smooth and is grooved for the obturator vessels and nerve. Its ventral surface is crossed by vascular grooves, below which there is a rough area, which is bounded medially by the psoas tubercle.

The Ischium

The **ischium** (Os ischii) forms the posterior part of the ventral wall or floor of the bony pelvis. It slopes a little downward and inward, but is practically horizontal in the longitudinal direction. The **body** or shaft of the ischium (Corpus ossis ischii) is irregularly quadrilateral, and may be described as having two surfaces, four borders, and four angles.

The **pelvic surface** (Facies pelvina) is smooth and slightly concave from side to side.

The **ventral surface** (Facies ventralis) is nearly flat, and is in great part roughened for the attachment of the adductor muscles of the thigh.

The **anterior border** forms the posterior margin of the obturator foramen.

The **posterior border** is thick and rough. It slopes medially and forward to meet the border of the other side, forming with it the **ischial arch** (Arcus ischiadicus).

The **medial border** meets the opposite bone at the symphysis ischii.

The **lateral border** is thick and rounded, but concave in its length; it forms the **lesser sciatic notch** (Incisura ischiadica minor), the lower boundary of the lesser sciatic foramen.

The **antero-medial angle** or **symphyseal branch** (Ramus symphyseos) meets the pubis, with which it forms the medial boundary of the obturator foramen.

The **antero-lateral angle** or **acetabular branch** (Ramus acetabularis) joins the other two bones at the acetabulum, of which it forms more than half. Dorsally it bears part of the **ischiatic spine** (Spina ischiadica), and medially it is grooved for the obturator vessels. The term **shaft** is often applied to the constricted part of the acetabular branch.

The **postero-medial angle** joins its fellow at the symphysis.

The **postero-lateral angle** is a thick, three-sided mass, the **tuber ischii** (Tuber ischiadicum); its lower border is the ventral ischiatic spine, to which the biceps femoris and semitendinosus muscles are attached.

The Pubis

The **pubis** (Os pubis) is the smallest of the three parts of the os coxæ. It forms the anterior part of the pelvic floor, and may be described as having two surfaces, three borders, and three angles.

The **pelvic surface** (Facies pelvina) is convex in the young subject and the stallion, concave and smooth in the mare and usually in the gelding also.[1]

The **ventral surface** (Facies ventralis) is convex, and in great part rough for muscular attachment. Near the anterior border it is crossed by the **pubic groove** (Sulcus pubis), the medial part of which is occupied by a large vein, the lateral part by the accessory ligament; the groove leads to the acetabular notch.

The **anterior border** is thin in its medial part (except in the young subject and the stallion), forming the **pecten ossis pubis**. Laterally it bears the rough **ilio-pectineal eminence** (Eminentia iliopectinea), beyond which it is continuous with the ilio-pectineal line. Near the symphysis is a variable prominence, the **tuberculum pubicum.**

The **medial border** joins the opposite bone at the symphysis pubis.

The **posterior border** forms the anterior margin of the obturator foramen, and is marked laterally by the obturator groove.

The **medial angle** meets its fellow at the anterior end of the symphysis. This part is very thick in the young subject and the stallion, but in the mare, and usually in the gelding also, it becomes thin with advancing age.

The **acetabular angle** joins the ilium and ischium at the acetabulum.

The **posterior angle** joins the ischium, with which it forms the inner boundary of the obturator foramen.

The pubis may conveniently be regarded as consisting of a **body** (Corpus ossis pubis) and two branches; the latter are termed the **acetabular branch** (Ramus acetabularis) and the **symphyseal branch** (Ramus symphyseos).

THE ACETABULUM

The **acetabulum** is a cotyloid cavity which lodges the head of the femur. It faces ventro-laterally, and consists of an articular and a non-articular part. The **articular part** (Facies lunata) is crescentic, and is cut into internally by a rough non-articular depression, the **acetabular fossa** (Fossa acetabuli). The medial part of the rim is correspondingly cut into by the **acetabular notch** (Incisura acetabuli), which is converted into a foramen by the transverse ligament in the fresh state, and transmits the accessory and round ligaments to the head of the femur.

THE OBTURATOR FORAMEN

The **obturator foramen** (Foramen obturatum) is situated between the pubis and ischium. It is oval in outline, the longer axis being directed forward and outward. Its margin is grooved antero-laterally for the obturator nerve and vessels.

Development.—Each division of the os coxæ ossifies from one chief center. The center for the ilium first appears near the acetabulum, followed quickly by one for the ischium, and a little later by the pubic center. Secondary centers appear for the crest and tuber coxæ of the ilium, the tuber and posterior border of the ischium, and the acetabular part of the pubis. The symphyseal branches of the pubis and ischium are usually united with each other before birth, but the three

---

[1] The pelvic surface of the pubis is quite variable. In the mare and in geldings which have been castrated early the two pubic bones form a central depression of variable depth and curvature. This depression is bounded posteriorly by two oblique convergent lines or ridges, to which the obturator internus muscle is attached. Not rarely small eminences may be present along the symphysis.

bones are not fused until the second year. The epiphyseal parts fuse with the main mass at four and a half to five years of age.

The acetabular part of the pubis ossifies from a separate center. It is most distinct in the embryo at three months, and is often called the **os acetabuli.** Martin says that the ilium has a center for the acetabular part, one for the shaft and wing, and a third for the crest. He also states that there is a special center for the acetabular part of the ischium, and a transitory nucleus in the symphyseal part of the pubis.

THE PELVIS

The bony **pelvis** is composed of the ossa coxarum, the sacrum, and the first three coccygeal vertebræ. The **dorsal wall** or **roof** is formed by the sacrum and first three coccygeal vertebræ, and the **ventral wall** or **floor** by the pubic and ischial

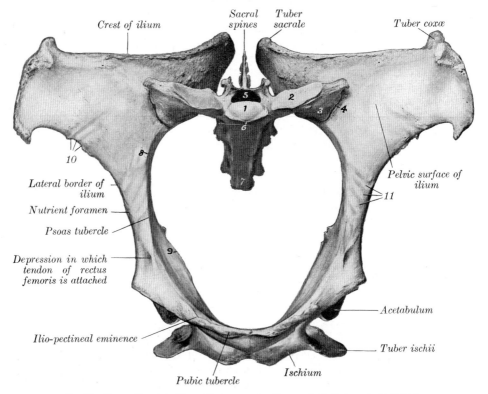

FIG. 88.—PELVIC BONES OF MARE, VIEWED FROM IN FRONT AND SOMEWHAT FROM BELOW.

1, Body of first sacral segment; 2, surface on wing of sacrum for articulation with like surface on transverse process of last lumbar vertebra; 3, wing of sacrum; 4, sacro-iliac articulation; 5, sacral canal; 6, promontory; 7, apex of sacrum; 8, ilio-pectineal line; 9, ischiatic spine; 10, grooves for ilio-lumbar vessels; 11, grooves for iliaco-femoral vessels.

bones. The **lateral walls** are formed by the ilia and the acetabular part of the ischia. The defect in the skeleton here is supplied in the fresh state by the sacrosciatic ligaments and semimembranosus muscles (Fig. 244).

The **anterior aperture** or **inlet** of the pelvis (Apertura pelvis cranialis) is bounded by the **terminal line** (Linea terminalis) or brim, which is composed of the base of the sacrum dorsally, the ilio-pectineal lines laterally, and the pecten pubis ventrally. It is almost circular in the mare, semi-elliptical in the stallion, and faces obliquely downward and forward. It has two principal diameters. Of these, the **conjugate** or sacro-pubic **diameter** (Conjugata anatomica) is measured from the sacral promontory to the anterior end of the symphysis. The **transverse diameter**

(Diameter transversa) is measured at the greatest width, *i. e.*, just above the psoas tubercle.

The **posterior aperture** or **outlet** of the pelvis (Apertura pelvis caudalis) is much smaller and is very incomplete in the skeleton. It is bounded dorsally by the

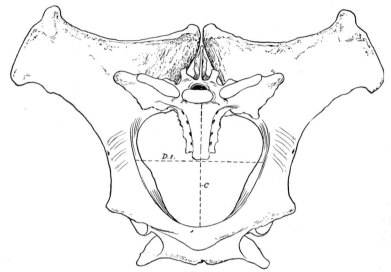

FIG. 89.—PELVIC BONES OF STALLION; FRONT VIEW.
C, Conjugate, *D.t.*, transverse diameter of pelvic inlet.

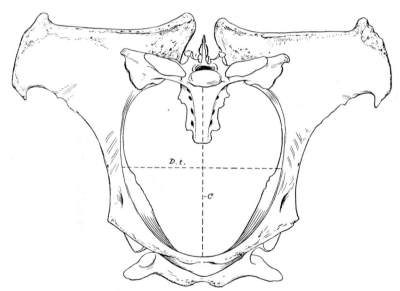

FIG. 90.—PELVIC BONES OF MARE; FRONT VIEW.
C, Conjugate, *D.t.*, transverse, diameter of pelvic inlet.

third coccygeal vertebra and ventrally by the ischial arch; in the fresh state it is completed laterally by the sacro-sciatic ligament and the semimembranosus muscle, thus inclosing the perineum.

The **axis** of the pelvis is an imaginary line drawn through the centers of the inlet, cavity, and outlet.

Sexual Differences.—Marked differences exist in the size and form of the pelvis in the two sexes. The average **conjugate diameter** is about 9½ inches (ca. 23 to

24 cm.) in the mare, 7½ inches (ca. 18.75 cm.) in the stallion. The **transverse diameter** of the inlet is about the same as the conjugate in the mare, but is about 8 inches (ca. 20 cm.) in the stallion. The **obliquity** of the inlet or **inclination of the pelvis** (Inclinatio pelvis) is greater in the female; the difference is indicated by the fact that a vertical plane from the pecten cuts the fourth sacral segment in the female, the second in the male. The **outlet** is also larger in the mare, the **ischial arch** being about one-third wider than in the stallion. The **cavity** is much more roomy in the female; the transverse diameter between the middles of the superior ischiatic spines is about 8 inches (20 cm.) in the mare, 6 inches (15 cm.) in the stallion. The pubic part of the **floor** in the female is concave and lies considerably lower than the ischiatic part, which is wide and almost flat. In the stallion the pubis is very thick medially, and this part of the floor is convex, while the ischial part is relatively narrow, and is concave from side to side. The **obturator foramina** are correspondingly larger in the female. The ilium is shorter, especially with regard to its shaft, and the greater sciatic notch is deeper and narrower in the male. The pelvis of the gelding, when castration has been performed early, resembles that of the mare; otherwise the male characters appear to be retained to a large degree.

THE FEMUR

The **femur** or thigh bone (Os femoris) is the largest and most massive of the long bones. It extends obliquely downward and forward, articulating with the acetabulum above and the tibia and patella below. The inclination on the horizontal plane is about 70–80 degrees. It presents for examination a shaft and two extremities.

The **shaft** (Corpus femoris) is, in general, cylindrical, but flattened behind, and larger above than below. The **anterior, medial,** and **lateral surfaces** are continuous and strongly convex from side to side; there is often a central vertical rough line on the proximal part, but otherwise these surfaces are smooth. They are covered by the quadriceps femoris muscle. The **posterior surface** is wide, flat, and smooth in its proximal fourth. Distal to this part there is a rough elevation laterally for the attachment of the femoral tendon of the biceps femoris, and a rough line medially to which the quadratus femoris is attached. The middle third is narrower, and is rough for the attachment of the adductor muscle. Just distal to this area an oblique groove crosses the surface, indicating the position of the femoral vessels. The **medial border** bears on its proximal part the **trochanter minor,** a thick rough ridge, to which the ilio-psoas muscle is attached. From this a rough line curves up to the front of the neck and indicates the posterior limit of the attachment of the vastus medialis muscle. A narrow rough area about the middle of the border gives attachment to the pectineus muscle, and the **nutrient foramen** is usually found just in front of this mark. The **medial supracondyloid crest** (Crista supracondyloidea medialis) is situated below the groove for the femoral vessels, and gives origin to the medial head of the gastrocnemius. The **lateral border** is prominent in its upper part, and bears at the junction of its proximal and middle thirds the **trochanter tertius;** this process is curved forward, and has a thick edge to which the tendon of the superficial gluteus muscle is attached. At the distal part is the **supracondyloid fossa** (Fossa supracondyloidea), in which the superficial digital flexor arises; it is bounded laterally by a thick, rough margin, the **lateral supracondyloid crest** (Crista supracondyloidea lateralis), to which the lateral head of the gastrocnemius muscle is attached.

The **proximal extremity** (Extremitas proximalis) is large and consists of the head, neck, and trochanter major. The **head** (Caput femoris) is placed at the medial side and is directed inward, upward, and somewhat forward. It is approximately hemispherical and articulates with the acetabulum. It is cut into

medially by a deep notch, the **fovea capitis,** in which the accessory and round ligaments are attached. The articular surface is surrounded by a distinct margin.
The **neck** (Collum femoris) is most distinct in front and medially. The **trochanter**
major is situated laterally; it presents three features. The **anterior part** or **con-**
vexity is situated opposite to the head and rises little above the level of the latter;
it gives attachment to the deep gluteus muscle, and in the fresh state its lateral
surface is coated with cartilage, over which a tendon of the middle gluteus passes,
to be inserted into the **crest,** which is placed below and behind the convexity.
The **posterior part** or **summit** is separated from the anterior part by a notch; it is
situated behind the plane of the head and rises to a much greater height. It

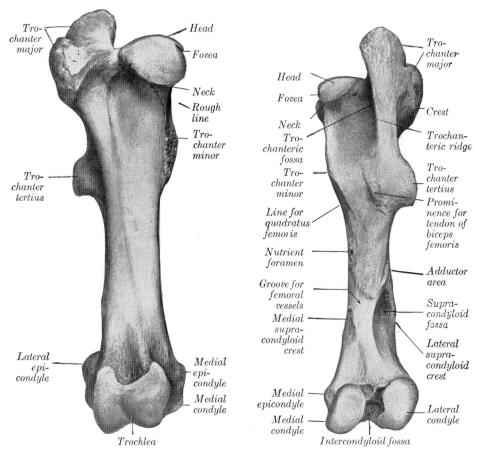

FIG. 91.—RIGHT FEMUR OF HORSE; FRONT VIEW.   FIG. 92.—RIGHT FEMUR OF HORSE; POSTERIOR VIEW.

furnishes insertion to part of the middle gluteus muscle. Its posterior border is
continued downward as the **trochanteric ridge** (Crista trochanterica), which forms
the lateral wall of the **trochanteric fossa** (Fossa trochanterica). A number of
foramina are found in the concave area medial to the convexity.

The **distal extremity** (Extremitas distalis) is large in both directions and comprises the trochlea in front and two condyles behind. The **trochlea** consists of two
ridges separated by a groove, and forms an extensive surface (Facies patellaris) for
articulation with the patella. It is very unsymmetrical; the medial ridge is much
wider, more prominent, and extends up higher than the lateral one, and the two
converge below. The **condyles, medial** and **lateral** (Condylus medialis, lateralis),

are separated by the deep **intercondyloid fossa** (Fossa intercondyloidea), and articulate with the condyles of the tibia and the menisci of the stifle joint. A ridge connects each condyle with the lower part of the corresponding ridge of the trochlea. The intercondyloid fossa lodges the spine of the tibia and the cruciate ligaments of the stifle joint, which are attached here.

The condyles are obliquely placed with their long axes directed downward, forward, and inward. The articular surface of the lateral condyle is more strongly convex from side to side than that of the medial one, and the ridge which connects it with the trochlea is much narrower.

The **medial epicondyle** (Epicondylus medialis) is a rounded prominence on the medial surface of the distal extremity, to which the collateral ligament and the adductor muscle are attached. The corresponding **lateral epicondyle** (Epicondylus

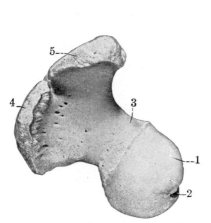

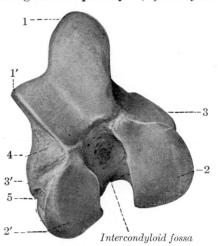

FIG. 93.—PROXIMAL EXTREMITY OF RIGHT FEMUR OF
HORSE; END VIEW.

1, Head; 2, fovea capitis; 3, neck; 4, 5, anterior and
posterior parts of trochanter major.

FIG. 94.—DISTAL EXTREMITY OF RIGHT FEMUR OF
HORSE; END VIEW.

1, 1′, Medial and lateral ridges of trochlea; 2, 2′,
medial and lateral condyles; 3, 3′, medial and lateral
epicondyles; 4, extensor fossa; 5, depression for origin
of popliteus.

lateralis) is less distinct; it presents a mark where the lateral ligament is attached, below and behind which there is a depression (Fossa musculi poplitei) in which the popliteus muscle arises. Between the lateral condyle and trochlea is the **extensor fossa** (Fossa extensoria), in which the common tendon of origin of the extensor digitalis longus and peroneus tertius is attached.

Development.—The shaft and the distal end each ossify from one center, but the proximal end has two centers, one of which is for the head and the other for the trochanter major. The edge of the trochanter tertius also has a separate center. The proximal end fuses with the shaft at three to three and a half years, the distal at about three and a half years.

THE TIBIA

The **tibia** is a long bone which extends obliquely downward and backward from the stifle to the hock. It articulates above with the femur, below with the tarsus, and laterally with the fibula. It possesses a shaft and two extremities.

The **shaft** (Corpus tibiæ), large and three-sided above, becomes smaller and flattened in the sagittal direction below, but widens at the distal end. It presents for notice three surfaces and three borders. The **medial surface** (Facies medialis) is broad above, where it presents rough prominences for the attachment of the medial ligament and the sartorius and gracilis muscles; below this it is narrower, convex from edge to edge and subcutaneous. The **lateral surface** (Facies lateralis) is smooth and somewhat spiral. It is wide and concave in its proximal fourth,

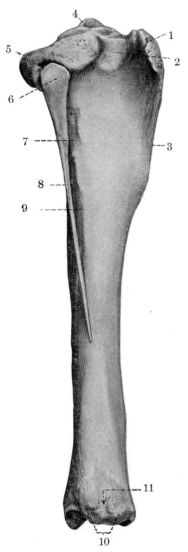

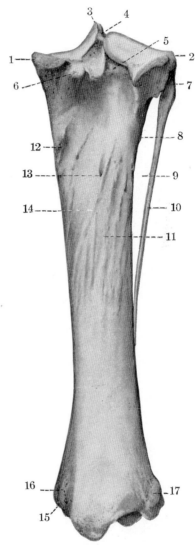

Fig. 95.—Right Tibia and Fibula of Horse; Lateral View.

1, Tuberosity; 2, sulcus muscularis; 3, crest; 4, spine; 5, lateral condyle; 6, head of fibula; 7, impression of anterior tibial vessels; 8, shaft of fibula; 9, lateral border of tibia; 10, lateral malleolus; 11, groove for lateral extensor tendon.

Fig. 96.—Right Tibia and Fibula of Horse; Posterior View.

1, Medial condyle; 2, lateral condyle; 3, spine; 4, fossa for anterior cruciate ligament; 5, popliteal notch; 6, tubercle for posterior cruciate ligament; 7, head of fibula; 8, vascular impression; 9, interosseous space; 10, shaft of fibula; 11, muscular lines; 12, tubercle; 13, nutrient foramen; 14, popliteal line; 15, medial malleolus; 16, groove for tendon of flexor digitalis longus; 17, lateral malleolus.

below which it becomes narrower and convex, and winds gradually to the front of the bone; near the distal end it widens a little, becomes flat, and faces forward. The **posterior surface** (Facies caudalis) is flattened, and is divided into two parts by the rough **popliteal line** (Linea poplitea), which runs obliquely from the proximal part of the lateral border to the middle of the medial border. The triangular area above the line is occupied by the popliteus muscle, while the area below is marked by rough lines (Lineæ musculares) to which the deep flexor muscle of the digit is attached; the lines fade out distally, where the surface is smooth and flat. The **nutrient foramen** is situated on or near the popliteal line. The **anterior border** is very prominent in its proximal third, forming the **crest** of the tibia (Crista tibiæ); distally it is reduced to a rough line, which ends at a small elevation near the distal end of the bone. The medial surface of the crest presents a rough prominence for the attachment of the tendon of the semitendinosus. The **medial border** (Margo medialis) is rounded in its proximal half, to which the popliteus muscle is attached, and a tubercle is found on this part. The distal part is a rough line on well-marked bones. The **lateral border** (Crista interossea) is concave in its proximal part and concurs with the fibula in the formation of the **interosseous space** of the leg (Spatium interosseum cruris); a smooth impression indicates the course of the anterior tibial vessels through the space to the front of the leg. About the middle of the bone the border divides and incloses a narrow triangular surface.

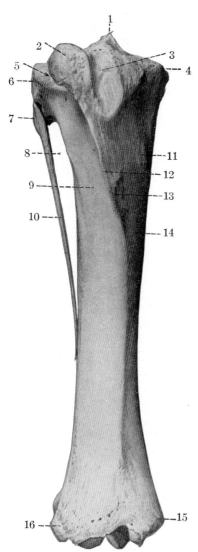

FIG. 97.—RIGHT TIBIA AND FIBULA OF HORSE; ANTERIOR VIEW.

1, Spine; 2, tuberosity; 3, groove for middle patellar ligament; 4, medial condyle; 5, sulcus muscularis; 6, lateral condyle; 7, head of fibula; 8, interosseous space; 9, lateral surface of tibia; 10, shaft of fibula; 11, imprint for attachment of gracilis; 12, crest; 13, prominence for attachment of semitendinosus; 14, medial surface of tibia; 15, medial malleolus; 16, lateral malleolus.

The **proximal extremity** (Extremitas proximalis) is large and three-sided. It bears two articular eminences, the **medial** and **lateral condyles** (Condylus medialis, lateralis). Each presents a somewhat saddle-shaped surface for articulation with the corresponding condyle of the femur and meniscus. The **spine** or **intercondyloid eminence** (Eminentia intercondyloidea) is the central prominence, upon the sides of which the articular surfaces are continued; it consists of a high medial part and a lower lateral part (Tuberculum intercondyloideum mediale, laterale). On, before, and behind the spine are the **intercondyloid fossæ,** in which the anterior cruciate ligament and the menisci are attached. The condyles are separated behind by the deep **popliteal notch** (Incisura poplitea), on the medial side of which there is a tubercle for the attachment of the posterior cruciate ligament. The lateral condyle has an overhanging outer margin (Margo infraglenoidalis), below which there is a **facet** (Facies articularis fibularis) for articulation with the fibula. The large anterior eminence is the **tuberosity** of the tibia (Tuberositas tibiæ). It is marked in front by a **groove** (Sulcus ligamenti), the lower part of which gives attachment to the middle patellar ligament, and the groove is flanked by rough areas for the attachment of the medial and lateral patellar ligaments. A semicircular smooth notch, the **sulcus muscularis,** separates the tuberosity from the lateral condyle, and gives passage to the common tendon of origin of the extensor digitalis longus and the peroneus tertius.

The **distal extremity** (Extremitas distalis) is much smaller than the proximal one; it is quadrangular in form and larger medially than laterally. It presents an **articular surface** (Cochlea tibiæ), which is adapted to the trochlea of the tibial tarsal bone, and consists of two grooves separated by a ridge. The ridge and grooves are directed obliquely forward and laterally, and are bounded on either side by the **malleoli,** to which the collateral ligaments of the hock joint are attached. A shallow synovial fossa is usually present on the middle of the articular ridge. The lateral groove is wider and shallower than the medial one; it is frequently marked by a line or groove which indicates the former demarcation between the tibia and fibula. The **medial malleolus** (Malleolus medialis) is the more prominent of the two, and forms the anterior boundary of a groove for the tendon of the flexor digitalis longus. The **lateral malleolus** (Malleolus lateralis) is broader, and is marked by a vertical groove for the passage of the lateral extensor tendon.

Development.—The tibia has the usual three chief centers of ossification and supplementary ones for the tuberosity and the lateral malleolus. The latter is really the distal end of the fibula; it is a separate piece at birth, and the line of union is commonly quite evident in the adult in the articular groove. The proximal end unites with the shaft at about three and a half years, and the distal end at about two years of age.

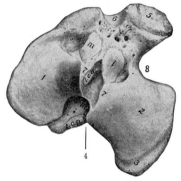

FIG. 98.—PROXIMAL EXTREMITY OF RIGHT TIBIA OF HORSE; END VIEW.

1, Medial condyle; 2, lateral condyle; 3, groove on 2 for popliteus tendon; 4, popliteal notch; 5, tuberosity; 6, groove for middle patellar ligament; 7, tubercles of spine; 8, sulcus muscularis; *l.c.a., l.c.p.,* depressions for attachment of anterior and posterior cruciate ligaments; *l, m, m,* depressions for attachment of menisci.

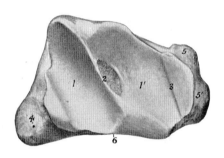

FIG. 99.—DISTAL EXTREMITY OF RIGHT TIBIA (AND FIBULA) OF HORSE; END VIEW.

1, 1', Articular grooves; 2, intermediate ridge and synovial fossa; 3, line of fusion of primitive distal end of fibula with tibia; 4, medial malleolus; 5, 5', lateral malleolus; 6, anterior border.

THE FIBULA

The **fibula** of the horse is a much reduced long bone, situated along the lateral border of the tibia.

The **shaft** (Corpus fibulæ) is a slender rod which forms the lateral boundary of the interosseous space of the leg; it usually terminates below in a pointed end about one-half to two-thirds of the way down the lateral border of the tibia.

The **proximal extremity** or **head** (Capitulum fibulæ) is relatively large, and is flattened transversely. Its medial surface presents a narrow area (Facies articularis capituli) along the upper border for articulation with the lateral condyle of the tibia. The lateral surface is rough and gives attachment to the lateral ligament of the stifle joint. It has rounded anterior and posterior borders.

The **distal extremity** is fused with the tibia, constituting the lateral malleolus.

Development.—This resembles that of the ulna. The embryonic cartilaginous fibula extends the entire length of the leg, but does not articulate with the femur. The distal part of the shaft is usually reduced to a fibrous band. Three centers of ossification appear, one each for the shaft and the extremities. The distal end unites early with the tibia, forming the lateral malleolus. It is interesting to note that in some cases the entire shaft of the fibula develops, a reversion to the condition in the Miocene ancestors of the horse.

THE PATELLA

The **patella** is a large sesamoid bone which articulates with the trochlea of the femur. It presents for description two surfaces, two borders, a base, and an apex.

The anterior, **free surface** (Facies libera) is quadrilateral, convex, and rough for muscular and ligamentous attachment.

The **articular surface** (Facies articularis) is also quadrilateral, but much less extensive. It presents a vertical rounded ridge, which corresponds to the groove

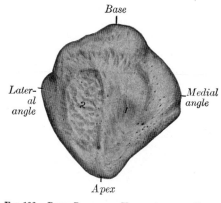

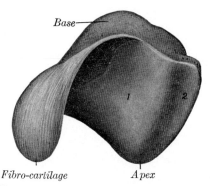

FIG. 100.—RIGHT PATELLA OF HORSE; ANTERIOR VIEW.

1, Attachment area of middle patellar ligament; 2, attachment area of lateral patellar ligament and biceps femoris.

FIG. 101.—RIGHT PATELLA OF HORSE; POSTERIOR VIEW.

1, Medial part, 2, lateral part, of articular surface.

on the trochlea of the femur, and separates two concave areas. Of the latter, the medial one is much the larger, and is not very well adapted to the corresponding ridge of the trochlea; in the fresh state, however, it is completed and rendered more congruent by the curved accessory fibro-cartilage.

In the natural standing position only a transverse area of the articular surface about one-half inch wide is in contact with the femur. The area on the patella is close to the distal border, and articulates with a corresponding area on the femur which is an inch or less below the proximal border of the trochlea.

The **borders,** medial and lateral, converge to the apex below, and each forms an angle at the base. The medial border is concave. The lateral border is rounded and its angle is less prominent. The medial angle and the adjacent part of the posterior margin of the base give attachment to the **fibro-cartilage of the patella** (Fibrocartilago patellæ).

The **base** (Basis patellæ) faces upward and backward, and is convex transversely, concave from before backward.

The **apex** (Apex patellæ) forms a blunt point directed distally.

Development.—The patella develops as a sesamoid bone from a single center in a cartilaginous deposit in the tendon of the quadriceps femoris muscle.

THE TARSAL BONES

The **tarsus** or hock of the horse usually comprises six short bones (Ossa tarsi), but exceptionally seven are present.

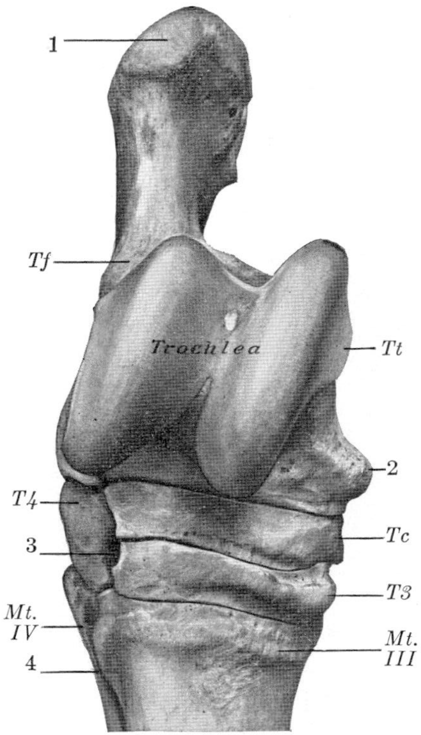

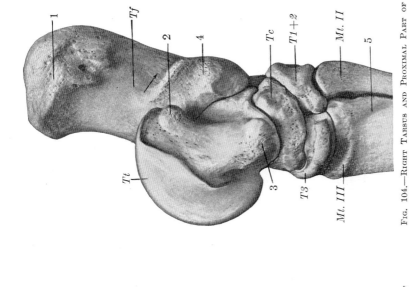

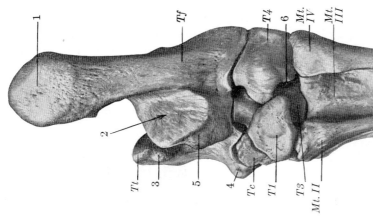

Fig. 102.—Right Tarsus and Proximal Part of Metatarsus of Horse; Anterior or Dorsal View.

Tt, Tibial tarsal bone; *Tf*, fibular tarsal; *Tc*, central tarsal; *T3*, third tarsal; *T4*, fourth tarsal; 1, tuber calcis; 2, distal tuberosity of tibial tarsal; 3, vascular canal; 4, groove for great metatarsal artery; *Mt. III, IV*, metatarsal bones.

Fig. 103.—Right Tarsus and Proximal Part of Metatarsus of Horse; Posterior or Plantar View.

Tt, Tibial tarsal bone; *Tf*, fibular tarsal (body); *Tc*, central tarsal; *T1*, first tarsal (fused with second); *T3*, third tarsal; *T4*, fourth tarsal; 1, tuber calcis; 2, tarsal groove for deep flexor tendon; 3, proximal tuberosity of tibial tarsal; 4, distal tuberosity of same; 5, sustentaculum; 6, vascular canal; *M. II, III, IV*, metatarsal bones.

Fig. 104.—Right Tarsus and Proximal Part of Metatarsus of Horse; Medial View.

Tt, Tibial tarsal (trochlea); *Tf*, fibular tarsal; *Tc*, central tarsal; *T1+2*, fused first and second tarsals (dotted line indicates division between two elements); *T3*, third tarsal; 1, tuber calcis; 2, 3, proximal and distal tuberosities of tibial tarsal; 4, sustentaculum; 5, groove for great metatarsal vein; *Mt. II, III*, metatarsal bones. Arrow indicates course of flexor tendon in tarsal groove.

The Tibial Tarsal Bone

The **tibial tarsal bone** (Os tarsi tibiale) is the medial bone of the proximal row. It is extremely irregular in form, but may be considered as offering six surfaces for description.

The **proximal** and **dorsal surfaces** are continuous, and form a **trochlea** (Trochlea tali) for articulation with the distal end of the tibia. The trochlea consists of two oblique ridges with a deep groove between them; these curve spirally forward, downward, and outward, forming an angle of 12 to 15 degrees with a sagittal plane. There is usually a shallow synovial fossa in the groove. The **distal surface** is convex from before backward. and most of it articulates with the central tarsal; laterally it has an oblique facet for the fourth tarsal, and a non-articular groove cuts into the surface to its middle. The **plantar surface** (Facies plantaris) is oblique and extremely irregular; it presents four facets for articulation with the fibular tarsal bone; the facets are separated by

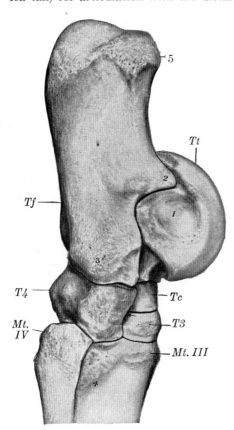

FIG. 105.—Right Tarsus and Proximal Part of Metatarsus of Horse; Lateral View.

Tt, Tibial tarsal (trochlea); *Tf*, fibular tarsal (body); *Tc*, central tarsal; *T3*, third tarsal; *T4*, fourth tarsal; 1, depression for attachment of lateral ligament; 2, processus cochlearis; 3, prominence for attachment of lateral ligament; 4, groove for great metatarsal artery; 5, tuber calcis; *Mt. III, IV*, metatarsal bones. Arrow points to vascular canal.

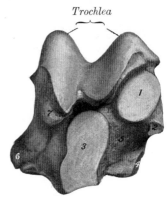

FIG. 106.—Right Tibial Tarsal Bone of Horse; Plantar View.

1–4, Facets for articulation with fibular tarsal; 5, fossa; 6, distal tuberosity; 7, proximal tuberosity.

rough excavated areas, and the largest fossa (Sulcus tali) forms with a corresponding one on the fibular tarsal a cavity termed the **sinus tarsi**. The **medial surface** bears on its distal part a large tuberosity and on its proximal part a small one for the attachment of the medial ligament of the hock joint. The **lateral surface** is smaller than the medial, and is marked by a wide rough fossa in which the lateral ligament is attached.

The Fibular Tarsal Bone

The **fibular tarsal bone** (Os tarsi fibulare) is the largest bone of the hock. It is elongated, flattened from side to side, and forms a lever for the muscles which extend the hock joint. It consists of a body and a medial process, the sustentaculum tali.

The **body** (Corpus) is enlarged at its proximal end to form the **tuber calcis** or "point of the hock"; the posterior part of this eminence gives attachment to the tendon of the gastrocnemius, while in front and on each side it furnishes insertion to tendons of the superficial digital flexor, biceps, and semitendinosus muscles. The **distal extremity** bears a concave facet for articulation with the fourth tarsal bone. The **medial surface** of the body has on its lower part a strong process, the **sustentaculum tali,** which projects inward. The process has a large, oval, slightly concave facet in front for articulation with the tibial tarsal, and sometimes a small articular surface below for the central bone. Its plantar surface forms with the smooth medial surface of the body a groove for the deep flexor tendon (Sulcus tarsi). Its medial surface has a prominence on the distal part for the attachment of the medial ligament. The **lateral surface** of the body is flattened, except below, where there is a rough prominence for the attachment of the lateral ligament. The **dorsal border** is concave in its length, smooth and rounded in its upper part. About its middle is a blunt-pointed projection (Processus cochlearis) which bears facets on its medial and lower surfaces for articulation with the tibial tarsal bone, and is roughened laterally for ligamentous attachment. Below this are two facets for the tibial tarsal, and an extensive rough fossa which concurs in the formation of the sinus tarsi. The **plantar border** is straight and broad, and widens a little at each end; it is rough, and gives attachment to the long plantar ligament.

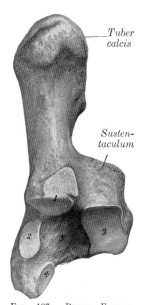

Tuber calcis

Sustentaculum

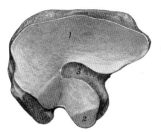

FIG. 107. — RIGHT FIBULAR TARSAL BONE OF HORSE; DORSAL VIEW.

1–4, Facets for articulation with tibial tarsal bone; 5, fossa.

FIG. 108.—RIGHT CENTRAL TARSAL BONE OF HORSE; PROXIMAL SURFACE.

1, Articular surface for tibial tarsal; 2, facet for fibular tarsal; 3, non-articular depression.

THE CENTRAL TARSAL BONE

The **central tarsal bone** (Os tarsi centrale) is irregularly quadrilateral, and is situated between the tibial tarsal and the third tarsal. It is flattened from above downward, and may be described as having two surfaces and four borders. The **proximal surface** is concave from before backward, and almost all of it articulates with the tibial tarsal; a non-articular depression cuts into its lateral part, and sometimes there is a facet for the fibular tarsal bone on the posterior angle. The **distal surface** is convex, and is crossed by a non-articular groove, which separates facets for articulation with the third and the first and second (fused) tarsals. The **dorsal border** and the **medial border** are continuous, convex, and rough. The **plantar border** bears two prominences, separated by a notch. The **lateral border** is oblique, and bears anterior and posterior facets for articulation with the fourth tarsal, between which it is excavated and rough.

First and Second Tarsal Bones

The **first** and **second tarsal bones** (Os tarsale primum et secundum) are usually fused in the horse, forming a bone of very irregular shape, situated in the medio-plantar part of the distal row, below the central and behind the third tarsal. It is the smallest of the tarsal bones, and may be described as having four surfaces and two extremities. The **medial surface** faces backward and inward, and is convex. Its anterior part is ridged, and gives attachment to the medial ligament, and its posterior part bears an imprint where the medial tendon of the tibialis anterior is inserted. The **lateral surface** is marked by a deep notch which indicates the division between the first and second tarsal elements; it bears on its anterior part a facet for the third tarsal. The **proximal surface** is concave and has two facets for articulation with the central tarsal; it is separated from the medial surface by a prominent border. The **distal surface** is broad in front, where it articulates with

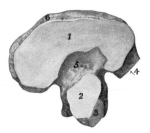

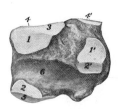

FIG. 109.—RIGHT FIRST AND SECOND (FUSED) TARSAL BONES OF HORSE; LATERAL SURFACE.

T1, T2, First and second tarsal bones; 1, 1′, articular surface for central tarsal; 2, facet for third tarsal; 3, facet for medial small metatarsal bone. Separation between two bones (when present) is indicated so far as visible by dotted line between 1 and 1′.

FIG. 110.—RIGHT THIRD TARSAL BONE OF HORSE; PROXIMAL SURFACE.

1, 2, Facets for central tarsal; 3, 4, facets for fourth tarsal; 5, non-articular depression; 6, dorsal ridge.

FIG. 111.—RIGHT FOURTH TARSAL BONE OF HORSE; MEDIAL SURFACE.

1, 1′, Facets for central tarsal; 2, 2′, facets for third tarsal; 3, facet for tibial tarsal; 4, 4′, facets for fibular tarsal; 5, facet for large metatarsal bone; 6, groove which concurs with central and third tarsals in formation of vascular canal of tarsus.

the large and medial small metatarsal bones. The **dorsal extremity** bears a ridge or tubercle. The **plantar extremity** is a blunt point.

In some cases the first and second tarsal bones remain separate—a remarkable reversion to the condition in the early ancestors of the horse. In such specimens the first tarsal is a discoid bone, articulating above with the central, below with the small metatarsal bone. The second tarsal is quadrangular, equivalent to the thick anterior part of the bone as described above, and overlapped in part by the first tarsal.

The Third Tarsal Bone

The **third tarsal bone** (Os tarsale tertium) resembles the central, but is smaller and triangular in outline. It is situated between the central above and the large metatarsal bone below. It possesses two surfaces and three borders.

The **proximal surface** is concave, and is crossed by a non-articular depression which divides it into two unequal facets; it articulates with the central tarsal. The **distal surface** is slightly convex, and rests on the large metatarsal bone; it has an extensive central rough excavation. The **dorsal border** is convex and bears a rounded ridge on its medial part. The **medial border** is deeply notched and has a small facet for the second tarsal on its anterior part. The **lateral border** is also divided by a notch into two parts, and bears two diagonally opposite facets for articulation with the fourth tarsal. In some cases there is a facet for the medial small metatarsal bone.

THE FOURTH TARSAL BONE

The **fourth tarsal bone** (Os tarsale quartum) is the lateral bone of the distal row, and is equal in height to the central and third together. It is cuboid in shape and presents six surfaces.

The **proximal surface** is convex from side to side, and articulates chiefly with the fibular tarsal, but to a small extent with the tibial tarsal also.

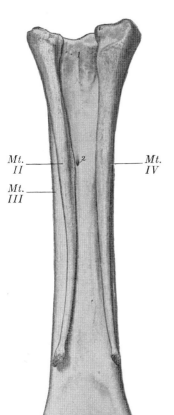

The **distal surface** rests on the large and lateral small metatarsal bones. The **medial surface** bears four facets for articulation with the central and third tarsal bones. It is crossed from before backward by a smooth groove, which by apposition with the adjacent bones forms the **canal of the tarsus** (Canalis tarsi) for the passage of the perforating tarsal vessels. The **dorsal, lateral,** and **plantar surfaces** are continuous and rough. A tuberosity behind gives attachment to the plantar ligament.

Development.—The fibular tarsal bone has two centers of ossification, one for the main mass and the other for the tuber calcis; the latter fuses with the rest of the bone at about three years of age. The first and second tarsals have separate centers, but fusion usually occurs before birth. Each of the other bones ossifies from a single center.

THE METATARSAL BONES

The **metatarsal bones** (Ossa metatarsalia), three in number, have the same general arrangement as

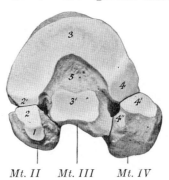

FIG. 112.—RIGHT METATARSAL BONES OF HORSE; PLANTAR VIEW.

1, Rough area for attachment of suspensory ligament; 2, nutrient foramen. Compare with Fig. 76.

FIG. 113.—PROXIMAL EXTREMITIES OF RIGHT METATARSAL BONES OF HORSE; END VIEW.

1, Facet for first tarsal; 2, 2', facets for second tarsal; 3, 3', facets for third tarsal; 4, 4', 4'', facets for fourth tarsal; 5, non-articular depression. Compare with Fig. 77.

the metacarpal bones, but present some important differences. Their direction is slightly oblique, downward, and a little forward.

The **third** or **large metatarsal bone** (Os metatarsale tertium) is about one-sixth longer than the corresponding metacarpal; in an animal of medium size the difference is about two inches. The **shaft** is more cylindrical, and is almost circular on cross-section, except in its distal part. At the proximal part of its lateral surface there is a groove, which is directed obliquely downward and backward, and is continued by the furrow formed by the apposition of the fourth or lateral metatarsal bone; it indicates the course of the great metatarsal artery. A shallow impression in a similar place on the medial side marks the position of the corresponding vein. The nutrient foramen is relatively higher than on the metacarpal bone. The **proximal extremity** is much wider from before backward than that of the metacarpal bone. Its articular surface is slightly concave, and is marked by a large central non-articular depression, continued outward by a deep notch. The greater part of the surface articulates with the third tarsal, but there is a lateral facet for the fourth, and usually a small facet postero-medially for the second tarsal bone. Posteriorly there are two pairs of facets for articulation with the small metatarsal bones. The front is crossed by a rough ridge for insertion, which becomes larger and turns downward on the lateral side behind the vascular groove. The **distal extremity** closely resembles that of the corresponding metacarpal bone.

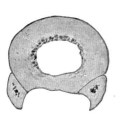
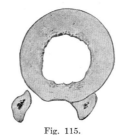

Fig. 114.   Fig. 115.

FIGS. 114, 115.—CROSS-SECTIONS OF LEFT METACARPAL AND METATARSAL BONES.

Sections are cut a little above middle of bones.

In some cases the distal part of the shaft is bent backward somewhat. The distal articular surface extends a little higher behind than in the case of the metacarpal bone. The large metatarsal bone is even more strongly constructed than the metacarpal. The shell of compact substance is very thick in the middle of the shaft, especially in front and medially.

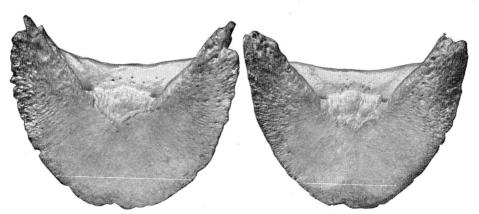

FIG. 116.—THIRD PHALANX OF THORACIC LIMB OF HORSE.   FIG. 117.—THIRD PHALANX OF PELVIC LIMB OF HORSE.

The **small metatarsal bones** (Ossa metatarsalia secundum et quartum) are a little longer than the corresponding metacarpals. The **lateral (fourth) metatarsal bone** is relatively massive, especially in its upper part. The proximal extremity is large and outstanding, and bears one or two facets above for the fourth tarsal, and two dorso-medially for articulation with the large metatarsal; elsewhere it is roughened for attachment. The **medial (second) metatarsal bone** is much more slender than the lateral one, especially in its proximal part. The latter bears two facets above for the first and second tarsals, and sometimes one for the third tarsal.

THE PHALANGES AND SESAMOID BONES

The axis of the phalanges of the hind limb forms with the ground plane an angle which is about five degrees greater than that of the fore limb, and the chief differences in the form and size of the bones are as follows:

The **first phalanx** is a little shorter, wider above, and narrower below.

The **second phalanx** is narrower and slightly longer.

The **third phalanx** is narrower, the angle of inclination of the dorsal surface is a little (ca. 5 degrees) greater, the plantar surface is more concave, and the angles are less prominent and closer together. The term plantar is to be substituted for volar in the designation of corresponding features.

The **proximal sesamoids** are a little smaller, except in thickness. The **distal sesamoid** is narrower and shorter.

SKELETON OF THE OX

VERTEBRAL COLUMN

The usual vertebral formula is $C_7T_{13}L_6S_5Cy_{18-20}$.

The **cervical vertebræ** are much shorter than those of the horse and are smaller in their other dimensions. The **articular processes** are smaller than in the horse, and a plate of bone connects each two of the same side. The **transverse processes** of the third, fourth, and fifth are double; the upper part projects backward, and is short and stout; the lower part is directed downward and forward, and is longer and more plate-like. The lower part of the sixth transverse process is a large, thick, quadrilateral and almost sagittal plate, directed ventrally. The seventh transverse process is single, short, and thick, and presents no foramen transversarium; it is in series with the upper part of the preceding processes. The **spinous processes** are well developed, and increase in height from before backward. They are directed upward and forward, with the exception of the last, which is nearly vertical and is about four or five inches (ca. 10 to 12 cm.) in height. The summit of that of the third vertebra is usually bifid. The **ventral spines** are prominent and thick in their posterior part; they are absent on the last two.

The **atlas** has a large rough **tuberosity** on its dorsal arch. The **ventral arch** is very thick. The **wings** are less curved than in the horse, and the foramen transversarium is absent.

Fig. 118.—Third Cervical Vertebra of Ox; Lateral View.

1, Spinous process; 2, 2', anterior and posterior articular processes; 3, 3', ends of body; 4, 4', transverse process; 5, foramen transversarium; 6, ventral spine.

The **anterior articular cavities** for the occipital condyles are partially divided into dorsal and ventral parts by a non-articular area, and are separated by a narrow interval below. The **posterior articular surfaces** are flattened behind and are continued into the vertebral canal, forming an extensive area for the dens of the axis.

The **axis** is short. The **spine** projects a little in front, and increases in height and thickness behind; its posterior border descends abruptly. The **dens** is wide, and its dorsal surface is deeply concave from side to side. The **intervertebral**

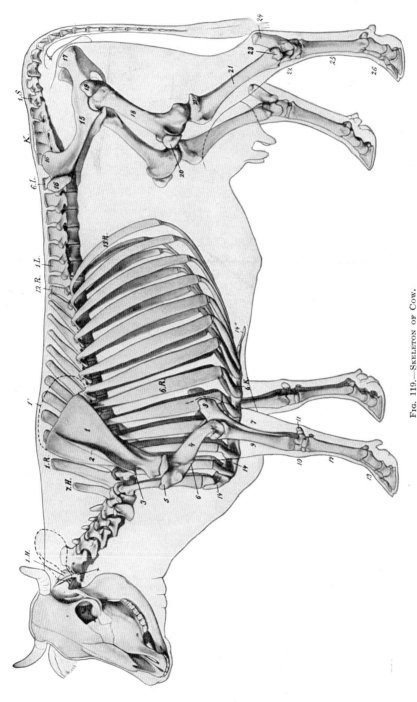

Fig. 119.—Skeleton of Cow.

1.H., Atlas; *7.H.*, seventh cervical vertebra; *1.R.*, first thoracic vertebra; *6.R.*, sixth rib; *12.R.*, twelfth thoracic vertebra; *13.R.*, last rib; *1.L.*, first, *6.L.*, last lumbar vertebra; *K*, sacrum *1.S.*, first coccygeal vertebra; *6.K.*, sixth costal cartilage; *X*, wing of atlas; *1*, scapula; *1'*, cartilage of scapula; *2*, spine of scapula; *3*, acromion; *4*, humerus; *4'*, lateral condyle of humerus; *5*, lateral tuberosity of humerus; *6*, deltoid tuberosity; *7*, ulna; *8*, olecranon; *9*, radius; *10*, carpus; *11*, accessory carpal bone; *12*, metacarpus; *13*, phalanges; *14*, sternum; *14'*, manubrium; *14''*, xiphoid cartilage; *15*, ilium; *16*, tuber coxae; *16'*, tuber sacrale; *17*, tuber ischii; *18*, femur; *19*, trochanter major; *20*, patella; *21*, tibia; *21'*, lateral condyle of tibia; *22*, tarsus; *23*, distal end of fibula; *24*, tuber calcis; *25*, metatarsus; *26*, phalanges.   The bones of the fore limb are placed too high in relation to the thorax.   (After Ellenberger-Baum, Anat. für Künstler.)

foramen is circular and not so close to the anterior border of the arch as in the horse. The **posterior notches** are not so deep. The **transverse processes** are stouter, but the **foramen transversarium** is small and sometimes absent.

The **thoracic vertebræ,** thirteen in number, are larger than those of the horse.

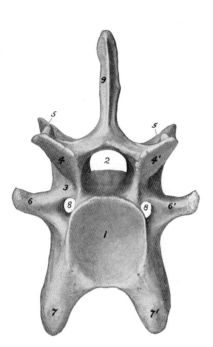

FIG. 120.—SIXTH CERVICAL VERTEBRA OF OX; POSTERIOR VIEW.

1, Posterior cavity of body; 2, vertebral foramen; 3, arch; 4, 4′, posterior articular processes; 5, 5, anterior articular processes; 6, 6′, lateral branches of transverse processes; 7, 7′, ventral branches of transverse processes; 8, foramen transversarium; 9, spinous process.

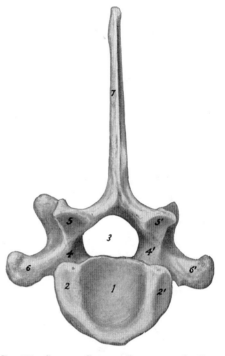

FIG. 121.—SEVENTH CERVICAL VERTEBRA OF OX; POSTERIOR VIEW.

1, Posterior cavity of body; 2, 2′, facets for head of first rib; 3, vertebral foramen; 4, 4′, arch; 5, 5′, articular processes; 6, 6′, transverse processes; 7, spinous process.

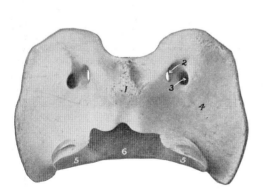

FIG. 122.—ATLAS OF OX; DORSAL VIEW.

1, Dorsal tubercle; 2, intervertebral foramen; 3, alar foramen; 4, wing; 5, 5, posterior articular surfaces; 6, ventral arch (surface for dens of axis).

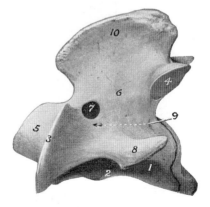

FIG. 123.—AXIS OF OX; LATERAL VIEW.

1, Body; 2, ventral spine; 3, anterior articular process; 4, posterior articular process; 5, dens; 6, arch; 7, intervertebral foramen; 8, transverse process; 9, foramen transversarium and canalis transversarius (dotted line); 10, spinous process.

The **body** is longer and is distinctly constricted in the middle. It bears a thin-edged ventral crest. The **arch**—in addition to the usual notches, which are shallow—is perforated in the posterior part by a foramen. The **transverse proc-**

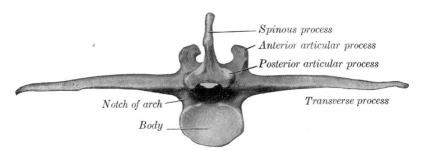

Spinous process
Anterior articular process
Posterior articular process

Notch of arch
Transverse process
Body

Fig. 124.—Fourth Lumbar Vertebra of Ox; Posterior View.

ess is thick and strong, and bears a rounded mammillary process (except at the posterior end of the series); the last two, although prominent, do not always articulate with the ribs. The **spinous process** is long. The first is much higher than in the horse, the next two are usually the most prominent, and behind this there is a very gradual diminution in height. The backward slope, slight at first, increases to the tenth; the last is vertical and lumbar in character. The summit is usually pointed on the first, and the thickening on those further back is less than in the horse. The width diminishes from the fifth to the eleventh usually. Both borders of the spines are in general thin and sharp, but the last three or four sometimes have thick posterior margins.

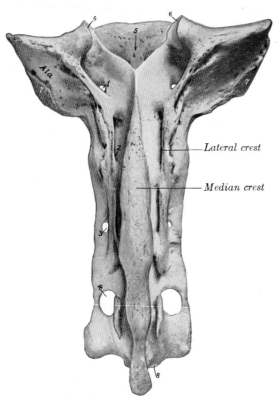

Lateral crest

Median crest

Fig. 125.—Sacrum of Ox; Dorsal View.
1–4, Dorsal sacral foramina; 5, sacral canal; 6, 6, articular processes; 7, auricular surface; 8, apex.

The **lumbar vertebræ,** six in number, are much longer than in the horse. The **body** is much constricted in the middle, expanded at either end, and bears a rudimentary ventral crest. The fourth and fifth are usually the longest. The **intervertebral foramina** are often double in the anterior part of the series, and are very large further back. The **articular processes** are large, and their facets are more strongly curved than in the horse. The **transverse proc-**

esses all curve forward. They are separated by considerable intervals, and form no articulations with each other or with the sacrum. Their borders are thin and irregular, and often bear projections of variable size and form. The first is the shortest and the length increases to the fifth, the last being considerably shorter. The **spinous processes** are relatively low and wide, the last being the smallest; their summits are moderately thickened.

The **sacrum** is longer than that of the horse. It consists originally of five segments, but fusion is more complete and involves the spinous processes, which are united to form a **median sacral crest** (Crista sacralis media), with a convex thick and rough margin. A **lateral sacral crest** is formed by the fusion of the articular processes. The **pelvic surface** is concave in both directions, and is marked by a central **groove** (Sulcus vasculosus), which indicates the course of the middle sacral artery. The **ventral sacral foramina** are large. The **wings** curve downward and forward; they are quad-

rangular, short, compressed from before backward, and high dorso-ventrally. They have an extensive anterior surface, which is concave from side to side and non-articular. The posterior surface is rough, and at its lower part there is a triangular area for articulation with the ilium. The body of the first segment is very wide, and the entrance to the sacral canal correspondingly wide and low. The **anterior articular processes** are large and widely separated; they are concave and semicylindrical in curvature medially. The **lateral borders** are thin, sharp, and irregular. The bone does not become narrower posteriorly, so that the **apex** is usually a little wider than the part just behind the wings; the posterior end of the median crest forms a pointed projection over the opening of the sacral canal.

The **coccygeal vertebræ** are longer and better devel-

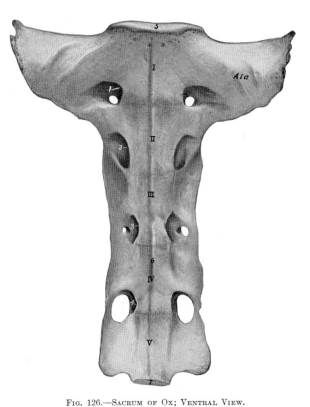

Fig. 126.—Sacrum of Ox; Ventral View.

I–V, Segments; 1–4, ventral sacral foramina; 5, anterior end of body of first sacral vertebra; 6, vascular groove; 7, posterior end of body of last sacral vertebra.

oped than in the horse. The first five or six have complete arches and spinous processes. The transverse processes are relatively large in the anterior part of the series, in which there are also anterior articular processes (which do not articulate), and a pair of ventral spines which form a groove (Sulcus vasculosus) for the middle coccygeal artery.

Vertebral Curves.—The cervical curve is very slight and is concave dorsally. The thoracic and lumbar regions form a gentle curve, concave ventrally. The promontory is more pronounced than in the horse, especially in subjects in which the sacrum is inclined upward behind. Another prominence occurs at the junction of the sacrum and first coccygeal vertebræ.

Length.—The following table gives the lengths (inclusive of the intervertebral fibro-cartilages) of the vertebral regions of a shorthorn cow of medium size:

Cervical	50 cm.
Thoracic	82 cm.
Lumbar	48 cm.
Sacral	25 cm.
Coccygeal	75 cm.
	280 cm.

Variations.—Sometimes fourteen thoracic vertebræ and fourteen pairs of ribs are present; reduction to twelve with the normal number of lumbar vertebræ is very rare. According to Franck there are sometimes seven lumbar vertebræ with the normal number in the thoracic region. The number of coccygeal vertebræ may vary from sixteen to twenty-one.

THE RIBS

Thirteen pairs of **ribs** are present normally, of which eight are sternal and five asternal. They are in general longer, wider, flatter, less curved, and less regular in form than in the horse. The eighth, ninth, and tenth are the longest and widest. The width of most of the ribs increases considerably in the middle, and

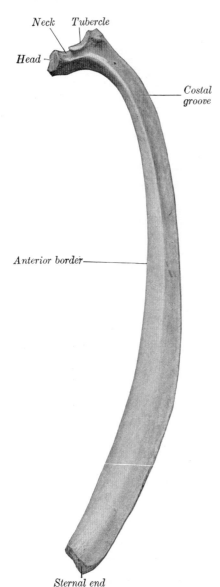

FIG. 127.—RIGHT EIGHTH RIB OF OX; MEDIAL VIEW.

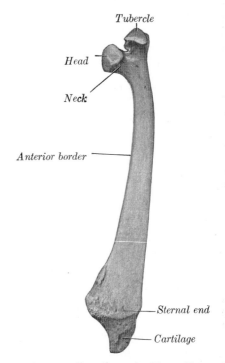

FIG. 128.—FIRST RIB OF OX; MEDIAL VIEW.

the breadth of the intercostal spaces is correspondingly diminished; this is not the case in the posterior part of the series, where the intercostal spaces are very wide.

The neck is long, and forms (except in the posterior part of the series) a smaller angle with the shaft than in the horse. The articular surface of the tubercle is concave transversely, except on the last two or three, where the facet is small and flat or absent. The ventral ends of the second to the tenth or eleventh inclusive form diarthrodial joints with the costal cartilages. The first costal cartilages are very short; they articulate by their medial surfaces with the sternum, but not with each other.

The presence of a fourteenth rib is quite common. It is usually floating and may correspond to an additional thoracic vertebra or to the first lumbar. Reduction of the thirteenth is more common. The eighth cartilage often does not reach the sternum, but articulates with the seventh.

THE STERNUM

The **sternum** consists of seven sternebræ, most of which are developed from two lateral centers. It is wider, flatter, and relatively longer than in the horse, and the ventral crest is absent. The manubrium is somewhat wedge-shaped and laterally compressed. Its base forms a diarthrodial joint with the body of the bone, and its upper part has a large facet on each side for articulation with the first costal cartilage. The body widens from before backward, but behind the last pair of costal facets it becomes much narrower. The ventral surface is very prominent in its anterior part, slightly concave further back. The lateral borders are notched for the passage of vessels. The cariniform cartilage is absent. The xiphoid cartilage is like that of the horse but is smaller.

THE THORAX

The bony thorax is shorter than in the horse. The inlet is higher. The roof is short, and the floor is wider and relatively longer. The transverse diameter is wider in the posterior part. The summits of the spinous processes are almost in a straight line from the second thoracic vertebra to the middle of the lumbar region.

In a subject of medium size the height of the thoracic inlet is 9 to 10 inches (ca. 22–25 cm.) and the greatest transverse diameter is about 4 inches (ca. 10 cm.). There is a pronounced "drop" or "offset" of the floor at the first intercostal space on account of the nearly upright position of the first sternebra. The second pair of costal cartilages form the lateral part of the socket on the manubrium which articulates with the corpus sterni. The height of the cavity from eighth thoracic vertebra to the last sternebra is about 21 inches (ca. 52 cm.). The length of the floor is about the same as the preceding.

THE SKULL

BONES OF THE CRANIUM

The **occipital bone** forms the lower part only of the posterior surface of the skull, and is separated from the highest part (the frontal eminence) by the parietal and interparietal bones. The supraoccipital, interparietals, and parietals fuse before birth or soon after, and the mass so formed is separated from the lateral parts of the occipital bone by a transverse suture in the skull of the calf. Above this suture is a central tuberosity, the external occipital protuberance, to which the ligamentum nuchæ is attached, and the surface on either side is depressed and rough for muscular attachment. There is commonly a median occipital crest which extends ventrally from the protuberance. Below the suture the bone is much wider than that of the horse. The foramen magnum is wide, so that the condyles are further apart, except below. The paramastoid processes are short and wide and are bent inward. Usually at least two foramina are found in the condyloid fossa; the ventral one is the hypoglossal, the other (often double) conducts a vein from the **condyloid canal.**[1] The latter passes upward from a foramen on the medial side of the condyle and opens into the temporal canal. The mastoid for-

[1] The number of foramina here is variable. In exceptional cases the foramen which opens into the condyloid canal is very small or absent; more often there are two, and sometimes three. In some cases there are two hypoglossal foramina. Thus as many as five foramina may be present.

amen is situated on each side, at the junction of the occipital and temporal bones; it communicates with the temporal and condyloid canals at their junction. The cerebral surface of the supraoccipital presents a central depression, and above this is a variable but never very pronounced eminence, the internal occipital protuberance. A groove on either side leads to the temporal canal. The basilar part is short and wide; its cerebral surface is deeply concave, and the internal spheno-occipital crest is prominent. Two large tubercles ventrally mark the junction with the sphenoid.

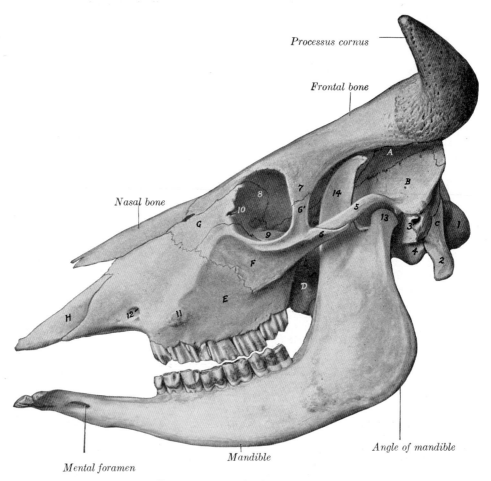

Fig. 129.—Skull of Ox; Lateral View.

The jaws are separated for the sake of clearness. *A*, Parietal bone; *B*, squamous temporal bone; *C*, occipital bone; *D*, perpendicular part of palatine bone; *E*, maxilla; *F*, malar bone; *G*, lacrimal bone; *H*, premaxilla; 1, occipital condyle; 2, paramastoid process; 3, meatus acusticus externus; 4, bulla tympanica; 5, zygomatic process of temporal bone; 6, 6', zygomatic and temporal processes of malar bone; 7, supraorbital process; 8, orbital part of lacrimal bone; 9, lacrimal bulla; 10, fossa sacci lacrimalis; 11, facial tuberosity; 12, infraorbital foramen; 13, condyle of mandible; 14, coronoid process of mandible.

The foramen lacerum is short and very narrow. In the adult animal the bone is excavated to contain an air-cavity which is regarded as a part of the frontal sinus.

The **sphenoid bone** is short. The cerebral surface of the body presents a deep sella turcica, in front of which it rises abruptly. The high anterior part bears a central ridge, the ethmoidal spine, which joins the ethmoidal crest. Two foramina occur on either side. Of these, the large anterior one is equivalent to the foramen rotundum, orbitale, and trochleare of the horse; it may be termed

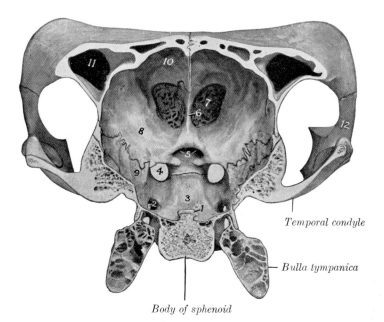

Temporal condyle

Bulla tympanica

Body of sphenoid

FIG. 130.—CROSS-SECTION OF CRANIUM OF OX.

The section cuts the posterior part of the temporal condyle and is viewed from behind. 1, Dorsum sellæ; 2, foramen ovale; 3, hypophyseal or pituitary fossa; 4, foramen orbito-rotundum; 5, optic foramina; 6, ethmoidal crest; 7, cribriform plate of ethmoid; 8, orbital wing of sphenoid; 9, temporal wing of sphenoid; 10, internal plate of frontal bone; 11, frontal sinus; 12, temporal process of malar bone.

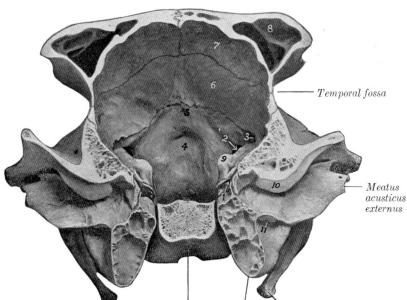

Temporal fossa

Meatus acusticus externus

Basilar part of occipital bone   Bulla tympanica   Paramastoid process

FIG. 131.—CROSS-SECTION OF CRANIUM OF OX.

The section cuts the posterior part of the temporal condyle and is viewed from in front. 1, Tympanic cavity; 2, internal opening of condyloid canal; 3, internal opening of temporal canal; 4, depression for vermis cerebelli; 5, internal occipital protuberance; 6, internal plate of parietal bone; 7, internal plate of frontal bone; 8, frontal sinus; 9, petrous temporal bone; 10, postglenoid process; 11, hyoid process.

the **foramen orbito-rotundum.** The posterior one is the **foramen ovale,** which transmits the mandibular nerve. The orbital wing is thick and is overlapped by the frontal in such manner as to appear externally to divide into two branches; the anterior part joins the ethmoid at the sphenopalatine foramen, and contains a small sinus which communicates with an ethmoidal meatus. The temporal wing is small, but forms a prominent thick pterygoid crest. The pterygoid process is wide, and there is no alar canal. The sphenoidal sinus is absent in the calf and small in the adult; it communicates by one or two small openings with an ethmoidal meatus, and so with the nasal cavity.

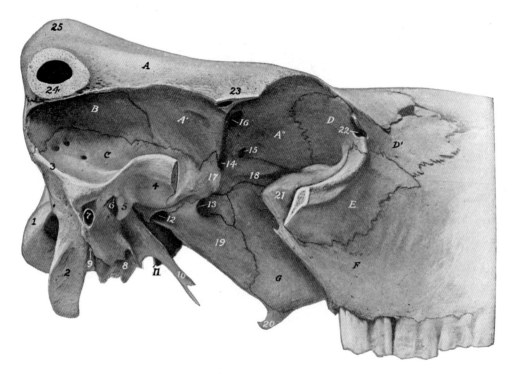

Fig. 132.—Cranial and Orbital Regions of Skull of Ox.

The horn core, supraorbital process, and greater part of zygomatic arch have been sawn off: *A*, Frontal bone; *A′*, *A″*, temporal and orbital parts of same; *B*, parietal bone; *C*, squamous temporal bone; *D*, *D′*, orbital and facial parts of lacrimal bone; *E*, malar bone; *F*, maxilla; *G*, perpendicular part of palatine bone; 1, occipital condyle; 2, paramastoid process; 3, temporal crest; 4, temporal condyle; 5, postglenoid process; 6, external opening of temporal canal; 7, meatus acusticus externus; 8, bulla tympanica; 9, stylo-mastoid foramen; 10, muscular process of temporal bone; 11, tip of basilar tubercle; 12, foramen ovale; 13, foramen orbito-rotundum; 14, optic foramen; 15, ethmoidal foramen; 16, orbital opening of supraorbital canal; 17, pterygoid crest; 18, ridge of orbital wing of sphenoid; 19, pterygoid process of sphenoid; 20, hamulus of pterygoid bone; 21, lacrimal bulla; 22, fossa sacci lacrimalis; 23, root of supraorbital process; 24, processus cornus (section); 25, frontal eminence.

The **ethmoid bone** has an extensive perpendicular plate. The lateral mass consists of five endoturbinates and eighteen ectoturbinates (Paulli). The largest ethmoturbinate is so extensive as to be termed a third or middle turbinate bone; it projects forward between the dorsal and ventral turbinates. The lamina lateralis appears to a small extent externally in the pterygo-palatine fossa, forming part of the dorsal margin of the sphenopalatine foramen.

The **interparietals** are primitively paired, but unite before birth. As already mentioned, fusion occurs before or shortly after birth with the parietals and supra-occipital. The bone has no intracranial projection.

The **parietal bones** do not enter into the formation of the roof of the cranium.

They constitute the upper part of the posterior wall, bend sharply forward along the lateral wall, and enter into the formation of the temporal fossa. The line of inflection is marked by the prominent **parietal crest,** which is continuous with the temporal crest below and the frontal crest anteriorly. The parietals are excavated to form part of the frontal sinuses in the adult animal.

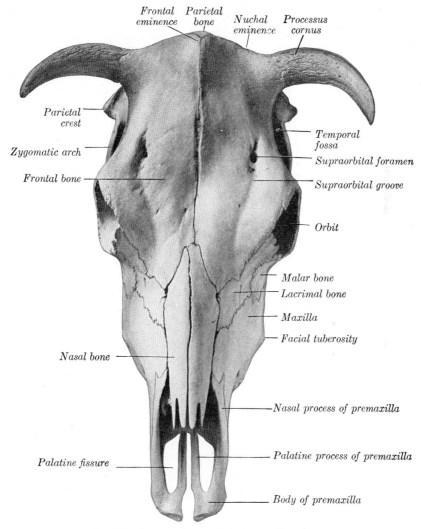

Frontal   *Parietal*
eminence   *bone*   *Nuchal*   *Processus*
            eminence   *cornus*

Parietal
crest

Zygomatic arch

Frontal bone

Temporal
fossa

Supraorbital foramen

Supraorbital groove

Orbit

Malar bone
Lacrimal bone

Maxilla

Facial tuberosity

Nasal bone

Nasal process of premaxilla

Palatine process of premaxilla

Palatine fissure

Body of premaxilla

Fig. 133.—Skull of Jersey Cow; Dorsal View.

The condition in the young subject is as follows: The two parietals are united with each other and also with the interparietal and supraoccipital. The resulting mass is somewhat horseshoe-shaped. Its occipital part (Planum occipitale) forms the greater part of the posterior wall of the cranium and bears about its center the tuberosity for the attachment of the ligamentum nuchæ. From either side of this a line curves outward and divides the surface into an upper smooth area and a lower area which is rough for muscular attachment. The upper border joins the frontal bone and concurs in the formation of the frontal eminence. The temporal parts (Plana temporalia) are much smaller and are concave externally; they join the frontal above and the squamous temporal below. A median occipital crest extends ventrally from the external occipital protuberance.

The **frontal bones** are very extensive, forming about one-half of the entire length of the skull, and all of the roof of the cranium. The posterior borders form with the parietals a large central **frontal eminence** (Torus frontalis), the highest point of the skull. At the junction of the posterior and the lateral border is the **processus cornus** or "horn core," for the support of the horn. These proc-

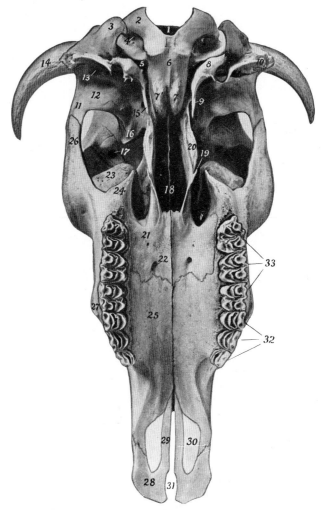

FIG. 134.—SKULL OF OX, WITHOUT MANDIBLE; VENTRAL VIEW.

1, Foramen magnum; 2, occipital condyle; 3, paramastoid process; 4, condyloid foramen; 5, foramen lacerum; 6, basilar part of occipital bone; 7, 7', basilar tubercles; 8, bulla tympanica; 9, foramen ovale (concealed by muscular process); 10, meatus acusticus externus; 11, zygomatic process of temporal bone; 12, condyle of same; 13, external opening of temporal canal; 14, processus cornus; 15, muscular process of temporal bone; 16, pterygoid crest; 17, orbital opening of supraorbital canal; 18, choanæ or posterior nares; 19, hamulus of pterygoid bone; 20, crest formed by pterygoid processes of sphenoid and palatine bones; 21, horizontal part of palatine bone; 22, anterior palatine foramen; 23. lacrimal bulla; 24, maxillary tuberosity; 25, palatine process of maxilla; 26, zygomatic process of malar bone; 27, facial tuberosity; 28, body of premaxilla; 29, palatine process of same; 30, palatine fissure; 31, incisive fissure; 32, premolars; 33, molars.

esses are of elongated conical form, and vary greatly in size, length, curvature, and direction. The external surface is rough and porous, marked by numerous grooves and foramina; in the fresh state it is covered by the corium of the horn. The base has a constriction, the neck. The interior is excavated to form a number of irregular spaces, partially divided by bony septa, and communicating with the frontal sinus. In the polled breeds these processes are absent, the skull is narrower here, and the frontal eminence more pronounced (Fig. 139). The supraorbital process is situated about half-way between the anterior and posterior margins; it is short and joins the frontal process of the malar bone. The **supraorbital foramen** (often double) is situated about an inch medially from the root of the process; it is the external orifice of the **supraorbital canal** (Canalis supraorbitalis), which passes downward and forward to the orbit. The foramen is in the course of the **supraorbital groove** (Sulcus supraorbitalis), which marks the course of the frontal vein. The anterior ends of the naso-frontal parts form a notch which receives the nasal bones, and sutural (or Wormian) bones are often found at this junction (naso-frontal suture). The orbital part is extensive; it is perforated behind by the orbital opening of the supraorbital canal, and below by the ethmoidal foramen. It does not articulate with the palatine bone, from which it is separated by the orbital wing of the sphenoid. The temporal part is also more extensive than in the horse. The frontal sinus is very extensive, being continued into the parietals and occipital, and the horn processes when present.

The **squamous** and **petrous parts** of the **temporal bone** fuse early—in fact union is nearly complete at birth. The squamous part is relatively small. Its lateral surface is divided into two parts by the prominent **temporal crest,** which is continuous with the parietal crest above and turns forward below, ending at a tubercle above the external acoustic meatus. The part behind the crest faces backward, and is partly free, partly united with the occipital. The area in front of the crest is concave and enters into the formation of the temporal fossa; it is perforated by foramina which communicate with the temporal canal. The zygomatic process is much shorter and weaker than in the horse, and articulates with the malar only. The condyle is convex in both directions. The postglenoid process is less prominent, and behind it is the chief external opening of the temporal canal. The cerebral surface is almost completely overlapped by the parietal and sphenoid. The petrous part is small, but the tympanic part is extensive. The external acoustic meatus is smaller than in the horse and is directed laterally. From it a plate projects downward and helps to inclose the deep depression in which the hyoid process is placed. Behind this plate is the stylo-mastoid foramen. The muscular process is large and often bifid at its free end. The bulla tympanica is large and laterally compressed. It is separated from the occipital bone by a narrow opening which is equivalent to part of the foramen lacerum of the horse. The temporal canal is formed entirely in the temporal bone. The facial canal, on the other hand, is bounded partly by the occipital bone.

BONES OF THE FACE

The **maxilla** is shorter but broader and relatively higher than in the horse. Its lateral surface bears the rough **facial tuberosity** (Tuber faciale), placed above the third and fourth cheek teeth; a rough line which extends backward from it to the upper part of the malar bone may be regarded as the facial crest. The infraorbital foramen—often double—is situated above the first cheek tooth. The tuber maxillare is small, laterally compressed, and usually bears a small pointed process (Processus pterygoideus). The zygomatic process is very small. The interalveolar border is concave, and there is no alveolus for a canine tooth. The palatine process is wider, but somewhat shorter than in the horse. It incloses a large air-space, which is continuous behind with a like cavity in the horizontal part of the palate bone, forming the **palatine sinus** (Sinus palatinus). This communicates laterally (over the infraorbital canal) with the maxillary sinus; in the macerated skull it communicates with the nasal cavity by a large oval opening, which is closed by mucous membrane in the fresh state. A median septum separates the two palatine sinuses. The alveoli for the cheek teeth increase in size from before backward. The maxillary sinus proper is small and is undivided. The maxillary foramen is a narrow fissure, deeply placed at the medial side of the lacrimal bulla. The maxilla takes no part in the formation of the palatine canal. Sutural (or Wormian) bones are often present at its junction with the lacrimal and malar bones.

The body of the **premaxilla** is thin and flattened, and has no alveoli, since the canine and upper incisor teeth are absent. A deep notch takes the place of the foramen incisivum. The nasal process is short, convex laterally, and does not reach to the nasal bone; the space between the two processes is greater than in the horse. The palatine process is narrow and is grooved on its nasal surface for the septal cartilage and the vomer. The palatine fissure is very wide.

The **palatine bone** is very extensive. The **horizontal part** forms one-fourth or

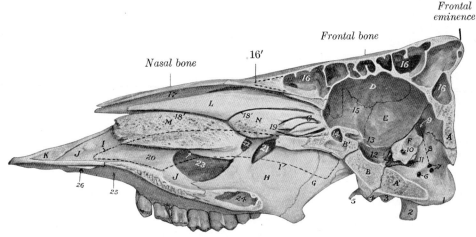

FIG. 135.—SAGITTAL SECTION OF SKULL OF OX, WITHOUT MANDIBLE.

A, A′, Squamous and basilar parts of occipital bone; B, B′, postsphenoid, presphenoid; C, lateral mass of ethmoid bone; D, internal plate of frontal bone; E, parietal bone; F, petrous temporal bone; G, pterygoid bone; H, perpendicular part of palatine bone; I, outline of vomer (dotted line); J, palatine process of maxilla; K, nasal process of premaxilla; L, dorsal turbinate bone; M, ventral turbinate bone; N, middle turbinate bone (great ethmo-turbinate); 1, occipital condyle; 2, paramastoid process; 3, bulla tympanica; 4, basilar tubercle; 5, muscular process; 6, hypoglossal foramen; 7, openings of condyloid canal; 8, direction of condyloid canal (dotted line); 9, internal opening of temporal canal; 10, meatus acusticus internus; 11, foramen lacerum; 12, sella turcica; 13, optic foramen; 14, sphenoidal sinus; 15, orbital wing of sphenoid bone; 16, frontal sinus; 16′, anterior limit of frontal sinus (dotted line); 17, dorsal nasal meatus; 18, middle nasal meatus; 18′, dorsal branch of middle meatus; 19, ethmoidal meatuses; 20, maxilla; 21, sphenopalatine foramen; 22, opening into maxillary sinus; 23, opening into palatine sinus, and arrow indicating communication of latter with maxillary sinus; 24, palatine sinus; 25, cross indicates anterior end of palatine sinus; 26, palatine fissure.

more of the hard palate. The anterior palatine foramen opens near the junction with the maxilla, about half an inch from the median palatine suture and crest. Accessory palatine foramina (Foramina palatina accessoria) are also present. The palatine groove is usually not very distinct. The palatine canal is formed entirely in this part, and there is no articulation with the vomer. A rounded ridge occurs on the nasal side of the median suture. The interior is hollow, forming part of the palatine sinus. The **perpendicular part** is an extensive, quadrilateral, thin plate, which forms the posterior part of the lateral wall of the nasal cavity and in part bounds the choanæ or posterior nares. Its nasal surface is nearly flat, and is smooth and free, except behind, where it is overlapped by the pterygoid bone. The lateral surface is attached to a small extent to the pterygoid process behind, and is free elsewhere. The sphenopalatine foramen is a long, elliptical opening, formed by a deep notch in the upper edge of the palate bone and completed by the ethmoid and sphenoid. The edge behind this foramen articulates with the orbital wing of the sphenoid, not the frontal, as in the horse.

The **pterygoid bone** is wider than in the horse, and forms the greater part of the lateral boundary of the posterior nares. Its lateral surface is almost entirely united to the palatine bone and the pterygoid process, but a small part is free in the pterygo-palatine fossa. The hamulus is distinctly hook-like, thin, and sharp.

The **nasal bone** is little more than half the length of that of the horse. It is straight in its length, but strongly curved from side to side. It does not fuse laterally with the adjacent bones, even in old age. The posterior extremity is pointed and fits into the notch between the frontal bones. The anterior end is broader, and is divided into two parts by a deep notch. In old animals there is a small extension of the frontal sinus into this bone.

The **lacrimal bone** is very large. The extensive facial part is concave in its length, and bears no lacrimal tubercle. The orbital margin is marked by several notches. The orbital part bears ventrally the remarkable **lacrimal bulla;** this is a large and very thin-walled protuberance, which bulges backward into the lower part of the orbit, and contains an extension of the maxillary sinus. The fossa for the lacrimal sac is small, and is just behind the orbital margin.

The **malar bone** is relatively long. The facial surface is extensive; it bears a curved crest (Crista facialis) just below the orbital margin which is continued on the maxilla, and below this it is concave dorso-ventrally. The zygomatic process divides into two branches; of these, the frontal branch (Processus frontalis) turns upward and backward and joins the supraorbital process of the frontal bone; the temporal branch (Processus temporalis) continues backward, and is overlapped by the zygomatic process of the temporal bone, completing the zygomatic arch.

The **dorsal turbinate bone** is less cribriform and fragile than in the horse, and is widest in its middle, small at either end. It is attached to the turbinate crest of the nasal bone, and curves downward, outward, and then upward to be applied outwardly to the frontal and lacrimal bones. It thus incloses a cavity which communicates with the middle meatus nasi. (In the macerated skull it opens into the frontal sinus, but this communication is closed by mucous membrane in the fresh state.)

The **ventral turbinate bone** is shorter but much broader than in the horse. It is attached to the maxilla by a basal lamella about an inch (ca. 2 to 3 cm.) wide, which slopes ventro-medially. At the inner edge of this it splits into two plates which are rolled in opposite directions, and inclose two separate cavities, subdivided by several septa. The dorsal one opens into the middle meatus, the ventral one into the ventral meatus nasi.

The **vomer** forms a wider and deeper groove than in the horse. Its anterior end rests in a groove formed by the ends of the palatine processes of the premaxillæ. The anterior third of its thin ventral edge fits into the nasal crest of the maxilla; behind this it is free and is separated by a considerable interval from the nasal floor.

The two halves of the **mandible** do not fuse completely even in advanced age, so that a symphysis mandibulæ is present. The symphyseal surfaces are extremely rough and are marked by reciprocal projections and cavities. The body is shorter, wider, and flatter than in the horse, and has eight round and relatively shallow alveoli for the lower incisors. The interalveolar border is long, curved, thin, and sharp. There are no alveoli for the canine teeth, which are absent. The anterior part of the ramus is narrow. The mental foramen is further forward than in the horse, and is in the posterior end of a fossa. The rami diverge more, so that the mandibular space is wider than in the horse. They are also more strongly curved, and the angle is more pronounced. The molar part is not so high, especially in its anterior part. Its ventral border is convex in its length. Its alveolar border bears six alveoli for the lower cheek teeth; the first is quite small, and they increase in size from before backward. The vertical part is much smaller than in the horse and its posterior border is relatively thin below, concave and wider above. The mandibular foramen is about in the middle of its medial surface, and a groove for

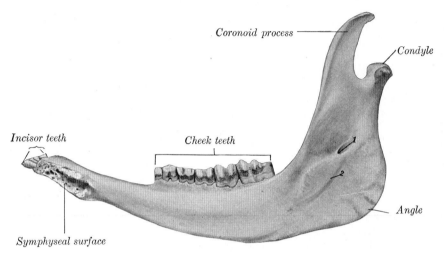

FIG. 136.—RIGHT HALF OF MANDIBLE OF OX; MEDIAL VIEW.
1, Mandibular foramen; 2, groove for lingual nerve.

the lingual nerve curves downward and forward from it. The condyle projects medially further than in the horse, and is concave from side to side. The coronoid process is extensive and curves backward.

The **hyoid bone** has a short tuberous lingual process. The middle cornua are almost as large as the small cornua. The great cornua are narrow, except at the ends. The upper end divides into two branches, which correspond to the two angles of that of the horse. The thyroid cornua do not fuse with the body except in old age.

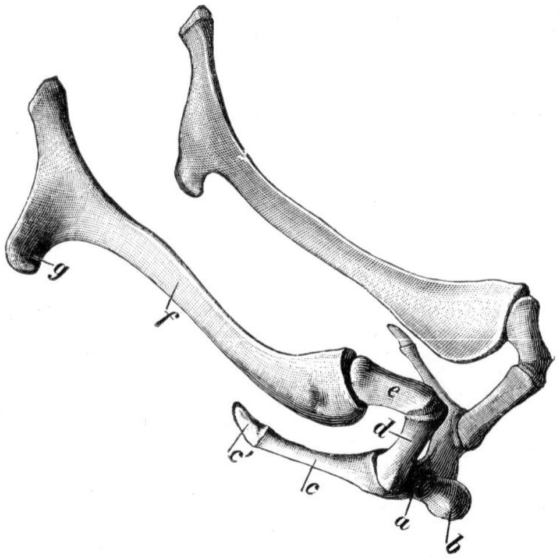

SKULL OF THE OX AS A WHOLE

The skull of the ox is more clearly pyramidal than that of the horse, and is shorter and relatively wider. The cranium is quadrangular and larger externally than in the horse; its large size is due mainly to the great extent of the frontal sinuses and does not affect the cranial cavity, which is smaller than in the horse.

FIG. 137.—HYOID BONE OF OX.

a, Body; b, lingual process; c, thyroid cornu and cartilage, c'; d, small cornu; e, middle cornu; f, great cornu; g, muscular angle. (Ellenberger-Baum, Anat. d. Haustiere.)

The **frontal surface** (Fig. 133) is formed by the frontals, nasals, and premaxillæ. The frontal part is quadrilateral and very extensive, the greatest width being at the orbits. It presents a central depression on its anterior part, and on either side are the supraorbital grooves and foramina. Behind is the median frontal eminence, and at the lateral angles the "horn cores" project in horned cattle. The nasal part is very short. The osseous nasal aperture is wide. The premaxillæ do not bend downward as in the horse; they are relatively thin and weak, and are separated by an interval which has a wide anterior part in place of the foramen incisivum.

The **lateral surface** (Fig. 129) is more triangular than in the horse. The temporal fossa is confined to this surface. It is deep and narrow, and its boundaries are more complete. It is limited dorsally by a crest which extends from the postero-lateral angle of the frontal bone to the supraorbital process, and is analogous to the parietal crest of the horse. It is bounded behind by the temporal crest. It is clearly marked off from the orbit by a rounded ridge and the pterygoid crest. The zygomatic arch is short, weak, and flattened, and is formed by the temporal and malar only. Its condyle is convex and is wide from before backward. The glenoid cavity and postglenoid process are small. The orbit is encroached upon below by the lacrimal bulla, and presents the orifice of the supraorbital canal behind. The orbital margin is completed behind by the frontal process of the malar; its lower part is prominent and rough, not smooth and rounded as in the horse. The pterygopalatine fossa is much larger, deeper, and more clearly defined. It has a long narrow recess between the vertical plate of the palate bone medially and the maxilla and lacrimal bulla laterally; thus the sphenopalatine and maxillary foramina are deeply placed. The preorbital region is short but relatively high. A tuberosity and curved line correspond to the facial crest of the horse. The infraorbital foramen is situated above the first cheek tooth and is often double.

The **basal surface** (Fig. 132) is short and wide, especially in its cranial part. The occipital condyles are limited in front by transverse ridges. The basilar tubercles at the junction of the occipital and sphenoid are large. The condyloid fossæ contain two foramina, the hypoglossal below and in front, and the condyloid above and behind; other inconstant ones occur. The paramastoid processes are short and convergent. The foramen lacerum is slit-like. The bulla tympanica is a large, laterally compressed prominence. The muscular processes are usually long and narrow triangular plates, with one or two sharp points. The external acoustic process is directed almost straight outward. A curved plate extends ventrally from it and joins the bulla ossea medially, completing the deep cavity which receives the articular angle of the hyoid bone. The chief external opening of the temporal canal is in front of this plate, and an accessory one lies behind it. The infratemporal fossa is small, and presents the foramen ovale. The posterior nares are very narrow, and the vomer does not reach to the level of their ventral margin. The hard palate is wide, and forms about three-fifths of the entire length of the skull. A small central part only of its posterior border enters into the formation of the posterior nares; the lateral parts are notched and just above them are the posterior palatine foramina. The anterior palatine foramina are an inch or more from the posterior margin, and about the same distance apart. The palatine grooves are distinct for a short distance only. Just beyond the cheek teeth the palate narrows and becomes concave; beyond this it widens and flattens.

The **nuchal surface** is extensive and somewhat pentagonal in outline in the adult. About its center is the external occipital protuberance for the attachment of the ligamentum nuchæ. From this a median occipital crest extends toward the foramen magnum, and laterally two lines (Lineæ nuchæ superiores) curve outward, marking the upper limit of the area which is roughened for muscular attachment. The surface above the lines is relatively smooth, and is covered only by the skin and the thin auricular muscles in the living animal. It is separated from the frontal surface by a thick border, which forms centrally the **frontal eminence,** and bears at its extremities the **processus cornus**—except in the polled breeds; midway between the frontal eminence and the processus cornus is the **nuchal eminence.**

The condyles are further apart, and the articular surfaces are more clearly divided into upper and lower parts than in the horse. The mastoid foramen is at the junction of the occipital and temporal bones; it is frequently very small.

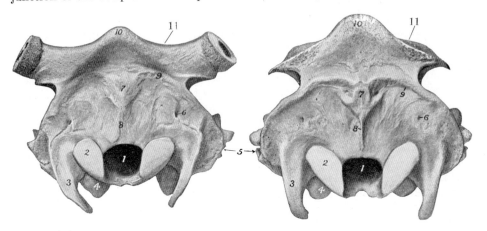

FIG. 138.—CRANIUM OF JERSEY COW, NUCHAL VIEW. THE GREATER PART OF THE PROCESSUS CORNUS HAS BEEN SAWN OFF.

FIG. 139.—CRANIUM OF POLLED ANGUS COW, NUCHAL VIEW.

1, Foramen magnum; 2, occipital condyle; 3, paramastoid process; 4, bulla tympanica; 5, meatus acusticus externus; 6, mastoid foramen; 7, external occipital protuberance; 8, median occipital crest; 9, linea nuchæ superior; 10, frontal eminence; 11, nuchal eminence.

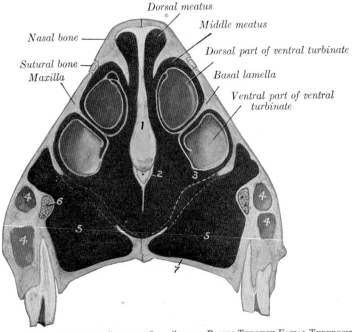

FIG. 140.—CROSS-SECTION OF NASAL REGION OF SKULL OF OX. SECTION PASSES THROUGH FACIAL TUBEROSITY AND THIRD CHEEK TOOTH.

1, Cartilage of septum nasi; 2, vomer; 3, ventral meatus; 4, anterior extremity of maxillary sinus; 5, palatine sinus; 6, infraorbital canal and nerve; 7, palatine process of maxilla. Dotted lines indicate mucous membrane which closes gap in bony floor of nasal cavity.

The **cranial cavity** is shorter and its long axis is more oblique than in the horse, but it is relatively high and wide. The anterior fossa lies at a much higher level than the rest of the floor. The ethmoidal fossæ are smaller, and the hypophyseal fossa or sella turcica is much deeper than in the horse. A deep groove leads from the petrous temporal forward over the foramen ovale to the foramen rotundum. Behind the sella there is often a distinct prominence (Dorsum sellæ). The internal parietal crest is prominent anteriorly, but subsides further back. A faintly marked elevation represents the internal occipital protuberance. The petrous temporal bone projects into the cavity laterally. The ridges and digital impressions are very pronounced. The temporal canal is formed entirely in the temporal bone, and opens internally at the apex of the petrous, where it is joined by the condyloid canal. The foramen lacerum is divided into two parts (For. lacerum orale et aborale).

The **nasal cavity** is incompletely divided by the septum, which does not reach

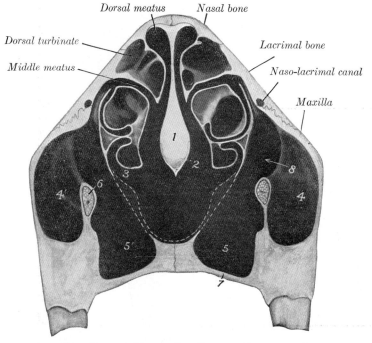

FIG. 141.—CROSS-SECTION OF NASAL REGION OF SKULL OF OX. SECTION IS CUT BETWEEN FOURTH AND FIFTH CHEEK TOOTH.

1, Cartilage of septum nasi; 2, vomer; 3, ventral meatus; 4, 4', maxillary sinuses; 5, 5', palatine sinuses; 6, infra-orbital canal and nerve; 7, horizontal part of palatine bone; 8, communication between maxillary and palatine sinuses. Dotted lines indicate mucous membrane which closes gap in bony floor of nasal cavity.

the floor posteriorly. The floor is relatively long, and is more concave from side to side than in the horse. In the dry skull it has a large oval opening (Hiatus maxillaris) into the palatine sinus, which is closed during life by mucous membrane. The middle meatus is divided behind into upper and lower branches by the great ethmoturbinate. The choanæ or posterior nares are narrow and oblique.

The **frontal sinus** is very large. It involves almost all of the frontal bone and a large part of the posterior wall of the cranium. It also extends for a variable distance into the horn processes when these are present. A complete median septum separates the right and left sinuses. The anterior limit is indicated by a transverse plane through the anterior margins of the orbits. It extends laterally to the crest, which limits the temporal fossa above, and into the root of the supraorbital process. At the highest part of the cranial cavity and at the external occipital protuberance the two plates of the bone usually come together. The cavity is divided into one major and one to four minor compartments on each side of the median plane. Each compartment has its own separate and distinct outlet from the floor, in its anterior part, leading into an ethmoidal meatus and thus indirectly into the upper division of the middle meatus.

The **major compartment** comprises that portion of the sinus lying posterior to the orbits. The supraorbital canal passes through this compartment. It usually

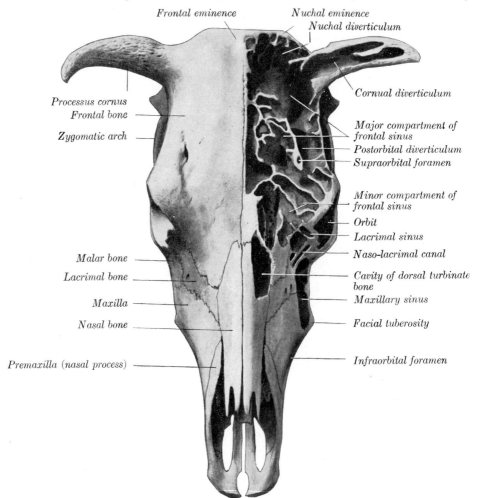

Frontal eminence   *Nuchal eminence*
Nuchal diverticulum

Processus cornus
Frontal bone

Zygomatic arch

Cornual diverticulum

Major compartment of frontal sinus
Postorbital diverticulum
Supraorbital foramen

Minor compartment of frontal sinus
Orbit
Lacrimal sinus
Naso-lacrimal canal

Malar bone
Lacrimal bone

Maxilla

Nasal bone

Cavity of dorsal turbinate bone
Maxillary sinus

Facial tuberosity

Premaxilla (nasal process)

Infraorbital foramen

FIG. 142.—SKULL OF OX; DORSAL VIEW; SINUSES OPENED.

has three diverticuli, the **nuchal diverticulum** in front of the nuchal eminence, the **postorbital diverticulum** behind the orbit and the **cornual diverticulum** which occupies the horn core when it is present. The outlet is a very small canal leading from the floor of the anterior part into an ethmoidal meatus.

The **minor compartments** lie in front of the major compartment and between the orbits. Each has its separate opening leading to the nasal cavity through an ethmoidal meatus. They vary in number and are named from their position. The communications with the cavity of the dorsal turbinate and with the lacrimal part of the maxillary sinus which are seen in the macerated skull are closed in the fresh state by mucous membrane.

The **maxillary sinus** is excavated chiefly in the maxilla, lacrimal, and malar, and is not divided by a septum as in the horse. It extends forward as far as the facial tuberosity, or a little further in old animals. Its dorsal limit is indicated approximately by a line drawn from the infraorbital foramen to the upper margin of the orbit. It is continued into the lacrimal bulla to a point nearly opposite to the bifurcation of the zygomatic process of the malar. It also extends upward and backward through a large opening into a cavity formed by the lacrimal, frontal, ethmoid, and turbinate bones, at the medial side of the orbit.[1] The floor of the cavity is irregular and the roots of the last three or four cheek teeth project up into it, covered by a plate of bone. The sinus communicates with the palatine sinus freely over the infraorbital canal through an oval opening about two to three inches (ca. 5 to 7.5 cm.) long. Above this it communicates by a shorter and much narrower opening with the middle meatus nasi.

The **palatine sinus** is excavated in the hard palate, and is separated from that of the opposite side by a median septum. It extends from the posterior border of the palate to a plane an inch or more (2.5 to 3 cm.) in front of the first cheek tooth. As mentioned above, there is a large communication with the maxillary sinus over

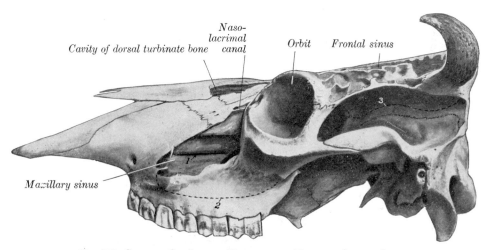

Naso-
lacrimal
Cavity of dorsal turbinate bone *canal*   *Orbit*   *Frontal sinus*

Maxillary sinus

Fig. 143.—Skull of Ox; Lateral View without Mandible; Sinuses Opened.
1, Communication between maxillary and palatine sinuses; 2, lowest extent of maxillary sinus; 3, lowest extent of frontal sinus.

the infraorbital canal, so that the cavity is sometimes regarded as a part of that sinus. The large defect in the bony roof of the sinus is closed by two layers of mucous membrane in the fresh state. The palatine canal passes obliquely through the posterior part of the sinus.

The **sphenoidal sinus** extends into the orbital wing of the sphenoid bone but does not communicate with the palatine sinus. It has one or two openings into the ventral ethmoidal meatuses. There is no cavity in the perpendicular part of the palate bone.

The **lacrimal sinus** is an excavation of the lacrimal bone producing a cavity which communicates freely with the posterior dorsal portion of the maxillary sinus.

BONES OF THE THORACIC LIMB

The **scapula** is more regularly triangular than in the horse, relatively wider at the vertebral end and narrower at the distal end. The scapular index is about

[1] This is termed the lacrimal sinus by some authors. It is similar in location and in the position of its orifice to the turbinate part of the frontal sinus of the horse with the important difference that it does not communicate with the frontal sinus in the ox.

1 : 0.6. The spine is more prominent and is placed further forward, so that the supraspinous fossa is narrow and does not extend to the lower part of the bone. The spine is sinuous, bent backward in its middle, forward below. Its free border is somewhat thickened in its middle, but bears no distinct tuber. Instead of subsiding below as in the horse, the spine becomes a little more prominent, and is prolonged by a pointed projection, the **acromion,** from which part of the deltoid muscle arises. The subscapular fossa is shallow. The areas for the attachment of the serratus muscle are not very distinct. The nutrient foramen is usually in the lower third of the posterior border. The glenoid cavity is almost circular and without any distinct notch. The tuberosity is small and close to the glenoid cavity.

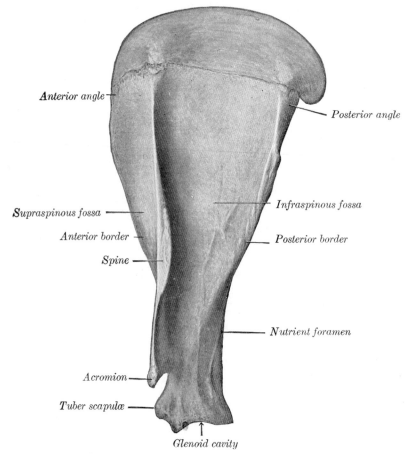

Anterior angle

Posterior angle

Supraspinous fossa

Infraspinous fossa

Anterior border

Posterior border

Spine

Nutrient foramen

Acromion

Tuber scapulæ

Glenoid cavity

FIG. 144.—LEFT SCAPULA OF OX; LATERAL VIEW.
Cartilage is shown but not marked.

The coracoid process is short and rounded. The cartilage resembles that of the horse. The tuberosity unites with the rest of the bone at seven to ten months.

The **humerus** has a shallow musculo-spiral groove. The deltoid tuberosity is less prominent than in the horse, and the curved line running from it to the neck bears a well-marked tubercle on its upper part. The nutrient foramen is usually in the distal third of the posterior surface. The lateral tuberosity is very large, and rises an inch or more (ca. 3 cm.) above the level of the head. Its anterior part curves medially over the intertuberal or bicipital groove, and below it laterally there is a prominent circular rough area for the insertion of the tendon of the infraspinatus. The anterior part of the medial tuberosity has a small projection which curves over the groove. The groove is undivided. The distal articular surface is decidedly oblique, and the grooves and ridge are very well marked. The coronoid and olecranon fossæ are deep and wide. The condyloid crest is represented by a rough raised area. The proximal end unites with the shaft at three and one-half to four years, and the distal at about one and one-half years.

The **radius** is short and relatively broad. It is somewhat oblique, the distal end being nearer the median plane than the proximal. The curvature is more pronounced below than above. The shaft is prismatic in its middle part and has

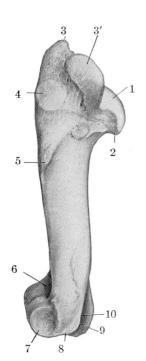

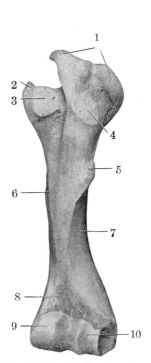

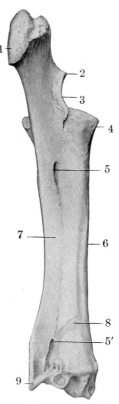

FIG. 145.—LEFT HUMERUS OF OX; LATERAL VIEW.

1, Head; 2, neck; 3, 3′, lateral tuberosity; 4, rough prominence for attachment of infraspinatus tendon; 5, deltoid tuberosity; 6, coronoid fossa; 7, lateral condyle; 8, lateral epicondyle; 9, medial epicondyle; 10, olecranon fossa.

FIG. 146.—LEFT HUMERUS OF OX; ANTERIOR VIEW.

1, Lateral tuberosity; 2, medial tuberosity; 3, intertuberal groove; 4, rough prominence for attachment of infraspinatus tendon; 5, deltoid tuberosity; 6, teres tubercle; 7, musculo-spiral groove; 8, coronoid fossa; 9, medial condyle; 10, lateral condyle.

FIG. 147.—LEFT RADIUS AND ULNA OF OX; POSTERO-MEDIAL VIEW.

1, Olecranon; 2, processus anconæus; 3, semilunar notch; 4, proximal extremity of radius; 5, 5′, proximal and distal interosseous spaces; 6, shaft of radius; 7, shaft of ulna; 8, vascular groove; 9, styloid process of ulna.

dorsal, volar, and lateral faces. There is a marked increase in width and thickness distally. The proximal articular surface presents a synovial fossa which extends medially from the deep groove between the two glenoid cavities. The radial tuberosity is represented by a slightly elevated rough area. The facets for the ulna are larger than in the horse. The two bones commonly fuse above the proximal interosseous space and always fuse below it, except near the distal end, where there is a small distal interosseous space. A groove connects the two spaces laterally. The distal extremity is large, and is thickest medially. Its articular surface is oblique in two directions, i. e., from within upward and backward. The grooves for the extensor tendons are shallow. The proximal end unites with the shaft at one to one and one-half years, and the distal at three and one-half to four years.

The approximation of the lower ends of the forearms and the carpi gives the "knock-kneed" appearance in cattle. The obliquity of the joint surfaces produces lateral deviation of the lower part of the limb in flexion. The facets for the radial and intermediate carpals are narrower than in the horse and run obliquely dorso-laterally. The surface for the ulnar carpal is extensive and saddle-shaped; its lateral part is furnished by the ulna.

The **ulna** is much less reduced than in the horse. The shaft is complete, three-sided, and strongly curved. It is fused with the radius in the adult, except at the two interosseous spaces mentioned above. Its proximal part contains a medullary cavity which extends somewhat into the proximal end. The olecranon is

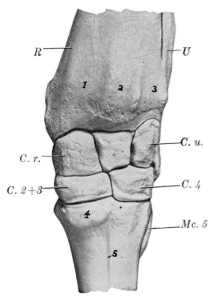

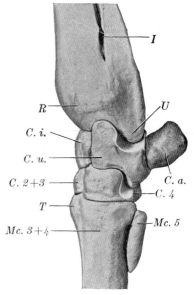

Fig. 148.—Left Carpus and Adjacent Bones of Ox; Front View.

R, Radius; *U*, ulna; *C. r.*, radial carpal; *C. u.*, ulnar carpal; *C. 2 + 3*, fused second and third carpals; *C. 4*, fourth carpal; *1, 2, 3*, grooves for extensor tendons; *4*, metacarpal tuberosity; *5*, vascular groove. Intermediate carpal bone (between radial and ulnar) not marked.

Fig. 149.—Left Carpus and Adjacent Bones of Ox; Lateral View.

R, Distal end of radius; *U*, styloid process of ulna; *I*, distal interosseous space; *C. i.*, intermediate carpal; *C. u.*, ulnar carpal; *C. a.*, accessory carpal; *C. 2 + 3*, fused second and third carpals; *C. 4*, fourth carpal; *Mc. 3 + 4*, fused third and fourth (large) metacarpal; *Mc. 5*, fifth (small) metacarpal; *T*, metacarpal tuberosity.

large and bears a rounded tuberosity. The distal end is fused with the radius; it projects below the level of the latter, forming the **styloid process** of the ulna (Processus styloideus ulnæ), which furnishes part of the facet for the ulnar carpal. The summit of the olecranon and the distal end unite with the shaft at three and one-half to four years.

The **carpus** consists of six bones, four in the proximal row and two in the distal. The proximal row is oblique in conformity with the carpal articular surface of the radius. The radial and intermediate resemble in general those of the horse, but are less regular in shape, and their long axes are directed obliquely backward and medially. The radial is narrower than in the horse and curves upward behind. The intermediate is constricted in its middle, and wider behind than in front. The ulnar is large and very irregular. Its proximal surface is extensive and sinuous and articulates with both radius and ulna; it has a large oval facet behind for articulation with the accessory carpal. The accessory is short, thick, and rounded; it articulates with the ulnar carpal only. The first carpal is absent. The second and third carpals are fused to form a large quadrilateral bone. The fourth carpal is a smaller quadrilateral bone.

The **metacarpus** consists of a large metacarpal and a lateral small metacarpal bone. The large metacarpal bone (Mc. 3 + 4) results from the fusion of the third and fourth bones of the fœtus, and bears evidences of its double origin even in the adult state. The shaft is shorter than in the horse, and is relatively wider and flatter. The dorsal surface is rounded, and is marked by a vertical vascular groove connecting two canals which traverse the ends of the shaft from before backward. The volar surface is flat and presents a similar but much fainter groove. The borders are rough in the proximal third. The proximal end bears two slightly concave facets for articulation with the bones of the lower row of the carpus; the medial area is the larger, and they are separated by a ridge in front and a notch behind. The lateral angle has a facet behind for the small metacarpal bone. The medial part of the extremity has anterior and posterior tuberosities. The distal end is divided into two parts by a sagittal notch. Each division bears an articular surface similar to that in the horse, but much smaller. The medullary cavity is divided into two parts by a vertical septum which is usually incomplete in the adult. The **small metacarpal** bone (Mc. 5) is a rounded rod about an inch and a half (ca. 3.5 to 4 cm.) in length, which lies against the proximal part of the lateral border of the large bone. Its proximal end articulates with the latter, but not with the carpus. The distal end is pointed.

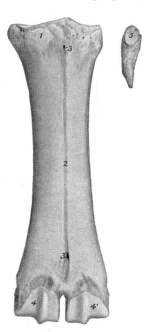

Four cartilaginous metacarpals are present in the early fœtal state, viz., the second, third, fourth, and fifth. The second commonly either disappears or unites with the third; sometimes it develops as a small rod of bone. The third and fourth gradually unite, but can be cut apart at birth. Each has three centers of ossification; the proximal epiphysis fuses with the shaft before birth, the distal at two to two and one-half years.

Four **digits** are present in the ox. Of these, two—the third and fourth—are fully developed and have three phalanges and three sesamoids each. The second and fifth are vestiges and are placed behind the fetlock; each contains one or two small bones which do not articulate with the rest of the skeleton.

The **first phalanx** is shorter and narrower than in the horse and is three-sided. The interdigital surface is flattened and its volar part bears a prominence for the attachment of the interdigital ligaments. The proximal extremity is relatively large, and is somewhat compressed from side to side. The articular surface is concave from before backward and is divided by a sagittal groove into two areas, of which the abaxial one is the larger and higher. Behind these are two facets for articulation with the sesamoid bones. The volar surface bears two tuberosities separated by a deep depression. The distal extremity is smaller than the proximal, especially in the dorso-volar direction. Its articular surface is divided by a sagittal groove into two convex facets, of which the abaxial one is decidedly the larger. There are depressions on either side for ligamentous attachment. The bone consists at birth of two pieces—the distal end and the fused shaft and proximal extremity. Union occurs at one and one-half to two years.

The **second phalanx** is about two-thirds of the length of the first and is dis-

FIG. 150.—LEFT METACARPAL BONES OF OX; FRONT VIEW. THE SMALL BONE HAS BEEN MOVED LATERALLY.

1, Metacarpal tuberosity; 2, vascular groove; 3, 3′, foramina; 4, 4′, condyles; 5, articular facet of fifth (small) metacarpal bone.

tinctly three-sided. The proximal articular surface is divided by a sagittal ridge into two glenoid cavities, of which the abaxial one is much the larger. There is a central dorsal prominence and two tubercles are present on the volar face. The distal extremity is smaller than the proximal. Its articular surface encroaches considerably on the dorsal and volar surfaces, and is divided into two parts by a sagittal groove. There is a deep depression for ligamentous attachment on the interdigital side. The bone contains a small medullary canal. The distal end unites with the rest of the bone about the middle of the second year.

The **third phalanges** resemble in a general way one-half of the bone of the horse. Each has four surfaces. The dorsal surface is marked in its distal part by a shallow groove, along which there are several foramina of considerable size; the posterior one of the series is the largest, and conducts to a canal in the interior of the bone. Distal to the groove the surface is prominent, rough, and porous.

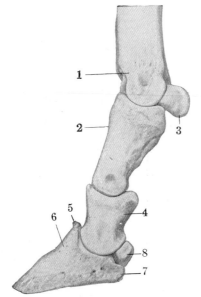

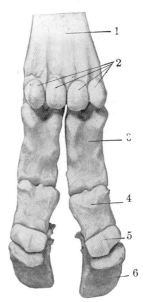

Fig. 151.—Bones of Distal Part of Fore Limb of Ox; Lateral View.

1, Distal end of metacarpal bone; 2, first phalanx; 3, proximal sesamoid bone; 4, second phalanx; 5, extensor process of third phalanx; 6, dorsal surface; 7, angle; 8, distal sesamoid bone.

Fig. 152.—Bones of Distal Part of Fore Limb of Ox; Volar View.

1, Metacarpal bone; 2, proximal sesamoid bones; 3, first phalanx; 4, second phalanx; 5, distal sesamoid bone; 6, third phalanx.

Near and on the extensor process are several relatively large foramina. The slope of the surface is very steep posteriorly, but in front it forms an angle of 25 to 30 degrees with the ground plane. The articular surface is narrow from side to side, and slopes downward and backward. It is also oblique transversely, the interdigital side being the lower. It is adapted to the distal surface of the second phalanx, with the exception of a facet behind for the distal sesamoid. The extensor process is very rough. The volar surface is narrow and slightly concave, and presents two or three foramina of considerable size. It is separated from the dorsal surface by a border which is sharp in front, rounded behind. There is no semilunar crest, since the deep flexor tendon is attached to the thick posterior border of the volar surface. The interdigital surface is smooth and grooved below, rough and porous above. At the proximal angle it is perforated by a large foramen, which is equivalent to the volar foramen of the horse and leads to a cavity in the middle of the bone. The surface is separated by a rounded border from the dorsal surface, and by a sharp edge from the volar surface. The angle is very short and blunt, and there is no cartilage.

Four **proximal sesamoids** are present, two for each digit. They are much smaller than in the horse. The bones of each pair articulate with the corresponding part of the distal end of the large metacarpal bone by their dorsal surfaces, with each other and with the first phalanx by small facets.

The two **distal sesamoids** are short and their ends are but little narrower than the middle.

BONES OF THE PELVIC LIMB

The **ilia** are almost parallel to each other and form a much smaller angle with the horizontal plane than in the horse. They are relatively small. The gluteal line is prominent and is nearly parallel to the lateral border; it joins the ischiatic spine. A rounded ridge separates the two parts of the pelvic surface. The surface

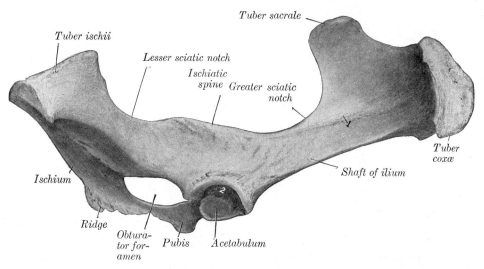

FIG. 153.—RIGHT OS COXÆ OF OX; LATERAL VIEW.
1, Gluteal line; 3, fossa acetabuli.

for articulation with the sacrum is triangular. The tuber sacrale is truncated, does not extend so high as the vertebral spines, and is separated from the opposite angle by a wider interval than in the horse. The tuber coxæ is relatively large and prominent; it is not so oblique as in the horse, and is wide in the middle, smaller at either end. The shaft is short and compressed from side to side.

The **ischium** is large. Its long axis is directed obliquely upward and backward, forming an angle of about 50 to 60 degrees with the horizontal plane. The transverse axis is oblique downward and inward at a similar angle, so that this part of the pelvic floor is deeply concave from side to side. The middle of the ventral surface bears a rough ridge or imprint for muscular attachment. The ischiatic spine is high and thin, and bears a series of almost vertical rough line laterally. The tuber ischii is large and three-sided, bearing dorsal, ventral, and lateral tuberosities. The ischial arch is narrow and deep. The symphysis bears a ventral ridge, which fades out near the ischial arch.

The acetabular branch of the **pubis** is narrow, and is directed laterally and a little forward. The anterior border is marked by a transverse groove which ends below the rough ilio-pectineal eminence. The symphyseal branch is wide and thin.

The **acetabulum** is smaller than in the horse. The rim is rounded and is usually marked by two notches. One of these is postero-medial and is narrow and deep; it leads to the deep acetabular fossa and is often almost converted into a foramen by a bar of bone. The other notch is antero-medial, small, and sometimes replaced by a foramen or absent.

The **obturator foramen** is large and elliptical; its medial border is thin and sharp.

Fusion of the three bones occurs at seven to ten months.

The **pelvic inlet** is elliptical and is more oblique than in the horse. In a cow

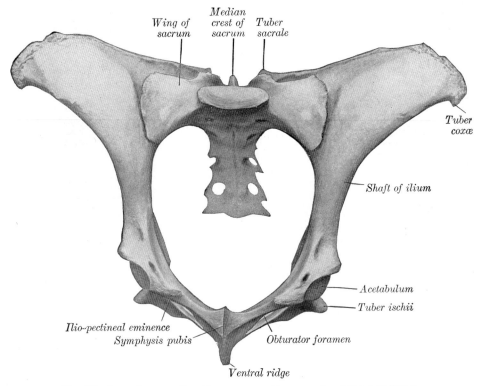

Fig. 154.—Pelvic Bones of Cow, Viewed from in Front and Somewhat from Below.

of medium size the **conjugate diameter** is about nine to ten inches, and the **transverse diameter** seven to eight inches (ca. 18 to 20 cm.). The **vertical diameter** measured from the anterior end of the symphysis to the junction of the third and fourth sacral segments is about nine inches (ca. 22 cm.). The **dorsal wall** or **roof** is concave in both directions. The **ventral wall** or **floor** is deeply concave, particularly in the transverse direction. The **cavity** is narrower and its **axis** is inclined strongly upward in the posterior part. The **outlet** has a vertical diameter of about nine inches (ca. 22 cm.), measured to the second coccygeal vertebra. The distance between the acetabulum and the tuber coxæ is only a little (ca. 3 to 4 cm.) more than the distance between the former and the tuber ischii.

The **femur** has a relatively small shaft, which is cylindrical in its middle, prismatic distally. The trochanter minor has the form of a rough tuberosity, and is situated higher up than in the horse and encroaches on the posterior surface. The trochanteric ridge (Crista intertrochanterica posterior) connects it with the trochanter major. The third trochanter is absent. The supracondyloid fossa is shallow. The proximal extremity is very wide. The head is smaller than in the horse, and the articular surface extends considerably on the upper surface of the neck. The fovea capitis is a small depression on the middle of the head for the attachment of the round ligament. The neck is well defined except above. The trochanter major is very massive and is undivided; its lateral surface is very rough.

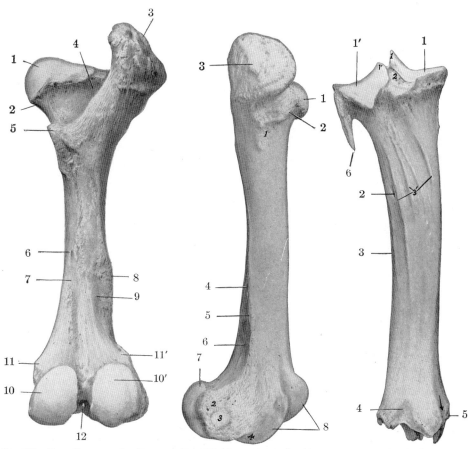

FIG. 155.—RIGHT FEMUR OF OX; POSTE-
RIOR VIEW.

1, Head; 2, neck; 3, trochanter major; 4, trochanteric fossa; 5, trochanter minor; 6, nutrient foramen; 7, vascular groove; 8, lateral supracondyloid crest; 9, supracondyloid fossa; 10, 10′, medial and lateral condyles; 11, 11′, medial and lateral epicondyles; 12, intercondyloid fossa.

FIG. 156.—RIGHT FEMUR OF OX; LATERAL VIEW.

Numbers around bone: 1, Head; 2, neck; 3, trochanter major; 4, lateral border; 5, lateral supracondyloid crest; 6, supracondyloid fossa; 7, lateral condyle; 8, trochlea. Numbers on bone: 1, Eminence for attachment of gluteus profundus; 2, lateral epicondyle; 3, depression for origin of popliteus muscle; 4, extensor fossa.

FIG. 157.—LEFT TIBIA AND PROX-
IMAL PART OF FIBULA OF OX;
POSTERIOR VIEW.

Numbers around bones: 1, 1′, Medial and lateral condyles of tibia; 2, nutrient foramen; 3, lateral border; 4, distal extremity; 5, medial malleolus; 6, shaft of fibula. Numbers on bone: 1, 1′, Tubercles of spine; 2, intercondyloid fossa; 3, muscular lines. Arrow indicates groove for flexor digitalis longus.

The trochanteric fossa is deep, but does not extend so far distally as in the horse. The distal end presents no very striking differential features, but the ridges of the trochlea are less oblique than in the horse, and converge very slightly below. The proximal extremity unites with the shaft at about three and one-half years, the distal at three and one-half to four years.

The **tibia** resembles that of the horse rather closely, but is somewhat shorter.

The shaft is distinctly curved, so that the medial side is convex. The posterior surface is not divided into two areas, and the lineæ musculares are fewer and extend up higher than in the horse. The articular grooves and ridge of the distal end are almost sagittal in direction, and present an extensive but shallow synovial fossa. The lateral groove is separated by a sharp ridge from an outer area which is for articulation with the lateral malleolus. The anterior part of the medial malleolus is prolonged downward and has a pointed end. The groove behind it is broad and well defined. Laterally there is a deep narrow groove which separates two prominences. The proximal extremity fuses with the shaft at three and one-half to four years, the distal at two to two and one-half years.

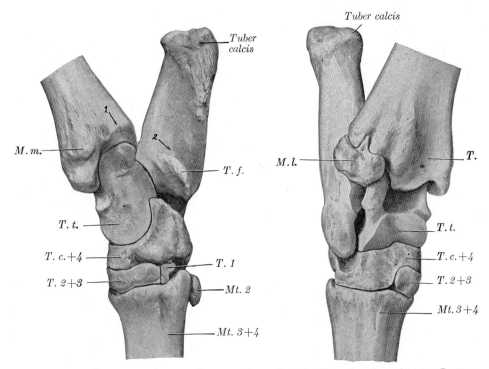

FIG. 158.—RIGHT TARSUS AND ADJACENT BONES OF OX; MEDIAL VIEW.

FIG. 159.—RIGHT TARSUS AND ADJACENT BONES OF OX; DORSO-LATERAL VIEW.

M. m., Medial malleolus; *M. l.*, lateral malleolus (distal end of fibula); *T*, tibia; *T. t.*, tibial tarsal bone; *T. f.*, fibular tarsal bone (sustentaculum); *T. c.+4*, fused central and fourth tarsal bones; *T. 1*, first tarsal bone; *T. 2+3*, fused second and third tarsal bones; *Mt. 2*, small or second metatarsal bone; *Mt. 3+ 4*, large metatarsal or fused third and fourth metatarsal bones; *1*, groove for tendon of flexor digitalis longus; *2*, groove for deep flexor tendon.

The **fibula** usually consists of the two extremities only. The head is fused with the lateral condyle of the tibia and is continued by a small, blunt-pointed prolongation below. The distal end remains separate and forms the lateral malleolus (sometimes called the os malleolare). It is quadrilateral in outline and compressed from side to side. The proximal surface articulates with the distal end of the tibia, and bears a small spine which fits into the groove on that bone. The distal surface rests on the fibular tarsal, and the medial articulates with the lateral ridge of the tibial tarsal bone. The lateral surface is rough and irregular.

The early cartilaginous fibula is complete, but later the shaft is reduced to the small prolongation noted in speaking of the head and a fibrous cord which connects it with the distal end (lateral malleolus). In some cases, however, the upper part undergoes partial ossification, forming a slender rod which is usually united with the lateral border of the tibia and is joined to the head by fibrous tissue.

The **patella** is long, narrow, and very thick. The free surface is strongly convex and very rough and irregular. The articular surface is convex from side to side and nearly straight in the vertical direction. The large prominence on the medial side for the attachment of the fibro-cartilage allows prompt determination of the side to which the bone belongs. The apex is more pointed than in the horse.

The **tarsus** consists of five pieces; the central and fourth and the second and third tarsal bones are fused.

The **tibial tarsal** bone is relatively long and narrow, and is somewhat flattened from before backward. It bears a trochlea at either end. The groove and ridges of the proximal trochlea are not spiral, but almost sagittal; the lateral ridge is the wider, and articulates with both tibia and fibula. The distal trochlea consists of two condyles divided by a groove, and articulates with the combined central and fourth tarsals. The plantar surface bears a large oval facet for articulation with the fibular tarsal; this occupies most of the surface, and is convex and grooved from above downward. The lateral surface presents two facets for articulation with the fibular tarsal, and is excavated and rough elsewhere. The medial surface bears a tuberosity at its upper part, and is flattened below.

The **fibular tarsal** bone is longer and more slender than in the horse. The distal part of the body is compressed laterally, and bears a projection in front which articulates with the lateral malleolus. The tuber calcis is marked posteriorly by a wide shallow groove, which is coated with cartilage in the fresh state.

The **central** and **fourth tarsals** are fused to form a large bone (Os centrotarsale quartum, scapho-cuboid), which extends across the entire width of the tarsus and articulates with all of the other bones. The greater part of the proximal surface is molded on the distal trochlea of the tibial tarsal, and its medial part rises high above the rest posteriorly. Laterally there is a narrow, undulating surface for articulation with the distal end of the fibular tarsal bone. The plantar surface bears two tuberosities, of which the lateral one is rounded, the medial more prominent and narrower.

The **first tarsal** bone is quadrilateral and small. It articulates with the central above, the metatarsus below, and the second tarsal in front.

The **second** and **third tarsals** are fused to form a rhomboid piece. The proximal surface is concavo-convex, and articulates with the central component. The distal surface is undulating and rests on the metatarsus. The lateral surface bears a small facet in front for the fourth tarsal component, and the plantar surface a very small one for the first tarsal bone.

Fig. 160.—LARGE METATARSAL BONE OF OX; DORSAL VIEW.

1, Vascular groove; 2, foramen; 3, 3′, condyles.

The **large metatarsal** bone is about one-seventh (ca. 3 cm.) longer than the corresponding metacarpal. Its shaft is compressed transversely and is distinctly four-sided. The groove on the dorsal surface is deep and wide. The plantar surface is marked by variable grooves. The proximal foramen on this surface does not perforate the shaft, but passes obliquely through the extremity, opening on the posterior part of its proximal surface. The medio-plantar angle of the proximal end bears a facet for articulation with the small metatarsal bone.

The **small metatarsal** bone is a quadrilateral disc a little less than an inch in width and height. Its anterior face bears a facet for articulation with the large metatarsal bone. It may be a sesamoid bone.

The large metatarsal bone is usually regarded as consisting of the fused third and fourth metatarsal bones, and the small bone as the second metatarsal. The medullary cavity is subdivided like that of the large metacarpal bone. Some anatomists, however, consider that the ridges at the upper end of each border represent the second and fifth metatarsals (Rosenberg and Retterer). On this basis the small bone might be the first metatarsal or a sesamoid.

The **phalanges** and **sesamoids** resemble those of the thoracic limb so closely as to render separate description unnecessary.

SKELETON OF THE SHEEP

VERTEBRAL COLUMN

The **vertebral formula** may be given as $C_7T_{13}L_{6-7}S_4Cy_{16-18}$, but it should be noted that, except in the cervical region, variation in number is common.

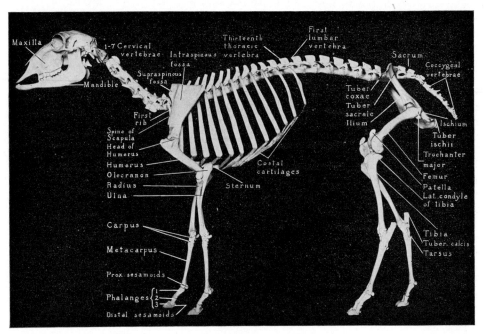

FIG. 160a.—SKELETON OF THE SHEEP.

It is not very rare to find twelve thoracic and seven lumbar, or an ambiguous intermediate vertebra. More commonly there are seven lumbar vertebræ without reduction in the thoracic region. In some cases there are fourteen thoracic and five or six lumbar vertebræ, and Lesbre records a case in which twelve thoracic and seven lumbar were present. In some cases the fourth sacral vertebra remains separate, and in others the first coccygeal unites with the sacrum, although the fusion here is rarely complete. Nathusius states that the number of coccygeal vertebræ varies from three to twenty-four or more.

The **cervical vertebræ** are relatively longer than those of the ox. The **atlas** differs chiefly in that the prominence on the dorsal arch is much less developed. The anterior articular cavities are often separated by a central ridge. The wings are produced to form blunt points behind. The spinous process of the **axis** is not enlarged posteriorly; those of the succeeding vertebræ are less developed than in the ox; they increase in length from the third to the last. The ventral spines are rudimentary. The arches are separated dorsally by interarcuate spaces.

The **thoracic vertebræ** are usually thirteen in number, but fourteen may be present, or, more rarely, only twelve. Their bodies are relatively wider and less constricted than those of the ox, and their extremities are not so strongly curved, especially toward the end of the series. The intervertebral foramina are larger, in correlation with the absence of the foramina which usually occur in the arches of these vertebræ in the ox.

The **lumbar vertebræ** number six or seven, the former being a little more frequent than the latter. It is not common to find the number reduced to five. In some cases there is an ambiguous vertebra at the junction of the thoracic and lumbar regions. The bodies are more flattened dorso-ventrally than those of the ox; their anterior ends are somewhat concave transversely, and the posterior ends are almost flat. The anterior articular processes are strongly curved and overlap the posterior ones. The transverse processes curve forward and have expanded ends.

The **sacrum** consists ordinarily of four segments, but the last vertebra may remain separate or undergo only partial fusion. There is no vascular groove on the pelvic surface. The spines are not fused, with the exception of the first and second, which may be partially united. The transverse processes of the last segment are distinct and outstanding.

The **coccygeal vertebræ** vary in number from three (in short-tailed sheep) to twenty-four or more. The bodies have no hemal processes on the ventral surface. The transverse processes are long and thin and project backward.

THE RIBS

The **ribs** usually number thirteen pairs, but the occurrence of fourteen pairs is common. The thirteenth rib is often floating and may have a cartilage only about an inch long. The fourteenth rib, when present, is floating. As compared with those of the ox, they are narrower and are more strongly curved in the anterior part of the series. The lateral surface is in general smooth and rounded. The second to the eleventh form diarthroses with their cartilages.

The thirteenth rib may be more or less rudimentary on one side or both, and may be fused with the corresponding vertebra; the latter may, therefore, be ambiguous in character.

THE STERNUM

The **sternum** resembles in general that of the ox. The number of segments may be reduced to six, and the primitive division of the next to the last sternebra into two lateral halves may persist for a long time. The first segment is cylindrical, with enlarged ends; the second and third are wide and flat; the last is long and narrow.

THE SKULL

The more important differences in the skull of the sheep as compared with that of the ox are in regard to the cranium. Viewed from above, the cranium is irregularly hexagonal in outline; it is widest in the frontal region, between the posterior parts of the orbits, and narrows greatly both anteriorly and posteriorly. In profile the roof of the cranium is strongly convex; the highest part of the curve coincides with the greatest width, and the posterior part slopes at an angle of about 45 degrees with the basal plane.

The **occipital bone** forms all of the nuchal surface of the cranium, except a small lateral area occupied by the mastoid part of the temporal bone. A narrow part (about 1.5 cm. in width) enters into the formation of the roof of the cranium also; it joins the parietal bones at a transverse suture. The parietal and nuchal surfaces are separated by a rough transverse ridge, the central part of which is united below with the external occipital protuberance, to which the ligamentum nuchæ is attached. The mastoid foramen is situated between the lateral border and the petro-mastoid part of the temporal bone. The paramastoid process is grooved laterally, has a concave anterior border, and tapers to a blunt point. The basilar part is wide; the tubercles at its junction with the sphenoid are placed laterally, and are broad and short.

The **sphenoid bone** resembles that of the ox. The posterior wall of the deep hypophyseal or pituitary fossa is formed by a plate (Dorsum sellæ) which is directed forward and upward, and bears a projection (Processus clinoideus posterior) at each side of its upper part. The sphenoidal sinus is commonly absent or rudimentary.

The **ethmoid bone** resembles that of the ox.

The **parietal bone** fuses soon after birth with its fellow and with the interparietal. From this union there result a central quadrilateral curved plate which forms part of the roof of the cranium, and, separated from it by a curved line, a narrower lateral part, which extends forward on either side as part of the medial

Fig. 161.—Skull of Sheep; Lateral View.

A, Occipital bone; *B*, parietal bone; *C*, squamous temporal bone; *D*, frontal bone; *E*, nasal bone; *F*, lacrimal bone; *G*, malar bone; *H*, maxilla; *I*, premaxilla; *J*, mandible; *K*, perpendicular part of palatine bone; *L*, hyoid bone; 1, occipital condyle; 2, paramastoid process; 3, mastoid process; 4, meatus acusticus externus; 5, bulla tympanica; 6, zygomatic process of temporal bone; 7, condyle of mandible; 8, coronoid process; 9, supraorbital process; 10, processus cornus; 11, 11', openings of supraorbital canal; 12, ethmoidal foramen; 13, optic foramen; 14, fossa sacci lacrimalis; 15, bulla lacrimalis; 16, external lacrimal fossa; 17, facial tuberosity; 18, infraorbital foramen; 10, mental foramen; 20, outline of maxillary sinus; 21, course of naso-lacrimal duct.

wall of the temporal fossa. The frontal sinus does not extend into the parietal bone. There is no internal occipital protuberance.

The **frontal bone** is relatively less extensive than in the ox. The naso-frontal part is strongly curved, but varies considerably in contour in different breeds. In horned breeds the processus cornus projects from the lateral part of the external surface a little (ca. 1.5 cm.) behind a transverse plane through the posterior margin of the orbit. The process varies in size and shape, and may, depending on the age, contain an extension of the frontal sinus. In other cases there is a rounded tuberosity or a slightly roughened elevation. The supraorbital foramen is further forward than in the ox, being just behind a transverse plane through the middle of the orbit; it is a little nearer to the orbital margin than to the median line. The groove which leads forward from it is often rather faint. The orbital part is deeply concave.

The infraorbital canal opens on the medial wall of the orbit as in the ox. The **frontal sinus** extends backward to a transverse plane through the posterior part of the temporal condyle, and forward to one through the anterior margin of the orbit. It is commonly divided into a major and a minor compartment each with its own distinct outlet into the nasal cavity. The orifices are somewhat elliptical in outline, and measure respectively, 2.5 mm. x 4.5 mm. and 3.5 mm. x 5.5 mm. in diameter. The **major compartment** is partially subdivided by numerous septa, one of which is important as the supraorbital canal passes through its anterior border; it extends backward and inward from the supraorbital foramen usually meeting the median plane on a line through the posterior limits of the orbits. The **minor compartment** may or may not be separate from the sinus of the dorsal turbinate.

The **temporal bone** consists of distinct squamous, tympanic, and petro-mastoid parts. The squamous part in general resembles that of the ox, but has, like that of the horse, a notch through which the external acoustic process protrudes. The root of the zygomatic process is perforated by a foramen which opens ventrally behind the postglenoid process, in front of the chief external opening of the temporal canal. The latter extends upward and backward between the petro-mastoid and squamous parts and the parietal bone, and opens into the cranial cavity in front of the apex of the petrous. The tympanic part includes the external acoustic process, the bulla tympanica, and the muscular process; the first resembles that feature in the horse, the others those of the ox, but the cavity of the bulla is undivided. The cerebral surface of the petrous part presents the floccular fossa on its upper part, and a round eminence behind the internal acoustic meatus.

The bones of the face present, aside from the difference in size, few important special features.

In regard to the **maxilla** it may be noted that the junction with the lacrimal and malar is less oblique than in the ox, since the facial parts of these bones are quadrilateral and not produced to a point anteriorly. The facial tuberosity and the infraorbital foramen are a little further back, and lie about over the fourth and second cheek tooth respectively. The **palatine sinus** is excavated in the palatine process of the maxilla and the horizontal portion of the palatine bone and situated medial to the infraorbital canal. It does not reach the median plane. It extends forward to a point opposite to the first upper cheek tooth and backward to a transverse plane through the anterior margin of the orbits. The sinus communicates freely with the maxillary sinus over the infraorbital canal with and the nasal cavity by way of the maxillary sinus and its orifice. The defect (in the dry skull) in its nasal wall is quite small—in marked contrast to that of the ox—since the basal lamella of the ventral turbinate bone curves ventro-medially, joins the palatine bone, and is separated only by a narrow hiatus from the nasal plate of the palatine process of the maxilla. The anterior palatine foramen is at the transverse palatine suture. The anterior end of the palatine process tapers to a point. The **maxillary sinus** resembles that of the ox, but is relatively small. The dorsal limit is approximately a line from the infraorbital foramen to a point below the medial canthus of the eye. The outlet extends upward, backward and inward from its upper part reaching the middle meatus beneath the anterior free end of the great ethmoturbinate bone, which partially blocks the orifice. The orifice is elliptical in outline measuring about 7 mm. x 9 mm.

The **premaxilla** has a narrow and pointed body. The palatine process is extremely narrow in front and is grooved laterally. The palatine fissure is long and narrows to a very acute angle behind.

The **palatine bone** resembles that of the ox, but there is no air-cavity in its vertical part. The sphenopalatine foramen is large and oval.

The **pterygoid bone** is very broad above and narrow below, where it ends in a sharp-pointed hamulus.

The **nasal bone** tapers to a point at its anterior end, which is not notched.

The facial part of the **lacrimal bone** has an elongated quadrilateral outline; in front of the orbit it forms, with the adjacent part of the malar, the **external lacrimal fossa** (Fossa lacrimalis externa) which lodges a cutaneous cul-de-sac known as the infraorbital or lacrimal pouch. The bone here may be more or less cribriform. The lacrimal bulla is relatively small, is usually cribriform, and has a pointed posterior end; the maxillary sinus extends into it. The orbital margin forms a distinct prominence, and behind the latter is the fossa for the lacrimal sac. The

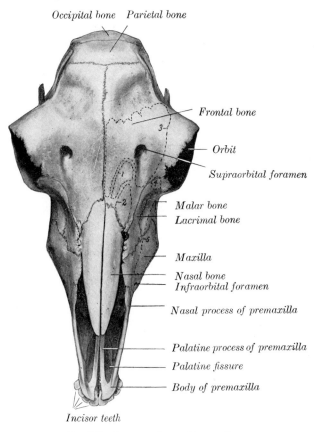

Occipital bone   Parietal bone

Frontal bone

Orbit

Supraorbital foramen

Malar bone
Lacrimal bone

Maxilla

Nasal bone
Infraorbital foramen

Nasal process of premaxilla

Palatine process of premaxilla

Palatine fissure

Body of premaxilla

Incisor teeth

FIG. 162.—SKULL OF SHEEP; DORSAL VIEW.

1, Outline of minor compartment of frontal sinus; 2, outline of sinus of dorsal turbinate; 3, outline of major compartment of frontal sinus; 4, outline of lacrimal sinus; 5, outline of maxillary sinus.

lacrimal sinus is very small, situated antero-medial to the orbit in the lacrimal bone. It has a very thin wall, usually partly mucous membrane, separating it from the major compartment of the frontal sinus. It has a separate orifice communicating with an ethmoidal meatus.

The facial part of the **malar bone** is extensive and quadrilateral. Its upper part concurs in the formation of the external lacrimal fossa; this area is limited below by a curved crest which continues backward on the zygomatic process. The latter divides into two branches, as in the ox.

The **turbinates** and the **vomer** resemble those of the ox. The **dorsal turbinate sinus** is located beneath the extreme anterior portion of the frontal bone. It and the minor compartment of the frontal sinus may form a common sinus. The outlet is into an ethmoid meatus.

The **mandible** differs from that of the ox chiefly in that the ventral border of the ramus, from the body to the angle, is only slightly curved.

On account chiefly of the limited extent of the frontal sinuses, the **cranial cavity** corresponds to the external form of the cranium more closely than is the case in the ox. It is ovoid, and is much longer relatively, but has a much shorter dorso-ventral diameter than that of the ox. The parietal bone forms a distinct ridge on the lateral wall between the cerebral and cerebellar compartments, but, on the other hand, the petrous temporal projects very little into the cavity.

The **nasal cavity** resembles that of the ox, but is relatively narrow (especially anteriorly), and there is no large hiatus in the nasal plate of the maxilla.

BONES OF THE THORACIC LIMB

The **scapula** differs chiefly from that of the ox in the following points: The vertebral border is longer and the neck narrower. The spine is less sinuous. The glenoid extremity is relatively long, since the tuber scapulæ is connected with the rim of the glenoid cavity. The subscapular fossa is more extensive.

The **humerus** is relatively longer and more slender than that of the ox. The anterior part of the lateral tuberosity is blunt and less incurved, while the posterior part is small. The deltoid tuberosity is nearer to the proximal end and is less prominent.

The bones of the forearm are relatively longer than those of the ox. The **radius** is a little more curved than that of the ox, and its dorsal surface is more regularly rounded. The shaft of the **ulna** is more slender, especially in its distal half; its fusion with the radius occurs later and is usually much less extensive than in the ox.

The **carpal bones** resemble those of the ox except in size. The accessory is long and less tuberous.

The **large metacarpal bone** (Mc. 3 + 4) is long and slender. The lateral **small metacarpal bone** (Mc. 5) is often absent or is represented by a ridge on the large metacarpal.

The **phalanges** of the chief digits are relatively long and narrow. The third phalanx in particular is much flattened on its abaxial side, so as to form a prominent dorsal border. Of the **proximal sesamoids,** the abaxial ones are compressed from side to side, and the axial ones from before backward. The flexor surface of the **distal sesamoids** forms a shallow groove, not divided by a ridge. The accessory digits usually have no phalanges.

BONES OF THE PELVIC LIMB

The **os coxæ** differs greatly from that of the ox. The long axis of the **ilium** is almost in a line with that of the ischium. The gluteal line appears as a ridge which is nearly parallel with the lateral border. The tuber coxæ is only slightly thickened, and the tuber sacrale is pointed. The crest is concave medially, convex laterally. The shaft is relatively long and is flattened laterally. The superior ischiatic spine is low and everted. The **pubis** resembles that of the ox, but its anterior border (pecten) is thin and sharp. The **ischium** slopes downward and backward, and forms a much larger angle with its fellow than in the ox. The lesser sciatic notch is very shallow. The tuber ischii is flattened and everted; it bears a long, blunt-pointed lateral process, and a very short and blunt dorsal prominence. There is a very low ventral ridge on the symphysis. The latter is not usually completely ossified, even in old animals. The acetabulum is further back than in the ox, and is relatively larger and deeper; it has a deep notch posteriorly. The **pelvic inlet** is very oblique, so that a vertical plane from the anterior end of the symphysis cuts the first coccygeal vertebra. The brim is elliptical; the conjugate diameter is about five inches (ca. 12 cm.), and the transverse about three and a half to four inches (ca. 9.5 cm.). The floor of the pelvic cavity is wide and shallow as compared with the ox, and the pelvic axis inclines downward posteriorly.

The shaft of the **femur** is slightly curved, the convexity being anterior. A distinct line separates the lateral and posterior surfaces. The supracondyloid fossa is very shallow. The head has a shallow fovea and the neck is distinct. The trochanter major is little higher than the head. The ridges of the trochlea are similar and parallel, but slightly oblique.

The **tibia** is long and slender, but otherwise resembles that of the ox. The **fibula** has no shaft, and its proximal end is represented by a small prominence below the lateral margin of the lateral condyle of the tibia; the distal end forms the lateral malleolus, as in the ox.

The **patella** is relatively longer and narrower than that of the ox.

The **tarsal bones** resemble those of the ox except in size.

The **metatarsal** and **digital bones** present special characters similar to those of the corresponding part of the thoracic limb.

SKELETON OF THE PIG

VERTEBRAL COLUMN

The **vertebral formula** is $C_7T_{14-15}L_{6-7}S_4Cy_{20-23}$.

The **cervical vertebræ** are short and wide. The bodies are elliptical in cross-section, the long diameter being transverse. The anterior articular surfaces are slightly convex from side to side and concave dorso-ventrally; the posterior ones

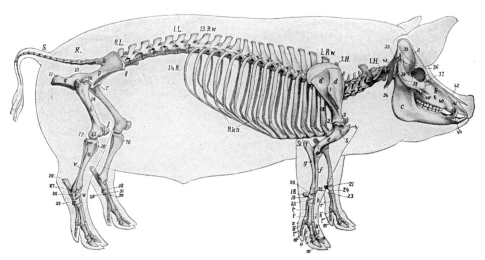

FIG. 163.—SKELETON OF PIG; LATERAL VIEW.

 a, Cranium; *b*, maxilla; *c*, mandible; *1H.–7H.*, cervical vertebræ; *1R.w.*, first thoracic vertebra; *13 R.w.*, thirteenth thoracic vertebra (next to last); *1L.*, first lumbar vertebra; *6L.*, sixth lumbar vertebra (next to last usually); *K.*, sacrum; *S.*, coccygeal vertebræ; *1R.*, first rib; *14R.*, last rib; *R.kn.*, costal cartilages; *St.*, sternum; *d*, supraspinous fossa; *d'*, infraspinous fossa; *1*, spine of scapula; *2*, neck of scapula; *e*, humerus; *3*, head of humerus; *4*, tuberosities of humerus; *5*, deltoid tuberosity; *6*, lateral epicondyle of humerus; *f*, radius; *g*, ulna; *7*, olecranon; *h*, carpus; *18–25*, carpal bones; *i–i''''*, metacarpus; *k–k''''*, proximal phalanges; *l–l''''*, middle phalanges; *m–m''''*, distal phalanges; *n, o*, sesamoids; *p*, ilium; *8*, tuber coxæ; *9*, tuber sacrale; *10*, superior ischiatic spine; *q*, ischium; *11*, tuber ischii; *r*, pubis; *12*, acetabulum; *s*, femur; *13*, trochanter major; *14*. trochanter minor; *15*, lateral epicondyle; *t*, patella; *u*, tibia; *16*, crest of tibia; *17*, lateral condyle of tibia; *v*, fibula; *w*, tarsus; *26–31*, tarsal bones; *26'*, tuber calcis. (After Ellenberger, in Leisering's Atlas).

are slightly concave. A ventral spine is not present. The arches are wide transversely, but the laminæ are narrow, so that a considerable interval (Spatium interarcuale) separates adjacent arches dorsally. The pedicles are perforated by a foramen in addition to the usual intervertebral foramina. The transverse processes divide into two branches, both of which increase in size from the third to the sixth. The dorsal branch projects outward and backward; it is short and is thickened at its free end. The other branch is a quadrilateral plate directed ventrally; each overlaps the succeeding one to a small extent, and the series forms the lateral boundary of a deep and wide ventral groove. The spines increase in height from the third to the last; the anterior ones are inclined backward, the posterior ones forward. The last cervical is recognized by the great length of its spine (ca. 10 cm. in the adult), the absence of the ventral plate of the transverse process, and the flatness of the body, which bears a pair of small facets on its posterior margin for the

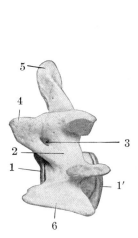

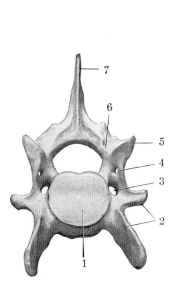

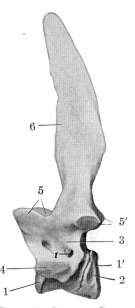

FIG. 164.—FOURTH CERVICAL VERTEBRA OF PIG; LATERAL VIEW.

1, 1', Anterior and posterior ends of body; 2, arch; 3, foramen of arch; 4, anterior articular process; 5, spinous process; 6, ventral branch of transverse process.

FIG. 165.—SIXTH CERVICAL VERTEBRA OF PIG; ANTERIOR VIEW.

1, Body; 2, transverse process; 3, foramen transversarium; 4, additional foramen of arch; 5, articular process; 6, arch; 7, spinous process.

FIG. 166.—SEVENTH CERVICAL VERTEBRA OF PIG; LATERAL VIEW.

1, 1', Anterior and posterior ends of body; 2, facet for head of first rib; 3, arch; 4, transverse process; 5, 5', articular processes; 6, spinous process; 1 (number on bone), foramina of arch.

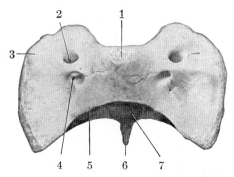

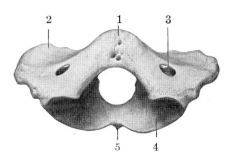

FIG. 167.—ATLAS OF PIG; DORSAL VIEW.

1, Dorsal tuberosity; 2, alar foramen; 3, wing; 4, intervertebral foramen; 5, dorsal arch; 6, ventral tubercle; 7, surface for dens.

FIG. 168.—ATLAS OF PIG; ANTERIOR VIEW.

1, Dorsal tuberosity; 2, wing; 3, alar foramen; 4, anterior articular cavity; 5, ventral tubercle.

heads of the first ribs. It has foramina transversaria, and usually two foramina in each side of the arch.

The dorsal tuberosity of the **atlas** is large. The ventral tubercle is long, compressed laterally, and projects back under the axis. The wing is flattened and bears a posterior tuberosity. The foramen transversarium passes through the

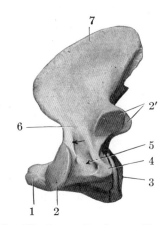

Fig. 169.—Axis of Pig; Lateral View.

1, Dens; 2, 2', anterior and posterior articular processes; 3, posterior end of body; 4, transverse process; 5, foramen transversarium; 6, arch; 7, spinous process. Arrow indicates intervertebral foramen.

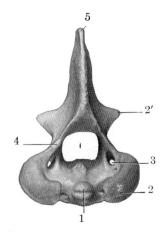

Fig. 170.—Axis of Pig; Anterior View.

1, Dens; 2, 2', anterior and posterior articular processes; 3, foramen transversarium; 4, arch; 5, spinous process.

posterior border of the wing to the fossa under the latter, and is not visible dorsally; it is sometimes very small or absent. The sides of the vertebral foramen bear two lateral projections which partially divide it into a ventral narrow part, which receives the dens, and a dorsal larger part for the spinal cord. In the fresh state the division is completed by the transverse ligament, which is attached to the projections.

The **axis** has a large spinous process, which is directed upward and backward. The dens is a thick cylindrical rod. The transverse process is very small and the foramen transversarium is often incomplete.

The **thoracic vertebræ** are commonly fourteen or fifteen in number. Their bodies are relatively long, constricted in the middle, and without ventral spines. Their extremities are elliptical, depressed in the middle, and prominent at the periphery. The arch is perforated by a foramen on each side and in most of the series there is also a foramen in the posterior part of the root of the transverse process which communicates with the former or with the posterior intervertebral foramen. Sometimes there is a foramen in the anterior part of the process also. There are **mammillary processes** except on the first two; in the posterior five or six vertebræ they project from the anterior articular processes. The facet for the tubercle of the rib is absent or fused with that for the head in the last five or six. The last trans-

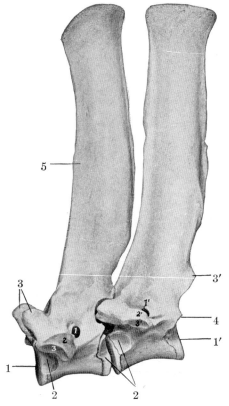

Fig. 171.—Second and Third Thoracic Vertebræ of Pig; Lateral View.

Numbers around bones: 1, 1', Anterior and posterior ends of bodies; 2, cavities for heads of ribs; 3, 3', articular process; 4, facet for head of rib; 5, spinous process. Numbers on bones: 1, 1', Foramina of arches; 2, 2', transverse processes; 3, 3', facets for tubercles of ribs.

verse process is lumbar in character, plate-like, and about an inch (2 cm.) long. Small **accessory processes** occur in the posterior part of the region. The first spinous process is broad, very high, and inclined a little forward. The others diminish very gradually in length to the tenth, beyond which they are about equal. The second to the ninth are inclined backward, the tenth is vertical (anticlinal), and the rest incline forward. The width decreases decidedly from the fourth to the tenth, beyond which there is a gradual increase. The summits are slightly enlarged and lie almost in a straight line.

The **lumbar vertebræ** are six or seven in number. The bodies are longer than in the thoracic region and bear a ventral crest. They become wider and flatter in the posterior part of the series. The arches are deeply notched, and are separated by an increasing space dorsally. The mammillary processes project outward and backward. The transverse processes are bent downward and incline a little forward. Their length increases to the fifth and is much diminished in the last. They form no articulation with each other or with the sacrum. The posterior edge of the root of the process is marked by a notch in the anterior part of the series, a fora-

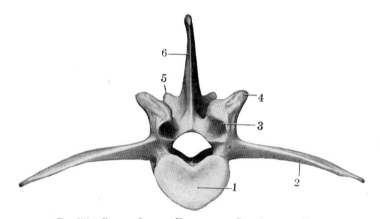

FIG. 172.—FOURTH LUMBAR VERTEBRA OF PIG; ANTERIOR VIEW.
1, Body; 2, transverse process; 3, anterior articular process; 4, mammillary process; 5, posterior articular process; 6, spinous process.

men in the posterior part. The spines are broad and incline forward, with the exception of the last, which is narrow and vertical.

Lesbre states that six and seven lumbar vertebræ occur with almost equal frequency. The number may be reduced to five, and the number of presacral vertebræ varies from twenty-six to twenty-nine.

The **sacrum** consists usually of four vertebræ, which fuse later and less completely than in the other domesticated animals. It is less curved than in the ox. The spines are little developed and commonly in part absent. The middle of the dorsal surface is flattened and smooth, and presents openings into the sacral canal between adjacent arches (Spatia interarcualia). On either side are the dorsal sacral foramina, and tubercles which indicate the fused articular processes. The wings resemble those of the ox. The anterior articular processes are very large. The pelvic surface resembles that of the ox, but is not so strongly curved, and the transverse lines are very distinct.

The **coccygeal vertebræ** are specially characterized by the presence of functional articular processes on the first four or five, beyond which these processes become non-articular and smaller. The arches of the first five or six are complete. The transverse processes are broad and plate-like in the anterior part of the series and diminish very gradually.   Not rarely the first coccygeal vertebra unites with the sacrum.

Vertebral Curves.—The cervical region is practically straight.   The thoracic and lumbar regions form a gentle curve, concave ventrally, the highest point of which is at the junction of the two regions.   The sacral promontory is not so pronounced as in the ox, and the sacral curve is flatter.

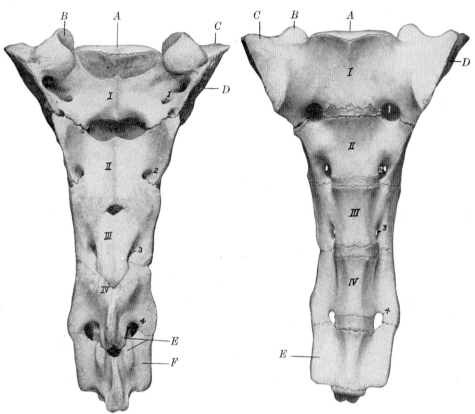

FIG. 173.—SACRUM AND FIRST COCCYGEAL VERTEBRA OF PIG; DORSAL VIEW.

I–IV, Arches of sacral vertebræ; 1, 2, 3, dorsal sacral foramina; 4, similar foramen between sacrum and first coccygeal vertebra; *A*, body of first sacral vertebra; *B*, articular process; *C*, wing; *D*, auricular surface; *E*, articular processes; *F*, first coccygeal vertebra.

FIG. 174.—SACRUM AND FIRST COCCYGEAL VERTEBRA OF PIG; VENTRAL VIEW.

I–IV, Sacral vertebræ (bodies); 1, 2, 3, ventral sacral foramina; 4, similar foramen between sacrum and first coccygeal vertebra; *A*, body of first sacral vertebra; *B*, articular process; *C*, wing; *D*, auricular surface; *E*, first coccygeal vertebra.

Length.—The regional lengths of the vertebral column of a large Berkshire sow were as follows: Cervical, 24 cm.; thoracic, 53.5 cm.; lumbar, 31 cm.; sacral, 17 cm.; coccygeal, 35 cm.

Variations.—The occurrence of fifteen thoracic vertebræ is quite common, and the existence of sixteen or even seventeen has been recorded.   Reduction to thirteen is very rare.   Six and seven lumbar vertebræ seem to occur with about equal frequency, and reduction to five is on record.   The number of coccygeal vertebræ varies from twenty to twenty-six according to the records of several observers.   Lesbre states that he has found twenty-three most frequently.

THE RIBS

The **ribs** number fourteen or fifteen pairs, of which seven are sternal and seven or eight asternal usually.   They are in general strongly curved in the improved breeds, so that there is a fairly distinct angle, except toward the end of the series.

The backward slope of the posterior ribs is slight. The first rib is prismatic, has a large sternal end, and a very short cartilage. The width is greatest in the third to the sixth, and the length in the sixth and seventh usually. The tubercle fuses with the head on the last five or six. The second to the fifth form diarthrodial joints with their cartilages, which are wide and plate-like.

The fifteenth rib, when present, may be fully developed and its cartilage enter into the formation of the costal arch; but in most cases it is floating, and in some cases it is only about an inch (ca. 2–3 cm.) in length.

THE STERNUM

The **sternum** consists of six segments and resembles that of the ox in general form. The first segment (Manubrium) is long, flattened laterally,

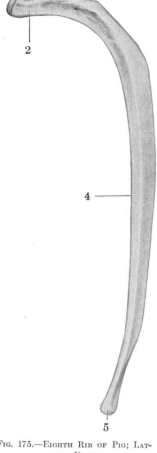

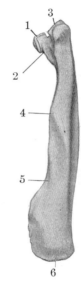

FIG. 175.—EIGHTH RIB OF PIG; LATERAL VIEW.
1, Head; 2, neck; 3, tubercle; 4, anterior border; 5, sternal extremity.

FIG. 176.—FIRST RIB OF PIG; LATERAL VIEW.
1, Head; 2, neck; 3, tubercle; 4, anterior border; 5, vascular impression; 6, sternal extremity.

and bears a blunt-pointed cartilage on its anterior end; its posterior end forms a diarthrodial joint with the body. The latter is flattened, wide in its middle, narrow at either end. The widest segments are formed of two lateral parts, which are not completely fused in the adult. The last segment has a long, narrow part which bears the xiphoid cartilage.

The **thorax** is long and is more barrel-shaped than in the horse or ox, since the ribs are more strongly curved and differ less in relative length.

BONES OF THE SKULL
CRANIUM

The **occipital bone** has an extensive squamous part, which forms a very broad and prominent nuchal crest. The latter is concave, and is thick and rough above, where it forms the highest part of the skull; laterally it becomes thinner, turns downward, and is continuous with the temporal crest. Two divergent ridges pass upward from the foramen magnum, and the surface between them is concave and smooth. The greater part of the cerebral surface of the squamous part is united with the parietal bones, but a ventral concave area faces into the cranial cavity. The foramen magnum is almost triangular, and is narrow above, where it is flanked by two small tuberosities. The paramastoid processes are extremely long and project almost straight ventrally. The hypoglossal foramen is at the medial side of the root of the process. The basilar part is short and wide; its ventral surface

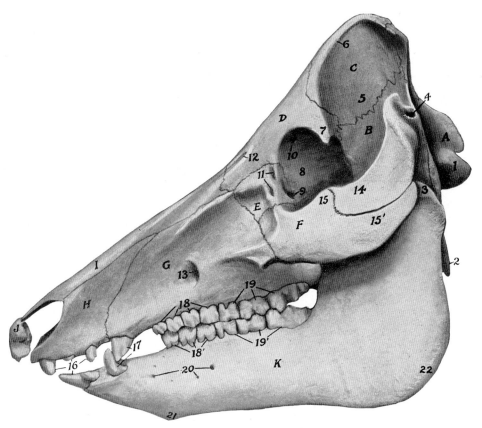

FIG. 177.—SKULL OF PIG; LATERAL VIEW.

A, Occipital bone; B, squamous temporal bone; C, parietal bone; D, frontal bone; E, lacrimal bone; F, malar bone; G, maxilla; H, premaxilla; I, nasal bone; J, os rostri; K, mandible; 1, occipital condyle; 2, paramastoid process; 3, condyle of mandible; 4, meatus acusticus externus; 5, temporal fossa; 6, parietal crest; 7, supraorbital process; 8, orbital part of frontal bone; 9, fossa for origin of ventral oblique muscle of eyeball; 10, orbital opening of supraorbital canal; 11, lacrimal foramina; 12, supraorbital foramen and groove; 13, infraorbital foramen; 14, zygomatic process of temporal bone; 15, temporal, and 15′, zygomatic, process of malar bone; 16, incisor teeth; 17, canine teeth; 18, 18′, premolars; 19, 19′, molars; 20, mental foramina; 21, mental prominence; 22, angle of mandible.

bears a thin median ridge and two lateral imprints or tubercles which converge at the junction with the sphenoid bone.

The **interparietal bone** fuses before birth with the occipital. The internal occipital protuberance is absent.

The **parietal bone** is overlapped by the occipital bone behind and concurs in the formation of the nuchal crest. Its external surface is divided by the parietal crest into two parts. The medial part (Planum parietale) faces upward and forward, and is flattened and smooth. Its medial border is short and straight and unites early with the opposite bone. Its anterior border is concave and joins the frontal bone. The lateral part (Planum temporale) faces outward and is more extensive; it is concave, forms a large part of the temporal fossa, and is overlapped ventrally by the squamous temporal. The parietal crest extends in a curve from the nuchal crest forward and outward to the supraorbital process. The cerebral surface is concave and is marked by digital impressions. The ventral border projects into the cranial cavity and forms a crest which separates the cerebral and cerebellar compart-

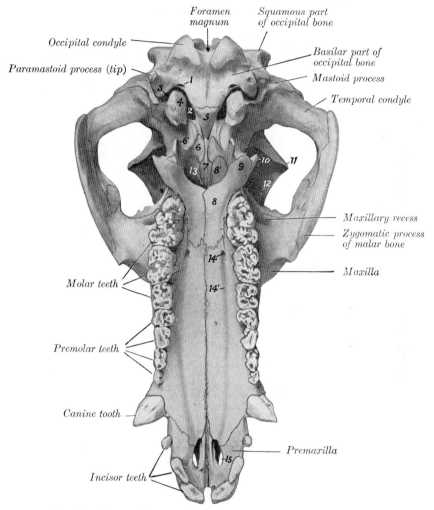

FIG. 178.—SKULL OF PIG; VENTRAL VIEW, WITHOUT MANDIBLE AND HYOID.

1, Hypoglossal foramen; 2, foramen lacerum anterius; 3, foramen lacerum posterius; 4, bulla tympanica; 5, body of sphenoid; 6, pterygoid bone, and 6′, hamulus of same; 7, vomer; 8, horizontal, and 8′, perpendicular, part of palatine bone; 9, pterygoid process of palatine bone; 10, pterygoid process of sphenoid bone; 11, supraorbital process; 12, orbital opening of supraorbital canal; 13, choanæ or posterior nares; 14, 14′, anterior palatine foramen and groove; 15, palatine fissure.

ments laterally. The interior is excavated and forms part of the frontal sinus in the adult. There is no temporal canal.

The **frontal bone** is long. The frontal surface slopes downward and forward, the inclination varying in different subjects. The anterior part is concave and is marked by the supraorbital foramen and the groove leading forward from the foramen to the nasal bone. The supraorbital canal opens into the orbit at the upper part of the medial wall of the latter. The supraorbital process is short and blunt-pointed, and is not connected with the zygomatic arch. The gap in the orbital margin is closed by the orbital ligament in the fresh state. The orbital part is extensive and forms the greater part of the medial wall of the orbit. Its upper part is perforated by the orbital orifice of the supraorbital canal, in front of which is the distinct fovea trochlearis. The ethmoidal foramen is situated in the ventral part near the junction with the orbital wing of the sphenoid. The temporal part is very narrow and is separated from the orbital plate by a ridge which joins the

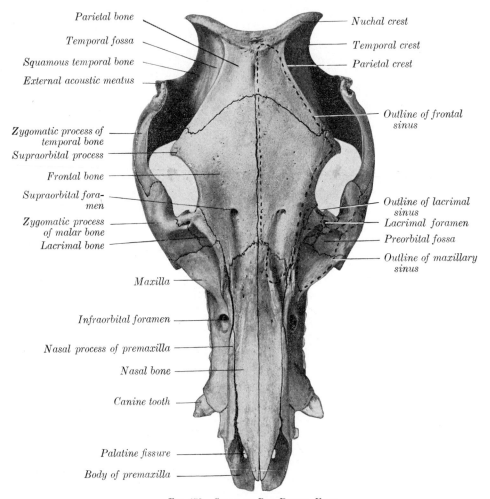

FIG. 179.—SKULL OF PIG; DORSAL VIEW.

pterygoid crest below. The interior of the bone is excavated by the frontal sinus in practically its entire extent in the adult. In the young subject the cavity is confined to the anterior part and the rest of the bone is thick.

The **temporal bone** has a general resemblance to that of the ox. The zygomatic process is short and stout and is bent at a right angle. The dorsal border of the process is thin; traced from before backward it curves sharply upward and forms a high prominence in front of the external acoustic meatus; beyond this it drops rather abruptly and is then continued upward to the nuchal crest. The anterior part of the ventral border joins the zygomatic process of the malar, which is deeply notched. The condyle is concave in the transverse direction. The post-glenoid process is absent, but the articular surface is bounded behind and medially by a crest. There is no temporal canal. The external acoustic meatus is very long and is directed dorso-laterally. The bulla tympanica is large, compressed laterally, and bears a pointed muscular process in front. A narrow space intervenes between the bulla and the basilar part of the occipital bone, so that the foramen lacerum resembles that of the horse. The small hyoid process is situated in a deep depression in front of the root of the paramastoid process, and the stylo-mastoid foramen is lateral to it. The petrous part presents no important differential features. The squamous part (including the root of the zygomatic process) contains an air-cavity, which is continuous with the sphenoidal sinus.

The **sphenoid bone** is short and resembles that of the ox in general. The body is narrow. The hypophyseal or pituitary fossa is very deep, and is limited behind by a prominent dorsum sellæ; the dorsum bears lateral projections, the **posterior clinoid processes** (Processus clinoidei aborales). The foramen ovale is absent, being included in the foramen lacerum anterius. The other foramina are like those of the ox. The pterygoid process is broad and twisted. Its base is not perforated and its free edge is thin and sharp. It concurs with the pterygoid and palate bones in the formation of the **pterygoid fossa** (Fossa pterygoidea), which opens backward and is not present in the horse or ox. The sphenoidal sinus is very large and occupies the body, the temporal wings, and a great part of the pterygoid processes in the adult; it is continued into the temporal bone as mentioned above.

The **ethmoid bone** has a relatively long perpendicular plate, which is marked by ridges corresponding to the ethmoidal meatuses. The cribriform plate is extensive and very oblique, so that it and the ethmoidal crest are almost in line with the basi-cranial axis. A linear series of relatively large foramina is found on either side of the crista. The lateral mass consists of five endoturbinates and eighteen ectoturbinates (Paulli). The lamina lateralis concurs in the formation of the pterygo-palatine fossa. The **lamina transversalis** separates the fundus of the nasal cavity from the naso-pharyngeal meatus.

FACE

The **maxilla** is extensive. Its facial surface forms a longitudinal groove, which is continued upon the premaxilla in front and the facial parts of the lacrimal and malar behind. The infraorbital foramen—sometimes double—is large and is situated above the third or fourth cheek tooth. The alveolus for the canine tooth produces a ridge (Juga canina) at the anterior end which is very pronounced in the boar. The facial crest extends forward from the root of the zygomatic process and fades out behind the infraorbital foramen; in some specimens it is prominent and thin-edged, in others it is rounded and projects little. The zygomatic process is short but stout and buttress-like; it is overlapped laterally by the malar. The maxillary tuberosity forms in the young subject a long bulla, which occupies most of the pterygo-palatine fossa and contains the developing permanent molars; after the eruption of the teeth the tuberosity flattens and joins the vertical part of the palate bone. The palatine process is very long and is marked in its anterior part by **transverse grooves** (Sulci palatini transversi) corresponding with those of the mucous membrane of the palate. The anterior palatine foramen is near the junction with the palate bone; from it the palatine groove can be traced distinctly along the entire length of the process. The alveolar border presents a large alveolus for the canine tooth at its anterior end; behind this are seven alveoli for the cheek teeth, which increase in size from first to last. The maxillary foramen and infraorbital canal are very large. The maxillary sinus is small.

The body of the **premaxilla** is narrow and prismatic. It presents three alveoli for the incisor teeth, which are separated by short intervals and diminish in size from before backward.   As in the ox, a narrow space separates the right and left bones and takes the place of the foramen incisivum.   The palatine process is long and narrow.   The nasal process is very extensive and is somewhat rhomboid in outline.   Its dorsal border forms a very long suture with the nasal bone, and the ventral articulates to about the same extent with the maxilla.   The palatine fissure is relatively wide.

The horizontal part of the **palatine bone** forms a fourth to a fifth of the length of the palate; its palatine surface is triangular, the apex being anterior; its nasal surface is deeply grooved and smooth.   A **pterygoid process** (Processus pyramidalis of man) projects backward and downward, and its thick rounded end is received between the pterygoid process of the sphenoid and the pterygoid bone.   The perpendicular part is largely overlapped laterally by the maxilla and concurs in

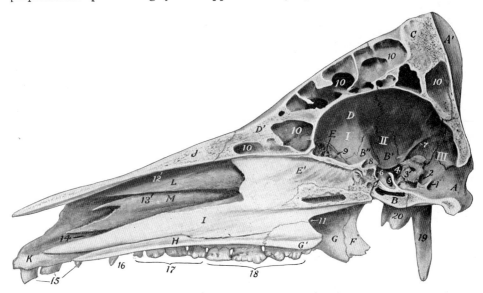

FIG. 180.—SAGITTAL SECTION OF SKULL OF PIG, WITHOUT MANDIBLE.

A, A', Basilar and squamous parts of occipital bone; *B*, body, *B'*, temporal wing, *B''*, orbital wing, of sphenoid bone; *C*, parietal bone; *D, D'*, internal and external plates of frontal bone; *E, E'*, cribriform and perpendicular plates of ethmoid bone; *F*, pterygoid bone; *G, G'*, perpendicular and horizontal parts of palatine bone; *H*, palatine process of maxilla; *I*, vomer; *J*, nasal bone; *K*, body of premaxilla; *L*, dorsal turbinate bone; *M*, ventral turbinate bone; *I, II, III*, fossæ cranii; 1, hypoglossal foramen; 2, foramen lacerum posterius; 3, meatus acusticus internus; 4, foramen lacerum anterius; 5, hypophyseal or pituitary fossa; 6, foramen orbito-rotundum; 7, lateral crest between cerebral and cerebellar parts of cranial cavity; 8, optic foramen; 9, ethmoidal foramen; 10, frontal sinus; 11, meatus nasopharyngeus; 12, 13, 14, dorsal, middle, and ventral nasal meatuses; 15, incisor teeth; 16, canine tooth; 17, premolar teeth; 18, molar teeth; 19, paramastoid process; 20, bulla tympanica.

forming part of the palatine canal.   The two plates separate dorsally and inclose an air-cavity which opens into an ethmoidal meatus.   The inner plate curves inward and unites with the vomer and ethmoid to form a horizontal plate, the **lamina transversalis,** which divides the posterior part of the nasal cavity into a dorsal olfactory part and a ventral respiratory part.

The **pterygoid bone** is nearly vertical in direction, and is narrow in its middle, wide at each end.   The lateral surface is free below and forms the medial wall of the pterygoid fossa.   The ventral end is notched and forms a distinct hamulus.

The **nasal bone** is very long and its width is almost uniform, except at the anterior end, which is pointed and reaches almost as far forward as the premaxilla. The facial surface is flattened from side to side.   In profile it is nearly straight in some subjects, variably concave in others.   The lateral border is free to a small extent in front only; otherwise it is firmly connected with the premaxilla and maxilla. In the adult the frontal sinus extends into the posterior part of the bone.

The **lacrimal bone** is very sharply bent. Its facial surface presents a deep depression, surmounted by a ridge or tubercle. On or close to the orbital margin are two **lacrimal foramina** which lead to the lacrimal canals. The orbital surface presents a fossa in which the inferior oblique muscle of the eyeball arises, and its lower part bears a crest, which is crossed obliquely by a vascular furrow. The dorsal border articulates with the frontal only. The bone concurs in the formation of the maxillary sinus.

The **malar bone** is strongly compressed from side to side. Its facial surface is small and presents a fossa which is continuous with the depressions of the maxilla and lacrimal. The orbital surface is still smaller and is smooth and deeply grooved. The zygomatic process is very extensive, especially in the vertical direction. Its lateral surface is convex and free, and bears a rough eminence in its middle. Its medial surface is concave; it is overlapped in front by the maxilla, and in the remainder of its extent is free and smooth. The dorsal border is thick and rounded in front, where it forms the lower part of the orbital margin; behind this it forms an extensive notch which receives the zygomatic process of the temporal. (It might be regarded as dividing into frontal and temporal branches.) The ventral border is convex and becomes thinner behind.

The **turbinate bones** resemble those of the ox. The dorsal turbinate is, however, relatively longer, less fragile, and more firmly attached to the nasal bone. There is no middle turbinate.

The **vomer** is very long. The anterior extremity reaches to the body of the premaxilla or very close to it. The ventral border is received into a groove formed by the nasal crest of the maxillæ and palatine bones and in front by the palatine processes of the premaxillæ. The posterior border is concave, thin, and sharp.

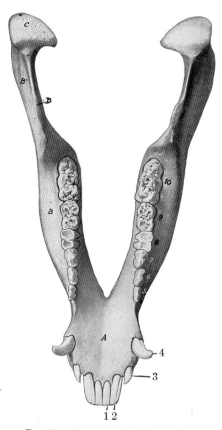

FIG. 181.—MANDIBLE OF PIG; DORSAL VIEW.

A, Body; B, B', horizontal and vertical parts of ramus; C, condyle; D, coronoid process; 1, 2, 3, incisor teeth; 4, canine tooth; 5, 6, 7, premolar teeth (first absent); 8, 9, 10, molar teeth.

The **os rostri** (or prenasal bone) is situated in the snout between the nostrils. It has the form of a short, three-sided prism. The dorsal surface is convex and is notched at each end. The lateral surfaces are concave, smooth, and converge below, forming a grooved ventral border. The posterior surface is triangular, notched centrally, and rough laterally. The anterior surface is deeply pitted and is surrounded by an irregular sharp border.

The **mandible** is very strong, and differs very much from that of the horse or ox. The body narrows decidedly in front; the lingual surface is deeply concave; the mental surface is strongly convex, slopes downward and backward, and forms a distinct prominence (Tuber mentale) at the point of divergence of the rami.

Above this prominence is a pair of foramina. The alveolar border presents six alveoli for the incisor teeth, and a little further back two large cavities for the canine teeth. There are two pairs of mental foramina of considerable size and a variable number of smaller ones. The rami diverge more than in the horse or ox, and the upper part is somewhat incurved. The horizontal part is very thick and strong. Its lateral surface is strongly convex from above downward. The medial surface is prominent over the roots of the molar teeth and overhangs the concave lower part. The alveolar border is thin in front and widens behind; it does not follow the axis of the ramus, but runs nearly straight and produces the marked overhang noted above. There are seven alveoli for the lower cheek teeth, which increase in size from before backward. The first is small, not always present in the adult, and is separated by short spaces from the second and the canine alveolus. The vertical part is relatively wide above. The condyle is convex in both directions, wide in front, narrow and declivitous behind. The very small and thin-edged coronoid process is not quite so high as the condyle, from which it is separated by a very wide notch. The mandibular foramen is large. The two halves of the bone unite soon after birth in the improved breeds.

The body of the **hyoid bone** is broad from before backward, short transversely, and bears on its ventral aspect a very short pointed lingual process. The thyroid cornua are wide and curved, concave and grooved dorsally; their ends are attached to the thyroid cartilage of the larynx by rather long bars of cartilage. The small cornua are short, wide, and flattened dorso-ventrally; they are attached to short bars which project from the junction of the body and thyroid cornua. The middle cornu is a little longer than the small cornu, but is relatively slender; it is largely cartilaginous in the young subject and does not ossify at either end. The great cornu is a very slender rod, slightly enlarged at either end; the dorsal extremity is attached to the hyoid process of the temporal by a rather long and wide bar of cartilage.

THE SKULL AS A WHOLE

The **length** and the **profile** vary greatly in different subjects. Primitively the skull is long—especially in its facial part—and the frontal profile is almost straight. The condition is very pronounced in wild or semi-feral pigs, and exists also—though in less degree—in the improved breeds during extreme youth. Most of the latter are decidedly brachycephalic when fully developed; the face is "dished" in a pronounced fashion. The frontal region slopes sharply upward, and the nasal region is shortened, and in some specimens even distinctly concave in profile. The supraorbital foramina are about midway between the orbital margin and the frontal suture. The supraorbital grooves extend forward from the foramina to the nasal region and turn ventro-laterally toward the infraorbital foramina over the ridges which separate the nasal and lateral regions.

The **lateral surface** is triangular when the mandible is included. The temporal fossa is entirely lateral and its long axis is almost vertical. It is bounded above by the nuchal crest, behind by the temporal crest, in front by the parietal crest, and is marked off from the orbital cavity by the supraorbital process and a curved crest which extends from it to the root of the pterygoid process. The zygomatic arch is strong, high, and flattened from side to side. Its root is notched dorsally and bears a projection ventrally. It curves sharply upward behind and forms a pointed recurved projection above and in front of the external acoustic meatus. The orbit is small. Its margin is deficient behind in the dry skull, thick and rounded in front and below. The cavity is limited below by a ridge on the frontal and lacrimal bones, and is separated by a crest from the temporal fossa. The medial wall is perforated above by the orbital opening of the supraorbital canal, and below by the optic and ethmoidal foramina; on its antero-inferior part is the fossa in which the inferior oblique muscle of the eye takes origin. Two lacrimal foramina are found on or close to the anterior margin. The pterygo-palatine fossa is well defined; its upper part forms a deep groove which leads from the foramen orbito-rotundum to the very large maxillary foramen. The preorbital region is deeply grooved in its length and is clearly marked off by a ridge from the nasal and frontal regions. The facial crest is short, usually thin-edged, and lies above the fifth and sixth cheek teeth. A little (ca. 2 cm.) in front of it is the infraorbital fora-

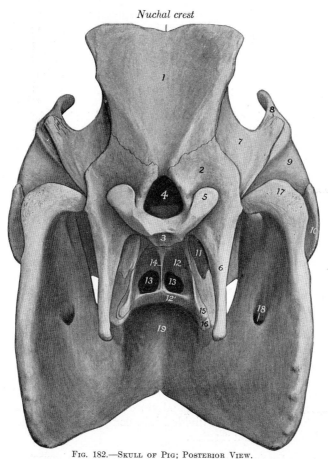

FIG. 182.—SKULL OF PIG; POSTERIOR VIEW.

1, 2, 3, Squamous, lateral, and basilar parts of occipital bone; 4, foramen magnum; 5, occipital condyle; 6, paramastoid process; 7, squamous temporal bone; 8, meatus acusticus externus; 9, temporal condyle; 10. zygomatic process of malar bone; 11, bulla tympanica; 12, 12′, perpendicular and horizontal parts of palatine bone; 13, 13′, choanæ or posterior nares; 14, vomer; 15, pterygoid process of sphenoid bone; 16, pterygoid process of palatine bone; 17, condyle of mandible; 18, mandibular foramen; 19, body of mandible.

men. There is a ridged prominence over the canine alveolus. In some skulls the anterior part of the upper jaw is inclined upward.

The most striking features of the **basal surface** are as follows: The basioccipital is wide and flattened; it bears a median crest and two lateral tubercles. The paramastoid process is extremely long, less flattened than in the horse and ox, and nearly vertical. At the medial side of its root is the hypoglossal foramen, and in front of it are the stylo-mastoid foramen and a deep cavity in which the hyoid process is concealed. The bulla tympanica is long, compressed laterally, and bears a sharp, short, muscular process. The posterior nares are small and are wider below than above. On either side of them is the tuberosity of the palate bone, and above this is the pterygoid fossa. The palate constitutes about two-thirds of the entire length of the skull, and is relatively narrow. It is widest between the canines and premolars and narrow at each end. It is marked by a crest medially and by the palatine foramen and groove laterally. The anterior part bears transverse ridges. It is moderately arched from side to side. In some specimens it is nearly straight or slightly concave in its length; in others it curves upward to a variable degree in front. The posterior end always slopes upward more or less.

The **nuchal surface** is remarkable for its height and the breadth of the nuchal crest. The central part above the foramen magnum is smooth and concave from side to side, and is bounded laterally by ridges, which converge ventrally and end on two tubercles at the upper margin of the foramen magnum. The surface is separated from the temporal fossæ by the temporal crests, which curve downward and outward and blend with the external acoustic meatus. The mastoid process has the form of a plate which overlaps the root of the paramastoid process and bears a crest on its anterior part.

The **cranial cavity** is small, in spite of the great size of the cranium; the discrepancy is due to the enormous development of the frontal sinuses in the adult. It is relatively longer, but much lower than that of the ox. Its width is greatly diminished between the orbits. The ethmoidal fossæ are extensive and very oblique. The floor resembles that of the ox, but the foramen ovale is absent, the dorsum sellæ is more developed, and the foramen lacerum is like that of the horse. Two oblique lateral crests clearly mark the limit between the cerebral and cerebellar compartments. The internal occipital protuberance and the temporal canal are absent.

The **nasal cavity** is very long. Its posterior part is divided by the lamina transversalis into olfactory and respiratory parts. The olfactory part or fundus is dorsal, and contains the ethmoturbinates and ethmoidal meatuses. The ventral part is continuous with the ventral meatus and leads to the pharyngeal orifice; hence it is called the naso-pharyngeal meatus. The bony roof is almost complete in front on account of the great length of the nasal bones.

The **frontal sinus** is a vast excavation in the adult animal. It involves all of the roof and almost all of the sides of the cranium, and extends forward into the roof of the nasal cavity a variable distance—sometimes as far as a transverse plane through the infraorbital foramina. The septum between the right and left sinuses is usually deflected in an irregular manner in its middle part, but is practically median at either end. Each sinus is subdivided by numerous septa, some of which are complete. Thus the sinus is divided into compartments, each of which communicates with an ethmoidal meatus.

In the young pig the sinus is small and is confined to the anterior part of the frontal bone. Later it extends backward, outward, and to a less extent forward. In the old subject it penetrates laterally into the supraorbital process and the root of the zygomatic process of the temporal bone, and behind almost down to the foramen magnum and the occipital condyles. It then consists of six to eight compartments usually.

The **maxillary sinus** is relatively small. Its anterior end is a little less than an inch (ca. 2 cm.) behind the infraorbital foramen, and it extends upward into the lacrimal and backward into the malar bone. The infraorbital canal passes along its floor, and the roots of the molar teeth do not project up into it. It does not communicate with the frontal and sphenoidal sinuses, but with the posterior part of the middle meatus nasi by means of a considerable orifice.

The **sphenoidal sinus** is very large. It involves the body, pterygoid processes, and temporal wings of the sphenoid bone, and extends into the squamous temporal. It communicates with the ventral ethmoidal meatus.

There is a small sinus in the perpendicular part of the palatine bone which communicates with an ethmoidal meatus.

BONES OF THE THORACIC LIMB

The **scapula** is very wide, the index being about 1 : 0.7. The spine is triangular and is very wide in its middle, which curves backward over the infraspinous fossa and bears a large tuberosity. Its lower part bears a small projection (rudimentary acromion). The anterior border is strongly convex in profile, sinuous when viewed from the front, and thick and rough in its middle. The posterior border is wide, slightly concave, and bears a rough outer lip. The vertebral border is convex, and the cartilage is not so extensive as in the horse and ox. The anterior angle is thin and bent medially a little. The posterior angle is thick and is about

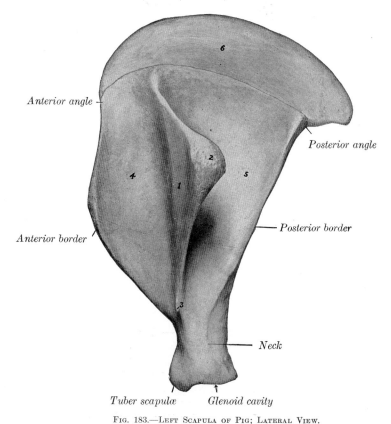

Anterior angle

Posterior angle

Anterior border

Posterior border

Neck

Tuber scapulæ   Glenoid cavity

Fig. 183.—Left Scapula of Pig; Lateral View.

1, Spine; 2, tuber spinæ; 3, acromion; 4, supraspinous fossa; 5, infraspinous fossa; 6, cartilage.

a right angle. The neck is well defined. The rim of the glenoid cavity is rounded and not notched. The tuber scapulæ is just above the antero-medial part of the glenoid cavity and bears no distinct coracoid process; it unites with the rest of the bone at about one year.

The **humerus** has an appearance in profile somewhat like an italic *f* minus the cross-bar; this is due to the marked backward and forward inclination of the proximal and distal ends respectively. The shaft is decidedly compressed from side to side. The medial surface is extensive and flattened; it is separated from the anterior surface by a distinct border, and bears no teres tubercle. The musculospiral groove is shallow. The deltoid tuberosity is small, and there is a larger rounded eminence midway between it and the lateral tuberosity. The nutrient foramen is on the posterior surface below its middle. The head is more strongly curved and the neck better marked than in the horse or ox. The lateral tuberosity is very large and extends upon the front of the extremity. It is divided into two high prominences by a wide deep groove. There is a third eminence below and laterally for the attachment of the supraspinatus muscle. The intertuberal or bicipital groove is at the front of the medial side; it is undivided and is almost converted into a canal. The lateral groove on the distal articular surface is so shallow as to give the appearance of two condyles of similar size. The olecranon fossa is very deep, and the plate of bone which separates it from the coronoid fossa is thin and sometimes perforated. The proximal end unites with the shaft at three and a half years, the distal at one year.

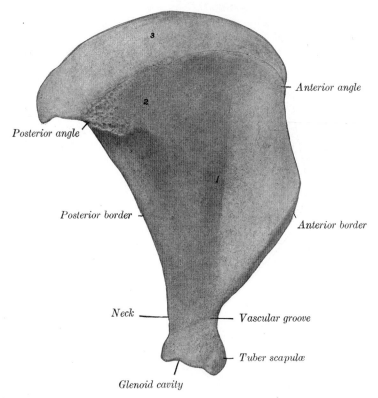

Fig. 184.—Left Scapula of Pig; Medial View.
1, Subscapular fossa; 2, serratus area; 3, cartilage.

The **radius** is short and narrow, but thick. The shaft increases in size distally. The greater part of the volar surface is in apposition with the ulna; this part is marked by a vascular furrow which runs distally from the proximal interosseous space, and has the nutrient foramen at its proximal end. The radial tuberosity is represented by a rough area. The distal end is relatively large. Its carpal surface consists of concavo-convex facets for the radial and intermediate carpal bones. There is a wide shallow groove on the middle of the front. The proximal end fuses with the shaft at one year, the distal at three and a half years.

The **ulna** is massive. It is much longer and considerably heavier than the radius. The shaft is curved. The dorsal surface is convex and most of it is rough and attached to the radius by the interosseous ligament. There is a smooth area on the upper third, which concurs with the radius in forming the proximal inter-

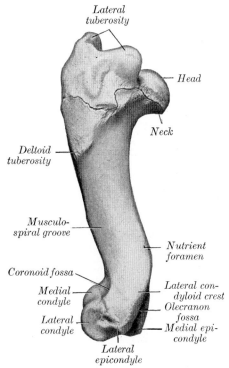

Lateral
tuberosity

Head

Neck

Deltoid
tuberosity

Musculo-
spiral groove

Nutrient
foramen

Coronoid fossa

Medial
condyle

Lateral con-
dyloid crest

Olecranon
fossa

Lateral
condyle

Medial epi-
condyle

Lateral
epicondyle

Fig. 185.—Left Humerus of Pig; Lateral View.

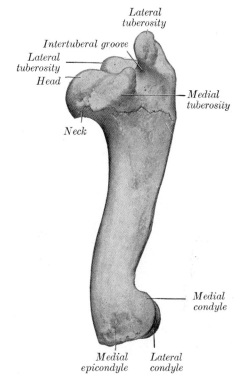

Lateral
tuberosity

Intertuberal groove

Lateral
tuberosity

Head

Medial
tuberosity

Neck

Medial
condyle

Medial
epicondyle

Lateral
condyle

Fig. 186.—Left Humerus of Pig; Medial View.

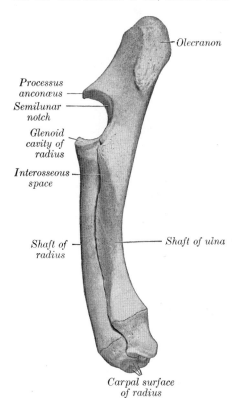

Olecranon

Processus
anconæus

Semilunar
notch

Glenoid
cavity of
radius

Interosseous
space

Shaft of
radius

Shaft of ulna

Carpal surface
of radius

Fig. 187.—Left Radius and Ulna of Pig; Lateral
View.

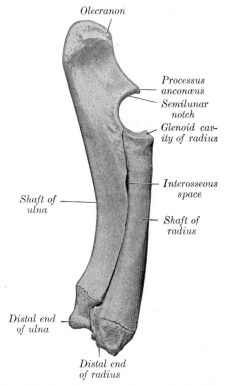

Olecranon

Processus
anconæus

Semilunar
notch

Glenoid cav-
ity of radius

Interosseous
space

Shaft of
ulna

Shaft of
radius

Distal end
of ulna

Distal end
of radius

Fig. 188.—Left Radius and Ulna of Pig; Medial
View.

osseous space, and is marked in its upper part by the nutrient foramen. From this space a vascular furrow descends to the distal part of the shaft, where there is often a distal interosseous space for the passage of vessels. The medial surface is extensive, concave, and smooth. The lateral surface is slightly convex, and its proximal part is marked by an oblique rough line or ridge. The proximal extremity is large and is bent medially somewhat; its length is more than one-third of that of the entire bone. The distal extremity is relatively small; it articulates with the ulnar and accessory carpal bones, and is notched in front to accommodate the ridge

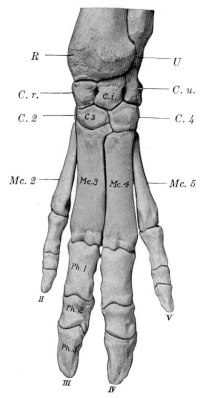 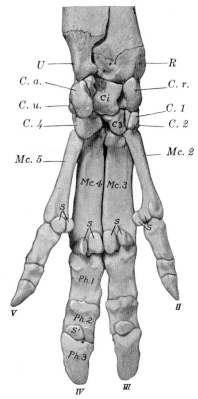

Fig. 189.—Skeleton of Distal Part of Left Thoracic Limb of Pig; Dorsal View.

R, Distal end of radius; U, distal end (styloid process) of ulna; C. r., radial carpal; C. i., intermediate carpal; C. u., ulnar carpal; C. 2, C. 3, C. 4, second, third, and fourth carpal bones; Mc. 2–5, metacarpal bones; Ph.1, Ph.2, Ph. 3, first, second, and third phalanges.

Fig. 190.—Skeleton of Distal Part of Left Thoracic Limb of Pig; Volar View.

R, Distal end of radius; U, distal end (styloid process) of ulna; C. r., C. i., C. u., C. a., radial, intermediate, ulnar, and accessory carpal bones; C. 1–4, first to fourth carpal bones; Mc. 2–5, metacarpal bones; Ph. 1, Ph. 2, Ph. 3, first, second, and third phalanges; S, proximal, and S', distal sesamoid bones.

on the radius. The bone contains a considerable medullary canal, and is consolidated at three to three and a half years.

The **carpus** comprises eight bones, four in each row. The bones of the proximal row resemble those of the ox, with the exception of the accessory, which is more like that of the horse, but has no lateral groove. The first carpal is small, elongated from before backward, rounded, and articulates in front with the second carpal. The latter is high and narrow, and articulates with the second and third metacarpal bones distally. The third carpal articulates with the radial and intermediate above, the third metacarpal bone below. The fourth is the largest bone of the row; it articulates with the intermediate and ulnar above, the fourth and fifth metacarpals below, and bears a tuberosity on its volar aspect.

Four **metacarpal bones** are present. The first is absent, the third and fourth are large and carry the chief digits, while the second and fifth are much smaller and bear the accessory digits. Their proximal ends articulate with each other and with the carpus as indicated above. The distal ends fuse with the shafts at about two years of age.

The third and fourth metacarpals are flattened from before backward, three-sided, and placed close together. The distal end of each bears a trochlea for articulation with the first phalanx and the sesamoids. The third is the wider of the two, and articulates with all of the distal row of the carpus except the first. The fourth articulates with the fourth carpal chiefly, but has a small facet for the third. The second and fifth metacarpals are placed further back than the chief bones. The fifth is considerably the thicker of the two. The proximal ends are small and articulate with the corresponding carpal and metacarpal bones. The distal end is relatively large; its articular surface is condyloid in front, trochlear behind.

Each chief digit comprises three **phalanges** and three **sesamoids**. The bones of the chief digits resemble those of the ox in form, but there is no foramen on the interdigital side of the extensor process and the proximal sesamoids are narrow and ridged behind. The phalanges of the accessory digits (which do not reach the ground ordinarily) are similar in form but much smaller. Fusion of the proximal ends with the shafts takes place at about two years for the first phalanges, at about one year for the second phalanges.

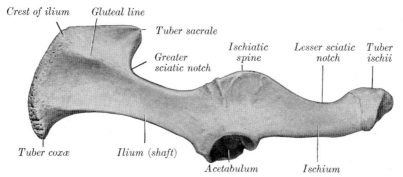

FIG. 191.—LEFT OS COXÆ OF PIG; LATERAL VIEW.

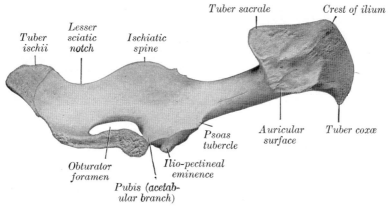

FIG. 192.—LEFT OS COXÆ OF PIG; MEDIAL VIEW.

BONES OF THE PELVIC LIMB

The **os coxæ** is long and narrow. The ilium and ischium are almost in line with each other and nearly sagittal in direction. The wing of the **ilium** bends outward much less than in the horse or ox. The gluteal surface is divided into two fossæ by a ridge, which is continuous with the superior ischiatic spine behind. The pelvic surface presents an extensive rough area behind, which is in apposition with the wing of the sacrum. The smooth iliac area is narrow, and is bounded above by a ridge. The crest is convex, and is thick, rough, and prominent in its middle, which forms the highest point of the bone. The tuber sacrale is lower than the crest, is directed backward, and articulates internally with the sacrum. The tuber coxæ is lower still and is very little thickened. The **ischia** in the female are some-what divergent and flattened behind. The tubera are everted and bear three prom-inences. There is a crest or tuberosity on the ventral surface. The superior ischiatic spine is like that of the cow, but is slightly incurved and the muscular

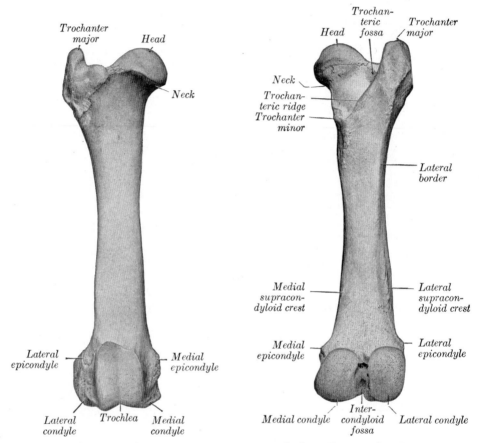

FIG. 193.—RIGHT FEMUR OF PIG; ANTERIOR VIEW.   FIG. 194.—RIGHT FEMUR OF PIG; POSTERIOR VIEW.

ridges on its lateral face are more pronounced. The symphyseal part of the **pubis** is thick and the two bones are almost in a horizontal plane. The ilio-pectineal eminence is prominent and the psoas tubercle is well marked.

The **acetabulum** is placed a little further back than in the ox. The rim is thick and is cut into posteriorly by a narrow fissure, which leads into the deep fossa acetabuli. The three pieces of the os coxæ are fused by the end of the first year, but the crest and the tuber ischii are partially separate till the sixth or seventh year. The symphysis does not usually undergo complete ankylosis. Interischial bones are present.

The **inlet** of the **pelvis** is elliptical and very oblique. In a sow of full size the **conjugate** diameter measures five to six inches (12.5–15 cm.), and the **transverse** about three and a half to four inches (ca. 8.75 to 10 cm.). In the female the floor is relatively wide and flattened, especially at the outlet, where the tubera are everted; it also has a decided ventral inclination behind. The pelvic axis is therefore correspondingly oblique. The ischial arch is wide. In the boar the pubis is much thicker and the ischia are not everted posteriorly. The inlet is smaller; the conjugate diameter is about four and a half to five inches (ca. 11–12.5 cm.), and the transverse three to three and a half inches (ca. 7.5–8.75 cm.). The floor is concave from side to side and slopes decidedly less than in the sow. The superior ischiatic spines are more incurved, and the ischial arch is much narrower and deeper.

The **femur** has a relatively wide and massive shaft, on which four surfaces might be recognized. The principal nutrient foramen is situated in the proximal

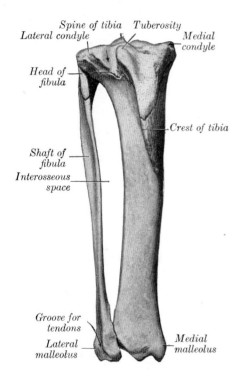

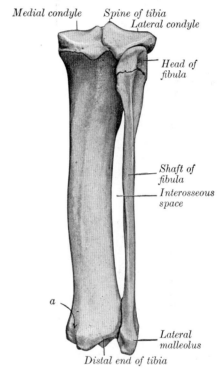

Fig. 195.—Right Tibia and Fibula of Pig; Anterior View.

Arrow indicates muscular notch of proximal end of tibia.

Fig. 196.—Right Tibia and Fibula of Pig; Posterior View.

a, Groove on medial malleolus for tendon of flexor digitalis longus.

third of the anterior surface. The posterior surface is wide, and is limited laterally by a ridge which extends from the trochanter major to the large lateral supracondyloid crest. There is no supracondyloid fossa. The head is strongly curved, and is marked toward the medial side by a rather large fovea for the attachment of the round ligament. The neck is distinct. The trochanter major, although massive, does not extend above the level of the head. The trochanteric ridge and fossa resemble those of the ox. The third trochanter is absent. The ridges of the trochlea are similar and almost sagittal. The extremities unite with the shaft at about three and a half years.

The shaft of the **tibia** is slightly curved, convex medially. The tuberosity is grooved in front, and a narrow sulcus separates it from the lateral condyle. The facet for the fibula is on the posterior border of the latter, and is bounded medially by an eminence. The proximal part of the crest is very prominent and curves outward. The distal end resembles in general that of the ox, but is relatively narrower transversely and thicker from before backward. The proximal end unites with the shaft at about three and a half years, the distal at about two years.

The **fibula** extends the entire length of the region, and is separated from the tibia by a wide interosseous space. The shaft is flattened from side to side; the proximal part is wide and deeply grooved laterally; the distal part is narrower

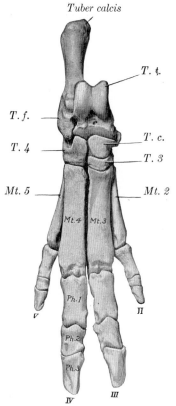

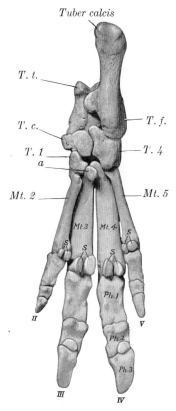

FIG. 197.—SKELETON OF RIGHT PES OF PIG; DORSAL VIEW.

　　T. t., Tibial tarsal; *T. f.*, fibular tarsal; *T. c.*, central tarsal; *T. 3*, third tarsal; *T. 4*, fourth tarsal; *Mt. 2–5*, metatarsal bones; *Ph. 1*, *Ph. 2*, *Ph. 3*, first, second, and third phalanges.

FIG. 198.—SKELETON OF RIGHT PES OF PIG; PLANTAR VIEW.

　　T. t., Tibial tarsal; *T. f.*, fibular tarsal; *T. c.*, central tarsal; *T.1*, *T.4*, first and fourth tarsal bones; *Mt. 2–5*, metatarsal bones; *Ph. 1*, *Ph. 2*, *Ph. 3*, first, second, and third phalanges; *S*, proximal sesamoid bones; distal sesamoids shown but not marked; *a*, sesamoid bone.

and thicker. The proximal end is flattened, grooved laterally, and articulates medially with the lateral condyle of the tibia. The distal end forms the lateral malleolus. It is grooved laterally, and articulates with the tibia and tibial tarsal medially, with the fibular tarsal bone distally. The proximal end unites with the shaft at about three and a half years, the distal at about two and a half years.

The **patella** is very much compressed transversely and presents three surfaces.

The **tarsus** comprises seven bones. The tibial and the fibular tarsals resemble in general those of the ox. The axis of the tibial is, however, slightly oblique (ventro-medial), and its distal end bears a double trochlea for articulation with the central and fourth tarsals. The tuber calcis is deeply grooved posteriorly. The central tarsal is narrow transversely and thick. Its proximal surface is deeply concave, and the plantar bears a large tubercle. The first tarsal is high and narrow; it articulates with the central and second tarsals and the second metatarsal bone. The second tarsal is small and somewhat prismatic; it articulates with the central above, the third in front, the first behind, and the second and third metatarsals below. The third tarsal is much larger, and is compressed from above downward, wide in front, narrow behind. It articulates with the central tarsal above, the third metatarsal below, the second tarsal medially, and the fourth tarsal laterally. The fourth tarsal is large. Its lateral face is crossed by an oblique groove for the tendon of the peroneus longus. The medial surface articulates with the central and third tarsals. The proximal surface supports the tibial and fibular tarsal bones, and the distal surface rests on the fourth and fifth metatarsals. It ossifies from two centers. The summit of the tuber calcis fuses with the rest of the bone at two to two and a half years.

The four **metatarsal bones** resemble the corresponding bones of the fore limb, but are somewhat longer. The proximal ends of the third and fourth each have a considerable plantar projection; the process on the third has a facet for articulation with a discoid sesamoid bone. The second and fifth are placed more toward the plantar aspect of the large bones than is the case in the fore limb.

The first and second **phalanges** are a little longer and narrower than those of the fore limb.

SKELETON OF THE DOG

VERTEBRAL COLUMN

The vertebral formula is $C_7T_{13}L_7S_3Cy_{20-23}$.

The **cervical vertebræ** are relatively longer than in the ox and the pig. The bodies of the typical vertebræ diminish in length from first to last and are compressed dorso-ventrally. The anterior extremity is moderately convex and the posterior slightly concave; both are oblique. The median ridge and lateral grooves on the dorsal surface of the body are very well marked. The second, third, and fourth have distinct ventral spines. The spinous process of the third has the form of a long low crest; in the remainder it is higher, blunt-pointed, and inclined forward. The transverse processes of the third, fourth, and fifth project ventrally and backward, and divide into two branches; of these, the anterior one is thin, and the posterior is thick and tuberculate at its free end. The process of the sixth has two parts; one of these is an extensive quadrilateral plate which is directed ventro-laterally and is ridged on its medial surface; the other part is short and blunt, and is directed outward and a little backward and upward. The seventh is readily distinguished by its shortness, the length of its spine, and the single transverse process. The posterior articular processes bear tubercles which are large on the third, fourth, and fifth.

The ventral arch of the **atlas** is narrow from before backward, and bears a small tubercle posteriorly. The dorsal surface of the dorsal arch is strongly convex and rough centrally. The wings are wide, flattened, and almost horizontal. The dorsal surface is rough. There is an **alar notch** (Incisura alaris) on the anterior border instead of the alar foramen. The foramen transversarium is present.

The body of the **axis** is flattened dorso-ventrally, especially in front. The dens is rounded and relatively long, reaching almost to the occipital bone; it is inclined upward a little. The articular surfaces which flank it are condyloid in form and very oblique. The ventral surface is wide, and is divided by a median

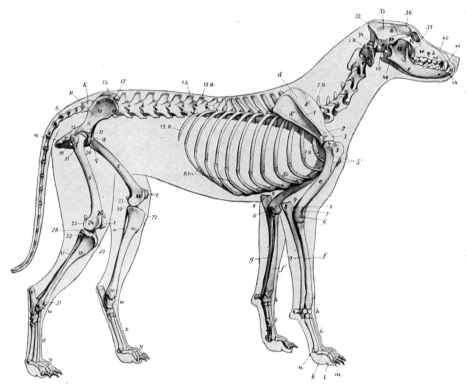

FIG. 199.—SKELETON OF DOG; LATERAL VIEW.

a, Cranium; *b*, face; *c*, mandible; *1H–7H*, cervical vertebræ; *13B*, last thoracic vertebra; *1L–7L*, lumbar verte-bræ; *K*, sacrum; *S*, coccygeal vertebræ; *1R–13R*, ribs; *R.kn.*, costal cartilages; *St.*, sternum; *d*, scapula; *d'*, supra-spinous fossa; *d''*, infraspinous fossa; *1*, spine of scapula; *2*, acromion; *3*, tuberosity of scapula; *3'*, articular end of scapula; *e*, humerus; *4*, head of humerus; *5*, lateral tuberosity of humerus; *5'*, deltoid ridge; *6, 6'*, epicondyles of humerus; *7*, lateral condyloid crest; *7'*, coronoid fossa; *f*, radius; *g*, ulna; *8*, olecranon; *9*, "beak" of ulna; *h*, carpus; *i*, metacarpus; *k*, proximal phalanges; *l*, middle phalanges; *m*, distal phalanges; *n*, sesamoid; *p*, ilium; *10*, wing of ilium; *11*, shaft of ilium; *12*, crest of ilium; *13*, tuber coxæ; *14*, tuber sacrale; *15*, superior ischiatic spine; *q*, pubis; *r*, ischium; *16*, tuber ischii; *17*, acetabulum; *s*, femur; *18*, head of femur; *19*, trochanter major; *20*, trochanter minor; *21*, trochanter tertius; *22, 23*, condyles; *24, 25*, epicondyles; *26*, trochlea; *t*, patella; *u*, tibia; *27*, tuberosity of tibia; *28, 29*, condyles of tibia; *30*, medial malleolus; *v*, fibula; *31*, lateral malleolus; *32*, head of fibula; *w*, tarsus; *x*, meta-tarsus; *y*, phalanges; *33*, occipital bone; *34*, paramastoid process; *35*, parietal bone; *36*, frontal bone; *37*, lacrimal bone; *38*, malar bone; *39*, squamous temporal; *40*, maxilla; *40'*, infraorbital foramen; *41*, premaxilla; *42*, nasal bone; *43*, external acoustic meatus; *44*, canine tooth; *45*, masseteric fossa; *46*, angular process of mandible. (After Ellen-berger, in Leisering's Atlas.)

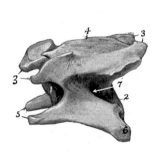

FIG. 200.—THIRD CERVICAL VERTEBRA OF DOG; LEFT LATERAL VIEW.

1, 2, Anterior and posterior ends of body; *3, 3,* articular processes; *4*, spinous process; *5, 6*, transverse process; *7*, foramen transversarium.

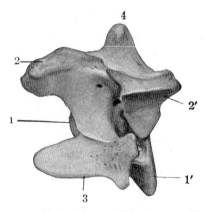

FIG. 201.—FOURTH CERVICAL VERTEBRA OF DOG; LEFT LATERAL VIEW.

1, 1', Anterior and posterior ends of body; *2, 2'*, articular processes; *3*, transverse process; *4*, spinous process.

crest into two fossæ. The transverse processes are single, pointed, directed backward and outward, and perforated by relatively large foramina transversaria. The spinous process is thin and of moderate height, but very long; it is prolonged forward so as to overhang the dorsal arch of the atlas, and is terminated behind by a tuberosity which is connected by two crests with the posterior articular processes. The anterior notches are large and are never converted into foramina.

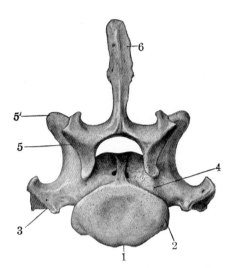

FIG. 202.—SEVENTH CERVICAL VERTEBRA OF DOG; POSTERIOR VIEW.

1, Body; 2, costal facet; 3, transverse process; 4, notch; 5, 5', articular processes; 6, spinous process.

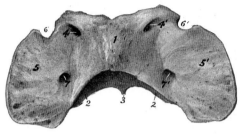

FIG. 203.—ATLAS OF DOG; DORSAL VIEW.

1, Dorsal arch; 2, 2, posterior articular cavities; 3, ventral tubercle; 4, 4' intervertebral foramina; 5, 5', wings; 6, 6', alar notches; 7, 7', foramina transversaria.

The bodies of the thirteen **thoracic vertebræ** are wide and compressed dorsoventrally, especially at each end of the region. Their convex anterior surfaces are depressed in the middle. The posterior facets for the heads of the ribs are absent on the last two or three. The transverse processes resemble those of the horse. They bear mammillary processes except at the anterior end of the region. The facets for the tubercles of the ribs are large and concave in the anterior part of the series, and become smaller and slightly convex further back.

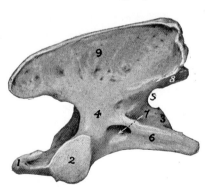

FIG. 204.—AXIS OF DOG; LEFT LATERAL VIEW.

1, Dens; 2, anterior articular process; 3, posterior end of body; 4, arch; 5, posterior notch; 6, transverse process; 7, intervertebral foramen; 8, posterior articular process; 9, spinous process.

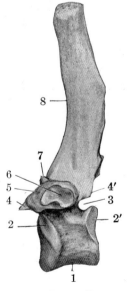

FIG. 205.—FOURTH THORACIC VERTEBRA OF DOG; LEFT VIEW.

1, Body; 2, 2', costal facets of body; 3, posterior notch; 4, 4', articular processes; 5, transverse process; 6, facet for tubercle of rib; 7, mammillary process; 8, spinous process.

The last three have accessory processes also. The first three or four spinous processes are about equal in length. Behind this they become gradually shorter to the tenth, and then remain equal. The backward slope is most marked in the ninth and tenth. The eleventh is practically vertical (anticlinal vertebra), and the last two incline slightly forward.

The bodies of the seven **lumbar vertebræ** are decidedly flattened dorso-ventrally, and increase in width from first to last. The length increases to the sixth. The transverse processes are plate-like and are directed forward and downward. Their length increases to the fifth and sixth. They form no joints with each other or with the sacrum. Their extremities are enlarged, with the exception of the last. The accessory processes project backward over the posterior notches of the first five. The anterior articular processes are large, compressed laterally, and bear mammillary processes. The spinous processes are broad below, narrower above, and with the exception of the last, incline a little forward. Their height diminishes behind the fourth.

The **sacrum** results from the early fusion of three vertebræ. It is short,

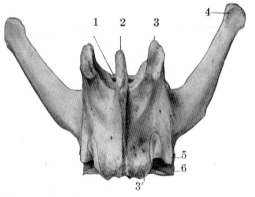

FIG. 206.—FIFTH LUMBAR VERTEBRA OF DOG; DORSAL VIEW.

1, Anterior end of body; 2, spinous process; 3, 3′, articular processes; 4, transverse process; 5, accessory process; 6, groove for spinal nerve.

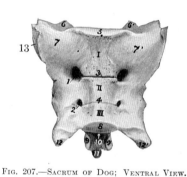

FIG. 207.—SACRUM OF DOG; VENTRAL VIEW.

I, II, III, Bodies of vertebræ; 1, 2, ventral sacral foramina; 3, 4, lineæ transversæ; 5, anterior end of body of first sacral vertebra; 6, 6′, anterior articular processes; 7, 7′, wings; 8, posterior end of body of last sacral vertebra; 9, 9′, posterior articular processes; 10, sacral canal; 11, spinous process; 12, 12′, transverse processes; 13, auricular surface.

wide, and quadrangular. The spines are fused to form a median crest, which is notched, however, between the summits of the spines. On either side are two tubercles, vestiges of the fused articular processes. The pelvic surface is deeply concave and presents two pairs of foramina. The wings are prismatic and very high. Their lateral surfaces are extensive, face almost directly outward, and bear an auricular surface on the lower part. The anterior surface of the body of the first vertebra is extensive, depressed in its middle, and bears a prominent lip below. The anterior articular processes are large and have extensive, slightly concave facets which face dorso-medially. The posterior articular processes are small. The transverse processes of the last vertebra project backward and may articulate or fuse with those of the first coccygeal. The sacral canal is strongly compressed dorso-ventrally.

The **coccygeal vertebræ** are fully developed in the anterior part of the region. The arch is complete in the first six usually. The first three or four have well developed articular processes at each end. Behind this the posterior processes quickly disappear, and the anterior ones become non-articular and gradually reduced in size. The transverse processes of the first five or six are relatively large; behind this they quickly disappear. **Hemal arches** (or chevron bones) in the form of a **V** or **Y** occur ventrally at the intercentral junctions of the third, fourth, and fifth usually. They transmit the middle coccygeal artery, which passes between pairs of ventral tubercles further back.

Curves.—A gentle curve, convex ventrally, is formed by the cervical and the anterior part of the thoracic region. The posterior thoracic and the lumbar vertebræ form a second curve, concave ventrally. The sacral promontory is well marked. The sacrum and the anterior part of the coccygeal region constitute a third and more pronounced curve, concave ventrally. In long-tailed dogs the sacro-coccygeal region is somewhat **S**-shaped.

Variations.—Numerical variations are not common except in the coccygeal region. The number of thoracic vertebræ may be twelve or fourteen, with or without compensatory change in the lumbar region. Girard recorded a case with eight lumbar and the usual number of thoracic vertebræ. Six lumbar with fourteen thoracic vertebræ have been met with. The first coccygeal sometimes unites with the sacrum.

THE RIBS

Thirteen pairs of ribs are present, of which nine are sternal and four asternal. They are strongly curved, narrow, and thick. Those in the middle of the series are the longest. The first eight or nine increase in width in their lower part. The last rib is usually floating. The heads of the last two or three articulate with only one vertebra. The costal cartilages are long and curve ventrally and forward; the length and curvature of the first pair are striking special features.

THE STERNUM

This is long, laterally compressed, and consists of eight sternebræ, which fuse only in exceptional cases and in extreme old age. The first segment is the longest; its anterior end is blunt-pointed and bears a short conical cartilage. It widens at the point of articulation of the first pair of cartilages. The last segment is also long, thinner than its predecessors, wide in front, and narrow behind, where it bears a narrow xiphoid cartilage.

The **thorax** is distinctly barrel-like and is not decidedly compressed anteriorly like that of the horse and ox. The inlet is oval and is relatively wide on account of the marked curvature of the first pair of ribs and cartilages.

BONES OF THE SKULL[1]

CRANIUM

The **occipital bone** is similar in position to that of the horse. The nuchal crest is prominent, angular, and directed backward. Just below the crest are two rough imprints or tubercles for muscular attachment. The surface below these is convex from side to side and concave dorso-ventrally. On each side, at the junction with the squamous temporal, is the mastoid foramen which opens into the cranial cavity. The condyles are somewhat flattened and are widely separated above; at the medial side of each is a short condyloid canal, which opens into the temporal canal. The paramastoid processes are very short. The basilar part is wide and joins the bulla tympanica on either side; its ventral surface is flattened and the tubercles are at the junction with the bulla. The hypoglossal foramen is small and is close to the foramen lacerum posterius; the latter is bounded in front by the bulla tympanica, behind and medially by the occipital bone.

[1] In the following descriptions of the separate bones an intermediate type—*e g.*, a fox terrier, —is selected, and the most striking differences in the brachycephalic and dolichocephalic breeds will be considered in the section on the skull as a whole.

The **interparietal bone** fuses with the occipital before birth. It bears the high posterior part of the parietal crest, and is wedged in between the two parietal bones. It forms the central part of the tentorium osseum, which is thin and curved, concave ventrally. Its base concurs with the occipital and parietal bones in the formation of a transverse canal which is continuous with the temporal canals.

The **parietal bone** is rhomboid in outline and is strongly curved. It is extensive and forms the greater part of the roof of the cranial cavity. At the junction of the right and left bones there is a prominent parietal crest which is continued upon the frontal bones. The ventral border articulates with the temporal wing of the sphenoid by its anterior part and with the squamous temporal in the remainder of its extent. The external surface enters into the formation of the temporal

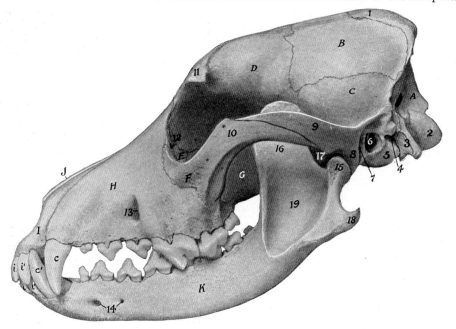

FIG. 208.—SKULL OF DOG; LATERAL VIEW.

A, Occipital bone; *B*, parietal bone; *C*, squamous temporal bone; *D*, frontal bone; *E*, lacrimal bone; *F*, malar bone; *G*, perpendicular part of palatine bone; *H*, maxilla; *I*, premaxilla; *J*, nasal bone; *K*, mandible; 1, parietal crest; 2, occipital condyle; 3, paramastoid process; 4, stylo-mastoid foramen; 5, bulla tympanica; 6, meatus acusticus externus; 7, external opening of temporal canal; 8, postglenoid process; 9, zygomatic process of temporal bone; 10, zygomatic process of malar bone; 11, supraorbital process; 12, entrance to lacrimal canal; 13, infraorbital foramen; 14, mental foramina; 15, condyle of mandible; 16, coronoid process; 17, mandibular notch; 18, angular process; 19, masseteric fossa; *i*, *i'*, incisor teeth; *c*, *c'*, canine teeth.

fossa. The cerebral surface is marked by digital impressions, and by grooves for the middle meningeal artery and its branches.

The external surface of the **frontal bone** is crossed by a frontal crest, which extends in a curve from the parietal crest to the supraorbital process, and separates the frontal and temporal parts. The frontal parts of the two bones form a central depression and slope downward and forward. The supraorbital process is very short, so that the supraorbital margin is incomplete as in the pig. The supraorbital foramen is absent. In front there is a narrow pointed nasal part which fits in between the nasal bone and the maxilla. The orbital and temporal parts are relatively extensive. Two ethmoidal foramina are commonly present. The frontal sinus is confined to the frontal bone.

The parts of the **temporal bone** fuse early. The zygomatic process curves widely outward and forward. Its anterior part is beveled ventrally and articulates extensively with the corresponding process of the malar. The articular surface for the condyle of the mandible consists of a transverse groove which is continued upon the front of the large postglenoid process. Behind the latter is the lower opening of the temporal canal. There is no condyle. The mastoid part is small, but bears a distinct mastoid process. The external acoustic meatus is wide and very short, so that one can see into the tympanum in the dry skull. The bulla tympanica is very large and is rounded and smooth; its medial side is united to the basilar part of the occipital bone. Above this junction and roofed in by the union of the petrous part and the basioccipital is the **petro-basilar canal** (Canalis petro-basilaris); this transmits a vein from the floor of the cranium to the foramen lacerum posterius. The latter opens into a narrow depression behind the bulla tympanica.

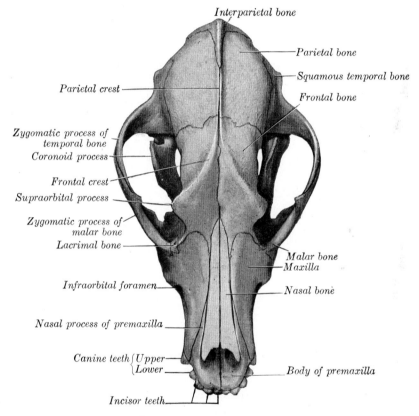

Interparietal bone

Parietal bone

Squamous temporal bone

Frontal bone

Parietal crest

Zygomatic process of temporal bone

Coronoid process

Frontal crest

Supraorbital process

Zygomatic process of malar bone

Lacrimal bone

Malar bone

Maxilla

Infraorbital foramen

Nasal bone

Nasal process of premaxilla

Canine teeth {Upper

{Lower

Body of premaxilla

Incisor teeth

FIG. 209.—SKULL OF DOG; DORSAL VIEW.

It transmits the ninth, tenth, and eleventh cranial nerves. The **carotid canal** branches off from the petro-basilar, passes forward lateral to it through the medial part of the bulla tympanica, and opens in front at the **carotid foramen;** it transmits the internal carotid artery. The Eustachian opening is immediately lateral to the carotid foramen. The muscular and hyoid processes are extremely rudimentary. The petrous part projects into the cranial cavity and forms a sharp prominent petrosal crest. The medial surface presents a deep **floccular fossa** above the internal acoustic meatus. The anterior surface is also free. The anterior angle is perforated by a **canal** for the trigeminal nerve (Canalis nervi trigemini).

The body of the **sphenoid bone** is flattened dorso-ventrally. The hypophyseal fossa is shallow, but the dorsum sellæ is well developed and bears **posterior clinoid processes.** A pair of **anterior clinoid processes** (Processus clinoidei orales) project back from the roots of the orbital wings. The latter are relatively small and are crossed laterally by a crest, which is continued forward upon the palatine bone. The temporal wings are extensive and articulate dorsally with the parietals. Perforating the roots of the wings are the following foramina, named from before backward: The optic passes through the orbital wing. The foramen orbitale is a little lower and is at the junction of the wings. The foramen rotundum opens into the alar canal, which passes through the root of the short but wide pterygoid process. The foramen ovale is near the posterior border of the temporal wing. There is no sphenoidal sinus.

The **ethmoid bone** is highly developed. The cribriform plate is extensive, and the olfactory fossæ are very deep. The ethmoidal crest is little developed, and often incomplete. The perpendicular plate is long. The lateral masses are greatly developed and project into the frontal sinus. There are four large endoturbinates

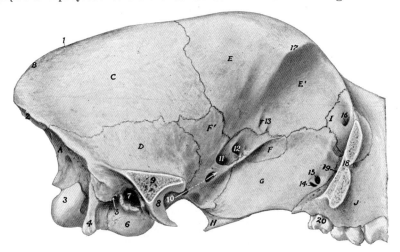

Fig. 210.—Cranial and Orbital Regions of Skull of Dog. The Zygomatic Arch Has Been Sawn Off.

A, Occipital bone; B, interparietal bone; C, parietal bone; D, squamous temporal bone; E, E', temporal and orbital parts of frontal bone; F, F', orbital and temporal wings of sphenoid bone; G, perpendicular part of palatine bone; H, pterygoid bone; I, lacrimal bone; J, maxilla; 1, parietal crest; 2, nuchal crest; 3, occipital condyle; 4, paramastoid process; 5, stylo-mastoid foramen; 6, bulla tympanica; 7, meatus acusticus externus; 8, articular surface for condyle of mandible; 9, section of root of zygomatic process of temporal bone; 10, alar canal; 11, foramen orbitale; 12, optic foramen; 13, ethmoidal foramen; 14, posterior palatine foramen; 15, sphenopalatine foramen; 16, entrance to lacrimal canal; 17, supraorbital process; 18, zygomatic process of malar bone (section); 19, maxillary foramen; 20, last molar tooth.

and six ectoturbinates. The lamina lateralis is extensive and forms the medial wall of the maxillary sinus. Its ventral border joins the palatine process of the maxilla and the horizontal part of the palate bone. A shelf-like plate extends inward from its lower part and concurs with the similarly incurved part of the palatine bone in forming the **lamina transversalis,** which divides the olfactory fundus of the nasal cavity from the naso-pharyngeal meatus.

FACE

The **maxilla** is short, but very high posteriorly. The facial crest is absent. The infraorbital foramen is over the alveolus for the third premolar. The **frontal process** fits into a deep notch between the nasal and orbital parts of the frontal bone, and the middle part of the posterior border lies along the orbital margin. There are more or less pronounced ridges, juga alveolaria, over the canine and molar teeth. The zygomatic process is short and thin; it is completely overlapped laterally by the malar, and is perforated by a number of foramina (Foramina alveolaria). A maxillary tuberosity is not present in the adult, but there is a pointed projection, the pterygoid process, behind the last alveolus. The nasal surface bears a short turbinate crest on its anterior part, behind which it is deeply concave and forms the lateral wall of the maxillary sinus. The palatine process is short, wide behind, and moderately arched from side to side. The anterior palatine

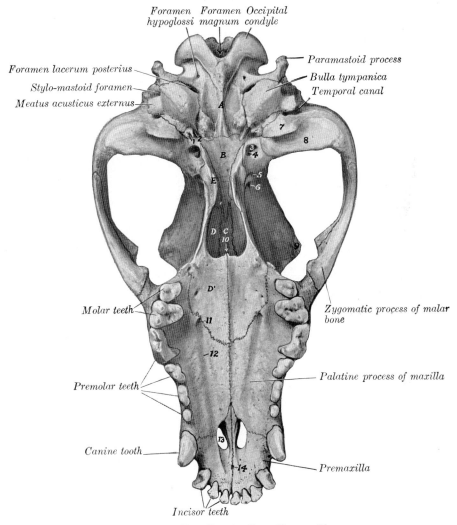

FIG. 211.—SKULL OF DOG; VENTRAL VIEW, WITHOUT MANDIBLE.

A, Basilar part of occipital bone; *B*, body of sphenoid bone; *C*, vomer; *D*, *D'*, perpendicular and horizontal parts of palatine bone; *E*, pterygoid bone; 1, Eustachian opening; 2, external carotid foramen; 3, foramen ovale; 4, 5, posterior and anterior openings of alar canal; 6, foramen orbitale; 7, postglenoid process; 8, articular groove of temporal bone; 9, supraorbital process; 10, meatus naso-pharyngeus; 11, anterior palatine foramen; 12, palatine groove; 13, palatine fissure; 14, foramen incisivum. There is a supernumerary incisor on the right side in this specimen.

foramen is situated at or close to the transverse palatine suture and about midway between the median suture and the alveolar border. The palatine groove is distinct. The large alveolus for the canine tooth is completed by the premaxilla. The small alveolus for the first premolar is separated from the preceding one by a small interval. The next two consist of anterior and posterior parts for the roots of the teeth. The fourth and fifth are much larger and are divided into three parts. The last is small and consists of three divisions. The infraorbital canal is short.

The body of the **premaxilla** is compressed dorso-ventrally, and contains three alveoli for the incisor teeth, which increase in size from first to third; it also completes the medial wall of the large alveolus for the canine tooth. The foramen incisivum is very small except in large skulls. The interalveolar border is wide and very short. The nasal process is wide at its origin and tapers to a sharp point behind; the anterior part curves upward, backward, and a little inward, and forms the lateral margin of the osseous nasal aperture; the posterior part extends backward a long distance between the nasal bone and the maxilla. The palatine process turns upward and outward, forming with its fellow a wide groove for the septal cartilage; the posterior end is pointed and fits into a notch between the palatine

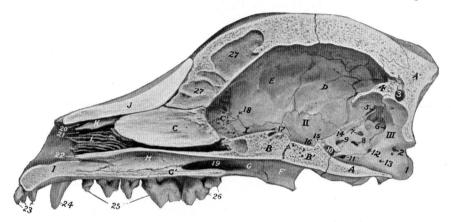

Fig. 212.—Sagittal Section of Skull of Dog, Without Mandible.

A, A′, Basilar and squamous parts of occipital bone; *B, B′*, presphenoid and postsphenoid; *C, C′*, perpendicular and cribriform plates of ethmoid bone; *D*, parietal bone; *E*, frontal bone; *F*, pterygoid bone; *G, G′*, vertical and horizontal parts of palatine bone; *H*, vomer; *I*, premaxilla; *J*, nasal bone; *K*, dorsal turbinate bone; *L*, ventral turbinate bone; *I, II, III*, anterior, posterior and middle fossæ of cranium; 1, occipital condyle; 2, opening of condyloid canal; 3, canal for intertransverse sinus of dura mater; 4, internal occipital protuberance; 5, internal opening of temporal canal; 6, mastoid foramen; 7, floccular fossa; 8, meatus acusticus internus; 9, canal for trigeminal nerve; 10, internal carotid foramen; 11, 12, openings into petro-basilar canal; 13, foramen hypoglossi; 14, petrosal crest; 15, dorsum sellæ; 16, hypophyseal or pituitary fossa; 17, optic foramen; 18, ethmoid foramen; 19, meatus naso-pharyngeus; 20, 21, 22, dorsal, middle, and ventral meatus nasi; 23, incisor teeth; 24, canine tooth; 25, premolar teeth; 26, molar teeth; 27, septum between frontal sinuses.

processes of the maxillæ, and supports the end of the vomer. The palatine fissure is short but wide.

The horizontal part of the **palatine bone** is extensive, forming about one-third of the hard palate. It presents a variable number of accessory palatine foramina. There is usually a pointed **posterior nasal spine** (Spina nasalis aboralis) at the end of the median suture. The palatine canal is sometimes formed entirely in this bone. The perpendicular part is even more extensive. Its lateral surface is chiefly free and forms most of the medial wall of the large pterygo-palatine fossa. The maxillary foramen is situated in a deep recess between this bone and the zygomatic process of the maxilla. Just above it there is commonly another foramen which opens into the nasal cavity. The posterior palatine and sphenopalatine foramina are situated further back and a little lower; the former is ventral to the latter. A horizontal plate extends from the nasal surface, meets that of the opposite bone, and completes the lamina transversalis spoken of in the description of the ethmoid bone. There is no palatine sinus.

The **pterygoid bones** are very wide and short. They form a considerable part of the lateral boundaries of the posterior nares. The lower and posterior borders are free and at their angle of junction there is a variable hamulus.

The **nasal bones** are (in most breeds) long and wider in front than behind. The facial surface is variably concave in its length and is inclined toward the median suture so as to form a central groove. The medial borders turn downward and form an internal nasal crest which becomes very prominent behind. The posterior parts fit into a notch formed by the frontal bones. The anterior ends form an almost semicircular nasal notch.

The **lacrimal bone** is very small. The facial part extends very little or not at all beyond the orbital margin. The orbital surface is small and triangular, and presents the entrance to the lacrimal canal.

The large zygomatic process constitutes the bulk of the **malar bone.** It is very long and is strongly curved. The dorsal border is convex, free in front, where it forms part of the orbital margin, beveled behind for articulation with the similar process of the temporal bone. Between these it bears an eminence, the processus frontalis, to which the orbital ligament is attached. The body of the bone may be considered to consist of a **lacrimal process** directed dorsally and fitting in between

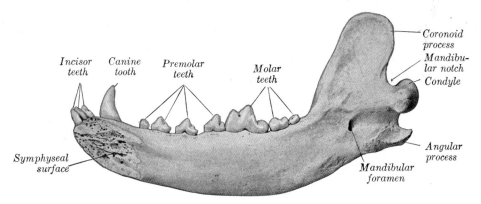

FIG. 213.—RIGHT HALF OF MANDIBLE OF DOG; MEDIAL VIEW.

the lacrimal and maxilla, and a **maxillary process** directed ventrally. The facial surface is convex.

The **dorsal turbinate bone** is in its anterior part a simple plate, attached by one edge to the nasal bone; it curves ventro-medially, and its free border is thickened and everted. The posterior part is wider and resembles the ethmoturbinates, with which it is connected.

The **ventral turbinate bone** is short and very complex. It is attached to the nasal surface of the maxilla by a basal lamina, which divides into two secondary lamellæ. The latter detach numerous tertiary lamellæ, which are coiled and have thick free edges.

The **vomer** is not in contact with the posterior part of the floor of the nasal cavity, and does not divide the posterior nares. The posterior end is narrow and deeply notched. Near the posterior nares the two plates curve outward and join the palatine bones and assist in forming the lamina transversalis.

The two halves of the **mandible** do not fuse completely even in old age, so that there is a permanent symphysis mandibulæ. The body presents six alveoli for the incisor teeth and two for the canines. The incisor alveoli increase in size from first to third. The canine alveoli extend deeply downward and backward. The rami diverge less than in the pig. The ventral border of the horizontal part is convex in its length and is thick and rounded. The alveolar border is slightly concave in its length and is a little everted, especially in its middle; it presents seven alveoli for the lower cheek teeth, which resemble those of the upper jaw except that the fourth and sixth are much smaller and the fifth is like the fourth of the upper series. The interalveolar space is very short or even absent. There are two or three mental foramina on either side. The vertical part is relatively small. Its lateral surface presents a deep **masseteric fossa** (Fossa masseterica) which encroaches on the coronoid process and is limited by ridges in front and below. The medial surface is convex and is marked by the usual mandibular foramen. At about the same level as the latter is the rough **angular process** (Processus angularis), which projects backward from the posterior border, and is equivalent to the angle of the other animals. The condyle is placed very low—not much higher than the apex of the canine tooth when the bone is resting on a flat surface. It is long transversely and the medial part of the articular surface is much the wider and extends over the posterior surface. Its long axis is a little oblique, the medial end being inclined somewhat downward and forward. The coronoid process is very extensive and is bent slightly outward and backward.

The body of the **hyoid bone** is a slightly curved transverse rod; it is compressed from before backward, and bears no lingual process. The thyroid cornua are permanently attached to the body by cartilage; they diverge widely, curve inward, and are compressed laterally. The small cornua are short, prismatic, and strong. The middle cornua are commonly a little longer than the great cornua; they are compressed laterally, and are slightly enlarged at the ends, which are joined by cartilage to the adjacent cornua. The great cornua are bent outward and are somewhat twisted.

THE SKULL AS A WHOLE

The different breeds of dogs display great variations in the form and size of the skull. Those which have a long narrow skull (*e. g.*, greyhound, collie) are designated **dolichocephalic**. Other dogs (*e. g.*, bulldog, small spaniels, pugs) have very broad, short skulls and are termed **brachycephalic**. Intermediate forms (*e. g.*, fox terrier, dachshund) are **mesaticephalic**.

The length is usually measured from the nuchal crest to the anterior end of the premaxillary suture, and the breadth between the summits of the zygomatic arches. The cephalic index is the relation of the breadth to the length, assuming the latter equal 100; the formula is: $\frac{breadth \times 100}{length}$ = cephalic index. The index of extreme dolichocephalic breeds is about 50, as in the greyhound, and that of brachycephalic specimens may be as high as 90, as in the pug and some toy terriers. Among the mesaticephalic types are the fox terrier, with an index of about 70, and the white Pomeranian, with one about 72 to 75. The cranio-facial index is the relation of the distance between the nuchal crest and the fronto-nasal suture to that between the latter and the nasal notch. It varies from 10 : 3 in extreme brachycephalic breeds to 10 : 7 in extreme dolichocephalic subjects.

The **frontal surface** shows the wide outward curve of the zygomatic arches and the great extent of the temporal fossæ. The latter are separated by the parietal crest, which in the larger breeds is very strong and prominent, and is continued by the diverging frontal crests to the supraorbital processes. The frontal and nasal regions are centrally depressed, and are more or less concave in profile. The nasal region is narrow and is terminated in front by a nasal notch. In the extreme brachycephalic breeds the differences are very striking. The cranium is strongly convex in both directions and is considerably longer than the face. The parietal crest is more or less effaced posteriorly and is formed by the interparietal only. The parietofrontal crests are separated by an interval behind and diverge to the supraorbital processes, so that the temporal fossæ are widely separated. The frontal region is wide, strongly convex, and has a shallow central depression. The nasal region is very short, relatively wide, and centrally depressed. In profile there is a marked depression at the fronto-nasal junction, producing what is termed by fanciers the "stop" of the face.

On the **lateral surface** the great extent of the temporal fossa is seen. The orbit communicates freely with the fossa, the posterior part of the orbital margin being absent in the dry skull. The axis of the orbital cavity forms a much smaller angle with the median plane than in the horse and ox. A distinct crest marks the limit between the orbital cavity and the extensive pterygo-palatine fossa. The preorbital region is somewhat triangular, concave in its length, and convex dorsoventrally; the infraorbital foramen is on its lower part above the third cheek tooth. In extreme brachycephalic breeds the orbit is relatively very large and the preorbital region extremely short but high. In the bulldog the lower jaw protrudes beyond the upper—a condition known as prognathism. The opposite condition, brachygnathism, is seen in the dachshund.

Striking features on the **basal surface** of the cranium are the width and flatness of the basilar part of the occipital bone, the small size of the paramastoid processes, the large size and

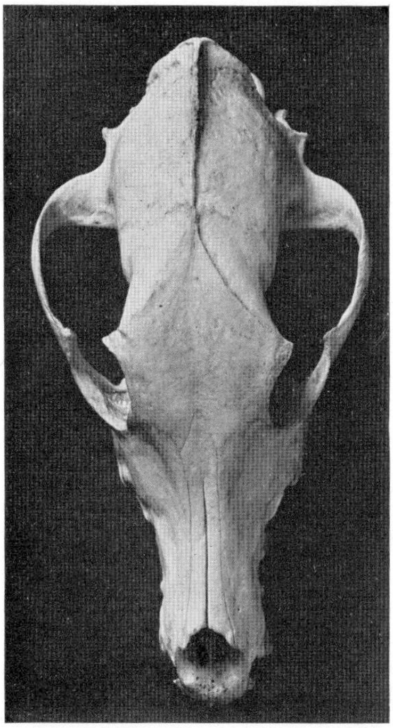

FIG. 214.—SKULL OF DOLICHOCEPHALIC DOG; DORSAL VIEW.

FIG. 215.—SKULL OF BRACHYCEPHALIC DOG; DORSAL VIEW.

rounded shape of the bulla tympanica, and the grooved form of the articular surfaces for the mandible. The posterior nares are long and narrow and are not divided by the vomer. The hard palate is usually about half the length of the skull. It is commonly marked by a median crest or rough line, and on each side are the anterior and accessory palatine foramina and the palatine grooves. The width is greatest between the fourth pair of cheek teeth, and here there is in most skulls a pronounced depression on either side. The length, width, and contour vary greatly in different breeds.

The angle of divergence of the rami of the mandible varies from 25 to 30 degrees; it is smallest in the greyhound, largest in extreme brachycephalic types, e. g., bulldog, pug.

The **nuchal surface** is somewhat triangular, with the base ventral. The summit is formed by the nuchal crest, which projects very strongly backward in the large breeds. Below it there are two very distinct rough imprints for muscular attachment. In some skulls there is a thin median occipital crest, in others a rounded elevation. Laterally are the temporal crests and the mastoid processes.

The mastoid foramen is at the junction of the occipital and temporal bones, above the root of the paramastoid process; it opens directly into the cranial cavity. The foramen magnum varies greatly in form; most often the transverse diameter is the greater, but in some skulls it is equaled or exceeded by the vertical diameter.

The **cranial cavity** (Fig. 212) corresponds in form and size with the cranium, especially in those breeds in which the various crests are more or less effaced and the frontal sinuses are small. The basi-cranial axis is almost parallel with the palate, and the floor is flattened. The anterior fossa is narrow and is only slightly higher than the middle one. The ethmoidal fossæ are very deep and the crest is little developed. The hypophyseal fossa is variable in depth, and the dorsum sellæ is relatively high and bears **clinoid processes** laterally. The cerebral and cerebellar compartments are well marked off laterally by the petrosal crests and dorsally by the tentorium osseum. The base of the latter is traversed by a canal which connects the two temporal canals. The anterior angle of the petrous temporal is perforated by a canal for the trigeminal nerve.

The **nasal cavity** (Fig. 212) conforms to the shape of the face. Its anterior aperture is large and nearly circular in most dogs. The complex ventral turbinates occupy the anterior part of the cavity to a large extent, except near the aperture. Behind the ventral turbinate is the large opening of the maxillary sinus. Behind this the cavity is divided by the lamina transversalis into a large upper olfactory region or fundus nasi and a lower naso-pharyngeal meatus. The fundus is occupied largely by the ethmoturbinates. The posterior nares are undivided and are in general long and narrow, but vary with the shape of the skull.

The **frontal sinus** is of considerable size in the large breeds, but is confined to the frontal bone. It is usually divided into a small anterior and a much larger posterior compartment, each of which opens into the dorsal ethmoidal meatus. The sinus is very small in extreme brachycephalic types.

The **maxillary sinus** is small, and is in such free communication with the nasal cavity as to make it rather a recess than a true sinus. It is bounded medially by the lamina lateralis of the ethmoid, and its lateral wall is crossed obliquely by the naso-lacrimal canal. The roots of the molar teeth do not project up into it.

BONES OF THE THORACIC LIMB

The **clavicle** is a small, thin, irregularly triangular bony or cartilaginous plate. It is embedded in the brachiocephalicus muscle in front of the shoulder-joint and forms no articulation with the rest of the skeleton. (It is nearly an inch long in a large cat and is a slender curved rod.)

The **scapula** is relatively long and narrow. The spine increases gradually in height from above downward and divides the lateral surface into two nearly equal fossæ. Its free edge is thick and rough above, and at the lower part is thin and bent backward. The **acromion** is short and blunt and is opposite the rim of the glenoid cavity. The subscapular fossa is very shallow and is marked by rough lines (Lineæ musculares). The rough area above it for the attachment of the serratus ventralis is large and quadrilateral in front, narrow and marginal behind. The anterior border is thin, strongly convex, and sinuous. The posterior border is straight and thick. The vertebral border is convex and thick and bears a band of cartilage. The anterior angle is rounded. The posterior angle is thick and square. The neck is well defined and bears a rough eminence posteriorly, from which the long head of the triceps arises. The glenoid cavity is continued forward upon the lower face of the tuber scapulæ, which is blunt and bears no coracoid process. The cervical angle is opposite the first thoracic spine; the dorsal angle lies above the vertebral end of the fourth rib, and the glenoid angle at a point just in front of the sternal end of the first rib in the ordinary standing position. The tuber scapulæ unites with the rest of the bone at six to eight months. The shoulder has a great range of movement on the chest wall.

The **humerus** is relatively very long, rather slender, and has a slight spiral twist. The shaft is somewhat compressed laterally, especially in its proximal two-thirds; this part is curved in varying degree, convex in front. The deltoid tuberosity has the form of a low ridge, and it is continued by a crest which runs upward and backward and bears a tubercle on its proximal part. Another line runs from it down the anterior aspect and forms the medial boundary of the very shallow musculo-spiral groove. The nutrient foramen is about in the middle of the posterior surface. A slight elevation on the proximal third of the medial surface represents the teres tubercle. The head is long and strongly curved from before backward. The neck is better marked than in the horse. The undivided lateral tuberosity is placed well forward and extends little above the level of the head. The medial tu-

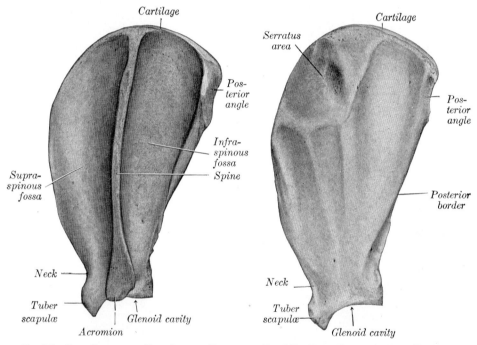

FIG. 216.—LEFT SCAPULA OF DOG; LATERAL VIEW.   FIG. 217.—RIGHT SCAPULA OF DOG; MEDIAL VIEW.

berosity is small. The intertuberal or bicipital groove is undivided and is displaced to the medial side by the extension forward of the lateral tuberosity. The distal end bears an oblique trochlear articular surface for articulation with the radius and ulna, the lateral part of which is the more extensive and is faintly grooved. The epicondyles are prominent. The coronoid and olecranon fossæ often communicate through a large **supratrochlear foramen.** The proximal end unites with the shaft at about one year, the distal at six to eight months.

The two bones of the forearm are relatively long and articulate with each other at each end in such a manner as to allow of slight movement. A narrow interosseous space separates their shafts. The **radius** is flattened from before backward and increases in size distally. The shaft forms two curves, so that it is convex dorsally and medially. The dorsal surface is convex in both directions and is marked in its distal half by a groove for the oblique extensor of the carpus. The volar surface presents the nutrient foramen in its proximal third, and bears a rough line (Crista interossea) laterally for the attachment of the interosseous ligament. The proximal end (Capitulum radii) is relatively small and is supported by a distinct neck (Collum radii). It bears a concave surface (Fovea capituli) for articulation with the humerus, and a convex marginal area (Circumferentia articularis) behind for the ulna. The radial tuberosity is small. There is a large lateral tuberosity and below this a rough eminence. The distal extremity is much wider. It has an extensive concave carpal articular surface. Its medial border projects downward, forming the **styloid process** of the radius. Laterally there is a concave facet (Incisura ulnaris radii) for articulation with the ulna. Dorsally are three distinct grooves for the extensor tendons. The **ulna** is well developed, but dimin-

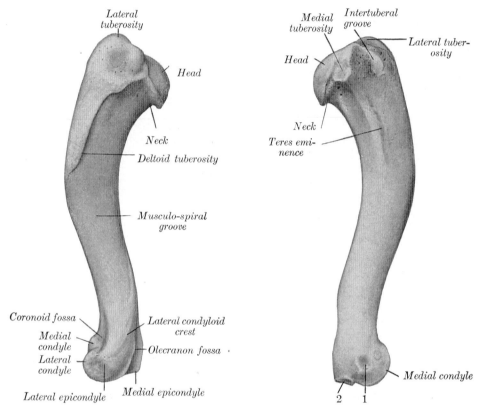

FIG. 218.—LEFT HUMERUS OF DOG; LATERAL VIEW.

FIG. 219.—LEFT HUMERUS OF DOG; MEDIAL VIEW.
1, Attachment of medial ligament of elbow joint; 2, attachment of flexor muscles to medial epicondyle.

ishes in size distally. It crosses the volar surface of the radius medio-laterally. The shaft is large and three-sided in its proximal two-thirds, smaller and more rounded below. Its dorsal surface is in general rough. The nutrient foramen is near the proximal end. A vascular groove descends from it and indicates the course of the interosseous artery. The proximal end is relatively short. It is concave and smooth medially, convex and rough laterally. The olecranon is grooved and bears three prominences, of which the posterior one is large and rounded. The semilunar notch is wide below and completes the surface for articulation with the trochlea of the humerus. Below it is a concave surface (Incisura radialis), which articulates with the back of the head of the radius, and below this is a fossa, which receives a tuberosity of the radius. The distal end (Capitulum ulnæ) is small and is produced to a blunt point (Processus styloideus ulnæ). It articulates with the ulnar carpal distally, and has a convex facet on its dorso-medial aspect for the radius. The proximal end of the radius unites with the shaft at six to eight months, the distal at about one and a half years of age. The olecranon and the distal end of the ulna fuse with the rest of the bone at about fifteen months.

The **carpus** comprises seven bones—three in the proximal row and four in the distal. The numerical reduction in the proximal row is apparently due to the fusion of the radial and intermediate, constituting a large bone (radio-intermediate) which articulates with almost all of the distal surface of the radius and with the bones of the distal row. It projects prominently on the volar surface of the carpus. The ulnar carpal is long; it articulates with the radius and ulna above and the accessory behind; below it rests on the fourth carpal and is prolonged downward to articulate with the fifth metacarpal also. The accessory is cylindrical, constricted in its middle and enlarged at each end; the anterior extremity articulates with the ulna and ulnar carpal bone. The first carpal is the smallest bone of the lower row; it articulates with the second carpal laterally and the first metacarpal distally. The second carpal is wedge-shaped, the base being posterior; its proximal surface is convex, and its distal is concave and rests on the second metacarpal. The third carpal is somewhat like the second; its distal surface is concave and articulates chiefly with the third metacarpal. The fourth carpal is the largest of the row; it articulates with the fourth and fifth metacarpals. Two small bones or cartilages may be found on the volar surface at the junction of the two rows, and a third small bone articulates with the medial side of the radio-intermediate.[1]

Five **metacarpal bones** are present. The first is much the shortest; the third and fourth are the longest, and are about one-fifth longer than the second and fifth. The fifth is the widest at the proximal end and is slightly shorter than the second. They are close together above, but diverge somewhat distally; the first is separated from the second by a considerable interosseous space. They are so arranged as to form a convex dorsal surface and a concave volar surface, which corresponds to the hollow of the palm of the hand in man. Each consists of a shaft and two extremities. The shaft is compressed from before backward. In the third and fourth it is almost four-sided, in the second and fifth three-sided, in the first rounded. The proximal ends (Bases) articulate with each other and with the corresponding

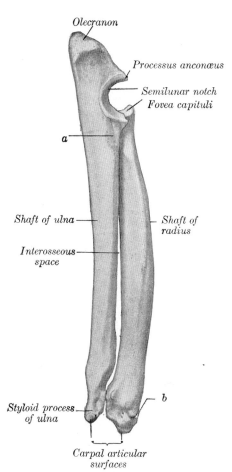

Olecranon

Processus anconæus

Semilunar notch
Fovea capituli

a

Shaft of ulna

Interosseous
space

Shaft of
radius

b

Styloid process
of ulna

Carpal articular
surfaces

FIG. 220.—LEFT RADIUS AND ULNA OF DOG; MEDIAL
VIEW.

a, Rough area for attachment of biceps brachii and brachialis muscles; b, groove for tendon of extensor carpi obliquus.

---

[1] The third bone was termed the phacoid in the cat by Strauss-Durckeim, and is regarded by some authors as the vestige of an additional digit, the prepollex.

carpal bones. The carpal articular surface formed by them is concave from side to side, convex from before backward. The distal ends (Capitula) have articular surfaces of the nature of a head, but bear a sagittal ridge on the volar aspect, except the first, which is grooved. Ossification is complete at five or six months of age.

The five **digits** have three phalanges each, except the first, which has two. The third and fourth digits are the longest; the first is very short and does not come in contact with the ground in walking. The **first phalanges** of the chief digits have four-sided shafts, which are slightly curved dorsally. The proximal end of each has a concave surface for articulation with the metacarpal bone and is deeply notched behind. The distal end has a trochlea for articulation with the second phalanx, and depressions on each side for ligamentous attachment. The **second phalanges** are about two-thirds of the length of the first phalanges. The proximal articular surface consists of two cavities separated by a sagittal ridge. The distal extremity is wider and flatter than that of the first. The **third phalanges** correspond in general to the form of the claws. The base has an articular surface adapted to the second phalanx and is encircled by a collar of bone (Crista unguicularis). The volar surface bears a wing or tuberosity, and on each side of this is a foramen. The ungual part is a curved rod with a blunt-pointed free end. It is rough and porous. Its base forms with the collar previously mentioned a deep groove, into which the proximal border of the claw is received. The two phalanges of the first digit resemble in arrangement the first and third phalanges of the other digits. Ossification is complete at five or six months.

Nine **volar sesamoids** are usually present. Two are found at each metacarpo-phalangeal joint of the chief digits. They are high and narrow, articulate with the distal end of the

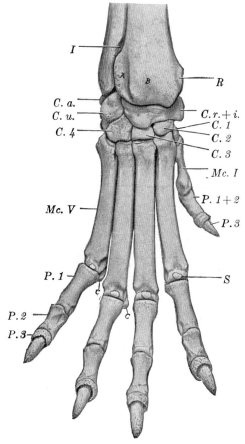

Fig. 221.—Skeleton of Distal Part of Right Thoracic Limb of Dog; Dorsal View.

The digits are spread. *I*, Distal end of interosseous space; *R*, distal end of radius; *C. r.+ i.*, radio-intermediate carpal; *C. u.*, ulnar carpal; *C. a.*, accessory carpal (very small part visible); *C. 1, C. 2, C. 3, C. 4*, first to fourth carpal bones; *Mc. I*, metacarpal bone of first digit; *P. 1+2*, fused first and second phalanges of same; *P. 3*, third phalanx of same; *Mc. V*, fifth metacarpal bone; *P. 1, P. 2, P. 3*, phalanges of fifth digit; *S*, dorsal sesamoid; *C, C*, volar sesamoids.

metacarpal bone in front, and have a small facet on the base for the first phalanx. On this joint of the first digit there is usually a single flattened sesamoid, but exceptionally two are present. The distal volar sesamoids remain cartilaginous. A nodular **dorsal sesamoid** occurs in the capsule of the metacarpo-phalangeal joints, and cartilaginous nodules are found in a similar position in connection with the joints between the first and second phalanges.

BONES OF THE PELVIC LIMB

The **ilium** is nearly parallel with the median plane and its axis is only slightly oblique with regard to the horizontal plane. The gluteal surface is concave. The pelvic surface is almost flat. The auricular surface faces almost directly inward, and in front of it there is an extensive rough area. The ilio-pectineal line is very distinct and is uninterrupted. The crest is strongly convex, thick, and rough. The tuber sacrale is represented by a thickened part which bears two eminences, homologous with the posterior superior and posterior inferior iliac spines of man. The tuber coxæ also has two prominences, which are equivalent to the two anterior spines present in man. The shaft is almost sagittal and is compressed laterally. It is smooth and rounded dorsally, and it bears a ventro-lateral crest (Linea glutæ ventralis), which terminates at a tuberosity in front of the acetabulum.

The **ischium** has a twisted appearance, owing to the fact that its acetabular part is nearly sagittal while the posterior part is almost horizontal. The two bones

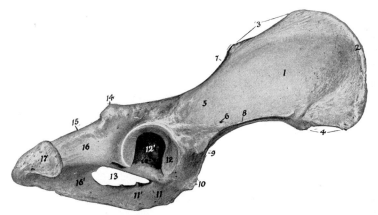

Fig. 222.—Right Os Coxæ of Dog; Lateral View.

1, Gluteal surface of ilium; 2, crest of ilium; 3, tuber sacrale; 4, tuber coxæ; 5, shaft of ilium; 6, nutrient foramen; 7, greater sciatic notch; 8, ventral gluteal line; 9, tubercle to which rectus femoris is attached; 10, ilio-pectineal eminence; 11, 11', acetabular and symphyseal branches of pubis; 12, articular surface of acetabulum; 12', fossa acetabuli; 13, obturator foramen; 14, ischiatic spine; 15, lesser sciatic notch; 16, 16', acetabular and symphyseal branches of ischium; 17, tuber ischii.

also diverge behind and the tubera are flattened and everted. The superior ischiatic spine is low and thick; its posterior part is marked by transverse grooves and has a prominent outer lip. The greater sciatic notch is elongated and very shallow. There is no lesser sciatic notch. The ischial arch is relatively small and is semi-elliptical.

The symphyseal part of the **pubis** is thick and fuses late with the opposite bone. There is no subpubic groove.

The **acetabulum** is about twice as far from the tuber coxæ as from the tuber ischii. The fossa acetabuli is deep, and is bounded medially by a flat plate of bone; its floor is so thin as to be translucent. There is a small notch behind.

The **obturator foramen** resembles in outline an equilateral triangle with the angles rounded off.

Union of the three parts of the os coxæ has usually taken place at six months, but the epiphyses of the ilium and ischium do not fuse with the main part of these bones till about the end of the second year.

The inlet of the **pelvis** is very oblique. It is almost circular in the female, but in the male it is elliptical and the conjugate diameter is the longer. The cavity is narrowest between the acetabula, and very wide behind. The floor is concave and relatively narrow in front, wide and flat behind.

The **femur** is relatively much longer than in the horse or ox. The shaft is regularly cylindrical, except near the extremities, where it is wider and compressed from before backward. It is strongly curved in its distal two-thirds, convex in front. The posterior surface is flattened transversely, narrow in the middle, and widens toward each end. It is bounded by two rough lines (Labium laterale, mediale) which diverge toward the extremities. The third trochanter and the supracondyloid fossa are absent. There are two supracondyloid crests, the medial one being small. The nutrient foramen is in the proximal third of the posterior surface. The head is a little more than a hemisphere and has a shallow fovea behind and lateral to its center. The neck is well defined. The trochanter major does not extend as high

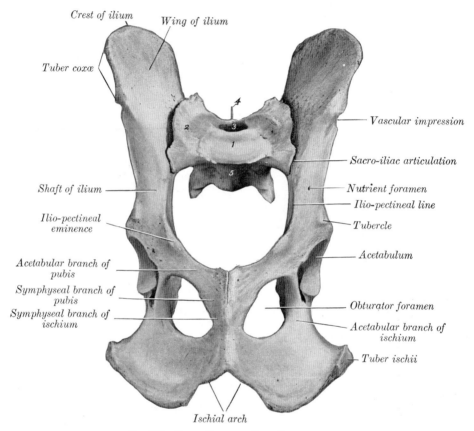

FIG. 223.—PELVIC BONES OF DOG; VENTRAL VIEW.

1, Body of first sacral vertebra; 2, wing of sacrum; 3, sacral canal; 4, median crest of sacrum; 5, pelvic surface of sacrum.

as the head; a thick ridge runs from its anterior surface to the neck. The trochanter minor has the form of a blunt tuberosity. The trochanteric fossa is round and deep. The ridges of the trochlea are practically sagittal in direction and are almost similar. The intercondyloid fossa is wide. Just above each condyle posteriorly there is a facet for articulation with the **sesamoid bone** which is developed in the origin of the gastrocnemius muscle. Union of shaft and extremities takes place at about one and a half years.

The **tibia** is about the same length as the femur. The shaft forms a double curve; the proximal part is convex medially, the distal part laterally. The proximal third is prismatic, but is compressed laterally and is long from before backward. The remainder is almost regularly cylindrical. The crest is short but very prominent. The nutrient foramen is usually in the proximal third of the lateral border. The tuberosity is not grooved, but bears a distinct mark where the ligamentum patellæ is attached. There is a small facet for the fibula on the postero-lateral part of the lateral condyle, and a small **sesamoid bone** in the tendon of origin of the popliteus is in contact with the posterior angle of the latter. The distal end is quadrangular and relatively small. The articular grooves and ridge are almost sagittal. There is a facet laterally for articulation with the fibula. There is a vertical groove medially and a shallower one behind—both for tendons. The proximal end unites with the shaft at about eighteen months, the distal at fourteen or fifteen months.

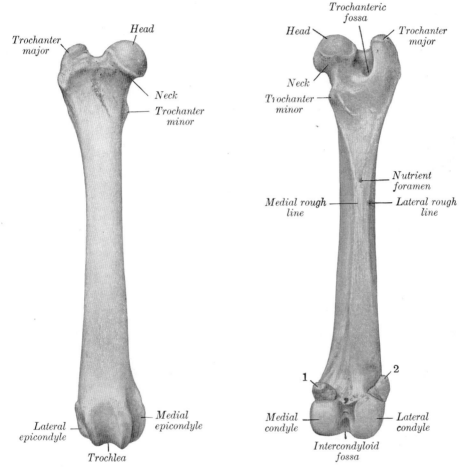

FIG. 224.—RIGHT FEMUR OF DOG; ANTERIOR VIEW. FIG. 225.—RIGHT FEMUR OF DOG; POSTERIOR VIEW.
1, 2, Sesamoid bones.

The **fibula** extends the entire length of the region. It is slender, somewhat twisted, and enlarged at either end. The proximal part of the shaft is separated from the tibia by a considerable interosseous space, but the distal part is flattened and closely applied to the tibia. The proximal extremity is flattened and articulates with the lateral condyle of the tibia. The distal end is somewhat thicker and forms the lateral malleolus. It articulates medially with the tibia and the tibial tarsal bone. Laterally it bears two tubercles.

The **patella** is long and narrow. The free surface is convex in both directions. The articular surface is convex from side to side and slightly concave from above downward.

The **tarsus** comprises seven bones. The tibial tarsal consists of a body, neck, and head, like the bone in man. The body presents a proximal trochlea for articulation with the tibia and fibula. The plantar surface has three facets for articulation with the fibular tarsal bone. The head is directed a little inward and articulates with the central. The fibular tarsal has a long anterior process or "beak," but the sustentaculum is short. The tuber calcis presents a sagittal groove. The central has a concave proximal surface adapted to the head of the tibial tarsal. Its distal surface articulates with the first, second, and third tarsals. It bears two plantar tubercles. The first tarsal is flattened and irregularly quadrangular; its proximal surface articulates with the central and the distal with the first metatarsal.

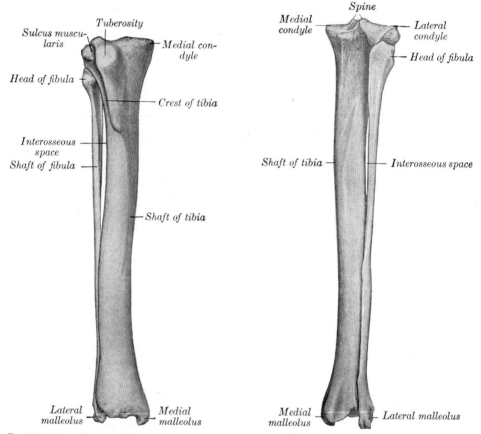

Fig. 226.—Right Tibia and Fibula of Dog; Anterior View.

Fig. 227.—Right Tibia and Fibula of Dog; Posterior View.

The second tarsal is the smallest and is wedge-shaped; it articulates distally with the second metatarsal bone. The third tarsal is also wedge-shaped, the base being in front; it articulates with the third metatarsal distally. The fourth tarsal is remarkably high, and resembles a quadrangular prism; its proximal surface articulates with the fibular tarsal, its distal with the fourth and fifth metatarsal, and the medial with the central and third tarsal bones. A groove for the tendon of the peroneus longus crosses its lateral and plantar surface, and above it are one or two tubercles. The tuber calcis fuses with the body of the bone at fourteen or fifteen months.

Five **metatarsal bones** are present. The first is commonly very small and has the form of a blunt cone, somewhat compressed laterally. It articulates with the first tarsal and furnishes insertion to the tibialis anterior muscle. In some cases it fuses with the first tarsal; when the first digit is well developed, its metatarsal may resemble the others (except in size) or be reduced in its proximal part to a fibrous band. The other metatarsals are a little longer than the corresponding metacarpals. Their proximal ends are elongated from before backward and have plantar projections, which in the case of the third and fourth usually have facets

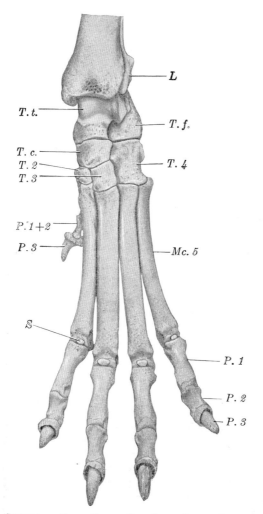

Fig. 228.—Skeleton of Distal Part of Left Pelvic Limb of Dog; Dorsal View.

L, Lateral malleolus (distal end of fibula); T. t., tibial tarsal bone: T. f., fibular tarsal bone; T. c., central tarsal bone; T. 2, T. 3, T. 4, second, third, and fourth tarsal bones; P. 1 + 2, fused first and second phalanges, and P. 3, third phalanx, of first digit; Mc. fifth metatarsal bone; P. 1, P. 2, P. 3, phalanges of fifth digit; S, dorsal sesamoid.

for articulation with two small rounded sesamoid bones. In other respects they resemble the metacarpals.

The first digit is often absent. When present, its development varies and it contains one or two phalanges. In other cases—especially in very large dogs—a sixth digit is present; it does not articulate with the metatarsus, but is attached by fibrous tissue. The phalanges of the other digits resemble those of the thoracic limb.

Ossification of the metatarsal bones and phalanges is complete at five or six months.

ARTHROLOGY

THE ARTICULATIONS OR JOINTS

An **articulation** or **joint** is formed by the union of two or more bones or cartilages by other tissue. Bone is the fundamental part of most joints; in some cases a bone and a cartilage, or two cartilages, form a joint. The uniting medium is chiefly fibrous tissue or cartilage, or a mixture of these. Union of parts of the skeleton by muscles (Synsarcosis), as in the attachment of the thoracic limb in the horse, will not be considered in this section.

Joints may be classified—(a) anatomically, according to their mode of development, the nature of the uniting medium, and the form of the joint surfaces; (b) physiologically, with regard to the amount and kind of movement or the absence of mobility in them; (c) by a combination of the foregoing considerations.

The classification of joints is still in a very unsatisfactory state, and unfortunately the same term is used in various senses by different authors. The two main subdivisions proposed by Hepburn are: (1) Those in which the uniting medium is coextensive with the opposed joint surfaces, and in which a direct union of these surfaces is thereby effected. (2) Those in which the uniting medium has undergone interruption in its structural continuity, and in which a cavity of greater or less extent is thus formed in the interior of the joint. This distinction is of considerable importance clinically.

Three chief subdivisions of joints are usually recognized—viz., **synarthroses, diarthroses,** and **amphiarthroses.**

SYNARTHROSES

In this group the segments are united by fibrous tissue or cartilage, or a mixture of the two in such a manner as practically to preclude movement; hence they are often termed fixed or immovable joints. There is no joint cavity. Most of these joints are temporary, the uniting medium being invaded by the process of ossification, with a resulting ankylosis or synostosis. The chief classes in this group of joints are as follows:

(1) **Suture.**—This term (Sutura) is applied to those joints in the skull in which the adjacent bones are closely united by fibrous tissue—the sutural ligament. In many cases the edges of the bones have irregular interlocking margins, forming the **sutura serrata,** e. g., the frontal suture. In others the edges are beveled and overlap, forming the **sutura squamosa,** e. g., the parieto-temporal suture. If the edges are plane or slightly roughened, the term **sutura harmonia** is applied to the joint, e. g., the nasal suture.

(2) **Syndesmosis.**—In these the uniting medium is white fibrous or elastic tissue or a mixture. As examples are the union of the shafts of the metacarpal bones and the attachments to each other of costal cartilages.

(3) **Synchondrosis.**—In these the two bones are united by cartilage, e. g., the joint between the basilar part of the occipital bone and the sphenoid bone. Very few of these joints are permanent.

(4) **Symphysis.**—This term is usually limited to a few median joints which connect symmetrical parts of the skeleton, e. g., symphysis pelvis, symphysis mandibulæ. The uniting medium is cartilage and fibrous tissue. In some cases a cleft-like rudimentary joint cavity occurs.

(5) **Gomphosis.**—This term is sometimes applied to the implantation of the teeth in the alveoli. The gomphosis is not, properly considered, a joint at all, since the teeth are not parts of the skeleton.

DIARTHROSES

These joints are characterized by the presence of a joint cavity with a synovial membrane in the joint capsule and by their mobility. They are often called movable or true joints. A **simple joint** (Articulatio simplex) is one formed by two articular surfaces; a **composite joint** (Articulatio composita), one formed by several articular surfaces. The following structures enter into their formation:

1. The **articular surfaces** (Facies articulares) are in most cases smooth, and vary much in form. They are formed of specially dense bone, which differs histologically from ordinary compact substance. In certain cases (*vide* Osteology) the surface is interrupted by non-articular cavities known as **synovial fossæ.**

2. The **articular cartilages** (Cartilagines articulares), usually hyaline in type, form a covering over the articular surfaces of the bones. They vary in thickness in different joints; they are thickest on those which are subject to the most pressure and friction. They usually tend to accentuate the curvature of the bone, *i. e.*, on a concave surface the peripheral part is the thickest, while on a convex surface the central part is the thickest. The articular cartilages are non-vascular, very smooth, and have a bluish tinge in the fresh state. They diminish the effects of concussion and greatly reduce friction.

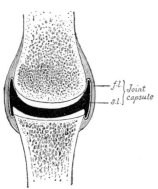

Fig. 229.—Diagram of Section of Diarthrosis.

f.l., Fibrous layer, *s.l.*, synovial layer of joint capsule. The articular cartilages are white, bones dotted, and the joint cavity black in the figure.

3. The **articular** or **joint capsule** (Capsula articularis) is, in its simplest form, a tube, the ends of which are attached around the articulating surfaces. It consists of two layers—an external one, composed of fibrous tissue, and an internal one, the synovial layer or membrane. The **fibrous layer** (Stratum fibrosum), sometimes termed the capsular ligament, is attached either close to the margins of the articular surfaces or at a variable distance from them. Its thickness varies greatly in different situations: in certain places it is extremely thick, and sometimes cartilage or bone develops in it; in other places it is practically absent, the capsule then consisting only of the synovial membrane. Tendons which pass over a joint may partially take the place of the fibrous layer; in these cases the deep face of the tendon is covered by the synovial layer. Parts of the capsule may undergo thickening and so form ligaments, which are not separable, except artificially, from the rest of the capsule. The **synovial layer** (Stratum synoviale) lines the joint cavity except where this is bounded by the articular cartilages; it stops normally at the margin of the latter. It is a thin membrane, and is richly supplied by close networks of vessels and nerves. It frequently forms **folds** (Plicæ synoviales) and **villi** (Villi synoviales), which project into the cavity of the joint. The folds commonly contain pads of fat, and there are in many places masses of fat outside of the capsule which fill up interstices and vary in form and position in various phases of movement. The synovial membrane secretes a fluid, the **synovia**, which lubricates the joint; it resembles white-of-egg, but has a yellowish tinge.[1] In many places the

---

[1] It is doubtful whether the synovia is a true secretion or a transudate containing products of friction. The view given above is that which is more commonly accepted. It contains albumen, mucin, and salts, and is alkaline. In it there are commonly cells derived from the synovial membrane, portions of cells, cells which have undergone fatty degeneration, particles of articular cartilage, etc.

membrane forms extra-articular pouches, which facilitate the play of muscles and tendons.

The **articular** or **joint cavity** (Cavum articulare) is enclosed by the synovial membrane and the articular cartilages. Normally, it contains only a sufficient amount of synovia to lubricate the joint.

The student must guard against a false conception of the joint cavity which may result from dissections and diagrams in which an actual cavity of considerable extent appears to exist. A correct idea of the intimate apposition of the parts is obtained from the study of frozen sections (Fig. 242). On the other hand, it is instructive to examine joints which have been injected so as to distend the capsule (Fig. 246). It is then seen that the cavity is often of much greater potential extent than one might suppose, and that the capsule is often very irregular in form, i. e., forms a variety of sacculations.

The foregoing are constant and necessary features in all diarthroses. Other structures which enter into the formation of these joints are ligaments, articular discs or menisci, and marginal cartilages.

4. **Ligaments.**—These (Ligamenta) are strong bands or membranes, usually composed of white fibrous tissue, which bind the bones together. They are pliable, but practically inelastic. In a few cases, however, e. g., the ligamentum nuchæ, they are composed of elastic tissue. They may be subdivided, according to position, into **periarticular** and **intraarticular.** Periarticular ligaments are frequently blended with or form part of the fibrous capsule; in other cases they are quite distinct. Those which are situated on the sides of a joint are termed **collateral ligaments** (Ligamenta collateralia). Strictly speaking, intra-articular ligaments, though within the fibrous capsule, are not in the joint cavity; the synovial membrane is reflected over them. The term seems justifiable, however, on practical grounds. Those which connect directly opposed surfaces of bones are termed **interosseous ligaments.** In many places muscles, tendons, and thickenings of the fasciæ function as ligaments and increase the security of the joint. Atmospheric pressure and cohesion play a considerable part in keeping the joint surfaces in apposition.

5. **Articular discs** or **menisci** (Disci s. menisci articulares) are plates of fibrocartilage or dense fibrous tissue placed between the articular cartilages, and divide the joint cavity partially or completely into two compartments. They render certain surfaces congruent, allow greater range or variety of movement, and diminish concussion.

6. A **marginal cartilage** (Labrum glenoidale) is a ring of fibro-cartilage which encircles the rim of an articular cavity. It enlarges the cavity and tends to prevent fracture of the margin.

Vessels and Nerves.—The **arteries** form anastomoses around the larger joints, and give off branches to the extremities of the bones and to the joint capsule. The synovial membrane has a close-meshed network of capillaries; the latter form loops around the margins of the articular cartilages, but do not usually enter them. The **veins** form plexuses. The synovial membrane is also well supplied with **lymph-vessels.** **Nerve-fibers** are especially numerous in and around the synovial membrane and there are special **nerve-endings,** e. g., Pacinian bodies and the articular end-bulbs described by Krause.

Movements.—The movements of a joint are determined chiefly by the form and extent of the joint surfaces and the arrangement of the ligaments. They are usually classified as follows:

1. **Gliding.**—This refers to the sliding of one practically plane surface on another, as in the joints between the articular processes of the cervical vertebræ.

2. **Angular Movements.**—In these cases there is movement around one or more axes. Motion which diminishes the angle included by the segments forming the joint is termed **flexion,** while that which tends to bring the segments into line with each other is called **extension.** With reference to the joints of the distal parts

of the limbs, it seems advisable to employ the terms **dorsal** and **volar** or **plantar flexion,** since these joints can be "overextended." Similarly the terms **dorsal** and **ventral flexion** are applied to the corresponding movements of the spinal column. The meaning of the term **lateral flexion** as applied to the vertebral column is evident. These movements are all rotations around axes which are approximately either transverse or vertical. Depression, elevation, and transverse movement of the lower jaw fall in this category.

3. **Circumduction.**—This designates movements in which the distal end of the limb describes a circle or a segment of one. In man such movement is easily performed, but in quadrupeds it is possible to a limited degree only, and is to be regarded usually as an indication of disease.

4. **Rotation.**—As a matter of convenience, this term is reserved to indicate rotation of one segment around the longitudinal axis of the other segment forming the joint. It is seen typically in the atlanto-axial joint.

5. **Adduction** and **abduction** designate respectively movement of a limb toward and away from the median plane, or of a digit toward and away from the axis of the limb.

Classification.—This is based on the form of the joint surfaces and the movements which occur. The following chief classes may be recognized:

1. **Arthrodia,** or gliding joint. In these the surfaces are practically flat, admitting of gliding movement. Examples: carpo-metacarpal joints; joints between the articular processes of the cervical and thoracic vertebræ.

2. **Ginglymus,** or hinge-joint. In this class the joint surfaces consist usually of two condyles, or of a segment of a cylinder or cone, which are received by corresponding cavities. In typical cases the movements are flexion and extension, *i. e.*, around a single transverse axis. Examples: atlanto-occipital and elbow joints.

3. **Trochoid,** or pivot joint. In these the movement is limited to rotation of one segment around the longitudinal axis of the other. Example: atlanto-axial joint.

4. **Enarthrosis,** or ball-and-socket joint. These are formed by a surface of approximately spherical curvature, received into a corresponding cavity. They are multiaxial, and allow of the greatest variety of movement, *e. g.*, flexion, extension, rotation, abduction, adduction, circumduction. Examples: hip and shoulder joints.[1]

AMPHIARTHROSES

These joints, as the name indicates, share some characters with both of the preceding groups. In them the segments are directly united by a plate of fibrocartilage, and usually by ligaments also. The amount and kind of movement are determined by the shape of the joint surfaces and the amount and pliability of the uniting medium.[2] These joints are nearly all medial in position, and are best illustrated by the joints between the bodies of the vertebræ. There is typically no joint cavity, but in certain situations one exists.

[1] This classification makes no claims to scientific accuracy, but is simply a statement of the terms in general use. A grouping based on mechanical principles might be desirable, but appears to be almost impossible on account of the great variety and irregularity of form of the articular surfaces.

[2] The movements in some of these joints are more extensive and varied than in some diarthroses. To illustrate this we may compare the movements of the cervical or coccygeal vertebræ with those possible in the carpo-metacarpal or the sacro-iliac joints.

THE ARTICULATIONS OF THE HORSE

JOINTS AND LIGAMENTS OF THE VERTEBRÆ

The movable vertebræ form two sets of articulations, viz., those formed by the bodies, and those formed by the articular processes of adjacent vertebræ; the former are termed **intercentral**, and the latter **interneural**. Associated with these are ligaments uniting the arches and processes; some of these are special, *i. e.*, confined to a single joint, while others are common, *i. e.*, extend along almost the entire vertebral column or a considerable part of it. The joints between the atlas and axis and between the former and the skull require separate consideration.

INTERCENTRAL ARTICULATIONS

These are **amphiarthroses,** formed by the junction of the extremities of the bodies of adjacent vertebræ. The **articular surfaces** in the cervical region consist of a cavity on the posterior end of the body of the anterior vertebra, and a corresponding convexity or head of the succeeding vertebra. In the other regions the surfaces are much flattened. The uniting media are:

1. The **intervertebral fibro-cartilages** (Fibrocartilagines intervertebrales). Each of these is a disc which occupies the space between the bodies of two adjacent vertebræ, to which it is intimately attached. The discs are thinnest in the middle of the thoracic region, thicker in the cervical and lumbar regions, and thickest in the coccygeal region.

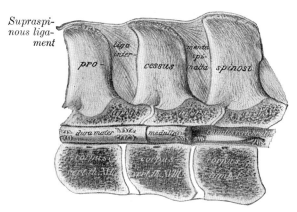

FIG. 230.—SAGITTAL SECTION OF LAST TWO THORACIC AND FIRST LUMBAR VERTEBRÆ, SHOWING LIGAMENTS AND SPINAL CORD (MEDULLA). (After Schmaltz, Atlas d. Anat. d. Pferdes.)

Each consists of a peripheral **fibrous ring** (Annulus fibrosus) and a soft central **pulpy nucleus** (Nucleus pulposus).

The fibrous ring consists of laminæ of fibrous tissue and fibro-cartilage, which pass obliquely between the two vertebræ and alternate in direction, forming an X-shaped arrangement. The central part of the ring is largely cartilaginous, and gradually assumes the character of the pulpy center. The latter is very elastic and is compressed, so that it bulges considerably from the surface of sections; it consists of white and elastic fibers, connective-tissue cells, and peculiar clear, transparent cells of various sizes. It is a remnant of the notochord. There are joint cavities in the cervical intercentral joints, in those between the last cervical and the first thoracic, and between the last lumbar and the sacrum.

2. The **ventral longitudinal ligament** (Lig. longitudinale ventrale) lies on the ventral surface of the bodies of the vertebræ and the intervertebral fibro-cartilages, to which it is firmly attached. It begins to be distinct a little behind the middle of the thoracic region, and is at first a narrow, thin band. Further back it becomes gradually thicker and wider, and terminates on the pelvic surface of the sacrum by spreading out and blending with the periosteum. It is strongest in the lumbar region, where the tendons of the crura of the diaphragm fuse with it.

3. The **dorsal longitudinal ligament** (Lig. longitudinale dorsale) lies on the floor of the vertebral canal from the axis to the sacrum. It is narrow over the middles of the vertebral bodies, and widens over the intervertebral fibro-cartilages, to which it is very firmly attached.

This ligament is in relation with the spinal veins on either side, and in the middle of each vertebra a transverse anastomotic vein passes under the ligament.

INTERNEURAL ARTICULATIONS

Each typical vertebra presents two pairs of articular processes, which form diarthroses with the two adjacent vertebræ. The **articular surfaces** are extensive, almost flat, and oval in the cervical region, small and flat in the thoracic region,

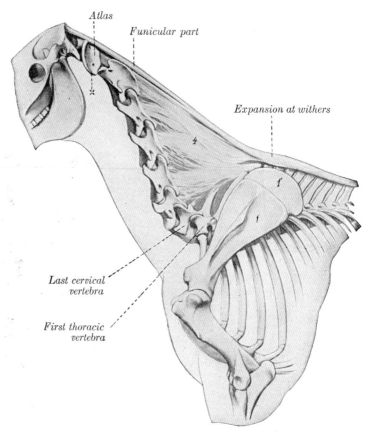

Atlas

Funicular part

Expansion at withers

Last cervical vertebra

First thoracic vertebra

Fig. 231.—Ligamentum Nuchæ of Horse.

1, Scapula; *1'*, cartilage of scapula; *4*, lamellar part of ligamentum nuchæ; *x*, wing of atlas. (After Ellenberger-Baum, Anat. für Künstler.)

while in the lumbar region the anterior ones are concave and the posterior convex. The **joint capsule** is strong and ample in the cervical region, in conformity with the large size and greater mobility of these joints in the neck. In the thoracic and lumbar regions the capsule is small and close. These joints are arthrodia in the neck and back, trochoid in the lumbar region.

Associated with these joints are the **ligamenta flava,** which connect the arches of adjacent vertebræ. They are membranous and consist largely of elastic tissue.

The **supraspinous ligament** (Lig. supraspinale) extends medially from the occipital bone to the sacrum. Behind the withers it consists of a strong cord of white fibrous tissue, attached to the summits of the vertebral spines. In the neck and withers it is remarkably modified to form the ligamentum nuchæ, which requires more extended notice.

The **ligamentum nuchæ** is a powerful elastic apparatus, the principal function of which is to assist the extensor muscles of the head and neck. It extends from the occipital bone to the withers, where it is directly continuous with the lumbo-dorsal part of the supraspinous ligament. It consists of two parts—funicular and lamellar. The **funicular part** (Pars occipitalis) arises from the external occipital protuberance and is inserted into the summits of the vertebral spines at the withers. At the occipital attachment it is flattened laterally and is an inch or more (ca. 3 cm.) in height, but quickly changes to a rounded shape about half as high. Two **bursæ** are usually found under it in the adult. The **atlantal bursa** lies between the ligament and the dorsal arch of the atlas. The **supraspinous bursa** is most commonly over the second thoracic spine, where there is a space between the funicular and lamellar parts that is occupied otherwise by fat and loose connective tissue. Other irregular bursæ often occur over the highest spines.[1] Another bursa may be present at the spine of the axis; this is between the funicular part and the large digitation attached to the axis. In the neck the funicular part consists for the greater part of two bands closely applied and attached to each other. Near and at the withers it broadens greatly, forming an expansion about five to six inches (ca. 12 to 15 cm.) in width, the lateral margins of which are thin and turn down over the trapezius and rhomboideus muscles. Behind the higher spines it becomes narrower and thinner, and is continued by the white fibrous lumbo-dorsal part.[2] A mass of fat and elastic tissue lies upon the ligament as far back as the withers. It varies greatly in amount in different subjects, and is most developed in stallions of draft breeds, in which it forms the basis of the so-called "crest." The **lamellar part** (Pars cervicalis) consists of two laminæ separated medially by a layer of loose connective tissue. Each lamina is formed of digitations which arise from the second and third thoracic spines and from the funicular part, are directed downward and forward, and end on the spines of the cervical vertebræ, except the first and last. The digitation which is attached to the spine of the axis is very thick and strong. Behind this they diminish in size and strength; the last one, which is attached to the sixth cervical vertebra, is quite thin and feeble, or may be absent.

The **interspinous ligaments** (Ligg. interspinalia) extend between the spines of contiguous vertebræ. In the cervical region they are narrow elastic bands, and in the thoracic and lumbar regions they consist of white fibers directed obliquely downward and backward except the first thoracic one, which is elastic and its fibers run downward and forward.

The **intertransverse ligaments** (Ligg. intertransversaria) are membranes which connect adjacent transverse processes in the lumbar region.

INTERTRANSVERSE ARTICULATIONS

These joints (peculiar to equidæ) are diarthroses formed by the transverse processes of the fifth and sixth lumbar vertebræ and between the latter and the alæ of the sacrum. A similar joint between the fourth and fifth lumbar processes is frequently present. The **articular surfaces** have an elongated oval form, the anterior one being concave and the posterior one convex. The capsule is tight, and is reinforced ventrally.

SACRAL AND COCCYGEAL ARTICULATIONS

In the foal the bodies of the five sacral vertebræ form joints which resemble somewhat those in the posterior part of the lumbar region. These joints are in-

---

[1] In dissecting-room subjects these bursæ and the adjacent structures are commonly the seat of pathological changes. They appear to be the starting-point of "poll evil" and "fistulous withers." Subcutaneous bursæ may be found over the ligament at the withers.

[2] No line of demarcation exists between the ligamentum nuchæ and the lumbo-dorsal part of the supraspinous ligament, since the change from the elastic to the white fibrous structure is gradual.

vaded by the process of ossification early, so that the consolidation of the sacrum is usually complete, or nearly so, at three years.

The coccygeal vertebræ are united by relatively thick intervertebral fibro-cartilages, which have the form of biconcave discs. Special ligaments are not present, but there is a continuous sheath of fibrous tissue. The movement in this region is extensive and varied. In old horses the first coccygeal vertebra is often fused with the sacrum.

MOVEMENTS OF THE VERTEBRAL COLUMN

The movements of the spine, exclusive of those at the atlanto-axial joint, are dorsal, ventral, and lateral flexion, and rotation. The range of movement at a single joint is small, but the sum of the movements is considerable. The movements are freest in the cervical and coccygeal regions. Rotation is extremely limited in the thoracic and lumbar regions.

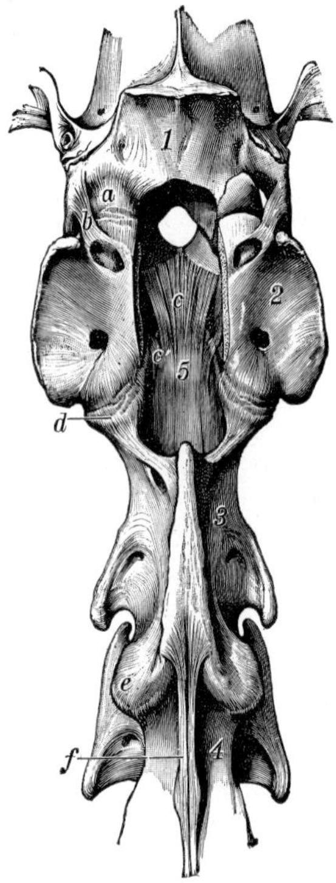

FIG. 232.—ATLANTO-OCCIPITAL AND ATLANTO - AXIAL JOINTS OF HORSE; DORSAL VIEW AFTER REMOVAL OF DORSAL ARCH OF ATLAS.

a, Joint capsule of left part of atlanto-occipital joint; b, lateral ligament of same; c, c′, ligament of the dens; d, atlanto-axial joint capsule; e, joint capsule of articulation between axis and third cervical vertebra; f, interspinous ligament; 1, occipital bone; 2, atlas; 3, axis; 4, third cervical vertebra; 5, dorsal longitudinal ligament. (Ellenberger-Baum, Anat. d. Haustiere.)

ATLANTO-AXIAL ARTICULATION

This is a trochoid or pivot joint of a rather peculiar character. The articular surfaces are: (1) On the lateral masses of the atlas, two somewhat saddle-shaped facets, which are separated by a wide notch above and a narrow one below; (2) on the axis, reciprocal saddle-shaped surfaces which extend upon the dens and are confluent on its ventral aspect. It will be observed that the joint surfaces are not at all accurately adapted to each other, so that only limited areas are in contact at any time.

The **joint capsule** is attached around the margins of the articular surfaces. It is loose and ample enough laterally to allow extensive movement.

The **dorsal atlanto-axial ligament** (Lig. interarcuale) is membranous and reinforces the capsule dorsally.

The **interspinous ligament** (Lig. interspinale) consists of two elastic bands which extend from the dorsal arch of the atlas to the spine of the axis.

The **ventral atlanto-axial ligament** (Lig. dentis externum) arises from the ventral tubercle of the atlas and is attached by two branches on the ventral spine of the axis.

The **ligament of the dens** (Lig. dentis internum) is short, very strong, and somewhat fan-shaped. It extends from the rough concave dorsal surface of the dens, widens in front, and is attached to the transverse rough area on the inner surface of the ventral arch of the atlas.

Movements.—The atlas and the head rotate upon the axis; the axis of rotation passes through the center of the body of the axis.

THE ATLANTO-OCCIPITAL ARTICULATION

This joint may be classed as a ginglymus. The **articular surfaces** of this joint are: (1) On the atlas, two deep oval cavities; (2) the corresponding condyles of the occipital bone.

The joint surfaces are oblique, coming very close to the median line ventrally, but separated by a considerable interval dorsally. A triangular rough area cuts into the medial part of each of the atlantal articular surfaces.

There are two roomy **joint capsules,** which sometimes communicate ventrally, especially in old subjects.

The **dorsal atlanto-occipital membrane** (Membrana atlanto-occipitalis dorsalis) extends from the dorsal arch of the atlas to the dorsal margin of the foramen magnum. It is blended with the capsules and contains many elastic fibers.

The **ventral atlanto-occipital membrane** (Membrana atlanto-occipitalis ventralis) extends from the ventral arch of the atlas to the ventral margin of the foramen magnum. It is narrower and thinner than the dorsal membrane, and also fuses with the joint capsules.

The **lateral atlantal ligaments** (Ligg. lateralia atlantis) are two short bands which are partially blended with the capsules. Each is attached to the border of the wing of the atlas near the intervertebral foramen, and to the lateral surface of the paramastoid process of the occipital bone.

Movements.—These are chiefly flexion and extension. A small amount of lateral oblique movement is also possible.

ARTICULATIONS OF THE THORAX
COSTO-VERTEBRAL ARTICULATIONS

Each typical rib forms two joints with the vertebral column, one by its head, and one by its tubercle. They are termed respectively costo-central and costo-transverse joints.

I. The **costo-central articulation** (Articulatio capituli) is a trochoid or rotatory joint, formed by the junction of the head of the rib with the bodies of two adjacent vertebræ and the intervertebral fibro-cartilage. The two facets on the head of the rib are separated by a non-articular groove, and correspond to the two concave facets (Foveæ costales) on the vertebral bodies. The **joint capsule** is rather tight, and is covered by the accessory ligaments, which are as follows: 1. The **radiate ligament** (Lig. capituli costæ radiatum) extends ventrally from the neck of the rib to spread out on the vertebral bodies and the intervertebral fibro-cartilage. 2. The **conjugal ligament** (Lig. conjugale) —absent from the first joint—is attached to the groove on the head of the rib, passes transversely into the vertebral canal, and divides under the dorsal longitudinal liga-

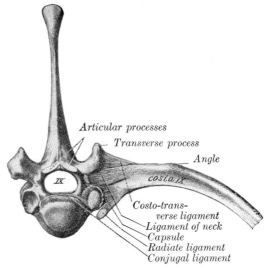

Articular processes

Transverse process

Angle

costa IX

IX

Costo-transverse ligament

Ligament of neck

Capsule

Radiate ligament

Conjugal ligament

Fig. 233.—Costo-vertebral Articulation; Anterior View.
(After Schmaltz, Atlas d. Anat. d. Pferdes.)

ment into two branches: one of these is attached to the body of the anterior vertebra; the other is continued across to the head of the opposite rib, and is also attached to the intervertebral fibro-cartilage. The joint cavity is divided into two compartments by the conjugal ligament. 3. The **ligament of the neck** of the rib (Lig. colli costæ) is a strong band which crosses the joint dorsally. It is attached on the vertebra above the costal facet and on the neck of the rib.

II. The **costo-transverse articulation** (Articulatio costo-transversaria). This is formed by the facet on the tubercle of the rib and on the transverse process of the vertebra. They are gliding joints. The **capsule** is reinforced by the **dorsal costo-transverse ligament** (Lig. costo-transversarium dorsale), a distinct strong band which arises on the transverse process and ends on the non-articular part of the tubercle. It is covered by the levator costæ muscle, and begins to be quite distinct at the fifth joint.

The cavity for the head of the first rib is formed by concave facets on the bodies of the last cervical and first thoracic vertebræ. The conjugal ligament is absent, but the ligament of the neck is short and strong. The radiate ligament is very strong, and consists of two parts. In the case of the last two or three ribs the costo-central and costo-transverse joints are confluent, and the soft structures are correspondingly modified.

Movements.—The chief movement is rotation around an axis which connects the centers of the head and tubercle of the rib. The movement is very limited in the anterior part of the series of joints, but very considerable in the posterior part.

In the case of the first rib the movement is evidently extremely limited. The facet for the tubercle of the rib is deeply concave, and the axis of rotation is almost transverse, so that the movement is chiefly sagittal in direction. Further back the facets on the transverse processes become flat, and the axis of rotation gradually approaches a longitudinal direction. This, in connection with the mobility of the ventral ends of the asternal ribs and their elasticity, allows a great increase here in the range of movement which is largely transverse, the effect being to enlarge (chiefly) the transverse diameter of the thorax.

COSTO-CHONDRAL ARTICULATIONS

The costo-chondral junctions are synarthroses. The rib has a concave surface which receives the convex end of the cartilage. They are united by the continuity of the strong periosteum and perichondrium.

CHONDRO-STERNAL ARTICULATIONS

These joints (Articulationes sternocostales) are diarthroses formed by the cartilages of the sternal ribs and the sternum. The articular ends of the cartilages (except the first) are somewhat enlarged, and present surfaces of cylindrical curvature. The articular surfaces on the sternum for the first pair of cartilages are placed close together on the dorsal border of the cariniform cartilage; the other seven are placed laterally at the junctions of the segments. The capsules are strong and tight; the first pair of joints has a common capsule, and the cartilages articulate with each other medially. The ventral ends of the first pair of cartilages articulate with the sternum and with each other; above this they are firmly attached to each other by dense fibrous tissue, which is prolonged forward along the upper margin of the cariniform cartilage and is continuous behind with the sternal ligament. Each of the other capsules is reinforced dorsally by the **radiate costo-sternal ligament** (Ligamentum sterno-costale radiatum), composed of radiating fibers which blend with the sternal ligament. Interarticular bands may be present. The movement is rotation around a nearly vertical axis, except in the case of the first pair of joints.

INTERCHONDRAL LIGAMENTS

The eighth and ninth costal cartilages are firmly united by fibrous tissue. The chondro-xiphoid ligament attaches the ninth costal cartilage to the xiphoid cartilage. The remaining cartilages are rather loosely attached to each other by elastic tissue.

STERNAL ARTICULATIONS

In the new-born foal the seven bony segments are united by persisting cartilage (Synchondroses intersternales). The last two segments coalesce within a few weeks after birth. In old subjects there is more or less ossification of the intersternebral cartilage, which may lead to fusion of adjacent segments, especially posteriorly. The **internal sternal ligament** (Lig. sterni proprium internum) lies on the thoracic surface of the sternum (Fig. 274). It arises on the first segment, and divides opposite the second chondro-sternal joint into three parts. The median branch passes backward and spreads out on the last segment and the xiphoid cartilage (Fig. 274). The lateral branches—thicker and wider—lie along the lateral borders above the chondro-sternal joints, and end at the cartilage of the eighth rib; they are covered by the transversus thoracis muscle.

THE ARTICULATIONS OF THE SKULL

MANDIBULAR ARTICULATION

This joint (Articulatio mandibularis) is a diarthrosis formed between the ramus of the mandible and the squamous temporal bone on either side.

The **articular surfaces** are dissimilar in form and size. That on the squamous temporal bone is concavo-convex, and the long axis is directed outward and somewhat forward; it consists of a condyle in front and a glenoid cavity, which is continued upon the postglenoid process behind. The mandible presents a transversely elongated condyle.

The **articular disc** (Discus articularis) is placed between the joint surfaces, which it renders congruent. Its surfaces are molded upon the temporal and mandibular surfaces respectively, and its circumference is attached to the joint capsule; thus it divides the joint cavity into upper and lower compartments, the former being the more roomy.

The **joint capsule** is strong and tight. It is reinforced by two ligaments. The **lateral ligament** (Lig. laterale) extends obliquely across the anterior part of the lateral surface of the capsule, from which it is not distinctly separable. The **posterior ligament** (Lig. posterius) is an elastic band which is attached above to the postglenoid process, and below to a line on the posterior face of the neck of the mandible.

Movements.—The chief movements take place around a transverse axis passing through both joints. Associated with this hinge-like action is slight gliding movement, as in opening and shutting the mouth. When the mouth is shut, the condyle of the mandible lies under the glenoid cavity. When the mandible is depressed, the condyle moves forward under the articular eminence of the temporal bone, carrying the disc with it. In protrusion and retraction of the lower jaw the gliding movement just described occurs without the hinge-like rotation of the condyle. These movements are similar in both joints. In the transverse movements (as usually performed in mastication) the action consists of rotation of the condyles around a vertical axis, while the disc glides forward on one side and backward on the other.

SYNARTHROSES OF THE SKULL

Most of the bones of the skull are united with the adjacent bones by **sutures;** a few are united by cartilage. The difference in the uniting medium depends on the fact that most of these bones are developed in membrane, but some are preformed in cartilage. Most of these joints are temporary, and are obliterated at various periods during development and growth. Their importance lies in the fact that so long as they persist, continuous growth is possible. They are usually designated according to the bones which enter into their formation, *e. g.*, spheno-squamous, naso-frontal, etc.

Detailed description of the sutures has not sufficient clinical value to justify much addition to the statements made in the osteology in this connection. The obliteration or closure of the sutures is, however, worthy of brief mention. The cranial sutures are usually all closed at seven years, but the apex only of the petrous temporal is fused with the occipital and squamous temporal. Most of the facial sutures are practically closed at ten years, although complete synostosis may in some be delayed for years or may not occur at all; the nasal suture, for example, usually persists even in advanced age, so far as its anterior part is concerned.

The principal **synchondroses** are: (1) That between the basilar part of the occipital bone and the body of the sphenoid (Synchondrosis spheno-occipitalis); (2) that between the presphenoid and postsphenoid (Synchondrosis intersphenoidalis); (3) those between the parts of the occipital bone (Synchondroses intraoccipitales). The first is ossified at four or five years, the second at three years, and the occipital bone is consolidated at two years.

The **symphysis mandibulæ** ossifies at one to six months.

THE HYOIDEAN ARTICULATIONS

The **temporo-hyoid articulation** is an amphiarthrosis, in which the articular angle of the dorsal end of the great cornu of the hyoid bone is attached by a short bar of cartilage to the hyoid process of the petrous temporal bone. The cartilage (Arthrohyoid) is about half an inch (ca. 1–1.5 cm.) in length. The chief movement is hinge-like, the axis of motion passing transversely through both joints.

The **intercornual articulation** is an amphiarthrosis formed by the junction of the ventral extremity of the great cornu with the dorsal end of the small cornu of the hyoid bone. They are united by a very short piece of cartilage, in which there is usually a small nodule of bone in the young subject. This nodule, the epihyoid or middle cornu, is usually fused with the great cornu in the adult. The chief movement here is also hinge-like, the angle between the cornua being increased or diminished.

The **basi-cornual articulation** is a diarthrosis formed by the junction of each small cornu with the body of the hyoid bone. The small cornu has a concave facet which articulates with the convex facet on either end of the dorsal surface of the body. The capsule is ample enough to allow considerable movement, which is chiefly hinge-like.

The movements of the hyoid bone are concerned chiefly in the acts of mastication and swallowing. In the latter the ventral parts of the hyoid bone are moved forward and upward, carrying the root of the tongue and the larynx with them, and then return to their former position.

THE ARTICULATIONS OF THE THORACIC LIMB

In the absence of the clavicle the thoracic limb forms no articulation with the trunk, to which it is attached by muscles. The movement of the shoulder on the chest-wall is chiefly rotation around a transverse axis passing through the scapula behind the upper part of the spine.

THE SHOULDER JOINT

The shoulder or scapulo-humeral joint (Articulatio scapulo-humeralis) is formed by the junction of the distal end of the scapula with the proximal end of the humerus. The **articular surfaces** are: (1) On the scapula, the glenoid cavity;

(2) on the humerus, the head. Both surfaces are approximately spherical and similar in curvature, but the humeral surface is about twice as extensive as that of the scapula.

The **joint capsule** is ample enough to allow the bones to be drawn apart about an inch (ca. 2–3 cm.); but this requires a very considerable amount of force unless air is admitted into the joint cavity. The fibrous layer is not attached to the margin of the joint surfaces, but at a distance of one to two centimeters from it. It is strengthened in front by two diverging elastic bands, which arise on the tuber scapulæ and end on the tuberosities of the humerus. A pad of fat is interposed between the capsule and the tendon of the biceps.

Ligaments are absent from this joint, but the muscles and tendons around it afford remarkable security, so that dislocation very seldom occurs. The large extent of the head of the humerus is also of importance in this regard.

The principal muscles which are attached around the joint and act as ligaments are: laterally, the supraspinatus, infraspinatus, and teres minor; medially, the subscapularis; in front, the biceps and supraspinatus; behind, the triceps. Fibers of the brachialis are attached to the lower edge of the posterior part of the joint capsule, and would evidently tense the latter. In some cases the joint cavity communicates with the bicipital or intertuberal bursa.

Movements.—While it is a typical enarthrosis in structure, and capable of the various movements of the ball-and-socket joint, the chief normal movements are flexion and extension. In the position of rest the angle formed between the scapula and humerus posteriorly is about 120° to 130°; in flexion it is reduced to about 80°, and in extension it is increased to about 145°. Adduction and abduction are very restricted, the former being limited chiefly by the infraspinatus, the latter by the subscapularis and the low insertion of the superficial pectoral muscles. Rotation is somewhat freer, but does not exceed 33° when all the muscles are removed (Franck).

THE ELBOW JOINT

This, the cubital articulation (Articulatio cubiti), is a ginglymus formed between the distal extremity of the humerus and the proximal ends of the radius and ulna.

The **articular surfaces** are: (1) A trochlear surface formed by the condyles of the humerus; (2) the corresponding glenoid cavities and ridge on the proximal extremity of the radius, together with the semilunar notch of the ulna.

The articular surface of the condyles does not extend upon the back of the extremity, but the groove which receives the semilunar notch of the ulna extends up into the olecranon fossa. In the fore part of the groove there is a synovial fossa. The surface on the lateral condyle is much smaller than that of the medial one, and is subdivided into two unequal parts by a shallow furrow. On the lower part of the semilunar notch and the adjacent part of the ridge on the radius are synovial fossæ.

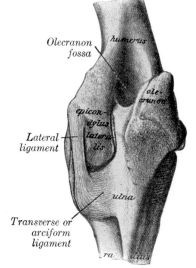

FIG. 234.—LEFT ELBOW JOINT OF HORSE; POSTERIOR VIEW. THE CAPSULE IS REMOVED. (After Schmaltz, Atlas d. Anat. d. Pferdes.)

The **joint capsule** is extremely thin behind, where it forms a pouch in the olecranon fossa under the anconeus muscle and a pad of fat. In front it is strengthened by oblique fibers (Lig. obliquum or anterior ligament), and on each side it fuses with the collateral ligaments. It also is adherent to the tendons of muscles which arise from the distal end of the humerus or end on the proximal end of the radius. The **synovial membrane** sends prolongations to the small radio-ulnar

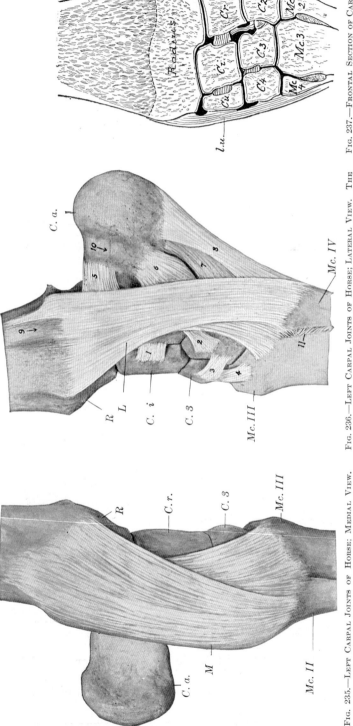

FIG. 237.—FRONTAL SECTION OF CARPAL JOINTS OF HORSE (RIGHT SIDE).

l.u., Lateral, *l.r.,* medial ligament; *Cr,* radial carpal; *Ci,* intermediate carpal; *Cu,* ulnar carpal; *C2,* second carpal; *C3,* third carpal; *C4,* fourth carpal; *Mc2,* second (medial) metacarpal; *Mc3,* third (large) metacarpal; *Mc4,* fourth (lateral) metacarpal. Distal epiphyseal line of radius is dotted.

FIG. 236.—LEFT CARPAL JOINTS OF HORSE; LATERAL VIEW. THE JOINT CAPSULE IS REMOVED.

R, Distal end of radius; *C. a.,* accessory carpal bone; *C. i.,* intermediate carpal bone; *C. 3,* third carpal bone; *Mc. III, Mc. IV,* metacarpal bones; *L,* lateral ligament; 1, dorsal ligament connecting intermediate and ulnar carpal; 2, dorsal ligament connecting ulnar and fourth carpal; 3, dorsal ligament connecting fourth and third carpal; 4, ligament connecting third carpal and metacarpal bone; 5, proximal ligament of accessory carpal bone; 6, middle ligament of same; 7, 8, distal ligaments of same; 9, groove for lateral extensor tendon; 10, groove for tendon of ulnaris lateralis; 11, interosseous metacarpal ligament.

FIG. 235.—LEFT CARPAL JOINTS OF HORSE; MEDIAL VIEW. THE JOINT CAPSULE IS REMOVED.

M, Medial collateral ligament; *R,* radius; *C. r.,* radial carpal bone; *C. 3,* third carpal bone; *C. a.,* accessory carpal bone; *Mc. II, Mc. III,* metacarpal bones.

joints and also pouches downward under the origins of the flexors of the digit and the lateral flexor of the carpus. There are two collateral ligaments.

The **medial ligament** (Lig. collaterale radiale) is attached above to an eminence on the medial epicondyle of the humerus, and divides into two parts: the long, superficial part ends on the medial border of the radius, just below the level of the interosseous space; the deep, short part is inserted into the medial tuberosity of the radius.

The **lateral ligament** (Lig. collaterale ulnare) is short and strong. It is attached above to a depression on the lateral epicondyle of the humerus, and below to the lateral tuberosity of the radius, just below the margin of the articular surface.

Movements.—This joint is a typical ginglymus, the only movements being flexion and extension around an axis which passes through the proximal attachments of the collateral ligaments. In the standing position the articular angle (in front) is about 150°. The range of movement is about 55° to 60°. Complete extension is prevented chiefly by the tension of the collateral ligaments and the biceps muscle. (The axis of movement is slightly oblique, so that in flexion the forearm is carried somewhat outward.)

THE RADIO-ULNAR ARTICULATION

In the foal the shaft of the ulna is attached to the radius above and below the interosseous space by the **interosseous ligament** of the forearm (Lig. interosseum antibrachii). Below the space the two bones become fused before adult age is reached. Above the space the ligament usually persists, but may undergo more or less ossification in extreme old age. The **transverse** or arciform **ligament** (Lig. transversum ulnare et radiale ulnæ et radii) consists of fibers which pass above the interosseous space from each border of the shaft of the ulna to the posterior surface of the radius. The **proximal radio-ulnar articulation** (Articulatio radio-ulnaris proximalis), formed by two small convex facets on the ulna and the corresponding facets on the posterior surface of the proximal extremity of the radius, is inclosed in the capsule of the elbow-joint and does not require separate consideration. The distal extremity of the ulna fuses early with the radius, and is therefore regarded usually as a part of the latter.

Movement.—This is inappreciable, the forearm being fixed in the position of pronation.

THE CARPAL JOINTS

These joints taken together constitute the composite **articulatio carpi,** or what is popularly termed the "knee-joint" in animals.[1] This consists of three chief joints, viz., (1) The **radio-carpal** or **antibrachio-carpal joint** (Articulatio radiocarpea) formed by the distal end of the radius and the proximal row of the carpus; (2) the **intercarpal joint** (Articulatio intercarpea), formed between the two rows of the carpus; (3) the **carpo-metacarpal joint** (Articulatio carpometacarpea), formed between the distal row of the carpus and the proximal ends of the metacarpal bones. The proximal and middle joints may be regarded as ginglymi, although they are not typical or pure examples of hinge-joints. The distal joint is arthrodial. In addition there are arthrodial joints formed between adjacent bones of the same row (Articulationes interosseæ). All these form a composite joint with numerous ligaments. The articular surfaces have been described in the Osteology.

The **joint capsule** may be regarded, so far as the fibrous part is concerned, as being common to all three joints. It is attached close to the margin of the articu-

---

[1] The term is a very unfortunate one, since it is a distinct misapplication of the name as it is used in regard to man. It is, however, very firmly established, and appears likely to persist indefinitely in the absence of a convenient popular equivalent.

lar surface of the radius above and the metacarpus below; its deep face is also attached to a considerable extent to the carpal bones and to the small ligaments. Its anterior part, the **dorsal carpal ligament,** is loose, except during flexion, and assists in forming the fibrous canals for the extensor tendons. Its posterior part, the **volar carpal ligament** (Lig. carpi volare), is very thick and dense, and is closely attached to the carpal bones. It levels up the irregularities of the skeleton here, and forms the smooth anterior wall of the carpal canal. It is continued downward to form the **subcarpal** or **inferior check ligament,** which blends with the tendon of the deep flexor of the digit about the middle of the metacarpus, and may well be regarded as the carpal (tendinous) head of that muscle.

The **synovial membrane** forms three sacs corresponding to the three joints. The **radio-carpal sac** is the most voluminous; it includes the joints formed by the accessory carpal bone, and also those between the proximal carpal bones as far as the interosseous ligaments. The **intercarpal sac** sends extensions upward and downward between the bones of the two rows as far as the interosseous ligaments; it communicates between the third and fourth carpal bones with the **carpo-metacarpal sac.** The latter is very limited in extent, and is closely applied to the bones; it incloses the carpo-metacarpal joint, and lubricates also the lower parts of the joints between the distal carpal bones and the inter-metacarpal joints.

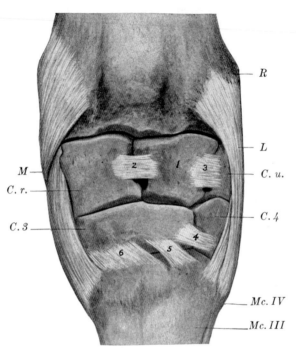

FIG. 238.—LEFT CARPAL JOINTS OF HORSE; DORSAL VIEW. THE JOINT CAPSULE IS REMOVED.

R, Lateral distal tuberosity of radius; *M,* medial ligament; *L,* lateral ligament; *C. r.,* radial carpal bone; *C. u.,* ulnar carpal bone; *C. 3,* third carpal bone; *C. 4,* fourth carpal bone; *Mc. III, Mc. IV,* metacarpal bones; *1,* intermediate carpal bone; *2–6,* dorsal ligaments.

The **lateral carpal ligament** (Lig. carpi collaterale ulnare) is attached above to the lateral tuberosity of the distal end of the radius. Its long superficial part is attached below to the proximal end of the lateral small metacarpal chiefly, but some fibers end on the large metacarpal bone. A canal for the lateral extensor tendon separates a short deep band which ends on the ulnar carpal bone. Other deep fibers connect the latter with the fourth carpal bone, and the fourth carpal with the metacarpus.

The **medial carpal ligament** (Lig. carpi collaterale radiale) resembles the preceding in general, but is stronger and wider distally. It is attached above to the medial tuberosity of the distal end of the radius and ends below on the proximal ends of the large and medial small metacarpal bones. Deep fasciculi are detached to the radial and second carpal bones. The first carpal bone, when present, is usually embedded in the posterior part of the distal end of the ligament. The posterior part of the ligament is fused with the transverse ligament of the carpus (Lig. carpi transversum), and concurs in the formation of a canal for the tendon of the flexor carpi radialis.

A number of special short ligaments connect two or more adjacent bones; only the most distinct of these will be described here.

The accessory carpal bone is connected with adjacent bones by three ligaments (Fig. 236). The proximal one is a short band which extends from the accessory carpal in front of the groove on its lateral face and is inserted into the distal end of the radius behind the groove for the lateral extensor tendon. A middle band connects the accessory with the ulnar carpal. The distal ligament consists of two strong bands which pass from the distal margin of the accessory to the fourth carpal and the proximal end of the fourth metacarpal bone; these bands transmit the action of the muscles which are inserted into the accessory carpal bone. The other bones of the proximal row are connected by two dorsal ligaments, which are transverse in direction, and two interosseous ligaments. An oblique ligament passes from an eminence on the volar surface of the radial carpal bone to a small depression on the radius medial to the facet for the accessory carpal bone.

Two ligaments connect the proximal and distal rows posteriorly. The medial one joins the radial to the second and third carpal, and the lateral one attaches the ulnar to the third and fourth carpals.

The bones of the distal row are connected by two strong transverse dorsal ligaments and two interosseous ligaments.

There are four carpo-metacarpal ligaments. Two oblique dorsal ligaments (Ligg. carpometacarpea dorsalia) connect the third carpal with the large metacarpal bone. Two interosseous ligaments pass downward from the interosseous ligaments of the distal row to end in depressions of the opposed surfaces of the proximal ends of the metacarpal bones. Volar ligaments (Ligg. carpometacarpea volaria) connect the second and third carpal bones with the metacarpus. Other short special ligaments have been described, but some of them at least are artefacts.

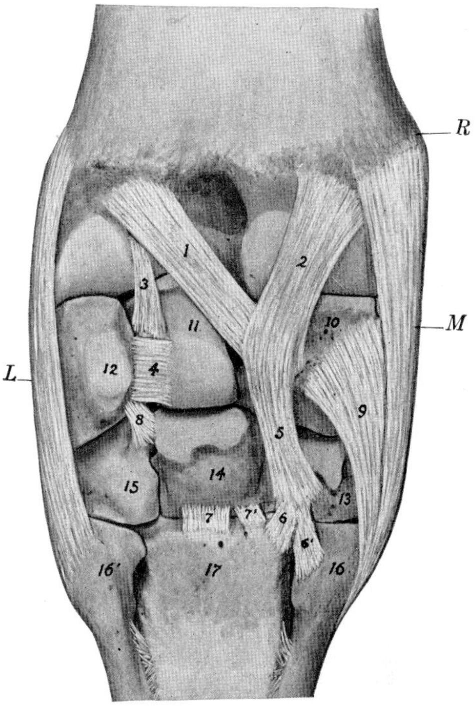

Fig. 239.—Left Carpal Joints of Horse; Volar View. Accessory Carpal and Capsule have been Removed.

R, Distal end of radius; M, medial ligament; L, lateral ligament; 1, 2, ligaments connecting radial carpal bone and radius; 3, ligament connecting intermediate carpal with radius; 4, stump of ligament connecting intermediate and accessory carpal; 5, ligament connecting radial and second carpal; 6, 6', ligaments connecting second carpal and metacarpal bones; 7, 7', ligaments connecting third carpal and metacarpal bone; 8, ligament connecting ulnar and third and fourth carpal bones; 9, deep short part of medial collateral ligament; 10, 11, 12, radial, intermediate, and ulnar carpal bones; 13, 14, 15, second, third, and fourth carpal bones; 16, 16', 17, metacarpal bones. (Of the preceding volar ligaments, 1, 3, and 8 are distinct from the capsule.)

Movements.—Taking the joint as a whole, the chief movements are flexion and extension. In the standing position the joint is extended. When the joint is flexed, slight transverse movement and rotation can be produced by manipulation. The dorsal part of the capsule is, of course, tense during flexion, the volar part in extension.

The movement practically all occurs at the radio-carpal and intercarpal joints, the articular surfaces of which are widely separated in front during flexion, but remain in contact behind. The distal row remains in contact with the metacarpus. The intermediate and ulnar carpals move together as one piece, but the radial does not move so far as the intermediate, so that the dorsal and interosseous ligaments connecting these bones become tense and oblique in direction.

INTERMETACARPAL JOINTS

The small joints formed between the proximal ends of the metacarpal bones (Articulationes intermetacarpeæ) are enclosed by the carpal joint capsule, as described above. The opposed surfaces of the shafts of the bones are closely united by an **interosseous metacarpal ligament** (Lig. interosseum metacarpi), which often undergoes more or less extensive ossification.

THE FETLOCK JOINT

This, the **metacarpo-phalangeal articulation** (Articulatio metacarpo-phalangea), is a ginglymus formed by the junction of the distal end of the large (third) metacarpal bone, the proximal end of the first phalanx, and the proximal sesamoid bones.

Articular Surfaces.—The surface on the large metacarpal bone is approximately cylindrical in curvature, but is divided into two slightly unequal parts by a sagittal ridge. This is received into a socket formed by the first phalanx below and the two sesamoids together with the intersesamoid ligament behind. The latter is a mass of fibro-cartilage in which the sesamoid bones are largely embedded. It extends above the level of the sesamoids, and is grooved to receive the ridge on the metacarpal bone; its volar surface forms a smooth groove for the deep flexor tendon.

The **joint capsule** is attached around the margin of the articular surfaces. It is thick and ample in front; here a bursa is interposed between it and the extensor tendons, but the tendons are also attached to the capsule. Posteriorly it forms a thin-walled pouch which extends upward between the metacarpal bone and the suspensory ligament about as high as the point of bifurcation of the latter.[1] The capsule is reinforced by two collateral ligaments.

The **collateral ligaments, medial** and **lateral** (Lig. collaterale ulnare, radiale), are partially divided into two layers: the **superficial layer** arises from the eminence on the side of the distal end of the large metacarpal bone, and passes straight to the rough area below the margin of the articular surface of the first phalanx; the **deep layer,** shorter and much stronger, arises in the depression on the side of the distal end of the metacarpal bone, and passes obliquely downward and backward to be inserted into the abaxial surface of the sesamoid and the proximal end of the first phalanx.

The capsule is further strengthened by a layer of oblique fibers which pass over the collateral ligament on either side and end on the extensor tendon and the proximal extremity of the first phalanx. It may properly be regarded as fascia rather than ligament.

Movements.—These are of the nature of flexion and extension, the axis of motion passing through the proximal attachments of the collateral ligaments. In the ordinary standing position the joint is in a state of partial dorsal flexion, the articular angle (in front) being about 140°. (In the hind limb it is about 5° greater.) Diminution of this angle (sometimes termed "overextension") is normally very limited on account of the resistance offered by the sesamoidean apparatus, but it varies considerably in amount in different subjects. Volar flexion is limited only by contact of the heels with the metacarpus. During volar flexion a small amount of abduction, adduction and rotation are possible.

THE SESAMOIDEAN LIGAMENTS

Under this head will be described a number of important ligaments which are connected with the sesamoid bones and form a sort of **stay apparatus** or brace.

The **intersesamoidean ligament** (Lig. intersesamoideum) not only fills the space between and unites the sesamoid bones, but also extends above them, entering into the formation of the articular surface of the fetlock joint. Other facts in regard to it have been given above.

The **collateral sesamoidean ligaments,** lateral and medial (Ligg. sesamoidea

[1] This pouch is in part bound down by a layer of elastic tissue which arises by two branches from the distal part of the volar surface of the shaft of the large metacarpal bone and ends on the intersesamoid ligament. It was first described by Skoda who terms it the lig. metacarpo-intersesamoideum.

ulnare et radiale), arise on the abaxial surface of each sesamoid bone, pass forward, and divide into two branches, one of which ends in the depression on the distal end of the large metacarpal bone, the other on the eminence on the proximal end of the first phalanx. They are partly covered by the branches of the suspensory or superior sesamoidean ligament.

The **suspensory ligament** or **interosseous tendon** (Tendo interosseus)[1] lies in great part in the metacarpal groove, where it has the form of a wide, thick band. It is attached above to the proximal part of the posterior surface of the large

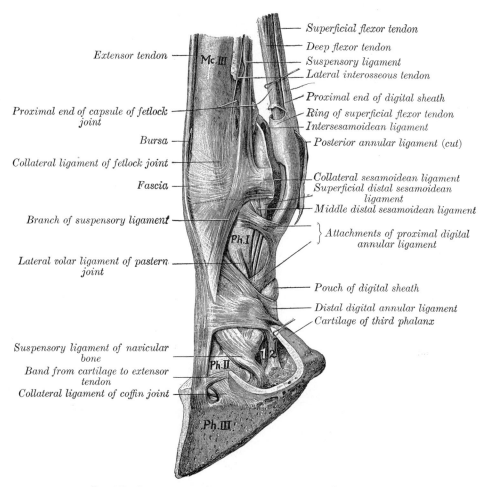

FIG. 240.—LIGAMENTS AND TENDONS OF DISTAL PART OF LIMB OF HORSE.

Mc.III, Large metacarpal bone; Ph.I, first phalanx; Ph.II, second phalanx; Ph.III, third phalanx; 1, deep flexor tendon; 2, band from first phalanx to digital cushion. (After Schmaltz, Atlas d. Anat. d. Pferdes.)

metacarpal bone and to the distal row of carpal bones. At the distal fourth of the metacarpus it divides into two diverging branches. Each branch passes to the abaxial face of the corresponding sesamoid, on which a considerable part is attached. The remainder passes obliquely downward and forward to the dorsal surface of the first phalanx, where it joins the extensor tendon; there is a bursa between this extensor branch and the proximal end of the first phalanx. This ligament possesses

[1] This is also known as the superior sesamoidean ligament; it is described here in deference to custom and on account of its ligamentous function.

considerable elasticity, and is the highly modified interosseous medius muscle. **It** consists mainly of tendinous tissue, but contains a variable amount of striped muscular tissue, especially in its deep part and in young subjects. Its principal function is to support the fetlock, *i. e.*, to prevent excessive dorsal flexion of the joint when the weight is put on the limb. The branches which join the common extensor tendon limit volar flexion of the interphalangeal joints in certain phases of movement.

The **distal sesamoidean ligaments** are three in number. The **superficial or**

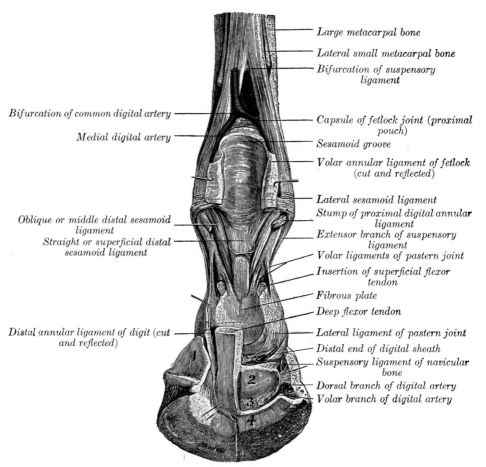

FIG. 241.—Deep Dissection of Distal Part of Right Fore Limb of Horse, Showing Joints and Ligaments; Posterior View.

1, Cartilage of third phalanx; 2, flexor surface of navicular bone; 3, distal navicular ligament; 4, insertion of deep flexor tendon. Small arrows point to openings made in capsules of pastern and coffin joints. (After Schmaltz, Atlas d. Anat. d. Pferdes.)

straight sesamoidean ligament (Lig. sesamoideum rectum) is a flat band and is somewhat wider above than below. It is attached above to the bases of the sesamoid bones and the intersesamoid ligament, below to the complementary fibrocartilage of the proximal end of the second phalanx. The **middle sesamoidean ligament** (Lig. sesamoideum obliquus) is triangular, with thick, rounded margins and a thin central portion. Its base is attached to the sesamoid bones and intersesamoid ligament, and its deep face to the triangular rough area on the volar surface of the first phalanx. The **deep** or **cruciate sesamoidean ligaments** (Ligg. sesamoidea cruciata) consist of two thin layers of fibers which arise on the base of the sesamoid bones, cross each other, and end on the opposite eminence on the proximal end of the first phalanx.

The two **short sesamoidean ligaments** (Ligg. sesamoidea brevia) are best seen

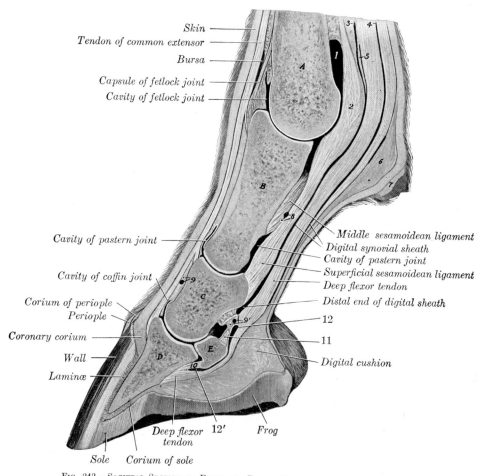

FIG. 242.—Sagittal Section of Digit and Distal Part of Metacarpus of Horse.

A, Metacarpal bone; *B*, first phalanx; *C*, second phalanx; *D*, third phalanx; *E*, distal sesamoid bone; 1, volar pouch of capsule of fetlock joint; 2, intersesamoidean ligament; 3, 4, proximal end of digital synovial sheath; 5, ring formed by superficial flexor tendon; 6, fibrous tissue underlying ergot; 7, ergot; 8, 9, 9′, branches of digital vessels; 10, distal ligament of distal sesamoid bone; 11, suspensory ligament of distal sesamoid bone; 12, 12′, proximal and distal ends of bursa podotrochlearis. By an oversight the superficial flexor tendon (behind 4) is not marked.

by opening the joint in front and pushing the sesamoid bones backward; they are covered by the synovial membrane. They are short bands which extend from the anterior part of the base of the sesamoid bones outward and inward, respectively, to the posterior margin of the articular surface of the first phalanx.

The distal sesamoidean ligaments may be regarded as digital continuations of the suspensory ligament, the sesamoid bones being intercalated in this remarkable stay apparatus, by which the fetlock is supported and concussion diminished.

THE PASTERN JOINT

This, the **proximal interphalangeal articulation** (Articulatio interphalangea proximalis), is a ginglymus formed by the junction of the distal end of the first phalanx and the proximal end of the second phalanx.

The **articular surfaces** are: (1) On the first phalanx, two slightly unequal convex areas with an intermediate shallow groove; (2) on the second phalanx, a corresponding surface, completed behind by a plate of fibro-cartilage.

The **joint capsule** is close-fitting in front and on the sides, where it blends with the extensor tendon and the collateral ligaments respectively. Behind it pouches upward a little and is reinforced by the straight sesamoidean ligament and the branches of the superficial flexor tendon.

There are two collateral and four volar ligaments.

The **collateral ligaments**, medial and lateral (Lig. collaterale radiale, ulnare), are very short and strong bands which are attached above on the eminence and depression on each side of the distal end of the first phalanx, and below on the eminence on each side of the proximal end of the second phalanx. The direction of the ligaments is about vertical and, therefore, does not correspond to the digital axis.

The **volar ligaments** (Ligg. volaria) consist of a central pair and lateral and medial bands which are attached below to the posterior margin of the proximal end of the second phalanx and its complementary fibro-cartilage. The lateral and medial ligaments are attached above to the middle of the borders of the first phalanx, the central pair lower down and on the margin of the triangular rough area.

These ligaments are very commonly thickened as a result of chronic inflammation, and then are not well defined. The central ones blend below with the branches of the superficial flexor tendon and with the straight sesamoidean ligament.

Movements.—These are very limited, and consist of flexion and extension. The axis of motion passes transversely through the distal end of the first phalanx. In the standing position the joint is extended. A small amount of volar flexion is possible, and in this position slight lateral and medial flexion and rotation can be produced by manipulation. Dorsal flexion is prevented by the lateral, volar, and straight sesamoidean ligaments.

THE COFFIN JOINT

This joint, the **distal interphalangeal articulation** (Articulatio interphalangea distalis), is a ginglymus formed by the junction of the second and third phalanges and the distal sesamoid bone.

Articular Surfaces.—The surface on the distal end of the second phalanx is convex in the sagittal direction, concave transversely. The articular surface of the third phalanx slopes sharply upward and forward; its central part is prominent, and is flanked by two glenoid cavities. It is completed behind by the articular surface of the distal sesamoid or navicular bone.

Joint Capsule.—This is attached around the margins of the articular surfaces. In front and on the sides it is tight, and is blended with the extensor tendon and the collateral ligaments respectively. It forms a considerable pouch behind, which extends upward to about the middle of the second phalanx, where it is separated by a fibrous membrane from the digital synovial sheath. On each side small pouches project (especially during volar flexion) against the cartilages of the third phalanx just behind the collateral ligaments.[1]

Ligaments.—The **collateral ligaments**, medial and lateral (Lig. collaterale

[1] This should be noted in regard to resection of the cartilage or other operations in this vicinity.

ulnare, radiale), are short, strong bands which are attached above in the depressions on either side of the lower part of the second phalanx, under cover of the cartilage of the third phalanx. They widen below and end in the depressions on either side of the extensor process and on the anterior ends of the cartilages.

The **collateral sesamoidean** or suspensory navicular **ligaments,** medial and lateral (Lig. sesamoideum collaterale ulnare, radiale), are strong, somewhat elastic bands, which form a sort of suspensory apparatus for the distal sesamoid. They are attached superiorly in and above the depressions on each side of the distal end of the first phalanx and are here partly blended with the collateral ligaments of the pastern joint. They are directed obliquely downward and backward, and end chiefly on the ends and proximal border of the distal sesamoid, but detach a branch to the axial surface of each cartilage and angle of the third phalanx.

The **phalango-sesamoidean** or **distal navicular ligament** (Lig. phalangeo-sesamoideum) reinforces the capsule distally. It is a strong layer of fibers which extend from the distal border of the distal sesamoid to the flexor surface of the third phalanx.

Movements.—The chief movements are flexion and extension. In the standing position the joint is extended. During volar flexion a very small amount of lateral movement and rotation can be produced by manipulation. Dorsal flexion is very limited.

Dorsal flexion appears to be checked mainly by the deep flexor tendon, since in cases of rupture of the latter the toe turns up. The mobility of the posterior part of the socket for the second phalanx (formed by the distal sesamoid) diminishes concussion when the weight comes on the foot.

LIGAMENTS OF THE CARTILAGES OF THE THIRD PHALANX

In addition to the bands mentioned above, which attach the cartilages to the extremities of the navicular bone, there are three ligaments on either side which attach the cartilages to the phalanges.

An ill-defined elastic band passes from the middle part of the border of the first phalanx to the upper part of the cartilage, detaching a branch to the digital cushion.

A short, strong band connects the anterior extremity of the cartilage with the rough eminence on the second phalanx in front of the attachment of the collateral ligament of the coffin joint.

The lower border of the cartilage is covered in part by fibers which attach it to the angle of the third phalanx.

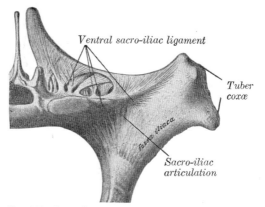

Fig. 243.—Left Sacro-iliac Articulation of Horse; Anterior View. (Adapted from Schmaltz, Atlas d. Anat. d. Pferdes.)

THE ARTICULATIONS OF THE PELVIC LIMB

THE SACRO-ILIAC ARTICULATION

This joint (Articulatio sacroiliaca) is a diarthrosis formed between the auricular surfaces of the sacrum and ilium. These surfaces are not smooth in the adult, but are marked by reciprocal eminences and depressions, and are covered by a thin layer of cartilage. The joint cavity is a mere cleft, and is often crossed by fibrous bands.

The **joint capsule** is very close fitting, and is attached around the margins of the articular surfaces. It is reinforced by the **ventral sacro-iliac ligament** (Lig. sacro-iliacum ventrale), which surrounds the joint; this is exceedingly strong above, where it occupies the angle between the ilium and the wing of the sacrum; it consists chiefly of nearly vertical fibers.

The **movements** are inappreciable in the adult—stability, not mobility, being the chief desideratum. The angle formed by the long axis of the ilium on the horizontal plane varies from 30° to 40°.

LIGAMENTS OF THE PELVIC GIRDLE

The following ligaments (Ligg. cinguli extremitatis pelvinæ) may be regarded as accessory to the sacro-iliac joint, although not directly connected with it:

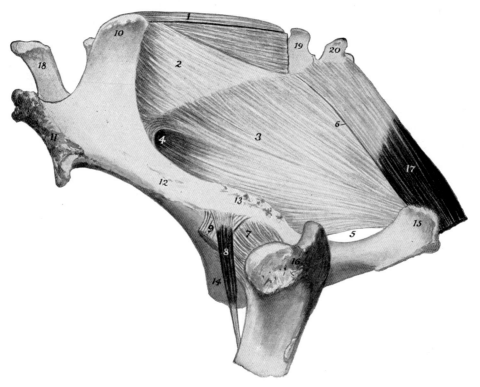

FIG. 244.—PELVIC LIGAMENTS AND HIP JOINT.

1, Dorsal sacro-iliac ligament; *2*, lateral sacro-iliac ligament; *3*, sacro-sciatic ligament; *4*, greater sciatic foramen; *5*, lesser sciatic foramen; *6*, line of attachment of intermuscular septum between biceps femoris and semitendinosus; *7*, capsule of hip joint; *8*, capsularis muscle; *9*, lateral tendon of origin of rectus femoris; *10*, tuber sacrale; *11*, tuber coxæ; *12*, shaft of ilium; *13*, superior ischiatic spine; *14*, pubis; *15*, tuber ischii; *16*, trochanter major; *17*, semimembranosus; *18*, fifth lumbar spine; *19, 20*, first and second coccygeal vertebræ.

The **dorsal sacro-iliac ligament** (Lig. sacro-iliacum dorsale breve) is a strong band which is attached to the tuber sacrale and the summits of the sacral spines.

The **lateral sacro-iliac ligament** (Lig. sacro-iliacum dorsale longum) is a triangular, thick sheet which is attached in front to the tuber sacrale and adjacent part of the medial border of the ilium above the great sciatic notch, and below to the lateral border of the sacrum. It blends above with the dorsal sacro-iliac ligament, below with the sacro-sciatic ligament, and behind with the coccygeal fascia.

The **sacro-sciatic ligament** (Lig. sacroischiadicum s. sacrospinosum et tuberosum) is an extensive quadrilateral sheet which completes the lateral pelvic wall.

Its dorsal border is attached to the border of the sacrum and the transverse processes of the first and second coccygeal vertebræ. Its ventral border is attached to the superior ischiatic spine and tuber ischii. Between these it bridges over the lateral border of the ischium and completes the **lesser sciatic foramen** (Foramen ischiadicum minus). The anterior border is concave, and completes the **greater sciatic foramen** (Foramen ischiadicum majus). The posterior border is fused with the vertebral head of the semimembranosus muscle.

The lesser sciatic foramen is closed, except where the tendon of the obturator internus and a vein pass through it, by a thin fibrous sheet given off from the sacro-sciatic ligament.

The **ilio-lumbar ligament** (Lig. ilio-lumbale) is a triangular sheet which attaches the ends of the lumbar transverse processes to the ventral surface of the ilium below the attachment of the longissimus muscle (Fig. 273).

SYMPHYSIS PELVIS

The **symphysis pelvis** is formed by the junction of the two ossa coxarum at the ventral median line. In the young subject the bones are united by a layer of cartilage (Lamina fibrocartilaginea); in the adult the latter is gradually replaced by bone, the process beginning in the pubic portion and extending backward, but commonly the ischia are in part not fused. The union is strengthened by white fibrous tissue dorsally and ventrally. A transverse band also covers the anterior border of the pubis, and other fibers (Lig. arcuatum ischiadicum) extend across at the ischial arch. No appreciable movement occurs even before synostosis takes place.

OBTURATOR MEMBRANE

This (Membrana obturatoria) is a thin layer of fibrous tissue which covers the obturator foramen, leaving, however, a passage (Canalis obturatorius) for the obturator vessels and nerve.

THE HIP JOINT

This joint (Articulatio coxæ) is an enarthrosis formed by the proximal end of the femur and the acetabulum.

Articular Surfaces.—The head of the femur presents an almost hemispherical articular surface, which is continued a short distance on the upper surface of the neck. It is more extensive than the socket which receives it. It is cut into medially by a deep notch for the attachment of the round and accessory ligaments. The acetabulum is a typical cotyloid cavity. Its articular surface is somewhat crescentic, being deeply cut into medially by the acetabular notch and fossa.

The acetabulum is deepened by a ring of fibro-cartilage, the **cotyloid ligament** (Labrum glenoidale), which is attached to the bony margin; that part of the ligament which crosses the notch is called the **transverse acetabular ligament** (Lig. transversum acetabuli) (Fig. 291).

The **joint capsule** is roomy. It is attached around the margin of the acetabulum and the neck of the femur. It is thickest laterally.

The attachment on the femur is about 1 cm. from the margin of the articular surface, except above, where 2 to 3 cm. of the neck is intracapsular. A thin, oblique band corresponding in direction with the capsularis muscle reinforces the antero-lateral part of the capsule; this appears to be the feeble homologue of the very strong ilio-femoral ligament of man. The capsule is very thin under the ilio-psoas, and is adherent to the muscle. Its fibrous part is perforated medially by the accessory and round ligaments and the articular vessels.

The **round ligament** (Lig. teres) is a short, strong band which is attached in the subpubic groove close to the acetabular notch, passes outward, and ends in the notch on the head of the femur (Fig. 581).

The **accessory ligament** (Lig. accessorium) does not occur in the domestic animals other than the equidæ. It is a strong band detached from the prepubic tendon of the abdominal muscles (Fig. 581). It is directed outward, backward, and upward, passes through the acetabular notch dorsal to the transverse ligament, and ends behind the round ligament in the notch on the head of the femur. The origin of the pectineus muscle is perforated by the ligament, which furnishes attachment to many fibers of the muscle.

The **synovial membrane** is reflected over the intracapsular parts of these ligaments and covers the fossa acetabuli. A pouch also extends from the acetabular notch for a variable distance along the subpubic groove above the accessory ligament.

Movements.—This joint is capable of all the movements of a ball-and-socket joint, viz., flexion, extension, abduction, adduction, rotation, and circumduction. The greatest range of movement is displayed in flexion and extension. When standing at rest, the joint is partially flexed, the articular angle (in front) being about 115°. The other movements occur to a very limited extent in normal action. Abduction appears to be checked by tension of the round and accessory ligaments. The accessory ligament is tensed so promptly by inward rotation of the thigh that this movement is almost nil.

THE STIFLE JOINT

This joint (Articulatio genu), which corresponds to the knee-joint of man, is the largest and most elaborate of all the articulations. Taken as a whole, it may be classed as a ginglymus, although it is not a typical example of the group. In reality it consists of two joints—the femoro-patellar and the femoro-tibial.

The **femoro-patellar articulation** (Articulatio femoro-patellaris) is formed between the trochlea of the femur and the articular surface of the patella.

Articular Surfaces.—The trochlea consists of two slightly oblique ridges, with a wide and deep groove between them. The medial ridge is much the larger of the two, especially at its proximal part, which is wide and rounded. The lateral ridge is much narrower, and is more regularly curved; its proximal part lies about an inch behind a frontal plane tangent to the medial one. The articular surface of the patella is much smaller than that of the trochlea. It is completed medially by a supplementary plate of fibro-cartilage (Fibrocartilago patellæ), which curves over the medial ridge of the trochlea. A narrow strip of cartilage is found along the lateral border also. The articular cartilage on the trochlea completely covers both surfaces of the medial ridge, but extends only a short distance on the lateral surface of the outer ridge.

Joint Capsule.—This is thin and is very capacious. On the patella it is attached around the margin of the articular surface, but on the femur the line of attachment is at a varying distance from the articular surface. On the medial side it is an inch or more from the articular cartilage; on the lateral side and above, about half an inch. It pouches upward under the quadriceps femoris for a distance of two or three inches, a pad of fat separating the capsule from the muscle. Below the patella it is separated from the patellar ligaments by a thick pad of fat, but inferiorly it is in contact with the femoro-tibial capsules. The joint cavity is the most extensive in the body. It usually communicates with the medial sac of the femoro-tibial joint cavity by a slit-like opening situated at the lowest part of the medial ridge of the trochlea. A similar, usually smaller, communication with the lateral sac of the femoro-tibial capsule is often found at the lowest part of the lateral ridge.

The medial communication is rarely absent in adult horses, but is liable to be overlooked on account of the fact that it is covered by a valvular fold of the synovial membrane. It is about half an inch wide, and lies under the narrow articular area which connects the trochlea and medial condyle. The lateral communication occurs in 18 to 25 per cent. of cases, according to Baum; in rare cases it is larger than the inner one. It is instructive to distend this capsule and thus obtain an idea of its potential capacity and relations (Fig. 246).

Ligaments.—The **femoro-patellar ligaments,** lateral and medial (Lig. femoro-patellare laterale, mediale) are two thin bands which reinforce the capsule on either

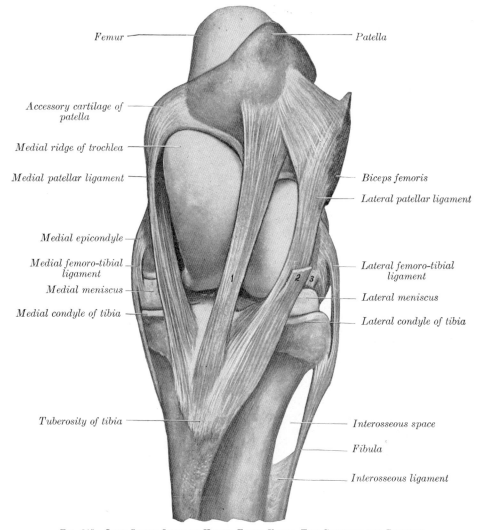

FIG. 245.—LEFT STIFLE JOINT OF HORSE; FRONT VIEW. THE CAPSULES ARE REMOVED.
1, Middle patellar ligament; 2, stump of fascia lata; 3, stump of common tendon of extensor longus and peroneus tertius.

side. The lateral ligament is fairly distinct; it arises from the lateral epicondyle of the femur just above the lateral femoro-tibial ligament, and ends on the lateral border of the patella. The medial ligament is thinner and is not distinct from the capsule; it arises above the medial epicondyle, and ends on the patellar fibro-cartilage.

The **patellar ligaments** (Ligg. patellæ) are three very strong bands which attach the patella to the tuberosity of the tibia. The **lateral patellar ligament** extends from the lateral part of the anterior surface of the patella to the lateral part of the tuberosity of the tibia. It receives a strong tendon from the biceps femoris muscle and also part of the fascia lata. The **middle patellar ligament** extends from the front of the apex of the patella to the distal part of the groove on the tuberosity of the tibia; a bursa is interposed between the ligament and the upper part of the groove, and a smaller one occurs between the upper part of the ligament and the apex of the patella. The **medial patellar ligament** is distinctly weaker

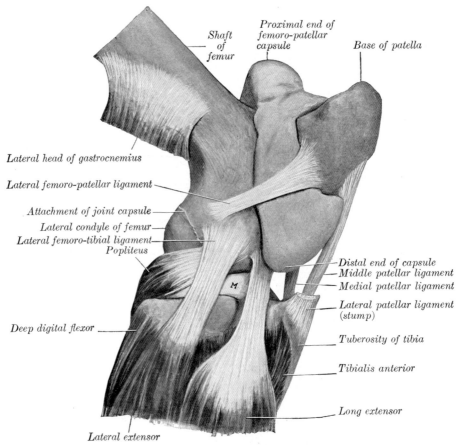

FIG. 246.—RIGHT STIFLE JOINT OF HORSE; LATERAL VIEW.

The femoro-patellar capsule was filled with plaster-of-Paris and then removed after the cast was set. The femoro-tibial capsule and most of the lateral patellar ligament are removed. *M*, lateral meniscus.

than the others; it is attached above to the patellar fibro-cartilage, and ends on the tuberosity of the tibia at the medial side of the groove. It is joined by the common aponeurosis of the gracilis and sartorius, and its proximal part furnishes insertion to fibers of the vastus medialis. These so-called ligaments are, in reality, the tendons of insertion of the quadriceps femoris and biceps femoris muscles, and transmit the action of the latter to the tibia; they also function similarly for the other muscles attached to them as noted above.

It will be noticed that the proximal attachments are further apart than the distal ones, so that the ligaments converge below. The medial ligament is especially oblique. The middle ligament is more deeply placed than the others, and therefore cannot usually be felt so distinctly in the living animal. The lateral ligament is very largely the tendon of the anterior part of the biceps femoris, but it also furnishes insertion to the tensor fasciæ latæ by means of the fascia lata, which blends with it. The fibro-cartilage is, in the author's opinion, to be regarded as part of the medial patellar ligament rather than part of the patella; it is not visible superficially.

The **femoro-tibial articulation** (Articulatio femoro-tibialis) is formed between the condyles of the femur, the proximal end of the tibia, and the interposed articular menisci or semilunar cartilages.

Articular Surfaces.—The condyles of the femur are slightly oblique in direction. The articular surface of the lateral one is more strongly curved than that of the medial one; the latter is confluent below with the medial ridge of the trochlea,

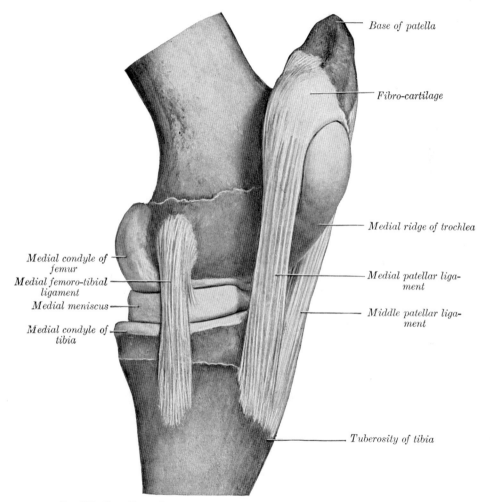

FIG. 247.—LEFT STIFLE JOINT OF HORSE; MEDIAL VIEW. THE CAPSULES ARE REMOVED.

while the narrow ridge which connects the lateral condyle with the trochlea is usually non-articular. The saddle-shaped surfaces of the condyles of the tibia are not adapted to the femoral condyles, and are in contact with only a small part of them.

The **menisci, lateral** and **medial** (Meniscus lateralis, medialis) (Fig. 250) are crescentic plates of fibro-cartilage which produce congruence in the articular surfaces. Each has a proximal concave surface adapted to the condyle of the femur, and a distal surface which fits the corresponding condyle of the tibia.

The lateral meniscus does not cover the lateral and posterior part of the tibial condyle, over which the tendon of origin of the popliteus muscle plays. The peripheral border is thick and convex, the central one very thin and concave. The fibrous ends or ligaments are attached to the tibia in front of and behind the spine. The lateral meniscus has a third attachment by means of an oblique band (Ligamentum femorale menisci lateralis) which passes from the posterior end to the posterior part of the intercondyloid fossa of the femur.

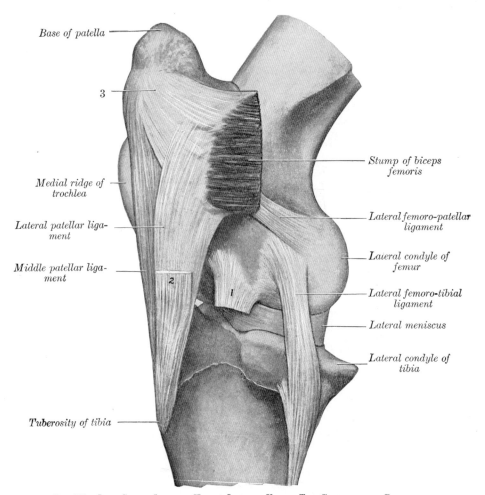

FIG. 248.—LEFT STIFLE JOINT OF HORSE; LATERAL VIEW. THE CAPSULES ARE REMOVED.

1, Stump of tendon of origin of extensor longus and peroneus tertius; 2, stump of fascia lata; 3, patellar attachment of biceps femoris and lateral patellar ligament.

The ligaments of the medial meniscus, anterior and posterior (Ligamenta tibialia anterius et posterius menisci medialis), are attached in front of and behind the medial eminence of the spine of the tibia. The anterior ligament of the lateral meniscus (Ligamentum tibiale anterius menisci lateralis) is attached in front of the lateral eminence of the spine. The posterior one bifurcates; the lower branch (Ligamentum tibiale posterius menisci lateralis) is inserted at the popliteal notch, the upper (Ligamentum femorale menisci lateralis) in a small fossa in the extreme posterior part of the intercondyloid fossa.

The **joint capsule** is attached to the margin of the tibial articular surface, but on the femur the line of attachment is for the greater part about half an inch (ca. 1 cm.) from the articular margin. It is also attached to the convex borders of the menisci and to the cruciate ligaments. It is thin in front, where it consists practically of the synovial layer only. It is much stronger posteriorly: here it is reinforced by what might be regarded as a posterior ligament. This is a strong, flat band which arises from the femur just lateral to the origin of the medial head of the gastrocnemius, and extends down to the posterior border of the medial condyle of the tibia; it is wider below than above. There are two synovial sacs, corresponding to the double nature of the articular surfaces; they do not usually communicate, and each is partially divided into an upper and a lower compartment by the meniscus. The medial sac pouches upward about half an inch over the con-

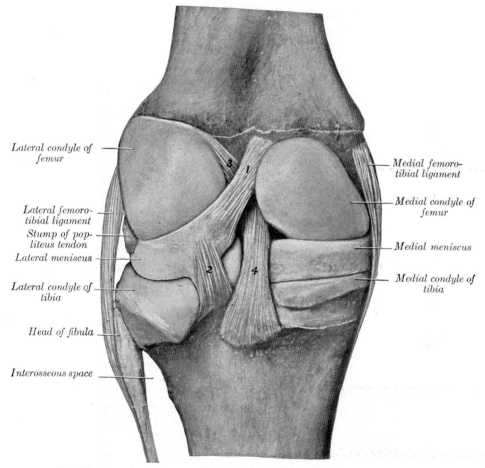

Lateral condyle of femur

Lateral femoro-tibial ligament

Stump of pop-liteus tendon

Lateral meniscus

Lateral condyle of tibia

Head of fibula

Interosseous space

Medial femoro-tibial ligament

Medial condyle of femur

Medial meniscus

Medial condyle of tibia

Fig. 249.—Left Stifle Joint of Horse; Posterior View. The Capsule is Removed.
1, Femoral ligament of lateral meniscus; 2, posterior ligament of lateral meniscus; 3, anterior cruciate ligament; 4, posterior cruciate ligament.

dyle of the femur. The lateral sac invests the tendon of origin of the popliteus muscle, and also pouches downward about three inches (ca. 7.5 cm.) beneath the peroneus tertius and extensor longus muscles. As stated above, the lateral sac sometimes communicates with the femoro-patellar joint cavity, and the medial sac usually does so in the adult.

Ligaments.—There are four of these—two collateral and two cruciate.

The **medial ligament** (Lig. collaterale mediale) is attached above to the prominent medial epicondyle of the femur, and below to a rough area below the margin of the medial condyle of the tibia.

The **lateral ligament** (Lig. collaterale laterale) is somewhat thicker; it arises from the upper depression on the lateral epicondyle, and ends on the head of the fibula.

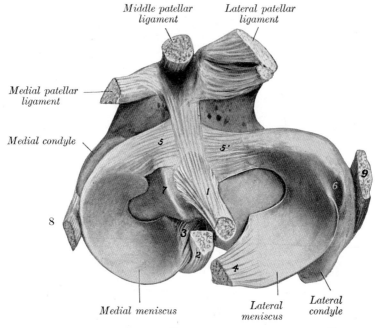

FIG. 250.—PROXIMAL END OF RIGHT TIBIA WITH MENISCI, ETC.

1, 2, Anterior and posterior cruciate ligaments; 3, posterior ligament of medial meniscus; 4, femoral ligament of lateral meniscus; 5, 5′, anterior ligaments of menisci; 6, groove for popliteus tendon; 7, spine of tibia; 8, 9, medial and lateral femoro-tibial ligaments.

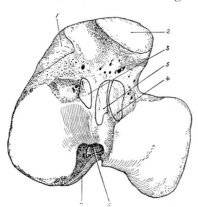

FIG. 251.—PROXIMAL END OF RIGHT TIBIA OF HORSE, WITH AREAS OF LIGAMENTOUS ATTACHMENT.

1, 2, Medial and lateral patellar ligaments; 3, 4, anterior ligaments of menisci; 5, 7, anterior and posterior cruciate ligaments; 6, posterior ligament of medial meniscus.

It covers the tendon of the origin of the popliteus muscle, a bursa being interposed between the two; another bursa is present between the lower part of the ligament and the margin of the lateral condyle of the tibia.

The **cruciate ligaments** are two strong rounded bands situated mainly in the intercondyloid fossa of the femur, between the two synovial sacs. They cross each other somewhat in the form of an **X**, and are named according to their tibial attachments. The **anterior cruciate ligament** (Lig. cruciatum anterius) arises in the central fossa on the tibial spine, extends upward and backward, and ends on the lateral wall of the intercondyloid fossa. The **posterior cruciate ligament** (Lig. cruciatum posterius) is medial to the preceding, and is somewhat larger. It is attached to an eminence at the popliteal notch of the tibia, is directed upward and forward, and ends in the anterior part of the intercondyloid fossa of the femur.

It may be added that these ligaments do not lie in a sagittal plane, but are somewhat twisted across each other; outward rotation of the leg untwists and slackens them.

Movements.—The principal movements of the stifle joint as a whole are flexion and extension. In the ordinary standing position the articular angle (behind) is about 150°. Flexion is limited only by contact of the leg with the thigh, if the hock is also flexed. Extension is incomplete, *i. e.*, the femur and tibia cannot be brought into the same straight line. Rotation is limited, and is freest during semiflexion. The patella glides on the femoral trochlea upward in extension, downward in flexion.

Extension is checked mainly by tension of the cruciate and collateral ligaments. In extreme extension, which is accompanied by slight outward rotation of the leg, the patella can be pushed upward and inward so that its fibro-cartilage hooks over the upper end of the medial ridge of the trochlea, but it will not remain there unless held in position. When pressure is removed, the base of the patella tips forward and the cartilage lies upon the most prominent part of the trochlear ridge. During flexion, which is accompanied by slight inward rotation of the leg, the condyles of the femur and the menisci glide backward on the tibia; the movement of the lateral condyle and meniscus is greater than that of the medial one. In extreme flexion the patellar and posterior cruciate ligaments are tense; the other ligaments are relaxed. The movement of the patella is gliding with coaptation, *i. e.*, different parts of the opposing articular surfaces come into contact successively. In the ordinary standing position the actual area of contact of the patella and femur is surprisingly small; it is a strip about 12–15 mm. (one-half inch or little more) in width. On the patella it corresponds closely with the distal border of the articular surface and is only 3–5 mm. distant from it. On the femur the area is ca. 2.5 cm. (an inch) medially and ca. 2 cm. laterally below the proximal margin of the trochlear articular surface. The area for the fibro-cartilage is on the proximal part of the medial surface of the medial ridge of the trochlea; it is oval and is about 3 cm. high and 2 cm. wide.

TIBIO-FIBULAR ARTICULATION

This joint (Articulatio tibiofibularis) is formed by the head of the fibula articulating with a crescentic facet just below the outer margin of the lateral condyle of the tibia. The **joint capsule** is strong and close. The shaft of the fibula is attached to the lateral border of the tibia by the **interosseous membrane of the leg** (Membrana interossea cruris); this is perforated about an inch from its proximal end by an opening which transmits the anterior tibial vessels to the front of the tibia. A fibrous cord usually extends from the distal end of the shaft of the fibula to the lateral malleolus. The latter is the distal end of the fibula which has fused with the tibia. No appreciable movement occurs in this joint.

THE HOCK JOINT

This is a composite joint made up of a number of articulations (Articulationes tarsi). These are: (1) The tibio-tarsal articulation; (2) the intertarsal articulations; (3) the tarso-metatarsal articulation.

The **tibio-tarsal articulation** (Articulatio talocruralis) is a typical ginglymus formed by the trochlea of the tibial tarsal bone and the corresponding surface of the distal end of the tibia. The ridges and grooves of these surfaces are directed obliquely forward and outward at an angle of about 12° to 15° with a sagittal plane. The trochlear surface is about twice as extensive as that on the tibia, and its ridges have a spiral curvature. The other articulations are arthrodia, which have joint surfaces and ligaments of such a nature as to allow only a minimal amount of gliding motion.

As in the case of the carpal joints, it is convenient to describe first the common capsule and ligaments, which are the more important practically, and then to consider very briefly the special ligaments.

The fibrous part of the **joint capsule** is attached around the margin of the tibial articular surface above and the metatarsal surfaces below; it is also attached in part to the surfaces of the bones which it covers, and blends with the collateral ligaments. Its dorsal part is rather thin; in distention of the capsule, as in "bog-spavin," its dorso-medial part, which is not bound down by the tendons passing over the joint, forms a fluctuating swelling over the medial ridge of the trochlea. The plantar part (plantar and tarso-metatarsal ligaments) is very thick below, and is intimately attached to the tarsal bones. It is in part cartilaginous, and forms a smooth surface for the deep flexor tendon. The proximal part pouches upward behind the distal end of the tibia for a distance of about two inches (ca. 5 cm.); here it is thin. It is continued downward to form the **subtarsal** or **check ligament,** which unites with the deep flexor tendon about the middle of the metatarsus.

There are four **synovial sacs:** 1. The **tibio-tarsal sac** lubricates the proximal joint, and is much the largest and most important.[1] 2. The **proximal intertarsal sac** lines the joints formed by the tibial and fibular tarsal bones above, and the central and fourth tarsals below; it communicates in front with the tibio-tarsal sac. 3. The **distal intertarsal sac** lubricates the joints formed between the central tarsal and the bones below and on either side. 4. The **tarso-metatarsal sac** lubricates

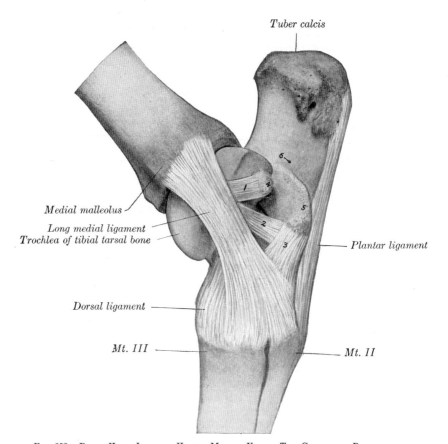

Tuber calcis

Medial malleolus
Long medial ligament
Trochlea of tibial tarsal bone

Plantar ligament

Dorsal ligament

Mt. III

Mt. II

Fig. 252.—Right Hock Joint of Horse; Medial View. The Capsule is Removed.

1, 2, Branches of short part of medial ligament; 3, tarso-metatarsal ligament; 4, proximal tuberosity of tibial tarsal bone; 5, sustentaculum; 6, groove for deep flexor tendon; *Mt. II, Mt. III,* metatarsal bones.

the joints formed between the tarsal and metatarsal bones, those between the proximal ends of the metatarsal bones, and those formed by the third tarsal with the bones on either side.

Common Ligaments.—The **lateral ligament** (Lig. collaterale fibulare) consists of two distinct bands which cross each other. The **long lateral ligament** (Lig. collaterale laterale longum) is superficial; it arises on the posterior part of the lateral malleolus, is directed almost straight downward, and is attached to the fibular and fourth tarsal bones and the large and lateral small metatarsal bones. It forms a

[1] It is this part of the capsule which is chiefly involved in distention by excess of fluid in the joint cavity (as in so-called "bog-spavin").

canal for the lateral extensor tendon. The **short lateral ligament** (Lig. collaterale laterale breve) is deeper; it arises on the anterior part of the lateral malleolus, is directed chiefly backward, and ends on the rough excavation on the lateral surface of the tibial tarsal and the adjacent surface of the fibular tarsal bone.

The **medial ligament** (Lig. collaterale tibiale) also consists of two parts which cross each other. The **long medial ligament** (Lig. collaterale mediale longum) is superficial; it arises on the posterior part of the medial malleolus, becomes wider below, and is attached on the distal tuberosity of the tibial tarsal, the large and medial small metatarsal bones, and the surface of the lower tarsal bones which it

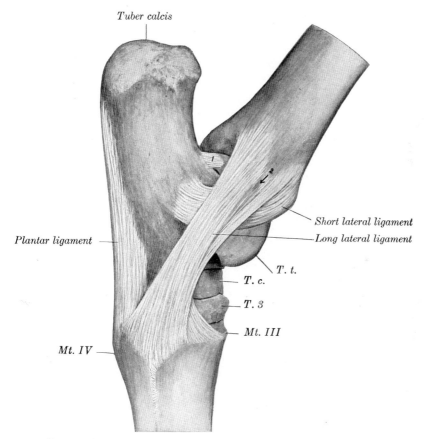

Tuber calcis

Plantar ligament

Short lateral ligament

Long lateral ligament

T. t.

T. c.

T. 3

Mt. III

Mt. IV

Fig. 253.—Right Hock Joint of Horse; Lateral View. The Capsule is Removed.

1, Ligament connecting lateral ridge of tibial tarsal with processus cochlearis of fibular tarsal bone; 2, groove for lateral extensor tendon; *T. t.*, lateral ridge of trochlea of tibial tarsal bone; *T. c.*, central tarsal bone; *T. 3*, third tarsal bone; *Mt. III*, *Mt. IV*, metatarsal bones.

covers. The **short medial ligament** (Lig. collaterale mediale breve) lies largely under cover of the long one. It extends from the anterior part of the medial malleolus, runs backward and somewhat downward, and divides into two branches; one of these ends on the proximal tuberosity on the medial surface of the tibial tarsal bone, the other on the sustentaculum tali.

The **plantar ligament** (Lig. tarsi plantare) is a very strong, flat band which covers the lateral part of the plantar surface of the tarsus. It is attached to the plantar surface of the fibular and fourth tarsal bones and the proximal end of the lateral metatarsal bone.

The **dorsal ligament** (Lig. tarsi dorsale) is a triangular sheet which is attached above to the distal tuberosity on the medial face of the tibial tarsal bone, and spreads out below on the central and third tarsal bones, and the proximal ends of the large and medial small metatarsal bones, to all of which it is attached.

Special Ligaments.—A considerable number of short bands which connect adjacent bones of the tarsus and metatarsus are described by various authors; some of these are quite distinct; others are difficult to isolate. Most of them are not of sufficient importance to justify detailed description.

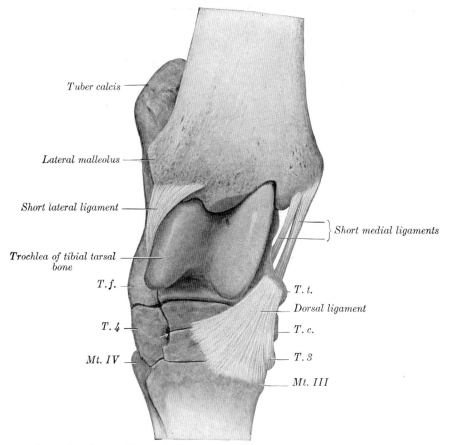

FIG. 254.—RIGHT HOCK JOINT OF HORSE. VIEWED FROM THE FRONT AND SLIGHTLY LATERALLY AFTER REMOVAL OF JOINT CAPSULE AND LONG COLLATERAL LIGAMENTS.

T. t., Tibial tarsal bone (distal tuberosity); *T. c.*, central tarsal bone; *T. 3*, ridge of third tarsal bone; *T. f.*, fibular tarsal bone (distal end); *T. 4*, fourth tarsal bone; *Mt. III*, *Mt. IV*, metatarsal bones. Arrow points to vascular canal.

(1) The **tibial** and **fibular tarsal** bones are united by four bands (astragalo-calcaneal ligaments). The **medial ligament** extends from the sustentaculum tali to the adjacent part of the tibial tarsal, blending with the short collateral ligament. The **lateral ligament** extends from the cochlear process of the fibular tarsal to the adjacent part of the lateral ridge of the trochlea. The **proximal ligament** extends from the posterior margin of the trochlea to the fibular tarsal. The **interosseous ligament** is deeply placed in the sinus tarsi between the two bones, and is attached in the rough areas of the opposed surfaces.

(2) The smaller bones are attached to each other as follows: The central and third tarsal are united by an interosseous and an oblique dorsal ligament (scaphoido-cunean ligaments). The central and fourth tarsal are united by an interosseous and a lateral transverse ligament (cuboido-scaphoid ligament). The third and fourth tarsals are similarly connected (cuboido-cunean ligaments). The third tarsal is joined by an interosseous (intercunean) ligament to the (fused) first and second tarsals; the latter are connected with the fourth tarsal by a plantar transverse ligament.

(3) The smaller bones are connected with the proximal row as follows: The central is

attached to the tibial by plantar and interosseous (astragalo-scaphoid) ligaments, and to the fibular tarsal by a short oblique (calcaneo-scaphoid) band. The fourth is attached to the fibular tarsal by interosseous and plantar (calcaneo-cuboid) ligaments. The (fused) first and second tarsals are connected with the fibular tarsal by a plantar (calcaneo-cunean) ligament.

(4) The distal tarsal bones are connected with the metatarsus by tarso-metatarsal ligaments, which are not distinct from the common ligaments, except in the case of the interosseous ligament between the third tarsal and metatarsal bones.

Movements.—These are flexion and extension, which take place at the tibio-tarsal joint. The movements between the tarsal bones, and between the latter and the metatarsus, are so limited as to be negligible so far as the action of the joint as a whole is concerned. In the standing position the articular angle (in front)

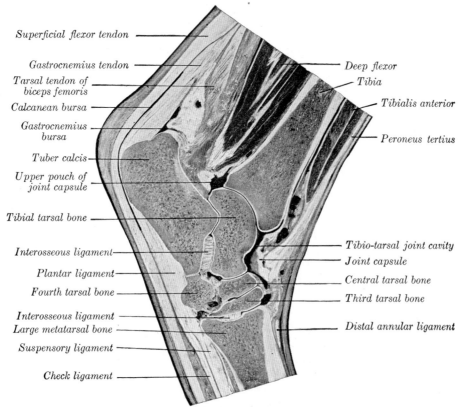

FIG. 255.—SAGITTAL SECTION OF HOCK OF HORSE. SLIGHTLY FLEXED.
The section is cut so far laterally that the deep flexor tendon does not show.

is about 150°. Complete extension is prevented by tension of the collateral ligaments. Flexion is checked only by contact of the metatarsus with the leg, provided the stifle joint is also flexed. Owing to the fact that the axis of motion is slightly oblique, the lower part of the limb deviates somewhat outward during flexion. The long collateral ligaments are tense in extension, the short ones in flexion, of the joint. The movements of the hock joint must correspond with those of the stifle on account of the tendinous bands in front and behind (peroneus tertius and flexor digitalis superficialis), which extend from the lower part of the femur to the tarsus and metatarsus.

The remaining joints differ in no material respect from those of the thoracic limb.

COMPARATIVE ARTHROLOGY[1]

JOINTS AND LIGAMENTS OF THE VERTEBRÆ

Ox.—The ligamentum nuchæ is better developed than in the horse. The funicular part is clearly divided into two lateral halves, which are round at their occipital attachment, but from the axis backward become rapidly wider and flat. This wide portion is almost sagittal, lies on either side of the vertebral spines, and is covered by the trapezius and rhomboideus muscles. From the highest part of the withers (third thoracic spine) it gradually diminishes in size and fades out in the lumbar region. The lamellar part is thick, and consists of anterior and posterior parts. The anterior part is double; its fibers proceed from the funicular part to the second, third, and fourth cervical spines. The posterior part is single; its fibers extend from the first thoracic spine to the fifth, sixth, and seventh cervical spines.

The ventral longitudinal ligament is very strong in the lumbar region.

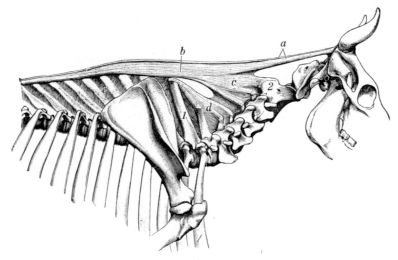

FIG. 256.—LIGAMENTUM NUCHÆ OF OX.

a, Funicular part; *b*, its wide portion; *c, d*, lamellar part; *e*, interspinous ligament; *1*, spinous process of first thoracic vertebra; *2*, axis   (Ellenberger-Baum, Anat. d. Haustiere.)

The intervertebral fibro-cartilages are thicker than in the horse.

The interspinous ligaments of the back and loins consist largely of elastic tissue.

There are no intertransverse joints in the lumbar region.

Pig.—The ligamentum nuchæ is represented by a fibrous raphé and thin layers of elastic tissue which extend between the cervical spines.

The atlanto-occipital and atlanto-axial joints resemble those of the dog.

The interspinous ligaments of the neck are elastic.

Dog.—The ligamentum nuchæ consists of a small fibrous band which extends from the spine of the axis to the anterior thoracic spines; it may be regarded as a mere fibrous raphé between the right and left muscles.

There are interspinous muscles instead of ligaments in the neck.

There are three ligaments in connection with the dens of the axis. The two **alar ligaments** (Ligg. alaria) arise on either side of the dens, diverge, and end on

[1] This section consists necessarily only of a brief statement of the most important differences in the joints of the other animals.

either side of the foramen magnum. The **transverse ligament** of the atlas (Lig. transversum atlantis) stretches across the dorsal surface of the dens and binds it down on the ventral arch of the atlas, a bursa being interposed. It is attached on either side to the lateral mass of the atlas.

The two capsules of the atlanto-occipital joint communicate with each other, and usually with the capsule of the atlanto-axial joint also.

ARTICULATIONS OF THE THORAX

Ox.—The second to the eleventh costo-chondral joints inclusive are diarthroses with close capsules, reinforced externally. (They are the same in the sheep.) The upper parts of the cartilages are attached to each other by distinct elastic ligaments (Ligg. intercostalia).

The first pair of chondro-sternal joints are separate from each other; a strong cruciate ligament unites the ventral ends of the first pair of ribs.

The first segment of the sternum forms with the body a diarthrodial **intersternal joint** (Articulatio intersternalis). The anterior joint surface is concave and is completed laterally by the second costal cartilages. There is a close capsule, and the joint surfaces are attached to each other by an interarticular ligament. Limited lateral movement is possible. (In the sheep the joint is a synchondrosis.) Both surfaces of the sternum are covered by a layer of fibrous tissue (Membrana sterni).

Pig.—The second to the fifth or sixth costo-chondral joints are diarthroses. The intersternal articulation and the sternal ligaments resemble those of the ox.

Dog.—The first chondro-sternal joints do not coalesce. The internal sternal ligament divides into three bands.

TEMPORO-MANDIBULAR ARTICULATION

Ox.—The articular surfaces are of such a character as to permit more extensive transverse movement than in the horse (*vide* Osteology). The posterior ligament is absent.

Pig.—The considerable longitudinal diameter of the temporal articular surfaces and the very small size of the postglenoid process allow great freedom of protraction and retraction of the lower jaw. Transverse movement is limited. The posterior ligament is absent.

Dog.—As the articular surfaces are cylindrical in curvature and the interarticular disc is very thin there is practically no transverse or gliding movement. The posterior ligament is absent.

The other articulations of the skull are sufficiently described in the Osteology.

ARTICULATIONS OF THE THORACIC LIMB

SHOULDER JOINT

Ox.—The articular angle is about 100°.

Pig and Dog.—The joint capsule communicates so freely with the bicipital bursa that the latter may well be regarded as a pouch of the capsule. There is a rudimentary marginal cartilage around the rim of the glenoid cavity. In the pig the front of the capsule is reinforced by cruciate bands. In the dog there is usually a strong band extending from the acromion to the lateral part of the capsule; another band (Ligamentum coraco-acromiale) often stretches between the scapular tuberosity and the acromion.

ELBOW JOINT

Ox.—No important differences exist. The upper part of the interosseous radio-ulnar ligament is commonly ossified in the adult.

Pig.—There are no important differences. The radius and ulna are so firmly united by the interosseous ligament as to prevent any appreciable movement between them.

Dog.—The joint capsule is reinforced in front by an oblique ligament which arises on the front of the lateral condyle of the humerus above the joint surface, and joins the terminal part of the biceps and brachialis below. There is a strong reinforcement of the postero-medial part of the capsule, which extends obliquely from the medial side of the olecranon fossa to the ulna, just above the processus anconeus. The lateral ligament is much stronger than the medial one. It is attached above to the lateral epicondyle of the humerus, and below chiefly to the eminence distal to the neck of the radius; but part of it inclines backward and is attached to the ulna. The middle part of the ligament is wide and forms a sort of cap over the proximal tuberosity of the radius. From this part a band, the **annular ligament** of the radius (Lig. annulare radii), extends across the front of the proximal end of the radius and ends on the ulna; although incorporated in the joint capsule it is easily defined. The medial ligament is more slender. It arises from the medial epicondyle of the humerus and passes deeply into the proximal part of the interosseous space, ending chiefly on the posterior surface of the radius a little medial to the attachment of the lateral ligament; there is also a small attachment to the interosseous border of the ulna. This ligament is very oblique. An elastic band (Ligamentum olecrani) extends from the lateral surface of the medial epicondyle to the anterior border of the ulna.

There are two radio-ulnar joints. The **proximal radio-ulnar joint** (Articulatio radioulnaris proximalis)is included in the capsule of the elbow, but is provided with an annular ligament, as described above. The **distal radio-ulnar joint** (Articulatio radioulnaris distalis) is formed by a concave facet on the radius and a convex one on the ulna, and is surrounded by a tight capsule. The interosseous membrane unites the shafts of the two bones; its proximal part is specially strong and is attached to prominences on both bones. The movements consist of limited rotation of the radius (ca. 20°), carrying the paw with it. The ordinary position is termed pronation; outward rotation is supination.[1]

THE CARPAL JOINTS

These have the same general arrangement as in the horse. Numerous minor differences naturally exist, but must be excluded from this brief account, which contains only important special features.

The lateral and medial movements are freer, especially in the dog, but flexion is not so complete: the anatomical explanation of these facts lies in the nature of the articular surfaces and certain ligamentous differences. The collateral ligaments are much weaker, the long lateral one being especially small in the ox. Two oblique, somewhat elastic bands cross the front of the radio-carpal and intercarpal joints. The proximal one is attached to the distal end of the radius and passes downward and outward to the ulnar carpal bone; the other one connects the radial and fourth carpal bones in a similar fashion.

In the ox the short collateral ligaments are well defined; a ligament connects the accessory carpal with the distal end of the ulna, and strong volar bands connect

---

[1] These movements are best seen in man, in whom the back of the hand may be turned forward (pronation) or backward (supination). In the dog the rotation is much restricted and is freest when the elbow is flexed.

the distal bones with the metacarpus. A strong oblique ligament connects the ulnar carpal bone with the metacarpus.

The dorsal, volar, and interosseous carpal ligaments vary with the number of carpal bones present in the different species.

In the dog there are six dorsal and six volar ligaments. The interosseous ligaments are not interordinal. The accessory carpal bone is attached by ligaments to the ulna, the radio-intermediate, and the third, fourth, and fifth metacarpal bones. The distal carpal bones are attached to the metacarpal bones by dorsal and volar ligaments.

INTERMETACARPAL JOINTS

In the ox the small (fifth) metacarpal bone articulates with the large metacarpal, but not with the carpus. The joint cavity is connected with that of the carpo-metacarpal sac. The proximal end of the small metacarpal bone is attached by a ligament to the fourth carpal, and another band extends from its distal part to the side of the large metacarpal. There is also an interosseous ligament, which is permanent and allows a small amount of movement.

The chief metacarpal bones of the pig, and the second to the fifth of the dog, articulate with each other at their proximal ends, and are connected by interosseous ligaments, which do not, however, unite them closely, as in the horse. There are feeble dorsal and volar ligaments (Ligg. basium) which unite the proximal ends of the metacarpal bones in the dog.

METACARPO-PHALANGEAL JOINTS

Ox.—There are two joints, one for each digit. The volar parts of the two joint capsules communicate. The two interdigital **collateral ligaments** (Ligg. collateralia interdigitalia) result from the bifurcation of a

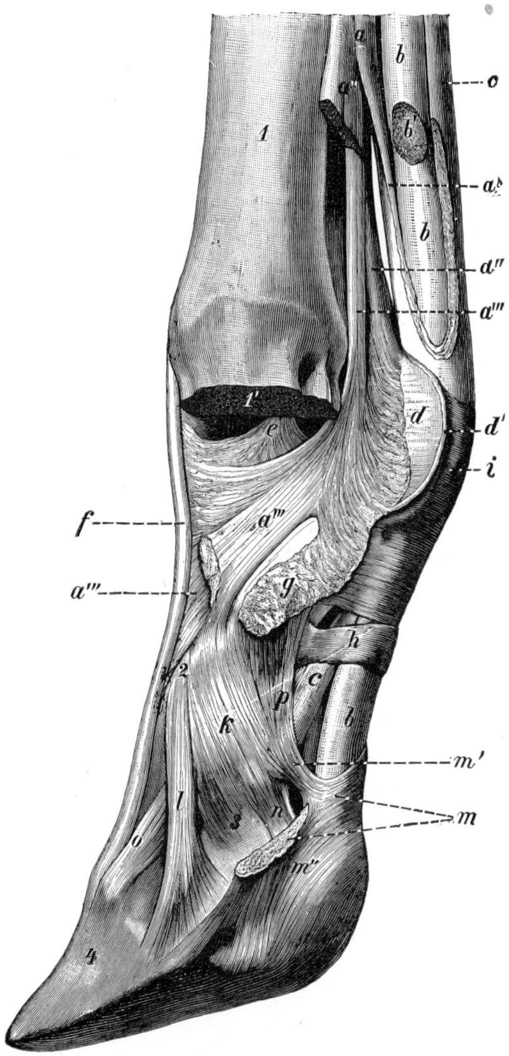

Fig. 257.—Distal Part of Limb of Ox, Showing Ligaments and Tendons. One Digit and Corresponding Articular Part of Metacarpal Bone are Removed.

a, Suspensory ligament; a′, branch of a to superficial flexor tendon; a″, a‴, lateral and central branches of a; b, deep flexor tendon; b′, branch of b to digit removed; c, c, superficial flexor tendon; d, d′, intersesamoid ligament (cut); e, interdigital collateral ligament of fetlock joint; f, tendon of common extensor; g, proximal interdigital ligament; h, digital annular ligament; i, posterior annular ligament of fetlock; k, collateral ligament of pastern joint; l, distal interdigital ligament; m, cruciate interdigital ligament (cut); m′, m″, attachments of m to second phalanx and distal sesamoid bone; n, suspensory ligament of distal sesamoid; o, dorsal elastic ligament; p, lateral volar ligament of pastern joint; 1, metacarpus, sawn off at 1′; 2, first phalanx; 3, second phalanx; 4, third phalanx. (Ellenberger-Baum, Anat. d. Haustiere.)

band which arises in the furrow between the divisions of the distal end of the large metacarpal bone; they spread out and end on the proximal ends of the first phalanges. The other collateral ligaments are arranged like those of the horse. A strong **interdigital ligament** (Lig. interdigitale), consisting of short intercrossing fibers, unites the middles of the interdigital surfaces of the first phalanges of the chief digits. It prevents undue divergence of the phalanges. It is not present in the sheep.

Cruciate ligaments (Ligg. phalango-sesamoideæ) connect the proximal sesamoids with the proximal end of the opposite first phalanx.

The intersesamoid ligament connects all four sesamoids, and extends upward much less than in the horse.

The laterate and medial sesamoidean ligaments end chiefly on the first phalanges, but also detach a small part to the large metacarpal bone.

The superficial or straight distal sesamoidean ligament is absent. The middle distal sesamoidean ligaments of each digit are two short, strong bands which extend from the distal margins of the proximal sesamoids to the proximal ends of the first phalanges. The deep distal sesamoidean ligaments are strong and distinctly cruciate.

The suspensory ligament or interosseus tendon contains more muscular tissue than in the horse—indeed, in the young animal it consists largely of muscular tissue. At the distal third of the metacarpus it divides into three branches. These give rise to five subdivisions, either by bifurcation of the lateral and medial branches or trifurcation of the middle branch. The two lateral and two medial bands end on the proximal sesamoid bones and the distal end of the large metacarpal bone, and detach slips to the extensor tendons. The middle band passes through the groove between the two divisions of the distal end of the metacarpus, and divides into two branches which join the tendons of the proper extensors of the digits; it sends fibers also to the interdigital collateral ligaments and to the central sesamoids. About the middle of the metacarpus the suspensory ligament detaches a band which unites lower down with the superficial flexor tendon, thus inclosing the tendon of the deep flexor of the digit; it also blends with the thick fascia of the region. The latter gives off a band on either side to the accessory digits, and a tendinous band descends from each accessory digit to the third phalanx and distal sesamoid bone, blending with the tendon of the corresponding proper extensor.

Pig.—There are four metacarpo-phalangeal joints, each of which has a capsule, collateral, intersesamoidean, and cruciate sesamoidean ligaments. Since distinct interosseous muscles are present, there are, of course, no suspensory ligaments.

Dog.—There are five metacarpo-phalangeal joints, each having its own capsule and indistinct collateral ligaments. A small sesamoid bone occurs in the anterior part of each capsule, over which the corresponding extensor tendon plays. The intersesamoidean ligaments do not extend above the sesamoids. The cruciate ligaments are present, as well as a fibrous layer which attaches the distal margins of the sesamoids to the posterior surface of the proximal end of the first phalanx.

INTERPHALANGEAL JOINTS

Ox.—The two proximal joints have separate capsules, and broad, but rather indistinct, collateral ligaments. Each joint has also central and collateral volar ligaments. The central ligaments are largely fused to form a strong band which is attached by two branches to the distal end of the first phalanx and to the depression on the volar surface of the proximal end of the second phalanx. The collateral ones extend from the borders of the first phalanx to the proximal end of the second phalanx; those on the interdigital side are weak and indistinct.

The distal interphalangeal joints have, in addition to the capsules and collateral ligaments, bands which reinforce them on either side. The interdigital pair arise in the depressions on the distal ends of the first phalanges, receive fibers from the second phalanges, and end on the interdigital surfaces of the third phalanges at the margin of the articular surface. The abaxial pair have a similar course, but are thinner, and end on the corresponding third sesamoid. An elastic band crosses the front of the second phalanx obliquely, from the distal end of the first phalanx to the extensor process of the third phalanx.

The **cruciate** or **distal interdigital ligaments** (Ligg. cruciata interdigitalia) are two strong bands which limit the separation of the digits. They are attached above to the abaxial eminences on the proximal ends of the second phalanges (blending with the collateral ligaments), cross the deep flexor tendon obliquely, and reach the

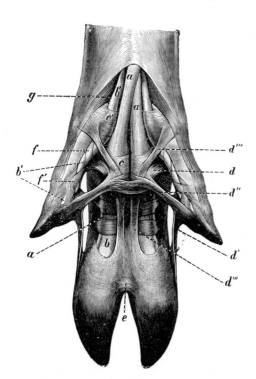

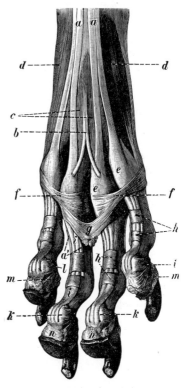

FIG. 258.—LIGAMENTS AND TENDONS OF DIGITS OF PIG; VOLAR VIEW.

a, Superficial flexor tendon; *b*, deep flexor tendon; *b'*, branches of *b* to accessory digits; *c, c'*, annular ligaments; *d–d'''*, ligaments of accessory digits; *e*, cruciate interdigital ligaments; *f, f'*, spiral band around the flexor tendons of the accessory digits; *g*, abductor of accessory digit. (Ellenberger-Baum, Anat. d. Haustiere.)

FIG. 259.—LIGAMENTS AND TENDONS OF DIGITS OF DOG, HIND LIMB; PLANTAR VIEW.

a, a', Superficial flexor tendon; *b*, tendon to large pad; *c*, lumbricales muscles; *d*, interossei muscles; *e, f*, annular ligaments at metatarsophalangeal joints; *g*, suspensory ligament of large pad; *h*, digital annular ligaments; *i*, deep flexor tendon; *k*, distal sesamoid; *l*, suspensory ligament of *k*; *m*, suspensory ligament of digital pad; *n*, digital pads. (Ellenberger-Baum, Anat. d. Haustiere.)

interdigital space, where they intercross and blend. Most of the fibers end on the distal sesamoid of the opposite side, but some are attached to the interdigital aspect of the second phalanx and the distal sesamoid of the same side. In the sheep there is, instead of the foregoing, a transverse ligament which is attached on either side to the interdigital surfaces of the second and third phalanges and the distal sesamoid bone. It is related below to the skin, above to a pad of fat.

Pig.—The interphalangeal joints of the chief digits resemble in general those of the ox. The distal interdigital ligament resembles, however, that of the sheep, and is intimately adherent to the skin. There is, besides, a remarkable arrangement of ligaments which connect the small digits with each other and with the chief digits (Fig. 258).

This apparatus is somewhat complex, but its chief features are as follows: A proximal interdigital ligament is attached on either side to the third phalanges of the small digits, while centrally it blends with the annular ligaments of the flexor tendons behind the metacarpo-phalangeal joints of the chief digits. Two bands (central longitudinal interdigital ligaments) arise on the bases of the small digits, cross the flexor tendons obliquely downward and centrally, pass through the proximal interdigital ligament, and blend below with the distal interdigital ligament. Two collateral bands (collateral longitudinal interdigital ligaments) are attached in common with the proximal interdigital ligaments to the third phalanges of the small digits, and blend below with the outer part of the distal interdigital ligament.

Dog.—Each joint has a capsule and two collateral ligaments. The distal joints have also two elastic **dorsal ligaments** (Ligg. dorsalia), which extend from the proximal end of the second phalanx to the ridge at the base of the third phalanx. They produce dorsal flexion of the joint, and thus raise or retract the claws when the flexor muscles relax. The distal sesamoids are represented by complementary cartilages attached to the volar margins of the articular surfaces of the third phalanges.

Three interdigital ligaments restrict the spreading apart of the digits (Fig. 259). Two of these cross the volar surface of the proximal parts of the chief digits, i. e., one for the second and third, the other for the fourth and fifth; they blend with the annular ligaments on either side. The third ligament is attached on either side to the foregoing ligaments and the annular ligaments of the third and fourth digits, and curves downward centrally, ending in the large pad on the paw.

ARTICULATIONS OF THE PELVIC LIMB

SACRO-ILIAC JOINT

This joint and the pelvic ligaments present no very striking differences in the other animals except that the sacro-sciatic ligament in the dog is a narrow but strong band which extends from the posterior part of the lateral margin of the sacrum to the tuber ischii; it is the homologue of the ligamentum sacro-tuberosum of man.

HIP JOINT

Ox.—The shallowness of the acetabulum is compensated by the greater size of the marginal cartilage, which is specially large laterally. The head of the femur has a smaller radius of curvature than that of the horse, and the articular surface extends a considerable distance outward on the upper surface of the neck. The round ligament is entirely intra-articular; it is small, and sometimes absent. The accessory ligament is absent.

There are no important differences in the other animals.

STIFLE JOINT

Ox.—There is a considerable communication between the femoro-patellar and medial femoro-tibial joint cavities; this is situated as in the horse, but is wider. A small communication with the lateral femoro-tibial capsule sometimes occurs. The two femoro-tibial capsules usually communicate. The middle patellar ligament is not sunken, as there is no groove on the tuberosity of the tibia where it is attached. The lateral patellar ligament fuses completely with the tendon of insertion of the biceps femoris, and a large synovial bursa is interposed between them and the lateral condyle of the femur.

Pig.—The femoro-patellar capsule is strongly reinforced on both sides by bands which blend with the collateral femoro-tibial ligaments. The cavity is continuous below with that of the femoro-tibial joint. A sagittal synovial fold (rudimentum septi) extends up a short distance from the anterior cruciate ligament. The suprapatellar pouch extends an inch or more (ca. 2–3 cm.) above the trochlea; from this a pouch extends up beneath the quadriceps femoris almost an inch and communicates through a large round opening with the joint cavity. There is a strong ligamentum patellæ, which has a bursa under its distal part. The tendon of the biceps femoris takes the place of the lateral patellar ligament. A small ligamentum transversum connects the anterior faces of the menisci.

Dog.—The joint in general resembles that of the pig. The posterior part of the capsule contains two sesamoid bones, which are imbedded in the origin of the gastrocnemius.

TIBIO-FIBULAR JOINTS

Ox.—The proximal end of the fibula fuses with the lateral condyle of the tibia. The distal end remains separate, and forms an arthrosis with the distal end of the tibia; the movement here is imperceptible, as the two bones are closely united by strong peripheral fibers.

Pig.—The proximal joint is provided with a capsule which is reinforced in front and behind by fibrous tissue. The interosseous ligament attaches the shaft of the fibula to the lateral border of the tibia. The distal joint is included in the capsule of the hock joint, and is strengthened by dorsal and plantar ligaments (Lig. malleoli lateralis dorsalis, plantaris), which extend almost transversely from one bone to the other. There is also an interosseous ligament.

Dog.—The arrangement is essentially the same as in the pig, but there is no interosseous ligament in the distal joint. Not uncommonly the distal part of the shaft of the fibula and tibia are ankylosed.

HOCK JOINT

Ox.—There is very considerable mobility at the proximal intertarsal joint, the capsule of which is correspondingly roomy. The short lateral ligament is attached distally on the tibial tarsal only. A strong transverse ligament attaches the lateral malleolus (distal end of the fibula) to the back of the tibial tarsal bone. The dorsal ligament is narrow and thin.

Pig.—The arrangement in general resembles that of the ox. The medial ligament consists of a thin superficial part which extends almost vertically from malleolus to metatarsus, and a very strong deep part, which runs from the malleolus backward and downward to the sustentaculum and tibial tarsal. The lateral ligament also consists of two parts. The small superficial part extends from the malleolus down to the lateral face of the body of the fibular tarsal bone. The stronger deep part arises from the anterior part of the malleolus, passes chiefly backward, widens, and ends on a ridge on the lateral surface of the fibular tarsal. A strong band extends from the lateral face of the medial malleolus to a depression on the medial surface of the proximal part of the tibial tarsal bone. An oblique dorsal band connects the central and fourth tarsal bones.

Dog.—The long collateral ligaments are very small, and the short ones double. The plantar ligament is weak, and ends on the fourth metacarpal bone. No distinct dorsal ligament is present, unless we regard as such a ligament which extends from the neck of the tibial tarsal to the fourth tarsal and third metatarsal bones.

The remaining joints resemble those of the thoracic limb.

MYOLOGY

Myology deals with the muscles and their accessory structures. The **muscles** (Musculi) are highly specialized organs, which are characterized by their property of contracting in a definite manner when stimulated. They are the active organs of motion. The contractile part of the muscle is the **muscular tissue.** Three kinds of muscular tissue are recognized, viz.: (1) **Striated** or striped; (2) **non-striated,** unstriped or smooth; (3) **cardiac,** which may be regarded as a specialized variety of striated muscle. Only the first of these will be considered in this section. The striated muscles are for the most part connected directly or indirectly with the skeleton, upon which they act, and are hence often designated as **skeletal muscles** (Musculi skeleti), in distinction from non-striated muscle, which is often spoken of as **visceral.** The striated muscles cover the greater part of the skeleton, and play an important part in determining the form of the animal. They are red in color, the shade varying in different muscles and under various conditions. Some are intimately associated with and attached to the skin, and are called **cutaneous muscles** (Musculi cutanei). The muscular part of each is composed of bundles of contractile fibers surrounded by a thin sheath of connective tissue, the **perimysium.**

The description of the muscles may be arranged under the following heads: (1) Name; (2) shape and position; (3) attachments; (4) action; (5) structure; (6) relations; (7) blood and nerve supply.

(1) The **name** is determined by various considerations, *e. g.*, the action, attachments, shape, position, direction, etc. In most cases two or more of these are combined to produce the name, *e. g.*, flexor carpi radialis, longus colli, obliquus externus abdominis.[1]

(2) The **shape** is in many cases sufficiently definite and regular to allow the use of such terms as triangular, quadrilateral, fan-shaped, fusiform, etc. Some muscles are characterized as long, broad, short, etc. Orbicular or ring-like muscles circumscribe openings; since the contraction of such a muscle closes the orifice, it is often termed a **sphincter.** The position and direction are usually stated with reference to the region occupied and to adjacent structures which may be presumed to be already known.

(3) The **attachments** are in most cases to bone, but many muscles are attached to cartilage, ligaments, fascia, or the skin. As a matter of convenience, the term **origin** (Origo) is applied to the attachment which always or more commonly remains stationary when the muscle contracts; the more movable attachment is termed the **insertion** (Insertio). Such a distinction is often quite arbitrary, and cannot always be made, as the action may be reversible or both attachments may be freely movable. With respect to the muscles of the limbs, the proximal attachment is regarded as the origin and the distal one as the insertion. In all cases the attachment is made by fibrous tissue, the muscular tissue not coming into direct relation with the point of attachment. But when the intermediate fibrous tissue is not evident to the naked eye, it is customary to speak of a "fleshy attachment." The term "tendinous attachment" is applied to those cases in which the intermediate fibrous tissue—tendon or aponeurosis—is evident. A **tendon** (Tendo) is a band of

[1] A satisfactory comparative nomenclature is exceedingly difficult to work out, and much confusion exists in this respect. This is due in great part to the lack of a uniform basis for the formation of names and the difficulty in determining homologies in various species.

dense white fibrous tissue by means of which a muscle is attached; an **aponeurosis** is a broad fibrous sheet which fulfils a similar function.

(4) The **action** belongs rather to physiological study, but the main points are usually given in anatomical descriptions. In some cases the action is simple, in others complex. Muscles which concur in action are termed synergists; those which have opposite actions are antagonists.

(5) The consideration of **structure** includes the direction of the muscular fibers, the arrangement of the tendons, the synovial membranes, and any other accessory structures. The terms fleshy and tendinous are sometimes used to indicate the relative amounts of muscular and fibrous tissue. In the case of the long muscles of the limbs, the origin is termed the **head** (Caput), and when the muscle is fusiform, the large fleshy part is often called the **belly** (Venter) of the muscle. Some muscles have two or more heads, and are hence designated as biceps, triceps, etc. A **digastric** muscle is one having two bellies and an intermediate tendon. In most muscles the muscle-fibers join the tendon at an acute angle, like the relation of the barbs of a feather to its shaft; hence the term **pennate** is applied to such an arrangement. When the fibers are so arranged on one side of the tendon the muscle is **unipennate** (M. unipennatus); while one in which this arrangement exists on both sides is **bipennate** (M. bipennatus). The structure may be still more complex, resulting in a **multipennate** muscle. The structure of many muscles, especially those of the limbs, is much more complex than a superficial examination would

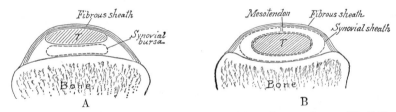

FIG. 260.—DIAGRAMS OF CROSS-SECTIONS OF SYNOVIAL BURSA (A) AND SYNOVIAL SHEATH (B); *T*, TENDON.
In both the synovial sac is represented for the sake of clearness as though somewhat distended.

lead one to suppose. Frequently they are intersected by tendinous layers or bands, known as **tendinous intersections.** Intersecting bands or tracts which appear on the surface—usually as zig-zag lines—are termed **tendinous inscriptions** (Inscriptiones tendineæ).

(6) The **relations** constitute a very important part of anatomical topography, and a knowledge of them is fundamental to further study in this respect.

(7) The **blood** and **nerve supply** are, of course, important on clinical grounds. The nerve supply is often of value in the determination of homologies. As might be expected, the muscles have a large blood supply. The nerves to the muscles are motor, sensory, and vasomotor in function.

The **accessory structures** associated with the muscles are the synovial membranes and the fasciæ.

The **synovial membranes** are thin-walled sacs, similar to the synovial membranes of the joints, and having a similar function. Two forms are recognized. A **synovial bursa** (Bursa synovialis) is a simple sac which is interposed at a point of unusual pressure between a tendon or muscle and some underlying structure, commonly a prominence of the skeleton. A **synovial sheath** (Vagina synovialis tendinis) differs from a bursa in the fact that the sac is folded around the tendon so that two layers can be distinguished: the inner one is adherent to the tendon, while the outer one lines the canal in which the tendon lies. The two layers are continuous along a fold termed the **mesotendon.** The arrangement is shown in the annexed diagrams. The synovial membranes of joints in some places form extra-articular pouches which act as bursæ. The student will note in dissection that intermediate forms of these sacs occur. A synovial sheath may belong to two or more tendons in common; in such cases the synovial membrane is reflected from one tendon to the other, forming a secondary mesotendon. In the normal state these sacs cannot be recognized on external examination of the subject. It is only when they are distended that their presence is evident. The synovial sheath is not to be confused with the **fibrous sheath** of a tendon (Vagina fibrosa tendinis).

The **fasciæ** are sheets of connective tissue, composed mainly of bundles of white fibers, with a greater or less admixture of elastic fibers in some cases. At least two layers may usually be distinguished. The **superficial fascia** (Fascia superficialis) is subcutaneous, and is composed of loose connective tissue which usually contains more or less fat. The **deep fascia** is composed of one or more layers of dense fibrous tissue. Its deep face may be very slightly adherent to the underlying structures, but in many places it is attached to the skeleton, ligaments, and tendons. In many places laminæ are given off from the deep face of the fascia, pass between muscles, and are attached to bones or ligaments; such layers are termed **intermuscular septa** (Septa intermuscularia). The groove in which a tendon lies is converted into a canal by a band or fascial sheet known as a **vaginal** or **annular ligament** (Lig. vaginale). Many fasciæ furnish origin or insertion to muscles and thus act as tendons; such are tendinous in structure, so as to render the distinction between fascia and aponeurosis in these cases arbitrary. Bursæ occur in certain situations between the fascia and underlying structures, and are distinguished as **subfascial bursæ.** Those between the fascia and the skin are **subcutaneous bursæ.**

FASCIÆ AND MUSCLES OF THE HORSE

The **cutaneus muscle** (Musculus cutaneus)[1] is a thin muscular layer developed in the superficial fascia. It is intimately adherent in great part to the skin, but has very little attachment to the skeleton. It does not cover the entire body, and may be conveniently divided into facial, cervical, omobrachial, and abdominal parts.

The facial part, **M. cutaneus faciei,** consists of a thin and usually incomplete muscular layer, which extends over the mandibular space and the masseter muscle. A distinct branch of it passes forward to the angle of the mouth and blends with the orbicularis oris. This part, the **M. cutaneus labiorum,** retracts the angle of the mouth, and has therefore been termed the retractor anguli oris.

The cervical part, **M. cutaneus colli,** is situated on the ventral region of the neck. It arises from the cariniform cartilage and a median fibrous raphé. The fibers are directed forward and diverge from the raphé to the sides of the neck in pennate fashion. It is thick at its sternal origin, but thins out in front and laterally. On the side of the neck it is attached to the cervical fascia, which acts as its aponeurosis. It is related deeply to the sterno-cephalicus, the brachio-cephalicus (in part) and the jugular vein. Some bundles extend upon the parotid gland, and in well-developed subjects it is continuous with the facial part.

The omo-brachial part, **M. cutaneus omo-brachialis,** covers the lateral surface of the shoulder and arm. Its fibers begin at the level of the tuber spinæ of the scapula and extend to the proximal part of the forearm. Most of its fibers are vertical, but posteriorly they become oblique and are continued by the abdominal part.

The abdominal part, **M. cutaneus trunci,** covers a large part of the body behind the shoulder and arm. Its fibers are largely longitudinal. It is continuous in front with the omo-brachial part. A thin tendon from it passes forward with

---

[1] Formerly termed the panniculus carnosus.

the posterior deep pectoral muscle to the medial tuberosity of the humerus and also blends with the tendon of the latissimus dorsi (Fig. 566). Posteriorly it forms a fold, which, covered by the skin, forms the fold of the flank, and ends on the fascia above the stifle. Dorsally the highest part of the muscle is about at the middle of the back, where it is only about two inches (ca. 5 cm.) from the median line. From here the dorsal border descends to the fold of the flank. Ventrally the two muscles are about a handbreadth apart in the umbilical region. Further forward they diverge, so as to overlap the posterior deep pectoral muscle only to a small extent. Here the cutaneus muscle is closely adherent to the pectoral and contains the external thoracic vein. Posteriorly they diverge to the fold of the flank. The muscle is in general closely adherent to the skin and its contraction twitches the skin, thus getting rid of insects or other irritants.

THE FASCIÆ AND MUSCLES OF THE HEAD

The muscles of the head (Mm. capitis) may be divided into four groups, viz.: (1) Superficial muscles, including the cutaneus muscle and those of the lips, cheeks, nostrils, eyelids, and external ear; (2) the orbital muscles; (3) the mandibular muscles; (4) the hyoid muscles.

The **superficial fascia** forms an almost continuous layer, but is very scanty around the natural orifices. It contains a number of the thin superficial muscles, so that care must be exercised in removing the skin. Over the frontal and nasal bones the fascia blends with the periosteum.

The **deep fascia** is of special interest in three regions. The **temporal fascia** (Fascia temporalis) covers the temporalis muscle, and is attached to the parietal and frontal crests medially, and to the zygomatic arch laterally. The **buccal fascia** (F. buccalis) covers the buccinator muscle and the free part of the outer surface of the ramus of the mandible. It is attached to the facial crest, and posteriorly it forms a band (Raphé pterygomandibulare) which stretches from the hamulus of the pterygoid bone to the mandible behind the last molar tooth. It is directly continuous with the **pharyngeal fascia** (F. pharyngea), which is attached to the great and thyroid cornua of the hyoid bone and the thyroid cartilage of the larynx; it covers the lateral walls of the pharynx, and blends dorsally with the median raphé of the constrictor muscles of the latter.

Cutaneus faciei.—This has been described (p. 256).

MUSCLES OF THE LIPS AND CHEEKS

1. **Orbicularis oris.**—This is the sphincter muscle of the mouth; it is continuous with the other muscles which converge to the lips. It lies between the skin and the mucous membrane of the lips, and is intimately adherent to the former. Most of the fibers run parallel to the free edges of the lips and have no direct attachment to the skeleton.

Action.—It closes the lips.

Blood-supply.—Palato-labial, facial, and mental arteries.

Nerve-supply.—Facial nerve.

2. **Levator nasolabialis.**—This thin muscle lies directly under the skin, and chiefly on the lateral surface of the nasal region.

Origin.—The frontal and nasal bones.

Insertion.—(1) The upper lip and the lateral wing of the nostril; (2) the commissure of the lips.

Action.—(1) To elevate the upper lip and the commissure; (2) to dilate the nostril.

Structure.—The muscle arises by a thin aponeurosis. The belly is also thin, and divides into two branches, between which the lateral dilator of the nostril passes. The dorsal branch reaches the nostril and upper lip, blending with the lateral dilator; the ventral one is much smaller, and blends at the labial commissure with the orbicularis and buccinator.

Relations.—Superficially, the skin, fascia, and lateral dilator (in part); deeply,

FIG. 261.—MUSCLES OF HEAD OF HORSE; LATERAL VIEW. THE M. CUTANEUS IS REMOVED.

a, Levator labii superioris proprius; *b*, levator nasolabialis; *c*, brachiocephalicus; *d*, sterno-cephalicus; *d'*, tendon of *d*; *e*, omo-hyoideus; *f*, dilatator naris lateralis; *g*, zygomaticus; *h*, buccinator; *i*, depressor labii inferioris; *k*, orbicularis oris; *l*, lateralis nasi, dorsal part; *m*, masseter; *n*, parotido-auricularis; *o*, zygomatico-auricularis; *p*, interscutularis; *p'*, fronto-scutularis, pars temporalis; *q*, cervico-auricularis profundus major; *r*, cervico-auricularis superficialis; *s*, obliquus capitis anterior; *t*, splenius; *v*, occipito-mandibularis; *y*, mastoid tendon of brachiocephalicus; *2*, posterior, *3*, anterior, border of external ear; *8*, scutiform cartilage; *9*, zygomatic arch; *10*, orbital fat; *18*, temporo-mandibular articulation; *27*, facial crest; *30'*, angle of jaw; *37*, external maxillary vein; *38*, jugular vein; *39*, facial vein; *40*, parotid duct; *41*, transverse facial vein; *42*, masseteric vein; *43*, facial nerve; *44*, parotid gland; *45*, chin; *x*, wing of atlas. By an oversight the superior buccal branch of the facial nerve is shown crossing over instead of under the zygomaticus. (After Ellenberger-Baum, Anat. für Künstler.)

the levator labii superioris proprius, lateral dilator (in part), buccinator, branches of the facial vessels and nerve, and the infraorbital artery and nerve.

Blood-supply.—Facial and palato-labial arteries.

Nerve-supply.—Facial nerve.

3. Levator labii superioris proprius.—This lies on the dorso-lateral aspect of the face, partly covered by the preceding muscle.

Origin.—The lacrimal, malar, and maxillary bones at their junction.

Insertion.—The upper lip, by a common tendon with its fellow.

Action.—Acting with its fellow, to elevate the upper lip. This action, if carried to the fullest extent, results in eversion of the lip. In unilateral action the lip is drawn upward and to the side of the muscle acting.

Structure.—The muscle has a short, thin tendon of origin. The belly is at first flattened, but becomes narrower and thicker, then tapers over the nasal diverticulum, to terminate in a tendon. The tendons of the two muscles unite over the alar cartilages of the nostrils, forming an expansion which spreads out in the substance of the upper lip.[1]

Relations.—Superficially, the skin, the levator nasolabialis, and the angular vessels of the eye; deeply, the lateralis nasi, the transversus nasi, and the infraorbital artery and nerve.

Blood-supply.—Facial artery.

Nerve-supply.—Facial nerve.

4. Zygomaticus.—This very thin muscle lies immediately under the skin of the cheek.

Origin.—The fascia covering the masseter muscle below the facial crest.

Insertion.—The commissure of the lips, blending with the buccinator.

Action.—To retract and raise the angle of the mouth.

Structure.—Fleshy, with a thin aponeurotic origin.

Relations.—Superficially, the skin; deeply, the buccinator.

Blood-supply.—Facial artery.

Nerve-supply.—Facial nerve.

5. Incisivus superior.—This lies under the mucous membrane of the upper lip.

Origin.—The alveolar border of the premaxilla from the second incisor to the first cheek tooth.

Insertion.—The upper lip.

Action.—To depress the upper lip.

6. Incisivus inferior.—This is arranged in the lower lip like the preceding muscle in the upper one.

Origin.—The alveolar border of the mandible from the second incisor to a point near the first cheek tooth.

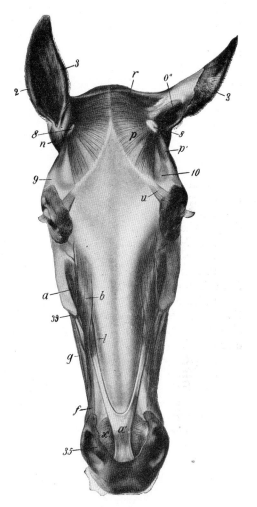

FIG. 262.—MUSCLES OF HEAD OF HORSE; DORSAL VIEW. THE M. CUTANEUS IS REMOVED.

a, Levator labii superioris proprius; *a′*, common tendon of *a* with opposite muscle; *b*, levator nasolabialis; *f*, dilatator naris lateralis; *g*, zygomaticus; *l*, lateralis nasi; *n*, parotido-auricularis; *o″*, scutulo-auricularis superficialis superior; *p*, interscutularis; *p′*, fronto-scutularis, pars temporalis; *r*, cervico-auricularis superficialis; *u*, corrugator supercilii; *x*, transversus nasi; *2*, posterior, *3*, anterior, border of external ear; *8*, scutiform cartilage; *9*, zygomatic arch; *10*, supraorbital depression; *35*, medial wing of nostril, containing lamina of alar cartilage; *39*, facial vein. (After Ellenberger-Baum, Anat. für Künstler.)

---

[1] In rare cases a branch is given off from the ventral border of the muscle. It passes forward and ends in the subcutaneous tissue at the posterior end of the diverticulum nasi.

Insertion.—The skin of the lower lip and the prominence of the chin.

Action.—To raise the lower lip. The two incisivi bring the lips together, concurring with the orbicularis oris in prehension of food.

7. Mentalis.—This is situated in the prominence of the chin. Its fibers arise from each side of the body of the mandible and are inserted into the skin of the chin. It is mingled with fat and strands of connective tissue, in which the roots of the tactile hairs are embedded. It raises and corrugates the skin to which it is attached.

8. Depressor labii inferioris.—This muscle lies on the lateral surface of the ramus of the mandible, along the ventral border of the buccinator.

Origin.—The alveolar border of the mandible near the coronoid process and the maxillary tuberosity, in common with the buccinator.

Insertion.—The lower lip.

Action.—To depress and retract the lower lip.

Structure.—The tendon of origin and the belly are fused with the buccinator as far forward as the first cheek tooth. From this point forward the belly is distinct and rounded, terminating in a tendon which spreads out in the lower lip, blending with the orbicularis and the muscle of the opposite side.

Relations.—Superficially, the skin, masseter, facial vessels, and parotid duct; deeply, the mandible and inferior labial artery.

Blood-supply.—Facial artery.

Nerve-supply.—Facial nerve.

9. Buccinator.—This muscle lies in the lateral wall of the mouth, extending from the angle of the mouth to the maxillary tuberosity.

Origin.—The lateral surface of the maxilla above the interalveolar space and the molar teeth; the alveolar border of the mandible at the interalveolar space and also posteriorly where it turns upward to the coronoid process; the pterygo-mandibular raphé.

Insertion.—The angle of the mouth, blending with the orbicularis oris.

Action.—To flatten the cheeks, thus pressing the food between the teeth; also to retract the angle of the mouth.

Structure.—Two layers may be recognized. The **superficial layer** (Pars buccalis) extends from the angle of the mouth to the masseter. It is incompletely pennate, having a longitudinal raphé on which most of the muscle-fibers converge. The upper fibers are directed chiefly downward and backward, the lower ones upward and backward. The **deep layer** (Pars molaris) consists mainly of longitudinal fibers. It blends in part with the superficial layer of the orbicularis; it has a small tendinous attachment to the coronoid process behind, and is united ventrally with the depressor labii inferioris.

Relations.—Superficially, the skin and fascia, the zygomaticus, levator nasolabialis, lateral dilator of the nostril, the superior buccal glands, the parotid duct, the facial vessels, and branches of the facial nerve; deeply, the mucous membrane of the mouth and the inferior buccal glands.

Blood-supply.—Facial and buccinator arteries.

Nerve-supply.—Facial nerve.

MUSCLES OF THE NOSTRILS

1. Levator nasolabialis.—This has been described (p. 257).

2. Dilatator naris lateralis (M. caninus).—This thin, triangular muscle lies on the lateral nasal region, and passes between the two branches of the levator nasolabialis.

Origin.—The maxilla, close to the anterior extremity of the facial crest.

Insertion.—The lateral wing of the nostril.

Action.—To dilate the nostril.

Structure.—The muscle has a flat tendon of origin, passes between the two branches of the levator nasolabialis, and spreads out in the lateral wing of the nostril. The lower fibers blend with the orbicularis oris.

Relations.—Superficially, the skin, fascia, and the labial branch of the levator nasolabialis; deeply, the maxilla and the nasal branch of the levator nasolabialis.

Blood-supply.—Facial artery.

Nerve-supply.—Facial nerve.

3. **Transversus nasi.**—This is an unpaired, quadrilateral muscle, which lies between the nostrils. It consists of two layers.

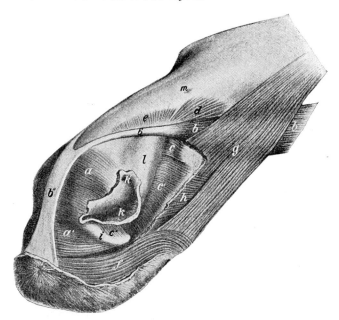

Fig. 263.—Nasal and Superior Labial Muscles of Horse.

a, a', Transversus nasi; *b*, levator labii superioris proprius; *b'*, tendon of *b; b''*, common tendon of two levatores labii superioris proprii; *c, c', c'', d*, ventral part of lateralis nasi; *e*, dorsal part of lateralis nasi; *f*, orbicularis oris; *g*, levator nasolabialis, a portion of which is removed; *h*, dilatator naris lateralis (the terminal part of which is removed); *i*, cornu of alar cartilage; *k*, nostril; *k'*, upper commissure of nostril; *l*, nasal diverticulum; *m*, nasal bone. (After Ellenberger-Baum, Top. Anat. d. Pferdes.)

Attachments.—Superficial layer, the superficial faces of the laminæ of the alar cartilages; deep layer, the convex edges of the cornua of the same.

Action.—To dilate the nostrils.

Structure.—It is composed of transverse fleshy fibers, which blend below with the orbicularis.

Relations.—Superficially, the skin, fascia, and tendinous expansion of the levator labii superioris proprius; deeply, the alar cartilages, the extremity of the septum nasi, and the palato-labial artery.

Blood-supply.—Palato-labial artery.

Nerve-supply.—Facial nerve.

Lateralis nasi.—This is situated along the margins of the naso-maxillary notch, and may be regarded as consisting of dorsal and ventral parts.

The **dorsal part** (Pars dorsalis m. lateralis nasi) is a thin layer which lies along the dorsal border of the naso-maxillary notch. Its fibers arise from the nasal bone and pass outward and downward to the parietal cartilage and the adjacent part of the soft lateral wall of the nasal cavity.

The **ventral part** (Pars ventralis m. lateralis nasi) is much thicker and lies along the ventral border of the notch. It arises from the nasal process of the premaxilla and the adjacent part of the maxilla, and its fibers curve inward to end on the cartilaginous prolongations of the turbinate bones (chiefly the ventral one) and on the lateral wall of the vestibule of the nasal cavity (Fig. 452). A few bundles pass from the cornu of the alar cartilage to the lateral wing of the nostril.

Action.—To dilate the vestibule of the nasal cavity, to rotate the turbinal cartilages outward, and to assist in dilating the nostril.

Relations.—Superficially, the skin, fascia, nasal diverticulum, the levator labii superioris proprius, the levator nasolabialis, and the lateral nasal artery; deeply, the nasal bone, the parietal cartilage, the maxilla, the premaxilla, the nasal mucous membrane, and the anterior nasal branch of the infraorbital nerve.

Blood-supply.—Facial and palato-labial arteries.

Nerve-supply.—Facial nerve.

The preceding muscle does not dilate the so-called "false nostril" or nasal diverticulum, as is commonly stated. It acts on the lateral wall of the vestibule of the nasal cavity so as to draw it outward, thus tending to constrict, rather than dilate, the nasal diverticulum. The thick part of the ventral muscle which is attached to the cartilage of the turbinate bone has a similar effect. When the nostril is fully dilated, the so-called "false nostril," *i. e.*, the entrance to the nasal diverticulum, is closed. Dilatation of the diverticulum is not produced by muscular action.

MUSCLES OF THE EYELIDS

1. **Orbicularis oculi.**—This is a flat, elliptical, sphincter muscle, situated in and around the eyelids, the portion in the upper lid being much broader than that in the lower. The chief attachment is to the skin of the lids, but some bundles are attached to the palpebral ligament at the medial canthus and to the lacrimal bone. Its action is to close the lids.

2. **Corrugator supercilii.**—This is a very thin, small muscle, which arises over the root of the supraorbital process and spreads out in the upper eyelid, blending with the orbicularis oculi (Fig. 262). Its action is to assist in raising the upper lid or, especially in pathological conditions, to wrinkle the skin.

3. **Malaris.**—This is a very thin muscle, which varies much in different subjects. It extends from the fascia in front of the orbit to the lower lid. Its action is to depress the lower lid.

The foregoing muscles receive their blood-supply from the facial, transverse facial, supraorbital, and infraorbital arteries; the nerve-supply is derived from the facial nerve.

4. **Levator palpebræ superioris.**—This slender, flat muscle is almost entirely within the orbit (Fig. 692). It arises on the pterygoid crest, passes forward above the rectus oculi superior and below the lacrimal gland, and terminates in a thin tendon in the upper lid.

Action.—To elevate the upper lid.

Blood-supply.—Ophthalmic artery.

Nerve-supply.—Oculomotor nerve.

MANDIBULAR MUSCLES

The muscles of this group (Mm. mandibulæ) are six in number in the horse. They arise from the upper jaw and the cranium, and are all inserted into the mandible.

1. **Masseter.**—This muscle extends from the zygomatic arch and facial crest over the broad part of the mandibular ramus. It is semi-elliptical in outline.

Origin.—By a strong tendon from the zygomatic arch and the facial crest.

Insertion.—The lateral surface of the broad part of the ramus of the mandible.

Action.—Its action is to bring the jaws together. Acting singly, it also carries the lower jaw toward the side of the contracting muscle.

Structure.—The superficial face of the muscle in its upper part is covered by a strong, glistening aponeurosis, and several tendinous intersections partially divide the muscle into layers. The fibers of the superficial layer take origin from the malar and maxilla only, and diverge somewhat to their insertion close to the thick ventral border of the lower jaw. The fibers of the deep layer arise from the entire area of origin, and pass straight to the border of the mandible; it will be noted that a small part, near the temporo-mandibular joint, is not covered by the superficial layer. The two layers are separable only above and behind; elsewhere they are fused.

Relations.—Superficially, the skin and cutaneus muscle, parotid gland, transverse facial and masseteric vessels, and the facial nerve; deeply, the ramus of the mandible, the buccinator and depressor labii inferioris muscles, the superior buccal glands, the buccinator vessels and nerve, and the vena reflexa, which joins the facial vein at the anterior edge of the muscle. The facial vessels and parotid duct run along the anterior edge of the muscle, but the duct inclines forward about the middle of the border and leaves the muscle.

Blood-supply.—Transverse facial and masseteric arteries.

Nerve-supply.—Mandibular nerve.

2. **Temporalis.**—This muscle occupies the temporal fossa.

Origin.—The rough part of the temporal fossa and the crests which limit it.

Insertion.—The coronoid process of the mandible, which it envelops.

Action.—Chiefly to raise the lower jaw, acting with the masseter and medial pterygoid muscles.

Structure.—The surface of the muscle is covered with a glistening aponeurosis, and strong tendinous intersections are found in its substance. The medial edge of the muscle is quite thin, but as the fibers converge toward the much smaller area of insertion, the muscle becomes nearly an inch thick. It fuses partly with the masseter.

Relations.—Superficially, the scutiform cartilage, the anterior muscles of the external ear, and the auricular and orbital fat; deeply, the temporal fossa and the deep temporal vessels and nerves.

Blood-supply.—Superficial and deep temporal, and posterior meningeal arteries.

Nerve-supply.—Mandibular nerve.

3. **Pterygoideus medialis.**—This muscle occupies a position on the medial surface of the ramus of the mandible similar to that of the masseter laterally.

Origin.—The crest formed by the pterygoid processes of the sphenoid and palatine bones.

Insertion.—The concave medial surface of the broad part of the ramus of the mandible and the medial lip of the ventral border.

Action.—Acting together, to raise the lower jaw; acting singly, to produce also lateral movement of the jaw.

Structure.—The muscle is capable of division into two parts. The principal part is medial, and its fibers are, for the most part, vertical in direction. It contains much tendinous tissue (septa). The smaller portion is lateral to the foregoing, and its fibers are directed downward and backward.

Relations.—Laterally, the ramus of the mandible, the lateral pterygoid muscle, the inferior alveolar vessels and nerve, and the lingual and mylo-hyoid nerves;

medially, the great cornu of the hyoid bone, the pharynx, the larynx, the tensor palati, mylo-hyoideus, digastricus, and stylo-hyoideus muscles, the guttural pouch, the external maxillary vessels, the ninth and twelfth nerves, the mandibular salivary gland, the mandibular and parotid ducts, and the mandibular and pharyngeal lymph-glands.

Blood-supply.—Internal maxillary, masseteric, and inferior alveolar arteries.

Nerve-supply.—Mandibular nerve.

4. **Pterygoideus lateralis.**—This muscle is considerably smaller than the preceding one, and is situated lateral to its upper part.

Origin.—The lateral surface of the pterygoid process of the sphenoid bone.

Insertion.—The medial surface of the neck, the medial part of the anterior border of the condyle of the mandible and the articular disc.

Action.—Acting together, to draw the lower jaw forward; acting singly, to

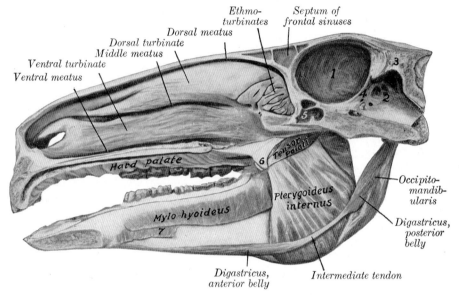

FIG. 264.—SAGITTAL SECTION OF HEAD OF HORSE, SHOWING DEEP PTERYGO-MANDIBULAR REGION AND NASAL AND CRANIAL CAVITIES.

1, Cerebral compartment of cranial cavity; *2*, cerebellar compartment of same; *3*, tentorium osseum; *4*, tentorium cerebelli; *5*, sphenoidal sinus; *6*, hamulus of pterygoid bone-tendon of tensor palati cut off short at anterior border of hamulus; *7*, mylo-glossus. The olfactory mucous membrane is shaded.

move the jaw also toward the side opposite to the muscle acting. The latter action is due to the fact that the origin is nearer to the median plane than the insertion.

Structure.—The muscle is almost entirely fleshy, and the fibers are almost longitudinal in direction. Some of them are inserted into the edge of the articular disc.

Relations.—Laterally, the temporo-mandibular articulation and the temporalis muscle; medially, the medial pterygoid and tensor palati muscles. The internal maxillary artery crosses the ventral face of the muscle and dips in between it and the tensor palati. The mandibular nerve lies on the ventral surface, and the buccinator nerve perforates the origin of the muscle.

Blood-supply.—Internal maxillary and inferior alveolar arteries.

Nerve-supply.—Mandibular nerve.

5. **Occipito-mandibularis.**—This is a short, fusiform muscle extending from

the paramastoid process of the occipital bone to the posterior border of the lower jaw; it is covered by the parotid gland.

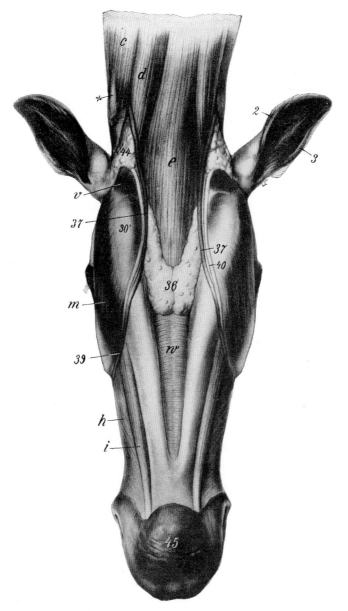

FIG. 265.—MANDIBULAR AND LARYNGEAL REGIONS OF HORSE, AFTER REMOVAL OF SKIN AND CUTANEUS.

c, Brachiocephalicus; *d*, sterno-cephalicus; *e*, omo-hyoideus and sterno-hyoideus; *h*, buccinator; *i*, depressor labii inferioris; *m*, masseter; *v*, occipito-mandibularis; *w*, mylo-hyoideus; *2*, posterior, *3*, anterior, border of external ear; *30'*, angle of jaw; *36*, mandibular lymph-glands; *37*, external maxillary vein; *39*, facial continuation of *37*; *40*, parotid duct; *44*, parotid gland; *45*, prominence of chin; *x*, wing of atlas. (After Ellenberger-Baum, Anat. für Künstler.)

Origin.—The paramastoid process of the occipital bone, in common with the posterior belly of the digastricus.

Insertion.—The posterior border of the ramus of the mandible.

Action.—To depress the lower jaw and open the mouth.

Structure.—The muscle contains a good deal of tendinous tissue. It blends with the posterior belly of the digastricus.

Relations.—Superficially, the parotid gland, the tendon of the sterno-cephalicus and the fibrous expansion which connects it with the tendon of the brachiocephalicus; deeply, the guttural pouch, the external carotid artery, the glosso-pharyngeal and hypoglossal nerves, the pharynx, and the mandibular salivary gland.

Blood-supply.—External carotid artery.

Nerve-supply.—Facial nerve.

6. **Digastricus.**—This muscle is composed of two fusiform, flattened bellies, united by a round tendon.

Origin.—The paramastoid process of the occipital bone, in common with the preceding muscle.

Insertion.—The medial surface of the ventral border of the molar part of the ramus of the mandible.

Action.—It assists in depressing the lower jaw and opening the mouth. If the mandible be fixed and both bellies contract, the hyoid bone and the base of the tongue are raised, as in the first phase of deglutition.

Structure.—The posterior belly has the appearance of a branch detached from the medial surface of the occipito-mandibularis. It passes downward and forward, and is succeeded by a small rounded tendon. The latter perforates the tendon of insertion of the stylo-hyoideus, and is provided with a **synovial sheath.** The anterior belly is larger and terminates by thin, tendinous bundles.

Relations.—The posterior belly has practically the same relations as the occipito-mandibularis. The intermediate tendon is in contact laterally with the medial pterygoid muscle, the mandibular gland and duct, and the external maxillary artery. The anterior belly lies in the mandibular space between the ramus of the jaw and the mylo-hyoideus muscle; the sublingual vessels run along its dorsal border.

Blood-supply.—External carotid and sublingual arteries.

Nerve-supply.—Facial and mandibular nerves.

THE HYOID MUSCLES

This group consists of eight muscles (Mm. ossis hyoidei), one of which, the hyoideus transversus, is unpaired.

1. **Mylo-hyoideus.**—This muscle, together with its fellow, forms a sort of sling between the rami of the mandible, in which the tongue is supported.

Origin.—The medial surface of the alveolar border of the mandible.

Insertion.—(1) A median fibrous raphé extending from the symphysis to the hyoid bone; (2) the lingual process, body, and thyroid cornu of the hyoid bone.

Action.—It raises the floor of the mouth, the tongue, and the hyoid bone.

Structure.—Each muscle consists of a thin curved sheet, the fibers passing ventrally from their origin and then curving toward the median raphé. It is chiefly fleshy, and is thickest behind. There is a tendinous intersection between this muscle and the omo-hyoideus, to which both muscles are attached. The anterior superficial part of the muscle is termed the mylo-glossus.

Relations.—On the superficial surface of the muscles are the ramus, the medial pterygoid and digastricus muscles, and the mandibular lymph-glands. The deep surface is in contact with the mucous membrane of the mouth, the stylo-glossus, hyo-glossus, and genio-hyoideus muscles, the sublingual gland and vessels, the mandibular duct, and the lingual and hypoglossal nerves. The sublingual vein passes through the posterior part.

Blood-supply.—Sublingual artery.

Nerve-supply.—Mylo-hyoid branch of the mandibular nerve.

2. **Stylo-hyoideus.**—This is a slender, fusiform muscle, having a direction nearly parallel to that of the great cornu of the hyoid bone (Fig. 332).

Origin.—The muscular angle of the dorsal extremity of the great cornu of the hyoid bone.

Insertion.—The anterior part of the thyroid cornu of the hyoid bone.

Action.—It draws the base of the tongue and the larynx upward and backward.

Structure.—It arises by a thin, short tendon, and has a fusiform belly. The tendon of insertion is perforated for the passage of the intermediate tendon of the digastricus, and at this point there is a small synovial sheath.

Relations.—Superficially, the medial pterygoid muscle and the parotid gland; deeply, the guttural pouch, the pharynx, the external carotid and maxillary arteries, and the hypoglossal nerve.

Blood-supply.—External carotid artery.

Nerve-supply.—Facial nerve (stylo-hyoid branch).

In rare cases an anomalous arrangement is present in which the stylo-hyoideus is not attached to the thyroid cornu but is continuous with the intermediate tendon of the digastricus, and no fibrous ring is formed. The posterior belly of the digastricus is inserted chiefly on the thyroid cornu, but also sends a delicate tendinous slip to the intermediate tendon.

3. **Occipito-hyoideus.**—This is a small triangular muscle, which lies in the space between the paramastoid process and the great cornu of the hyoid bone.

Origin.—The paramastoid process of the occipital bone.

Insertion.—The dorsal extremity and ventral edge of the great cornu of the hyoid bone.

Action.—It carries the ventral extremity of the great cornu backward.

Structure.—The muscle is somewhat triangular, its fibers being longer as the ventral border is approached. It blends with the posterior belly of the digastricus.

Relations.—Superficially, the parotid gland; deeply, the guttural pouch.

Blood-supply.—Occipital artery.

Nerve-supply.—Facial nerve.

4. **Genio-hyoideus.**—This is a long, spindle-shaped muscle, which lies under the tongue in contact with its fellow of the opposite side (Figs. 330, 333).

Origin.—A small depression on the medial surface of the ramus of the mandible, close to the symphysis.

Insertion.—The extremity of the lingual process of the hyoid bone.

Action.—It draws the hyoid bone and tongue forward.

Structure.—The muscle arises by a short tendon, which is succeeded by the belly, composed of long bundles of parallel fibers.

Relations.—Ventrally, the mylo-hyoideus; dorsally, the hyo-glossus, styloglossus, genio-glossus, the sublingual gland, mandibular duct, and the lingual nerve.

Blood-supply.—Sublingual artery.

Nerve-supply.—Hypoglossal nerve.

5. **Kerato-hyoideus.**—This small triangular muscle lies in the space between the thyroid and small cornu, under cover of the hyo-glossus (Figs. 332, 333).

Origin.—The posterior edge of the small cornu and the adjacent part of the ventral border of the great cornu.

Insertion.—The dorsal edge of the thyroid cornu.

Action.—It raises the thyroid cornu and the larynx.

Relations.—The muscle is crossed laterally by the lingual artery.

Blood-supply.—Lingual artery.

Nerve-supply.—Glosso-pharyngeal nerve.

6. **Hyoideus transversus.**—This is a small, unpaired muscle, which extends transversely between the two small cornua of the hyoid bone.

Attachments.—The small cornua close to the junction with the great cornua.

Action.—When relaxed its dorsal surface is concave; when it contracts, it elevates the root of the tongue.

Structure.—Fleshy, composed of parallel transverse bundles.

Blood-supply.—Lingual artery.

Nerve-supply.—Glosso-pharyngeal nerve.

7. **Sterno-thyro-hyoideus,** and

8. **Omo-hyoideus.**—These are described with the muscles on the ventral surface of the neck (p. 270).

THE FASCIÆ AND MUSCLES OF THE NECK

It is convenient to divide the muscles of the neck (Mm. colli) into ventral and lateral groups, the two lateral groups being separated from each other by the ligamentum nuchæ.

THE FASCIÆ OF THE NECK

The **superficial fascia** is in part two-layered, and contains the cervical cutaneous muscle. The fasciæ of the right and left sides are attached along the dorsal line of the neck to the ligamentum nuchæ, while along the ventral line they meet in a fibrous raphé. A deep layer is detached which passes underneath the cutaneous muscle, bridges over the jugular furrow, and crosses over the deep face of the brachiocephalicus and omo-hyoideus to join the superficial layer. It again separates to pass under the cervical trapezius, and become attached to the ligamentum nuchæ. Along the ventral line a septum is detached which separates the sterno-cephalici. Two other layers in front of the shoulder enclose the prescapular lymph-glands.

The **deep fascia** also forms two layers. The **superficial layer** is attached to the wing of the atlas and the ventral edge of the longissimus capitis et atlantis and scalenus. Passing downward it encloses the trachea, and, together with the deep layer, furnishes sheaths for the vagus and sympathetic nerves and the carotid artery. Passing upward it detaches septa between the extensor muscles of the spine. Anteriorly it covers the thyroid gland, the guttural pouch, the adjacent vessels and nerves, and the larynx, and is attached to the mastoid process of the temporal bone and the thyroid cornu of the hyoid bone. Posteriorly it is attached to the first rib and the cariniform cartilage of the sternum. The **deep layer** (prevertebral fascia) covers the ventral surface of the longus colli, and encloses the trachea and œsophagus. Anteriorly it forms, with the corresponding layer of the opposite side, a septum between the guttural pouches; posteriorly it becomes continuous with the endothoracic fascia. A **fascia propria** forms a tubular sheath around the trachea, enclosing also the recurrent nerves.

VENTRAL CERVICAL MUSCLES

This group consists of twelve pairs of muscles which lie ventral and lateral to the vertebræ.

1. **Cutaneus colli.**—This has been described (p. 256).

2. **Brachiocephalicus.**—This is described on p. 296.

3. **Sterno-cephalicus.**[1]—This is a long, narrow muscle which extends along the ventral and lateral aspects of the trachea from the sternum to the angle of the jaw. It forms the ventral boundary of the jugular furrow.

---

[1] This muscle is probably the homologue of the sternal part of the sterno-cleido-mastoid of man. On account of the differences in its insertion in the various animals, it seems desirable to adopt the name sterno-cephalicus. It is also known as the sterno-mandibularis.

Origin.—The cariniform cartilage of the sternum.

Insertion.—The posterior border of the ramus of the mandible.

Action.—Acting together, to flex the head and neck; acting singly, to incline the head and neck to the side of the muscle contracting.

Structure.—The two muscles are fused at their origin, which is fleshy. Near

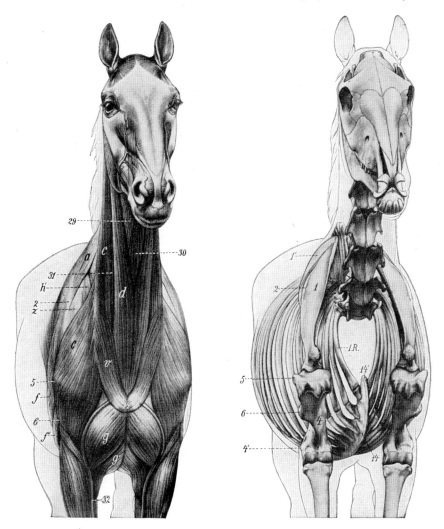

Fig. 266.—Antero-lateral View of Muscles and Skeleton of Horse.

a, Trapezius; *c*, brachiocephalicus; *d*, sterno-cephalicus; *f*, long head of triceps; *f'*, lateral head of triceps; *g*, anterior superficial pectoral muscle; *g'*, posterior superficial pectoral; *h'*, anterior deep pectoral; *v*, cutaneus colli; *z*, supraspinatus; *29*, omo-hyoideus; *30*, sterno-thyro-hyoideus; *31*, jugular vein; *32*, cephalic vein; *1*, scapula; *1'*, cartilage of scapula; *2*, spine of scapula; *4*, shaft of humerus; *4'* lateral epicondyle; *5*, lateral tuberosity of humerus; *6*, deltoid tuberosity; *14*, ventral border ("keel") of sternum; *14'*, cariniform cartilage; *1.R.*, first rib. (After Ellenberger-Baum, Anat. für Künstler.)

the middle of the neck they separate, and, becoming narrower and thinner, each muscle passes under the parotid gland and terminates by a flat tendon. The latter is connected by a thin aponeurosis with that of the brachiocephalicus.

Relations.—Superficially, the cutaneous muscle; deeply, the sterno-thyro-hyoideus and omo-hyoideus muscles. The dorsal edge of the muscle is related to the jugular vein, which lies in the jugular furrow. The carotid artery, the vagus, sympathetic, and recurrent nerves also lie along the upper edge at the root of the neck. The tendon passes under the external maxillary vein and the parotid gland, having the mandibular gland and occipito-mandibularis muscle on its medial side.

Blood-supply.—Carotid artery.

Nerve-supply.—Ventral branch of the spinal accessory nerve.

4. **Sterno-thyro-hyoideus** (Sterno-thyreoideus et sterno-hyoideus).—This is a long, slender, digastric muscle, applied to the ventral surface of the trachea and its fellow of the opposite side.

Origin.—The cariniform cartilage of the sternum.

Insertion.—(1) A prominence on the posterior border of the lamina of the thyroid cartilage of the larynx at the ventral end of the oblique line; (2) the body and lingual process of the hyoid bone.

Action.—To retract and depress the hyoid bone, the base of the tongue, and the larynx, as in deglutition. It may also fix the hyoid bone when the depressors of the tongue are acting, as in sucking.

Structure.—The origin of the muscle is fleshy, and as far as the middle of the neck, it blends with its fellow. The common belly is then interrupted by a tendon, or sometimes two tendons, from which arise three or four fleshy bands. The lateral small bands (Sterno-thyroidei) diverge to reach their insertion into the thyroid cartilage by a delicate tendon; while the medial and larger bands (Sterno-hyoidei), closely applied to each other and blending with the omo-hyoideus, pass straight forward to reach the ventral surface of the hyoid bone.

Relations.—At the root of the neck the common belly is related ventrally to the sterno-cephalicus, and the carotid arteries and recurrent nerves dorsally. Further forward the trachea becomes the dorsal relation, and near the head the omo-hyoideus, skin and fascia, the ventral one.

Blood-supply.—Carotid artery.

Nerve-supply.—Ventral branches of the first and second cervical nerves.

5. **Omo-hyoideus.**[1]—This is a thin, ribbon-like muscle, almost entirely fleshy, which crosses the trachea very obliquely.

Origin.—The subscapular fascia close to the shoulder joint.

Insertion.—The body and adjacent part of the lingual process of the hyoid bone, in common with the hyoid branch of the preceding muscle.

Action.—To retract the hyoid bone and the root of the tongue.

Structure.—The muscle is composed of parallel fleshy fibers, except at its origin, where it has a thin tendon.

Relations.—The posterior part of the muscle is related laterally to the supraspinatus, anterior deep pectoral, and brachiocephalicus and the prescapular lymphglands; and medially to the scalenus. It is intimately adherent to the brachiocephalicus. In the middle of the neck it is related superficially to the brachiocephalicus, sterno-cephalicus, and the jugular vein; deeply, to the rectus capitis ventralis major, the carotid artery, the vagus, sympathetic, and recurrent nerves, the trachea, and, on the left side, the œsophagus. In its anterior part the muscle blends with the sterno-hyoideus, the two covering the sterno-thyroideus, the thyroid gland in part, and the ventral face of the larynx.

Blood-supply.—Carotid and inferior cervical arteries.

Nerve-supply.—Ventral branch of the first cervical nerve.

6. **Scalenus** (M. scalenus primæ costæ).—This muscle is deeply situated on the side of the posterior half of the neck. It is composed of two parts, between which the cervical roots of the brachial plexus of nerves emerge.

Origin.—The anterior border and lateral surface of the first rib.

Insertion.—(1) The dorsal (smaller) part (M. scalenus dorsalis) is attached to the transverse process of the seventh cervical vertebra; (2) the ventral part (M.

---

[1] Also termed the subscapulo-hyoideus.

scalenus ventralis) is attached to the transverse processes of the sixth, fifth, and fourth cervical vertebræ.

Action.—The neck is flexed or inclined laterally, according as the muscles act together or singly. If the neck be the fixed point, the muscle may have a respiratory action by pulling forward or fixing the first rib.

Structure.—The dorsal part is composed of several small fleshy bundles. The ventral portion, which is much larger, is almost entirely fleshy, and not so divided.

Relations.—Superficially, the anterior deep pectoral, brachiocephalicus, and omo-hyoideus muscles, the phrenic nerve, and branches of the brachial plexus; deeply, the vertebræ, the longus colli and intertransversales muscles, the œsophagus (on the left side), the trachea (on the right side), the vertebral vessels, the vagus, sympathetic, and recurrent nerves. The roots of the brachial plexus form a flat anastomosis, which lies between the two parts of the muscle. The brachial vessels cross the ventral edge close to the first rib.

Blood-supply.—Carotid, vertebral, and inferior cervical arteries.

Nerve-supply.—Ventral branches of the cervical nerves.

7. Cervicalis ascendens.[1]—This muscle is the cervical continuation of the longissimus costarum, and is sometimes regarded as a part of the scalenus, with which it is partially united. It consists of three or four bundles which are attached to the transverse processes of the last three or four cervical vertebræ and the first rib.

Action.—To extend the neck or to flex it laterally.

Relations.—Superficially, the brachiocephalicus and anterior deep pectoral; deeply, the scalenus and intertransversales.

Blood-supply.—Vertebral artery.

Nerve-supply.—Cervical nerves.

8. Rectus capitis ventralis major (M. longus capitis).—This is the largest of the three special flexors of the head, and lies along the ventro-lateral surface of the anterior cervical vertebræ and the base of the cranium.

Origin.—The transverse processes of the fifth, fourth, and third cervical vertebræ.

Insertion.—The tubercles at the junction of the basilar part of the occipital bone with the body of the sphenoid.

Action.—Acting together, to flex the head; acting singly, to incline it to the same side also.

Structure.—The origin of the muscle is by fleshy digitations. The belly increases in size by the union of these digitations, reaching its maximum at the axis. It then diminishes, passes toward the median plane, and terminates on a rounded tendon.

Relations.—Superficially, the brachiocephalicus and omo-hyoideus, the mandibular gland, the carotid artery (which lies along the ventral border), the occipital and internal carotid arteries, and the tenth, eleventh, and sympathetic nerves; deeply, the vertebræ, the longus colli, intertransversales, and the rectus capitis ventralis minor. The terminal part of the muscle lies in contact with its fellow above the pharynx and between the guttural pouches.

Blood-supply.—Carotid, vertebral, and occipital arteries.

Nerve-supply.—Ventral branches of the cervical nerves.

9. Rectus capitis ventralis minor (M. rectus capitis ventralis).—This is a small muscle which lies dorsal to and under cover of the preceding one.

Origin.—The ventral arch of the atlas.

Insertion.—The basilar part of the occipital bone, close to the preceding muscle.

Action.—To flex the atlanto-occipital articulation.

Structure.—Fleshy.

---

[1] This muscle is also known as the ilio-costalis cervicis.

Relations.—Ventrally, to the preceding muscle; dorsally, to the atlas, atlanto-occipital articulation, and the basilar part of the occipital bone; laterally, to the rectus capitis lateralis and the guttural pouch.

Blood-supply.—Occipital artery.

Nerve-supply.—Ventral branch of the first cervical nerve.

10. **Rectus capitis lateralis.**—This is a still smaller muscle, which lies for the most part under the obliquus capitis anterior.

Origin.—The atlas, lateral to the preceding muscle.

Insertion.—The paramastoid process of the occipital bone.

Action.—The same as the preceding muscle.

Structure.—Fleshy.

Relations.—Superficially, the obliquus capitis anterior, the occipital vessels, and the ventral branch of the first cervical nerve.

Blood-supply.—Occipital artery.

Nerve-supply.—Ventral branch of the first cervical nerve.

11. **Longus colli.**—This muscle covers the ventral surfaces of the vertebræ from the fifth or sixth thoracic to the atlas, and is united with its fellow. It consists of two parts, thoracic and cervical.

Origin.—(1) Thoracic part, the bodies of the first five or six thoracic vertebræ; (2) cervical part, the transverse processes of the cervical vertebræ.

Insertion.—(1) Thoracic part, the bodies and transverse processes of the last two cervical vertebræ; (2) cervical part, the bodies of the cervical vertebræ and the ventral tubercle of the atlas.

Action.—To flex the neck.

Structure.—The muscle is composed of a succession of bundles. The largest of these constitute the thoracic part of the muscle, which has a strong tendon inserted into the last two cervical vertebræ. A bursa is interposed between the tendon and the spine at the first costo-vertebral articulation. The cervical part consists of a number of smaller bundles, each of which passes from its origin on the transverse process of one vertebra forward and medially to its insertion into a vertebra further forward. The most anterior bundle is inserted by a strong tendon into the ventral tubercle of the atlas.

Relations.—The principal relations of the two muscles in the thorax are: ventrally, the pleura, and, further forward, the trachea and œsophagus; dorsally, the vertebræ and the costo-vertebral joints; laterally, the dorsal, deep cervical, and vertebral vessels, the sympathetic nerve, and the thoracic roots of the brachial plexus. In the neck important relations are: ventrally, the trachea and œsophagus, the carotid artery, the vago-sympathetic nerve trunk; dorsally, the vertebræ and, in the middle third of the neck, the intertransversales muscles; laterally, the scalenus, the rectus capitis ventralis major, and the intertransversales (in the anterior third). The terminal part of the muscle is separated from the trachea by the œsophagus, which is here median in position.

Blood-supply.—Subcostal and vertebral arteries.

Nerve-supply.—Ventral branches of the spinal nerves.

12. **Intertransversales colli** (Mm. intertransversarii cervicis).—These are six fasciculi which occupy the spaces between the lateral aspects of the vertebræ and the transverse and articular processes. There is thus a bundle for each intervertebral articulation except the first. Each bundle consists of a dorsal and ventral part.

Attachments.—The dorsal bundles pass from transverse process to articular process; the ventral bundles extend between adjacent transverse processes.

Action.—To flex the neck laterally.

Structure.—They contain strong tendinous intersections.

Relations.—Superficially, the brachiocephalicus, rectus capitis ventralis major, obliquus capitis posterior, complexus, longissimus capitis et atlantis, splenius, scalenus, and longissimus dorsi et costarum muscles; deeply, the vertebræ, the longus colli muscle, and the vertebral vessels. The muscles are perforated by branches of these vessels and by the primary branches of the cervical nerves.

Blood-supply.—Vertebral artery.

Nerve-supply.—The cervical nerves.

LATERAL CERVICAL MUSCLES

This group consists of twelve pairs of muscles arranged in layers.

FIRST LAYER

1. **Trapezius cervicalis.**—Described on p. 295.

SECOND LAYER

2. **Rhomboideus cervicalis.**—Described on p. 295.
3. **Serratus cervicis.**—Described on p. 299.

THIRD LAYER

4. **Splenius.**—This is an extensive, flat, triangular muscle, partly covered by the preceding three muscles.

Origin.—The third, fourth, and fifth thoracic spines by means of the dorso-scapular ligament and the funicular part of the ligamentum nuchæ.

Insertion.—The nuchal crest, the mastoid process, the wing of the atlas, and the transverse processes of the third, fourth, and fifth cervical vertebræ.

Action.—Acting together, to elevate the head and neck; acting singly, to incline the head and neck to the side of the muscle acting.

Structure.—The muscle arises in the withers from the anterior part of the dorso-scapular ligament, which also affords attachment to the rhomboideus, serratus dorsalis, and complexus muscles. The fibers pass upward and forward toward the head and the first cervical vertebra. The insertion on the occipital bone and the mastoid process is by means of a thin aponeurosis common to the brachiocephalicus and longissimus capitis. The atlantal insertion is by a strong, flat tendon, in common with the longissimus atlantis and the brachiocephalicus. The remaining insertions are fleshy digitations.

Relations.—Superficially, the skin and fascia, the trapezius, rhomboideus cervicalis, serratus ventralis, and posterior auricular muscles· deeply the complexus and longissimus dorsi muscles.

Blood-supply.—Deep cervical and dorsal arteries.

Nerve-supply.—Dorsal branches of the last six cervical nerves.

FOURTH LAYER

5. **Longissimus capitis et atlantis.**—This muscle consists of two parallel, fusiform portions. It lies between the deep face of the splenius and the ventral part of the complexus.

Origin.—(1) The transverse processes of the first two thoracic vertebræ; (2) the articular processes of the cervical vertebræ.

Insertion.—(1) The mastoid process; (2) the wing of the atlas.

Action.—Acting together, to extend the head and neck; acting singly, to flex the head and neck laterally or to rotate the atlas.

Structure.—The origin from the thoracic vertebræ is by aponeurotic slips which blend with the complexus. The succeeding fleshy part, in passing along the neck, receives fasciculi from each of the cervical vertebræ except the first two. The dorsal division of the muscle (M. longissimus capitis) is inserted into the mastoid process by a flat tendon which fuses with that of the splenius; the ventral division (M. longissimus atlantis) is inserted into the

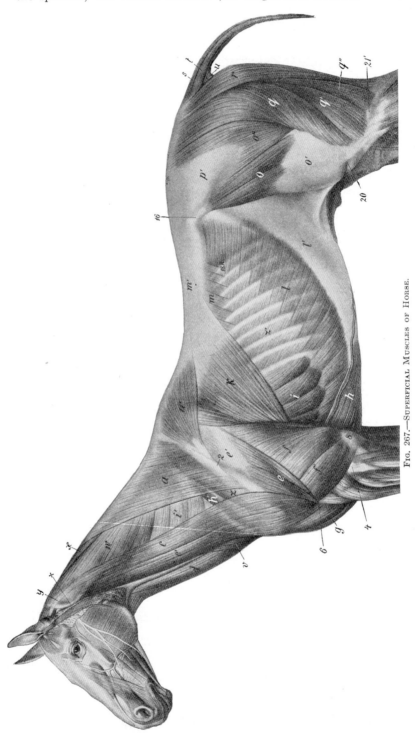

Fig. 267.—Superficial Muscles of Horse.

The cutaneus muscle, except the cervical part, has been removed. *a*, Trapezius cervicalis; *a'*, trapezius thoracalis; *c*, *c'*, brachiocephalicus; *e*, deltoid; *f*, long head of triceps; *f'*, lateral head of triceps; *g*, anterior superficial pectoral; *h*, posterior deep pectoral; *h'*, anterior deep pectoral; *i'*, serratus cervicis; *k*, latissimus dorsi; *l*, obliquus abdominis externus; *l'*, aponeurosis of *l*; *m*, serratus dorsalis; *m'*, lumbo-dorsal fascia; *o*, tensor fasciæ latæ; *o'*, fascia lata; *o''*, gluteus superficialis; *p'*, gluteal fascia; *q*, *q'*, *q''*, biceps femoris; *r*, semitendinosus; *s*, sacro-coccygeus dorsalis; *t*, sacro-coccygeus lateralis; *u*, coccygeus; *v*, cervical cutaneus muscle; *w*, splenius; *x*, rhomboideus; *y*, tendon of longissimus capitis et atlantis and brachiocephalicus; *z*, supraspinatus; *z'*, external intercostal; ✕, wing of atlas; *2*, spine of scapula; *4'*, lateral epicondyle of humerus; *6*, deltoid tuberosity; *8*, olecranon; *16*, tuber coxæ; *20*, patella; *21'*, lateral condyle of tibia. The tensor fasciæ antibrachii, which projects behind the long head of the triceps (*f*), is shown but not marked. (After Ellenberger-Baum, Anat. für Künstler.)

wing of the atlas by a ribbon-like tendon in common with the splenius and brachiocephalicus.

Relations.—Superficially, the splenius muscle and dorsal branches of the cervical nerves; deeply, the complexus, the spinalis colli, and the oblique muscles of the head. The deep cervical vessels cross the deep face of the muscle obliquely at the level of the sixth and seventh cervical vertebræ.

Blood-supply.—Vertebral and deep cervical arteries.

Nerve-supply.—Dorsal branches of the last six cervical nerves.

6. **Complexus** (M. semispinalis capitis).—This is a large triangular muscle which lies chiefly on the ligamentum nuchæ, under cover of the splenius.

Origin.—(1) The third, fourth, and fifth thoracic spines by means of the dorso-scapular ligament; (2) transverse processes of the first six or seven thoracic vertebræ; (3) the articular processes of the cervical vertebræ.

Insertion.—A rough area on the occipital bone just ventral to the nuchal crest.

Action.—It is the chief extensor of the head and neck. Acting singly, the muscle inclines the head to the same side.

Structure.—The muscle consists of two parts, which are, however, largely fused. The dorsal part (M. biventer cervicis) has an aponeurotic origin at the withers and is crossed by four or five oblique tendinous intersections. The ventral part (M. complexus) is pennate and consists of bundles which arise from the transverse processes of the first six or seven thoracic vertebræ and the articular processes of the cervical vertebræ and run obliquely forward and upward. The insertion is by a strong tendon.

Relations.—Superficially, the rhomboideus, serratus ventralis, splenius, and longissimus capitis et atlantis; deeply, the ligamentum nuchæ, the multifidus cervicis, longissimus dorsi, and the oblique and dorsal straight muscles of the head, the deep cervical vessels, and the dorsal cutaneous branches of the cervical nerves.

Blood-supply.—Deep cervical, vertebral, and occipital arteries.

Nerve-supply.—Dorsal branches of the last six cervical nerves.

7. **Multifidus cervicis.**—This muscle lies on the arches of the last five cervical vertebræ. It consists of five or six segments.

Origin.—The articular processes of the last four or five cervical and the first thoracic vertebræ.

Insertion.—The spinous and articular processes of the cervical vertebræ.

Action.—Acting together, to extend the neck; acting singly, to flex the neck on the side of the muscle contracting and to rotate the neck to the opposite side.

Structure.—The muscle is composed of two sets of bundles. The superficial bundles are directed obliquely forward and inward, each passing from an articular process to the spine of the preceding vertebra. The deep bundles are shorter and run straight from an articular process to that of the preceding vertebra.

Relations.—Superficially, the complexus, longissimi, and obliquus capitis posterior; deeply, the spinalis, the ligamentum nuchæ, and the arches of the vertebræ.

Blood-supply.—Deep cervical and vertebral arteries.

Nerve-supply.—Dorsal branches of the last six cervical nerves.

8. **Spinalis.**—Described with the longissimus on p. 280.

9. **Obliquus capitis posterior** (s. caudalis).—This is a strong, quadrilateral muscle, which covers the dorso-lateral aspect of the atlas and axis.

Origin.—The side of the spine and the posterior articular process of the axis.

Insertion.—The dorsal surface of the wing of the atlas.

Action.—Chiefly to rotate the atlas, and with it the head, to the same side; also to assist in extending and fixing the atlanto-axial joint.

Structure.—The muscle is composed almost entirely of parallel fleshy fibers directed obliquely forward and outward. It is covered by a special fascia.

Relations.—Superficially, the splenius, complexus, longissimus capitis, and brachiocephalicus muscles; deeply, the arch and spine of the axis, the wing of the atlas, the atlantoaxial joint, the rectus capitis dorsalis minor, the occipital and vertebral vessels, and the first and second cervical nerves. The terminal part of the vertebral artery joins the posterior branch of the occipital artery under cover of the muscle.

Blood-supply.—Occipital and vertebral arteries.

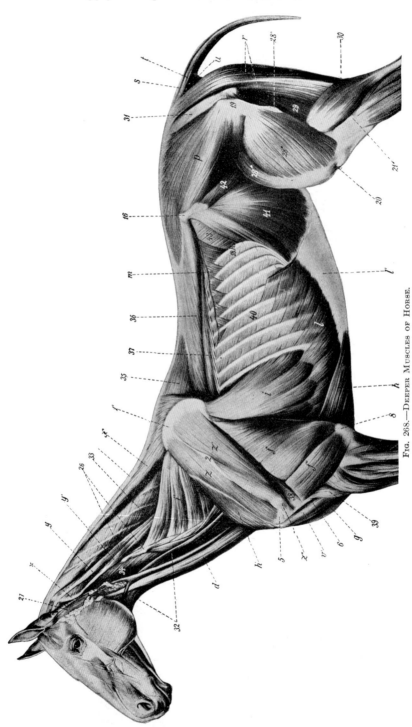

FIG. 268.—DEEPER MUSCLES OF HORSE.

d, Sterno-cephalicus; *f*, long head of triceps; *f'*, lateral head of triceps; *g*, anterior superficial pectoral; *h*, posterior deep pectoral; *h'*, anterior deep pectoral; *i*, serratus thoracis; *i'*, serratus cervicis; *l*, obliquus abdominis externus, and *l'*, its aponeurosis, the posterior part of which has been removed; *m*, serratus dorsalis posterior; *p*, gluteus medius; *r*, semitendinosus; *s*, sacro-coccygeus dorsalis; *t*, sacro-coccygeus lateralis; *u*, coccygeus; *v'*, biceps brachii; *z*, rhomboideus; *y*, *y'*, longissimus capitis et atlantis; *z*, supraspinatus; *z'*, infraspinatus; *z''*, tendon of *z'*; *1'*, cartilage of scapula; *2*, spine of scapula; *5*, lateral tuberosity of humerus; *6*, deltoid tuberosity; *8*, olecranon; *16*, tuber coxæ; *19*, trochanter major; *20*, patella; *21'*, lateral condyle of tibia; *26*, transverse processes of cervical vertebræ; *27*, paratido-auricularis; *28*, vastus lateralis; *28'*, rectus femoris; *28''*, trochanter tertius; *29*, semimembranosus; *30*, gastrocnemius; *31*, sacro-sciatic ligament; *32*, omo-hyoideus; *33*, complexus; *34*, rectus capitis ventralis major; *35*, spinalis dorsi; *36*, longissimus dorsi; *37*, longissimus costarum; *38*, teres minor; *39*, brachialis; *40*, external intercostal; *41*, obliquus abdominis internus; *42*, iliacus; *43*, transversus abdominis. (After Ellenberger-Baum, Anat. für Künstler.)

Nerve-supply.—Dorsal branch of the second cervical nerve.

10. **Obliquus capitis anterior** (s. cranialis).—This short, thick, quadrilateral muscle lies on the side of the atlantooccipital articulation.

Origin.—The anterior edge and ventral surface of the wing of the atlas.

Insertion.—The paramastoid process and nuchal crest of the occipital bone and the mastoid process.

Action.—Acting together, to extend the head on the atlas; acting singly, to flex the head laterally.

Structure.—The muscle contains a good deal of tendinous tissue. The direction of its fibers is forward, upward, and inward.

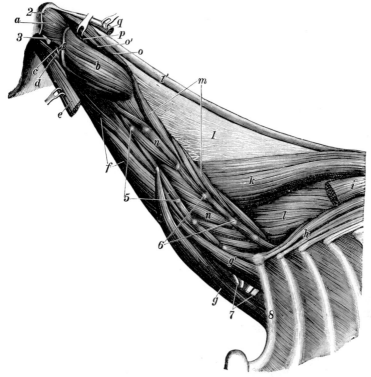

FIG. 269.—DEEPEST LAYER OF MUSCLES OF NECK OF HORSE.

a, Obliquus capitis anterior; *b,* obliquus capitis posterior; *c,* rectus capitis lateralis; *d,* rectus capitis ventralis minor; *e,* rectus capitis ventralis major; *f,* longus colli; *g, g',* scalenus; *h,* longissimus costarum; *i,* longissimus dorsi; *k,* spinalis et semispinalis; *l,* multifidus dorsi; *m,* multifidus cervicis; *n,* intertransversales; *o, o',* rectus capitis dorsalis major; *p,* rectus capitis dorsalis minor; *q,* tendon of insertion of complexus; *1,* lamellar part, *1',* funicular part of ligamentum nuchæ; *2,* nuchal crest; *3,* paramastoid process; *4,* edge of wing of atlas; *5,* transverse, and *6,* articular processes of cervical vertebræ; *7,* nerves of brachial plexus (cut); *8,* first rib. (Ellenberger-Baum, Anat. d. Haustiere.)

Relations.—Superficially, the complexus, the aponeurosis of the splenius, longus capitis, and brachiocephalicus, overlying which are the posterior auricular muscles, artery, and nerve, and the parotid gland; deeply, the dorsal straight muscles, the occipito-hyoideus, the atlanto-occipital articulation, the posterior meningeal artery, and a branch of the occipital nerve.

Blood-supply.—Occipital artery.

Nerve-supply.—Dorsal branch of the first cervical nerve.

11. **Rectus capitis dorsalis major.**—This muscle extends from the axis to the occipital bone, in contact with the ligamentum nuchæ.

Origin.—The edge of the spinous process of the axis.

Insertion.—The occipital bone, below the complexus; the tendon of insertion of the complexus.

Action.—To extend the head.

Structure.—The muscle is fleshy and may be divided into two parallel parts, superficial and deep. The former blends somewhat with the terminal part of the complexus. The deep part may be termed the rectus capitis dorsalis medius. Bundles frequently arise from the fascia over the obliquus capitis posterior.

Relations.—Superficially, the obliquus capitis anterior, splenius, and complexus; medially, the ligamentum nuchæ; deeply, the atlas, the atlanto-occipital articulation, and the rectus capitis dorsalis minor. The dorsal branch of the first cervical nerve appears between this muscle and the obliquus capitis anterior.

Blood-supply.—Occipital artery.

Nerve-supply.—Dorsal branch of the first cervical nerve.

12. **Rectus capitis dorsalis minor.**—This small muscle lies under cover of the preceding.

Origin.—The dorsal surface of the atlas.

Insertion.—The occipital bone beneath the preceding muscle and lateral to the funicular part of the ligamentum nuchæ.

Action.—To assist the preceding muscle.

Structure.—It is fleshy and varies a good deal in volume, being sometimes small and difficult to recognize.[1] On the other hand, it is sometimes double.

Relations.—Superficially, the preceding muscle and the obliquus capitis anterior; deeply, the atlas and the atlanto-occipital articulation.

Blood-supply.—Occipital artery.

Nerve-supply.—Dorsal branch of the first cervical nerve.

THE FASCIÆ AND MUSCLES OF THE BACK AND LOINS
(FASCIÆ ET MUSCULI DORSI ET LUMBORUM)

The **superficial fascia** presents no special features. The **lumbo-dorsal fascia** (Fascia lumbo-dorsalis) closely invests the muscles, but is easily stripped off the longissimus. It is attached medially to the supraspinous ligament and the spinous processes of the vertebræ; it divides laterally into two layers. The superficial layer is practically the aponeurosis of the latissimus dorsi. The deep layer gives origin to the serratus dorsalis, the lumbar part of the obliquus abdominis externus, the transversus abdominis, and the retractor costæ. Its lateral edge curves under the longissimus and is attached to the ribs and lumbar transverse processes. Posteriorly it is continuous with the gluteal fascia. At the withers it forms an important structure, the so-called **dorso-scapular ligament.** This is attached to the third, fourth, and fifth thoracic spines. Its upper part is very thick and gives origin superficially to the rhomboideus thoracalis, deeply to the complexus, and anteriorly to the splenius. The lower part is thin and elastic, and furnishes numerous lamellæ which intersect the scapular part of the serratus ventralis and are attached to the scapula. Three lamellæ are detached from the ligament. The deepest of these passes between the longissimus and spinalis and is attached to the transverse processes of the first seven thoracic vertebræ; it gives attachment to the complexus. The middle one dips in between the longissimus dorsi and longissimus costarum. The superficial one gives origin to the serratus dorsalis. A strong fascial layer, the ilio-lumbar ligament, extends from the last rib to the tuber coxæ.

There are nine pairs of muscles in this region, arranged in four layers.

---

[1] This seems due to pressure produced by pathological changes in the atlantal bursa, and the ligamentum nuchæ which are frequently extensive in dissecting-room subjects.

<h2>First Layer</h2>

1. Trapezius thoracalis.
2. Latissimus dorsi.

<h2>Second Layer</h2>

3. **Rhomboideus thoracalis.**

The foregoing are described with the other muscles which attach the thoracic limb to the trunk (p. 295).

4. **Serratus dorsalis anterior** (s. cranialis).—This is a thin quadrilateral muscle, named from its serrated ventral border. It lies under cover of the rhomboideus, serratus ventralis, and latissimus dorsi.

Origin.—The lumbo-dorsal fascia and dorso-scapular ligament.

Insertion.—The lateral surfaces of the fifth or sixth to the eleventh or twelfth ribs inclusive.

Action.—To draw the ribs on which it is inserted forward and outward, thus assisting in inspiration.

Structure.—The muscle arises by means of a thin aponeurosis. The muscle-fibers pass ventrally and backward to be attached to the ribs by seven or eight digitations below the lateral edge of the longissimus costarum.

Relations.—Superficially, the rhomboideus, serratus ventralis, latissimus dorsi, and serratus dorsalis posterior; deeply, the longissimus dorsi, longissimus costarum, external intercostal muscles, and the ribs.

Blood-supply.—Intercostal arteries.

Nerve-supply.—Thoracic nerves.

5. **Serratus dorsalis posterior** (s. caudalis).—This muscle resembles the preceding one, which it partly covers.

Origin.—The lumbo-dorsal fascia.

Insertion.—The lateral surfaces of the last seven or eight ribs.[1]

Action.—To draw the ribs backward, thus assisting in expiration.

Structure.—Similar to the preceding muscle. The fibers are directed ventrally and forward and terminate in seven or eight digitations, one or two of which cover the posterior teeth of the anterior muscle. The aponeurosis blends with that of the latissimus dorsi.

Relations.—Superficially, the latissimus dorsi and external oblique; deeply, the longissimus dorsi, longissimus costarum, external intercostals, serratus dorsalis anterior, and the ribs.

Blood-supply.—Intercostal and lumbar arteries.

Nerve-supply.—Thoracic nerves.

<h2>Third Layer</h2>

6. **Longissimus costarum.**[2]—This long, segmental muscle extends across the series of ribs, in contact with the outer edge of the longissimus dorsi.

Origin.—(1) The deep layer of the lumbo-dorsal fascia as far back as the third or fourth lumbar transverse process. (2) The anterior borders and lateral surface of the last fifteen ribs.[3]

Insertion.—The posterior borders of the ribs and the transverse processes of the last cervical vertebra.

Action.—Chiefly to depress and retract the ribs and so help in expiration.

---

[1] There may be nine digitations, especially if a nineteenth rib is present.

[2] This muscle is also known as the long costal, ilio-costalis, or transversalis costarum.

[3] The lumbar part of this muscle is subject to variation. It may, in quite exceptional cases, extend as far as the ilium, and sometimes, on the other hand, it does not arise quite so far back as given above. In some subjects the origin can be traced distinctly to the tips of lumbar transverse processes.

Acting together, they may assist in extending the spine, acting singly in inclining it laterally.

Structure.—This muscle presents a distinct segmental arrangement. It is composed of a series of bundles, the fibers of which are directed forward and a little ventro-laterally. From these are detached two sets of tendons. The superficial tendons spring from the lateral edge of the muscle. They are flat and each crosses two or three intercostal spaces, to be inserted on the posterior border of a rib. The deep tendons are detached from the dorsal part of the deep face of the muscle. Each passes backward across one or two intercostal spaces to its origin on the anterior border or lateral surface of a rib. Small bursæ may be found between the ribs and tendons.

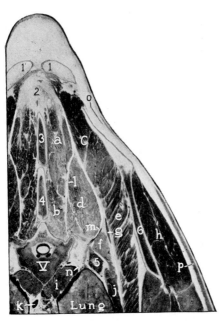

FIG. 270.—RIGHT PORTION OF CROSS-SECTION OF WITHERS OF HORSE. SECTION CUT THROUGH FIFTH THORACIC VERTEBRA.

1, 1, Ligamentum nuchæ; 2, summit of second thoracic spine; 3, 4, sections of spinous processes of third and fourth thoracic vertebræ; 5, fifth rib; *V*, fifth thoracic vertebra; 6, scapula; *a*, spinalis; *b*, multifidus; *c*, rhomboideus; *d*, longissimus dorsi; *e*, serratus ventralis; *f*, levator costæ; *g*, serratus dorsalis; *h*, infraspinatus; *i*, longus colli; *j*, external intercostal; *k*, ductus thoracis; *l*, tendon of complexus; *m*, middle layer of lumbo-dorsal fascia; *n*, sympathetic trunk; *o*, trapezius; *p*, omo-brachialis.

Relations.—Superficially, the dorsal and ventral serrati; deeply, the external intercostals and the ribs. The lumbar origin is covered by the longissimus dorsi. The deep cervical and dorsal vessels cross the surface of the muscle at the first and second intercostal spaces respectively, and branches of the intercostal vessels and nerves emerge between it and the longissimus dorsi; here a fascial layer dips in between the two.

Blood-supply.—Intercostal arteries.

Nerve-supply.—Thoracic nerves.

7. Longissimus dorsi.[1]—This is the largest and longest muscle in the body. It extends from the sacrum and ilium to the neck, filling up the space between the spinous processes medially and the lumbar transverse processes and the upper ends of the ribs ventrally; consequently it has the form of a three-sided prism.

Origin.—(1) The tubera, crest, and adjacent part of the ventral surface of the ilium; (2) the first three sacral spines; (3) the lumbar and thoracic spines and the supraspinous ligament.

Insertion.—(1) The lumbar transverse and articular processes; (2) the thoracic transverse processes; (3) the spinous and transverse processes of the last four cervical vertebræ; (4) the lateral surfaces of the ribs, except the first.

Action.—Acting with its fellow, it is the most powerful extensor of the back and loins; by its cervical attachment it assists in extending the neck. By its costal attachment it may also assist in expiration. Acting singly, it flexes the spine laterally.

Structure.—This is quite complex. The posterior part of the muscle is greatly developed and constitutes the common mass of the loins. This is covered by a strong aponeurosis which blends with the supraspinous and sacro-iliac ligaments, and is attached to the crest and sacral angle of the ilium and the first and second sacral spines; it furnishes origin to the lumbar portion of the middle gluteus. In

[1] The muscle as here described includes the longissimus dorsi et cervicis and the spinalis and semispinalis components, as the separation of these is largely artificial in the horse.

its course further forward the muscle receives fasciculi from the lumbar and thoracic spines, but diminishes somewhat in volume. About the twelfth thoracic vertebra it divides into two parts. The **dorsal division** (M. spinalis et semispinalis dorsi), reinforced by bundles from the first four thoracic spines, passes forward under the semispinalis capitis to be inserted into the spines of the last four cervical vertebræ. The **ventral division** (M. longissimus cervicis) passes forward and downward underneath the serratus ventralis to be inserted into the ribs and the transverse processes of the last four cervical vertebræ. This division arises in part from the thin tendon of the semispinalis capitis attached to the transverse processes. Three sets of fasciculi may be distinguished, viz.: (1) spinal, which are superficial and medial; (2) transverse, attached to the transverse and articular processes, which are medial and deep; (3) costal, which are lateral.

Relations.—Superficially, the middle gluteus, the lumbo-dorsal fascia, the latissimus dorsi, serratus dorsalis, serratus ventralis, and complexus; deeply, the multifidus, intertransversales, external intercostals, levatores costarum, the ligamentum nuchæ, and its fellow of the opposite side (in the neck).

Blood-supply.—Dorsal, deep cervical, intercostal, and lumbar arteries.

Nerve-supply.—Dorsal branches of the thoracic and lumbar nerves.

8. Multifidus dorsi.—This is a long segmental muscle which lies along the sides of the spinous processes of the vertebræ from the sacrum to the neck.

Origin.—(1) The lateral part of the sacrum; (2) the articular processes of the lumbar vertebræ; (3) the transverse processes of the thoracic vertebræ.

Insertion.—The spinous processes of the first two sacral, the lumbar, thoracic, and last cervical vertebræ.

Action.—Acting with its fellow, it is an extensor of the spine; acting singly, it flexes it laterally.

Structure.—It is composed of a series of bundles which are directed obliquely forward and upward. Each fasciculus passes over several vertebræ to its insertion. In the posterior part of the series the bundles cross two or three vertebræ and are inserted into the summits of the spines. From the twelfth thoracic vertebra forward the bundles have a more horizontal direction and are inserted on the sides of the spines below their summits. A further complication consists in the fusion of several bundles into a common insertion.

Relations.—Superficially, the longissimus dorsi; deeply, the vertebral spines.

Blood-supply.—Intercostal and lumbar arteries.

Nerve-supply.—Dorsal branches of the thoracic and lumbar nerves.

9. Intertransversales lumborum.—These are very thin muscular and tendinous strata, which occupy the spaces between the transverse processes of the lumbar vertebræ except the fifth and sixth.

Action.—To assist in flexing the loins laterally or in rendering the region rigid.

Relations.—Superficially, the longissimus dorsi; deeply, the quadratus lumborum.

Blood-supply.—Lumbar arteries.

Nerve-supply.—Lumbar nerves.

THE FASCIA AND MUSCLES OF THE TAIL

(FASCIA ET MUSCULI CAUDÆ)

The muscles of the tail are inclosed in the strong **coccygeal fascia,** which is continuous in front with the gluteal fascia and blends with the lateral sacro-iliac ligament. At the root of the tail it is loosely attached to the subjacent muscles, but further back it is intimately adherent to them. From its deep face are detached septa which pass between the muscles to become attached to the vertebræ.

1. Coccygeus.—This is a flat, triangular muscle which lies chiefly between the sacro-sciatic ligament and the rectum.

Origin.—The pelvic surface of the sacro-sciatic ligament near the ischiatic spine.
Insertion.—The first four coccygeal vertebræ and the coccygeal fascia.

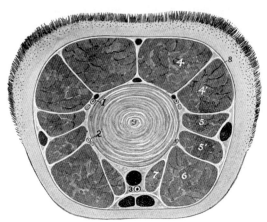

FIG. 271.—CROSS-SECTION OF TAIL OF HORSE.

1, 2, Branches of lateral coccygeal vessels and nerve; 3, middle coccygeal artery; 4, sacro-coccygeus dorsalis; 4', sacro-coccygeus lateralis; 5, 5', intertransversales; 6, sacro-coccygeus ventralis; 7, recto-coccygeus; 8, coccygeal fascia; 9, fibro-cartilage between fourth and fifth coccygeal vertebræ. The veins are black.

Action.—Acting together, to depress (flex) the tail, compressing it over the perineum; acting singly, to depress and incline it to the same side.

Structure.—The origin of the muscle is aponeurotic. Becoming fleshy, its fibers pass upward and backward and divide into two layers. The lateral layer is attached to the vertebræ, the medial to the fascia; included between the two lie the intertransversales. When the tail is raised, the ventral edges of the muscles produce a distinct ridge at either side of the anus.

Relations. — Laterally, the sacro-sciatic ligament and the semi-membranosus; medially, the rectum and the sacro-coccygeus ventralis muscle. The internal pudic artery crosses the origin of the muscle.

2. Sacro-coccygeus dorsalis (M. sacro-coccygeus dorsalis medialis).—This muscle lies along the dorso-median aspect of the tail, in contact with its fellow.

Origin.—The last three sacral spines and some of the coccygeal spines.

Insertion.—The dorsal surface of the coccygeal vertebræ.

Action.—Acting together, to elevate (extend) the tail; acting singly, to elevate and incline it laterally.

Structure.—The muscle has a strong rounded belly. It is inserted by means of short tendons which fuse with those of the next muscle.

Relations.—Superficially, the coccygeal fascia; medially, its fellow; laterally, the sacro-coccygeus lateralis; deeply, the vertebræ.

3. Sacro-coccygeus lateralis (M. sacro-coccygeus dorsalis lateralis).—This muscle lies immediately lateral to the preceding.

Origin.—The sides of the sacral spines, with the multifidus, and the transverse processes of the sacral and coccygeal vertebræ.

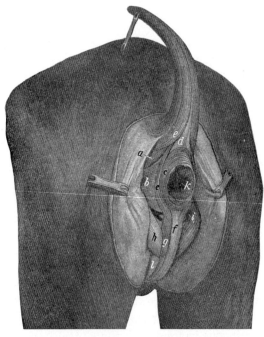

FIG. 272.—MUSCLES OF PERINEUM OF HORSE.

a, Coccygeus; *b*, retractor ani; *c, c'*, sphincter ani externus *d*, recto-coccygeus; *e*, sacro-coccygeus ventralis lateralis; *f*, retractor penis; *g*, bulbo-cavernosus; *h*, ischio-cavernosus; *i*, internal pudic artery; *k*, anus; *l*, penis. (After Ellenberger-Baum, Top Anat. d. Pferdes.)

Insertion.—The lateral surface of the coccygeal vertebræ, except the first four.

Action.—Acting with its fellow, to assist the preceding muscle in elevating the tail; acting singly, to incline it to the same side.

Structure.—This muscle appears to be a direct continuation of the multifidus dorsi. The belly is fusiform and receives reinforcing fasciculi from the transverse processes of the sacrum. This is succeeded by bundles of tendons, as many as four lying alongside of each other.

Relations.—Superficially, the lateral sacro-iliac ligament and the coccygeal fascia; dorsally, the sacro-coccygeus dorsalis; ventrally, the intertransversales; deeply, the vertebræ and a branch of the lateral coccygeal artery and accompanying vein and nerve.

4. **Intertransversales caudæ** (Mm. intertransversarii caudæ).—These consist of muscular bundles which lie on the lateral aspect of the tail, between the preceding muscle and the sacro-coccygeus ventralis. They begin on the lateral edge of the sacrum and occupy the spaces between the transverse processes, to which they are attached. They are, however, not arranged in a strict segmental manner.

Action.—Acting together, to fix the coccygeal vertebræ; acting singly, to assist in lateral flexion.

5. **Sacro-coccygeus ventralis** (M. sacro-coccygeus ventralis).—This muscle lies on the ventral aspect of the sacrum and coccyx. It is composed of two parts, described by Bourgelat and the German anatomists as separate muscles.

(*a*) The **lateral part** (M. coccygeus ventralis lateralis) is much the larger of the two. It arises from the lateral part of the ventral surface of the sacrum, about as far forward as the third foramen, and is inserted into the transverse processes and ventral surface of the coccygeal vertebræ.

(*b*) The **medial part** (M. sacro-coccygeus ventralis medialis) arises from the ventral surface of the sacrum medial to the preceding muscle and the first eight coccygeal vertebræ, and is inserted into the ventral surfaces of the coccygeal vertebræ.

Action.—Acting together, to depress (flex) the tail; acting singly, to incline it laterally also.

Structure.—The lateral part has a somewhat compressed belly, and receives bundles from the transverse processes of the coccygeal vertebræ. The medial part is much smaller and shorter, reaching only about to the middle of the tail.

Relations.—Ventrally, the pelvic and coccygeal fasciæ; dorsally, the sacrum, coccygeal vertebræ, and the intertransversales; laterally, the sacro-sciatic ligament, the coccygeus, and the coccygeal fascia; medially, its fellow, the recto-coccygeus, and the middle coccygeal vessels. Branches of the lateral coccygeal vessels and nerves lie between the lateral division of the muscle and the intertransversales.

Blood-supply.—Middle and lateral coccygeal arteries.

Nerve-supply.—Coccygeal nerves.

THE MUSCLES OF THE THORAX
(MUSCULI THORACIS)

These consists of seven muscles or sets of muscles, which are attached to the thoracic vertebræ, to the ribs and their cartilages, and to the sternum. They are muscles of respiration.

1. **Levatores costarum.**—These constitute a series of small muscles which occupy and overlie the dorsal ends of the intercostal spaces.

Origin.—The transverse processes of the thoracic vertebræ.

Insertion.—The lateral surfaces and anterior borders of the upper ends of the ribs posterior to the vertebral origin.

Action.—To draw the ribs forward in inspiration or to produce rotation and lateral flexion of the spine.

Structure.—Arising by tendinous fibers, each muscle passes backward and outward and expands at its insertion. Some fibers pass over one rib and are inserted on a succeeding one. At the beginning and end of the series the muscle cannot be

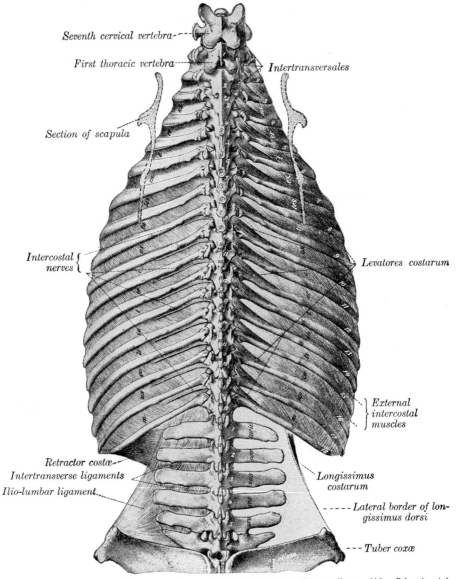

Seventh cervical vertebra

First thoracic vertebra

Intertransversales

Section of scapula

Intercostal nerves

Levatores costarum

External intercostal muscles

Retractor costæ

Intertransverse ligaments

Ilio-lumbar ligament

Longissimus costarum

Lateral border of longissimus dorsi

Tuber coxæ

Fig. 273.—Deep Dissection of Dorsal and Lumbar Regions of Horse; Dorsal View. (After Schmaltz, Atlas d. Anat. d. Pferdes.)

distinguished from the external intercostal, of which it is in reality only a specially developed part.

Relations.—Superficially, the longissimus dorsi; deeply, the ribs, internal intercostal muscles, and the intercostal vessels and nerves.

Blood-supply.—Intercostal arteries.

Nerve-supply.—Intercostal nerves.

2. **External intercostals** (Mm. intercostales externi).—Each of these occupies an intercostal space, from the levatores to the sternal extremity of the rib. They do not occupy the intercartilaginous spaces.

Origin.—The posterior borders of the ribs.

Insertion.—The anterior borders and lateral surfaces of the succeeding ribs.

Action.—To draw the ribs forward in inspiration.

Structure.—The fibers are directed downward and backward. There is a considerable admixture of tendinous tissue. The thickness of the muscles gradually diminishes toward the lower ends of the spaces.

Relations.—Superficially, the serratus ventralis, latissimus dorsi, serratus dorsalis, longissimus dorsi, longissimus costarum, rectus thoracis, deep pectoral, obliquus abdominis externus, and cutaneous muscles; deeply, the internal intercostals and (in the upper part of the spaces) the intercostal vessels and nerves.

Blood-supply.—Intercostal and internal thoracic arteries.

Nerve-supply.—Intercostal nerves.

3. **Internal intercostals** (Mm. intercostales interni).—These extend the entire length of the intercostal spaces, including their interchondral portion.

Origin.—The anterior borders of the ribs and their cartilages.

Insertion.—The posterior borders of the preceding ribs and cartilages.

Structure.—The fibers are directed obliquely downward and forward. There is a smaller amount of tendinous tissue than in the external set, and the thickness diminishes dorsally. In the upper part of the spaces fibers sometimes cross a rib in a fashion similar to the subcostals of man. A thin fascia separates the internal from the external intercostal muscle in each space.

Relations.—Superficially, the levatores costarum and the external intercostals; deeply, the endothoracic fascia and pleura, the transversus thoracis, diaphragm, transversus abdominis, and the internal thoracic and musculo-phrenic vessels. In the upper part of the intercostal spaces the intercostal vessels and nerves lie between the internal and external intercostal muscle, but below they lie chiefly on the deep face of the internal muscle.

Blood-supply.—Intercostal and internal thoracic arteries.

Nerve-supply.—Intercostal nerves.

Action.—It is commonly stated that the external intercostal muscles pull the ribs forward in inspiration, while the internal set have the opposite action. But apparently they act together, and it would seem that their chief function is to narrow the intercostal spaces and to prevent the wall here being pushed out or pulled in during respiration.

The muscles in connection with the costal cartilages are sometimes distinguished as Mm. intercartilaginei; their direction is similar to that of the internal intercostal, and they cover the cartilages of the asternal ribs more or less. At the ventral ends of some of the intercostal spaces there is a layer of longitudinal muscle.

4. **Retractor costæ.**—This is a small triangular muscle which lies behind the last rib, chiefly under cover of the serratus dorsalis.

Origin.—The transverse processes of the first three or four lumbar vertebræ by means of the lumbar fascia.

Insertion.—The posterior border of the last rib.

Action.—To retract the last rib.

Structure.—The muscle arises by a thin aponeurosis. Its fibers are parallel to those of the adjacent internal oblique.

Relations.—Superficially, the serratus dorsalis and external oblique; deeply, the transversus abdominis.

Blood-supply.—Lumbar arteries.

Nerve-supply.—Lumbar nerves.

5. **Rectus thoracis.**—This is a thin muscle which lies under cover of the deep

pectoral muscles. It is directed obliquely backward and downward, and crosses the lower part of the first three intercostal spaces.

Origin.—The lateral surface of the first rib, below the scalenus.

Insertion.—The cartilage of the fourth rib. The aponeurosis usually joins the rectus abdominis. It may reach the fifth rib or the sternum.

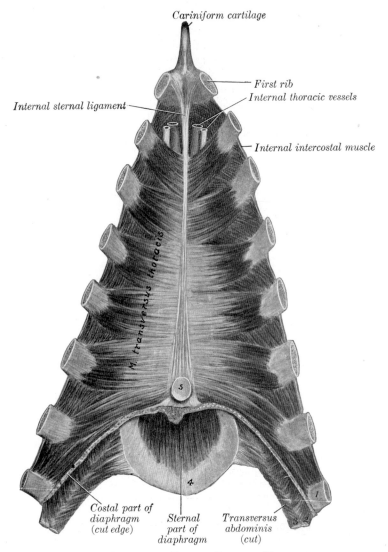

FIG. 274.—DISSECTION OF FLOOR OF THORAX OF HORSE.

The ribs have been sawn off near their sternal ends and the diaphragm and transversus abdominis cut off close to their attachment.

1, Eighth rib; 2, 3, cartilages of ninth and tenth ribs; 4, xiphoid cartilage; 5, apex of pericardium.

Action.—It may assist in inspiration or concur with the rectus abdominis.

Relations.—Superficially, the deep pectoral muscles; deeply, the intercostal muscles and the ribs.

Blood-supply.—Internal and external thoracic arteries.

Nerve-supply.—Intercostal nerves.

6. **Transversus thoracis.**—This is a flat muscle situated on the thoracic surface of the sternum and the cartilages of the sternal ribs.

Origin.—The sternal ligament, meeting the opposite muscle.

Insertion.—The cartilages of the ribs, from the second to the eighth inclusive, and the adjacent part of some of the ribs.

Action.—It draws the ribs and costal cartilages inward and backward, thus assisting in expiration.

Structure.—Each muscle has the form of a scalene triangle, of which the base is the strongly serrated lateral border. The muscle contains a good deal of tendinous tissue. The anterior bundles are directed forward and outward; the posterior, backward and outward.

Relations.—Dorsally, the endothoracic fascia and pleura; ventrally, the costal cartilages, the internal intercostal muscles, and the internal thoracic vessels.

Blood-supply.—Internal thoracic artery.

Nerve-supply.—The intercostal nerves.

7. **Diaphragm.**—This is a broad, unpaired muscle which forms a partition between the thoracic and abdominal cavities.[1] In outline it has some resemblance to a palm-leaf fan. In form it is dome-shaped, compressed laterally. On a median section it is seen to have a general direction downward and forward from the lumbar vertebræ to the xiphoid cartilage. The thoracic surface is strongly convex, and is covered by the pleura. The abdominal surface is deeply concave, and is covered for the most part by the peritoneum. The muscle consists of a fleshy rim which may be subdivided into costal and sternal parts; a lumbar part, composed of two crura; and a tendinous center.

Attachments.—(1) **Costal part** (Pars costalis): The cartilages of the eighth, ninth, and tenth ribs, and behind this to the ribs at an increasing distance from their sternal ends.

(2) **Sternal part** (Pars sternalis): The upper surface of the xiphoid cartilage.

(3) **Lumbar part** (Pars lumbalis): (*a*) The **right crus** (Crus dextrum) is attached to the ventral longitudinal ligament, and by this means to the first four or five lumbar vertebræ. (*b*) The **left crus** (Crus sinistrum) is attached in a similar fashion to the first and second lumbar vertebræ.

Action.—It is the principal muscle of inspiration and increases the longitudinal diameter of the chest. The contraction produces a general lessening of the curvature of the diaphragm. In the expiratory phase the costal part and crura lie almost entirely on the body walls, so that the bases of the lungs are in contact with the tendinous center almost exclusively. In ordinary inspiration the fleshy rim recedes from the chest-wall, so that the bases of the lungs move backward to a line about parallel with the costal arches, and about four or five inches (ca. 10–12 cm.) therefrom.

It is stated by Sussdorf and others that the inspiratory movement affects the tendinous center much less than the fleshy part, and that the foramen venæ cavæ scarcely moves at all, since the posterior vena cava is firmly attached to it. It should be noted, however, that the direction of the thoracic part of the vena cava in the expiratory phase is oblique, upward and backward. Thus it would seem that there is no anatomical reason why the diaphragm should not move as a whole in ordinary inspiration at least; examination of formalin-hardened subjects in which the diaphragm appears to be fixed in the inspiratory phase indicates that such is the case.

Structure.—The **costal part** consists of a series of digitations which meet, or are separated by a very narrow interval from, the transversus abdominis; between the two are the musculo-phrenic vessels. From the tenth rib backward the attachments to the ribs are at an increasing distance above the costo-chondral junctions. Thus at the last rib the upper limit of the attachment is four to five inches (10–12 cm.) from the ventral end. Anteriorly the origin extends along the ninth

[1] It should be noted, however, that in the embryo the diaphragm appears as a paired structure, extending from the lateral walls of the cœlom to fuse with the septum transversum.

costal cartilage to the xiphoid cartilage. From these points of origin the fibers curve dorso-medially and forward to join the tendinous center.[1] The **right crus** is about twice as thick as the left one and is also longer. It arises by a strong tendon

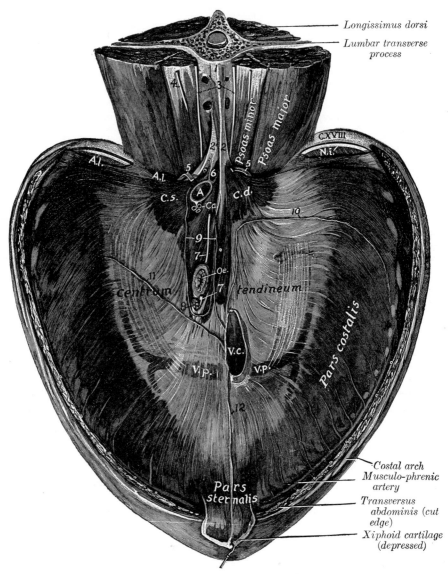

FIG. 275.—DIAPHRAGM OF HORSE; ABDOMINAL SURFACE.

1, Ventral longitudinal ligament; *2*, *2'*, tendons of crura; *3*, lumbar sympathetic trunks; *4*, external spermatic nerve; *5, 5*, great splanchnic nerves; *6*, cisterna chyli (opened); *7, 7*, œsophageal continuations of vagus nerves; *8*, lymph-gland; *9*, gastro-phrenic ligament (cut); *10*, right lateral ligament of liver (cut); *11*, left lateral ligament of liver (cut); *12*, falciform ligament of liver (cut); *A.l.*, lumbo-costal arch; *N.i.*, intercostal nerve; *C.d.*, right crus; *C.s.*, left crus; *A*, aorta; *Ca*, cœliac artery; *Oe*, œsophagus; *V.c.*, posterior vena cava; *V.p.*, phrenic veins. (After Schmaltz, Atlas d. Anat. d. Pferdes.)

which blends with the ventral longitudinal ligament. The tendon is succeeded by a rounded belly which leaves the vertebral column at the last thoracic vertebra.

[1] It is interesting to note that when a nineteenth rib is present the diaphragm usually has no connection with it, but ends on the eighteenth rib at a point a little more ventral than usual; sometimes, however, an additional digitation is present.

Passing downward and forward, its fibers spread out and join the tendinous center. The **left crus** arises by a thin tendon from the ventral longitudinal ligament at the first and second lumbar vertebræ. This is succeeded by a triangular belly which joins the central tendon. Between the crura and the attachment to the last rib the edge of the muscle crosses the ventral surface of the psoas muscles, the sympathetic trunk and splanchnic nerve without attachment, forming the so-called **lumbo-costal arch** (Arcus lumbocostalis); here the thoracic and abdominal cavities are separated only by the serous membranes and some areolar tissue. The **tendinous center** (Centrum tendineum) resembles the periphery in outline, but is more elongated. It is partially divided into right and left parts by the descent of the crura into it. It is composed largely of radiating fibers, but many interlace in various directions; this is specially evident around the foramen venæ cavæ, which is encircled by fibers. A strong tendinous layer extends across below the hiatus œsophageus.

Schmaltz and others describe the lumbar part as consisting of four crura, two medial and two lateral. On this basis the left crus of the preceding description becomes the **crus laterale sinistrum,** and the corresponding part of the right side is the **crus laterale dextrum.** The central part is divided by the hiatus œsophageus and the slit which extends from it dorsally into a **crus mediale dextrum** and a **crus mediale sinistrum.** Both modes of division are in part artificial.

It is noticeable that the cupola formed by the most anterior part of the diaphragm is not symmetrical. On the right side it extends forward to a transverse plane through the anterior border of the ventral part of the sixth rib, while on the left side it is usually about an inch (ca. 2–3 cm.) further back. Thus there are two prominences with an almost central depression which corresponds to the posterior part of the pericardium and heart.

The diaphragm is pierced by three foramina. (1) The **hiatus aorticus** is an interval between the two crura and below the last thoracic vertebra. It contains the aorta, vena azygos, and cisterna chyli. (2) The **hiatus œsophageus** perforates the right crus near its junction with the tendinous center. It is situated a little to the left of the median plane and about a handbreadth ventral to the thirteenth and fourteenth thoracic vertebræ. It transmits the œsophagus, the vagus nerves, and the œsophageal branch of the gastric artery; a serous sac, or bursa, is ventral and to the right of the œsophagus, which extends forward from the stomach into the mediastinum about three or four inches (ca. 7.5–10 cm.). (3) The **foramen venæ cavæ** pierces the tendinous center about an inch (ca. 2–3 cm.) to the right of the median plane, and about six to eight inches (ca. 15–20 cm.) below the eleventh and twelfth thoracic vertebræ. The vena cava is firmly attached to the margin of the opening.

In order to get a clear idea of the relative positions of these foramina and of the form of the diaphragm, the thoracic surface of the latter should be examined in properly preserved subjects while the abdominal viscera remain *in situ*. It will be observed that the distances of the hiatus œsophageus and foramen venæ cavæ from the vertebral column vary according to the fulness of the abdominal viscera and the degree of contraction of the diaphragm. The statements given above are averages.

Relations.—The thoracic surface is related to the endothoracic fascia, pleuræ, pericardium, the bases of the lungs, and the ribs in part. The abdominal surface is in great part covered by the peritoneum, and is related chiefly to the liver, stomach, intestine, spleen, pancreas, kidneys and adrenals. The sympathetic trunk and splanchnic nerve pass between the crus and the psoas muscles on each side. The musculophrenic vessels perforate the edge of the muscle at the ninth costo-chondral joint.

Blood-supply.—Phrenic and musculo-phrenic arteries.

Nerve-supply.—Phrenic nerves.

THE ABDOMINAL FASCIÆ AND MUSCLES
(FASCIÆ ET MUSCULI ABDOMINUS)

The **superficial fascia** of the abdomen is in part fused dorsally with the lumbo-dorsal fascia; in front it is continuous with the superficial fascia of the shoulder and arm, behind with that of the gluteal region. In the inguinal region it forms part of the fascia of the penis or of the mammary glands. At the lower part of the flank it forms a fold which is continuous with the fascia of the thigh near the stifle joint. In this fold are the prefemoral lymph-glands. Medially it blends with the linea alba. It contains the abdominal cutaneous muscle (described on p. 256).

The **deep fascia** is represented chiefly by the **abdominal tunic** (Tunica flava abdominis). This is a sheet of elastic tissue which assists the muscles in supporting the great weight of the abdominal viscera. It is practically coextensive with the obliquus externus, which it covers. Ventrally it is thick, and is intimately adherent to the aponeurosis of the muscle. Laterally it becomes thinner and is more easily separated, although fibers from it dip in between the muscle-bundles. It is continued for some distance upon the intercostals and serratus ventralis. Traced forward, it passes as a thin layer beneath the posterior deep pectoral muscle. Posteriorly it is attached to the tuber coxæ. In the inguinal region it forms the deep fascia of the prepuce or of the mammary glands.

The **linea alba** is a median fibrous raphé which extends from the xiphoid cartilage to the prepubic tendon. It is formed chiefly by the junction of the aponeuroses of the oblique and transverse muscles, but partly by longitudinal fibers. A little behind its middle (about in a transverse plane tangent to the last pair of ribs) is a cicatrix, **the umbilicus,** which indicates the position of the umbilical opening of the foetus.

1. **Obliquus abdominis externus.**—This is the most extensive of the abdominal muscles. It is a broad sheet, irregularly triangular in shape, widest behind. Its fibers are directed chiefly downward and backward.

Origin.—(1) The lateral surfaces of the ribs behind the fourth and the fascia over the external intercostal muscles; (2) the lumbo-dorsal fascia.

Insertion.—(1) The linea alba and the prepubic tendon; (2) the tuber coxæ and shaft of the ilium; (3) the medial femoral fascia.

Action.—(1) To compress the abdominal viscera, as in defecation, micturition, parturition, and expiration; (2) to flex the trunk (arch the back); (3) acting singly, to flex the trunk laterally.

Structure.—The muscle is composed of a muscular part and an aponeurosis. The **muscular part** lies on the lateral wall of the thorax and abdomen. It arises by a series of digitations, the anterior four of which alternate with those of the serratus ventralis. The origin may be indicated by a slightly curved line (concave dorsally) drawn from the lower part of the fifth rib to the tuber coxæ. The fibers are directed downward and backward and terminate on the aponeurosis, except in the upper part of the flank, where they are less oblique in direction and end on the tuber coxæ. The line of junction is a curve (concave dorsally) extending from the upper edge of the posterior deep pectoral muscle toward the point of the hip. The **aponeurosis** is intimately attached to the abdominal tunic, and its fibers are largely interwoven ventrally with those of the aponeurosis of the internal oblique. By this fusion is formed the outer sheath of the rectus abdominis, which blends at the linea alba with that of the opposite side. In the inguinal region the aponeurosis divides into two chief layers; one of these curves dorsally and backward and is inserted into the tuber coxæ and the prepubic tendon. Between these points the aponeurosis is much strengthened and is called the **inguinal ligament** (Ligamentum inguinale).[1] This curves upward and somewhat forward, becomes thin, and blends with the iliac fascia. It forms the posterior wall of the inguinal canal. About an inch (ca. 2 to 3 cm.) in front of the pubis and about two inches (ca. 4 to 5 cm.) from the median plane the aponeurosis is pierced by a slit-like opening, the **subcutaneous** or **external inguinal ring** (Annulus inguinalis subcutaneus).[2] This is

---

[1] Also commonly known as Poupart's ligament—based on a false historical allusion. It is in no proper sense a ligament, but is the inguinal part of the aponeurosis of the obliquus externus; it might therefore well be termed the lamina inguinalis.

[2] It is narrow and slit-like in the natural condition, but may appear oval in the dissecting-room, especially if the hind limb is drawn back and abducted.

the external orifice of the inguinal canal. Its long axis is directed outward, forward, and somewhat ventrally, and is four to five inches (ca. 10–12 cm.) in length.

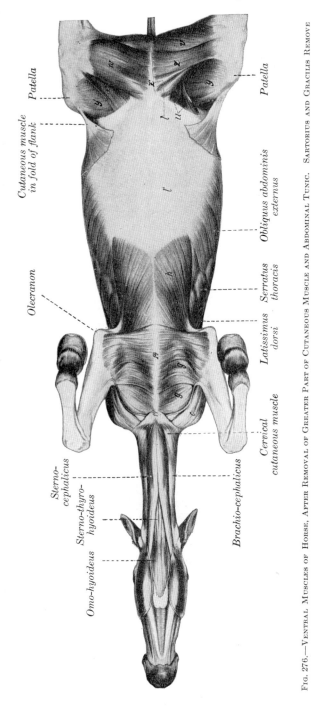

Fig. 276.—Ventral Muscles of Horse, After Removal of Greater Part of Cutaneous Muscle and Abdominal Tunic. Sartorius and Gracilis Removed from Right Thigh.

c, Brachiocephalicus; b, anterior superficial pectoral; b', posterior superficial pectoral; h, posterior deep pectoral; l', aponeurosis of obliquus abdominis externus; t, pectineus; u, ilio-psoas; v, semimembranosus; w, gracilis; x, sartorius; y, vastus medialis; y, sartorius; z, z', adductor; 14, sternum; 14', cariniform cartilage. (After Ellenberger-Baum, Anat. f. Künstler.)

The medial angle is rounded and is well defined by the junction of the aponeurosis with the prepubic tendon, but the lateral angle is not so sharply defined. The borders or crura are constituted by arciform fibers of the aponeurosis (Crus mediale, laterale). The **femoral lamina** of the aponeurosis (Lamina femoralis) passes on to the medial surface of the thigh, where it blends with the femoral fascia. A thin **iliac lamina** (Lamina iliaca) passes over the lateral margin of the iliacus and is attached to the lateral border of the ilium.

Relations.—Superficially, the skin, the abdominal cutaneus, the abdominal tunic, and the posterior deep pectoral muscle; deeply, the ribs and their cartilages, the intercostal muscles, the obliquus abdominis internus, the contents of the inguinal canal, and the sartorius and gracilis.

Blood-supply.—Intercostal and lumbar arteries.

Nerve-supply.—Intercostal and lumbar nerves.

2. **Obliquus abdominis internus.**—This muscle is situated under the preceding one. Its fibers are directed downward, forward, and inward. It forms a triangular curved sheet with the base behind.

Origin.—The tuber coxæ and the adjacent part of the inguinal ligament.

Insertion.—(1) The cartilages of the last four or five ribs; (2) the linea alba and the prepubic tendon.

Action.—Similar to that of the preceding muscle.

Structure.—Like the external oblique, it is composed of a fleshy portion and an aponeurosis. The muscular part is fan-shaped, and is situated chiefly in the flank. At its iliac origin it is covered by a glistening aponeurosis. Traced medially and ventrally along the abdominal surface of the inguinal ligament, the muscular origin is found to become much thinner, and also becomes loosely attached to the ligament. This medial part of the muscle forms the anterior wall of the inguinal canal. The abdominal orifice of the canal, the **abdominal** or **internal inguinal ring** (Annulus inguinalis abdominalis), is found here. It is normally a narrow slit, bounded in front by the edge of the internal oblique, and behind by the inguinal ligament. The term "ring" is rather misleading as applied to the abdominal opening of the canal, since normally it is a mere dilatable slit. The ring-like constriction that exists here in the male is constituted by the peritoneum, which descends into the canal to form the tunica vaginalis. This peritoneal ring is termed the **vaginal ring** (Annulus vaginalis), and must not be confused with the subperitoneal ring, *i. e.*, the abdominal or internal inguinal ring. The internal inguinal ring is six or seven inches (ca. 16 cm.) in length. Its direction corresponds approximately to a line from the lateral margin of the prepubic tendon to the ventral part of the tuber coxæ. Near the last rib the muscle divides into two parts. The small dorsal part is inserted by four or five thin tendinous strips to the medial surface of the last four or five costal cartilages. The aponeurosis of the large ventral part is to a great extent blended with that of the external oblique, being, indeed, considerably interwoven with it ventrally. Where it covers the rectus abdominis it is attached to the tendinous inscriptions of that muscle. It may be noted that the dorsal margin of the aponeurosis varies in different subjects in the fact that it may cover the costal arch or lie ventral to it.

Relations.—Superficially, the obliquus externus; deeply, the rectus abdominis, transversus abdominis, and the peritoneum.

Blood-supply.—Circumflex iliac, lumbar, and intercostal arteries.

Nerve-supply.—Ventral branches of the lumbar nerves.

3. **Rectus abdominis.**—This muscle is confined to the ventral part of the abdominal wall; it extends from the sternal region to the pubis.

Origin.—The cartilages of the fourth or fifth to the ninth ribs inclusive, and the adjacent surface of the sternum.

Insertion.—The pubis, by means of the prepubic tendon.

Action.—Similar to that of the oblique muscles. It is especially adapted to flex the lumbo-sacral joints and the lumbar and thoracic parts of the spine.

Structure.—The fibers of the muscle are directed longitudinally. Nine to eleven transverse bands of fibrous tissue extend in an irregular manner across the muscle. These are termed **inscriptiones tendineæ.** They strengthen the muscle and serve to prevent separation of its fibers. The width of the muscle is greatest about its middle. The anterior part blends with the rectus thoracis.

Relations.—Superficially, the aponeuroses of the oblique muscles (which constitute the external rectus sheath) and the posterior deep pectoral; deeply, the transversus abdominis, intercostals, the cartilages of the ribs, and the sternum. The posterior abdominal artery runs along the lateral edge of the muscle posteriorly, and the anterior abdominal artery on or in its anterior part.

Blood-supply.—Anterior and posterior abdominal arteries.

Nerve-supply.—Intercostal and lumbar nerves.

4. **Transversus abdominis.**—This muscle, named from the general direction of its fibers, is a triangular curved sheet. Its lateral part is muscular, its ventral aponeurotic.

Origin.—(1) The medial surfaces of the ventral ends or the cartilages of the asternal ribs, meeting the costal attachment of the diaphragm; (2) the transverse processes of the lumbar vertebræ, by means of the deep layer of the lumbo-dorsal fascia.

Insertion.—The xiphoid cartilage and the linea alba.

Action.—Similar to that of the oblique muscles.

Structure.—The **muscular part** is a sheet of parallel bundles of fibers, directed ventro-medially. It is thickest along the cartilages of the ribs, and from here it thins out greatly toward the aponeurosis and the lumbar region. The fibers of the **aponeurosis** directly continue those of the fleshy part. Posteriorly it becomes extremely thin and fades out without reaching the pelvis. It covers the deep face of the rectus, so forming the internal rectus sheath.

Relations.—Superficially, the oblique and straight muscles, the retractor costæ, the cartilages of the asternal ribs, and the internal intercostal muscles; deeply, the fascia transversalis and the peritoneum. The **fascia transversalis** is little developed in the horse, and is very thin in emaciated subjects, but in animals in good condition it contains a good deal of fat. It blends with the iliac fascia and descends into the inguinal canal. The musculo-phrenic artery runs along the interval between the origin of the transversus and the costal part of the diaphragm. The intercostal nerves pass down over the lateral surface of the muscle, to which they give branches. Branches of the first three lumbar nerves are similarly disposed further back.

Blood-supply.—Intercostal, lumbar, and musculo-phrenic arteries.

Nerve-supply.—Intercostal and lumbar nerves.

5. **Cremaster externus.**—This small muscle may be regarded as a detached portion of the obliquus abdominis internus, with which it blends at its origin (Figs. 370, 575).

Origin.—The iliac fascia, near the origin of the sartorius.

Insertion.—The tunica vaginalis communis.

Action.—To raise the tunica vaginalis, and with it the testicle.

Structure.—The muscle arises by a thin aponeurosis which is succeeded by a flat muscular belly about two inches (ca. 5 cm.) in width in the stallion. It passes down the inguinal canal on the postero-lateral surface of the tunica vaginalis, to which it is very loosely attached. On reaching the point where the tunic is reflected on to the tail of the epididymis, the muscle is inserted into the outer surface of the tunic by short tendinous fibers. As might be expected, the cremaster usually undergoes atrophy and is paler in the castrated subject. In the mare the muscle is very small, and ends in the connective tissue in the inguinal canal.

Relations.—The muscle lies between the peritoneum and the fascia transversalis in front and the iliac fascia and inguinal ligament behind. On reaching the abdominal ring it descends the inguinal canal on the postero-lateral surface of the tunica vaginalis communis.

Blood-supply.—External spermatic artery.

Nerve-supply.—External spermatic nerve.

The Inguinal Canal.—This term (Canalis inguinalis) is applied to an oblique passage through the posterior part of the abdominal wall. It begins at the abdominal inguinal ring, and extends obliquely ventro-medially, and somewhat forward, to end at the subcutaneous inguinal ring. Its anterior wall is formed by the fleshy posterior part of the internal oblique muscle, and the posterior wall by the strong tendinous inguinal ligament. The term canal is somewhat misleading; it is rather a slit-like passage or space between the two oblique muscles, since the inguinal ligament is that part of the aponeurosis of the external oblique muscle which stretches between the tuber coxæ and the prepubic tendon. The average length of the canal, measured along the spermatic cord, is about four inches (ca. 10 cm.). The **abdominal** or **internal inguinal ring** (Annulus inguinalis abdominalis) is the internal opening of the canal; it is bounded in front by the thin margin of the internal oblique muscle, and behind by the inguinal ligament. It is directed from the edge of the prepubic tendon approximately toward the tuber coxæ. Its length is about six or seven inches (ca. 15–17.5 cm.). The edge of the muscle is attached to the surface of the ligament here by delicate connective tissue, except where structures intervene between the walls of the canal. The lateral limit of the ring is determined by the muscle becoming firmly attached to the ligament, *i. e.*, actually arising from the latter. The **subcutaneous** or **external inguinal ring** (Annulus inguinalis subcutaneus) is a well-defined slit in the aponeurosis of the external oblique muscle, lateral to the prepubic tendon. Its long axis is directed from the edge of the prepubic tendon outward, forward, and slightly ventrally, and its length is about four or five inches (ca. 10–12 cm.). The canal contains in the male the spermatic cord, the tunica vaginalis, the external cremaster muscle, the external pudic artery (and inconstantly a small satellite vein), and the inguinal lymph vessels and nerves. In the female it contains the external pudic vessels and nerves; in the bitch it also lodges the round ligament of the uterus, enclosed in a tubular process of peritoneum.

The two rings do not correspond in direction, but diverge laterally, so that the length of the canal varies greatly when measured at different points. The medial angles of the two rings are separated only by a distance equal to the thickness of the prepubic tendon (about a centimeter), but the lateral angles are about seven inches (ca. 17.5 cm.) apart. The distance measured along the spermatic cord is about four inches (ca. 10 cm.). The medial angle of the subcutaneous ring is well defined and distinctly palpable at the side of the prepubic tendon; from here the direction of the ring is traceable.

The Prepubic Tendon.—The **prepubic tendon** (Tendo præpubicus) is essentially the tendon of insertion of the two recti abdominis, but also furnishes attachment to the obliqui, the graciles, and the pectinei. It is attached to the anterior borders of the pubic bones, including the ilio-pectineal eminences. It has the form of a very strong thick band, with concave lateral borders which form the medial boundaries of the subcutaneous inguinal rings. Its direction is obliquely upward and backward. The obliquity of the tendon and the angle which it forms with the pelvic floor are of clinical importance in regard to manipulation of the fœtus in obstetrical cases. The slope varies in different subjects. In some cases the tendon forms about a right angle with the pubic bones. Its structure is somewhat complex. Most of the fibers of the posterior part extend from one ilio-pectineal eminence to the other. The fibers which belong to the recti curve in to the median line. The aponeuroses of the internal oblique muscles are inserted into its abdominal surface, and the inguinal ligaments are attached to and continue across it in arciform fashion. The anterior part of the tendon of origin of the gracilis is fused with it ventrally, and many of the fibers of the pectineus arise from it. It gives off on either side a strong round band, the so-called **accessory ligament,** which is inserted into the fovea of the head of the femur with the round ligament (*vide* hip joint). A band from the ventral surface extends backward and blends with the tendon of origin of the gracilis on each side.

THE MUSCLES OF THE THORACIC LIMB

I. THE MUSCLES OF THE SHOULDER GIRDLE (Figs. 266, 267, 268, 276)

This group (Mm. cinguli extremitatis thoracalis) consists of those muscles which connect the thoracic limb with the head, neck, and trunk. It may be regarded as consisting of two divisions—dorsal and ventral.[1]

A. DORSAL DIVISION

This division consists of two layers which overlie the proper muscles of the neck and back.

FIRST LAYER

1. **Trapezius.**—This is a flat, triangular muscle, the base of which extends along the supraspinous ligament. It is divided by an aponeurotic portion into two parts:

(a) **Trapezius cervicalis.**—*Origin.*—The funicular part of the ligamentum nuchæ, from the second cervical to the third thoracic vertebra.

Insertion.—The spine of the scapula and the fascia of the shoulder and arm.

(b) **Trapezius thoracalis** (s. dorsalis).—*Origin.*—The supraspinous ligament, from the third to the tenth thoracic vertebra.

Insertion.—The tuber spinæ of the scapula.

Action.—Acting as a whole, to elevate the shoulder; the cervical part draws the scapula forward and upward and the thoracic part draws it backward and upward.

Structure.—The muscle arises by a narrow, thin aponeurosis, from which the fibers of the flat fleshy part converge to the spine of the scapula and the aponeurosis which separates the two portions. The cervical fascia joins the ventral edge of the cervical portion to the brachiocephalicus, or the two muscles may unite or overlap here.

Relations.—Superficially, the skin and fascia; deeply, the rhomboideus, latissimus dorsi, supraspinatus, infraspinatus, deltoid, splenius, serratus ventralis, and anterior deep pectoral muscles, and the cartilage of the scapula.

Blood-supply.—Dorsal, deep cervical and intercostal arteries.

Nerve-supply.—Spinal accessory nerve.

SECOND LAYER

This consists of two muscles—the rhomboideus and latissimus dorsi.

2. **Rhomboideus.**—This consists of two parts:

(a) **Rhomboideus cervicalis.**—*Origin.*—The funicular part of the ligamentum nuchæ, from the second cervical to the second thoracic vertebra.

Insertion.—The medial surface of the cartilage of the scapula.

(b) **Rhomboideus thoracalis** (s. dorsalis).—*Origin.*—The spinous processes of the second to the seventh thoracic vertebra by means of the dorso-scapular ligament.

---

[1] The terms dorsal and ventral are here used in the topographic and not in the morphological sense; all the muscles of the group are ventral in the latter sense.

Insertion.—The medial surface of the cartilage of the scapula.

Action.—To draw the scapula upward and forward.   When the limb is fixed the cervical part will elevate the neck.

Structure.—The cervical part is narrow, pointed at its anterior extremity, and lies along the funicular part of the ligamentum nuchæ, to which it is attached by short tendon bundles.   The fibers are directed for the most part longitudinally. The thoracic part is quadrilateral in shape, and its fibers are nearly vertical.   Its deep face is intimately attached to the dorso-scapular ligament.

Relations.—Superficially, the skin and fascia (over a small area in front), the trapezius, and the cartilage of the scapula; deeply, the dorso-scapular ligament, the splenius, complexus, longissimus dorsi, and serratus dorsalis.

Blood-supply.—Dorsal and deep cervical arteries.

Nerve-supply.—Sixth and seventh cervical nerves.

3. Latissimus dorsi.—This is a wide muscle which has the form of a right-angled triangle.   It lies for the most part under the skin and cutaneus muscle, on the lateral wall of the thorax, from the spine to the arm.

Origin.—The lumbo-dorsal fascia—and by this means from the lumbar and thoracic spines as far forward as the highest point of the withers.

Insertion.—The teres tuberosity of the humerus, in common with the teres major.

Action.—To draw the humerus upward and backward and flex the shoulder-joint.   If the limb is advanced and fixed, it draws the trunk forward.

Structure.—The muscle arises by a wide aponeurosis, which fuses with that of the serratus dorsalis and with the lumbo-dorsal fascia.   The muscular part is at first rather thin, but by the convergence of its fibers becomes thicker as it approaches the arm.   The anterior fibers pass almost vertically downward over the dorsal angle of the scapula and its cartilage.   The posterior fibers are directed downward and forward.   The thick belly formed by the convergence of these passes under the triceps to end on the flat tendon of insertion, which is common to this muscle and the teres major.   The tendon of insertion furnishes origin to the anterior part of the tensor fasciæ antibrachii.

Relations.—Superficially, the superficial fascia, skin, cutaneus, trapezius, and triceps; deeply, the cartilage of the scapula, the rhomboideus, the serrati, the external intercostals, and the lumbo-dorsal fascia.

Blood-supply.—Subscapular, intercostal, and lumbar arteries.

Nerve-supply.—Thoraco-dorsal nerve.

B. Ventral Division

1. Brachiocephalicus.—This muscle extends along the side of the neck from the head to the arm.   It is incompletely divisible into two portions.

Origin.—(1) The mastoid process of the temporal bone and the nuchal crest; (2) the wing of the atlas and the transverse processes of the second, third, and fourth cervical vertebræ.

Insertion.—The deltoid tuberosity and crest of the humerus, and the fascia of the shoulder and arm.

Action.—When the head and neck are fixed, to draw the limb forward, extending the shoulder joint.   When the limb is fixed, to extend the head and neck, if the muscles act together; acting separately, to incline the head and neck to the same side.   By means of its attachment to the strong fascia which extends from the deltoid tuberosity to the outer face of the elbow the muscle also acts as an extensor of the elbow joint (*e. g.*, in standing).

Structure.—As already mentioned, the muscle is capable of incomplete division into two parts, the line of division being indicated by the emergence of superficial branches of the ventral divisions of the cervical nerves. The mastoid part (M. cleido-mastoideus) partly overlaps the other (M. cleido-transversarius), which lies dorsal to it. The former is attached to the mastoid process and the occipital bone by a broad tendon which fuses at its terminal part with that of the splenius and longissimus capitis and is also connected with the tendon of insertion of the sterno-cephalicus by aponeurosis. The dorsal part is attached to the transverse processes by four fleshy digitations. The belly of the muscle is adherent superficially to the cervical fascia and the cutaneus muscle, and deeply to the omo-hyoideus. In front of the shoulder its deep face may present a tendinous intersection of variable development.[1] Here the muscle becomes wider, covers the shoulder joint, passes between the brachialis and biceps, and is inserted by means of a wide tendon which it shares with the superficial pectoral muscle.

Relations.—Superficially, the skin, cervical fascia, parotid gland, cutaneus, and brachialis muscles, and branches of the cervical nerves; deeply, the splenius, longissimus capitis et atlantis, rectus capitis ventralis major, omo-hyoideus, serratus ventralis, anterior deep pectoral and biceps muscles, the inferior cervical artery, the prescapular lymph glands, and branches of the cervical nerves. The ventral edge of the muscle forms the dorsal boundary of the jugular furrow. The dorsal border may be in contact with the cervical trapezius, or be separated from it by a variable interval.

Blood-supply.—Inferior cervical, carotid, and vertebral arteries.

Nerve-supply.—Spinal accessory, cervical, and axillary nerves.

The **pectoral fascia** is a thin membrane covering the surface of the pectoral muscles, to which it is, for the most part, closely attached. It detaches a layer which passes between the superficial and deep pectorals. At the posterior edge of the triceps another layer is given off, which passes on the lateral surface of this muscle to blend with the scapular fascia; the deeper layer becomes continuous with the subscapular and cervical fasciæ.

The **pectoral muscles** form a large fleshy mass which occupies the space between the ventral part of the chest-wall and the shoulder and arm. They are clearly divisible into a superficial and a deep layer. The superficial layer may be subdivided into two parts by careful dissection; the deep layer is made up of two distinct muscles.

2. **Superficial pectoral muscle** (M. pectoralis superficialis).

(a) **Anterior superficial pectoral muscle** (pars descendens).—This is a short, thick, somewhat rounded muscle, which extends from the manubrium sterni to the front of the arm. It forms a distinct prominence on the front of the breast, which is easily recognized in the living animal.

Origin.—The cariniform cartilage of the sternum.

Insertion.—(1) The deltoid tuberosity and crest of the humerus with the brachiocephalicus; (2) the fascia of the arm.

Action.—To adduct and advance the limb.

Structure.—The belly of the muscle is convex on its superficial face, but deeply it is flattened where it overlaps the posterior superficial pectoral. Here the two muscles are usually closely attached to each other, and care must be exercised in making the separation. The tendon of insertion blends with that of the brachio-cephalicus and with the fascia of the arm. At the middle line of the breast a furrow occurs between the two muscles; laterally, another furrow, containing the cephalic vein, lies between the muscle and the brachiocephalicus.

Relations.—Superficially, the skin, fascia, and cutaneus muscle; deeply, the

---

[1] This is regarded as a vestige of the clavicle. On this basis the portion of the muscle from the vestige to the arm represents the clavicular part of the deltoid and perhaps the clavicular part of the pectoralis major of man.

posterior division, the deep pectoral, and the biceps. The cephalic vein lies in the groove between this muscle and the brachiocephalicus.

(b) **Posterior superficial pectoral muscle** (pars transversa).—This is a wide muscular sheet which extends from the ventral edge of the sternum to the medial surface of the elbow.

Origin.—(1) The ventral edge of the sternum as far back as the sixth cartilage; (2) a fibrous raphé common to the two muscles.

Insertion.—(1) The fascia on the proximal third of the forearm; (2) the curved line of the humerus with the preceding muscle.

Action.—To adduct the limb and to tense the fascia of the forearm.

Structure.—It is thin and pale, and mixed with a good deal of fibrous tissue. The right and left muscles fuse at a median fibrous raphé. The tendon of insertion unites with the fascia on the medial side of the forearm for the most part; only a small part in front, about an inch in width, is attached to the humerus.

Relations.—Superficially, the skin, fascia, and the preceding muscle: deeply, the deep pectoral, the biceps, and the brachialis; at the elbow, the median vessels and nerve, and the medial and middle flexors of the carpus.

3. **Deep pectoral muscle** (M. pectoralis profundus).—This muscle is much thicker and more extensive in the horse than the superficial pectoral. It consists of two distinct parts.

(a) **Anterior deep pectoral muscle** (pars scapularis).—This is prismatic and extends from the anterior part of the lateral surface of the sternum to the cervical angle of the scapula.

Origin.—The anterior half of the lateral surface of the sternum and the cartilages of the first four ribs.

Insertion.—The aponeurosis which covers the supraspinatus at its dorsal end, and the scapular fascia.

Action.—To adduct and retract the limb; when the limb is advanced and fixed, to draw the trunk forward.

Structure.—The muscle is almost entirely fleshy. It describes a curve (convex anteriorly), passing at first forward, then upward over the front of the shoulder, a little to its medial side, and finally inclines somewhat backward along the anterior border of the supraspinatus. It is loosely attached to the latter muscle, and terminates in a pointed end which becomes more firmly attached near the cervical angle of the scapula.

Relations.—Superficially, the skin and fascia, the cutaneus, superficial pectoral, trapezius, and brachiocephalicus muscles, the cephalic vein, the inferior cervical artery and the prescapular lymph glands; deeply, the posterior deep pectoral, biceps, supraspinatus, omo-hyoideus, and serratus ventralis muscles, the brachial vessels, and the branches of the brachial plexus of nerves.

(b) **Posterior deep pectoral muscle** (pars humeralis s. ascendens).—This is much the largest of the pectoral group in the horse. It is somewhat triangular or fan-shaped.

Origin.—(1) The abdominal tunic; (2) the xiphoid cartilage and ventral aspect of the sternum; (3) the cartilages of the fourth to the ninth ribs.

Insertion.—(1) The anterior part of the medial tuberosity of the humerus; (2) the anterior part of the lateral tuberosity of the humerus; (3) the tendon of origin of the coraco-brachialis.

Action.—To adduct and retract the limb; if the limb is advanced and fixed, to draw the trunk forward.

Structure.—This muscle is almost entirely fleshy. Its posterior part is wide and thin, but as the muscle is traced forward, it becomes narrower and much thicker. It passes forward and slightly upward in a gentle curve to its insertion. The humeral insertion is just below that of the medial division of the supraspinatus. Part of the fibers are inserted by means of a tendinous band which binds down the tendon of the biceps and is attached to the lateral lip of the intertuberal or bicipital groove, and a small part is attached to the tendon of origin of the coraco-brachialis.

Relations.—Superficially, the skin, cutaneus, and superficial pectoral; deeply, the abdominal tunic, the external oblique, the rectus abdominis et thoracis, the brachial vessels, external thoracic artery, and branches of the brachial plexus of nerves. The external thoracic vein lies along the lateral border.

Blood-supply.—Internal and external thoracic, inferior cervical, anterior circumflex, and intercostal arteries.

Nerve-supply.—Pectoral nerves, from the brachial plexus.

4. **Serratus ventralis** (Figs. 267, 268).—This is a large, fan-shaped muscle, situated on the lateral surface of the neck and thorax. It derives its name from the serrated ventral edge of its thoracic portion. It consists of cervical and thoracic parts.

(a) **Serratus cervicis.**

Origin.—The transverse processes of the last four or five cervical vertebræ.

Insertion.—The anterior triangular area on the costal surface of the scapula (facies serrata) and the adjacent part of the cartilage.

(b) **Serratus thoracis.**

Origin.—The lateral surfaces of the first eight or nine ribs.

Insertion.—The posterior triangular area on the costal surface of the scapula (facies serrata) and the adjacent part of the cartilage.

Action.—The two muscles form an elastic support, which suspends the trunk between the two scapulæ.[1] Contracting together, they raise the thorax; contracting singly, the weight is shifted to the limb on the side of the muscle acting. The two parts can act separately and are antagonistic in their effect on the scapula. The cervical part draws the base of the scapula toward the neck, while the thoracic part has the opposite action; these effects concur in the backward and forward swing of the limb respectively. With the limb fixed, the cervical part extends (raises) the neck or inclines it laterally. The thoracic part may act as a muscle of forced inspiration.

Structure.—In the domesticated animals there is no such clear division of the muscle as is found in man and the apes. On account of the difference in action, however, it seems desirable to distinguish the two portions. The serratus cervicis is thick and almost entirely fleshy. The serratus thoracis has on its superficial face a thick, tendinous layer which may sustain the weight of the trunk when the muscle substance relaxes. The ventral edge presents distinct digitations, the last four of which alternate with those of the obliquus externus abdominis, and are covered by the abdominal tunic. The fifth digitation extends to the sternal end of the rib. The ninth digitation is small and may be absent. Exceptionally, additional digitations may be attached to the tenth or eleventh rib or to the fascia over the intercostal muscles. The fibers converge to the insertion, which is thick and is intersected by elastic lamellæ derived from the dorso-scapular ligament.

Relations.—Superficially, the brachiocephalicus, trapezius, deep pectoral, subscapularis, teres major, latissimus dorsi, cutaneus, the abdominal tunic, the brachial vessels, and the long thoracic nerve; deeply, the splenius, complexus,

---

[1] It has been commonly stated that these muscles form a sort of sling in which the trunk is suspended. This is not quite correct, as the two muscles do not meet ventrally. The arrangement is admirable, since the pull of the thorax on the muscles presses the scapulæ against the body wall.

serratus dorsalis, longissimi, the ribs and external intercostal muscles, and branches of the deep cervical and dorsal arteries.

Blood-supply.—Deep cervical, dorsal, vertebral, and intercostal arteries.

Nerve-supply.—Fifth to eighth cervical nerves.

II. THE MUSCLES OF THE SHOULDER

The muscles of this group (Mm. omi) arise on the scapula and end on the arm; they may be divided into two groups—one covering the lateral, the other the costal, surface of the scapula.

The **superficial fascia** of the shoulder and arm contains the cutaneous muscle of this region (*vide* p. 256), and may be considered to be continued on the medial side of the limb by the subscapular fascia.

The **deep fascia** of the shoulder and arm (Fascia omobrachialis) is strong and tendinous, and is intimately adherent to the muscles on the lateral surface of the scapula, between which it detaches **intermuscular septa,** which are attached to the spine and borders of the scapula.   The brachial portion is, for the most part, only loosely attached to the underlying muscles, for which it forms sheaths; it is attached to the proximal and deltoid tuberosities of the humerus.   A specially strong part extends from the deltoid tuberosity to the lateral surface of the elbow; it furnishes insertion to part of the brachiocephalicus and gives origin to fibers of the lateral head of the triceps and of the extensor carpi radialis.   The fascia blends distally with the tendon of insertion of the biceps, and is continued by the antibrachial fascia.

A. Lateral Group (Figs. 267, 268)

1. **Deltoideus.**—This lies partly on the triceps in the angle between the scapula and humerus, partly on the infraspinatus and teres minor.

Origin.—(1) The upper part of the posterior border of the scapula; (2) the spine of the scapula, by means of the strong aponeurosis which covers the infraspinatus.

Insertion.—The deltoid tuberosity and the brachial fascia.

Action.—To flex the shoulder joint and abduct the arm.

Structure.—The origin of the muscle is partly aponeurotic, partly fleshy. The aponeurosis fuses with that which covers the infraspinatus; the posterior part is attached to the scapula immediately in front of the origin of the long head of the triceps.   The belly of the muscle lies for the most part in a cavity formed in the triceps.   It is widest about its middle.

Relations.—Superficially, the skin, fascia, cutaneus, and brachiocephalicus; deeply, the infraspinatus, teres minor, triceps, and brachialis muscles, and branches of the posterior circumflex artery and axillary nerve.

Blood-supply.—Subscapular artery (chiefly through the posterior circumflex).

Nerve-supply.—Axillary nerve.

2. **Supraspinatus.**—This muscle occupies the supraspinous fossa, which it fills, and beyond which it extends, thus coming in contact with the subscapularis.

Origin.—The supraspinous fossa, the spine, and the lower part of the cartilage of the scapula.

Insertion.—The anterior parts of the proximal tuberosities of the humerus.

Action.—To extend the shoulder joint.   It also assists in preventing dislocation.

Structure.—The surface of the muscle is covered by a strong aponeurosis, from the deep face of which many fibers arise.   The muscle is thin at its origin from the cartilage, but becomes considerably thicker distally.   At the neck of the scapula it divides into two branches, between which the tendon of origin of the biceps emerges. These branches, fleshy superficially, tendinous deeply, are united by a fibrous membrane already mentioned in connection with the deep pectoral muscle; some fibers are attached to this membrane and the capsule of the shoulder joint. A **bursa** is often present under the muscle at the tuber scapulæ.

Relations.—Superficially, the skin, fascia, cutaneus, trapezius, and brachiocephalicus; deeply, the scapula and its cartilage, the subscapularis muscle, and the suprascapular vessels and nerve; in front, the anterior deep pectoral muscle; behind, the spine of the scapula and infraspinatus muscle.

Blood-supply.—Suprascapular and posterior circumflex arteries.

Nerve-supply.—Suprascapular nerve.

3. **Infraspinatus.**—This muscle occupies the greater part of the infraspinous fossa and extends beyond it posteriorly.

Origin.—The infraspinous fossa and the scapular cartilage.

Insertion.—(1) The lateral tuberosity of the humerus, distal to the lateral insertion of the supraspinatus; (2) the posterior eminence of the lateral tuberosity.

Action.—To abduct the arm and rotate it outward.[1] It also acts as a lateral ligament.

Structure.—This muscle is also covered by a strong aponeurosis, from which many fibers arise, and by means of which the deltoid is attached to the spine of the scapula. A thick tendinous layer partially divides the muscle into two strata, and, coming to the surface at the shoulder joint, constitutes the chief means of insertion. This tendon, an inch or more (3 cm.) in width, passes over the posterior eminence of the lateral tuberosity of the humerus; it is bound down by a fibrous sheet, and a **synovial bursa** is interposed between the tendon and the bone. The portion of the tendon which crosses the lateral tuberosity is in part cartilaginous. When the long insertion is cut and reflected, the short insertion, partly tendinous, partly fleshy, is exposed.

Relations.—Superficially, the skin, fascia, cutaneus, trapezius, and deltoid; deeply, the scapula and its cartilage, the shoulder joint and capsule, the long head of the triceps, the teres minor, and branches of the posterior circumflex artery of the scapula.

Blood-supply.—Subscapular artery.

Nerve-supply.—Suprascapular nerve.

4. **Teres minor.**—This is a much smaller muscle than the foregoing. It lies chiefly on the triceps, under cover of the deltoid and infraspinatus.

Origin.—(1) The rough lines on the distal and posterior part of the infraspinous fossa; (2) a small part of the posterior border of the scapula, about its middle; (3) a tubercle near the rim of the glenoid cavity.

Insertion.—The deltoid tuberosity and a small area just above it.

Action.—To flex the shoulder joint and to abduct the arm; also to assist in outward rotation.

Structure.—The muscle is not rounded, but flat and triangular in the horse. Its origin from the posterior border of the scapula is by means of a fascicular aponeurosis which also gives origin to fibers of the infraspinatus and triceps. The short, deep part of the muscle which lies on the joint capsule behind the lateral tuberosity of the humerus is covered at its origin by the distal edge of the tendon of origin of the long head of the triceps. A **bursa** is commonly found between the terminal part of the muscle and the capsule of the shoulder joint, and is often continuous with that of the infraspinatus.

Relations.—Superficially, the deltoid and infraspinatus muscles; deeply, the scapula, the shoulder joint, and the triceps muscle.

Blood-supply.—Subscapular artery.

Nerve-supply.—Axillary nerve.

---

[1] Günther states that this muscle assists in extension or flexion according to the position of the head of the humerus relative to the glenoid cavity.

B. Medial Group

1. **Subscapularis.**—This muscle occupies the subscapular fossa, beyond which, however, it extends both before and behind.

Origin.—The subscapular fossa.

Insertion.—The posterior eminence of the medial tuberosity of the humerus.

Action.—To adduct the humerus.

Structure.—The muscle is flat and triangular. The base is thin and inter-digitates with the scapular attachments of the serratus ventralis. Distally the belly thickens and becomes narrower. It is covered by an aponeurosis, and contains a considerable amount of tendinous tissue. The tendon of insertion is crossed by the tendon of origin of the coraco-brachialis; it is intimately adherent to the capsule of the shoulder joint, and may be regarded as replacing the medial ligament of the latter. A small bursa usually is present between the tendon and the tuberosity of the humerus.

Relations.—Superficially, the scapula and shoulder joint, the supraspinatus, triceps, and teres major muscles; deeply, the serratus ventralis muscle, the brachial vessels, and the chief branches of the brachial plexus. The subscapular vessels run along or near the posterior edge of the muscle.

Blood-supply.—Subscapular artery.

Nerve-supply.—Subscapular nerves.

2. **Teres major.**—This muscle is flat, widest about its middle, and lies chiefly on the medial face of the triceps.

Origin.—The posterior angle and the adjacent part of the posterior border of the scapula.

Insertion.—The teres tuberosity of the humerus, in common with the latissimus dorsi.

Action.—To flex the shoulder joint and adduct the arm.

Structure.—It is for the most part fleshy, but the origin consists of an aponeurosis which blends with that of the tensor fasciæ antibrachii. The insertion is by a flat tendon which fuses with that of the latissimus dorsi.

Relations.—Laterally, the triceps; medially, the serratus ventralis. The subscapular vessels lie in a groove between the anterior edge of this muscle and the posterior border of the subscapularis; near the shoulder joint the posterior circumflex artery and the axillary nerve emerge between the two muscles. The medial face of the muscle is crossed by the thoracic branches of the brachial plexus, and by the artery which supplies the latissimus dorsi.

Blood-supply.—Subscapular artery.

Nerve-supply.—Axillary nerve.

3. **Coraco-brachialis.**—This muscle lies on the medial surface of the shoulder joint and the arm.

Origin.—The coracoid process of the scapula.

Insertion.—(1) A small area above the teres tuberosity of the humerus; (2) the middle third of the anterior surface of the humerus.

Action.—To adduct the arm and to flex the shoulder joint.

Structure.—The long tendon of origin emerges between the subscapularis and the medial branch of the supraspinatus. It passes over the terminal part of the subscapularis and is provided with a **synovial bursa.** The belly spreads out and divides into two parts. The small, short part is inserted into the proximal third of the medial surface of the shaft of the humerus; the large, long part is inserted into the middle third of the humerus, in front of the teres tuberosity and the medial head of the triceps.

Relations.—Laterally, the subscapularis, the brachialis, the tendon of insertion of the latissimus dorsi, and the humerus; medially, the deep pectoral; in front, the biceps brachii. The anterior circumflex artery and the nerve to the biceps pass between the two parts, or between the muscle and the bone, and the brachial vessels lie along the posterior border of the muscle.

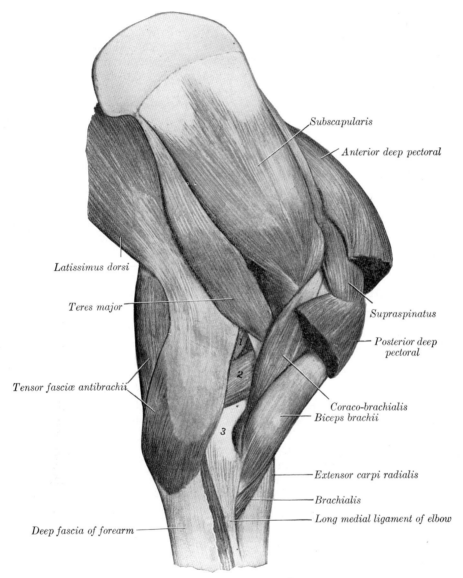

Fig. 277.—Muscles of Shoulder and Arm of Horse; Medial View.

1, Long head of triceps brachii; 2, medial head of triceps; 3, distal end of humerus.

Blood-supply.—Anterior circumflex artery.

Nerve-supply.—Musculo-cutaneous nerve.

4. **Capsularis.**—This is a very small muscle, which lies on the flexion surface of the capsule of the shoulder joint.

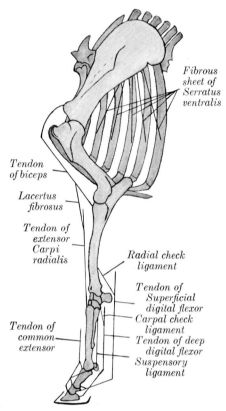

Tendon
of biceps

Lacertus
fibrosus

Tendon of
extensor
Carpi
radialis

Tendon of
common
extensor

*Fibrous
sheet of
Serratus
ventralis*

*Radial check
ligament*

*Tendon of
Superficial
digital flexor*

*Carpal check
ligament*

*Tendon of deep
digital flexor*

*Suspensory
ligament*

Fig. 277*a*.—DIAGRAM OF THORACIC LIMB OF THE HORSE.
Structures making up the "Stay Apparatus"
which enables the horse to stand while he sleeps.
Lateral view.

Origin.—The scapula, just above the posterior part of the rim of the glenoid cavity.

Insertion.—The posterior surface of the shaft of the humerus, a short distance below the head.

Action.—It has been held that it tenses the capsule of the shoulder joint and prevents its being pinched during flexion, but there does not appear to be any attachment of the muscle to the joint capsule.

Structure.—It is fleshy and commonly about one half inch wide, but it may consist of only a few bundles of fibers; sometimes it is double. It passes through the origin of the brachialis muscle to reach its insertion.

Relations.—Superficially, the long head of the triceps, the posterior circumflex vessels of the humerus and the axillary nerve; deeply, the capsule of the joint.

Blood-supply.—Posterior circumflex artery.

Nerve-supply.—Axillary nerve.

III. THE MUSCLES OF THE ARM

This group consists of five muscles (Mm. brachii) which are grouped around the humerus. They arise from the scapula and the humerus, and are inserted into the forearm. They act on the elbow joint and the fascia of the forearm.

1. **Biceps brachii.**—This is a strong fusiform muscle, which lies on the anterior surface of the humerus (Fig. 277).

Origin.—The tuber scapulæ.

Insertion.—(1) The radial tuberosity; (2) the medial ligament of the elbow joint; (3) the fascia of the forearm and the tendon of the extensor carpi radialis.

Action.—To flex the elbow joint; to fix the shoulder and elbow in standing; to assist the extensor carpi radialis, and to tense the fascia of the forearm.

Structure.—The muscle is inclosed in a double sheath of fascia, which is attached to the tuberosities and the deltoid ridge of the humerus. The tendon of origin is molded on the intertuberal or bicipital groove; it is very strong and dense and is partly cartilaginous. It is bound down here by a tendinous layer which furnishes attachment to part of the posterior deep pectoral muscle. Its play over the groove is facilitated by the large **intertuberal** or **bicipital bursa** (Bursa intertubercularis); the synovial membrane extends somewhat around the edges to the superficial face of the tendon. A well-marked tendinous intersection runs through the muscle and divides distally into two portions (Fig. 277*a*). Of these, the short, thick one is inserted into the radial tuberosity and detaches fibers to the medial ligament of the elbow joint. The long tendon (Lacertus fibrosus) is thinner, blends with the fascia of the forearm, and joins the tendon of the extensor carpi radialis; thus the action is continued to the metacarpus.

Relations.—Laterally, the brachiocephalicus and brachialis muscles; medially, the posterior deep pectoral and the superficial pectoral muscles; in front, the anterior deep pectoral muscle; behind, the humerus, the coraco-brachialis muscle, anterior circumflex and anterior radial vessels, and the musculo-cutaneous nerve.

Blood-supply.—Branches of the brachial and anterior radial arteries.

Nerve-supply.—Musculo-cutaneous nerve.

2. **Brachialis.**—This occupies the musculo-spiral groove of the humerus.

Origin.—The proximal third of the posterior surface of the humerus.

Insertion.—The medial border of the radius under cover of the long collateral ligament and the transverse radio-ulnar ligament.

Action.—To flex the elbow joint.

Structure.—The peculiar spiral course of this muscle gave rise to the name often applied to it—humeralis obliquus. Beginning on the posterior surface of the shaft, close to the head of the humerus, it winds over the lateral surface, crosses the biceps very obliquely, and finally reaches the medial side of the forearm by passing between the biceps and the extensor carpi. It is entirely fleshy, with the exception of its relatively slender tendon of insertion; there is a bursa under the tendon. Some fibers at the proximal end are attached to the capsule of the shoulder joint, which may thereby be tensed during flexion.

Relations.—Laterally, the skin and fascia, the teres minor, deltoid, triceps (lateral head), and brachiocephalicus muscles. Deeply, the teres major, the biceps, and the humerus. The anterior radial artery crosses the deep face of the muscle in its distal third, and the radial nerve accompanies the muscle in the distal half of the musculo-spiral groove.

Blood-supply.—Brachial artery.

Nerve-supply.—Median nerve; frequently radial nerve also.

3. **Tensor fasciæ antibrachii** (Fig. 277).—This is a thin muscle which lies chiefly on the medial surface of the triceps.

Origin.—The tendon of insertion of the latissimus dorsi and the posterior border of the scapula.

Insertion.—(1) The deep fascia of the forearm; (2) the olecranon.

Action.—(1) To tense fascia of the forearm and to extend the elbow joint.

Structure.—The origin consists of a very thin aponeurosis which blends with those of the caput longum and the latissimus dorsi. In most cases there is a distinct division into anterior and posterior heads. The muscular portion is thin in its anterior part, somewhat thicker behind, and is narrower than the aponeurotic origin. It is succeeded by an aponeurotic insertion, which ends chiefly by blending with the fascia of the forearm a little below the elbow. There is, however, a small but constant tendinous attachment to the olecranon.

Relations.—Laterally, the cutaneus, triceps (long and medial heads), the flexor carpi radialis and flexor carpi ulnaris, and the ulnar vessels and nerve; medially, the latissimus dorsi, serratus ventralis, and posterior pectoral muscles.

Blood-supply.—Subscapular, ulnar, and deep brachial arteries.

Nerve-supply.—Radial nerve.

4. **Triceps brachii** (Figs. 267, 268, 277).—This, together with the preceding muscle, constitutes the large muscular mass which fills the angle between the posterior border of the scapula and humerus. It is clearly divisible into three heads.

(a) **Long head** (Caput longum tricipitis).—This, the largest and longest of the three heads, is a powerful, thick, triangular muscle, which extends from the posterior border of the scapula to the olecranon.

Origin.—The posterior border of the scapula.

Insertion.—The lateral and posterior part of the summit of the olecranon.

Action.—(1) To extend the elbow joint; (2) to flex the shoulder joint.

Structure.—The muscle arises by a wide, strong aponeurosis from the posterior border of the scapula. From this the bundles of the fleshy portion converge to the short, strong tendon of insertion. A careful examination will show that the muscle is penetrated by a tendinous intersection from which many fibers take origin obliquely. The superficial face is covered by an aponeurosis specially developed at its distal part. A small **bursa** occurs under the tendon of insertion.

Relations.—Laterally, the cutaneus, deltoid, infraspinatus, teres minor, and the lateral head; medially, the tensor fasciæ antibrachii, teres major, latissimus dorsi and posterior deep pectoral muscles, and the subscapular vessels; in front, the brachialis and the medial head, the deep brachial and posterior circumflex vessels, and the axillary and radial nerves; behind, the skin and fascia.

Blood-supply.—Subscapular and deep brachial arteries.

Nerve-supply.—Radial nerve.

(b) Lateral head (Caput laterale tricipitis).—This is a strong, quadrilateral muscle, which lies on the lateral surface of the arm. Its proximal third is covered by the deltoid and teres minor muscles, the remainder only by the thin cutaneus muscle and the skin.

Origin.—(1) The deltoid tuberosity and the curved rough line which extends from it to the neck of the humerus; (2) the strong fascia which extends from the deltoid tuberosity to the lateral surface of the elbow joint.

Insertion.—(1) A small prominent area on the lateral surface of the olecranon; (2) the tendon of the long head.

Action.—To extend the elbow joint.

Structure.—The origin consists of short tendinous fibers. The belly is thick, and is composed of parallel bundles which are directed obliquely downward and backward. They are inserted partly into the tendon of the long head and partly into the olecranon below and in front of that tendon.

Relations.—Laterally, the deltoid, teres minor, and cutaneus muscles; medially, the long and medial heads and the brachialis muscle. Branches of the circumflex vessels and axillary nerve emerge between the posterior edge of the muscle and the long head. The deep face of the muscle is related to the branches of the deep brachial artery and of the radial nerve.

Blood-supply.—Posterior circumflex and deep brachial arteries.

Nerve-supply.—Radial nerve.

(c) Medial head (Caput mediale tricipitis) (Fig. 277).—This is much the smallest of the three heads. It is situated on the medial surface of the arm, and extends from the middle third of the humerus to the olecranon.

Origin.—The middle third of the medial surface of the shaft of the humerus, behind and below the teres tuberosity.

Insertion.—The medial and anterior part of the summit of the olecranon, between the insertion of the long head and the origin of the ulnar head of the deep digital flexor.

Action.—To extend the elbow joint.

Structure.—The muscle is fleshy except at its insertion, where it has a flat tendon, under which there is usually a small bursa.

Relations.—Laterally, the humerus, brachialis, anconeus, and the lateral head; medially, the posterior deep pectoral, coraco-brachialis, teres major, latissimus dorsi, and tensor fasciæ antibrachii muscles, the brachial and deep brachial vessels, and the median and ulnar nerves; behind, the long head, branches of the deep brachial vessels, and the radial nerve.

Blood-supply.—Deep brachial and ulnar arteries.

Nerve-supply.—Radial nerve.

5. Anconeus.—This is a small muscle which covers the olecranon fossa and is covered by the triceps. It is somewhat difficult to separate from the lateral head.

Origin.—The distal third of the posterior surface of the humerus.

Insertion.—The lateral surface of the olecranon.

Action.—To extend the elbow joint, and to raise the capsule of the joint and prevent its being pinched during extension.

Structure.—It is almost entirely fleshy. The deep face is adherent to the capsule of the elbow joint.

Relations.—Superficially, the triceps muscle; deeply, the humerus and the elbow joint.

Blood-supply.—Deep brachial artery.

Nerve-supply.—Radial nerve.

IV. FASCIÆ AND MUSCLES OF THE FOREARM AND MANUS
(FASCIÆ ET MUSCULI ANTIBRACHII ET MANUS)

The forearm is covered on three sides by the muscles of this group, leaving the medial surface of the radius for the most part subcutaneous. The extensors of the carpus and digit lie on the dorsal and lateral parts of the region, while the flexors occupy the volar surface.

The **fascia of the forearm** (Fascia antibrachii) forms a very strong and complete investment for all the muscles of the region. The **superficial fascia** is thin, and blends at the carpus with the deep fascia; it furnishes insertion to the posterior superficial pectoral muscle. The **deep fascia** is very strong and tendinous in character. It furnishes insertion at its proximal and medial part to the tensor fasciæ antibrachii muscle; at its proximal anterior and lateral part to the brachiocephalicus and biceps. It is attached at the elbow to the lateral tuberosities of the humerus and radius, to the ulna, and to the collateral ligaments. On the medial surface of the forearm it blends with the periosteum on the subcutaneous surface of the radius. It is closely adherent to the surface of the extensor muscles, but is rather loosely attached to the flexors; near the carpus it blends with the tendons attached to the accessory carpal bone. From its deep face are detached **intermuscular septa,** which form sheaths for the muscles and are attached to the underlying bones. The principal septa are: (*a*) One which passes between the common digital extensor and the lateral extensor and ulnaris lateralis; (*b*) one between the common extensor and the extensor carpi radialis; (*c*) one between the medial and middle flexors of the carpus.

The **carpal fascia** (Fascia carpi) is a direct continuation of that of the forearm. It is attached chiefly to the tuberosities at the distal end of the radius, to the accessory carpal bone, and to the carpal collateral ligaments. In front it forms the so-called **dorsal annular ligament** of the carpus (Lig. carpi dorsale), bridging over

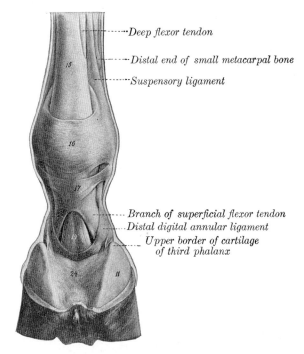

······Deep flexor tendon

······Distal end of small metacarpal bone

······Suspensory ligament

······Branch of superficial flexor tendon
····Distal digital annular ligament
Upper border of cartilage of third phalanx

Fig. 278.—Digit of Horse; Volar View.

14, Deep flexor tendon; *15,* superficial flexor tendon; *16,* volar annular ligament of fetlock; *17,* proximal digital annular or vaginal ligament; *11,* cartilage of third phalanx; *24,* digital cushion. (After Ellenberger-Baum, Anat. für Künstler.)

the grooves and binding down the extensor tendons and their synovial sheaths.   Behind it is greatly thickened and forms the **volar annular** or **transverse ligament** of the carpus (Lig. carpi transversum).   This stretches across from the accessory carpal bone to the medial collateral ligament and the proximal extremity of the medial metacarpal bone.   It thus completes the **carpal canal** (Canalis carpi), in which lie the flexor tendons, the carpal synovial sheath, the common digital artery, and the medial volar nerve.

The **superficial fascia** of the **metacarpus** and **digit** presents no special features, but the **deep fascia** (Fascia metacarpea et digitalis) is complicated by the existence of several annular ligaments.   In the metacarpus it is hardly distinguishable from the periosteum in front.   On the proximal part of the volar surface it forms a strong and close sheath for the flexor tendons, and is attached to the metacarpal bone on each side.   Lower down and between the annular ligaments it is thin.   On the flexion surface of the fetlock joint it is much thickened by fibers passing transversely from one sesamoid bone to the other, forming the **volar annular ligament** of the fetlock, which binds down the flexor tendons in the sesamoid groove and converts the latter into a canal.   Distal to this is a second thick quadrilateral sheet, the **proximal digital annular ligament** (Lig. vaginale), which covers and is adherent to the tendon of the superficial flexor.   It is attached on either side by two bands to the ends of the borders of the first phalanx, thus firmly binding down the flexor tendons. A little further down a crescentic fibrous sheet, the **distal digital annular ligament,** covers the terminal expansion of the deep flexor tendon (Fig. 654).   It is attached on either side by a strong band to the side of the first phalanx about its middle; its superficial face is largely covered by the digital cushion and its deep surface is in great part adherent to the deep flexor tendon.   It is also connected with the so-called **tendon** or **ligament of the ergot** (Fig. 572).   This is a thin and narrow fibrous band, which begins in the fibrous basis of the ergot, as the mass of horn at the fetlock is called.   It descends to the side of the pastern joint, crossing over the digital artery and nerve; here it widens out and blends with the fibro-elastic sheet just described.

A. Extensor Division

1. **Extensor carpi radialis.**—This is the largest muscle of the extensor division, and lies on the dorsal surface of the radius.

Origin.—(1) The lateral condyloid crest of the humerus; (2) the coronoid fossa; (3) the deep fascia of the arm and forearm and the intermuscular septum between this muscle and the common extensor.

Insertion.—The metacarpal tuberosity.

Action.—To extend and fix the carpal joint and to flex the elbow joint.

Structure.—The tendon of origin blends with that of the common extensor and is adherent to the capsule of the elbow joint.   The belly of the muscle is rounded and runs out to a point at the distal third of the forearm.   The tendon, which runs nearly the whole length of the fleshy portion, appears on the surface of the latter about its middle; here the muscle shows a distinctly pennate arrangement.   The tendon passes through the middle groove at the distal extremity of the radius and over the capsule of the carpal joint, bound down by the dorsal annular ligament and invested with a **synovial sheath.**   The latter begins three to four inches (ca. 8–10 cm.) above the carpus and extends to the middle of the carpus.   Distal to this the tendon is attached to the joint capsule, but there is usually a small bursa at the level of the third carpal bone.   In the distal half of the forearm the deep fascia blends with the tendon, and here the latter is joined by the long tendon of the biceps.

Relations.—Superficially, the skin, fascia, and the oblique extensor; deeply, **the** capsule of the elbow joint, the short biceps tendon, the radius, the carpal joint capsule, the anterior radial artery, and the radial nerve; laterally, the common extensor; medially, at the elbow, the brachialis and biceps.

Blood-supply.—Anterior radial artery.

Nerve-supply.—Radial nerve.

2. **Common digital extensor** (M. extensor digitalis communis).—This muscle lies lateral to the foregoing, which it resembles in general form, although less bulky.

Origin.—(1) The front of the distal extremity of the humerus, in and lateral to the coronoid fossa; (2) the lateral tuberosity on the proximal extremity of the radius, the lateral ligament of the elbow, and the lateral border of the radius at the junction of its proximal and middle thirds; (3) the lateral surface of the shaft of the ulna; (4) the fascia of the forearm.

Insertion.—(1) The extensor process of the third phalanx; (2) the dorsal surface of the proximal extremities of the first and second phalanges.

Action.—To extend the digital and carpal joints, and to flex the elbow joint.

Structure.—The muscle is a compound one, representing the common extensor, together with vestiges of the proper extensors of the digits. Usually at least two heads may be distinguished, although the division is always more or less artificial so far as the muscular part is concerned. The **humeral head** (Caput humerale), which constitutes the bulk of the muscle, arises from the front of the lateral epicondyle of the humerus in common with the extensor carpi; the tendon of origin is adherent to the capsule of the elbow joint. Its belly is fusiform, and terminates in a point near the distal third of the radius. The tendon appears on the surface of the muscle about the middle of the belly, the arrangement being pennate. The tendon passes downward through the outer of the two large grooves on the front of the distal end of the radius, and over the capsule of the carpal joint. Passing down over the front of the metacarpus, it gradually inclines medially, reaching the middle line of the limb near the fetlock. A little below the middle of the first phalanx it is joined by the branches of the suspensory ligament, and the tendon thus becomes much wider. Two synovial membranes facilitate the play of the tendon. The proximal one is a **synovial sheath** which begins about three inches (ca. 7–8 cm.) above the carpus, and terminates at the proximal end of the metacarpus. At the fetlock a **bursa** occurs between the tendon and the joint capsule, but otherwise the two are adherent. The smaller head, arising chiefly from the radius and ulna, is often divisible into two parts (Fig. 568). The larger of these is the **radial head** (Caput radiale);[1] it arises from the lateral tuberosity and border of the radius, and from the lateral ligament of the elbow joint. The flat belly is succeeded by a delicate tendon, which accompanies the principal tendon over the carpus (included in the same sheath), and then passes outward to fuse with the tendon of the lateral extensor, or it may continue downward between the common and lateral extensor tendons to the fetlock. Usually a slip is detached which is inserted on the proximal extremity of the first phalanx, or ends in the fascia here. The smaller and deeper division is the **ulnar head** (Caput ulnare);[2] it is usually somewhat difficult to isolate. It arises from the ulna close to the interosseous space. It has a small rounded belly and is provided with a delicate tendon which may fuse with the principal tendon or may be inserted into the joint capsule and the fascia in front of the fetlock joint.

Relations.—The chief relations of the belly of the muscle are: superficially, the skin and fascia; deeply, the elbow joint, the radius and ulna, the extensor carpi obliquus, and the anterior radial vessels and radial nerve; in front and medially,

[1] This (formerly called the muscle of Phillips) is considered to represent the part of the common extensor for the fourth and fifth digits.

[2] Martin considers that this muscle (formerly termed the muscle of Thiernesse) represents the extensor indicis proprius and the part of the common extensor for the second digit.

the extensor carpi radialis; behind, the lateral extensor and the interosseous vessels.

Blood-supply.—Radial and interosseous arteries.

Nerve-supply.—Radial nerve.

Lesbre reports that he has found in one case a **brachioradialis** muscle in the horse. It was a delicate fleshy bundle, superposed on the medial border of the common extensor, and extended from the lateral condyloid crest to the distal part of the medial border of the radius.

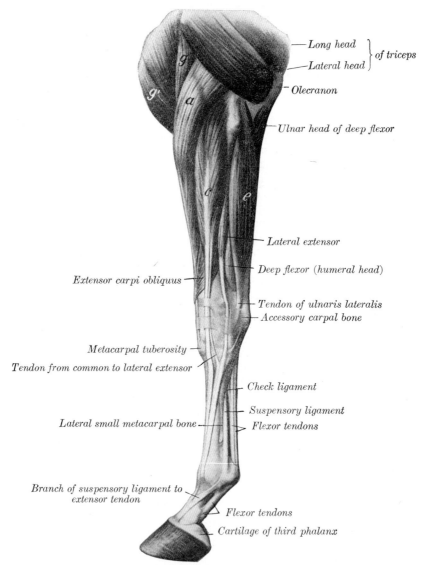

FIG. 279.—MUSCLES OF LEFT THORACIC LIMB OF HORSE FROM ELBOW DOWNWARD; LATERAL VIEW.

a, Extensor carpi radialis; *g*, brachialis; *g'*, anterior superficial pectoral; *c*, common digital extensor; *e*, ulnaris lateralis. (After Ellenberger-Baum, Anat. für Künstler.)

3. **Lateral digital extensor** (M. extensor digitalis lateralis s. digiti quinti proprius).—This muscle is much smaller than the preceding, behind which it is situated.

Origin.—The lateral tuberosity of the radius and the lateral ligament of the elbow joint, the shaft of the ulna, the lateral border of the radius, and the intermuscular septum.

Insertion.—An eminence on the front of the proximal extremity of the first phalanx.

Action.—To extend the digit and carpus.

Structure.—The muscle is pennate, and is enclosed in a sheath formed by the deep fascia, from which many fibers arise. The belly is thin and fusiform and terminates at the distal third of the forearm. From here the tendon (at first small and round) passes downward through the groove on the lateral tuberosity of the distal end of the radius, then over the carpus, and, gradually inclining toward

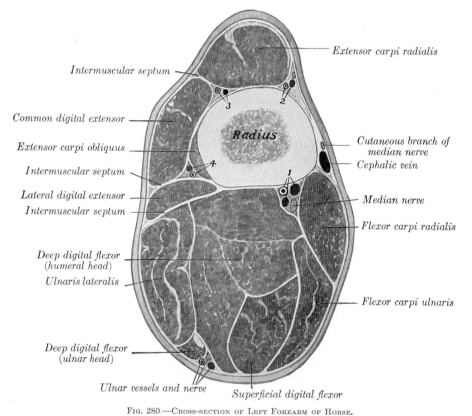

Intermuscular septum

Common digital extensor

Extensor carpi obliquus

Intermuscular septum

Lateral digital extensor
Intermuscular septum

Deep digital flexor
(humeral head)

Ulnaris lateralis

Deep digital flexor
(ulnar head)

Ulnar vessels and nerve

Extensor carpi radialis

Radius

Cutaneous branch of
median nerve
Cephalic vein

Median nerve

Flexor carpi radialis

Flexor carpi ulnaris

Superficial digital flexor

Fig. 280.—Cross-section of Left Forearm of Horse.

Section is cut a little above middle of region and the figure is a proximal view.
1, Median artery and satellite veins; 2, 3, branches of deep brachial and anterior radial vessels; 4, dorsal interosseous vessels.

the front, but not reaching the middle line of the limb, it passes over the metacarpus and fetlock to its insertion. Two synovial membranes occur in connection with the tendon. A **synovial sheath** envelops the tendon, beginning about three inches (ca. 6–8 cm.) above the carpus, and reaching to the proximal end of the metacarpus. At the fetlock a small **bursa** lies between the tendon and the joint capsule, but otherwise the tendon is adherent to the capsule. The tendon becomes flat and much larger below the carpus, having received the tendon of the radial head of the common extensor and a strong band from the accessory carpal bone.

Relations.—Superficially, the skin and fascia; deeply, the lateral face of the radius and ulna; in front, the common extensor, the oblique extensor, and the interosseous artery; behind, the lateral flexor of the carpus and the deep flexor of the digit.

Blood-supply.—Interosseous artery.

Nerve-supply.—Radial nerve.

4. **Extensor carpi obliquus** (M. abductor pollicis longus et extensor pollicis brevis).—This is a small muscle which curves obliquely over the distal half of the radius and the carpus.

Origin.—The lateral border and adjacent part of the dorsal surface of the radius (the attachment area beginning at a point above the middle of the bone and extending down to its distal fourth).

Insertion.—The head of the medial (second) metacarpal bone.

Action.—To extend the carpal joint.

Structure.—The muscle is pennate and has a flat belly which curves downward, forward, and medially over the distal part of the radius. The tendon continues the direction of the muscle, and passes over the tendon of the extensor carpi radialis; it then occupies the oblique groove at the distal end of the radius, and crosses the medial face of the carpus. It is provided with a **synovial sheath.**

Relations.—Superficially, the skin and fascia, the lateral extensor, and the common extensor; deeply, the radius, the extensor carpi radialis, the carpal joint capsule, and the medial ligament of the carpus.

Blood-supply.—Interosseous and anterior radial arteries.

Nerve-supply.—Radial nerve.

B. Flexor Division

1. **Flexor carpi radialis** (or medial flexor of the carpus).—This muscle lies on the medial surface of the forearm, behind the border of the radius.

Origin.—The medial epicondyle of the humerus, below and behind the collateral ligament.

Insertion.—The proximal end of the medial (second) metacarpal bone.

Action.—To flex the carpal joint and to extend the elbow.

Structure.—The muscle has a short tendon of origin, which is succeeded by a somewhat flattened, fusiform belly. The tendon of insertion begins near the distal fourth of the radius and descends in a canal in the transverse carpal ligament. It is provided with a **synovial sheath** which begins two or three inches (ca. 5–8 cm.) above the carpus and extends almost to the insertion of the tendon.

Relations.—Superficially, the skin and fascia, the posterior superficial pectoral, and the tensor fasciæ antibrachii; deeply, the elbow joint, the radius, the deep flexor, the flexor carpi ulnaris, the median vessels, and the median nerve. At the elbow the artery and nerve lie in front of the muscle, but below they dip beneath it.

Blood-supply.—Median artery.

Nerve-supply.—Median nerve.

On removing the deep fascia on the medial surface of the elbow the student may notice a small muscle lying along the collateral ligament. This is the **pronator teres,** which is usually not present or a mere vestige in the horse. It arises by a small, flat tendon from the medial epicondyle of the humerus, and is inserted into the medial ligament of the elbow. On account of its small size and the fact that the forearm is fixed in the position of pronation, the muscle can have no appreciable function. It is usually represented by a tendinous band.

2. **Flexor carpi ulnaris** (or middle flexor of the carpus).—This muscle lies on the medial and posterior aspect of the forearm, partly under, partly behind, the preceding muscle. It arises by two heads—humeral and ulnar.

Origin.—(1) The medial epicondyle of the humerus just behind the preceding muscle; (2) the medial surface and posterior border of the olecranon.

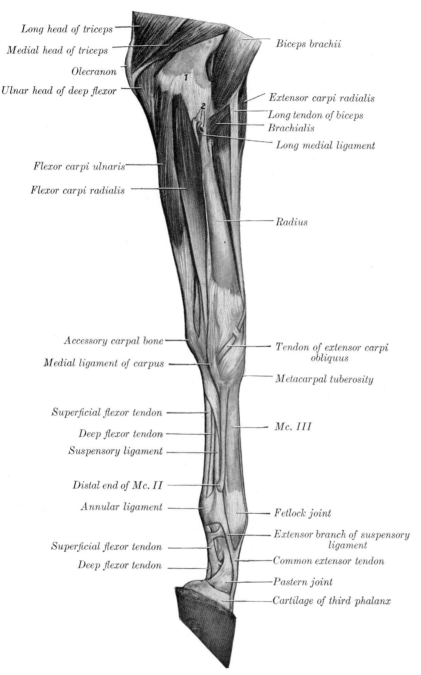

Long head of triceps

Medial head of triceps

Olecranon

Ulnar head of deep flexor

Biceps brachii

Extensor carpi radialis

Long tendon of biceps

Brachialis

Long medial ligament

Flexor carpi ulnaris

Flexor carpi radialis

Radius

Accessory carpal bone

Medial ligament of carpus

Tendon of extensor carpi obliquus

Metacarpal tuberosity

Superficial flexor tendon

Deep flexor tendon

Suspensory ligament

Mc. III

Distal end of Mc. II

Annular ligament

Fetlock joint

Extensor branch of suspensory ligament

Superficial flexor tendon

Deep flexor tendon

Common extensor tendon

Pastern joint

Cartilage of third phalanx

FIG. 281.—MUSCLES OF LEFT THORACIC LIMB OF HORSE FROM ELBOW DOWNWARD; MEDIAL VIEW. The fascia and the ulnar head of the flexor carpi ulnaris have been removed. 1, Distal end of humerus; 2, median vessels and nerve.

Insertion.—The proximal edge of the accessory carpal bone.

Action.—To flex the carpal joint and to extend the elbow.

Structure.—The humeral head is much the larger, constituting, in fact, the bulk of the muscle. It is flattened, curved, and tapers at both ends. The ulnar head, much smaller and very thin, is covered by an aponeurosis from which many of its fibers arise. It joins the large head a little above the middle of the forearm.

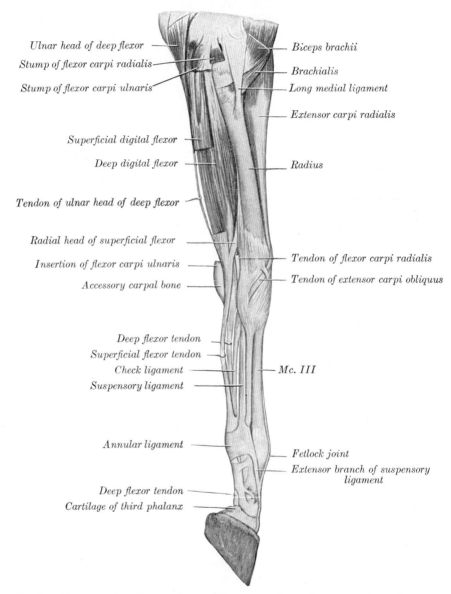

Ulnar head of deep flexor

Stump of flexor carpi radialis

Stump of flexor carpi ulnaris

Superficial digital flexor

Deep digital flexor

Tendon of ulnar head of deep flexor

Radial head of superficial flexor

Insertion of flexor carpi ulnaris

Accessory carpal bone

Deep flexor tendon
Superficial flexor tendon
Check ligament
Suspensory ligament

Annular ligament

Deep flexor tendon
Cartilage of third phalanx

Biceps brachii

Brachialis

Long medial ligament

Extensor carpi radialis

Radius

Tendon of flexor carpi radialis

Tendon of extensor carpi obliquus

Mc. III

Fetlock joint
Extensor branch of suspensory ligament

Fig. 282.—Muscles of Left Thoracic Limb of Horse, from Elbow Downward; Medial View. Parts of superficial muscles have been removed, carpal canal opened up, and flexor tendons drawn backward.

The tendon of insertion is short and strong; it blends with the posterior annular ligament of the carpus.

Relations.—Superficially, the tensor fasciæ antibrachii, superficial pectoral, and flexor carpi radialis, the skin and fascia, and cutaneous branches of the ulnar nerve; deeply, the superficial and deep flexors of the digit. In the distal half of the forearm the ulnar vessels and nerve lie between the lateral edge of this muscle and the lateral flexor of the carpus.

Blood-supply.—Ulnar and median arteries.

Nerve-supply.—Ulnar and median nerves.

3. **Ulnaris lateralis** (or lateral flexor of the carpus).[1]—This muscle lies on the lateral face of the forearm, behind the lateral extensor of the digit.

Origin.—The lateral epicondyle of the humerus, behind and below the lateral ligament.

Insertion.—(1) The lateral surface and proximal border of the accessory carpal bone; (2) the proximal extremity of the lateral (fourth) metacarpal bone.

Action.—To flex the carpal joint and to extend the elbow.

Structure.—The belly of the muscle is flattened and is intersected by much tendinous tissue. There are two tendons of insertion. The short tendon is inserted into the accessory carpal bone. The long tendon is detached just above the carpus; it is smaller and rounded; it passes downward and a little forward through a groove on the lateral surface of the accessory carpal bone, enveloped by a **synovial sheath,** to reach its insertion on the lateral metacarpal bone. A synovial pouch lies under the origin of the muscle at the elbow joint, with the cavity of which it communicates.

Relations.—Superficially, the skin, fascia, and cutaneous branches of the ulnar nerve; deeply, the elbow joint, the ulna, and the flexors of the digit; in front, the lateral extensor of the digit; behind, the flexor carpi ulnaris, the ulnar head of the deep flexor, and the ulnar vessels and nerve.

Blood-supply.—Interosseous, ulnar, and median arteries.

Nerve-supply.—Radial nerve.

4. **Superficial digital flexor**[2] (M. flexor digitalis superficialis).—This muscle is situated in the middle of the flexor group, between the flexor carpi ulnaris and the deep digital flexor.

Origin.—(1) The medial epicondyle of the humerus; (2) a ridge on the posterior surface of the radius, below its middle and near the medial border.

Insertion.—(1) The eminences on the proximal extremity of the second phalanx, behind the collateral ligaments; (2) the distal extremity of the first phalanx, also behind the collateral ligaments.

Action.—To flex the digit and carpus and to extend the elbow.

Structure.—The fleshy part of the muscle is the **humeral head** (Caput humerale); it takes origin from the humerus. The **radial head** (Caput tendineum) consists of a strong fibrous band, usually termed the **radial** or **superior check ligament,** which fuses with the tendon near the carpus. The belly of the muscle is multipennate, and fuses more or less with that of the deep flexor, from which it is therefore somewhat difficult to separate. Near the carpus it is succeeded by a strong, thick tendon which passes down through the carpal canal and is enveloped by a synovial sheath in common with the deep flexor. This, the **carpal synovial sheath** (Vagina carpea), begins three or four inches (8–10 cm.) above the carpus, and extends downward to the middle of the metacarpus. Below the carpus the tendon becomes flattened and broader and at the fetlock it widens greatly. Near the fetlock it forms a ring through which the tendon of the deep flexor passes (Fig. 286). Here the two tendons are bound down in the sesamoid groove by the volar annular ligament, which fuses more or less with the superficial flexor tendon. At the distal end of the first phalanx the tendon divides into two branches which diverge to reach their points of insertion, and between these branches the tendon of

---

[1] Also known as the extensor carpi ulnaris. Morphologically it belongs to the extensor group.

[2] Also commonly known as the flexor perforatus or superficial flexor of the phalanges.

the deep flexor emerges (Fig. 278). A second synovial membrane, the **digital synovial sheath** (Vagina digitalis), begins at the distal fourth of the metacarpus,

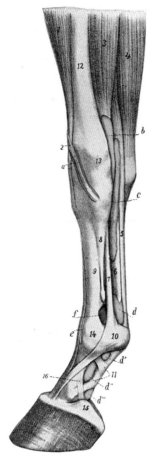
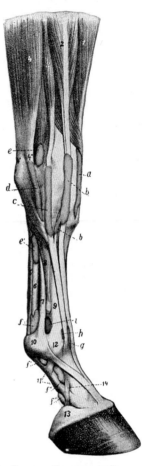

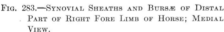

FIG. 283.—SYNOVIAL SHEATHS AND BURSÆ OF DISTAL PART OF RIGHT FORE LIMB OF HORSE; MEDIAL VIEW.

FIG. 284.—SYNOVIAL SHEATHS AND BURSÆ OF DISTAL PART OF RIGHT FORE LIMB OF HORSE; LATERAL VIEW.

The synovial sheaths (colored yellow) and the joint capsules (colored pink) are injected.

a, Sheath of extensor carpi obliquus; *b*, sheath of flexor carpi radialis; *c*, carpal sheath; *d, d', d'', d'''*, digital sheath; *e*, bursa under common extensor tendon; *f*, capsule of fetlock joint; *1*, extensor carpi radialis; *2*, tendon of extensor carpi obliquus; *3*, flexor carpi radialis; *4*, flexor carpi ulnaris; *5*, superficial flexor tendon; *6*, deep flexor tendon; *7*, suspensory ligament; *8*, small metacarpal bone; *9*, large metacarpal bone; *10*, volar annular ligament of fetlock; *11*, proximal digital annular ligament; *12*, radius; *13*, radiocarpal joint; *14*, fetlock joint; *15*, cartilage of third phalanx; *16*, band from first phalanx to cartilage. (After Ellenberger, in Leisering's Atlas.)

a, Sheath of extensor carpi radialis; *b*, sheath of common extensor; *c*, sheath of lateral extensor; *d*, sheath of long tendon of ulnaris lateralis; *e, e'*, carpal sheath; *f, f', f''*, digital sheath; *g*, bursa under common extensor tendon; *h*, bursa under lateral extensor tendon; *i*, capsule of fetlock joint; *1*, extensor carpi radialis; *2*, common digital extensor; *3*, lateral digital extensor; *4*, ulnaris lateralis; *4', 4''*, tendons of *4*; *5*, superficial flexor tendon; *6*, deep flexor tendon; *7*, suspensory ligament; *8*, lateral metacarpal bone; *9*, large metacarpal bone; *10*, volar annular ligament of fetlock; *11*, digital annular ligament; *12*, fetlock joint; *13*, cartilage of third phalanx; *14*, band from first phalanx to cartilage. (After Ellenberger, in Leisering's Atlas.)

two or three inches (ca. 5–8 cm.) above the fetlock, and extends to the middle of the second phalanx.

Relations.—The belly of the muscle is related superficially to the ulnar head of the deep flexor, the flexor carpi ulnaris, and, at its origin, to the ulnar vessels and nerve; deeply, to the humeral head of the deep flexor. The tendon is related superficially to the skin and fascia; deeply, to the deep flexor tendon.

Blood-supply.—Median artery.

Nerve-supply.—Ulnar and median nerves.

5. **Deep digital flexor**[1] (M. flexor digitalis profundus).—The fleshy part of this muscle lies on the posterior surface of the radius, and is almost entirely under cover of the preceding muscles. It is the largest muscle of the flexor group.

Origin.—(1) The medial epicondyle of the humerus; (2) the medial surface of the olecranon; (3) the middle of the posterior surface of the radius and a small adjacent area of the ulna.

Insertion.—The semilunar crest and the adjacent surface of the cartilage of the third phalanx.

Action.—To flex the digit and carpus and to extend the elbow.

Structure.—This muscle consists of three heads. The **humeral head** (Caput humerale) constitutes the bulk of the muscle. It is marked by tendinous intersections, and is separable into three subdivisions. A synovial pouch from the elbow joint descends under its origin about two inches. The **ulnar head** (Caput ulnare) is much smaller, and is at first superficially situated between the lateral and middle flexors of the carpus. The **radial head** (Caput radiale) is the smallest, and is not always present; it is situated on the distal two-thirds of the posterior surface of the radius, under the humeral head. Each of these heads is provided with a tendon. The principal tendon—that of the humeral head—appears about three or four inches (8–10 cm.) above the carpus and is joined at the carpus by the tendons of the other two heads. The conjoined tendon passes downward through the

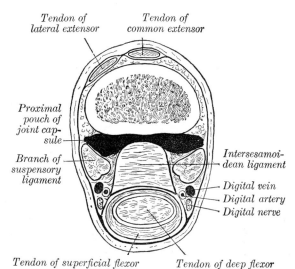

Tendon of lateral extensor

Tendon of common extensor

Proximal pouch of joint capsule

Branch of suspensory ligament

Intersesamoidean ligament

Digital vein

Digital artery

Digital nerve

Tendon of superficial flexor

Tendon of deep flexor

Fig. 285.—Cross-section of Distal Part of Left Metacarpus of Horse, Just Above Sesamoids.

carpal canal, being included in the **carpal synovial sheath** with the superficial flexor tendon, as previously described. The tendon is at first broad and three-sided, but becomes narrower and rounded below. Continuing downward, it is joined about the middle of the metacarpus by a strong fibrous band, the so-called **inferior check ligament** (Caput carpale s. tendineum). This is a direct continuation of the posterior ligament of the carpus. It may appropriately be termed the carpal head or tendinous head. At its upper end it is broad, occupying the entire width of the space between the small metacarpal bones; below it becomes narrower and thicker. It is related in front to the suspensory ligament, and its posterior face, which is related to the deep flexor tendon, is covered by the deep layer of the carpal sheath. Below this the tendon passes through the ring formed by the superficial flexor tendon, then in succession over the sesamoid groove, the distal sesamoidean ligaments, and the flexor surface of the distal sesamoid, to its insertion (Figs. 241 and 242). At the fetlock it widens considerably, narrows again in the middle of the digital region, again widens at the pulley of the second phalanx,

[1] Also commonly known as the flexor perforans or deep flexor of the phalanges.

and forms a terminal fan-like expansion. At the pulleys of the digit the tendon contains cartilage and is thickened. From the distal fourth of the metacarpus to the middle of the second phalanx it is inclosed in the **digital synovial sheath** described in connection with the superficial flexor. The **bursa podotrochlearis** or **navicular bursa** is found between the tendon and the distal sesamoid or navicular bone; it extends about half an inch (ca. 1–1.5 cm.) above the navicular bone and down to the insertion of the tendon. The terminal part of the tendon is bound down by the distal digital annular ligament described with the fascia.

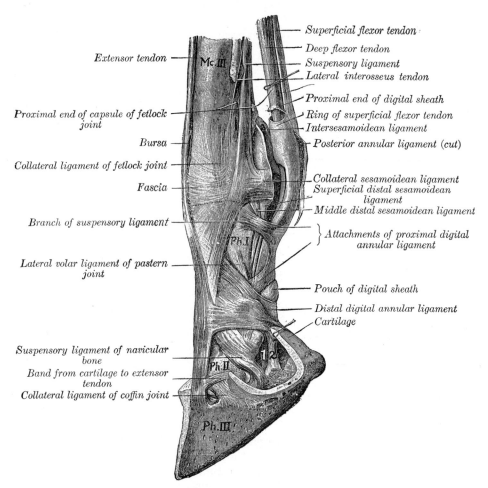

FIG. 286.—LIGAMENTS AND TENDONS OF DISTAL PART OF LIMB OF HORSE.

Mc. III, Large metacarpal bone; Ph. I, first phalanx; Ph. II, second phalanx; Ph. III. third phalanx; 1, deep flexor tendon; 2, band from first phalanx to digital cushion. (After Schmaltz, Atlas d. Anat. d. Pferdes.)

Relations.—The belly of the muscle is related posteriorly to the superficial digital flexor and to the flexor carpi ulnaris; medially, to the flexor carpi radialis, the radial check ligament, and the median vessels and nerve; laterally, to the ulnaris lateralis; anteriorly, to the radius and ulna and branches of the median artery and nerve. Below the carpus the tendon is accompanied by the vessels and nerves of the digit. It may also be noted that the muscle is not entirely covered by the other flexors; it comes in contact with the skin and fascia on the postero-lateral aspect of the proximal half of the forearm, and also on the lateral aspect of the distal fourth.

Blood-supply.—Median and ulnar arteries.

Nerve-supply.—Median and ulnar nerves.

6, 7. **Lumbricales** (medialis et lateralis).—These are two very slender fusiform muscles which lie on either side of the flexor tendons above the fetlock. They arise from the deep flexor tendon, and end in the fibrous tissue which lies under the nodule of horn at the fetlock which is known as the ergot (Fig. 572). Their action is inappreciable. The size of these muscles is subject to much variation. Often very little muscular tissue can be found, but the small tendon is constantly present.

Blood-supply.—Volar metacarpal arteries.

Nerve-supply.—Median and ulnar nerves.

8, 9, 10. **Interossei.**—These are three in number in the horse, and are situated chiefly in the metacarpal groove. Two, the **medialis** and **lateralis,** are very small muscles, each of which arises from the corresponding small metacarpal bone near its proximal extremity, and is provided with a delicate tendon which is usually lost in the fascia at the fetlock (Fig. 240). They have no appreciable action. Their blood- and nerve-supply is the same as that of the preceding muscles.

The **interosseus medius** is so much modified that it is usually termed the **suspensory** or **superior sesamoidean ligament.** It contains little muscular tissue, being transformed very largely into a strong tendinous band (Tendo interosseus), bifurcate below, and having for its chief function the supporting of the fetlock. It has been described, in deference to common usage, with the ligaments.

FASCIÆ AND MUSCLES OF THE PELVIC LIMB

THE FASCIÆ

The **iliac fascia** (Fascia iliaca) covers the ventral surface of the iliacus and psoas muscles, over which it is tightly stretched (Fig. 575). It is attached medially to the tendon of the psoas minor; laterally it is attached to the tuber coxæ and blends with the deep layer of the lumbo-dorsal fascia. Its anterior part is thin. Posteriorly it is continuous with the inguinal ligament and the pelvic fascia. It furnishes surfaces of origin for the sartorius, cremaster externus, and transversus abdominis muscles.

The **pelvic fascia** (Fascia pelvis) lines the cavity as the parietal layer and at the pelvic outlet is reflected on the viscera to form the visceral layer. Laminæ are detached from it to strengthen the various peritoneal folds.

The **superficial fascia** of the **gluteal region** is thin and is closely adherent to the deep fascia. A subcutaneous bursa may be found on the tuber coxæ. The **gluteal fascia** (Fascia glutæa) covers the superficial muscles of the region, and detaches intermuscular septa, which pass between the muscles. It is attached to the sacral spines, the dorsal sacro-iliac ligament, and the tubera of the ilium, and is continuous in front with the lumbo-dorsal fascia, behind with the coccygeal fascia. Its deep face gives origin to fibers of the superficial and middle glutei, the biceps femoris, and the semitendinosus, so that care is necessary in dissecting it off these muscles. The chief **intermuscular septa** are: (1) One which passes between the superficial gluteus and the biceps femoris; (2) one between the biceps and semitendinosus, from which a lamella is detached which passes between the middle and posterior parts of the biceps and is attached to the tuber ischii; (3) one between the semitendinosus and semimembranosus, which is attached to the sacro-sciatic ligament and tuber ischii; it furnishes origin for fibers of the long head of the semimembranosus.

The **superficial fascia of the thigh** presents no exceptional features, but the **deep**

fascia is very thick and strong on the front and lateral surface. This part, the **fascia lata** (Fig. 267), is continuous with the gluteal fascia; it is tendinous in character, and easily separable from the underlying muscles. It furnishes insertion to the tensor fasciæ latæ and to the biceps femoris (in part), by both of which it is tensed. At the stifle it is attached to the patella and the lateral and medial patellar ligaments. Medially it is continuous with the medial femoral fascia. It furnishes the following **intermuscular septa:** (1) One which passes between the vastus lateralis and biceps femoris to be attached to the third trochanter of the femur; (2) two which pass between the three branches of the biceps femoris; (3) a fourth between the biceps femoris and semitendinosus. The **medial femoral fascia** (Fascia femoralis medialis) covers the superficial muscles on the medial surface of the thigh. At its upper part it is joined by the femoral lamina of the aponeurosis of the external oblique muscle (Fig. 575). The posterior part is thin. It is continuous with the fascia lata in front and the fascia cruris below. At the stifle it fuses with the tendons of the sartorius and gracilis.

The **fascia cruris,** or fascia of the leg, consists of three layers. Two of these invest the entire region and may, therefore, be termed the **common fasciæ.** The superficial layer is a continuation of that of the thigh, while the second layer may be regarded chiefly as a continuation of the tendons of the superficial muscles of the hip and thigh (biceps femoris, semitendinosus, tensor fasciæ latæ, sartorius, and gracilis). The two layers frequently fuse, and are attached chiefly to the medial and lateral patellar ligaments and the crest and medial surface of the tibia. About the middle of the leg the two layers unite behind the deep flexor of the digit and form a strong band which passes downward in front of the tendons of the gastrocnemius and superficial flexor, to be attached with the latter to the anterior and medial part of the tuber calcis. This constitutes a tarsal tendon of insertion of the biceps femoris and semitendinosus. A strong band, about two inches in width, arises from the lateral supracondyloid crest, descends over the lateral head of the gastrocnemius, and blends with the foregoing and the superficial flexor tendon. The third layer forms sheaths for the muscles, furnishing origin in part to their fibers. Two important **intermuscular septa** are detached, viz.: (1) One which passes between the long and lateral digital extensors to be attached to the fibula and the lateral border of the tibia; (2) one between the lateral digital extensor and the deep digital flexor.

The **tarsal fascia** (Fascia tarsi) fuses with the ligaments and bony prominences of the region. It is strong and tendinous in front, and joins the tendon of the long extensor below the joint. On the sides it is thin and fuses with the ligaments. Posteriorly it is very thick and strong, forming an annular ligament which stretches from the medial ligament to the fibular tarsal bone and the plantar ligament. This converts the groove at the back of the hock into a canal, in which are the deep flexor tendon with its synovial sheath and the plantar vessels and nerves. In this vicinity there are three **annular ligaments** (Ligamenta transversa). The proximal one binds down the tendons of the long extensor, peroneus tertius, and tibialis anterior on the distal end of the shaft of the tibia. The middle one is attached to the fibular tarsal bone and the lateral tendon of the peroneus tertius, forming a loop around the tendon of the long extensor. The distal band stretches across the proximal extremity of the large metatarsal bone and incloses the tendons (and sheaths) of the two extensors of the digit.

The **metatarsal** and **digital fasciæ** do not differ materially from those of the corresponding regions of the thoracic limb.

THE MUSCLES[1]

I. THE SUBLUMBAR MUSCLES (Figs. 287, 575)

The muscles of this group are not confined to the sublumbar region, but extend beyond it both before and behind. Their chief function is to flex the hip joint. Two, however,—the psoas minor and the quadratus lumborum,—have not this action.

1. **Psoas minor.**—This is a fusiform, flattened, pennate muscle, which lies along the ventro-lateral aspect of the bodies of the last three thoracic and the lumbar vertebræ.

Origin.—The bodies of the last three thoracic and first four or five lumbar vertebræ, and the vertebral ends of the sixteenth and seventeenth ribs.[2]

Insertion.—The psoas tubercle on the shaft of the ilium.

Action.—To flex the pelvis on the loins, or to incline it laterally.

Structure.—The muscle arises by a series of digitations which pass backward and outward to join the tendon at an acute angle. The latter lies along the lateral border of the fleshy portion and is flattened. It appears on the surface of the muscle at the third lumbar process and increases gradually in width until it reaches the pelvic inlet, where it becomes narrower.

Relations.—The ventral surface of the thoracic part of the muscle is related to the pleura, crura of the diaphragm, and sympathetic and splanchnic nerves. In the abdomen the chief ventral relations are the peritoneum, the vena cava (right side), the aorta and left kidney (left side), the sympathetic nerves, and the ureters. Dorsally, the chief relations are the vertebræ, the psoas major, and lumbar nerves. The lumbar arteries pass through the medial edge. Near its insertion the tendon is crossed medially by the external iliac artery, and laterally by the femoral nerve.

Blood-supply.—Intercostal and lumbar arteries.

Nerve-supply.—Lumbar nerves.

2. **Psoas major.**—This is much larger than the preceding muscle, by which it is partly covered. It is triangular, with the base anterior.

Origin.—The ventral surfaces of the transverse processes of the lumbar vertebræ and the last two ribs.

Insertion.—The trochanter minor of the femur, by a common tendon with the iliacus.

Action.—To flex the hip joint and to rotate the thigh outward.

Structure.—The origin of the muscle is fleshy, the belly being in general flattened, thick in its middle, thin at its edges. The thoracic part is small, the abdominal part much thicker and wider, extending laterally beyond the extremities of the lumbar transverse processes. From the lumbo-sacral articulation it lies in a deep groove formed in the iliacus (with which it is partly united), becomes smaller and rounded, and passes downward and backward to terminate by a strong tendon common to it and the iliacus. On account of the intimate union between the psoas major and iliacus they are frequently considered a single muscle, to which the name **ilio-psoas** is applied; some anatomists include the psoas minor also under this term.

Relations.—Dorsally, the last two ribs and thoracic vertebræ, the lumbar vertebræ, the internal intercostals, quadratus lumborum, longissimus dorsi, and iliacus, and the lumbar vessels and nerves; ventrally, the pleura and peritoneum, the iliac fascia, inguinal ligament, the diaphragm, psoas minor and sartorius, and the circumflex iliac vessels.

---

[1] On account of the very slight mobility of the sacro-iliac articulation, the muscles of the pelvic girdle are much reduced, and almost all of those which might be included in this group extend to the femur or even to the leg. It seems undesirable, therefore, to attempt a morphological grouping.

[2] It may be attached to the fifteenth rib also.

Blood-supply.—Lumbar and circumflex iliac arteries.

Nerve-supply.—Lumbar and femoral nerves.

3. **Iliacus.**—This muscle covers the ventral surface of the ilium lateral to the sacro-iliac articulation, and extends beyond the lateral border of the bone, underneath the middle gluteus.

Origin.—The ventral surface of the ilium lateral to the ilio-pectineal line, the ventral sacro-iliac ligament, the wing of the sacrum, and the tendon of the psoas minor.

Insertion.—The trochanter minor of the femur, by a common tendon with the psoas major.

Action.—To flex the hip joint and to rotate the thigh outward.

Structure.—The belly of the muscle is so deeply grooved for the psoas major as to give the appearance of being completely divided into medial and lateral parts. When the psoas is removed, it is seen, however, that the two heads are not entirely separated. The lateral, larger head arises from the wing of the ilium chiefly; the medial, smaller head arises chiefly from a small area on the shaft of the ilium, between the psoas tubercle and the depression for the medial tendon of the rectus femoris, and from the tendon of the psoas minor. The two parts inclose the psoas major in front of the hip joint.

Relations.—Dorsally, the ilium, sacrum, sacro-iliac articulation, the gluteus medius, the ilio-lumbar and external circumflex vessels; ventrally, the iliac fascia, inguinal ligament, the psoas major, sartorius, and abdominal muscles. At the level of the hip joint the chief relations are: medially, the femoral vessels, the femoral nerve, and the sartorius muscle; laterally, the rectus femoris and tensor fasciæ latæ; in front, the abdominal muscles; behind, the hip joint.

Blood-supply.—Lumbar, circumflex iliac, and deep femoral arteries.

Nerve-supply.—Lumbar and femoral nerves.

4. **Quadratus lumborum.**—This thin muscle lies on the lateral part of the ventral surfaces of the lumbar transverse processes.

Origin.—The ventral surface of the upper part of the last two ribs and the lumbar transverse processes.

Insertion.—The ventral surface of the wing of the sacrum and the ventral sacro-iliac ligament.

Action.—Acting together, to fix the last two ribs and the lumbar vertebræ; acting singly, to produce lateral flexion of the loins.

Structure.—The muscle is pennate, and is curved with the convexity lateral. It is thin, largely mixed with tendinous fibers, and is, in general, little developed in the horse in comparison with some of the other animals (*e. g.*, dog, sheep).

Relations.—Ventrally, the psoas major and the last thoracic and first three lumbar nerves; dorsally, the last two ribs, the lumbar transverse processes, and the lateral branches of the lumbar arteries.

Blood-supply.—Lumbar arteries.

Nerve-supply.—Lumbar nerves.

5. **Intertransversales lumborum.**—(See p. 281).

II. THE LATERAL MUSCLES OF THE HIP AND THIGH

Under this head the muscles of the lateral surface of the pelvis and thigh, and those which form the posterior contour of the latter, will be described.

1. **Tensor fasciæ latæ** (Fig. 267).—This is the most anterior muscle of the superficial layer. It is triangular in form, with its apex at the tuber coxæ.

Origin.—The tuber coxæ.

Insertion.—The fascia lata and thus indirectly to the patella, the lateral patellar ligament, and the crest of the tibia.

Action.—To tense the fascia lata, flex the hip joint, and extend the stifle joint.

Structure.—The muscle arises by a rather small head, about two inches (ca. 5 cm.) wide, on the antero-inferior eminence of the tuber coxæ. Below this the belly spreads out and terminates in the aponeurosis about midway between the point of the hip and the stifle. Many fibers arise from an intermuscular septum between this muscle and the superficial gluteus; this septum is attached to the lateral border of the ilium. The aponeurosis fuses with the fascia lata, which may be regarded practically as the tendon of insertion; it detaches a lamina which passes with the tendon of insertion of the superficial gluteus to the lateral border of the femur.

Relations.—Laterally, the skin and fascia; medially, the obliquus abdominis externus, the iliacus, superficial gluteus, rectus femoris, and vastus lateralis, branches of the circumflex iliac, ilio-lumbar, and iliaco-femoral arteries, and the anterior gluteal nerve; anteriorly, the prefemoral lymph-glands. A considerable quantity of connective tissue is found between the deep face of the muscle and the abdominal wall.

Blood-supply.—Circumflex iliac, ilio-lumbar, and iliaco-femoral arteries.

Nerve-supply.—Anterior gluteal nerve.

2. **Gluteus superficialis** (Fig. 267).—This muscle lies behind and partly underneath the tensor fasciæ latæ. It is triangular and consists of an anterior and a posterior head united by the gluteal fascia.

Origin.—(1) The tuber coxæ and the adjacent part of the lateral border of the ilium; (2) the gluteal fascia.

Insertion.—The third trochanter of the femur.

Action.—To abduct the limb, flex the hip joint, and tense the gluteal fascia.

Structure.—The anterior head of the muscle is not completely separable (except artificially) from the tensor fasciæ latæ, since both muscles are attached to an intermuscular septum. The attachment to the border of the ilium is by means of an intermuscular septum, which passes beneath the thick lateral border of the gluteus medius and furnishes origin to fibers of both muscles. The posterior head arises from the deep face of the gluteal fascia, and so indirectly from the dorsal sacro-iliac ligament. The two heads unite and terminate on a strong flat tendon, which is inserted into the edge of the third trochanter of the femur, under cover of the biceps femoris.

Relations.—Superficially, the skin, fascia, and biceps femoris; deeply, the gluteus medius, iliacus, rectus femoris, and branches of the iliaco-femoral vessels; in front, the tensor fasciæ latæ; behind, the biceps femoris.

Blood-supply.—Gluteal and iliaco-femoral arteries.

Nerve-supply.—Anterior and posterior gluteal nerves.

3. **Gluteus medius** (Figs. 268, 580).—This is a very large muscle which covers the gluteal surface of the ilium and the greater part of the lateral wall of the pelvis, and extends forward also on the lumbar part of the longissimus dorsi.

Origin.—(1) The aponeurosis of the longissimus dorsi, as far forward as the first lumbar vertebra; (2) the gluteal surface and tubera of the ilium; (3) the dorsal and lateral sacro-iliac and sacro-sciatic ligaments, and the gluteal fascia.

Insertion.—(1) The summit of the trochanter major of the femur; (2) the crest below the trochanter; (3) the lateral aspect of the trochanteric ridge.

Action.—To extend the hip joint and abduct the limb. By its connection with the longissimus a muscular mass is formed which is one of the chief factors in rearing, kicking, and propulsion.

Structure.—The anterior extremity of the muscle is narrow and thin, and lies in a depression on the surface of the longissimus, from the strong aponeurosis of which the fibers take origin. The pelvic portion of the muscle is very voluminous, and forms the bulk of the muscular mass which gives the haunch its rounded contour. This part of the muscle is intersected by several tendinous sheets. One of these is particularly distinct, and is attached to the gluteal line on the ilium. This divides the muscle incompletely into superficial and deep strata. The superficial part is inserted by a strong tendon into the summit of the great trochanter, and by a pointed fleshy mass with a tendinous border into the lateral surface of the trochanteric ridge. The deep part is termed the **gluteus accessorius;** it is smaller, and arises entirely from the ilium between the gluteal line and the tuber coxæ (Fig. 580). It has a strong flat tendon which passes over the anterior part or convexity of the trochanter to be inserted into the crest below it. The trochanter is covered here with cartilage, and the **trochanteric bursa** (Bursa trochanterica) is interposed between the tendon and the cartilage.[1]

Relations.—Superficially, the skin, lumbo-dorsal and gluteal fasciæ, the tensor fasciæ latæ, gluteus superficialis, and biceps femoris; deeply, the longissimus, the ilium, sacro-iliac and sacro-sciatic ligaments, the gluteus profundus, iliacus and rectus femoris, the iliaco-femoral vessels, the gluteal and internal pudic vessels and nerves, and the great sciatic nerve.

Blood-supply.—Gluteal, ilio-lumbar, lumbar, and iliaco-femoral arteries.

Nerve-supply.—Gluteal nerves.

4. **Gluteus profundus.**[2]—This much smaller quadrilateral muscle lies under the posterior part of the preceding muscle, and extends over the hip joint, from the superior ischiatic spine to the anterior part of the trochanter major (Fig. 580).

Origin.—The superior ischiatic spine and the adjacent part of the shaft of the ilium.

Insertion.—The edge of the anterior part or convexity of the trochanter major of the femur.

Action.—To abduct the thigh and to rotate it inward.

Structure.—The muscle is short and thick and contains numerous tendinous intersections. The fibers are directed almost transversely outward over the capsule of the hip joint and converge at the convexity of the trochanter.

Relations.—Superficially, the gluteus medius and branches of the gluteal vessels and nerves; deeply, the shaft of the ilium, the hip joint, and the rectus femoris and capsularis.

Blood-supply.—Gluteal artery.

Nerve-supply.—Anterior gluteal nerve.

5. **Biceps femoris.**[3]—This large muscle lies behind and in part upon the superficial and middle glutei. It extends in a curved direction from the sacral and coccygeal spines to the lateral surface of the stifle and leg (Figs. 267, 292, 580).

Origin.—(1) The dorsal and lateral sacro-iliac ligaments, the gluteal and coccygeal fasciæ, and the intermuscular septum between this muscle and the semitendinosus; (2) the tuber ischii.

Insertion.—(1) A rough eminence on the posterior surface of the femur near the trochanter tertius; (2) the free (anterior) surface of the patella and the lateral patellar ligament; (3) the tibial crest; (4) the crural fascia and the tuber calcis.

Action.—The action is somewhat complex, because the muscle is composed of three parts, has several points of insertion, and acts on all the joints of the limb except those of the digit. The general action is to extend the limb, as in propelling the body, rearing or kicking, and to abduct it. The anterior part, by its attachment to the posterior surface of the femur and to the patella, would extend

---

[1] By most anatomists the portion inserted into the crest is termed the gluteus accessorius, but Lesbre considers this to be the deep gluteus, homologous with the gluteus minimus of man. The portion inserted into the trochanteric ridge apparently represents the piriformis of man.

[2] Lesbre considers this to be the scansorius.

[3] Apparently the muscle represents the biceps, together with part of the gluteus superficialis of man. Hence the names gluteo-biceps and paramero-biceps have been suggested.

the stifle and hip joints and abduct the limb. The middle part, being inserted chiefly on the tibial crest and the lateral patellar ligament, would extend the hip, and may, with the semitendinosus, flex the stifle. The posterior part, by virtue of its attachment to the tuber calcis, assists in extending the hock. It is to be noted, however, that extension of the hock joint can occur only when the stifle is also extended, and vice versâ.

Structure.—The muscle has two heads of origin. The long or vertebral head arises chiefly from the dorsal and lateral sacro-iliac ligaments, the coccygeal fascia, and the intermuscular septum. There is often a large **bursa** between this head and the trochanter major. The short or ischiatic head arises by a strong tendon from the ventral spine on the tuber ischii, which also furnishes origin to part of the semitendinosus. They unite, and a short tendon, detached from the deep face of the muscle, is inserted into the posterior surface of the femur near the third trochanter; here a **bursa** is interposed between the tendon and the bone. The muscle then divides into three parts, which terminate on a strong aponeurosis over the junction of the thigh and leg. The anterior part is directed toward the patella, the middle one toward the tibial crest, while the posterior one assists in the formation of the posterior contour of the limb. The aponeurosis blends with the deep layer of the fascia cruris, as already described. A synovial **bursa** occurs under the patellar insertion, and in some cases there is also one between the muscle and the third trochanter.

Relations.—Superficially, the skin and fascia; deeply, the sacro-iliac and sacrosciatic ligaments, the coccygeal fascia, the femur, the gluteus medius, obturator, gemellus, quadratus femoris, adductor, semimembranosus, vastus lateralis, and gastrocnemius muscles, branches of the lateral sacral, gluteal, obturator, femoral and deep femoral vessels, the great sciatic, tibial, peroneal, and posterior gluteal nerves; in front, the superficial and middle glutei; behind and medially, the semitendinosus.

Blood-supply.—Gluteal, obturator, deep femoral and posterior femoral arteries.

Nerve-supply.—Posterior gluteal, great sciatic and peroneal nerves.

6. **Semitendinosus.**—This is a long muscle which extends from the first two coccygeal vertebræ to the proximal third of the medial surface of the tibia. It lies at first behind the biceps, then passes downward on the back of the thigh, between that muscle and the semimembranosus (Figs. 268, 288, 580). It has two heads of origin.

Origin.—(1) The transverse processes of the first and second coccygeal vertebræ, the coccygeal fascia, and the intermuscular septum between this muscle and the biceps femoris; (2) the ventral surface of the tuber ischii.

Insertion.—(1) The tibial crest; (2) the crural fascia and the tuber calcis.

Action.—To extend the hip and hock joints, acting with the biceps and semimembranosus in propulsion of the trunk, rearing, etc.; also to flex the stifle and rotate the leg inward.[1]

Structure.—The long or vertebral head is small at its origin, but becomes larger by the accession of fibers arising on the intermuscular septum. Below the tuber ischii it unites with the short head, which arises partly by fleshy fibers, partly by a common tendon with the biceps. The muscle then passes downward on the back of the thigh, and terminates on a wide tendon on the medial surface of the proximal third of the leg. A distinct band passes forward to be inserted on the tibial crest (a **bursa** lying between the tendon and the tibia), part fuses with the fascia of the leg, while the remainder joins the biceps tendon and concurs in the formation of the tendinous band, which, as before described, terminates on the tuber calcis (Fig. 583). A **bursa** may occur under the long head where it passes over the tuber ischii.

[1] It should be remembered, however, that the stifle can be flexed only when the hock is also flexed and vice versâ.

Relations.—Laterally, the skin and fascia, the biceps, and the medial head of the gastrocnemius; medially, the coccygeal fascia, the sacro-sciatic ligament, the semimembranosus; anteriorly, the biceps femoris, branches of the femoral artery, and the great sciatic nerve.

Blood-supply.—Posterior gluteal, obturator, deep and posterior femoral arteries.

Nerve-supply.—Posterior gluteal and great sciatic nerves.

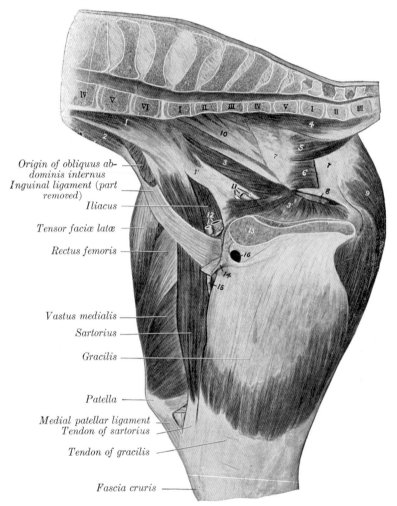

Origin of obliquus ab-
dominis internus
Inguinal ligament (part
removed)
Iliacus
Tensor faciæ latæ
Rectus femoris
Vastus medialis
Sartorius
Gracilis
Patella
Medial patellar ligament
Tendon of sartorius
Tendon of gracilis
Fascia cruris

Fig. 287.—Muscles of Pelvis and Thigh of Young Horse, Right Side; Medial View.

1, Psoas minor, and 1′, its insertion; 2, psoas major; 3, 3′, heads of obturator internus; 4, sacro-coccygeus ventralis; 5, coccygeus; 6, retractor ani (cut); 7, sacro-sciatic ligament; 8, lesser sciatic foramen; 9, semimembranosus; 10, lumbo-sacral plexus; 11, obturator nerve and vessels (cut); 12, femoral vessels (origin); 13, pubis; 14, prepubic tendon; 15, deep inguinal lymph glands; 16, opening for external pudic vein. Vertebræ are numbered by regions.

7. Semimembranosus[1] (Figs. 276, 287, 288, 576).—This very large, three-sided muscle lies on the medial surface of the preceding muscle and the gastrocnemius, and has two heads of origin.

Origin.—(1) The posterior border of the sacro-sciatic ligament; (2) the ventral surface of the tuber ischii.

[1] This muscle was incorrectly designated the adductor magnus by Percivall and Strangeways. Its name, however, is not at all descriptive of its structure in the domesticated animals

Insertion.—The medial epicondyle of the femur, behind the collateral ligament.

Action.—To extend the hip joint and to adduct the limb.

Structure.—The long head, small and pointed above, extends toward the root of the tail, fusing with the sacro-sciatic ligament. Passing downward, it becomes larger and covers in part the posterior aspect of the tuber ischii. A **bursa** may be found here. Below this it joins the short head, which is larger. The large belly so formed passes downward and forward, covered in great part by the gracilis, and terminates on a short, flat tendon of insertion at the distal end of the femur.

Relations.—The upper part of the muscle concurs with the sacro-sciatic ligament in forming the lateral boundary of the pelvic outlet. It is related posteriorly and laterally to the skin and fascia and the semitendinosus; medially, to the anus and its muscles, the vulva in the female, and the internal pudic artery and nerve (Figs. 577, 578). Below the pelvis the chief relations are: laterally, the semitendinosus, biceps, and gastrocnemius, branches of the obturator, femoral, and posterior femoral arteries, and the great sciatic nerve and its chief branches; medially, the crus penis and ischio-cavernosus muscle (in the male) and the gracilis; in front, the adductor and the femoral vessels; behind, the skin and fascia.

Blood-supply.—Obturator, posterior gluteal and femoral arteries.

Nerve-supply.—Great sciatic nerve.

III. THE MEDIAL MUSCLES OF THE THIGH

The muscles of this group are arranged in three layers.

First Layer

1. **Sartorius** (Figs. 287, 288, 576).—This long and rather narrow muscle is the most anterior one of the first layer. It extends from the posterior part of the sublumbar region to the lower and medial part of the stifle, and is directed downward and somewhat backward.

Origin.—The iliac fascia and the tendon of the psoas minor.

Insertion.—The medial patellar ligament and the tuberosity of the tibia.

Action.—To flex the hip joint and adduct the limb.

Structure.—The muscle is thin at its origin, but becomes thicker, narrower, and three sided distally. It terminates near the stifle joint on an aponeurosis which blends with that of the gracilis and with the fascia of the leg.

Relations.—Medially, the inguinal ligament, the abdominal muscles, the skin and fascia; laterally, the ilio-psoas, quadriceps femoris, and femoral nerve. It forms the anterior boundary of the femoral canal, in which the femoral artery and vein and the deep inguinal lymph glands are situated (Fig. 576).

Blood-supply.—Femoral artery.

Nerve-supply.—Saphenous nerve.

A rare variation is the existence of a small accessory head which arises from the anterior border of the pubis or from the prepubic tendon and joins the normal muscle near the middle of the thigh.

2. **Gracilis** (Figs. 276, 287, 575).—This is a wide, quadrilateral muscle, which is situated behind the sartorius, and covers the greater part of the medial surface of the thigh.

Origin.—The middle third of the pelvic symphysis, the prepubic tendon and accessory ligament, and the ventral surface of the pubis behind the prepubic tendon.

Insertion.—The medial patellar ligament, the medial surface of the tibia in front of the medial femoro-tibial ligament, and the crural fascia.

Action.—To adduct the limb.

Structure.—The muscle arises by a strong tendon, chiefly in common with the opposite muscle. Its direct attachment to the ventral surface of the pelvis is not so extensive as a superficial inspection would suggest. The tendon of origin presents anteriorly a foramen for the passage of the external pudic vein. The belly is composed of parallel bundles, and is marked by a superficial furrow which, however, does not indicate a muscular division. It terminates on the medial surface of the stifle on a thin wide tendon which blends in front with that of the sartorius, below with the crural fascia.

Relations.—Superficially, the skin and fascia, the penis or mammary gland, and the saphenous vessels and nerve; deeply, the pectineus, adductor, semimembranosus and semitendinosus, and, at the middle of the femur, the femoral vessels; anteriorly, the sartorius. In the proximal third of the thigh the sartorius and gracilis are separated by a triangular interval (femoral triangle), in which lie the deep inguinal lymph glands and the femoral vessels.

Blood-supply.—Femoral and deep femoral arteries.

Nerve-supply.—Obturator nerve.

Second Layer

1. **Pectineus** (Figs. 276, 288, 576).—This muscle is fusiform and extends from the anterior border of the pubis to the middle of the medial border of the femur.

Origin.—The prepubic tendon, the accessory ligament, and the anterior border of the pubis.

Insertion.—The middle of the medial border of the femur, near the nutrient foramen.

Action.—To adduct the limb and flex the hip joint.

Structure.—The belly is cylindrical and contains little fibrous tissue. Its origin is perforated by the accessory ligament—from which many fibers arise—and is thus divided into two unequal parts. The large upper part arises largely from the prepubic tendon—only a small part gaining direct attachment to the pubis. The small lower part does not reach the bone. The insertion is pointed and tendinous.

Relations.—Medially, the gracilis; laterally, the femur, the vastus medialis, the terminal part of the psoas major and iliacus, and the deep femoral artery; anteriorly, the sartorius, the femoral vessels, the saphenous nerve, and the deep inguinal lymph glands; posteriorly, the adductor and obturator externus, and the obturator nerve (anterior division).

Blood-supply.—Femoral and deep femoral arteries.

Nerve-supply.—Obturator nerve.

The **femoral canal** is exposed in the dissection of the preceding muscles (Figs. 288, 290). It is bounded anteriorly by the sartorius, posteriorly by the pectineus, and laterally by the ilio-psoas and vastus medialis. Its medial wall is formed by the femoral fascia and the gracilis. Its upper or abdominal opening, the femoral ring (Lacuna vasorum), lies behind the medial part of the internal inguinal ring and is bounded anteriorly by the inguinal ligament, posteriorly by the anterior border of the pubis, and laterally by the tendon of the psoas minor. The canal terminates below at the insertion of the pectineus. It contains the deep inguinal lymph glands, the femoral artery and vein, and the saphenous nerve.

2. **Adductor**[1] (Figs. 276, 288, 576).—This fleshy, prismatic muscle lies behind the pectineus and vastus medialis. It extends downward and forward from the ventral surface of the pelvis to the medial epicondyle of the femur.

Origin.—The ventral surface of the pubis and ischium and the tendon of origin of the gracilis.

---

[1] It has been customary to describe two adductors—a parvus or brevis, and a longus or magnus. This division is partly artificial, and has been abandoned in the new nomenclature—a return to the views of Bourgelat and Girard.

Insertion.—(1) The posterior surface of the femur from the level of the third trochanter to the groove for the femoral vessels; (2) the medial epicondyle of the femur and the medial ligament of the stifle joint.

Action.—To adduct the limb and extend the hip joint. It also rotates the femur inward.

Structure.—It is almost entirely fleshy, and is composed of parallel bundles

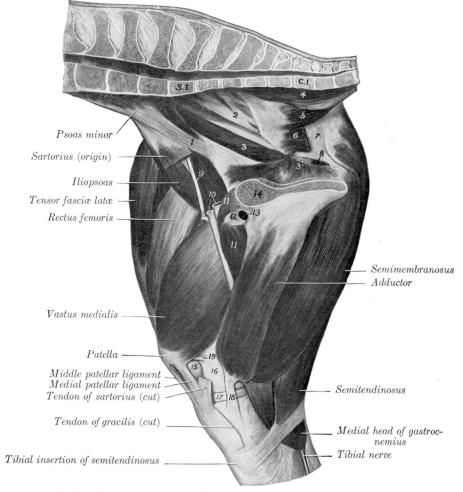

FIG. 288.—MUSCLES OF PELVIS AND THIGH OF HORSE, RIGHT SIDE; MEDIAL VIEW.
Figure represents deeper dissection of specimen shown in preceding figure.

1, Tendon of insertion of psoas minor; 2, lumbo-sacral plexus; 3, 3′, heads of obturator internus; 4, sacro-coccygeus ventralis; 5, coccygeus; 6, retractor ani (origin); 7, sacro-sciatic ligament; 8, lesser sciatic foramen; 9, femoral nerve; 10, femoral vessels; 11, 11, pectineus; 12, accessory ligament; 13, external pudic vein; 14, pubis; 15, femoro-patellar joint capsule; 16, distal end of femur; 17, medial meniscus; 18, medial ligament of stifle joint; 19, medial femoro-patellar ligament.

united rather loosely. It is usually possible to separate from the principal mass a small anterior short part, which is inserted into the femur behind the pectineus. The principal mass is perforated just below the insertion of the pectineus by an opening for the femoral vessels (hiatus adductorius), and is thus divided into two branches.   The lateral branch is inserted into the back of the femur with the short portion, while the medial branch is attached to the medial epicondyle and collateral ligament.   There is often a superficial slip which ends partly on the femoro-patellar joint capsule and may reach the accessory cartilage or medial ligament of the patella.   Some fibers pass under the collateral ligament and end on the tendon of the semimembranosus.

Relations.—Medially, the gracilis, and branches of the femoral artery and of the obturator nerve; laterally, the femur, the obturator externus, quadratus femoris, biceps femoris, and the femoral, deep femoral, and obturator arteries; anteriorly, the pectineus, vastus medialis, and a large branch of the obturator nerve; posteriorly, the semimembranosus and the great sciatic nerve.

Blood-supply.—Femoral, deep femoral, and obturator arteries.

Nerve-supply.—Obturator nerve.

3. **Semimembranosus.**—Described on p. 326.

Third Layer

1. **Quadratus femoris.**—This is a narrow, three-sided muscle, which lies under cover of the upper part of the adductor (Fig. 581).

Origin.—The ventral surface of the ischium, just in front of the semimembranosus.

Insertion.—An oblique line on the posterior surface of the femur, near the lower part of the trochanter minor.

Action.—To extend the hip joint and to adduct the thigh.

Structure.—It is composed of parallel bundles of fibers directed downward, forward, and outward.

Relations.—Postero-medially, the adductor, semimembranosus, and the obturator vessels; antero-laterally, the obturator externus and biceps femoris, the deep femoral vessels, and the great sciatic nerve.

Blood-supply.—Deep femoral and obturator arteries.

Nerve-supply.—Great sciatic nerve.

2. **Obturator externus** (Fig. 581).—This is a pyramidal muscle which extends across the back of the hip joint from the ventral surface of the pelvis around the obturator foramen to the trochanteric fossa.

Origin.—The ventral surface of the pubis and ischium, and the margin of the obturator foramen.

Insertion.—The trochanteric fossa.

Action.—To adduct the thigh and to rotate it outward.

Structure.—It is almost entirely fleshy, the muscle-bundles being rather loosely connected.   The insertion is pointed, flattened, and partly tendinous.   The origin is perforated by the obturator vessels and nerve.

Relations.—Medially, the adductor and quadratus femoris and the deep femoral vessels; laterally, the gemellus, the tendon of the obturator internus, the biceps femoris, and the great sciatic nerve; anteriorly, the hip joint, the pectineus, and the external pudic vein.

Blood-supply.—Deep femoral and obturator arteries.

Nerve-supply.—Obturator nerve.

3. **Obturator internus** (Fig. 288).—This arises within the pelvic cavity by two heads, the tendon emerging through the lesser sciatic foramen.

Origin.—(1) The pelvic surface of the pubis and ischium around the obturator foramen; (2) the pelvic surface of the shaft of the ilium and the wing of the sacrum.

Insertion.—The trochanteric fossa.

Action.—To rotate the femur outward.

Structure.—The ischio-pubic head lies on the pelvic floor and covers the obturator foramen. It is thin and fan-shaped. The iliac head extends along the lateral wall of the pelvis, and is pennate, with a central tendon throughout. Both terminate on a flat tendon which passes outward through the lesser sciatic foramen to be inserted into the trochanteric fossa. The tendon furnishes insertion to fibers of the gemellus. A synovial **bursa** facilitates the play of the tendon over the lateral border of the ischium.[1]

Relations.—The pelvic surface is covered by the pelvic fascia and in part by the peritoneum. The obturator vessels and nerve lie between the two heads, and the internal pudic vessels and nerve lie along the dorsal edge of the iliac head. The tendon is crossed by the great sciatic nerve.

Blood-supply.—Obturator and internal pudic arteries.

Nerve-supply.—Great sciatic nerve.

4. **Gemellus**[2] (Fig. 580).—This is a thin, triangular muscle, which extends from the lateral border of the ischium to the trochanteric fossa and ridge.

Origin.—The lateral border of the ischium near the ischiatic spine.

Insertion.—The trochanteric fossa and ridge.

Action.—To rotate the femur outward.

Structure.—The thin tendon of origin is attached to a line on the lateral border of the ischium, which begins just below the posterior end of the superior ischiatic spine. Many superficial fibers are inserted into the tendon of the obturator internus.

Relations.—Superficially, the biceps femoris, the tendon of the obturator internus, the gluteus medius, and the great sciatic nerve; deeply, the obturator externus and the hip joint.

Blood-supply.—Obturator artery.

Nerve-supply.—Great sciatic nerve.

IV. ANTERIOR MUSCLES OF THE THIGH

This group consists of the sartorius, quadriceps femoris, and capsularis.

1. **Sartorius.**—This is described on p. 327.

2. **Quadriceps femoris** (Figs. 268, 289, 291).—This constitutes the large muscular mass which covers the front and sides of the femur. It has four heads, one of which, the rectus, arises from the ilium; the other three arise from the femur. All are inserted into the patella.

(1) **Rectus femoris.**—This is fusiform and rounded. It arises by two tendons.

Origin.—Two depressions on the shaft of the ilium above and in front of the acetabulum.

Insertion.—The base and anterior surface of the patella.

Action.—To extend the stifle joint and to flex the hip joint.

Structure.—It has two short strong tendons of origin; beneath the lateral one is a **bursa**. The belly is rounded and rests in a groove formed by the other portions of the quadriceps. Its sides are covered by a strong tendinous layer which fur-

---

[1] The iliac head has been described as a separate muscle, and termed the piriformis. This does not seem desirable, especially since it is probable that the homologue of the piriformis of man is that portion of the middle gluteus which is inserted into the trochanteric ridge.

[2] The name is based on the arrangement in man, in whom the muscle usually consists of two fasciculi forming a groove between them for the tendon of the obturator internus. In the horse it is usually undivided at its origin, but toward the insertion the upper part is separated from the rest of the muscle or is readily isolated. The muscle is subject to much variation in size. When well developed, the insertion extends from the proximal end of the trochanteric fossa to a point just above the femoral attachment of the biceps femoris; in such cases the upper part, which occupies the space behind the hip joint between the gluteus profundus and obturator externus, is much thicker than the remainder, which covers the latter muscle. The gemellus may be regarded as the extrapelvic head of the obturator internus (Gegenbaur).

nishes insertion to fibers of the vasti. The tendon of insertion is formed by the union of these tendinous layers on the lower part of the muscle. The lower portion of the muscle is pennate, the fibers on either side converging on the tendon at an acute angle.

Relations.—Medially, the iliacus, sartorius, and vastus medialis; laterally, the tensor fasciæ latæ, glutei, and vastus lateralis; posteriorly, the hip joint and the vastus intermedius; anteriorly, the fascia lata and the skin. The anterior femoral artery and branches of the femoral nerve descend into the interspace be-

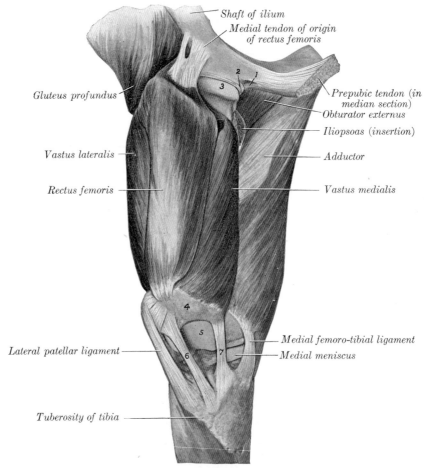

Fig. 289.—Muscles of Right Thigh of Horse, Deep Dissection. The Preparation is Viewed from in Front and Somewhat Medially.

1, Accessory ligament of hip joint; 2, transverse ligament of same; 3, head of femur; 4, patella; 5, trochlea of femur; 6, 7, middle and medial patellar ligaments.

tween the upper part of the rectus and the vastus medialis; similarly, the iliaco-femoral artery dips in between the rectus femoris and vastus lateralis.

Blood-supply.—Femoral and iliaco-femoral arteries.

Nerve-supply.—Femoral nerve.

(2) **Vastus lateralis.**—This lies on the lateral surface of the femur, extending from the great trochanter to the patella. It is wide in its middle, smaller at each end.

Origin.—The lateral border and surface of the femur, from the trochanter major to the supracondyloid fossa.

Insertion.—(1) The lateral part of the anterior surface of the patella; (2) the tendon of the rectus femoris.

Action.—To extend the stifle joint.

Structure.—The fibers are directed downward and forward, many being inserted into the tendinous sheet which covers the side of the rectus. A bursa is usually present between the distal end and the patella.

Relations.—Laterally, the fascia lata and skin, tensor fasciæ latæ, superficial

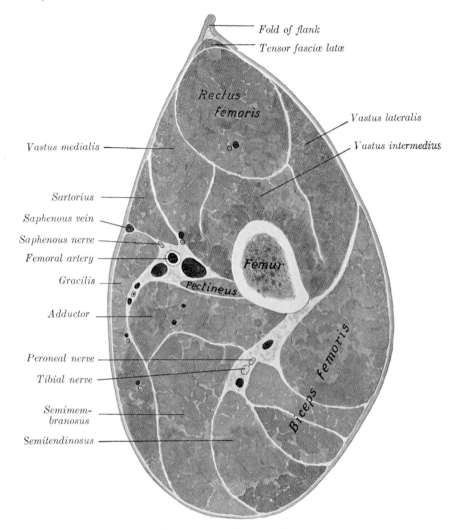

FIG. 290.—CROSS-SECTION OF MIDDLE OF RIGHT THIGH OF HORSE.

gluteus, and biceps femoris; medially, the femur and femoro-patellar joint capsule, the rectus femoris, vastus intermedius, and the iliaco-femoral artery.

Blood-supply.—Iliaco-femoral and popliteal arteries.

Nerve-supply.—Femoral nerve.

(3) **Vastus medialis.**—This resembles the preceding muscle, and lies in a similar position on the medial side of the femur.

Origin.—The medial surface of the femur, from the neck to the distal third.

Insertion.—(1) The medial border of the patella and its cartilage, and the proximal part of the medial patellar ligament. (2) The tendon of the rectus femoris.

Action.—To extend the stifle joint.

Structure.—This is very similar to that of the vastus lateralis. It is, however, more difficult to separate from the intermedius, because many fibers of the latter arise on the tendinous sheet which covers the contact surface of the medial

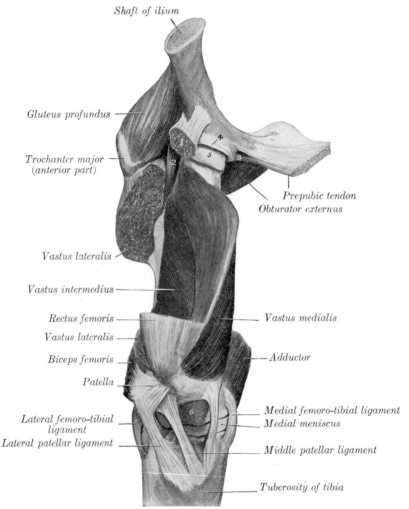

Shaft of ilium

Gluteus profundus

Trochanter major (anterior part)

Prepubic tendon
Obturator externus

Vastus lateralis

Vastus intermedius

Rectus femoris

Vastus lateralis

Biceps femoris

Patella

Vastus medialis

Adductor

Medial femoro-tibial ligament
Medial meniscus

Lateral femoro-tibial ligament

Lateral patellar ligament

Middle patellar ligament

Tuberosity of tibia

FIG. 291.—MUSCLES OF RIGHT THIGH OF HORSE; DEEP DISSECTION.

The preparation is viewed from the front and somewhat medially. Most of rectus femoris and vastus lateralis has been removed. 1, Stump of origin of rectus femoris; 2, capsularis; 3, accessory ligament; 4, cotyloid ligament; 5, head of femur; 6, trochlea of femur.

vastus. Its insertion into the patella is chiefly by means of a broad, strong tendon. From the deep face fleshy fibers are inserted also into the femoro-patellar joint capsule.

Relations.—Medially, the skin and fascia, the iliacus, sartorius, pectineus, and adductor, the femoral vessels, and saphenous nerve; laterally, the femur, femoro-patellar joint capsule, rectus femoris, and vastus intermedius, the anterior femoral artery, and branches of the femoral nerve.

Blood-supply.—Femoral and anterior femoral arteries.

Nerve-supply.—Femoral nerve.

(4) **Vastus intermedius.**—This muscle is deeply situated on the anterior face of the femur, and is entirely covered by the preceding heads.

Origin.—(1) The anterior surface of the femur, from the proximal to the distal fourth; (2) the tendinous covering of the vastus medialis.

Insertion.—(1) The base of the patella; (2) the femoro-patellar joint capsule.

Action.—(1) To extend the stifle joint; (2) to tense (raise) the femoro-patellar capsule during extension of the joint.

Structure.—The muscle is usually quite difficult to isolate from the other vasti, so that many since Günther have declared it an artefact.[1] It is entirely fleshy, and is small at its proximal end, but when traced downward increases in bulk by the accession of fibers arising on the femur and the tendinous covering of the vastus medialis. The terminal part is intimately adherent to the femoro-patellar joint capsule, where the latter bulges above the level of the patella.

Relations.—Medially, the vastus medialis; laterally, the vastus lateralis; anteriorly, the rectus; posteriorly, the femur and femoro-patellar capsule.

Blood-supply.—Iliaco-femoral and anterior femoral arteries.

Nerve-supply.—Femoral nerve.

The patellar ligaments are to be regarded as tendons of the quadriceps which communicate the action of the latter to the tibia, the patella being intercalated as a sesamoid bone.

3. **Capsularis coxæ** (Fig. 291).— This is a small fusiform muscle (hardly as large as one's finger), which arises by a thin tendon on the ilium immediately above the outer tendon of the rectus femoris. Its delicate tendon of insertion dips in between the vastus intermedius and lateralis and is attached to the proximal third of the anterior surface of the femur. It passes over the outer side of the hip joint, to the capsule of which some fibers are attached. Sometimes the muscle has two distinct heads, in which case the additional head arises between the two tendons of origin of the rectus femoris. Its action may be to raise the capsule during flexion of the joint. It is related laterally to the gluteus profundus and vastus lateralis, medially to the rectus femoris and vastus intermedius and the hip joint.

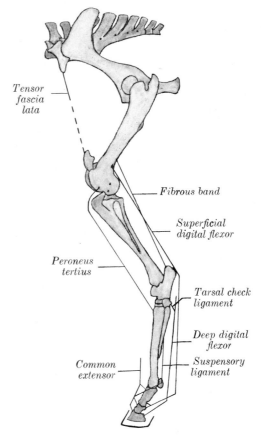

FIG. 291*a*.—DIAGRAM OF PELVIC LIMB OF THE HORSE. Structures making up the "Stay Apparatus" which enables him to stand while he sleeps. Lateral view.

V. THE MUSCLES OF THE LEG AND FOOT

The muscles of this region cover almost all of the tibia except its medial face, which is largely subcutaneous. As in the forearm, the muscles fall into two groups, a dorsolateral and a plantar. The muscles

[1] While it is true that the separation of the intermedius is never entirely a natural one in the horse, it varies in individual cases, and is usually clear on cross-sections. In some subjects it is possible to separate another slip which may represent the articularis genu of man.

of the first group are extensors of the digit and flexors of the hock, those of the second have the opposite action.

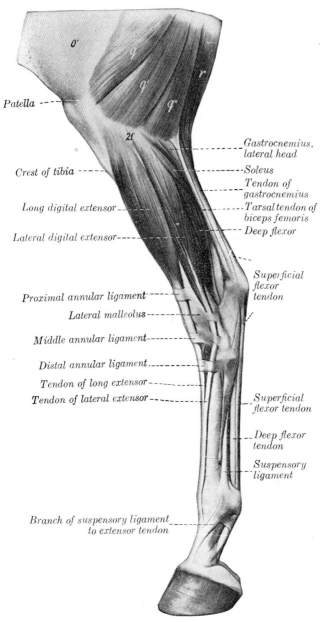

FIG. 292.—MUSCLES OF LOWER PART OF THIGH, LEG, AND FOOT OF HORSE; LATERAL VIEW.

o', Fascia lata; *q, q', q''*, biceps femoris; *r*, semitendinosus; *21'*, lateral condyle of tibia. The extensor brevis is visible in the angle between the long and lateral extensor tendons, but by an oversight it is not marked. (After Ellenberger-Baum, Anat. für Künstler.)

A. DORSO-LATERAL GROUP

1. Long digital extensor (M. extensor digitalis longus).—This muscle is situated superficially on the dorso-lateral aspect of the leg, and is provided with a long tendon which passes down over the front of the tarsus, metatarsus, and digit.

Origin.—The extensor fossa of the femur.

Insertion.—(1) The extensor process of the third phalanx; (2) the dorsal surface of the proximal extremities of the first and second phalanges.

Action.—To extend the digit and flex the hock. It also assists in fixing the stifle joint.

Structure.—The origin is by means of a strong tendon in common with the peroneus tertius, on which also many fibers arise. The common tendon passes downward in the groove between the lateral condyle and the tuberosity of the tibia, where a pouch from the femoro-tibial capsule descends about three inches (ca. 7 to 8 cm.) beneath the tendon. The belly is fusiform and somewhat flattened. The long tendon of insertion begins in the belly about its middle, and is clear of the

fleshy part near the tarsus. It passes downward over the front of the hock, bound
down by the three annular ligaments already described (see tarsal fascia), and enveloped by a **synovial sheath** which begins a little above the level of the lateral
malleolus, and extends nearly to the junction with the lateral extensor tendon.
This union occurs usually about a hand's breadth below the tarsus. In the angle
of union the extensor brevis also joins the principal tendon. Beyond this point
the arrangement is the same as in the fore limb.

Relations.—Superficially, the skin and fascia; deeply, the femoro-tibial joint,
peroneus tertius, and tibialis anterior; behind, the lateral extensor and the superficial and deep peroneal nerves. In front of the tarsus the anterior tibial artery
crosses the deep face of the tendon (Fig. 585).

Blood-supply.—Anterior tibial artery.

Nerve-supply.—Peroneal nerve.

2. **Lateral digital extensor** (M. extensor digitalis lateralis).[1]—This muscle lies
on the lateral surface of the leg, behind the preceding one.

Origin.—The lateral ligament of the stifle joint, the fibula, the lateral border
of the tibia, and the interosseous ligament.

Insertion.—The tendon of the long extensor, about a third of the way down
the metatarsus.

Action.—To assist the long extensor.

Structure.—The belly is fusiform, flattened, and pennate. The tendon runs
through the entire length of the belly and becomes free from it at the distal fourth
of the tibia. It descends through the groove on the lateral malleolus, bound down
by an annular ligament, and, inclining forward, blends (usually) with the tendon
of the long extensor. It is provided with a **synovial sheath,** which begins about
an inch (ca. 2 to 3 cm.) above the lateral malleolus and ends about one and one-
half inches (ca. 3 to 4 cm.) above the junction. Sometimes the fusion does not
occur; the tendon then descends alongside of that of the long extensor, and is inserted into the first phalanx like the corresponding muscle of the thoracic limb.

Relations.—Laterally, the skin and fascia and the superficial peroneal nerve;
medially, the tibia and fibula; anteriorly, the intermuscular septum, the long
extensor, and the tibialis anterior; posteriorly, the deep digital flexor and the soleus.

Blood-supply.—Anterior tibial artery.

Nerve-supply.—Peroneal nerve.

3. **Peroneus tertius** (Tendo femoro-metatarseus).—This consists in the horse
of a strong tendon which lies between the long extensor and the tibialis
anterior.

Origin.—The extensor fossa (between the lateral condyle and the trochlea
of the femur), in common with the long extensor.

Insertion.—(1) The proximal extremity of the large (third) metatarsal bone
and the third tarsal bone; (2) the fibular and fourth tarsal bones.

Action.—Mechanically to flex the hock when the stifle joint is flexed.

Structure.—It is entirely tendinous. The proximal end and the underlying
prolongation of the synovial membrane of the femoro-tibial joint have been mentioned in the description of the long extensor. The superficial face gives origin
to fibers of the long extensor in the upper part of the leg, and the deep face is fused
with the tibialis anterior except at either end of the region. At the distal end of the
tibia the tendon is perforated for the emergence of the tendon of the tibialis anterior
and divides into two branches. The anterior branch is attached to the third tarsal
and third metatarsal bones, while the lateral one curves outward, bifurcates, and
is inserted into the fibular and fourth tarsal bones. The lateral tendon blends

---

[1] Also known as the peroneus or the lateral extensor of the phalanges. Lesbre considers it
to be the homologue of the peroneus brevis of man and other pentadactyls.

with the middle annular ligament which forms a loop around the long extensor tendon.

Relations.—Superficially, the long extensor; deeply, the tibialis anterior. The anterior tibial vessels cross the deep face of the lateral branch.

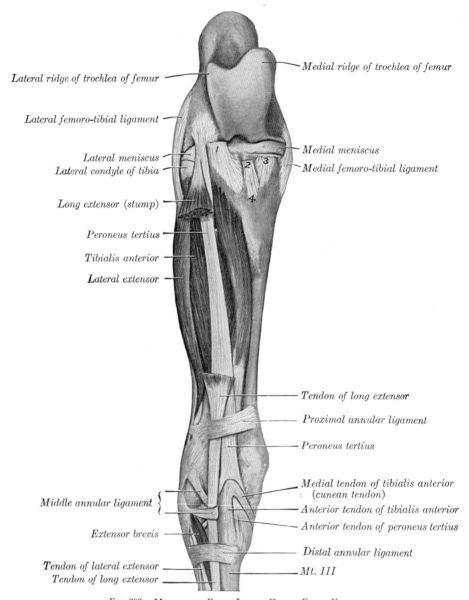

Lateral ridge of trochlea of femur

Lateral femoro-tibial ligament

Lateral meniscus
Lateral condyle of tibia

Long extensor (stump)

Peroneus tertius

Tibialis anterior

Lateral extensor

Medial ridge of trochlea of femur

Medial meniscus
Medial femoro-tibial ligament

Tendon of long extensor

Proximal annular ligament

Peroneus tertius

Medial tendon of tibialis anterior (cunean tendon)

Middle annular ligament

Anterior tendon of tibialis anterior

Anterior tendon of peroneus tertius

Extensor brevis

Distal annular ligament

Tendon of lateral extensor
Tendon of long extensor

Mt. III

FIG. 293.—MUSCLES OF RIGHT LEG OF HORSE; FRONT VIEW.

The greater part of the long extensor has been removed. 1, 2, 3, Stumps of patellar ligaments; 4, tuberosity of tibia. Small cross near end of leader line for peroneus tertius indicates distal limit of underlying pouch of femoro-tibial joint capsule.

4. **Tibialis anterior.**—This lies on the dorso-lateral face of the tibia; it is wide and flattened above, narrow below.

Origin.—The lateral condyle and border of the tibia and a small area on the lateral surface of the tuberosity; the crural fascia.

Insertion.—(1) The ridge on the front of the proximal end of the large metatarsal bone; (2) the first tarsal bone.

Action.—To flex the hock joint.

Structure.—The origin is fleshy, and forms a groove in which lie the common tendon of the long extensor and peroneus tertius and a synovial pouch which descends from the femoro-tibial joint. Many superficial fibers arise from the deep fascia at the proximal part of the leg and thus from the tibial crest. Passing downward on the tibia, the belly is united by tendinous and fleshy fibers with the peroneus tertius, and terminates close to the tarsus in a point on the tendon of inser-

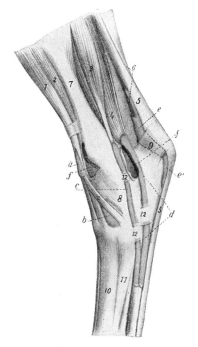

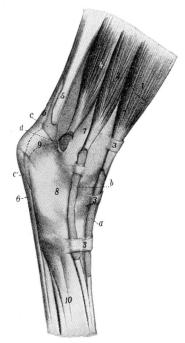

FIG. 294.—INJECTED SYNOVIAL SHEATHS AND BURSÆ OF TARSAL REGION OF HORSE; MEDIAL VIEW.

a, Synovial sheath of peroneus tertius and tibialis anterior; *b*, bursa under medial tendon of tibialis anterior; *c*, synovial sheath of flexor longus; *d*, tarsal sheath of deep flexor; *e*, *e'*, bursa under superficial flexor tendon; *f*, *f'*, tibio-tarsal joint capsule; *1*, long extensor; *2*, tibialis anterior; *2'*, medial tendon of *2*; *3*, flexor longus; *4*, deep digital flexor; *5*, superficial flexor tendon; *6*, gastrocnemius tendon; *7*, tibia; *8*, tarsus; *9*, tuber calcis; *10*, large metatarsal bone; *11*, medial small metatarsal bone; *12*, *12'*, fascial bands. (After Ellenberger, in Leisering's Atlas.)

FIG. 295.—INJECTED SYNOVIAL SHEATHS AND BURSÆ OF TARSAL REGION OF HORSE; LATERAL VIEW.

a, Synovial sheath of long digital extensor; *b*, synovial sheath of lateral digital extensor; *c*, *c'*, bursa under superficial flexor tendon; *d*, capsule of hock joint; *1*, long extensor; *2*, lateral extensor; *3*, *3*, *3*, annular ligaments; *4*, deep digital flexor; *5*, tendon of gastrocnemius; *6*, superficial flexor tendon; *7*, tibia; *8*, tarsus; *9*, tuber calcis; *10*, metatarsus. (After Ellenberger, in Leisering's Atlas.)

tion. The latter emerges between the branches of the peroneus tertius and bifurcates, the anterior branch being inserted into the large metatarsal bone, the medial one into the first tarsal bone. The tendon is provided with a **synovial sheath** at its emergence, and a **bursa** is interposed between the medial branch and the medial ligament of the hock.[1]

Relations.—Superficially, the long and lateral extensors, the peroneus tertius, and the deep peroneal nerve; deeply, the tibia, the deep flexor, and the anterior tibial vessels.

[1] In surgical works the medial branch is commonly termed the cunean tendon; it is sometimes resected for the relief of bone spavin.

Blood-supply.—Anterior tibial artery.

Nerve-supply.—Peroneal nerve.

B. PLANTAR GROUP

1. **Gastrocnemius** (Figs. 268, 292, 296).—This muscle extends from the distal third of the femur to the point of the hock. It arises by two heads.

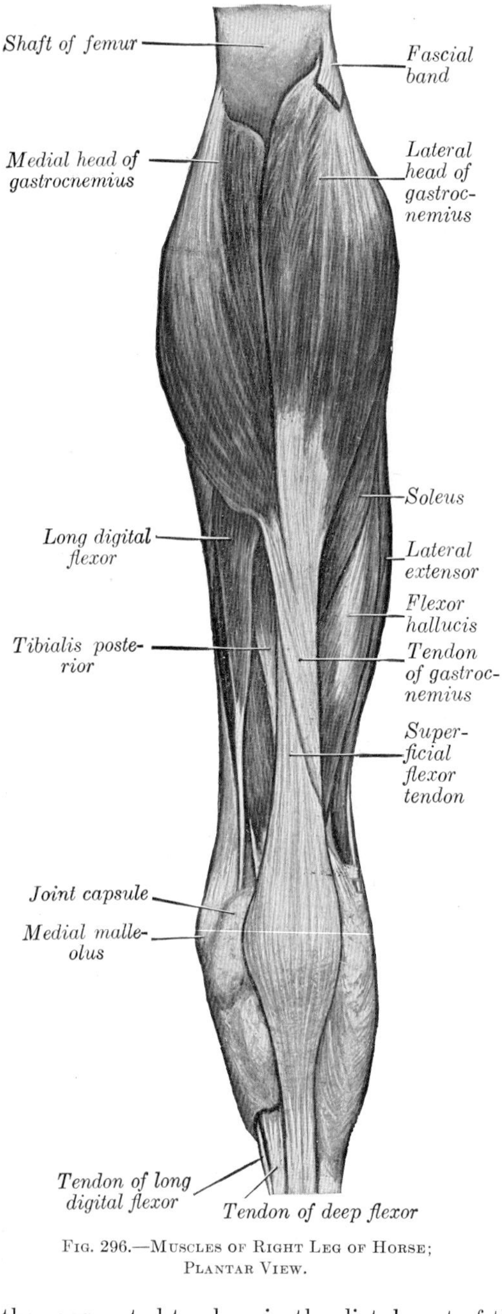

Origin.—(1) Lateral head, from the lateral supracondyloid crest (margin of the supracondyloid fossa); (2) medial head, from the medial supracondyloid crest.

Insertion.—The posterior part of the tuber calcis.

Action.—To extend the hock and to flex the stifle joint; these two actions, however, cannot occur simultaneously.

Structure.—The two bellies are thick, fusiform, and somewhat flattened. They are covered by a strong aponeurosis and contain tendinous intersections. They terminate toward the middle of the leg on a common tendon, which at first lies posterior to that of the superficial flexor, but, by a twist in both, comes to lie in front of the latter. The deep fascia blends with the tendon throughout its length, and the soleus muscle is inserted into its anterior edge. A strong fascial band, about two inches in width, arises from the lateral supracondyloid crest, descends over the lateral head of the gastrocnemius muscle forming a groove in the fleshy part of the muscle, and fuses with the tarsal tendon of the biceps femoris and semitendinosus muscles, thus becoming a part of the stay apparatus of the pelvic limb (Fig. 291a). A small **bursa** (Bursa tendinis m. gastrocnemii) lies in front of the insertion on the tuber calcis, and a large **bursa** (calcanea subtendinea) is interposed between the two tendons from the twist downward to the middle of the hock. The superficial digital flexor lies between the two heads and is adherent to the lateral one (Fig. 584). The term **tendo calcaneus** or **tendo Achillis** is a convenient designation for the aggregated tendons in the distal part of the leg which are attached to the tuber calcis.

Fig. 296.—MUSCLES OF RIGHT LEG OF HORSE; PLANTAR VIEW.

Relations.—Anteriorly, the stifle joint, the superficial digital flexor, popliteus, deep digital flexor, popliteal vessels, and tibial nerve; medially (above), the semitendinosus, semimembranosus, and adductor, (below) the fascia and skin; laterally (above), the biceps femoris and peroneal nerve, (below) the fascia and skin. The popliteal lymph glands lie on the upper part of the muscle.

Blood-supply.—Popliteal artery.

Nerve-supply.—Tibial nerve.

2. **Soleus** (Fig. 296).—This muscle is very small in the horse. It lies along the lateral border of the gastrocnemius under the common deep fascia, on the proximal half of the lateral surface of the leg.

Origin.—The head of the fibula.

Insertion.—The tendon of the gastrocnemius, at the distal fourth of the leg.

Action.—To assist the gastrocnemius.

Structure.—It is a thin, fleshy band, usually about an inch (ca. 2 to 3 cm.) in width, and terminates on a thin tendon which fuses with that of the gastrocnemius.[1]

Relations.—Superficially, the skin, fascia, and peroneal nerve; deeply, the lateral extensor and deep flexor.

Blood-supply.—Posterior tibial artery.

Nerve-supply.—Tibial nerve.

3. **Superficial digital flexor** (M. flexor digitalis pedis superficialis) (Figs. 292, 296, 297).—The proximal part of this muscle lies between and under cover of the two heads of the gastrocnemius. It consists almost entirely of a strong tendon, the belly being very little developed.

Origin.—The supracondyloid fossa of the femur.

Insertion.—(1) The tuber calcis; (2) the eminences on each side of the proximal extremity of the second phalanx, and the distal extremity of the first phalanx behind the collateral ligaments of the pastern joint.

Action.—To flex the digit and extend the hock joint. On account of the exceedingly small amount of muscular tissue the action is to be regarded chiefly as a mechanical effect which results from the action of other muscles on the stifle joint.

Structure.—The origin is by means of a strong round tendon which is incompletely covered with fleshy fibers as far as the upper third of the leg. Here it is intimately attached to the gastrocnemius, especially to the lateral head. At the distal third of the tibia it winds around the medial surface of the gastrocnemius tendon, and then occupies a position behind the latter. At the point of the hock it widens out, forming a sort of cap over the tuber calcis, and detaches on either side a strong band which is inserted into the tuber calcis with the tarsal tendons of the biceps and semitendinosus. It then passes downward over the plantar ligament, becomes narrower, and is arranged distally as in the thoracic limb. A large **synovial bursa** (B. calcanea subtendinea) lies under the tendon from the distal fourth of the tibia to the middle of the tarsus. A **subcutaneous bursa** (B. calcanea subcutanea) is sometimes present on the wide part of the tendon at the point of the hock.

Relations.—Posteriorly, the gastrocnemius, fascia, and skin; anteriorly, the femoro-patellar capsule, the popliteus, the deep flexor, and the popliteal vessels; medially, the tibial nerve.

Blood-supply.—Posterior femoral artery.

Nerve-supply.—Tibial nerve.

4. **Deep digital flexor** (M. flexor digitalis pedis profundus) (Figs. 292, 298).— The belly of this muscle lies on the posterior surface of the tibia, and is divisible into three heads, which, however, finally unite on a common tendon of insertion.

Origin.—(1) The posterior edge of the lateral condyle of the tibia; (2) the border of the lateral condyle of the tibia, just behind the facet for the fibula; (3)

---

[1] The soleus is sometimes included with the two heads of the gastrocnemius under the name triceps suræ.

the middle third of the posterior surface and the upper part of the lateral border of the tibia, the posterior border of the fibula, and the interosseous ligament.

Insertion.—The semilunar crest and the adjacent surface of the cartilage of the third phalanx.

Action.—To flex the digit and to extend the hock joint.

Structure.—(1) The medial head is termed the **long digital flexor** (M. flexor digitalis longus); it is easily isolated (Figs. 298, 584). It has a fusiform belly, which crosses the leg obliquely and lies in a groove formed by the other heads and the

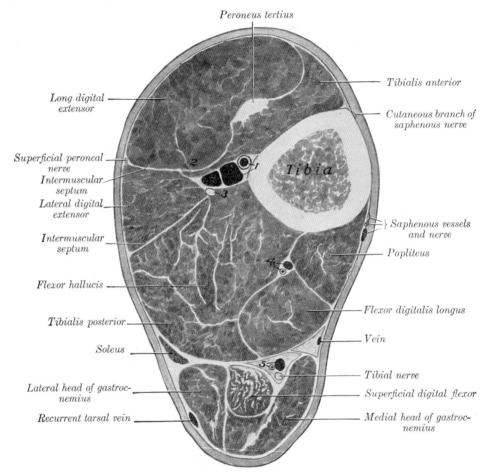

FIG. 297.—CROSS-SECTION OF LEFT LEG OF HORSE.

The section is cut about the junction of the proximal and middle thirds of the region. 1, Anterior tibial vessels; 2, deep peroneal nerve; 3, fibula; 4, posterior tibial vessels; 5, recurrent tibial vessels. A cutaneous branch of the saphenous nerve is shown medial to the popliteus, but is not marked.

popliteus. This terminates near the lower third of the tibia on a round tendon which descends in a canal in the medial ligament of the hock, and joins the common tendon about a third of the way down the metatarsus. In its course over the medial surface of the hock the tendon is provided with a **synovial sheath** which extends from the distal fourth of the tibia to the junction with the principal tendon. (2) The superficial head is the **tibialis posterior** (M. tibialis posterior); it is only partially separable from the deep head. It has a flattened belly, terminating near the distal third of the tibia on a flat tendon which soon fuses with the principal tendon. (3) The deep head, the **flexor hallucis** (M. flexor hallucis longus), is much the largest. It lies on the posterior surface of the tibia, from the popliteal line outward and downward. The belly contains much tendinous tissue, and terminates behind the distal end of the tibia on a strong round ten-

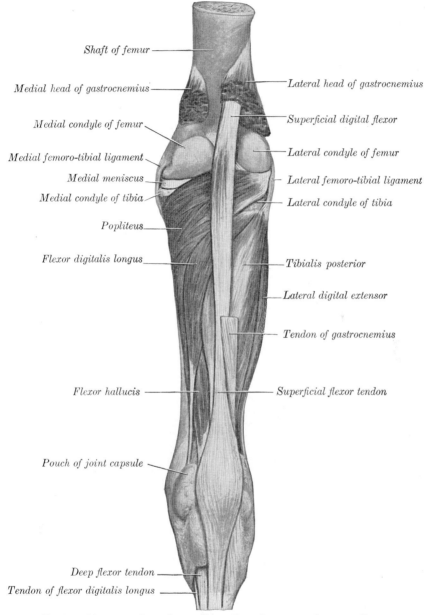

Shaft of femur

Medial head of gastrocnemius

Medial condyle of femur

Medial femoro-tibial ligament

Medial meniscus

Medial condyle of tibia

Popliteus

Flexor digitalis longus

Flexor hallucis

Pouch of joint capsule

Deep flexor tendon

Tendon of flexor digitalis longus

Lateral head of gastrocnemius

Superficial digital flexor

Lateral condyle of femur

Lateral femoro-tibial ligament

Lateral condyle of tibia

Tibialis posterior

Lateral digital extensor

Tendon of gastrocnemius

Superficial flexor tendon

Fig. 298.—Muscles of Right Leg of Horse, Deep Dissection; Posterior View.

don. The latter receives the tendon of the tibialis posterior, descends in the tarsal groove, bound down by the strong plantar annular ligament (Ligamentum laciniatum) and enveloped in a synovial sheath, receives the tendon of the medial head below the hock, and, a little further down, the so-called **check ligament** (Caput tendineum). The tendon is partly cartilaginous where it plays over the fibular tarsal bone.   The **tarsal sheath** (Vagina tarsea) begins two to three inches (ca. 5 to 7.5 cm.) above the level of the medial malleolus, and extends about one-fourth of the way down the metatarsus.   The check ligament resembles that of the fore limb, except that it is longer and very much weaker; it may be absent.[1]   In the mule it is usually absent.   The remainder of the tendon is arranged like that of the thoracic limb.

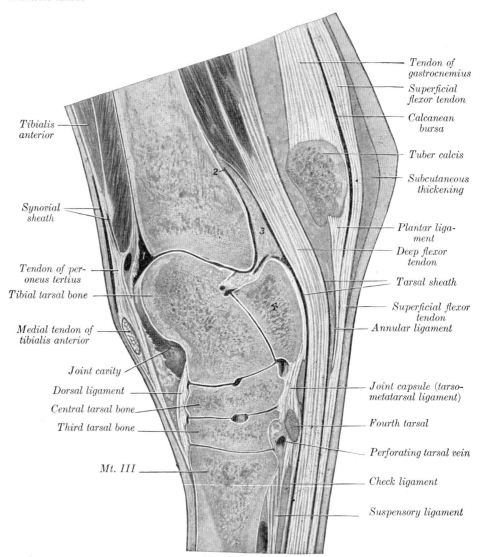

Tibialis anterior

Synovial sheath

Tendon of peroneus tertius

Tibial tarsal bone

Medial tendon of tibialis anterior

Joint cavity

Dorsal ligament

Central tarsal bone

Third tarsal bone

Mt. III

Tendon of gastrocnemius

Superficial flexor tendon

Calcanean bursa

Tuber calcis

Subcutaneous thickening

Plantar ligament

Deep flexor tendon

Tarsal sheath

Superficial flexor tendon

Annular ligament

Joint capsule (tarsometatarsal ligament)

Fourth tarsal

Perforating tarsal vein

Check ligament

Suspensory ligament

FIG. 299.—SAGITTAL SECTION OF RIGHT HOCK OF HORSE.

The section passes through the middle of the groove of the trochlea of the tibial tarsal bone.   1, 2, Proximal ends of cavity of hock joint; 3, thick part of joint capsule over which deep flexor tendon plays; 4, fibular tarsal bone (sustentaculum).   A large vein crosses the upper part of the joint capsule (in front of 1).

Relations.—Anteriorly, the tibia and fibula, the popliteus, lateral extensor, tibialis anterior, and the tibial vessels; posteriorly, the gastrocnemius, superficial flexor, and the tibial nerve; laterally, the fascia, skin, and the soleus; medially, the fascia and skin.

[1] This might well be called the tarsal (tendinous) head of the deep flexor.

Blood-supply.—Posterior tibial artery.

Nerve-supply.—Tibial nerve.

5. **Popliteus** (Fig. 298).—This thick, triangular muscle lies on the posterior surface of the tibia above the popliteal line.

Origin.—A small depression on the lateral epicondyle of the femur, close to the articular surface and under the lateral ligament.

Insertion.—A triangular area on the posterior surface of the tibia, proximal and medial to the popliteal line; also the proximal half of the medial border and a narrow adjacent part of the medial surface of the tibia.

Action.—To flex the femoro-tibial joint and to rotate the leg inward.

Structure.—The strong tendon of origin lies at first under the lateral ligament, and curves backward and inward over the lateral condyle of the tibia in contact with the lateral meniscus; it is invested by a reflection of the synovial membrane of the joint (Fig. 584). The tendon is succeeded by a thick triangular belly, the fibers of which are directed medially in the proximal part, but incline downward below.

Relations.—Superficially, the fascia and skin, semitendinosus, gastrocnemius, superficial flexor; deeply, the femoro-tibial joint, the tibia, the popliteal vessels and their divisions. The saphenous vessels and nerve lie along the medial border of the muscle, separated from it, however, by the deep fascia.

Blood-supply.—Popliteal and posterior tibial arteries.

Nerve-supply.—Tibial nerve.

MUSCLES OF THE METATARSUS AND DIGIT

Extensor digitalis brevis.—This small muscle lies in the angle of union of the tendons of the long and lateral extensors of the digit. (Fig. 293.)

Origin.—The lateral tendon of the peroneus tertius, the middle annular ligament, and the lateral ligament of the hock.

Insertion.—The tendons of the long and lateral extensors.

Action.—To assist the long extensor.

Structure.—It is principally fleshy, having a superficial origin from the annular ligament, and a deep one (by a thin tendon) from the lateral tendon of the peroneus tertius. The insertion is by a thin tendon.

Relations.—Superficially, the skin and fascia and the tendons of the long and lateral extensors; deeply, the tarsal joint capsule, the great metatarsal artery, and the deep peroneal nerve.

Blood-supply.—Great metatarsal artery.

Nerve-supply.—Deep peroneal nerve.

The **interossei** and **lumbricales** are arranged like those of the thoracic limb, the only noticeable difference being the greater development of the lumbricales in the pelvic limb.

THE MUSCLES OF THE OX

MUSCLES OF THE FACE

The **cutaneus faciei** presents as a special feature the extensive **frontalis** muscle, which covers the frontal and nasal regions.

The **orbicularis oris** does not form a complete ring, the defect being in the middle of the upper lip.

The **levator nasolabialis** is extensive, thin, and not very distinct from the frontalis; it divides into two layers, between which the levator labii superioris proprius and the lateral dilator of the nostril pass. The superficial layer ends in the nostril and upper lip, the deep layer on the parietal nasal cartilages and on the nasal process of the premaxilla.

The **levator labii superioris proprius** arises on and before the facial tuberosity and terminates by several tendons in the muzzle. It passes between the two layers of the preceding muscle, blending in part with the deep layer.

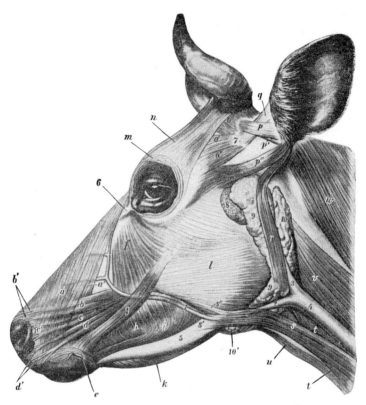

FIG. 300.—MUSCLES OF THE HEAD OF THE OX; LATERAL VIEW.

a, a′, Levator nasolabialis; b, b′, levator labii superioris proprius and tendon; c, c′, dilator naris lateralis and tendon; d, d′, depressor labii superioris and tendon; e, orbicularis oris; f, malaris; g, zygomaticus; h, buccinator; i, depressor labii inferioris; k, mylohyoideus; l, masseter; m, orbicularis oculi; n, frontalis; o, o′, o″, scutularis; p, scutulo-auricularis superficialis superioris; p′, middle scutulo-auricularis superficialis; p″, zygomatico-auricularis and scutulo-auricularis inferioris; q, scutulo-auricularis superficialis accessorius; r, parotido-auricularis; s, s′, s″, sterno-cephalicus and tendons (mandibular branch); t, sterno-cephalicus (mastoid branch); u, sterno-hyoideus; v, cleido-mastoideus; w, cleido-occipitalis. 1, Facial vein; 2, external maxillary vein; 3, internal maxillary vein; 4, jugular vein; 5, mandible; 6, medial palpebral ligament; 7, scutiform cartilage; 8, parotid lymph gland; 9, 9′, parotid and 10, 10′, mandibular salivary gland. (Ellenberger and Baum, Vergleichenden Anatomie d. Haustiere.)

The **zygomaticus** is much stronger than in the horse. It arises on the masseteric fascia, and ends chiefly in the upper lip.

The **depressor labii superioris** arises just in front of the facial tuberosity, and divides usually into two branches, which terminate in a number of tendons that form a network in the muzzle and upper lip.

The **incisivus inferior** is a small, rounded muscle, which arises on the body of the mandible below the second and third incisors, and ends in the lower lip, blending with the orbicularis.

The **depressor labii inferioris** is thin, and does not extend so far backward as in the horse; only the anterior end is distinct from the buccinator.

The **buccinator** shows no marked variation, but its superficial layer is well developed.

The **dilatator naris lateralis** arises in front of the facial tuberosity, passes forward between the branches of the levator nasolabialis, and terminates in the lateral wing of the nostril.

The **dilatator naris apicalis** is situated in the muzzle and joins its fellow at a median raphé. It arises on the border and upper surface of the body of the pre-

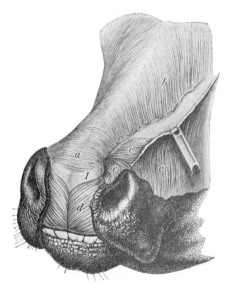

Fig. 301.—Nasal Muscles of the Ox.

a, Apical part of the levator nasolabialis; *b*, levator nasolabialis; *c*, nasal section and *c′*, maxillary section of the levator nasolabialis; *d*, dilator naris apicalis; *e*, dilator naris medialis; *1*, parietal cartilage. (Ellenberger and Baum, Vergleichenden Anatomie d. Haustiere.)

maxilla, the fibers passing obliquely upward and outward to the medial wing of the nostril.

The **dorsal part** of the **lateralis nasi** arises from the anterior part of the dorsal parietal cartilage and ends in the medial wing of the nostril.

The **ventral part** of the **lateralis nasi** consists of two layers which arise on the nasal process of the premaxilla and the ventral parietal cartilage and end in the lateral wing of the nostril.

The **orbicularis oculi** is well developed.

The corrugator supercilii is not present as a separate muscle, its place and function being taken by the frontalis.

The **malaris** is broad, and spreads out below on the fascia over the buccinator and masseter; it is divided into two parts.

MANDIBULAR MUSCLES

The **masseter** is not so large as in the horse; a considerable part of it arises on the facial tuberosity and is directed obliquely backward and downward, so that it would draw the lower jaw forward as well as upward.

The **temporalis** conforms to the temporal fossa, and is therefore longer and entirely lateral in position.

The **pterygoideus medialis** arises from the lateral surface of the perpendicular part of the palatine bone and from the pterygoid process. Since the origin is nearer the median plane and the insertion further from it than in the horse, the muscle produces more marked lateral movement of the mandible.

The **pterygoideus lateralis** is flattened transversely, wide and thin in front, narrower and thicker behind. It has an extensive origin in the pterygo-palatine fossa, where it is partly covered by the pterygoideus medialis.

The **occipito-mandibularis** is absent.

The **digastricus** has a tendinous origin on the paramastoid process of the occipital bone; its bellies are short and thick. The intermediate tendon is round and thick; it does not perforate the stylo-hyoideus. The anterior bellies are connected beneath the root of the tongue by a layer of transverse muscle-fibers termed the transversus mandibulæ.

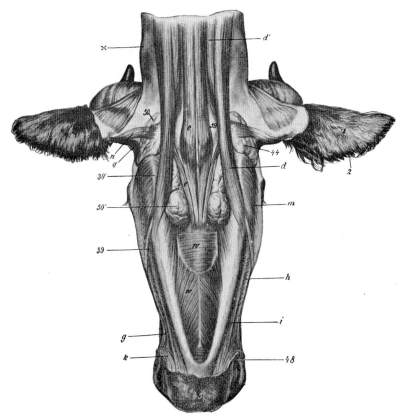

Fig. 302.—Muscles of Head of Ox; Ventral View.

d, *d'*, Sterno-cephalicus; *e* (opposite *59*), sterno-hyoideus; *e* (lower), omo-hyoideus; *g*, zygomaticus; *h*, buccinator; *i*, depressor labii inferioris; *k*, orbicularis oris; *m*, masseter; *n*, parotido-auricularis; *o'*, zygomatico-auricularis; *w*, mylo-hyoideus; *1*, concha, convex surface; *2*, anterior border of concha; *30'*, angle of jaw; *39*, facial vein; *44*, parotid gland; *45*, lower lip; *48*, angle of mouth; *50, 50'*, mandibular gland; *59*, larynx; ×, wing of atlas. (After Ellenberger-Baum, Anat. für Künstler.)

HYOID MUSCLES

The **mylo-hyoideus** is thicker and more extensive than in the horse.

The **stylo-hyoideus** has a long, slender tendon of origin which is attached to the muscular angle of the great cornu of the hyoid bone. The insertion is fleshy and is not perforated by the digastricus.

The **genio-hyoideus** is much more developed than in the horse.

The **kerato-hyoideus** has an additional attachment on the middle cornu of the hyoid bone.

The **hyoideus transversus** is bifid.

The **sterno-thyro-hyoideus** has no intermediate tendon and is thicker.

The **omo-hyoideus** arises as a thin band from the fascia over the third and fourth cervical vertebræ. It blends here with the rectus capitis ventralis major.

The **occipito-hyoideus** is thick. Its large lateral part entirely covers the paramastoid process (from which it arises) and is inserted into the muscular angle of the great cornu. The smaller medial part arises from the ventral end of the paramastoid process and ends on the medial face of the great cornu below the dorsal end.

MUSCLES OF THE NECK

A. VENTRAL GROUP

The **cervical cutaneus** is absent.

The **sterno-cephalicus** consists of two muscles which arise from the manubrium sterni and first costal cartilage. The superficial muscle, the **sterno-mandibularis,** is inserted on the anterior border of the masseter, the ramus of the mandible, and the buccal fascia. The deep muscle is the **sterno-mastoideus;** it crosses under the preceding and ends on the mastoid processes, the mandible, and, in common with the rectus capitis ventralis major, on the basilar part of the occipital bone.

There are two scaleni. The **scalenus ventralis** (s. primæ costæ) arises from the transverse processes of the third to the seventh cervical vertebræ and ends on the first rib. It is traversed by the roots of the brachial plexus, which divide it into bundles. The **scalenus dorsalis** (s. supracostalis) arises usually on the transverse processes of the fourth, fifth, and sixth cervical vertebræ. Its wide posterior part lies on the ventral part of the serratus ventralis; and ends on the fourth rib.

The **rectus capitis ventralis major** arises on the third to the sixth cervical transverse processes, and blends at its insertion with the sterno-mastoideus and the cleido-mastoideus.

The **rectus capitis ventralis minor** is larger than in the horse.

The **rectus capitis lateralis** and **longus colli** resemble those of the horse.

The **intertransversales** are large. From the sixth cervical vertebra forward they form a muscular mass (M. intertransversarius longus) which is inserted into the wing of the atlas.

B. LATERAL GROUP

The **splenius** is thin. It arises directly from the first three or four thoracic spines, and ends by a thin tendon on the occipital bone, the wing of the atlas, and the transverse process of the axis, blending with the brachiocephalicus, longissimus capitis et atlantis, and omo-transversarius. The complexus arises as far back as the eighth or ninth thoracic vertebra.

MUSCLES OF THE THORAX

The **levatores costarum** number ten or eleven pairs.

The **external intercostal** muscles are thick; they terminate at the costochondral junctions. The **internal intercostals** are specially thick in relation to the cartilages of the sternal ribs; here there exist bundles (comparable to the levatores costarum) which are attached in front to the sternum, behind to a costal cartilage. The interosseous part thins toward the upper end of the spaces.

The **diaphragm** presents several important differential features. Its slope is much steeper and its width is greater than in the horse. The upper limit of the costal attachment extends almost in a straight line from the last rib about a handbreadth below its vertebral end to the junction of the eighth rib with its cartilage,

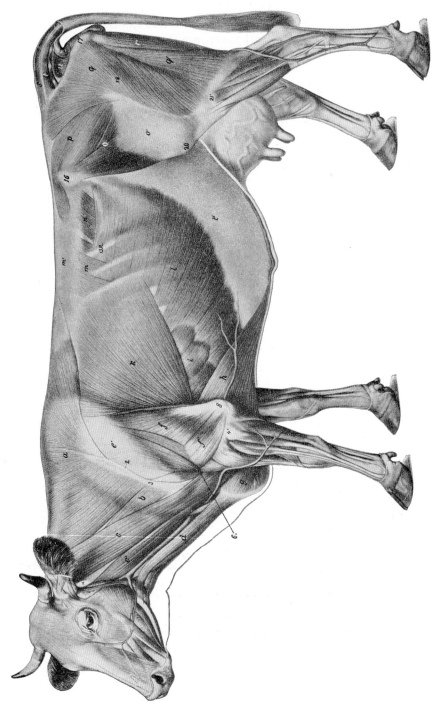

FIG. 303.—SUPERFICIAL MUSCLES OF OX, AFTER REMOVAL OF CUTANEOUS MUSCLE.

a, Trapezius; b, omo-transversarius; c, c', brachiocephalicus (c, cleido-occipitalis; c', cleido-mastoideus); d, sterno-cephalicus; e, deltoid; f, long head; f', lateral head of triceps; g, superficial pectoral; h, deep pectoral; i, serratus ventralis; k, latissimus dorsi; l, obliquus abdominis externus; l', aponeurosis of l; m, serratus dorsalis; m', lumbo-dorsal fascia; n, obliquus abdominis internus; o, tensor fasciæ latæ; o', fascia lata; p, gluteus medius; q, q', biceps femoris; r, semitendinosus; s, sacro-coccygeus dorsalis; t, sacro-coccygeus lateralis; u, coccygeus. (After Ellenberger-Baum, Anat. f. Künstler.)

and along the latter to the sternum. In exceptional cases there is no attachment to the twelfth rib. The midline slopes from the twelfth thoracic vertebra obliquely as far as the foramen venæ cavæ, beyond which it is almost vertical. The right crus divides into two branches, which circumscribe the hiatus œsophageus, unite below, and then spread out in the tendinous center. The left crus is small. The hiatus œsophageus is situated about a handbreadth (10 cm.) below the eighth thoracic vertebra, a little to the left of the median plane. A serous sac or bursa is located to the right of and ventral to the œsophagus. The foramen venæ cavæ is a little more ventral and almost in the median plane.[1]

In the **sheep** the costal attachment differs from that of the ox. The upper limit of the attachment extends in a gentle curve (convex ventrally) from the last rib about the junction of its middle and ventral thirds to the ventral end of the ninth rib.

Muscles of the Back and Loins

The **serratus dorsalis anterior** is very thin. It is inserted on the fifth to the eighth ribs when fully developed, but it may be reduced to two or three digitations or may be absent. The **serratus dorsalis posterior** is inserted on the last three or four ribs by wide digitations.

The **longissimus costarum** has a lumbar portion which is attached to the lumbar transverse processes and the tuber coxæ.

The **longissimus dorsi** resembles that of the horse, but it is more fleshy anteriorly, and the spinalis dorsi is clearly distinguishable from the common mass. In the lumbar region the tendons meet across the summits of the spines.

Intertransversales are present in the back, and **interspinales** in the back and loins.

Muscles of the Tail

These resemble in general those of the horse; the **coccygeus** is, however, much more developed.

Abdominal Muscles

The **obliquus abdominis externus** is somewhat thinner and has a less extensive origin, which begins at the lower part of the fifth intercostal space and ends on the last rib above its middle. The direction of the fibers in the flank is horizontal, and they do not reach to the tuber coxæ, nor as high as the lumbar transverse processes. (In this region the abdominal tunic has a strong attachment to the point of the hip and the lumbo-dorsal fascia.) The external inguinal ring is less oblique than in the horse. There is a lateral lamina of fascia extending to the skin on the udder of the cow and the scrotum in the bull.

The **obliquus abdominis internus** is more developed and has an additional origin from the lumbo-dorsal fascia. The aponeurosis blends with that of the external oblique near the linea alba, and detaches a layer which assists in the formation of the internal sheath of the rectus abdominis.

The **rectus abdominis** arises on the lateral border of the sternum as far forward as the third costal cartilage. The two muscles are separated, except near the pelvis, by an interval varying from two to four inches (ca. 5 to 10 cm.), so that this part of the abdominal wall is entirely fibrous. (The umbilicus is in a transverse plane through the third lumbar vertebra.) There are five tendinous inscriptions, near the second of which usually there is a foramen for the passage of the subcutaneous abdominal vein. The prepubic tendon has, in addition to lateral

---

[1] The sternal part is clearly separable from the costal part. The costal attachment in some cases only extends to the twelfth rib. The last digitation is thus some seven or eight inches (ca. 18 to 20 cm.) above the corresponding digitation of the transversus abdominis. There are small intermediate digitations at the last two intercostal spaces.

branches inserted into the ilio-pectineal eminences, a strong attachment to the symphysis pelvis, a structure about four inches wide (ca. 10 cm.) whose fibers are directed downward and forward from the symphysis to the prepubic tendon, so that the abdominal wall is strongly retracted and almost vertical at its junction with the pubis.

The **transversus abdominis** presents no striking differential features. The transversalis fascia is strong and distinct except over the diaphragm.

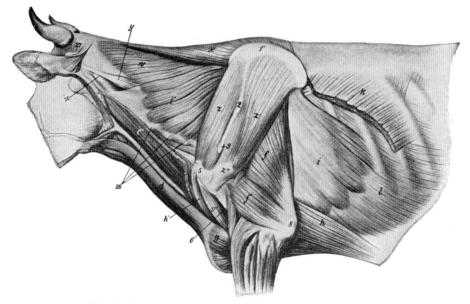

FIG. 304.—DEEPER MUSCLES OF NECK, SHOULDER, AND THORAX OF OX.

c', Cleido-occipitalis muscle; d, sterno-cephalicus; f, f', long and lateral heads of triceps; g, superficial pectoral muscle; h, h', deep pectoral muscle; i, i', serratus ventralis; k, latissimus dorsi; l, obliquus abdominis externus; v', biceps brachii; w, splenius; x, rhomboideus; y, longissimus capitis et atlantis; z, supraspinatus; z', infraspinatus; z'', tendon of insertion of z'; $1'$, cartilage of scapula; 2, tuberosity of spine of scapula; 3, acromion; 5, lateral tuberosity of humerus; 6, deltoid tuberosity; 8, olecranon; 26, transverse processes of cervical vertebræ; 27, posterior auricular muscles· $\times$, wing of atlas. (After Ellenberger-Baum, Anat. für Künstler.)

MUSCLES OF THE THORACIC LIMB

I. MUSCLES OF THE SHOULDER GIRDLE

The **trapezius** is thick, wide and undivided. It arises on the ligamentum nuchæ and supraspinous ligament, from the atlas to the twelfth thoracic vertebra and ends on the scapular spine.

The **omo-transversarius** arises on the wing of the atlas, and, inconstantly, the transverse process of the axis, and is inserted into the scapular spine and fascia.

The **rhomboideus** arises on the ligamentum nuchæ from the second cervical to the eighth thoracic vertebra.

The **latissimus dorsi** has a broad tendon of origin, which blends with the lumbo-dorsal fascia; it is also attached to the tenth and eleventh ribs, also the ninth or twelfth, and the fascia over the external intercostal and oblique abdominal muscles. The anterior fibers end on the tendon of the teres major, the middle part on an aponeurosis on the medial surface of the caput longum, and the posterior part on a tendon which is common to this muscle and the deep pectoral.

The **brachiocephalicus** has two distinct parts. The dorsal division, the **cleido-occipitalis,** arises on the occipital bone and the ligamentum nuchæ. The ventral part, the **cleido-mastoideus,** is smaller and arises by a round tendon on the mastoid process and the rectus capitis ventralis major, and by a thin tendon on the mandible.

The **superficial pectoral** muscle is thinner than in the horse and its two parts are not so clearly separable. The **deep pectoral** muscle arises as far forward as the second costal cartilage and is undivided. Some authors consider that the scapular portion is represented by a small muscle which arises from the cartilages and sternal end of the first rib and passes upward to end on the deep face of the brachiocephalicus in front of the shoulder joint; it seems quite plausible, however, that this is the homologue of the **subclavius** muscle of man. A tendon along the dorsal edge of the deep pectoral blends with the latissimus dorsi and coraco-brachialis.

The **serratus ventralis** is clearly divided into cervical and thoracic parts. The former is large and extends from the third (or second) cervical vertebra to the fifth rib, being overlapped behind by the thoracic part. It is inserted on a large triangular area on the antero-superior part of the costal surface of the scapula. The thoracic part is relatively thin and is covered by a very strong aponeurosis; it is attached to the fourth to the ninth ribs by six digitations, and is inserted by a flat tendon which insinuates itself between the middle and posterior parts of the subscapularis to end on a rough line—equivalent to the posterior serratus area of the horse—and also on the cartilage of the scapula in continuity with this line.

II. MUSCLES OF THE SHOULDER

The **deltoid** is clearly divided into acromial and scapular parts. The former (Pars acromialis) arises on the acromion, the latter (Pars scapularis) on the posterior border of the scapula and the aponeurotic covering of the infraspinatus. The scapular part of the muscle is largely inserted into the fascia covering the triceps.

The **supraspinatus, infraspinatus,** and **teres minor** do not differ materially from those of the horse.

The **subscapularis** consists of three parts with a common tendon of insertion.

The **teres major** and **coraco-brachialis** resemble those of the horse.

The **capsularis** is absent.

III. MUSCLES OF THE ARM

The **biceps** is smaller and less tendinous, and is situated more medially than in the horse. The tendon of origin is flat, and is bound down in the intertuberal or bicipital groove by a fibrous band. The tendon to the extensor carpi radialis is less distinct than in the horse. (In the sheep the tendon of origin is round and is invested by the synovial membrane of the shoulder joint. The tendon of insertion bifurcates; one branch ends on the tuberosity of the radius, the other on the ulna.)

The medial head of the **triceps** is more developed than in the horse, and extends up to the neck of the humerus.

The **tensor fasciæ antibrachii** is a slender muscle which lies along the posterior border of the triceps.

IV. MUSCLES OF THE FOREARM AND MANUS

A. EXTENSOR DIVISION

The **extensor carpi radialis** is like that of the horse. There is sometimes a small muscle lying along its medial border, which may represent the extensores pollicis.

There are three digital extensors: 1. The **common digital extensor** (M. extensor digitalis communis) arises by two heads from the lateral epicondyle of the humerus and from the ulna. The heads fuse about the middle of the forearm, and terminate soon on a tendon which passes over the carpus and metacarpus, gradually inclining forward. At the fetlock joint it divides into two branches, each of which is inserted into the extensor process of the corresponding third phalanx. 2. The **medial digital extensor** (M. extensor digiti tertii proprius) arises on the lateral epicondyle, and is inserted by two branches into the second and third phalanges of the medial digit. The tendon receives two reinforcing slips from the suspensory ligament. 3. The **lateral digital extensor** (M. extensor digitalis lateralis s. digiti quarti proprius) is stronger than that of the horse; it arises from the lateral liga-

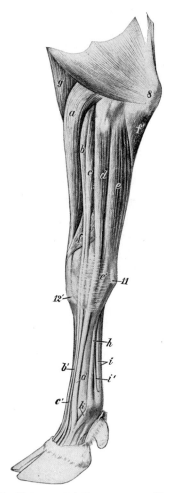

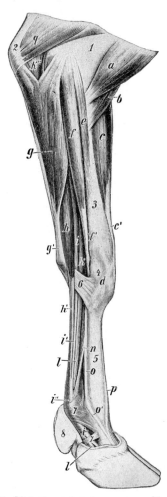

Fig 305.—Muscles of Antibrachium and Manus of Ox; Lateral View.

a, Extensor carpi radialis; *b*, extensor digiti tertii, and *b'*, its tendon; *c*, extensor dig. communis, and *c'*, its tendon; *d*, extensor digiti quarti; *e*, ulnaris lateralis, and *e'*, its lateral tendon; *f*, extensor carpi obliquus; *f'*, ulnar head of deep flexor; *g*, brachialis; *h*, interosseus medius or suspensory ligament; *i*, flexor tendons; *i'*, branch of *h* to superficial flexor tendon; *k*, branch of *h* to *d*; *8*, olecranon; *11*, accessory carpal bone; *12'*, metacarpal tuberosity. (Ellenberger-Baum, Anat. der Haustiere.)

Fig. 306.—Muscles of Antibrachium and Manus of Ox; Medial View.

a, Biceps brachii; *b*, brachialis; *c*, extensor carpi radialis, and *c'*, its tendon; *d*, tendon of extensor carpi obliquus; *e*, pronator teres; *f*, flexor carpi radialis; *g*, flexor carpi ulnaris, and *g'*, its tendon; *h*, *i*, superficial and deep heads of superficial digital flexor; *h'*, *i'*, *i''*, superficial flexor tendons; *k*, deep digital flexor, and *l*, its tendon; *n*, check ligament; *o*, interosseus medius, and *o'*, its extensor branch; *p*, tendon of extensor digiti tertii; *q*, medial head of triceps; *1*, humerus; *2*, olecranon; *3*, radius; *4*, carpus; *5*, metacarpus; *6*, lig. carpi volare; *7*, annular lig. of fetlock; *8*, accessory digit. (Ellenberger-Baum, Anat. d. Haustiere.)

ment of the elbow joint, the lateral tuberosity of the radius, and the ulna. The tendon terminates like that of the preceding muscle.[1]

The **extensor carpi obliquus** resembles that of the horse.

[1] It may be remarked that, in addition to the extension action, the common extensor approximates the digits, while the others tend to abduct them.

The extensor tendons are bound down at the carpus by an annular ligament, and are furnished with synovial sheaths (Figs. 307, 308).

B. FLEXOR DIVISION

The three **flexors of the carpus** are like those of the horse, but the long tendon of the lateral flexor ends on the large metacarpal bone, not on the small one. The tendon of the medial flexor naturally ends on the medial part of the large metacarpal bone.

The **superficial digital flexor** is somewhat blended at its origin with the middle flexor of the carpus. It divides into two bellies, superficial and deep, terminating

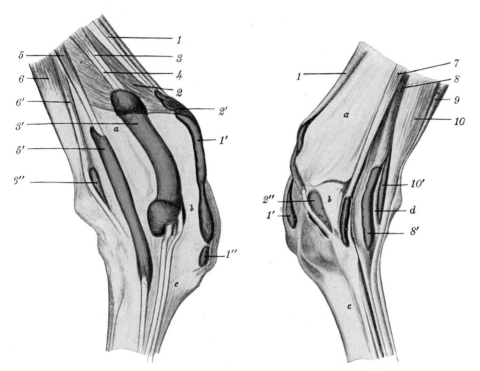

FIG. 307.—RIGHT CARPUS OF OX WITH BURSÆ AND   FIG. 308.—RIGHT CARPUS OF OX WITH BURSÆ AND
     SYNOVIAL SHEATHS INJECTED; LATERAL VIEW.   SYNOVIAL SHEATHS INJECTED; MEDIAL VIEW.

1, Extensor carpi radialis, with synovial sheath (*1'*) and bursa (*1''*); *2*, extensor carpi obliquus, with synovial sheath (*2'*) and bursa (*2''*); *3*, extensor digiti tertii proprius; *4*, extensor digitalis communis; *3'*, common synovial sheath of *3* and *4*; *5*, extensor digiti quarti proprius, with synovial sheath (*5'*); *6*, *6'*, ulnaris lateralis, with bursa (*6''*); *7*, flexor carpi radialis, with synovial sheath; *8*, deep digital flexor, with synovial sheath (*8'*); *9*, flexor carpi ulnaris; *10*, superficial digital flexor, with synovial sheath, *10'*; *a*, radius; *b*, carpus; *c*, metacarpus; *d*, cut edge of annular ligament. (After Schmidtchen.)

on tendons at the distal part of the forearm. The superficial tendon passes over the posterior annular ligament (Lig. carpi transversum), perforates the metacarpal fascia, and joins the deep tendon about the middle of the metacarpus. The deep belly is connected with the deep flexor by a strong fibrous band. Its tendon passes under the annular ligament of the carpus in a groove on the deep flexor, from which it receives fibers. The conjoined tendon soon bifurcates, each branch receiving a reinforcing band from the suspensory ligament, and forming near the fetlock a ring for the corresponding branch of the deep flexor tendon. Passing under two digital annular ligaments, they are inserted into the volar surfaces of the second phalanges by three slips.

The **deep digital flexor** has the same heads as in the horse, the humeral head, as before mentioned, being connected with the deep part of the superficial flexor. The tendon, which is not reinforced by a check ligament as in the horse, divides near the distal end of the metacarpus into two branches which are inserted into the volar surfaces of the third phalanges.

The synovial sheaths at the carpus present the following special features: One is found in connection with the tendon of the superficial part of the superficial flexor of the digits. There is a common sheath for the tendons of the common extensor and the medial extensor.

Bursæ may occur under the tendons of the proper extensors of the digits at the fetlock; they are constant only in old animals. The branches of the tendon of the common extensor are provided with synovial sheaths from their origin to the middle of the second phalanx. There are two digital synovial sheaths for the flexor tendons; they may communicate at their upper part, and they extend from the distal third of the metacarpus nearly to the distal sesamoids. Bursæ occur between the latter and the branches of the deep flexor tendon.

A feeble **pronator teres** is present on the medial surface of the elbow along the medial collateral ligament.

The fascia on the volar face of the metacarpus and digit is very thick. It is continuous above with the ligamentum carpi transversum, and is attached on either side to the metacarpal bone. At the fetlock it forms the fibrous basis for the small claws, and below this it detaches two strong bands which diverge to be inserted into the second and third phalanges, blending with the collateral ligaments.

The **lumbricales** are absent, unless we regard as such the muscular bundles which arise on the deep flexor and are inserted into the superficial flexor tendon at the carpus.

The **interosseus medius,** or suspensory ligament, is somewhat more muscular than in the horse; indeed, in the young subject it may be almost entirely fleshy. Its arrangement is somewhat complex. Single at its origin, it detaches about the middle of the metacarpus a band which joins the tendon of the superficial flexor and concurs near the fetlock in the formation of the ring for the deep flexor tendon.[1] A little lower down it divides into three and then into five branches. The abaxial branches (two pairs) are attached to the corresponding sesamoids and tendons of the proper extensors, while the middle branch passes through the sulcus at the distal end of the metacarpus and bifurcates, each division fusing with the tendon of the corresponding proper extensor.

The Muscles of the Pelvic Limb

I. THE SUBLUMBAR MUSCLES

The **psoas minor** begins at the disc between the twelfth and thirteenth thoracic vertebræ.

The **psoas major** has a fleshy origin on the posterior border of the last rib, and a thin tendon attached to the twelfth rib; it is relatively narrower than in the horse and does not entirely cover the quadratus lumborum.

The **iliacus** begins under the body of the sixth lumbar vertebra, and is more closely united with the psoas major than in the horse.

The **quadratus lumborum** extends as far forward as the body of the tenth or eleventh thoracic vertebra. It is wider than in the horse and extends beyond the lateral border of the psoas major.

---

[1] Lesbre regards this band as the subcarpal check ligament, which on this basis is blended with the suspensory ligament above.

II. LATERAL MUSCLES OF THE HIP AND THIGH (Figs. 303, 309)

The **tensor fasciæ latæ** is large, and the fleshy part extends further down than in the horse.

The gluteus superficialis is not present as such; apparently its anterior part has fused with the tensor fasciæ latæ and its posterior part with the biceps femoris.

The **gluteus medius** is small, the lumbar part being insignificant and extending forward only to the fourth lumbar vertebra. Its deep portion (gluteus accessorius) is easily separable, and its strong tendon is inserted into the femur below the trochanter major, under cover of the upper part of the vastus lateralis.

The **gluteus profundus** is thin, but extensive, arising as far forward as the tuber coxæ, and from the lower part of the sacro-sciatic ligament. The fibers converge on a broad, strong tendon which passes under the upper part of the vastus lateralis, and is inserted into a tubercle a short distance below the great trochanter.

The **biceps femoris** is very wide at its upper part, having apparently absorbed the posterior part of the superficial gluteus. It arises from the sacral spines, sacro-sciatic ligament, and tuber ischii. It is divided by a fibro-elastic septum in the thigh into two portions, which end in front and below on a wide aponeurosis; the latter is attached to the patella and its lateral ligament and blends with the fascia cruris and fascia lata. There is no femoral attachment, but many fibers go to the fascia lata. A large bursa occurs between the muscle and the great trochanter in the adult. The part of the tendon which fuses with the lateral patellar ligament presents a fibro-cartilaginous thickening, and an extensive bursa is interposed between it and the lateral condyle of the femur.

A layer derived from the fascia lata is intimately adherent to the deep face of the muscle, and cases occur in which this fascia is ruptured by the trochanter major, thus fixing the muscle behind the trochanter.

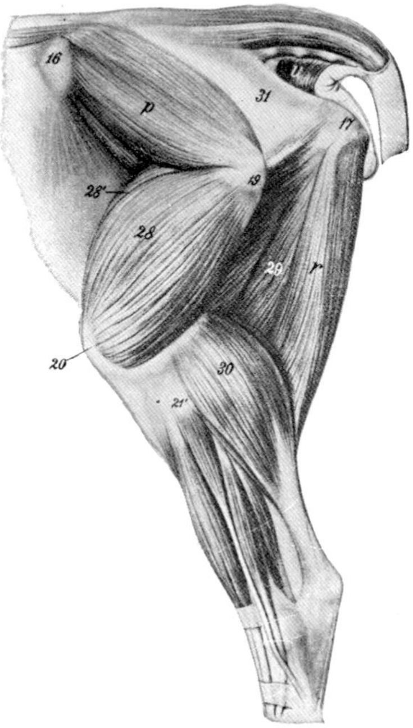

Fig. 309.—Gluteal, Femoral, and Crural Regions of Ox, After Removal of Superficial Muscles.

p, Gluteus medius; *r*, semitendinosus; *u*, coccygeus; *28*, vastus lateralis; *28'*, rectus femoris; *29*, semimembranosus; *30*, gastrocnemius; *31*, sacro-sciatic ligament: *16*, tuber coxæ; *17*, tuber ischii; *19*, trochanter major; *20*, patella; *21'*, lateral condyle of tibia. (After Ellenberger-Baum, Anat. für Künstler.)

The **semitendinosus** and **semimembranosus** arise on the ischium only. The latter is very large and has a branch attached to the medial condyle of the tibia.

III. ANTERIOR MUSCLES OF THE THIGH

The **quadriceps femoris** resembles that of the horse; but the vasti (and especially the medial one) are not so thick, and the vastus intermedius is more clearly separable, and consists of two parts. Bursæ occur under the insertions of the medial and lateral vasti, and often under the end of the rectus in the adult.

The **articularis genu** is a small muscle which lies under the distal part of the vastus intermedius, and is partly inserted on the suprapatellar cul-de-sac of the synovial membrane of the stifle joint.

The **capsularis** is absent.

IV. MEDIAL MUSCLES OF THE THIGH

The **sartorius** arises by two heads, one from the tendon of the psoas minor and the iliac fascia, the other from the shaft of the ilium. The femoral vessels pass between them.

The **gracilis** is more extensively united with its fellow at its origin than in the horse.

The **pectineus** is large, and arises by a single head from the pubis and prepubic tendon. It divides into two branches, one of which is inserted as in the horse, while the other extends to the medial epicondyle of the femur.

The **adductor** resembles that of the horse, but does not reach to the medial condyle of the femur.

The **quadratus femoris** and **obturator externus** resemble those of the horse.

The **obturator internus** has no iliac head, and its tendon passes through the obturator foramen.

The **gemellus** is large; some of its fibers of origin join the obturator internus through the lesser sciatic foramen.

V. MUSCLES OF THE LEG AND FOOT

A. DORSO-LATERAL GROUP

There are four digital extensors, two of which are fused with each other and the peroneus tertius in the upper third of the leg.

1. The **long digital extensor** (M. extensor digitalis longus) arises in common with the peroneus tertius and the medial extensor in the extensor fossa of the femur, and separates from the other muscles near the middle of the leg. At the distal end of the tibia it terminates on a tendon which passes down over the hock (bound down by two annular ligaments) and ends like that of the thoracic limb.

2. The **medial digital extensor** (M. extensor digiti tertii proprius) arises in common with the preceding muscle and the peroneus tertius, and is covered by them to the distal third of the tibia. Its tendon passes under the annular ligaments between those of its cogeners and ends on the second phalanx of the medial digit.

3. The **lateral digital extensor** (M. extensor digitalis lateralis s. digiti quarti proprius)[1] arises on the lateral ligament of the stifle joint and the lateral condyle of the tibia. Its tendon passes over the lateral surface of the hock, and terminates on the dorsal surface of the second phalanx of the lateral digit.

The reinforcing bands from the suspensory ligament are arranged as in the forelimb.

4. The **short digital extensor** (M. extensor digitalis brevis) resembles that of the horse; it is inserted on the tendon of the long extensor.

The **peroneus longus** (not present in the horse) is situated in front of the lateral extensor. It arises on the lateral condyle of the tibia and the fibrous band which represents the shaft of the fibula. Its tendon passes downward and backward over the lateral surface of the hock, crosses over that of the lateral extensor and under the lateral ligament, and ends on the first tarsal bone and the proximal end of the large metatarsal bone. It is enveloped by a synovial sheath. It would apparently act as an inward rotator at the hock joint.

The **peroneus tertius** is a well-developed muscle which arises on the common tendon with the long and medial extensors. It has a large, fusiform belly, which is superficially situated on the front of the leg. Close to the tarsus it ends on a flat tendon, which is perforated by that of the tibialis anterior, and ends on the proximal end of the large metatarsal and second and third (fused) tarsal bones.

[1] Lesbre regards this muscle as the homologue of the peroneus brevis of man and other pentadactyls.

The **tibialis anterior** is smaller, and arises by two heads. The larger head springs from the lateral surface of the tuberosity and crest of the tibia; the lateral, smaller one (M. extensor hallucis longus), arises from the upper part of the lateral

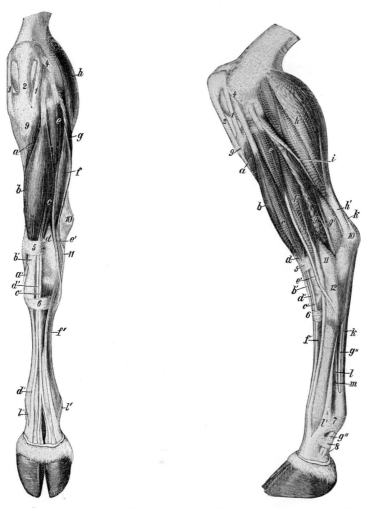

FIG. 310.—MUSCLES OF LEG AND FOOT OF OX; FRONT VIEW.   FIG. 311.—MUSCLES OF LEG AND FOOT OF OX; LATERAL VIEW.

a, Tibialis anterior, and *a′*, its tendon; *b*, peroneus tertius; and *b′*, its tendon; *c*, long extensor, and *c′*, its tendon; *d*, medial extensor, and *d′*, its tendon; *e*, peroneus longus, and *e′*, its tendon; *f*, lateral extensor, and *f′*, its tendon; *g*, flexor hallucis; *g′*, tibialis posterior; *g″*, deep flexor tendon; *h*, gastrocnemius, and *h′*, its tendon; *i*, soleus; *k*, superficial flexor tendon; *l*, interosseus medius (or suspensory ligament); *l′*, extensor branch of *l*; *m*, flexor branch of *l*; *1*, *2*, *3*, patellar ligaments; *4*, femoro-patellar ligament; *5*, *6*, *7*, *8*, annular ligaments; *9*, tibial tuberosity; *10*, tuber calcis; *11*, lateral malleolus; *12*, lateral ligament of hock. (Ellenberger-Baum, Anat. d. Haustiere.)

border of the tibia and the fibrous band which replaces the shaft of the fibula. The tendon perforates that of the preceding muscle, passes to the medial face of the hock, and ends on the metatarsal and second and third tarsal bones.

B. PLANTAR GROUP

The **gastrocnemius** and **soleus** resemble those of the horse.

The **superficial digital flexor** is more fleshy than in the horse. Its tendon terminates as in the fore limb.

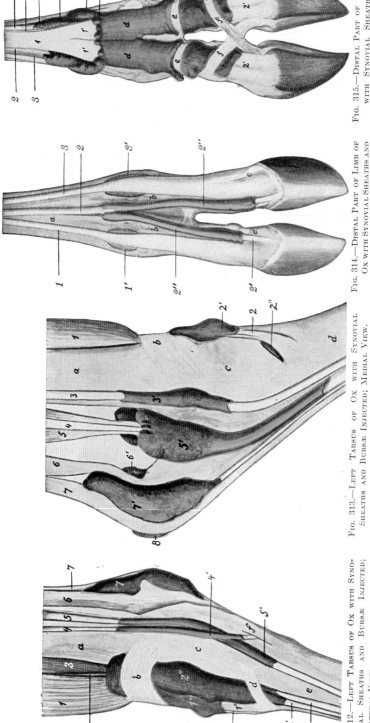

FIG. 312.—LEFT TARSUS OF OX WITH SYNO-
VIAL SHEATHS AND BURSÆ INJECTED;
LATERAL VIEW.

1, Peroneus tertius; 1', tendon of 1 and
its sheath, 1''; 2, extensor digiti tertii proprius; 2', tendon of 2; 2'', common sheath of
tendons of extensor digiti tertii and extensor
digitalis longus (3, 3'); 4, peroneus longus and
its sheath, 4'; 5, extensor digiti quarti and its
sheath, 5'; 6, tendon of gastrocnemius; 7,
superficial digital flexor and its sheath, 7';
8, tendon of tibialis anterior; a, tibia; b, proximal annular ligament; c, tarsus; d, distal annular ligament; e, metatarsus; f, lateral ligament. (After Schmidtchen.)

FIG. 313.—LEFT TARSUS OF OX WITH SYNOVIAL
SHEATHS AND BURSÆ INJECTED; MEDIAL VIEW.

1, Peroneus tertius; 2, tendon of tibialis anterior
with sheath, 2', and bursa, 2''; 3, long digital flexor
and 3', its sheath; 4, tibialis posterior; 5, deep digital
flexor and its sheath, 5'; 6, tendon of gastrocnemius
and bursa, 6'; 7, superficial digital flexor and its bursa,
7'; 8, subcutaneous bursa; a, tibia; b, proximal annular ligament; c, tarsus; d, metatarsus. (After
Schmidtchen.)

FIG. 314.—DISTAL PART OF LIMB OF
OX WITH SYNOVIAL SHEATHS AND
BURSÆ INJECTED; DORSAL VIEW.

1, Tendon of extensor digiti tertii,
with bursa (1'); 2, tendon of common
extensor; 2', branch of 2, with synovial sheath (2''); 3, tendon of extensor
digiti quarti, with bursa (3'); a, metatarsus; b, first phalanx; c, second
phalanx. (After Schmidtchen.)

FIG. 315.—DISTAL PART OF LIMB OF OX
WITH SYNOVIAL SHEATHS INJECTED;
PLANTAR VIEW.

1, Superficial flexor tendon; 1', 1',
branches of 1; 1'', 1''', upper part of synovial sheaths of 1', 1'; 2, deep flexor tendon;
2', 2'', branches of 2; 2'', upper part of
synovial sheath of 2'; 3, 3, abaxial branches
of interosseus medius or suspensory ligament; 3', branch of same to superficial
flexor tendon; a, fetlock joint; b, pastern
joint; c, coffin joint; d, e, annular ligaments; f, cruciate interdigital ligament.
(After Schmidtchen.)

The **deep digital flexor** in general resembles that of the horse, but the tibialis posterior (superficial head) is distinct and is relatively larger than in the horse. The flexor digitalis longus (medial head) is also larger, while the flexor hallucis longus (deep head) is smaller. The common tendon ends like that on the fore limb.

The synovial sheaths and bursæ of the muscles of the leg and foot are shown in Figs. 312–315.

THE MUSCLES OF THE PIG

Muscles of the Face

The **facial cutaneus** is pale, thin, and difficult to separate from the skin.

The **orbicularis oris** is little developed.

The **levator nasolabialis** is thin and pale, and is undivided.

The **levator labii superioris proprius** may well be termed the **levator rostri**. It has a large pennate belly, which arises in the preorbital fossa. The tendon ends on the anterior part of the os rostri. A muscular slip connects it with the premaxilla.

The **zygomaticus** arises on the fascia over the masseter and ends at the angle of the mouth.

The **depressor labii inferioris** separates from the buccinator only near the angle of the mouth; it ends by a number of tendinous branches in the lower lip.

The **dilatator naris lateralis** is well developed. It arises under the levator rostri and ends by a tendinous network around the nostril.

The **transversus nasi** is represented only by a few fibers which cross over the os rostri.

The **depressor rostri** arises on the facial crest. It has a long strong tendon which passes below the nostril and turns dorso-medially to meet the tendon of the opposite side and end in the skin of the snout. It depresses the snout and contracts the nostril.

The malaris is absent, and the other palpebral muscles present no special features.

MANDIBULAR MUSCLES

The **masseter** is thick.

The **pterygoideus medialis** is wide at its insertion.

The **pterygoideus lateralis** is large and distinct.

The **occipito-mandibularis** arises on the paramastoid process of the occipital bone and ends on the medial and lower surface of the mandible in front of the groove for the facial vessels.

HYOID MUSCLES

The **mylo-hyoideus** consists of two more or less distinct layers, the superficial one being the transversus mandibulæ.

The **occipito-hyoideus** and **kerato-hyoideus** are small.

The **hyoideus transversus** is absent.

The **omo-hyoideus** and **sterno-hyoideus** are referred to in connection with the muscles of the neck.

MUSCLES OF THE NECK

The **cutaneus** consists of two layers which cross each other obliquely. The fibers of the superficial layer are directed nearly vertically, those of the deep layer toward the face, on which they are continued to form the facial portion.

The **brachiocephalicus** is described with the other muscles of the shoulder girdle.

The **sterno-cephalicus** arises on the sternum and is inserted by a long round tendon on the mastoid process.

The thyroid part of the **sterno-thyro-hyoideus** has a peculiar arrangement. It arises (separately from the opposite muscle) on the manubrium sterni. About the middle of the neck it has an oblique tendinous intersection, beyond which it

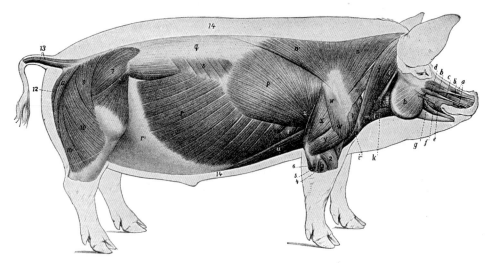

FIG. 316.—SUPERFICIAL MUSCLES OF PIG, AFTER REMOVAL OF M. CUTANEUS.

a, Levator nasolabialis; *b*, levator labii superioris proprius; *b'*, fleshy slip of *b* which comes from premaxilla; *c*, dilatator naris lateralis; *d*, depressor rostri; *e*, orbicularis oris; *f*, depressor labii inferioris; *g*, zygomaticus; *h*, masseter; *i i', i''*, brachiocephalicus (cleido-occipitalis, cleido-mastoideus, pars clavicularis deltoidei); *k*, sterno-cephalicus; *l*, sterno-hyoideus; *m*, omo-transversarius; *n, n'*, trapezius; *o*, anterior deep pectoral; *p*, latissimus dorsi; *q*, lumbo-dorsal fascia; *r*, obliquus abdominis externus; *r'*, aponeurosis of *r*; *s*, serratus dorsalis; *t*, serratus ventralis; *u*, posterior deep pectoral; *v*, supraspinatus; *w, w'*, deltoideus; *x*, long head of triceps; *y*, lateral head of triceps; *z*, tensor fasciæ antibrachii; *1*, brachialis; *2*, extensor carpi radialis; *3*, extensor digiti quarti; *4*, extensor digiti quinti; *5*, extensor carpi ulnaris; *6*, ulnar head of deep flexor; *7*, gluteus medius; *8*, tensor fasciæ latæ; *9, 10, 10'*, biceps femoris; *11*, semitendinosus; *12*, semimembranosus; *13*, caudal muscles; *14*, panniculus adiposus in section. (After Ellenberger, in Leisering's Atlas.)

divides into two branches: one of these is inserted in the usual fashion, the other ends on the laryngeal prominence. The hyoid part is well developed.

The **omo-hyoideus** is thin. It arises as in the horse, but has no connection with the brachiocephalicus nor with the opposite muscle.

The **omo-transversarius** arises on the first or second cervical vertebra (under cover of the brachiocephalicus), and is inserted into the lower part of the scapular spine.

There are two **scaleni**. The **scalenus ventralis** (s. primæ costæ) resembles that of the ox, is attached to the last four cervical vertebræ, and is perforated by the nerves of the brachial plexus. The **scalenus dorsalis** (s. supracostalis) arises on the transverse processes of the third to the sixth cervical vertebræ, and ends on the third rib.

The **ventral muscles of the head** present no special features.

The **longus colli** is separated from the opposite muscle, so that part of the bodies of the cervical vertebræ is exposed as in man.

The **intertransversales** resemble those of the ox.

The **splenius** is thick and extensive. It ends in three parts on the occipital, the temporal, and the wing of the atlas (inconstant).

The **longissimus capitis et atlantis** is small, and its atlantal part is blended with the longissimus cervicis.

The **complexus** is large, and is clearly divided into two parts: the dorsal part (Biventer cervicis) is marked by several tendinous intersections; the ventral part is the complexus proper.

The **obliquus capitis posterior** is relatively thin.

The **recti capitis dorsales** are thick and more or less fused.

Muscles of the Thorax

The **levatores costarum** and **rectus thoracis** present no special features.

The **external intercostal** muscles are absent under the serratus dorsalis and the digitations of the external oblique.

The **internal intercostals** are thick between the cartilages of the sternal ribs.

The **retractor costæ** and the **transversus thoracis** resemble those of the horse; the latter extends back to the eighth cartilage and fuses with the transversus abdominis.

The **diaphragm** has seven costal digitations on each side, the posterior ones being attached to the ribs at some distance (ca. one-third to one-fourth of rib-length) from the costo-chondral junction.[1] The line of attachment reaches the latter at the tenth rib, and passes along the eighth cartilage to the xiphoid process. The tendinous center is more rounded than in the horse. The crura are well developed. The right crus is very large, and is perforated by the extensive slit-like hiatus œsophageus, which is median in position, and lies about two and one-half to three inches (ca. 6 to 8 cm.) below the twelfth thoracic vertebra. A serous sac is found in the hiatus œsophageus, usually to the right and ventral to the œsophagus, extending from the stomach forward between the pleuræ a distance of three or four inches (ca. 7.5–10 cm.); this sac may be in the form of a synovial sheath in older subjects and be of greater extent both anteriorly and posteriorly. The hiatus aorticus is between the crura.

Abdominal Muscles

The **abdominal tunic** is little developed.

The **obliquus abdominis externus** has an extensive fleshy portion and a correspondingly narrow aponeurosis; the latter does not detach a femoral lamina, but is reflected in toto to form the inguinal ligament.

The **obliquus abdominis internus** resembles that of the ox; a small fusiform muscle, which crosses the inguinal canal obliquely and is attached on the abdominal surface of the inguinal ligament, is apparently a detached slip of the internal oblique.

The **rectus abdominis** is extensive and thick. It has seven to ten inscriptions. Its tendon of insertion fuses largely with the common tendon of the graciles, and does not give off an accessory band to the head of the femur.

The fleshy part of the **transversus abdominis** is well developed. It blends in front with the transversus thoracis.

The **cremaster externus** is present in the female as well as in the male.

Muscles of the Back and Loins

The **serratus dorsalis anterior** is inserted into the fifth to the eighth ribs inclusive, the **serratus dorsalis posterior** into the last four or five ribs. There are usually no digitations attached to the ninth and tenth ribs.

---

[1] It is interesting to note that the diaphragm has no attachment to the fifteenth rib, which is often present and well developed.

The **longissimus costarum** extends to the wing of the atlas.

The **spinalis et semispinalis** can be separated without much difficulty from the longissimus dorsi, the division from the common mass of the loins beginning about the first lumbar vertebra.

The **multifidus** resembles that of the horse.

Interspinales are present, as well as distinct **intertransversales** of the back and loins.

MUSCLES OF THE TAIL

The dorsal and lateral **sacro-coccygei** arise as far forward as the last lumbar vertebra. Gurlt explains the twist of the tail as being due to the spiral arrangement of the insertions of the tendons.

MUSCLES OF THE THORACIC LIMB

MUSCLES OF THE SHOULDER GIRDLE

The **trapezius** is very wide, its line of origin extending from the occipital bone to the tenth thoracic vertebra. There is no clear division between its two parts, which are both inserted into the scapular spine.

The **omo-transversarius** resembles that of the ox.

The **rhomboideus** consists of three parts. The **cervical part** (Rhomboideus cervicalis) is greatly developed, its origin extending from the second cervical to the sixth thoracic vertebra. The **cephalic part** (Rhomboideus capitis) arises with the splenius on the occipital bone, and is inserted with the cervical part. The **thoracic part** (Rhomboideus thoracalis) extends as far back as the ninth or tenth thoracic vertebra.

The **latissimus dorsi** is attached to the four ribs preceding the last. It is inserted into the medial tuberosity of the humerus.

The **brachiocephalicus** divides into two parts, the **cleido-mastoideus** and **cleido-occipitalis,** which arise on the mastoid process and nuchal crest respectively, and unite at the fibrous vestige of the clavicle.

The **anterior superficial pectoral** muscle is thin. The **posterior superficial pectoral** muscle is divided into two parts, one of which ends on the humerus, the other on the fascia of the forearm. The **anterior deep pectoral** muscle resembles that of the horse, but its origin does not extend behind the first two chondro-sternal joints. The **posterior deep pectoral** muscle is very long.

The cervical part of the **serratus ventralis** is greatly developed, its origin extending from the wing of the atlas to the upper part of the fifth rib, and passing under the thoracic part; the latter resembles that of the ox.

MUSCLES OF THE SHOULDER

The **deltoid** is undivided; it arises from the aponeurosis covering the infraspinatus, and it ends largely on the deltoid ridge, but partly on the fascia of the arm.

The **supraspinatus** is large; it has a small attachment to the medial tuberosity and ends chiefly on the lateral tuberosity of the humerus. There is a bursa between the tendon and the anterior part of the lateral tuberosity.

The **infraspinatus** is wide; it is inserted into a depression below the posterior division of the lateral tuberosity. There is a bursa between the tendon and the tuberosity.

The **teres minor** is large and rounded; it ends on a tubercle between the lateral and deltoid tuberosities of the humerus.

The **subscapularis** is very broad at its upper part.   It extends posteriorly up to the dorsal angle of the scapula, but anteriorly only about two-thirds of the way up to the vertebral border.

The **teres major** presents nothing remarkable.

The **coraco-brachialis** is short, wide, and undivided.   There is a bursa between its broad tendon of origin and the tendon of insertion of the subscapularis.

The **capsularis** is variable; it may be half an inch wide or very small and is frequently absent.

MUSCLES OF THE ARM

The **biceps brachii** is fusiform and not greatly developed.   Its tendon of origin is rounded and the underlying bursa communicates so freely with the shoulder joint as to be regarded as an evagination of the synovial membrane of the latter.   A small band binds down the tendon in the bicipital groove.   The tendon of insertion divides into two branches.   One branch passes back across the medial surface of the neck of the radius to end on the proximal extremity of the ulna.   The other is attached to the radius under cover of the brachialis tendon.

The **brachialis** is large.   Its tendon of insertion divides.   The small branch is inserted into the medial border of the radius distal to the biceps tendon.   The large branch crosses the medial border of the radius and ends on the medial surface of the ulna distal to the biceps tendon; there is a bursa under this tendon.

The **tensor fasciæ antibrachii** resembles that of the horse, but is very wide and bends around the posterior border of the triceps.

The **long head** of the **triceps** is inserted into the summit of the olecranon by two tendons, between which there is a synovial bursa.   The **lateral head** is inserted into a crest on the lateral surface of the olecranon by a thin tendon, under which there is a bursa.   The **medial head** arises from the proximal third of the medial surface of the humerus; it is inserted into the medial surface of the olecranon by a short tendon, under which there is a small bursa.

There are two **anconei.**

MUSCLES OF THE FOREARM AND MANUS

The **extensor carpi radialis** is a strong, fleshy muscle, the tendon of which is inserted into the proximal end of the third metacarpal bone.   It may be divided into two parts (M. extensor carpi radialis longus, brevis).

The **extensor carpi obliquus** is well developed; it arises from the distal two-thirds of the lateral surface of the radius and ulna and ends on the second metacarpal bone.

The **common digital extensor** (M. extensor digitalis communis) arises on the lateral epicondyle of the humerus and the lateral ligament of the elbow, and divides into three parts.   The tendon of the medial head ends chiefly on the third digit, but commonly sends a small branch to the second.   The tendon of the middle head divides lower down into two branches for the third and fourth (chief) digits; above this bifurcation it detaches a small branch to the second digit, which usually unites with the tendon of the extensor digiti secundi.   The tendon of the deep head divides into two branches, the medial one joining the tendon of the middle head, while the lateral one ends on the fifth digit.

The **extensor of the second digit** (M. extensor digiti secundi proprius) is covered by the preceding muscle, with which it is partially fused.   It arises on the ulna. Its delicate tendon usually unites with the tendon of the middle head of the common extensor which goes to the second digit.

The **lateral digital extensor** (M. extensor digitalis lateralis) consists of two distinct parts: (1) The large dorsal muscle is the extensor digiti quarti proprius; it has a long tendon which ends on the fourth digit, and often sends a slip to the fifth digit. (2) The small volar muscle is the extensor digiti quinti proprius; it ends by a long tendon on the lateral aspect of the fifth digit.

The **supinator,** when present, is a pale, thin muscular slip which arises on the lateral border of the radius just above the interosseous space, extends medially and downward across the dorsal surface of the bone to its medial border, where it blends with the radial head of the deep flexor.

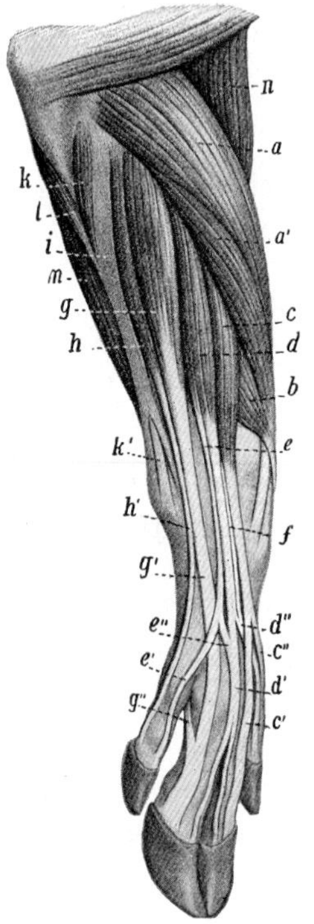

FIG. 317.—MUSCLES OF ANTI-
BRACHIUM AND MANUS
OF PIG; DORSO-LATERAL
VIEW.

a, a', Extensor carpi
radialis; *b*, extensor carpi
obliquus (s. abductor pollicis
longus); *c, d, e*, common digital extensor; *c', c''*, tendons of
insertion of *c; d', d''*, tendons
of *d; e', e''*, tendons of *e; f*,
tendon of extensor digiti secundi; *g*, extensor digiti quarti;
h, extensor digiti quinti; *h'*,
tendon of *h; i*, tendinous, and
k,, fleshy, part of ulnaris lateralis; *k'*, tendon of *k; l*, ulnar
head of deep digital flexor; *m*,
superficial digital flexor; *n*,
brachialis. (After Ellenberger,
in Leisering's Atlas.)

The **pronator teres** is a delicate, fusiform muscle which lies along the medial surface of the elbow and proximal part of the forearm. It arises from the medial epicondyle and collateral ligament of the elbow and is inserted by a thin tendon to the medial border of the radius about its middle.

The **flexor carpi radialis** is well developed. It arises on the medial epicondyle of the humerus, and is inserted into the third metacarpal bone.

The **flexor carpi ulnaris** is narrow and usually has no ulnar head. It runs obliquely down the back of the fore-arm in the furrow between the superficial and deep flexors of the digit. It arises from the medial epicondyle of the humerus and ends on the accessory carpal bone.

The **ulnaris lateralis** (M. extensor carpi ulnaris) is covered by a tendinous band, which is a thickened part of the fascia of the forearm and extends from the lateral epicondyle to the accessory carpal bone and lateral aspect of the carpus. The belly of the muscle is round: its ten-don of insertion perforates this band in the distal part of the forearm and ends on the proximal end of the fifth metacarpal bone.

The **superficial digital flexor** arises from the medial epicondyle of the humerus and consists of two parts. The tendon of the superficial head passes down behind the pos-terior annular ligament of the carpus (bound down by a special annular ligament), forms a ring at the fetlock for a tendon of the deep flexor, and ends by two branches on the second phalanx of the fourth digit. It receives a small band from the accessory carpal bone. The tendon of the deep head, after detaching a strong branch to the tendon of the deep flexor, passes down with the latter (for which it forms a ring), and ends on the third digit.

The **deep digital flexor** has three heads—humeral, ulnar, and radial. The **humeral head** is very large and forms the greater part of the contour of the volar face of the forearm. It consists of two parts—a large superficial part, and a much smaller deep part which arises with the superficial flexor. Each ends at the distal part of the fore-arm on a short tendon. These unite and receive the ten-dons of the radial and ulnar heads and a branch from the superficial flexor tendon. The **ulnar head** has a short, thick, prismatic belly which arises from the medial surface of the proximal part of the ulna. Its long, thin tendon passes down on the humeral head and joins the tendon of the latter at the level of the accessory carpal bone. The **radial head** is small. It arises from the upper part of the medial border of the radius and from the deep fascia, and its tendon joins that of the humeral head at the distal end of the forearm. The common tendon divides into four branches, the larger central pair ending on the third phalanges of the principal digits, the smaller abaxial pair on the accessory digits. The latter are bound down by a peculiar spiral band. There is no subcarpal check ligament. The carpal sheath envelops the tendon of the deep flexor and that of the deep part of the superficial flexor. It extends from the distal third of the forearm to the distal third of the metacarpus. At the proximal part of the metacarpus a small muscular band extends from the deep flexor tendon to the tendon of the deep part of the superficial flexor. Another muscular bundle passes from the deep flexor tendon to the second digit.

The **lumbricales** are represented by bundles which extend from the deep flexor tendon to the tendon of the deep head of the superficial flexor.

The third and fourth **interossei** are present. Each sends two slips to the corresponding sesamoid bones and extensor tendon.

There are **flexors, adductors,** and **abductors** of the **second** and **fifth digits.**

Muscles of the Pelvic Limb

SUBLUMBAR MUSCLES

The **psoas minor** is intimately united with the psoas major in front, and has a long small tendon which ends on the psoas tubercle. It has no thoracic part.

The **psoas major** is large and rounded. It begins at the last rib.

The **quadratus lumborum** is well developed, and extends to the last three or four thoracic vertebræ.

MUSCLES OF THE HIP AND THIGH

The **tensor fasciæ latæ** is broad, and its fleshy part reaches almost to the patella.

The **gluteus superficialis** has a sacral head only; it blends with the biceps femoris.

The **gluteus medius** has a small lumbar part which does not extend so far forward as in the horse. The deep part (Gluteus accessorius) is pretty clearly marked.

The **gluteus profundus** is extensive, reaching nearly to the tuber coxæ.

The **biceps femoris** has a narrow origin from the sacro-sciatic ligament and tuber ischii. It ends below like that of the ox.

The **semitendinosus** has two heads like that of the horse.

The **semimembranosus** arises from the tuber ischii and has two insertions as in the ox.

The **sartorius** has two heads of origin, between which the external iliac vessels are situated. The medial one arises from the tendon of the psoas minor, the lateral one from the iliac fascia.

The **graciles** are united at their origin even more than in the ox.

The **pectineus** is well developed and is flattened from before backward.

The **adductor** shows no division and is partially fused with the gracilis. It ends on the femur just above the origin of the gastrocnemius.

The **quadratus femoris** is large.

The **obturator externus** resembles that of the horse.

The **obturator internus** is extensive and strong; its tendon emerges through the obturator foramen.

The **gemellus** is fused in part with the obturator internus.

The **quadriceps femoris** is more clearly divided than in the horse, and its action is transmitted by a single patellar ligament.

The **capsularis** is absent.

MUSCLES OF THE LEG AND FOOT

The **peroneus tertius** is a well-developed muscle which is in great part superficially situated on the front of the leg. It covers the long digital extensor, with which it is united except in the distal third of the leg. It arises from the extensor fossa of the femur by a common tendon with that muscle, a synovial pouch from the femoro-tibial joint extending down under the origin.

This sac is an inch and a half or more (ca. 3 to 4 cm.) in length in large subjects and extends around the lateral edge of the tendon to its superficial face, so as to make a partial sheath and underlie the origin of the peroneus longus also.

The muscle is continued at the distal end of the leg by a strong tendon which passes over the flexion surface of the hock, between the tendon of the long extensor (lateral) and that of the tibialis anterior (medial), all three being bound down by a strong annular ligament which extends across from one malleolus to the other. It ends by two or more branches on the first and second tarsal and third metatarsal bones. Not rarely there is a thin tendon inserted into the fourth metatarsal bone. The tendon usually receives a small branch from that of the tibialis anterior at the annular ligament.

The **tibialis anterior** is smaller than the preceding. It arises from the lateral surface of the tuberosity and lateral condyle of the tibia. At the distal end of the leg the tendon passes under the annular ligament mentioned above (where it detaches a small branch to the peroneus tertius), and ends on the second tarsal and the proximal end of the second metatarsal bone. The terminal part passes under a superficial layer of the medial ligament of the hock, and is provided with a bursa.

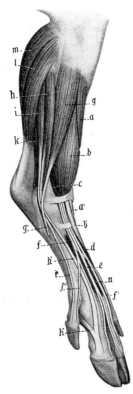

Fig. 318.—Muscles of Leg and Foot of Pig; Dorso-lateral View.

a, Tibialis anterior; a', tendon of preceding; b, peroneus tertius; b', tendon of b; c, long digital extensor; d, e, f, f', f'', tendons of c; g, peroneus longus; g', tendon of g; h, extensor digiti quarti; h', tendon of h, which receives h'' from the interosseus medius; i, extensor digiti quinti; k, deep digital flexor; l, soleus; m, gastrocnemius; n, extensor digitalis brevis. (After Ellenberger, in Leisering's Atlas.)

The **peroneus longus** descends in front of the fibula and the lateral extensor. It arises chiefly from the lateral condyle of the tibia. The tendon of insertion descends through a groove on the lateral malleolus, crosses over the tendons of the lateral extensor, then under the lateral ligament to the plantar surface of the hock, to end on the first tarsal bone. There is a bursa under the tendon where it lies in the groove on the fourth tarsal. The muscle is a flexor of the hock.

The **long digital extensor** arises in common with the peroneus tertius, by which it is largely covered and with which it is united to the distal third of the leg. Three tendons appear at the proximal annular ligament and extend downward and a little medially over the flexion surface of the hock. Here they are bound down by an annular ligament given off from the tendon of the peroneus tertius and attached laterally to the distal end of the fibular tarsal bone. The tendons gradually diverge as they descend the metatarsus. The central one divides at the distal end of the metatarsus into two branches which end on the third phalanges of the chief (third and fourth) digits. This tendon is joined before bifurcating by the tendon of the extensor digitalis brevis. The medial tendon ends on the second and third phalanges of the medial chief (third) digit. It receives a branch from the interosseus at the distal end of the first phalanx, and may detach a tendon to the second digit. The lateral tendon is smaller. Its branches end on the third phalanges of the accessory (second and fifth) digits and on the lateral chief (fourth digit); there may be a branch to the third digit, and the branch for the fourth may go to the corresponding branch of the central tendon. Other variations occur.

The synovial sheath for the tendons of the extensor longus and peroneus tertius at the hock extends nearly half an inch (ca. 1 cm.) above the proximal annular ligament and an inch or more (ca. 2 to 3 cm.) below the distal annular ligament in a large adult.

The **lateral digital extensor** lies on the lateral face of the leg, behind the peroneus longus. It arises from the lateral surface of the fibula, the lateral femorotibial ligament, and the intermuscular septum between this muscle and the deep digital flexor. It consists of two parts. The larger anterior muscle (extensor digiti quarti) has a tendon which appears a little distal to the middle of the leg, descends on the grooved lateral surface of the fibula, inclines forward, crossing under the tendon of the peroneus longus, and ends on the extensor process of the third phalanx of the lateral chief (fourth) digit. It receives an interosseus tendon at the first phalanx. The tendon of the posterior muscle (extensor digiti quinti) accompanies that of the anterior one to the tarsus and descends to the lateral accessory (fifth) digit.

The two tendons are bound down at the lateral malleolus by an annular ligament. The anterior tendon may receive a branch of the long extensor tendon and send a tendon to the fifth digit. The posterior tendon may send a reinforcing branch to the tendon of the long extensor for the fifth digit. There may be a third small head which arises from the middle of the fibula and sends a delicate tendon to join that of the posterior head.

The **extensor hallucis longus** is a small, fusiform muscle which is covered by the extensor longus and peroneus longus. It arises from the proximal end of the fibula and its delicate tendon descends at first under that of the peroneus tertius, inclines medially at the hock, and ends on the medial accessory (second) digit.

The **extensor digitalis brevis** is a well-developed muscle which lies on the dorsal face of the distal part of the tarsus and on the chief metatarsal bones. It arises from the neck of the tibial tarsal and the body of the fibular tarsal bone, and is partially divided into three parts. The tendon of the superficial part joins that of the long extensor for the chief digits. The deep part has two tendons which join those of the long extensor for the accessory digits.

The **gastrocnemius** has short but wide and thick heads. The lateral one is the larger and is united with the superficial digital flexor to the distal third of the leg. The tendon forms a groove for the superficial flexor tendon above the hock and is inserted chiefly into the prominences on each side of the notch of the tuber calcis.

The **soleus** is thick and wide and blends with the lateral head of the gastrocnemius. It arises from the lateral epicondyle of the femur and the deep fascia at the stifle. Its tendon joins that of the gastrocnemius.

The **popliteus** presents nothing remarkable.

The **superficial digital flexor** has a belly of considerable size. It arises with the lateral head of the gastrocnemius, with which it is fused to the distal third of the leg. The tendon is almost entirely enclosed by the twist of the gastrocnemius in the lower part of the leg. At the tuber calcis it is thick and largely cartilaginous, and is molded on the groove and ridges of the bone. It is attached by a strong band to each side of the tuber calcis. A large bursa under the tendon extends upward in the groove formed by the gastrocnemius almost to the muscular part and downward to the middle of the fibular tarsal bone. The tendon divides distally into two branches which go to the chief digits. It also detaches from its plantar surface two bands which join the fascia of the accessory digits.

The **deep digital flexor** presents three distinct heads: (1) The **tibialis pos-**

terior is the smallest. It has a fusiform belly in the proximal half of the leg and arises from the grooved plantar surface of the fibula. The tendon joins that of the flexor hallucis at the distal end of the leg. (2) The **flexor digitalis longus** is much larger and has a fusiform, pennate belly which extends obliquely across the proximal two-thirds of the leg. It arises from the proximal end of the fibula, the popliteal line, the middle third of the medial part of the plantar surface of the tibia, and the intermuscular septum between this muscle and the flexor hallucis. The tendon (which has a synovial sheath) descends in a groove behind the medial malleolus, bound down by an annular ligament, inclines laterally on the joint capsule, and joins the tendon of the flexor hallucis. (3) The **flexor hallucis** has a large fusiform belly which extends almost to the distal end of the leg. It arises from the greater part of the plantar surface of the tibia, the medial surface and plantar border of the fibula, and the interosseous membrane. The tendon descends in the tarsal canal, receiving the tendons of the other heads, and ends like the corresponding one of the forelimb. The tarsal synovial sheath begins at the distal end of the muscular part and extends to the middle of the metatarsus.

The **lumbricales** are absent, but there are four **interossei.** Rudimentary **adductors** of the **second** and **fifth digits** may be found.

THE MUSCLES OF THE DOG

MUSCLES OF THE FACE

The **cutaneus** of the face is well developed. Most of it is a continuation of the cervical cutaneus; the bundles extend forward over the lower part of the lateral surface of the face to the angle of the mouth and the upper lip. Other bundles extend upward; some of these spread out on the cheek and lateral nasal region, and a thin layer passes toward the lower eyelid, blending with the orbicularis oculi and constituting a malaris muscle. Another stratum is attached to the scutiform cartilage and spreads out on the masseter.

The **orbicularis oris** is poorly developed. In the upper lip it is divided centrally, and in the lower lip it is distinct only near the angles of the mouth.

The **levator nasolabialis** is wide and undivided. It has an extensive origin on the frontal and nasal bones. The fibers run downward and forward to the lateral wing of the nostril and the upper lip.

The **levator labii superioris proprius** arises behind the infraorbital foramen, runs forward under the preceding muscle, and ends in numerous small tendons which are in part inserted around the nostril, in part blend with those of the opposite side.

The **zygomaticus** is narrow and very long; it arises on the scutiform cartilage, and ends at the angle of the mouth.

The **depressor labii inferioris** is absent.

There are no special **nasal muscles.** The homologue of the lateral dilator is triangular; it is small at its origin just ventral to the levator labii superioris proprius, and ends almost entirely in the upper lip.

The **buccinator** is wide and very thin, and the two planes of fibers cross each other.

The **palpebral muscles** present no very noteworthy special characters. Two small muscles act on the upper eyelid. One of these, the corrugator supercilii, arises from the fascia on the frontal bone and ends near the medial canthus. The other arises from the zygomatic arch and ends near the lateral canthus.

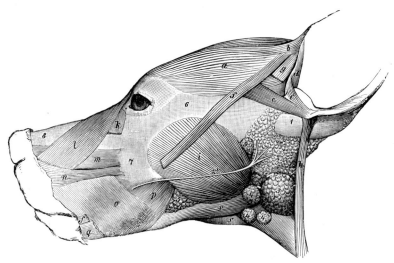

FIG. 319.—MUSCLES OF HEAD OF DOG.

a, Scutularis; *b, c*, anterior auricular muscles; *d*, helicis; *e*, antitragicus; *f, f*, zygomaticus, out of which a portion is cut; *g*, stump of cutaneus attached to scutiform cartilage; *h*, parotido-auricularis; *i*, masseter; *k*, malaris; *l*, levator nasolabialis; *m*, levator labii superioris proprius; *n*, dilatator naris lateralis; *o, p*, buccinator (buccalis, molaris); *q*, retractor anguli oris (from cutaneus); *r*, occipito-mandibularis; *s*, mylo-hyoideus; *1*, base of concha; *2*, parotid gland; *2'*, parotid duct; *3*, mandibular gland; *4*, mandibular lymph glands; *5*, buccal glands; *6*, zygomatic arch; *7*, maxilla; *8*, dorsum nasi; *9*, parotid lymph gland. (Ellenberger-Baum, Anat. d. Hundes.)

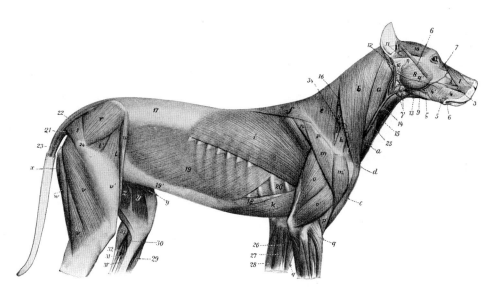

FIG. 320.—SUPERFICIAL MUSCLES OF DOG, AFTER REMOVAL OF M. CUTANEUS.

1, Levator nasolabialis; *2*, levator labii superioris proprius; *3*, dilatator naris lateralis; *4, 4'*, buccinator; *5*, retractor anguli oris; *6*, zygomaticus; *7*, malaris; *8*, masseter; *9*, occipito-mandibularis; *10*, scutularis; *11*, other auricular muscles; *12*, parotido-auricularis; *13*, mylo-hyoideus; *14*, sterno-hyoideus; *15*, sterno-thyroideus; *16*, splenius; *17*, lumbo-dorsal fascia; *18*, rectus abdominis; *19*, obliquus abdominis externus; *19'*, aponeurosis of preceding; *20*, intercostal muscle; *21*, sacro-coccygeus accessorius; *22*, sacro-coccygeus dorsalis; *23*, sacro-coccygeus ventralis; *24*, great trochanter; *25*, jugular vein; *a, b, c*, brachiocephalicus; *d*, clavicle; *e, f*, trapezius; *g*, serratus cervicis; *h*, omo-transversarius; *i*, latissimus dorsi; *k*, posterior deep pectoral; *l*, supraspinatus; *m, m'*, deltoid; *n*, infraspinatus; *o*, triceps, long head; *o'*, triceps, lateral head; *p*, brachialis; *q*, extensor carpi radialis; *r*, gluteus medius; *s*, gluteus superficialis; *t, t'*, tensor fasciæ latæ; *u*, sartorius; *v*, biceps femoris; *v'*, fascia lata; *w*, semitendinosus; *x*, semimembranosus; *y*, sartorius; *z*, gracilis; *26*, pronator teres; *27*, flexor carpi radialis; *28*, flexor carpi ulnaris; *29*, tibialis anterior; *30*, popliteus; *31, 31'*, deep digital flexor; *32*, superficial digital flexor; *33*, gastrocnemius; *34*, spine of scapula; *a*, parotid gland, with *a'*, its duct; *β*, mandibular gland; *δ*, mandibular lymph glands; *η*, parotid lymph gland; *ʓ*, inferior buccal glands. (After Ellenberger, in Leisering's Atlas.)

MUSCLES OF THE MANDIBLE

The **masseter** is thick and its superficial face is strongly convex. It arises from the zygomatic arch, and extends beyond the branch of the jaw below and behind. Three partly separate strata may be recognized in its structure.

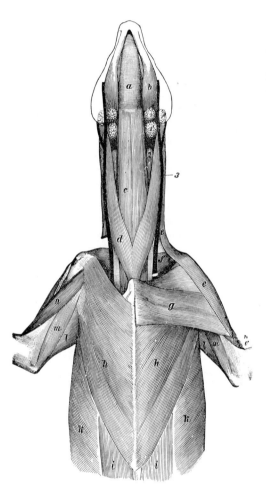

The **temporalis** is very large and strong, and contains much tendinous tissue. It arises from the temporal fossa and the orbital ligament and ends on the coronoid process of the mandible. It blends in part with the masseter.

The **pterygoideus lateralis** is not distinct from the **medialis**.

The **digastricus** is absent.

The **occipito-mandibularis** is a strong, round, fleshy muscle, which arises on the paramastoid process and is inserted into the border and medial surface of the ramus of the mandible at the level of the last molar teeth; it sometimes has a tendinous intersection.

HYOID MUSCLES

The **mylo-hyoideus** is well developed.

The **stylo-hyoideus** is very slender, and is inserted into the body of the hyoid bone.

The hyoideus transversus and omo-hyoideus are absent.

The **sterno-thyro-hyoideus** is large and arises chiefly on the first costal cartilage. It is clearly divided into **sterno-thyroideus** and **sterno-hyoideus.**

Fig. 321.—Ventral Muscles of Head, Neck, and Thorax of Dog.

a, Mylo-hyoideus; b, occipito-mandibularis; c, sterno-hyoideus; c', sterno-thyroideus; d, sterno-cephalicus; e, brachio-cephalicus; f, subscapularis; g, superficial pectoral; h, deep pectoral; i, rectus abdominis; k, obliquus abdominis externus; l, long head of triceps; m, medial head of triceps; n, biceps brachii; o, brachialis; 1, 1', 1'', mandibular lymph glands; 2, thyroid gland; 3, external jugular vein. (Ellenberger-Baum, Anat. d. Hundes.)

MUSCLES OF THE THORACIC LIMB

The **trapezius** is thin, and is divided into cervical and thoracic portions by a narrow aponeurotic part. Its line of origin extends from about the middle of the dorsal border of the neck to the ninth or tenth thoracic spine, the right and left muscles meeting (except at their posterior part) on a median fibrous raphé. It is inserted into the entire length of the spine of the scapula.

The **omo-transversarius** arises by a tendon on the lower part of the spine of the scapula (where it is often partially blended with the trapezius), and is inserted into the wing of the atlas.

The **rhomboideus** consists of three parts. The **rhomboideus thoracalis** is small; it arises from the fourth to the sixth or seventh thoracic spine, and is inserted into the medial surface (chiefly) of the dorsal angle of the scapula. The **rhomboideus cervicalis** arises from the ligamentum nuchæ as far forward as the second or third cervical vertebra, and is inserted into the medial surface of the cervical angle of the scapula. The **rhomboideus capitis** is a narrow band which is given off laterally from the preceding; it is inserted into the nuchal crest.

The **latissimus dorsi** is extensive; it has an attachment to the last two ribs and also to the upper part of the spine of the scapula in addition to the origin from the lumbo-dorsal fascia. Its lower edge blends near the shoulder with the cutaneus.

The **brachiocephalicus** contains in front of the shoulder a tendinous intersection and a fibrous mass in which the clavicle is embedded. Anterior to this it separates into two diverging parts. The dorsal part is the **cleido-cervicalis,** which widens above and is attached to the median raphê of the neck and to the occipital bone. The ventral part is the **cleido-mastoideus;** it is narrow and is attached to the mastoid process. The common mass posterior to the clavicle and the fibrous intersection, which is attached to the humerus, is homologous with the clavicular part of the deltoid of man.

The **superficial pectoral** muscle is small. It arises on the sternum from the manubrium as far back as the third costal cartilage, and is inserted into the humerus at the border between the medial and anterior surfaces. A superficial slip detached from it is inserted into the fascia of the forearm. The **deep pectoral** has no scapular part. It arises on the sternum and costal cartilages from the second costal to the xiphoid cartilage, and from the aponeurosis of the obliquus abdominis externus. It is inserted chiefly into the medial tuberosity of the humerus, but also by small slips into the lateral tuberosity and the fascia of the arm.

The **serratus ventralis** shows no clear division into cervical and thoracic parts. It arises from the last five cervical vertebræ and the first eight ribs, and is inserted into the upper part of the costal surface of the scapula.

The **deltoid** is clearly divided into scapular and acromial parts. The scapular part is triangular and arises from almost the entire length of the spine of the scapula; it is inserted largely into the fascia on the lateral surface of the arm. The acromial part is short, thick, and fusiform; it arises from the lower edge of the acromion, and ends on the deltoid tuberosity.

The **supraspinatus** is large; it ends chiefly on the lateral tuberosity of the humerus, but has a small attachment to the medial tuberosity also.

The **infraspinatus** is bipennate. The tendon of insertion passes in a groove on the lateral tuberosity of the humerus, to end on a well-defined mark on the same; a large bursa lies under the tendon.

The **teres minor** is short and fusiform; it arises on a tubercle on the posterior border of the scapula, just above the glenoid cavity, and is inserted into a tubercle on the upper part of the deltoid ridge.

The **subscapularis** is wide and is multipennate in structure, being intersected by fibrous septa which are attached to the rough lines on the costal surface of the scapula. It is inserted into the medial tuberosity of the humerus.

The **teres major** is thick. It arises on the upper part of the posterior border of the scapula and on the subscapularis, and is inserted into an eminence (tuberositas teres) on the proximal third of the medial surface of the humerus by a common tendon with the latissimus dorsi.

The **coraco-brachialis** has a short and undivided belly. It arises from a small depression on the medial surface of the tuber scapulæ, and ends on the proximal third of the humerus, just medial to the brachialis. The tendon of origin has a synovial sheath.

The **capsularis** is absent.

The **biceps brachii** lies almost entirely on the medial surface of the humerus. It is long and fusiform. The tendon of origin is round, and is bound down in the intertuberal groove by an annular ligament. It is enveloped by an extension of the synovial membrane of the shoulder joint. The tendon of insertion is bifid;

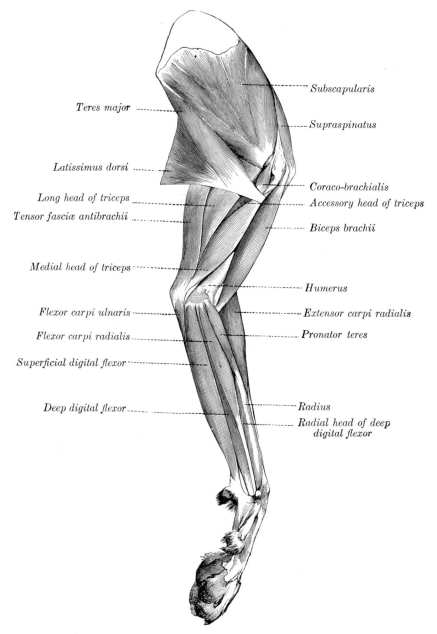

FIG. 322.—MUSCLES OF THORACIC LIMB OF DOG; MEDIAL VIEW.   (Ellenberger-Baum, Anat. des Hundes.)

one branch is attached to a rough mark on the lateral surface of the ulna, just below the semilunar notch; the other branch ends on a distinct mark on the postero-medial aspect of the proximal part of the shaft of the radius, one to two inches below the head.

The **brachialis** is very little curved. Its tendon of insertion passes over the medial ligament of the elbow and under the ulnar tendon of the biceps and ends just proximal to the latter. The tendon of the biceps forms a partial sheath for that of the brachialis.

The **tensor fasciæ antibrachii** is thin and narrow. It arises on the tendon and lateral surface of the latissimus dorsi, and ends on the olecranon and the fascia of the forearm.

The **triceps** has an additional deep head (Caput accessorium), which arises just below the head of the humerus. The medial head is very long; it arises from a mark on the proximal fourth of the medial surface of the humerus, just behind the insertion of the teres major and latissimus dorsi. A bursa lies on the olecranon in front of the common tendon of insertion.

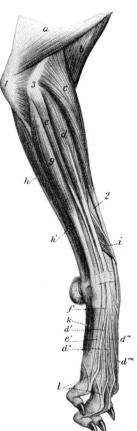

The **brachioradialis** is a long, narrow, delicate muscle, situated superficially on the dorsal surface of the forearm. It arises with the extensor carpi on the crest above the lateral epicondyle of the humerus, and is inserted into the distal part of the medial border of the radius. It is often much reduced, and is sometimes absent. It rotates the forearm and paw outward.

The **extensor carpi radialis** arises on the lateral condyloid crest and divides into two parts. The larger lateral part, the **extensor carpi radialis brevis,** ends on the proximal end of the third metacarpal bone. The medial and more superficial part, the **extensor carpi radialis longus,** ends on the second metacarpal bone. (A tendon to the fourth metacarpal may occur.)

The **extensor carpi obliquus** or **abductor pollicis longus** arises from the lateral border and dorsal surface of the ulna, the interosseous ligament, and the proximal part of the lateral border of the radius. It is inserted into the first metacarpal bone by a tendon which contains a small sesamoid bone. It abducts the first digit.

There are three (or four) extensors of the digits.

1. The **common digital extensor** (M. extensor digitalis communis) arises on the lateral epicondyle of the humerus and the lateral ligament of the elbow joint. It has four bellies, each of which has a tendon of insertion. These end on the third phalanges of the second, third, fourth, and fifth digits.

2. The **extensor of the first and second digits** (M. extensor pollicis longus et extensor indicis proprius) is small, and is covered by the common and lateral extensors. It arises on the proximal half of the ulna. Its tendon descends with that of the common extensor and divides into two branches. The delicate medial branch ends on the first digit, while the larger lateral one ends with the tendon of the common extensor for the second digit.

FIG. 323.—MUSCLES OF ANTIBRA-CHIUM AND MANUS OF DOG; LATERAL VIEW.

a, Triceps brachii; *b,* brachialis; *c,* extensor carpi radialis; *d,* common digital extensor; *d', d'',* *d''', d''''*, tendons of preceding; *e,* lateral digital extensor; *e', f,* tendons of preceding; *g,* ulnaris lateralis; *h,* ulnar head, *h',* humeral head of flexor carpi ulnaris; *i,* extensor carpi obliquus (s. abductor pollicis longus); *k,* interossei; *l,* branches from preceding to extensor tendons; *1,* olecranon; *2,* radius; *3,* lateral epicondyle of humerus. (After Ellenberger, in Leisering's Atlas.)

3. The **lateral digital extensor** (M. extensor digitalis lateralis) consists of two muscles which are not rarely fused. They arise on the lateral epicondyle of the humerus and the lateral ligament of the elbow joint. The larger superficial muscle is the **extensor of the third and fourth digits** (M. extensor digiti tertii et quarti);

its tendon divides at or near the carpus into two branches, which are inserted into the third phalanges of the third and fourth digits, blending with the corresponding tendons of the common extensor. The posterior muscle is the **extensor of the fifth digit** (M. extensor digiti quinti); its tendon fuses with that of the common extensor for the fifth digit.

The **ulnaris lateralis** or **extensor carpi ulnaris** is a large flat muscle which lies on the lateral surface of the ulna. It arises on the lateral epicondyle of the humerus, and is inserted into the proximal end of the fifth metacarpal and the accessory carpal bone. It is chiefly an abductor of the paw.

The **flexor carpi ulnaris** consists of two quite distinct heads. The larger **humeral head** arises on the medial epicondyle, while the smaller, superficial **ulnar head** arises on the posterior border of the ulna. The tendons of the two end on the accessory carpal bone and have a bursa between them.

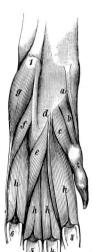

FIG. 324.—VOLAR MUS-CLES OF LEFT FORE-PAW OF DOG.

a, Abductor pollicis brevis et opponens pollicis; b, flexor pollicis brevis; c, adductor pollicis; d, adductor digiti secundi; e, adductor digiti quinti; f, flexor digiti quinti brevis; g, abductor digiti quinti; h, interossei; 1, accessory carpal bone; 2, first digit; 3–6, sesamoids of metacarpo-phalangeal joints. (Ellenberger-Baum, Anat. d. Hundes.)

The **flexor carpi radialis** arises on the medial epicondyle of the humerus and is inserted by a bifid tendon into the second and third metacarpal bones.

The tendons of the foregoing eight muscles are provided with synovial sheaths at the carpus.

The **pronator teres** is a fusiform muscle, which is situated superficially on the proximal part of the medial border of the radius. It arises on the medial epicondyle of the humerus, and is inserted into the dorsal surface and medial border of the radius almost half way to the carpus. It is related deeply to the radial vessels, the median nerve, and the tendon of the biceps. Its action is to flex the elbow and rotate the forearm inward (pronation).

The **superficial digital flexor** is situated superficially on the medio-volar surface of the forearm. It arises on the medial epicondyle of the humerus and terminates near the carpus on a tendon which passes downward outside of the carpal canal and receives below the carpus two reinforcing bands, one from the accessory carpal, the other from the sesamoid bone at the medial side of the carpus. It divides distally into four branches, which are inserted into the second phalanges of the second, third, fourth, and fifth digits.

The **deep digital flexor** has **humeral**, **ulnar**, and **radial heads;** the radial head arises from the medial border of the radius. They unite on a common tendon which passes down through the carpal canal, gives off a branch to the first digit, and divides into four branches. These perforate the tendons of the superficial flexor and are inserted into the third phalanges of the second to the fifth digits. The tendons are provided with synovial sheaths from the middle of the metacarpus downward, and are held in place by three digital annular ligaments.

The **palmaris longus**[1] is a small muscle which arises from the deep digital flexor below the middle of the forearm, and ends by two tendons which unite with those of the superficial flexor for the third and fourth digits.

The **supinator** is a short, flat, fusiform muscle which arises from the front of the lateral epicondyle of the humerus with the lateral ligament, and from the lateral prominence of the head of the radius, and is inserted into the proximal fourth of the

---

[1] The homology here is doubtful. Sussdorf regards the ulnar head of the deep digital flexor as the homologue of the palmaris longus of man, while Alexais considers that the latter is represented by the superficial digital flexor.

dorsal surface and the medial border of the radius. (A pouch of the capsule of the elbow joint lies under the tendon of origin.) Its action is to rotate the forearm outward (supination).

The **pronator quadratus** consists of a thin layer of fibers which cross the volar surface of the radius and the interosseous ligament of the forearm, except at the two extremities of the latter. The fibers extend from the medial border of the radius backward and outward to the interosseous border of the ulna. It rotates the forearm inward (pronation).

The **palmaris brevis** (?) is a very small muscle, which arises on the tendon of the superficial digital flexor at the carpus, and is inserted at the fifth metacarpophalangeal joint into the sheath and annular ligament of the deep flexor.

The **lumbricales** are three very delicate muscles, which arise on the volar surface of the tendons of the deep flexor, and are inserted into the first phalanges of the third, fourth, and fifth digits.

The **abductor pollicis brevis et opponens pollicis,** a very small pale muscle, arises on the fibrous band which connects the superficial flexor tendon with the medial carpal sesamoid, and ends on the distal end of the first metacarpal bone and the first phalanx of the first digit. It abducts the first digit.[1]

The **flexor pollicis brevis** arises on the volar carpal ligament over the second metacarpal bone, and ends on the volar sesamoid of the first digit.

The **adductor pollicis,** situated lateral to the preceding, is the largest of the thumb muscles. It arises between the preceding and the second interosseous muscle, and is inserted into the first phalanx of the first digit.

The **adductor digiti secundi** is situated between the second interosseous muscle and the adductor digiti quinti. It arises on the volar carpal ligament, and ends on the first phalanx of the second digit.

The **adductor digiti quinti** arises close to the preceding muscle, and passes outward to end on the first phalanx of the fifth digit.

The **flexor digiti quinti** arises on the ligament connecting the accessory carpal to the third and fourth metacarpal bones, crosses the corresponding interosseous muscle, and ends on the fifth digit with the next muscle.

The **abductor digiti quinti** is larger than the two preceding muscles; it arises on the accessory carpal bone, and ends on the lateral sesamoid of the fifth digit and on the lateral ligament.

There are four **interossei** which lie on the volar surface of the metacarpus. They are well developed and fleshy. They arise on the distal row of the carpus and on the proximal ends of the metacarpals. Each divides distally into two branches, which are inserted by small tendons on the corresponding sesamoid bones, and detach slips to the extensor tendons.

The chief facts with regard to the synovial membranes in connection with the muscles of the forearm and manus are as follows: The tendons of the extensor carpi radialis frequently have a synovial sheath at the distal part of the forearm, and there may be one or two bursæ at the carpus. The tendons of the extensor digitalis communis have a synovial sheath which extends from the distal part of the forearm to the carpus or to the proximal part of the metacarpus. The tendons of the extensor digitalis lateralis have in about half of the cases a synovial sheath at the distal part of the forearm and at the carpus. The tendon of insertion of the extensor carpi obliquus has a synovial sheath. The tendon of insertion of the ulnaris lateralis sometimes has a bursa between it and the styloid process of the ulna. The tendon of insertion of the flexor carpi radialis has a synovial sheath. There is a bursa between the two tendons of the flexor carpi ulnaris at their insertion; it usually communicates with a subfascial bursa which lies on the accessory carpal bone. The superficial digital flexor has a bursa under its origin; this communicates with another bursa which lies between the deep digital flexor and the flexor carpi ulnaris. The tendons of the digital flexors for the second to the fifth digits have a common sheath for each digit which begins at the distal part of the metacarpus. The tendon of the deep flexor for the first digit has a synovial sheath.

---

[1] Movements of individual digits are specified with regard to the axis of the manus (paw), and not to the median plane of the body.

Muscles of the Neck

The **cervical cutaneus** consists of two strata.   One of these is composed of thin bundles which curve across the ventral region of the neck and fade out laterally. The other layer is thicker and more extensive.   Its bundles begin at the dorsal margin of the neck, are directed obliquely over the sides, and are for the most part continued by the facial part as previously described.

The **sterno-cephalicus** is well developed.   It arises on the manubrium sterni, diverges from its fellow, and ends on the mastoid process, blending with the cleido-cervicalis.   It may be termed the sterno-mastoideus.   It is crossed superficially by the external jugular vein.

The **scalenus ventralis** (s. primæ costæ) arises on the last four cervical transverse processes, and is inserted into the first rib.

The **scalenus dorsalis** (s. supracostalis) is large.   It blends with the preceding muscle in front, and divides into two parts posteriorly.   The dorsal part is inserted on the third and fourth ribs, the ventral part by a long, thin tendon on the seventh or eighth rib.

The **longus colli** resembles that of the horse.

The **rectus capitis ventralis major** arises on the transverse processes of the second to the sixth cervical vertebræ and ends as in the horse.   The **rectus capitis ventralis minor** and **rectus capitis lateralis** resemble those of the horse.

The **intertransversales** resemble those of the ox.

The **splenius** is strong and extensive.   It arises on the first four or five thoracic spines and the median raphé of the neck, and is inserted into the nuchal crest and mastoid process.

The **complexus** is composed of dorsal and ventral parts—the biventer cervicis and the complexus major.   The **biventer cervicis** arises from the transverse processes of the fifth and sixth, and the spines of the second to the fifth (or sixth) thoracic vertebræ, from the ligamentum nuchæ, and the median raphé.   It has four oblique tendinous intersections.   The **complexus major** arises on the transverse processes of the first three or four thoracic vertebræ and the articular processes of the last five cervical.   Both end on a strong common tendon which is inserted into the nuchal crest and the depression below it.

The **longissimus capitis et atlantis** consists of two unequal parts.   The large dorsal part, the **longissimus capitis,** arises from the transverse processes of the first four thoracic and the articular process of the last three or four cervical vertebræ, and ends with the splenius on the mastoid process of the temporal bone.   The small ventral part, the **longissimus atlantis,** arises from the articular processes of the third, fourth, and fifth cervical vertebræ, and ends on the wing of the atlas.

The other muscles present no striking differential features, but it may be noted that distinct **interspinales** are present.   There are also small muscular bundles which lie beneath the multifidus in the back.   These extend from the transverse process of one vertebra to the spine of the preceding one, and are appropriately termed the **submultifidus.**

Muscles of the Thorax

There are twelve pairs of **levatores costarum** and **intercostales.   The external intercostal muscles** do not occupy the spaces between the costal cartilages anteriorly, but further back they do so in varying degree; where they are deficient there are (in most of the spaces) thick **intercartilaginei;** the fibers are almost longitudinal.

The **diaphragm** is very strongly curved, and has a small tendinous center. The hiatus œsophageus is between the crura and is ventral to the twelfth thoracic vertebra.   The costal part is attached to the lower (horizontal) part of the ninth costal cartilage, to the tenth and eleventh cartilages a little (ca. 1 to 2 cm.) below the junction with the rib, to the twelfth rib at its ventral end and to the last rib below its middle. The cupola is very unsymmetrical; on the left side it is opposite the sixth rib, while on the right it is an intercostal space further back.

MUSCLES OF THE BACK AND LOINS

The **serratus dorsalis anterior** arises from the median raphé of the neck and the first six or seven thoracic spines, and is inserted into the second to the ninth ribs. It is well developed. The **serratus dorsalis posterior**—much weaker—arises from the lumbo-dorsal fascia, and is inserted into the last three or four ribs. Thus one or two ribs intervene between the two.

The **longissimus costarum** is well developed, and extends from the ilium to the sixth, fifth, or fourth cervical vertebra.

The **longissimus dorsi** resembles that of the other animals, but the spinalis et semispinalis separates clearly from the longissimus proper at the sixth or seventh thoracic vertebra. It is inserted into the articular and spinous processes of the last six cervical vertebræ. It has no depression in the lumbar region for the gluteus medius.

The **intertransversales** are fleshy, as in the ox.

The **interspinales** are distinct and are most developed in the lumbar region.

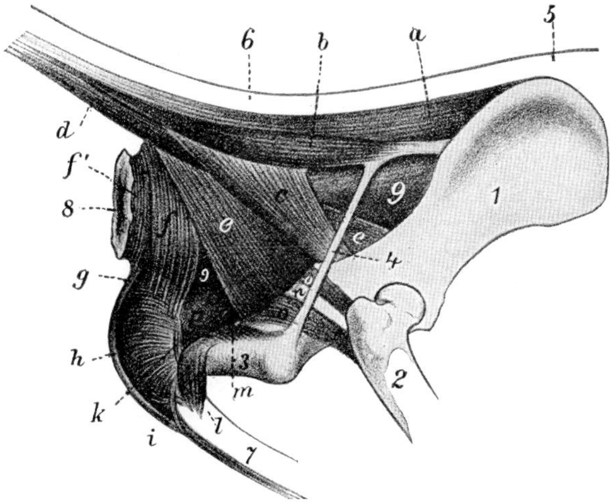

MUSCLES OF THE TAIL

These present the same general arrangement as in the horse. The **sacrococcygei,** however, arise on the lumbar vertebræ also, and the **coccygeus** on the ischiatic spine. There is a **sacro-coccygeus accessorius,** which arises on the medial border of the ilium, the edge of the sacrum, and the transverse processes of

FIG. 325.—MUSCLES OF TAIL, ANUS, AND GENITAL ORGANS OF DOG.

1, Ilium; 2, femur; 3, tuber ischii; 4, sacro-sciatic ligament; 5, sacral region; 6, tail; 7, penis; 8, anus; 9, rectum; a, sacro-coccygeus dorsalis; b, sacro-coccygeus accessorius; c, coccygeus; d, sacro-coccygeus ventralis; e, retractor ani; f, f′, sphincter ani externus; g, retractor penis; h, bulbocavernosus; i, transversus perinei (?); k, m, ischio-urethrales; l, ischiocavernosus; n, tendon of obturator internus; o, [gemellus, p, urethral muscle. (After Ellenberger, in Leisering's Atlas.)

the first coccygeal vertebræ, and is inserted between the dorsal and lateral sacrococcygei. It is homologous with the intertransversales.

MUSCLES OF THE ABDOMEN

The abdominal tunic is practically absent.

The **obliquus abdominis externus** has an extensive fleshy part. It arises from the last eight or nine ribs and the lumbo-dorsal fascia.

The **obliquus abdominis internus** arises from the tuber coxæ and the lumbo-dorsal fascia. The fibers have an almost vertical direction, and there is a fleshy attachment to the last rib. The anterior part of the aponeurosis divides into two layers, which concur in the formation of the internal and external sheaths of the rectus.

The **rectus abdominis** is attached by a long tendon on the first five or six costal cartilages, and by fleshy fibers on the xiphoid cartilage. It usually has five tendinous inscriptions. The two recti diverge very gradually in front, so that they are about half an inch (ca. 1 cm.) apart in the xiphoid region.

The **transversus abdominis** presents no special features except that the posterior part of its aponeurosis splits into two layers which include the rectus between them.

Muscles of the Pelvic Limb

The **psoas minor** arises from the bodies of the last three or four thoracic and first three or four lumbar vertebræ, and is inserted into the iliopectineal line. Its anterior part blends with the quadratus lumborum.

The **psoas major** is relatively small and short; it arises from the last three or four lumbar vertebræ.

The lateral head of the **iliacus** is small, while the medial head is large and fuses with the psoas major to constitute an **ilio-psoas.**

The **quadratus lumborum** is well developed, and extends laterally beyond the edge of the ilio-psoas. It arises from the last three or four thoracic vertebræ in common with the psoas minor, and from the last rib and the lumbar transverse processes, and ends on the pelvic surface of the wing of the ilium.

The **tensor fasciæ latæ** arises from the lateral border of the ilium and the gluteus medius; it consists of two parts. The anterior part is long and rounded; the posterior is shorter and fan-like.

The **gluteus superficialis** is small. It arises from the gluteal fascia, the lateral part of the sacrum, first coccygeal vertebra, and sacro-sciatic ligament. It is inserted below and behind the trochanter major of the femur, on the lateral branch of the linea aspera. In some cases there is a bursa between the tendon and the trochanter major.

The **gluteus medius** has no lumbar portion. It is inserted into the trochanter major by a strong tendon. There is a bursa under the tendon of insertion which also extends under the gluteus profundus.

The **gluteus profundus** is broad and fan-shaped. It arises on the superior ischiatic spine and on the ilium as far forward as the gluteal line, and is inserted into the trochanter major below the medius.[1]

The **piriformis** is not blended with the gluteus medius. It arises from the border and ventral surface of the sacrum and from the sacro-sciatic ligament, and ends on the trochanter major with or close to the gluteus medius.

The **obturators, gemellus,** and **quadratus femoris** resemble in arrangement those of the horse, and present no notable special features. There is a large bursa under the tendon of the obturator internus.

The **biceps femoris** has two heads of origin which soon fuse. The larger head arises from the sacro-sciatic ligament and tuber ischii, the smaller one from the tuber ischii. The aponeurosis of insertion ends on the patella, the patellar ligament, the fascia lata, and the tibial crest. There is also a tendinous band, which comes from the deep face of the muscle and terminates at the tarsus, as in the horse. There is usually a bursa between the muscle and the trochanter major.

The **abductor cruris posterior** may be regarded as an accessory head of the biceps femoris. It is a thin muscular band which arises from the sacro-sciatic

---

[1] Lesbre maintains that this is the scansorius, and that the gluteus profundus is so intimately united with the medius as to have been regarded by anatomists as part of the latter.

ligament, passes downward between the biceps and semimembranosus, and ends by
blending with the former.

The **semitendinosus** arises from the tuber ischii only.   It ends on the crest and
medial surface of the tibia.

The **semimembranosus** is large and arises from the ischium only.   It divides
into two parts: the anterior part ends on the tendon of the pectineus, on the femur
above the medial condyle, and on the medial sesamoid bone; the posterior part

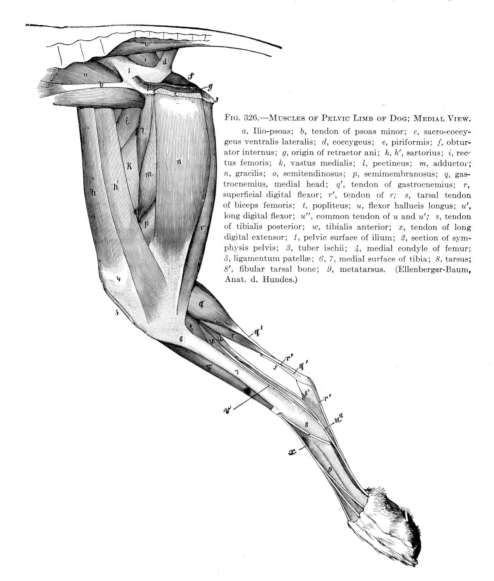

FIG. 326.—MUSCLES OF PELVIC LIMB OF DOG; MEDIAL VIEW.

a, Ilio-psoas; *b*, tendon of psoas minor; *c*, sacro-coccygeus ventralis lateralis; *d*, coccygeus; *e*, piriformis; *f*, obturator internus; *g*, origin of retractor ani; *h, h'*, sartorius; *i*, rectus femoris; *k*, vastus medialis; *l*, pectineus; *m*, adductor;
n, gracilis; *o*, semitendinosus; *p*, semimembranosus; *q*, gastrocnemius, medial head; *q'*, tendon of gastrocnemius; *r*,
superficial digital flexor; *r'*, tendon of *r*; *s*, tarsal tendon
of biceps femoris; *t*, popliteus; *u*, flexor hallucis longus; *u'*,
long digital flexor; *u''*, common tendon of *u* and *u'*; *v*, tendon
of tibialis posterior; *w*, tibialis anterior; *x*, tendon of long
digital extensor; *1*, pelvic surface of ilium; *2*, section of symphysis pelvis; *3*, tuber ischii; *4*, medial condyle of femur;
5, ligamentum patellæ; *6, 7*, medial surface of tibia; *8*, tarsus;
8', fibular tarsal bone; *9*, metatarsus. (Ellenberger-Baum,
Anat. d. Hundes.)

ends on the medial condyle of the tibia, the tendon passing under the medial ligament of the stifle joint.

It is not possible clearly to separate the **quadriceps femoris** into four heads.
The **vastus lateralis** is so much larger than the **vastus medialis** as to indicate that
the **vastus intermedius** is incorporated with the former.   The **rectus femoris** has
only one tendon of origin.   There is a bursa under the muscle at the distal third
of the femur.   The single patellar ligament acts as the tendon of insertion of the
quadriceps.

The **capsularis** is usually present, but is small and pale.

The **sartorius** consists of two parts. The anterior part arises from the tuber coxæ and its flat tendon ends on the patella. The posterior part arises from the lateral border of the ilium and ends on the medial surface of the tibia, its tendon blending with that of the gracilis. The anterior part is superficial in front of the tensor fasciæ latæ and forms here the anterior contour of the thigh.

The **graciles** are not so much fused at their origin as in the other animals. Its anterior part is thin. Its broad tendon is inserted into the tibial crest, and blends with those of the sartorius and semitendinosus.

The **pectineus** is long and slender. It arises from the ilio-pectineal eminence and ends on the medial branch of the linea aspera above the distal end of the femur.

The **adductor femoris** is a large muscle which arises on the ventral surface of the pubis and ischium; it ends on the linea aspera of the femur and the medial surface of the stifle. It is commonly separable into two parts.

The **peroneus tertius** is represented by a tendinous band which arises on the medial surface of the tibia below the crest. It passes on the medial surface of the tibialis anterior, blends with the annular ligament above the tarsus, and is attached to the joint capsule and the proximal end of the third metatarsal bone.

Arloing and Lesbre say: "The third peroneus is a proper extensor of the fifth digit; it is a very feeble, fleshy band, situated behind the peroneus brevis, which it partially covers. It is attached to the upper part of the fibula, and is continued by a long, delicate tendon which passes in the same malleolar groove with the muscle mentioned; it then crosses behind the tendon of the peroneus longus and extends to the phalanges of the outer digit, where it joins one of the branches of the common extensor."

The **tibialis anterior** is large and superficial. It arises on the lateral condyle and crest of the tibia, and is inserted into the first metatarsal bone, or into the first tarsal and second metatarsal.

There are four extensors of the digits.

1. The **long digital extensor** (M. extensor digitalis longus) is fusiform, and lies largely under the preceding muscle. It arises from the extensor fossa of the femur. The tendon is bound down by two annular ligaments: the proximal one, at the distal end of the tibia, encloses also the tendon of the tibialis anterior; the distal one is at the lower part of the tarsus. The tendon divides at the tarsus into four branches, which end on the distal phalanges of the digits (second to fifth).

2. The **lateral digital extensor** (M. extensor digitalis pedis lateralis s. digiti quinti) has a small, unipennate belly which is covered by the peroneus longus and the deep digital flexor. It arises on the fibula below the head. The tendon descends behind that of the peroneus longus, inclines forward under the lateral ligament of the tarsus and the peroneus tendon, and joins the branch of the tendon of the long extensor for the fifth digit.

3. The **extensor hallucis longus** is a very thin muscle which arises from the fibula under the long extensor. Its delicate tendon accompanies that of the tibialis anterior to the first metatarsal bone, or becomes lost in the fascia.

4. The **extensor digitalis brevis** has three divisions. It arises on the fibular tarsal bone and the adjacent ligaments. The three tendons are inserted into the second, third, and fourth digits, blending with the interossei. (Sometimes there is a tendon for the rudimentary first digit, which may represent the extensor hallucis brevis. There may be a fourth belly for the tendon to the second digit.)

The **peroneus longus** arises on the lateral condyle of the tibia, the head of the fibula, and the lateral ligament. The belly does not extend to the middle of the leg, and the long tendon passes down the leg parallel to the fibula. It is bound down in the groove of the lateral malleolus by an annular ligament, crosses the plantar surface of the tarsus transversely, and ends on the first metatarsal bone.

The **peroneus brevis** is unipennate and arises from the distal half or **more** of the lateral face of the tibia and the fibula. Its tendon accompanies that of the lateral extensor over the lateral malleolus, and ends on the proximal end of the fifth metatarsal bone.

The soleus is absent. (It is present and large in the cat.)

The **gastrocnemius** arises from the rough lines above the condyles of the femur. The origin of each head contains a sesamoid bone about the size of a pea (Os sesamoideum m. gastrocnemii), which articulates with the corresponding condyle of the femur. The tendon comports itself as in the horse.

The **superficial digital flexor** has a large round belly. It arises in common with the lateral head of the gastrocnemius from the lateral rough line and sesamoid bone, and from the aponeurosis of the vastus lateralis. The tendon winds around that of the gastrocnemius, passes over the tuber calcis (where it is arranged as in the horse), and divides below the tarsus into two branches. Each of these divides into two branches which end as in the forelimb. The lateral and medial branches detach slips to the suspensory ligaments of the large digital pad. Muscle-fibers often occur in the tendon in the metatarsal region.

The **deep digital flexor** has two heads. The large lateral head, the **flexor hallucis longus,** arises from the posterior surface of the tibia and fibula, filling the interosseous space. The small medial head, **flexor digitalis pedis longus,** also arises from the tibia and fibula; its tendon passes through the groove on the medial malleolus, inclines backward in its descent over the tarsus, and joins that of the large head below the tarsus. The common tendon detaches a branch to the large digital pad and terminates as in the forelimb.

The **tibialis posterior** is a very small but distinct muscle, which arises on the proximal part of the fibula. The delicate tendon accompanies that of the flexor longus and ends on the medial ligament of the tarsus.

The tendon of origin of the **popliteus** contains a small sesamoid bone.

The **adductors of the second and fifth digits,** the **lumbricales,** and the **interossei** are arranged as in the thoracic limb.

The **quadratus plantæ** arises on the lateral surface of the distal end of the fibular tarsal bone and on the lateral tarsal ligament, passes downward and inward, and terminates on a thin tendon which fuses with that of the deep flexor.

The **abductor digiti quinti** is a very small muscle which consists of two parts. One of these is a tendinous slip which extends from the plantar surface of the proximal part of the fibular tarsal bone to the head of the fifth metatarsal bone; the other part arises from the medial surface of the fibular tarsal bone (or from the tendinous part) and ends on the first phalanx of the fifth digit.

In case the skeleton of the first digit is well developed, there are three muscles

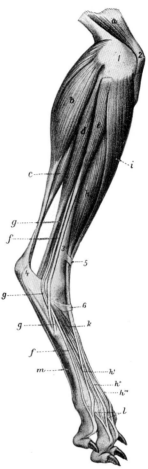

FIG. 327.—MUSCLES OF LEG AND FOOT OF DOG; LATERAL VIEW.

a, Quadriceps femoris; b, gastrocnemius, lateral head; c, superficial digital flexor; d, deep digital flexor; e, peroneus longus; f, tendon of lateral extensor; g, peroneus brevis; h, long digital extensor; h', h'', h''', tendons of preceding; i, tibialis anterior; k, extensor brevis; l, slips from interossei (m); 1, lateral condyle of femur; 2, patella; 3, tibia; 4, tuber calcis; 5, 6, annular ligaments. (After Ellenberger, in Leisering's Atlas.)

which are homologous with those of the same digit in the forelimb. These are the **abductor hallucis, adductor hallucis, and flexor hallucis brevis.**

The principal bursæ and synovial sheaths of the muscles of the leg and foot are as follows: The tibialis anterior has a bursa under its tendon at the tarsus. A pouch of the synovial membrane of the stifle joint underlies the tendon of origin of the extensor digitalis longus, and is partially reflected upon the superficial face of the tendon; the tendons of insertion are provided with a synovial sheath which begins at the end of the muscular part and extends to the proximal part of the metatarsus. The tendons of the lateral digital extensor and peroneus brevis have a common synovial sheath at the distal end of the leg and proximal part of the tarsus. The tendon of the peroneus longus has a synovial sheath which begins an inch or more above the lateral malleolus (in a good-sized dog) and extends about to the middle of the tarsus; another sheath envelops the tendon to the point where it bends round to the plantar surface of the hock; a bursa lies between the tendon and the joint capsule and fourth tarsal bone, and communicates with the joint cavity. A bursa underlies the terminal part of the tendon of the peroneus brevis. There is a bursa in front of the distal part of the tendon of the gastrocnemius; it extends an inch or more (in large dogs) above the tuber calcis. A bursa underlies the superficial flexor tendon at the tarsus; in large dogs it extends about an inch above and below the tuber calcis. The tendon of the tibialis posterior has a synovial sheath at the distal end of the leg. The tendon of the flexor digitalis longus has a synovial sheath which begins a little above the medial malleolus and extends to the junction with the tendon of the flexor hallucis. The tarsal sheath of the flexor hallucis begins (in large dogs) about an inch and a half above the level of the medial malleolus and extends to the distal end of the tarsus; it communicates with the tibio-tarsal joint cavity. The synovial apparatus in the distal part of the limb resembles that of the forelimb.

SPLANCHNOLOGY

This branch deals with the viscera of the digestive, respiratory, and uro-genital systems.[1] Each of these systems consists fundamentally of a tube or tract which is lined with **mucous membrane** (Tunica mucosa) and communicates with the exterior at one end or both. Thus the epithelium of the mucous membranes is continuous with the epidermis at the various natural openings. In addition to this fundamental part there are to be considered aggregations of secreting cells known as glands, muscular tissue, fibrous membranes, serous membranes, vessels and nerves.

Mucous Membranes.—These vary much in thickness, color, and other char-acters. In many places they form **folds** (Plicæ mucosæ) which may be temporary or permanent. In other places they form ridges (Rugæ). With certain excep-tions they are moistened by a viscid secretion, termed **mucus,** which is derived from glands or goblet cells of the epithelium. The membrane consists of two dis-tinct parts: the **epithelium,** which forms the free surface and is protective and secre-tory; and the **lamina propria,** a layer of connective tissue which contains and sup-ports the peripheral ramifications of the vessels and nerves. The mucous mem-brane is connected with surrounding structures by areolar **submucous tissue** (Tela submucosa). In many places there is a layer of unstriped muscle, the **mus-cularis mucosæ,** in the deepest part of the mucous membrane. In many situa-tions the tunica propria presents numerous elevations, known as **papillæ.** When small (microscopic), the papillæ do not modify the surface of the mucous membrane, since the epithelium levels up the depressions between them, but when large (ma-croscopic), they are conspicuous surface features, and are named according to their shape as conical, foliate, etc.

Glands.—The term gland (Glandula) is usually understood to mean an aggre-gation of epithelial cells, the secretion of which is extruded on the free surface of the membrane, or is conveyed away in the blood or lymph stream; the latter are known as **ductless glands** or glands of internal secretion.[2] Glands are divided according to their form into two chief classes, **tubular** and **alveolar,** each of which may be **simple** or **compound;** many, however, combine the characters of both types and are termed **tubulo-alveolar** or **alveolo-tubular.** A simple tubular gland is a cylindrical de-pression lined by epithelium which is continuous with that of the surrounding mucous membrane, from which it developed originally as an outgrowth. The deeper part of such a gland is termed the **fundus,** and here the epithelium is differ-entiated and has taken on secretory function. The more superficial part which conveys the secretion to the surface is called the **duct;** in it the epithelium resembles more or less closely that of the surrounding surface. Many glands are microscopic, while others are large organs. The larger ones are composed of subdivisions known as **lobules** (Lobuli), which are held together by areolar **interlobular tissue;** each lobule has its duct and by the union of these ducts there is formed an **excretory**

---

[1] The term viscus is applied in general to the organs which are contained in the body cavities. It is usual to exclude the heart, except when considering the thoracic organs topographically. Certain other organs which do not belong to these systems are usually considered with them as a matter of convenience.

[2] But unicellular glands are recognized in lower forms, and in higher forms the goblet-cells of many mucous membranes have the same function. Other organs which are not epithelial in structure are commonly classed as glands; such, for example, are the lymph glands and nodules and the spleen; they are usually termed ductless or vascular glands, and are described with the organs with which they are associated anatomically.

duct (Ductus excretorius), through which the secretion is conveyed. Some glands consist of divisions of a larger order which are known as **lobes** (Lobi); these may be separated by layers of connective tissue (Septa interlobares) or by fissures (Incisuræ interlobares).

There is no correspondence between the size of a gland and the number of its excretory ducts. Thus the largest gland in the body, the liver, has a single excretory duct, while some small glands have many.

In the group of **ductless glands** there are those, other than the lymph glands and spleen, which are known as glands of internal secretion or **endocrine glands.** These glands originate in the embryo through invagination of an epithelial sheet in the same manner as do the glands with a well developed duct; but the connection with the epithelial surface is later cut off, so their secretions leave the gland by passing into the blood or lymph vessels which supply them, and are carried to all parts of the body or may leave by rupture of the glandular structure (ovary). The following glands comprise this group: thyroid, parathyroids, thymus, adrenals, hypophysis cerebri, epiphysis cerebri, the gonads, islets of Langerhans in the pancreas, liver, carotid, and coccygeal. They are usually described with the organs with which they are associated topographically.

Muscular Tissue.—Most of the hollow organs are provided with a **muscular coat** (Tunica muscularis) outside of the mucous membrane. This is in great part composed of strata of unstriped muscle, but in certain places—and especially in the vicinity of the natural apertures—it consists of striped muscle. Some of the solid organs contain muscular tissue in their capsule or stroma.

Fibrous Membranes.—Many viscera are enclosed by a **fibrous coat** (Tunica fibrosa). In the case of glands such an enveloping membrane is usually called the **capsule.** Other membranes of a like character are known as a tunica albuginea or tunica adventitia; the former consist mainly of dense white fibrous tissue, while the latter usually contain many elastic fibers and are looser in texture.

Serous Membranes.—These are thin membranes which line the body-cavities and cover more or less the external surface of the viscera contained therein.[1] They include the peritoneum in the abdomen, and the pleura and the deep layer of the pericardium in the thorax. Their free surface is formed by a **mesothelium** of flat cells; it is smooth and glistening and is moistened by a film of serum, thus reducing friction to a minimum. The external surface is in most places connected with the structure covered by areolar **subserous tissue** (Tela subserosa) which often contains fat. The part which lines the wall of a cavity is termed the **parietal layer** (Lamina parietalis), while the **visceral layer** (Lamina visceralis) is that which forms the serous coat (Tunica serosa) of the viscera. Double layers which connect viscera with the wall or with each other are in general called **serous folds** (Plicæ serosæ) or **serous ligaments** (Ligamenta serosa), but many special terms are in use and will be referred to later.

[1] The serous membranes form closed sacs, except in the female, in which case the uterine tubes open into the peritoneal cavity and also communicate indirectly with the exterior.

THE DIGESTIVE SYSTEM

This apparatus (Apparatus digestorius) consists of the organs directly concerned in the reception and digestion of the food, its passage through the body, and the expulsion of the unabsorbed portion. These organs are conveniently grouped under two heads, viz.: (1) the **alimentary canal;** (2) the **accessory organs.**

The **alimentary canal** (Tractus alimentarius) is a tube which extends from the lips to the anus. It has a complete lining of mucous membrane, external to which is an almost continuous muscular coat. The abdominal portion of the tube is largely covered with a serous membrane—the visceral peritoneum. The canal consists of the following consecutive segments: (1) The mouth; (2) the pharynx; (3) the œsophagus; (4) the stomach; (5) the small intestine; (6) the large intestine.

The **accessory organs** are the teeth, tongue, salivary glands, liver, and pancreas.

DIGESTIVE SYSTEM OF THE HORSE

THE MOUTH

The **mouth**[1] (Cavum oris) is the first part of the alimentary canal. It is bounded laterally by the cheeks; dorsally, by the palate; ventrally, by the body of the mandible and the mylo-hyoid muscles; behind, by the soft palate. In the horse it is a long, cylindrical cavity, and when closed, it is almost entirely filled up by the contained structures; a small space remains between the root of the tongue, the soft palate, and the epiglottis; this may be termed the glosso-epiglottic space. The entrance to the mouth (Rima oris) is closed by the lips.

The cavity of the mouth is subdivided into two parts by the teeth and alveolar processes. The space external to these and inclosed by the lips and cheeks is termed the vestibule of the mouth (Vestibulum oris). In the resting state of the parts the walls of this cavity are in contact, and the space is practically obliterated. Its existence becomes very evident in facial paralysis, when the food tends to collect in it laterally, pouching out the cheeks. The space within the teeth and alveolar processes is termed the mouth cavity proper (Cavum oris proprium). When the teeth are in contact, it communicates with the vestibule only by the interdental spaces and the intervals behind the last molar teeth. Posteriorly it communicates with the pharynx through the **isthmus faucium.**

The **mucous membrane** of the mouth (Tunica mucosa oris) is continuous at the margin of the lips with the common integument, and behind with the mucous lining of the pharynx. During life it is chiefly of a pink color, but may be more or less pigmented.

The **lips** (Labia oris) are two musculo-membranous folds which surround the orifice of the mouth. Their angles of union (Anguli oris s. commissuræ labiorum) are situated near the first cheek tooth and are rounded. Each lip presents two surfaces and two borders. The external surface is covered by the skin, which presents long tactile hairs in addition to the ordinary fine hair. The upper lip has a shallow median furrow (Philtrum), the lower a rounded prominence, the chin

---

[1] The term "mouth" is commonly used to signify either the cavity (Cavum oris) or the entrance to it (Rima oris).

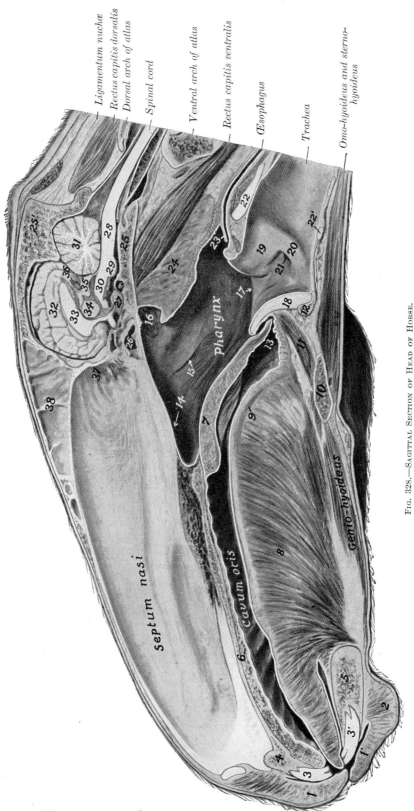

Fig. 328.—Sagittal Section of Head of Horse.

The section is cut about one centimeter to the left of the median plane. 1, 1′, Lips; 2, chin; 3, 3′, incisor teeth; 4, body of premaxilla; 5, body of mandible; 6, hard palate; 7, soft palate; 8, m. genio-glossus; 9, m. longitudinalis linguæ; 10, hyoid bone; 11, m. hyo-epiglotticus; 12, body of thyroid cartilage; 13, glosso-epiglottic space; 14, nasal cavity; 15, pharyngeal opening of auditive or Eustachian tube; 16, pharyngeal recess; 17, aditus laryngis; 18, epiglottis; 19, arytenoid cartilage; 20, vocal cord; 21, lateral ventricle of larynx; 22, 22′, lamina and arch of cricoid cartilage; 23, junction of posterior pillars of soft palate over entrance to œsophagus; 24, septum between guttural pouches; 25, 25′, basilar and squamous parts of occipital bone; 26, sphenoidal sinus; 27, hypophysis cerebri or pituitary body; 28, medulla oblongata; 29, pons; 30, cerebral peduncle; 31, cerebellum; 32, cerebral hemisphere; 33, corpus callosum and septum pellucidum; 34, thalamus; 35, corpora quadrigemina; 36, pineal body; 37, olfactory mucous membrane; 38, septum between frontal sinuses.

(Mentum). The internal surface is covered with mucous membrane which is commonly more or less pigmented. The small papillæ on the surface show on their summits the openings of the ducts of the labial glands. Small folds of mucous membrane which pass from the lip to the gum form the **frænula labii** (superioris, inferioris). The free border of the lip is dense and bears short, very stiff hairs. The attached border is continuous with the surrounding structures.

Structure.—The lips are covered externally by the skin, and are lined by mucous membrane; between these are muscular tissue, glands, vessels, and nerves. The skin lies directly on the muscles, many fibers of which are inserted into it. The muscles have been described (p. 257). The **labial glands** (Glandulæ labiales) form a compact mass at the commissures; they are numerous in the upper lip, fewer in the lower. The mucous membrane is often pigmented, and is reflected upon the bones of the jaws to form the gums.

Vessels and Nerves.—The arteries are derived from the superior and inferior labial and palato-labial arteries. The veins go chiefly to the external maxillary vein. The lymph vessels go to the mandibular lymph glands. The sensory nerves come from the trigeminus, and the motor nerves from the facial nerve.

The **cheeks** (Buccæ) form the sides of the mouth, and are continuous in front with the lips. They are attached to the alveolar borders of the bones of the jaws.

Structure.—This comprises: (1) The skin; (2) the muscular and glandular layer; (3) the mucous membrane. The skin is rather thin and pliable. The muscular tissue is formed mainly by the buccinator, but also by parts of the cutaneous, zygomaticus, dilatator naris lateralis, levator nasolabialis, and depressor labi inferioris. The buccal glands (Glandulæ buccales) (Fig. 646) are arranged in two rows. The **superior buccal glands** lie on the outer surface of the buccinator muscle, near its upper border. The anterior part of the row consists of scattered lobules; the posterior part, which lies under cover of the masseter muscle, is more developed and compact. The **inferior buccal glands,** less voluminous than the superior, are situated in the submucous tissue at the lower border of the buccinator muscle. The mucous membrane is reflected above and below upon the gums, and is continuous behind with that of the soft palate. It is reddish in color and frequently shows pigmented areas. The parotid duct usually opens opposite the third upper cheek tooth on a papilla (Papilla salivalis); exceptionally the opening may be opposite to the anterior part of the second tooth. Linear series of small papillæ above and below indicate the orifices of the small ducts of the buccal glands.

Vessels and Nerves.—The blood-supply is derived from the facial and buccinator arteries, and the blood is carried away by veins of the same name. The lymph vessels go to the mandibular lymph glands. The sensory nerves come from the trigeminus and the motor nerves from the facial nerve.

The **gums** (Gingivæ) are composed of a dense fibrous tissue which is intimately united with the periosteum of the alveolar processes, and blends at the edges of the alveoli with the alveolar periosteum; the latter fixes the teeth in their cavities. They are covered by a smooth mucous membrane, destitute of glands, and of a low degree of sensibility.

The **hard palate** (Palatum durum) is bounded in front and on the sides by the alveolar arches, and is continuous with the soft palate behind. Its osseous basis is formed by the premaxilla, maxilla, and palatine bones. The mucous membrane is smooth, and is attached to the bones by a submucosa which contains in its anterior part an exceedingly rich venous plexus, constituting an erectile tissue. A central **raphé** (Raphé palati) divides the surface into two equal portions. Each of these presents about eighteen transverse curved ridges (Rugæ palatini) which have their concavity and their free edges directed backward. They are further apart and more prominent anteriorly. The central prominence just behind the first pair of incisors is the **papilla incisiva;** it is margined by a fissure on each side. There are no glands in the submucosa. The **ductus incisivus** is a small tube of mucous membrane which extends very obliquely through the palatine fissure. Its ventral or palatine end is blind and lies in the submucous tissue of the palate. The dorsal or nasal end communicates with the nasal cavity (in common with the vomero-nasal organ) by a slit-like opening in the anterior part of the ventral nasal meatus.

Vessels and Nerves.—The blood-supply is derived chiefly from the palatine arteries and the veins go to the vena re-flexa. The nerves come from the trigeminus.

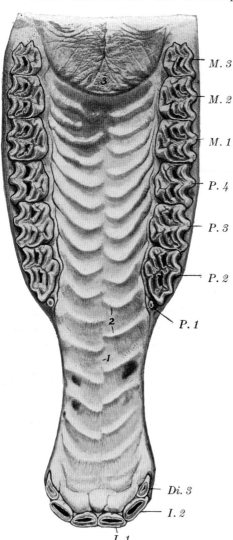

The **soft palate** (Palatum molle) is a musculo-membranous curtain which separates the cavity of the mouth from that of the pharynx, except during swallowing. It slopes downward and backward from its junction with the hard palate. The **oral surface** faces ventrally and somewhat forward, and is covered with a mucous membrane continuous with that of the hard palate. It presents a rounded, median ridge, flanked usually by a sagittal fold on either side. Numerous small ducts of the palatine glands open on this surface. On each side a short, thick fold passes to the lateral border of the tongue; this is the **anterior pillar** of the soft palate (Arcus glossopalatinus). The **pharyngeal surface** faces dorsally and a little backward and is covered by a mucous membrane continuous with that of the nasal cavity. The **free border** (Arcus palatinus) is concave and thin; it is in contact (except during deglutition) with the epiglottis. It is continued by a fold of the mucous membrane, which passes on each side along the lower part of the lateral wall of the pharynx and unites with the opposite fold over the beginning of the œsophagus; this fold is termed the **posterior pillar** of the soft palate (Arcus pharyngopalatinus). The space between the diverging anterior and posterior pillars (Sinus tonsillaris) is occupied by the **tonsil** (Tonsilla palatina). In the horse, however, there is not a compact tonsil, as in man, dog, etc., but a series of masses of lymphoid tissue and mucous glands which extend backward from the root of the tongue on either side a distance of about four inches (ca. 10 cm.). These cause elevations of the surface, on which there are depressions (crypts) in which the gland ducts open. The soft palate is greatly developed in equidæ, its average length, measured medially, being about six inches (15 cm.). Its length and contact with the epiglottis may account for the fact that in these animals mouth-

Fig. 329.—Hard Palate and Adjacent Part of Soft Palate of Horse.

1, Raphé of palate; 2, ridges of palate; 3, soft palate; *I. 1, I. 2,* first and second incisor; *Di. 3,* deciduous third incisor; *P. 1–4,* premolars; *M. 1–3,* molars.

breathing does not occur under normal conditions, and that in vomiting the ejected matter escapes usually through the nasal cavity.[1]

Structure.—The soft palate consists of: (1) The oral mucous membrane, continuous with that of the hard palate, which it resembles; it covers also a narrow marginal area of the pharyngeal surface along the free border; (2) the **palatine glands** (Glandulæ palatinæ), which form a layer about half an inch in thickness; (3) the aponeurotic and muscular layer; (4) the pharyngeal mucous membrane, continuous with that of the nasal cavity, which it resembles.

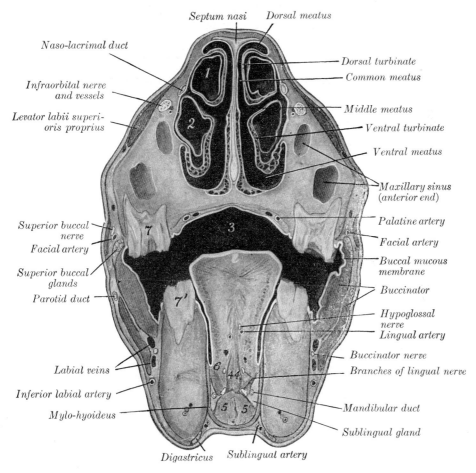

Fig. 330.—Cross-section of Head of Horse at Anterior End of Facial Crest.

1, Cavity of dorsal turbinate; *2*, cavity of ventral turbinate; *3*, cavum oris; *4, 4*, genio-glossi; *5, 5*, genio-hyoidei; **6,** hyo-glossus; *7*, upper, *7'*, lower, fourth cheek tooth. Line to facial artery crosses zygomaticus.

The **muscles** proper to the soft palate are the palatinus, the levator palati, and the tensor palati.

The **palatinus** (M. palatinus) consists of two small muscular bundles which lie together at the median line. It is attached through the medium of the palatine aponeurosis to the palatine bones, and terminates near the free edge of the soft palate. Usually a bundle from it is continued a short distance into the posterior pillar. Its action is to shorten the soft palate.

The **levator palati** (M. levator veli palatini) arises from the muscular process

[1] The epiglottis may be either on the oral (prevelar) or pharyngeal (postvelar) side of the soft palate as shown in Figs. 328 and 349.

of the petrous temporal bone and from the lateral lamina of the Eustachian tube, and passes at first forward, lateral to the latter; it then inclines ventrally across the deep face of the anterior pharyngeal muscles and turns medially into the soft palate, in which it spreads out above the glandular layer. It raises the soft palate, thus closing the posterior nares during deglutition.

The **tensor palati** (M. tensor veli palatini) is larger than the levator, and is fusiform and flattened. It arises from the muscular process of the petrous temporal bone, the pterygoid bone, and the lateral lamina of the Eustachian tube, and passes forward, lateral to the levator, across the medial surface of the origin of the pterygoideus medialis. Its tendon is then reflected around the hamulus of the pterygoid bone, where it is held in position by a fibrous band and lubricated by a bursa, turns inward and expands in the aponeurosis of the soft palate. It tenses the soft palate.

Vessels and Nerves.—The blood-supply of the soft palate is derived from the internal and external maxillary arteries and the blood is carried away by the corresponding veins. The lymph vessels go to the pharyngeal lymph glands. The nerves come from the trigeminus, vagus, and glosso-pharyngeal nerves.

The **floor** of the mouth in its anterior part is free and is formed by the body of the mandible, covered by mucous membrane. The remainder is occupied by the attached portion of the tongue in the undisturbed state of the parts. The following features are exposed by raising the tongue and drawing it to one side. About opposite the canine tooth on each side is a papilla, the **caruncula sublingualis,** through which the duct of the mandibular gland opens. Just behind these papillæ is a median fold of mucous membrane which passes to the ventral surface of the tongue, constituting the **frenum linguæ.** On either side is the **sublingual fold** (Plica sublingualis) which extends from the frenum to the level of the fourth cheek tooth. The fold indicates the position of the underlying sublingual gland, and presents numerous small papillæ, through which the ducts open. Behind the last tooth a vertical fold of the mucous membrane passes from upper to lower jaw. This is termed the **plica pterygomandibularis;** it contains a ligament of like name.

The **isthmus faucium** is the orifice of communication between the mouth and the pharynx. It is bounded above by the soft palate, below by the root of the tongue, and laterally by the anterior pillars of the soft palate. It is relatively small and not very dilatable in the horse, and is closed by the soft palate under normal conditions, except during deglutition.

THE TONGUE

The **tongue** (Lingua) is situated on the floor of the mouth, between the rami of the mandible, and is supported mainly in a sort of sling formed by the mylo-hyoid muscles. Its posterior part, the **root** (Radix linguæ), is attached to the hyoid bone, soft palate, and pharynx. Only the upper surface of this part is free, and slopes downward and backward. The middle part, the **body** (Corpus linguæ), has three free surfaces. The dorsal surface is slightly rounded. The lateral surfaces are nearly flat for the most part, but anteriorly become rounded and narrower. The ventral surface is related to the genio-hyoid and mylo-hyoid muscles. The **apex** or tip (Apex linguæ) is free, spatula-shaped, and presents upper and lower surfaces and a rounded border. The term **dorsum linguæ** is applied to the dorsal surface; it is free throughout, and when the mouth is closed is in contact with the palate except at the glosso-epiglottic space.

Structure.—The tongue consists of: (1) The mucous membrane; (2) the glands; (3) the muscles; (4) vessels and nerves.

The **mucous membrane** (Tunica mucosa linguæ) adheres intimately to the subjacent tissue, except on the lower part of the lateral surfaces of the body and the ventral surface of the tip. It varies considerably in thickness. On the dorsum it is very thick and dense; underneath this part there is a dense fibrous cord, which extends medially a distance of five or six inches forward from the vallate papillæ. On the sides and ventral surface of the tongue the membrane is much thinner and smooth, and can more readily be dissected off the muscular tissue.[1] From the lower surface of the free part of the tongue a fold of the mucous membrane passes to the floor of the mouth, forming the **frenum linguæ.** Posteriorly a fold passes on each side from the edge of the dorsum to join the soft palate, forming the anterior pillars of the latter. A thick central **glosso-epiglottic fold** (Plica glossoepiglottica) passes from the root to the base of the epiglottis; this encloses the hyoepiglottic muscle. The mucous membrane presents numerous **papillæ,** which are of four kinds—filiform, fungiform, vallate, and foliate. The **filiform papillæ** (Papillæ filiformes) are fine, thread-like projections which stud the dorsum and the sides of the tip; they are absent on the root. On the anterior part they are so small as to be scarcely visible, but on the posterior part they are much larger and give the surface a distinct pile. The **fungiform papillæ** (Papillæ fungiformes) are larger and easily seen; they are rounded at the free end, which is supported by a neck. They occur principally on the lateral part of the tongue, but are also found scattered over the dorsum. The **vallate papillæ** (Papillæ vallatæ) are usually two or three in number. The two constant ones are a quarter of an inch or more (ca. 6 to 7 mm.) in diameter, and are found on the posterior part of the dorsum, one on each side of the median plane, about an inch (ca. 3 cm.) apart. The third, when present, is behind these, is centrally situated, and is always smaller. Rarely a fourth may be found. They are rounded, broader at their exposed than at their attached surfaces, and are sunk in a depression which is bounded by an annular wall. Their free surface

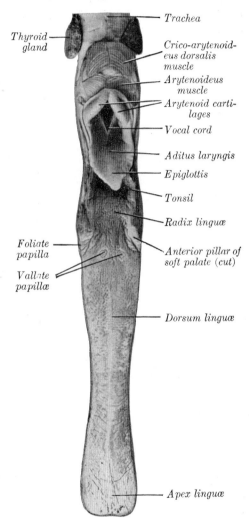

FIG. 331.—TONGUE, LARYNX, AND PART OF TRACHEA OF HORSE; DORSAL VIEW.

Labels: Trachea, Thyroid gland, Crico-arytenoideus dorsalis muscle, Arytenoideus muscle, Arytenoid cartilages, Vocal cord, Aditus laryngis, Epiglottis, Tonsil, Radix linguæ, Foliate papilla, Anterior pillar of soft palate (cut), Vallate papillæ, Dorsum linguæ, Apex linguæ

is tuberculate, i. e., bears small, round secondary papillæ. The **foliate papillæ** (Papillæ foliatæ) are situated just in front of the anterior pillars of the soft palate, where they form a rounded eminence about an inch (ca. 2 to 3 cm.) in length, marked by transverse fissures. The last three varieties are covered with microscopic secondary papillæ and are furnished with taste-buds. The mucous membrane of the root of the tongue presents numerous folds and rounded elevations.

[1] The mucous membrane is thick and closely adherent where food naturally comes in contact with the tongue.

The latter are marked by crypts and consist essentially of a mass of lymphoid tissue; they are known as **lingual follicles** (Folliculi linguales), and taken together form what is sometimes called the lingual tonsil. The **lingual glands** (Glandulæ linguales) constitute a thick layer in the loose submucous tissue and also lie between the muscle bundles. Mucous glands are found also in part of the dorsum and sides of the tongue.

The **lingual muscles** (Mm. linguæ) may be divided into intrinsic and extrinsic. The intrinsic musculature consists, not of distinct muscles, but rather of systems of fibers which run longitudinally, vertically, and transversely, blending with the extrinsic muscles, which are now to be described.[1]

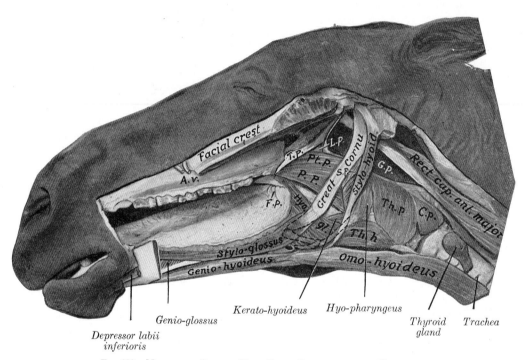

FIG. 332.—MUSCLES OF TONGUE, HYOID BONE, PHARYNX, ETC., OF HORSE.

T. p., Tensor palati; *L. p.*, levator palati; *Pt. p.*, pterygo-pharyngeus; *P. p.*, palato-pharyngeus; *S. p.*, stylo-pharyngeus; *Th. p.*, thyro-pharyngeus; *C. p.*, crico-pharyngeus; *Th. h.*, thyro-hyoideus; *Hyo. gl.*, hyo-glossus; *G. p.*, space occupied by guttural pouch; *F. p.*, foliate papilla; *A. v.*, facial artery and vein. Most of the left ramus of the mandible is removed. The concealed parts of the hyoid bone are indicated by dotted lines.

1. **Stylo-glossus.**—This is a long, thin muscle, which lies along the lateral part of the tongue. It arises by a thin tendon from the lateral surface of the great cornu of the hyoid bone, near the articulation with the small cornu. It terminates near the tip of the tongue by blending with its fellow of the opposite side and with the intrinsic musculature. The action is to retract the tongue. Unilateral contraction would also draw the tongue toward the side of the muscle acting.

A small muscular band sometimes arises on the thyroid cornu of the hyoid bone and ends on the tendon of origin of the stylo-glossus. In some cases a similar band arises higher up, with and on the hyo-glossus.

2. **Hyo-glossus.**—This is a wide, flat muscle, somewhat thicker than the pre-

[1] This distinction is more or less conventional. It is evident that much of what may appear on cross-sections of the tongue to be intrinsic muscle is in reality a part of the extrinsic musculature. The arrangement is further complicated by the existence of bundles running in various directions, intercrossing of bundles, and the breaking up of the systems by masses of fat.

ceding. It lies in the lateral part of the root and body of the tongue, partly under cover of the preceding muscle. Its deep face is related to the genio-glossus. It

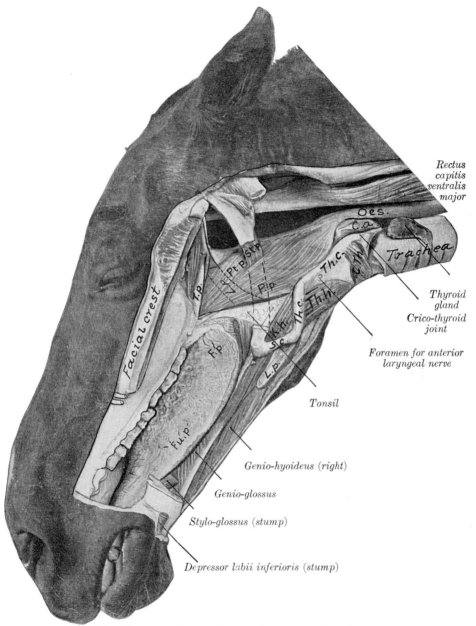

Fig. 333.—Muscles of Tongue, Pharynx, Larynx, etc.; Deep Dissection.

T. p., Tensor palati; *L. p.*, levator palati, concealed part indicated by dotted line; *Pt. p.*, pterygo-pharyngeus; *P. p.*, palato-pharyngeus; *St. p.*, stylo-pharyngeus; *C. a.*, crico-arytenoideus dorsalis; *C. th.*, crico-thyroideus; *Th. c.*, thyroid cartilage (lamina); *Th. h.*, thyro-hyoideus; *K. h.*, kerato-hyoideus; *Th. c.*, thyroid cornu; *S. c.*, small cornu; *L. p.*, lingual process; *F. p.*, foliate papilla; *Fu. p.*, fungiform papillæ. Part of great cornu is removed and indicated by dotted lines. The guttural pouch has been removed.

arises from the lateral aspect of the hyoid bone, from the lingual process to the oral extremity of the great cornu, and from the thyroid cornu. The fibers pass obliquely forward and upward, and for the most part turn toward the median plane of the dorsum of the tongue. Its action is to retract and depress the tongue.[1]

3. **Genio-glossus.**—This is a fan-shaped muscle, which lies parallel to the median plane of the tongue. It is separated from the muscle of the opposite side by a layer of fat and areolar tissue. It arises from the medial surface of the ramus of the mandible just behind the symphysis. From the tendon the fibers pass in a radiating manner, some curving forward to the tip, others pass toward the dorsum, and others toward the root of the tongue; some fibers pass from the posterior end of the tendon to the body and small cornu of the hyoid bone. The muscle as a whole is a depressor of the tongue, and especially of its middle portion; when both muscles act, a median groove is formed on the dorsum. The posterior fibers protrude the tongue, the middle fibers depress the tongue, and the anterior fibers retract the tip of the tongue.

In some cases there is a small anomalous muscle which arises by a delicate tendon with the genio-glossus and is attached behind with the genio-hyoideus.

Vessels and Nerves.—The arteries of the tongue are the lingual and sublingual branches of the external maxillary artery. The veins go to the internal and external maxillary veins. The lymph vessels go chiefly to the pharyngeal lymph glands. The sensory nerves are the lingual and glosso-pharyngeal, and the muscles are innervated by the hypoglossal nerve.

THE TEETH IN GENERAL

The teeth are hard white or yellowish-white structures implanted in the alveoli of the bones of the jaws. Morphologically they are large calcified papillæ. Functionally they are organs of prehension and mastication, and may serve as weapons. The domesticated mammals have two sets of teeth. The teeth of the first set appear during early life and are known as **deciduous** or **temporary** teeth (Dentes decidui),[2] since they are replaced during the period of growth by the **permanent teeth** (Dentes permanentes). They are classified according to form and position as follows:

1. The **incisor teeth** (Dentes incisivi) are situated in front and are implanted in the premaxilla and mandible.

2. The **canine teeth** (Dentes canini) are situated a little further back, and interrupt the interalveolar space.

3. The **premolar** and **molar teeth** (Dentes præmolares et molares) form the sides of the dental arch. The premolars form the anterior part of the series; they appear in both sets. The molars appear only in the permanent dentition. The term **cheek teeth** is used to include both premolars and molars.

The interval between the incisors and premolars is the interalveolar or interdental space.

As the teeth of the two sides of the jaw are alike in number and character (in normal cases), the complete dentition may be briefly indicated by a **dental formula** such as the following:

$$2\left(I\ \frac{2}{2}\ C\ \frac{1}{1}\ P\ \frac{2}{2}\ M\ \frac{3}{3}\right) = 32.$$

In this formula the letters indicate the kinds of teeth, and the figures above and below the lines give the number of teeth of one side in the upper and lower jaw respectively in man.

[1] It may be possible to recognize in this muscle three parts, which would correspond to the baseo-, kerato-, and chondro-glossus of man.

[2] They are also popularly spoken of as "milk" teeth.

The individual teeth of each group are designated numerically, the starting-point being the middle line; thus the incisor on either side of the middle line is the first incisor, and may be conveniently indicated by the notation I^1. The deciduous teeth may be designated in a similar manner, prefixing D (for deciduous) to the letter indicating the kind of tooth. In addition to the above systematic method of notation other terms have received the sanction of popular usage. Thus the first incisors are commonly called middle incisors, "pinchers," or "nippers"; the second, intermediate; and the third, corner teeth. The canines, when highly developed, may be termed tusks or fangs. The vestigial and inconstant first premolar of the horse is popularly termed the "wolf-tooth."

Each tooth presents for description a part coated with enamel, termed the **crown** (Corona dentis), and a part covered with cement, termed the **root** (Radix dentis). The line of union of these parts is the **neck** (Collum dentis).[1] In many teeth the neck is distinct and is embraced by the gum, e. g., the teeth of the dog and the deciduous incisors of the horse. In other teeth no constriction is present, e. g., the permanent incisors of the horse. Between these extremes are the molars of the horse, in which the neck is seen only in advanced age.

The **surface** of a tooth directed toward the lips is termed **labial;** that toward the cheek, **buccal;** and that toward the tongue, **lingual** (Facies labialis, buccalis, lingualis). The surface opposed to a neighboring tooth of the same dental arch is termed the **contact surface** (Facies contactus). The **masticatory surface** (Facies masticatoria) is that which comes in contact with a tooth or teeth of the opposite jaw.[2]

Structure.—Teeth are composed of four tissues, which are considered here from within outward. The **pulp** of the tooth (Pulpa dentis) is a soft, gelatinous tissue, which occupies a space in the central part of the tooth termed the **pulp cavity** (Cavum dentis). The pulp is well supplied with blood-vessels and nerves. It occupies a relatively large space in young growing teeth, but later the dentine deposited on its surface gradually encroaches on it until, in advanced age, the cavity is much reduced or obliterated. The **dentine** (Substantia eburnea) forms the bulk of most teeth, covering the surface of the pulp. It is hard, and is yellowish-white in color. The **enamel** (Substantia adamantina), the hardest tissue of the body, constitutes a layer of varying thickness covering the dentine of the crown of the tooth. It is easily distinguished by its clear, bluish-white appearance and its extreme density. The **cement** (Substantia ossea) is the outermost tooth substance. In simple teeth it forms usually a thin layer on the surface of the root only, but in complex teeth it exists in considerable quantity, tending to fill in the spaces between the enamel folds of the crown also. Its structure is practically the same as that of bone without Haversian canals, and even these occur where the cement forms a thick layer. The embedded part of the tooth is attached to the alveolus by a vascular layer of connective tissue, the **alveolar periosteum** (Periosteum alveolare); this is the periosteum of the alveolus and performs a like function with regard to the embedded part of the tooth. The name pericementum has also been applied to it.

[1] It will be noted that this definition of crown and root does not agree exactly with the popular view that the crown is the free part and the root the embedded part. The objection to the latter statement lies in the fact that it is not capable of general application. Thus the morphological crown of the permanent molars in the horse is extremely long, and is, for the most part, embedded in the bone in the young animal. The root proper begins to form at four or five years of age, and continues its growth for about eight years. As the exposed part of the crown wears down, the embedded part erupts, thus preventing deficiency of length. On the old basis we should have to say that successive portions of the root become crown, while in point of fact it is only in very extreme age that the true root comes into wear. This difficulty does not arise in cases in which the eruption of the teeth is completed rapidly, e. g., man, dog. In such brachydont forms the short crown is clearly marked off from the root or roots by a neck, which is embraced by the gum. The opposite extreme is seen in the incisors of typical rodents, which grow continuously and have no roots.

[2] This is popularly termed the grinding surface or "table" of the tooth.

The **blood-supply** to the pulp is derived from the infraorbital and mandibular alveolar branches of the internal maxillary artery; the **nerve-supply** comes from corresponding branches of the trigeminus.

THE TEETH OF THE HORSE[1]

THE PERMANENT TEETH

The formula of the permanent teeth of the horse is:

$$2\left(I\ \frac{3}{3}\ C\ \frac{1}{1}\ P\ \frac{3\ or\ 4}{3}\ M\ \frac{3}{3}\right) = 40\ or\ 42$$

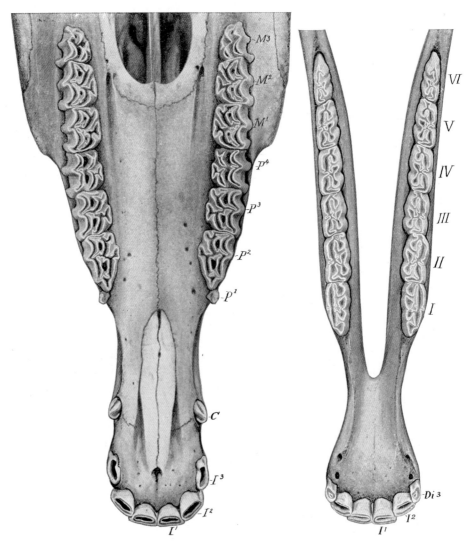

FIG. 334.—UPPER TEETH OF HORSE, ABOUT FOUR AND ONE-HALF YEARS OLD.

I^1, I^2, I^3, Incisors; C, canine; P^1, P^2, P^3, P^4, premolars; M^1, M^2, M^3, molars. The eruption of the third incisor is not complete and the tooth is unworn.

FIG. 335.—LOWER TEETH OF HORSE, FOUR YEARS OF AGE.

I^1, I^2, First and second permanent incisors; Di^3, third deciduous incisor. The cheek teeth are numbered according to popular usage

[1] Other figures illustrating the teeth are to be found in the description of the skull.

In the mare the canines usually are very small and do not erupt, reducing the number to 36 or 38.[1]

Incisor Teeth.—These are twelve in number. The six in each jaw are placed close together, so that their labial edges form almost a semicircle in the young horse. They have the peculiarity (not found in existing mammals other than the equidæ) of presenting, instead of the simple cap of enamel on the crown, a deep invagination, the **infundibulum,** which becomes partly filled up with cement. Hence as the tooth wears, the masticatory surface (or "table") has a central ring of enamel surrounding this cavity in addition to the peripheral enamel. The cavity becomes darkened by deposits from the food, and is commonly termed the "cup" or "mark." Each tooth is curved so that the labial surface is convex

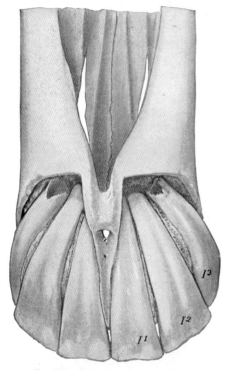
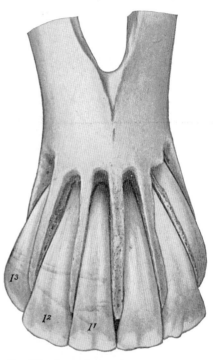

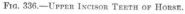

FIG. 336.—UPPER INCISOR TEETH OF HORSE.   FIG. 337.—LOWER INCISOR TEETH OF HORSE.

The labial surfaces of the teeth have been exposed by removal of the bone. Subject was five years old.

and the embedded parts converge. The average total length of an incisor at five or six years of age is about two and a half to three inches (ca. 7 cm.). They taper regularly from exposed crown to apex, without any constriction, and in such a manner that in young horses the masticatory surface is broad transversely; toward the middle the two diameters of a cross-section are about equal; near the apex the antero-posterior diameter is considerably greater than the transverse.

This fact is of value in the determination of age by the teeth, since the masticatory surfaces at different ages represent a series of cross-sections. As the exposed crown wears down, the embedded part (reserve crown) emerges from the

[1] Ellenberger found, as the result of extensive observations (8000 subjects), that about 2 to 3 per cent. of mares have erupted canines in both jaws; that 6 to 7 per cent. have them in the upper jaw; while 20 to 30 per cent. have them in the lower jaw. The numerical variation in the above formula results from the fact that the first premolar ("wolf-tooth") is often absent in the adult and further that it is doubtful to what set it belongs when present. It is commonly not included in the enumeration.

alveolus, so that the masticatory surfaces of the first and second lower incisors are at first oval, with the long diameter transverse; later—at about fourteen years usually for the first lower incisors—they are triangular, with the base at the labial edge. At the same time the infundibulum or "cup" becomes smaller, approaches the lingual border, and finally disappears; it remains longer on the upper incisors, as it is deeper in them. Another marked feature in old age is the progressive approach to a horizontal direction as seen in profile; at the same time the exposed crowns of the teeth become parallel and finally convergent.

Canine Teeth.—These are four in number in the male; in the mare they are usually absent or rudimentary.[1] They interrupt the interdental space, dividing it into unequal parts. The upper canine

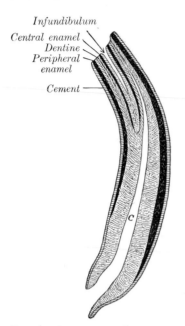

Infundibulum
Central enamel
Dentine
Peripheral enamel
Cement

c

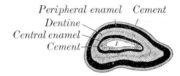

Peripheral enamel   Cement
Dentine
Central enamel
Cement
i

FIG. 338.—LONGITUDINAL SECTION OF LOWER INCISOR TOOTH OF HORSE.

C, Pulp cavity. Cement is shown in the infundibulum, but is not marked.

FIG. 339.—CROSS-SECTION OF LOWER INCISOR TOOTH OF HORSE.
I, Infundibulum.

is situated at the junction of the premaxilla and the maxilla; the lower canine is nearer the corner incisor. The canines are simple teeth, smaller than the incisors,

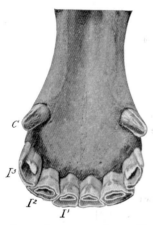

C

I³

I²

I'

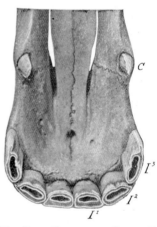

C

I³

I²

I'

FIG. 340.—LOWER INCISOR AND CANINE TEETH OF HORSE, FIVE YEARS OLD.

FIG. 341.—UPPER INCISOR AND CANINE TEETH OF HORSE, FIVE YEARS OLD.

The lingual border of the third lower incisor is unworn. *I¹, I², I³*, Incisors; *C*, canine.

and are curved with the concavity directed backward. The exposed crown in the young subject is compressed, convex and smooth laterally, concave with a median

[1] It is interesting to notice that vestigial canines are not at all uncommon in mares, especially in the lower jaw. They are very small, and do not usually erupt; their presence is indicated in the latter case by a prominence of the gum. This is in conformity with the fact that they were present in both sexes in Eocene and Miocene ancestors of existing equidæ.

ridge medially; its edge is sharp in the unworn tooth. The embedded part (usually called the root) is round and the pulp cavity is large, persisting to advanced

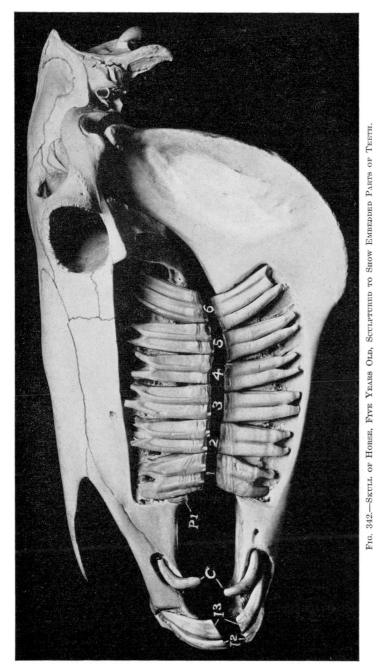

FIG. 342.—SKULL OF HORSE, FIVE YEARS OLD, SCULPTURED TO SHOW EMBEDDED PARTS OF TEETH.

The jaws are separated for the sake of clearness. I_2, I_3, Incisors; C, canines. The cheek teeth are numbered without reference to the first premolar, which is marked P_1. In this subject the lengths of the upper cheek teeth in centimeters enumerated from before backward were: 6.5, 8.3, 8.5, 7.8, 8.5, 8.0. The smallest distance between the first pair was 5.5 cm. and between the last 7.5 cm. The lengths of the lower cheek teeth were: 6.5, 7.6, 8.2, 8.0, 8.5, 7.5. The distances between the first and last pairs were 4.0 and 6.5 respectively.

age. In old subjects, when the compressed part of the crown has worn away, the exposed part is rounded and blunt.

Cheek Teeth (Premolars and Molars).[1]—The constant number of these is

[1] It is common in veterinary works to apply the term "molar" to all the cheek teeth, since, in the horse particularly, the premolars are molariform, *i. e.*, do not differ materially from the true molars in size or form. The term cheek teeth conveniently includes the premolars and molars.

twenty-four—twelve in each jaw. Quite commonly, however, the number is increased by the presence in the upper jaw of the so-called "wolf-tooth." This tooth, the first premolar, is usually situated just in front of the first well-developed tooth; it is a much-reduced vestige, not often more than one-half or three-fourths of an inch (ca. 1 to 2 cm.) in length. (It is interesting as being the remnant of a tooth which was well developed in the Eocene ancestors of the horse.) It may erupt during the first six months, and is often shed about the same time as the milk-tooth behind it, but may remain indefinitely. The occurrence of a similar tooth in the lower jaw—which rarely erupts—increases the dental formula to 44, which is considered the typical number for mammals.[1] The cheek teeth are very large, prismatic in form, and quadrilateral in cross-section, except the first and last of the series, which are three-sided. The crown is remarkably long, most of it being embedded in the bone or projecting into the maxillary sinus in the young horse. As the exposed part wears away the embedded part erupts to replace it, so that a functional crown of about four-fifths of an inch (ca. 2 cm.) is maintained.[2] The root begins to grow at about five years of age, and is complete at twelve to fourteen, although the deposition of cement may continue indefinitely.

The **maxillary** or **upper cheek teeth** are embedded in the alveolar processes of the max-

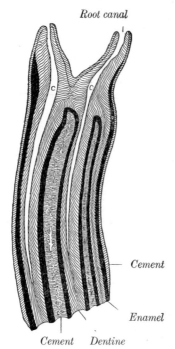

Root canal

Cement

Enamel

Cement   Dentine

Fig. 343.—Frontal Section of Upper Cheek Tooth of Horse.

C, C, Pulp cavities.   Infundibulum filled with cement.

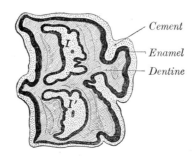

Cement

Enamel

Dentine

Fig. 344.—Cross-section of Upper Cheek Tooth of Horse.

Buccal (lateral) surface to left.   *I,* Anterior, *I ',* posterior infundibulum, both almost filled up with cement.

illa. The exposed parts of the crowns are normally in close contact, forming a continuous row which is slightly curved, with the convexity toward the cheek. The embedded parts diverge as shown in the annexed figures (Figs. 342, 347). Thus the long axis of the first is directed upward and a little forward, that of the second may be vertical or incline slightly backward, the third curves backward more, while the fourth is often about vertical. The last tooth curves strongly backward in the adult, but the inclination of the fifth is much less. The **buccal surface** presents a central ridge running lengthwise and separating two grooves; the first tooth has, in addition, a less prominent ridge in front of the primary one. The **lingual surface** is marked by a wide, rounded ridge, the accessory pillar or column, which separates two very shallow grooves. The **masticatory surface** presents

[1] The question to which set these teeth belong is an open one.
[2] For teeth of this kind it is convenient to employ the terms functional crown and reserve crown.

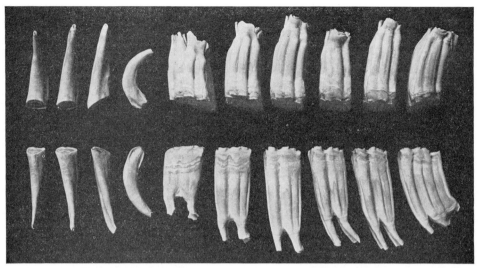

FIG. 344a.—TEETH OF HORSE, SIX YEARS OLD, RIGHT SIDE; MEDIAL VIEW.

two infundibula, anterior and posterior. It slopes obliquely downward and outward, so that the buccal edge is prominent and sharp. Its average width, except

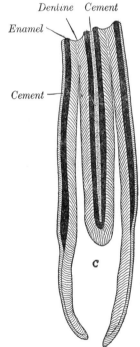

FIG. 345.—FRONTAL SECTION OF LOWER CHEEK TOOTH OF HORSE.
C, Pulp cavity. Infundibulum filled with cement.

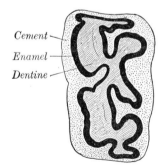

FIG. 346.—CROSS-SECTION OF LOWER CHEEK TOOTH OF HORSE.
Buccal surface to left.

at each end of the series, is about an inch (ca. 2.5 cm.). The first and last teeth have three roots, the remainder four or three. The individual teeth differ in length as shown in Fig. 342.

The position of the embedded crowns and roots of the last four varies at different ages and in different subjects. Two factors in this variation may be noted. All of these teeth are developed in the posterior part of the body of the maxilla. As growth proceeds the teeth move forward, so that commonly only the last three, but sometimes also the third, project into the maxillary sinus. The second cause of variation is the fact that the anterior limit of the maxillary sinus may be at the extremity of the facial crest, or about an inch beyond it. In the latter case the third tooth projects into the sinus.[1]

The **mandibular** or **lower cheek teeth** are implanted in the rami of the mandible, forming two straight rows which diverge behind. The space between the rows is considerably less than that separating the upper teeth, especially in the middle of the series. The length of the lower teeth is about the same as that of the upper set. Their direction is also similar, but the embedded portions diverge even more, with the exception of the first and second. The long axis of the first is vertical; the remainder project downward and backward in a gradually increasing obliquity. The **buccal surface** has a longitudinal furrow; the last molar has a secondary shallower furrow in addition. The **lingual surface** is uneven, but the grooves are not regular; there are usually three on the first and last tooth. The **masticatory surface** is oblique, sloping upward and inward in correspondence with the opposing tooth; thus the lingual edge is prominent. Its average width (except at each end of the series) is somewhat less than three-fourths of an inch (ca. 1.8 cm.). The first five have two roots, while the sixth commonly has three. The width of the lower molars is a little less than two-thirds of that of the upper.

The **structure** is quite complex. Two infundibula run vertically through the entire length of the crown; these become filled with cement. In the upper teeth there are five main divisions of the pulp-cavity and five enamel folds, four of which are arranged symmetrically, while the fifth is an outgrowth from the antero-medial fold. In the lower teeth the infundibula are open along the lingual surface until closed by deposit of cement. The pulp-cavity has two main divisions (anterior and posterior) and three or four secondary diverticula. The enamel folds correspond, forming a pattern even more complicated than on the upper teeth. On the exposed crown of the unworn tooth the enamel folds form rounded ridges covered with a thin layer of cement. After the tooth comes into wear the enamel on the masticatory surface stands out in the form of sharp, prominent ridges.[2] Progressive cementation of the periphery of the tooth takes place, thus leveling up the irregularities of surface to a considerable extent.

The lengths of the lower teeth shown in Fig. 342 were in centimeters: 5.7, 7.9, 9.0, 8.5, 8.2 7.6. The distance between the two rows was 4.7 cm. at the anterior end and 7 cm. at the posterior end.

THE DECIDUOUS TEETH

The **deciduous teeth** are smaller and fewer than those of the permanent set. The formula is:

$$2 \left(\mathrm{Di}\, \frac{3}{3} - \mathrm{Dc}\, \frac{0}{0} - \mathrm{Dp}\, \frac{3}{3} \right) = 24$$

The **deciduous incisors** are much smaller than the permanent ones and have a distinct **neck** at the junction of the crown and root. The **crown** is short; its labial surface presents five ridges and grooves, but later becomes smooth and white. The **infundibulum** is shallow. The **root** is flattened; it undergoes absorption as the

[1] The student is advised to amplify these very general statements by the examination of heads of subjects of varying ages. It may also be noted that the position of the septum between the two divisions of the sinus varies much.

[2] It is estimated that the enamel ridges of an upper cheek tooth of a young adult horse, if straightened out, would form a line more than a foot long. The extent diminishes with age.

permanent tooth develops behind it. The **deciduous canines** are quite vestigial. They occur in both sexes as slender spiculæ about a quarter of an inch in length, but do not erupt. The lower one develops close to the corner incisor. They are not usually included in the formula, as they are never functional. The **deciduous premolars** differ from the permanent set chiefly in that they have much shorter crowns than the latter. The roots form early, so that a distinct neck occurs.

Vessels and Nerves.—The blood supply of the teeth is derived from the infraorbital and alveolar branches of the internal maxillary artery. The lymph

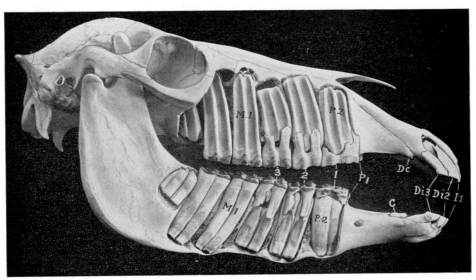

Fig. 347.—Skull of Colt, Two and One-half Years Old, Sculptured to Show Embedded Parts of Teeth.

Both permanent and deciduous cheek teeth are shown. *I1*, first permanent incisor; *Di. 2, Di. 3*, second and third deciduous incisors; *Dc.*, deciduous canine; *C*, permanent canine; *P1*, first premolar ("wolf-tooth"); *1, 2, 3*, deciduous premolars; *P2*, first permanent premolar; *M1*, first molar.

vessels go to the mandibular and pharyngeal lymph glands. The nerves come from the trigeminus.

Eruption of the Teeth

The subjoined table indicates the average periods of the eruption of the teeth:

	TEETH		ERUPTION
A. *Deciduous:*			
	1st incisor	(Di 1)	Birth or first week.
	2nd "	(Di 2)	4–6 weeks.
	3rd "	(Di 3)	6–9 months.
	Canine	(Dc)	
	1st premolar	(Dp2)	Birth or first
	2nd "	(Dp3)	two weeks.
	3rd "	(Dp4)	
B. *Permanent:*			
	1st incisor	(I1)	2½ years.
	2nd "	(I2)	3½ years.
	3rd "	(I3)	4½ years.
	Canine	(C)	4–5 years.
	1st premolar (or wolf-tooth)	(P1)	5–6 months.
	2nd "	(P2)	2½ years.
	3rd "	(P3)	3 years.
	4th "	(P4)	4 years.
	1st molar	(M1)	9–12 months.
	2nd "	(M2)	2 years.
	3rd "	(M3)	3½–4 years.

(The periods given for P 3 and 4 refer to the upper teeth; the lower ones may erupt about six months earlier.)

THE SALIVARY GLANDS

This term is usually restricted to the three pairs of large glands situated on the sides of the face and the adjacent part of the neck—the parotid, mandibular, and sublingual. Their ducts open into the mouth.

The **parotid gland** (Glandula parotis) (Fig. 560)—so named from its proximity to the ear—is the largest of the salivary glands in the horse. It is situated chiefly in the space between the ramus of the mandible and the wing of the atlas. It has a long quadrilateral outline, the dorsal end partially embracing the base of the external ear. Its length is about eight to ten inches (ca. 20 to 25 cm.), and its average thickness nearly an inch (ca. 2 cm.). Its average weight is about seven ounces (ca. 200 to 225 g.). It presents for description two surfaces, two borders, a base, and an apex. The **lateral** (or superficial) **surface** is covered by the parotid fascia and the cutaneous and parotido-auricularis muscles. It is crossed obliquely by the jugular vein, which is largely embedded in the gland. It is also related to the great auricular vein, the cervical branch of the facial nerve, and branches of the second cervical nerve. The **medial** (or deep) **surface** is very uneven and has numerous important relations. Some of these are: the guttural pouch and the great cornu of the hyoid bone; the masseter, occipito-mandibularis, digastricus and occipito-hyoideus muscles; the tendons of the brachiocephalicus and sterno-cephalicus (which separate the parotid from the underlying mandibular gland); the external carotid artery and some of its branches; the facial nerve; the pharyngeal lymph glands. The **anterior** or **facial border** is closely attached to the ramus of the mandible and the masseter muscle; it overlaps the latter to a varying extent.[1] The **posterior** or **cervical border** is concave, and is loosely attached to the underlying muscles. The **ventral border** or **base** is related to the external maxillary vein. The **dorsal extremity** or **apex** forms a deep notch into which the base of the external ear fits. The gland has a yellowish-gray color and is distinctly lobulated. It is inclosed in a capsule formed by the fascia. The **parotid duct** (Ductus parotideus) is formed at the ventral part of the gland, near the facial edge, by the union of three or four radicles. It leaves the gland about an inch (ca. 2 to 3 cm.) above the external maxillary vein, crosses the tendon of the sterno-cephalicus, and gains the medial face of the pterygoideus medialis. It then runs forward in the mandibular space below the external maxillary vein and winds around the ventral border of the mandible behind the vein, passes upward between the vein and the masseter muscle for about two inches (ca. 5 cm.), turns forward underneath the facial vessels, and perforates the cheek obliquely opposite the third upper cheek tooth. Before piercing the cheek it is somewhat dilated, but its termination is small, and is surrounded by a circular mucous fold (Papilla salivalis). (In exceptional cases the opening may be a little further forward.) The gland belongs to the compound alveolar glands of the serous type.

Blood-supply.—Branches of the carotid and maxillary arteries.

Nerve-supply.—Trigeminal, facial, and sympathetic nerves.

The **mandibular** or submaxillary **gland** (Glandula mandibularis) is much smaller than the parotid. It is long, narrow, and curved, the dorsal edge being concave. It extends from the fossa altantis to the body of the hyoid bone, so that it is covered partly by the parotid gland, partly by the lower jaw (Fig. 646). Its length is eight to ten inches (ca. 20 to 25 cm.), its width an inch to an inch and a half (ca. 2.5 to 3 cm.), and its thickness about half an inch (ca. 1 cm.). It weighs

---

[1] In some cases there is a well-marked triangular facial process, which covers the temporo-mandibular joint, the facial nerve, and the transverse facial vessels. The width of the ventral end also varies; in some cases there is marked deficiency at the retromandibular (Viborg's) triangle; this may be compensated by increase in size at the venous angle, so that the gland overlies the external maxillary vein to a variable extent.

about one and a half to two ounces (ca. 45 to 60 g.). It is often divisible into two parts. It presents for description two surfaces, two borders, and two extremities. The **lateral surface** is covered by the parotid gland, the occipito-mandibularis, digastricus, and pterygoideus medialis muscles. The tendon of the sterno-cephalicus crosses this surface, and, together with the aponeurosis connecting it with that of the brachiocephalicus, is a useful guide in separating the parotid gland from it. The **medial surface** is related to the rectus capitis ventralis major, the guttural pouch, the larynx, the division of the carotid artery, and the tenth, eleventh, and sympathetic nerves. The **dorsal border** is concave and thin. It is related to the guttural pouch and the duct of the gland. The **ventral border** is convex and thicker. It is related to the external maxillary vein and often to the thyroid gland. The **posterior extremity** is loosely attached in the fossa atlantis. The **anterior extremity** lies at the side of the root of the tongue, and is crossed laterally by the external maxillary artery. The **mandibular** or submaxillary **duct** (Ductus mandibularis) is formed by the union of small radicles which emerge along the concave edge. It runs forward along this border, and, after leaving the anterior extremity, crosses the intermediate tendon of the digastricus, passes between the hyo-glossus and mylo-hyoideus, and gains the medial surface of the sublingual gland. Its terminal part lies on the body of the mandible, under the mucous membrane, which it pierces opposite the canine tooth. The orifice is at the end of a flattened papilla, the **caruncula sublingualis.** The gland differs from the parotid in possessing serous, mucous, and mixed alveoli.

Blood-supply.—Occipital, external carotid, and external maxillary arteries.

Nerve-supply.—Chorda tympani and sympathetic nerves.

The **sublingual gland** (Glandula sublingualis) (Figs. 330, 561) is situated beneath the mucous membrane of the mouth, between the body of the tongue and the ramus of the mandible. It extends from the symphysis to the fourth or fifth lower cheek tooth. Its length is about five or six inches (ca. 12 to 15 cm.) and its weight about half an ounce (ca. 15 to 16 g.). It is flattened laterally, and has a thin **dorsal border** which underlies the sublingual fold of the mucous membrane of the floor of the mouth. The **lateral surface** is related to the mylo-hyoideus muscle, and the **medial surface** to the genio-glossus and stylo-glossus, the mandibular duct, and branches of the lingual nerve. The **ventral border** is related to the geniohyoid muscle. The **sublingual ducts** (Ductus sublinguales), about thirty in number, are small, short, and twisted; they open on small papillæ on the sublingual fold. The gland has mixed alveoli.

Blood-supply.—Sublingual artery.

Nerve-supply.—Trigeminal and sympathetic nerves.

THE PHARYNX

The pharynx is a musculo-membranous sac which belongs to the digestive and respiratory tracts in common. It is somewhat funnel-shaped, the large anterior part joining the mouth and nasal cavity, while the small end is continued by the œsophagus. Its long axis is directed obliquely downward and backward, and has a length of about six inches (ca. 15 cm.). The pharynx is attached by its muscles to the palatine, pterygoid, and hyoid bones, and to the cricoid and thyroid cartilages of the larynx.

Its principal **relations** are: dorsally, the base of the cranium and the guttural pouches; ventrally, the larynx; laterally, the medial pteryoid muscle, the great cornu of the hyoid bone, the external carotid and external maxillary arteries, the glosso-pharyngeal, anterior laryngeal, and hypoglossal nerves, the mandibular salivary gland, and the parapharyngeal lymph glands.

The cavity of the pharynx (Cavum pharyngis) presents **seven openings.** Through the **posterior nares** or **choanæ** it communicates dorsally with the nasal cavity. The **pharyngeal orifices** of the two **Eustachian tubes** (Ostia pharyngea

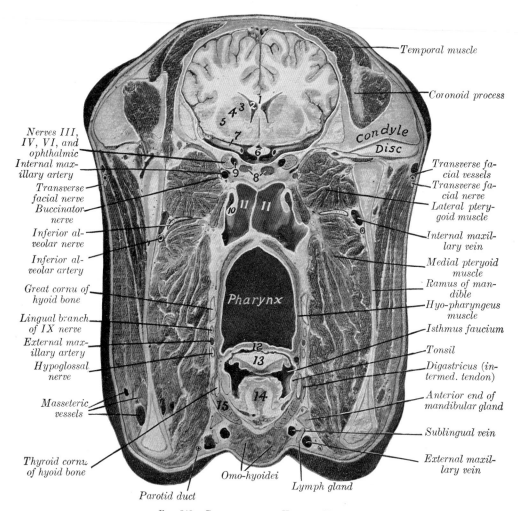

FIG. 348.—CROSS-SECTION OF HEAD OF HORSE.

The section passes through the anterior part of the temporo-mandibular articulation, but is slightly oblique, passing a few millimeters further forward on left side than on right. *1,* Corpus callosum; *2,* lateral ventricle of brain; *3,* caudate nucleus; *4,* internal capsule; *5,* lenticular nucleus; *6,* optic chiasma; *7,* middle cerebral artery; *8,* sphenoidal sinuses; *9,* cavernous sinus; *10,* Eustachian tube, medial lamina; *11, 11,* guttural pouches; *12,* soft palate; *13,* epiglottis; *14,* hyo-epiglottic muscle; *15,* thyro-hyoid muscle. The tensor palati (not marked) lies medial to the pterygoideus lateralis, and medial to the tensor is the levator palati, which blends above with the outer lamina of the Eustachian tube.

tubæ auditivæ) are situated on the lateral wall behind the posterior nares just below the level of the ventral nasal meatus. They are slit-like openings, directed obliquely downward and backward, and are a little more than an inch (ca. 3 cm.) in length. They are bounded medially by a fold which encloses the expanded extremity of the cartilaginous Eustachian tube. The **isthmus faucium** is the oral opening; it is closed by the soft palate except during swallowing. The **aditus** laryngis occupies the greater part of the ventral wall or floor of the pharynx; it is open except during deglutition. Behind this is the **aditus œsophagi,** the entrance to the œsophagus.

The wall of the pharynx comprises, from without inward, the muscles, the pharyngeal aponeurosis, and the mucous membrane.

The **muscles** of the pharynx (Mm. pharyngis) (Figs. 332, 333) are covered by the pharyngeal fascia, which is attached to the base of the skull, the great cornu of the hyoid bone, and the thyroid cartilage of the larynx. They are as follows:

1. The **stylo-pharyngeus** arises from the medial surface of the dorsal third of the great cornu of the hyoid bone, passes ventro-medially, and enters the wall of the pharynx by passing between the pterygo-pharyngeus and palato-pharyngeus. Its fibers radiate, many bundles passing forward, others inward or backward beneath the hyo-pharyngeus. It raises and dilates the pharynx to receive the bolus in swallowing.

2. The **palato-pharyngeus** arises chiefly by means of the aponeurosis of the soft palate from the palatine and pterygoid bones; some fibers are attached to the anterior wide part of the Eustachian tube. Its fibers pass backward on the lateral wall of the pharynx, and are inserted in part into the upper edge of the thyroid cartilage, in part turn inward to end at the median fibrous raphé. Its action is to shorten the pharynx, and to draw the larynx and œsophagus toward the root of the tongue in swallowing.

3. The **pterygo-pharyngeus** is flat and triangular. It lies on the anterior part of the lateral wall of the pharynx. It arises from the pterygoid bone above the preceding muscle,—from which it is not distinctly separated,—crosses the levator palati, and is inserted into the median raphé. Its action is similar to the preceding.

4. The **hyo-pharyngeus** may consist of two parts:

(*a*) The **kerato-pharyngeus** is a small and inconstant muscle which arises from the medial surface of the great cornu of the hyoid bone near its ventral end. It passes upward and backward on the lateral face of the palato-pharyngeus, turns toward the raphé, and spreads out under the next muscle.

(*b*) The **chondro-pharyngeus,** broad and fleshy, arises from the thyroid cornu of the hyoid bone and by a thin fasciculus from the lamina of the thyroid cartilage. The bundles spread out and end at the median raphé. The posterior part dips under the thyro-pharyngeus, while the anterior part overlies the pterygo- and palato-pharyngeus.

5. The **thyro-pharyngeus** arises from the lateral surface of the lamina of the thyroid cartilage on and behind its oblique line. Its fibers pass forward and medially to the median raphé.

6. The **crico-pharyngeus** arises from the lateral part of the arch of the cricoid cartilage and ends at the raphé. The fibers are directed upward, forward, and inward; they blend behind with the longitudinal fibers of the œsophagus.

The last three muscles are constrictors of the pharynx.

The **pharyngeal aponeurosis** is attached to the base of the cranium. It is well developed on the medial face of the palato-pharyngeus muscle and forms a median **raphé pharyngis** dorsally, which is wide in its posterior part.

The **mucous membrane** of the pharynx is continuous with that of the several cavities which open into it. It is thin and closely adherent to the base of the skull in the vicinity of the posterior nares, where the muscular wall is absent. Behind the Eustachian openings there is a median cul-de-sac, the **pharyngeal recess** (Recessus pharyngeus). The recess is somewhat variable, but is usually about an inch in depth and will admit the end of the finger. In the ass and mule it is much deeper. Here also the muscular wall is absent and the mucous membrane lies against the guttural pouches. From the Eustachian opening a fold of the mucous membrane (Plica salpingo-pharyngea) passes toward, but does not reach, the aditus laryngis. A horizontal fold, the **posterior pillar of the soft palate** (Arcus pharyngo-palatinus), passes along the ventral part of the lateral wall and unites with its fellow over the entrance to the œsophagus. The dorsal part of the cavity (Pars respiratoria) is lined with a ciliated epithelium, while the ventral part (Pars digestoria) has a stratified squamous epithelium. The communication between the two is oval and is bounded by the free edge of the soft palate and its posterior pillars; it is termed the **pharyngeal isthmus.** On either side of the aditus laryngis is a narrow deep depression, the **piriform recess** (Recessus piriformis).

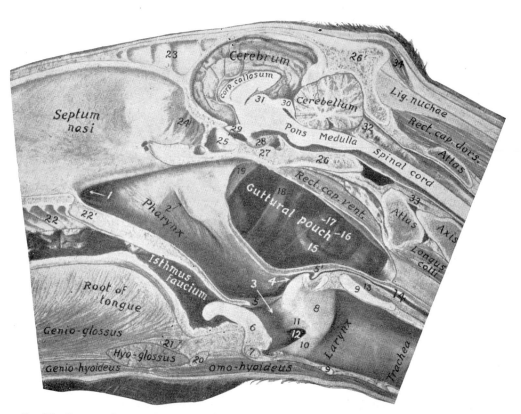

Fig. 349.—Posterior Part of a Sagittal Section of Head and Part of Neck of Horse, Cut about 1 cm. to the Left of the Median Plane.

1, Posterior nares: *2*, pharyngeal orifice of Eustachian tube; *3*, aditus laryngis; *4*, aditus œsophagi; *5*, posterior pillar of soft palate; *5'*, junction of *5* with its fellow over entrance to œsophagus; *6*, epiglottis; *7*, body of thyroid cartilage: *8*, arytenoid cartilage: *9, 9*, cricoid cartilage; *10*, true vocal cord; *11*, false vocal cord; *12*, lateral ventricle of larynx; *13*, crico-arytenoideus dorsalis; *14*, œsophagus; *15*, external carotid artery; *16*, hypoglossal nerve; *17*, glosso-pharyngeal nerve; *18*, great cornu of hyoid bone; *19*, Eustachian tube; *20*, body of hyoid bone; *21*, hyoideus transversus; *22*, ridges of hard palate; *22'*, soft palate; *23*, septum between frontal sinuses; *24*, olfactory mucous membrane; *25*, sphenoidal sinus; *26*, basilar part of occipital bone; *26'*, supra-occipital; *27*, body of sphenoid bone; *28*, pituitary body; *29*, chiasma opticum; *30*, corpora quadrigemina; *31*, thalamus; *32*, arachnoid; *33*, odontoid ligament; *34*, posterior auricular muscles.

The submucous tissue contains numerous mucous **glands** (Glandulæ pharyngeæ). In the young subject the lymph follicles are numerous and form a collection dorsally and between the Eustachian openings, known as the pharyngeal tonsil (Tonsilla pharyngea).

Vessels and Nerves.—The arteries are derived from the common carotid, external carotid, and external maxillary arteries. The lymph vessels pass to the pharyngeal and anterior cervical lymph glands. The nerves are derived from the trigeminus, glosso-pharyngeus, and vagus.

THE ŒSOPHAGUS

The œsophagus is a musculo-membranous tube, about 50 to 60 inches (ca. 125 to 150 cm.) in length, which extends from the pharynx to the stomach. In its course it shows several changes of direction. It begins in the median plane above the anterior border of the cricoid cartilage of the larynx. At the fourth cervical vertebra it has passed to the left side of the trachea, and continues this relation as far as the third thoracic vertebra. With the head held in the usual standing position, at the fourth cervical vertebra it is passing obliquely across the left surface of the trachea and usually reaches the median plane ventral to the trachea at the posterior end of the sixth cervical vertebra (Fig. 349a), then passes dorsally and backward through the thoracic inlet between the left face of the trachea and first

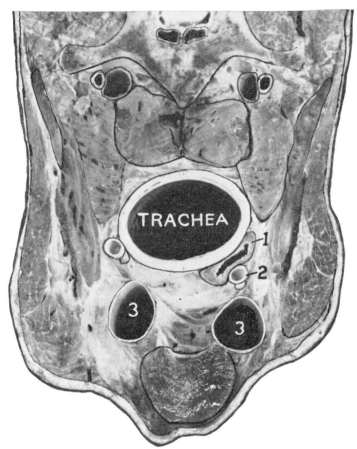

Fig. 349a.—Cross Section of Neck of Horse through Seventh Cervical Vertebra.
1, Esophagus; 2, common carotid with vagus nerve contacting it; 3, jugular vein.

rib, reaching the dorsal surface of the trachea at the third thoracic vertebra, and passing backward, crosses the aortic arch, by which it is pushed over to the right of the median plane. Here it gains the dorsal surface of the trachea, and, passing backward, crosses the aortic arch, by which it is pushed over to the right of the median plane (Figs. 469, 470). It continues in the mediastinum between the lungs, backward and a little dorsally, inclining gradually to the left, and reaches the hiatus œsophageus of the diaphragm. Passing through this it terminates at once at the cardiac orifice of the stomach, a little to the left of the median plane, and about four or five inches (ca. 10 to 12 cm.) ventral to the vertebral end of the fourteenth rib.

Viewed with reference to the horizontal plane, its course is downward and backward till it enters the thorax and passes upward to gain the dorsal face of the trachea. Then for a short distance (*i. e.*, to the root of the lung) its direction is almost horizontal; behind this it passes somewhat upward to its termination. The **cervical part** (Pars cervicalis) of the tube is about four to six inches (10 to 15 cm.) longer than the **thoracic part** (Pars thoracalis), while the so-called **abdominal part** (Pars abdominalis) is about an inch (2 to 3 cm.) long.

The principal **relations** of the œsophagus at its origin are: to the cricoid cartilage and dorsal crico-arytenoid muscles ventrally; to the guttural pouches and the ventral straight muscles dorsally; and to the carotid arteries laterally. In the middle of the neck the relations are: to the left longus colli muscle dorsally; to the trachea medially; to the left carotid artery, vagus, sympathetic, and recurrent nerves laterally. Near the thoracic inlet the œsophagus is usually in contact with the left jugular vein for a short distance. At its entrance into the thorax it has the trachea on its medial side; the first rib, the roots of the brachial plexus of nerves, and the left posterior cervical ganglion laterally. After gaining the dorsal surface of the trachea, it has the aorta on its left and the vena azygos and right vagus nerve on its right side. In its course through the posterior mediastinum the œsophageal trunks of the vagus nerves lie above and below it, and the œsophageal artery is dorsal to it, a bursa is provided ventrally and to the right as it passes through the hiatus œsophageus.

Structure.—The wall is composed of four coats: (1) A fibrous sheath termed the tunica adventitia; (2) the muscular coat; (3) a submucous layer; (4) the mucous membrane. The **muscular coat** is of the striped variety as far as the base of the heart, where it rapidly changes to the unstriped type. In addition to this change, the muscular coat becomes much thicker and firmer, while the lumen is diminished. Except at each end of the tube the muscular coat consists chiefly of two layers of fibers arranged spirally or elliptically, which intercross dorsally and ventrally. At the origin two bundles nearly an inch (ca. 2 cm.) wide arise from the wide posterior part of the pharyngeal raphé and from a tendon common to the crico-pharyngeus and thyro-pharyngeus. These bundles, which blend and decussate at their origin, diverge and pass to each side of the œsophagus. In the angle between them a deeper layer of circular fibers is visible. Two small ventral bundles emerge from the depression between the lamina of the cricoid cartilage and the arytenoid cartilages. These curve around to the side of the œsophagus and blend with the dorsal bundles before described. In the terminal part there is an external longitudinal layer and an internal circular layer, the latter being extremely thick. The **mucous membrane** is pale, and is covered with squamous stratified epithelium. It is loosely attached to the muscular coat by an abundant submucosa, and lies in longitudinal folds which obliterate the lumen except during deglutition.

Blood-supply.—Carotid, broncho-œsophageal, and gastric arteries.

Nerve-supply.—Vagus, glosso-pharyngeal, and sympathetic nerves.

THE ABDOMINAL CAVITY

The abdominal cavity (Cavum abdominis) is the largest of the body cavities. It is separated from the thoracic cavity by the diaphragm and is continuous behind with the pelvic cavity. The line of demarcation between the abdominal and pelvic cavities is known as the **terminal line,** or brim of the pelvis; it is formed by the base of the sacrum dorsally, the ilio-pectineal lines laterally, and the anterior borders of the pubic bones ventrally.

The cavity is ovoid in form, but is somewhat compressed laterally. Its long axis extends obliquely from the center of the pelvic inlet to the sternal part of the diaphragm. Its dorso-ventral diameter is greatest at the first lumbar vertebra, while its greatest transverse diameter is a little nearer the pelvis.

The **dorsal wall** or roof is formed by the lumbar vertebræ, the lumbar muscles, and the lumbar part of the diaphragm.

The **lateral walls** are formed by the oblique and transverse abdominal muscles, the abdominal tunic, the anterior parts of the ilia with the iliacus muscles, the cartilages of the asternal ribs, and the parts of the posterior ribs which are below the attachment of the diaphragm.

The **ventral wall** or floor consists of the two recti, the aponeuroses of the oblique and transverse muscles, the abdominal tunic, and the xiphoid cartilage.

The **anterior wall** is formed by the diaphragm, which is deeply concave, thus greatly increasing the size of the abdomen at the expense of the thorax.

The muscular walls are lined by a layer of fascia, distinguished in different parts as: (1) The diaphragmatic fascia; (2) the transversalis fascia; (3) the iliac fascia; (4) the deep layer of the lumbo-dorsal fascia.

The **subserous tissue** (Tela subserosa) unites the fascia and peritoneum. It is areolar tissue, and is more or less loaded with fat according to the condition of the subject, except over the diaphragm. It sends laminæ into the various peritoneal folds.

The peritoneum, the serous membrane lining the cavity, will be described later.

The abdominal walls are pierced in the adult by five apertures. These are the three foramina of the diaphragm and the inguinal canals, which have been described. In the fœtus there is the umbilical opening also. This transmits the urachus, a tube which connects the bladder with the allantois; the two umbilical arteries, which carry blood from the fœtus to the placenta; and the umbilical vein, which returns blood from the placenta to the liver of the fœtus. After birth the orifice is closed by fibrous tissue, leaving a scar, the **umbilicus,** which is more or less distinctly visible in the median ventral line in a transverse plane about tangent to the ventral end of the last rib.

The cavity contains the greater part of the digestive and urinary organs, part of the internal genital organs, numerous nerves, blood vessels, lymph vessels and glands, ductless glands (spleen and adrenal bodies), and certain fœtal remains.

For topographic purposes the abdomen is divided into nine regions by imaginary planes. Two of these planes are sagittal and two are transverse. The sagittal planes cut the middles of the inguinal ligaments; the transverse planes pass through the last thoracic and fifth lumbar vertebræ, or the ventral end of the fifteenth rib and the tuber coxæ respectively. The transverse planes divide the adbomen into three zones, one behind the other, viz., **epigastric, mesogastric,** and **hypogastric:** these are subdivided by the sagittal planes as indicated:

Left parachondriac..........Xiphoid.................Right parachondriac
Left lumbar...............Umbilical...............Right lumbar
Left iliac..................Prepubic...............Right iliac

Other useful regional terms are: sublumbar, diaphragmatic, inguinal. The first two require no explanation. The **inguinal regions** (right and left) (Inguina) lie in front of the inguinal ligament. The **flank** (Latus) is that part of the lateral wall which is formed only of soft structures. The triangular depression on its upper part is termed the **paralumbar fossa;** this is bounded dorsally by the lateral border of the longissimus, ventrally by the upper border of the obliquus abdominis internus, and in front by the last rib.

THE PERITONEUM

The peritoneum is the thin serous membrane which lines the abdominal cavity and the pelvic cavity (in part), and covers to a greater or less extent the viscera contained therein. In the male it is a completely closed sac, but in the female there are two small openings in it; these are the abdominal orifices of the uterine or Fallopian tubes, which at their other ends communicate with the uterus, and so indirectly with the exterior. The **peritoneal cavity** (Cavum peritonæi) is only a potential one, since its opposing walls are normally separated only by the thin film of serous fluid (secreted by the membrane) which acts as a lubricant.

The free surface of the membrane has a glistening appearance and is very smooth. This is due to the fact that this surface is formed by a layer of flat mesothelial cells, and is moistened by the peritoneal fluid. Friction is thus reduced to a minimum during the movements of the viscera. The outer surface of the peritoneum is related to the subserous tissue, which attaches it to the abdominal wall or the viscera.

In order to understand the general disposition of the peritoneum, we may imagine the abdominal cavity to be empty and lined by a simple layer of peritoneum, termed the **parietal layer** (Lamina parietalis). We may further imagine the organs as beginning to develop in the subserous tissue, enlarging, and migrating into the abdominal cavity to a varying extent. In doing so they carry the peritoneum before them, producing introversion of the simple sac, and forming folds which connect them with the wall or with each other. The viscera thus receive a complete or partial covering of peritoneum, termed the **visceral layer** (Lamina visceralis). The connecting folds are termed **omenta, mesenteries, ligaments, etc.** They contain a varying quantity of connective tissue, fat, and lymph glands, and furnish a path for the vessels and nerves of the viscera. Some contain unstriped muscular tissue. An **omentum** is a fold which passes from the stomach to other viscera. There are three of these, namely: (1) The **lesser omentum** (Omentum minus),[1] which passes from the lesser curvature of the stomach to the liver; (2) the **gastro-splenic omentum** (Ligamentum gastrolienale), which extends from the greater curvature of the stomach to the spleen; (3) the **greater omentum** (Omentum majus),[2] which passes from the greater curvature of the stomach and from the spleen to the terminal part of the great colon and the origin of the small colon. It does not pass directly from one organ to the other, but forms an extensive loose sac (Figs. 377, 378). A **mesentery** (Mesenterium) is a fold which attaches the intestine to the dorsal wall of the abdomen. There are two mesenteries in the horse: (1) The **great mesentery** connects the greater part of the small intestine with the dorsal abdominal wall; (2) the **colic mesentery** attaches the small colon to the dorsal abdominal wall. In some animals (e. g., the dog) there is a common mesentery for the whole intestine. **Ligaments** are folds which pass between viscera other than parts of the digestive tube, or connect them with the abdominal wall. The term is also applied to folds which attach parts of the digestive tract to the abdominal wall, but do not contain their blood-vessels and nerves. Some (e. g., the lateral and coronary ligaments of the liver) are strengthened by fibrous tissue; others (e. g., the broad ligaments of the uterus) contain also unstriped muscular tissue.

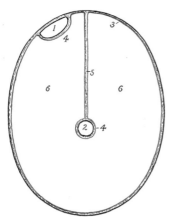

Fig. 350.—Diagrammatic Cross-section of Abdomen.

To show arrangement of peritoneum when reduced to its simplest form. The external black line indicates the body-wall. 1, Organ (e. g., kidney) in contact with wall; 2, organ (e. g., small intestine) at a distance from wall; 3, parietal peritoneum; 4, 4, visceral peritoneum; 5, mesentery; 6, peritoneal cavity.

THE PELVIC CAVITY

The pelvis is the posterior part of the trunk. It incloses the pelvic cavity (Cavum pelvis), which communicates in front with the abdominal cavity, the line of demarcation being the terminal line or pelvic brim.

The **dorsal wall** or roof is formed by the sacrum and first three coccygeal vertebræ. The **lateral walls** are formed by the parts of the ilia behind the ilio-

[1] Also known as the gastro-hepatic omentum.
[2] Also known as the gastro-colic omentum.

pectineal lines and the sacro-sciatic ligaments. The **ventral wall** or floor is formed by the pubic and ischial bones. The boundary of the **outlet** is formed by the third coccygeal vertebra dorsally, the ischial arch ventrally, and the posterior edges of the sacro-sciatic ligaments and the semi-membranosus muscles laterally, thus inclosing the perineum. The outlet is closed by the **perineal fascia;** this consists of superficial and deep layers which are attached around the margin of the outlet and centrally to the organs at the outlet—the anus and its muscles, the vulva (in the female), and the root of the penis (in the male).

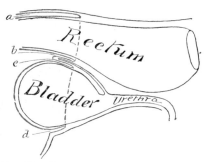

The cavity contains the rectum, parts of the internal genital and urinary organs, some fœtal remnants, muscles, vessels, and nerves. It is lined by the **fascia pelvis,** and in part by the peritoneum.

FIG. 351.—DIAGRAM OF SAGITTAL SECTION OF MALE PELVIS TO SHOW DISPOSITION OF PERITONEUM.

a, Sacro-rectal pouch, continuous laterally with *b,* recto-genital pouch; *c,* vesico-genital pouch; *d,* vesico-pubic pouch. The lateral line of reflection of the peritoneum is dotted.

The **pelvic peritoneum** is continuous in front with that of the abdomen. It lines the cavity for a variable distance backward, and is then reflected on to the viscera, and from one organ to another. We may therefore distinguish an anterior, peritoneal, and a posterior, retroperitoneal, part of the cavity. Along the mid-dorsal line it forms a continuation of the colic mesentery, the **mesorectum,** which attaches the first or peritoneal part of the rectum to the roof. In animals in fair condition a consider-

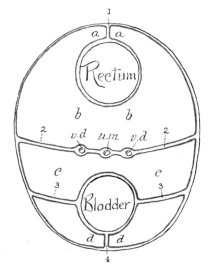

FIG. 352.—SCHEMATIC CROSS-SECTION TO SHOW ARRANGEMENT OF PELVIC PERITONEUM IN THE MALE.

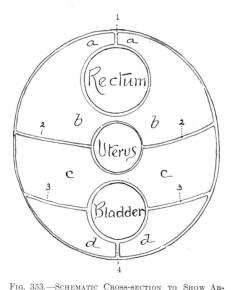

FIG. 353.—SCHEMATIC CROSS-SECTION TO SHOW ARRANGEMENT OF PELVIC PERITONEUM IN THE FEMALE.

a, b, Recto-genital pouch; *c, c,* vesico-genital pouch; *d, d,* vesico-pubic pouch; 1, mesorectum; 2, 2, genital folds in male, broad ligaments of uterus in female; 3, 3, lateral ligaments of bladder; 4, middle ligament of bladder; *v.d.,* ductus deferentes; *u.m.,* uterus masculinus.

able quantity of subserous and retroperitoneal fat is found on the walls and in the various interstices.

In the male the general disposition of the peritoneum here is as follows. If traced along the dorsal wall, it is reflected from the sacrum on to the rectum, forming the visceral peritoneum for the first part of that tube. The point at which the reflection takes place is quite variable, and apparently depends chiefly on the amount of feces in the rectum. When the bowel is very full the reflection may be little behind the promontory; when it is empty, the reflection may be at the posterior end of the sacrum. Laterally it is reflected in a similar fashion. If the rectum be raised, it will be seen that the peritoneum passes from its ventral surface and forms a transverse fold which lies on the dorsal surface of the bladder (Fig. 370). This is the **genital fold** (Plica genitalis). Its concave free part passes on either side into the inguinal canal. The ventral layer of this fold is reflected on to the dorsal surface of the bladder. Thus there is formed a pouch between the rectum and bladder—the **recto-vesical pouch** (Excavatio recto-vesicalis), which is partially subdivided by the genital fold into recto-genital and vesico-genital cavities. The

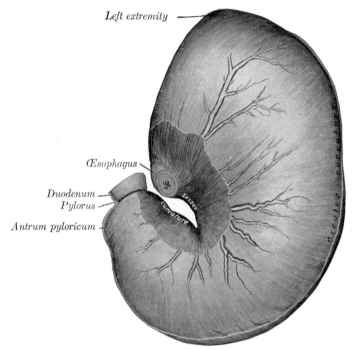

Left extremity

Œsophagus

Duodenum
Pylorus

Antrum pyloricum

FIG. 354.—STOMACH OF HORSE; PARIETAL SURFACE.

The organ was fixed *in situ* when well filled. The lesser curvature has been opened up slightly and the peritoneum, etc., in this vicinity removed. The larger branches of the anterior gastric artery and vein are visible.

fold contains the ductus deferentes, part of the vesiculæ seminales, and the uterus masculinus (a fœtal remnant). If the bladder is now raised, it is seen that the peritoneum passes from its ventral surface on to the pelvic floor, forming centrally the **median umbilical fold** or **middle ligament** of the bladder (Plica umbilicalis media). It also passes from each side of the bladder to the lateral pelvic wall and forms thus the **lateral umbilical fold** or **ligament** of the bladder (Plica umbilicalis lateralis); this contains in its edge the so-called **round ligament** of the bladder (Ligamentum teres vesicæ)—the partially occluded umbilical artery, which is a large vessel in the fœtus. In the fœtus and new-born foal these three folds extend to the umbilicus in conformity with the abdominal position of the bladder. When the latter becomes a pelvic organ, the lateral folds conform to the change and end at the vertex of the bladder. The median fold may still be traceable to the umbilicus.

In the female the arrangement is modified by the presence of the uterus;

the genital fold is enlarged, so as to inclose the uterus and a small part of the vagina. It forms two extensive folds, the **broad ligaments of the uterus** (Ligamenta lata uteri), which attach that organ to the sides of the pelvic cavity and the lumbar part of the abdominal wall (Fig. 530). It thus divides the recto-vesical pouch completely into dorsal and ventral compartments—the **recto-genital pouch** (Excavatio recto-uterina) and the **vesico-genital pouch** (Excavatio vesico-uterina).

Further details will be given in the description of the pelvic viscera.

THE STOMACH

The stomach (Ventriculus) is the large dilatation of the alimentary canal behind the diaphragm which intervenes between the œsophagus and the small intestine. It is a sharply curved, J-shaped sac, the right part being very much shorter

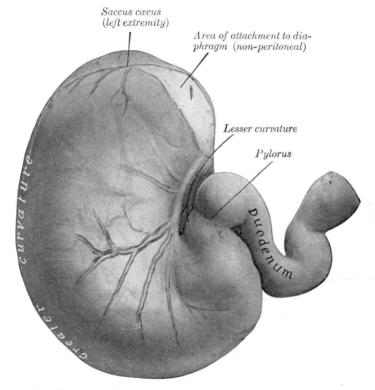

FIG. 355.—STOMACH OF HORSE; VISCERAL SURFACE, WITH FIRST PART OF DUODENUM.
Fixed *in situ* when full but not distended. The posterior gastric artery and its larger branches with two satellite veins are shown.

than the left one. The convexity is directed ventrally. When moderately distended, there may be a slight constriction which indicates the division into right and left sacs. It is relatively small, and is situated in the dorsal part of the abdominal cavity, behind the diaphragm and liver, mainly to the left of the median plane.

It presents for description two surfaces, two curvatures, and two extremities. The **parietal surface** (Facies parietalis) is convex and is directed forward, upward, and toward the left; it lies against the diaphragm and liver. The **visceral surface** (Facies visceralis), also convex, faces in the opposite direction; it is related to the terminal part of the large colon, the pancreas, the small colon, the small intestine, and the greater omentum. The borders between these surfaces are termed the curvatures. The **lesser curvature** (Curvatura ventriculi minor) is very short, extending from the termination of the œsophagus to the junction with the small intestine. When the stomach is *in situ*, its walls are here in contact, and the cardia and pylorus close together.[1] The **greater curvature** (Curvatura ventriculi major) is very extensive. From the cardia it is first directed dorsally and curves over the left extremity; it then descends, passes to the right, crosses the median plane, and curves upward to end at the pylorus. Its left part is related to the spleen, while its ventral portion rests on the left parts of the great colon. The **left extremity** (Extremitas sinistra) has the form of a rounded cul-de-sac termed the **saccus cæcus;** it lies ventral to the left crus of the diaphragm, and so beneath the dorsal part of the sixteenth and seventeenth ribs. It is related to the pancreas and the termination of the great colon behind and the base of the spleen laterally. The **right** or **pyloric extremity** (Extremitas dextra) is much smaller and is continu-

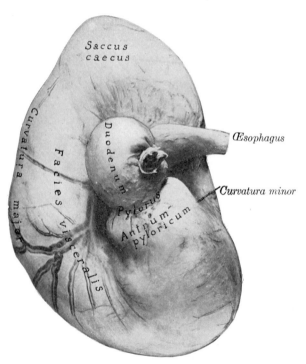

FIG. 356.—STOMACH OF HORSE; RIGHT VIEW.

ous with the duodenum, the junction being indicated by a marked constriction. It lies just to the right of the median plane, and about two inches (ca. 5 cm.) lower than the cardia; it is in contact with the visceral surface of the liver. About two or three inches (ca. 5 to 8 cm.) from the pylorus there is a constriction which marks off the **antrum pyloricum** from the rest of the right sac. The œsophageal orifice is termed the **cardia;** it is situated at the left end of the lesser curvature, but about eight to ten inches (ca. 20 to 25 cm.) from the left extremity.[2] The œsophagus joins the stomach very obliquely. The opening is closed by the sphincter cardiæ and numerous folds of mucous membrane. The **pylorus** is the opening into the

intestine. Its position is indicated externally by a distinct constriction. Internally it presents a circular ridge caused by a ring of muscular tissue—the **sphincter pylori.**

The stomach is held in position mainly by the pressure of the surrounding viscera and by the œsophagus. The following peritoneal folds connect it with the adjacent parts:

1. The **gastro-phrenic ligament** (Lig. gastrophrenicum) connects the greater curvature, from the cardia to the left extremity, with the crura of the diaphragm. This leaves a narrow area uncovered by peritoneum, and here the stomach is attached to the diaphragm by areolar tissue (Fig. 355).

---

[1] The more expressive term "incisura angularis" has been suggested and is worthy of adoption.

[2] The position of the cardia varies of course with the excursion of the diaphragm. It is usually an inch or more (ca. 3 cm.) to the left of the median plane and ventral to the vertebral end of the fourteenth rib. When the diaphragm is contracted the cardia may be six inches (ca. 15 cm.) below the level of the spine; when the diaphragm is relaxed, the interval may be reduced to about two inches (ca. 5 cm.).

The use of the term ligament in regard to the arrangement here is somewhat misleading, since the stomach is attached to the crus of the diaphragm by areolar tissue; the peritoneum passes from the diaphragm to the stomach on each side of the area of adhesion. In soft material there is the appearance of a ligament composed of two layers of peritoneum, but this is an artefact.

2. The **lesser omentum** (Omentum minus) connects the lesser curvature and the first part of the duodenum with the liver below the œsophageal notch and the portal fissure.

The part of the omentum which extends from the liver to the stomach is designated the lig. hepato-gastricum, and the remainder which goes to the duodenum as the lig. hepato-duodenale.

3. The **gastro-splenic omentum** (Lig. gastrolienale) passes from the left part of the greater curvature to the hilus of the spleen; it is continuous ventrally with the greater omentum.

4. The **greater omentum** (Omentum majus) connects the ventral part of the greater curvature and the first curve of the duodenum with the terminal part of the great colon and the initial part of the small colon. It does not pass directly between these parts but forms a large sac, which will be described later (p. 445).

5. The **gastro-pancreatic fold** (Plica gastropancreatica) extends from the left sac above the cardia to the duodenum. It is attached dorsally to the liver and vena cava, ventrally to the pancreas.

The stomach of the equidæ is relatively small, its capacity varying from two to four gallons (ca. 8 to 15 liters).

The size, form, and position of the stomach are subject to considerable variation. When the stomach is nearly empty, the saccus cæcus contains only gas and is strongly contracted; the middle part (physiological fundus) contains the ingesta and preserves its rounded character, while the pyloric part is contracted. In this state coils of small intestine usually lie ventral to the stomach and may separate it entirely from the colon. In exceptional cases, when the organ is empty and contracted, even the pyloric end is to the left of the median plane. When distended, the middle part settles down some four or five inches, pushing back coils of the small intestine which may lie between the greater curvature and the large colon, and also pushing to one side the left dorsal part of the great colon; the spleen, small colon, and small intestine are pushed back by the distention of the left sac. When the stomach is moderately full, its most ventral part lies opposite to the ninth intercostal space and tenth rib, about a handbreadth above the level of the left costal arch.

Structure.—The wall is composed of four coats—serous, muscular, submucous, and mucous. The **serous coat** (Tunica serosa) covers the greater part of the organ and is closely adherent to the muscular coat except at the curvatures. It partially bridges over the lesser curvature, and covers here elastic tissue which assists in retaining the bent form of the stomach. The peritoneal folds have been described. The **muscular coat** (Tunica muscularis) consists of three incomplete layers, an external of longitudinal, a middle of circular, and an internal of oblique fibers. The layer of **longitudinal fibers** (Stratum longitudinale) is very thin and exists only along the curvatures and at the antrum. It is not present on the saccus cæcus, and about the middle of the greater curvature it is almost entirely replaced by elastic fibers to the antrum pylori. At the lesser curvature it is continuous with the longitudinal fibers of the œsophagus. On the antrum pylori it forms a well-developed complete layer which is separate from that of the curvatures. The layer of **circular fibers** (Stratum circulare) exists only on the glandular part. At the pyloric orifice it forms a thick ring—the **pyloric sphincter** (Sphincter pylori). Another ring, the antral sphincter, is found at the left end of the antrum pylori. The **oblique fibers** (Fibræ obliquæ) are arranged in coarse bundles in two layers. The external stratum covers the left sac and is largely a continuation of the longitudinal fibers of the œsophagus. The internal stratum is found also on the left sac; it is continuous with the circular fibers of the œsophagus and stomach and exchanges fibers with the external oblique layer. It forms a remarkable loop around the cardiac orifice, constituting a powerful **cardiac sphincter** (Sphincter cardiæ). The **submucous coat** (Tela submucosa) is a layer of loose connective

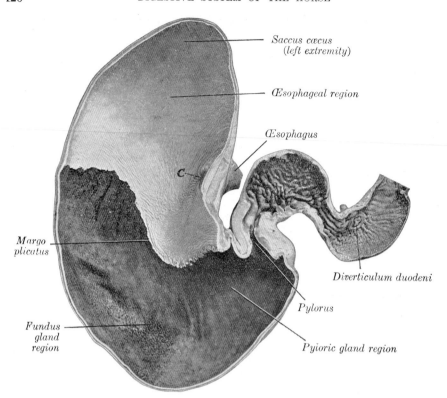

FIG. 357.—FRONTAL SECTION OF STOMACH AND FIRST PART OF DUODENUM OF HORSE.
C, Cardiac orifice.   Photograph of specimen fixed *in situ.*

tissue which connects the muscular and mucous coats; in it the vessels and nerves ramify before entering the mucosa. The **mucous coat** (Tunica mucosa) is clearly divided into two parts. That which lines the greater part of the left sac resembles the œsophageal mucous membrane, and is termed the **œsophageal part** (Pars œsophagea). It is white in color, destitute of glands, and covered with a thick, squamous, strati-

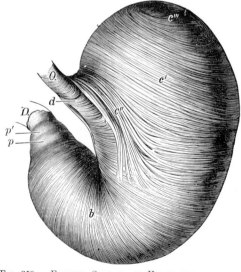

FIG. 358*a.*—EVERTED STOMACH OF HORSE FROM WHICH
THE MUCOUS MEMBRANE HAS BEEN REMOVED.

O, Œsophagus; *D,* duodenum; *b,* circular layer; *c′,* internal oblique fibers; *c″,* loop around cardia; *c‴,* transition of internal to external oblique fibers; *d,* fibers connecting the two branches of the cardiac loop; *p,* antral sphincter; *p′,* pyloric sphincter.   (Ellenberger-Baum, Anat. d. Haustiere.)

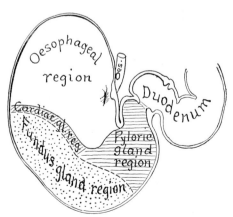

FIG 358.—DIAGRAM OF ZONES OF MUCOUS MEMBRANE
OF STOMACH OF HORSE.

fied epithelium. At the cardiac orifice it presents numerous folds which oc-clude the opening.[1] It terminates abruptly, forming an irregular, sinuous, raised edge, termed the **margo plicatus** (or cuticular ridge). Below and to the right of this line the mucous membrane has a totally different character, being soft and velvety to the touch, and covered by a mucoid secretion. It contains the **gastric glands** (Glandulæ gastricæ), and is therefore termed the **glandular part** (Pars glandularis). It is subdivided into three zones according to the types of glands which it contains, but no distinct lines of demarcation exist. A narrow zone along the margo plicatus, but not extending to the greater curvature, has a yellowish-gray color, and contains short tubular **cardiac glands** (cardiac gland region). Next to this is a large area which has a mottled, reddish-brown color, and contains **fundus glands** (fundus gland region); these glands have two distinct types of cells. This part of the mucous membrane is thick and very vascular, and corresponds to the fundus of the stomach in man and the dog. The remainder of the mucous mem-brane is thinner, has a reddish-gray or yellowish-gray color, and contains **pyloric glands,** which have a single type of cells corresponding to the chief cells of the fundus glands (pyloric gland region); it corresponds to the pyloric portion of man and the dog. The folding of the stomach wall at the lesser curvature produces a prominent ridge which projects into the cavity of the stomach. The circular fold which covers the pyloric sphincter is termed the **pyloric valve** (Valvula pylori).

The œsophageal part constitutes one-third to two-fifths of the mucous membrane. The cardiac gland region is extremely narrow (ca. 0.5 to 1 mm.) at the greater curvature, but becomes about an inch wide toward the pyloric part. Since the majority of the glands here are not typical cardiac glands, like those of the pig and other animals, but are intermediate in type between these and pyloric glands, the term intermediate zone might well be used.

Vessels and Nerves.—The stomach receives blood from all the branches of the cœliac artery. The **gastric veins** drain into the portal vein. The **lymph vessels** go chiefly to the gastric lymph glands, thence to the cisterna chyli. The **nerves** are derived from the vagus and sympathetic nerves.

THE SMALL INTESTINE

The **small intestine** (Intestinum tenue) is the tube which connects the stomach with the large intestine. It begins at the pylorus and terminates at the lesser curvature of the cæcum. Its average length is about seventy feet (ca. 22 meters), and when distended its diameter varies from three to four inches (7.5 to 10 cm.). Its capacity is about twelve gallons (40 to 50 liters).

It is clearly divisible into a **fixed** and a **mesenteric** part. The fixed part is termed the duodenum, while the mesenteric part (Intestinum tenue mesenteriale) is arbitrarily divided into parts termed the jejunum and ileum.[2]

The **duodenum** is about three to four feet (ca. 1 m.) long. Its shape is some-what like a horseshoe, the convexity being directed toward the right. The **first part** (Pars prima duodeni) is directed to the right and forms an ∽-shaped curve. The convexity of the first part of the curve is dorsal, of the second, ventral. It is in contact with the middle and right lobes of the liver, and presents two am-pullæ with a constriction between them. The duodenal angle (or head) of the pancreas is attached to the concavity of the second curve, and here, five to six inches (ca. 12 to 15 cm.) from the pylorus, the pancreatic duct and the bile duct pierce the bowel wall. The **second part** (Pars secunda duodeni) passes upward and backward on the right dorsal part of the colon and ventral to the right lobe of the liver and, on reaching the right kidney and the base of the cæcum, it curves toward the median plane, opposite the last rib. The **third part** (Pars tertia duo-

[1] This occlusion is usually so complete that distention of the stomach by air or fluid forced in through the pylorus may be carried far enough to rupture the stomach without ligating the œsophagus.
[2] No natural line of demarcation exists, but there is a marked increase of the thickness of the wall toward the terminal part. Other differences will be noted in the further description.

deni) passes from right to left behind the attachment of the base of the cæcum, crosses the median plane behind the root of the great mesentery, and turns forward to become continuous with the mesenteric part under the left kidney.[1] The sacculations of the first part have a diameter of three to four inches (ca. 7.5 to 10 cm.). It is attached by a short peritoneal fold termed the **mesoduodenum.** This fixes the first part of the duodenum closely to the liver and the second to the right dorsal colon; the remainder is somewhat less closely attached by it to the base of the cæcum and right kidney, the sublumbar muscles, and (more closely) to the terminal part of the great colon and the first part of the small colon.[2]

The **mesenteric part,** or jejuno-ileum, has been conventionally subdivided into the jejunum and ileum, but no distinct point exists at which to make the demarcation. With the exception of the origin and the last two or three feet, the mesenteric part of the intestine varies so much in position that only a general statement can be made. It lies in numerous coils, mingled with those of the small colon, chiefly in the dorsal part of the left half of the abdomen, from the visceral surface

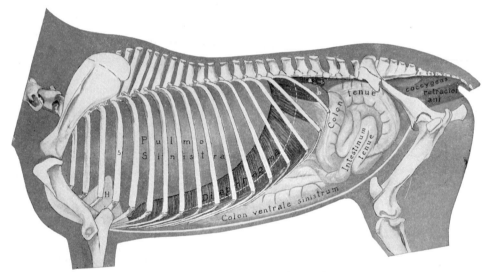

Fig. 359.—Topography of Viscera of Horse; Left View.
a, Left kidney; b, spleen; 5, fifth rib; H, pericardium. Phrenico-costal line dotted.

of the stomach to the pelvis. It may insinuate itself between the left parts of the colon and the abdominal wall; also between the ventral parts of the colon, reaching the floor of the abdomen. In some cases coils of it lie against the right flank when the cæcum contains little material. The terminal part of the intestine (ileum) passes to the medial (left) surface of the cæcum and joins the lesser curvature of its base. The average diameter of the jejuno-ileum is about two and a half to three inches (ca. 6 to 7 cm.). In the cadaver one often finds much of the tube presenting irregular constricted and dilated parts which are not to be mistaken for permanent conditions. The last three or four feet (ca. 1 m.) are usually tightly contracted, resembling somewhat the terminal part of the œsophagus. This part may be termed the ileum.

The mesenteric part is connected with the dorsal abdominal wall by the **great mesentery.** This is a wide, fan-shaped fold, consisting of two layers of peritoneum,

[1] The duodenum commonly curves around the periphery of the right kidney, from which it is separated by the base of the cæcum, but in some cases it is in contact with the ventral surface of the kidney. It may cross the median plane ventral to the second lumbar vertebra or further back, depending apparently on the fulness of the cæcum.

[2] It will be noticed that the mesoduodenum is not continuous with the great mesentery, but ends by a free edge. The mesentery begins on the opposite surface of the end of the duodenum, so that the bowel is attached by two peritoneal folds at this point.

between which the vessels and nerves reach the bowel; it also contains the mesenteric lymph glands and some fat. The visceral border of the mesentery contains the intestine, while the parietal border or **root of the mesentery** (Radix mesenterii) is attached to a small area around the great mesenteric artery under the first and second lumbar vertebræ. The root is thick, as it contains a large number of vessels and nerves placed close together. The mesentery is short at first, but soon reaches a length of one and a half to two feet (ca. 50 cm.)—sufficient to allow coils of the intestine to reach the abdominal floor, the pelvic cavity, or even to descend into the scrotum through the inguinal canal. Near its termination the intestine leaves the border of the mesentery, so that the latter has a free edge which passes to the cæcum. Thus there is formed the **ileo-cæcal fold** (Plica ileocæcalis), which attaches the ileum to the lesser curvature of the cæcum.

Structure.—The wall consists of four coats—serous, muscular, submucous, and mucous. The **serous coat** is complete except at the mesenteric edge, where the vessels and nerves reach the bowel. The **muscular coat** consists of an external longitudinal and an internal circular layer, the latter being the thicker. In the last few feet of the intestine the muscular coat is very thick, and being usually firmly contracted in the dead subject, gives the impression that this part of the bowel is of smaller caliber; such, however, is not the case during life. The **sub-mucous coat** is a layer of areolar tissue in which the vessels and nerves ramify. It contains also the duodenal glands and the bases of the solitary and aggregated lymph nodules. The **mucous membrane** is soft and velvety. It has a grayish or yellowish-red color and is very vascular. About five or six inches from the pylorus it forms a pouch, the **diverticulum duodeni,** in which the pancreatic and hepatic ducts open. On a small papilla nearly opposite this is the termination of the accessory pancreatic duct. At the ileo-cæcal opening the mucous membrane projects slightly into the

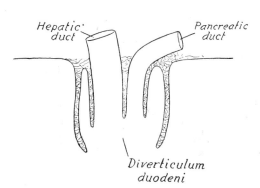

FIG. 360.—DIAGRAM OF SECTION OF DIVERTICULUM DUODENI OF HORSE.

Solid line indicates mucous membrane; muscular and serous layers are not shown.

cavity of the cæcum, forming the **ileo-cæcal valve.** The free surface is thickly beset with **villi,** small projections of the mucous membrane which can be seen well by placing a piece of the membrane in water. They are relatively short and thick in the horse. Each contains a central lymph-vessel (lacteal), and around this a plexus of capillaries, lymphoid tissue, and unstriped muscle-fibers. They are important agents in absorption from the contents of the intestine. The epithelium is columnar, with many goblet cells. Underneath the basement membrane is a layer of unstriped muscle-fibers, the **muscularis mucosæ.** The glands of the small intestine are of two kinds; their secretion, also that of the glands of the large intestine, is termed the **succus entericus.**

1. The **intestinal glands** (Glandulæ intestinales) are present throughout. They are simple tubular glands which open between the villi.

2. The **duodenal glands** (Glandulæ duodenales)[1] are present in the first twenty feet or more (ca. 6 to 7 m.) of the bowel. They are branched tubulo-alveolar glands, and are situated in the submucosa, so that their ducts perforate the muscularis mucosæ and the mucous membrane.

---

[1] These were formerly known as Brunner's glands, but in the B. N. A. are termed glandulæ duodenales. On account of their extension beyond the duodenum and their submucous position, Ellenberger has suggested the name glandulæ submucosæ.

Lymphoid tissue occurs in the form of distinct nodules (Noduli lymphatici), which are either scattered or in groups. In the former case they are termed **solitary nodules** (Noduli lymphatici solitarii), in the latter **aggregated nodules** or **Peyer's patches** (Noduli lymphatici aggregati). The solitary nodules are about the size of a millet-seed or a small sago grain. The patches are situated chiefly along the surface opposite to the mesenteric attachment and begin about three or four feet from the pylorus. They number one to two hundred, and are usually one to two inches (2 to 5 cm.) long and a quarter of an inch to one-half inch (ca. 2 to 14 mm.) wide. Larger ones occur in the terminal part, where one patch may have a length of seven to fifteen inches (ca. 17 to 38 cm.) and a width of half an inch to one inch (ca. 5 to 25 mm.) in young horses (Ellenberger). They vary much in number, size, and distribution in different individuals, and undergo atrophy in old subjects.

Vessels and Nerves.—The **arteries** of the small intestine come from the cœliac and anterior mesenteric arteries. The **veins** go to the portal vein. The **lymph-vessels** are numerous and go to the mesenteric lymph glands, thence to the

Fig. 361.—Large and Small Aggregated Nodules or Peyer's Patches of Small Intestine of Horse.

cisterna chyli. The **nerves** are derived from the vagus and sympathetic through the cœliac plexus.

THE LARGE INTESTINE

The large intestine (Intestinum crassum) extends from the termination of the ileum to the anus. It is about twenty-five feet (ca. 7.5 to 8 m.) in length. It differs from the small intestine in its greater size, in being sacculated for the most part, possessing longitudinal bands, and having a more fixed position. It is divided into cæcum, great colon, small colon, and rectum.

THE CÆCUM

The **cæcum** (Intestinum cæcum) is a great cul-de-sac intercalated between the small intestine and the colon. It has a remarkable size, shape, and position in the horse. Its average length is about four feet (ca. 1.25 m.), and its capacity about seven to eight gallons (ca. 25 to 30 liters).[1] It is curved somewhat like a comma.

[1] The length given here is measured from end to end along the side and midway between the curvatures.

It is situated chiefly to the right of the median plane, extending from the right iliac and sublumbar regions to the abdominal floor behind the xiphoid cartilage. Both extremities are blind, and the two orifices are placed two or three inches apart at the concave curvature. It presents for description a base, a body, and an apex. The **base** (Basis cæci s. Saccus cæcus) extends forward on the right side as far as the fourteenth or fifteenth rib, about a handbreadth below its middle, and backward to the tuber coxæ.[1] It is strongly curved, the greater curvature being dorsal, the lesser ventral; connected with the latter are the termination of the ileum and the origin of the colon. The rounded blind end is directed ventrally. The **body** (Corpus cæci) extends downward and forward from the base and rests largely on the ventral wall of the abdomen. Its lesser curvature is about parallel with the costal arch and some five to six inches (10 to 15 cm.) ventral to it. The **apex** (Apex cæci) lies on the

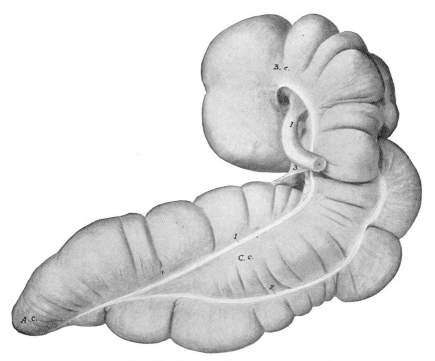

FIG. 362.—CÆCUM OF HORSE; LEFT VIEW.

B. c., Base; C. c., body; A. c., apex; I, ileum; 1 medial band; 2, ventral band; 3, ileo-cæcal fold. The cæcal vessels and lymph glands have been removed to expose the medial band (1)

abdominal floor, usually to the right of the median plane, and about a hand's length behind the xiphoid cartilage.

The right or parietal surface of the cæcum is related chiefly to the right abdominal wall, the diaphragm, duodenum, and liver. The left or visceral surface lies against the left and terminal parts of the colon, the root of the great mesentery, and the small intestine.

The base is attached dorsally by connective tissue and peritoneum on the ventral surface of the pancreas and right kidney, and a small area of the abdominal wall behind these; it is attached medially to the terminal part of the great colon, and ventrally to the origin of the great colon. The body is attached dorso-laterally

[1] The forward extent of the base of the cæcum is subject to some variation. It may be noted that the blind end is not the most anterior part. The extent of the contact of the base with the right flank varies; statements concerning this feature are given in the description of the great colon.

to the first part of the colon by the **cæco-colic fold**.   The apex is free, and consequently may vary in position.

The cæcum has four **longitudinal bands** (Tæniæ cæci), situated on the dorsal, ventral, right, and left surfaces; these cause four rows of **sacculations** (Haustra).

The **ventral band** is almost entirely exposed or free (Tænia libera); it begins on the highest part of the base, extends along the medial side of the greater curvature, and joins the medial band near the apex.   It is concealed only at its origin where the bowel is attached to the wall.   The **dorsal band** extends along the lesser curvature from the termination of the ileum to the apex. The **medial band** extends along the medial part of the lesser curvature of the base, inclines ventrally further forward, and ends by joining the ventral band.   It is covered at its origin by the adhesion to the right dorsal part of the great colon and beyond this by the cæcal vessels and lymph glands.   Medial to the termination of the ileum it projects from the wall of the bowel as a falciform band which can be felt distinctly although covered by vessels and fat.   The **lateral band** is continuous with that of the right ventral part of the colon.   It is covered by vessels, lymph glands and fat, but can be felt in its posterior part, where it forms a concave projecting edge.   It inclines ventrally in front and may extend to the apex or fade out without reaching it.

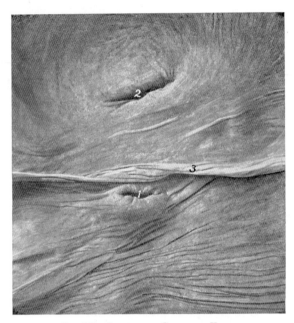

Fig. 363.—Orifices of Cæcum of Horse.
1, Ileo-cæcal orifice; 2, cæco-colic orifice; 3, intervening fold.

The **ileo-cæcal orifice** (Ostium ileocæcale) is situated in the lesser curvature of the base, about two or three inches (ca. 5 to 7.5 cm.) to the right of the median plane, and in a transverse plane through the first or second lumbar vertebra.   The end of the ileum is partially telescoped into the cæcum, so that the orifice is surrounded by a fold of mucous membrane which encloses a thick circular muscular layer, the **sphincter ilei.**

The **cæco-colic orifice** (Ostium cæcocolicum) is lateral to the preceding one; the interval between them is only about two inches (ca. 5 cm.), and they are separated by a large fold which projects into the interior of the cæcum.   The orifice is small in relation to the size of the cæcum and colon.   It is slit-like, or has a narrow oval outline, and is about two inches (ca. 5 cm.) long.   It has a thick **valvular fold** (Valvula cæcocolica) at its ventral margin and is encircled by a muscular ring, the sphincter cæci.[1]   Large crescentic or semilunar folds (Plicæ cæci) project into the cavity of the bowel, and between these are large pouches (Cellulæ cæci).

[1] The anatomical arrangement gives no support to the view which is sometimes expressed that ingesta may pass directly from the ileum to the colon.

It is somewhat difficult to get a correct idea of the cæcal orifices. The cæcum is sharply curved here and a large fold projects into its interior, somewhat like a shelf, and separates the two orifices. The ileo-cæcal orifice faces chiefly dorsally, while the cæco-colic orifice faces forward into the cæcum and is bounded ventrally by a thick fold of the bowel wall.

THE GREAT COLON

The **great colon** (Colon crassum) begins at the cæco-colic orifice, and terminates by joining the small colon behind the saccus cæcus of the stomach. It is ten to twelve feet (ca. 3 to 3.7 m.) long, and its average diameter (exclusive of its narrowest part) is about eight to ten inches (ca. 20 to 25 cm.). Its capacity is more than double that of the cæcum. When removed from the abdomen, it consists of two parallel parts, which are connected by peritoneum and partially by areolar and muscular tissue also. *In situ* it is folded so that it consists of four parts, which are designated according to their position or numerically. The three bent connecting parts are termed the flexures. The first part, the **right ventral colon** (Colon ventrale dextrum), begins at the lesser curvature of the base of the cæcum, about opposite the ventral part of the last rib or intercostal space. It forms an initial curve, the convexity of which is directed upward and backward; this part is in contact with

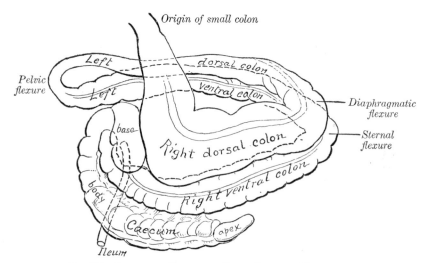

FIG. 364.—DIAGRAM OF CÆCUM AND LARGE COLON OF HORSE.

the upper part of the right flank. It then passes downward and forward along the right costal arch and then along the floor of the abdomen. Over the xiphoid cartilage it bends sharply to the left and backward, forming the **sternal flexure** (Flexura sternalis s. diaphragmatica ventralis). The second part, the **left ventral colon** (Colon ventrale sinistrum), passes backward on the abdominal floor, to the left of the first part and the cæcum and, on reaching the pelvic inlet, bends sharply dorsally and forward, forming the **pelvic flexure** (Flexura pelvina). This is continued by the third part, the **left dorsal colon** (Colon dorsale sinistrum), which passes forward dorsal or lateral to the left ventral part, and on reaching the diaphragm and the left lobe of the liver, turns to the right and backward, forming the **diaphragmatic flexure** (Flexura diaphragmatica dorsalis). The fourth part, the **right dorsal colon** (Colon dorsale dextrum), passes backward dorsal to the first part, and on reaching the medial surface of the base of the cæcum it turns to the left and dorsally behind the left sac of the stomach; here it becomes constricted, and joins the small colon below the left kidney.

The position of the origin of the great colon is variable, and one may easily get a wrong impression on account of the peculiar arrangement of the bowel here. The colon usually presents

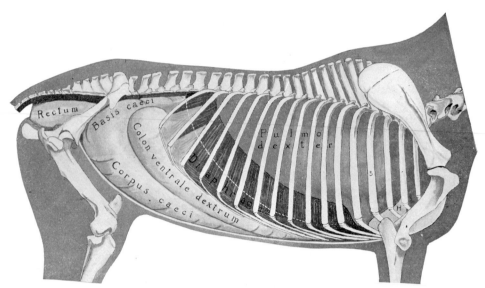

FIG. 265.—TOPOGRAPHY OF VISCERA OF HORSE; RIGHT VIEW.
5, Fifth rib; *H*, pericardium.   Phrenico-costal line dotted.

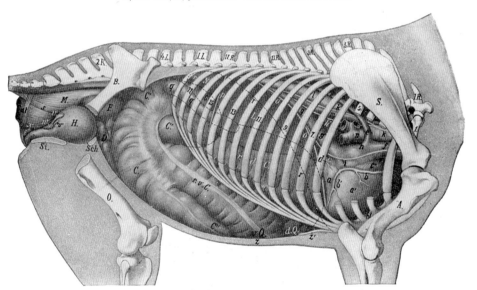

FIG. 366.—TOPOGRAPHY OF VISCERA OF HORSE; RIGHT SIDE, DEEPER VIEW.

1.R., First thoracic vertebra; *1.L.*, first lumbar vertebra; *2.K.*, second sacral spine; *S.*, scapula; *A.*, humerus; *B.*, ilium; *O.*, femur; *Sch.*, pubis; *Si.*, ischium; *St.*, sternum; *L.*, right lobe of liver; *r.N.*, right kidney; *C.*, body, *C'.*, base, *C''.*, apex of cæcum; *r.v.C.*, right ventral colon; *v.Q.*, sternal flexure of colon; *d.Q.*, diaphragmatic flexure of colon; *r.d.C.*, right dorsal colon; *F.*, pelvic flexure of colon; *D.*, small intestine; *H.*, urinary bladder; *M.*, rectum; *a*, left ventricle; *a'*, right ventricle; *b, b'*, right coronary artery; *c*, left atrium; *c'*, right atrium; *d*, left coronary artery, circumflex branch; *e*, vena azygos; *f*, anterior vena cava; *g*, posterior vena cava; *h*, sinus venosus; *i*, right phrenic nerve; *k*, right vagus, with its dorsal (*k'*) and ventral (*k''*) divisions; *l*, aorta; *m*, œsophagus; *n*, trachea; *o*, diaphragm (median section); *p*, right lateral ligament of liver; *q*, duodenum; *r*, dotted line indicating position in median section of diaphragm in inspiratory phase; *s*, recto-coccygeus muscle; *t*, suspensory ligament of rectum; *u*, sphincter ani; *v*, vesicula seminalis; *w*, prostate; *x*, bulbo-urethral gland; *y*, urethra; *z*, abdominal wall; *z'*, xiphoid cartilage.   (After Ellenberger, in Leisering's Atlas, reduced.)

a saccular dilatation at the lesser curvature of the base of the cæcum, which may be mistaken for its origin.   The real origin is a constricted part or neck anterior to the sacculation.   Thus the colon passes at first backward and then curves sharply downward and forward.   Schmaltz has proposed the name "vestibulum coli" for this sacculation.   In some cases it is large enough to displace the cæcum in large part from contact with the wall at the paralumbar fossa. In other subjects the sacculation is very slight or even practically absent; in such cases the bowel appears to have been fixed in a contracted state.

The sternal flexure extends forward to a point opposite to the ventral part of the seventh rib, and the diaphragmatic flexure as far as the sixth intercostal space on the right of the median plane.

The **caliber** of the great colon varies greatly at different points. At its origin it is only about two to three inches (ca. 5 to 7.5 cm.) in diameter.[1] This soon

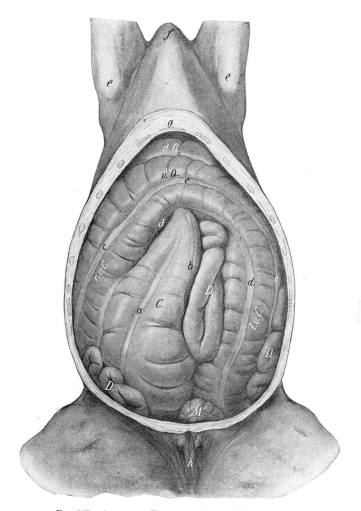

FIG. 367.—ABDOMINAL VISCERA OF HORSE; VENTRAL VIEW.

The ventral wall and part of the lateral walls of the abdomen are removed. *C.*, Cæcum; *r.v.C.*, right ventral part of colon; *v.Q.*, sternal flexure of colon; *l.v. C.*, left ventral part of colon; *d.Q.*, diaphragmatic flexure of colon; *D.*, small intestine; *M.*, small colon; *a*, ventral free band of cæcum; *b*, medial band of cæcum; *c*, lateral band of ventral part of colon *d*, ventral band of ventral part of colon; *e*, point of elbow; *f*, anterior end of sternal region; *g*, xiphoid cartilage; *h*, teats. (After Ellenberger-Baum, Top. Anat. d. Pferdes.)

increases to about eight to ten inches (ca. 20 to 25 cm.) for the ventral parts. Beyond the pelvic flexure the diameter is reduced to about three or four inches (ca. 8 to 9 cm.). Toward the diaphragmatic flexure the caliber rapidly increases, and reaches its maximum in the last part, where it forms a large sacculation, which may have a diameter of about twenty inches (50 cm.). This is succeeded by a funnel-shaped terminal contraction.

[1] Usually there is sacculation of considerable size which succeeds the constricted origin.

The right ventral part of the great colon is attached to the lesser curvature of the cæcum by two layers of peritoneum which form the **cæco-colic fold** (Plica cæcocolica). The right parts are united by peritoneum on either side and also by areolar tissue and muscular fibers, the surface of adhesion being about four or five inches (ca. 10 to 12 cm.) wide; the left parts are attached to each other in a similar fashion near the anterior flexures, but further back the connection is a peritoneal fold which gradually becomes wide enough to allow them to be drawn apart about six inches (ca. 15 cm.) near the pelvic flexure. The terminal part of the colon is attached by peritoneum and areolar tissue to the ventral surface of the pancreas

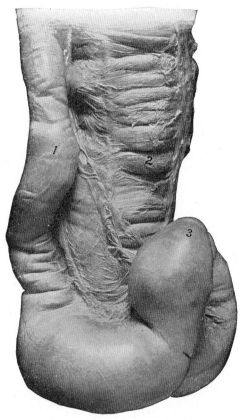

FIG. 368.—POSTERIOR PORTION OF LEFT PARTS OF COLON OF HORSE; DORSAL VIEW.
1, Left dorsal part; *2*, left ventral part; *3*, pelvic flexure.

dorsally and to the base of the cæcum laterally. It is connected indirectly with the diaphragm and liver by means of a fold derived from the right lateral ligament of the liver.

The **relations** are complex, and the more important facts follow. The ventral parts have extensive contact with the abdominal wall ventrally and laterally. On the right side the colon is usually almost entirely excluded from contact with the flank, by the cæcum, but exceptions to this are not uncommon.[1] On the left side it lies against the ventral part of the flank. Dorsally the chief relations are to the stomach, duodenum, liver, pancreas, small colon, small intestine, aorta, posterior vena cava, and portal vein. Since there are no transverse attachments of the right and left parts, and the latter have no attachment to the wall, they are subject to considerable displacement. The pelvic flexure is variable in position, but usually

[1] The colic vestibule may be of sufficient size to exclude the base of the cæcum largely from contact with the flank.

it is directed against the posterior part of the right flank or lies in the right inguinal region.[1]

The **bands of the colon** (Tæniæ coli) vary in number on the different parts. The ventral parts have four bands. The pelvic flexure has a band along its lesser

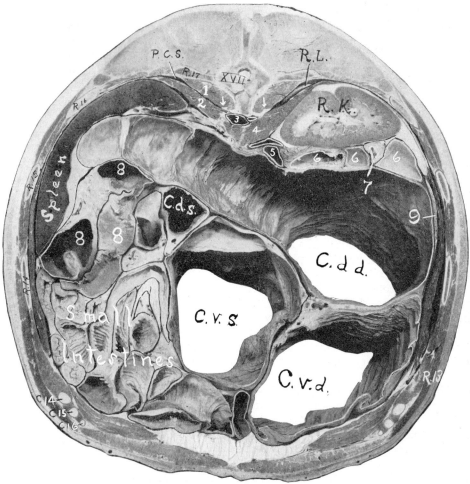

Fig. 368a.—Cross-section of Abdomen of Horse. Cut Through the Seventeenth Thoracic Vertebra.

1, Psoas muscles; *2,* left crus of diaphragm; *3,* aorta; *4,* right crus of diaphragm (thoracic duct above *4* and to right of *3*); *5,* portal vein (vena cava [collapsed] above *5*); *6, 6, 6,* cæcum; *7,* duodenum turning medially; *8, 8, 8,* small colon; *9,* liver, posterior part of right lobe; *C. 14, C. 15, C. 16,* costal cartilages fourteen, fifteen, and sixteen; *R. 13,* ventral end of thirteenth rib on right side; *R. 14, R. 15, R. 16, R. 17,* ribs fourteen, fifteen, sixteen and seventeen; *XVII,* seventeenth thoracic vertebra; *C. d. d.,* right dorsal colon; *C. d. s.,* left dorsal colon; *C. v. d.,* right ventral colon; *C. v. s.,* left ventral colon; *P. C. S.,* left pleural cavity (left lung ends about one and one-half inches anterior to surface); *R. K.,* right kidney; *R. L.,* right lung (about 1 cm. anterior to surface); *S. I.,* small intestines. Most posterior part of the stomach was ventral to rib seventeen, about 2 cm. in front of plane of section, concealed by transverse part of colon. Arrows on psoas muscle point to great splanchnic nerve.

curvature. The left dorsal colon has at first only one band, which is a continuation of the preceding one; further forward two other bands appear, and the three are

[1] The length of the left parts varies and this appears partly to account for the differences to be found in the arrangement of their posterior parts and the pelvic flexure. In subjects in which these parts of the colon are relatively long, their posterior ends are usually bent to the right across the pelvic inlet so that the pelvic flexure lies to the right of the inlet; it may even have extensive contact with the flank as high as the paralumbar fossa. In rare cases the left parts of the colon seem relatively short and the pelvic flexure lies in the pelvic cavity. Other dispositions are encountered. In many subjects the left dorsal part inclines medially over the ventral part, and exaggeration of this arrangement may lead to torsion of the left parts sufficient to produce death if not reduced.

continued on the right dorsal part. The ventral parts have alternate constrictions and sacculations (Haustra coli).

On the right ventral colon two bands are dorsal, and extend along the medial and lateral sides of the attachment to the right dorsal colon. The medial one is covered by the colic vessels, etc., and the lateral one is concealed entirely or almost entirely by the attachment to the right dorsal part. A lateral band comes from the lesser curvature of the cæcum and becomes ventral at the sternal flexure; it is free except that it is often covered for a short distance by the artery and vein of the arch and some fat. The ventral band is also free. On the left ventral colon also two bands are dorsal. Of these, the medial one is covered by the vessels and lymph glands and in the anterior part also by the adhesion to the left dorsal part. At the pelvic flexure it is continued along the concave face of the bowel to the left dorsal part; it is important clinically as being the only distinct band on the flexure and may be felt per rectum. The dorso-lateral band is largely free, but is covered in front by the attachment to the left dorsal part. It fades out at the pelvic flexure. The ventro-medial and ventro-lateral bands are free and fade out at the pelvic flexure. The left dorsal colon has at first only one band, which is the continuation of the one along the lesser curvature of the pelvic flexure; it extends along the ventral surface and is continued on the right dorsal colon. Beyond the middle of the left dorsal colon two dorsal bands begin, diverge very gradually, and are continued on the right dorsal colon; both are free and broaden at the diaphragmatic flexure. On the right dorsal colon the ventral band is concealed by the attachment to the right ventral colon and by the vessels and lymph glands. The two dorsal bands are free except at the parietal attachment of the bowel; the lateral one is very wide and somewhat indistinct; the medial one is narrower and more distinct, and is continued along the mesenteric border of the small colon.

THE SMALL COLON

The **small colon** (Colon tenue) begins at the termination of the great colon, behind the saccus cæcus of the stomach and ventral to the left kidney, and is continued by the rectum at the pelvic inlet.[1] Its length is about ten to twelve feet (ca. 3.5 m.), and its diameter three to four inches (ca. 7.5 to 10 cm.).

Its coils lie chiefly in the space between the stomach and the pelvic inlet, dorsal to the left parts of the great colon. They are mingled with those of the small intestine, from which they are easily distinguished by the bands and sacculation.

It is attached to the sublumbar region by the **colic mesentery,** and to the termination of the duodenum by the narrow **duodeno-colic fold** of peritoneum (Lig. duodeno-colicum). The greater omentum is also attached to the initial part of the bowel. The colic mesentery is narrow at its origin, but soon reaches a width of about three feet (ca. 80 to 90 cm.). Its parietal border is attached along a line extending from the ventral surface of the left kidney to the sacral promontory; it is continuous in front with the root of the great mesentery, and behind with the mesorectum.

There are two **longitudinal bands** (tæniæ) and two rows of sacculations. One of the bands is free, the other is concealed by the mesentery. When the bowel is hardened *in situ* its lumen between the pouches is reduced to a narrow slit.

THE RECTUM

The **rectum** (Intestinum rectum) is the terminal part of the bowel; it extends from the pelvic inlet to the anus.[2] Its length is about one foot (ca. 30 cm.). Its direction may be straight or oblique. The first or peritoneal part of the rectum is like the small colon, and is attached by a continuation of the colic mesentery termed the **mesorectum.** The second or retroperitoneal part forms a flask-shaped dilatation termed the **ampulla recti;** it is attached to the surrounding structures by connective tissue and muscular bands.

The first part of the rectum commonly lies along the left wall of the pelvic cavity, but may be about median or (more rarely) deflected to the right. It is related to coils of the small colon and (inconstantly) to the left parts or pelvic

[1] The position of the funnel-shaped termination of the great colon and the origin of the small colon is fixed, and this fact is of clinical importance in regard to impaction, which is not rare here. In horses of medium size this part of the bowel can be palpated per rectum when distended.

[2] There is no natural line of demarcation between the small colon and rectum: the plane of the pelvic inlet is selected as the division for convenience of description.

flexure of the great colon; ventrally to the bladder (when full) or to the uterus. The second part of the rectum is related dorsally and laterally to the pelvic wall. Ventrally the relations differ in the two sexes. In the male they are the bladder, the terminal parts of the ductus deferentes, the vesiculæ seminales, the prostate, the bulbo-urethral glands and the urethra. In the female they are the uterus, vagina, and vulva.[1]

STRUCTURE OF THE LARGE INTESTINE

The **serous coat** covers the different parts in varying degree. It does not cover (a) the opposed surfaces of the cæcum and colon which are between the layers

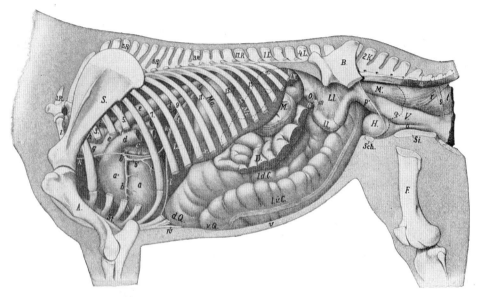

Fig. 369.—Topography of Viscera of Mare; Left Deep View.

1R., First thoracic vertebra; *1L.,* first lumbar vertebra; *2K.,* second sacral spine; *S.,* scapula; *A.,* humerus; *B.,* ilium; *F.,* femur; *Sch.,* pubis; *Si.,* ischium; *L.,* liver (left lobe); *Ma.,* stomach, the posterior contour of which is indicated by dotted line *x; Mi.,* spleen; *l.N.,* left kidney, concealed part indicated by dotted line; *M.,* small colon; *D.,* small intestine, parts of which have been removed; *l.d.C.,* left dorsal colon; *l.v.C.,* left ventral colon; *v.Q.,* sternal flexure; *d.Q.,* diaphragmatic flexure; *O.,* left ovary; *U.,* horn of uterus; *L.l.,* broad ligament of uterus; *M'.,* rectum; *V.,* vagina; *H.,* bladder; *a,* left ventricle; *a',* right ventricle; *b,* left coronary artery with descending (*b'*) and circumflex (*b''*) branches; *c,* left auricle; *d,* pulmonary artery (cut); *e,* aorta; *f,* ligamentum arteriosum; *g,* brachiocephalic trunk (anterior aorta); *h,* trachea; *i,* œsophagus; *k,* left phrenic nerve; *l,* diaphragm in median section; *m,* uterine tube; *n,* bursa ovarica; *o,* urethra; *p,* cut edge of broad ligament; *q,* line of reflection of pelvic peritoneum; *r,* recto-coccygeus; *s,* suspensory ligament of rectum; *t,* sphincter ani internus; *u,* sacro-coccygeus ventralis; *v,* abdominal wall in section; *w,* xiphoid cartilage. (After Ellenberger, in Leisering's Atlas.)

of the cæco-colic fold and mesocolon; (b) the areas of parietal attachment of the cæcum and colon; (c) the retroperitoneal part of the rectum.

The **muscular coat** consists of longitudinal and circular fibers. The bulk of the former is in the bands of the cæcum and colon. It is to be noted, however, that the bands of the cæcum and the ventral parts of the great colon are largely composed of elastic tissue. The bands of the dorsal parts of the colon are largely muscular, and those of the small colon are almost entirely muscular. Some of the circular fibers pass from one part of the colon to another, where they are attached to each other, forming the fibræ transversæ coli. The muscular coat of the ampulla of the rectum presents special features. The longitudinal layer of fibers is very

---

[1] The anterior part of the rectum is variable in position and relations. The amount covered by peritoneum dorsally and laterally is very variable, and appears to be in inverse proportion to the fulness of the bowel.

thick and consists of large bundles which are rather loosely united. A large band, the **recto-coccygeus,** is detached from it on either side, and passes upward and backward to be inserted into the fourth and fifth coccygeal vertebræ.

The **submucous tissue** is abundant in the wall of the rectum, so that the mucous

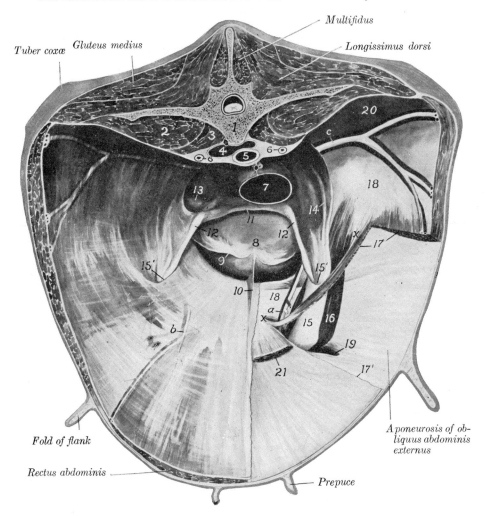

Fig. 370.—Pelvic Inlet and Posterior Part of Abdominal Wall of Stallion, Viewed from the Front.

On left side of figure the wall is undisturbed. On right side of figure most of rectus and obliquus abdominis internus have been removed, leaving stumps of their origin and narrow strip of obliquus internus which forms margin of internal inguinal or abdominal ring. *1,* Fifth lumbar vertebra; *2,* m. psoas major; *3,* m. psoas minor; *4,* posterior vena cava; *5,* aorta; *6, 6,* ureters; *7,* rectum; *8,* urinary bladder (vertex); *9,* round ligament in edge of lateral ligament of bladder; *10,* middle ligament of bladder; *11,* genital fold; *12,* ductus deferens in its fold; *13,* vesicula seminalis; *14,* internal spermatic artery in vascular fold; *15,* tunica vaginalis; *15',* vaginal ring; *x, x,* angles of internal inguinal or abdominal ring; *16,* m. cremaster externus; *17,* m. obliquus abdominis internus; *17',* cut edge of aponeurosis of *17; 18,* inguinal ligament; *19,* lateral angle of external inguinal ring; *20,* iliac fascia; *21,* m. rectus abdominis; *a,* external pudic artery; *b,* posterior abdominal vessels (stumps of same opposite "*a*"); *c,* circumflex iliac artery.

membrane is loosely attached to the muscular coat, and forms numerous folds when the bowel is empty.

The **mucous membrane** of the large intestine is thicker and darker in color than that of the small intestine. It forms large crescentic or semilunar **folds** (Plicæ semilunares), corresponding to the external constrictions. It has no villi nor duodenal glands. The **intestinal glands** are large and numerous. **Solitary** nodules are numerous, and there are **aggregated lymph nodules** at the apex of the cæcum and in the pelvic flexure and the adjacent portion of the left dorsal part of the colon.

Vessels and Nerves.—The **arteries** come from the anterior and posterior mesenteric and internal pudic arteries. The **veins** go to the portal and internal pudic veins. The **lymph vessels** of the cæcum and colon go to the cæcal and colic lymph glands, thence to the cisterna chyli. Those of the rectum go to the internal iliac and lumbar glands. The **nerves** are derived from the mesenteric and pelvic plexuses of the sympathetic.

THE ANUS

The **anus** is the terminal part of the alimentary canal. It is situated below the root of the tail where it forms a round projection, with a central depression when contracted. It is ventral to the fourth coccygeal vertebra. It is covered externally by an integument which is thin, hairless, and provided with numerous sebaceous and sweat glands. Its lumen, the **anal canal** (Pars analis recti), is about two inches (ca. 5 cm.) long; except during defecation it is closed by the contraction of the sphincter muscles and folds of the mucous lining. The mucous membrane is pale, glandless, and covered with a thick, squamous, stratified epithelium. The muscular arrangement is as follows: The **sphincter ani internus** is the terminal thickening of the circular coat of the bowel. The **sphincter ani externus** is a broad ring of striped muscle-fibers outside the internal sphincter. Some fibers are attached to the coccygeal fascia above, others to the perineal fascia below (Figs. 577, 578). Its action is to close the anus. The **retractor ani** is a flat muscle which lies between the rectum and the sacro-sciatic ligament; its fibers are directed backward and somewhat upward. It arises from the superior ischiatic spine and the sacro-sciatic ligament, and ends under the sphincter ani externus (Figs. 287, 577). Its action is to reduce the partial prolapse which the anus undergoes during defecation. The **suspensory ligament of the anus** (Lig. suspensorium ani) is a band of unstriped muscle which arises from the first coccygeal vertebra, passes downward under cover of the retractor ani, and unites with its fellow below the anus (Fig. 576). In the male it is largely continued by the retractor penis muscle; in the female it blends with the constrictor vulvæ. It may act as an accessory sphincter of the anus.

Vessels and Nerves.—The blood-supply comes from the internal pudic arteries, and the veins go to the internal pudic vein. The lymph vessels go to the anal lymph glands. The nerves come from the pudic nerve.

THE PANCREAS

The **pancreas** is situated transversely on the dorsal wall of the abdomen, the greater part being to the right of the median plane. Its central part lies under the seventeenth thoracic vertebra. When fresh, it has a reddish cream color, but if left in the unpreserved cadaver, it rapidly decomposes and becomes dark. It resembles the salivary glands in appearance, but is softer, and its lobules are more loosely united. Its average weight is about twelve ounces (ca. 350 g.). When hardened *in situ* its shape is very irregular. It is triangular in outline and presents for description two surfaces, three borders, and three angles.

The **dorsal surface** (Facies dorsalis) faces dorsally and forward. It is partially covered by peritoneum. It is related chiefly to the ventral surface of the right kidney and adrenal, the posterior vena cava, the portal vein, the cœliac artery and its divisions, the gastro-phrenic ligament and the saccus cæcus of the stomach, the right and caudate lobes of the liver, and the gastro-pancreatic fold. There are grooves for the divisions of the cœliac artery and a large one for the splenic vein. The **ventral surface** (Facies ventralis) faces ventrally and backward; it is in general concave. It presents two impressions, separated by an oblique ridge. The smaller of these (Impressio cæcalis) lies to the right, and is caused by the pressure of the base of the cæcum; the larger one (Impressio colica) indicates the area of contact with the terminal part of the great colon and its junction with the small colon. It has usually no peritoneal covering except over a small area at the duodenal angle.

The **right border** is nearly straight; it is related to the second part of the duodenum. The **left border** is slightly concave, and is related to the first part of the duodenum, the left sac of the stomach, and the splenic vessels. The **posterior border** presents a deep notch (Incisura pancreatis) where the root of the great mesentery is in contact with the gland. To the right the portal vein lies in the notch, and passes through the gland very obliquely; there is a thin bridge of gland tissue dorsal to the vein, thus forming the **portal ring** (Annulus portæ).

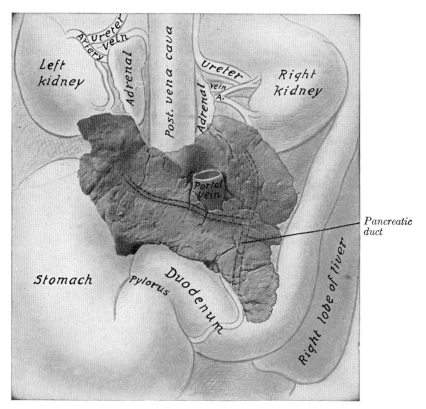

FIG. 371.—PANCREAS OF HORSE WITH CHIEF RELATIONS; VENTRAL VIEW.
The pancreatic duct and its two chief radicles are indicated by dotted lines, since they are in the substance of the gland.

The **anterior** or **duodenal angle** (Angulus cranialis)[1] is the most ventral part of the gland; it is attached to the concavity of the second curve of the duodenum and the adjacent part of the right lobe of the liver. The ducts leave at this extremity. The **left** or **splenic angle** (Angulus sinister)[2] fits into the space between the saccus cæcus of the stomach in front, the left kidney behind, the base of the spleen dorsally, and the termination of the great colon ventrally. The **right angle** (Angulus dexter) is rounded, and lies on the ventral surface of the right kidney and adrenal body.

The pancreas is attached dorsally by connective tissue to the kidneys and adrenal bodies, the gastro-phrenic ligament, the suspensory ligament of the spleen,

[1] This corresponds to the head of the pancreas of man.
[2] This corresponds to the tail of the pancreas of man.

the posterior vena cava, the portal fissure, and the gastro-pancreatic fold. The ventral surface is mainly attached by areolar tissue to the base of the cæcum and the terminal part of the great colon.

There are almost invariably two **ducts**. The large one is termed the **pancreatic duct** (Ductus pancreaticus). It is formed by the union of two radicles which come from the right and left extremities, passes through the duodenal angle, pierces the wall of the duodenum obliquely and opens into the duodenal diverticulum alongside of the bile-duct. The duct is nearly half an inch (ca. 1 cm.) wide, and is very thin walled. It is situated in the substance of the gland near its dorsal surface; none of it is free. The **accessory pancreatic duct** (Ductus pancreaticus accessorius) arises either from the chief duct or its left radicle, and ends on a papilla in the duodenum opposite the chief duct.

Structure.—The pancreas belongs to the class of tubulo-alveolar glands, the alveoli being long, like those of the duodenal glands; in other respects it resembles the serous salivary glands very closely. It has no proper capsule and the lobules are rather loosely united.

Vessels and Nerves.—The arteries of the pancreas come from the branches of the cœliac and anterior mesenteric arteries. The veins go to the portal vein. The nerves are derived from the cœliac and mesenteric plexuses of the sympathetic.

THE LIVER

The **liver** (Hepar) is the largest gland in the body. It is situated obliquely on the abdominal surface of the diaphragm. Its highest point is at the level of the right kidney, its lowest on the left side, usually about three or four inches (ca. 8 to 10 cm.) from the abdominal floor, opposite the ventral end of the seventh or eighth rib. The greater part of it lies to the right of the median plane, except when the right lobe is atrophic.

It is red-brown in color and is rather friable. Its average weight is about ten to twelve pounds (ca. 5 kg.), but in a large draft horse it weighs about twenty pounds. When in the body, or if hardened *in situ*, it is strongly curved and accurately adapted to the abdominal surface of the diaphragm. When removed in the soft state, it flattens out into a cake-like form quite different from its natural shape. It presents for description two surfaces, and four borders.

The **parietal surface** (Facies diaphragmatica) is strongly convex and lies against the diaphragm. It faces chiefly dorsally and forward. Its most anterior part is opposite the ventral third of the sixth intercostal space or seventh rib. It presents, just to the right of the median plane, a sagittal groove, the **fossa venæ cavæ,** in which the posterior vena cava is embedded.

The **visceral surface** (Facies visceralis) faces in general ventrally and backward; it is concave and irregular, being molded on the organs which lie against it. It presents the following features: (1) The **portal fissure** (Porta hepatis) is a depression above the middle of the surface and a little to the right of the median plane; through it the portal vein, hepatic artery, and hepatic plexus of nerves enter, and the hepatic duct and lymph vessels leave the liver. The hepatic lymph glands are also found here. The pancreas is attached at and to the right of the fissure, and the lesser omentum around it. Above the fissure is the **caudate lobe** (Lobus caudatus), which is continued to the right by the pointed **caudate process** (Processus caudatus). (2) The **gastric impression** (Impressio gastrica) is an extensive concave area which is the surface of contact with the stomach. (3) Leading from this to the right of the portal fissure and dorsally is the **duodenal impression** (Impressio duodenalis). (4) The **colic impression** (Impressio colica) is situated ventrally and to the right of the gastric and duodenal impressions, from which it is separated by a ridge; it corresponds to the extensive contact of the diaphragmatic flexure and right dorsal part of the colon. (5) **A cæcal impression** (Impressio cæcalis) may be found dorsal to the preceding; it corresponds to the anterior part of the base of the cæcum.[1] Coils of the small intestine may also lie on this surface, and the apex of the spleen may reach to it when the stomach is empty.

The **dorsal border** (Margo dorsalis s. obtusus) is thick for the most part. It presents from right to left: (1) The right lateral ligament; (2) the **renal impression** for the right kidney (Impressio renalis); (3) a notch, which is the dorsal end of the fossa venæ cavæ; (4) the deep **œsophageal notch** (Impressio œsophagea), which is occupied partly by the end of the œsophagus, but mainly by the thick margin of the hiatus œsophageus; (5) the left lateral ligament.

The **ventral border** (Margo ventralis) is thin, and is marked by two deep **interlobar fissures** or **incisures** (Incisuræ interlobares), which partially divide the

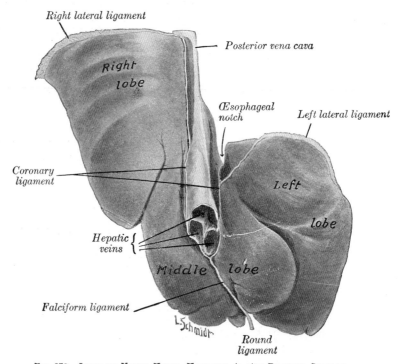

FIG. 372.—LIVER OF YOUNG HORSE, HARDENED *in situ;* PARIETAL SURFACE.

organ into three principal **lobes**—**right, middle** and **left**. The right lobe is the largest, except in old subjects, in which it is frequently much atrophied. The middle lobe is the smallest. It is marked by several small fissures and by the **umbilical fissure** (Incisura umbilicalis); the latter contains the umbilical vein in the fœtus, which is transformed into the round ligament after birth.

The **right border** (Margo dexter) is thin and long; it extends backward usually to the sixteenth rib, a little below its middle.

The **left border** (Margo sinister) is thin and convex. It begins at the left side of the œsophageal notch, about a handbreadth ventral to the fourteenth thoracic vertebra. It curves downward, outward, and somewhat forward to a point opposite the ventral end of the ninth rib, and then runs forward about parallel with the

---

[1] These impressions are not evident on the soft organ. In hardened material they are clearly mapped out, although, of course, variable in size, in conformity with the degree of fulness of the various hollow viscera. The cæcal impression may not be evident, if as often happens in old horses, the right lobe of the liver is much atrophied.

costal arch as far as the ventral end of the seventh rib. The ventral and lateral borders together constitute the margo acutus.

The form and size of the liver vary much and certain differences in the relations of the gland are correlated with this fact. In the young adult the right lobe is usually the largest and its dorsal border is about parallel with the dorsal half of the sixteenth rib; in such cases the visceral surface of the lobe usually presents a cæcal impression corresponding with the most

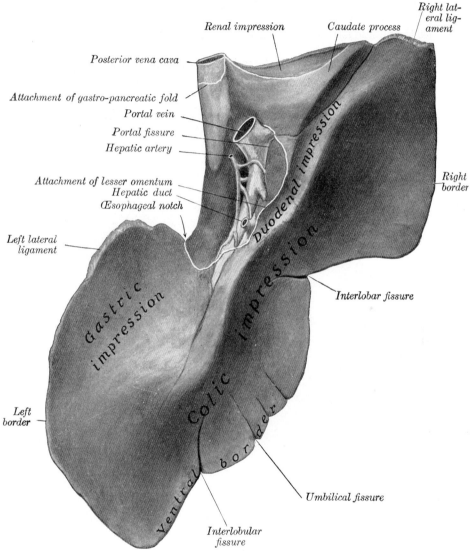

FIG. 373.—LIVER OF HORSE; VISCERAL SURFACE.

Specimen from middle-aged subject, hardened *in situ.* The fissure between the left and middle lobes is shown but not marked.

anterior part of the base of the cæcum. In many subjects—especially old ones—the right lobe has undergone more or less atrophy and a portion of it has become fibrous (appendix fibrosa hepatis); in pronounced cases there is no cæcal impression. Reduction of the middle lobe is also common, and the bulk of the gland may be formed by the left lobe. The latter is then likely to have more or less contact with the abdominal floor. Atrophy of the left lobe is rare.

The liver is held in position largely by the pressure of the other viscera and by its close application and attachment to the diaphragm. It has six ligaments.

1. The **coronary ligament** (Lig. coronarium hepatis) attaches it closely to the diaphragm. It consists of two strong laminæ. The right one is attached to the right of the fossa venæ cavæ; the left one begins to the left of the vena cava and passes dorsally and laterally, becoming continuous with the left lateral ligament at the left margin of the œsophageal notch; it detaches a middle fold which extends to the œsophageal notch and is continuous with the lesser omentum. The two laminæ unite below the vena cava to form the next ligament.

2. The **falciform ligament** (Lig. falciforme hepatis) is a crescentic fold which attaches the middle lobe to the sternal part of the diaphragm and to the abdominal floor for a variable distance.

3. The **round ligament** (Lig. teres hepatis) is a fibrous cord in the concave

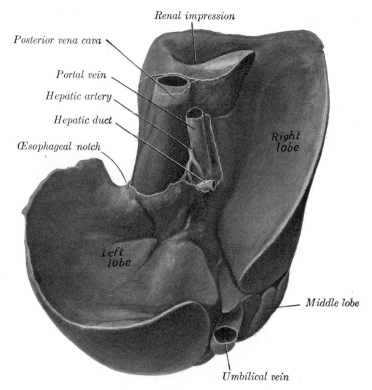

FIG. 374.—LIVER OF NEW-BORN FOAL, HARDENED *in situ*; VISCERAL SURFACE.
The differences, when compared with the organ in the adult, are very striking.

edge of the falciform ligament which extends from the umbilical fissure to the umbilicus; it is the vestige of the umbilical vein, which in the fœtus carries the blood from the placenta to the liver.[1]

4. The **right lateral ligament** (Lig. triangulare dextrum) attaches the dorsal border of the right lobe closely to the costal part of the diaphragm.

5. The **left lateral ligament** (Lig. triangulare sinistrum) is a triangular fold which attaches the dorsal edge of the left lobe to the tendinous center of the diaphragm.

6. The **hepato-renal** or **caudate ligament** (Lig. hepatorenale) attaches the caudate process to the right kidney and the base of the cæcum.

The lesser omentum and the first part of the mesoduodenum are formed by the

[1] It is to be noted that a remnant of the lumen of the vein is usually present, but has no endothelial lining.

peritoneum leaving the visceral surface at the portal fissure and along a curved line which extends from the fissure to the œsophageal notch. They pass to the lesser curvature of the stomach and the first part of the duodenum.

As stated above, the liver is divided by fissures into three principal lobes—right, middle, and left. The **right lobe** (Lobus dexter) is the largest in the young subject and is irregularly quadrilateral in form. On its dorsal part is the **caudate lobe** (Lobus caudatus), which ends in a pointed **caudate process** directed outward and assists in forming the cavity for the right kidney. The **central** or **middle lobe** (Lobus centralis) is normally much the smallest. The **left lobe** (Lobus sinister) is oval in outline and thickest centrally. In old or middle-aged subjects it commonly exceeds the right one in size, and in many cases constitutes the bulk of the gland. In some cases the atrophy of the right lobe is so extreme that the middle lobe may exceed it in size.[1]

The **hepatic duct** (Ductus hepaticus) is formed at the ventral part of the portal fissure by the union of right and left chief lobar ducts. It is about two inches (ca. 5 cm.) long and about half an inch (ca. 1 to 1.5 cm.) wide. It passes between the two layers of the mesoduodenum, and pierces the wall of the duodenum five or six inches (ca. 12 to 15 cm.) from the pylorus, alongside of the pancreatic duct. The ducts pass obliquely through the wall of the duodenum for about half an inch (ca. 1 cm.) before opening into the diverticulum duodeni. The arrangement forms a valve, which prevents regurgitation from the intestine. There is no gall-bladder.

In the new-born foal the liver presents striking differences when compared with the gland of the adult. It is relatively large and weighs 2½ to 3 pounds (ca. 1.25 kg.). It is thick and is strongly curved, and a considerable part of the parietal surface is in contact with the floor of the abdomen. The umbilical fissure is large and contains the umbilical vein. The latter is a very large vessel which carries blood from the placenta and joins the portal vein in the substance of the liver; it is in the edge of the falciform ligament, which at this time extends to the umbilicus. The visceral surface is deeply concave and is in contact chiefly with the stomach and duodenum.

Structure.—The liver is covered by an external serous, and an internal fibrous, coat. The **serous coat** (Tunica serosa) covers the gland except at the attachment of the pancreas and at the portal fissure; it is reflected from it to form the ligaments and the lesser omentum. The **fibrous capsule** (Capsula fibrosa) is in general thin; it sends laminæ into the ligaments, and also trabeculæ into the gland. At the portal fissure it is abundant and surrounds the vessels and ducts, which it accompanies in the portal canals of the gland substance.

The gland substance is composed of the parenchyma and the interstitial tissue. The **parenchyma** is made up of polygonal **lobules** (Lobuli hepatis), about 1.5 mm. in diameter, which are held together by a small amount of interlobular connective tissue. On account of the very small amount of the latter, the lobulation of the horse's liver is not usually at all distinct; for the same reason the organ is also quite friable. The lobules are composed of the polyhedral liver cells, a delicate reticulum, the bile capillaries, a plexus of blood capillaries, and a central vein.

Vessels and Nerves.—The **portal vein** enters at the portal fissure. It conveys blood from the stomach, intestine, and spleen, which contains various products of digestion and numerous white blood-cells. The **hepatic artery** also enters at the portal fissure; it may be termed the nutrient vessel. All the blood is returned from the liver to the posterior vena cava by the hepatic veins. The portal vein and the hepatic artery, both divide into interlobular branches, which run together in the portal canals of the interlobular tissue. The branches of the portal vein (Venæ

[1] Flower and Ruge describe the mammalian liver as being primarily divided by the umbilical fissure into two parts, the right and left lobes. Secondary fissures on either side may subdivide each of these primary lobes. On this basis we may recognize in the liver of the horse right lateral, right central, left central, and left lateral lobes. In the young foal these four lobes are distinctly recognizable. The two central lobes would correspond to the central or middle lobe of the foregoing description, and the right central lobe would be the equivalent of the quadrate lobe of man.

interlobulares) give off intralobular branches which form plexuses of capillaries (sinusoids) in the lobules and give rise to a central vein (Vena centralis). The interlobular branches of the hepatic artery (Rami arteriosi interlobulares) are of relatively small size. They supply mainly (if not exclusively) the interlobular tissue, the capsule, and the walls of the vessels and ducts. The **hepatic veins**[1] (Venæ hepaticæ) empty into the posterior vena cava as it lies in the fossa of the gland. Their ultimate radicles are the central lobular veins (Venæ centrales), which emerge from the bases of the lobules and join the sublobular veins (Venæ sublobulares); the latter unite to form the hepatic veins. The largest hepatic veins, three or four in number, join the posterior vena cava just before it leaves the liver to pass through the diaphragm. The **lymph vessels** go largely to the hepatic glands at the portal fissure, thence to the cysterna chyli; others pass by the ligaments to the diaphragm and through the hiatus œsophageus to the mediastinal glands.

The **nerves** come from the **hepatic plexus,** which is composed of branches from the vagus and sympathetic nerves.

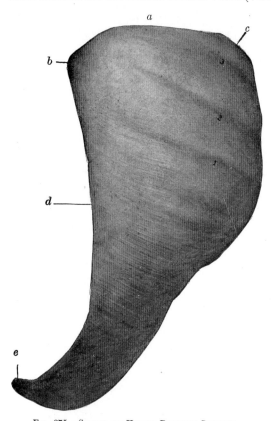

Fig. 375.—Spleen of Horse; Parietal Surface.

a, Dorsal extremity or base; *b, c,* anterior and posterior basal angles; *d,* anterior border; *e,* ventral extremity or apex; *1, 2, 3,* impressions of last three ribs.

THE SPLEEN

The **spleen** (Lien) is the largest of the heterogeneous group of organs which are usually designated ductless glands.[2] It is situated chiefly in the left parachondriac region, in close relation to the left part of the great curvature of the stomach, to which its long axis corresponds. Its size and weight vary greatly in different subjects, and also in the same subject under different conditions, depending chiefly on the great variability of the amount of blood contained in it. The average weight is about 35 to 40 ounces (ca. 1 kg.), its length about 20 inches (ca. 50 cm.), and its greatest width about 8 to 10 inches (ca. 20 to 25 cm.). It is usually bluish-red or somewhat purple in color. In the natural state it is soft and yielding, but not friable.

The weight, which is extremely variable, appears to range ordinarily from about one to eight pounds, although even the latter figure may be exceeded without any apparent evidence of disease. It is generally believed this variation is due to its physiological activity influenced by gastric

---

[1] The hepatic veins may be recognized on section from the fact that they remain open being connected closely with the parenchyma.

[2] The ductless glands include the lymph glands, which are described with the organs of circulation; the thyroid and thymus bodies, described usually with the respiratory organs; the adrenal or suprarenal bodies, described with the urinary organs; the pineal and pituitary bodies, described with the brain; and the spleen, described with the digestive system as a matter of convenience. The spleen is not, strictly speaking, a gland at all; it is not epithelial in origin or structure, but is mesenchymatous.

digestion. The author recently observed in a horse, which weighed about 1200 pounds, a spleen which weighed 10¼ pounds, and measured 26 inches in length and 11 inches in width at the base. The ventral end was situated opposite the lower part of the seventh intercostal space. In the new-born foal the weight is about 10 to 12 ounces (ca. 300 gm.). There does not seem to be any con-stant relation to the body-weight. For example, the spleen of a colt of medium size about ten months old weighed three and a half pounds, while it often weighs less than two pounds in horses weighing 1000 to 1200 pounds. The chief variation in outline consists of increase of width, especially of the dorsal part.

It extends obliquely in a curved direction, corresponding to the left part of the greater curvature of the stomach, from the left crus of the diaphragm to the ventral third of the tenth or eleventh rib. It presents for description two surfaces, two borders, and two extremities.

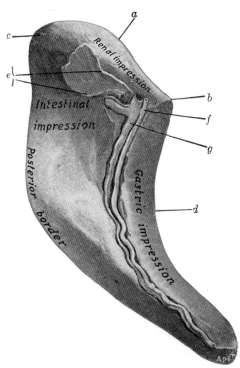

FIG. 376.—SPLEEN OF HORSE, HARDENED *in situ;* VIS-CERAL SURFACE.

a, Dorsal extremity or base; *b, c,* anterior and poste-rior basal angles; *d,* anterior border; *e,* cut edge of sus-pensory ligament; *f, g,* splenic artery and vein in hilus. The area marked intestinal impression is related to the first coil of the small colon. The area enclosed by the suspensory ligament is non-peritoneal.

The **parietal** or **lateral surface** (Fa-cies parietalis) is convex in adaptation to the diaphragm with which it is in con-tact; usually a small part lies against the flank at the angle beween the last rib and the longissimus muscle.

The **visceral** or **medial surface** (Fa-cies visceralis) is in general concave. It is divided into two unequal parts by a longitudinal ridge; on this is a groove, the **hilus,** in which the vessels and nerves are situated. The area in front of the ridge (Facies gastrica) is molded on the greater curvature of the stomach; it is about two inches (ca. 5 cm.) wide. The area behind the ridge (Facies intes-tinalis) is much more extensive; it is related to the small colon, the left parts of the great colon, the small intestine, and the great omentum. It may be marked by one or two fissures.

The **anterior border** (Margo crani-alis) is concave and thin, being wedged in between the diaphragm and the greater curvature of the stomach.

The **posterior border** (Margo cau-dalis) is convex and thin.

The **dorsal extremity** or **base** (Ex-tremitas dorsalis) is beveled, and fits into the interval between the left crus of the diaphragm and sublumbar muscles above, and the saccus cæcus of the stomach and the left kidney below. When hardened *in situ,* it shows an impression (Facies renalis) where it lies against the kidney. The left extremity of the pancreas touches it also. The anterior basal angle fits in between the saccus cæcus of the stomach and the left kidney at the seventeenth thoracic vertebra; the posterior basal angle usually lies against the upper part of the left flank, just behind the last rib.[1]

The **ventral extremity** or **apex** (Extremitas ventralis) is small and varies in position. It is commonly found opposite the tenth or eleventh rib, a handbreadth or more above the costal arch, but may be further forward and higher.

[1] It is uncommon to find the spleen extending more than two or three inches behind the last rib; on the other hand the posterior basal angle may lie just at the last rib. It must also be re-membered in this connection that the occurrence of a nineteenth rib is not rare.

The position of the ventral part depends largely upon two factors—the degree of fulness of the stomach and the size of the spleen. When the stomach is empty or nearly so and the spleen small (contracted), the latter is strongly curved, and its ventral end may be between the left lobe of the liver and the left dorsal part of the great colon. When the stomach is full, it pushes the spleen backward, affecting most the ventral part of the latter. Of course the spleen is affected by the respiratory movements, as may be readily observed by examination per rectum of the living subject.

The spleen is attached by two peritoneal folds, the suspensory ligament and the gastro-splenic omentum. The **suspensory ligament of the spleen** (Lig. suspensorium lienis) attaches the dorsal end to the left crus of the diaphragm and the left kidney; it contains a quantity of elastic tissue. The dorsal layer of the ligament, which passes to the diaphragm, is the ligamentum phrenico-lienale, and blends with the gastro-phrenic ligament; the ventral part, which goes to the kidney, is termed the ligamentum renolienale. The **gastro-splenic omentum** (Lig. gastro-lienale) passes from the hilus to the left part of the greater curvature of the stomach. It is narrow dorsally, where it joins the suspensory ligament; ventrally it becomes much wider and is continuous with the great omentum.

Small globular or lenticular masses of splenic tissue may be found in the gastro-splenic omentum. They are termed **accessory spleens** (Lienes accessorii).

Structure.—The spleen has an almost complete **serous coat** (Tunica serosa). Subjacent to this and intimately united with it is a **capsule** of fibrous tissue (Tunica albuginea), which contains many elastic fibers and some unstriped muscular tissue. Numerous **trabeculæ** (Trabeculæ lienis) are given off from the deep face of the capsule and ramify in the substance of the organ to form a supporting network. In the interstices of this framework is the **spleen pulp** (Pulpa lienis), a dark red, soft, grumous material. This is supported by a delicate reticulum, and contains numerous leukocytes, the large splenic cells, red blood-corpuscles, and pigment. The pulp is richly supplied with blood. The branches of the splenic artery enter at the hilus and pass along the trabeculæ. The arteries which enter the pulp have a sheath of lymphoid tissue, which collects on the vessel wall at certain points, forming small **splenic lymph nodules** (Noduli lymphatici lienales). These are visible to the naked eye as white spots, about as large as the head of a pin. The blood passes into cavernous spaces lined by endothelium which is continuous with the cells of the reticulum of the pulp. From these the veins arise. The splenic vein runs in the hilus in company with the artery and nerves, and joins the posterior gastric vein to form a large radicle of the portal vein.

Vessels and Nerves.—The **arteries** are derived from the splenic artery, which is the largest branch of the cœliac artery. The **splenic vein** lies behind the artery in the hilus; it goes to the portal vein. The **lymph vessels** go to the splenic lymph glands. The **nerves,** derived from the cœliac plexus of the sympathetic, accompany the vessels.

THE PERITONEUM

The general disposition of the peritoneum has been described, and other facts in regard to it were mentioned incidentally in the description of the viscera. It is now desirable to study it as a continuous whole[1] (Figs. 351, 352, 353, 377, 378).

We may consider the peritoneum as consisting of two sacs—a greater and a lesser. The **greater sac** lines the greater part of the abdominal cavity, and covers most of the viscera which have a peritoneal investment. The **lesser sac** is an introversion or invagination of the greater sac, formed during the development of the viscera. The two sacs communicate by a relatively narrow passage, termed

---

[1] The student is strongly recommended to study the peritoneum of a foal or other small subject when the opportunity occurs, as in these the viscera are easily handled, and the course of the peritoneum can be followed without difficulty.

the **epiploic foramen** (Foramen epiploicum).[1] This opening is situated on the visceral surface of the liver dorsal to the portal fissure. It can be entered by passing the finger along the caudate lobe of the liver toward its root. Its dorsal wall is formed by the caudate lobe and the posterior vena cava. Its ventral wall consists of the pancreas, the gastro-pancreatic fold, and the portal vein. The walls are normally in contact, and the passage merely a potential one. It is usually about four inches (ca. 10 cm.) in length. It is narrowest at the lateral extremity, where it is about an inch (ca. 2.5 to 3 cm.) wide.[2] If the finger is passed into the foramen from right to left, it enters the cavity of the lesser sac. If now an opening is made in the great omentum and the other hand introduced through it, the fingers of the two hands can touch each other over the lesser curvature of the stomach. The formation and boundaries of the lesser sac should now be examined by spreading out the great omentum. It will be found that the latter now encloses a considerable cavity behind the stomach; this is termed the **omental cavity** (Bursa omentalis). Passing forward over the lesser curvature of the stomach, we enter another space, the **vestibule** of the omental cavity (Vestibulum bursæ omentalis). This space is

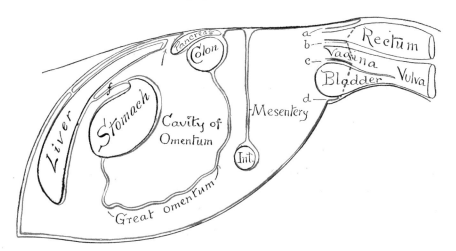

Fig. 377.—Diagram of General Arrangement of Peritoneum (of Mare) in Sagittal Tracing.
a, Sacro-rectal pouch, continuous with *b,* recto-genital pouch; *c,* vesico-genital pouch; *d,* pubo-vesical pouch; *f,* lesser omentum; *Int.,* small intestine. The arrow points to the epiploic foramen.

closed on the left by the gastro-phrenic ligament, ventrally and on the right by the lesser omentum, and dorsally by the gastro-pancreatic fold, which is attached to the dorsal border of the liver and to the posterior vena cava. Above the œsophageal notch there is a recess, into which the fingers can be passed around the border of the liver and the vena cava till the coronary ligament is encountered. Thus the vestibule is closed except—(1) on the right, where it communicates with the cavity of the greater sac by the epiploic foramen; and (2) behind, where it communicates with the cavity of the omentum.

The general arrangement of the **greater omentum** has already been indicated. We may now trace its line of attachment, which would correspond to the mouth of the sac. Beginning at the ventral part of the greater curvature of the stomach, it passes to the ventral face of the pylorus, then crosses obliquely the first part of the duodenum to the point where the pancreas is adherent to it. Here it passes to the anterior face of the terminal part of the great colon, runs along this transversely (from right to left), and continues for some ten or twelve inches (ca. 25

[1] Also known as the foramen of Winslow. Foramen omentale would be better.
[2] The passage is subject to a good deal of variation in caliber and is sometimes occluded.

to 30 cm.) on the small colon. It then forms an acute angle, passes medially and forward along the small colon to the dorsal part of the hilus of the spleen, where it blends with the suspensory ligament of the latter, and forms a recess (Recessus lienalis) behind the saccus cæcus of the stomach. It now passes along the hilus of the spleen, and is continued to the greater curvature of the stomach by the gastro-splenic omentum. It is convenient to regard the spleen as being intercalated in the left part of the greater omentum; on this basis the gastro-splenic omentum would be that part of the greater omentum which connects the hilus of the spleen with the greater curvature of the stomach. The greater omentum is relatively small in the horse, and is usually not visible when the abdomen is opened. It is generally folded up in the space between the visceral surface of the stomach and the intestine.[1]

The lesser sac furnishes the peritoneal covering for: (1) the visceral surface of the stomach and a small area of the first curve of the duodenum; (2) a large part of the dorsal surface of the pancreas and portal vein; (3) a small part of the visceral surface of the liver above the attachment of the lesser omentum and the portal fissure; (4) the posterior vena cava, from the level of the epiploic foramen to its passage through the diaphragm (in so far as it is not embedded); (5) the part of the parietal surface of the liver between the right and middle divisions of the coronary ligament; (6) the corresponding part of the diaphragm, and the right part of the right crus of the same; (7) part of the anterior surface of the terminal part of the great colon, and the origin of the small colon; (8) the left extremity of the pancreas (inconstant); (9) the spleen.

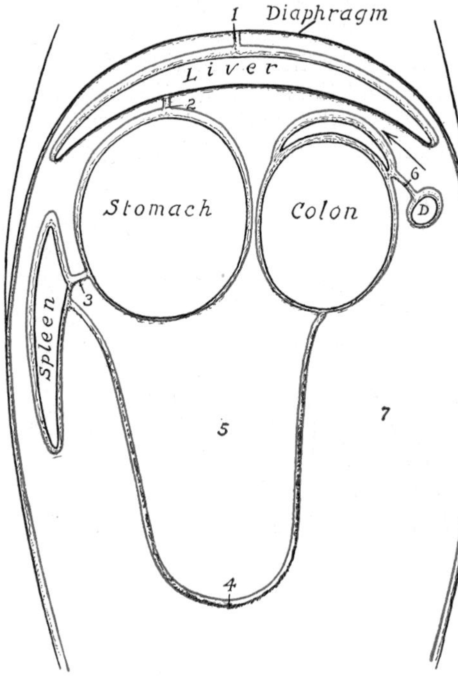

We may now trace the peritoneum in a longitudinal direction, beginning in front. It is reflected from the ventral abdominal wall and the diaphragm upon the liver, forming the ligaments and serous coat of the gland. It leaves the visceral surface of the liver as lesser omentum, and the crura of the diaphragm as the gastrophrenic ligament, reaches the saccus cæcus and lesser curvature of the stomach and the first curve of the duodenum, covers these organs, and is continued by the greater omentum.

On the left it passes from the left crus of the diaphragm and the left kidney to form the suspensory ligament of the spleen, clothes that organ, and leaves it to be continued by the greater and gastro-splenic omenta.

On the right it passes from the right crus of the diaphragm and the dorsal border of the liver to the concave border of the duodenum, forming the gastropancreatic fold (second part of the mesoduodenum), and covering part of the dorsal surface of the pancreas. From the margin of the pancreas, the right kidney, and a small area of the sublumbar region behind the latter, it passes on to the base of

Fig. 378.—Diagram of Abdominal Peritoneum in Frontal (or Horizontal) Tracing.

D, Duodenum; 1, falciform ligament; 2, lesser omentum; 3, gastro-splenic omentum; 4, greater omentum; 5, cavity of omentum; 6, mesoduodenum; 7, general peritoneal cavity. Arrow indicates epiploic foramen. By an oversight the pancreas, in front of the colon, is not marked.

[1] In dissecting-room subjects (which are usually aged) the omentum often exhibits pathological changes, such as adhesions, rents, tumors, formation of twisted strands, etc.

the cæcum and the terminal part of the great colon. From these it passes on the right to the duodenum, forming the third part of the mesoduodenum. On the left it covers part of the ventral surface and the lateral border of the left kidney, from which it passes to the base of the spleen, forming the ventral layer of the suspensory ligament of the latter. Behind the terminal part of the great colon it is reflected from the abdominal wall around the great mesenteric artery to form the great mesentery. Behind this it is reflected almost transversely from the roof of the cavity and from the origin of the small colon on to the duodenum, forming the terminal part of the mesoduodenum. The line of origin of the colic mesentery begins on the medial part of the ventral surface of the left kidney, and extends to the sacral promontory, where the mesorectum begins. At the termination of the latter the peritoneum is reflected from the rectum on to the dorsal and lateral walls of the pelvic cavity. Below the rectum it forms the genital fold, and passes on to the dorsal surface of the bladder, covers its anterior part, and is reflected on to the body-wall laterally and ventrally, forming the lateral and middle ligaments of the bladder. In the female the broad ligaments of the uterus replace the genital fold, with which they are homologous.

In the new-born foal certain folds are specially large. The falciform ligament of the liver extends to the umbilical opening, and contains in its free edge the large umbilical vein. The bladder—at this time an abdominal organ—has a ventral median fold (Plica umbilicalis media), which connects it and the urachus with the abdominal floor. This is flanked on either side by a fold (Plica umbilicalis lateralis), which also extends to the umbilicus, and contains the large umbilical artery.

DIGESTIVE SYSTEM OF THE OX

THE MOUTH

The **cavity of the mouth** is shorter and wider than that of the horse, and the vestibule is more capacious (Figs. 381, 386).

The **lips** are thick, wide, and comparatively immobile. The middle part of the upper lip and the surface between the nostrils is bare, and is termed the muzzle (Planum nasolabiale). It is smooth, and (in health) is kept cool and moist by a clear fluid secreted by the **naso-labial** glands (Glandulæ nasolabiales); they form a subcutaneous layer about half an inch (ca. 1.5 cm.) thick. It shows irregular lines, mapping out small polygonal areas on which the orifices of the gland ducts are visible. There is also a narrow bare strip along the edge of the lower lip. The remainder of the integument is provided with ordinary and tactile hairs. The free edge and the adjacent part of the lining membrane bear short, blunt, horny **papillæ**; toward the angles the papillæ become longer and sharp-pointed. The **labial glands** occur only near the angles, where they form compact masses (Fig. 385).

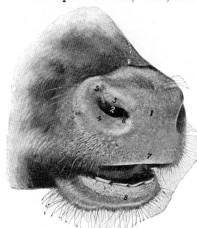

FIG. 379.—LIPS AND MUZZLE OF OX.

1, Muzzle; 2, nostril; 3, 4, wings of nostril; 5, 6, commissures of nostril; 7, 8, upper and lower lip.

The **cheeks** are more capacious than in the horse. The mucous membrane presents large pointed **conical papillæ** (Papillæ conicæ), which are directed toward the isthmus faucium and are covered with a horny epithelium. The largest of these have a length of about half an inch (ca. 1 to 1.5 cm.) and are situated around the angle of the mouth and parallel with the cheek teeth. The orifice of the parotid duct is opposite the fifth upper cheek tooth. The **buccal glands** (Fig. 385) are very

well developed, and are arranged in three parts. The dorsal part extends from the angle of the mouth to the maxillary tuberosity; its lobules are of a light yellow color. The ventral part consists of a compact brownish mass which reaches from the angle of the mouth a short distance under the masseter muscle. The middle part consists of loosely arranged yellow lobules. The small ducts of these glands open between the papillæ of the cheek.

A linear series of large papillæ exists on the floor of the mouth on each side of the frenum linguæ. Near these are found the openings of the small ducts of the sublingual gland. The caruncula sublingualis, the papilla on which the mandibular duct opens, is wide, hard, and has a serrated edge (Fig. 383).

The **hard palate** is wide, and is usually more or less pigmented. The body of the premaxilla is covered with a thick layer of dense connective tissue, which has a thick, horny epithelial covering—forming the so-called dental plate or pad. The palatine ridges extend from this backward about two-thirds of the length of the hard palate; they number 15 to 19. They are nearly straight, and, with the exception of a few at the poste-

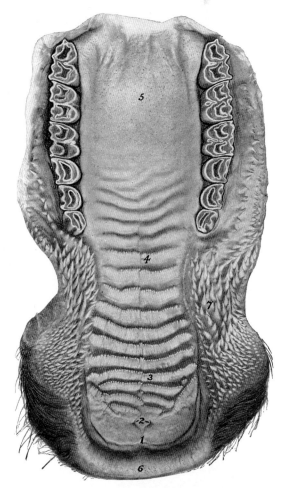

FIG. 380.—HARD PALATE OF OX.

1, Dental pad or plate; 2, placed on papilla incisiva with lines to orifices of ductus incisivi; 3, ridge of palate; 4, raphé of palate; 5, smooth part of palate showing orifices of palatine glands; 6, upper lip; 7, conical papillæ of cheek.

rior end of the series, are serrated on the free edge. A median raphé extends between the ridges. The posterior third of the palate is smooth. Between the dental plate and the first ridge is the triangular **papilla incisiva**; on either side of this is a deep furrow, in which is the oral opening of the **ductus incisivus**.[1] The duct is two inches or more (ca. 5 to 6 cm.) in length and opens on the floor of the nasal cavity; it also communicates by a slit-like opening with the vomeronasal organ.

[1] This is also known as the naso-palatine canal.

The **soft palate** is somewhat shorter than that of the horse, but is long enough to close the isthmus faucium. The posterior pillars do not extend to the origin of the œsophagus. The palatinus muscle is much better developed than in the horse. The fibrous aponeurosis is for the most part replaced by muscular tissue.

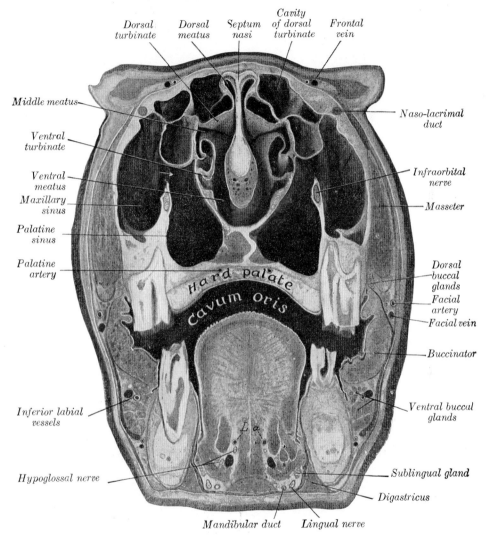

FIG. 381.—CROSS-SECTION OF HEAD OF OX.

The section passes through the medial canthi. *L. a.*, Lingual arteries. The arrow indicates the communication between the maxillary and palatine sinuses.

The **isthmus faucium** is wide and dilatable. On either side, behind the anterior pillar of the soft palate, there is a deep depression, the **tonsillar sinus** (Sinus tonsillaris); lateral to this is the compact, bean-shaped tonsil, which is about one to one and a half inches (ca. 3 to 4 cm.) in length. The tonsil does not project into the isthmus faucium, but outward instead: hence it does not occupy the tonsillar sinus, and is not visible internally, as is the case in most animals.

THE TONGUE

The tongue of the ox is often variably pigmented. The root and body are wider than that of the horse, but the tip is pointed and has a rather narrow edge. The posterior part of the dorsum forms an elliptical prominence, which is defined in front by a transverse depression. In front of this prominence there are large and horny filiform and conical papillæ with sharp points directed backward; they impart to the tip especially its rasp-like roughness and thus make it very efficient

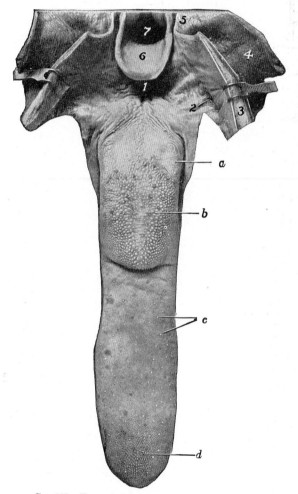

Fig. 382.—Tongue and Fauces of Ox; Dorsal View.

The pharynx and soft palate are cut dorsally and reflected. *a*, Vallate papillæ; *b*, prominence of dorsum with broad, flattened papillæ; *c*, fungiform papillæ; *d*, filiform papillæ of tip; *1*, glosso-epiglottic space; *2*, tonsillar sinus; *3*, cut surface of soft palate; *4*, pharynx; *5*, posterior pillar of soft palate; *6*, epiglottis; *7*, aditus laryngis.

in the prehension of food. The papillæ on the prominence are large, broad, and horny; some have a blunt, conical form, others are rounded or flattened and are termed **lenticular papillæ** (Papillæ lenticulares). The fungiform papillæ are numerous and distinct; they are scattered over the dorsum and edges of the free part. The vallate papillæ number 8 to 17 on each side; they are smaller than those of the horse, and form a long, narrow group on either side of the posterior part of the prominence of the dorsum. The foliate papillæ and the lingual fibrous cord are absent. There are lingual follicles in the posterior part of the root and on each side of the glosso-epiglottic fold. The muscles are well developed, and resemble in general those of the horse; the hyo-glossus arises by additional portions from the great and middle cornua of the hyoid bone. The tongue is highly protractile and is the chief organ of prehension.

THE TEETH[1]

The formula of the permanent teeth of the ox is:

$$2\left(I\ \frac{0}{4}-C\ \frac{0}{0}-P\ \frac{3}{3}-M\ \frac{3}{3}\right)=32$$

The **incisors** are absent from the upper jaw. There are eight incisors in the lower jaw, arranged in a somewhat fan-like manner. They are simple teeth, without infundibulum. The crown is white, short, and shovel-shaped; it has labial and lingual surfaces, which meet at a sharp edge in front. The crown is at first entirely covered with enamel, but later as a masticatory surface is developed through wear, the dentine comes into view on that surface. The root is rounded, and is

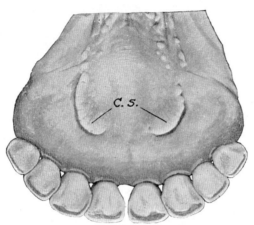

Fig. 383.—Incisor Teeth of Ox; Lingual Aspect.
C. s., Carunculæ sublinguales.

embedded in the jaw in such a manner as to allow a small amount of movement. There is a distinct neck. In addition to the simple numerical designation, the following terms are commonly applied to the individual teeth: central, first intermediate, second intermediate, and corner incisors. It is probable that the latter are much modified canines. The incisors of the adult ox do not undergo continued eruption, as is the case in the horse; in old age, however, the gum retracts so that the roots are partly exposed and may come into wear.[2] The **deciduous incisors** differ from the permanent set chiefly in being much smaller. The crowns are narrower and diverge more.

The **canines** are absent (unless the fourth incisors be considered to represent them in the lower jaw).[3]

The **cheek teeth** (Figs. 134, 384) resemble those of the horse in number and general arrangement. They are, however, smaller, and also differ in the fact that they progressively increase in size from before backward. This feature is so marked that the first tooth is quite small, and the space occupied by the first three (*i. e.* the premolars) is only about one-half of that required for the posterior three (*i. e.,* the molars). The enamel folds stand out even more prominently in relief on the masticatory surface than in the horse. The occurrence of wolf-teeth is rare.

[1] Other figures which show the teeth are to be found in the description of the skull.

[2] The reader will note here the difference between the structure and behavior of the brachydont (short-crowned) incisors of the ox and the hypsodont (long-crowned) type of the horse.

[3] According to A. Hoffman, the anlagen of the upper canines are present in the foetus, but soon disappear.

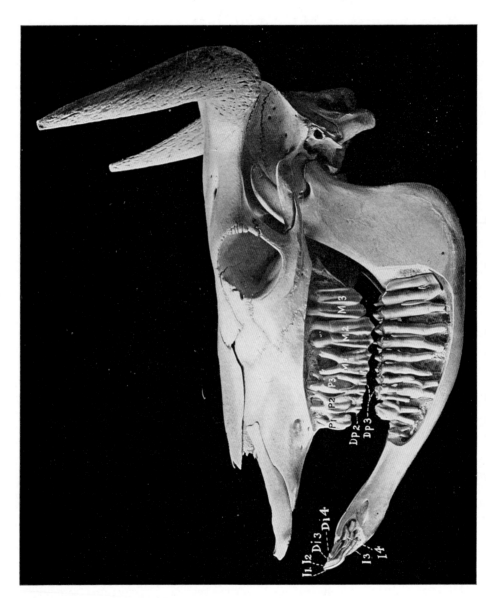

Fig. 384.—Skull of Ox Two Years of Age, Sculptured to Show the Embedded Parts of the Teeth.

I1–4, Permanent incisor teeth, the third and fourth not erupted; *Di. 3, 4*, third and fourth deciduous incisors; *P1–3*, upper permanent premolars, only first erupted; *Dp. 2, 3*, deciduous premolars; *M1–3*, molars.

The formula of the deciduous teeth is:

$$2\left(\text{Di}\,\frac{0}{4} - \text{Dc}\,\frac{0}{0} - \text{Dp}\,\frac{3}{3}\right) = 20$$

TABLE OF AVERAGE PERIODS OF ERUPTION OF THE TEETH IN THE OX

Teeth	Eruption
A. Temporary:	
First incisor (Di 1)	
Second incisor (Di 2)	
Third incisor (Di 3)	Birth to 2 weeks.
Fourth incisor (Di 4)	
First cheek tooth (Dp 1)	Birth to 2 weeks.
Second cheek tooth (Dp 2)	
Third cheek tooth (Dp 3)	Birth to few days.
B. Permanent:	
First incisor (I 1)	1½ to 2 years.
Second incisor (I 2)	2 to 2½ years.
Third incisor (I 3)	3 years.
Fourth incisor (I 4)	3½ to 4 years.
First cheek tooth (P 1)	2 to 2½ years.
Second cheek tooth (P 2)	1½ to 2½ years.
Third cheek tooth (P 3)	2½ to 3 years.
Fourth cheek tooth (M 1)	5 to 6 months.
Fifth cheek tooth (M 2)	1 to 1½ years.
Sixth cheek tooth (M 3)	2 to 2½ years.

The eruption of the deciduous teeth varies somewhat. About 75 percent of well-bred calves have all incisors erupted at birth.

Fig. 385.—Salivary Glands of Ox.

a, Parotid gland; *b*, mandibular gland; *c*, ventral, *d*, middle, and *e*, dorsal buccal glands; *f*, labial glands; *g*, buccinator nerve; *h*, buccinator vein; *1*, masseter (cut); *2*, ramus of mandible; *3*, zygomaticus muscle; *4*, conical papillæ of lip; *5*, buccinator muscle. (After Ellenberger, in Leisering's Atlas.)

The eruption of the permanent teeth is subject to great variation. The above figures are the average of observations of improved breeds under favorable conditions.

THE SALIVARY GLANDS

The **parotid gland** is smaller and denser in texture than that of the horse, and is light red-brown in color; its average weight is about four ounces (ca. 115 g.). It has somewhat the form of a very narrow long triangle, and lies chiefly on the posterior part of the masseter muscle. The dorsal part is wide and thick; its anterior border partly covers the parotid lymph gland. The small ventral end is bent forward and fits into the angle of union of the jugular and external maxillary veins; it lies on the mandibular gland. The parotid duct leaves the ventral part of the deep face; it follows in its course the ventral and anterior borders of the masseter, lying between the muscle and the external maxillary vein, and pierces the cheek opposite the fifth upper cheek tooth.

The **mandibular gland** is larger than the parotid, and is pale yellow in color; its average weight is about five ounces (ca. 140 g.). It is covered to a small extent by the parotid. Its general form resembles that of the horse, but its ventral end is large and rounded, and is separated by a small interval only from the gland of the other side (Fig. 302). This part can be felt in the living animal, and is related laterally to the mandibular lymph gland. The duct leaves the middle of the concave border of the gland, crosses the stylohyoideus and the intermediate tendon of the digastricus, and ends at the caruncula sublingualis.

The **sublingual gland** consists of two parts. The dorsal part (Glandula sublingualis parvicanalaris) is long, thin, and pale yellow in color. It extends from the anterior pillar of the soft palate about to the symphysis of the mandible. It has numerous small tortuous ducts (Ductus sublinguales minores), which open between the papillæ under the side of the tongue. The ventral part (Glandula sublingualis grandicanalaris) is shorter and thicker, and lies ventral to the anterior portion of the dorsal part; it is salmon pink in color. It has a single duct (Ductus sublingualis major), which either opens alongside of or joins the mandibular duct.

THE PHARYNX (Figs. 386, 476, 478)

The pharynx is short and wide. The vault (Fornix pharyngis) is divided into two culs-de-sac by a median fold of mucous membrane (Septum nasi membranaceum), which is a continuation of that of the septum nasi; on the lateral wall of each is the relatively small opening of the Eustachian tube, which is covered by a simple fold of mucous membrane. The choanæ or posterior nares are small. The entrance to the œsophagus is large.

On the dorsal wall of the pharynx there are two large suprapharyngeal lymph glands, which, when enlarged, cause difficulty in swallowing and breathing (Fig. 386).

THE ŒSOPHAGUS

This is much shorter, wider, and more dilatable than that of the horse. Its average diameter (when moderately inflated) is about two inches (ca. 5 cm.), and its length in an animal of medium size is about three to three and a half feet (ca. 90 to 105 cm.). The wall is relatively thin, and the muscular tissue is striped throughout. The latter consists, in the greater part of the tube, of two strata of spiral fibers, except near the stomach, where they are longitudinal and circular. Fibers are continued into the wall of the stomach for some distance. The mucous membrane forms a prominence at the ventral side of the pharyngeal end of the tube which contains glands; elsewhere it is non-glandular. There is not terminal dilatation, and no part in the abdominal cavity.

A very large mediastinal lymph gland lies above the posterior part of the œsophagus and may, if enlarged, obstruct it (Fig. 389a).

THE ABDOMINAL CAVITY

The abdominal cavity of the ox is very capacious, both absolutely and relatively, as compared with that of the horse.   This is due to several factors.   The lumbar part of the spine is about one-fourth longer than that of the horse.   The transverse diameter between the last ribs is greater.   The costal attachment of the diaphragm rises very steeply from the ventral part of the eighth rib to the dorsal

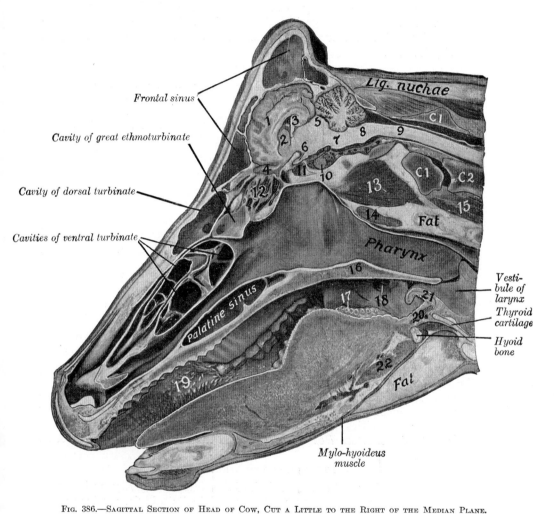

Fig. 386.—Sagittal Section of Head of Cow, Cut a Little to the Right of the Median Plane.

1, Cerebral hemisphere; *2*, corpus striatum; *3*, hippocampus; *4*, olfactory bulb; *5*, corpora quadrigemina; *6*, optic nerve; *7*, pons; *8*, medulla oblongata; *9*, spinal cord; *10*, pituitary body; *11*, sphenoidal sinus; *12*, lateral mass of ethmoid; *13*, ventral straight muscles; *14*, suprapharyngeal lymph gland; *15*, longus colli; *16*, soft palate; *17*, vallate papillæ; *18*, tonsillar sinus; *19*, conical papillæ of cheek; *20*, hyo-epiglotticus muscle; *21*, epiglottis; *22*, hyoglossus muscle; *C1, C2*, atlas, axis.   Subject was hardened with mouth open.

fourth of the last.[1]   Thus the abdomen is increased at the expense of the thorax, and the last four ribs enter more largely into the formation of the abdominal wall than in the horse.   The flank is also much more extensive.   The ilia, on the other hand, do not extend forward beyond a transverse plane through the middle of the last lumbar vertebra.   The chief differential features in the arrangement of the

[1] The costal part of the diaphragm may end at the twelfth rib.

peritoneum will be described with the viscera. The subperitoneal tissue is more abundant than in the horse, and in general contains a much larger amount of fat.

THE PELVIC CAVITY

The pelvic cavity is relatively long and narrow. The inlet is more oblique than that of the horse; it is elliptical in outline and the transverse diameter is smaller than that of the horse. The pubic part of the floor is about horizontal, but the ischiatic part slopes dorsally to a marked degree and is also deeply concave transversely. The roof is concave in both directions. The peritoneum extends backward as far as the first coccygeal vertebra, so that the retroperitoneal part of the cavity is short.

THE STOMACH

General Arrangement.—The stomach of the ox is very large, and occupies nearly three-fourths of the abdominal cavity. It fills the left half of the cavity (except the small space occupied by the spleen and a few coils of small intestine) and extends considerably over the median plane into the right half. It is compound, and consists of four parts, viz., **rumen, reticulum, omasum,** and **abomasum,**[1] and takes its form very early in fetal life (Fig. 386a). The division is indicated externally by furrows or constrictions. The first three parts are often regarded as **proventriculi** or œsophageal sacculations, since they are lined with a mucous membrane which is covered with squamous stratified epithelium and is nonglandular, which condition exists when they take their form. The abomasum, on the other hand, has a glandular mucous membrane and hence is popularly termed the "true stomach." The œsophagus opens into the stomach on a sort of dome, the **atrium ventriculi.** The abomasum joins the small intestine.

Capacity.—The capacity of the stomach varies greatly, depending on the age and size of the animal. In cattle of medium size it holds 30 to 40 gallons, in large animals 40 to 60, in small, 25 to 35. The relative sizes of the four parts vary with age, in correlation with the nature of the food. In the new-born calf the rumen and reticulum together are about half as large as the abomasum; in ten or twelve weeks this ratio is reversed. During this period the omasum appears to be contracted and functionless. At four months the rumen and reticulum together are about four times as large as the omasum and abomasum together, but are collapsed and functionless. At about one and one-half years the omasum equals or closely approaches the abomasum in capacity. The four parts have now reached their definitive relative capacities, the rumen constituting about 80 per cent., the reticulum 5 per cent., the omasum 7 or 8 per cent., and the abomasum 8 or 7 per cent. of the total amount.

EXTERIOR AND RELATIONS

The **rumen** occupies most of the left half of the abdominal cavity, and extends considerably over the median plane ventrally and in its middle. Its long axis reaches from a point opposite the ventral part of the seventh or eighth intercostal space almost to the pelvic inlet. It is somewhat compressed from side to side and may be described as having two surfaces, two curvatures or borders, and two extremities. The **parietal** (or left) **surface** (Facies parietalis) is convex and is related to the diaphragm, left wall of the abdomen, and spleen. The **visceral** (or right) **surface** (Facies visceralis) is somewhat irregular, and is related chiefly to the omasum and abomasum, the intestine, the liver, pancreas, left kidney, the left adrenal, the aorta and the posterior vena cava. The **dorsal curvature** (Curvatura dorsalis) follows the curve formed by the left part of the crura of the diaphragm and the sublumbar muscles; it is firmly attached to these by peritoneum and con-

---

[1] In popular language these are regarded as so many stomachs, and are often designated numerically. Other names are in common use, e. g., paunch, honeycomb, manifold or manyplies, and rennet or true stomach.

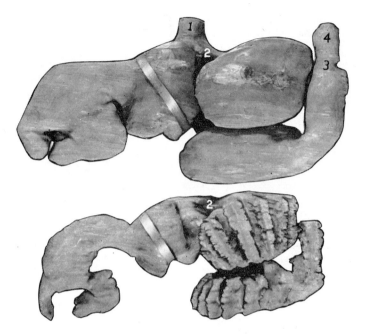

FIG. 386a.—MODELS OF THE EXTERIOR, *above*, AND OF THE CAVITY, *below*, OF THE STOMACH FROM A 48 MM. CALF EMBRYO 12.5X.

1, œsophagus; 2, reticulum; 3, pylorus; 4, duodenum. (Dr. H. M. Amstutz, M.D.)

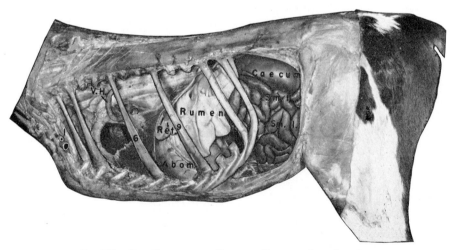

FIG. 386b.—DEEP DISSECTION OF NEW-BORN GUERNSEY CALF; LEFT SIDE.

Left lung, diaphragm and spleen have been removed. Part of wall of rumen and reticulum cut away. 1, First **rib**, (brachial vessels below 1); 6, 9, sixth and ninth ribs; Abom., abomasum; Ret., reticulum; Sm. I., small intestines; V. H., vena hemiazygos

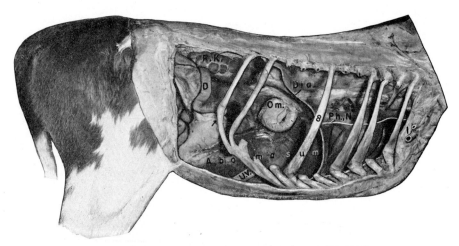

Fig. 386c.—Deep Dissection of a New-born Guernsey Calf: Right Side.

Right lung, liver and diaphragm removed. The right portion of the omasum has been cut away. 1, First rib, (brachial vessels at right of 1); 8, eighth rib; D, duodenum; Dia., cut edge of diaphragm; Om., omasum; Ph. N., right phrenic nerve; R. K., right kidney; U. V., umbilical vein; Arrow indicates pylorus.

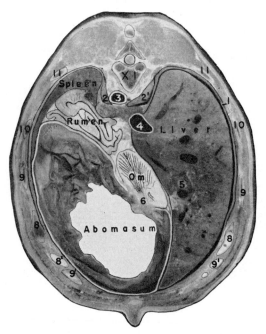

Fig. 386d.—Cross Section of a New-born Guernsey Calf.

The section is cut at the eleventh thoracic vertebra. 1, Cut edge of diaphragm; 2, 2′, tips of left and right lungs; 3, aorta; 4, posterior vena cava; 5, venous sinus of the liver; 6, omasal-abomasal orifice; 8, 8′, eighth rib and its costal cartilage; 9, 9′, ninth rib and its costal cartilage: 10, 11, tenth and eleventh ribs; Om., omasum.

nective tissue as far back as the fourth lumbar vertebra. The **ventral curvature** (Curvatura ventralis) is also convex and lies on the floor of the abdomen. The surfaces are marked by the **right** and **left grooves** (Sulcus ruminis dexter, sinister), which indicate externally the division of the rumen into dorsal and ventral sacs.[1] The **reticular** (or anterior) **extremity** (Extremitas reticularis) is divided ventrally by a transverse **anterior groove** (Sulcus ruminis cranialis) into two sacs. The dorsal sac is the longer of the two, and curves ventrally over the round, blind end of the ventral sac. The former is continuous with the reticulum, the external line of demarcation being the **rumino-reticular groove** (Sulcus rumino-reticularis). The groove is deep ventrally and is distinct on part of the lateral surface, but dorsally no natural separation exists, the rumen and reticulum together forming a dome-like vestibule (Atrium ventriculi) on which the œsophagus terminates. The **pelvic**

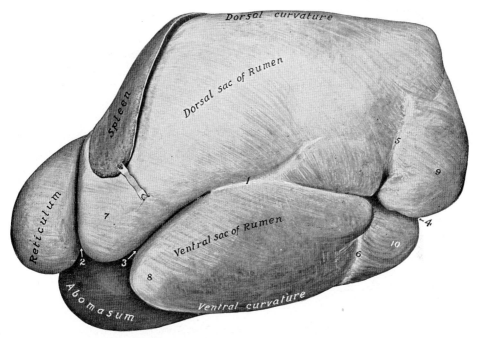

Fig. 387.—Stomach and Spleen of Ox; Left View.

1, Left groove of rumen; 2, rumino-reticular groove (not so distinct dorsally as shown here); 3, anterior groove of rumen; 4, posterior groove of rumen; 5, 6, coronary grooves; 7, 8, anterior, 9, 10, posterior, blind sacs of rumen.

(or posterior) **extremity** (Extremitas pelvina), extends nearly to the pubis; it is related to the intestine and bladder. It is divided into **dorsal** and **ventral blind sacs** (Saccus cæcus caudalis dorsalis, ventralis) by a deep transverse **posterior groove** (Sulcus ruminis caudalis), which connects the longitudinal grooves. The blind sacs are marked off from the remainder of the rumen by the **dorsal** and **ventral coronary grooves** (Sulcus coronarius dorsalis, ventralis).

The left groove begins at the anterior transverse groove, passes somewhat dorsally and backward and divides into two grooves. The ventral one is the chief groove, and passes backward and is continuous with the posterior groove. The dorsal (accessory) groove curves dorsally and then backward to terminate in the dorsal coronary sulcus. On the right surface there are two grooves. The dorsal one is the chief sulcus. It extends in a curved direction (the con-

---

[1] It has been customary to term the sacs left and right respectively, but these terms do not indicate well the relations as they exist *in situ* and as they are presented on frozen sections. When the stomach is removed in the soft state, it loses its shape and the dorsal and ventral sacs of the rumen become left and right.

vexity being dorsal), and is continuous with the transverse grooves between the dorsal and ventral blind sacs at each end. The ventral groove (Sulcus accessorius) curves somewhat ventrally and backward and joins the chief sulcus.

In many subjects, especially those well fed, the ventral sac has considerable contact with the ventral part of the right flank; it is then separated from the abdominal wall by the greater omentum.

The **reticulum** is the most anterior and the smallest of the four divisions; it is opposite to the ribs from the sixth to the seventh or eighth. The greater part of it lies on the left of the median plane. It is somewhat piriform, but compressed from before backward. The **parietal** or **diaphragmatic surface** (Facies diaphragmatica) faces forward; it is convex and lies against the diaphragm and liver.[1] The **visceral**

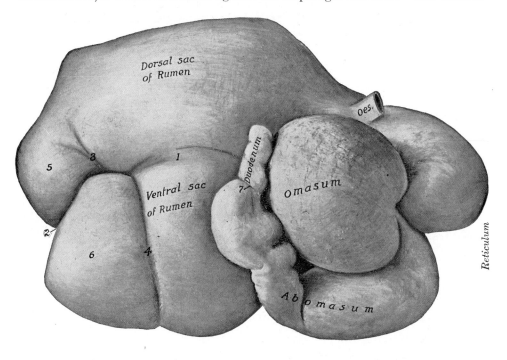

FIG. 388.—STOMACH OF OX; RIGHT VIEW.

Oes., Œsophagus; 1, right longitudinal groove of rumen; 2, posterior groove of rumen; 3, 4, coronary grooves; 5, 6, posterior blind sacs of rumen; 7, pylorus.

or **ruminal surface** (Facies ruminalis) faces backward; it is flattened more or less by the pressure of the other three compartments; it ends dorsally by joining the wall of the rumen, the concave line of junction corresponding to a ridge in the interior of the stomach which forms the lower margin of the large rumino-reticular orifice. The **lesser curvature** faces to the right and dorsally, and is connected with the omasum. The **greater curvature** faces to the left and ventrally; it lies against the diaphragm, opposite the sixth and seventh ribs. The **right extremity** or **fundus reticuli** forms a rounded cul-de-sac, which is in contact with the sternal part of the diaphragm, the liver, omasum, and abomasum; it is opposite to the ventral end of the sixth intercostal space.

The **omasum** is ellipsoidal in form and somewhat compressed between the pari-

[1] It is important to notice that the most anterior part of the reticulum is in contact with the diaphragm which in turn is in contact here with the pericardium and lungs. Foreign bodies which are often swallowed by cattle commonly lodge in the reticulum, and not rarely (if sharp) perforate the reticulum and diaphragm. When the reticulum is full its visceral surface is opposite to the eighth rib.

etal and visceral surfaces, the long axis is nearly vertical. It is clearly marked off from the other divisions. It lies chiefly to the right of the median plane, opposite the seventh to the eleventh ribs inclusive. The **parietal** (right) **surface** faces obliquely to the right and forward, and is related chiefly to the diaphragm and liver; below the latter a small area lies against the lateral wall at the ventral part of the ribs from the eighth to the tenth, from which it is separated by the lesser omentum and the diaphragm in part. The **visceral** (left) **surface** faces in the opposite direction and is in contact with the rumen, reticulum and abomasum. The **greater curvature** faces backward and to the right. The **lesser curvature** is relatively very short and faces forward and to the left so that it is visible from the left side after removal of the rumen and reticulum. It is connected in its upper part with the reticulum by a very short, narrow **neck of the omasum** (Collum omasi). Below this it is crossed by a deep indentation, which corresponds to the thick muscular omasal pillar to be seen in the interior. Immediately below the indentation is the extensive junction with the abomasum. The junction is much more extensive than the lumen of the orifice of the communication between the two sacs.[1]

The **abomasum** is an elongated sac which lies chiefly on the abdominal floor. The anterior blind end, the **fundus,** is in the xiphoid region in relation to the reticulum to which it is in part attached. The **body** of the sac extends backward between the ventral sac of the rumen and the omasum, and turns to the right behind the latter. The terminal, smaller **pyloric part** inclines dorsally and joins the duodenum at the pylorus, which is usually situated at or near the ventral part of the ninth or tenth rib. The **parietal surface** is in contact mainly with the abdominal floor, while the **visceral surface** is for the most part related to the rumen and omasum. The **greater curvature** gives attachment to the superficial part of the greater omentum, except at the fundus, which is adherent to the rumen. The **lesser curvature** is related to the omasum to which it is attached by peritoneum and connective tissue with more or less fat, except at the pyloric part, which is attached to the liver by the lesser omentum.

The form and position of the abomasum are variable. The turn to the right is often about at a right angle, but may be even sharper. In other cases the sac gradually inclines toward the right costal arch. These variations are chiefly due to the amount of fulness of the other divisions of the stomach.

The rumen is attached by peritoneum and connective tissue to the crura of the diaphragm and sublumbar muscles, from the hiatus œsophageus backward to the fourth or fifth lumbar vertebra. A small area of the anterior part of the visceral surface of the rumen is adherent to the adjacent surface of the abomasum. The greater part of the lesser curvature of the omasum is attached by connective tissue to the abomasum.[2]

The **lesser omentum** attaches the ventral part of the parietal surface of the omasum and the pyloric part of the abomasum to the visceral surface of the liver.

INTERIOR

The cavity of the rumen is partially divided into dorsal and ventral sacs by the **pillars** (Pilæ ruminis); these are folds of the wall, strengthened by additional muscular fibers, and correspond with the grooves on the outside. The two extensive chief pillars project like shelves into the anterior and posterior ends of the cavity, forming the blind sacs at either extremity. The **anterior pillar** (Pila cranialis) projects obliquely backward and upward from the ventral wall, and has a thick,

[1] The most ventral part of the omasum is in contact with the abdominal floor over a small area between the right costal arch, the xiphoid cartilage, and the lesser curvature of the abomasum.

[2] Adhesion of the reticulum to the diaphragm or liver is common in adult cattle, but is pathological.

concave free edge which is opposite to the eleventh and twelfth ribs. Its width from the middle of the free edge to its attached border is about eight to ten inches (ca. 20 to 25 cm.). It is continued on either side by the relatively narrow **right** and **left**

FIG. 389.—DISSECTION OF HOLSTEIN COW; LEFT SIDE.

1, First rib (brachial vessels at left of *1*); *2,* transversus abdominis showing through space between dorsal and ventral parts of obliquus abdominis internus; *3,* portion of aponeurosis of obliquus abdominis externus; *4,* m. iliacus; *5,* œsophagus; *6,* cut edge of diaphragm; *7,* seventh rib; *L.L.,* left lung; *Lgg.,* supramammary lymph glands; *M,* mediastinum removed exposing apical lobe of right lung; *P,* pericardium; *R,* rumen; *Re,* reticulum; *S,* spleen. The second, fourth, sixth and eighth ribs have been removed. Dotted line denotes the phrenico-costal line.

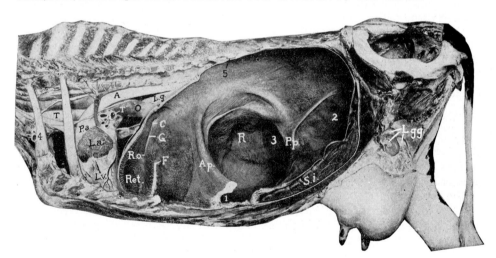

FIG. 389*a.*—DEEP DISSECTION OF HOLSTEIN COW; LEFT SIDE.

The lungs and pericardium have been removed. Most of the left wall of the rumen and reticulum has been cut away. *1, 2, 3,* Blind sacs of rumen; *4,* first rib (brachial vessels at left of *4*); *5,* vertebral end of thirteenth rib; *A,* aorta; *Ap., P.p.,* anterior and posterior pillars of rumen; *C,* cardia; *F,* rumino-reticular fold; *G,* reticular groove; *L.a.,* left auricle; *L.g.,* posterior mediastinal lymph gland (large one); *Lgg.,* supramammary lymph glands; *L.V.,* left ventricle; *O,* œsophagus; *P.a.,* pulmonary artery; *P.p.,* posterior pillar of rumen; *R,* rumen; *Ret.,* reticulum; *R.O.,* reticulo-omasal opening; *S.i.,* small intestines; *T,* trachea; *T′,* left bronchus.

pillars (Pila dexter, sinister). The **posterior pillar** (Pila caudalis) is more nearly horizontal than the anterior one, and separates the large dorsal and ventral posterior blind sacs. Its concave anterior border is about a handbreadth in front of a transverse plane through the tuber coxæ. It branches on either side to form the **dorsal** and **ventral coronary pillars** (Pila coronaria dorsalis, ventralis), which mark off the posterior blind sacs from the general cavity on the sides and ventrally. It will be noticed that the ventral coronary pillar is complete, while the dorsal one

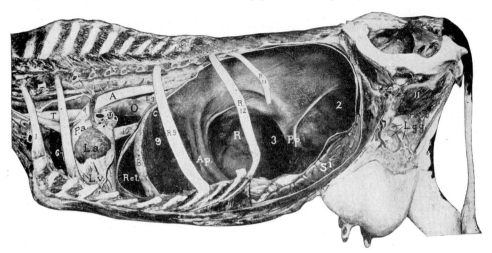

Fig. 390.—Deep Dissection of Holstein Cow; Left Side. Ribs Nine, Twelve and Thirteen (Rib Thirteen had no Costal Cartilage) Retained for Landmarks on Rumen.

A, Aorta; *A.p.*, anterior pillar of rumen; *C*, cardia; *L.a.*, left auricle; *L.g.*, posterior mediastinal lymph gland; *L.v.*, left ventricle; *O*, œsophagus; *P.a.*, pulmonary artery; *P.p.*, posterior pillar of rumen; *R*, rumen; *Ret.*, reticulum; *R.9, R.12, R.13*, ribs nine, twelve and thirteen; *S.i.*, small intestine; *T*, trachea; *U*, left bronchus (opening of pulmonary artery to left of *U*); *1*, first rib (brachial vessels to left of *1*); *2, 3*, posterior blind sacs of rumen; *4*, vagus nerve (recurrent branching off and passing over the ligamentum arteriosum below *4*); *5*, thoracic duct; *6*, right auricle; *7*, pulmonary veins; *8*, lateral attachment of rumino-reticular fold; *9*, rumino-reticular opening; *10*, posterior vena cava; *11*, tendo subpelvina.

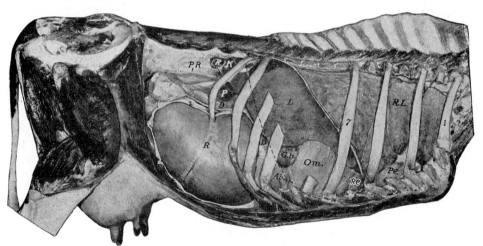

Fig. 390a.—Dissection of Holstein Cow; Right Side.

1, First rib; *2*, deep part of greater omentum; *7*, seventh rib; *Ab.*, abomasum (pyloric part); *D, D*, duodenum; *G.b.*, gall-bladder; *L*, liver; *Om.*, omasum; *P*, pancreas; *Pe*, Pericardium; *P R.*, peritoneal reflection in right flank; *R*, rumen (ventral sac); *Re.*, reticulum; *R.K.*, right kidney; *R.L.*, right lung. The superficial part of the greater omentum was removed to expose the rumen. Phrenico-costal line dotted.

fades out above. Another branch from the left part of the posterior pillar extends forward and upward a short distance and subsides gradually. The right pillar is in part double; its ventral division fades out about the middle of the surface, while the dorsal one joins the posterior pillar. The left pillar fades out near the posterior dorsal blind sac. The distance between the middles of the anterior and posterior pillars is only about sixteen to eighteen inches (ca. 40 to 45 cm.) in a cow of medium size. In this space the dorsal and ventral sacs communicate freely.

The anterior end of the dorsal sac of the rumen is separated in its ventral part from the reticulum by an almost vertical fold formed by the apposition of the walls of the two compartments. This **rumino-reticular fold** (Pila rumino-reticularis) corresponds to the rumino-reticular groove and is opposite to the seventh or eighth rib.[1] Its free dorsal edge is concave and forms the ventral and lateral margin of the large, oval **rumino-reticular orifice** (Ostium rumino-reticulare). The lateral part of the fold fades out an inch or two lateral to and behind the cardia. The medial part of the fold ends just behind the reticular groove and about three inches (ca. 7-8 cm.) below the level of the cardia, so that in the vicinity of the cardia there is no demarcation between rumen and reticulum; hence this part of the stomach may be termed the **atrium ventriculi.**

If an imaginary line be drawn completing the margin of the rumino-reticular fold the cardia and the reticular groove could be regarded as belonging to the reticulum and the term "atrium" might be dispensed with. But food or water swallowed with even a small degree of force passes first into the rumen. Foreign bodies (which are commonly swallowed by cattle) are, however, found in the reticulum chiefly.

The **cardia** is four or five inches (ca. 10-12 cm.) ventral to the vertebral end of the eighth or ninth rib and usually about an inch (ca. 2.5 cm.) to the left of the median plane. Its position, of course, varies with the excursion of the diaphragm, and is affected by the degree of fulness of the rumen and reticulum. The opening is usually slit-like and is about an inch (ca. 2-3 cm.) in height. The funnel-like termination of the œsophagus commonly seen in soft material is due to postmortem relaxation and distention.

The mucous membrane of the rumen is brown in color, except on the margins of the pillars, where it is pale. It is for the most part thickly studded with large papillæ, many of which are nearly half an inch (ca. 1 cm.) long. The edges of the chief pillars and a large part of the wall of the middle of the dorsal sac are, however, not papillated. The papillary arrangement is most developed in the blind sacs. The papillæ vary much in size and form; the largest are foliate, many are narrow or filiform, and others are conical or club-shaped. The mucous membrane on the medial wall of the atrium is finely wrinkled and non-papillated, while dorsally and laterally it is papillated. The papillary arrangement also extends over the edge of the rumino-reticular fold an inch or two (ca. 2 to 5 cm.).

The **reticular** or œsophageal **groove** (Sulcus reticuli) begins at the cardia and passes ventrally on the medial wall of the atrium and reticulum to end at the reticulo-omasal orifice. It is about seven or eight inches (ca. 18-20 cm.) in length. Its direction is chiefly dorso-ventral, but usually it inclines somewhat forward and medially in its ventral part; the ventral end, which is at the reticulo-omasal orifice, is commonly an inch or two (ca. 2.5-5 cm.) in front of the plane of the cardia and to the right of the median plane. The groove is twisted in a spiral fashion, so that its thickened edges or lips project first backward, then to the left, and finally forward. The twist involves chiefly the left lip, and the relative position of the lips is reversed at the ventral end. The mucous membrane on the lips of the reticular groove is brown and wrinkled; in the bottom of the groove it is pale, like that of the œsophagus, marked by longitudinal folds, and presents pointed, horny papillæ on its ventral part.

In the **reticulum** the mucous membrane is raised into folds about half an inch high, which enclose four-, five-, or six-sided spaces or cells (Cellulæ reticuli); this peculiar arrangement suggested the scientific name, and also the popular term

---

[1] The position of this fold naturally varies with the degree of fulness of the reticulum and rumen. When the latter is full, it may extend back in part to the eighth intercostal space.

"honey-comb." These cells are subdivided by smaller folds, and the bottoms are studded with pointed, horny papillæ. The cells grow smaller and gradually disappear near the reticular groove and the edge of the rumino-reticular fold; an inch or two from the latter the mucous membrane has the papillary arrangement of the rumen. At the reticulo-omasal orifice there are peculiar horny papillæ, which are curved and resemble the claws of a small bird; hence they are termed unguiform (Papillæ unguiformes). The **reticulo-omasal orifice** (Ostium reticulo-omasicum) is situated in the lesser curvature of the reticulum, five or six inches above the bottom of the latter, and just to the right of the median plane. It is rounded, and is limited below and on the sides by the lips of the reticular groove.

The cavity of the **omasum** is occupied to a considerable extent by about a hundred longitudinal folds, the **laminæ omasi,** which spring from the greater curva-

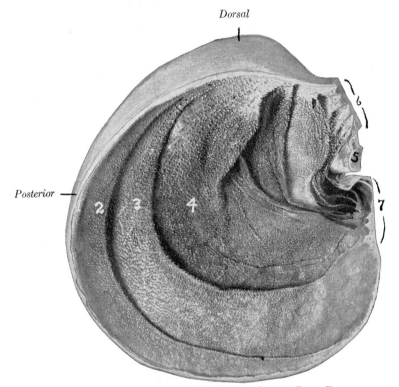

Fig. 391.—Omasum of Ox, Sagittal Section; Right View.

1, 2, 3, 4, Laminæ of various orders; 5, muscular pillar; 6, neck connecting with reticulum; 7, connection with abomasum.

ture and the sides. The largest of these—a dozen or more in number—have a convex attached edge, and a thick, concave free edge, which reaches to within a short distance of the lesser curvature. If these are drawn apart or a cross-section is made (Fig. 392, it will be seen that there is a second order or shorter laminæ, and a third and fourth still shorter; finally there is a series of very low folds or lines. The food is pressed into thin layers in the narrow spaces between the laminæ (Recessus interlaminares), and reduced to a fine state of division by being ground down by the numerous rounded, horny papillæ which stud the surfaces of the folds. A groove, the **sulcus omasi,** extends from the reticulo-omasal opening to the omaso-abomasal opening; it is about four inches (ca. 10 cm.) long, and is directed ventrally and slightly backward and medially. It is free from laminæ, but presents usually slight folds and small papillæ; it may function as a direct path from the reticulum to the abomasum for fluid and finely divided food. In the neck of the omasum the laminæ change to thick folds, and there are a number of the peculiar unguiform papillæ already mentioned as occurring in the lower part of the reticular groove. The **omaso-abomasal orifice** (Ostium omaso-abomasicum) is oval, and is about four inches (ca. 10 cm.) long. It is bounded in front by the thick muscular **omasal pillar** (Pila omasi), the fibers of which spread out above in the sides of the omasum. The mucous membrane of the abomasum forms an extensive fold on each side of the opening; these folds may act as valves (Valvulæ terminales), which probably prevent regurgitation of the contents of the abomasum.

The cavity of the **abomasum** is divided by a constriction into two areas. The first of these (fundus gland region) is lined with a soft glandular mucous membrane, which forms a dozen or more extensive **spiral folds** (Plicæ spirales). The second part (pyloric region) is much narrower and resembles in appearance the corresponding region of the horse's stomach. A small cardiac gland zone surrounds the omaso-abomasal orifice. The pyloric orifice is small and round.

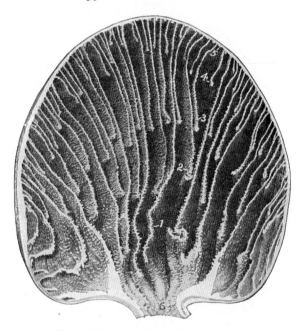

Fig. 392.—Cross-section of Omasum of Ox.
1–5, Laminæ of various orders; 6, neck connecting with reticulum.

Structure.—The **serous coat** invests all of the free surface of the stomach. The surface of the rumen which is attached to the dorsal abdominal wall is, of course, uncovered, as well as the adjacent area to which the spleen is attached. The furrows are bridged over by the peritoneum and superficial muscle-fibers, and contain fat and (in most cases) branches of the gastric arteries.

The **lesser omentum** leaves the visceral surface of the liver along a line extending from the œsophageal notch to the portal fissure. It passes over the parietal surface of the omasum and is attached along the area of adhesion of that sac to the abomasum, the pyloric part of the abomasum and the first part of the duodenum.

The **greater omentum** conceals the greater part of the intestine on the right side, with the exception of the duodenum, and covers the ventral sac of the rumen almost entirely. It is not lace-like, as in the horse, and contains a large amount of fat in animals in good condition. It may be conveniently described as consisting of two parts, each composed of two layers of peritoneum; the two serous layers enclose a variable amount of fat. The **superficial part** extends from the left groove of the rumen ventrally around the ventral sac and ascends on the right side, covering the deep part. It ends along the second part of the duodenum and the greater curvature of the abomasum. The **deep part** is attached along the visceral (right) surface of the rumen ventral to the right groove, and curves around the intestinal mass to the right side, where it is covered by the superficial part. It ends chiefly by blending with the medial layer of the mesoduodenum, but anteriorly is attached on the first bend of the colon and the visceral surface of the liver along the ventral border of the pancreas. The two parts are continuous at the attachment along the posterior groove of the rumen. They also join at the iliac flexure of the duodenum and at the origin of the colon. The **epiploic foramen** is almost sagittal in direction.

The **muscular coat of rumen** consists of two layers. The fibers of the external layer are in general longitudinal; those of the thicker internal layer are largely

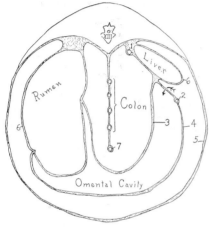

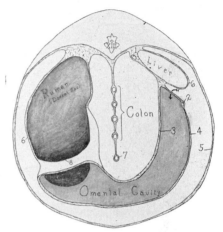

FIG. 392a.—DIAGRAM SHOWING ARRANGEMENT OF THE OMENTUM IN THE OX IN CROSS SECTION.

1, Duodenum (third part); 2, duodenum (second part); 3, greater omentum (deep part); 4, greater omentum (superficial part); 5, parietal peritoneum; 6, visceral peritoneum; 7, small intestine; XIII, thirteenth thoracic vertebra. Arrow in mesoduodenum is in the foramen epiploicum.

FIG. 392b.—DIAGRAM SHOWING ARRANGEMENT OF THE OMENTUM IN THE OX PARTLY CUT AWAY TO SHOW THE OMENTUM EXTENDING THROUGH THE POSTERIOR GROOVE OF THE RUMEN WITH OMENTAL CAVITY OPEN.

1, Duodenum (third part); 2, duodenum (second part); 3, greater omentum, (deep part); 4, greater omentum (superficial part); 5, parietal peritoneum; 6, visceral peritoneum; 7, small intestine: 8, posterior groove of the rumen; XIII, thirteenth thoracic vertebra. Arrow in mesoduodenum is in foramen epiploicum.

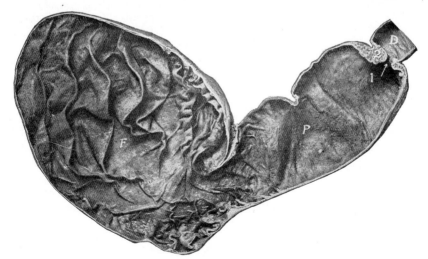

FIG. 393.—INTERIOR OF ABOMASUM OF OX.

F, Fundus gland region with large spiral folds; *P*, pyloric region; *D*, duodenum; 1, pylorus; 2, torus pyloricus.

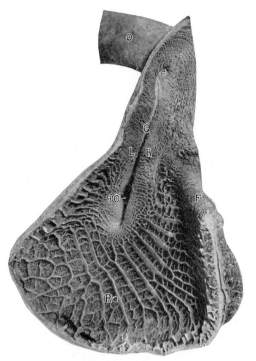

Fig. 394.—Section of Reticulum of the Cow Showing the Reticular Groove.

Fig. 394a.—Dissection of the Reticular Groove of
the Cow.

The mucous membrane has been removed. The
lips of the groove are separated to show the arrangement of the muscular tissue.

C Cardia; *F*, rumino-reticular fold; *G*, bottom of groove; *L, R*, left and right lips of groove; *O*, œsophagus; *Re.*, reticulum; *R.O.*, reticulo-omasal opening.

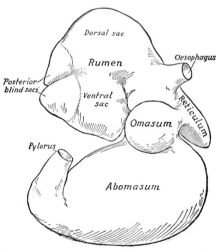

Fig. 395.—Stomach of New-born Calf; Right View.
The rumen is raised.

circular in direction. The latter forms
the bulk of the chief pillars, where it is
about one-half to one inch (ca. 1 to 2 cm.)
thick. Scattered bundles of striped muscle-fibers radiate from the cardia in the
wall of the atrium and extend also along
the reticular groove.

The **muscular coat of the reticulum**
consists of two chief layers which begin
and end at the œsophageal groove; they
pass in a circular or oblique fashion
around the sac, the fibers of the two layers
crossing each other at varying angles.
The walls of the cells contain a central
muscular layer. The lips of the reticular
groove consist chiefly of a thick layer of
longitudinal fibers, which are largely continuous above the cardia. Those of the
right spread out ventrally as internal
fibers of the reticulum, while those of the
left lip go mainly to the omasum. The bottom of the groove has two layers of

oblique, unstriped muscle-fibers, with a variable outer layer of striped muscle continuous with that of the œsophagus.

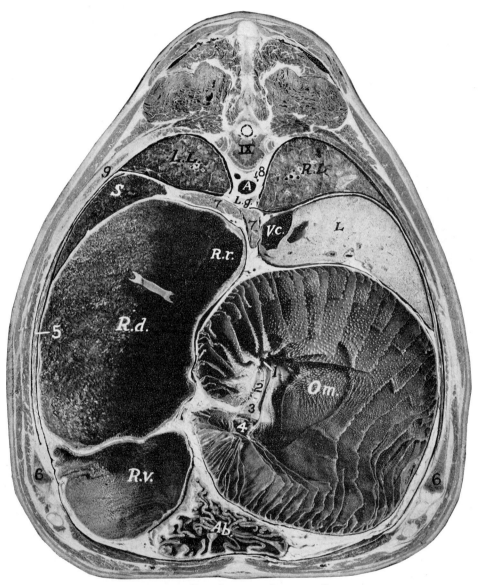

FIG. 395a.—CROSS SECTION OF SHORTHORN COW.

The section is cut through the ninth thoracic vertebra and heads of the tenth ribs. Parts of the omasal laminæ have been cut away to show the orifices and groove. *1*, Reticulo-omasal opening; *2*, omasal groove; *3*, omasal pillar; *4*, omaso-abomasal opening; *5*, diaphragm; *6, 6*, sternal ends of ninth ribs; *7, 7*, crura of the diaphragm; *8*, thoracic duct; *9*, ninth rib; *IX*, ninth thoracic vertebra; *A*, aorta; *Ab.*, abomasum; *L*, liver; *L.g.*, posterior mediastinal lymph gland; *L. L.*, left lung; *Om.*, omasum; *R.d.*, right dorsal sac; *R.L.*, right lung; *R.r.*, rumino-reticular opening; *R.v.*, anterior part of ventral sac of rumen; *V.c.*, posterior vena cava.

The external muscular layer of the œsophagus is in part continued down along the reticular groove (*i. e.*, along the lesser curvature of the reticulum), but in greater part spreads out on the wall of the rumen and reticulum.

The **muscular coat of the omasum** consists of a thin external longitudinal layer and a thick internal circular layer. At the omasal groove there is an incomplete inner layer of oblique fibers. The larger laminæ contain three muscular strata. The fibers of the central layer extend from the attached edge toward the free edge, but do not reach the latter; here there is a marginal band of longitudinal fibers. The central layer is continuous with the inner circular layer of the wall. On either side there is a layer of longitudinal fibers, which are continuous at the attached border with the muscularis mucosæ.

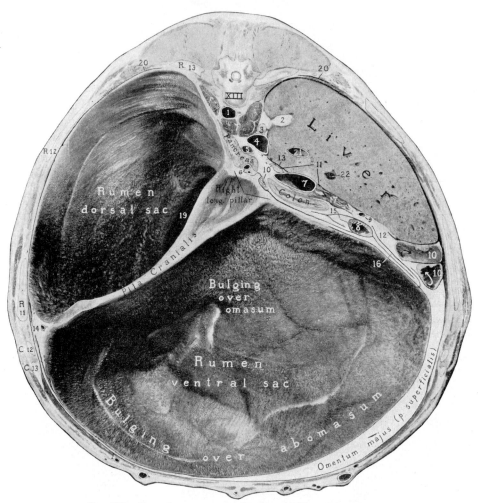

Fig. 395b.—Cross Section of Holstein Cow. Viewed from Behind.

The section cuts the thirteenth thoracic vertebra near the anterior end. *1*, Aorta (thoracic duct to right of aorta); *2*, perirenal fat; *3*, right adrenal; *4*, posterior vena cava (small vessel below vena cava is gastric lymph trunk); *5*, cœliac artery; *6*, right ruminal vessels; *7*, origin of portal vein; *8*, jejunum; *9*, ductus choledochus; *10, 10*, duodenum (first part); *10'*, duodenum (near termination) (hepatic artery just above *10'*); *11*, hepatic lymph glands; *12*, lesser omentum; *13*, epiploic foramen; 14, left ruminal vessels; *15*, mesentery; *16*, omentum majus (pars profundus); *17*, pancreas (right branch); *18, 18'*, left and right crura of diaphragm; *19*, rumino-reticular opening; *20, 20'*, left and right pleural sacs; *21*, branch to hepatic vein; *22*, branch from portal vein; *XIII*, thirteenth thoracic vertebra; *C. 12, C. 13*, costal cartilages twelve and thirteen; *R. 11, R. 12, R. 13*, ribs eleven, twelve and thirteen.

The **muscular coat of the abomasum** consists of longitudinal and circular layers; the latter forms a well-developed pyloric sphincter.

The **mucous membrane** of the first three divisions is destitute of glands, and is covered with a thick, stratified, squamous epithelium; the superficial part of the latter is horny, and is shed in large patches in the rumen and omasum. The tunica propria is papillated. The mucous membrane of the abomasum is glandular, and corresponds to that of the right sac of the stomach of the horse. The fundus glands (which are relatively short) occur in that part which presents the large folds, while the long pyloric glands are found in the remainder, except about the omaso-abomasal orifice, where cardiac glands occur. The mucosa of the fundus gland region is very thin as compared with that of the horse; toward the pylorus there is

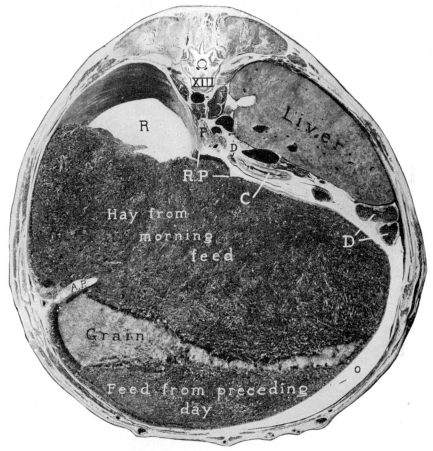

Fig. 395c.—Cross Section of Holstein Cow; Viewed from Behind.

The section cuts the last thoracic vertebra near the anterior end. This animal was well fed the evening before embalming; the following morning a feed of cracked corn, followed by all the hay she desired, then embalmed, frozen and sectioned. *XIII*, Last thoracic vertebra; *A.P.*, Left part of anterior pillar; *C*, most anterior part of colon; *D, D*, duodenum; *O*, greater omentum containing fat; *P*, pancreas; *R*, rumen; *R.P.*, right pillar double.

an increase in thickness. There is a round prominence (Torus pyloricus) on the upper part of the pyloric valve.

Vessels and Nerves.—The blood supply is derived from the cœliac artery, and the veins to go the portal vein. The nerves come from the vagus and sympathetic. Numerous ganglia are present in the submucous and intermuscular tissue, especially in the reticulum and œsophageal groove.

THE INTESTINE

The intestine of the ox is about twenty times the length of the body. It lies almost entirely to the right of the median plane, chiefly in contact with the right face of the rumen. It is attached to the sublumbar region by a common mesentery.

The **small intestine** has an average length of about 130 feet (ca. 40 m.) and a diameter of about two inches (ca. 5 to 6 cm.). The **duodenum** is about three or four feet (ca. 1 m.) in length. Beginning at the pylorus (usually at the ventral end of the tenth rib or ninth intercostal space), the first part passes dorsally and forward to the visceral surface of the liver; here it forms an S-shaped curve (Ansa sigmoidea). The second part runs backward almost to the tuber coxæ, where it turns forward, forming the iliac flexure. The third part extends forward in contact with the terminal part of the colon, and joins the mesenteric part. It is attached to the liver by the lesser omentum; the remainder of the mesoduodenum is a narrow fold which is largely derived from the right layer of the common mesentery, but at the

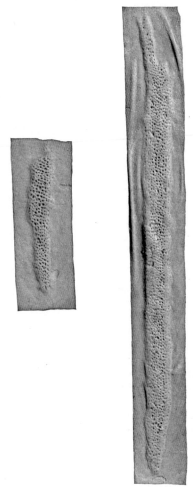

Fig. 396.—Large and Small Aggregated Nodules or Peyer's Patches of Small Intestine of Ox (about ⅓ natural size).

iliac flexure it comes directly from the sublumbar region. The **bile duct** opens in the ventral part of the S-shaped curve. The **pancreatic duct** opens about a foot (ca. 30 cm.) further back.

The remainder of the small intestine is arranged in numerous very close coils, which form a sort of festoon at the edge of the mesentery. It lies chiefly in the space bounded medially by the right face of the ventral sac of the rumen, laterally and ventrally by the abdominal wall, dorsally by the large intestine, and anteriorly by the omasum and abomasum. It is not subject to much variation in position, but a few coils may find their way behind the blind sacs of the rumen at the left side. The terminal part leaves the edge of the mesentery and runs forward between the cæcum and colon, to both of which it is adherent. The orifices of the pancreatic duct and the bile duct are on papillæ or thick folds, no diverticulum being present. There are permanent transverse folds of the mucous membrane (Plicæ circulares). Duodenal glands occur in the first twelve to fifteen feet (4 to 4.5

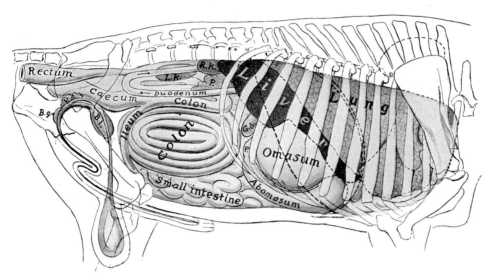

FIG. 397,—PROJECTION OF VISCERA OF BULL ON BODY-WALL; RIGHT SIDE.

P., Pylorus; *G.b.*, gall-bladder; *R.K.*, right kidney; *L.K.*, left kidney; *P.* (above duodenum), pancreas; *Bl.*, urinary bladder; *V.s.*, vesicula seminalis; *B.g.*, bulbo-urethral (Cowper's) gland. Costal attachment and median line of diaphragm are indicated by dotted lines.

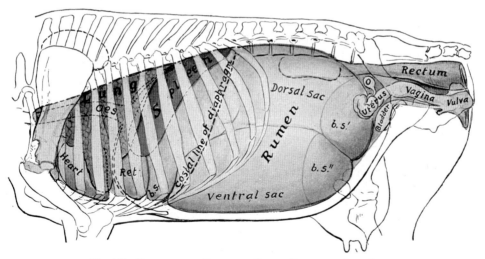

FIG. 398.—PROJECTION OF VISCERA OF COW ON BODY-WALL; LEFT SIDE.

Oes, œsophagus; *Ret.*, reticulum; *b. s.*, anterior blind sac; *b. s.'*, *b. s.''*, posterior blind sacs of rumen; *O*, ovary. The left kidney, concealed by the dorsal sac of the rumen, is indicated by dotted line. The median line of the diaphragm is dotted.

m.), intestinal glands throughout. The aggregated follicles or Peyer's patches are larger and more prominent and distinct than in the horse, and vary greatly in size and number; in adult cattle there are eighteen to forty; in calves twenty to fifty-eight have been counted. They usually have the form of narrow bands. There is a patch close to the ileo-cæcal valve.

The **large intestine** is much smaller in caliber than that of the horse, has no bands, and is not sacculated. Most of it is situated between the layers of the common mesentery in the right dorsal part of the abdominal cavity. It is related on the right to the lateral abdominal wall, from which, however, it is almost completely separated by the greater omentum. On the left it is chiefly related to the rumen. The average length of the **cæcum** is about thirty inches (ca. 75 cm.), and the diameter is about five inches (ca. 12 cm.). It is directly continuous in front with the colon, the conventional demarcation being the junction of the ileum with the large intestine.[1] From this junction, which is on the medial side and usually near the ventral end of the last rib, the cæcum extends backward and upward along the right flank (from which it is separated by the greater omentum), and its rounded blind end commonly lies at the right side of the pelvic inlet. The cæcum is attached along its medial side to the mesentery, except the posterior third, which is free and variable in position. The terminal part of the ileum runs forward along the medial surface of the cæcum and is attached to the latter. The dorsal surface is attached by areolar tissue and peritoneum to the colon. The **colon** is about thirty-five feet (ca. 10 m.) in average length. Its diameter is at first the same as that of the cæcum, but diminishes to about two inches (ca. 5 cm.). The greater part of it is arranged in double elliptical coils between the layers of the mesentery; the coils are attached to each other by areolar tissue. It begins as the direct continuation of the cæcum, runs forward a short distance (5–10 cm.), and turns dorsally and backward opposite to the ventral part of the last two ribs. It continues backward, in relation to the right flank laterally and the cæcum ventrally, to the posterior part of the sublumbar region. Here it turns forward and runs parallel with the second part as far forward as the second lumbar vertebra, turns backward, and is continued by the spiral part (Ansa spiralis). The coils of this are alternately centripetal and centrifugal (Gyri centripetales et centrifugales); they are best seen from the left side. The bowel gradually diminishes in caliber, and the terminal part (Ansa distalis) leaves the spiral mass, passes forward to the great mesenteric artery, and runs backward dorsal to the terminal part of the duodenum. It inclines to the right in relation to the ventral surface of the right kidney, forms an **S**-shaped curve near the pelvic inlet, and joins the rectum; this part is attached to the sublumbar region by a narrow mesentery, and is also attached to the recurrent part of the duodenum.

The **rectum** is somewhat shorter than that of the horse, and is usually covered with peritoneum as far back as the first coccygeal vertebra. The retroperitoneal part is surrounded by a quantity of fat. The anus is not prominent.

The **serous coat** is of course absent on the adherent surfaces of the spiral part of the colon. There is a large amount of fat in the mesentery. The longitudinal fibers of the muscular coat are evenly distributed, consequently there is no sacculation of the bowel. There is a valvular mucous fold at the ileo-cæcal orifice. A Peyer's patch occurs in the beginning of the cæcum and one in the first part of the colon.

THE LIVER

The liver lies almost entirely to the right of the median plane. Its long axis is directed obliquely downward and forward, about parallel with the median plane, and corresponds to the curvature of the right portion of the diaphragm. It is less extensive, but thicker than that of the horse. Its average weight is about 10 to 12 pounds (ca. 4.5 to 5.5 kg.).

[1] In formalin-hardened material there is sometimes a constriction in front of the termination of the ileum. This might be regarded as the demarcation between the cæcum and colon. The opening of the ileum is directly forward, so that material from it enters the origin of the colon. The posterior free part of the cæcum is naturally variable in position; it may be bent dorsally or ventrally, so that the blind end faces forward.

In small subjects the weight (according to Schmaltz) varies from 6½ to 10 pounds (ca. 3 to 4.5 kg.), in large subjects from 11 to 13 pounds (ca. 5 to 6 kg.). According to Schneider, the average weight is about 13 pounds (ca. 6 kg.)—a little over 1 per cent. of the live weight and about 2 per cent. of the dressed carcass.

When hardened *in situ*, it is seen to be adapted accurately to the structures with which it is in contact.

The **parietal surface** is convex and is for the most part applied to the right part of the diaphragm, but a small part of it is in direct contact with the last two or three ribs and (inconstantly) with the flank at the lumbo-costal angle. It faces dorsally, forward, and to the right.

The curvature of the parietal surface is not quite regular. It is marked, except in its ventral part, by a blunt oblique ridge which divides the surface into two areas. Of these, the lateral one

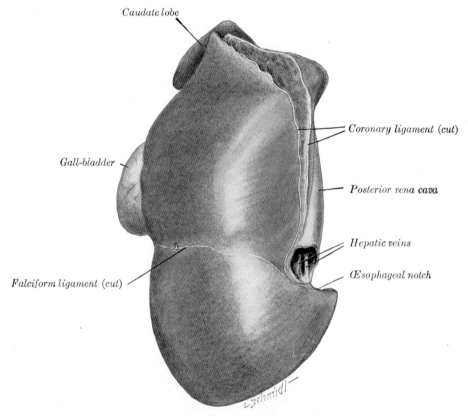

FIG. 399.—LIVER OF OX, PARIETAL SURFACE; HARDENED *in situ*.

is directed outward, is only slightly convex, and often shows impressions of the last three ribs; it is in contact in part directly with the right abdominal wall, in part with the costal part of the diaphragm which is in contact ordinarily with the lateral wall. The medial area presents a depression produced by the right crus of the diaphragm, and otherwise is regularly convex and adapted to the tendinous center and sternal part of the diaphragm. The falciform ligament is attached to the surface from the œsophageal notch to the umbilical fissure. There is a triangular area of considerable size on the dorso-medial part of the surface which is without a peritoneal covering, since it is adherent to the diaphragm.

The **visceral surface** is concave and very irregular; it presents impressions of the chief organs which are in contact with it—the omasum and reticulum. It is also related to the pancreas and duodenum.

The following markings are quite distinct on the visceral surface of well-hardened specimens: (1) The omasal impression (Impressio omasica) is a deep central cavity below the portal fissure. (2) The reticular impression (Impressio reticularis) is a smaller marginal depression below the œsophageal notch and the medial part of the preceding, from which it is separated by a rounded ridge. (3) The abomasal impression (Impressio abomasica), present only in the young subject

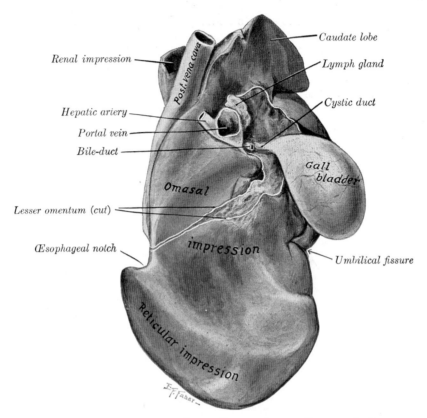

FIG. 400.—LIVER OF HEIFER, VISCERAL SURFACE; HARDENED *in situ.*
The abomasal impression is shown to the right of the reticular impression, but by an oversight is not marked.

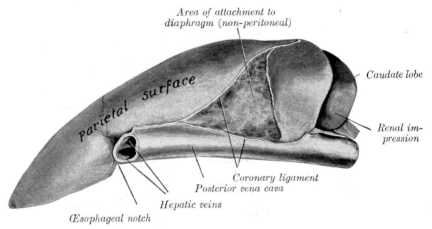

FIG. 401.—LIVER OF OX, LEFT MARGINAL VIEW; HARDENED *in situ.*

usually, corresponds to the fundus of the abomasum. It lies along the ventral part of the surface and is separated by ridges from the preceding impressions. It usually disappears as the omasum and reticulum increase in size and displace the abomasum from contact with the liver. (4) Shallow grooves for the S-shaped portion of the duodenum (Impressio duodenalis) may be found ventral and lateral to the portal fissure. (5) The fossa of the gall-bladder (Fossa vesicæ felleæ) is distinct when that organ is full. In the calf the omasal impression is small, and the abomasal one large in correspondence with the relative sizes of these two sacs.

The **portal fissure** is a well-defined rounded depression, situated dorsal to the omasal impression. It contains, besides the vessels and duct, several large hepatic lymph glands. Dorsal and lateral to it a part of the pancreas is attached.

The **dorsal border** is short and thick; it usually extends backward a short distance beyond the upper part of the last rib. It presents the large, thick, quadrilateral **caudate lobe,** and a deep depression for the right kidney and adrenal.

The **ventral border** is short and thin and has no interlobar incisures.

The **right** (or lateral) **border** is marked by the umbilical fissure, in which the ligamentum teres is attached in the young subject.

The **left border** presents the œsophageal notch below its middle; the notch is much shallower than in the horse. Above this it is practically median in position, and lodges the posterior vena cava, which is partially embedded in the gland. Below the notch the border extends an inch or two (ca. 2.5 to 5 cm.) to the left of the median plane, opposite the ventral third of the sixth rib or intercostal space.

The right lateral ligament attaches the dorsal border to the anterior part of the sublumbar region. The ligament of the caudate lobe passes to the ventral surface of the right kidney. There is no left lateral ligament. The falciform ligament may be present, but it and the ligamentum teres are usually found only in young subjects. The lesser omentum leaves the liver along a line extending from the œsophageal notch to the portal fissure. The only distinct lobes in the adult are the caudate and papillary. The latter is best seen in the soft specimen; it is a tongue-like mass which partly overlaps the portal vein and fissure.[1]

A **gall-bladder** (Vesica fellea) is present. This is a pear-shaped sac, four to six inches (ca. 10 to 15 cm.) long, which lies partly in contact with the visceral surface of the liver (to which it is attached), but largely against the abdominal wall at the ventral part of the tenth or eleventh intercostal space. It may be regarded as a diverticulum of the bile-duct, enlarged to form a reservoir for the bile. Its neck is continued by the **cystic duct** (Ductus cysticus), which joins the hepatic duct at an acute angle just outside of the portal fissure, to form with it the **bile-duct** (Ductus choledochus). The latter is short and enters the second bend of the **S**-shaped curve of the duodenum, i. e., about two feet (ca. 60 cm.) from the pylorus. The opening of the duct is at the end of a papilla or ridge-like fold. Several small ducts (Ductus hepatocystici) open directly into the gall-bladder.

The wall of the gall-bladder consists of serous, muscular, and mucous coats. The muscular tissue consists of unstriped fibers which run in various directions; externally many are longitudinal, while internally (and especially at the neck) they are chiefly circular. The mucous membrane is covered by a cylindrical epithelium and contains numerous groups of branched tubular glands. The cystic and bile ducts have a similar structure.

In the new-born calf the liver is relatively much larger than in the adult. The visceral surface presents, below the portal fissure, a rounded eminence, which is caused by the presence in the underlying gland substance of a large venous sinus into which the umbilical and portal veins empty. A large vessel, the **ductus venosus,** leads from this sinus directly to the posterior vena cava. The umbilical fissure is deep and partially divides the gland into two chief lobes.

THE PANCREAS

The pancreas of the ox is irregularly quadrilateral in form, and lies almost entirely to the right of the median plane. Its weight is about twelve ounces (ca. 350 gm.). Its dorsal surface is related to the liver, right kidney, crura of the diaphragm, posterior vena cava, and cœliac and anterior mesenteric arteries; it is

---

[1] The liver of the ox might be regarded as consisting of dorsal, ventral, caudate, and papillary lobes. Pathological adhesions of the ventral part of the liver to the diaphragm and reticulum are often present in dissecting-room subjects.

covered to a large extent by peritoneum. It is attached to the liver at and lateral to the portal fissure, and to the crura of the diaphragm. Between these adhesions it is free and forms the ventral wall of the epiploic foramen. On the right side it extends backward beyond the caudate lobe of the liver between the layers of the mesoduodenum; here it is in contact with the upper part of the flank at the lumbocostal angle, and is related dorsally to the right kidney and by its ventro-lateral

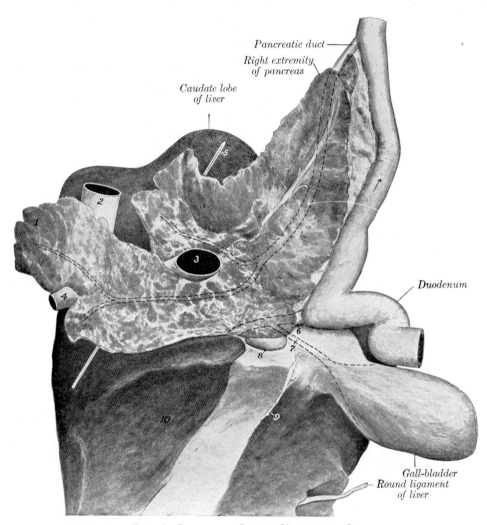

Fig. 402.—Pancreas and Related Structures of Ox.

1, Left extremity of pancreas; 2, posterior vena cava; 3, portal vein; 4, gastro-splenic vein; 5, probe in epiploic foramen; 6, bile duct; 7, cystic duct; 8, pancreatico-intestinal lymph gland; 9, cut edge of lesser omentum; 10, omasal impression of liver. Intraglandular part of pancreatic duct and its chief radicles are shown by dotted lines. Concealed parts of bile duct, cystic duct, and neck of gall-bladder are similarly indicated.

border to the second part of the duodenum. The ventral or gastro-intestinal surface is in contact with the dorsal curvature of the rumen and the intestine. There is a deep notch (Incisura pancreatis) for the portal vein and hepatic artery, and several lymph glands are present here. The left extremity is small and quadrilateral and turns upward; it is attached dorsally to the crus of the diaphragm and the cœliac and anterior mesenteric arteries, and is adherent ventrally to the rumen.

The right or posterior part is wide and thin and is often divided into two branches. The duct leaves the posterior part of the ventro-lateral (or right) border and enters the duodenum about twelve inches (ca. 30 cm.) further back than the bile-duct.

THE SPLEEN

The spleen has an elongated, elliptical outline, both extremities being thin, rounded, and similar in size.

Its average weight is about two pounds (ca. 900 gm.), or about ⅙ per cent. of the body-weight. Its average length is about 20 inches (ca. 50 cm.), its width about 6 inches (ca. 15 cm.), and in the middle its thickness is about an inch (ca. 2 to 3 cm.).

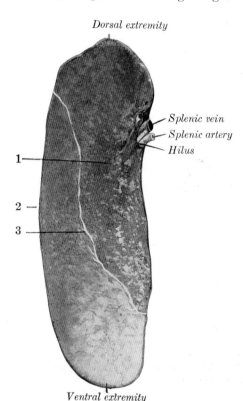

Dorsal extremity

Splenic vein
Splenic artery
Hilus

1
2
3

Ventral extremity

FIG. 403.—SPLEEN OF OX; VISCERAL SURFACE.

1, Area of attachment to rumen (non-peritoneal); *2*, posterior border; *3*, line of peritoneal reflection.

The **dorsal extremity** lies under the dorsal ends of the last two ribs, and may extend back as far as the first lumbar transverse process. The **ventral extremity** varies in position, but is commonly opposite the eighth or ninth rib, about a hand-breadth above its sternal end. The **parietal surface** is convex, and is related to the diaphragm. The **visceral surface** is concave, and is related chiefly to the left face of the rumen, but also usually to a narrow adjacent area of the reticulum. The dorsal part is attached to the left crus of the diaphragm and the left surface of the rumen by peritoneum and connective tissue; the ventral part is free. The **hilus** is situated on the dorsal third of the visceral surface, near the anterior border.

About one-half of the visceral surface of the spleen is attached directly to the stomach and is therefore not covered by peritoneum; the line of reflection of the latter crosses the surface obliquely, from the upper part of the posterior border to the anterior border below its middle. Similarly there is a narrow uncovered area on the upper part of the parietal surface along the anterior border. The hilus is not a groove, but a simple depression. When hardened *in situ*, the organ is seen to be somewhat twisted, so that the upper part of the parietal surface faces dorsally and forward, while below it is directed laterally. In some cases the spleen is considerably longer than is stated above, and may extend to the ventral end of the seventh or eighth rib. Not uncommonly there are pathological adhesions of the ventral part of the spleen to adjacent structures.

DIGESTIVE SYSTEM OF THE SHEEP

The **lips** are thin and mobile; the upper one is marked by a very distinct philtrum, and otherwise is not bare.

The anterior part of the **hard palate** is prominent and smooth, forming the so-called dental pad or plate. On the posterior part of this area there are two narrow depressions in the form of a V and separated by the central papilla incisiva, at the deep anterior ends of which the incisive or naso-palatine ducts open. The ridges of the palate, some fourteen in number, are irregular and their edges are smooth; most of them alternate with those of the opposite side, from which they are separated by the median raphé palati. The posterior third or rather more is not ridged and presents numerous orifices of ducts of the palatine glands. The mucous membrane is often more or less pigmented. The soft palate resembles that of the ox.

The mucous membrane of the **cheeks** is covered with large papillæ, many of which are long and sharp-pointed, while others are short and blunt. There is also

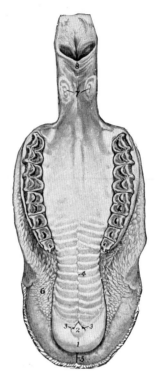

Fig. 404.—Palate of Sheep.

1, Dental pad; 2, papilla incisiva; 3, 3, openings of incisive ducts; 4, raphé palati; 5, philtrum; 6, conical papillæ of cheek; 7, tonsils; 8, palatine arch.

a series of conical papillæ on the floor of the mouth, under the lateral part of the tongue.

The **tongue** resembles that of the ox in form, but the tip is comparatively smooth; the papillæ here are very numerous, but short and blunt. This difference is in conformity with the dissimilarity in the mode of prehension of the two species. The prominence of the dorsum is commonly not so pronounced nor so sharply marked off in front as in the ox. The root is smooth. The mucous membrane of the dorsum is often pigmented in spots.

The **dental formula** is the same as that of the ox.[1] The **incisor teeth** form a narrow and strongly curved arch. The crowns are long and narrow; their labial surfaces are strongly convex and end at a sharp edge which is used in cropping the grass. The roots are more firmly embedded than in the ox. The **cheek teeth** resemble those of the ox, but have a thinner layer of cement, which is often blackened by deposits from the food. The average periods of eruption of the teeth are indicated in the table on opposite page.

[1] A lateral view of the teeth is given in the description of the skull.

Teeth	Temporary	Permanent
I₁	At birth or first week	1 to 1½ years
I₂	First or second week	1½ to 2 years
I₃	Second or third week	2½ to 3 years
I₄	Third or fourth week	3½ to 4 years
P₁		
P₂	2 to 6 weeks	1½ to 2 years
P₃		
M₁		3 months (lower), 5 months (upper)
M₂		9 to 12 months
M₃		1½ to 2 years

The **salivary glands** resemble those of the ox in general. The parotid gland is darker in color and more compact in texture than the mandibular. It is rounded in outline, but has a pointed cervical angle at which the external jugular vein emerges. The duct leaves the lower part of the anterior border of the gland and runs forward over the masseter muscle, about an inch and a half (ca. 3.4 cm.)

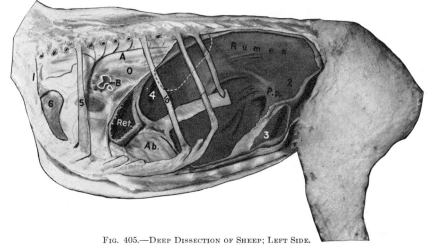

Fig. 405.—Deep Dissection of Sheep; Left Side.

The left lung, diaphragm and spleen have been removed. The left wall of the rumen and reticulum has been cut away. 1, First rib; 2, 3, blind sacs of rumen; 4, rumino-reticular opening; 5, fifth rib; 6, mediastinum removed showing apical lobe of right lung; 10. tenth rib; *A*, aorta; *Ab.*, abomasum; *B*, left bronchus; *O*, œsophagus; *P.p.*, posterior pillar of rumen; *Ret.*, reticulum. Dotted line indicates position of the spleen.

above the ventral border of the ramus; it opens opposite the third or fourth cheek tooth.

The **tonsil** is bean-shaped and about half an inch (ca. 12 mm.) in length. It does not project into the isthmus faucium. The mucous membrane of the latter presents two deep and very narrow tonsillar sinuses on either side.

The fornix of the **pharynx** presents a median plicated fold which is a continuation of the septum nasi. The pharyngeal orifice of the Eustachian tube has the form of a crescentic slit, placed about on a level with the ventral nasal meatus. There are two large lymph nodes and a number of hæmal nodes above the pharynx.

The **œsophagus** has a lumen of about an inch (ca. 2.5 cm.) when moderately distended; otherwise it resembles that of the ox.

The **stomach** is like that of the ox in its general arrangement. Its average capacity is about four gallons (ca. 15 liters). The **cardia** is opposite the eighth intercostal space; it is just to the left of the median plane, and about two inches (ca. 5 cm.) below the vertebral column. The dorsal sac of the **rumen** is a little longer than the ventral sac and extends considerably (ca. 7.8 cm.) further forward than the latter. The ventral sac is relatively larger and more of its volume extends to the right of the median plane than in the ox; its posterior blind sac extends further (ca. 6–8 cm.) back than that of the dorsal sac. The parietal attachment of the dorsal sac extends back to the second lumbar vertebra. The left longitudinal groove extends upward and backward for a short distance only, and therefore does not connect with the posterior groove. There are two longitudinal grooves on the right side which join at each end, thus enclosing a long, narrow prominent area; the dorsal one contains the right ruminal artery, and the ventral one corresponds to the pillar. The left coronary grooves do not extend to the curvatures. There is no dorsal coronary groove on the right side, but the ventral one is very distinct and extends to the curvature. The arrangement of the pillars corresponds to these external features. The papillæ of the rumen are relatively large and somewhat tongue-like; the largest are about a fourth of an inch (ca. 6 mm.) in length. The dorsal part is papillated, not glabrous, as in the ox. The lateral part of the rumino-

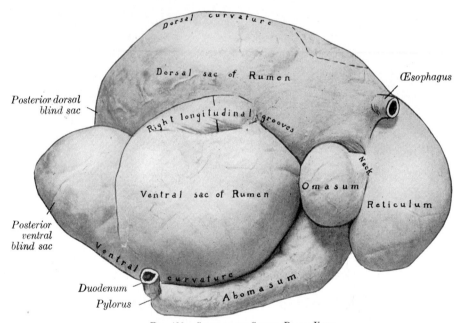

Fig. 406.—Stomach of Sheep; Right View.
From photograph of specimen hardened *in situ*. Dotted line indicates position of spleen.

reticular fold ends half an inch or more (ca. 1.5 cm.) behind the cardia. The **reticulum** is relatively larger than in the ox. Its ventral part curves more backward and less to the right than in the ox. The parietal surface extends forward as far as the sixth rib or intercostal space, and is related to the diaphragm and liver. The fundus lies on the sternal part of the diaphragm and is in contact behind with the abomasum. The **reticular groove** is disposed in general like that of the ox, and is about four to five inches (ca. 8 to 10 cm.) long.

There are, however, several marked differences in the arrangement of the groove. Its ventral part curves backward, so that the reticulo-omasal orifice is directed dorsally and lies in a transverse plane about an inch (ca. 2–3 cm.) behind one passing through the cardia. These differences are correlated with the small size of the omasum and the large size of the reticulum. Tubuloalveolar glands have been found by Thanhofer and others; they occur chiefly in the submucous tissue at the angle of junction of the lips and bottom of the groove.

The folds surrounding the cells of the reticulum are only 2 to 3 mm. in height, and have serrated edges. The dorsal part of this sac has, in the vicinity of the rumino-reticular orifice, a papillated mucous membrane just like that of the rumen. The **omasum** is much smaller than the reticulum, its capacity being only about one pint. It is oval and compressed laterally. It is situated almost entirely to the right of the median plane, opposite to the ninth and tenth ribs,

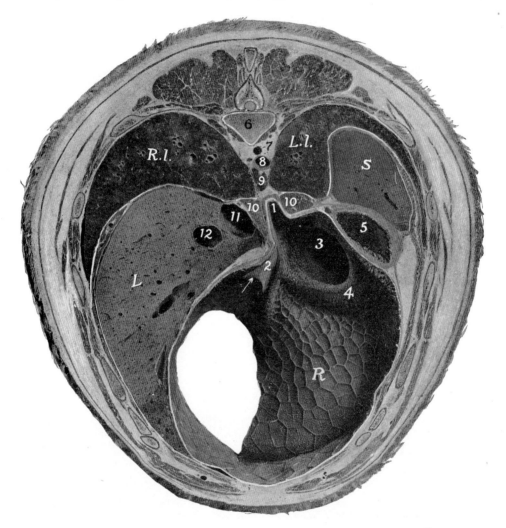

Fig. 407.—Cross-section of Sheep, through Ninth Thoracic Vertebra; Anterior View.

1, Cardia; *2*, reticular groove; *3*, rumino-reticular orifice; *4*, rumino-reticular fold; *5*, dorsal sac of rumen; *6*, body of ninth thoracic vertebra; *7*, vena hemiazygos; *8*, aorta; *9*, posterior mediastinal lymph gland; *10, 10*, crura of diaphragm; *11*, posterior vena cava; *12*, portal vein; *R.l.*, right lung; *L.l.*, left lung; *S*, spleen; *L*, liver; *R*, reticulum (posterior wall). Arrow points to reticulo-omasal orifice. The spleen is cut so obliquely as to appear much thicker than it really is.

higher than in the ox, and has no contact with the abdominal wall. It is related on the right to the liver and gall-bladder, on the left to the rumen, and ventrally to the abomasum. The laminæ are less numerous than in the ox; in the neck which connects the omasum with the reticulum they have the form of low, thick ridges, and bear long, pointed, horny papillæ. The **abomasum** is relatively larger and longer than in the ox. Its capacity is about twice that of the reticulum and averages about two quarts (ca. 1.75 to 2 liters). The blind anterior end lies almost centrally in the xiphoid region, in relation to the liver and reticulum. Its body extends backward a little ventral to and almost parallel with the right costal arch. The pylorus is usually opposite the ventral end of the eleventh or twelfth intercostal space. At the reticulo-omasal opening and on the adjacent part of the laminæ of the omasum are large, pointed, horny papillæ.

The general arrangement of the **intestine** is like that of the ox. The **small**

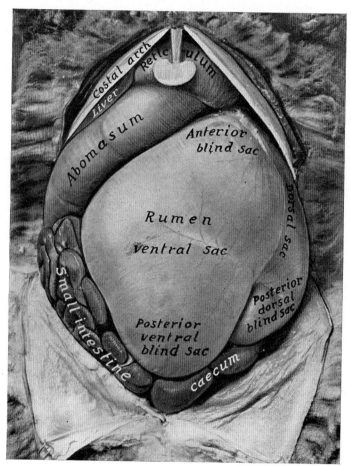

Fig. 408.—Abdominal Viscera of Sheep; Superficial Ventral View.

intestine is about 80 feet (ca. 24 to 25 m.) long; its average diameter is about an inch (ca. 2 to 3 cm.), the caliber increasing in its terminal part, where a very extensive Peyer's patch is found. Duodenal glands occur for a distance of two feet or more (ca. 60–70 cm.) beyond the pylorus. The **cæcum** is about 10 inches (ca. 25 cm.) long, 2 inches (ca. 5 cm.) wide, and has a capacity of about a quart (ca. 1 liter); only about two inches (ca. 5 cm.) of it is free. The **colon** is about 15 feet (ca. 4 to 5 m.) long. Its caliber is at first about the same as that of the cæcum, but diminishes to about the width of the small intestine.

The **liver** weighs about 20 to 25 ounces (ca. 550 to 700 gm.). It lies entirely to the right of the median plane. The parietal surface is related almost exclusively to the right part of the diaphragm. The visceral surface presents extensive reticular and abomasal impressions, and a small omasal impression medial to the portal fissure. The umbilical fissure is deep and partially divides the gland into two chief lobes, dorsal and ventral. The caudate lobe is prismatic and blunt-pointed. The œsophageal notch is represented by a slight impression. The gall-bladder is long and narrow. The bile-duct joins the pancreatic duct to form a **common bile-duct** (Ductus choledochus communis), which opens into the duodenum about one foot (ca. 30 cm.) from the pylorus.

The **pancreas** is arranged as in the ox. Its duct unites with the bile-duct.

The **spleen** (Fig. 405) is approximately triangular, with the angles rounded off;

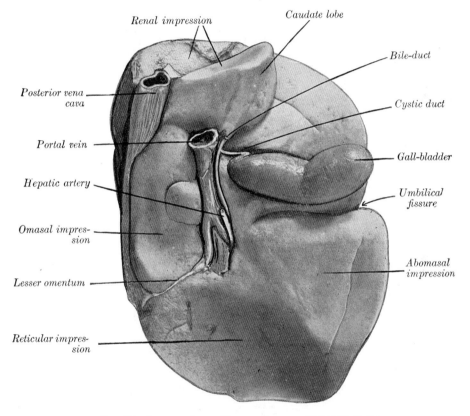

FIG. 409.—LIVER OF SHEEP, VISCERAL SURFACE; HARDENED *in situ.*

the wider end or base is dorsal. It weighs about three or four ounces (ca. 100 grams). Its length is about five to six inches (ca. 12 to 15 cm.), and its greatest width three to four inches (ca. 7.5–10 cm.). The long axis is oblique, and corresponds to a line drawn from the vertebral end of the last rib to about the middle of the tenth intercostal space. The parietal surface is convex and is related to the diaphragm, to which rather more than the anterior third is adherent; when hardened *in situ*, it often shows impressions of the upper parts of the last three ribs. The visceral surface is concave, and its anterior half is attached to the dorsal curvature of the rumen. The borders are thin, the posterior one often being crenated. The dorsal end or base is attached to the left crus of the diaphragm under the last two ribs;

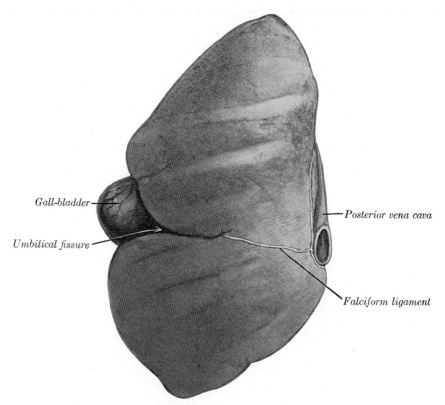

Gall-bladder
Umbilical fissure
Posterior vena cava
Falciform ligament

Fig. 410.—Liver of Sheep, Parietal Surface; Hardened *in situ*.

it usually extends about an inch (ca. 3 cm.) behind the last rib. The hilus is on the visceral surface, close to the anterior basal angle; it is a round depression, not a groove. The ventral end is narrower and thinner than the base; it is usually situated opposite the tenth intercostal space or eleventh rib, a little above its middle.

DIGESTIVE SYSTEM OF THE PIG

THE MOUTH

The **rima oris** is extensive, the angles of the mouth being situated far back. The **upper lip** is thick and short, and is blended with the snout; the **lower lip** is small and pointed. The labial glands are few and small.

The mucous membrane of the **cheeks** is smooth. The **buccal glands** are compactly arranged in two rows opposite the cheek teeth. The **parotid duct** opens opposite the fourth or fifth cheek tooth.

The **hard palate** is long and narrow; it is marked by a median furrow, on each side of which are twenty or more ridges. On its anterior part there is a long narrow prominence, the incisive papilla, at the posterior part of which the incisive or naso-palatine ducts open. There is a round prominence in front of the first pair of incisors.

The **soft palate** is very thick; its length in an animal of medium size is about two and a half inches (ca. 5 cm.). Its direction almost continues that of the hard palate, *i. e.*, it is nearly horizontal. It extends to the middle of the oral surface of the epiglottis. It has in many cases a small median prolongation termed the **uvula.** The oral surface presents a median furrow, on either side of which is an oval raised area, marked by numerous crypts; these elevations are the **tonsils.** Tonsillar tissue also occurs in the lateral walls of the isthmus faucium and the root of the tongue.

The **tongue** is long and narrow and the apex is thin. Two or three vallate

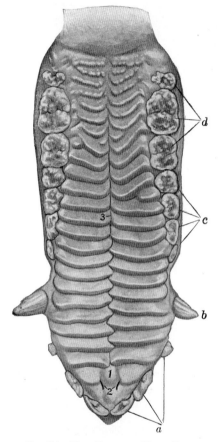

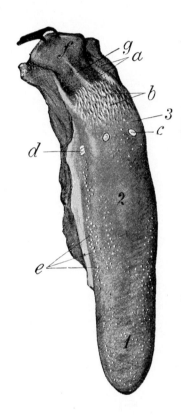

FIG. 411.—HARD PALATE OF YOUNG PIG.

1, Papilla incisiva; 2, openings of ductus incisivi; 3, raphé of palate; *a*, incisor teeth; *b*, canine tooth; *c*, premolar teeth; *d*, molar teeth.

FIG. 412.—TONGUE OF PIG.

1, Apex; *2*, dorsum; *3*, root; *a*, orifices of ducts of lingual glands; *b*, papillæ of root; *c*, vallate papilla (not really so distinct as in figure); *d*, foliate papilla; *e*, fungiform papillæ; *f*, epiglottis (pulled back); *g*, median glosso-epiglottic fold. (Ellenberger-Baum, Anat. d. Haustiere.)

papillæ are present. The fungiform papillæ are small and are most numerous laterally. The filiform papillæ are soft and very small. On the root there are soft, long, pointed papillæ, directed backward. Foliate papillæ are also present.

There is a well-marked median glosso-epiglottic fold, on either side of which is a depression (Vallecula epiglottica). The frenum linguæ is double.

The **dental formula**[1] of the pig is:

$$2\left(I\frac{3}{3} - C\frac{1}{1} - P\frac{4}{4} - M\frac{3}{3}\right) = 44$$

[1] Several figures in the osteology also illustrate the teeth.

The formula for the temporary teeth is:

$$2\left(\mathrm{Di}\,\frac{3}{3} - \mathrm{Dc}\,\frac{1}{1} - \mathrm{Dp}\,\frac{4}{4}\right) = 32$$

The **upper incisors** are small; they are separated from each other by spaces, and from the canines by a larger interval. The first incisors are the largest; they are flattened and strongly curved, and the crowns are convergent; they have no

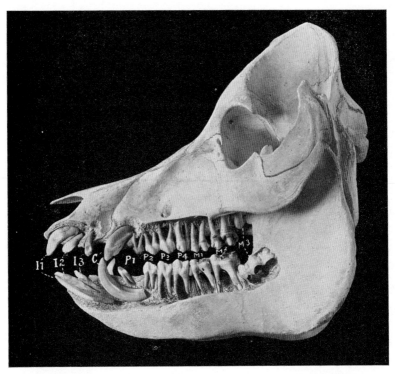

Fig. 413.—Skull of Pig about a Year and a Half Old, Sculptured to Show the Embedded Parts of the Teeth. *I1–3*, Incisors; *C*, canines; *P1–4*, premolars; *M1–3*, molars. The third molar has not erupted and its roots are not yet formed.

distinct neck. The convex labial surface has an extensive covering of enamel, but the latter covers only a small marginal area on the lingual surface. The second are much shorter and are only slightly curved; they have a short flattened crown and a rounded root. The third incisors are much smaller, are flattened laterally, and have three small eminences on the crown. The **lower incisors** are almost horizontal and are convergent and close together. The first and second are about equal in size, are rod-like, very slightly curved, and deeply implanted in the jaw. The labial surface is slightly convex, the lingual concave and marked near its extremity by a ridge. The third incisor is much shorter and is somewhat flattened; it has a short narrow crown and a distinct neck.

Cement Enamel Dentine

Fig. 414.—Cross-section of Lower Canine Tooth of Pig.

c, Pulp cavity.

The **canine teeth** or **tusks** of the male are greatly developed and project out of the mouth. The upper canine of the boar may be three or four inches (ca. 8 to 10 cm.) long. The crown is conical and is curved somewhat backward and outward; the embedded part is curved and has a large pulp eavity. The lower canine may reach a length of eight inches or more (ca. 20 cm.); the crown is prismatic and is curved backward and outward in front of the upper one, so that the friction between the two keeps a sharp edge on the lower tooth. In the sow they are much smaller.[1]

The **cheek teeth** increase in size from before backward. They have (with certain exceptions noted below) complex tuberculate crowns; the term bunodont is applied to this condition, as distinguished from the lophodont and selenodont structure in horses and cattle, in which there are prominent ridges of enamel.

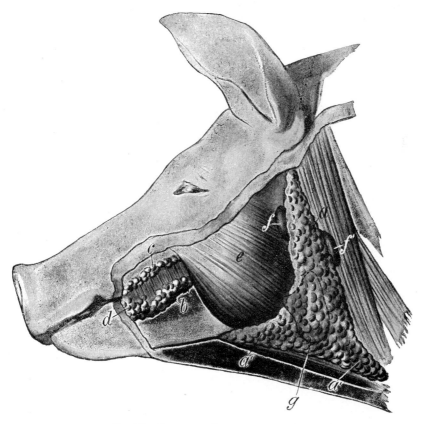

FIG. 415.—SUPERFICIAL GLANDS OF HEAD OF PIG.

a, Parotid gland; *a′, a″,* cervical and mandibular angles of *a; b, c,* ventral and dorsal buccal glands; *d,* labial glands; *e,* masseter muscle; *f, f′,* lymph glands; *g,* dotted line indicating outline of mandibular gland, which is concealed. (Ellenberger-Baum, Anat. d. Haustiere.)

They are short-crowned teeth with a distinct neck and round, pointed roots. The first tooth in each jaw is small, simple, and appears only once; in the lower jaw it is near the canine; in the upper, near the second cheek tooth.[2] The next two teeth are larger, laterally compressed, and sectorial. The fourth tooth below is larger, but otherwise like the preceding ones, while the upper one is much wider and is tuberculate. The first premolar has two roots, the others three or four. The molars have four roots, but the anterior pair may be largely fused.

[1] The canines of the pig are "permanent pulp" teeth and therefore capable of continued growth, and are without roots in the strict sense. The convex surface is covered with enamel, the concave with cement.

[2] It is often absent in the lower jaw.

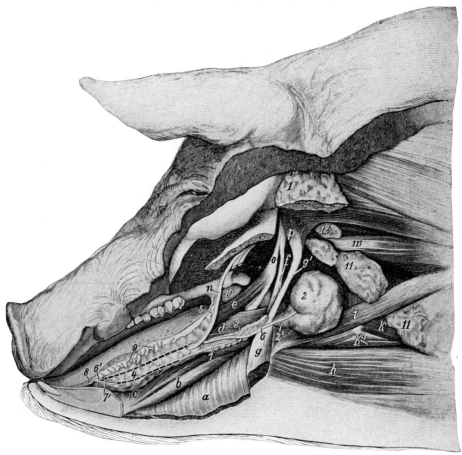

Fig. 416.—Dissection of Mouth and Pharyngeal Region of Pig.

1, Dorsal end of parotid gland; 2, 2′, mandibular gland; 3, 4, posterior and anterior parts of sublingual gland; 5, palatine glands; 6, 6′, mandibular duct (dotted part concealed); 7, 7′, ductus sublingualis major (dotted part concealed); 8, opening of 6 and 7; 9, ductus sublinguales minores; 10, tonsil; 11, thymus; 12, pharyngeal lymph gland; a, m. mylo-hyoideus (reflected); b, m. genio-hyoideus; c, m. genio-glossus; d, m. hyo-glossus; e, m. stylo-glossus; f, m. stylo-hyoideus; g, m. digastricus (cut), and g′, its tendon of origin; h, m. sterno-hyoideus; i, m. omo-hyoideus; k, k′, m. sterno-thyroideus; m, m. rectus capitis ventralis major; n, lingual nerve; o, great cornu of hyoid bone; p, paramastoid process. (Ellenberger-Baum, Anat. d. Haustiere.)

The average periods of **eruption** of the teeth are given in the subjoined table:

Tooth	Eruption	Change
I_1	2 to 4 weeks	12 months
I_2	upper 2 to 3 months lower 1½ to 2 months	16 to 20 months
I_3	Before birth	8 to 10 months
C	Before birth	9 to 10 months
P_1	5 months	
P_2	5 to 7 weeks	
P_3	upper 4 to 8 days lower 2 to 4 weeks	12 to 15 months
P_4	upper 4 to 8 days lower 2 to 4 weeks	
M_1	4 to 6 months	
M_2	8 to 12 months	
M_3	18 to 20 months	

The **parotid gland** is large and distinctly triangular. It extends very little on to the masseter muscle, and its upper angle does not quite reach the base of the ear. It is pale in color, and is embedded in fat in animals in good condition. On its deep face are several large subparotid lymph glands, some of which are only partially covered by the parotid. The **parotid duct** arises on the deep face, has a course similar to that of the ox, and perforates the cheek opposite the fourth or fifth upper cheek tooth. Small **accessory parotid glands** (Glandulæ parotideæ accessoriæ) may be found along the course of the duct.

The **mandibular** or submaxillary **gland** is small, reddish in color, and oval in outline; it is covered by the parotid. Its superficial face is convex, and is marked by rounded prominences. From its deep face a narrow process extends forward about two or three inches (ca. 5 to 7.5 cm.) beneath the mylo-hyoideus muscle along with the duct. The latter opens near the frenum linguæ, but there is no papilla.

The **sublingual gland** has an arrangement similar to that of the ox. The posterior part (Glandula sublingualis grandicanalaris) is reddish-yellow in color, and is about two inches (ca. 5 cm.) long and half an inch wide; its posterior end is in relation to the mandibular gland and its duct. The anterior part (Gl. sublingualis parvicanalaris) is much larger, being two or three inches (ca. 5 to 7 cm.) long and about twice the width and thickness of the posterior part. All or most of the ducts from the posterior part unite to form the **ductus sublingualis major,** which opens near the ductus mandibularis. Eight or ten **ductus sublinguales minores** convey the secretion from the anterior part through the floor of the mouth.

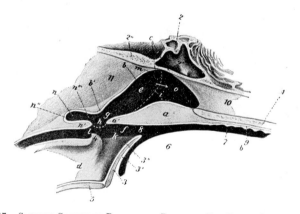

FIG. 417.—SAGITTAL SECTION OF PHARYNGEAL REGION OF PIG, PARTLY SCHEMATIC.

1, Palatine bone; *2*, sphenoid bone; *2'*, sphenoidal sinus; *2''*, occipital bone; *3*, epiglottis; *4*, arytenoid cartilage; *5*, thyroid cartilage; *6*, root of tongue; *7*, mouth cavity; *8*, isthmus faucium; *9*, hard palate; *10*, septum nasi; *11*, ventral muscles of head; *a*, soft palate; *a'*, free edge of *a;* *b*, dorsal wall of pharynx; *c*, fornix of pharynx; *d*, cavity of larynx; *e, g*, naso-pharynx; *f*, oro-pharynx; *h*, posterior pillar of soft palate; *i*, dotted line indicating lateral boundary between nasal cavity and pharynx; *k*, aditus laryngis; *l*, aditus œsophagi; *m*, Eustachian orifice; *n*, pharyngeal diverticulum; *o*, posterior naris. (After Ellenberger, in Leisering's Atlas.)

THE PHARYNX

The **pharynx** presents in its posterior part a median cul-de-sac about an inch and a half (ca. 3 to 4 cm.) long, which is situated between the ventral straight muscles of the head and the origin of the œsophagus; this is termed the **diverticulum pharyngeum.** Its ventral margin is formed by the junction of the posterior pillars of the soft palate, which contain muscular tissue derived from the palatinus and palato-pharyngeus. The fornix of the pharynx is divided by a median fold of mucous membrane which is a direct continuation of the septum nasi. On either side of this is an infundibulum in which the Eustachian tube opens.

THE ŒSOPHAGUS

The **œsophagus** is short and nearly straight. It has (according to Rubeli) a potential caliber in the adult of nearly 3 inches (ca. 7 cm.) at either end, and about $1\frac{7}{10}$ inches (ca. 4.2 cm.) in its middle part.[1] The muscular coat is striated, except near the cardia, where the deep part is unstriped. There are numerous tubulo-alveolar glands in the anterior half of the tube; further back they occur in decreasing numbers. Many lymph nodules and much lymphoid tissue are present.

THE STOMACH

The **stomach** is large; its average capacity is about 1½ to 2 gallons (ca. 5.7 to 8 liters). When full, its long axis is transverse and its greater curvature extends backward on the floor of the abdomen a little further than a point midway

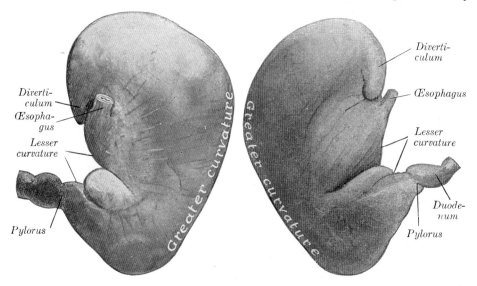

FIG. 418.—STOMACH OF PIG; PARIETAL SURFACE.
The organ contained a rather small amount of ingesta and hence is somewhat contracted.

FIG. 419.—STOMACH OF PIG; VISCERAL SURFACE.
Organ was fixed *in situ* and is somewhat contracted.

between the xiphoid cartilage and the umbilicus. The left part is large and rounded, while the right part (Pars pylorica) is small, and bends sharply upward to join the small intestine. The parietal surface faces chiefly forward, and is related to the liver and diaphragm. The visceral surface faces chiefly backward, and is related to the intestine, greater omentum, mesentery, and pancreas. The greater curvature is related to the diaphragm, spleen, liver, and abdominal floor. The pyloric end lies against the right lateral lobe of the liver, about opposite to the middle of the thirteenth intercostal space. The left extremity is ventral to the upper part of the thirteenth rib and intercostal space, and is related to the dorsal end of the spleen and the left extremity of the pancreas; it presents a flattened conical blind pouch, the **diverticulum ventriculi,** the apex of which projects backward. The œsophagus joins the stomach very obliquely just to the left of the median plane, and about two or three inches (ca. 6 to 10 cm.) ventral to the thirteenth thoracic vertebra. The cardiac opening is slit-like and is bounded above and to the left by a fold which contains a thickening of the internal oblique layer of the muscular coat. The opening into the diverticulum is situated above and a little to the left of the car-

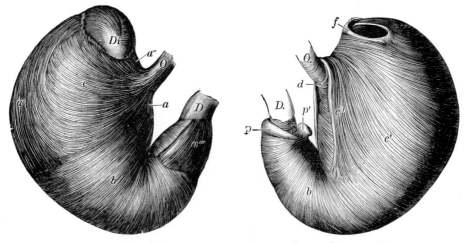

FIG. 420.—STOMACH OF PIG, FROM WHICH THE SEROUS COAT HAS BEEN REMOVED.

FIG. 421.—EVERTED STOMACH OF PIG, FROM WHICH THE MUCOUS MEMBRANE HAS BEEN REMOVED.

O, Œsophagus; *D*, duodenum; *Di*, diverticulum; *a, a', a'', a'''*, longitudinal fibers; *b*, circular fibers; *c*, external oblique fibers; *c'* internal oblique fibers; *c''*, cardiac loop; *d*, fibers which connect branches of cardiac loop; *f*, fold at entrance to diverticulum; *p*, pyloric sphincter; *p'*, pyloric prominence. (Ellenberger-Baum, Anat. d. Haustiere.)

dia; it is oval, and is bounded by a thick fold which contains spirally arranged muscular fibers. The mucous membrane may be divided into four regions (Fig. 422). Over a quadrilateral area around the cardia (which extends to the margin of the diverticulum on the left) it is **œsophageal** in character, glandless, and presents a number of folds. A sharp line of demarcation separates this

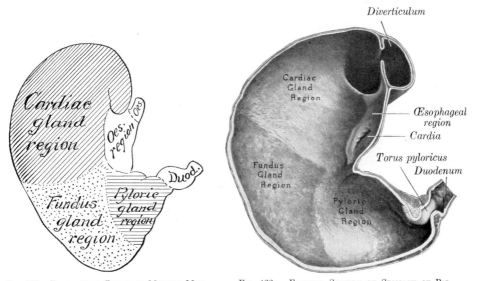

FIG. 422.—DIAGRAM OF ZONES OF MUCOUS MEMBRANE OF STOMACH OF PIG.

FIG. 422*a*.—FRONTAL SECTION OF STOMACH OF PIG.

from the rest of the mucous membrane, which is soft and glandular. The **cardiac** gland region is pale gray in color and thin (ca. 0.5 to 1 mm.); it extends about to the middle of the stomach. The **fundus** gland region is readily distinguished by its thickness (ca. 3 mm.) and its brownish-red, mottled appearance.[1] The **pyloric** region is pale, thinner than the preceding, and presents a number of irregular folds.[2] At the pylorus a remarkable prominence (Torus pyloricus) projects from the wall of the lesser curvature and diminishes considerably the size of the orifice. It is about an inch and a half (ca. 3 to 4 cm.) long and nearly half an inch (ca. 1 cm.) high. Sometimes it is a grooved ridge; in other cases it

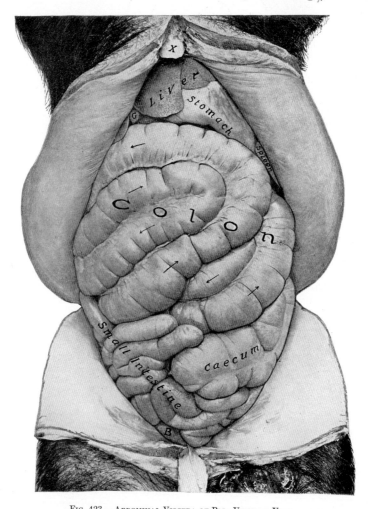

Fig. 423.—Abdominal Viscera of Pig; Ventral View.

The greater omentum has been removed. *B*, urinary bladder; *G*, gall-bladder; *X*, xiphoid cartilage. Arrows indicate course of coils of colon. The spleen was contracted.

has the form of a rounded eminence attached by a pedicle to the wall. It consists largely of fat, but fibers from the circular muscular coat extend into it. The arrangement of the muscular coat is shown in Figs. 420, 421.

---

[1] It will be noted that the fundus gland region does not extend up to the lesser curvature; here the cardiac gland region joins the pyloric.

[2] Microscopic examination shows that these regions are not sharply marked off from each other; instead, there are intermediate zones in which glands of both the adjacent regions are present, and also glands of intermediate histological character.

THE INTESTINE

The intestine is about fifteen times the length of the body.

The **small intestine** is 50 to 65 feet (ca. 15 to 20 m.) long. The mesentery of about the first two feet (ca. 60 cm.) is two to two and a half inches (ca. 5 to 6 cm.)

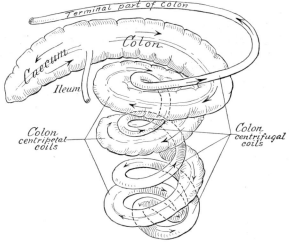

Fig. 424.—Diagram of Cæcum and Colon of Pig.
Coils of colon have been pulled apart.

long; this part may be termed duodenum. The first part of the duodenum turns sharply medially on the visceral surface of the liver to the right of the portal fissure. The second part passes backward, in relation to the medial part of the right kidney dorsally and the colon ventrally, and about the middle of the sublumbar region

Fig. 425.—Ileo-cæcal Opening of Pig.
1, Ileo-cæcal opening; 2, 2, frenulum ilei.

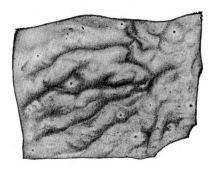

Fig. 426.—Solitary Nodules of Large Intestine of Pig. (Ellenberger-Baum, Anat. d. Haustiere.)

turns across the median plane and runs (as the third part) forward to be continued by the mesenteric part of the intestine. The right end of the pancreas is attached to the first part, and here the pancreatic duct opens into the bowel. The remainder of the bowel (Jejuno-ileum) has a mesentery about six to eight inches (ca. 15 to

20 cm.) long which is thick and contains a quantity of fat, and numerous large lymph glands at its root; the root is attached in the sublumbar region behind the stomach and blends here with the mesentery of the large intestine. The mesenteric part is arranged in close coils and lies mainly above the colon and cæcum, from the stomach to the pelvis; many coils lie against the right flank and on the posterior part of the floor of the abdomen. The opening of the **bile duct** is one or two inches (ca. 2.5 to 5 cm.) from the pylorus, and that of the **pancreatic duct** about four or five inches (ca. 10–12 cm.) beyond it. **Aggregated lymph nodules** or **Peyer's patches** and **solitary nodules** are numerous and very distinct. The patches are usually band-like and prominent; their number has been found to vary from 16 to 38. They begin 8 to 20 inches (ca. 20 to 50 cm.) from the pylorus. The last long one is continued a variable distance in the cæcum. The solitary nodules

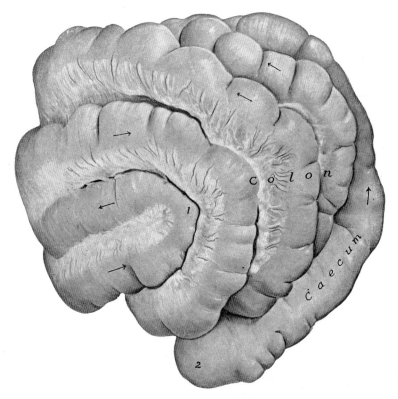

Fig. 427.—Cæcum and Colon of Pig; Left Ventral View.
1, Apex of spiral coil of colon; 2, apex of cæcum.

are distinct (except in the duodenum), but are only about a millimeter high. The duodenal glands extend some 10 to 16 feet (ca. 3–5 m.) from the pylorus.

The **large intestine** is about 12 to 15 feet (ca. 4 to 4.5 meters) in length, and is for the most part much wider than the small intestine; it is connected by a mesentery with the dorsal abdominal wall between the kidneys. The **cæcum** is cylindrical, about 8 to 12 inches (ca. 20 to 30 cm.) long, and 3 to 4 inches (ca. 8 to 10 cm.) wide. It lies against the upper and anterior part of the left flank, and extends ventrally, backward, and medially behind the coiled part of the colon, so that its ventral blind end usually lies on the floor of the abdomen, near the median plane, and at a variable point between the umbilicus and the pelvic inlet (Fig. 423). Its dorsal end is directly continued by the colon, the line of demarcation being indicated by the termination of the small intestine. The ileum joins the cæcum obliquely and projects considerably into the latter. A fold of mucous membrane (Frenulum ilei) passes from each side of the ileo-cæcal opening. The **colon** has at first about the same caliber as the cæcum, but becomes gradually smaller. It lies chiefly to the left of the median plane, behind the stomach. Most of it is arranged in three close, double spiral coils in the mesentery, in relation with the floor of the abdomen ventrally, the stomach and liver in front, the cæcum and small intestine behind, and the small intestine on the right. On emerging from this spiral laby-rinth it passes at first forward in the sublumbar region to the right of the median plane, and, on reaching the stomach and right end of the pancreas, turns to the left. It then passes backward, on the ventral surface of the pancreas, and in relation to the medial part of the left kidney, inclines medially, and is continued at the pelvic inlet by the rectum. This terminal part is closely attached by a short mesentery to the sublumbar region. The **rectum** is usually surrounded by a quantity of fat. The cæcum has three longitudinal muscular bands and three rows of sacculations, which are continued a short distance on the colon. The spiral colon has two bands and two series of sacculations, which, however, gradually disappear in the centrif-ugal part. The solitary nodules are numerous, and appear as round prominences, 2 to 3 mm. in diameter, often with a crater-like depression. The last Peyer's patch of the small intestine is continued a variable distance in the cæcum, and there are often patches in the first part of the colon.

THE LIVER

The liver is relatively large, its average weight in the adult being about four pounds (ca. 1.5 to 2 kg.). It is thick centrally, but the circumference is thin. It is

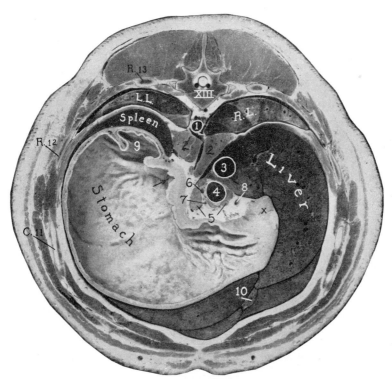

FIG. 427a.—CROSS SECTION OF PIG; POSTERIOR VIEW.

Section is cut through posterior end of the thirteenth thoracic vertebra. *1*, Aorta (thoracic duct to upper right of aorta); *2, 2′*, left and right crura of diaphragm; *3*, posterior vena cava; *4*, portal vein; *5*, hepatic lymph glands; *6*, hepatic artery; *7*, gastric branch; *8*, ductus choledochus; *9*, diverticulum ventriculi; *10*, gall-bladder; *C. 11*, cartilage of eleventh rib; *R. 12, R. 13*, ribs twelve and thirteen; *XIII*, thirteenth thoracic vertebra; *L. L.*, left lung; *R. L.*, right lung; arrow points to cardia.

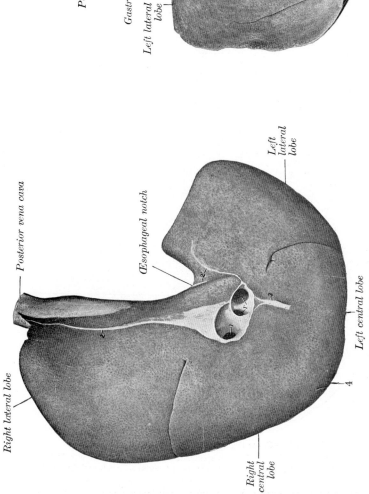

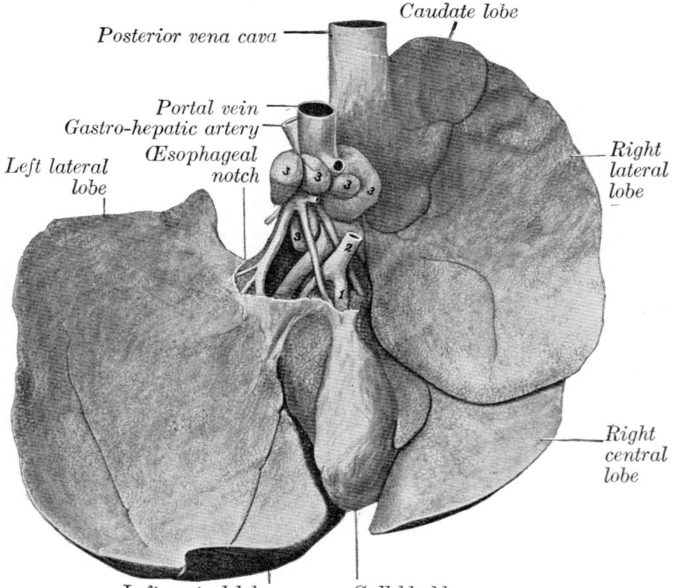

FIG. 429.—LIVER OF PIG; VISCERAL SURFACE.

The peritoneum and fat have been removed from the vicinity of the portal fissure. 1, Cystic duct; 2, bile-duct; 3, lymph-glands.

FIG. 428.—LIVER OF PIG; PARIETAL SURFACE.

1, 1′, Large hepatic veins opening into posterior vena cava; 2, 2′, coronary ligament; 3, falciform ligament. Only a very small part of the umbilical fissure between the right and left central lobes is visible above 4.

divided by three deep interlobar incisures into four principal lobes—**right lateral, right central, left central, left lateral**; the last of these is usually considerably the largest. On the upper part of the right lateral lobe, is the **caudate lobe,** which is clearly marked off by a fissure and is often partially subdivided by a secondary fissure. That part of the right central lobe which lies below the portal fissure and to the left of the gall-bladder and cystic duct is homologous with the quadrate lobe of man. Much the greater part is to the right of the median plane. The parietal surface is extremely convex in conformity with the curvature of the diaphragm, to which it is chiefly related.[1] A small part of the surface is in contact with the abdominal floor in the xiphoid region and ventral to the right costal arch. Its most anterior part reaches to a transverse plane through the ventral part of the sixth rib or intercostal space. The visceral surface is deeply concave; most of it is related to the stomach, for which there is a correspondingly large and deep gastric impression. There may be a duodenal impression on the upper part of the right lateral lobe, but no renal impression exists, as the right kidney does not touch the liver. The fossa for the gall-bladder (Fossa vesicæ felleæ) is mainly on the right central lobe, but also in part on the adjacent surface of the left central lobe. The

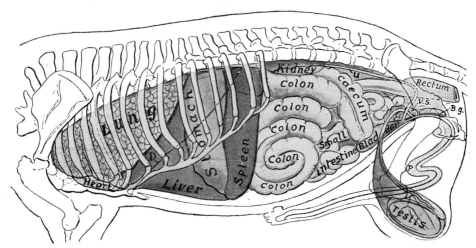

FIG. 430.—PROJECTION OF VISCERA OF PIG ON BODY-WALL; LEFT SIDE.

D, Costal line of diaphragm; *U,* ureter; *V.S.,* vesicula seminalis; *B.g.,* bulbo-urethral gland; *P,* penis.

posterior vena cava enters the dorsal border of the caudate lobe and soon becomes entirely embedded in the gland substance, emerging only at its passage through the diaphragm. The œsophageal notch is large and is occupied mainly by the large right crus of the diaphragm. The right lateral border extends backward to the upper part of the last intercostal space. The left lateral border is chiefly opposite the ninth intercostal space and tenth rib. The ventral border lies on the abdominal floor a short distance (ca. 3 to 5 cm.) behind the xiphoid cartilage.

The coronary ligament resembles that of the horse. The falciform ligament is very short or absent in the adult, and is attached to the diaphragm just below the foramen venæ cavæ. The round ligament is present in the young subject. Neither lateral nor caudate ligaments are present.

The **gall-bladder** is attached in the fossa vesicæ felleæ; its fundus does not reach to the ventral border. The cystic duct joins the hepatic duct at an acute

---

[1] The description here given is based on the appearance of the organ as hardened *in situ,* which differs radically from that of the soft organ. It also differs much in shape in young and adult subjects.

angle immediately after the emergence of the latter from the portal fissure. The **bile duct** (Ductus choledochus) opens at the papilla duodeni about one or two inches (ca. 2.5 to 5 cm.) from the pylorus; an ampulla may be formed.

Owing to the large amount of interlobular tissue, the **lobules** are mapped out sharply; they are polyhedral in form, and are 1 to 2.5 mm. in diameter. For the

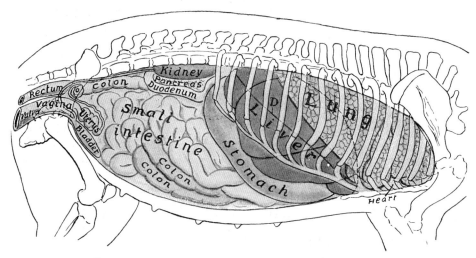

FIG. 431.—PROJECTION OF VISCERA OF PIG ON BODY-WALL; RIGHT SIDE.

D, Costal line of diaphragm; *O,* ovary. The pancreas and duodenum are not in contact with the flank, as would naturally be inferred from this figure, but are situated more medially and are covered laterally by small intestine.

same reason the gland is much less friable than that of the other animals, from which it is easily distinguished.

THE PANCREAS

The **pancreas** extends across the dorsal wall of the abdominal cavity behind the stomach. It is triradiate or triangular. The right extremity is attached to the first curve (Flexura portalis) of the duodenum, and here the duct passes to the bowel. The left extremity is related to the left extremity of the stomach, the dorsal end of the spleen, and the anterior pole of the left kidney. The middle or posterior extremity or lobe is practically median and is related to the portal vein and the root of the mesentery. The **pancreatic duct** passes from the right extremity directly through the duodenal wall, opening about four or five inches (ca. 10 to 12 cm.) from the pylorus. The interlobular tissue usually contains a good deal of fat.

THE SPLEEN

The **spleen** is long and narrow. Its long axis is nearly dorso-ventral in direction, and is curved to conform to the left part of the greater curvature of the stomach. The dorsal end lies under the vertebral ends of the last three ribs; it is related to the stomach in front, the left kidney behind, and the left extremity of the pancreas medially. The visceral surface has a longitudinal ridge on which the hilus is situated; this divides the surface into nearly equal gastric and intestinal areas, which are in contact with the stomach and colon respectively. The parietal surface is convex and is related to the left lateral and ventral wall of the abdomen. The ventral end is smaller than the dorsal one; it lies on the abdominal floor, usually in the umbilical region. The spleen is attached so loosely to the stomach that it may be regarded as being intercalated in the great omentum.

In large subjects it may reach a length of about 25 inches (ca. 60 cm.) and a width of 3 to 4 inches (ca. 8 to 10 cm.), and a weight of 10 to 15 ounces (ca. 350 gm.). Accessory spleens (Lienes accessorii) may be found in the gastro-splenic omentum.

The position of the spleen varies according to the fulness of the stomach and its own size. The dorsal end varies little. But the ventral end has a wide range, as might be expected; it may be in contact with the left lobe of the liver or may be centrally situated just in front of the um-

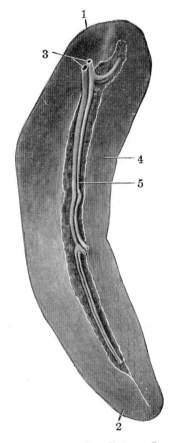

Fig. 432.—Spleen of Pig; Visceral Surface.

1, Dorsal end, 2, ventral end; 3, stumps of splenic vessels; 4, gastric surface; 5, hilus with vessels.

bilicus. As in other animals, the size of the spleen is extremely variable. Even in a large adult it may be only a little more than a foot (ca. 35 cm.) long, two and a half inches wide, and weigh six or seven ounces (ca. 200 gm.).

DIGESTIVE SYSTEM OF THE DOG

THE MOUTH

The size and form of the **mouth** vary greatly in different breeds, the cavity being in some long and narrow, in others short and wide. The **rima oris** is very extensive, so that the labial commissure is opposite the third or fourth cheek tooth. The **lips** are thin and mobile, and present numerous tactile hairs. The upper lip has a small, central, bare area which forms part of the muzzle, and is marked by a central groove, the philtrum, or (as in the bull-dog) a fissure, giving the appearance of harelip. The lateral borders of the lower lip are flaccid and denticulated. The mucous membrane is usually pigmented and forms distinct frena labiorum. The labial glands are small and scanty.

The **cheeks** are loose and capacious, and their mucous lining is smooth and more or less pigmented. The **parotid duct** opens usually opposite the third upper cheek tooth. Near the last tooth are the openings of the four or five ducts from the zygomatic gland. This gland may be regarded as the homologue of the dorsal

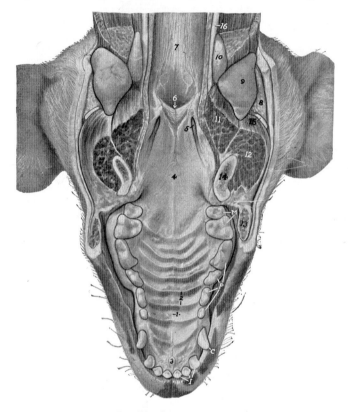

FIG. 433.—PALATE OF DOG.

The lower jaw and related structures have been removed by sawing through the rami of the mandible and cutting the soft structures horizontally.

1, Raphé of palate; 2, ridges of palate; 3, papilla incisiva; 4, soft palate; 5, tonsil; 6, meatus naso-pharyngeus; 7, dorsal wall of pharynx; 8, parotid gland; 9, mandibular gland; 10, pharyngeal lymph gland; 11, m. occipito-mandibularis (cut); 12, m. masseter (cut); 13, cheek (cut); 14, ramus of mandible (section); 15, parotid lymph gland; 16, carotid artery; *I*, incisor teeth; *C*, canine tooth; *P*, premolar teeth; *M*, molar teeth.

buccal glands of the other animals; it will be described later. The ventral buccal glands are opposite the cheek teeth and in series with the inferior labial glands.

The **hard palate** is widest between the fourth pair of cheek teeth. It has eight to ten curved ridges on either side of the median raphé; the latter may be indistinct or scarcely recognizable. Behind the first pair of incisor teeth is the rounded or triangular papilla incisiva, at which the incisive or naso-palatine ducts open. The mucous membrane is usually pigmented.

The **soft palate** (Figs. 433, 488) is thick, except at its margins. In the resting state of the parts it comes in contact with the epiglottis.[1] Between its anterior and

---

[1] It is usually stated that it is in contact with the oral surface of the epiglottis, but the epiglottis may be ventral to the soft palate (Fig. 488).

posterior pillars on either side is a marked tonsillar sinus, in which an elongated, fusiform **tonsil** is situated; this is reddish in color, about an inch long, and is largely or completely concealed between two folds of mucous membrane. The posterior pillar is double; the upper fold passes to the dorsal wall of the pharynx, where it subsides; the lower fold goes to the side of the epiglottis.

The **tongue** is wide and thin in front, thicker posteriorly; it is very mobile. It is not pigmented, but has a bright red color. The dorsum is marked by a median groove (Sulcus medianus linguæ), and is thickly beset with short, pointed, filiform papillæ, the free ends of which are directed backward. On the root there are long conical papillæ which are soft, and point backward; similar papillæ occur on the lateral walls of the isthmus faucium. The fungiform papillæ are small, and are scattered over the dorsum and sides of the tongue, but are absent on the posterior part of the dorsum and on the root, where the conical papillæ occur. There are usually two or three vallate papillæ on either side on the posterior part of the dorsum, where the conical papillæ begin. Small foliate papillæ are also present just in front of the anterior pillars of the soft palate; they are oval and are crossed by about half a dozen fine fissures. In the inferior part of the tip of the tongue is the **lyssa**, a fusiform cord, composed of fibrous tissue, muscular tissue, and fat. In large dogs it is about two inches (ca. 4 to 5 cm.) long. The lingual muscles present no remarkable special characters.

THE TEETH

The formula of the permanent teeth is:

$$2 \left(I \frac{3}{3} - C \frac{1}{1} - P \frac{4}{4} - M \frac{2}{3} \right) = 42$$

All of the teeth have short crowns and distinct necks; they erupt rapidly. The crowns are white, being destitute of cement.

The **incisors** are placed almost vertically and close together in the jaw bones. They do not correspond to an opposing tooth, but rather to parts of two teeth of the other jaw. They increase in size from the first to the third. The crowns are trituberculate, the central projection being the largest. The labial surface is convex; the lingual surface is slightly concave, and is marked off from the neck by a **V**-shaped ridge, the cingulum. The roots are narrow transversely. The lower incisors

Fig. 434.—Tongue, Pharynx, Larynx, etc., of Dog; Dorsal View.

The pharynx and soft palate have been cut medially and reflected, and the œsophagus cut off.

1, Median groove of tongue; 2, long conical papillæ of root of tongue; 3, vallate papillæ; 4, tonsil (drawn out of tonsillar sinus; 5, floor of pharynx (prominence here caused by cricoid cartilage and m. crico-arytenoideus dorsalis); 7, vestibule of larynx; 8, epiglottis; 9, arytenoid cartilage; 10, trachea (membranous part); 11, 11, lateral lobes of thyroid gland; 12, 12', anterior and posterior thyroid vessels.

are smaller than the upper ones. One or two supernumerary teeth may be present.

The **canine teeth** are large, conical, and curved. The upper canine is separated from the corner incisor by an interval into which the lower canine is received when the jaws are closed. The lower canine is close to the corner incisor. The root is about an inch (ca. 2 to 3 cm.) long and is flattened laterally.

The **cheek teeth** are typically $\frac{6}{7}$, but in brachycephalic breeds they are commonly reduced to $\frac{5}{7}$, and in extreme cases even to $\frac{4}{5}$. The reduction occurs at either end or at both ends of the series. The first tooth appears only once. The fourth tooth of the upper row and the fifth of the lower row are much larger than the rest,

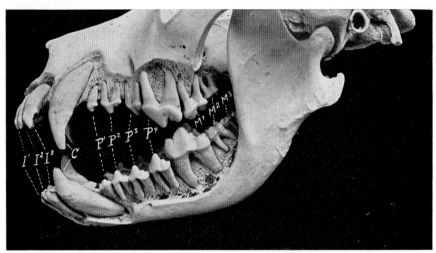

Fig. 435.—Jaws of Adult St. Bernard Dog, Sculptured to Show the Embedded Parts of the Teeth.
I1–3, Incisors; *C,* canines; *P1–4,* premolars; *M1–3,* molars.

and are termed **sectorial** or **carnassial** teeth. From these the teeth diminish in size both forward and backward. The upper and lower teeth do not correspond, but

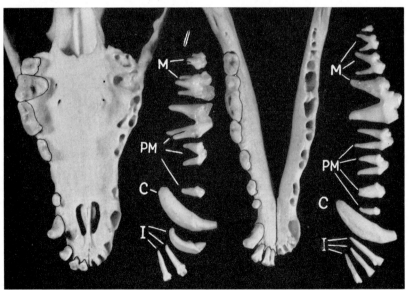

Fig. 435a—Showing Teeth of Dog of Upper and Lower Jaws Removed from Their Alveoli.
I, Incisors; C, canine; P.M., premolars; M, molars. The lower jaw shows a supernumerary molar present on one side and the third molar missing on the opposite side. The second premolar is missing on both upper jaws.

rather dovetail. The teeth behind the sectorial ones are tuberculate, *i. e.,* have rounded eminences on the masticatory surface. The others are all sectorial in character, *i. e.,* have sharp-edged, pointed projections, the middle one being the most prominent. The premolars are laterally compressed, and are separated by intervals from the canines and from each other, except in the brachycephalic breeds. The upper molars have wide, somewhat quadrangular crowns, and three roots. The crown of the upper fourth premolar (Dens sectorius) is divided into two pointed lobes and has an antero-medial tubercle; it has three roots. The crown of the first lower molar (Dens sectorius) is compressed laterally and has two pointed, sharp-edged lobes, behind which are one or two tubercles; it has two roots.

The average periods of eruption are given below.

Tooth	Eruption	Change
I_1	4 to 5 weeks	
I_2	4 to 5 weeks	4 to 5 months
I_3	4 weeks	
C	3 to 4 weeks	4 to 5 months
P_1	4 to 5 months	
P_2	4 to 5 weeks	5 to 6 months
P_3	3 to 4 weeks	
P_4	3 to 4 weeks	
M_1	4 months	
M_2	upper 5 to 6 months; lower 4½ to 5 months	
M_3	6 to 7 months	

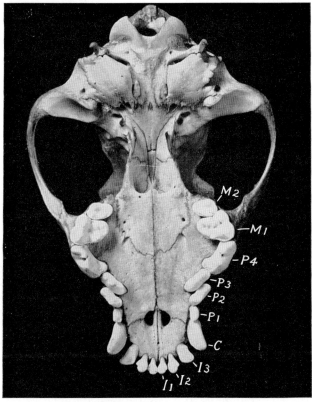

FIG. 436.—BASE OF SKULL OF COCKER SPANIEL.
I1–3, Incisors; *C*, canine; *P1–4*, premolars; *M1–2*, molars. Note the crowding of the canines and premolars on account of the shortness of the jaw.

THE SALIVARY GLANDS

The **parotid gland** is small and is irregularly triangular. Its dorsal end is wide and is divided into two parts by a deep notch into which the base of the ear is received. The ventral end is small and overlaps the mandibular gland. The **parotid duct** leaves the gland at the lower part of the anterior border, crosses the masseter muscle, and opens into the mouth opposite the third upper cheek tooth.

Small accessory parotid glands (Glandulæ parotideæ accessoriæ) are sometimes found along the course of the duct.

The **mandibular gland** is usually larger than the parotid. In large dogs it is about two inches (ca. 5 cm.) long and an inch or more (ca. 3 cm.) wide. It is rounded in outline, pale yellow in color, and is enclosed in a fibrous capsule. Its upper part is covered by the parotid, but it is otherwise superficial, and is palpable in the angle of junction of the jugular and external maxillary veins. The **mandibular duct** leaves the deep face of the gland, passes along the surface of the occipito-mandibularis and stylo-glossus, and opens into the mouth on a very indistinct papilla near the frenum linguæ.

The **sublingual gland** is pink in color and is divided into two parts. The posterior part (Glandula sublingualis grandicanalaris) lies on the occipito-man-

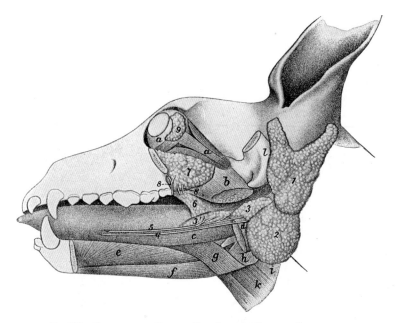

FIG. 437.—DISSECTION OF HEAD OF DOG, SHOWING SALIVARY GLANDS, ETC.

a, Ocular muscles; *b*, pterygoideus medialis (cut); *c*, stylo-glossus; *d*, occipito-mandibularis (cut); *e*, genio-glossus; *f*, genio-hyoideus; *g*, hyo-glossus; *h*, thyro-pharyngeus; *i*, crico-pharyngeus; *k*, thyro-hyoideus; *l*, zygomatic process of temporal (sawn off); *1*, parotid gland; *2*, mandibular gland; *3*, posterior part of sublingual gland; *3′*, anterior part of same; *4*, mandibular duct; *5*, ductus sublingualis major; *6*, palatine glands; *7*, zygomatic gland; *8*, ducts of *7*; *9*, lacrimal gland. (After Ellenberger, in Leisering's Atlas.)

dibularis muscle in intimate relation with the mandibular gland, but is clearly separable from it after removal of the common fibrous capsule. It has a pointed anterior process. Its **duct** (Ductus sublingualis major) accompanies the mandibular duct, and either opens beside it or joins it. The anterior part (Glandula sublingualis parvicanalaris) is long and narrow; it lies between the mucous membrane of the mouth and the mylo-hyoideus, dorsal to the stylo-glossus muscle. It has a number (8 to 12) of small **ducts** (Ductus sublinguales minores), some of which open directly into the mouth, while others join the large duct.

The **zygomatic gland** (Glandula zygomatica)[1] (Fig. 437) is situated in the anterior part of the pterygo-palatine fossa. It is related superficially to the zygomatic arch and the masseter and temporal muscles. Its deep face is in contact with the periorbita, the pterygoid muscle, the internal maxillary artery, and the

_____

[1] Also known as the orbital gland.

maxillary nerve. It has four or five **ducts** which open near the last upper cheek tooth; one of them (Ductus glandulæ zygomaticæ major) is almost as large as the parotid duct; the others (Ductus glandulæ zygomaticæ minores) are small.

THE PHARYNX (Fig. 434)

The fornix is narrow. The pharyngeal orifices of the auditive or Eustachian tubes are small and slit-like; the end of the tube causes a rounded projection of the mucous membrane (Torus tubarius). The œsophageal aditus is relatively small and is well defined by a transverse fold of the mucous membrane. The muscles present no marked differential features, but the hyo-pharyngeus muscle is clearly divided into a kerato-pharyngeus and a chondro-pharyngeus.

THE ŒSOPHAGUS

The **œsophagus** is relatively wide and dilatable except at its origin, where there is a constriction termed the **isthmus œsophagi.** This initial narrowness of the lumen is caused by a prominence of the ventral part of the mucous membrane, underlying which is a thick layer of mucous glands (Fig. 490). The cervical part is at first median and is dorsal to the trachea, but in the posterior part of the neck it lies to the left of the trachea. The thoracic part continues in this position and ventral to the left longus colli to the base of the heart; here it inclines medially, having the aortic arch on its left, and passes back over the bifurcation of the trachea. Continuing backward between the lungs it usually inclines slightly to the left, passes through the hiatus œsophageus, and joins the stomach just to the left of the median plane and ventral to the eleventh or twelfth thoracic vertebra. The muscular tissue is striated and consists mainly of two layers of spiral fibers which cross each other; near the cardia, however, the fibers are longitudinal and circular. There are tubulo-alveolar glands (Gl. œsophagæ) in the submucosa throughout.

THE STOMACH

The **stomach** is relatively large. Its capacity in a dog of average size is about five pints.

Colin estimates the average capacity at about 3 liters (ca. 6½ pints), with a range between 0.6 and 8 liters (ca. 1⅓ to 17½ pints). Neumayer gives the capacity as 100 to 250 c.c. per kilogram of body-weight (ca. 2.7 ounces per pound). Hall and Wigdor estimate the capacity at about a quart (ca. 1 liter) for a dog of average weight (ca. 10 kg.).

When full, it is irregularly piriform. The left or cardiac part (Fundus et corpus ventriculi) is large and rounded, while the right or pyloric part (Pars pylorica) is small and cylindrical. When empty, or nearly so, the left sac is strongly contracted; the pyloric part is much less affected by variations in the amount of ingesta.

The parietal surface of the full stomach is very extensive, strongly convex, and faces partly forward, but largely ventrally and to the left. It is related to the liver, the left part of the diaphragm, and the left and ventral abdominal wall as far back as a transverse plane through the second or third lumbar vertebra. The visceral surface is much less extensive and is considerably flattened; it faces chiefly dorsally and to the right, and is related to the intestine, pancreas, and left kidney.

The upper part of the lesser curvature is nearly straight and vertical, but the lower part forms a deep, narrow angle (Incisura angularis), due to the fact that the pyloric part is directed sharply forward and upward. The greater curvature is nearly four times as long as the lesser curvature. In the full stomach it extends considerably behind the left costal arch; ventrally it lies on the abdominal wall about midway between the xiphoid cartilage and the pubis.

The left extremity or fundus is large and rounded; it is the most dorsal part of the organ, and lies under the vertebral ends of the eleventh and twelfth ribs. The pyloric extremity is small and is directed forward and dorsally; it lies usually opposite to the ventral part of the ninth rib or intercostal space, and at a variable distance to the right of the median plane. It is related to the portal fissure of the liver and to the pancreas. The cardia is situated about two to three inches (ca. 5 to 7 cm.) from the left extremity, and is oval; it lies just to the left of the median plane, ventral to the eleventh or twelfth thoracic vertebra.

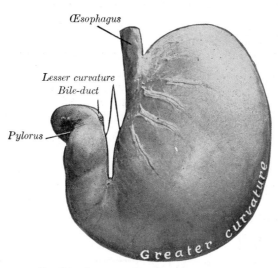

FIG. 438.—STOMACH OF DOG; PARIETAL SURFACE.
Organ fixed *in situ* when well filled.

When empty, or nearly so, the stomach is separated from the ventral abdominal wall by the liver and intestine, and the greater curvature extends back on the left side to the eleventh or twelfth rib. In this state there is commonly a marked constriction between the pyloric part and the body.

The preceding topographic statements are based on observations made on a considerable number of formalin-hardened subjects, and are to be regarded as average findings in dogs of

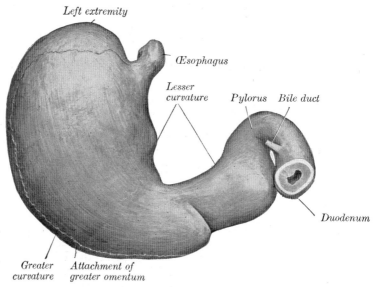

FIG. 439.—STOMACH OF DOG; VISCERAL SURFACE.
Organ fixed in situ when it contained small amount of ingesta.

medium size. The cardiac and pyloric ends vary least in position, but the former varies the length of one vertebra and the latter as much as two intercostal spaces. This variation appears to be due, not only to the amount of ingesta in the stomach, but also to the phase in which the diaphragm is fixed.

The serous coat is almost complete. Along the curvatures it leaves the stomach to form the omenta. The longitudinal muscular fibers are chiefly along the curvatures and on the pyloric part; they are continuous with the external layer of the œsophagus. The oblique fibers are arranged in two layers: the external layer is largely a continuation of the longitudinal fibers of the œsophagus to the body and fundus. The circular layer covers the whole stomach except the fundus, and forms a pyloric sphincter and an antral sphincter. The internal oblique layer is arranged as in the horse, and forms a similar loop-like, cardiac sphincter. Three regions of the mucous membrane exist. Cardiac glands are found in a very narrow pale zone around the cardiac opening, and also scattered along the lesser curva-

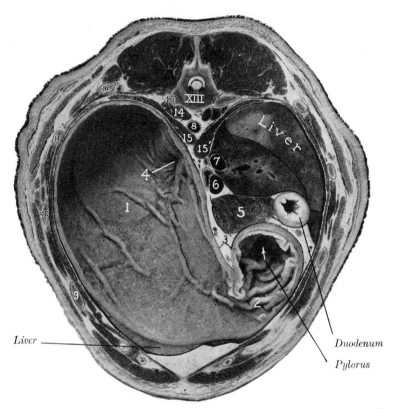

Fig. 439a.—Cross Section of Dog Through Thirteenth Thoracic Vertebra; Anterior End.

1, Fundus gland region; *2*, pyloric part; *3*, lesser curvature; *4*, cardia; *5*, pancreas; *6*, portal vein (medial to this is right adrenal); *7*, posterior vena cava; *8*, aorta; *9, 10, 11, 12, 13*, sections of ribs (sternal end of 9th and costo-vertebral articulation of 13th); *14*, psoas minor; *15, 15'*, left and right crura of diaphragm.

ture. The fundus gland region has a thick, reddish-brown mucous membrane, which lines about two-thirds of the organ. The pyloric mucous membrane is thinner and pale; in the dead subject it is often stained by regurgitated bile.

The **greater omentum** is very extensive, and in well-nourished subjects it contains much fat arranged in interlacing strands. Viewed ventrally it covers the entire intestinal mass, extending from the greater curvature of the stomach to the pelvic inlet. It is attached to the greater curvature of the stomach, the left part of the colon, the left branch of the pancreas, and the hilus of the spleen.

The **lesser omentum** extends from the lesser curvature of the stomach to the portal fissure; to reach the latter it passes in great part between the papillary and left lateral lobes of the liver.

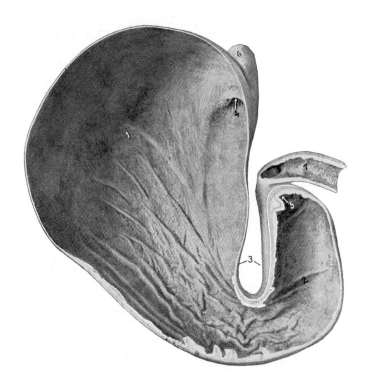

FIG. 440.—STOMACH OF DOG; FRONTAL SECTION.

1, Fundus gland region; 2, pyloric part; 3, lesser curvature; 4, cardia; 5, pylorus; 6, œsophagus; 7, duodenum.

THE INTESTINE

The intestine is short—only about five times the length of the body.

The **small intestine** has an average length of about thirteen feet (ca. 4 meters). It occupies most of the abdominal cavity behind the liver and stomach. The duodenum begins at the pylorus and passes backward and somewhat dorsally, at first on the visceral surface of the liver, then in contact with the right flank. Near the pelvis it turns medially and passes forward along the medial side of the left part of the colon and the left kidney, bends ventrally, and joins the jejunum to the left of the root of the mesentery.[1] The mesoduodenum is given off from the right side of the common mesentery; it is a relatively wide fold. The left part of the duodenum is connected with the mesocolon by a peritoneal fold; this fold has a free posterior border which is clearly seen when the posterior flexure of the duodenum is drawn away from the sublumbar region. The first part of the mesoduodenum contains the right branch of the pancreas. Its root is blended with the mesocolon to form a common mesentery. The remainder of the small intestine forms numerous coils, and is attached by a wide mesentery to the sublumbar region. The terminal part (ileum) passes forward in the sublumbar region along the medial surface of the cæcum and opens into the beginning of the colon at the **ileo-colic orifice** (Ostium ileocolicum). The bile duct and smaller pancreatic duct open into the duodenum about two or three inches (ca. 5 to 8 cm.) from the pylorus; the larger pancreatic duct opens an inch or two (ca. 2.5 to 5 cm.) further back. The mucous membrane has very long, thin villi. The duodenal glands occur only close to the pylorus. Aggregated lymph nodules or Peyer's patches are numerous (about twenty in

[1] The duodenum might be regarded as consisting of a first or retrograde part, an iliac flexure, and a second or recurrent part; the terminal bend is the duodeno-jejunal flexure.

young subjects), and begin in the duodenum. They are usually elliptical in outline, but the last one is band-like, reaches to the end of the ileum, and is four to sixteen inches (ca. 10 to 40 cm.) long in young dogs (Ellenberger). There is an ileo-colic valve.[1] The muscular coat is relatively thick.

The **large intestine** is two to two and a half feet (ca. 60 to 75 cm.) long in

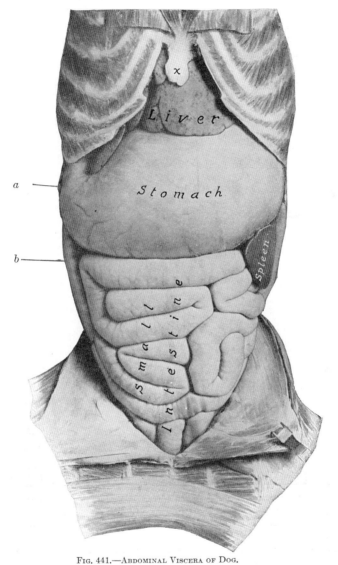

FIG. 441.—ABDOMINAL VISCERA OF DOG.

Ventral view after removal of greater omentum. The stomach is full.
a, Cartilage of last rib; b, duodenum; x, xiphoid cartilage.

average. Its caliber is about the same as that of the small intestine, and it has neither longitudinal bands nor sacculations.

The **cæcum** averages about five or six inches (ca. 12.5 to 15 cm.) in length, and

---

[1] The valve does not seem always to be efficient, since experience shows that rectal injections can be made to pass beyond it. This may be partly due also to the fact that the terminal part of the ileum runs horizontally forward, and its orifice faces forward into the beginning of the colon.

is flexuous (Fig. 442). The flexures are maintained by the peritoneum, which attaches it also to the ileum. It is situated usually about midway between the right flank and the median plane, ventral to the duodenum and the right branch of the pancreas.[1] Its anterior end opens into the origin of the colon, lateral to the ileo-colic orifice. The other end is pointed and blind.

The **colon** is attached to the sublumbar region by a mesentery—the mesocolon. It presents three parts, which correspond to the ascending, transverse, and descending colon of man. The first or right part (Colon dextrum s. ascendens) is very short. It passes forward along the medial surface of the first part of the duodenum and the right branch of the pancreas till it reaches the pyloric part of the stomach;

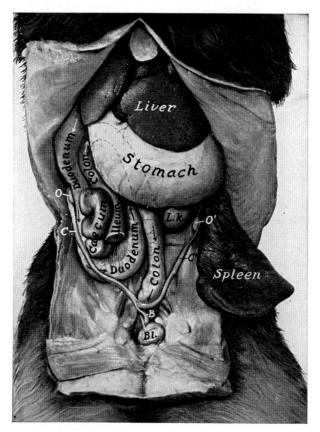

FIG. 442.—DEEP DISSECTION OF ABDOMINAL VISCERA OF DOG (FEMALE).

Bl., Bladder; *B,* body, *C, C',* cornua of uterus; *O, O',* ovaries; *L. k.,* left kidney. The concealed part of the colon is indicated by dotted lines. The spleen is drawn backward and outward.

here it turns to the left and crosses the median plane, forming the transverse part (Colon transversum). The third or left part (Colon sinistrum s. descendens) passes backward in the sublumbar region along the medial border or ventral surface of the left kidney; it then inclines toward the median plane and is continued by the rectum. The caliber of the colon is about the same throughout. It has no bands

[1] In large dogs (e. g., St. Bernard or Great Dane) the cæcum may reach a length of 45 cm. (measured along its curves) and a diameter of 3 cm. Its position is somewhat variable. It may be closer to the lateral wall, or more medial than is stated above. Its anterior end is usually in a transverse plane through the ventral end of the last rib if the stomach is not very full; it is often in contact with the right kidney.

nor sacculations. The mesentery of the colon is termed the **mesocolon**; it is given off from the left side of the common mesentery.[1]

The mucous membrane of the cæcum contains numerous solitary lymph nodules which are circular, with a central depression; some are present also in the first part of the colon.

The **rectum** is almost completely covered with peritoneum, the line of peritoneal reflection being under the second or third coccygeal vertebra. At the junction of the rectum and anus the mucous membrane has a stratified squamous epithelium, and contains the **anal glands.** A small opening on either side leads into two lateral **anal sacs** (Sinus paranales); these are usually about the size of a hazel-nut, and contain a dirty gray, fatty substance, which has a peculiar and very unpleasant odor. The skin which lines these pouches contains

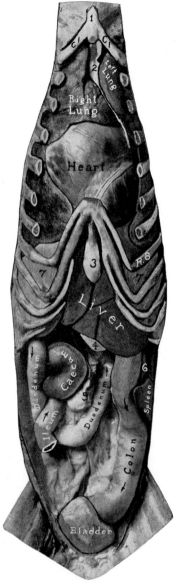

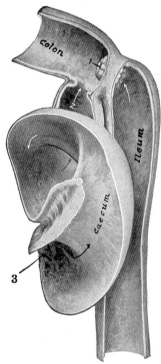

FIG. 443.—SECTIONAL VIEW OF ILEUM, CÆCUM, AND COLON OF DOG.

1, Ileo-colic orifice; 2, cæco-colic orifice; 3, apex of cæcum.

FIG. 443a.—DEEP DISSECTION OF ABDOMINAL VISCERA OF DOG; VENTRAL VIEW.

1, Cariniform cartilage; *2*, mediastinum; *3*, xiphoid cartilage; *4*, stomach; *5*, stump of mesentery; *6*, left kidney; *7, 7*, diaphragm; *C. 1*, first costal cartilage; *R. 8*, eighth rib.

coil-glands. Further back the skin contains large sebaceous glands and peculiar **circumanal glands.**

[1] The arrangement of the colon is variable. The transverse part may extend across from the angle of junction of the two branches of the pancreas to the dorsal end of the spleen. On the other hand a transverse part may be absent, the colon forming instead an acute angle or flexure. When the stomach is empty and contracted, the transverse colon may be separated from the ventral wall by the omentum only.

The **retractor ani muscle** is extensive. It arises from the shaft of the ilium, the pubis, and the symphysis pelvis, and passes upward and backward to end on the first coccygeal vertebræ and the sphincter ani externus. The retractors, together with the coccygei, form a sort of pelvic diaphragm, analogous to that of man.

THE LIVER

The liver is relatively large, weighing usually about 3 per cent. of the body-weight. It is divided into five chief **lobes** by fissures which converge at the portal fissure. When the gland is examined in the soft condition the lobes may be spread out so as to be all visible (Fig. 444), but when the organ is hardened *in situ* the lobes overlap to a considerable extent (Figs. 445, 446).

The **left lateral lobe** is the largest, and is oval in outline. The **left central lobe** is smaller and is prismatic. The **right central lobe** is second in size, and presents a somewhat tongue-shaped quadrate lobe, marked off by the deep fossa in which the gall-bladder lies. The **right lateral lobe** is third in size, and is oval in outline. On its visceral surface is the large **caudate lobe;** this consists of two parts—on the right, the caudate process, on the left, the papillary process, both often being subdivided by secondary fissures.

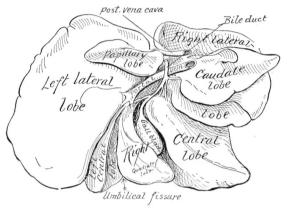

FIG. 444.—LIVER OF DOG.
Soft specimen sketched with lobes drawn apart.

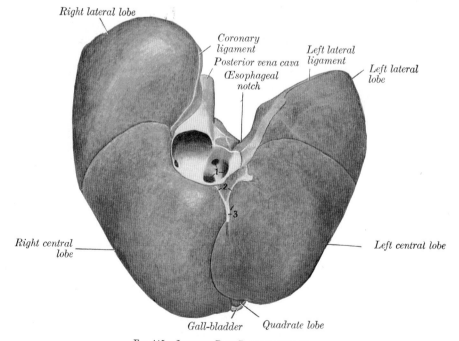

FIG. 445.—LIVER OF DOG; PARIETAL SURFACE.
1, Hepatic veins opening into posterior vena cava; 2, coronary ligament; 3, falciform ligament.

When hardened *in situ*, the gland presents the following characters:

The parietal surface is strongly convex in conformity with the curvature of the diaphragm and the adjacent part of the ventral wall of the abdomen, with which it is in contact.

The visceral surface is in general concave, but is irregular in adaptation to the viscera in contact with it. The largest of these is the stomach, and the configuration of the liver varies greatly in accordance with the degree of fulness of that viscus. When the stomach is well filled, there is a ridge on the liver which corresponds to the lesser curvature. To the left of this is a large concavity adapted to the body and fundus of the stomach; and on the right is a smaller impression of the pyloric part of the stomach, the first part of the duodenum, and the anterior part of the

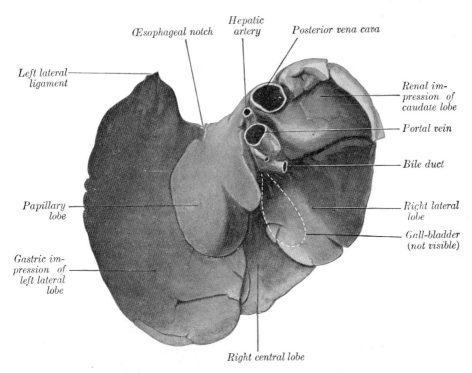

FIG. 446.—LIVER OF DOG, VISCERAL SURFACE; HARDENED *in situ*.
Left central lobe, gall-bladder, and great part of right central lobe not visible.

right branch of the pancreas. Dorsal to the cavity for the pyloric part of the stomach is a deep depression, and at the bottom of this is the portal fissure. To see the latter the papillary and caudate lobes must be drawn apart. The hepatic artery enters the liver at the dorsal part of the fissure, the portal vein enters centrally, and the hepatic duct emerges at the ventral part. The gall-bladder is not visible till the right lateral and central lobes are drawn apart.

When the stomach is empty and contracted, the visceral surface of the liver is strikingly different. There is then a shallow impression for the left part of the stomach on the left lobe and a large convex area, related to the small intestine and a mass of omentum. The pyloric and duodenal impressions are not much changed.

The dorsal border presents a deep renal impression on its right part. The posterior vena cava passes ventrally and forward, at first in a deep groove on the caudate lobe, then largely embedded in the parietal surface of the right lateral lobe; it receives two or three large hepatic veins just before piercing the diaphragm.

The œsophageal notch is large, and is occupied on the right by the thick margin of the hiatus œsophagus. The remainder of the circumference is thin, and is cut into by deep fissures which separate the lobes. The ventral border lies on the abdominal wall, a variable distance behind the xiphoid cartilage. The left border is also variable, but usually extends back ventrally as far as the tenth intercostal space or eleventh rib. The right border corresponds more or less closely in direction with the costal arch; the end of the caudate process is ventral to the right kidney, opposite to, or a little behind, the last rib.

The **gall-bladder** lies in the fossa vesicæ felleæ, between the two parts of the right central lobe; usually it does not reach to the ventral border of the liver. The cystic duct joins the hepatic duct at the ventral part of the portal fissure, forming with it the bile duct (Ductus choledochus); the latter passes to the right and opens into the duodenum, about two or three inches (ca. 5 to 8 cm.) from the pylorus.

Of the ligaments, the coronary and right

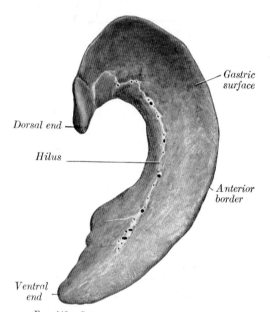

Dorsal end

Posterior border

Ventral end

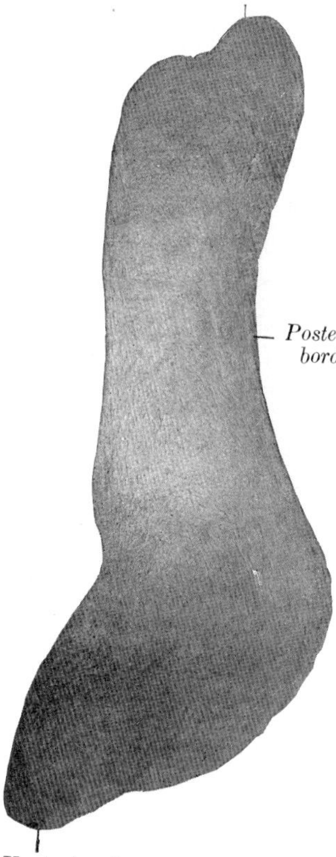

Fig. 447.—Spleen of Dog; Parietal Surface.

Gastric surface

Dorsal end

Hilus

Anterior border

Ventral end

Fig. 448.—Spleen of Dog; Visceral Surface.

Fig. 447 is from subject in which the stomach was full, while the organ shown in Fig. 448 was fixed *in situ* when the stomach contained little food.

lateral are well developed, but the left lateral and falciform are small; a ligament extends from the caudate process to the right kidney.

THE PANCREAS

The **pancreas** is **V**-shaped, consisting of two long narrow branches, which meet at an acute angle behind the pylorus. The **right branch** extends backward above the first part of the duodenum, below the caudate lobe of the liver and the right kidney, and ends usually a short distance behind the latter; it is enclosed by the mesoduodenum. The **left branch** passes to the left and backward between the visceral surface of the stomach and the transverse colon, and ends at the anterior pole of the left kidney. There are usually two **pancreatic ducts.** The smaller one opens into the duodenum with the bile duct or close to it; the larger one opens into the bowel an inch or two (ca. 3–5 cm.) further back.

THE SPLEEN

The **spleen** is bright red in color in the fresh state. It is somewhat falciform, long, and narrow; the ventral part is the widest. Its weight in a dog of medium

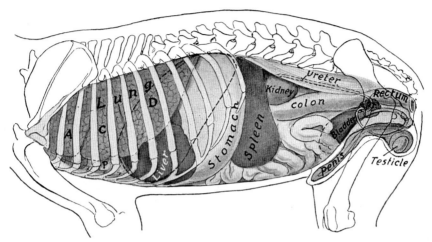

FIG. 449.—PROJECTION OF VISCERA OF DOG (MALE) ON BODY WALL; LEFT SIDE.

A, C, D, Apical, cardiac, and diaphragmatic lobes of lung; *P,* pericardium; *Pr,* prostate. Costal attachment and median line of diaphragm are dotted.

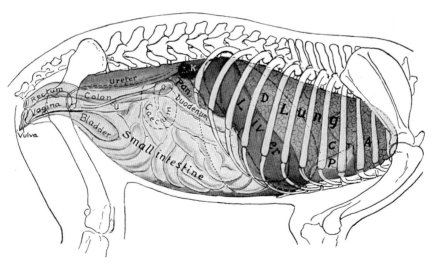

FIG. 450.—PROJECTION OF VISCERA OF DOG (FEMALE) ON BODY WALL; RIGHT SIDE.

A, C, D, Apical, cardiac, and diaphragmatic lobes of right lung; *P,* pericardium; *K,* right kidney; *Pan.,* right branch of pancreas; *O,* ovary; *U,* cornu of uterus. Costal attachment and median line of diaphragm are dotted; also posterior contour of stomach.

size is 1½–2 ounces (ca. 50 gm.). It is freely movable, and, with the exception of its dorsal end, varies much in position and shape. The dorsal end is ventral to the vertebral end of the last rib and the first lumbar transverse process; it fits into the interval between the left crus of the diaphragm, the left end of the stomach, and the left kidney. When the stomach is full, the long axis of the spleen corresponds to the direction of the last rib. Its parietal surface is convex and lies largely against the left flank. The visceral surface is concave in its length, and is marked by a longitudinal ridge, on which the vessels and nerves are situated, and to which the greater omentum is attached. The spleen is so loosely attached by the omentum as to be regarded as an appendage of the latter.

The dorsal end of the spleen does not vary notably in position, but the rest of the organ is very variable. When the stomach is full, the part of the visceral surface of the spleen in front of the hilus is usually in apposition with the left part of the greater curvature of the stomach (as in the horse). It may have a similar position when the stomach is not full, and may be in contact with the latter only to a small extent dorsally. It is not rare to find the spleen lying along the dorsal part of the left flank, with its long axis almost longitudinal; this is liable to be the case when the stomach is empty and contracted. In this condition the spleen shuts the left kidney entirely off from contact with the flank.

THE RESPIRATORY SYSTEM

The **respiratory apparatus** (Apparatus respiratorius) comprises the nasal cavity,[1] the pharynx, the larynx, the trachea, the bronchi, and the lungs. The lungs are the central organs in which the exchange of gases between the blood and the air takes place; the other parts of the system are passages by which the air passes to and from the lungs. The nasal cavity opens externally at the nostrils, and communicates behind with the pharynx through the choanæ or posterior nares; it contains the peripheral part of the olfactory apparatus, which mediates the sense of smell. The pharynx is a common passage for the air and food—a remnant of the primitive embryonic arrangement; it has been described with the digestive tube. The larynx is a complex valvular apparatus which regulates the volume of air passing through the tract; it is also the chief organ of voice. The trachea and the bronchi formed by its bifurcation are permanently open conducting tubes. The thorax, the pleural sacs which it contains, and the muscles which increase or diminish the size of the cavity are also parts of the system. The bones, joints, and muscles of the thorax have already been described.

For topographic reasons two ductless glands, the thyroid and the thymus, are usually described in this section, although they are in no sense a part of the respiratory system.

RESPIRATORY SYSTEM OF THE HORSE

THE NASAL CAVITY

The **nasal cavity** (Cavum nasi), the first segment of the respiratory tract, is a long, somewhat cylindrical passage, enclosed by all the facial bones except the mandible and hyoid. It is separated from the mouth ventrally by the palate. It opens externally at the nostrils, and communicates posteriorly with the pharynx through the posterior nares or choanæ.

The **nostrils** (Nares) are somewhat oval in outline, and are placed obliquely, so that they are closer together below than above. They are bounded by two **alæ** or **wings** (Alæ nasi), which meet above and below, forming the **commissures**. The lateral ala is concave; the medial one is convex above, concave below. The prominence of the medial ala is caused by the lamina of the alar cartilage; this prominence, together with the alar fold which extends backward from it, partially divides the nostril into a large lower part and a small upper part, which are popularly distinguished as the "true" and "false" nostril.[2] The superior commissure is narrow, the inferior one wide and rounded. If the finger is passed into the nostril at the upper commissure, it enters a blind cutaneous pouch. This cul-de-sac, the **diverticulum nasi**, extends backward to the angle of junction of the nasal bone and the nasal process of the premaxilla. In order to enter the nasal cavity the finger should be introduced at the inferior commissure and directed toward the septum nasi. The **naso-lacrimal orifice** (Ostium nasolacrimale), the external opening of

[1] A nose (Nasus externus), such as exists in man, forming a projection distinctly marked off from the rest of the face, does not exist in the domesticated animals.

[2] These terms should be abandoned, as they tend unnecessarily to complicate the description as well as to misconception with regard to function.

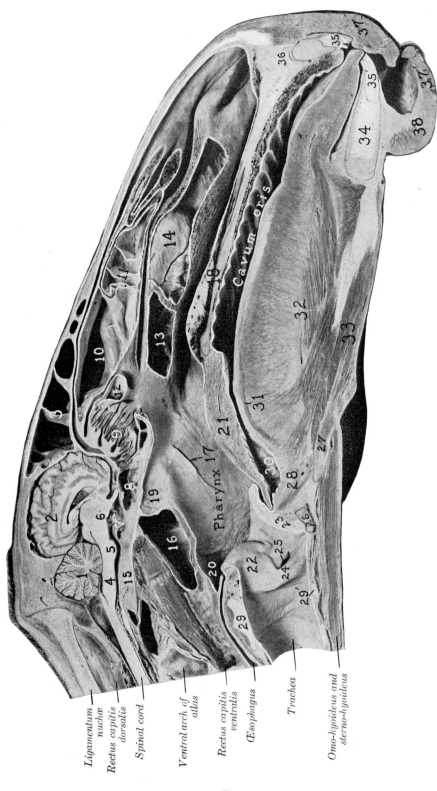

Fig. 450a.—Sagittal Section of Head of Horse.

1, Cerebellum; 2, cerebral hemisphere; 3, frontal sinus; 4, medulla oblongata; 5, pons; 6, cerebral peduncle; 7, hypophysis cerebri; 8, sphenoidal sinus; 9, lateral mass of ethmoid bone; 10, turbinate portion of frontal sinus; 11, scrolled portion of dorsal turbinate; 12, cavity of great ethmo-turbinate; 13, sinus portion of ventral turbinate; 14, large bulla of middle portion ventral turbinate; 1', basilar part of occipital bone; 16, guttural pouch; 17, pharyngeal opening of Eustachian tube; 18, hard palate; 19, pharyngeal recess; 20, junction of posterior pillars of soft palate over entrance to œsophagus; 21, soft palate; 22, arytenoid cartilage; 23, epiglottis; 24, vocal cord; 25, lateral ventricle of larynx; 26, body of thyroid cartilage; 27, hyoid bone; 28, m. hyo-epiglotticus; 29, 29', lamina and arch of cricoid cartilage; 30, glosso-epiglottic space; 31, m. longitudinalis linguæ; 32, m. genio-glossus; 33, genio-hyoideus; 34, body of mandible; 35, 35', incisor teeth; 36, body of premaxilla above foramen incisivum; 37, 37', lips; 38, chin. The section is cut to the left of the median plane.

the **naso-lacrimal duct,** is seen when the nostril is dilated; it is situated on the floor of the vestibule, about two inches (ca. 5 cm.) from the lower commissure, perforating the skin close to its junction with the mucous membrane. (It is not rare to find one or two accessory orifices further back.)

Structure.—The **skin** around the nostrils presents long tactile hairs as well as the ordinary ones. It is continued around the alæ and lines the vestibule. The skin of the diverticulum is thin and usually black, and is covered with very fine hairs; it is provided with numerous sebaceous glands. The medial wing is supported by the **alar cartilage** (Cartilago alaris), which is

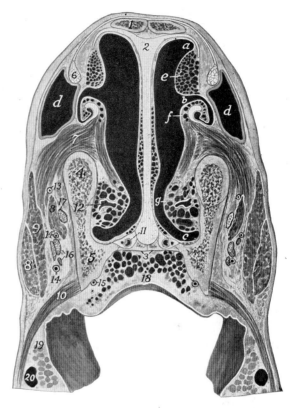

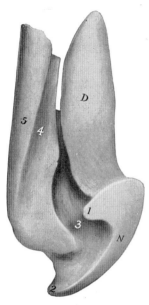

FIG. 451.—CAST OF LEFT NOSTRIL, NASAL DIVERTICULUM, AND NASAL VESTIBULE OF HORSE; DORSAL VIEW.

N, Nostril; *D,* diverticulum; 1, superior commissure of nostril; 2, inferior commissure; 3, space occupied by alar fold; 4, groove occupied by dorsal turbinate fold; 5, dorsal meatus.

FIG. 452.—CROSS-SECTION OF NASAL REGION OF HORSE.

The section is cut about two inches (5 cm.) behind the nostrils and a little more than half an inch behind the labial commissure.

a, Dorsal meatus; *b,* middle meatus; *c,* ventral meatus; *d,* diverticulum nasi; *e,* dorsal turbinate fold; *f,* ventral turbinate fold; *g,* prominence caused by venous plexus which extends back on lower part of ventral turbinate; 1, nasal bone; 2, cartilage of septum nasi; 3, 4, palatine and nasal processes of premaxilla; 5, maxilla; 6, tendon of levator labii superioris proprius; 7, part of lateralis nasi muscle which goes to cartilage of ventral turbinate; 8, 8′, levator nasolabialis; 9, dilator naris lateralis; 10, buccinator; 11, vomero-nasal organ; 12, nasolacrimal duct (wide part); 13, lateral nasal artery; 14, 14′, branches of superior labial artery; 15, palatine artery; 16, labial branches of infraorbital nerve; 17, external nasal nerve; 18, hard palate; 19, cheek; 20, superior labial vein. The veins (black) are filled by a natural injection.

shaped somewhat like a comma, the convex margin being medial (Fig. 453). The cartilages are attached by fibrous tissue to the extremity of the septal cartilage. Each consists of an upper, quadrilateral curved plate, the **lamina,** and a narrow **cornu** which curves ventro-laterally, supporting the medial wing and the inferior commissure, but not entering into the formation of the lateral wing. The lamina causes the projection of the upper part of the medial wing, from which the thick **alar fold** (Plica alaris) passes backward along the lateral wall of the nasal cavity to join the mucous fold which encloses the cartilaginous prolongation of the ventral turbinate bone.[1] The extremity of the cornu usually causes a slight projection of the skin a short distance behind and below the inferior commissure.

The muscles of the nostrils have been described (p. 260).

Vessels and Nerves.—The **arteries** are branches of the palato-labial, superior labial, and lateral nasal arteries, and the blood is conveyed away by corresponding veins. The **lymph vessels** go to the mandibular lymph glands. The **nerves** are derived from the infraorbital nerve (sensory) and from the facial nerve (motor).

The nasal cavity is divided into two similar halves by the median **septum nasi** (Figs. 452, 455, 456). The **osseous septum** (Septum nasi osseum) is formed by the perpendicular plate of the ethmoid behind and by the vomer ventrally. A few ridges on the former correspond to the ethmoidal meatuses. The major part of it, however, is formed by the **cartilage of the septum nasi** (Cartilago septi nasi). The surfaces of the cartilage are marked by faint grooves for the vessels and nerves which course over it. The dorsal border is attached along the frontal and nasal sutures, and extends beyond the apices of the nasal bones about two inches (ca. 5 cm.). From this border a thin, narrow plate, the **parietal cartilage** (Cartilago parietalis) curves outward for a short distance on either side. Near the nostrils these plates are somewhat wider, partially making good the defect (naso-maxillary notch) in the bony wall of the cavity in this situation. The ventral border is thick and rounded; it lies in the groove of the vomer and the palatine processes of the premaxillæ; its anterior part occupies the space between the premaxillary bones. A process from it extends into the palatine fissure, which it almost completely fills; the palatine end of the process lies in the

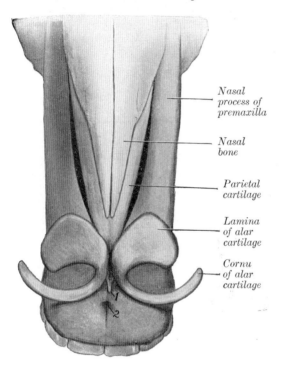

Nasal process of premaxilla

Nasal bone

Parietal cartilage

Lamina of alar cartilage

Cornu of alar cartilage

FIG. 453.—NASAL CARTILAGES OF HORSE; DORSAL VIEW.
1, Anterior extremity of cartilage of septum nasi; 2, foramen incisivum.

submucous tissue of the hard palate, and the palatine artery turns medially between the cartilage and the bone. The posterior border is continuous with the perpendicular plate of the ethmoid bone.[2] The alar cartilages are attached to the anterior extremity by fibrous tissue in such a manner as to allow very free movement—in fact an actual joint may be present. The ventral part of the cartilage is about half an inch (ca. 1 cm.), the middle part about one-tenth of an inch (ca. 2.5 mm.), and the dorsal part about a quarter to a third of an inch (ca. 6 to 8 mm.) in thickness.

[1] When the nostril is fully dilated it is circular in outline, and the so-called false nostril is effaced by the lamina of the alar cartilage being brought in contact with the superior commissure.

[2] The cartilage is to be regarded as an unossified part of the mesethmoid. It will be noted that the line of demarcation between the bone and the cartilage is irregular and varies with age; extensive ossification (or calcification) of the cartilage is commonly found in old animals. The process often results in the formation of calcareous islands in the cartilage.

The two turbinate bones project from the lateral wall, and divide the outer part of the cavity into three **meatuses**—dorsal, middle, and ventral (Figs. 454, 455, 456).

The **dorsal nasal meatus** (Meatus nasi dorsalis) is a narrow passage, bounded dorsally by the roof of the cavity, and ventrally by the dorsal turbinate bone; its posterior end is closed by the junction of the inner plate of the frontal bone with the cribriform plate and lateral mass of the ethmoid. It transmits air to the olfactory region.

The **middle nasal meatus** (Meatus nasi medius) is between the two turbinate bones. It is somewhat larger than the dorsal meatus, and does not extend back so far; it ends near the great ethmoturbinate and the ethmoidal meatuses. In its posterior part is the extremely narrow, slit-like interval by which the maxillary sinus communicates with the nasal cavity—the **naso-maxillary opening** (Aditus naso-maxillaris). The opening, which is normally a mere fissure, is not visible from the nasal side, being concealed by the overhanging dorsal turbinate. A fine flexible probe, passed outward and somewhat backward between the turbinate

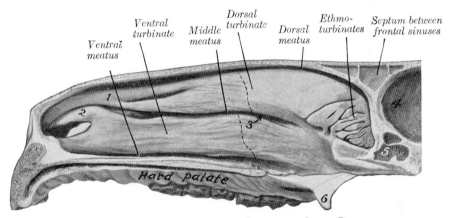

FIG. 454.—NASAL CAVITY OF HORSE; SAGITTAL SECTION WITH SEPTUM REMOVED.

1, Dorsal turbinate fold; *2*, alar fold, containing cartilaginous prolongation of ventral turbinate; *3*, arrow pointing to naso-maxillary opening, which is concealed by dorsal turbinate bone; *4*, cranial cavity; *5*, sphenoidal sinus; *6*, hamulus of pterygoid bone. The olfactory mucous membrane is shaded. Dotted lines indicate anterior limit of uncoiled parts of turbinate bones, which inclose parts of frontal and maxillary sinuses.

bones, enters the maxillary sinus; if introduced a little further in the same direction, it usually passes through the orifice of communication between the maxillary sinus and the frontal sinus and enters the latter. A small part of the fissure usually brings the anterior division of the maxillary sinus into communication with the nasal cavity. The spaces enclosed by the coiled parts of the turbinates also open into the middle meatus. This passage may be characterized as the sinus-meatus, but it also conducts air to the olfactory region.

The **ventral nasal meatus** (Meatus nasi ventralis) is situated between the ventral turbinate and the floor of the cavity. It is much larger than the other two, and is the direct passage between the nostrils and the pharynx. The small, slit-like orifice of the vomero-nasal organ and the incisive or naso-palatine duct is situated in the floor of the anterior end of the meatus.

The **common nasal meatus** (Meatus nasi communis) is situated between the septum and the turbinates, and is continuous laterally with the other meatuses. It is very narrow dorsally, but widens ventrally.

The lateral masses of the ethmoid bone project forward into the posterior part (fundus) of the nasal cavity. Between the ethmoturbinates, of which each mass is composed, there are three principal and numerous small passages, the **ethmoidal meatuses** (Meatus ethmoidales).

The **choanæ** or **posterior nares** are two elliptical orifices by which the nasal cavity and pharynx communicate.   They are in the same plane as the floor of the

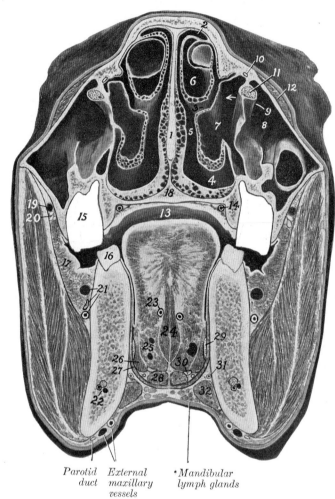

Parotid   External   •Mandibular
    duct   maxillary   lymph glands
                 vessels

FIG. 455.—CROSS-SECTION OF HEAD OF HORSE.

The section is cut midway between the medial canthus and the anterior end of the facial crest and is a front view.

1, Septum nasi; 2, 3, 4, dorsal, middle, and ventral meatus nasi; 5, common meatus nasi; 6, cavity of dorsal turbinate bone (*i. e.*, turbinate part of frontal sinus); 7, cavity of ventral turbinate bone (*i. e.*, turbinate part of maxillary sinus); 8, maxillary sinus; 9, communication between 7 and 8 over infraorbital canal; 10, naso-lacrimal duct; 11, infraorbital nerve and canal; 12, m. levator labii superioris proprius; 13, mouth cavity; 14, palatine artery; 15, fifth upper cheek tooth (posterior part); 16, sixth lower cheek tooth (anterior part); 17, m. buccinator; 18, hard palate; 19, vena reflexa; 20, superior buccal glands; 21, buccinator vessels and nerve; 22, alveolar vessels and nerve of mandible; 23, lingual artery; 24, mm. genio-glossi; 25, m. hyo-glossus (number placed between two radicles of lingual vein); 26, m. stylo-glossus; 27, m. mylo-hyoideus; 28, m. genio-hyoideus; 29, lingual nerve; 30, hypoglossal nerve; 31, sublingual artery; 32, m. digastricus (anterior belly). The mandibular duct is shown in the fat lateral to the genio-hyoideus but is not marked.

nasal cavity, and are separated from each other by the vomer.   They are, taken together, about two inches (ca. 5 cm.) wide and three to four inches (ca. 8 to 10 cm.) long.

The **nasal mucous membrane** (Membrana mucosa nasi) is thick, highly vascular, and is, in general, firmly attached to the underlying periosteum and perichondrium. It is continuous in front with the skin which lines the nostrils, and behind with the mucous membrane of the pharynx. It is also continuous at the naso-maxillary opening with the very thin and much less vascular mucous membrane which lines the paranasal sinuses. In the anterior part of the cavity it forms prominent thick folds on the lateral wall, which extend from the turbinate bones to the nostril. There are usually two **dorsal turbinate folds** which unite anteriorly.

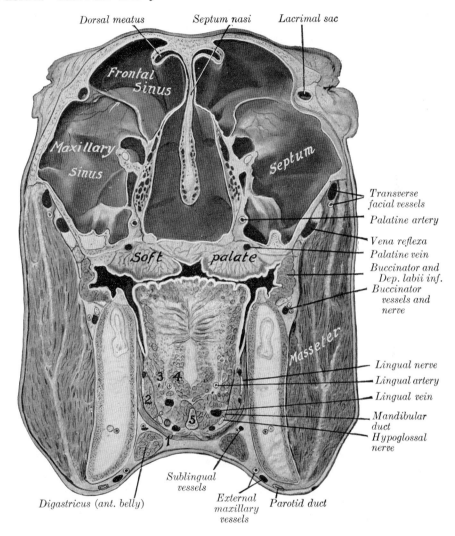

FIG. 456.—CROSS-SECTION OF HEAD OF HORSE. THE SECTION PASSES THROUGH THE MEDIAL CANTHI AND IS VIEWED FROM BEHIND.

1, Mylo-hyoideus; *2*, stylo-glossus; *3*, hyo-glossus; *4*, genio-glossus; *5*, lingual process of hyoid bone. An arrow points to the naso-maxillary opening. The projecting edge just above the arrow point is the anterior margin of the fronto-maxillary opening.

The upper one encloses a thin plate of cartilage which is continuous with the dorsal turbinate bone. The **ventral turbinate fold** is curved, and encloses an ⌣ shaped cartilaginous plate which prolongs the ventral turbinate bone; this fold is continuous with the alar fold of the nostril, and forms with it the upper margin of the entrance from the nostril to the nasal cavity. Below this there is a rounded ridge produced by the nasal process of the premaxilla. The mucous membrane of the greater part of the cavity (Regio respiratoria) is red in color, and is covered with a stratified ciliated epithelium. It contains numerous tubulo-alveolar **nasal glands** (Glandulæ nasales). The submucosa contains rich venous plexuses which form in certain situations a sort of cavernous tissue (Plexus cavernosus nasalis), composed of several strata of freely anastomosing veins, between which there are unstriped muscle-fibers. This arrangement is most marked in the turbinate folds, on the lower part of the ventral turbinate bone, and the lower part of the septum. The mucous membrane of the vestibule presents numerous small depressions (openings of gland ducts), and is covered with stratified squamous epithelium. On the posterior part of the lateral masses of the ethmoid and the adjacent part of the dorsal turbinate and the septum (Regio olfactoria) the mucous membrane is brownish-yellow in color and thicker; it contains the olfactory nerve-endings in a special non-ciliated epithelium. In it are numerous **olfactory glands** (Glandulæ olfactoriæ); these are long, tubular, and often branched.

The **vomero-nasal organ** (Organon vomeronasale)[1] is situated on the floor of the nasal cavity, on either side of the ventral border of the septum (Fig. 452). It consists of a tubular cartilage (Cartilago vomeronasalis) lined with mucous membrane (Ductus vomeronasalis), to which fibers of the olfactory nerve may be traced. Its anterior part communicates with the nasal cavity by a slit-like orifice in common with the incisive or naso-palatine duct. The posterior blind end is in a transverse plane through the second or third cheek tooth. The average length of the organ is about five inches (ca. 12 cm.).

The **ductus incisivus** (or naso-palatine duct) is a small mucous tube, an inch or more (ca. 2.5–3 cm.) in length, which extends obliquely through the palatine fissure. Its nasal end communicates with the nasal cavity through a slit-like opening in common with the vomero-nasal organ. The palatine extremity ends blindly in the submucous tissue of the hard palate.

The **paranasal sinuses** are described in the Osteology.

Vessels and Nerves.—The **arteries** are branches of the ethmoidal, sphenopalatine, palatine, superior labial, and lateral nasal arteries. The blood is carried away by corresponding **veins**. The **lymph vessels** go to the mandibular and pharyngeal lymph glands. The **nerves** come from the olfactory and trigeminal nerves.

THE LARYNX

The **larynx** is a short tube which connects the pharynx and trachea. It is a complex valvular apparatus, which regulates the volume of air in respiration, prevents aspiration of foreign bodies, and is the chief organ of voice.

It is situated partly between the medial pterygoid muscles, partly in the neck between the parotid glands.[2] Its long axis is practically horizontal in the ordinary position of the head and neck. It is related dorsally to the pharynx and the origin of the œsophagus. Ventrally it is covered by the skin, fascia, and sterno-hyoid and omo-hyoid muscles. Laterally it is related to the parotid and mandibular glands and to the medial pterygoid, occipito-mandibularis, digastricus, stylo-hyoid, and pharyngeal constrictor muscles. It is attached to the body and thyroid cornua of the hyoid bone, and thus indirectly to the base of the cranium. Its cavity communicates dorsally with the pharynx, posteriorly with the trachea. The skeleton of the larynx consists of a framework of cartilages, which are connected by joints and ligaments or membranes, and moved by extrinsic and intrinsic muscles. It is lined with mucous membrane.

---

[1] Commonly known as the organ of Jacobson.

[2] In the ordinary position of the head and neck more than half of the larynx lies between the branches of the mandible; when the head and neck are extended, proportionately more of the larynx lies behind a plane through the posterior borders of the rami.

CARTILAGES OF THE LARYNX

There are three single cartilages and one pair; the single cartilages are the cricoid, thyroid, and epiglottic; the arytenoid cartilages are paired.

The **cricoid cartilage** (Cartilago cricoidea) is shaped like a signet ring. The dorsal part is a broad, thick, quadrilateral plate termed the **lamina;** the external (dorsal) surface of this is marked by a median ridge (Crista mediana) separating two shallow cavities, from which the dorsal crico-arytenoid muscles arise. On either side of these depressions are two articular facets. The **anterior facet** (Facies articularis arytænoidea) is at the anterior border, is oval and convex, and articulates with the arytenoid cartilage. The **posterior facet** (Facies articularis thyreoidea) is situated on the front of a ridge, a short distance from the posterior border; it is concave, and articulates with the posterior cornu of the thyroid cartilage. The ventral and lateral parts of the ring are formed by a curved band, called the **arch** (Arcus), which is narrowest ventrally. The lateral surfaces of the arch are grooved

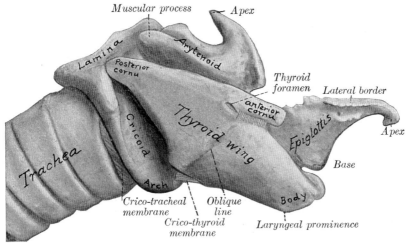

FIG. 457.—LARYNGEAL CARTILAGES AND PART OF TRACHEA OF HORSE; RIGHT VIEW.
For "thyroid wing" read "thyroid lamina."

for the crico-thyroid muscle. The anterior border of the lamina is thick and slightly concave; the posterior border is thin and irregular. The anterior border of the arch is concave ventrally and gives attachment to the crico-thyroid membrane; laterally it is thicker and gives attachment to the crico-arytenoideus lateralis muscle. The posterior border of the cartilage is attached to the first ring of the trachea by the crico-tracheal membrane. The internal surface is smooth and is covered with mucous membrane.

The **thyroid cartilage** (Cartilago thyreoidea) consists of a median thickened portion, termed the body, and two lateral laminæ. The **body** forms ventrally a slight prominence (Prominentia laryngea), which can be felt, but is not visible in the living subject; it is related dorsally to the base of the epiglottis, which is attached to it by an elastic ligament. The **laminæ** spring from the body on either side and form a large part of the lateral wall of the larynx. Each is a rhomboid plate, presenting a slightly convex lateral surface, which is divided into two areas by an oblique line (Linea obliqua), on which the thyro-hyoid and thyro-pharyngeus muscles meet. The dorsal border is nearly straight; it gives attachment to the pharyngeal fascia and the palato-pharyngeus muscle, and bears a cornu at each end. The **anterior cornu** (Cornu orale) articulates with the cartilage of the thyroid cornu of the hyoid bone; below it is a fissure (Fissura thyreoidea), which is converted into a foramen (Foramen thyreoideum) by a fibrous band, and transmits the anterior laryngeal nerve to the interior of the larynx. The **posterior cornu** (Cornu aborale) articulates with the cricoid cartilage. The ventral border joins the body in front, and behind diverges from its fellow to inclose a triangular space, the **thyroid notch** (Incisura thyreoidea aboralis), which is occupied by the crico-thyroid membrane. The ante-

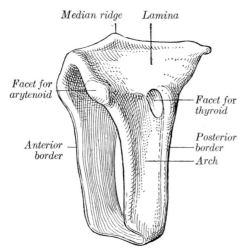

FIG. 458.—CRICOID CARTILAGE OF HORSE; LEFT ANTERO-
LATERAL VIEW.

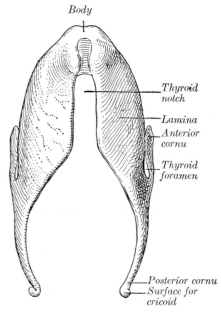

FIG. 459.—THYROID CARTILAGE OF HORSE; VENTRAL
VIEW.

rior border is slightly convex, and is attached to the hyoid bone by the thyro-hyoid membrane. The posterior border overlaps the arch of the cricoid cartilage, and

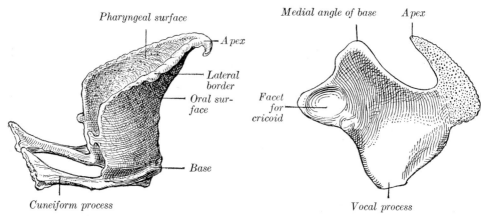

FIG. 460.—EPIGLOTTIC CARTILAGE OF HORSE; RIGHT
LATERAL VIEW.

FIG. 461.—LEFT ARYTENOID CARTILAGE OF HORSE;
MEDIO-VENTRAL VIEW.

gives attachment to the crico-thyroid muscle. The medial surface is concave, and is related to the laryngeal saccule and internal laryngeal muscles.

The **epiglottic cartilage** (Cartilago epiglottica), usually called the epiglottis for the sake of brevity, is situated above the body of the thyroid cartilage and curves toward the root of the tongue.   It is shaped somewhat like a pointed ovate leaf, and presents two surfaces, two borders, a base, and an apex.   The **oral** (or anterior) **surface** is concave in its length, convex transversely; the **pharyngeal** (or posterior) **surface** has the reverse configuration.   The **borders** are thin, irregular, and somewhat everted.   The **base** is thick, and is attached to the dorsal surface of the body of the thyroid cartilage by elastic tissue.   From each side of it a cartilaginous bar projects upward and backward; these are the **cuneiform processes** (Processus cuneiformes) and correspond to the cuneiform cartilages of man.   The **apex** is pointed and curved ventrally.   The greater part of the epiglottic cartilage is covered with mucous membrane.   It may project into the isthmus faucium, or be on the pharyngeal side of the soft palate (Figs. 349, 464)—*vide* footnote page 391.

The **arytenoid cartilages** (Cartilagines arytenoideæ) are situated on either side, in front of the cricoid, and partly medial to the laminæ of the thyroid cartilage. They are somewhat pyramidal in form, and may be described as having three surfaces, three borders, a base, and an apex.   The **medial surface** is concavo-convex, but very slightly curved, and is smooth and covered by mucous membrane. The **lateral surface** is concave and is separated from the lamina of the thyroid cartilage by the crico-arytenoideus lateralis and vocalis muscles, and the laryngeal saccule.   The **dorsal surface** is also concave, and is covered by the arytenoideus muscle, which is attached to it.   The dorsal and lateral surfaces are separated (except in front) by a ridge which increases in size toward the lateral angle of the base, where it forms a rounded prominence, the **muscular process** (Processus muscularis).   The **anterior** and **posterior borders** are convex; they converge ventrally to a thin, wide angle, the **vocal process** (Processus vocalis). The process is so named because it furnishes attachment to the vocal ligament. The **dorsal border** forms a deep notch with the apex.   The **base** is concave and faces chiefly backward; it presents laterally an oval concave **facet** (Facies articularis) for articulation with the anterior border of the lamina of the cricoid cartilage.   The medial angle of the base is attached to its fellow by the transverse arytenoid ligament.   The **apex** (Cartilago corniculata) curves upward and backward, forming with its fellow the pitcher-shaped lip from which the cartilages derive their name.

The cricoid and thyroid cartilages and the greater part of the arytenoid cartilages are hyaline.   The apices and vocal processes of the arytenoid and the epiglottis (including the cuneiform processes) consist of elastic cartilage; they show no tendency toward ossification at any age.   The thyroid and cricoid cartilages regularly undergo considerable ossification; the process begins in the body of the thyroid, and often involves the greater part of the cartilage.[1]

JOINTS, LIGAMENTS, AND MEMBRANES OF THE LARYNX

The **crico-thyroid joints** (Articulationes crico-thyreoideæ) are diarthroses formed by the apposition of the convex facets on the ends of the posterior cornua of the thyroid cartilage with corresponding facets on the sides of the cricoid cartilage.   The **capsule** is thin, but is strengthened by accessory bands dorsally, laterally, and medially.   The movements are chiefly rotation around a transverse axis passing through the centers of the two joints.

The **crico-arytenoid joints** (Articulationes crico-arytænoidea) are also diarthrodial.   They are formed by the apposition of the convex facets on the anterior border of the cricoid cartilages with the concave facets on the bases of the arytenoid cartilages.   Each has a very thin, loose **capsule**, strengthened by accessory bundles

---

[1] Calcareous deposits are present in the body of the thyroid cartilage even before adult age is reached.   Scheier (by use of X-rays) found complete calcification of the thyroid in two mares eight and ten years of age; in the former the process also involved a large part of the lamina and the adjacent part of the arch of the cricoid.

dorsally and medially. The most important movement is rotation of the arytenoid cartilage about a longitudinal axis so that the vocal process swings outward (abduction) or inward (adduction), carrying the vocal fold with it. Another movement here is rotation about a transverse axis, in which the apical part of the cartilage is raised or lowered. The arytenoid is also capable of slight inward or outward gliding movement.

The **thyro-hyoid joints** (Articulationes hyo-thyreoideæ) are formed by the anterior cornua of the thyroid cartilage and the cartilaginous extremities of the thyroid cornua of the hyoid bone. They are diarthroses and the joint capsule is reinforced by a relatively strong thyro-hyoid ligament. The thyroid cornu has here a cartilaginous prolongation about a quarter of an inch (ca. 6 mm.) in length. The chief movement is rotation around a transverse axis passing through the two joints.

The **crico-thyroid membrane** (Membrana crico-thyreoidea) occupies the thyroid notch and extends backward to the arch of the cricoid cartilage. It is triangular in form, and is attached by its base to the anterior border of the arch of the cricoid cartilage, while its borders are attached to the margins of the thyroid notch. It is strong, tightly stretched, and composed largely of elastic tissue. It is reinforced ventrally by longitudinal fibers, dorsally by fibers which stretch across the thyroid notch.

The **thyro-hyoid membrane** (Membrana hyo-thyreoidea) connects the body and anterior borders of the thyroid cartilage with the body and thyroid cornua of the hyoid bone.

The **hyo-epiglottic ligament** (Lig. hyo-epiglotticum) attaches the lower part of the oral surface of the epiglottis to the body of the hyoid bone. It forms an elastic sheath for the hyo-epiglottic muscle. Ventrally it blends with the thyrohyoid membrane, and dorsally it is not well defined.

The **thyro-epiglottic ligament** (Lig. thyreo-epiglotticum) is strong and thick; it is composed chiefly of elastic tissue. It connects the base of the epiglottis with the body and the adjacent medial surfaces of the laminæ of the thyroid cartilage. Other fibers attach the cuneiform processes somewhat loosely to the thyroid laminæ.

The **transverse arytenoid ligament** (Lig. arytænoideum transversum) is a slender band which connects the medial angles of the bases of the arytenoid cartilages.

The **vocal** (or posterior thyro-arytenoid) **ligament** (Lig. vocale) underlies and is intimately adherent to the mucous membrane of the vocal fold. It is thin and elastic and is attached ventrally to the body of the thyroid cartilage and the crico-thyroid membrane close to its fellow of the opposite side, and ends dorsally on the processus vocalis of the arytenoid cartilage.

The **ventricular** (or anterior thyro-arytenoid) **ligament** (Lig. ventriculare) is included in the ventricular fold. It consists of loosely arranged bundles which arise chiefly from the cuneiform process and end on the lateral surface of the processus vocalis and adjacent part of the arytenoid cartilage.

The **crico-tracheal membrane** (Membrana crico-trachealis) connects the cricoid cartilage with the first ring of the trachea.

MUSCLES OF THE LARYNX

A. EXTRINSIC MUSCLES

The **sterno-thyro-hyoideus** is described on p. 270.

The **thyro-hyoideus** (M. hyo-thyreoideus) is a flat, quadrilateral muscle, which lies on the lateral surface of the thyroid lamina and the lateral part of the thyrohyoid membrane. It arises from the body and thyroid cornu of the hyoid bone (almost meeting the opposite muscle), and ends on the oblique line on the lamina of the thyroid cartilage. Its action is to draw the larynx toward the root of the tongue. It is related laterally to the external maxillary vein and the anterior part of the mandibular gland.

The **hyo-epiglotticus** is a feeble muscle which occupies a median position above the central part of the thyro-hyoid membrane, enclosed by an elastic sheath, the hyo-epiglottic ligament. It arises from the body of the hyoid bone by two branches which unite and are inserted into the front of the base of the epiglottis. Its action is to draw the epiglottis toward the root of the tongue.

B. Intrinsic Muscles

The **crico-thyroideus** is a short muscle which fills the groove on the lateral surface of the cricoid cartilage; its fibers are directed dorsally and somewhat forward. It arises from the ventral part of the lateral surface and posterior edge of the cricoid cartilage, and is inserted into the posterior border and adjacent part

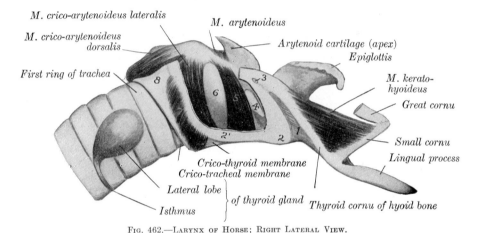

FIG. 462.—LARYNX OF HORSE; RIGHT LATERAL VIEW.

1, Thyro-hyoid membrane; *2,* body, *2′,* lamina of thyroid cartilage; *3,* thyroid foramen; *4,* cuneiform process; *5,* m. ventricularis; *6,* laryngeal saccule; *7,* m. crico-thyroideus; *8,* cricoid cartilage.

of the lateral surface of the lamina of the thyroid cartilage. Its action is to draw the thyroid cartilage and the ventral part of the cricoid cartilage together. In this action the cricoid cartilage is probably rotated about a transverse axis through the crico-thyroid joints, carrying the bases of the arytenoid cartilages with it and thus tensing the vocal folds.

The **crico-arytenoideus dorsalis** is a strong, somewhat fan-shaped muscle, which, with its fellow, covers the dorsal surface of the lamina of the cricoid cartilage. It is partially divisible into two layers. It has a broad origin on half of the lamina of the cricoid cartilage, including the median ridge, and its fibers converge to be inserted into the processus muscularis of the arytenoid cartilage. Its action is to dilate the rima glottidis by rotating the arytenoid cartilage so as to carry the vocal process and fold outward (abduction).

The **crico-arytenoideus lateralis** lies on the medial face of the thyroid lamina. It arises from the anterior border of the lateral part of the arch of the cricoid cartilage. The fibers pass in a dorsal direction and converge on the processus muscularis of the arytenoid cartilage. It closes the rima glottidis by rotating the arytenoid cartilage inward (adduction).

The **arytenoideus transversus** is an unpaired muscle which stretches across the concave dorsal surface of the arytenoid cartilages. Its fibers are attached on either side to the processus muscularis and the ridge which extends forward from it. The right and left parts of the muscle meet at a fibrous raphé, which is connected with the transverse arytenoid ligament. Fibers of the ventricularis muscle overlap its anterior part. It narrows the rima by drawing the arytenoid cartilages together (adduction).

The **ventricularis**[1] lies in the lateral wall of the larynx, covered by the lamina of the thyroid cartilage. It arises from the anterior part of the crico-thyroid membrane and the ventral border of the thyroid lamina. Its fibers pass upward and backward

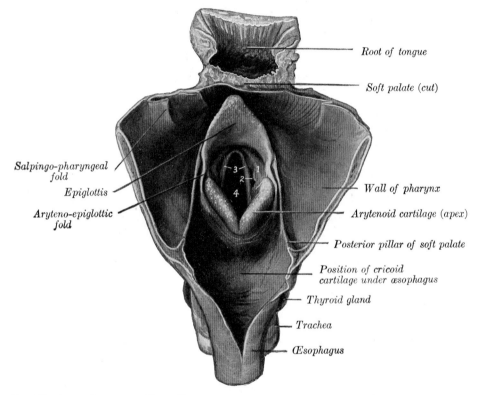

FIG. 463.—ADITUS LARYNGIS OF HORSE, EXPOSED BY OPENING PHARYNX AND BEGINNING OF ŒSOPHAGUS ALONG MEDIAN DORSAL LINE.

1, Ventricular fold; *2*, lateral ventricle; *3*, vocal folds or cords; *4*, rima glottidis.

to end partly on the processus muscularis, partly on the arytenoideus transversus, meeting its fellow.

The **vocalis**[1] is also medial to the lamina of the thyroid cartilage, and is largely separated from the preceding muscle by the laryngeal saccule. It has an extensive origin on the crico-thyroid membrane. Its direction corresponds with that of the vocal fold. It is inserted into the lateral surface of the arytenoid cartilage below the processus muscularis.

The two preceding muscles close the rima glottidis and slacken the vocal folds. With the arytenoideus transversus and crico-arytenoideus lateralis they form a sphincter vestibuli which closes the entrance to the larynx in swallowing.

In this action the ventricularis rotates the arytenoid so as to bring the apical

[1] These two muscles are also taken together as parts of the thyro-arytenoideus muscle.

part of the cartilage in contact with the epiglottis. In some cases there is a small **thyro-arytenoideus externus** muscle which arises from the medial face of the lamina of the thyroid cartilage near the dorsal border, passes upward and backward, and blends with the arytenoideus transversus.

CAVITY OF THE LARYNX

The **cavity** of the larynx (Cavum laryngis) is smaller than one would naturally expect from its external appearance. On looking into it through the pharyngeal end two folds are seen projecting from each lateral wall. The anterior pair are the

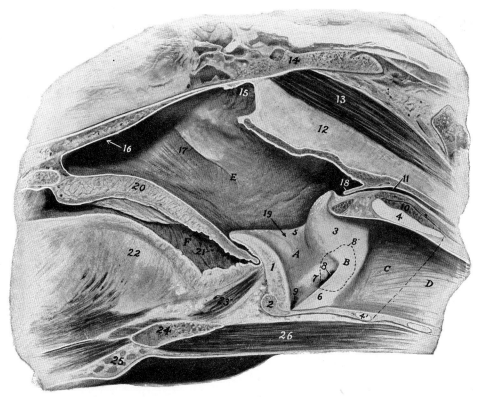

Fig. 464.—Part of Sagittal Section of Head of Horse.

Section is cut just to left of median plane.

1, Epiglottis; 2, body of thyroid cartilage; 3, arytenoid cartilage; 4, 4', lamina and arch of cricoid cartilage; 5, ary-epiglottic fold; 6, vocal fold; 7, ventricular fold; 8, lateral ventricle of larynx; 8', dotted line indicating contour of laryngeal saccule; 9, middle ventricle of larynx; 10, m. crico-arytenoideus dorsalis; 11, œsophagus; 12, septum of areolar tissue between guttural pouches; 13, m. rectus capitis ventralis; 14, body of sphenoid bone; 15, pharyngeal recess; 16, arrow points into nasal cavity; 17, pharyngeal opening of auditive or Eustachian tube; 18, posterior pillars of soft palate united over aditus œsophagi; 19, arrow points into vestibule of larynx; 20, soft palate; 21, tonsil; 22, root of tongue; 23, m. hyo-epiglotticus; 24, hyoid bone; 25, mandibular lymph glands; 26, mm. omo-hyoideus and sterno-hyoideus; A, vestibule of larynx; B, glottis; C, post-glottic part of larynx; D, trachea; E, pharynx; F, isthmus faucium.

ventricular folds and the posterior are the vocal folds; the narrow part of the cavity between the latter is the rima glottidis. Thus it is convenient to recognize three divisions of the cavity.

The **aditus laryngis,** or pharyngeal aperture, is a large, oblique, oval opening, which faces into the ventral part of the pharynx. It is bounded in front by the epiglottis, behind by the arytenoid cartilages, and laterally by the **ary-epiglottic folds** of mucous membrane (Plicæ aryepiglotticæ), which stretch between the edges of the epiglottis and the arytenoid **cartilages.**

The **vestibule** of the larynx (Vestibulum laryngis) is that part of the cavity which extends from the aditus to the vocal folds. On its lateral walls are the **ventricular folds** (Plicæ ventriculares), each of which consists of a fold of mucous membrane covering the ventricular ligament and the cuneiform process.[1] Behind them there is a pocket-like depression termed the **lateral ventricle of the larynx** (Ventriculus lateralis laryngis). This is the entrance to the **laryngeal saccule** (Sacculus laryngis), a cul-de-sac of the mucous membrane which is an inch or more (ca. 2.5 to 3 cm.) long and extends upward and backward on the medial surface of the thyroid lamina. There is a small **middle ventricle** (Ventriculus laryngis medianus) at the base of the epiglottis.

The term "laryngeal saccule" seems decidedly preferable to the "appendix ventriculi laryngis" of the B. N. A. The saccule is in relation with the ventricular vocal and lateral crico-

FIG. 466.—CAST OF RIGHT LATERAL VENTRICLE AND SACCULE OF HORSE; MEDIAL VIEW.

1, Ventricle; 2, saccule. Figure is a little less than three-fourths of natural size.

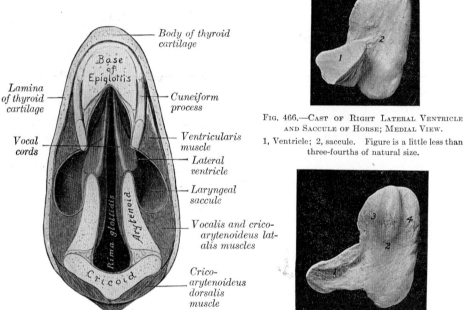

FIG. 465.—SECTION OF LARYNX OF HORSE.
The section cut is parallel with the vocal cords.

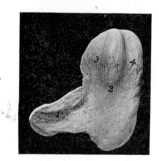

FIG. 467.—CAST OF LEFT LATERAL VENTRICLE AND SACCULE OF LARYNX OF HORSE; LATERAL VIEW.

1, Ventricle; 2, saccule; 3, impression of ventricularis muscle; 4, impression of vocalis muscle.

arytenoid muscles, and when these are atrophic (as in hemiplegia laryngis or "roaring"), the pouch is considerably larger on the affected side, having occupied the space vacated by the muscles. The blind end of the saccule lies just below the level of the muscular process of the arytenoid cartilage. It is loosely attached to the contiguous structures. The average capacity of the saccule is about 5 to 6 c.c.

The middle, narrow part of the cavity is termed the **glottis** or **rima glottidis**. It is bounded on either side by the vocal fold and the medial surface of the arytenoid cartilage. The **vocal folds** (Labia vocalia), or true vocal cords, are situated behind the false cords and the lateral ventricles. They extend from the angle of junction of the body and laminæ of the thyroid cartilage to the vocal processes of the arytenoid cartilages. They are prismatic in cross-section, and their free edges look forward and somewhat upward. The mucous membrane of the cord (Plica vocalis) is very thin and smooth, and is intimately attached to the underlying vocal

[1] These are commonly known as the "false vocal cords."

ligament. In ordinary breathing the rima is somewhat lanceolate in form (Fig. 465); when dilated, it is diamond-shaped, the widest part being between the vocal processes. The narrow part of the glottis between the vocal cords is termed the pars intermembranacea, while the wider part between the arytenoid cartilages is the pars intercartilaginea.

In the revised nomenclature the terms "true" and "false" vocal cords have been replaced by "labium vocale" and "plica ventricularis." The labium vocale consists of the plica vocalis, lig. vocale, and m. vocalis; the last forms the bulk of the projection.

The **posterior compartment** of the laryngeal cavity is directly continuous with the trachea. It is enclosed by the cricoid cartilage and the crico-thyroid membrane. It is clearly marked off laterally by the vocal cord and the projection caused by the posterior border of the arytenoid cartilage. It is oval in form, the transverse diameter being an inch and a half to two inches (ca. 4 to 5 cm.), and the dorso-ventral diameter two to two and a half inches (ca. 5 to 6 cm.).

The **mucous membrane** of the larynx (Tunica mucosa laryngis) is reflected around the margin of the aditus to become continuous with that of the pharynx, and is continuous behind with that which lines the trachea. It is closely attached to the epiglottis, except at the base, but elsewhere in the aditus and vestibule it is loosely attached by submucous tissue which contains many elastic fibers. It is thin and very closely adherent over the vocal cords and the medial surfaces of the arytenoid cartilages. The epithelium is of the stratified squamous type from the aditus to the glottis, beyond which it is columnar ciliated in character. There are numerous mucous **laryngeal glands** (Glandulæ laryngeæ), except in the glottis and the pharyngeal surface of the epiglottis, in which situations they are scanty. Lymph nodules (Noduli lymphatici laryngei) are also present, especially at the lateral ventricle.

Vessels and Nerves.—The **arteries** are derived from the laryngeal and ascending pharyngeal arteries. The **veins** correspond to the arteries. The **lymph-vessels** go to the anterior cervical and pharyngeal lymph glands. The **nerves** come from the vagus. The recurrent or posterior laryngeal is the motor nerve to the muscles with the exception of the crico-thyroideus. The anterior laryngeal is the sensory nerve; it commonly supplies the nerve to the crico-thyroideus.

THE TRACHEA

The **trachea** extends from the larynx to the hilus of the lungs, where it divides into the right and left bronchi. It is kept permanently open by a series of fifty to sixty incomplete cartilaginous rings embedded in its wall. It occupies a median position, except near its termination, where it is pushed a little to the right by the arch of the aorta. It is approximately cylindrical, but its cervical part is for the most part depressed dorso-ventrally by contact with the longus colli muscle, so that the dorsal surface is flattened. Its average length is about 30 to 32 inches (ca. 75 to 80 cm.). The average caliber is about two to two and one-half inches (ca. 5 to 6 cm.), but in the greater part of the neck the transverse diameter is greater and the dorso-ventral smaller.[1] It is enclosed by a fascia propria.

In its **cervical part** (Pars cervicalis) the trachea is related dorsally to the œsophagus for a short distance, but chiefly to the longus colli muscles. It is related laterally to the lateral lobes of the thyroid gland, the carotid artery, the jugular vein, the vagus, sympathetic, and recurrent laryngeal nerves, and the tracheal

[1] At its origin the trachea is almost circular in cross-section and the average diameter is about two and a quarter inches (ca. 5.5 cm.). It soon becomes flattened dorso-ventrally, so that the transverse diameter may be nearly three inches (ca. 7 cm.) and the dorso-ventral about two inches (ca. 5 cm.). In the thorax the diameters become more nearly equal, and sometimes the dorso-ventral diameter is the greater; this is the case where the aorta crosses the trachea.

lymph ducts and cervical lymph glands.   The œsophagus lies on its left face from
the third cervical vertebra backward.   The sterno-cephalicus muscles cross it very
obliquely, passing from the ventral surface forward over its sides, and diverging to
reach the angles of the jaw.   The omo-hyoidei also cross it very obliquely, passing
over the lateral surfaces of the tube, and converging ventrally in the laryngeal
region.   The sterno-thyro-hyoideus lies on the ventral surface.[1]   The scaleni lie on
either side near the entrance to the thorax.

The **thoracic part** (Pars thoracalis) of the trachea (Figs. 553, 554) passes back-

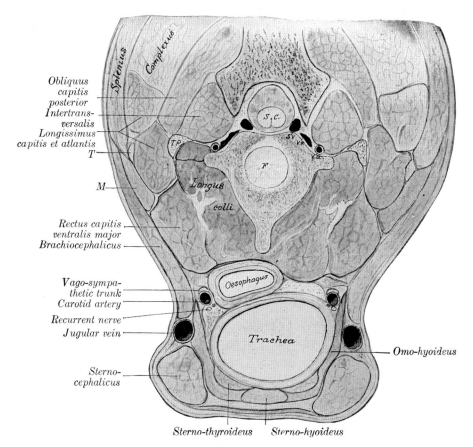

FIG. 468.—CROSS-SECTION OF VENTRAL PART OF NECK OF HORSE.

This section is cut at right angles to the long axis of the neck, passing through the junction of the second and third
cervical vertebræ.   S.c., Spinal cord; S.v., spinal vein; V.v., V.a., vertebral vein and artery; T.p., transverse process
(tip); F, intervertebral fibro-cartilage; T, atlantal tendon common to brachiocephalicus, splenius, and longissimus
atlantis; M, digitation of brachiocephalicus inserted by T.

ward between the pleural sacs and divides into two bronchi over the left atrium of the
heart. It is related dorsally to the longus colli for a short distance, and beyond this to
the œsophagus. Its left face is crossed by the aortic arch, the left brachial artery, and
the thoracic duct.   Its right face is crossed by the vena azygos, the dorso-cervical
and vertebral vessels, and the right vagus nerve.   Ventrally it is related to the
anterior vena cava, the brachiocephalic and common carotid trunks, and the cardiac and left recurrent nerves.

[1] The arrangement of the muscles should be noted, since the space enclosed by the divergence
of the sterno-cephalici and the convergence of the omo-hyoidei is the area of election for the opera-
tion of tracheotomy.

The **bifurcation** of the trachea (Bifurcatio tracheæ) is situated opposite to the fifth rib or intercostal space, and about four or five inches (ca. 10 to 12 cm.) ventral to the sixth thoracic vertebra.

The trachea is composed of—(1) the cartilaginous rings; (2) a fibro-elastic membrane which encloses and connects the rings; (3) a muscular layer; (4) the mucous membrane. The **elastic membrane** is intimately attached to the perichondrium of the rings. In the intervals between the latter it constitutes the **tracheal annular ligaments** (Ligamenta annularia trachealia). The **rings** of the trachea (Cartilagines tracheales) are composed of hyaline cartilage. They are incomplete dorsally, and when their free ends are drawn apart, resemble somewhat the letter C. In the cervical part the free ends overlap, while in the thoracic part they do not meet; here the deficiency is made up by thin plates of variable size and form, embedded in a membrana transversa. Ventrally the rings are about one-half inch (ca. 1.5 cm.) wide, while dorsally they are wider and thinner. The first ring is attached to the cricoid cartilage by the crico-tracheal membrane, and is often fused dorsally with the second ring. Various irregularities, such as partial bifurcation or partial or complete fusion of adjacent rings, are common. The arrangement in the terminal part is very irregular. The **trachealis muscle** (M. trachealis) consists of unstriped fibers which stretch across the dorsal part of the tube. It is separated from the ends of the rings and the membrana transversa by a quantity of areolar tissue. When it contracts the caliber of the tube is diminished. The **mucous membrane** is pale normally, and presents numerous fine longitudinal folds, in which are bundles of elastic fibers. The epithelium is stratified columnar ciliated. Numerous **tracheal glands** (Glandulæ tracheales) are present; they are tubulo-alveolar and mixed in type.

Vessels and Nerves.—The **arteries** are derived chiefly from the common carotid arteries, and the **veins** go mainly to the jugular veins. The **lymph-vessels** go to the cervical and mediastinal lymph glands. The **nerves** come from the vagus and sympathetic.

THE BRONCHI

The two **bronchi,** right and left (Bronchus dexter, sinister), are formed by the bifurcation of the trachea. Each passes backward and outward to the hilus of the corresponding lung. The right bronchus is a little larger and less oblique in direction than the left. They are related ventrally to the divisions of the pulmonary artery, and dorsally to the branches of the bronchial artery and the bronchial lymph glands. Their structure is similar to that of the trachea, but the cartilaginous framework consists chiefly of plates instead of rings.

THE THORACIC CAVITY

The **thoracic cavity** (Cavum thoracis) is the second in point of size of the body cavities. In form it is somewhat like a truncated cone, much compressed laterally in its anterior part, and with the base cut off very obliquely. The **dorsal wall** or **roof** is formed by the thoracic vertebræ and the ligaments and muscles connected with them. The **lateral walls** are formed by the ribs and the intercostal muscles. The **ventral wall** or **floor** is formed by the sternum, the cartilages of the sternal ribs, and the muscles in connection therewith. It is about one-half as long as the dorsal wall. The **posterior wall,** formed by the diaphragm, is very oblique and is strongly convex. The **anterior aperture** or **inlet** (Apertura thoracis cranialis) is relatively small, and of narrow, oval form. It is bounded dorsally by the first thoracic vertebra and laterally by the first pair of ribs. It is occupied by the longus colli muscles, the trachea, œsophagus, vessels, nerves, and lymph glands.

A longitudinal septum, termed the **mediastinum thoracis** or **septum medias-**

tinale, extends from the dorsal wall to the ventral and posterior walls, and divides the cavity into two lateral chambers. Each of these chambers is lined by a serous membrane called the pleura, and is termed a **pleural cavity** (Cavum pleuræ). The mediastinum is, for the most part, not median in position, as might be inferred from its name; this is correlated with the fact that the largest organ contained in it, the heart, is placed more on the left side than on the right; consequently the right pleural cavity and lung are larger than the left. Practically all of the organs in the thorax are in the mediastinal space between the pleuræ, with the exception of the lungs, the posterior vena cava, and the right phrenic nerve. The part in which the heart and the pericardium are situated, together with that dorsal to it, is usually called the **middle mediastinal space** (Cavum mediastinale medium); the parts before and behind this are termed respectively the anterior and posterior mediastinal spaces (Cavum mediastinale craniale, caudale).

THE PLEURÆ

The **pleuræ** are two serous membranes, right and left, which enclose on each side a **pleural cavity** (Cavum pleuræ). They line the walls of the thorax, form the lateral laminæ of the mediastinum, and are reflected from the latter upon the lungs. We therefore distinguish **parietal, mediastinal,** and **pulmonary** or **visceral** parts of the pleuræ.

The **parietal pleura** (Pleura parietalis) is attached to the thoracic wall by the endothoracic fascia. On the lateral thoracic wall it is adherent to the ribs and intercostal muscles and is termed the **costal pleura** (Pleura costalis). Behind it is closely attached to the diaphragm, forming the **diaphragmatic pleura** (Pleura diaphragmatica).

The **mediastinal pleura** (Pleura mediastinalis) covers the organs in the mediastinal space and is in part in apposition with the opposite sac. The part which is adherent to the pericardium is distinguished as **pericardiac pleura** (Pleura pericardiaca).[1]

From the mediastinum each pleura is reflected upon the corresponding lung, which it covers, constituting the **pulmonary** or **visceral pleura** (Pleura pulmonalis). The reflection occurs around and behind the hilus of the lung, and is in great part direct, so that a portion of the mediastinal surface of each lung has no pleural covering. Behind the hilus of the lung a considerable triangular area is not covered by the pleura, the two lungs being attached to each other by a thin layer of connective tissue in this situation.[2] Posteriorly the reflection is not direct, so that there is a fold formed by the reflection of the pleura from the mediastinum and the diaphragm to the lung, behind the triangular area of adhesion just mentioned; it is seen when the base of the lung is drawn outward. This fold, the **pulmonary ligament** (Lig. pulmonale), consists of two layers of pleura, between which there is elastic tissue, especially abundant in its posterior part; it also contains branches of the esophageal artery.

The right pleura forms a special sagittal fold about a handbreadth to the right of the median plane, which encloses the posterior vena cava in its upper edge; it is therefore called the **fold of the vena cava** (Plica venæ cavæ). It gives off a small accessory fold for the right phrenic nerve. The fold arises from the pericardium and from the diaphragm below the foramen venæ cavæ, and intervenes between the intermediate lobe and the body of the right lung. It is delicate and lace-like.

The posterior mediastinum is very delicate ventral to the œsophagus, and

---

[1] The student should bear in mind that these terms are employed simply as a matter of convenience in description; all the parts of each pleural sac, though differently named, form a continuous whole.

[2] Here the mediastinal pleura does not extend continuously from the dorsal to the ventral wall, but consists of dorsal and ventral parts.

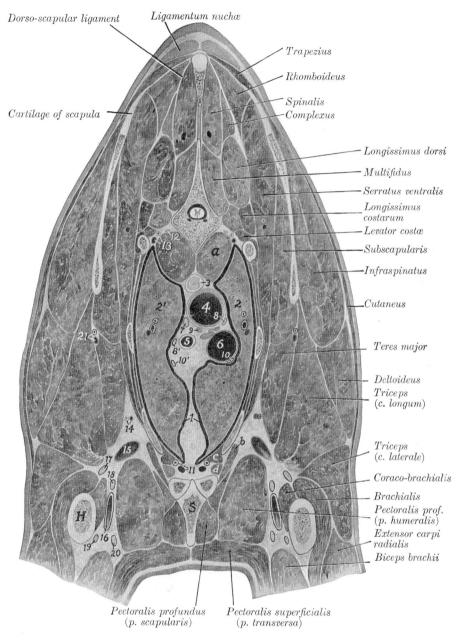

Dorso-scapular ligament

Ligamentum nuchæ

Trapezius

Rhomboideus

Spinalis
Complexus

Cartilage of scapula

Longissimus dorsi

Multifidus

Serratus ventralis

Longissimus
costarum

Levator costæ

Subscapularis

Infraspinatus

Cutaneus

Teres major

Deltoideus
Triceps
(c. longum)

Triceps
(c. laterale)

Coraco-brachialis

Brachialis

Pectoralis prof.
(p. humeralis)

Extensor carpi
radialis

Biceps brachii

Pectoralis profundus
(p. scapularis)

Pectoralis superficialis
(p. transversa)

Fig. 469.—Section of Thorax of Horse.

The section is cut in an oblique direction corresponding with the spine of the scapula. It passes through the fourth thoracic vertebra and a little more than an inch behind the shoulder joint. It cuts the fourth, third and second ribs and the first chondro-sternal joints. The pleural cavities, indicated by wide black lines, are exaggerated for the sake of clearness.

1, Pleural cavities (number is placed in mediastinum); 2, 2′, lungs; 3, œsophagus; 4, trachea; 5, brachiocephalic trunk; 6, anterior vena cava; 7, thoracic duct; 8, 8′, vagi; 9, left recurrent nerve; 10, 10′, phrenic nerves; 11, internal thoracic vessels; 12, sympathetic trunk; 13, subcostal-vessels; 14, external thoracic vessels; 15, brachial vein; 16, brachial artery; 17, radial nerve; 18, ulnar nerve; 19, musculo-cutaneous nerve; 20, median nerve; 21, subscapular vessels; a, m. longus colli; b, m. rectus thoracis; c, m. transversus thoracis; d, m. intercostalis internus; S, sternum; H, humerus. Ventral to the trachea there are shown, but not marked on account of lack of space, two cardiac nerves and a mediastinal lymph gland.

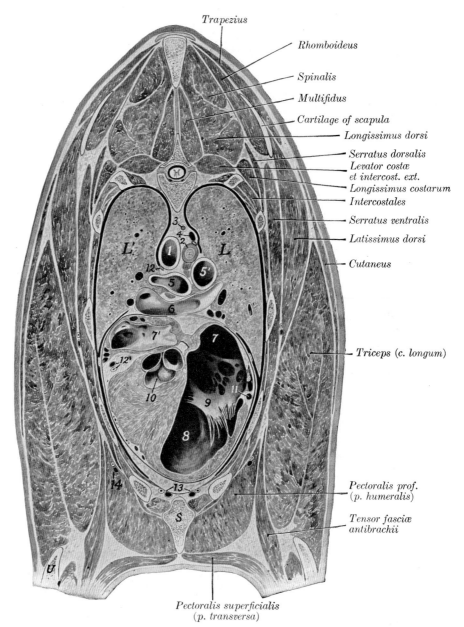

Trapezius

Rhomboideus

Spinalis

Multifidus

Cartilage of scapula

Longissimus dorsi

Serratus dorsalis
Levator costæ
et intercost. ext.
Longissimus costarum
Intercostales

Serratus ventralis

Latissimus dorsi

Cutaneus

Triceps (c. longum)

Pectoralis prof.
(p. humeralis)

Tensor fasciæ
antibrachii

Pectoralis superficialis
(p. transversa)

FIG. 470.—SECTION OF THORAX OF HORSE.

The section is cut in an oblique direction corresponding with the spine of the scapula. It cuts the body of the seventh thoracic vertebræ and the seventh rib dorsally and the fourth rib and its cartilage ventrally. The pleural and pericardiac cavities, represented by wide black lines, are exaggerated for the sake of clearness.

L, L', lungs; 1, aorta; 2, œsophagus; 3, thoracic duct; 4, vena azygos; 5, 5', bronchi; 6, bifurcation of pulmonary artery; 7, 7', right and left atria; 8, right ventricle; 9, tricuspid valve; 10, origin of aorta; 11, right coronary artery; 12, left vagus nerve; 12', left coronary artery (circumflex branch) and satellite vein; 13, internal thoracic vessels; 14, external thoracic vessels; S, sternum; U, ulna. The following structures are shown, but not marked on account of lack of space: The right vagus is on the œsophagus and ventral to the vena azygos. The phrenic nerves are on the upper part of the pericardium on each side. The sympathetic trunks are on each side of the body of the vertebra. The number 10 is placed on the ventricular septum. Bronchial lymph-glands are shown ventral to the œsophagus and the left bronchus.

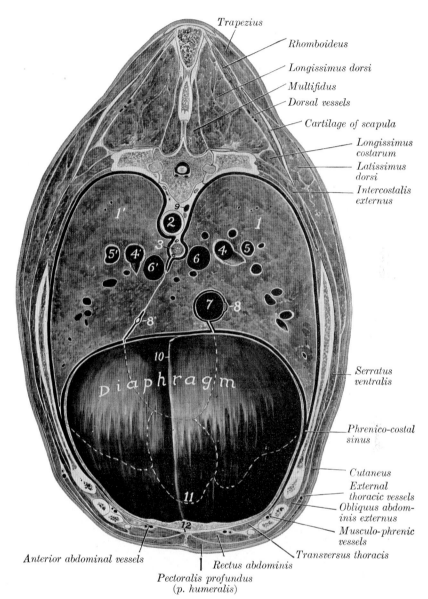

Trapezius

Rhomboideus

Longissimus dorsi

Multifidus

Dorsal vessels

Cartilage of scapula

Longissimus costarum

Latissimus dorsi

Intercostalis externus

Serratus ventralis

Phrenico-costal sinus

Cutaneus

External thoracic vessels

Obliquus abdominis externus

Musculo-phrenic vessels

Transversus thoracis

Anterior abdominal vessels

Rectus abdominis

Pectoralis profundus (p. humeralis)

FIG. 471.—CROSS-SECTION OF BODY OF HORSE.

The section is cut through the eighth thoracic vertebra and the anterior part of the xiphoid cartilage. It cuts the vertebral end of the eighth rib and a little more than half of the seventh rib. The flexures of the great colon and a small part of the liver, which lay in the concavity of the diaphragm, have been removed. The dotted lines indicate the contour of the bases of the lungs and the apex of the heart, which are concealed by the diaphragm. The pleural cavities, indicated by wide black lines, are exaggerated for the sake of clearness.

1, 1′, Lungs; 2, aorta; 3, œsophagus; 4, 4′, stem bronchi; 5, 5′, pulmonary arteries; 6, 6′, large pulmonary veins; 7, posterior vena cava; 8, 8′, phrenic nerves; 9, vena azygos; 10, falciform and round ligaments of liver; 11, position of apex of heart; 12 (placed on cut surface of sternal part of diaphragm), xiphoid cartilage. The sympathetic trunks (not marked) are shown on each side of the body of the vertebra. The œsophageal trunks of the vagi (not marked) are shown in relation to the œsophagus. The thoracic duct is ventral to the vena azygos.

usually appears fenestrated; when these apertures are present, the two pleural cavities communicate with each other.[1]

The pleural sacs contain a clear serous fluid, the **liquor pleuræ;** in health there is only a sufficient amount to moisten the surface, but it accumulates rapidly after death. It should be borne in mind that the pleural cavity is normally a capillary space between the parietal and visceral parts of the pleura, and contains a film of serous fluid. In illustrations it is necessary, for the sake of clearness, to exaggerate the space.

The pleura resembles the peritoneum in structure and appearance. It is attached to the structures which it covers by subserous tissue, which is elastic and in some situations contains fat. In the case of the parietal pleura the subserous tissue is termed the **endothoracic fascia.** This lines the thoracic walls, but is practically absent over the tendinous center of the diaphragm. A strong layer descends from it in the mediastinum and blends with the fibrous part of the pericardium. The subserous tissue under the pulmonary pleura is continuous with the interlobular tissue of the lung.

The pleura receives an abundant blood supply which is derived chiefly from the intercostal, internal thoracic, bronchial, and œsophageal arteries. Lymph vessels are very numerous in the pleura and subserous tissue; they go chiefly to the intercostal and mediastinal glands.

Lines of Pleural Reflection.—The parietal pleura is reflected along three lines which are known as the **lines of pleural reflection,** these may be termed vertebral, sternal, and diaphragmatic. The **vertebral line of pleural reflection** is that along which the costal pleura turns ventrally to form the mediastinal pleura; it extends along the longus colli and the bodies of the thoracic vertebræ to the vertebral end of the last intercostal space, where it joins the line of diaphragmatic reflection. The **sternal line of pleural reflection** is that along which the costal pleura is reflected dorsally to become the mediastinal pleura. Anteriorly the two lines are close together along the middle of the floor of the thorax, but further back they diverge to each side of the sternal attachment of the pericardium. The reflection is at an acute angle and the narrow angular recess of the pleural cavity here is termed the **costo-mediastinal sinus** (Sinus costomediastinalis). The **diaphragmatic line of pleural reflection** is that along which the costal pleura passes from the lateral wall to the diaphragm. This line is important clinically, since it is, from the standpoint of physical diagnosis, the demarcation between the thoracic and abdominal cavities. It extends along the eighth and ninth costal cartilages, crosses the sternal end of the ninth rib, and passes backward and upward in a gentle curve and at a gradually increasing distance from the sternal ends of the ribs, so that its most posterior part is at about the middle of the anterior border of the last rib; this is the posterior limit of the pleural cavity. Here it turns medially and a little forward and ends at the vertebral end of the last intercostal space. This reflection is also at an acute angle and the costal and diaphragmatic pleuræ are in contact over an area of variable width along this line. The narrow angular recess of the pleural cavity here is termed the **phrenico-costal sinus** (Sinus phrenicocostalis); and the line just described might well be designated similarly as the **linea phrenico-costalis.**

The **cupola pleuræ** or apex of each pleural sac lies at the anterior aperture of the thorax. On the right side it forms two culs-de-sac; one of these may extend forward more than an inch (ca. 3 cm.) beyond the first rib in contact with the deep face of the scalenus; the other is ventral to the anterior vena cava and may extend about an inch (ca. 2.5 cm.) beyond the first rib. The left cupola usually does not extend beyond the plane of the first rib.

THE LUNGS

The **lungs,** right and left (Pulmo dexter, sinister), occupy much the greater part of the thoracic cavity. They are accurately adapted to the walls of the cavity and the other organs contained therein. The two lungs are not alike in form or size, the right one being considerably larger than the left; the difference is chiefly in width, in conformity with the projection of the heart to the left. The lung is soft, spongy, and highly elastic. It crepitates when pressed between the finger and thumb, and floats in water. When the thoracic cavity of the unpreserved subject is opened, the lung collapses immediately to about one-

---

[1] The apertures do not exist in the fœtus, and are sometimes absent in the adult subject. Some of them are doubtless produced in dissection by the necessary disturbance of the parts, as the membrane is very delicate and easily damaged. Careful examination shows that the appearance of an opening may be produced by transparent thinness of the membrane.

third of its original size, and loses its proper form; this is due to its highly elastic character and the fact that the tension of the lung tissue caused by the air pressure in its cavities has been relieved by the external air pressure.[1] The **color** varies according to the amount of blood contained in the lung. During life the lung has a pink color, but in subjects which have been bled for dissection it is light gray or faintly tinged with red. In unbled subjects it is dark red; the depth of color varies, and is often locally accentuated by gravitation of blood to the most dependent parts (hypostasis). The **fœtal lung,** since it contains no air and has a relatively small blood-supply, differs from that of an animal which has breathed in the following respects: (1) It is much smaller; (2) it is firmer and does not crepitate; (3) it sinks in water; (4) it is pale gray in color. In **form** the lungs are like casts of the cavities in which they are situated. When well hardened *in situ,* their surfaces present

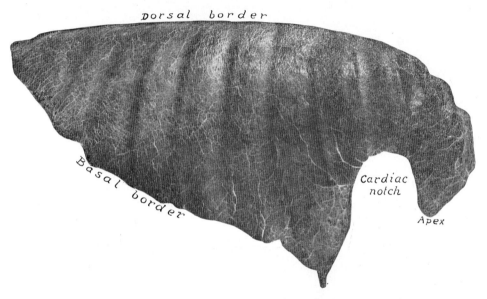

FIG. 472.—RIGHT LUNG OF HORSE; COSTAL SURFACE.
Specimen hardened *in situ.*

impressions and elevations corresponding exactly to the structures with which they are in contact. Each lung presents two surfaces, two borders, a base, and an apex.

The **costal surface** (Facies costalis) is convex, and lies against the lateral thoracic wall, to which it is accurately adapted; it presents impressions of the ribs.

The **mediastinal surface** (Facies mediastinalis) is much less extensive than the costal surface. It is molded on the mediastinum and its contents. It presents a large cavity adapted to the pericardium and heart; this is termed the **cardiac impression** (Impressio cardiaca). Above and behind this is the **hilus of the lung** (Hilus pulmonis), at which the bronchus, vessels, and nerves enter and leave the lung; the bronchial lymph glands are also found here. Behind this the two lungs are adherent to each other over a triangular area. Above this there is a groove for the œsophagus, which is deepest on the left lung. A groove for the aorta (Sulcus aorticus) curves upward and backward over the hilus, and passes backward near the dorsal border of the lung; the curved part of the groove for the aortic arch is

---

[1] No idea of the natural form and size of the lung can be obtained from a specimen in this state, nor can an accurate conception be gained by examination of the soft inflated organ. The lungs should be hardened *in situ* for this purpose, and if the process has been successful they conform in every detail to the structures with which they were in contact.

absent on the right lung, on which there is a groove for the vena azygos. Anteriorly there are grooves for the trachea, the brachiocephalic trunk, the anterior vena cava, and other vessels.

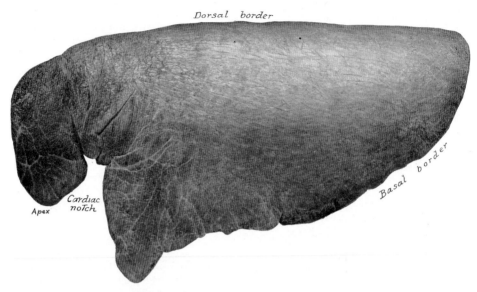

Fig. 473.—Left Lung of Horse; Costal Surface.
Specimen hardened *in situ.*

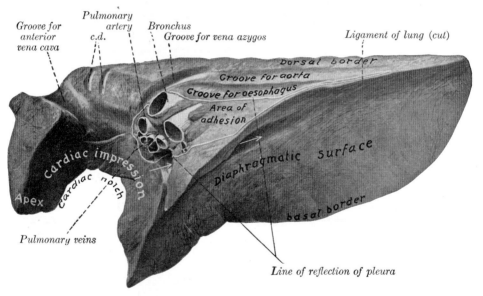

Fig. 474.—Right Lung of Horse; Mediastinal and Diaphragmatic Surfaces.

Organ hardened *in situ.* *c, d,* Grooves for deep cervical and dorsal veins. Arrows indicate canal for posterior vena cava between intermediate lobe and main part of lung. By an oversight the impression of the trachea is unmarked; it is dorsal to the groove for the vena cava.

The **dorsal border** (Margo dorsalis) is long, thick, and rounded; it lies in the groove alongside of the bodies of the thoracic vertebræ.[1]

[1] In some cases this border is cut into by a fissure which partly marks off the apex from the body of the lung.

The **ventral border** (Margo ventralis) is thin and short; it occupies the angular space between the mediastinum and the ventral parts of the sternal ribs (Recessus costo-mediastinalis). It presents, opposite to the heart, the **cardiac notch** (Incisura cardiaca). On the left lung this notch is opposite to the ribs from the third to the sixth, so that a considerable area of the pericardium here lies in direct contact with the chest-wall. On the right lung the notch is much smaller, and extends from the third rib to the fourth intercostal space.

The left cardiac notch is usually quadrilateral; its highest part is about four inches (ca. 10 cm.) above the sternal end of the fourth rib. The anterior border usually extends from the third intercostal space to the second, about two inches (ca. 5 cm.) above the sternal end of the third rib. The posterior border crosses very obliquely the fifth rib and space and ends at the sternal end of the sixth rib. The right notch is usually triangular; its apex is about three or four inches (ca. 8 to 10 cm.) above the level of the sternal end of the ribs at the third intercostal space or fourth rib. Its anterior border extends commonly to the ventral end of the second intercostal space, and its posterior margin to the ventral end of space five. In some cases a fissure partially marks off the apex from the body of the lung.

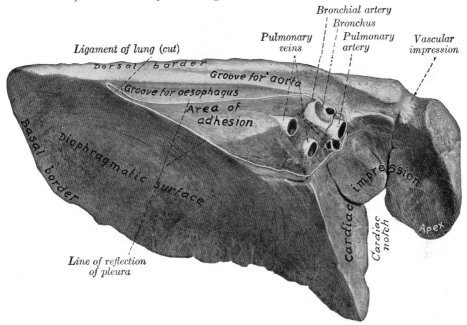

Fig. 475.—LEFT LUNG OF HORSE; MEDIASTINAL AND DIAPHRAGMATIC SURFACES.
Organ hardened *in situ.* Vascular impression for common dorso-cervico-vertebral vein.

The **base** of the lung (Basis pulmonis) is oval in outline; its surface (Facies diaphragmatica) is deeply concave in adaptation to the thoracic surface of the diaphragm. Laterally and dorsally it is limited by a thin convex **basal border** (Margo basalis) which fits into the narrow recess (Sinus phrenico-costalis) between the diaphragm and the lateral chest-wall. The position of this border, of course, varies during respiration. In the deepest inspiration it may reach the bottom of this recess. In dissecting-room subjects the distance between the border and the diaphragmatic line of reflection of the pleura increases from about two inches (ca. 5 cm.) at the seventh rib to about six or seven inches (ca. 16 to 18 cm.) at the fifteenth, and then decreases. The dorsal end of the base is usually at the vertebral end of the sixteenth intercostal space or seventeenth rib.[1]

The **apex** of the lung (Apex pulmonis) is prismatic, narrow, and flattened transversely. It is partially marked off from the rest of the lung by the cardiac

[1] The ventral and basal borders may be taken together under the term margo acutus.

notch. It curves downward, and is related deeply to the anterior mediastinum and (indirectly) to the anterior part of the pericardium.

The lungs of the horse are not divided into lobes by deep fissures, as is the case in most mammals. The left lung may be regarded as consisting of a chief part, the **body of the lung** (Corpus pulmonis), and the **apex** (Apex pulmonis). But in addition to these the right lung has an **intermediate lobe** (Lobus intermedius),[1] which is separated from the body of the lung by a fissure which forms in its dorsal part a canal for the posterior vena cava and the right phrenic nerve, enclosed in the plica venæ cavæ.[2]

The **root of the lung** (Radix pulmonis) is composed of the structures which enter or leave the lung at the hilus on the mediastinal surface. These are: (1) The **bronchus;** (2) the **pulmonary artery;** (3) the **pulmonary veins;** (4) the **bronchial artery;** (5) the **pulmonary nerves;** (6) the **pulmonary lymph vessels,** which go to the bronchial lymph glands. The bronchus is situated dorsally, with the bronchial artery on its upper surface and the pulmonary artery immediately below it. The pulmonary veins lie chiefly below and behind the artery.

The **lobulation** of the lungs is not very evident on account of the small amount of interlobular tissue. The lobules appear on the surface or on sections as irregular polygonal areas of different sizes.[3]

Bronchial branches.—Each bronchus at its entrance into the lung gives off a branch to the apex of the lung (Bronchus apicalis). It is then continued backward as the main stem bronchus, parallel with the dorsal border of the lung, giving off branches (Rami bronchiales) dorsally and ventrally; these branch similarly and reach all parts of the lung. The right bronchus gives off a special branch to the intermediate lobe. The apical bronchus of the right lung is larger than that of the left lung. A large ventral bronchial branch (Bronchus cardiacus) is given off from each stem bronchus to the part of the lung which is homologous with the cardiac lobe of other animals.

The **structure** of the larger bronchial tubes is, in general, similar to that of the trachea. Their walls contain irregular plates of cartilage instead of rings. There is a continuous layer of unstriped muscle, composed of circularly arranged bundles. The mucous membrane presents numerous longitudinal folds; it contains many elastic fibers, mucous glands, and lymph nodules, and is lined by ciliated columnar epithelium. As the tubes diminish in size the coats become thinner and the cartilages smaller; in tubes about 1 mm. in diameter the cartilages and mucous glands are absent.

By repeated branching the **interlobular bronchi** are formed, and from these arise the **lobular bronchioles.** The latter enter a lobule and branch within it, forming the **respiratory bronchioles** (Bronchioli respiratorii); these give off the **alveolar ducts** (Ductuli alveolares), the walls of which are pouched out to form hemispherical diverticula, the **alveoli** or air-cells (Alveoli pulmonum).

A **pulmonary lobule** (Lobulus pulmonis), the unit of lung structure, is made up of a lobular bronchiole with its branches and their air-cells, blood- and lymphvessels, and nerves. Between the lobules is the **interlobular tissue,** which forms the supporting framework of the lung.

Vessels and Nerves.—The branches of the **pulmonary artery** carry venous blood to the lungs. They accompany the bronchi, and form rich capillary plexuses

---

[1] This is also commonly called the mediastinal lobe.

[2] Some authors consider each lung to be divided into anterior and posterior lobes by the cardiac notch, so that the right lung would have three lobes and the left lung two lobes. Not rarely a fissure or notch in the dorsal border partially marks off the apex from the body of the lung, and in some cases there is a corresponding fissure in the ventral border.

[3] In fœtal lung the lobulation is much more distinct. Pigmentation of the lung is sometimes seen in horses, and in such cases the pigment is deposited mainly in the interlobular tissue, thus mapping out the lobules.

on the walls of the alveoli. Here the blood is arterialized, and is returned to the heart by the **pulmonary veins.** The **bronchial arteries** are relatively small vessels which carry arterial blood for the nutrition of the lungs. The branches of these arteries accompany the bronchial ramifications as far as the alveolar ducts, but do not extend to the alveoli. The œsophageal branches of the **broncho-œsophageal** and **gastric arteries** also supply pulmonary branches (in the horse) which reach the lung by way of the ligament of the lung. These branches vary much in size, and ramify chiefly in the subpleural tissue of the basal part of the lungs.[1] The **lymph vessels** are numerous, and are arranged in two sets. The superficial set forms close networks in and under the pleura, while the deep set accompanies the bronchi and pulmonary vessels. Most of them converge to the root of the lung and enter the bronchial lymph glands, but some go to the mediastinal lymph glands. The **pulmonary nerves** come from the vagus and sympathetic nerves. They enter at the hilus and supply branches to the bronchial arteries and the air-tubes.

THE THYROID GLAND

The **thyroid gland** (Glandula thyreoidea) is situated on the anterior part of the trachea, to which it is loosely attached. It is a very vascular ductless gland, and is firm in texture and dark red-brown in color. It consists of two lateral lobes and a very narrow connecting isthmus (Figs. 332, 649).

The **lateral lobes** (Lobus dexter, sinister) are situated on each side of the trachea near to or in contact with the larynx. Their position is indicated approximately by the angle of junction of the jugular and external maxillary veins. Each is oval in outline and is about as large as a plum of medium size. The superficial surface is convex and is covered by the cervical angle of the parotid gland and the sterno-cephalicus and omo-hyoideus. The deep surface is adapted to the trachea. About the lobe are the anterior cervical lymph glands. The anterior pole is large and rounded, while the posterior is smaller and often tapers to a tail-like process which is continuous with the isthmus.

The **isthmus** (Isthmus gl. thyreoideæ) extends across the ventral face of the trachea, connecting the two lobes. It is usually extremely narrow in the adult horse and is often reduced in great part to a small strand of fibrous tissue.

The lateral lobes are very variable in size and position, and are usually unsymmetrical. The average length is about two inches (ca. 5 cm.). The greatest height averages a little more than an inch (ca. 2.7 cm.), and the greatest width a little less than an inch (ca. 1.5-2 cm.). The average weight is about half an ounce (ca. 15 gm.). The right lobe is commonly in contact with the crico-pharyngeus or crico-thyroideus, but may be about a finger's breadth from the larynx. The left lobe may be an inch or more (ca. 4 cm.) from the larynx, but in some cases is in contact with it. The position varies considerably in the dorso-ventral direction also, irrespective of the ventral displacement noted in enlargement of the gland. The most common form is oval, with a smaller posterior pole which tapers to the isthmus. But the isthmus is sometimes connected with the middle of the ventral border of one lobe or both, so that the two poles are about alike. Many irregularities may be observed. Cases occur in which a variable posterior process is connected with the body of the gland by a sort of neck. A complete glandular isthmus is not rare, although it is usually very narrow and may easily escape notice; in quite exceptional cases it may be 6-8 mm. in width. Its connection with the lateral lobes and crossing of the trachea are quite variable. Most often it is connected with the posterior poles and passes almost directly between the two. But it may run backward and cross much further back; in one case (personal observation) the crossing was at the space between the ninth and tenth tracheal rings. In the foal the isthmus is relatively large and entirely glandular. In the ass and mule there is almost always a well-developed isthmus. Extending from it there is sometimes a narrow band of thyroid tissue which reaches to the body of the hyoid bone; this is the lobus pyramidalis.

Structure.—The gland is enveloped by a thin fibro-elastic **capsule,** from which trabeculæ pass into the substance of the organ. The gland tissue is compact and

---

[1] It must not be inferred from the necessarily brief account here given that the two sets of vessels are quite distinct. On the contrary, competent observers state that numerous small branches of the bronchial arteries anastomose with pulmonary vessels.

consists of **lobules** (Lobuli gl. thyreoideæ), which are embedded in a **stroma** of strands of fibrous tissue. The stroma contains numerous vessels. The lobules consist of non-communicating **alveoli** or **follicles** of varying form and size. The alveoli are lined by cubical or columnar epithelium, and contain a viscid colloid substance. The thyroid arises as a median evagination of the entodermal lining of the floor of the embryonic pharynx. For a time there is a thyro-glossal duct which opens on the posterior part of the dorsum linguæ; it disappears normally in early fœtal life.

Vessels and Nerves.—The **arteries** are relatively very large; there are usually two thyroid arteries, which arise from the carotid; their branches enter the gland chiefly at or near the ends and the dorsal border. The **veins** are also large; they go to the jugular vein; the largest one leaves the gland at its posterior pole. The **lymph vessels** go to the cervical lymph glands. The **nerves** are derived from the sympathetic system.

Nodules of thyroid tissue of variable size, sometimes as large as a pea, may be found near the anterior extremity of the lateral lobes, on the course of the anterior thyroid artery or on the trachea, even at a considerable distance from the thyroid region. They are termed **accessory thyroids** (Glandulæ thyreoideæ accessoriæ).

The **parathyroids** are small glandular bodies found in the thyroid region. They are paler and not so dense as the thyroid tissue, but often cannot be differentiated by their naked-eye appearance. In the horse there is usually only one on each side in the connective tissue over the dorsal border or anterior extremity of the lateral lobe of the thyroid. One may be embedded in the deep face of the lateral lobe of the thyroid. They resemble in structure embryonic thyroid tissue.

THE THYMUS GLAND

The **thymus** is a ductless gland which has a close resemblance to the lymphoid tissues. It is well developed only in late fœtal life and for a few months after birth. After this it undergoes rapid atrophy, fatty infiltration, and amyloid degeneration, so that in the adult it is usually represented by a thin remnant in the ventral part of the anterior mediastinum or has entirely disappeared. In the new-born foal it is of a grayish-pink color, and consists of right and left **lobes** (Lobus dexter, sinister). The greater part of the gland is situated in the anterior mediastinum ventral to the trachea and large vessels, but the two lobes are continued into the neck by a chain of lobules which lie on the trachea along the course of the carotid artery, extending sometimes as far as the thyroid gland.[1]

Structure.—The thymus is enclosed in a thin and loose fibro-elastic **capsule,** and consists of secondary **lobules** (Lobuli thymi), of varying shape and size, held together by areolar tissue and fat, and connected with a strand of connective tissue termed the **tractus centralis.** These lobules are subdivided into polyhedral primary lobules, which are composed of lymphoid tissue, and present a dark, vascular **cortex,** and a lighter **medulla** that contains small masses of concentrically arranged, flattened cells; these are known as concentric corpuscles.

Vessels and Nerves.—The **arteries** are derived from the internal thoracic and common carotid. The **nerves** come from the sympathetic and vagus.

---

[1] The cervical part of the gland is very variable. The thoracic lobe of one side may have no cervical continuation; the other lobe may then give off a single prolongation which bifurcates. The thoracic part in the new-born foal occupies most of the space which is later taken up by the apices of the lungs. Its two lobes are in contact, and its deep surface is molded on the anterior part of the pericardium and the large vessels. In exceptional cases a considerable remnant of the thymus is present in adult or even old subjects; this is usually true only of the thoracic part, but it may extend into the neck a short distance; but a large lymph gland must not be mistaken for thymus. Strictly speaking there are two thymus glands, right and left. They arise as ventral diverticula of the third pharyngeal pouches, which, however, soon lose their connection with the pouches. The gland becomes essentially lymphoid in character, but it appears to produce an internal secretion which has an influence on normal growth and sexual development.

RESPIRATORY SYSTEM OF THE OX

THE NASAL CAVITY

The **nostrils** (Fig. 379), situated on either side of the muzzle, are relatively small, and are much less dilatable than those of the horse. The alæ are thick and firm. The superior commissure is narrow. There is no diverticulum nasi. The skin is smooth, bare, and moist, and there is no clear line of demarcation between it and the nasal mucosa. The opening of the naso-lacrimal duct is not visible, as

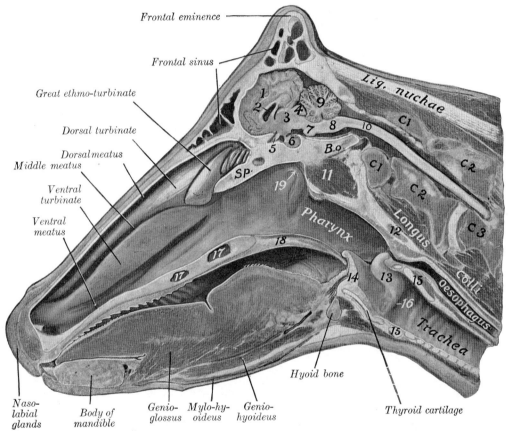

FIG. 476.—SAGITTAL SECTION OF HEAD OF COW.

1, Cerebral hemisphere; *2*, lateral ventricle; *3*, thalamus, *4*, corpora quadrigemina; *5*, optic chiasma; *6*, pituitary body; *7*, pons; *8*, medulla oblongata; *9*, cerebellum; *10*, spinal cord; *11*, ventral straight muscles; *12*, pharyngeal lymph gland; *13*, arytenoid cartilage; *14*, epiglottis; *15*, cricoid cartilage; *16*, vocal cord; *17*, palatine sinus; *18*, soft palate; *19*, Eustachian opening; *C1, C2, C3*, first, second, and third cervical vertebræ; *B.o.*, basioccipital; *Sp.*, presphenoid.

it is on the lateral wall of the nostril, and is concealed by the cartilaginous prolongation of the ventral turbinate. There are two **parietal cartilages** on either side, united by fibrous tissue. The dorsal cartilages are thin laminæ which curve ventro-laterally from the dorsal margin of the septal cartilage; they are prolongations of the nasal bones, and carry the alar cartilages on their anterior extremities. The ventral pair are lateral continuations of the basal lamellæ of the ventral turbinates. They lie along the nasal processes of the premaxillæ; anteriorly they become thicker, turn a little upward, and each blends with the cartilaginous prolongation of the upper coil of the ventral turbinate. The **alar cartilages** are of peculiar form. The lamina is oblong, and curves ventro-laterally from the anterior extremity of the dorsal parietal cartilage, with which it is connected. The cornu springs from the lateral part of the lamina and curves dorso-laterally into the outer wing of the nostril; it carries on its extremity a small transverse bar, thus having some resemblance to the fluke of an anchor.

The **nasal cavity** is short, wide anteriorly, narrow behind. It is not completely divided by the septum, which in its posterior third is separated from the floor of the cavity by an interval that increases from before backward (Figs. 140, 141). The middle meatus is very narrow, and divides posteriorly into two branches; the upper division leads to the ethmoidal meatuses, and communicates with the frontal sinus and the cavity of the dorsal turbinate. Anterior to the division are communications with the upper cavity of the ventral turbinate and the maxillary sinus. The main facts in regard to the sinuses were stated in the Osteology.

THE LARYNX

The **larynx** is more compact than in the horse, and presents numerous differential features. The **cricoid cartilage** is compressed laterally. The lamina is not distinctly marked off from the arch; it slopes downward and backward and has a

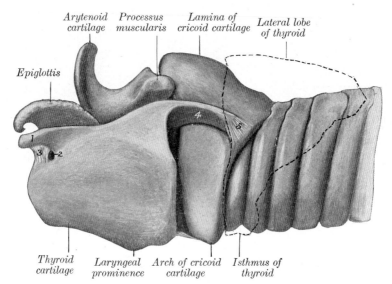

FIG. 477.—CARTILAGES OF LARYNX AND PART OF TRACHEA OF OX; LEFT VIEW.
Outline of thyroid gland indicated by dotted line.

1, Anterior cornu of thyroid cartilage; 2, thyroid foramen; 3, ligament converting notch into foramen; 4, posterior cornu of thyroid cartilage; 5, capsule of crico-thyroid joint.

large median ridge. The **thyroid cartilage** is complete ventrally, *i. e.*, the laminæ are united to form a long plate which is notched in front and behind; the laryngeal prominence is small and is situated posteriorly. The height and thickness of the cartilage increase from before backward. The posterior cornua are curved and are about an inch long; they form syndesmoses with the cricoid cartilage. The short anterior cornua unite similarly with the hyoid bone; near them there is a foramen or a notch on each side for the passage of the anterior laryngeal nerve. The **epiglottis** is short, oval in outline, and its apex is rounded; its base rests on the thyrohyoid membrane, to which it is rather loosely attached. The cuneiform cartilages are absent. The **arytenoid cartilages** present only slight differences. The muscular process is well developed, and the vocal process is narrow and long. The **vocal cords** are short and project very little from the wall, so that the **rima glottidis** is wide; the vocal ligament is attached ventrally to the crico-thyroid membrane and has the form of a half tube, open behind. The **lateral ventricle** is represented by a very shallow depression, and the saccule is absent. The thyro-arytenoideus muscle

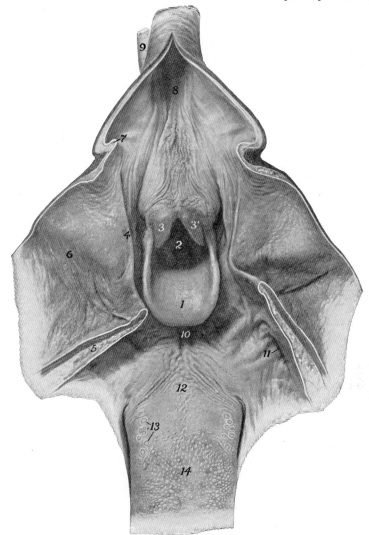

FIG. 478.—ADITUS LARYNGIS AND ADJACENT STRUCTURES OF OX.

The pharynx, soft palate, and origin of œsophagus have been cut along the dorsal median line and reflected.

1, Epiglottis; 2, aditus laryngis; 3, 3', apices of arytenoid cartilages; 4, posterior pillar of soft palate; 5, cut surface of soft palate; 6, pharynx; 7, limen œsophagi; 8, œsophagus; 9, trachea; 10, glosso-epiglottic space; 11, tonsillar sinus; 12, root of tongue; 13, vallate papillæ; 14, dorsum linguæ.

is equivalent to the vocalis and ventricularis of the horse; it is fan-shaped, thick, and narrow dorsally; it is attached ventrally to the base of the epiglottis, the angle of the union of the thyroid laminæ, and the crico-thyroid membrane. The hyo-epiglotticus muscle is large and bifid; it arises from the small cornua and at their articulation with the body of the hyoid bone, and thus may take the place of the hyoideus transversus in its action on the small cornua.

THE TRACHEA

The trachea is shorter than that of the horse, the average length being about 26 inches (ca. 65 cm.). Its caliber is relatively small, the width being about an inch and a half (ca. 4 cm.) and the height about two inches (ca. 5 cm.). The rings are smaller, and number about fifty. At the beginning of the tube their free ends are separated by a varying interval, so that the tube is flattened and membranous dorsally; but further back the ends are in apposition, so that they form a ridge dorsally. The trachea is adherent to the right lung from the third rib backward. The bifurcation is opposite the fifth rib, about a handbreadth (ca. 8 to 10 cm.) below the vertebral column.

In the **sheep** the average length of the trachea is about nine or ten inches (ca. 25 cm.) and its caliber a little less than an inch (ca. 2 cm.).

THE BRONCHI

There are three chief bronchi. The bronchus for the apical lobe of the right lung (Bronchus apicalis) is given off from the trachea opposite to the third rib or intercostal space.

THE THORACIC CAVITY AND PLEURÆ

The thoracic cavity is relatively small; it is short dorsally, and is much diminished laterally by the mode of attachment of the diaphragm to the ribs (*vide* p. 349). The endothoracic fascia is better developed than in the horse, and is distinctly elastic. The pleura is also thick, and there are no perforations of the mediastinum. The pleural sacs are even more unequal in extent than in the horse, and the ventral part of the mediastinum is further to the left; in front of the pericardium it is for the most part in contact with the left wall of the chest.

The diaphragmatic line of pleural reflection or linea phrenico-costalis differs considerably from that of the horse in conformity with the difference in the costal attachment of the diaphragm. Traced from the ventral end of the eighth rib, it extends in a very slight curve upward and backward, so that it reaches the twelfth rib about six inches (ca. 15 cm.) from its vertebral end; it may extend to the last rib at the lateral border of the longissimus muscle or may not quite reach to the twelfth rib.

The pleura forms a cul-de-sac alongside of the body of the last thoracic vertebra. The right pleural sac may extend forward on the deep face of the scalenus a short distance beyond the first rib.

THE LUNGS

The difference in size between the two lungs is greater than in the horse, the right lung weighing about half as much again as the left one. The average weight of the lungs is about 7½ pounds (ca. 3 to 4 kg.); they form about $\frac{1}{170}$ of the body weight. They are divided into lobes by deep **interlobar fissures** (Incisuræ interlobares). The **left lung** is divided into **three lobes,** named from before backward **apical, cardiac,** and **diaphragmatic** (Lobus apicalis, cardiacus, diaphragmaticus). The **right lung** may be regarded as having either **four** or **five lobes.** The **apical lobe** is much larger than that of the left lung, and occupies the space in front of the pericardium, pushing the mediastinum against the left wall; it is usually subdivided into anterior and posterior parts by a deep fissure. The other lobes are the **cardiac, diaphragmatic,** and **intermediate,** the last resembling that of the horse.[1] The apical lobe of the right lung receives a special bronchus from the trachea oppo-

[1] It has been customary to consider the cardiac lobe to consist of two parts; but the apical bronchus divides into two branches, the posterior of which goes to that division of the lung which has been regarded as belonging to the cardiac lobe; furthermore, these parts of the lung are sometimes fused. It therefore appears desirable to include both as apical lobe.

site the third rib or space, and is adherent to the trachea from here backward. The two lungs are not adherent to each other behind the root as in the horse, but

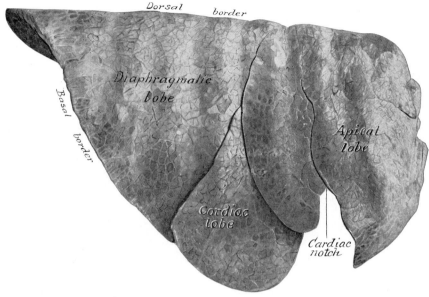

Fig. 479.—Right Lung of Ox; Costal Surface.

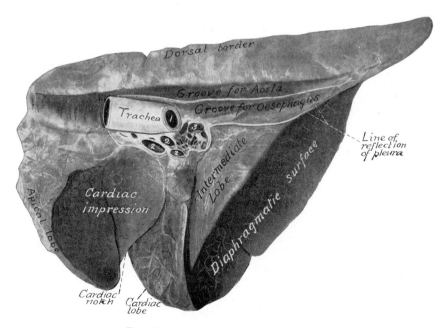

Fig. 480.—Right Lung of Ox; Medial View.
1, Left bronchus; *2*, pulmonary veins; *3*, pulmonary artery.

are in contact with the œsophagus; above and below the latter the pleura is reflected, as shown in Fig. 480.

The interlobar fissures begin at the ventral margin of the lung and pass toward the root. Those of the left lung lie opposite to the fourth and sixth ribs. The diaphragmatic lobe is the largest, and has the form of a three-sided pyramid with its base resting on the diaphragm.   The cardiac lobe is prismatic and forms the posterior margin of the cardiac notch; its long axis corresponds to the fifth rib.   The apical lobe of the left lung is small and pointed; its ventral margin

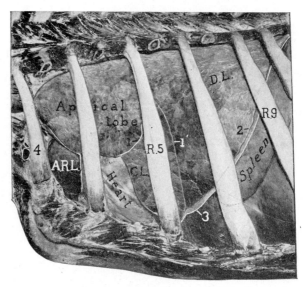

FIG. 481.—LEFT LUNG OF OX IN SITU; LATERAL VIEW.

1, 1′, Interlobar fissures; *2*, basal border; *3*, cut edge of diaphragm; *4*, first rib (brachial vessels at left of *4*); *R.5*, *R.9*, fifth and ninth ribs; *A.R.L.*, apical lobe of right lung, exposed by removal of mediastinum; *C.L.*, cardiac lobe; *D.L.*, diaphragmatic lobe. The pericardium has not been opened. The second, fourth, sixth and eighth ribs have been removed.

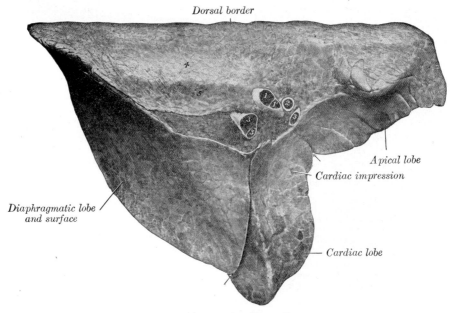

FIG. 482.—LEFT LUNG OF OX; MEDIAL VIEW.

1, Stem bronchus; *1′*, bronchial branch for apical and cardiac lobes; *2*, pulmonary artery; *3, 3, 3*, pulmonary veins; *4*, groove for aorta; *5*, groove for œsophagus.   Arrows indicate interlobar fissures.

lies at the level of the pulmonary and brachiocephalic arteries.   The apical lobe of the right lung occupies the space in front of the pericardium.   In some cases additional fissures partially subdivide the apical lobe, and on the other hand the apical lobe of the right lung may be undivided. On the left side the cardiac notch leaves the greater part of the pericardium in contact with the

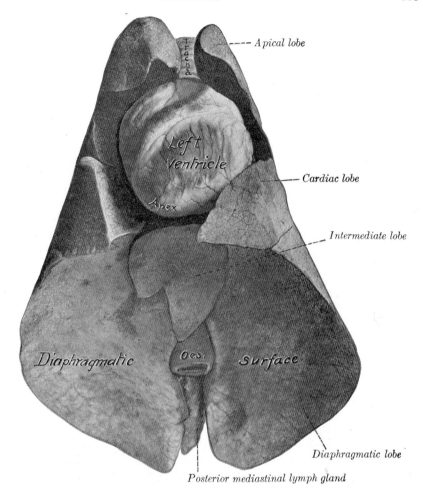

FIG. 483.—LUNGS AND HEART OF SHEEP; VENTRAL VIEW.

Specimen hardened *in situ*. Space between heart and lungs was occupied by pericardium and fat.

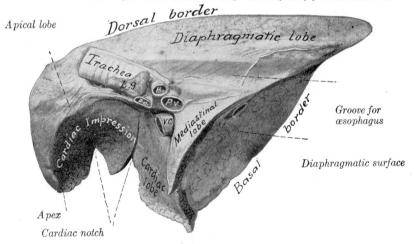

FIG. 484.—RIGHT LUNG OF SHEEP; MEDIASTINAL ASPECT.

Hardened *in situ*. *B*, Bronchus; *P.a.*, pulmonary artery; *P.v.*, pulmonary vein; *V.c.*, posterior **vena cava**; *L.g.*, bronchial lymph gland. Mediastinal lobe=intermediate lobe.

chest wall as far back as the fourth intercostal space. On the right side the lung may cover the pericardium, so that the latter has no contact with the lateral wall of the thorax. But in many cases (as in the annexed figures) there is a small cardiac notch at the ventral part of the fourth rib and adjacent intercostal spaces. In formalin-hardened subjects the basal border usually begins at the space between the fifth and sixth costal cartilages, crosses the ventral part of the sixth rib, and is then about parallel with the diaphragmatic line of pleural reflection. It crosses the ninth rib about its middle and ends at the vertebral end of the eleventh intercostal space or twelfth rib.

The **lobulation** is very distinct on account of the extremely large amount of interlobular tissue.

In the **sheep** the lungs resemble those of the ox in lobation, but differ from them considerably in shape. They are relatively somewhat longer, and the basal border differs in conformity with the diaphragmatic line of pleural reflection. There is usually a small triangular cardiac notch on the right lung opposite to the ventral part of the fourth and fifth ribs; its greatest height is about two inches (ca. 5 cm.). The left lung leaves the greater part of the pericardium uncovered as far back as the fifth intercostal space. The lobulation of the lung is much less distinct than in the ox. The pleural sacs form a cul-de-sac on each side of the first lumbar vertebra.

In the sheep the diaphragmatic line of pleural (Linea phrenico-costalis) reflection differs from that of the ox. After crossing the sterno-costal angle the line extends along the eighth and ninth costal cartilages, crosses the tenth rib close to its ventral end, the eleventh about an inch (ca. 2.5 cm.), the twelfth about an inch and a half (ca. 3 to 4 cm.), and the thirteenth about two inches (ca. 5 cm.) above the ventral end. It reaches as far back as the anterior border of the first lumbar transverse process.

THE THYROID GLAND

The thyroid gland is softer in texture than in the horse and is pale in color in the adult; in the calf it is dark red in color. The lateral lobes are irregularly triangular in outline and are more extensive and flatter than in the horse. In addition to their contact with the trachea they are related deeply to the œsophagus and the crico-pharyngeus muscle to a varying extent. The superficial face is related to the sterno-thyro-hyoideus, sterno-cephalicus, the carotid artery, internal jugular vein, and the vagus and sympathetic nerves. The isthmus is constantly present and glandular; it is band-like and is commonly about half an inch (ca. 1 cm.) in width.

The lateral lobes average about three inches or more (ca. 8 cm.) in length and about half an ounce (ca. 14 to 15 gm.) in weight. They are so soft and loose in texture that their true shape is seen only in specimens hardened *in situ*. In soft material they appear oval in outline. The isthmus may be connected with the ventral margin or the posterior end of the lateral lobes; it is relatively large in the calf, and is very evident on account of its dark color.

In the **sheep** the thyroid gland is dark red in color. The lateral lobes have a long elliptical outline and lie on each side of the first five or six rings of the trachea; they are two inches or more (ca. 5 to 6 cm.) in length and half an inch or more (ca. 1.5 cm.) in height. They are connected by a flat glandular isthmus a quarter of an inch or more (ca. 6 to 8 mm.) in width; the isthmus is connected with the lateral lobe at or near the posterior end of the latter, and crosses the trachea about the fifth ring.

Accessory thyroids may be found, and parathyroids also occur near the posterior extremity or on the deep surface of the lateral lobes of the thyroid.

THE THYMUS GLAND

The **thymus** is pale and distinctly lobulated. It is much larger in the calf than in the foal, weighing at five or six weeks about 15 to 25 ounces (ca. 425 to 600 gm.). At the period of its greatest development it occupies the greater part of the anterior mediastinal space, reaching back to the pericardium, pulmonary artery, and aortic arch. Its left face (covered by the mediastinal pleura) is in contact with the chest-wall and apical lobe of the left lung as far back as the third rib. Its right face is largely molded on the great vessels in front of the heart. The cervical part forms the bulk of the gland; it consists of right and left lobes which extend along the trachea and œsophagus from the thoracic inlet to the thyroid gland. The two lobes are large at the root of the neck, where they are in apposition

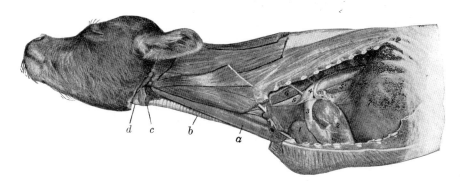

FIG. 485.—THYMUS OF YOUNG CALF.

a, Thymus (cervical part); *b*, trachea; *c*, isthmus of thyroid gland; *d*, laryngeal prominence; *1*, apical lobe of right lung; *2*, heart (left ventricle); *3*, pulmonary artery; *4*, aorta; *5, 5'*, œsophagus; *6*, m. longus colli; *7*, diaphragm.

and cover the trachea, œsophagus, carotid artery, and vago-sympathetic trunk. Further forward they gradually diminish in size and diverge to the sides of the trachea. They are related superficially to the sterno-cephalicus, sterno-thyro-hyoideus, and external jugular vein. It undergoes atrophy slowly and remnants of the thoracic part often remain even in advanced age.

RESPIRATORY SYSTEM OF THE PIG

THE NASAL CAVITY

The **nostrils** are small, and are situated on the flat anterior surface of the **rostrum** or snout (Rostrum suis). The latter is a short cylindrical projection, with which the upper lip is fused, and is circumscribed by a prominent circular margin. The skin on the snout is thin and highly sensitive; it presents small pores, and scattered over it are fine short hairs. In the snout between the nostrils is the **os rostri,** which is to be regarded as a special development of the extremity of the septum nasi in adaptation to the habit of burrowing or rooting. A plate of cartilage, representing the lamina of the alar cartilage of the horse, curves ventro-laterally from the dorsal part of the os rostri, and a pointed bar of cartilage curves upward from the lower part of the bone in the lateral wing of the nostril. The notch between the nasal bone and the premaxilla is closed in by parietal cartilages which resemble those of the ox.

The **nasal cavity** (Fig. 180) is long and narrow. It is divided behind by the lamina transversalis into an upper olfactory part, which leads to the ethmoidal meatuses, and a lower respiratory part, which is a direct continuation of the ventral meatus. The posterior part of the septum is membranous. The **turbinate bones** resemble in general those of the ox. The **dorsal meatus** is exceedingly small. The **middle meatus** is a deep fissure between the two turbinates: it divides posteriorly into two branches: one of these extends upward and backward between the lateral mass of the ethmoid bone and the dorsal turbinate; the other widens and joins the ventral meatus. The opening between the maxillary sinus and the middle meatus lies in a transverse plane through the last cheek teeth. The middle meatus is continuous with the space enclosed by the dorsal part of the ventral turbinate and with the cavity of the dorsal turbinate. The dorsal division of the middle meatus presents several openings into the frontal sinus. The **ventral meatus** is relatively roomy; it communicates with the space enclosed by the lower coil of the ventral turbinate. The opening of the naso-lacrimal duct is in the posterior part of the ventral meatus. The incisive duct and the vomero-nasal organ resemble those of the ox.

THE LARYNX

The larynx is remarkable for its great length and mobility. The cartilages are more loosely attached to each other than in the other animals. The **cricoid cartilage** is thick and compressed laterally; its lamina is long and narrow; its arch is directed obliquely downward and backward. The **thyroid cartilage** is very long; its laminæ are united ventrally and form a median ridge. The anterior cornua are absent, and no joints are formed with the hyoid bone. The posterior cornua are broad, bent inward, and articulate with the cricoid cartilage. The **epiglottis** is relatively very large, and is more closely attached to the hyoid bone than to the rest of the larynx. The middle part of its base is turned forward, and rests on the thyro-hyoid membrane; it is closely connected with the body of the hyoid bone by the hyo-epiglottic ligament and the strong hyo-epiglottic muscle.[1] The apex of the **arytenoid cartilage** is very large, and is divided into two parts at its extremity; the medial part is fused with that of the opposite cartilage. There is a small **interarytenoid cartilage** in the transverse ligament. The **rima glottidis** is very narrow. The **vocal cords** are directed obliquely downward and backward; and each is pierced by a long, slit-like opening, which leads into the large laryngeal saccule. The vocal ligament is similarly divided into a larger anterior and a smaller posterior part. There is a middle ventricle near the base of the epiglottis. The thyro-arytenoid muscle is very strong and is undivided; it is equivalent (as in the ox) to the vocalis and ventricularis muscles of the horse. The arytenoideus transversus is very small. The crico-thyroid consists of two strata: the superficial layer corresponds to the muscle of the other animals; the deep part consists of transverse fibers.

TRACHEA AND BRONCHI

The trachea is about six to eight inches (ca. 15–20 cm.) long, and contains thirty-two to thirty-five rings, which overlap dorsally. It is slightly depressed dorsally, except the terminal part, which is circular in cross-section. A special bronchus is detached for the apical lobe of the right lung, as in the ox. In the right lung the stem-bronchus sends branches (one each) to the cardiac and intermediate lobes and continues backward in the diaphragmatic lobe, in which it ramifies. In the left lung the stem-bronchus gives off a bronchus which divides into two branches for the anterior part of the lung (fused apical and cardiac lobes), and continues backward in the diaphragmatic lobe.

---

[1] The arrangement here is one of the most striking features of the pig's larynx. The short and thick middle hyo-epiglottic ligament and the anterior part of the thyro-hyoid membrane are inelastic, while the posterior part of the membrane is thin and elastic and allows the epiglottis to be separated by a considerable interval from the thyroid cartilage. Moreover, the borders of the epiglottis are connected with the thyroid cornua of the hyoid bone by lateral hyo-epiglottic ligaments.

THE THORAX AND PLEURÆ

The ribs are, in general, strongly curved in most of the improved breeds, so that the thorax is rounded. The pleural sacs extend forward to the first intercostal space. The diaphragmatic line of pleural reflection (Linea phrenico-costalis) begins at or a little above the sternal end of the seventh rib, and extends in a gentle curve to about the middle of the last rib, along the medial face of which it continues. (When a fifteenth rib is present—a very common occurrence—it does not affect the arrangement of the pleura or diaphragm).

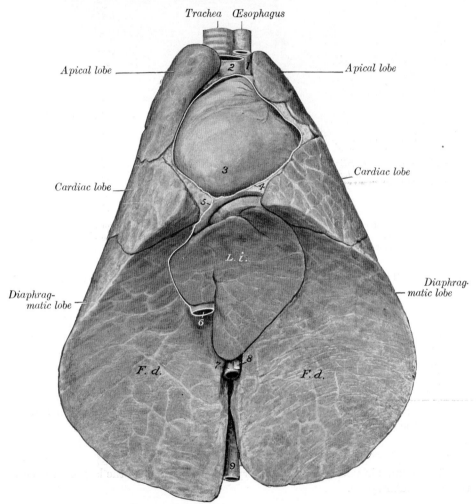

FIG. 486.—LUNGS AND HEART OF PIG; VENTRAL VIEW.

L. i., Intermediate lobe of right lung; *F. d.*, diaphragmatic surface of lungs; *1*, left brachial artery; *2*, brachiocephalic artery; *3*, apex of heart; *4*, pericardium (cut edge); *5*, plica venæ cavæ; *6*, posterior vena cava; *7*, œsophagus; *8*, ventral œsophageal nerve trunk; *9*, aorta.

THE LUNGS

The **right lung** has **four lobes—apical, cardiac, diaphragmatic,** and **intermediate.** In some cases the apical lobe is divided by a fissure into two parts; sometimes it is fused with the cardiac lobe. The **left lung** may be regarded as having **two** or **three lobes.** The **diaphragmatic lobe** is clearly marked off by a fissure. The part anterior to the fissure represents the **apical** and **cardiac lobes,** which are, however, separated only by the cardiac notch, not by an interlobar fissure, as is usual in the

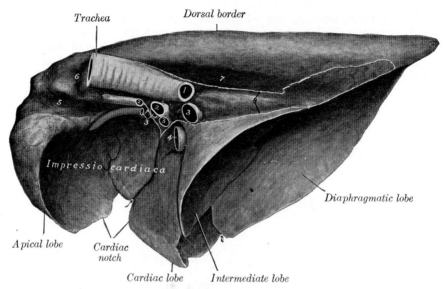

FIG. 487.—RIGHT LUNG OF PIG; MEDIAL VIEW.

1, Left bronchus (cut off); *2, 2,* pulmonary arteries; *3, 3, 3,* pulmonary veins; *4,* posterior vena cava; *5,* groove for anterior vena cava; *6,* groove for vena azygos; *7,* groove for aorta; *8* (placed on groove for œsophagus), lines of pleural reflection. Arrows indicate interlobar fissures.

right lung. The lobulation is distinct, but the interlobular septa are thinner than in the ox.

THE THYROID GLAND

The **thyroid gland** is large and is situated usually at a considerable distance from the larynx, but may be in contact with it. The lateral lobes are irregularly triangular in outline, and are two inches or more (ca. 5–6 cm.) in length in a large adult. They are united to a considerable extent ventrally, so that an isthmus cannot be distinguished. The gland is related deeply to the sides and ventral face of the trachea, and is in contact dorsally with the œsophagus. The chief artery enters at the posterior extremity.

THE THYMUS

The **thymus** in young subjects is very large, extending to the larynx or even to the mandibular space.

RESPIRATORY SYSTEM OF THE DOG

THE NASAL CAVITY

The **nostrils** are situated on the muzzle, with which the upper lip blends. They are shaped somewhat like a comma, with the broad part next to the septum and the narrow part directed backward and outward. The skin around the nostrils is bare, usually black, and in health moist and cool. The muzzle is marked by a median furrow (philtrum), or a deep fissure in some breeds. The cartilaginous framework is formed essentially by the septal cartilage and the parietal cartilages which proceed from it. The septal cartilage projects beyond the premaxilla, and

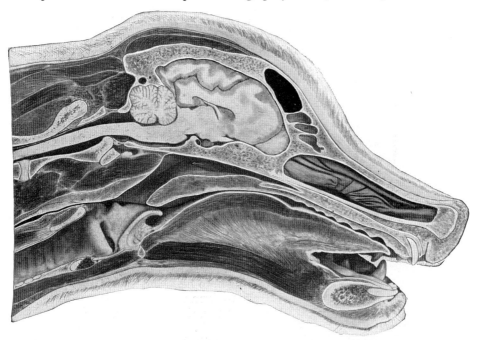

FIG. 488.—SAGITTAL SECTION OF HEAD AND PART OF NECK OF DOG.

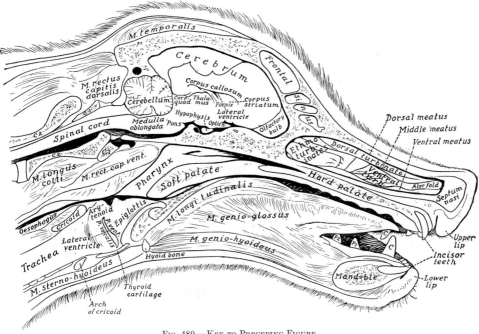

FIG. 489.—KEY TO PRECEDING FIGURE.

is much thickened at its extremity; it gives off from its margins the two parietal cartilages, which curve laterally and toward each other. A grooved plate extends outward from the septal cartilage in the floor of the nostril, and another lamina supports the alar fold of the ventral turbinate bone; these may be termed accessory nasal cartilages (Cartilagines nasi accessoriæ).

The length of the **nasal cavity** varies greatly in different breeds, corresponding, of course, to the length of the face. The cavity is roomy, but is very largely occupied by the turbinates and the lateral masses of the ethmoid bone. The **middle meatus** is short and narrow, and divides posteriorly into two branches: the upper branch leads to the ethmoidal meatuses; the lower branch joins the ventral meatus. The **ventral meatus** is very small in its middle part, owing to the great development here of the ventral turbinate. The posterior part of the nasal cavity is divided by the lamina transversalis into an upper olfactory part and a lower respiratory part. The sinuses have been described (*vide* Osteology).

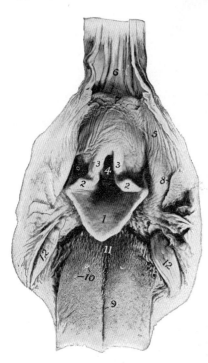

FIG. 490.—ADITUS LARYNGIS AND RELATED STRUCTURES OF DOG.

The pharynx and œsophagus have been cut along the mid-dorsal line and reflected.

1, Epiglottis; *2, 2*, corniculate cartilages; *3, 3*, arytenoid cartilages; *4*, glottis; *5*, wall of pharynx; *6*, œsophagus; *7*, limen œsophagi; *8*, posterior pillar of soft palate; *9*, median sulcus of tongue; *10*, vallate papillæ; *11*, conical papillæ of root of tongue; *12, 12*, tonsils (shown by opening up tonsillar sinus).

THE LARYNX

The larynx is relatively short. The lamina of the **cricoid cartilage** is wide; the arch is grooved laterally. The laminæ of the **thyroid cartilage** are high, but short; they unite ventrally to form the body, on which there is anteriorly a marked prominence, and posteriorly a deep notch. The oblique line on the lateral surface of the lamina is prominent. There is a rounded notch (Fissura thyreoidea) below the short anterior cornu for the passage of the anterior laryngeal nerve. The posterior cornu is strong, and has a rounded surface for articulation with the cricoid cartilage. The **arytenoid cartilages** are relatively small, and have between them a small **interarytenoid cartilage.** The **epiglottis** is quadrilateral; its lower part or stalk (petiolus) is narrow, and fits into the angle of the thyroid cartilage. The **cuneiform cartilages** (Cartilagines cuneiformes) are large and somewhat crescent shaped; they are not fused with the epiglottis.

The **false vocal cords** extend from the cuneiform cartilages to the thyroid. The **true vocal cords** are large and prominent. The large **lateral ventricle** is a long slit parallel with the anterior margin of the true vocal cord (Fig. 489). The **laryngeal saccule** is extensive and lies lateral to both true and false vocal cords.

The crico-thyroid muscle is thick. The hyo-epiglotticus is well developed, and is double at its hyoid attachment. The ventricularis or anterior part of the thyro-arytenoideus arises on the cuneiform cartilage. Hence Lesbre has suggested the name cuneo-arytenoideus for it.

THE TRACHEA AND BRONCHI

The trachea is practically circular in cross-section at its ends, but the intervening part is very slightly flattened dorsally. It contains about forty to forty-five C-shaped rings; the ends of the rings do not meet dorsally, so that here the trachea has a membranous wall (Paries membranacea), and is composed of a layer of transverse smooth muscle-fibers outside of the rings, the fibrous membrane, and the mucous membrane. The bifurcation is opposite to the fifth rib.

The stem-bronchi diverge at an obtuse angle, and each divides into two branches before entering the lung, but the ramification differs in the two lungs. In the right lung the anterior bronchus goes to the apical lobe, and the stem-bronchus gives off a branch to the cardiac lobe and another to the intermediate lobe. In the left lung the anterior bronchus divides into two branches for the apical and cardiac lobes. The anterior branch of the left bronchus crosses under the pulmonary artery.

THE LUNGS

The lungs differ in shape from those of the horse and ox in conformity with the shape of the thorax, which is relatively very wide in the dog; the lateral thoracic walls are strongly curved, and the costal surface of the lungs is correspondingly convex.[1]

The right lung is much (ca. 25 per cent.) larger than the left. It is divided

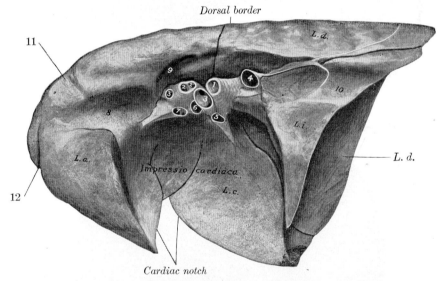

Fig. 491.—Right Lung of Dog; Medial View.

L. a., Apical lobe; *L. c.*, cardiac lobe; *L. d.*, diaphragmatic lobe; *L. i.*, intermediate lobe; *1*, stem-bronchus; *2, 2'*, bronchi of apical lobe; *3, 3'*, divisions of pulmonary artery; *4–7*, pulmonary veins; *8*, groove for anterior vena cava; *9*, groove for vena azygos; *10*, groove for œsophagus; *11*, groove for trunk of vertebral, cervical, and dorsal veins; *12*, groove for internal thoracic vessels.

into four lobes by deep fissures which extend to the root. The lobes are the **apical, cardiac, diaphragmatic,** and **intermediate.** The apical lobe extends considerably over the median plane in front of the pericardium. The intermediate lobe has the form of an irregular, three-sided pyramid, with its base against the diaphragm and its apex at the root; on its lateral face there is a deep groove which contains the posterior vena cava and right phrenic nerve, enclosed in a special pleural fold. The cardiac impression of the right lung is much deeper than that of the left. The

[1] The costal attachment of the diaphragm is lower than in the other animals, thus further increasing the capacity of the thorax (*vide* diaphragm).

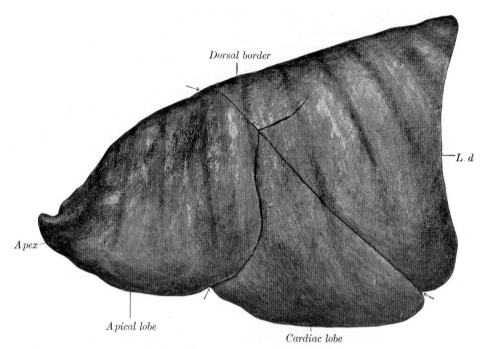

Dorsal border

L. d

Apex

Apical lobe

Cardiac lobe

FIG. 492.—LEFT LUNG OF DOG; COSTAL SURFACE.
L. d., Diaphragmatic lobe.   Arrows indicate interlobar fissures.

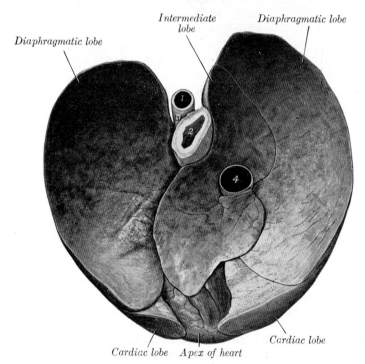

Intermediate lobe

Diaphragmatic lobe

Diaphragmatic lobe

Cardiac lobe   *Apex of heart*

Cardiac lobe

FIG. 493.—DIAPHRAGMATIC SURFACE OF LUNGS AND HEART OF DOG.
1, Aorta; 2, œsophagus; 3, œsophageal nerve trunk; 4, posterior vena cava.

cardiac notch is triangular and allows the pericardium to come in contact with the lateral wall at the fourth and fifth interchondral spaces.

The left lung is divided into three lobes—**apical, cardiac,** and **diaphragmatic.** The cardiac impression is shallow, and a distinct cardiac notch is not present, but the pericardium is in contact with the lateral wall along a narrow area at the ventral part of the fifth and sixth interchondral spaces. The apical lobe has a small, blunt-pointed apex which lies over the manubrium sterni. On account of the small amount of interlobular tissue the lobulation is not distinct. Pigmentation of the interlobular tissue is usual in dogs kept in town.

Accessory fissures may partially subdivide some of the lobes; this is most common in regard to the apical lobe. When the lungs have been successfully hardened *in situ*, additional markings are seen on the mediastinal surface. On the right lung there are: (1) A groove for the anterior vena cava in front of the root; (2) a groove for the vena azygos which curves upward and backward over the root; (3) a shallow groove for the aorta above the posterior part of the root; (4) a groove for the œsophagus behind the root; (5) a groove for the internal thoracic vessels curving downward and backward over the apex; (6) a groove for the right phrenic nerve in the upper part of the cardiac impression; (7) grooves for the dorso-cervical and vertebral veins running from the dorsal border to the groove for the vena cava. On the left lung there are: (1) A well-marked groove for the aorta, which curves over the root and runs back just below the dorsal border; (2) a shallow groove for the œsophagus behind the root; (3) grooves on the apical lobe for the left brachial and brachiocephalic arteries; (4) grooves near the apex for the internal thoracic vessels; (5) a groove for the left phrenic nerve is more or less evident; it passes downward and backward over the middle of the apical lobe, then runs backward over the cardiac and diaphragmatic lobes.

The diaphragmatic line of pleural reflection (Linea phrenico-costalis) extends along the lower part of the ninth costal cartilage, crosses the tenth cartilage a little (ca. 1 to 2 cm.) below the costo-chondral junction, and the eleventh rib at the costo-chondral junction; it then curves up to the last rib, just above its middle, and passes medially and backward to the second lumbar transverse process. In a good-sized dog (*e. g.*, bull-terrier) the apex of the left pleural sac extends about an inch (ca. 2.5 cm.) anterior to the plane of the first rib.

THE THYROID GLAND

The **lateral lobes** of the thyroid gland are long and narrow, and have a flattened, ellipsoidal form; they are situated on the lateral surfaces of the trachea near the larynx, extending along the first six or seven rings (Fig. 434). The extremities, are small, the posterior one often being pointed. The **isthmus** is inconstant and variable; in large dogs it has the form of a glandular band which may be nearly half an inch (ca. 1 cm.) wide; in medium-sized dogs it is often absent, and in small dogs it is usually absent. **Accessory thyroids** are frequently present; three or four may be found on either side, as well as a median one near the hyoid bone.

The **parathyroids,** about the size of millet or hemp seed, are four in number usually. Two are situated on the deep face of the thyroid lobes, in which they are often embedded; the others are placed laterally near the anterior extremity of the thyroid.

THE THYMUS

The thymus is relatively small, and is situated almost entirely in the thorax. The left lobe is much larger than the right, and extends back on the pericardium as far as the sixth rib at the time of its greatest size. According to Baum, the gland increases in size during the first two weeks after birth, and atrophies rapidly in the next two or three months. Traces of it are present at two or three years of age, and may be found even in old subjects.

THE UROGENITAL SYSTEM

The urogenital apparatus (Apparatus urogenitalis) includes two groups of organs, the urinary and the genital. The **urinary organs** elaborate and remove the chief excretory fluid, the urine. The **genital organs** serve for the formation, development, and expulsion of the products of the reproductive glands. In the higher vertebrates the two apparatus are independent except at the terminal part, which constitutes a urogenital tract, and includes the vulva in the female and the greater part of the urethra in the male.

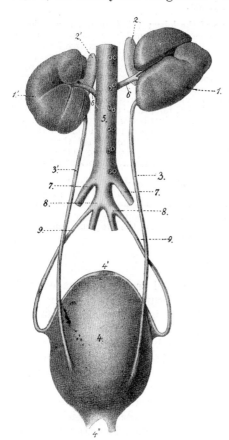

FIG. 494.—GENERAL DORSAL VIEW OF URINARY ORGANS OF HORSE.

1, Right kidney; *1'*, left kidney; *2, 2'*, adrenal bodies; *3, 3'*, ureters; *4*, urinary bladder; *4'*, anterior end of bladder with cicatricial remnant of urachus; *4''*, urethra; *5*, aorta; *6, 6*, renal arteries; *7, 7*, external iliac arteries; *8, 8*, internal iliac arteries; *9, 9*, umbilical arteries. (After Leisering's Atlas.)

THE URINARY ORGANS

The **urinary organs** (Organa uropoiëtica) are the kidneys, ureters, bladder, and urethra. The **kidneys** are the glands which secrete the urine; they are red-brown in color, and are situated against the dorsal wall of the abdomen, being in most animals almost symmetrically placed on either side of the spine. The **ureters** are tubes which convey the urine to the **urinary bladder**. The latter is an ovoid or piriform sac, which is situated on the pelvic floor when empty or nearly so; it is a reservoir for the urine. The urine accumulates in the bladder and is then expelled through the **urethra.**

THE URINARY ORGANS OF THE HORSE

THE KIDNEYS

Each kidney presents two surfaces, two borders, and two extremities or poles, but they differ so much in form and position as to require a separate description of each in these respects.

The **right kidney** (Ren dexter) in outline resembles the heart on a playing card, or an equilateral triangle with the angles rounded off. It lies ventral to the upper parts of the last two or three ribs and the first lumbar transverse process. The **dorsal surface** (Facies dorsalis) is strongly convex; it is related chiefly to the diaphragm, but also to a small extent posteriorly to the iliac fascia and psoas muscles. In well-hardened specimens, especially those from thin subjects, impressions of the last two ribs and the tip of the first lumbar transverse process are usually visible.[1] The **ventral surface** (Facies ventralis) is in general slightly concave, and is related to the liver, pancreas, cæcum, and right adrenal; it either has no peritoneal covering, or only a narrow peritoneal area laterally.[2] The **medial border** (Margo medialis) is convex and rounded; it is related to the right adrenal and the posterior vena cava. It presents about its middle a deep notch, the **renal hilus** (Hilus renalis); this is bounded by rounded margins, and leads into a space termed the **renal sinus** (Sinus renalis). The vessels and nerves reach the kidney at the hilus, and the sinus contains the renal pelvis or dilated origin of the ureter. The **lateral border** (Margo lateralis) is rounded, and is thinner than the medial one.

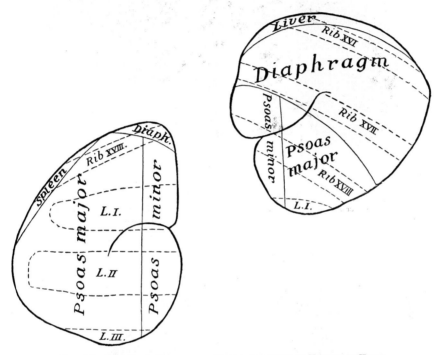

FIG. 495.—DIAGRAM OF POSITION AND DORSAL RELATIONS OF KIDNEYS OF HORSE.
Areas of direct relations are enclosed by continuous lines; parts of skeleton which overlie the kidneys are indicated by dotted lines. *L.I.—L.III*, lumbar transverse processes.

It consists of two parts, anterior and posterior, which meet at a lateral angle; the anterior part fits into the renal impression of the liver. The duodenum curves around the lateral border. The **anterior extremity** or **pole** (Extremitas cranialis), thick and rounded, lies in the renal impression of the liver. The **posterior extremity** or **pole** (Extremitas caudalis) is thinner and narrower.

The **left kidney** (Ren sinister) is bean shaped. It is considerably longer and narrower than the right one, and is situated nearer the median plane and further back, so that the hilus of the left kidney is usually about opposite to the posterior extremity of the right one. It is usually ventral to the last rib and the first two

[1] The dorsal surface, being largely in contact with the diaphragm, slopes downward in front; thus its anterior part is about three inches (ca. 6–8 cm.) ventral to the dorsal part of the seventeenth rib.

[2] In exceptional cases a considerable area—as much as the outer and posterior third—of the surface may have a peritoneal covering. In the new-born foal a large part is so covered; this is apparently due to the small size of the cæcum and the small area of attachment of its base.

or three lumbar transverse processes. The **dorsal surface** is convex, and is related to the left crus of the diaphragm, the iliac fascia and psoas muscles, and the dorsal end

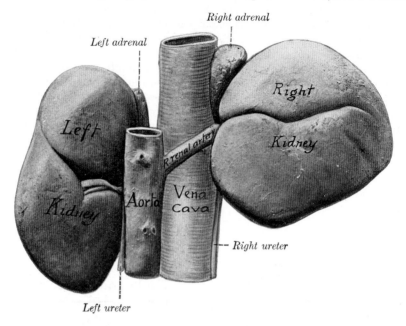

FIG. 496.—KIDNEYS AND ADRENALS OF HORSE; DORSAL VIEW.

Hardened *in situ.* Impression of seventeenth rib on right kidney is indicated by small cross. The left kidney was a little further forward in this subject than is usual.

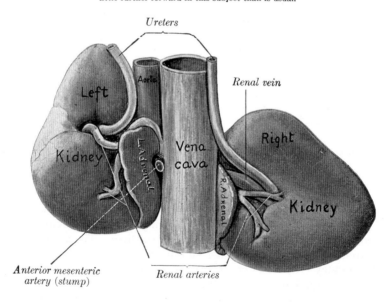

FIG. 497.—KIDNEYS AND ADRENALS OF HORSE; VENTRAL VIEW.

Hardened *in situ.* Left renal vein (not marked) is seen curving round posterior end of left adrenal.

of the spleen. The **ventral surface** is convex and irregular; the greater part of it is covered by the peritoneum. It is in relation with the origin of the small colon, the terminal part of the duodenum, the left adrenal, and the left extremity of the pancreas. The **medial border** is longer, straighter, and thicker than that of the right kidney. It is related to the posterior aorta, the adrenal, and the ureter. The **lateral border** is related chiefly to the base of the spleen. The **anterior extremity** or **pole** extends almost to the saccus cæcus of the stomach; it is related to the left end of the pancreas and the splenic vessels. The **posterior extremity** or **pole** is usually larger than the anterior one.

The form of the left kidney is variable. In some cases its outline is similar to that of the right kidney, but its ventral surface is convex and is often marked by several furrows which diverge from the hilus. In well-hardened specimens the three areas of the dorsal surface are often distinct. The psoas area (Impressio muscularis) is flat, parallel with the medial border, and widens behind. The diaphragmatic area is small and convex; it is crescentic and is confined to the anterior end. The lateral splenic area is somewhat flattened and is often so extensive and distinct as really to constitute a third surface as in Fig. 496.

Fixation.—The kidneys are held in position chiefly by the pressure of adjacent organs and by the renal fascia. The latter is a special development of the sub-

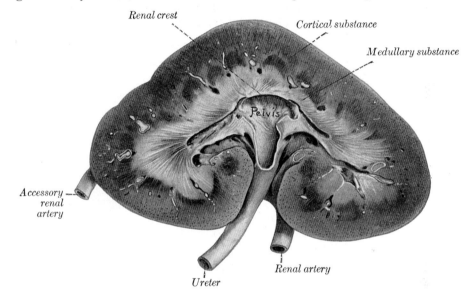

Fig. 498.—Frontal (Horizontal) Section of Kidney of Horse.
The renal vein is removed. A large accessory renal artery entered the posterior pole. Sections of arteries in limiting layer between cortical and medullary substance are white in figure.

peritoneal tissue, which splits into two layers to enclose the kidney, together with the perirenal fat, which is termed the **capsula adiposa.**[1] On account of its relations with the liver, pancreas, and base of the cæcum, the right kidney is much more strongly attached than the left one. It is, therefore, not surprising that the latter varies somewhat in position; its posterior extremity may be ventral to the third or fourth lumbar transverse process. The position of the right kidney, excluding its movements during respiration, seems to be very constant.

Weight and Size.—The average weight of the kidney is about 24 to 25 ounces (ca. 700 gm.). The right one is commonly an ounce or two heavier than the left, but the reverse relation is frequent, and there is often no material difference in weight. The relation of the weight of both kidneys to the body-weight is about 1:300–350. In the new-born foal the kidney weighs about 6 ounces (ca. 170 gm.).

[1] The amount of perirenal fat varies; in animals in good condition it may entirely conceal the kidneys; in such cases the impressions produced by contact of the kidney with contiguous structures may be indistinct.

Chauveau gives as an average 750 grams for the right kidney and 710 grams for the left. Ellerberger and Baum (24 cases) give the right kidney as varying between 430 and 840 grams; and the left between 425 and 780; this is an average of 635 grams (about 22½ ounces) for the right kidney, and 602.5 grams (about 21½ ounces) for the left. They give the relation of the weight of both kidneys to the body-weight as 1:255–344. In a Percheron mare weighing about 2000 pounds the right kidney weighed 4 pounds 3 ounces, and the left one 4 pounds. In a horse of medium size the right kidney is about six inches (ca. 15 cm.) in length, about the same in width, and about two inches (ca. 5 cm.) thick. The left kidney is about seven inches (ca. 18 cm.) long, four to five inches (ca. 10 to 12 cm.) wide, and two to two and a half inches (ca. 5 to 6 cm.) thick.

Structure.—The surface of the kidney is covered by a thin but strong **fibrous capsule** (Tunica fibrosa), which is in general easily stripped off the healthy kidney; it is continued into the renal sinus, where it is attached. Sections through the kidney show it to consist of an external cortical substance and an internal medullary substance. The **cortical substance** (Substantia corticalis) is red brown in color and has a granular appearance. It is dotted over with minute dark points; these are the **renal corpuscles** (Corpuscula renis),[1] each consisting of the dilated origin of a renal tubule (Capsula glomeruli), with an invaginated tuft of capillaries (Glomerulus) enclosed by it. The **medullary substance** (Substantia medullaris)

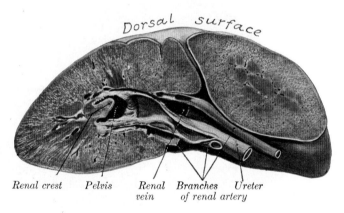

FIG. 499.—TRANSVERSE SECTION OF RIGHT KIDNEY OF HORSE PASSING THROUGH THE HILUS.
Posterior portion of organ hardened *in situ*. Note curvature of dorsal surface.

is more resistant and presents a distinct radial striation. Its central part is pale, but its periphery, the **intermediate zone,** is of a deep red color; in the latter are seen, at fairly regular intervals, sections of the relatively large arciform vessels, which are taken to represent the demarcation between the primitive lobes.[2] Between the vessels the medulla is prolonged somewhat toward the periphery, forming the bases of the **renal pyramids** (Pyramides renales). These are not very pronounced in the kidney of the horse, especially as the gland is not papillated. Between the bases of the pyramids processes of the cortex dip in toward the sinus, forming the **renal columns** (Columnæ renales).[3] The inner central part of the medulla forms a concave ridge which projects into the pelvis of the kidney. This projection is termed the **renal crest;** it presents numerous small openings at which renal tubules open into the pelvis of the kidney, and hence the surface here is known as the **area cribrosa.**

[1] Also known as Malpighian corpuscles.

[2] The fœtal kidney is divided by furrows into a number of polygonal areas, each of which is the base of a pyramidal lobe or renculus. These furrows usually disappear before or soon after birth in the foal, although traces of them are sometimes seen in the adult.

[3] In the kidney of the horse the renal columns dip in between the pyramids very superficially as compared with the arrangement in the human kidney. Breuer states that the pyramids are 40 to 64 in number, and are arranged in four rows. Only the middle ones are distinct.

Examination with a pocket lens shows that the cortex is imperfectly divided into **lobules** (Lobuli corticales). Each lobule consists of an axial **radiate part** (Pars radiata), surrounded by a **convoluted part** (Pars convoluta). The former appear as ray-like prolongations from the bases of the pyramids (hence also termed medullary rays), and consist largely of narrow, straight or slightly flexuous tubules (limbs of the loops of Henle). The convoluted part is granular in appearance, and consists largely of the renal corpuscles and convoluted tubules.

The **renal pelvis** (Pelvis renalis) is the dilated origin of the excretory duct. It lies in the sinus of the kidney, and it is funnel-shaped, but flattened dorso-ventrally. The **renal crest**[1] (Crista renalis) projects into the outer part of the pelvis in the form of a horizontal ridge with a concave free edge. The tubules of the middle part of the medullary substance open on this crest into the pelvis. The tubules from each end of the kidney do not open into the pelvis proper (Recessus medius), but into two long, narrow diverticula (Recessus terminales), which proceed from it toward the poles of the kidney. The wall of the pelvis consists of three layers. The external **fibrous coat** or adventitia is continuous with the supporting tissue of the kidney. The **muscular coat** consists of longitudinal and

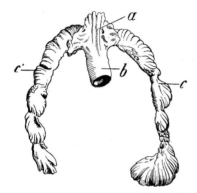

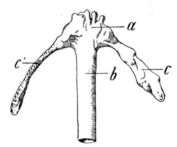

FIG. 500.—CAST OF RIGHT RENAL PELVIS (a), RECESSES (c, c'), AND ORIGIN OF URETER (b) OF HORSE. (After Dumont.)

FIG. 501.—CAST OF LEFT RENAL PELVIS (a), RECESSES (c, c'), AND ORIGIN OF URETER (b) OF HORSE. (After Dumont.)

circular fibers. The **mucous coat** does not cover the renal crest nor is it continued into the diverticula of the pelvis. It has a yellowish tinge, and forms numerous folds. It contains compound tubular **glands** (Glandulæ pelvis renalis), which secrete the thick, viscid mucus always found in the pelvis.[2]

Renal Tubules.—The parenchyma or proper substance of the kidney is composed of the small **renal** or **uriniferous** tubules (Tubuli renales), which are very close together and have a complicated course. Each tubule begins in a thin-walled, spherical dilatation or **capsule** (Capsula glomeruli), which is invaginated to receive a tuft of looped capillaries termed a **glomerulus**; these two structures constitute a **renal corpuscle**; the corpuscles are visible as minute red or dark spots in the convoluted part of the cortex. Succeeding this is a short narrow neck, beyond which the tubule becomes wide and convoluted, forming the proximal convoluted tubule, and enters the radiate portion of the cortex. It then gradually narrows and enters the intermediate zone; becoming very narrow and nearly straight, it descends for a variable distance into the medullary substance, turns sharply upon itself, and returns to the cortex, forming thus the loop of Henle, with its descending and ascending limbs. In the convoluted part of the cortex it widens and becomes tortuous, constituting the distal convoluted tubule. The tubule then narrows, enters a medullary ray, and opens with other tubules into a straight collecting tubule; this passes axially through a pyramid, and unites with other collecting tubules to form the relatively large papillary ducts, which open into the renal pelvis.

Stroma.—The interstitial tissue forms a reticulum throughout which supports the tubules

[1] The crest is the result of fusion of the papillæ or apices of the pyramids in the embryo and is therefore also known as the papilla communis.

[2] There are goblet cells in the epithelium of the pelvis which doubtless concur in the secretion of mucus.

and blood-vessels. It is very scanty in the cortex, much more abundant in the medulla, in which it increases in amount toward the pelvis.

Vessels and Nerves.—The kidneys receive a large amount of blood through the **renal arteries** which come from the aorta.[1] Branches of these enter at the hilus and on the ventral surface of the gland, and reach the intermediate zone, where they form anastomotic arches (Arteriæ arciformes). From these arciform arteries branches pass into the cortex and medulla. The cortical branches (Arteriæ interlobulares) have in general a radial course between the cortical lobules, and give off short lateral branches, each of which ends as the **afferent vessel** (Vas afferens) of a renal corpuscle. The blood is carried from the glomerulus by a smaller **efferent**

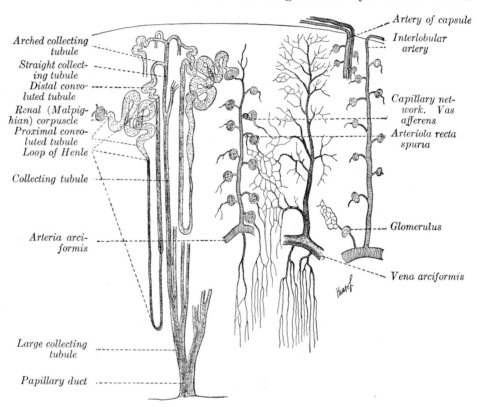

Arched collecting tubule

Straight collecting tubule

Distal convoluted tubule

Renal (Malpighian) corpuscle

Proximal convoluted tubule

Loop of Henle

Collecting tubule

Arteria arciformis

Large collecting tubule

Papillary duct

Artery of capsule

Interlobular artery

Capillary network. Vas afferens

Arteriola recta spuria

Glomerulus

Vena arciformis

Fig. 502.—Diagrammatic Scheme of Uriniferous Tubules and Blood-vessels of Kidney.
Drawn in part from the descriptions of Golubew (Böhm, Davidoff, and Huber).

vessel, which breaks up immediately into capillaries which form networks around the tubules. The medullary branches descend in the pyramids, forming in them bundles of straight twigs (Arteriolæ rectæ). The **renal veins** are large and thin-walled; they go to the posterior vena cava. In the superficial part of the cortex the veins form star-like figures (Venæ stellatæ) by the convergence of several small radicles to a common trunk. The **lymph-vessels** form two networks, capsular or superficial, and parenchymatous or deep. On leaving the hilus they go to lymph glands in this vicinity which are known as the renal lymph glands.

The **nerves** are derived from the renal plexus of the sympathetic, which enlaces the renal artery.

[1] The occurrence of accessory renal arteries is not at all rare. They may come from various branches of the aorta (e. g., posterior mesenteric, spermatic, circumflex iliac) and enter the posterior part of the gland.

THE URETERS

The **ureter** is the narrow part of the excretory duct of the kidney. Each begins at the renal pelvis and terminates at the bladder. It is about ⅓ to ¼ inch (ca. 6 to 8 mm.) in diameter, and its average length is about 28 inches (ca. 70 cm.). The **abdominal part** (Pars abdominalis) of each ureter emerges ventrally from the hilus of the kidney, and curves backward and medially toward the lateral face of the posterior vena cava (right side) or the aorta (left side). They then pass almost straight backward in the subperitoneal tissue on the surface of the psoas minor, cross the external iliac vessels, and enter the pelvic cavity. The **pelvic part** (Pars pelvina) passes backward and a little ventrally on the lateral wall of the pelvic cavity, turns medially, and pierces the dorsal wall of the bladder near the neck. In the male the pelvic part enters the genital fold and crosses the ductus deferens. In the female the ureter is situated in most of its course in the dorsal part of the broad ligament of the uterus.

The wall of the ureter is composed of three coats. The external **fibrous coat** (Tunica adventitia) contains many elastic fibers. The **muscular coat** consists of internal and external layers of longitudinal fibers, with a stratum of circular fibers between them. The **mucous membrane** is covered with transitional epithelium; glands (Glandulæ mucosæ ureteris) resembling those of the renal pelvis occur in the first three or four inches of the ureter.

The **blood-supply** is derived from the renal, internal spermatic, and umbilical arteries. The **nerves** come from the cœliac and pelvic plexuses; many minute ganglia are present.

THE URINARY BLADDER

The **urinary bladder** (Vesica urinaria) (Figs. 366, 369, 370) differs in form, size, and position according to the amount of its contents. When empty and contracted, it is a dense, piriform mass, about the size of a fist, and lies on the ventral wall of the pelvic cavity at a variable distance behind the inlet. When moderately filled, it is ovoid in form, and extends a variable distance along the ventral abdominal wall. Its physiological capacity varies greatly, but may be estimated approximately at about three or four quarts.

The anterior rounded blind end is termed the **vertex;**[1] on its middle is a mass of cicatricial tissue (Centrum verticis), a vestige of the urachus, which in the fœtus forms a tubular connection between the bladder and the allantois. The middle part or **body** (Corpus vesicæ) is rounded, and is somewhat flattened dorso-ventrally, except when distended. It presents two surfaces, dorsal and ventral, the former being the more strongly convex, especially in its posterior part in front of the entrance of the ureters.[2] The posterior narrow extremity, the **neck** (Collum vesicæ), joins the urethra.

The **relations** of the bladder vary according to the degree of fulness of the organ, and also differ in important respects in the two sexes. The **ventral surface** (Facies ventralis) lies on the ventral wall of the pelvis, and extends forward on the abdominal wall as the bladder fills. The **dorsal surface** (Facies dorsalis) in the male is related to the rectum, the genital fold, the terminal parts of the ductus deferentes, the vesiculæ seminales, and the prostate; in the female it is in contact with the body of the uterus and the vagina (Fig. 530). The vertex of the full bladder has variable relations with coils of the small intestine and small colon, and the left parts of the large colon.

Fixation.—Displacement of the bladder is limited chiefly by three peritoneal

[1] This is often termed the fundus by veterinarians, but is not the homologue of the fundus of the human bladder.
[2] This would correspond to the fundus vesicæ of man.

folds, termed the middle and lateral ligaments (Figs. 352, 370). The **middle ligament** (Plica umbilicalis media) is a median triangular fold, formed by the reflection of the peritoneum from the ventral surface of the bladder on to the ventral wall of the pelvis and abdomen. In the new-born animal it is extensive and reaches to the umbilicus; in the adult it is usually much reduced in length relatively. It contains elastic and muscular fibers in its posterior part. The **lateral ligaments** (Plicæ umbilicales laterales) stretch from the lateral aspects of the bladder to the lateral pelvic walls. Each contains in its free edge a round, firm band, the **round ligament** (Lig. teres vesicæ); this is the remnant of the large fœtal umbilical artery, the lumen of which in the adult is very small. The retroperitoneal part of the bladder is attached to the surrounding parts by loose connective tissue, in which there is a quantity of fat. It is evident that the posterior part of the bladder has a definite fixed position, while its anterior part is movable.

Structure.—The wall of the bladder consists of a partial peritoneal investment, the muscular coat, and the mucous lining. The **serous coat** (Tunica serosa) covers the greater part of the dorsal surface, from which it is reflected in the male to form the genital fold; in the female it passes on to the vagina, forming the vesico-genital pouch. Ventrally the peritoneum covers only the anterior half or less of the bladder, and is reflected posteriorly on to the pelvic floor. The **muscular coat** (Tunica muscularis) is relatively thin when the bladder is full. It is unstriped, pale, and not clearly divided into layers, but has rather a plexiform arrangement. Longitudinal fibers occur on the dorsal and ventral surfaces, but laterally they become oblique and decussate with each other. A distinctly circular arrangement is found at the neck, where the fibers form a **sphincter vesicæ.** The **mucous coat** (Tunica mucosa) is pale and thin. It is in general attached by a highly elastic submucosa to the muscular coat, and forms numerous folds when the organ is empty and contracted. It is modified dorsally in the vicinity of the neck over a triangular area, termed the **trigonum vesicæ;** the angles of this space lie at the orifices of the two ureters and the urethra, which are close together. Here the mucous membrane is closely attached and does not form folds. From each **ureteral orifice** (Orificium ureteris) a fold of mucous membrane (Plica ureterica) passes backward and inward, uniting with its fellow to form a median crest (Crista urethralis) in the first part of the urethra. The ureteral orifices are a little more than an inch (ca. 3 cm.) apart. The terminal part of the ureter, after piercing the muscular coat of the bladder, passes for a distance of about an inch (ca. 2 to 3 cm.) between the muscular and mucous coats before piercing the latter; this arrangement constitutes a valve which prevents absolutely the return of the urine from the bladder into the ureter. The **internal urethral orifice** (Orificium urethræ internum) lies at the apex of the trigonum, and is about an inch and a half (ca. 4 cm.) behind the ureteral orifices. The mucous membrane is covered with transitional epithelium like that of the ureter and renal pelvis. It contains lymph nodules.

Vessels and Nerves.—The **arteries** are derived chiefly from the internal pudic, but branches also come from the obturator and umbilical arteries. The **veins** terminate chiefly in the internal pudic veins. They form plexuses posteriorly. The **lymph-vessels** form plexuses on both surfaces of the muscular coat. They go to the internal iliac and lumbar glands. The nerves are derived from the pelvic plexus (sympathetic and ventral branches of third and fourth sacral nerves). They form a plexus in the submucosa which presents microscopic ganglia.

In the fœtus and new-born animal the bladder is situated chiefly in the abdomen. It is long, narrow, and fusiform. Its abdominal end lies at the umbilicus, through which it is continued by the urachus to the extra-embryonic part of the allantois. The lateral ligaments also extend to the umbilicus and each contains in its edge the large umbilical artery. As the pelvis increases in size and the large intestine grows, the bladder retracts into the pelvis and changes its form.

The **urethra** will be described with the genital organs.

THE ADRENAL BODIES

The **adrenal bodies** or **glands** (Glandulæ adrenales)[1] are two small, flattened organs, which lie in contact with the anterior part of the medial border of the kidneys (Figs. 496, 497). They are ductless. In the horse they are red-brown in color, about three and a half to four inches (ca. 9 to 10 cm.) long, one to one and a half inches (ca. 3 to 4 cm.) wide, and about half an inch or more (ca. 1.5 cm.) in thickness. The weight varies from one to two ounces (ca. 28 to 56 gm.).

The **right adrenal body** is related medially to the posterior vena cava, to which it is adherent. Its anterior part curves dorsally around the medial border of the right kidney. Its posterior part is flattened and is related ventrally to the pancreas and cæcum, dorsally to the right renal vessels. The anterior extremity is concealed in the renal impression of the liver; the posterior is related to the ureter.

The **left adrenal body** is a little shorter than the right one, and its extremities are rounded; it is usually curved, so that its medial border partly embraces the anterior mesenteric artery. Its dorsal surface is related to the kidney, the renal artery, the aorta, and the left cœliaco-mesenteric ganglion. The ventral surface is in relation with the left extremity of the pancreas and the root of the great mesentery. The posterior extremity often curves inward behind the anterior mesenteric artery; it is related behind to the left renal vein.

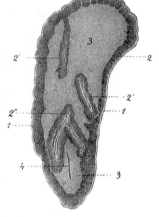

When hardened *in situ* the adrenals present several features not evident in the soft organs. The anterior part of the right adrenal is twisted dorso-laterally over the medial margin of the kidney, so that this part is prismatic and has three surfaces; of these, the concave lateral one is applied to the kidney, the dorsal one is related to the right crus of the diaphragm and the liver, and the medial one is in contact with the posterior vena cava. The anterior mesenteric artery is nearly always more or less enlarged as a result of verminous arteritis, and the form and degree of curvature of the left adrenal seem to vary in conformity with the condition of the artery.

Structure.—The **fibrous capsule** adheres intimately to the surface of the organ. It contains elastic fibers, and in its deep part unstriped muscle-fibers. From it trabeculæ pass radially into the substance, blending with the fine supporting reticulum. The **parenchyma** consists of a cortical and a medullary part. The **cortical substance** (Substantia corticalis) is red-brown in

Fig. 503.—Adrenal Body of Horse; Horizontal Section, Reduced.

1, Capsule; *2*, *2'*, cortical substance; *3*, medullary substance; *4*, blood-vessel in section. (From Leisering's Atlas, reduced.)

color, and is clearly distinguishable from the yellow **medullary substance** (Substantia medullaris). A large **central vein** (Vena centralis) is visible on cross-sections.

The cells of the cortex are arranged in chains of one or two rows. In the peripheral portion the cells are of high cylindrical shape, and the chains form connecting loops; Günther has proposed the name zona arcuata for this part, instead of the usual term zona glomerularis. More deeply the chains are distinctly palisade-like, and this region is called the zona fasciculata. Next to the medulla is the zona reticularis, in which the chains form a network. The cells in these two zones are polygonal and contain a brown pigment. The cells of the medulla are arranged in irregular groups or form sheaths around the veins. They react to chromic salts by assuming a yellow or yellow-brown color, and are termed chromaffin cells; they share this peculiarity with certain cells of the sympathetic ganglia and paraganglia, with which they are probably related genetically. The alkaloid adrenalin appears to be formed in the medullary cells.

Vessels and Nerves.—The adrenals receive a relatively large blood-supply through the **adrenal arteries,** which arise from the renal arteries or from the aorta directly. The **veins** terminate in the posterior vena cava and the left renal vein.

[1]From the standpoint of comparative anatomy the term "adrenal" is decidedly preferable to "suprarenal."

The **lymph-vessels** go to the renal lymph glands. The numerous **nerves** are derived from the sympathetic system through the cœliac and renal plexuses. The fibers form a rich interlacement, especially in the medullary substance. Ganglion cells are found chiefly in the medulla, but also occur in the deeper part of the cortex. The cortex of the adrenal is derived from the cœlomic mesothelium, while the medulia is formed by sympatho-chromaffin cells which migrate into the developing cortex.

URINARY ORGANS OF THE OX AND SHEEP

The **kidneys** of the ox are superficially divided into polygonal lobes by fissures of variable depth. The lobes vary in size, and are commonly about twenty in number. The fissures are filled with fat.

The **right kidney** has an elongated elliptical outline, and is flattened dorso-ventrally. It commonly lies ventral to the last rib and the first two or three lumbar

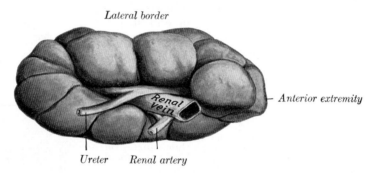

Fig. 504.—Right Kidney of Ox; Ventral Face.
Organ hardened *in situ*. Fat has been removed from fissures between lobes.

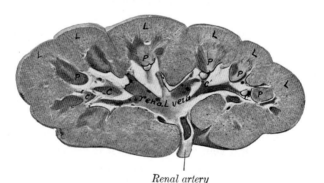

Fig. 505.—Frontal Section of Kidney of Ox.
L, Lobes of cortex; *P*, papillæ; *C*, calyx major; *c'*, calyces minores.

transverse processes, but its extremities may be ventral to the first and fourth lumbar transverse processes. The dorsal surface is rounded, and is in contact chiefly with the sublumbar muscles. The ventral surface is less convex, and is related to the liver, pancreas, duodenum, and colon. The hilus is situated on the anterior part of this surface, near the medial border. The medial border is nearly straight, and lies parallel with the posterior vena cava. The lateral border is convex. The anterior extremity occupies the renal impression of the liver, and is capped by the adrenal body.

The **left kidney** occupies a remarkable position, and when hardened *in situ* differs strongly in form from the right one. When the rumen is full, it pushes the kidney backward and across the median plane, so that it is situated on the right side, behind, and at a lower level than, the right kidney. It then lies usually ventral to the third, fourth, and fifth lumbar vertebræ. When the rumen is not full, the left kidney may lie partly to the left of the median plane. It has three surfaces. The dorsal surface is convex, and presents on its antero-lateral part the hilus, which opens laterally. The ventral surface is related to the intestine. The third face is more or less flattened by contact with the rumen, and may be termed the ruminal surface. The anterior extremity is small, the posterior large and rounded.[1]

The kidneys are embedded in a large amount of perirenal fat termed the capsula adiposa. The weight of a kidney of an adult animal is about 20 to 25 ounces (ca. 600–700 gm.), the left one being usually an ounce or more the heavier. The two form about $\frac{1}{5}$ per cent. of the body-weight.

The right kidney measures about 8 or 9 inches (ca. 20–22.5 cm.) in length, 4 to 5 inches (ca. 10–12 cm.) in width, and 2½ to 3 inches (ca. 5–6 cm.) in thickness. The left kidney is one or two inches (ca. 2 to 5 cm.) shorter, but its posterior part is much thicker than the right one.

Structure.—The hilus is equivalent to the hilus and sinus of the kidney of the

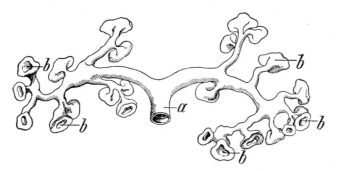

Fig. 506.—Cast of Origin of Ureter (*a*), Calyces majores, and Calyces minores (*b*) of Ox. (After Dumont.)

horse; in the right kidney it is an extensive elliptical cavity; in the left one it is a deep fissure. The pelvis is absent. The ureter begins at the junction of two wide, thin-walled tubes, the **calyces majores;** the anterior calyx is usually the larger. Each calyx major gives off a number of branches, and these divide into several funnel-shaped **calyces minores,** each of which embraces a renal papilla. The space not occupied by the calyces and vessels is filled with fat.

On section through the kidney the **renal pyramids** are easily made out. The blunt apex of each pyramid, the **renal papilla** (Papilla renalis), projects into a calyx minor. On each papilla are small orifices (Foramina papillaria) by which the papillary ducts (Ductus papillares) open into the calyx. The renal columns are much more distinct than in the horse.

At the hilus the renal artery is dorsal, the vein in the middle, and the ureter ventral; a quantity of fat surrounds these structures in the hilus.

[1] The above statements refer to the adult subject, and are based on investigations made on living subjects, and studies of frozen sections and material hardened *in situ*. In the new-born calf the kidneys are almost symmetrically placed, but as the rumen grows it pushes the left kidney to the right and backward *pari passu*. It also usually causes a rotation of the kidney, so that the primary dorsal surface comes to lie almost in a sagittal plane. Further, the gland is bent so that the hilus is largely closed up and faces outward (to the right). In very fat subjects the three-sided appearance of the kidney may be absent, and about one-third or more may remain to the left of the median plane, even where the rumen is pretty well filled.

The **kidneys** of the **sheep** are bean-shaped and smooth, without any superficial lobation. The soft organ is regularly elliptical in form, with convex dorsal and ventral surfaces and rounded extremities; its length is about 3 inches (ca. 7.5 cm.), its width about 2 inches (ca. 5 cm.), and its thickness a little more than 1 inch (ca. 3 cm.). They are embedded in fat normally. In position they resemble those of the ox, except that the right one is usually a little further back, and lies under the first three lumbar transverse processes.[1] The average weight of each is about four ounces. The hilus is in the middle of the medial border. There is a renal crest or common papilla formed by the fusion of twelve to sixteen pyramids.

The **ureters** are, in general, like those of the horse, except in regard to the first part of the left one, which has a peculiar course, in conformity with the remarkable position of the kidney. It begins at the ventral part of the hilus (which faces

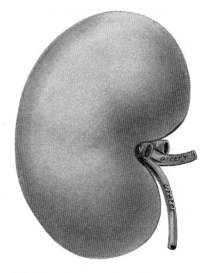

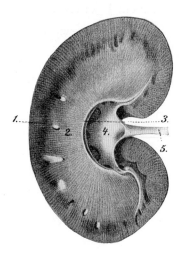

FIG. 507.—RIGHT KIDNEY OF SHEEP; VENTRAL VIEW.

V.V., Branches of renal vein.

FIG. 508.—KIDNEY OF SHEEP; HORIZONTAL SECTION.

1, Cortical substance; *2*, medullary substance; *3*, renal crest; *4*, renal pelvis; *5*, ureter. (From Leisering's Atlas, reduced.)

toward the right), curves over the lateral aspect of the kidney to its dorsal surface, crosses the median plane, and runs backward on the left side.

The **bladder** is longer and narrower than that of the horse, and extends further forward on the abdominal floor. The peritoneal coat extends backward further than in the horse.

THE ADRENAL BODIES

The **right adrenal** lies against the medial part of the anterior pole of the right kidney. When hardened *in situ*, it is pyramidal in form. Its medial surface is flattened and is in contact with the right crus of the diaphragm. The lateral surface is convex and lies in the renal impression of the liver. The ventral surface is grooved for the posterior vena cava; on this surface a relatively large vein emerges near the apex. The base is concave and rests obliquely against the anterior pole of the kidney. The apex fits into the angle between the posterior vena cava and

---

[1] When the rumen is full, the left kidney (which is attached by a short mesentery) usually lies entirely to the right of the median plane, and is ventral to the third, fourth, and fifth lumbar transverse processes. The primitive dorsal surface has become ventro-medial, and is somewhat flattened by contact with the rumen.

the dorsal border of the liver. The **left adrenal** lies on the medial face of the posterior vena cava, just behind the anterior mesenteric artery, and is therefore practically median in position. It is flattened, and irregularly triangular or heart-shaped in outline. Its left face is related to the dorsal sac of the rumen. Its right face is related to the vena cava, and presents a large emergent vein. The posterior border or base is deeply notched. The left adrenal does not migrate with the kidney, but retains its primitive position; it lies usually two or three inches (ca. 5–8 cm.) in front of a transverse plane through the anterior pole of the left kidney.

The **adrenals** of the **sheep** are both bean-shaped. The right one lies along the anterior part of the medial border of the kidney, at the angle of the junction of the right renal vein and the posterior vena cava. It is a little over an inch (ca.

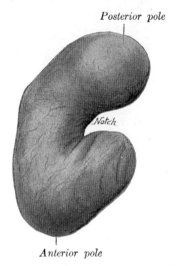

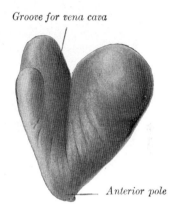

Fig. 509.—Left Adrenal of Ox; Ventral View.
Hardened *in situ*.

Fig. 510.—Right Adrenal of Ox; Ventral View.
Hardened *in situ*.

3 cm.) long, and about half as wide. The left adrenal is usually longer, and is flatter and somewhat bent. It lies across the left renal vein, to which it is attached; it is not in contact with the kidney, from which it may be separated by a distance of nearly two inches (ca. 4 cm.).

URINARY ORGANS OF THE PIG

The **kidneys** are smooth and bean-shaped; they are more flattened dorso-ventrally, more elongated, and smaller at the extremities than those of the dog. The length is about twice the width. They are usually almost symmetrically placed ventral to the transverse processes of the first four lumbar vertebræ, but the left kidney is often a little further forward than the right one. The lateral border lies against the flank parallel with the edge of the longissimus muscle. The posterior extremity is usually about midway between the last rib and the tuber coxæ. The anterior extremity of the right kidney has no contact with the liver.

Variations in position are not rare, and involve the left kidney oftener than the right; the former has been found near the pelvic inlet. When a fifteenth rib is present the anterior end of the kidney is usually ventral to it. The right kidney is usually separated from the liver by an interval of an inch or more. Absence of the left kidney has been recorded.

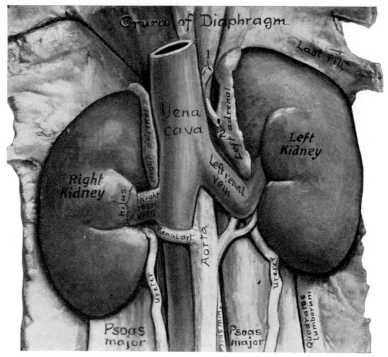

FIG. 511.—KIDNEYS OF PIG *in situ;* VENTRAL VIEW.
1, Hepatic artery; 2, gastro-splenic artery.

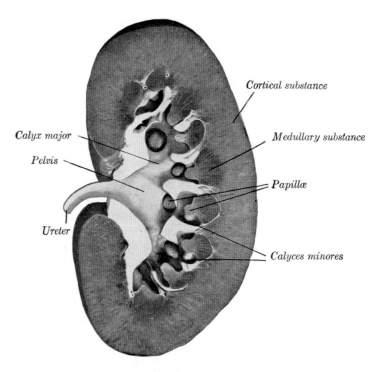

FIG. 512.—FRONTAL SECTION OF KIDNEY OF PIG.

The weight of the kidney of an adult pig is about seven to nine ounces (200 to 250 grams). The ratio of their combined weight to that of the body is about 1 : 150–200. The length in an adult of good size is about five inches (ca. 12.5 cm.) and the greatest width about two and a half inches (ca. 6–6.5 cm.).

Structure.—The hilus is about in the middle of the medial border. The pelvis is funnel-shaped, and divides into two calyces majores, which pass in a curve forward and backward respectively, and give off some eight to twelve short calyces minores; each of the latter contains a papilla. Some papillæ are narrow and conical, and correspond to a single pyramid; others are wide and flattened, and result from the fusion of two or more pyramids; some project directly through the wall of the renal pelvis without the formation of a calyx. The renal pyramids are distinct, but it is apparent that some are compound, i. e., formed by fusion of primitively separate pyramids. The renal vessels enter the ventral part of the hilus, and the ureter leaves it dorsally.

The **adrenals** are long and narrow. Each lies along the medial border of the corresponding kidney from the hilus forward; they are in contact medially with the crus of the diaphragm and the posterior vena cava.

The only special features in regard to the **ureter** are that it is at first relatively wide and gradually diminishes in caliber, and that it is slightly flexuous.

The **bladder** is relatively very large; when full, it lies chiefly in the abdominal cavity. The dorsal surface is almost completely covered with peritoneum, but the serous covering does not extend so far back ventrally.

URINARY ORGANS OF THE DOG

The **kidneys** (Fig. 624) are relatively large, forming about $\frac{1}{150}$ to $\frac{1}{200}$ of the body-weight; the weight of the kidney of a medium-sized dog is about two ounces (ca. 50 to 60 grams). They are both bean-shaped, thick dorso-ventrally, with a rounded ventral surface and a less convex dorsal surface; the surfaces are smooth.

The **right kidney** is not subject to much variation in position; it is situated usually opposite to the bodies of the first three lumbar vertebræ, but may be as far forward as the last thoracic. Its anterior half or more lies in the deep renal impression of the liver; its posterior part is related to the sublumbar muscles dorsally, and the right branch of the pancreas and duodenum ventrally.

The **left kidney** is subject to some variation in position; this is due to the fact that it is loosely attached by the peritoneum, and is affected by the degree of fulness of the stomach. When the stomach is nearly empty, the kidney usually corresponds to the bodies of the second, third, and fourth lumbar vertebræ, so that its anterior pole is opposite to the hilus of the right kidney; exceptionally the anterior pole may be opposite the posterior end of the first lumbar vertebra. When the stomach is full, the left kidney is usually the length of one vertebra further back, so that its anterior pole may be opposite the posterior pole of the right kidney. The dorsal surface is related to the sublumbar muscles. The ventral surface is in contact with the left part of the colon. The lateral border is related to the spleen and the flank. The anterior extremity touches the stomach and the left extremity of the pancreas.

The lateral border of the left kidney usually has considerable contact with the flank, and hence it may be palpated more or less distinctly in the living animal, about half-way between the last rib and the crest of the ilium. But in some cases the spleen assumes an almost longitudinal direction, thus intervening between the kidney and the flank.

Structure.—The hilus is in the middle of the medial border and is relatively wide.   Cortex, limiting zone, and medulla are clearly defined.   On frontal sections it is seen that the medullary substance forms a horizontal renal crest like that of the horse, but with the important difference that curved ridges proceed dorsally and ventrally from the crest somewhat like buttresses.   Sections above or below the renal crest often cut these ridges in such a manner as to give the appearance of conical papillæ, and thus tend strongly to produce a false impression.   The pelvis is adapted to this arrangement of the medullary substance.   It encloses a central cavity into which the renal crest projects, and is prolonged outward between the ridges, forming cavities for the latter, thus simulating the appearance of calyces which do not exist.

The **ureters** present no special features.

The **bladder,** when full, is abdominal in position, the neck lying at the anterior border of the pubic bones.   It is relatively large, and when distended, the vertex may reach to the umbilicus.   When empty and contracted, it is usually entirely in the pelvic cavity.   It has a practically complete peritoneal coat.

THE ADRENALS

The **right adrenal** lies between the anterior part of the medial border of the kidney and the posterior vena cava.   It is somewhat prismatic, and is pointed at either end.   The **left adrenal** lies along the posterior aorta, from the renal vein forward, but is not in contact with the kidney.   It is elongated and flattened dorsoventrally.   (There is a furrow on the ventral surface for the phrenico-abdominal vein which crosses it; the part in front of this furrow is discoid, and may be taken for the entire organ in a fat subject.)   The cortex is pale yellow in color, the medulla dark brown.

THE MALE GENITAL ORGANS

The **male genital organs** (Organa genitalia masculina) are: (1) The two **testicles,** the essential reproductive glands, with their coverings and appendages; (2) the **ductus deferentes,** the ducts of the testicles; (3) the **vesiculæ seminales;** (4) the **prostate,** a musculo-glandular organ; (5) the two **bulbo-urethral** (or Cowper's) **glands;** (6) the male **urethra,** a canal which transmits the generative and urinary secretions; (7) the **penis,** the male copulatory organ. The vesiculæ seminales, the prostate, and the bulbo-urethral glands discharge their secretions into the urethra, where they mix with the fluid secreted by the testicles; hence they are often termed the accessory sexual glands.

GENITAL ORGANS OF THE STALLION

THE TESTICLES

The **testicles** (Testes) are situated in the prepubic region, enclosed in a diverticulum of the abdomen termed the scrotum. Their long axes are nearly longitudinal.[1] They are ovoid in form, but considerably compressed from side to side. Each presents two surfaces, two borders, and two extremities. The **medial and lateral surfaces** (Facies medialis, lateralis) are convex and smooth; the former is somewhat flattened by contact with the septum scroti. The **free border** (Margo liber) is ventral and is convex. The **attached** or **epididymal border** (Margo epididymidis) is dorsal; it is nearly straight, and is the one by which the gland is suspended in the scrotum by the spermatic cord; the epididymis is attached to this border and overlies it laterally. The **anterior** and **posterior extremities** (Extremitas capitata, caudalis) are rounded.

At the anterior extremity there is often a sessile or pedunculated sac which contains a clear fluid; this is the **appendix testis,** from which a thread-like process extends backward toward the ductus deferens. It is regarded as a remnant of the Müllerian duct of the embryo.

A testicle of average size of an adult stallion is about four or five inches (ca. 10 to 12 cm.) long, two and a half to three inches (ca. 6 to 7 cm.) high, and two inches (ca. 5 cm.) wide; it weighs about eight to ten ounces (ca. 225–300 grams). They vary much in size in different subjects, and are commonly of unequal size, the left one being more often the larger.

The **epididymis** is adherent to the attached border of the testicle, and overlaps somewhat the lateral surface. Its anterior enlarged end is termed the **head** (Caput epididymidis); and its posterior, slightly enlarged end is the **tail** (Cauda epididymidis); the intermediate narrow part is the **body** (Corpus epididymidis). The head is closely connected with the testicle by the efferent ducts of the latter, by connective tissue, and by the serous membrane. The body is less closely attached by the serous covering, which forms laterally a pocket beneath the epididymis termed the sinus epididymidis. The tail is continued by the ductus deferens; it is attached to the posterior extremity of the testicle by the **ligament of the epididymis** (Lig. epididymidis), which is formed by a short thick fold of the tunica vaginalis and contains smooth muscle-fibers.

[1] When the testicle is drawn up or has not completed its descent into the scrotum, its long axis is almost vertical.

Structure of the Testicle and Epididymis.—The greater part of the surface of the testicle is covered by a serous membrane, the **tunica vaginalis propria,** which is the visceral layer of the serous envelop of the cord and testicle; this is reflected from the attached border of the gland, leaving an uncovered area at which the vessels and nerves in the spermatic cord reach the testicle.[1]   Beneath this serous covering is the **tunica albuginea,** a strong capsule composed of dense white fibrous tissue and unstriped muscle-fibers.   When the tunic is cut, the gland substance, which is soft and reddish gray in color, protrudes.   From the attached border and from the deep face of the tunica albuginea trabeculæ and septa of connective tissue

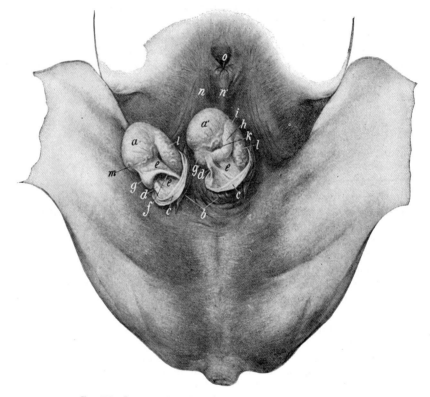

FIG. 513.—INGUINAL REGION OF STALLION, WITH TESTICLES EXPOSED.

a, a′, Testicles; *b,* scrotum, opened and reflected; *c,* tunica vaginalis communis, opened and reflected; *d,* reflection of tunica vaginalis enclosing scrotal ligament; *e,* tunica vaginalis propria (mesorchium); *f,* ductus deferens; *g, g′,* tail of epididymis; *h,* body of same; *i,* head of same; *k,* sinus epididymidis; *l,* spermatic vessels showing through tunica vaginalis propria; *m,* spermatic artery; *n,* prepuce; *n′,* raphé; *o,* preputial orifice. (After Ellenberger-Baum, Top. Anat. d. Pferdes.)

and unstriped muscle (Septula testis) pass into the gland and subdivide the parenchyma into lobules (Lobuli testis).   The larger trabeculæ radiate from the attached border into the central part of the gland.

A distinct mediastinum testis, such as is present in man and many animals, does not exist in the horse.   The trabeculæ and interlobular septa form a network which shows no special condensation in any part of the gland.   In correlation with this is the absence of a rete testis, formed by the anastomosis of the seminiferous tubules in the mediastinum.

The spaces imperfectly marked off by the septa contain the **parenchyma testis,** which consists of **seminiferous tubules** (Tubuli seminiferi), supported

[1] In the normal state the surface of the testicle is quite smooth on account of the serous covering.   Frequently, and especially in old subjects, local inflammation has produced roughening of the surface and thread-like proliferations.

by loose intralobular connective tissue. The tubules are at first very tortuous (Tubuli contorti); then they unite with other tubules, forming larger straight tubules (Tubuli recti). The latter unite with adjacent tubules and converge toward the anterior part of the attached border of the gland. In this way there are formed more than a dozen larger **efferent ducts** (Ductuli efferentes), which pierce the albuginea at a small area (about a centimeter in diameter) at the anterior part of the attached border and enter the head of the epididymis.

The **epididymis** is covered by the tunica vaginalis propria and a thin albuginea. Its head consists of a dozen or more coiled tubules, which are grouped into **lobules** (Lobuli epididymidis). The tubules of a lobule (four or five in number) unite to form a single tube, and by the union of the latter with those of the other lobules there is formed a single tube, the **duct of the epididymis** (Ductus epididymidis),

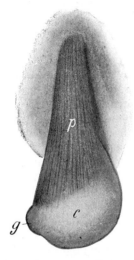

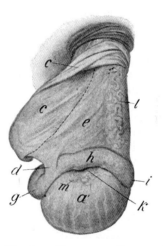

FIG. 514.—RIGHT TESTICLE AND SPERMATIC CORD OF HORSE, ENCLOSED IN TUNICA VAGINALIS.

c, Tunica vaginalis communis; g, prominence caused by tail of epididymis; p, cremaster externus muscle. (After Ellenberger-Baum, Top. Anat. d. Pferdes.)

FIG. 515.—RIGHT TESTICLE AND SPERMATIC CORD OF HORSE, EXPOSED.

a', Lateral surface of testicle; c, tunica vaginalis, cut and reflected; d, reflection of tunica vaginalis; e, mesorchium; g, tail, h, body, i, head, of epididymis; k, sinus epididymidis; l, spermatic vessels showing through tunica vaginalis propria; m, end of spermatic artery. Dotted line indicates position of ductus deferens on other side of mesorchium. (After Ellenberger-Baum, Top. Anat. d. Pferdes.)

which, by its complex coils, forms the body and tail of the epididymis and terminates in the ductus deferens. The tubules and the coils of the duct of the epididymis are held together by connective tissue and unstriped muscle-fibers. The tubules and duct are lined with ciliated epithelium, and the duct has a muscular coat which consists of longitudinal and circular fibers.

Several fœtal remnants in connection with the epididymis and adjacent part of the spermatic cord have been described in man. The **appendix epididymidis** is a small, piriform body, 3–4 mm. long, which is attached to the head of the epididymis. The **paradidymis** consists of a number of tubules which lie in the lower part of the spermatic cord close to the head of the epididymis. Most of the tubules are blind and disappear in early life, but one or more may communicate with the epididymis or rete testis; the latter may give rise to cysts. The **ductuli aberrantes** are tubules that extend upward from the canal of the epididymis and end blindly. Similar structures have been mentioned as occurring in the domestic animals, but authentic data in regard to them are lacking.

Vessels and Nerves.—The testicle is richly supplied with blood by the **spermatic artery,** a branch of the posterior aorta. The artery descends in the anterior part of the spermatic cord, and is very tortuous near the testicle; on reaching the attached border of the gland it passes backward in a flexuous manner, giving branches to the testicle and epididymis, turns around the posterior extremity, and runs forward on the free border to the anterior extremity. It is partially embedded in the tunica albuginea, and detaches lateral branches which ascend and descend in a tortuous fashion on each surface of the testicle; these give off small branches which enter the gland on the trabeculæ and septa. The veins on leaving the testicle, form a network, the **pampiniform plexus,** around the artery in the spermatic cord. The **spermatic vein,** which issues from this plexus, usually joins the posterior vena cava on the right side, the left renal vein on the left side. The **lymph-vessels** follow in general the course of the veins and enter the lumbar lymph glands. The **nerves,** derived from the renal and posterior mesenteric plexuses, form the **spermatic plexus** around the vessels, to which they are chiefly distributed.

THE SCROTUM

The **scrotum,** in which the testicles and the adjacent parts of the spermatic cords are situated, is somewhat globular in form, but is commonly asymmetrical, since one testicle—more often the left—is the larger, more dependent and placed a little further back. It varies in form and appearance in the same subject, according to the condition of its subcutaneous muscular tissue. The latter contracts on exposure to cold, so that the scrotum is drawn up and becomes thicker and wrinkled; when relaxed under the influence of heat or fatigue, or from debility, it becomes smooth and pendulous, with a constriction or neck superiorly. It consists of layers, which correspond with those of the abdominal wall; considered from without inward, these are:

(1) The **skin,** which is thin, elastic, usually dark or black in color, and smooth and oily to the touch. It presents scattered short fine hairs, and is abundantly supplied with very large sebaceous and sweat glands. It is marked centrally by a longitudinal **raphé scroti;** this is continued forward on the prepuce and behind on the perineum.

(2) The **dartos** (Tunica dartos) is reddish in color and is closely adherent to the skin except superiorly. It consists of fibro-elastic tissue and unstriped muscle. Along the raphé it forms a median partition, the **septum scroti,** which divides the scrotum into two pouches. Dorsally the septum divides into two layers which diverge on either side of the penis to join the abdominal tunic. At the bottom of the scrotum fibers connect the dartos closely with the tunica vaginalis (and thus indirectly with the tail of the epididymis), constituting the **scrotal ligament.**[1] Elsewhere the dartos is loosely connected with the underlying tunic by areolar tissue which contains no fat.

(3) The scrotal **fascia,** which is apparently derived from the oblique abdominal muscles.

It has been customary to describe three layers of fascia, in conformity with the accounts given in text-books of human anatomy. These are: (1) The intercolumnar or spermatic fascia, derived from the margin of the external inguinal ring; (2) the cremasteric fascia, derived from the internal oblique muscle; (3) the infundibuliform fascia, derived from the fascia transversalis. The first two cannot be distinguished by dissection and the third is (in the scrotum) fused with the parietal peritoneum of the tunica vaginalis.

(4) **The parietal layer of the tunica vaginalis.**—This is a fibro-serous sac which is continuous with the parietal peritoneum of the abdomen at the internal inguinal ring. It is thin above, but is thick in its scrotal part, where it is strengthened by fibrous tissue (Lamina fibrosa) derived from the fascia transversalis. It will be described further under the caption tunica vaginalis.[2]

[1] This is a remnant of the gubernaculum testis of the fœtus.

[2] The tunica vaginalis is not a part of the scrotum in the strict or narrow sense of that term, but is included here on practical grounds.

Vessels and Nerves.—The blood supply is derived from the **external pudic artery,** and the veins go chiefly to the **external pudic vein.** The **nerves** are derived from the ventral branches of the second and third lumbar nerves.

THE DUCTUS DEFERENS

This tube, also commonly termed the vas deferens, extends from the tail of the epididymis to the pelvic part of the urethra. It ascends in the inguinal canal, enclosed in a fold detached from the medial surface of the mesorchium, near the posterior (attached) border of the latter. At the vaginal ring it separates from the other constituents of the spermatic cord, and turns backward and medially into the pelvic cavity (Fig. 370). For some distance it lies in the free edge of the genital fold, by which it is attached to the inguinal part of the abdominal wall and the ventral part of the lateral wall of the pelvis. In its further course (over the dorsal surface of the bladder) it leaves the edge of the fold and inclines medially between its layers, and comes in contact with the medial face of the vesicula seminalis. Over the neck of the bladder the two ducts lie very close together, flanked laterally by the necks of the vesiculæ seminales, and having the uterus masculinus between them. They then disappear under the isthmus of the prostate, and are continued through the wall of the urethra to open in a small diverticulum on the colliculus seminalis with the excretory duct of the vesicula seminalis. The common opening is the **ejaculatory orifice** (Orificium ejaculatorium).

It has been customary to describe a short tube, the ejaculatory duct, as resulting from the union of the ductus deferens and the duct of the corresponding vesicula seminalis. Such a duct, about 18–20 mm. (ca. ¾ in.) long, exists in man as the morphological continuation of the ductus deferens. In the domestic animals it is not present, since the ductus deferens and duct of the vesicula seminalis open either in common or alongside of each other in a diverticulum or evagination of the mucous membrane on the side of the colliculus seminalis.

From its origin until it reaches the dorsal surface of the bladder the ductus deferens has a uniform diameter of about a quarter of an inch (ca. 6 mm.). It then forms a fusiform enlargement, the **ampulla ductus deferentis** (Fig. 517); this part is about six to eight inches (ca. 15 to 20 cm.) long, and in its largest part nearly an inch (ca. 2 cm.) in diameter in the stallion; in geldings the enlargement is usually not very pronounced. Beyond the ampulla the duct abruptly diminishes in size.[1]

Structure.—The wall of the ductus deferens is thick and the lumen very small, so that the tube has a firm and cord-like character. It is covered with peritoneum, except in the last few inches of its course. The loose **adventitia** contains numerous vessels and nerves. The thick **muscular coat** consists of longitudinal and circular fibers. The **mucous membrane** has an epithelium of short columnar cells. In the posterior part of the tube, and especially in the ampulla, there are numerous glands.

Vessels and Nerves.—The **arteries** are branches of the spermatic, umbilical, and internal pudic arteries, and the **nerves** come from the pelvic plexus of the sympathetic.

THE SPERMATIC CORD

The **spermatic cord** (Funiculus spermaticus) consists of the structures carried down by the testicle in its migration through the inguinal canal from the abdominal cavity to the scrotum. It begins at the abdominal inguinal ring, where its constituent parts come together, extends obliquely downward through the inguinal canal, passes over the side of the penis, and ends at the attached border of the testicle. It consists of the following structures:

(1) The **spermatic artery.**

[1] The term "ampulla" is not entirely satisfactory, since it is likely to be interpreted to mean a dilatation. There is no increase here in the lumen of the tube, and the increase in size is caused by a thickening of the wall, due to the presence of numerous branched tubular glands. The term "pars glandularis," suggested by Schmaltz, seems worthy of adoption.

(2) The **spermatic veins,** which form the pampiniform plexus around the artery.

(3) The **lymphatics,** which accompany the veins.

(4) Sympathetic **nerves,** which run with the artery.

(5) The **ductus deferens.**

(6) The **internal cremaster muscle,** which consists of bundles of unstriped muscular tissue about the vessels.

(7) The **visceral layer** of the **tunica vaginalis.**

The first four of these constituents are gathered into a rounded mass which forms the anterior part of the cord; they are united by connective tissue, interspersed with which are bundles of the cremaster internus. The ductus deferens is situated postero-medially, enclosed in a special fold detached from the medial surface of the tunic; hence it is not visible laterally.

The term spermatic cord is to a certain extent misleading as applied to most animals, while in man the structure is distinctly cord-like. In the horse, when the tunica vaginalis is slit open and the "cord" stretched out, the latter is seen to have the form of a wide sheet, the mesorchium, which has a thick, rounded anterior edge, the so-called "vascular part" of the cord. The posterior edge of the mesorchium is continuous with the parietal layer of the tunic; its medial surface presents posteriorly the fold of the ductus deferens (Plica ductus deferentis). Between the two layers of the mesorchium are bundles of unstriped muscle (cremaster internus) and small vessels.

THE TUNICA VAGINALIS

The **tunica vaginalis** is a flask-like serous sac which extends through the inguinal canal to the bottom of the scrotum. Like the abdominal peritoneum, of which it is an evagination, it consists of two layers—parietal and visceral. The **parietal layer** or **tunica vaginalis communis** lines the scrotum below; its narrow, tubular part lies in the inguinal canal, and is directly continuous with the parietal peritoneum of the abdomen at the abdominal inguinal ring. The **cavity** of the tunica vaginalis (Cavum vaginale) is a diverticulum of the general peritoneal cavity, with which it communicates through the **vaginal ring** (Annulus vaginalis); it contains normally a small quantity of serous fluid. The parietal layer is reflected from the posterior wall of the inguinal canal around the structures of the cord, forming the **mesorchium,** a fold analogous to the mesentery of the intestine. The **visceral layer**

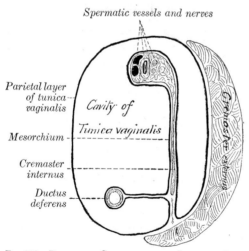

Spermatic vessels and nerves

Parietal layer of tunica vaginalis

Cavity of Tunica vaginalis

Mesorchium

Cremaster internus

Ductus deferens

Cremaster externus

FIG. 516.—DIAGRAM OF CROSS-SECTION OF SPERMATIC CORD AND TUNICA VAGINALIS; LATTER REPRESENTED AS DISTENDED.

or **tunica vaginalis propria** covers the spermatic cord, testicle, and epididymis.

The **external cremaster muscle** (M. cremaster externus) lies on the lateral and posterior part of the tunic, to the scrotal part of which it is attached.

Confusion has arisen from the use of the term abdominal or internal inguinal ring in two senses. The term is used to designate the abdominal opening of the inguinal canal, but it is also often applied to the opening of the cavity of the tunica vaginalis. It should not be used in the latter sense. The peritoneal ring at which the cavity of the tunica vaginalis opens into the general peritoneal sac is distinguished by the name **vaginal ring.** It is four or five inches (ca. 10 to 12 cm.) from the linea alba, and two or three inches (ca. 6 to 8 cm.) in front of the ilio-pectineal eminence. In stallions it will usually admit the end of the finger readily, but it may be abnormally large and allow a loop of bowel to enter the cavity of the tunica vaginalis. It is large in the young foal. In the gelding it is smaller and sometimes partially occluded. In man the cavity is almost always obliterated early, except in its scrotal portion, thus abolishing the vaginal ring and the inguinal part of the cavity.

DESCENT OF THE TESTICLES

During early fœtal life the testicle is situated against the dorsal wall of the abdominal cavity, in contact with the ventral surface of the corresponding kidney. As growth proceeds it gradually migrates from this primitive position, and finally passes down the inguinal canal into the scrotum. Previous to its descent through the abdominal wall the testicle is attached to the sublumbar region by a fold of peritoneum, termed the **mesorchium.** This fold contains the vessels and nerves of the testicle in its anterior border. In its posterior edge is the elongated tail of the epididymis, and two cords of fibrous tissue and unstriped muscle. One of these cords is short and connects the tail of the epididymis with the testicle; later it becomes shorter, and is termed the ligament of the epididymis. The other cord, the **gubernaculum testis,** extends from the tail of the epididymis to the subperitoneal tissue in the vicinity of the future vaginal ring. The **fold of the ductus deferens** (Plica ductus deferentis) is given off from the medial face of the mesorchium, and joins the genital fold posteriorly. The body of the epididymis at this time lies in the edge of an oblique fold formed by the lateral layer of the mesorchium. After the middle of fœtal life a pouch of the peritoneum, the **processus vaginalis,** grows downward through the inguinal canal, carrying with it cremaster fibers derived from the internal oblique muscle and a layer from the transversalis fascia. It is accompanied by an inguinal extension of the gubernaculum testis. The latter blends below with the subcutaneous tissue which later becomes the dartos. The tail of the epididymis first enters the processus vaginalis, followed by the testicle with its mesorchium, which descends within this diverticulum of the peritoneum until it reaches the scrotum. The ductus deferens and its fold descend synchronously with the epididymis and testicle. In the foal the descent of the testicles is often complete at birth, but it frequently happens that one testicle or both may be retained in the inguinal canal or in the abdomen for some months. In other cases the testicle may return into the canal or abdomen, since in the young foal the vaginal ring is large and the testicle small and soft, and not yet closely anchored by the scrotal ligament. In rare cases the descent may be completed as late as the fourth year.

The mechanical factors concerned in the migration of the testicle are matters on which much uncertainty still exists. That the gubernaculum exerts sufficient traction to guide the epididymis and testicle to the inguinal canal seems plausible. The abdominal inguinal ring may constitute a locus minoris resistentiæ in the abdominal wall, especially after the descent of the processus vaginalis. Progressive shortening of the gubernaculum was formerly considered to be the chief cause of the descent through the abdominal wall. Increase in the intra-abdominal pressure is probably an important factor.

Indefinite retention of one testicle or both in the abdominal cavity or inguinal canal is not rare in horses; this condition is termed **cryptorchism.** Abdominal retention is the more usual form of cryptorchism in adult horses, inguinal retention being usually temporary. The retained testicle is usually, but not always, small, thin, soft, and flabby, and is non-spermiogenic. The processus vaginalis and the inguinal part of the gubernaculum are usually present, but may be rudimentary. The ligament of the epididymis and the corresponding part of the mesorchium are often so long that the tail of the epididymis may be several inches distant from the testicle. The abdominal part of the gubernaculum may be eight to ten inches (ca. 20 to 25 cm.) long, and the ligament of the epididymis much elongated (10 to 15 cm. in length, according to Vennerholm); thus the testicle may have a wide range. The vaginal ring is sometimes closed.

In many mammals the testicles normally remain in the abdominal cavity; such animals are termed testiconda, and include the elephant, some insectivora, hyrax, sloths, ant-eaters, armadillos, and cetacea. In others the testicles descend periodically during the period of œstrum, and then return into the abdomen, or they may be extruded and retracted voluntarily; this is true of most rodents, many insectivora (moles, shrews, hedgehog), and bats.

THE VESICULÆ SEMINALES

The **vesiculæ seminales** (Fig. 517) are two elongated and somewhat piriform sacs, which lie on each side of the posterior part of the dorsal surface of the bladder. They are partly enclosed in the genital fold, and are related to the rectum dorsally. Their long axes are parallel with the ductus deferentes and converge posteriorly. Each consists of a rounded blind end, the **fundus;** a middle, slightly narrower part, the **body;** and a posterior constricted part, the **neck** or **duct.**

In the stallion they are about six to eight inches (ca. 15 to 20 cm.) long, and their greatest diameter is about two inches (ca. 5 cm.); in the gelding they are normally much smaller.[1]

The vesiculæ are chiefly retroperitoneal, but the fundus extends forward into the genital fold and hence has a serous covering. The **excretory duct** (Ductus excretorius) dips under the prostate, and opens in common with or alongside of the ductus deferens in a pouch of the mucous membrane on the side of the colliculus seminalis.

Structure.—The wall, exclusive of the partial serous coat, consists of a fibrous **adventitia,** a middle **muscular coat,** and a **mucous lining.** The muscular coat is thickest at the fundus, and consists of two planes of longitudinal fibers with a circular layer between them. The mucous membrane is thin, and is arranged in numerous folds and projections which form a network; the spaces so enclosed present the openings of tubulo-alveolar glands. The epithelium is columnar. The **blood-supply** is derived from the **internal pudic artery.**

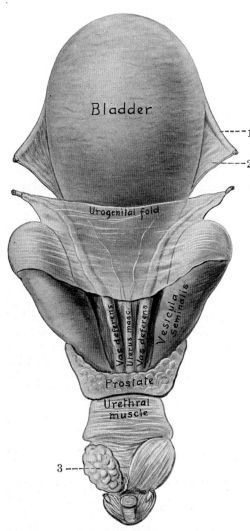

FIG. 517.—INTERNAL GENITAL ORGANS OF STALLION; DORSAL VIEW.

On left side urethral muscle has been removed over bulbo-urethral gland. Cornua of uterus masculinus are indicated in genital fold. The posterior limit of the peritoneum is shown but not marked. 1, Round ligament and, 2, lateral ligament of bladder; 3, bulbo-urethral gland; 4, artery of the bulb. For "vas" read "ductus" and for "urogenital" read "genital."

THE PROSTATE

The **prostate** (Prostata) is a lobulated gland which lies on the neck of the bladder and the beginning of the urethra, ventral to the rectum. It consists of

---

[1] Sometimes one or both of the vesiculæ are very large in the gelding. The writer has seen four cases in the dissecting room, three of which were bilateral, the other unilateral. The vesicula resembled the urinary bladder in appearance and contained about a quart of thick, amber-colored secretion.

two lateral lobes and a connecting isthmus. The **lateral lobes,** right and left (Lobus dexter et sinister), are somewhat prismatic in form, and are directed forward, laterally, and somewhat upward. The deep surface of each lobe is concave and partly embraces the corresponding vesicula seminalis. The dorsal surface is concave and is in relation with the rectum. The ventral surface is convex and lies on the obturator internus muscle and fat. The apex is pointed and lies near the posterior end of the superior ischiatic spine. The **isthmus** is a thin, transverse band, about four-fifths of an inch (ca. 2 cm.) wide. It lies over the junction of the bladder with the urethra, the uterus masculinus, the terminal parts of the ductus deferentes, and the ducts of the vesiculæ seminales. Dorsally it is partly covered by fibers of the urethral muscle.

Structure.—The prostate is enclosed in a **capsule** of fibrous tissue, with an admixture of unstriped muscle fibers. The gland substance is divided into spheroidal or ovoid **lobules** by trabeculæ which consist to a large extent of unstriped muscle. Each lobule is traversed by an axial duct, which gives off numerous tubular branches and these ramify further in the lobule. The tubules are thickly beset with saccular diverticula, giving the gland a branched, tubulo-alveolar structure. The ducts and tubules are lined with cubical or columnar epithelium. The prostatic secretion (Succus prostaticus) is milky in appearance and has a characteristic odor. There are fifteen to twenty **prostatic ducts** (Ductus prostatici) on either side, which perforate the urethra and open lateral to the colliculus seminalis (Fig. 521). The **blood-supply** is derived from the **internal pudic artery.**

The surface of the prostate is commonly tuberculate in old subjects, and amyloid bodies and calcareous concretions may be found in it.

THE UTERUS MASCULINUS

The **uterus masculinus** or utriculus prostaticus is a fœtal remnant of variable size and form, which is situated centrally on the posterior part of the dorsal surface of the bladder. When well developed, it consists of a median flattened tube, some three or four inches (ca. 7.5 to 10 cm.) long, and about half an inch (ca. 1 to 1.5 cm.) wide, the anterior part of which lies in the genital fold and gives off two slender processes or cornua; the latter curve forward and outward in the fold a variable distance, being sometimes traceable as far as the anterior end of the ampulla of the ductus deferens. The posterior extremity of the tube passes under the isthmus of the prostate, and opens into the urethra on the summit of the colliculus or joins a duct of a vesicula seminalis or has a blind end. It has a muscular coat and a mucous lining. In many cases it consists merely of a very small central tubule with a blind anterior end, or a band, not sharply marked off from the adjacent tissue; in other cases it cannot be recognized. It is a remnant of the ducts of Müller and the homologue of the uterus and vagina.

THE BULBO-URETHRAL GLANDS

The **bulbo-urethral glands** (Glandulæ bulbourethrales)[1] are two in number, and are situated on either side of the pelvic part of the urethra close to the ischial arch (Fig. 577). They are covered by the urethral muscle, from which bundles enter the larger trabeculæ of the gland. They are ovoid in form, somewhat depressed dorso-ventrally, and their long axes are directed obliquely forward and outward. In the stallion they may measure nearly two inches (ca. 4 cm.) in length, and about an inch (ca. 2.5 cm.) in width. In the gelding they are about the size of an average hazel-nut.

Structure.—They resemble the prostate in general structure, but the inter-

[1] Also termed Cowper's glands.

stitial tissue is much less abundant, and contains much less muscular tissue; hence the lobulation is not very distinct. The parenchyma consists of large collecting tubules, into which numerous side branches open; these are lined with cuboid epithelium. In the larger septa there are striped muscle-fibers. Each gland has six to eight **excretory ducts** (Ductus excretorii) which open into the urethra on a series of small papillæ behind the prostatic ducts and close to the median plane (Fig. 521). The **blood-supply** comes from the **internal pudic artery** which overlies the gland.

THE PENIS

The **penis,** the male organ of copulation, is composed essentially of erectile tissue, and encloses the extrapelvic part of the urethra. It extends from the ischial arch forward between the thighs to the umbilical region of the abdominal wall. It is supported by the fascia penis and the skin, and its prescrotal portion is situated in a cutaneous pouch, the prepuce or sheath. It is cylindrical in form, but much compressed laterally in the greater part of its extent. In the quiescent state it is about 20 inches (ca. 50 cm.) long; of this, about 6 to 8 inches (ca. 15 to 20 cm.)

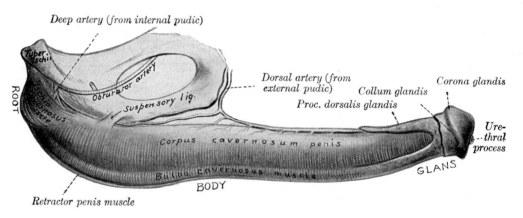

FIG. 518.—PENIS OF HORSE; LATERAL VIEW.

is free in the prepuce. In erection it increases 50 per cent. or more in length. It may be divided into root, body, and glans.

The **root** of the penis (Radix penis) is attached to the lateral parts of the ischial arch by two **crura,** which converge and unite below the arch (Fig. 577). The urethra passes over the ischial arch between the crura, and curves sharply forward to become incorporated with the penis. The **body** of the penis (Corpus penis) begins at the junction of the crura and constitutes the bulk of the organ. At its origin it is attached to the symphysis ischii by two strong flat bands, the **suspensory ligaments** of the penis (Ligamenta suspensoria penis), which blend with the tendon of origin of the graciles muscles (Figs. 518, 576). This part of the penis is flattened laterally for the most part, but becomes rounded and smaller anteriorly. It presents four surfaces. The **dorsum penis** is narrow and rounded; on it are the dorsal arteries and nerves of the penis and a rich venous plexus. The **urethral surface** (Facies urethralis) is ventral; it is rounded, and along it runs the urethra, embedded in the deep urethral groove of the corpus cavernosum. The **lateral surfaces** are high and flattened, except anteriorly, where they are lower and rounded; they are covered to a large extent by a plexus of veins. The **glans penis** is the enlarged free end of the organ. Its anterior surface or base is surrounded by a prominent, denticulated margin, the **corona glandis.** The surface is convex; its lower part slopes backward, and presents a deep depression, the **fossa glandis,** in which the urethra protrudes for about an inch (ca. 2.5 cm.) as a free tube, the **urethral process** (Processus urethræ), covered by a thin integument. The urethra is thus surrounded by a circular fossa, which opens superiorly into the **urethral sinus,** a bilocular diverticulum lined by thin skin. This diverticulum is filled sometimes with a caseous mass of sebaceous matter and epithelial débris. Behind the corona glandis there is a constriction, the **collum glandis.** It is to be noted, however, that this does not indicate the demarcation between the glans and corpus penis, since the former extends backward above the corpus cavernosum a distance of about four inches (ca. 10 cm.), forming the processus dorsalis glandis (Fig. 518).

Structure.—The penis consists essentially of two erectile bodies, the corpus cavernosum penis and the corpus cavernosum urethræ.

The **corpus cavernosum penis** forms the greater part of the bulk of the penis except at its free extremity. It arises from each side of the ischial arch by a **crus penis,** which is embedded in the ischio-cavernosus muscle. Below the ischial arch the crura unite to form the laterally compressed body of the corpus cavernosum; this presents ventrally the **urethral groove** (Sulcus urethralis), which contains the urethra and corpus cavernosum urethræ. Anteriorly the corpus cavernosum penis divides into three processes—a long central one, which is capped by the glans penis, and two short blunt lateral ones. The corpus cavernosum is enclosed by the **tunica albuginea,** a thick capsule of fibrous tissue which contains some elastic fibers. Externally the fibers are chiefly longitudinal; internally they are mainly circular and are looser in arrangement. Numerous **trabeculæ** pass inward from the tunic and form a framework in the interior of the corpus cavernosum. Enclosed by this framework is the erectile tissue, which is readily distinguished from the fibrous trabeculæ by its reddish-gray color and softer texture. It is composed largely of strands of unstriped muscle, between which there are cavernous spaces (Cavernæ). These spaces may be regarded as greatly enlarged capillaries; they contain blood, are lined with flat endothelial cells resting upon a layer of delicate connective tissue, and are directly continuous with the veins of the penis. Erection is produced by distention of these spaces with blood; at other times the spaces are mere slits.

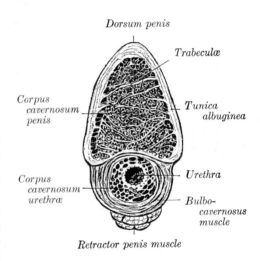

FIG. 519.—CROSS-SECTION OF BODY OF PENIS OF HORSE.

In man there are two distinct corpora cavernosa, separated by a median septum penis, which is complete except in the middle part of the organ, where the septum is composed of vertical trabeculæ, between which are slit-like intervals; through the latter the blood-spaces of the two corpora cavernosa communicate. In the horse no distinct septum exists except near the root, but in the anterior and posterior parts of the corpus cavernosum there are vertical trabeculæ which form an arrangement like the septum pectiniforme of man.

The **corpus cavernosum urethræ** (or corpus spongiosum) forms a tube around the urethra, and is continuous at its anterior end with the glans penis. It forms a slight enlargement at the root of the penis, which is termed the **bulb** (Bulbus urethræ). In the body of the penis it forms a thinner layer dorsally than on the sides and ventrally. The structure of the corpus cavernosum urethræ is somewhat like that of the corpus cavernosum penis, but the trabeculæ are much finer; they consist of fibrous tissue, much of which is elastic, and of bundles of unstriped muscle which are chiefly longitudinal in direction. The spaces are numerous and large.

In the glans penis the trabeculæ are highly elastic, and the spaces are large and very distensible; the latter are specially wide in the posterior part of the processus dorsalis, where they communicate with large veins on the dorsum penis. There is a partial septum glandis. The skin covering the glans is thin, destitute of glands, and richly supplied with nerves and special nerve-endings.

Vessels and Nerves.—The penis is supplied with blood by three **arteries,** viz., the internal pudic, obturator, and external pudic. The terminal part of the internal pudic artery enters the root as the artery of the bulb and breaks up in the bulb into numerous branches. The obturator artery gives off the large arteria profunda penis, which enters the crus penis and ramifies in the corpus cavernosum. The external pudic artery gives off the dorsal arteries of the penis, branches from which pass through the tunica albuginea. The **veins** form a rich plexus on the dorsum and sides of the penis, which is drained by the external pudic and obturator veins; from the root the blood is carried by the internal pudic veins.[1] The **lymph vessels** run with the veins and go to the superficial inguinal glands. The **nerves** are derived chiefly from the pudic nerves and the pelvic plexus of the sympathetic. The former supply the dorsal nerves of the penis; special nerve-endings, the end-bulbs (of Krause), occur in the skin of the glans penis. The sympathetic fibers supply the unstriped muscle of the vessels and the erectile tissue.

MUSCLES OF THE PENIS (Figs. 272, 576, 577, 581)

1. The **ischio-cavernosus**[2] is a short but strong, paired muscle, which arises from the tuber ischii and the adjacent part of the sacro-sciatic ligament, and is inserted on the crus and adjacent part of the body of the penis. It is somewhat fusiform, encloses the crus as in a sheath, and is situated in a deep depression in the semimembranosus muscle. It pulls the penis against the pelvis, and assists in producing and maintaining erection by compressing the dorsal veins of the penis. Its blood-supply is derived from the obturator artery, and the nerve-supply from the pudic nerve.

2. The **retractor penis** is an unstriped muscle which is a continuation of the suspensory ligaments of the anus. The latter arise on the ventral surface of the first and second coccygeal vertebræ and pass downward over the sides of the rectum to meet below the anus. Here there is a decussation of fibers, thus forming a sort of suspensory apparatus for the posterior part of the rectum and the anus. From the decussation the muscle passes for a short distance between superficial and deep layers of the bulbo-cavernosus, and then along the ventral surface of the penis, to which it is loosely attached. Near the glans penis it splits up into bundles which pass through the bulbo-cavernosus and are attached to the tunica albuginea. Below the anus the muscle is attached to the sphincter ani externus. On the penis the right and left muscles are adherent to each other. Their action is to withdraw the penis into the sheath after erection or protrusion.

THE PREPUCE

The **prepuce** (Præputium), popularly called the "sheath," is a double invagination of the skin which contains and covers the free or prescrotal portion of

---

[1] It has been shown that the cavernous spaces of the glans penis receive blood exclusively from veins which come from the penile layer of the prepuce. This may account for the fact that the glans reaches its extreme size during erection later than the corpus cavernosum penis.

[2] Also termed the erector penis.

the penis when not erect. It consists of two parts, external and internal. The external part or sheath extends from the scrotum to within two or three inches of the umbilicus, where the external layer is reflected dorsally and backward, forming the thick margin of the **preputial orifice** (Ostium præputiale); dorsally it is directly continuous with the integument of the abdominal wall. It is marked by a median **raphé præputii,** a continuation of the scrotal raphé. At the lower margin of the preputial orifice there are often in the stallion two papillæ, which are regarded as rudimentary teats. The internal layer passes backward from the preputial orifice a distance of about six to eight inches (ca. 15 to 20 cm.), lining the cavity of the external part of the prepuce, and is then reflected forward until it approaches the orifice, where it is again reflected backward. It thus forms within the cavity of the sheath a secondary tubular invagination, the prepuce proper, in which the anterior part of the penis lies. This tubular cavity is closed behind by the reflection of the internal layer on to the penis to form the penile layer of the prepuce. Its orifice is

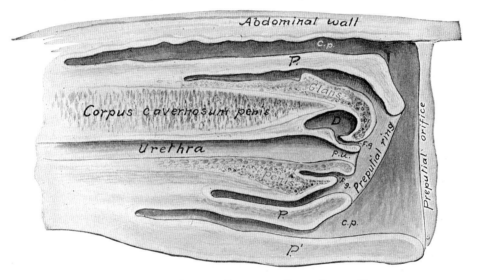

Fig. 520.—Sagittal Section of Prepuce and Part of Penis of Horse.

P, Internal part of prepuce or prepuce proper; *P′,* external part of prepuce or sheath; *C.p.,* preputial cavity; *F.g.,* fossa glandis; *D,* diverticulum of fossa glandis; *P.u.,* processus urethræ.

surrounded by a thick margin, the **preputial ring** (Annulus præputialis), which is connected ventrally with the external part by the **preputial frenum** (Frenulum præputii).

The arrangement differs from that found in man in the fact that the inner part of the prepuce as described above is equivalent to the entire human prepuce. This part, the prepuce proper, is well seen on sagittal sections, and can be demonstrated by pulling the penis, enclosed in this prepuce, out of the cavity of the sheath; the arrangement of the free part of the penis and prepuce is then like that in man. (In paraphimosis the penis is strangulated by the preputial ring.) The external part might be distinguished as the sheath or vagina penis.

Structure.—The outer skin of the external part resembles that of the scrotum. The internal layers of skin, as far as the preputial ring, are almost hairless, variable in color, and often irregularly pigmented; they form irregular folds, and are supplied with numerous large sebaceous glands and coil glands, which reach their greatest size at the ring. Beyond this the glands are absent, and the skin resembles a nonglandular mucous membrane. The secretion of the **preputial glands** (Glandulæ præputiales), together with desquamated epithelial cells, forms the fatty **smegma præputii,** which has a strong, unpleasant odor, and often accumulates in considerable amount. Beneath the skin there is a large amount of loose connective tissue, except over the glans penis, where the skin is closely attached to the tunic of the erectile tissue. The external part of the prepuce is strengthened by a layer of elastic tissue, derived from the abdominal tunic, and termed the suspensory ligament of the prepuce.

Vessels and Nerves.—The **arteries** are branches of the external pudic artery, and the **veins** go chiefly to the external pudic vein. The **lymph vessels** go to the superficial inguinal and lumbar lymph glands. The **nerves** are derived from the pudic, ilio-hypogastric, and ilio-inguinal nerves.

THE MALE URETHRA

The **male urethra** (Urethra masculina) is the long mucous tube which extends from the bladder to the glans penis. It passes backward on the floor of the pelvis,

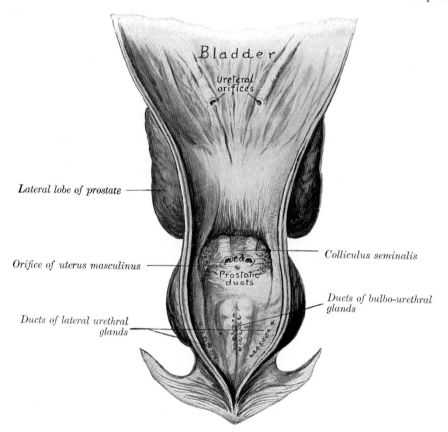

Fig. 521.—Pelvic Urethra and Posterior Part of Bladder of Horse Slit Ventrally and Laid Open.
e.d., openings of ductus deferentes and ducts of vesiculæ seminales.

turns around the ischial arch, forming a sharp bend, and passes forward as a part of the penis, enclosed in the corpus cavernosum urethræ. It may, therefore, be divided into two parts, pelvic and extrapelvic.

The **pelvic part** (Pars pelvina) is four or five inches (ca. 10 to 12 cm.) long. At its origin it is not distinguishable from the neck of the bladder in size or structure; in fact, no line of demarcation exists between the two. Behind the prostate the tube dilates to a potential width of two inches or more (ca. 5 to 6 cm.). Near the ischial arch, between the bulbo-urethral glands, it contracts again, forming the **isthmus urethræ.** It is related dorsally to the rectum and the prostate, ventrally to the internal obturator muscles, and laterally to the bulbo-urethral glands. It is enclosed, except at its origin, by the urethral muscle.[1]

The **extrapelvic part** (Pars externa) passes between the two crura of the penis and runs along the groove on the ventral surface of the corpus cavernosum penis, enclosed by the corpus cavernosum urethræ and the bulbo-cavernosus muscle. It passes through the glans penis and projects forward about an inch in the fossa glandis as a free tube, the **processus urethræ;** this part is covered by a delicate integument, under which there is a thin layer of erectile tissue.

The lumen of the tube is largely obliterated in the inactive condition of the parts. When moderately distended, its dimensions in a horse of medium size are as follows: At its origin the diameter is about half an inch (1 to 1.5 cm.). The pelvic dilatation at its widest part measures one and a half to two inches (ca. 3.5 to 5 cm.) transversely, and about an inch (2 to 3 cm.) vertically; it is elliptical in cross-section when fully distended. The isthmus at the ischial arch is a little smaller than the initial part. Beyond this the lumen is about one-half to three-fourths of an inch (ca. 1.5 cm.) in diameter, and is fairly uniform to the glans penis. Here there is a slight fusiform dilatation (Fossa navicularis), beyond which the tube contracts.

The opening from the bladder into the urethra is termed the **internal urethral orifice** (Orificium urethræ internum); it is closed except during urination. The terminal opening is the **external urethral orifice** (Orificium urethræ externum) or meatus urinarius. The **colliculus seminalis** is a rounded prominence, situated medially on the dorsal wall, about two inches (ca. 5 cm.) behind the internal urethral orifice. On either side of the colliculus there is a small diverticulum, in which the ductus deferens and the duct of the vesicula seminalis open. The small orifice of the uterus masculinus is placed centrally on the colliculus; it is inconstant. The orifices of the **prostatic ducts** are on two groups of small papillæ, placed lateral to the ejaculatory openings. The **ducts** of the **bulbo-urethral glands** open on two lateral series of small papillæ, about an inch (ca. 2.5 cm.) further back and close to the median line. The small orifices of the **lateral urethral glands** are situated laterally in the wide pelvic portion.

Structure.—The **mucous membrane** contains a large amount of fine elastic fibers, and in its pelvic part there are tubulo-alveolar **urethral glands** (Glandulæ urethrales).[2] The epithelium is at first like that of the bladder, then becomes cylindrical, and in the terminal part is stratified squamous. In the dorsal wall the membrane forms a median ridge, the **urethral crest** (Crista urethralis); this terminates about two inches from the internal urethral orifice in the colliculus seminalis.

At the origin of the urethra there is a layer of circular **unstriped muscle-fibers** outside of the mucous coat. Beyond this the latter is enclosed by a layer of **erectile tissue** (Stratum cavernosum), which contains plexuses of veins supported by trabeculæ of elastic and unstriped muscular tissue; in its peripheral part there are numerous small arteries. There is a slight thickening of the erectile tissue at the ischial arch, producing an enlargement known as the **bulb of the urethra** (Bulbus urethræ). This is continued by the corpus cavernosum urethræ. Outside of the erectile tissue there is a continuation of the intrinsic unstriped muscular coat, consisting of external and internal longitudinal strata, with a layer of circular fibers between them.

[1] It has been customary to divide the pelvic part of the urethra into prostatic and membranous parts. These terms apply well in human anatomy, but have no special value in comparative anatomy. In the horse a prostatic part hardly exists, unless we assume that it and the neck of the bladder together are only about an inch in length. There is no membranous part in the sense in which that term is used in regard to man, since the tube has a continuous envelop of erectile tissue.

[2] Two sets of glands can be distinguished in the pelvic part of the urethra. Two rows of dorsal glands occur close to the median plane; their ducts open into those of the bulbo-urethral glands. A series of lateral glands extends on either side from a point near the prostatic ducts to the end of the pelvic urethra; their ducts open laterally, as mentioned above.

Except at its origin and termination the urethra is provided with a continuous layer of striped muscle, placed outside of the erectile tissue. This is described as consisting of two parts or muscles.

(1) The **urethral muscle** (M. urethralis)[1] encloses the wide pelvic part of the urethra, and covers the bulbo-urethral glands. It consists of longitudinal and transverse fibers. It is a compressor of the pelvic part of the urethra and the bulbo-urethral glands. By its forcible contraction it plays an important rôle in the ejaculation of the seminal fluid, and also in evacuating the last of the urine in micturition.

(2) The **bulbo-cavernosus muscle** (M. bulbocavernosus)[2] is the continuation of the urethral muscle on the extrapelvic part of the urethra; it extends from the ischial arch to the glans penis. At the root of the penis it is the thickest, and forms a complete layer of circular fibers which enclose the corpus cavernosum urethræ. Beyond this it diminishes very gradually in thickness, and consists of fibers which arise on a median ventral raphé and curve around the corpus cavernosum urethræ to end on the tunica albuginea of the corpus cavernosum. Its action is to empty the extrapelvic part of the urethra.

The **ischio-urethral muscles** (Fig. 577) are small bands which arise on the ischial arch and crura of the penis and pass forward to become lost on the ventral layer of the urethral muscle. They may assist in erection of the penis by exerting pressure on the dorsal veins.

GENITAL ORGANS OF THE BULL

The **scrotum** is situated somewhat further forward than in the horse. It is ovoid, but compressed from before backward, is long and pendulous, and has a well-marked neck when not contracted. The skin here is usually flesh-colored, but in some breeds it is more or less pigmented; it is sparsely covered with short hairs. Just in front of it are four (sometimes only two) rudimentary teats.

The **testicles** are relatively larger than those of the horse, and have an elongated, oval outline. The long axis is vertical, the attached border being posterior. The medial surface is somewhat flattened. A testicle of an adult bull measures on the average about four or five inches (10 to 12 cm.) in length, exclusive of the epididymis; with the latter the length is about six inches (15 cm.). The width is about two and a half to three inches (ca. 6 to 8 cm.), and the anterior-posterior diameter about the same. The weight is about ten to twelve ounces (ca. 300 grams). The tunica albuginea is thin; it contains many elastic fibers, but no unstriped muscle. The parenchyma is yellowish in color. The mediastinum testis is an axial strand of connective tissue (about 5 mm. in thickness), which descends from the upper part of the attached border deeply into the gland. From it the chief trabeculæ radiate, but distinct interlobular septa are not present. The seminiferous tubules form in the mediastinum a network, the **rete testis**. The efferent ducts from the rete, a dozen in number, leave at the upper end of the mediastinum.

The **epididymis** is very closely attached to the testicle along the posterior border of the latter. The head is long; it curves over the upper extremity and about a third of the way down the anterior border of the testicle; it is covered by an extension of the tunica albuginea. The body is very narrow, and lies along the lateral part of the posterior border of the testicle, to which it is attached by a narrow peritoneal fold. The tail is large and is closely attached at the lower extremity of the testicle.

The **spermatic cord** and the **tunica vaginalis** are much longer than in the horse;

---

[1] Formerly termed Wilson's muscle.   [2] Formerly called the accelerator urinæ.

the extra-inguinal part of the cord is about eight to ten inches (20 to 25 cm.) in length. The **cremaster externus** is well developed, and almost completely encloses the tunic to the neck of the scrotum; it is inserted about at the level of the upper pole of the testicle. The **vaginal ring** is relatively very small, and is about four inches (ca. 10 cm.) from the linea alba. The cremaster internus is feeble.

The spermatic cords emerge through the lateral angles of the subcutaneous inguinal rings, and curve downward and inward to the neck of the scrotum. The rings are about four inches (ca. 10 cm.) long, and are two and a half to three inches (6 to 8 cm.) apart. In animals in good condition there is a large mass of fat above the neck of the scrotum, between the spermatic cords. The mesorchium extends to the bottom of the tunica vaginalis, forming a narrow fold (ca. 1 cm. wide) which attaches the epididymis to the posterior part of the tunic.

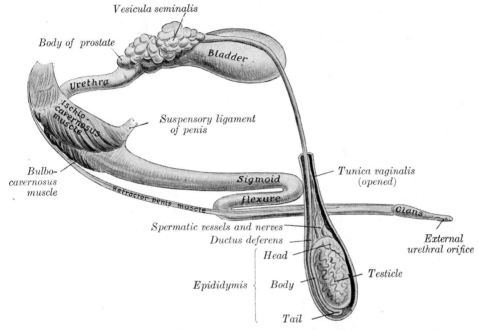

FIG. 522.—GENERAL VIEW OF GENITAL ORGANS OF BULL

The inguinal canal presents several special features in the bull. The abdominal ring is very long. Its anterior border, formed by the edge of the internal oblique, is decidedly concave and is tendinous in its medial part. The long axis of the subcutaneous ring is directed outward, forward, and downward. The spermatic cord lies in its lateral part, the external pudic vessels in its middle. A muscular band about an inch wide, detached from the internal oblique muscle, crosses the lateral side of the vaginal ring.

The **ductus deferens** is small in caliber and has a much thinner wall than that of the horse. At first it pursues a flexuous course upward along the posterior border of the testicle, then becomes straight and lies in the posterior part of the spermatic cord. The genital fold is narrow, so that the ducts are closer together in it than in the horse. On reaching the posterior part of the bladder they are in apposition for a distance of about four inches (10 cm.), flanked and overlapped by the vesiculæ seminales. They form ampullæ about four or five inches (10 to 12 cm.) long and half an inch (1.2 to 1.5 cm.) wide, the mucous lining of which is plicated. They then pass under the body of the prostate and end, just medial to the ducts of the vesiculæ seminales, as slit-like openings on either side of the colliculus seminalis.

The **vesiculæ seminales** are not bladder-like sacs, as in the horse, but are compact glandular organs with a lobulated surface. In the adult they measure about four or five inches (ca. 10 to 12 cm.) in length, two inches (5 cm.) in width in their largest part, and an inch or more (ca. 3 cm.) in thickness.   The dorsal surface of each faces upward and medially and is partially covered with peritoneum.   The ventral surface faces in the opposite direction and is non-peritoneal.   Each may be regarded as consisting of a very thick-walled, sacculated tube, bent on itself in a tortuous manner.   This tube, if straightened out, would be about ten inches (25

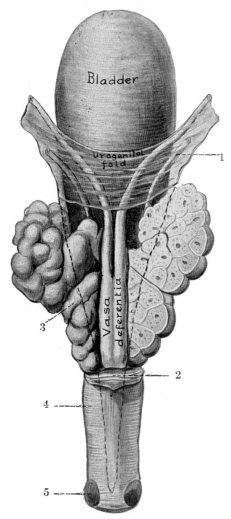

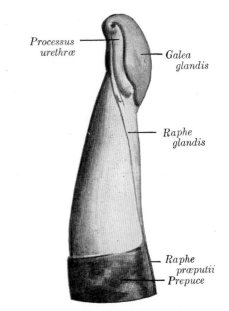

FIG. 524.—ANTERIOR EXTREMITY OF PENIS OF BULL; LEFT VIEW.   (After Böhm.)

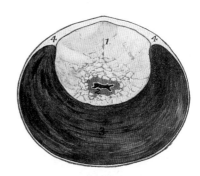

FIG. 523.—INTERNAL GENITAL ORGANS OF BULL; DORSAL VIEW.

The right vesicula is sectioned frontally.   The dotted line indicates the backward extension of the peritoneum. 1, Ureter; 2, body of prostate; 3, vesicula seminalis; 4, urethral muscle; 5, bulbo-urethral gland.

FIG. 525.—CROSS-SECTION OF PELVIC URETHRA OF BULL.

1, Prostate gland (pars disseminata); 2, urethra; 3, urethral muscle; 4, aponeurosis. The lumen of the urethra is black and the shaded area around the urethral lumen is the stratum cavernosum.

cm.) in length.   They are commonly unsymmetrical in size and shape.   Short branches are often given off from the chief tube.   The excretory duct opens at the colliculus seminalis, just lateral to the ductus deferens.

The structure of the vesicula is masked by a thick capsule of fibrous tissue and unstriped muscle, which maintains it in its bent condition and also sends trabeculæ between the alveoli. There is a central canal into which the secretion formed in the alveoli passes.   The cavities (central canal and alveoli) are lined with columnar epithelium.   On account of this structure the term glandulæ vesiculares is preferred by some anatomists.

The **prostate** is pale yellow in color, and consists of two parts, which are, however, continuous with each other. The **body** (Corpus prostatæ) is a small mass which stretches across the dorsal surface of the neck of the bladder and the origin of the urethra. It measures about an inch and a half (ca. 3.5 to 4 cm.) transversely, and about half an inch (ca. 1 to 1.5 cm.) in width and thickness. The **pars disseminata** surrounds the pelvic part of the urethra; dorsally it forms a layer about half an inch (ca. 10 to 12 mm.) thick, but ventrally it is quite thin (ca. 2 mm.). It is concealed by the urethral muscle and its aponeurosis; hence it often escapes notice, but is very evident on cross-section (Fig. 525). It has a branched tubular structure, and the interlobular tissue contains a large amount of unstriped muscle. The **prostatic ducts** open into the urethra in rows, two of which are between two folds of the mucous membrane that proceed backward from the colliculus seminalis; two other series occur on either side, lateral to the folds.

The **uterus masculinus** appears to be absent usually. Ellenberger states that it opens between the ejaculatory orifices, while Martin says that it usually has two orifices at the colliculus, but that it often unites with the ductus deferens.

The **bulbo-urethral glands** are somewhat smaller than in the stallion. They are liable to escape notice, since they are covered by a thick layer of dense fibrous tissue and also partially by the bulbo-cavernosus muscle. Each has a single duct which opens into the urethra under cover of a fold of the mucous membrane. This forms a blind pouch one-half inch deep, on the wall of the urethra.

The **penis** is cylindrical, and is longer and of very much smaller diameter than in the horse. Just behind the scrotum it forms an S-shaped curve, the **sigmoid flexure**; thus about one foot of the penis is folded up when it is fully retracted. The flexure is effaced during erection. The **glans penis** is about three inches (ca. 8 cm.) in length. It is flattened dorso-ventrally, and its extremity is pointed and twisted. The **external urethral orifice** is situated at the end of a groove formed by this twist; it is only large enough to admit a probe of medium size. Even in the non-erect state the penis is remarkably dense and firm. The **tunica albuginea** is very thick, and encloses the urethra; it is composed of dense white fibrous tissue. In the first part, as far as the first curve, there is a thick median **septum penis.** Beyond this there is a central axial band of dense fibrous tissue from which numerous strong trabeculæ radiate. The erectile tissue is small in amount, except in the root, so that the organ undergoes very little enlargement in erection, the chief effect being increased rigidity. The walls of the cavernous spaces are fibro-elastic, not muscular.

The length of the penis in the adult is about three feet (ca. 90 cm.). The crura are flattened laterally; they contain a well-developed corpus cavernosum and numerous helicine arteries, some of which open directly into the cavernous spaces. The suspensory ligaments are attached to the ventral ridge on the symphysis pelvis. The body is somewhat flattened dorso-ventrally beyond the first curve. The extremity of the glans is unsymmetrical, the urethral orifice being situated ventro-laterally. The glans contains only a thin superficial stratum of erectile tissue, and hence undergoes little enlargement in erection. In the body of the penis there is a longitudinal vein on either side in the ventral part of the corpus cavernosum.

The **bulbo-cavernosus muscle** presents several remarkable features. It is for the greater part an inch or more (ca. 3 cm.) in thickness, but its length is only six to eight inches (15 to 20 cm.). It is covered by a strong aponeurosis, and is divided by a median raphé into two lateral halves, except at its origin. It diminishes in size from behind forward, and its anterior extremity is pointed.[1]

The **ischio-cavernosus muscle** resembles in general that of the horse, but is flattened laterally. It is covered by a tight aponeurosis.

The **retractor penis** muscle resembles that of the horse in origin. Its two parts

[1] In the sheep and sometimes in the ox there is a m. ischio-bulbosus which consists of fibers that extend across the initial part of the bulbo-cavernosus. Fibers which extend from the ischial arch over the bulbourethral gland form the m. ischio-glandularis. A urethro-cavernosus muscle is sometimes present; it consists of fibers which arise on the urethra near the origin of the bulbo-cavernosus and end on the latter and the ischio-cavernosus.

are about an inch (ca. 2 to 5 cm.) apart on the root of the penis, where they lie in a groove on either side of the bulbo-cavernosus.   They then come close together and pass on either side of the ventral curve of the sigmoid flexure.   Further forward they are on the ventral surface of the penis, and end about five or six inches (ca. 12 to 15 cm.) behind the glans.

The **prepuce** is very long and narrow.   Its orifice is about two inches (ca. 5 cm.) behind the umbilicus; it is only large enough to admit a finger readily, and is surrounded by long hairs.   The preputial cavity is about fifteen inches (35 to 40 cm.) long and a little over an inch (ca. 3 cm.) in diameter.   The lining membrane forms longitudinal folds; it is covered with squamous stratified epithelium, and has coiled tubular glands.   The penile layer is glandless, and is reddish in color. It presents lymph nodules in its posterior part.

There are two pairs of preputial muscles which are derivatives of the cutaneus muscle.   The **anterior preputial muscles** or **protractors** of the prepuce (Mm. præputiales craniales) are two flat bands, two inches or more (5 to 6 cm.) in width, which arise close together in the xiphoid region, about eight inches (20 cm.) in

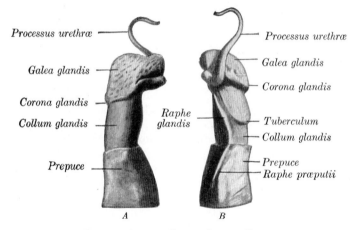

Processus urethræ — — — Processus urethræ

Galea glandis — — Galea glandis

— Corona glandis

Corona glandis —

Collum glandis — — Raphe — — Tuberculum
glandis — Collum glandis

Prepuce — — Prepuce
— Raphe præputii

A   B

FIG. 526.—ANTERIOR PART OF PENIS OF RAM.
A, Right side; B, left side.   (After Böhm.)

front of the preputial orifice.   Traced backward they diverge, leaving the umbilicus and an area about one and a half inches wide free, and then unite behind the preputial orifice.   They draw the prepuce forward.   The **posterior preputial muscles** or **retractors** of the prepuce (Mm. præputiales caudales) arise in the inguinal region and converge on the anterior part of the prepuce.   They draw the prepuce backward.[1]

The **urethra** in its pelvic part is about five inches (12 cm.) long, and is of relatively small and uniform caliber.   The **urethral muscle** encloses the tube ventrally and laterally; it is very thick, crescentic in cross-section, and is covered by an aponeurosis.   Dorsally the aponeurosis is thick and the muscle absent. Inside of these the pars disseminata of the prostate surrounds the urethra as far back as the bulbo-urethral glands.   The **colliculus seminalis** is a rounded prominence about an inch (ca. 2.5 cm.) in length.   On it there are two slit-like openings, situated close together.   These are the ejaculatory orifices, at which the ductus deferens and the excretory duct of the vesicula seminalis open.   The urethral

[1] These muscles are subject to a good deal of variation.   The retractor may be absent.   Many fibers come in from the cutaneus on either side, dip under the protractor, and are inserted into the skin just behind the preputial opening.   The homologue of the protractor is present in the cow.

crest extends forward from the colliculus, and two mucous folds pass backward from it and diverge. The mucous membrane behind the colliculus is red in color. The extrapelvic part has an enlargement, the **bulb,** at its origin; it then gradually diminishes in diameter, and is relatively very small at its termination. Other features have been mentioned in preceding paragraphs.

The bulb of the urethra has a thick tunica albuginea, enclosing a highly developed erectile tissue. The cavernous spaces are wide; their walls are relatively thin and consist of fibrous tissue and unstriped muscle. On cross-section many arteries are visible laterally. Further forward the urethra is surrounded by a well-developed corpus cavernosum, which is thickest ventrally; here an artery of considerable size occurs on each side.

In the **ram** the genital organs resemble in general those of the bull. But the testicles are relatively much larger; a testicle of an adult ram may be four inches (ca. 10 cm.) long and weigh about nine to ten ounces (ca. 250–300 gm.). They are broader in proportion to their length. The prostate is entirely disseminate. The bulbo-urethral glands are relatively very large. The peculiar character of the terminal part of the penis is shown in the annexed figure. The urethra lies in a groove on the ventral surface of the corpus cavernosum. Its terminal part projects commonly about an inch and a half (ca. 3–4 cm.) beyond the glans penis, forming a twisted processus urethræ.

GENITAL ORGANS OF THE BOAR

The **scrotum** is situated a short distance from the anus, and is not so sharply defined from the surrounding parts as in the other animals.

The **testicles** are very large and are regularly elliptical in contour. They are placed so that the long axis is directed upward and backward, the free border being superficial and the tail of the epididymis highest. They are comparatively soft in texture. The tunica albuginea contains much elastic tissue, but no muscular fibers. The mediastinum testis is an axial strand of fibro-elastic tissue, from which interlobular septa radiate. Other septa are given off from the deep face of the tunica albuginea. The interlobular tissue is abundant, and the lobulation correspondingly distinct. The parenchyma is gray and often dark in fat animals. There is a rete testis from which seven or eight efferent ducts proceed to the epididymis. The epididymis is closely attached to the testicle; its tail is very large and forms a blunt conical projection at the posterior end of the testicle.

The **spermatic cord** is necessarily very long (20 to 25 cm. in a boar of medium size). The **ductus deferens** in its testicular part is flexuous, and is closely attached by the tunica vaginalis; it forms no distinct ampulla. The **cremaster externus** is well developed, and extends to about the middle of the scrotal part of the tunic.

The **vesiculæ seminales** are exceedingly large, and extend into the abdominal cavity. They are three-sided pyramidal masses, are in apposition with each other medially, and cover the posterior part of the bladder and the ureters, the ductus deferentes, the body of the prostate, and the anterior part of the urethra and bulbo-urethral glands. They are pale pink in color, distinctly lobate and glandular in structure, and are enclosed in a thin fibrous capsule. Half a dozen or more large, thin-walled ducts emerge from the medial surface of each and converge to a much smaller excretory duct. The latter passes back lateral to the ductus deferens, and terminates at a slit-like opening on the colliculus seminalis. The two ducts may unite.

In the adult boar the vesiculæ are about five to six inches (ca. 12 to 15 cm.) long, two to three inches (ca. 5 to 8 cm.) wide, and one and a half to two inches (ca. 4 to 5 cm.) thick; they weigh about 6 to 8 ounces each. They have a branched tubular structure and are distinctly divided into lobules. Many of the tubules are extremely wide (as much as 2 mm. in diameter), and are beset with bay-like extensions and short, wide branches. These axial spaces of the lobules are succeeded by the efferent ducts. The cavities are lined by a single layer of columnar cells. The secretion is thick and turbid, and has an acid reaction.

The **prostate** consists of two parts, as in the ox. The **body** is about an inch (2.5 cm.) wide, and overlies the neck of the bladder and the urethra at their junction. It is concealed by the vesiculæ seminales. The **pars disseminata** forms a layer which surrounds the pelvic part of the urethra, and is covered by the urethral muscle, except dorsally.

The **uterus masculinus** is small, and appears to be inconstant.

The **bulbo-urethral glands** are very large and dense. They are somewhat cylindrical, and lie on either side of and upon the posterior two-thirds of the pelvic urethra.[1] In a large boar they are about five inches (ca. 12 cm.) in length and an inch or more (ca. 2.5 to 3 cm.) in width. They are partially covered with a layer of striated muscle (M. bulbo-glandularis), and have a lobulated surface. Each gland has a large excretory duct which leaves at the deep face of the posterior part, perforates the dorsal wall of the urethra at the ischial arch, and opens in a cul-de-sac covered by a fold of mucous membrane.

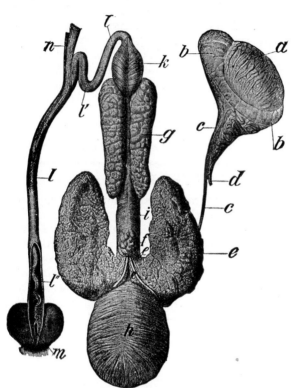

FIG. 527.—GENITAL ORGANS OF BOAR.

a, Testicle; *b*, epididymis; *c*, ductus deferens; *d*, spermatic artery; *e*, vesicula seminalis; *e′*, excretory ducts of vesiculæ; *f*, body of prostate; *g*, bulbo-urethral gland; *h*, urinary bladder; *i*, urethral muscle; *k*, bulbo-cavernosus muscle; *l*, penis; *l′*, sigmoid flexure of penis; *l″*, spiral anterior part of penis, exposed by slitting open prepuce; *m*, orifice of preputial pouch; *n*, retractor penis muscle. The vesiculæ seminales are drawn outward to show the structures which, in the natural position, are covered by them. (Ellenberger-Baum, Anat. d. Haustiere.)

It is to be noted that these accessory glands are very small in animals which have been castrated early; the bulbo-urethral glands may be only about an inch long in such subjects.

The **penis** resembles in general that of the ox. The sigmoid flexure is, however, prescrotal. The anterior part has no glans, and is spirally twisted, especially in erection. The external urethral orifice is slit-like and is situated ventro-laterally, close to the pointed extremity. The penis in the adult boar measures about 18 to 20 inches (ca. 45 to 50 cm.) in length. Its muscles resemble those of the bull. The bulbo-cavernosus is very strong but short. The retractor penis arises from the third and fourth sacral segments; its two parts run backward and a little ventrally on each side of the rectum to the perineum, where they reach the urethral surface of the penis; they end on the ventral curve of the sigmoid flexure of the penis.

---

[1] When hardened *in situ*, they are in great part three sided, with rounded edges. They are in contact with each other to a considerable extent and cover the urethra dorsally and laterally. The urethral muscle partly covers their lateral surfaces.

The **prepuce** has a narrow orifice, around which there are stiff hairs. The cavity is very long, and is partially divided by a circular fold into a posterior narrow part and a much wider anterior part. The lining membrane of the posterior part is papillated, and is in close contact with the penis; it contains numerous lymph nodules, the largest of which occur in the fundus. In the dorsal wall of the wide part there is a circular opening which leads into a cul-de-sac, the **preputial diverticulum.** This pouch is ovoid in form (when distended), and varies greatly in size in different subjects. It extends for the most part backward over the narrow part of the prepuce. Its cavity is partially divided by a narrow septum. It contains usually decomposing urine and macerated epithelium, which have a characteristic and very unpleasant odor. Concrements have been found in it.

Oehmke found that a cast of the pouch in a Yorkshire boar weighing about 500 pounds measured 9 cm. in length, 12½ cm. in breadth, and 6 cm. in height. The opening into the prepuce will admit two fingers in the adult, but is ordinarily closed by folds of the lining membrane. The sac is much smaller in animals which were castrated young, and the opening is vertical and further back; in them it is often empty or contains only a little clear urine. The pouch is glandless, but contains many small lymph nodules; it is covered by a layer of striped muscle which is mainly derived from the homologue of the protractor of the prepuce of ruminants.

The **urethra** has a very long pelvic part (ca. 15 to 20 cm. long in the adult); it is covered (with the pars disseminata of the prostate) by a thick **urethral muscle,** except dorsally, where there is a dense fibrous layer. Surrounding the mucous membrane there is a rich venous plexus, which is regarded as a stratum cavernosum. Outside of this the pars disseminata of the prostate is easily distinguished on cross-section by its yellow color. The prostatic ducts are numerous and small. The ductus deferentes and the excretory ducts of the vesiculæ seminales have slit-like openings close together in small diverticula on either side of the colliculus seminalis. The latter has the form of a round prominence. A small **uterus masculinus** may occur in the colliculus between the ducts, but it is often absent. There is a distinct **bulb** at the root of the penis. It has a dense covering, which in part resembles fibro-cartilage. The erectile tissue here is highly developed. The cavernous spaces are large, and the trabeculæ contain much unstriped muscle; between the spaces there are numerous arteries. The penile part is of small caliber, and is surrounded by erectile tissue which, however, does not extend to the extremity of the penis.

MALE GENITAL ORGANS OF THE DOG

The **scrotum** is situated about half way between the inguinal region and the anus. The skin covering it is pigmented and is covered sparsely with fine hairs. The raphé is not very distinct.

The **testicles** are relatively small, and have a round-oval form. The long axis is oblique, and is directed upward and backward. The mediastinum testis is central and is well developed. The epididymis is large, and is closely attached along the dorsal part of the lateral surface of the testicle.

The **spermatic cord** and the **tunica vaginalis** are long; they cross the side of the penis very obliquely. The upper end of the tunic is sometimes closed, so that there is then no vaginal ring. The **ductus deferentes** have narrow ampullæ.

The **vesiculæ seminales** are absent.

The **prostate** is relatively large; it is yellowish in color, dense in structure, and lies at or near the anterior border of the pubis. It is globular, and surrounds the neck of the bladder and the urethra at their junction. A median furrow indicates a division into two lateral lobes. The capsule and stroma contain a large amount of unstriped muscle. The ducts are numerous. Lobules of prostatic

tissue (pars disseminata) are also found in the wall of the urethra for a short distance
further back.   The gland is subject to much variation in size, and is often enlarged,
especially in old subjects.

The position of the prostate varies.   When the bladder is empty and contracted, the gland
is entirely in the pelvic cavity and may be an inch or more behind the anterior border of the
pubis.   When the bladder is full, the prostate is often largely or entirely prepubic.

The **uterus masculinus** is a small compressed saccule in the colliculus seminalis.
The **bulbo-urethral glands** are absent.[1]

The **penis** presents several special features.   In its posterior part there are two
distinct corpora cavernosa, separated by a median **septum penis.**   In its anterior
part there is a bone, the **os penis,** which in large dogs reaches a length of four inches
(ca. 10 cm.) or more.   It is regarded as a part of the corpus cavernosum which has

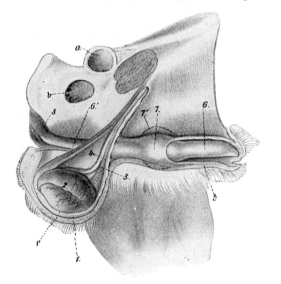

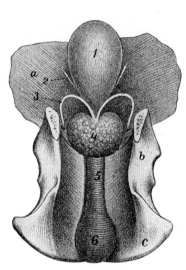

Fig. 528.—External Genital Organs of Male Dog; Ventro-
lateral View of Preparation.

1, Scrotum; *1',* tunica vaginalis; *2,* epididymis; *3,* vascular
part of spermatic cord; *4,* ductus deferens; *5,* prepuce; *6,*'pars longa
glandis; *6',* corpus cavernosum penis; *7,* bulbus glandis; *7',* contour of bulbus in erection; *8,* ischio-cavernosus muscle; *a,* acetabulum; *b,* obturator foramen. (After Ellenberger, in Leisering's
Atlas.)

Fig. 529.—Internal Genital Organs of
Male Dog; Dorsal View.

1, Urinary bladder; *2,* ureter; *3,* ductus
deferens; *4,* prostate; *5,* urethral muscle; *6,*
bulb of urethra; *a,* abdominal wall; *b,* ilium;
c, ischium. (After Ellenberger, in Leisering's
Atlas.)

ossified.   Ventrally it is grooved for the urethra; dorsally it is convex, and anteriorly it becomes smaller and has a curved fibrous prolongation.[2]   The **glans
penis** is very long, extending over the entire length of the os penis; its anterior
part, the **pars longa glandis,** is cylindrical, with a pointed free end; behind this
there is a rounded enlargement, the **bulbus glandis.**   Both are composed of erectile
tissue.   The two dorsal veins arise from the bulbus glandis, pass backward on the
dorsum penis, and unite at the ischial arch.   A small muscle (M. compressor venæ
dorsalis penis) arises from the tuber ischii on either side; the two converge on the
dorsum penis near the bulbus glandis.   They compress the dorsal veins, and may
also tend to elevate the penis and thus assist in copulation.   The other muscles
offer no features worthy of special description.

[1] They are present in the cat, and are the size of a pea.

[2] In the young subject it has a prolongation composed of hyaline cartilage, which becomes
fibrous later.

The cavernous spaces of the glans penis are venous in character. Von Frey has shown that the spaces of the pars longa are continuous with veins which come from the penile layer of the prepuce, and have no arterial blood supply. The erectile tissue of the bulbus glandis receives its blood by veins which come from the pars longa. This arrangement is considered to account for the erection of the bulbus during copulation, and the slowness with which erection subsides.

The **prepuce** forms a complete sheath around the anterior part of the penis. The outer layer is ordinary integument. The inner layers are thin, reddish in color, and glandless. The penile layer is closely attached to the pars longa glandis, more loosely to the bulbus glandis. There are many lymph nodules in these layers, which are specially large and often prominent in the fundus of the preputial cavity. The protractor muscles arise in the xiphoid region and decussate posteriorly around the extremity of the prepuce.

The pelvic part of the **urethra** is relatively long. Its first part is enclosed in the prostate.[1] At the ischial arch the urethra has a well-developed **bulb,** formed by an enlargement here of the corpus cavernosum urethræ. It is divided by a median furrow and septum (Septum bulbi urethræ) into two lateral **lobes** or **hemispheres** (Hemispheria bulbi urethræ), and is covered by the strong but short **bulbocavernosus muscle.** The other erectile bodies have been described. The **urethral muscle** is very strong; it encircles the urethra from the prostate backward and has a median raphé dorsally. The **ischio-urethral muscle** arises from the tuber ischii and ends on a fibrous ring at the symphysis ischii which encircles the dorsal veins of the penis.

[1] This is clinically important, since enlargement of the prostate may interfere with micturition.

THE FEMALE GENITAL ORGANS

The **female genital organs** (Organa genitalia feminina) are: (1) The two **ovaries,** the essential reproductive glands, in which the ova are produced; (2) the **uterine** or **Fallopian tubes,** which convey the ova to the uterus; (3) the **uterus,** in which the ovum develops; (4) the **vagina,** a dilatable passage through which the fœtus is expelled from the uterus; (5) the **vulva,** the terminal segment of the genital tract, which serves also for the expulsion of the urine; (6) the **mammary glands,** which are in reality glands of the skin, but are so closely associated functionally with the generative organs proper that they are usually described with them.

GENITAL ORGANS OF THE MARE

THE OVARIES

The **ovaries** (Ovaria) of the mare are bean-shaped, and are much smaller than the testicles. Their size varies much in different subjects, and they are

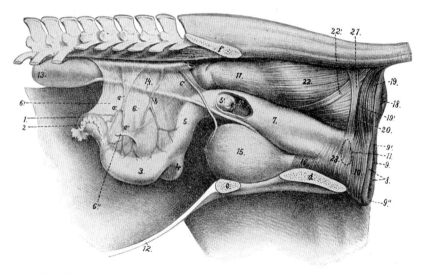

Fig. 530.—Lateral View of Genital Organs and Adjacent Structures of Mare.

It is to be noted that the removal of the other abdominal viscera has allowed the ovaries and uterus to sink down; this has, however, the advantage of showing the broad ligaments of the uterus. *1,* Left ovary; *2,* uterine or Fallopian tube; *3,* left cornu uteri; *4,* right cornu uteri; *5,* corpus uteri; *5',* portio vaginalis uteri, and *5",* os uteri, seen through window cut in vagina; *6,* broad ligament of uterus; *6",* round ligament of uterus; *7,* vagina; *8,* labia vulvæ; *9,* rima vulvæ; *9',* dorsal commissure, and *9",* ventral commissure, of vulva; *10,* constrictor vulvæ; *11,* position of vestibular bulb; *12,* ventral wall of abdomen; *13,* left kidney; *14,* left ureter; *15,* urinary bladder; *16,* urethra; *17,* rectum; *18,* anus; *19, 19',* unpaired and paired parts of sphincter ani externus; *20,* retractor ani cut at disappearance under sphincter ani externus; *21,* suspensory ligament of anus; *22,* longitudinal muscular layer of rectum; *22',* recto-coccygeus; *23,* constrictor vaginæ; *a,* utero-ovarian artery, with ovarian (*a'*) and uterine (*a"*) branches; *b,* uterine artery; *c,* umbilical artery; *d,* ischium; *e,* pubis; *f,* ilium. (After Ellenberger, in Leisering's Atlas.)

normally larger in young than in old animals; one ovary is often larger than the other. They are about three inches (ca. 7 to 8 cm.) long and an inch to an inch and a half (ca. 3–4 cm.) thick. The weight is about two and a half to three ounces (ca. 70–80 grams).

Each presents for description two surfaces, two borders, and two extremities. The **surfaces** are termed **medial** and **lateral** (Facies medialis, lateralis); they are both smooth and rounded.[1] The **attached** or **mesovarial border** (Margo mesovaricus) is convex. It is enclosed in a part of the broad ligament termed the mesovarium; the vessels and nerves reach the gland at this border. The **free border** (Margo liber) is marked by a notch which leads into a narrow depression, the **ovulation fossa.** The **tubal** or anterior **extremity** (Extremitas tubaria) is rounded, and is related to the fimbriated end of the uterine tube. The **uterine** or posterior **extremity** (Extremitas uterina) is also round, and is connected with the horn of the uterus by the ovarian ligament.

The ovaries are situated in the sublumbar region, and are usually ventral to the fourth or fifth lumbar vertebra. They are usually in contact with the lumbar wall of the abdomen. The average distance from the ovaries to the vulvar orifice is about twenty to twenty-two inches (ca. 50–55 cm.) in a mare of medium size.

The position of the ovaries is very inconstant, as might be expected from their mode of attachment. Either ovary or both may be deflected transversely in either direction to the full limit allowed by the mesovarium. The so-called medial and lateral surfaces are usually dorsal and ventral, or vice versâ, according to the direction of the deflection. The range of variation in the longitudinal direction is greater than was formerly thought to be the case. The right ovary is often about six inches (ca. 15 cm.) behind the corresponding kidney, but the distance between them may be nearly twice as great or may be only about two inches (ca. 5 cm.). The left ovary is usually a little (ca. 2–3 cm.) further back than the right one, but is usually nearer the corresponding kidney, the average distance between them being about four inches (ca. 10 cm.). They may be about two inches (ca. 5 cm.) from the extremity of the corresponding cornu of the uterus or in contact with it. Except during pregnancy, they are almost always in contact with the lumbar abdominal wall, and do not hang down among the adjacent viscera.

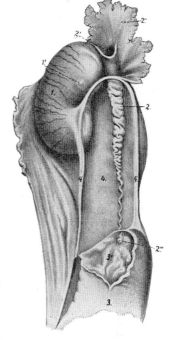

Fig. 531.—Right Ovary of Mare, with Adjacent Structures.

The extremity of the cornu is opened. *1*, Ovary; *1'*, corpus luteum; *2*, uterine or Fallopian tube, with its ostium abdominale (*2'*), fimbriæ (*2''*), and ostium uterinum (*2'''*); *3*, cornu uteri with its mucous lining (*3'*) exposed; *4*, ligament of ovary; *4'*, mesosalpinx. (After Ellenberger, in Leisering's Atlas, reduced.)

The ovary is attached to the sublumbar region by the anterior part of the broad ligament of the uterus; this part of the ligament, the **mesovarium**, is about three or four inches (ca. 8 to 10 cm.) wide, measured from the ovary directly to the parietal attachment. The uterine extremity of the ovary is connected with the extremity of the cornu of the uterus by the **ligament of the ovary** (Lig. ovarii proprium); this is a band of unstriped muscle enclosed between the layers of the broad ligament.

Structure.—The greater part of the surface of the ovary has a covering of peritoneum. The peritoneal investment is absent at the attached border where the vessels and nerves enter; this area is termed the **hilus** of the ovary (Hilus ovarii), although there is no depression here. The ovulation fossa is covered by a layer of short polygonal cells, a remnant of the primitive germinal epithelium.

---

[1] These terms apply properly only when the adjacent viscera are removed and the ovaries are actually "suspended" by the broad ligaments. When the ovary is in its natural position, the surfaces are usually dorsal and ventral, the former corresponding to the "lateral" surface if the free border is directed outward, to the "medial" if the free edge is medial.

The **stroma** of the ovary (Stroma ovarii) is a network of connective tissue. In the meshes of the stroma there are (in young subjects) numerous **ovisacs** or **folliculi oöphori,** containing **ova** (Ovula) in various stages of development. The immature ovum is surrounded by follicle cells; those more advanced in development are enclosed by several (5–8) layers of follicle cells, forming the **stratum granulosum,** and by a condensation of the stroma termed the **theca folliculi;** within the theca is a quantity of fluid, the **liquor folliculi.** At one point the follicle cells are heaped up as a sort of mound (Cumulus oöphorus), in which the ovum is enclosed. Such sacs are termed folliculi oöphori vesiculosi;[1] they enlarge as they mature, becoming visible to the naked eye as vesicles with a diameter of a centimeter or more. When fully developed the follicles are superficially situated and often project slightly from the surface of the ovary. At intervals follicles rupture and their contents escape. This process, which sets free the ovum, is termed **ovulation;** it takes place in the mare only at the ovulation fossa, and occurs during the periods of œstrum.

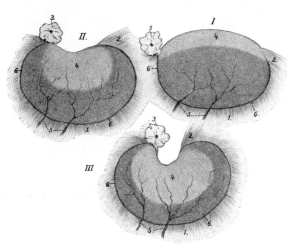

FIG. 532.—SCHEMATIC REPRESENTATION OF CHANGES IN OVARY OF MARE FROM FŒTAL TO ADULT STATE. (After Born.)

The changes affect chiefly the free border (upper in figure) and the extent and form of the area covered by germinal epithelium (*4*). *1*, Peritoneum (broad ligament); *2*, ligament of ovary; *3*, fimbria of uterine tube; *4*, germinal epithelium; *5*, vessels, which reach the ovary at the attached border (*6*). The latter represents the hilus, while the deep depression at the free border is the ovulation fossa. (Ellenberger, in Leisering's Atlas.)

The structure of the ovary of the mare is peculiar and differs from that of other animals in the fact that it does not consist of a cortex (zona parenchymatosa), in which the follicles are situated, and a medulla (zona vasculosa), which contains the vessels and nerves. This arrangement is present in the fœtus, but later the follicles become distributed throughout the interior of the gland, and the vascular zone is superficial.

After rupture of a follicle, its cavity is partly occupied by a blood-clot, constituting what may be termed a **corpus rubrum.** By proliferation and enlargement and fatty changes, the follicle cells are transformed into lutein cells, forming a yellow mass known as a **corpus luteum.** If impregnation takes place, the accompanying increase in vascularity of the organs may cause the corpus luteum to reach a large size; if impregnation does not occur, it is much smaller, and is sooner replaced by scar tissue, forming the **corpus albicans s. fibrosum.**

It should be noted that in the mare corpora lutea do not project from the surface of the ovary as is the case in the cow and pig, but are embedded in the ovary.

In the new-born foal the ovaries are large and oval in form. The free border is convex and is covered by germinal epithelium, which extends over a large part of the surfaces also. This area is distinguishable by its dull gray appearance from the peritoneal surface, which has the usual smooth glistening character. The limit of the peritoneal epithelium is a distinct line, termed by Waldeyer the margo limitans peritonæi. As growth proceeds the ovary gradually becomes bent until it assumes its definitive curved shape. The germinal epithelium is then limited to the ovulation fossa. The ovary migrates somewhat during development from its primitive position, which is the same as that of the testicle.

In old animals the ovaries commonly consist largely of fibrous tissue, in which there are often cysts of various sizes. The ova, present in enormous number at birth, have then been extruded, or destroyed by phagocytic action or degeneration.

Vessels and Nerves.—The **arteries** of the ovary are derived from the ovarian artery. The artery is relatively large and is flexuous; it reaches the attached border of the ovary by passing between the layers of the mesovarium. The **veins** are large and numerous. They form a plexus somewhat like that of the spermatic

---

[1] Also known as Graafian follicles.

cord. The **lymph vessels** pass to the lumbar glands. The **nerves** are derived from the sympathetic system through the renal and aortic plexuses. They accompany the arterial branches.

THE UTERINE TUBES

The **uterine** or **Fallopian tubes** (Tubæ uterinæ) act as excretory ducts of the ovaries, since they convey the ova from the reproductive glands to the uterus. They are not, however, in direct continuity with the glands, but rather partly in contiguity with, and partly attached to, them.[1] They are two flexuous tubes, eight to twelve inches (ca. 20 to 30 cm.) long, which extend from the extremities of the uterine cornua to the ovaries. The tube is very small at its uterine end (ca. 2–3 mm. in diameter), but toward the ovary it widens considerably (4–8 mm. in diameter), forming the ampulla tubæ. Each is enclosed in a peritoneal fold, derived from the lateral layer of the broad ligament, and termed the **mesosalpinx.** This largely covers the lateral aspect of the ovary, and forms with it and the broad ligament a pouch called the **bursa ovarica.** The **uterine extremity** (Extremitas uterina) of the tube communicates with the cavity of the cornu by a minute orifice, the **ostium uterinum tubæ.** The **ovarian extremity** is expanded and somewhat funnel shaped, and is therefore termed the **infundibulum tubæ uterinæ.** The margin of the latter is slit into irregular processes, the **fimbriæ,** some of which, the **fimbriæ ovaricæ,** are attached in the ovulation fossa. About the middle of the infundibulum is a small opening, the **ostium abdominale tubæ,** by which the tube communicates with the peritoneal cavity. The ovarian extremity of the tube appears normally to be applied to the ovary, so that the extruded ova pass into it and are conveyed to the uterus.[2]

Pedunculated cysts, the **hydatides terminales,**[3] are often found on one or more of the fimbriæ. In the mesosalpinx are blind flexuous tubules, which constitute the **paroöphoron,** a remnant of the Wolffian body. They are most evident in the young adult, and tend to disappear with increasing age. Not uncommonly they give rise to cysts.

Structure.—The tube is covered externally by a **serous coat** formed by the mesosalpinx. The serous membrane is continued on the fimbriæ, and meets the mucous lining on them. The fibrous **adventitia** is continuous with the fibrous lamina of the broad ligament. The **muscular coat** consists chiefly of circular fibers, outside of which there are longitudinal fibers derived from the broad ligament; the thickness of the muscular coat diminishes toward the ovarian extremity. The **mucous coat** is thin and is much plicated. The folds (Plicæ tubariæ) are chiefly longitudinal, but in the wide part of the tube (Ampullæ tubæ) they are very complex, so that on cross-sections the spaces between the folds may be mistaken for branched tubular glands. The folds are continued on to the fimbriæ. The epithelium is a single layer of columnar ciliated cells, the cilia producing a current directed toward the uterus. At the ovarian extremity this epithelium passes gradually into the squamous type of the serous coat.

Vessels and Nerves.—The **arteries** are derived from the utero-ovarian artery. The **veins** are satellites of the arteries. The **lymph vessels** pass with the ovarian vessels to the lumbar glands. The **nerves** have a similar origin to those of the ovary.

THE UTERUS

The **uterus** is a hollow muscular organ, which is continuous with the uterine tubes anteriorly and opens into the vagina posteriorly. It is situated chiefly in the

---

[1] The tubes may be regarded, both in origin and structure, as prolongations of the uterus.

[2] The arrangement is the only exception to the general rule that the serous cavities are closed. In this case the mucous membrane of the infundibulum is continuous with the adjacent peritoneum, a persistence of the embryonic relations of the Müllerian duct.

[3] Also known as hydatids of Morgagni.

abdominal cavity, but extends a short distance into the pelvic cavity. It is attached to the sublumbar region and the lateral walls of the pelvic cavity by two folds of peritoneum termed the broad ligaments. It consists of two horns, the body, and the neck.

The **horns** or **cornua** of the uterus (Cornua uteri) are situated entirely in the abdomen. They appear to vary considerably in position; commonly they are pressed up against the sublumbar muscles by the intestine (cæcum, left parts of

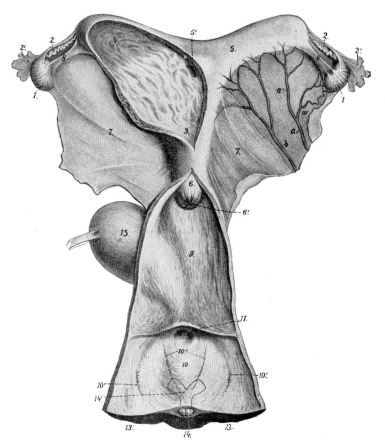

FIG. 533.—GENITAL ORGANS OF MARE; DORSAL VIEW

The left horn and adjacent part of the body of the uterus and the vagina and vulva are opened up. *1*, Ovary; *2*, uterine tube, with *2′*, its ovarian end; *3*, cavity of body of uterus; *4*, cavity of left horn; *5*, right horn, with *5′*, its communication with the body; *6*, portio vaginalis uteri; *6′*, external orifice of uterus; *7*, broad ligament of uterus; *8*, ligament of ovary; *9*, vagina; *10*, vulva; *10′*, orifices of ducts of glandulæ vestibulares majores; *10″*, orifices of ducts of glandulæ vestibulares minores; *11*, transverse fold; *12*, external urethral opening; *13, 13′*, labia vulvæ; *14*, glans clitoridis; *14′*, junction of crura to form corpus clitoridis indicated by dotted lines; *15*, urinary bladder; *a*, utero-ovarian artery with ovarian (*a′*) and uterine (*a″*) branches; *b*, middle uterine artery. (After Ellenberger, in Leisering's Atlas.)

large colon, small colon, and small intestine). They are cylindrical when moderately distended, and are about ten inches (ca. 25 cm.) in length. The anterior extremity of each forms a blunt point which receives the uterine tube. Posteriorly they increase somewhat in caliber, converge, and unite with the body. The **dorsal border** (Margo mesometricus) is slightly concave and is attached to the sublumbar region by the broad ligament. The **ventral border** (Margo liber) is convex and free.

When a soft uterus is distended, its horns are strongly curved, but this does not represent the natural form. When fixed *in situ*, the horns are either slightly curved or nearly straight.

The two horns are commonly unsymmetrical in length and diameter in mares which have borne young.

The **body** of the uterus (Corpus uteri) is situated partly in the abdominal, partly in the pelvic cavity. It is cylindrical, but considerably flattened dorso-ventrally, so that in cross-section it is elliptical. Its average length is seven or eight inches (ca. 18–20 cm.), and its diameter, when moderately distended, about four inches (10 cm.). Its **dorsal surface** (Facies dorsalis) is related to the rectum and other parts of the intestine. Its **ventral surface** (Facies ventralis) is in contact with the bladder, and has inconstant relations with various parts of the intestine. The term **fundus uteri** is applied to the wide anterior part from which the cornua diverge.

The position of the body of the uterus is variable, especially in regard to its anterior part. It is often pressed up against the rectum, and may be deflected to either side—most frequently to the left—by the pelvic flexure of the great colon or coils of the small colon.

The **neck** or **cervix** of the uterus (Cervix uteri) is the constricted posterior part which joins the vagina. It is about two to three inches (5–7.5 cm.) in length, and an inch and a half (3.5–4 cm.) in diameter. Part of it (Portio vaginalis uteri) projects into the cavity of the vagina; it is therefore not visible externally, but may be felt through the vaginal wall.

Attachments.—The body and horns are attached to the abdominal and pelvic walls by two extensive peritoneal folds, the **broad ligaments of the uterus** (Ligamenta lata uteri). These extend on either side from the sublumbar region and the lateral pelvic walls to the dorsal border of the cornua and the lateral margins of the body of the uterus. They contain the vessels and nerves of the uterus and ovaries, connective tissue, and a large amount of unstriped muscular fibers which are continuous with those of the uterus. The ureters are situated along their parietal margins. The lateral layer of each gives off a fold, the **round ligament of the uterus** (Ligamentum teres uteri), which blends with the parietal peritoneum over the abdominal inguinal ring; its anterior extremity is situated above the extremity of the cornu and forms a long round appendix. It contains muscular tissue, vessels, and nerves, and is the homologue of the gubernaculum testis. The anterior part of the neck is continuous with the vagina, and thus has a more fixed position than the rest of the organ.

The **cavity** of the uterus (Cavum uteri) is largely obliterated in the non-pregnant state by the contraction of the wall and by folds of the mucous lining. At the extremity of each cornu it communicates with the uterine tube by a minute opening on a small papilla. The cavity of the neck is termed the **cervical canal** (Canalis cervicis); it is closed ordinarily by mucous folds and a plug of mucus. It opens into the vagina by the **orificium externum uteri,**[1] and into the body by the **orificium internum uteri.**

Structure.—The wall of the uterus consists of three coats. The **serous coat** (Perimetrium) is, for the most part, closely adherent to the muscular coat. It is continuous with the broad ligaments. The **muscular coat** consists essentially of two layers, a thin external stratum of longitudinal fibers, and a thick internal layer of circular fibers. Between these is a very vascular layer (Stratum vasculare) of connective tissue with circular and oblique muscular fibers in it. The circular coat is very thick in the neck, where it forms a sphincter half an inch or more (ca. 1.5 cm.) in thickness. The **mucous membrane** rests directly on the muscular coat, and is brownish-red in color, except in the neck, where it is pale. It is covered by a single layer of high columnar cells, and contains numerous long, branched tubular **uterine glands** (Glandulæ uterinæ); these are absent in the cervix.

Vessels and Nerves.—The chief **arteries** are the uterine and the uterine branch of the utero-ovarian, which have a flexuous course in the broad ligaments;

[1] This is frequently designated the os uteri.

there is also a branch from the internal pudic artery.   The **veins** form pampiniform plexuses and accompany the arteries.   The **lymph vessels** are numerous and
go to the internal iliac and lumbar glands.   The **nerves** are derived from the
sympathetic through the uterine and pelvic plexuses.

The foregoing statements refer to the non-gravid uterus.   In the pregnant state it undergoes important changes in size, position, and structure.   The increase in size affects chiefly the
gravid horn (except in the case of twins) and the body.   The horn attains a length of about
two and a half to three feet (ca. 80 to 90 cm.), and a corresponding diameter; in this process it
extends much beyond the ovary and the broad ligament.   The gravid uterus is entirely abdominal
in position, and extends along the ventral wall, chiefly to the left of the median plane.   It weighs
about nine pounds (ca. 4 kg.), according to Ellenberger.   The broad ligaments increase greatly
in size and contain more muscular tissue.   The vessels are greatly enlarged and form new branches.
The muscular coat, in spite of the increase in size and number of the fibers, is somewhat thinner,
except in the neck.   The mucous membrane is thicker and more vascular.

THE VAGINA

The **vagina** is the passage which extends horizontally through the pelvic
cavity from the neck of the uterus to the vulva.   It is tubular, is about six to eight
inches (ca. 15–20 cm.) in length, and, when slightly distended, about four or five
inches (ca. 10–12 cm.) in diameter.   Its dilatability appears to be limited only by
the pelvic wall.   There is no external line of demarcation between the vagina
and the uterus or the vulva.

It is related dorsally to the rectum, ventrally to the bladder and urethra, and
laterally to the pelvic wall.   The recto-genital pouch of the peritoneum commonly
extends between the vagina and rectum for a distance of about two inches (5 cm.),
and ventrally the vesico-genital pouch passes backward somewhat further between
the vagina and bladder.   Thus most of the vagina is retroperitoneal and is surrounded by a quantity of loose connective tissue, a venous plexus, and a variable
amount of fat.[1]

Structure.—With the exception of the short peritoneal part, as indicated above,
the proper wall of the vagina is composed of muscular and mucous coats.   The
muscular coat is composed of a thin layer of longitudinal fibers, and a thicker layer
of circular fibers; it is covered externally by a fibrous adventitia, and there is a
large amount of intermuscular connective tissue.   The **mucous coat** is highly
elastic, and is covered with a stratified—but not squamous—epithelium.   It has
no glands.

Under usual conditions the cavity is practically obliterated by apposition of
the walls, so that the lumen is a transverse slit; this condition is pronounced when
the rectum is full.   The anterior end of the vagina is largely occupied by the intravaginal part of the neck of the uterus, so that the cavity is here reduced to an annular recess termed the **fornix vaginæ.**   The posterior part is directly continuous
with the vulva without any line of demarcation except the transverse fold which
covers the external urethral orifice; in very young subjects this fold is continued
on either side, forming the **hymen,** which narrows the entrance to the vagina (In-
troitus vaginæ).[2]

Vessels and Nerves.—The **arteries** are branches of the internal pudic arteries.
The **veins** form a rich plexus which is drained by the internal pudic veins.   The
lymph vessels go to the internal iliac lymph glands.   The **nerves** are derived from
the sympathetic through the pelvic plexus; numerous ganglia are present in the
adventitia.

[1] The amount of the vagina which is covered by peritoneum varies, depending apparently
on the degree of fullness of the rectum and bladder.   When these organs are empty, the peritoneum
may cover the vagina for a distance of three or four inches (ca. 8–10 cm.); when they are full, the
vagina may be completely retroperitoneal or nearly so.

[2] In formalin-hardened subjects there is frequently a pronounced ring-like constriction at the
junction of the vulva and vagina.

THE VULVA

The **vulva** or **urogenital sinus** (Vestibulum vaginæ) is the terminal part of the genital tract.[1] It is continuous in front with the vagina, and opens externally at the vulvar cleft two or three inches (ca. 5–7 cm.) below the anus. There is no external line of demarcation between the vagina and vulva. The tube is four or five inches (ca. 10–12 cm.) in length, measured from the external urethral orifice to the ventral commissure; dorsally (from a point vertically opposite to the external urethral orifice) it is considerably shorter. It is related dorsally to the rectum and anus, ventrally to the pelvic floor, and laterally to the sacro-sciatic ligament, the semimembranosus muscle, and the internal pudic artery. The external orifice, the **vulvar cleft** (Rima vulvæ), has the form of a vertical slit, five or six inches (ca. 12.5–15 cm.) high, and is margined by two prominent rounded lips, the **labia vulvæ.** The labia meet above at an acute angle, forming the **dorsal commissure** (Commissura dorsalis), which is two inches (ca. 5 cm.) below the anus. They unite below to form the thick, rounded **ventral commissure** (Commissura ventralis), which lies about two inches (ca. 5 cm.) behind and below the ischial arch. When the labia are drawn apart, a rounded body, about an inch (ca. 2.5 cm.) wide, is seen occupying a cavity in the ventral commissure; this is the **glans clitoridis,** the homologue of the glans penis, and the cavity in which it lies is the **fossa clitoridis.** The roof of the fossa is formed by a thin fold (Frenulum clitoridis), which overlies the glans clitoridis and is attached centrally to it. At the anterior extremity of the ventral wall of the vulva, i. e., four or five inches (ca. 10–12 cm.) from the ventral commissure, is the **external urethral orifice** (Orificium urethræ externum).[2] It readily admits the finger and is very dilatable. It is covered by a fold of mucous membrane, the free edge of which is directed backward (Fig. 533).

Structure.—The labia are covered by thin, pigmented, smooth skin, which is richly supplied with sebaceous and sweat glands. This is continuous at a distance of about half an inch (ca. 1–1.5 cm.) from the free edge with a thin, glandless mucous membrane. Under the skin there is a layer of striped muscle, the **constrictor vulvæ;** this fuses above with the sphincter ani, and embraces the clitoris below, spreading out laterally at the ventral commissure. It constricts the vulvar orifice and elevates the clitoris. The **constrictor vestibuli** muscle embraces the vulva in front of the preceding; it is deficient dorsally and is joined on either side by a band of unstriped muscle, the suspensory ligament of the anus. It constricts the vulva. Within this there is an unstriped muscular coat, most of the bundles of which are circular. Chiefly between this coat and the mucous membrane there is in the lateral wall, just in front of the labia, a flattened, oval body, the **bulbus vestibuli** (Fig. 578); this is an erectile structure, homologous with the corpus cavernosum urethræ of the male. It is about two and a half to three inches (ca. 6–8 cm.) long, and an inch or more (ca. 3 cm.) wide. It is similar in structure to the bulb of the corpus cavernosum urethræ of the male, and is supplied with blood by a large branch of the internal pudic artery. The **mucous membrane** of the vulva is reddish in color, and forms longitudinal and transverse folds. It presents ventrally two linear series of small papillæ which converge toward the ventral commissure; these mark the orifices of the ducts of the **glandulæ vestibulares minores.** On either side of the dorsal wall is a group of eight to ten larger prominences on which the ducts of the **glandulæ vestibulares majores** open (Fig. 533).

Quite exceptionally there may be found on either side of the urethral orifice the openings of the canals of Gartner (Ductus epoöphori longitudinales).

[1] The term vulva is used here in the sense in which it is understood generally by English and French veterinarians. In the German works it is applied only to the labia and other structures around the external orifice of the urogenital sinus, while the sinus itself is termed the vestibule of the vagina (Vestibulum vaginæ).

[2] Also termed the meatus urinarius.

The **clitoris** is the homologue of the penis and consists of similar parts (minus the urethra and its muscle). The **corpus clitoridis** is about two inches (ca. 5 cm.) long, and its diameter about that of one's little finger. It is attached to the ischial arch by two **crura** (Crura clitoridis). The **glans clitoridis** is the rounded and enlarged free end of the organ which was noted above as occupying the fossa clitoridis in the ventral commissure of the vulva. It is covered by a thin pigmented integument, similar to and continuous with that which lines the fossa; these constitute the **prepuce of the clitoris** (Præputium clitoridis). The organ is composed of erectile tissue similar to the corpus cavernosum penis. The **ischio-cavernosus** is the homologue of the muscle of the same name of the male; it is a very feeble muscle. The veins of the clitoris communicate by an intermediate plexus on either side with the bulbus vestibuli.

THE FEMALE URETHRA

The female **urethra** (Urethra feminina) represents only that part of the canal of the male which lies between the internal urethral orifice and the colliculus seminalis. Its length is two to three inches (5–7.5 cm.), and its lumen is sufficient to allow easily the introduction of the finger; it is, however, capable of remarkable dilatation if sufficient care and patience are exercised in the process. It lies centrally on the pelvic floor, and is related dorsally to the vagina, to which it is in part attached. The external orifice is at the anterior end of the vulva, as described above.

Structure.—The intrinsic **muscular coat** consists of external longitudinal and internal circular fibers; it is absent where the urethra is attached to the vagina. The **mucous membrane** is thrown into longitudinal folds when the canal is closed; it is highly elastic, and is covered with stratified epithelium. There is a rich submucous network of veins, forming a sort of corpus cavernosum.

The **urethral muscle** (M. compressor urethræ) embraces the urethra and is continuous with the constrictor vestibuli. It is covered by a fibro-elastic membrane.

THE MAMMARY GLANDS

The **mammary glands** (Glandulæ lactiferæ) are modified cutaneous glands which are so closely associated functionally with the genital organs as to be considered accessory to them.

In the mare they are two in number, and are placed on either side of the median plane in the prepubic region. Each gland has the form of a very short, flattened cone, much compressed transversely, and having a flat medial surface. It consists of the glandular mass or **body** of the gland (Corpus mammæ) and the **papilla or teat** (Papilla mammæ). The base is related to the abdominal wall, to which it is attached by areolar tissue, which contains a venous plexus, the superficial inguinal lymph glands, and a variable amount of fat. The apex is constituted by the teat, which is also flattened transversely and varies in length from one to two inches (ca. 2.5 to 5 cm.). Between the bases of the teats is the intermammary groove. On the apex of each teat there are usually two small orifices placed close together; these are the openings of the lactiferous ducts.

Structure.—The **skin** covering the glands is thin, pigmented, chiefly hairless, and supplied with numerous large sebaceous and sweat glands. Under this are two layers of **fascia,** except on the teats. The superficial fascia presents no special features. The deep fascia consists of elastic tissue; centrally two laminæ detached from the abdominal tunic descend on either side of the median plane, forming a **septum** between the two glands, and constituting their ligamentum suspensorium.[1]

The **gland substance** or **parenchyma** is pinkish gray in color, and of firmer

---

[1] These laminæ are separated almost completely by a layer of areolar tissue, so that it is possible to remove a diseased gland by careful dissection between the layers of the septum.

consistence than the fat which is found around and within the gland. It is enclosed by a fibro-elastic capsule which sends inward numerous trabeculæ; these form the **interstitial tissue,** and divide the gland into **lobes** and **lobules.** In the latter are the secretory **tubules** and **alveoli,** which unite to form the larger **ducts.** Each lobe has a duct, which opens at the base of the teat into a space called the **lactiferous sinus** (Sinus lactiferus), and from this two (or three) **lactiferous ducts** (Ductus lactiferi) pass through the extremity of the teat. These ducts are lined with a non-glandular mucous membrane, which is covered with stratified squamous epithelium. They are surrounded by unstriped muscular tissue, the bulk of the fibers being arranged in a circular manner to form a **sphincter.**

The size and form of the mammary glands are subject to much variation. In the young subject, before pregnancy, they are small and contain little gland tissue. During the latter part of gestation, and especially during lactation, they increase greatly in size, and the gland tissue is highly developed. After lactation the secretory structures undergo marked involution, and the gland is much reduced in size. The relative amounts of gland substance and interstitial tissue vary greatly; in some cases a gland of considerable size contains little parenchyma and is consequently functionally deficient.

Vessels and Nerves.—The **arteries** are derived from the external pudic artery, which enters the gland at the posterior part of its base. The **veins** form a plexus on either side of the base of the gland, which is drained by the external pudic vein chiefly. The **lymph vessels** are numerous and pass to the superficial inguinal and lumbar lymph glands. The **nerves** are derived from the inguinal nerves and the posterior mesenteric plexus of the sympathetic system.

GENITAL ORGANS OF THE COW

The **ovaries** of the cow are much smaller than those of the mare; they measure usually about one and a half inches (ca. 3.5–4 cm.) in length, an inch (ca. 2.5 cm.) in width and a little more than half an inch (ca. 1.5 cm.) thick in their largest part; the weight is half an ounce or more (ca. 15–20 gm.).[1] They are oval in form, pointed at the uterine end, and have no ovulation fossa. They are situated usually near the middle of the lateral margin of the pelvic inlet in front of the external iliac artery in the non-pregnant subject, but may be further forward, es-

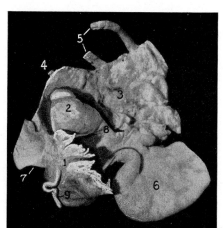

FIG. 534.—LEFT OVARY AND ADJACENT STRUCTURES FROM A PREGNANT COW.

The ovary is turned dorsally from beneath fimbriæ ovaricæ.

1, Fimbria; *2*, ovary (above *2*, a corpus luteum); *3*, broad ligament of uterus; *4*, ovarian artery; *5*, branches of anterior uterine artery; *6*, cornu uteri; *7*, anterior free border of broad ligament; *8*, ligament of ovary; *9*, uterine or Fallopian tube. The ostium abdominale tubæ is on the opposite surface of fimbria from the figure *1*. The uterine tube winds around pouch-like development in free border of the broad ligament.

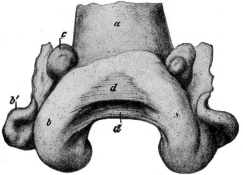

FIG. 535.—UTERUS OF COW, CONTRACTED; DORSAL VIEW.

a, Body of uterus; *b, b',* horn of uterus; *c,* ovary; *d, d,* triangular folds connecting horns of uterus (Ligg. intercornualia). (After Zieger.)

[1] Hess gives the following average measurements of the ovaries of 95 cows: Length of right, 4.3 cm.; of left, 3.71 cm.; width of right, 2.8 cm.; of left, 2.36 cm. Zieger found that the right one was larger than the left in 65 out of 75 cases.

pecially in cows which have been pregnant. They are thus about 16 to 18 inches (ca. 40–45 cm.) from the vulvar opening in a cow of medium size. The greater part of the surface of the gland is covered with germinal epithelium, the peritoneal epithelium being limited to a narrow zone along the attached border. Follicles of various sizes are often seen projecting from the surface, as well as corpora lutea; a corpus luteum of pregnancy has a pronounced yellow color, and may reach a width of half an inch or more (ca. 1–1.5 cm.). It should be noted that in many cases only a small part of the corpus luteum shows on the surface of the ovary, the bulk of it being concealed in the interior of the latter. The size of the ovary is affected by the corpus luteum.

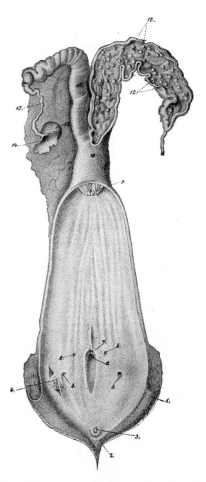

The **uterine** or **Fallopian tubes** are long (ca. 20–25 cm.) and less flexuous than in the mare. They follow a course over a pouch, formed by a folding over of the free edge of the broad ligament, which envelops the ovary. The fimbria is attached to the free margin of this pouch (Fig. 534). The junction with the cornu of the uterus is not so abrupt as in the mare, since the extremities of the horns are pointed. The uterine ori-

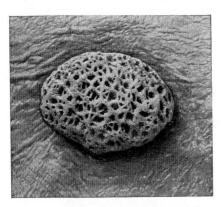

FIG. 536.—COTYLEDON OF GRAVID UTERUS OF COW.

The photograph is about three-fourths natural size of a specimen of medium size.

FIG. 537.—GENITAL ORGANS OF COW; DORSAL VIEW.

The right uterine cornu and the vagina and vulva are opened up: *1*, Labium vulvæ; *2*, ventral commissure; *3*, glans clitoridis; *4*, glandula vestibularis major, exposed by slit in mucous membrane; *5*, pouch in which the ducts of the preceding open; *6*, suburethral diverticulum; *7*, external urethral opening; *8*, openings of canals of Gartner; *9*, orificium uteri externum; *10*, corpus uteri; *11*, cornu uteri; *12*, cotyledons; *13*, uterine tube; *14*, ostium abdominale tubæ; *15*, ovary. (From Leisering's Atlas, reduced.)

fice of the tube is rather large and funnel-shaped. The fimbriæ are not so extensive as in the mare.

The **uterus** lies almost entirely within the abdominal cavity in the adult. The **body** is only about an inch and a half (ca. 3–4 cm.) in length, although externally it appears to be about five or six inches long. This false impression is due to the fact that the posterior parts of the cornua are united by connective and muscular tissue and have a common peritoneal covering. The **cornua** are, therefore, really more extensive than they appear externally and have an average length of about fifteen inches (ca. 35–40 cm.). They taper gradually toward the free end, so that the junction with the uterine tubes is not abrupt, as in the mare. The free part of the horn curves at first downward, forward, and outward, and then turns backward and upward, forming a spiral coil. In some cases the curvature resembles the letter S. The **cervix** is about four inches (ca. 10 cm.) long; its wall is very dense, and may be more than an inch (ca. 3 cm.) in thickness. Its lumen, the **cervical canal,** is spiral, and is ordinarily tightly closed and difficult to dilate; it is clearly marked off from the body of the uterus and the vagina, so that the external and internal orifices are both quite distinct. The vaginal part of the uterus is so fused ventrally with the vagina, that the fornix vaginæ is an inch or more (ca. 3.5 cm.) deep dorsally, while ventrally it is extremely shallow or even practically absent. The **muscular coat** of the uterus is thicker than in the mare. It consists of an external longitudinal layer and two circular strata. The inner circular layer is about a fourth of an inch (ca. 6 mm.) thick in the cervix. The other layers are continued in the vagina. The **mucous membrane** of the horns and body presents as a characteristic feature the **uterine cotyledons** (Cotyledones uterinæ).[1] These are oval prominences, about a hundred in number, which are either irregularly scattered over the surface or arranged in rows of about a dozen.

In the non-gravid uterus they average about half an inch or more (ca. 15 mm.) in length, and a little less in width and thickness. During pregnancy they become greatly enlarged and pedunculated. The larger ones then measure about four or five inches (10 to 12 cm.) in length, an inch and a half (3 to 4 cm.) in width, and an inch (2 to 2.5 cm.) in thickness. The deep face has a hilus at which the vessels enter. The rest of the surface has a spongy appearance, due to numerous crypts which receive the villi of the chorion.

The **uterine glands** are long and branched. The mucous membrane of the cervix is pale, glandless, and forms numerous folds. The latter are arranged in several series which obliterate the lumen. At the external uterine orifice the folds (Plicæ palmatæ) form rounded prominences arranged circularly, which project into the cavity of the vagina. There are no glands in the cervix, but a thick mucus is secreted by goblet cells.

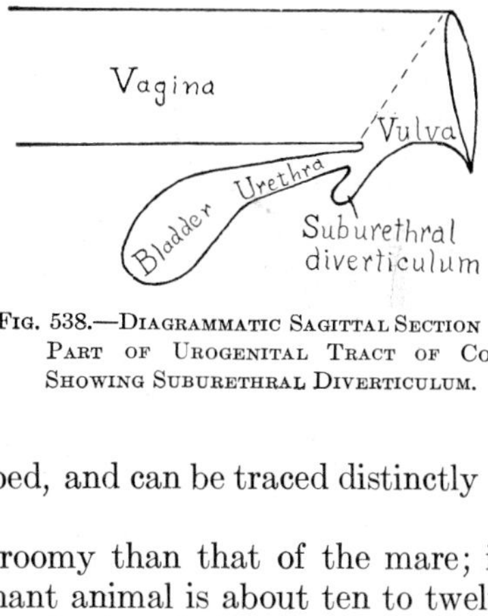

The **broad ligaments** are not attached in the sublumbar region as in the mare, but to the upper part of the flanks, about a handbreadth below the level of the tuber coxæ. They contain a conspicuous amount

FIG. 538.—DIAGRAMMATIC SAGITTAL SECTION OF PART OF UROGENITAL TRACT OF COW, SHOWING SUBURETHRAL DIVERTICULUM.

of unstriped muscle, especially in their anterior part. The **round ligaments** are well developed, and can be traced distinctly to the vicinity of the abdominal inguinal ring.

The **vagina** is somewhat longer and more roomy than that of the mare; its wall is also thicker. Its length in the non-pregnant animal is about ten to twelve inches (ca. 25–30 cm.); but in the pregnant cow the length increases somewhat. The recto-genital pouch of peritoneum extends backward about five inches (ca. 12 cm.) on the dorsal surface, while ventrally the serous coat only extends backward about two inches (ca. 5 cm.). In the ventral wall of the vagina, between the muscular and mucous coats, there are commonly present the two **canals of Gartner** (Ductus epoöphori longitudinales). When well developed, they may attain the diameter of a goose quill, and may be traced forward to the anterior part of the vagina or even further. They open posteriorly near the external urethral orifice.[2]

[1] Also known as carunculæ uterinæ.

[2] These tubes are remnants of the Wolffian ducts, and, like other fœtal vestiges, are very variable. Röder states that the right canal was absent in over 52 per cent., the left in only 22 per cent., of the cows examined by him. In some cases they may be traced in the broad ligaments for a variable distance toward the ovary. They are of clinical interest in that cysts frequently form along their course.

The **vulva** has thick, wrinkled labia, and both commissures are acute; the ventral one is pointed, and has on it a number of long hairs; it lies about two inches (5 cm.) behind, and about the same distance below the level of, the ischial arch. The **external urethral orifice** is about four inches (10 cm.) from the ventral commissure; it has the form of a longitudinal slit about an inch (ca. 2.5 cm.) long. Beneath it is a blind pouch, the **suburethral diverticulum,** which is about an inch and a half (ca. 3.5 cm.) long, and readily admits the end of a finger.[1] The two **glandulæ vestibulares majores** are situated in the lateral walls of the vulva, under the constrictor vulvæ. They are little over an inch (ca. 3 cm.) long and about half an inch (ca. 1.5 cm.) in width. Each has two or three ducts which open into a small pouch of the mucous membrane; the cul-de-sac opens on the floor of the vulva, about an inch and a half (ca. 3–4 cm.) lateral to and behind the external urethral orifice. The gland consists of lobules separated by relatively thick trabeculæ of connective tissue and unstriped muscle. The **glandulæ vestibulares minores** occur along the median ventral groove. Numerous lymph nodules are present in the mucous membrane, especially in the ventral part; they may be large enough to cause visible prominences.

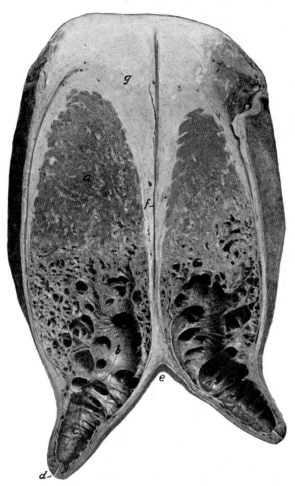

FIG. 539.—CROSS-SECTION OF MAMMARY GLANDS OF COW.

a, Body of gland; *b,* lactiferous sinus; *c,* cavity of teat; *d,* lactiferous duct; *e,* intermammary groove; *f,* septum between glands; *g,* supramammary fat.

The **clitoris** has very short crura, but the body is four or five inches (ca. 10–12 cm.) long and is flexuous. Only the pointed end of the glans is visible in the ventral commissure of the vulva.

The **urethra** is four or five inches (10–12 cm.) in length; it is narrower and much less dilatable than that of the mare. It is fused dorsally with the wall of the vagina, while laterally and ventrally it is covered by the constrictor vaginæ muscle.

The **mammary glands,** normally four in number, are popularly termed the udder. They are very much larger than in the mare, and the body of each is somewhat ellipsoidal in form, but flattened transversely. The base of each gland is slightly concave and slopes obliquely downward and forward in adaptation to

---

[1] The form and position of this pouch should be carefully noted on account of the difficulty it causes in catheterizing the bladder. If the catheter is passed along the ventral wall of the vulva (as in the mare), it will always enter the pouch instead of the urethra.

the abdominal wall, to which it is attached by means of a well-developed **suspensory apparatus** (Lig. suspensorium mammaricum) which extends backward and

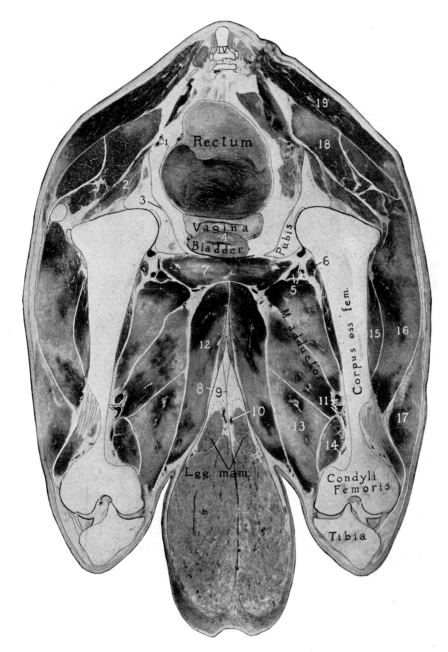

Fig. 539a.—Cross Section of Cow; Posterior View.

Cuts fourth sacral vertebra posterior end and just misses central part of pecten pubis.

1, Internal iliac vessels; *2*, gluteus profundus; *3*, obturator nerve; *4*, ureters; *5*, deep femoral vessels; *6*, iliopsoas; *7*, obturator externus; *8, 9*, lateral and medial sheets of tendo subpelvinea; *10*, perineal veins; *11*, femoral vessels; *12*, gracilis; *13*, semimembranosus; *14*, gastrocnemius; *15*, vastus intermedius; *16*, vastus lateralis; *17, 19*, biceps; *18*, gluteus medius.

is attached to the symphysis pelvis by means of the strong plate of tendinous tissue (Tendo subpelvina). This plate of tissue attaches the prepubic tendon to the ventral part of the symphysis. The **suspensory apparatus** consists essentially of four sheets of tissue two of which are well developed and median in position and are chiefly yellow elastic tissue; the two glands are separated by this double septum which attaches to the medial flat surface of each gland. The lateral sheets (containing less elastic tissue), arise from the subpelvic tendon posterior to the udder; on reaching the abdominal floor they diverge and pass laterally to the external inguinal ring. They extend downward over the udder and divide into superficial and deep layers: the superficial layer attaches to the skin where it reflects off the udder to the medial face of the thigh, and the deep layer is thicker and attaches to the convex lateral surface of the udder by numerous lamellæ which pass into

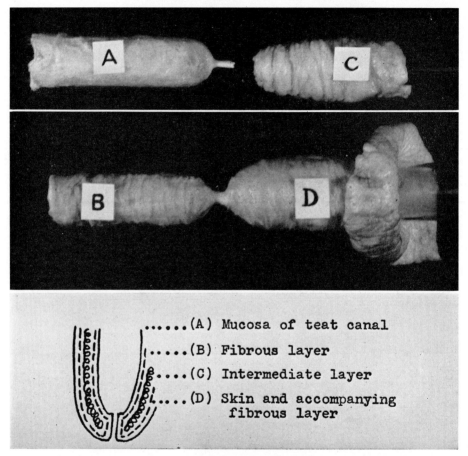

......(A) Mucosa of teat canal

......(B) Fibrous layer

.....(C) Intermediate layer

.....(D) Skin and accompanying fibrous layer

FIG. 539b.—DISSECTIONS AND DIAGRAM SHOWING STRUCTURES AND THEIR ARRANGEMENT IN THE TEAT WALL.
A, mucosa of teat cavity and outlet; B, inner fibrous layer; C, intermediate layer; D, skin and accompanying fibrous layer (inside out). (Drs. W. D. Pounden and James D. Grossman.)

the gland. It is in relation posteriorly to the large supramammary lymph nodes and a quantity of fat. The lateral surface is convex. Four well-developed teats are present; they average about three inches (ca. 7–8 cm.) in length. It is customary to consider the udder to consist of four "quarters"; there is no septum nor visible division between the two quarters of the same side, but, on the other hand, injections of fluids of different colors into the two teats of the gland demonstrate that the cavities drained by them do not communicate.

Each teat has a single lactiferous duct (Ductus lactiferus) which widens superiorly into a roomy lactiferous sinus (Sinus lactiferus), popularly known as the milk cistern. The lower part of the duct, the outlet, is narrow and is closed by a sphincter of unstriped muscle and elastic tissue. The lactiferus duct is lined through the outlet by a stratified squamous epithelium, which changes abruptly inside the outlet into a cuboidal type of epithelium which is usually two layered and continues into the lactiferous sinus. The wall of the teat is composed of five distinct layers from without inward: the skin, outer fibrous layer, intermediate layer, inner fibrous layer and the mucosa (Fig. 539b).

Vessels and Nerves.—The **arteries** are derived from the external pudic and perineal arteries. The **veins** form a circle at the base of the udder, from which the blood is drained by three trunks, viz., the very large subcutaneous abdominal, the external pudic, and the perineal vein. The **lymph vessels** are numerous, and pass to the supramammary glands chiefly. The **nerves** are derived from the inguinal nerves and the posterior mesenteric plexus of the sympathetic.

GENITAL ORGANS OF THE EWE

The genital organs of the ewe resemble in general those of the cow, but a few special features may be noted.

The **ovaries** are almond shaped and are half an inch or more (ca. 1.5 cm.) long.

There is no demarcation between the **uterine tube** and the horn of the uterus; the tube is very flexuous near the infundibulum.

The **uterus** resembles that of the cow. The **horns** are four or five inches (ca. 10–12 cm.) long and taper in such a manner to their junction with the uterine tubes that no clear distinction between the two exists. They are coiled in a close spiral, and an inch or more of their posterior parts are united. The **body** is less than an inch (ca. 2 cm.) long. The cotyledons are much smaller than those of the cow and have a depression on the free surface. The cervix is about an inch and a half (ca. 4 cm.) long; its lumen is closed by reciprocal prominences and depressions of the mucous membrane. The external uterine orifice is in the ventral part of the vagina.

The **vagina** is three or four inches (ca. 8 cm.) long. Its ventral part contains numerous lymph follicles.

The **vulva** is an inch or more (ca. 2.5–3 cm.) in length. There is a very small diverticulum below the urethral orifice which is similar in the goat. The glandulæ vestibulares majores are inconstant; when present, they may be about the size of a small bean. The labia are thick and the ventral commissure is pointed and projects downward.

The **clitoris** is short, and the glans is concealed in the fossa clitoridis.

The **mammary glands,** two in number, are relatively large, and are approximately globular, but flattened on the septal side.

GENITAL ORGANS OF THE SOW

The **ovaries** are concealed in the bursa ovarii, owing to the large extent of the mesosalpinx. They are more rounded than in the bitch, and have a distinct hilus. They may be situated at or near the lateral margin of the pelvic inlet, as in the cow; but their position is quite variable in animals which have borne young and they may be only an inch or two behind the kidney. The surface commonly presents rounded prominences, so that the gland usually has an irregular lobulated appearance; the projections are large follicles and corpora lutea. Mature follicles may have a diameter of about a third of an inch (ca. 7–8 mm.), and corpora lutea may be found which measure half an inch or more (ca. 12–15 mm.).

The **uterine** or **Fallopian tubes** are long (ca. 15–30 cm.), and less flexuous than in the mare. The fimbriated extremity forms an ampulla and has a large abdominal opening. The uterine end shades insensibly into the small extremity of the cornu.

The **uterus** presents several striking features. The **body** is only about two inches (ca. 5 cm.) long. The **horns** are extremely long and flexuous, and are freely movable, on account of the large extent of the broad ligaments. In the non-pregnant animal they are arranged in numerous coils and appear somewhat like thick-walled small intestine. They may be four or five feet (1.2–1.5 m.) in length. The extremities of the horns taper to about the diameter of the uterine tubes. The **neck** is remarkable for its length (ca. 10 cm.) and the fact that it is directly continued by the vagina without forming any intravaginal projection. When slit open, peculiar rounded prominences are seen on its interior; some of these dovetail and occlude the cervical canal. They are continuous behind with folds of the mucous membrane of the vagina. The broad ligaments contain a large amount of unstriped muscle; they also contain a large lymph gland near the ovary.[1] In the upper part of the ligament the muscular tissue forms a rounded band termed the round ligament. In an adult sow of full size it is about six inches (ca. 15 cm.) long; its anterior end forms a blunt projection and posteriorly it ends in the subserous tissue at the internal inguinal ring. The medial layer of the broad ligament is continuous with the lateral ligament of the bladder.

The **vagina** is about four or five inches (ca. 10–12 cm.) long in a sow of medium size. It is small in caliber, and has a thick muscular coat which consists of circular

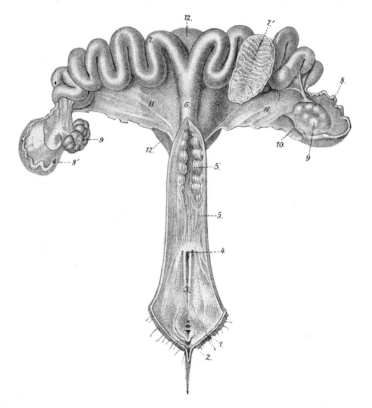

FIG. 540.—GENITAL ORGANS OF SOW; DORSAL VIEW. THE VULVA, VAGINA, AND CERVIX UTERI ARE SLIT OPEN.

1, Labium vulvæ; 2, glans clitoridis; 3, vulva; 4, external urethral orifice; 5, vagina; 5′, cervix uteri; 6, corpus uteri; 7, cornua uteri, one of which is opened at 7′ to show folds of mucous membrane; 8, uterine tube; 8′, abdominal opening of tube; 9, 9, ovaries; 10, ovarian bursa; 11, 11, broad ligaments of uterus; 12, urinary bladder. (From Leisering's Atlas.)

fibers between two layers of longitudinal fibers. The mucous membrane is plicated, and is intimately united with the muscular coat.

The **vulva** is about three inches (7.5 cm.) in length. The labia are thick and are covered with a wrinkled integument. The dorsal commissure is rounded, but the ventral one is produced to form a long pointed projection. The fossa clitoridis is nearly an inch (ca. 2 cm.) anterior to the ventral commissure. Above it the glans clitoridis forms a pointed projection, from which a mucous fold extends laterally and backward on each side. There is a deep central depression about half way between the fossa clitoridis and the external urethral orifice. The latter

---

[1] The changes in form and position of the uterus during pregnancy are similar to those mentioned later in the case of the bitch (p. 624).

is bounded on each side by a thick fold which extends backward for a variable distance. Lateral to this fold is a depression in which the ducts of vestibular glands open.

On either side of the anterior part of the floor of the vulva there is a cul-de-sac and a deep groove leading back from it; these are bounded medially by a longitudinal fold. Ductus epoophori (canals of Gartner) may be found opening anterior to the external urethral orifice.

The **clitoris** is long and flexuous; its glans forms a pointed projection over the fossa clitoridis.

The **urethra** is about three inches (7–8 cm.) long. Its posterior part is fused with the vagina and produces a corresponding elevation of the floor of the latter.

The **mammary glands** are usually ten or twelve in number, and are arranged in two rows, as in the bitch. Each teat has commonly two ducts.

GENITAL ORGANS OF THE BITCH

The **ovaries** (Fig. 442) are small, elongated-oval in outline, and flattened. The average length is a little less than an inch (ca. 2 cm.). Each ovary is commonly situated a short distance (ca. 1–2 cm.) behind, or in contact with, the posterior pole of the corresponding kidney, and thus lies opposite to the third or fourth lumbar vertebra, or about half way between the last rib and the crest of the ilium. The right one lies between the right part of the duodenum and the lateral abdominal wall. The left one is related laterally to the spleen. Each is concealed in a peritoneal pouch, the **bursa ovarii,** which has a slit-like opening ventrally. The two layers which form this pouch contain a quantity of fat and unstriped muscle. They are continued to the cornu of the uterus, constituting the **mesosalpinx** and the **ligament of the ovary.** The surface of the ovary presents prominences caused by projecting follicles. Many follicles contain several ova. There is no distinct hilus.

The **uterine** or **Fallopian tubes** are small and average two or three inches (ca. 5–8 cm.) in length. Each passes at first forward in the lateral part of the bursa ovarii, and then runs backward in the medial part of the pouch; it is only slightly flexuous. The pouch is thus a part of the mesosalpinx. The fimbriated extremity lies chiefly in the bursa ovarii, but part of it often protrudes through the slit-like opening of the bursa; it has a rather large abdominal opening. The uterine orifice is very small.

The **uterus** has a very short body and extremely long narrow horns. In a bitch of medium size the body is about an inch (ca. 2–3 cm.) and the cornua five or six inches (ca. 12–15 cm.) long. The horns are of uniform diameter, are nearly straight, and lie entirely within the abdomen. They diverge from the body in the form of a V toward each kidney. Their posterior parts are united by the peritoneum. The neck is very short and has a thick muscular coat. Dorsally there is no line of demarcation between uterus and vagina, but the cervix uteri is much thicker than the vagina. Ventrally the cervix forms a cylindrical projection which lies in a depression of the vaginal wall. The mucous membrane of the uterus has long uterine glands and also short tubular crypts.

The **broad ligaments** contain much fat and some unstriped muscle. They are much wider in the middle than at either end. The posterior part is attached to the anterior part of the vagina. The **round ligaments** are contained in the free edge of folds given off from the lateral face of the broad ligaments. They are bands of unstriped muscle and fat. Each passes through the inguinal canal, enveloped by a peritoneal pouch (processus vaginalis). A ligamentous fold extends forward from the bursa ovarii lateral to the kidney and is attached to the abdominal wall at the middle of the last rib.

The horns of the gravid uterus present dilatations, the **ampullæ,** which contain the fœtuses, and are separated by constrictions. The gravid uterus lies on the ventral abdominal wall, and toward the end of gestation extends forward to the stomach and liver.

The **vagina** is relatively long. It is narrow anteriorly, and has no distinct fornix. The muscular coat is thick and consists chiefly of circular fibers. The mucous membrane forms longitudinal folds. The canals of Gartner are usually absent.

The **vulva** has thick labia which form a pointed inferior commissure. The mucous lining is smooth and red. It frequently presents small prominences caused

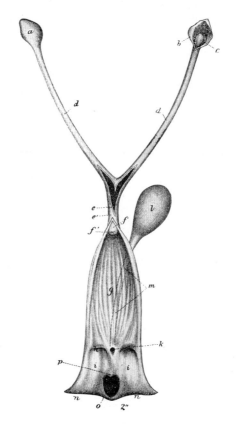

Fig. 541.—Genital Organs of Bitch.

Vulva, vagina, and uterus (in part) are slit open. *a*, Ovarian bursa; *b*, same opened to show the right ovary, *c;* *d*, *d*, horns of uterus; *e*, *e'*, body of uterus; *f*, neck of uterus; *f'*, external uterine orifice; *g*, vagina; *h*, hymen; *i*, vulva; *k*, external urethral orifice; *l*, urinary bladder; *m*, urethra; *n*, *n*, labia vulvæ; *o*, fossa clitoridis; *p*, central projection of fold of mucous membrane which conceals the clitoris. (After Ellenberger, in Leisering's Atlas.)

by lymph follicles. On either side of the urethral orifice there is a small depression. The glandulæ vestibulares majores are absent, but the smaller glands are often present, and their ducts open ventrally on either side of a median ridge. The vestibular bulbs are relatively large and are commonly united ventrally by a sort of isthmus. The constrictor muscle is strong and divides into two layers which enclose the vestibular bulb. The body of the **clitoris** is broad and flat, and is about an inch and a half (ca. 3–4 cm.) long in a subject of medium size. It is not erectile in structure, but is infiltrated with fat. It is enclosed by a fibrous albuginea and contains large arteries and numerous nerves in its ventral part. The glans clitoridis is composed of erectile tissue and is situated in a large fossa clitoridis. A fold of mucous membrane extends backward over the glans and fossa; a central projection of this fold may be mistaken for the glans clitoridis.

The **mammary glands** are usually ten in number, and are arranged in two series, extending from the posterior part of the pectoral region to the inguinal region; they are, therefore, designated according to location as **pectoral, abdominal,** and **inguinal.** The teats are short, and present on their apices six to twelve small orifices of the excretory ducts.

ANGIOLOGY

Angiology is the description of the organs of circulation of the blood and lymph —the heart and vessels. The **heart** is the central hollow muscular organ which functions as a suction and force pump; the differences in pressure caused by its contraction and relaxation chiefly determine the circulation of the blood and lymph. It is situated in the middle mediastinal space of the thorax and is enclosed in a fibro-serous sac—the pericardium. The vessels are tubular and run through almost all parts of the body. They are designated according to their contents as **blood-** and **lymph-vessels.**

THE BLOOD-VASCULAR SYSTEM

The **blood-vascular system** consists of: (1) The **arteries,** which convey blood from the heart to the tissues; (2) the **capillaries,** microscopic tubes in the tissues, which permit of the necessary interchange between the blood and the tissues; (3) the **veins,** which convey the blood back to the heart.

The blood-vessels are divided into the **pulmonary** and the **systemic.** The **pulmonary artery** conveys the blood from the right ventricle of the heart to the lungs, where it is arterialized, and is returned by the **pulmonary veins** to the left atrium of the heart, and passes into the left ventricle. The **systemic arteries** convey the blood from the left ventricle all over the body, whence it is returned by the **venæ cavæ** to the right atrium, and passes into the right ventricle.[1]

The term **portal system** is often applied to the portal vein and its tributaries which come from the stomach, intestine, pancreas, and spleen. The vein enters the liver, where it branches like an artery, so that the blood in this subsidiary system passes through a second set of capillaries (in the liver) before being conveyed to the heart by the hepatic veins and the posterior vena cava.

The **arteries** (Arteriæ), as a rule, divide at an acute angle, giving off finer and finer branches. In some cases branches come off at a right angle, and others are recurrent, *i. e.,* run in a direction opposite to that of the parent stem. The intercommunication of branches of adjacent arteries is termed **anastomosis.** Most commonly the connections are made by a network of numerous fine branches which constitute a **vascular plexus** (Plexus vasculosus). Relatively large communicating branches occur in certain places; they may be transverse or in the form of arches. Wide-meshed networks of vessels are termed **retia vasculosa. Terminal** or **end arteries** are such as form isolated networks, *i. e.,* do not anastomose with adjacent arteries; such are the interlobular arteries of the kidney. A **rete mirabile** is a network intercalated in the course of an artery. A **collateral vessel** (Vas collaterale) is one which pursues a course near and similar to that of a larger vessel.

The **veins** (Venæ) are, in general, arranged like the arteries, but are usually of greater caliber. When a vein accompanies an artery, it is termed a **vena comitans** or **satellite vein** and is usually homonymous; in many places two veins accompany an artery. The primitive venous trunks do not run with the arteries, and most of the superficial veins (Venæ cutaneæ) pursue independent courses. They anastomose even more freely than the arteries, and large communicating branches are very common. **Venous plexuses** (Plexus venosi) occur in many places. Some veins which are enclosed by dense membranes and run usually in bony grooves are

---

[1] It should be noted, however, that the lungs also receive arterial blood through the systemic bronchial arteries. This blood is returned mainly, if not exclusively, by the pulmonary veins to the left atrium.

termed **venous sinuses**; their wall consists of endothelium only; examples of this are the sinuses of the dura mater of the brain. A vein which connects one of these sinuses with veins outside of the cranium is termed an **emissarium.**

A **corpus cavernosum** is an erectile structure which consists essentially of intercommunicating blood-spaces enclosed by unstriped muscle and fibro-elastic tissue. These spaces (Cavernæ) are lined with endothelium and contain blood. Some are to be regarded as greatly enlarged capillaries, since minute arteries open into them and they are drained by veins; others are intercalated in the course of veins. Distention of the cavernæ with blood produces the enlargement and hardening of the corpus cavernosum which is termed erection.

Structure of Arteries.—The wall consists of three coats. The **external coat** or **adventitia** (Tunica externa) consists chiefly of fibrous connective tissue. In the deeper part are some elastic fibers, and in some arteries there are also longitudinal unstriped muscle-fibers. The **middle coat** (Tunica media) is composed of unstriped muscle and elastic tissue in medium-sized arteries. In small vessels there is chiefly muscular tissue, and in the largest trunks almost exclusively elastic tissue. The **internal coat** or **intima** (Tunica intima) consists of a layer of endothelial cells, resting on an elastic membrane. The **sheath of the vessel** (Vagina vasis) is a condensation of the surrounding connective tissue, and is attached more or less closely to the external coat.

Structure of Veins.—The walls of veins are similar in structure to those of the arteries, but are very much thinner, so that veins collapse more or less completely when empty, while arteries do not. The **middle coat** is very thin and consists to a large extent of ordinary fibrous tissue. The **internal coat** is also less elastic than in the arteries. In many veins this coat forms semilunar **valves,** the free edges of which are directed toward the heart. They are most numerous in the veins of the skin and of the extremities (except the foot), while in most veins of the body cavities and viscera they are absent or occur only where the veins open into larger ones or where two veins join.

The walls of the vessels are supplied with blood by numerous small arteries, called **vasa vasorum.** These arise from branches of the artery which they supply or from adjacent arteries, ramify in the external coat, and enter the middle coat also. The **nerves** of the vessels (Nervi vasorum) consist of both medullated and non-medullated fibers. They are derived from the sympathetic system, either directly or by way of cerebrospinal nerves. They form plexuses around the vessels, from which fibers pass mainly to the muscular tissue of the middle coat; on account of their function they are termed vasomotor nerves.

THE LYMPHATIC SYSTEM

The **lymphatic system** (Systema lymphaticum) is subsidiary to the venous part of the circulatory system, from which it arises in the embryo. It consists of the lymph vessels and glands.

The **lymph vessels** (Vasa lymphatica) contain a colorless fluid, the **lymph,** in which are numerous lymphocytes.[1] They resemble the veins in structure but have thinner walls and are provided with more numerous valves. The vessels are sacculated opposite the segments of the valves and have a characteristic beaded appearance when distended. The collecting lymph vessels do not usually form rich plexuses, as veins often do, their branching is more limited and less tree-like than that of the blood-vessels, and their caliber therefore increases less from the periphery toward their termination. Nearly all of the lymph is ultimately carried into the venous system by two trunks, the **thoracic duct** and the **right lymphatic duct.**

[1] The term chyle is often applied to the lymph carried by the efferent vessels of the intestine when it contains products of digestion, and these vessels may be designated accordingly as lacteals or chyle vessels.

Almost all of the lymph passes through at least one group of lymph glands before entering the blood-vascular system.

The **lymph glands** or **nodes** (Lymphoglandulæ) are intercalated in the course of the lymph vessels. They vary widely in size, some being microscopic, others several inches in length. In form they may be globular, ovoid and flattened, elongated, or irregular. In certain situations they are aggregated into groups, and a knowledge of the position of these and the territory drained into them is important. It is convenient, when possible, to indicate their position with regard to arteries on the course of which they are placed. In color they are usually gray or yellowish-brown in the dead subject, pink or reddish-brown during life, but this varies according to their position and functional state. The bronchial glands are often blackened by infiltration with carbon. The mesenteric glands are creamy or white while the chyle is passing through, but pink at other times. Vessels which carry lymph to a gland are called **afferent;** the **efferent** vessels which convey it away are larger and fewer. Each gland has a depression, the **hilus,** at which the blood-vessels enter and the efferent lymph vessels emerge.

Lymph nodules or **follicles** (Noduli lymphatici) are minute masses of lymphoid tissue which occur in certain mucous membranes. They may be solitary, as in the solitary nodules of the intestine, or aggregated into masses or patches, as in the tonsils and the aggregate masses or so-called Peyer's patches.

The **lymph nodule** or **follicle** is the unit of structure of the lymph gland. It consists essentially of an artery surrounded by a **reticulum** of connective tissue, the meshes of which contain numerous **lymphocytes.** Surrounding this is a rich plexus of lymph vessels, forming the so-called **sinus,** enclosed in some cases by a fibrous capsule. The gland consists of a mass of follicles, enclosed in a fibrous **capsule,** from which **trabeculæ** pass in and unite the follicles. Beneath the capsule is the **peripheral sinus,** which consists of a very rich plexus of lymph vessels; to this the afferent vessels pass at various points of the surface. In the **cortical substance** the cells are in rounded masses, the cortical nodules, while in the **medullary substance** they lie around the arteries, forming the so-called medullary cords. The medulla is redder than the cortex, since it is more vascular; it contains the **central lymph sinuses,** which have a similar structure to the peripheral sinus.

The **hæmal nodes** or **hæmolymph glands** differ from the lymph glands in color and structure and the absence of afferent and efferent lymph vessels. They are of a deep red color or even black and are not usually larger than a pea. They have a well-developed peripheral sinus which contains blood. From this, secondary sinuses extend into the interior, and form an intercommunicating system of blood spaces. There is no clear division into cortical and medullary substance, and the trabeculæ contain smooth muscle-cells. They resemble the spleen in some respects, but their significance is not yet clear. They are numerous in the ox and sheep, much fewer in the dog, and apparently are absent in the horse and pig. They occur especially along the course of the aorta, in the perineal fat, at the portal fissure, and with the gastric and mesenteric lymph glands. In the ox they are also found under the trapezius muscle, under the skin of the upper part of the flank, and in other places less constantly. The **red lymph-glands** of the pig have very commonly been mistaken for hæmal nodes. Intermediate types between lymph-glands and hæmal nodes occur.

The **tissue spaces** are interstices of varying size between cells or in the meshes of connective tissue. They contain a fluid derived from the blood-plasma, which is termed **tissue fluid;** in the lymphoid tissues it is lymph. They are drained by the veins and lymph vessels. The large serous sacs are often included in this category.

The exact relationship between the lymphatic capillaries and the tissue spaces is a matter of controversy. It is still held by some that the lymph vessels are in direct communication with the tissue spaces, but recent investigators indicate that the lymphatics are complete closed tubes. Communication between the spaces and vessels is in general very free. Mall has shown that granules injected into the hepatic artery are returned by the lymphatics as well as by the veins, and intramuscular injections will enter the lymph vessels of the tendon in spite of the fact that the presence of lymphatics in muscle is doubtful.

BLOOD-VASCULAR SYSTEM OF THE HORSE

THE PERICARDIUM

The **pericardium** is the fibro-serous sac which encloses the heart, and in part also the great vessels in connection with it. Its form is in general similar to that of the heart. The **fibrous layer** is relatively thin, but strong and inelastic. It is attached dorsally to the large vessels at the base of the heart, and is continued in part up to the longus colli muscle. It is firmly attached ventrally to the middle of the posterior half of the thoracic surface of the sternum. The **serous layer** is a closed sac, surrounded by the fibrous pericardium, and invaginated by the heart. It is smooth and glistening, and contains a small amount of clear serous fluid, the **liquor pericardii**. Like other serous membranes, it may be regarded as consisting of two parts, parietal and visceral. The **parietal part** lines the fibrous layer, to which it is closely attached. The **visceral part** covers the heart and parts of the great vessels, and is therefore also termed the **epicardium.** The serous pericardium is composed of a connective-tissue membrane, rich in elastic fibers, and covered on its free surface by a layer of flat mesothelial cells.

The pericardium is covered by the pericardiac part of the mediastinal pleura (Pleura pericardiaca), and is crossed laterally by the phrenic nerves. Its lateral surfaces are related chiefly to the lungs, but the lower part is in partial contact with the chest-wall. On the left side the area of contact is from the third rib to the sixth rib and intercostal space. On the right side the contact is smaller and is chiefly opposite the ventral part of the third and fourth intercostal spaces and intervening rib. The anterior end of its base is opposite to the second intercostal space or third rib, and the posterior border is opposite to the sixth rib and space. The base is related to the great vessels, the trachea and its bifurcation, the bronchial lymph glands, and the vagus, left recurrent, and cardiac nerves.

The extent of contact of the pericardium with the lateral wall of the thorax, which is designated clinically as the **superficial cardiac area** is determined by the cardiac notch of the lung. On the left side the anterior margin of the notch is at the third rib and the posterior margin is at the sixth rib dorsally and sixth intercostal space ventrally. The greatest height of the notch is at the fourth rib and intercostal space, where it is a handbreadth or more (ca. 10–12 cm.) above the sternal end of the rib. The notch is quadrilateral, but much narrower above than below. On the right side the notch is usually triangular and is much smaller. Its anterior margin begins at the third intercostal space, about three inches (ca. 7–8 cm.) above the sternal ends of the third and fourth ribs and runs obliquely to the sternal end of the third rib. The posterior margin begins at the same point and extends to the ventral end of the fourth intercostal space or of the anterior border of the fifth rib.

The two parts of the serous pericardium are, of course, continuous with each other at the line of reflection on to the great vessels. The latter are covered in varying degree by the visceral layer. The aorta and pulmonary artery are enclosed in a complete common sheath as far as the bifurcation of the latter. The membrane passes inward between the pulmonary artery and the left auricle, and is continued between the right auricle and the aorta, thus forming the **transverse sinus of the pericardium** (Sinus transversus pericardii). The posterior vena cava is covered on the right and ventrally for a distance of an inch or a little more (ca. 3 cm.). The pulmonary veins have practically no serous covering. The epicardium is closely adherent to the muscular tissue of the heart, but is attached to the vessels by areolar tissue and fat, and hence is easily dissected off them.

THE HEART

The **heart** (Cor) occupies the greater part of the middle mediastinal space. Its shape is that of an irregular and somewhat flattened cone. It is attached at its base by the great vessels, but is otherwise entirely free in the pericardium. It is asymmetrical in position, the amounts (by weight) on the right and left of the median plane being about as 4 : 5. The long axis (from the middle of the base to the apex) is directed ventrally and backward. The **base of the heart** (Basis cordis) is directed dorsally and its highest part lies about at the junction of the dorsal and middle thirds of the dorso-ventral diameter of the thorax. It is opposite to the lateral wall of the thorax, from the second intercostal space or third rib to the sixth rib or intercostal space.[1] The **apex** (Apex cordis) lies centrally above the last segment of the sternum; it is half an inch or less (ca. 1 cm.) above the sternum and about an inch (ca. 2–3 cm.) from the sternal part of the diaphragm. The **anterior border** (Margo cranialis) is strongly convex and curves ventrally and backward; the greater part is parallel with the sternum. The **posterior border** (Margo caudalis) is much shorter, is nearly vertical, and is opposite to the sixth rib and intercostal space. The **surfaces, right** and **left** (Facies dextra, sinistra), are convex and

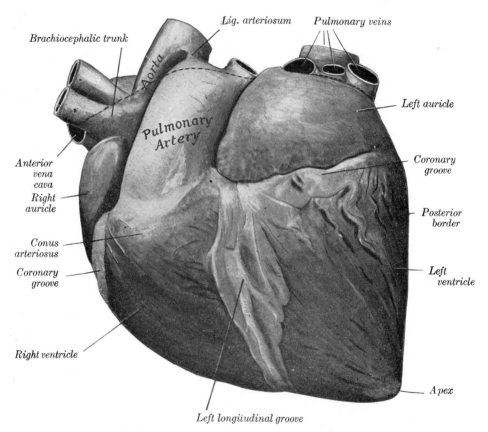

FIG. 542.—HEART OF HORSE; LEFT VIEW. HARDENED *in situ.*
The dotted line indicates the line of reflection of the serous pericardium. The epicardium and subepicardial fat have not been removed.

are marked by grooves which indicate the division of the heart into four chambers, the two atria above and two ventricles below. The left surface (covered by the pericardium) is related to the lower third of the chest-wall from the third to the sixth rib. On the right side the cardiac notch of the lung is smaller, so that the area of relation to the chest-wall extends from the third to the fourth intercostal space.[2]

[1] The size and form of the heart vary according to the degree of its contraction and relaxation (systole and diastole). In subjects which have been bled and preserved by intravascular injection of formalin solution the right side is usually fixed in diastole while the left is more or less strongly contracted. The base may extend back to the seventh rib.

[2] The arrangement in this regard has been stated at greater length in the descriptions of the lungs and the pericardium.

The **coronary groove** (Sulcus coronarius) indicates the division between the atria and the ventricles. It almost completely encircles the heart, but is interrupted at the origin of the pulmonary artery. The **longitudinal grooves,** right and left, correspond to the septum between the ventricles. The **left longitudinal groove** (Sulcus longitudinalis sinister) is left-anterior in position. It begins at the coronary groove, behind the origin of the pulmonary artery, and descends almost parallel to the posterior border. The **right longitudinal groove** (Sulcus longitudinalis dexter) is right-posterior in position. It begins at the coronary groove, below the termina-

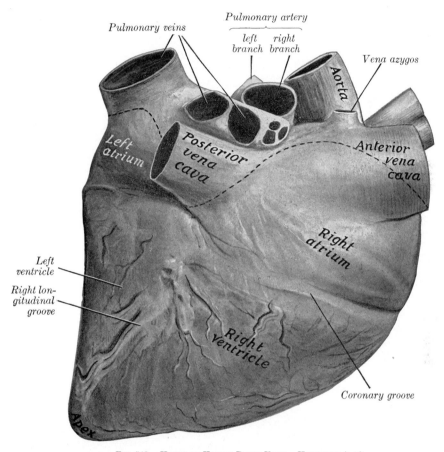

FIG. 543.—HEART OF HORSE; RIGHT VIEW. HARDENED *in situ.*
Line of reflection of serous pericardium dotted. Epicardium and subepicardial fat have not been removed from heart. Left ventricle is considerably contracted.

tion of the posterior vena cava and passes toward the apex, but ends about an inch and a half (ca. 3–4 cm.) above the latter. Thus the two grooves do not meet. The grooves are occupied by the coronary vessels and a variable quantity of fat.

The left groove is opposite to the fourth rib or intercostal space, and the right one is opposite to the fifth intercostal space above and the sixth rib below.

Size and Weight.—The average weight of the heart is about nine pounds (ca. 4 kg.) and is about 0.7 per cent. of the body-weight. There is, however, great range of variation in apparently normal specimens.

As might be expected, race horses have hearts which are larger than the average, both absolutely and relatively. The heart of the celebrated thoroughbred **Eclipse** weighed a little over fourteen pounds (6.5 kg.). In fat subjects the ratio to the body-weight may be about 0.4 per cent., and, on the other hand, it is commonly 1 per cent. or more in light horses which are not fat.

The following average measurements were obtained in medium-sized hearts:

Sagittal diameter of base.................................... 25 cm.
Greatest width of base.................................... 18 to 20 cm.
Circumference at coronary groove.......................... 65 to 70 cm.
Distance between origin of pulmonary artery and apex.......... 25 cm.
Distance between termination of posterior vena cava and apex..... 18 to 20 cm.

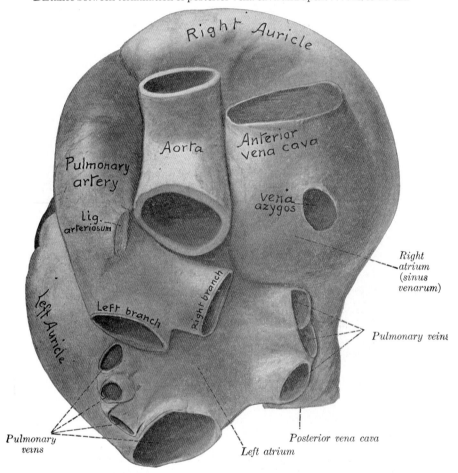

Fig. 544.—Base of Heart of Horse with Large Vessels: Dorsal View. Specimen Hardened *in situ.*

THE RIGHT ATRIUM

The **right atrium** (Atrium dextrum)[1] forms the right-anterior part of the base of the heart, and lies above the right ventricle. It consists of a **sinus venarum,** into which the veins open, and an **auricle**[2] (Auricula dextra). The latter is a conical diverticulum which curves around the right and anterior surfaces of the aorta, its blind end appearing on the left side in front of the origin of the pulmonary artery; it **is** the most anterior part of the heart.

There are five chief openings in the right atrium. The **opening of the anterior vena cava** (Ostium venæ cavæ cranialis) is in the dorsal part, and is chiefly opposite to the fourth rib. The **opening of the posterior vena cava** (Ostium venæ cavæ

[1] Also termed the right auricle.   [2] Also termed the auricular appendix.

caudalis) is at the posterior part, opposite to the fifth intercostal space or sixth rib. Between the two the wall pouches upward somewhat, and here the **vena azygos** opens. The **coronary sinus** opens ventral to the posterior vena cava; the orifice is provided with a small semilunar valve (Valvula sinus coronarii). The small coronary vein has a separate opening in some cases close to that of the coronary sinus. The **right atrio-ventricular orifice** (Ostium atrio-ventriculare dextrum) is in the ventral part, and leads into the right ventricle. In addition to the

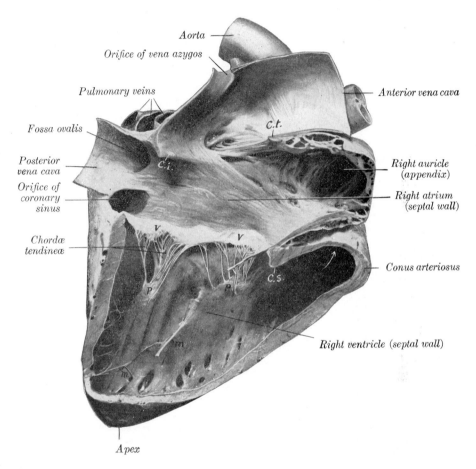

FIG. 545.—RIGHT SIDE OF HEART OF HORSE OPENED UP BY REMOVAL OF GREATER PART OF RIGHT WALL. ORGAN HARDENED *in situ.*

The right ventricle was in diastole. *C.i.,* Intervenous crest; *V, V,* tricuspid valve; *P, P,* papillary muscles; *m, m,* moderator bands; *C.S.,* crista supraventricularis; *C.t.,* crista terminalis. Arrow points into origin of pulmonary artery.

foregoing there are several small orifices of the venæ cordis parvæ; these are concealed in the depressions between the musculi pectinati.

In common with all the cavities of the heart the atrium is lined with a glistening membrane, the **endocardium.** Its walls are smooth except on the right and in the auricle, where it is crossed in various directions by muscular ridges, the **musculi pectinati.** Small bands extend across some of the spaces enclosed by the musculi pectinati. The latter terminate above on a curved crest, the **crista terminalis,** which indicates the junction of the primitive sinus reuniens of the embryo with the atrium proper, and corresponds with the sulcus terminalis externally.

The openings of the venæ cavæ are valveless. A ridge, the **intervenous crest** (Crista intervenosa), projects downward and forward from the dorsal wall just in front of the opening of the posterior vena cava; it tends to direct the flow of blood from the anterior vena cava to the atrio-ventricular opening. The **fossa ovalis** is a diverticulum in the septal wall, at the point of entrance of the posterior vena cava, bounded laterally by a concave margin (Limbus fossæ ovalis). The fossa is the remnant of an opening in the septum, the **foramen ovale,** through which the two atria communicate in the fœtus.

The fossa varies in form and size. It is commonly about an inch deep and permits introduction of the end of one's finger. It is directed forward and somewhat medially. In some cases

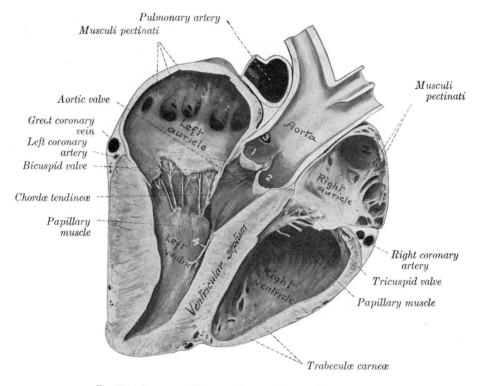

Pulmonary artery
Musculi pectinati
Musculi pectinati
Aortic valve
Great coronary vein
Left coronary artery
Bicuspid valve
Chordæ tendineæ
Papillary muscle
Right coronary artery
Tricuspid valve
Papillary muscle
Trabeculæ carneæ

FIG. 546.—SECTION OF HEART OF HORSE. SPECIMEN HARDENED *in situ.*

The section is cut nearly at right angles to the ventricular septum, and is viewed from the right and posteriorly. *1, 2,* Sinuses of aorta; *3,* origin of left coronary artery; *4,* moderator band.

it is shallower and only large enough to admit a lead pencil. The interatrial septum is very thin here, and in some cases the foramen ovale fails to close entirely.

THE RIGHT VENTRICLE

The **right ventricle** (Ventriculus dexter) constitutes the right anterior part of the ventricular mass. It forms almost all of the anterior border of the heart, but does not reach the apex, which is formed entirely by the left ventricle. It extends from the third rib to the fourth rib or intercostal space on the left side, to the fifth intercostal space on the right side. It is somewhat triangular in outline, and is crescentic in cross-section. Its base is connected largely with the **right atrium,** with which it communicates through the right atrio-ventricular orifice; but its left part projects higher and forms the **conus arteriosus,** from which the pulmonary artery arises. Its apex is two inches or more (ca. 5–6 cm.) above the apex of the heart. On opening the cavity it is seen that the atrio-ventricular orifice and the cavity of the conus arteriosus are separated by a thick ridge, the **crista supraventricularis.** The axis of the cavity, taken from the conus arteriosus to the apex, forms a spiral curve to the right downward and backward. The septal wall is convex and faces obliquely forward and to the right.

The **right atrio-ventricular orifice** is oval and is chiefly opposite to the fourth and fifth ribs and the intervening space.[1] The plane of the opening is oblique, much lower in front than behind. Its height above the sternal end of the fourth rib is about three inches (ca. 7 cm.).

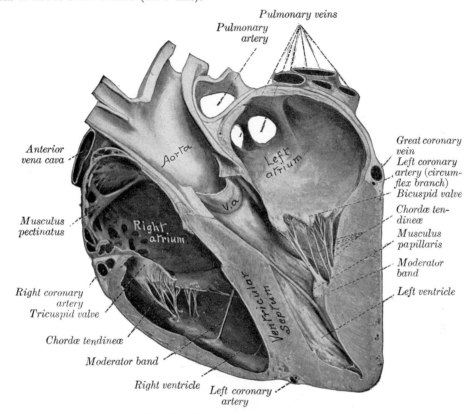

FIG. 547.—SECTION OF HEART OF HORSE.

Specimen hardened *in situ* and cut nearly at right angles to the ventricular septum. The left ventricle is contracted, but not *ad maximum. V.a.,* Segment of aortic valve. Compare Fig. 542.

The anterior part of the orifice is usually only about two inches (ca. 5 cm.) above the level of the ventral end of the fourth rib, while the posterior part is about three inches (ca. 8 cm.) above the sternal end of the fifth rib. It may extend back almost to the sixth rib.

It is guarded by the **tricuspid valve** (Valvula tricuspidalis); of the three large cusps of this valve, one is between the atrio-ventricular opening and the conus arteriosus, one is septal, and the third is on the right margin. Small intermediate cusps intervene between the large ones. The peripheral edges of the cusps are attached to the fibrous ring at the atrio-ventricular opening. The central edges are

___

[1] The extent of the atrio-ventricular orifices, of course, varies with the phase in which the heart is fixed. In subjects which are preserved by intravascular injection of formalin solution the right side of the heart is usually in diastole, while the left side is more or less contracted.

irregular and hang down into the ventricle; they give attachment to chordæ tendineæ. The auricular surfaces are smooth. The ventricular surfaces are rough and furnish attachment to interlacing branches of the chordæ tendineæ. The valves are folds of the endocardium, strengthened by fibrous tissue and at the periphery by muscular fibers also. The **chordæ tendineæ** are attached below to the three **musculi papillares,** which project from the ventricular wall; superiorly they divide into branches which are inserted into the ventricular surfaces and the free

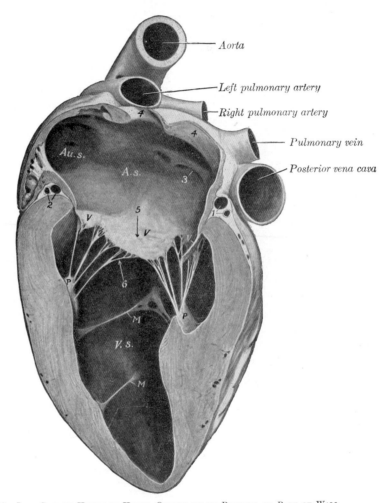

FIG. 548.—LEFT SIDE OF HEART OF HORSE, OPENED UP BY REMOVAL OF PART OF WALL.

A.s., Left atrium; *Au.s.,* left auricle; *V, V, V,* bicuspid valve; *V.s.,* left ventricle; *M, M,* moderator bands; *P, P,* papillary muscles; *1, 2,* great cardiac vein and circumflex branches of coronary arteries; *3,* position of foramen ovale of fœtus; *4, 4,* openings of pulmonary veins (chiefly cut away); *5,* atrio-ventricular orifice; *6,* arrow points to aortic vestibule.

edges of the valves. Each cusp of the valve receives chordæ tendineæ from two papillary muscles. Of the latter, two are on the septum and the third and largest springs from the anterior wall.

The **pulmonary orifice** (Ostium arteriæ pulmonalis) is circular and is at the summit of the conus arteriosus, opposite to the third rib and intercostal space.

The position of the orifice is somewhat variable. Its anterior margin may extend as far forward as the second intercostal space, and the posterior part is often opposite to the fourth rib. It is about two inches (ca. 5 cm.) above the sternal end of the third rib. The plane of the orifice is somewhat oblique, highest in front and medially.

It is guarded by the **pulmonary valve,** composed of three semilunar cusps (Valvulæ semilunares arteriæ pulmonalis); of these, one is medial, one lateral, and the third posterior.[1] The convex peripheral border of each cusp is attached to the fibrous ring at the junction of the pulmonary artery and the conus arteriosus. The central border is free and concave. Each cusp consists of a layer of endo-cardium on its ventricular surface, a continuation of the inner coat of the artery on its arterial surface, and an intermediate layer of fibrous tissue. The edge of the conus arteriosus forms three arches with intermediate projecting angles or horns, to all of which the cusps are attached; and the artery forms opposite each cusp a pouch, the sinus of the pulmonary artery.

The walls of the ventricle (except in the conus arteriosus) bear muscular ridges and bands, termed **trabeculæ carneæ.** These are of three kinds, viz., (1) ridges or columns in relief; (2) **musculi papillares,** somewhat conical flattened projections, continuous at the base with the wall and giving off the chordæ tendineæ to the tricuspid valve; (3) **moderator bands** (Musculi transversi cordis) which extend from the septum to the opposite wall. The latter are partly muscular, partly tendinous, and vary in different subjects. The strongest one is usually about midway between the base and apex and extends from the septum to the base of the lateral musculus papillaris (Fig. 547). It is considered that they tend to prevent overdistention.

The Left Atrium

The **left atrium** (Atrium sinistrum) forms the posterior part of the base of the heart. It lies behind the pulmonary artery and the aorta and above the left ven-tricle. The **auricle** (Auricula sinistra) extends outward and forward on the left side, and its pointed, blind end is behind the origin of the pulmonary artery. The **pulmonary veins,** usually seven or eight in number, open into the atrium behind and on the right side. The cavity of the atrium is smooth, with the exception of the auricle, in which the musculi pectinati are present. In some cases there is a depression on the septal wall opposite the fossa ovalis, bounded above by a fold which is the remnant of the valve of the foramen ovale of the fœtus. The **left atrio-ventricular opening** (Ostium atrio-ventriculare sinistrum) is situated below and in front; it usually appears smaller than the right one on account of the con-traction of the left ventricle in the dead subject. The apertures of small veins of the heart are found in the spaces enclosed by the musculi pectinati.

The number and the arrangement of the pulmonary veins are variable. They may be five to nine in number. The largest vein is posterior; it is formed by the union of veins from both lungs. Usually three veins of considerable size, which lie above the posterior vena cava, enter close together on the right, and three or four open close to the ridge which projects from the roof at the base of the auricle.

The Left Ventricle

The **left ventricle** (Ventriculus sinister) forms the left posterior part of the ventricular mass. It is more regularly conical than the right ventricle, and its wall is much thicker except at the apex. It forms all of the posterior contour of the ventricular part and the apex of the heart. Its base is largely continuous with the left atrium, with which it communicates through the left atrio-ventricular opening, but its anterior part opens into the aorta. The cavity usually appears smaller than that of the right ventricle in the dead subject, on account of the greater contraction of its wall. It is almost circular in cross-section.

[1] In some cases there are four cusps, and very rarely only two.

The **left atrio-ventricular orifice** is chiefly opposite to the fifth rib and inter-costal space.

It often extends back to the sixth rib, and its anterior margin may be at the posterior border of the fourth rib.   It is three or four inches (ca. 8–10 cm.) above the sternal end of the fifth rib. The plane of the opening is somewhat oblique, and is higher behind than in front.

It is almost circular and is guarded by the **bicuspid valve** (Valvula bicus-pidalis).[1] The cusps of this valve are larger and thicker than those of the right

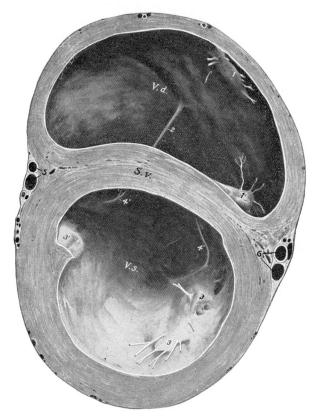

Fig. 549.—Cross-section of Ventricular Part of Heart of Horse.

The section is cut about 5 cm. from the coronary groove.   The ventricles are moderately distended.   *V. d.*, Right ventricle; *V. s.*, left ventricle; *S. v.*, ventricular septum; 1, 1', papillary muscles of right ventricle; *2*, large moderator band of right ventricle; 3, 3, 3', papillary muscles of left ventricle; 4, 4', moderator bands of left ventricle; 5, descend-ing branch of left coronary artery and great cardiac vein; 6, right coronary artery and small cardiac vein, The an-terior septal papillary muscle of the right ventricle is not visible, and the right one of the left ventricle is double.

side of the heart.   The large anterior cusp (Fig. 548) separates the atrio-ventricular orifice from the aortic vestibule.   The other is posterior, and between it and the anterior one there are usually accessory cusps.

The **aortic orifice** (Ostium aorticum) is directed upward and slightly forward (Figs. 546, 550).   It is chiefly opposite to the fourth rib and intercostal space, but often extends backward to the fifth rib.   It is three to four inches (ca. 8–10 cm.) above the sternal end of the fourth rib.[2]   It is guarded by the **aortic valve,** com-posed of three semilunar cusps (Valvulæ semilunares aortæ); one cusp is anterior, the others right and left posterior.   They are similar to those of the pulmonary

[1] Also termed the mitral valve.
[2] It may be noted that the aortic opening is posterior medial to the orifice of the pulmonary artery; this explains the mixing of the two sounds here as noted in auscultation.

valve, but are much stronger. The free edge of each contains a central nodule of fibrous tissue (Nodulus valvulæ semilunaris).

The chordæ tendineæ are fewer but larger than those of the right ventricle. There are two large **musculi papillares,** one on each side; they are usually compound. The moderator bands are variable. Commonly two larger ones (which are often branched) extend from the musculi papillares to the septum. Smaller ones may be found in various places, especially at the apex. The other trabeculæ are fewer and less prominent than in the right ventricle.

The **ventricular septum** (Septum ventriculorum) is the partition which separates the cavities of the two ventricles. It is placed obliquely, so that one surface, which is convex, faces forward and to the right, and bulges into the right ventricle; the other surface, which faces into the left ventricle, is concave and looks backward

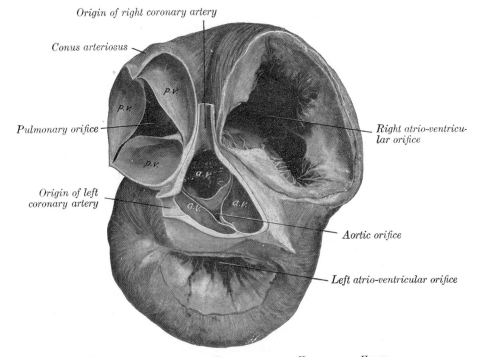

FIG. 550.—THE BASES OF THE VENTRICLES OF THE HEART OF THE HORSE.
The atria have been removed and the aorta and pulmonary artery cut off short. The right ventricle is dilated and the left ventricle is contracted. *p.v.,* Pulmonary valve; *a.v.,* aortic valve.

and to the left. The greater part of the septum is thick and muscular (Septum musculare), but a very small part is thin and membranous (Septum membranaceum). The latter intervenes between the aortic vestibule on the one hand, and the right ventricle and atrium on the other.

STRUCTURE OF THE HEART

The heart-wall consists mainly of peculiar striped muscle, the myocardium, which is covered externally by the visceral part of the serous pericardium or epicardium, and is lined by the endocardium.

The **epicardium** is, in general, closely attached to the muscular wall, but is loosely attached over the coronary vessels and the associated subepicardial fat.

It consists of a layer of flat polygonal cells, resting on a membrane of white and elastic fibers.

The **myocardium** consists of planes of fibers arranged in a somewhat complicated manner. The muscular tissue of the atria is almost completely separated from that of the ventricles by the fibrous rings around the atrio-ventricular orifices.

The connection between the musculature of the atria and that of the ventricles is established by the **atrio-ventricular bundle** (Fasciculus atrio-ventricularis). This begins as a network of fibers about the opening of the coronary sinus and the adjacent atrial wall. The fibers converge to a flat, irregular mass at the upper border of the ventricular septum. From this two chief divisions proceed. One of these descends on the right side of the ventricular septum and passes by the moderator band to the lateral papillary muscle. The other branch descends on the left side of the septum and ramifies on the wall of the ventricle. The left branch is somewhat difficult to follow, since it is thin and reticulate and is covered in great part by a layer of ventricular muscle fibers. The right branch is subendocardial. The bundle and its divisions are enclosed in a fibrous sheath. The functional importance of the bundle in mediating the contraction wave was shown by Erlanger, who found that clamping the bundle caused heart-block.

In the atria the muscle bands fall naturally into two groups—superficial and deep. The former are common to both atria, the latter special to each. The **superficial** or **common fibers** for the most part begin and end at the atrio-ventricular rings, but some enter the interatrial septum. The **deep** or **special bundles** also form two sets. Looped fibers pass over the atria from ring to ring, while annular or spiral fibers surround the ends of the veins which open into the atria, the auricles, and the fossa ovalis.

The muscular wall of the ventricles is much stronger than that of the atria. That of the left ventricle is in general about three times as thick as that of the right one, but is thin at the apex. The **superficial fibers** are attached above to the atrio-ventricular fibrous rings and pass in a spiral toward the apex. Here they bend upon themselves and pass deeply upward to terminate in a papillary muscle of the ventricle opposite to that in which they arose. The loops so formed at the apex constitute a whorl, the **vortex cordis.** The **deep fibers,** although they appear to be proper to each ventricle, have been shown by MacCallum to be in reality almost all common to both. Their arrangement is scroll-like. They begin on one side, curve around in the wall of that ventricle, then pass in the septum to the opposite side, and curve around the other ventricle. There is a layer of deep fibers which is confined to the basal part of the left ventricle; it is attached to the left atrio-ventricular ring.

Four **fibrous rings** (Annuli fibrosi) surround the orifices at the bases of the ventricles. The atrio-ventricular rings separate the musculature of the atria from that of the ventricles. Those which surround the origins of the pulmonary artery and aorta are festooned in conformity with the attached borders of the valves. The aortic ring contains on the right side a plate of cartilage (Cartilago cordis), which frequently becomes more or less calcified in old animals. Sometimes a smaller plate is present on the left side.

The **endocardium** lines the cavities of the heart and is continuous with the internal coat of the vessels which enter and leave the organ. Its free surface is smooth and glistening and is formed by a layer of endothelial cells. The latter rest on a thin layer of fibro-elastic tissue, which is connected with the myocardium by a subendocardial elastic tissue containing vessels and nerves.

Vessels and Nerves.—The heart receives a large blood-supply through the two **coronary arteries** which arise from the aorta opposite to the anterior and left cusps of the aortic valve. Most of the blood is returned by the **coronary veins,** which open into the right atrium by the coronary sinus.[1] A few small veins open directly into the right atrium, and others are said to open into the left atrium and the ventricles. The **lymph-vessels** form a subepicardial network which communicates

[1] These vessels will be described later in their systematic order.

through stomata with the cavity of the pericardium. There is a less distinct subendocardial network. The vessels converge usually to two trunks, which accompany the blood-vessels in the grooves and enter the glands at the bifurcation of the trachea. The **nerves** are derived from the **vagus** and **sympathetic** through the cardiac plexus.

THE ARTERIES

THE PULMONARY ARTERY

The **pulmonary artery** (A. pulmonalis) springs from the conus arteriosus at the left side of the base of the right ventricle. It curves upward, backward, and medially, and divides behind the arch of the aorta into right and left branches. It is related in front to the right auricle, behind to the left auricle, and medially to the aorta. It is enveloped with the latter in a common sheath of the visceral layer of the serous pericardium. Near the bifurcation it is connected with the arch of the aorta by a fibrous band about half an inch (ca. 1.2 cm.) in width; this is the **ligamentum arteriosum** (Fig. 542), a remnant of the large **ductus arteriosus,** which conducts most of the blood from the pulmonary artery to the aorta in the foetus.[1] The artery is bulbous at its origin, and forms three pouches, the **sinuses of the pulmonary artery,** which correspond to the cusps of the pulmonary valve. Beyond this it gradually diminishes in caliber.

In a horse of medium size the artery is about seven inches (ca. 17–18 cm.) long. At the origin it is about two and a half inches (ca. 6–6.5 cm.) in width; at the bifurcation its caliber is about one and a half inches (ca. 3.5–4 cm.). The wall is relatively thin, especially at the origin.

The **right branch** (Ramus dexter) of the pulmonary artery is longer and a little wider than the left one. It passes over the forepart of the left atrium and under the bifurcation of the trachea to the hilus of the right lung, and enters the latter below the right bronchus. In the lung it passes to the ventro-lateral side of the stem-bronchus and accompanies it to the base of the organ. The branches correspond to the ramification of the bronchi. The **left branch** (Ramus sinister) is very short. It passes backward and enters the lung below the left bronchus. Its branches within the lung are arranged like that of the right one.

THE SYSTEMIC ARTERIES

The **aorta** is the main systemic arterial trunk. It begins at the base of the left ventricle and is almost median at its origin. Its first part, the **ascending aorta** (Aorta ascendens), passes upward and forward between the pulmonary artery on the left and right atrium on the right. It then curves sharply backward and dorsally, inclines somewhat to the left, forming the **arch of the aorta** (Arcus aortæ), and reaches the ventral surface of the spine at the eighth or ninth thoracic vertebra. After passing backward along the ventral aspect of the bodies of the vertebræ and between the lungs, it traverses the hiatus aorticus and enters the abdominal cavity, where it lies ventral to the vertebral bodies and the psoas minor, just to the left of the median plane. It divides under the fifth or sixth lumbar vertebra into the two internal iliac arteries.

From the bifurcation a small vessel, the **middle sacral artery** (A. sacralis media), sometimes passes backward on the pelvic surface of the sacrum. It becomes lost in the periosteum or joins the coccygeal artery, or in exceptional cases is traceable to the sphincter ani externus.

The caliber of the aorta is greatest at its origin, which is termed the **bulbus**

---

[1] There is a depression in the interior of the artery which corresponds to the attachment of the lig. arteriosum, and in some cases the latter has a very small lumen.

aortæ. Here it forms three pouch-like dilatations, the **sinuses of the aorta.** These correspond to the cusps of the aortic valve, and the coronary arteries arise from the left posterior and anterior sinuses. At the arch the diameter is about two inches (ca. 5 cm.), and beyond this it diminishes rather rapidly in width.

It is convenient to divide the aorta into thoracic and abdominal parts. The **thoracic aorta** (Aorta thoracica) (Figs. 553, 554) lies within the pericardium to the point of attachment of the ligamentum arteriosum, and is enclosed with the pulmonary artery in a prolongation of the epicardium. Beyond this it is between the two pleural sacs. It is crossed on the right by the œsophagus and trachea, on the left by the left vagus nerve. The left recurrent nerve winds around the concavity

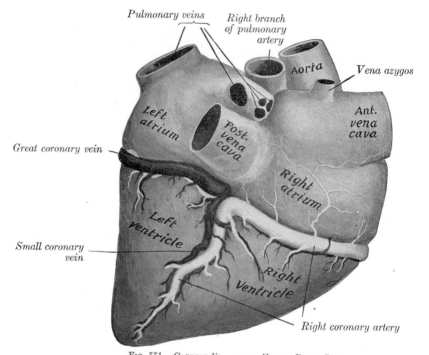

FIG. 551.—CARDIAC VESSELS OF HORSE; RIGHT SIDE.
Veins are black, arteries white, The circumflex branch of the coronary artery is largely concealed by the great coronary vein.

of the arch from the lateral to the medial side, and the vena azygos and thoracic duct lie along the dorsal part of its right face. The trachea causes it to deviate to the left, but beyond this it becomes median. The **abdominal aorta** (Aorta abdominalis) (Fig. 575) is related dorsally to the lumbar vertebræ, the ventral longitudinal ligament, and the left psoas minor muscle; in the hiatus aorticus it is related to the cisterna chyli. On its right is the posterior vena cava, and on its left the left kidney and ureter.

BRANCHES OF THE THORACIC AORTA

I. CORONARY ARTERIES

The two coronary arteries, right and left, are distributed almost entirely to the heart, but send some small twigs to the origins of the great vessels.

The **right coronary artery** (A. coronaria dextra) arises from the anterior sinus of the aorta. It passes forward and somewhat downward between the conus arteriosus and the right auricle to the coronary groove, in which it curves around to the right and backward. It then descends in the right longitudinal groove almost to the apex of the heart. It usually gives off a **circumflex branch** as it turns downward; this branch (Ramus circumflexus) passes back in the coronary groove, and anastomoses with the corresponding branch of the left artery.

The **left coronary artery** (A. coronaria sinistra) arises from the left posterior sinus of the aorta, emerges behind the origin of the pulmonary artery, and divides into two branches. The **descending branch** (Ramus descendens) passes down the

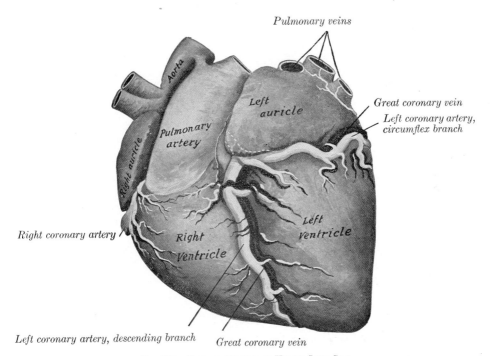

Fig. 552.—Cardiac Vessels of Horse; Left Side.
The dotted lines indicate part of the left coronary artery which is concealed by the left auricle. The ligamentum arteriosum is shown but not marked.

left longitudinal groove toward the apex. The **circumflex branch** (Ramus circumflexus) runs backward in the coronary groove, in which it winds around to the right side.

2. COMMON BRACHIOCEPHALIC TRUNK

The **common brachiocephalic trunk** (Truncus brachiocephalicus communis) is a very large vessel which arises from the convexity of the arch of the aorta within the pericardium. It is directed forward and upward. Its apparent length in horses of medium size is usually about two inches (ca. 5 cm.), but it may be only half an inch long, or absent. It is crossed on the left by the left vagus and cardiac nerves, and the left recurrent nerve runs between it and the trachea. It divides opposite to the second intercostal space or third rib into the brachiocephalic and left brachial arteries.

The **brachiocephalic artery** (A. brachiocephalica) is directed forward and somewhat dorsally in the anterior mediastinum, beneath the trachea. Opposite the first rib it gives off the bicarotid trunk and is continued as the **right brachial artery.** The latter (A. subclavia dexter) turns ventrally and bends around the anterior border of the first rib and the insertion of the scalenus muscle above the brachial vein. Its course and branches beyond this point will be described with the vessels of the thoracic limb.

The **left brachial artery** (A. subclavia sinistra) is longer than the right one and rises to a higher level. It forms an almost semicircular curve, the concavity being ventral. It is related medially to the œsophagus, trachea, and thoracic duct; and the left vagus, phrenic, and cardiac nerves cross under its origin.[1] It emerges from the thorax like the artery of the right side. There is thus a difference at first

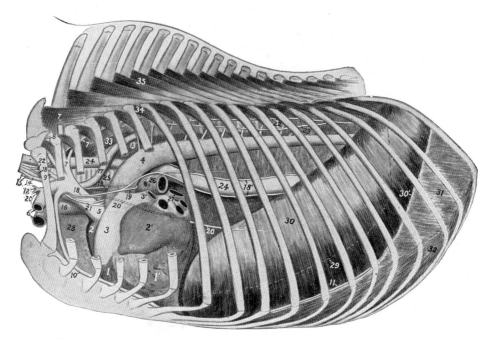

FIG. 553.—TOPOGRAPHY OF THORAX OF HORSE, LEFT SIDE, AFTER REMOVAL OF LUNG, PERICARDIUM, AND GREATER PART OF MEDIASTINAL PLEURA.

1, Right ventricle; 1', left ventricle; 2, right auricle; 2', left auricle; 3, pulmonary artery; 3', left branch of 3; 4, aorta; 5, brachiocephalic trunk; 6, left brachial vessels; 7, dorsal artery; 7', subcostal artery; 8, deep cervical artery; 9, vertebral artery; 10, internal thoracic artery; 11, musculo-phrenic artery; 12, inferior cervical artery; 13, intercostal artery; 14, bicarotid trunk; 15, common carotid arteries; 16, anterior vena cava; 17, thoracic duct; 18, left vagus; 18', œsophageal continuations of vagi; 19, left recurrent nerve; 20, left phrenic nerve (part which crosses pericardium indicated by dotted line); 21, cardiac nerve; 22, sympathetic trunk; 23, great splanchnic nerve; 24, œsophagus; 25, trachea; 26, left bronchus; 27, pulmonary veins; 28, apical lobe of right lung; 29, basal border of left lung indicated by dotted line; 30, diaphragm; 30', diaphragmatic line of pleural reflection; 31, 32, external and internal intercostal muscles; 33, longus colli; 34, levator costæ; 35, multifidus dorsi.

between the trunks of opposite sides, but beyond this their course and distribution are similar.

The left brachial and brachiocephalic arteries give off within the thorax the dorsal, deep cervical, vertebral, and internal thoracic arteries. At the first rib each gives off the external thoracic and inferior cervical arteries.

1. The **dorsal** or **costo-cervical artery** (A. costo-cervicalis) of the left side passes dorsally across the left face of the trachea and œsophagus toward the second intercostal space. The right artery arises usually by a common trunk with the deep cervical, crosses the right face of the trachea, and has no contact with the œsophagus. Both detach small branches to the trachea, mediastinal lymph glands, and pleura, and on reaching the longus colli divide into two branches. Of these, the

---

[1] In some cases the artery is too low to touch the œsophagus.

subcostal artery (A. intercostalis suprema) is the smaller. It passes backward along the lateral border of the longus colli with the sympathetic trunk. It gives off the second, third, and fourth intercostal arteries, and ends at the fifth space, where it anastomoses with the first aortic intercostal artery, or constitutes the fifth intercostal artery, or dips into the longissimus muscle. It also gives off spinal branches and twigs to the longus colli and the pleura. The other branch (A. transversa colli) is the direct continuation of the trunk. It emerges through the

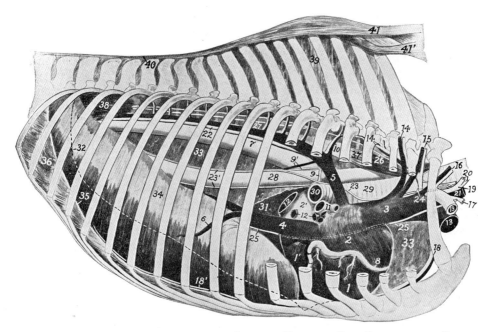

Fig. 554.—Topography of Thorax of Horse, Right Side, after Removal of Lung, Pericardium, and Greater Part of Mediastinal Pleura.

1, Right ventricle; 1', left ventricle; 2, right atrium; 2', left atrium; 3, anterior vena cava; 4, posterior vena cava; 5, vena azygos; 6, phrenic vein; 7, aorta; 8, right coronary artery; 9, bronchial artery; 9', œsophageal artery and vein; 10, first aortic intercostal artery and vein; 11, right pulmonary artery; 12, pulmonary veins; 13, right brachial vessels; 14, dorsal vessels; 14', subcostal vessels; 15, deep cervical vessels; 16, vertebral vessels; 17, inferior cervical artery; 18, internal thoracic vessels: 18', musculo-phrenic artery; 19, bicarotid trunk; 20, common carotid arteries; 21, jugular vein; 22, thoracic duct; 23, right vagus; 23', œsophageal continuations of vagi; 24, right recurrent nerve; 25, right phrenic nerve (part which crosses pericardium indicated by dotted line); 26, sympathetic trunk; 27, great splanchnic nerve; 28, œsophagus; 29, trachea; 30, right bronchus; 31, left lung; 32, basal border of right lung indicated by dotted line; 33, mediastinal pleura; 34, diaphragm; 35, diaphragmatic line of pleural reflection; 36, intercostal muscle; 37, longus colli; 38, psoas; 39, interspinous ligament; 40, supraspinous ligament; 41, funicular part, 41', lamellar part, of ligamentum nuchæ.

dorsal end of the second intercostal space, passes across the longissimus costarum and longissimus dorsi toward the withers, and divides into several diverging branches. An anterior branch passes upward and forward between the splenius and complexus and anastomoses with branches of the deep cervical artery; the others ascend on the dorso-scapular ligament under cover of the serratus ventralis and rhomboideus to the withers, supplying the muscles and skin of this region.

The left dorsal artery sometimes arises with the deep cervical by a common trunk; this arrangement is usual on the right side, and there may be a common stem for the dorsal, deep cervical and vertebral arteries. Occasionally the artery arises from the brachiocephalic trunk. Sometimes it emerges through the third space. The subcostal may arise independently behind the dorsal or from the deep cervical artery.

2. The **deep** or superior **cervical artery** (A. cervicalis profunda) arises in front of the dorsal or by a common trunk with it. It crosses the œsophagus (left side),

the trachea (right side), and the longus colli, and emerges from the thoracic cavity by passing through the space behind the first costo-transverse articulation.[1] In the thorax it gives off a small **mediastinal branch** (A. mediastini cranialis) to the mediastinum and the pericardium; also the **first intercostal artery** (A. intercostalis prima), a very small vessel which passes down in the first intercostal space. After leaving the thorax the artery passes upward and forward on the spinalis muscle and the lamellar part of the ligamentum nuchæ, covered by the complexus. Its terminal branches anastomose with branches of the occipital and vertebral arteries in the region of the axis. Numerous collateral branches are detached to the lateral muscles of the neck, the ligamentum nuchæ, and the skin, and anastomoses occur with the dorsal artery also.

3. The **vertebral artery** (A. vertebralis) arises from the brachial on the left side, the brachiocephalic on the right; it begins opposite the first intercostal space and passes upward and forward. On the left side it crosses the œsophagus, on the right, the trachea. Emerging from the thorax it passes between the longus colli medially and the scalenus laterally, under the transverse process of the seventh cervical vertebra, and continues along the neck through the series of foramina transversaria, between which it is covered by the intertransversales colli.[2] Emerging

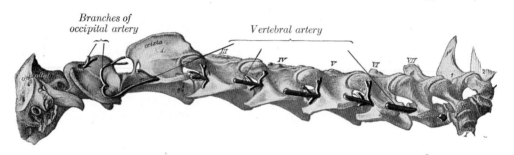

FIG. 555.—VERTEBRAL ARTERY OF HORSE. (After Schmaltz, Atlas d. Anat. d. Pferdes.)

from the foramen of the axis, it crosses the capsule of the atlanto-axial joint, and joins the recurrent branch of the occipital artery under cover of the obliquus capitis posterior. At each intervertebral foramen a **spinal branch** (Ramus spinalis) is given off which enters the vertebral canal and reinforces the ventral spinal artery. It also gives off series of dorsal and ventral **muscular branches** (Rami musculares). The dorsal branches are the larger; they supply the deep extensor muscles of the head and neck, and anastomose with the deep cervical and occipital arteries. The ventral branches supply chiefly the scalenus, longus colli, intertransversales, and rectus capitis ventralis major. The artery is accompanied by the vertebral vein and a sympathetic nerve trunk (Nervus transversarius).

4. The **internal thoracic artery** (A. thoracica interna) is a large vessel which arises from the ventral side of the brachial opposite the first rib. It curves downward and backward, being at first on the medial surface of the rib, and then crosses the ventral part of the first intercostal space and passes under the transversus thoracis muscle. It runs backward under cover of that muscle over the chondro-sternal joints to the eighth costal cartilage, where it divides into musculo-phrenic and anterior abdominal branches. At each intercostal space two collateral branches are detached. The **intercostal branches** (Rami intercostales) ascend in the intercostal spaces and anastomose with homonymous descending arteries. The ventral

[1] The artery sometimes emerges through the second intercostal space.

[2] In some cases the last cervical transverse process has a foramen transversarium, through which the artery passes.

branches detach small twigs to the transversus thoracis, pleura, and pericardium, and pass out between the costal cartilages as **perforating branches** (Rami perforantes) to supply the pectoral muscles and skin, anastomosing with the external thoracic artery. A very small **pericardiaco-phrenic artery** (A. pericardiaco-phrenica) ascends in the mediastinum on the left side, in the caval fold of pleura on the right side; it supplies fine twigs to the pericardium and pleura and accompanies the phrenic nerve to the diaphragm. In the young subject it gives small branches, the **thymic arteries** (Aa. thymicæ), to the thymus gland. The **musculo-phrenic** or asternal **artery** (A. musculophrenica) passes along the groove between the eighth and ninth costal cartilages and continues along the costal attachment of the transversus abdominis (Fig. 275). It gives off intercostal branches which anastomose with those descending from the thoracic aorta, and twigs to the diaphragm and transversus abdominis. The **anterior abdominal artery** (A. abdominalis cranialis) is the direct continuation of the internal thoracic. It passes between the ninth costal cartilage and the xiphoid cartilage, runs backward on the abdominal surface of the rectus abdominis, and then becomes embedded in the muscle (Fig. 590). It supplies the ventral wall of the abdomen and anastomoses with the posterior abdominal artery.

5. The **external thoracic artery** (A. thoracica externa) is given off from the ventral aspect of the brachial, usually at the medial surface or anterior border of the first rib. It turns around the first rib ventral to the brachial vein (when given off within the thorax), and passes backward under cover of the deep pectoral muscle; it is continued as a small vessel in the cutaneous muscle, where it accompanies the external thoracic vein. It gives branches to the pectoral muscles and the axillary lymph glands and terminates in the cutaneous muscle and the skin of the ventral wall of the abdomen.

This artery varies in origin and size. It may come from the internal thoracic or from the brachial outside of the thorax (even as far distally as the teres tuberosity), or may arise by a common trunk with the inferior cervical. It may be very small or even absent, in which case the perforating branches of the internal thoracic compensate.

6. The **inferior cervical artery** (Truncus omo-cervicalis) arises usually from the dorsal surface of the brachial artery opposite the first rib or where that vessel winds around the rib. It is directed downward and a little forward across the lateral surface of the terminal part of the jugular vein and the deep face of the scalenus among the posterior cervical lymph glands, and divides into ascending and descending branches. The **ascending branch** (A. cervicalis ascendens) passes upward and forward along the lateral surface of the jugular vein, then turns sharply backward and runs upward along the anterior border of the anterior deep pectoral muscle, between the omo-hyoideus and brachiocephalicus and in relation to the prescapular lymph glands; it gives branches to these muscles and the posterior cervical and prescapular lymph glands. The **descending branch** (A. transversa scapulæ) passes ventro-laterally across the surface of the anterior deep pectoral and then runs in the groove between the anterior superficial pectoral muscle and the brachiocephalicus in company with the cephalic vein. It supplies branches to these muscles and the skin of the breast.[1]

THE COMMON CAROTID ARTERY

The two common carotid arteries arise from the brachiocephalic artery by a common trunk. This stem, the **truncus bicaroticus,** is detached from the medial face of the brachiocephalic opposite the first rib and passes forward on the ventral face of the trachea. It is related ventrally to the posterior cervical lymph glands, the terminal parts of the jugular veins, and the anterior vena cava, and

[1] In rare cases the two branches arise separately.

laterally to the vagus and recurrent nerves. It is commonly two or three inches (ca. 5–7 cm.) in length, but it may vary between one and eight inches (ca. 2.5–20 cm.).[1]

The **right common carotid artery** (A. carotis communis dextra) passes obliquely from the ventral face of the trachea to its right side and continues in this position, but inclines toward the dorsal surface of the trachea near its termination. It

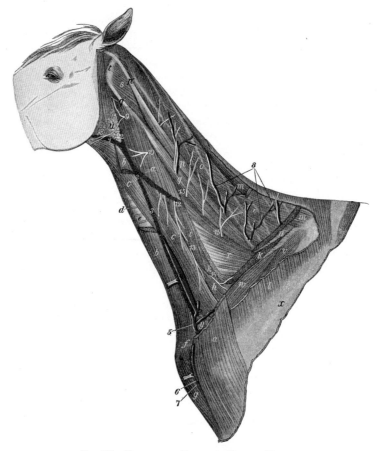

FIG. 556.—VESSELS AND NERVES OF NECK OF HORSE.

a, Brachiocephalicus; *b*, sterno-cephalicus; *c*, omo-hyoideus; *d*, sterno-thyro-hyoideus; *e*, trachea; *f*, position of cariniform cartilage; *g*, anterior superficial pectoral muscle; *h*, scalenus; *i*, intertransversales; *k*, insertion of serratus cervicis; *l*, remnant of trapezius; *m*, rhomboideus; *n*, splenius; *o*, complexus; *p*, *q*, longissimus capitis et atlantis; *p′*, *q′*, tendons of same; *r*, longissimus; *s*, obliquus capitis posterior; *t*, wing of atlas; *u*, parotid gland; *v*, supraspinatus; *w*, anterior deep pectoral; *x*, spine of scapula; *y*, prescapular lymph glands; *1*, external maxillary vein; *2*, *3*, jugular vein; *4*, carotid artery, exposed by drawing jugular vein aside; *5*, *6*, ascending and descending branches of inferior cervical artery; *7*, cephalic vein; *8*, branches of deep cervical artery; *9–14*, ventral branches of second to seventh cervical nerves; *15*, branches of dorsal divisions of cervical nerves. (Ellenberger-Baum, Top. Anat. d. Pferdes.)

divides at the crico-pharyngeus muscle and under cover of the mandibular gland into external carotid, internal carotid, and occipital arteries. A small nodule is present in the angle of division. This is the carotid body or **glomus caroticum.** It is enclosed in a fibrous sheath, and is accompanied dorsally by the vagus and sympathetic nerves, ventrally by the recurrent nerve. In the posterior part of the neck it is in contact superficially with the jugular vein, but further forward

---

[1] In very rare cases there is no truncus bicaroticus. The two carotid arteries then arise separately from the brachiocephalic, the left one first, and the right one an inch or more further forward.

the omo-hyoideus muscle intervenes between the artery and vein. Near its termination the artery becomes more deeply placed and is related laterally to the

mandibular and parotid glands, medially to the œsophagus. In some cases it is in contact ventrally with the lateral lobe of the thyroid gland, especially when the latter is more dorsally situated or larger than usual.

The **left common carotid artery** (A. carotis communis sinistra) differs from the right one in that it is related deeply to the œsophagus also, which usually separates it from the trachea in part of its course.

The left carotid is commonly in contact with the trachea for a short distance (ca. 8–10 cm.) at the root of the neck, but this contact may be even less when the œsophagus is more ventral than usual and the bicarotid trunk long. On the other hand, the relation to the trachea may be more extensive.

The collateral branches of the common carotids are in the main small. They commonly comprise the following:

1. **Muscular branches** (Rami musculares) of variable size go to the ventral muscles of the neck and the skin.

2. **Œsophageal** and **tracheal branches** (Rami œsophagei et tracheales). Small twigs go to the cervical lymph glands also.

3. The **parotid artery** (A. parotidea) comes off near the termination and enters the ventral part of the parotid gland. It also sends twigs to the adjacent lymph glands, and sometimes detaches a branch to the mandibular gland. It is inconstant.

4. The **anterior thyroid** or **thyro-laryngeal artery** (A. thyreoidea cranialis), the largest collateral branch of the carotid, arises from the latter two or three inches before it divides. It curves over the anterior end of the thyroid gland, into which it sends several branches. It gives off the **laryngeal artery** (A. laryngea), which sends branches to the external muscles of the larynx and the constrictors of the pharynx, passes between the cricoid and thyroid cartilages, and supplies the internal muscles and the mucous membrane of the larynx. A small **pharyngeal branch** (A. pharyngea ascendens) runs upward and forward to the crico-pharyngeus, and supplies twigs to the posterior part of the pharynx and the origin of the œsophagus. Small innominate twigs are given off to the trachea, the œsophagus, and the sterno-thyro-hyoideus and omo-hyoideus muscles.

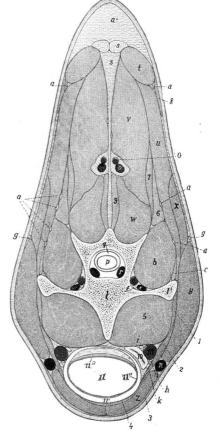

FIG. 557.—Cross-section of Neck of Horse, Passing through Fifth Cervical Vertebra; Anterior View.

a, Branches of cervical nerves; *a'*, nuchal fat; *b,* intertransversalis muscle; *c,* longissimus muscle; *d,* vertebral artery; *e,* vertebral vein; *f,* nervus transversarius; *g,* spinal accessory nerve (dorsal division); *h,* recurrent nerve; *i,* vago-sympathetic trunk; *k,* tracheal lymph duct; *l,* body of fifth cervical vertebra; *l'*, transverse process of same; *m,* common carotid artery; *n,* jugular vein; *o,* deep cervical artery; *o'*, satellite vein of *o;* *p,* spinal cord; *q,* dura mater; *r,* spinal vein; *s,* ligamentum nuchæ; *t,* rhomboideus muscle; *u,* splenius; *v,* complexus; *w,* multifidus; *x,* serratus cervicis; *y,* brachiocephalicus; *z,* sterno-cephalicus; *1,* rectus capitis ventralis major; *2,* omo-hyoideus; *3,* cutaneus; *4,* sterno-thyro-hyoideus; *5,* longus colli; *6, 7,* longissimus capitis et atlantis; *8,* trapezius; *9,* spinalis; *10,* œsophagus; *11,* trachea, with cartilaginous ring (*11'*), mucous membrane (*11''*), and muscular layer (*11'''*). (After Ellenberger, in Leisering's Atlas.)

　　In some cases the thyroid and laryngeal arteries arise from the carotid separately or by a short common stem. A laryngeal branch is often detached from the carotid in front of the thyrolaryngeal and enters the larynx with the anterior laryngeal nerve. The pharyngeal branch frequently comes directly from the carotid.

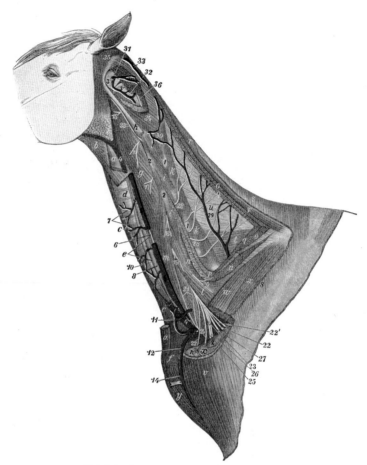

FIG. 558.—DEEP DISSECTION OF NECK OF HORSE.

　　a, a, Ends of sterno-cephalicus; *b,* anterior part of omo-hyoideus; *c,* sterno-thyro-hyoideus; *d,* trachea; *e,* œsophagus; *f,* cariniform cartilage; *g,* rectus cap. ventralis major; *h,* stump of longissimus atlantis; *i,* intertransversales; *k,* multifidus; *l, m,* scalenus; *n,* serratus cervicis; *o, o,* stumps of splenius; *p,* longissimus cervicis; *q,* complexus (most of which is removed); *r,* rhomboideus; *s,* trapezius; *t,* spinalis et semispinalis; *u,* lamellar part of lig. nuchæ; *v,* brachiocephalicus; *w,* anterior deep pectoral; *x,* supraspinatus; *y,* anterior superficial pectoral; *z,* tuber scapulæ; *1, 1,* articular processes of cervical vertebræ; *2, 2,* transverse processes of same; *3,* atlas; *3',* axis; *4, 4,* jugular vein (remainder removed); *5,* common carotid artery, from which a piece is removed to show the accompanying nerves and the œsophagus; *6,* vago-sympathetic trunk; *7, 7,* tracheal and muscular branches of carotid artery; *8,* recurrent nerve; *10,* left tracheal lymph-duct; *11, 12,* ascending and descending branches of inferior cervical artery (*13*); *14,* cephalic vein; *15–20,* ventral branches of second to seventh cervical nerves; *21,* roots of phrenic nerve; *22,* pectoral nerves; *22',* nerve to serratus ventralis; *23,* musculo-cutaneous nerve; *24,* median nerve; *25,* ulnar nerve; *26,* radial nerve; *27,* axillary nerve; *28,* dorsal branches of cervical nerves; *28',* accessory nerve (cut); *29,* deep cervical artery; *30,* muscular branch of vertebral artery; *31,* posterior branch of occipital artery; *32,* vertebral artery; *33,* muscular branches of occipital artery; *34,* obliquus capitis post.; *35,* obl. cap. ant.; *36,* twig from dorsal branch of third cervical nerve. (After Ellenberger-Baum, Top. Anat. des Pferdes.)

　　5. The **posterior thyroid artery** (A. thyreoidea caudalis) is a small and inconstant vessel which arises from the carotid at a variable distance behind the anterior thyroid or from the latter or the parotid artery. It sends branches into the posterior part of the thyroid gland, and detaches small tracheal and muscular twigs. In some cases it is distributed chiefly or entirely to the adjacent muscles.

THE OCCIPITAL ARTERY

The **occipital artery** (A. occipitalis) is usually the second in size of the terminals of the carotid. It arises commonly just in front of the internal carotid, but in some cases with that artery by a common trunk of variable length. It pursues a somewhat flexuous course to the fossa atlantis, where it divides into anterior and posterior branches. It is related superficially to the mandibular gland and the brachiocephalicus, and deeply to the guttural pouch and the rectus capitis ventralis major.[1]

The internal carotid artery, the ventral cerebral vein, and the accessory, vagus, and sympathetic nerves cross its deep face. It gives off twigs to the mandibular gland, the ventral straight muscles of the head, the guttural pouch and the adjacent lymph glands, and two named collateral branches.[2] The **condyloid artery** (A. condyloidea) is a small vessel which passes upward and forward on the guttural pouch, and divides into muscular and meningeal branches. The latter enter the cranium through the foramen lacerum and hypoglossal foramen and are distributed to the dura mater. This artery is very variable in its origin; it often comes from the posterior meningeal. The **posterior meningeal artery** (A. meningea aboralis) is a much larger vessel, which runs upward and forward between the obliquus capitis anterior and the paramastoid process, passes through the mastoid foramen into the temporal canal, enters the cranial cavity, and is distributed to the dura mater. It gives collateral branches to the atlanto-occipital articulation and the adjacent muscles.

The **posterior** or **recurrent branch** (Ramus recurrens) of the occipital passes up through the

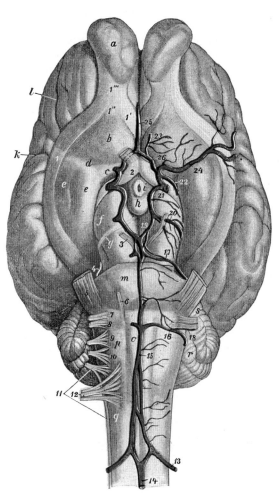

FIG. 559.—VESSELS AND NERVES OF BASE OF BRAIN OF HORSE.

13, Cerebro-spinal artery; *14*, ventral spinal artery; *15*, basilar artery; *16*, posterior cerebellar artery; *17*, anterior cerebellar artery; *18*, internal auditory artery; *19*, posterior cerebral artery; *20*, deep cerebral artery; *21*, stump of internal carotid artery; *22*, anterior chorioid artery; *23*, anterior meningeal artery; *24*, middle cerebral artery; *25*, artery of corpus callosum; *26*, anterior cerebral artery; *1*, *1'*, *1''*, olfactory striæ; *1'''*, olfactory tract; *2–12*, cranial nerves; *a*, olfactory bulb; *b*, trigonum olfactorium; *c*, lamina perforata anterior; *d*, fossa lateralis; *e*, piriform lobe; *f*, cerebral peduncle; *g*, tractus transversus; *h*, corpus mammillare; *i*, tuber cinereum; *k*, lateral fissure (of Sylvius); *l*, presylvian fissure; *m*, pons; *o*, pyramid; *p*, facial eminence; *q*, corpus restiforme; *r*, cerebellum; *s*, middle peduncle of cerebellum. (After Ellenberger-Baum, Top. Anat. d. Pferdes.)

[1] The relation to the guttural pouch is not constant. In some cases —especially when the head and neck are extended—the artery lies behind the pouch. The backward extension of the latter is variable.

[2] The branch to the mandibular gland (A. glandulæ mandibularis dorsalis) may come from the external carotid or the posterior meningeal artery.

foramen transversarium of the atlas and joins the vertebral artery. It gives branches to the obliquus capitis posterior, which covers it.

The **anterior** or **occipital branch** (Ramus occipitalis) passes through the alar foramen of the atlas and supplies the muscles and skin of the poll, anastomosing with the deep cervical artery and its fellow of the opposite side. In the alar furrow it gives off the **cerebrospinal artery** (A. cerebrospinalis), which enters the spinal canal through the intervertebral foramen of the atlas, perforates the dura mater, and divides into cerebral and spinal branches. The **cerebral branch** (Ramus cerebralis) unites with that of the opposite side to form the **basilar artery,** and the **spinal branch** (Ramus spinalis) similarly forms by union with its fellow the **ventral spinal artery.**

The **basilar artery** (A. basilaris cerebri) passes forward in the median groove on the ventral surface of the medulla oblongata and pons and divides into the two posterior cerebral arteries. The collateral branches of the basilar are:

1. Medullary branches (Rami medullares), ten or twelve in number, distributed to the medulla oblongata.

2. Posterior cerebellar arteries (Aa. cerebelli aborales), which pass outward around the medulla behind the pons to the cerebellum, to which they are distributed after giving twigs to the medulla and pons.

3. The small auditory artery (A. auditiva interna) accompanies the acoustic nerve to the internal ear. It often arises from the posterior cerebellar.

4. Anterior cerebellar arteries (Aa. cerebelli orales). These are very variable in number and origin. There are often two or three on either side, and they frequently arise from the posterior cerebral. They pass outward in front of the pons and supply the anterior part of the cerebellum.

The **posterior cerebral arteries** (Aa. cerebri aborales) diverge at an acute angle and join the posterior communicating branches of the internal carotid arteries on the ventral surface of the cerebral peduncles. They are connected by a transverse branch and by a network of fine twigs which form often a rete mirabile.

The **ventral spinal artery** (A. spinalis ventralis) runs along the ventral median fissure of the spinal cord, which it supplies. It is reinforced along its course by branches from the vertebral, intercostal, lumbar, and lateral sacral arteries, which enter the vertebral canal through the intervertebral foramina.

THE INTERNAL CAROTID ARTERY (Figs. 559, 561, 562)

This artery (A. carotis interna) is usually somewhat smaller than the occipital. It usually arises just behind that artery, crosses its deep face, and runs upward and forward on the guttural pouch to the foramen lacerum. Not rarely it arises with the occipital artery from a common trunk of variable length. It is closely related to the vagus nerve and the anterior cervical ganglion of the sympathetic nerve, fibers from which accompany it. It is crossed laterally by the ninth and twelfth cranial nerves and the pharyngeal branch of the vagus. It passes through the ventral petrosal sinus and enters the cavernous sinus, within which it forms an S-shaped curve. It is connected with the opposite artery by a transverse branch, the **intercarotid artery** (A. intercarotica), which lies in the intercavernous sinus behind the pituitary body. A branch (A. caroticobasilaris) often connects it with the basilar artery. It then perforates the dura mater, gives off the posterior communicating artery, and passes forward and divides at the side of the optic chiasma into anterior and middle cerebral arteries.

The **posterior communicating artery** (A. communicans aboralis) turns backward and joins the posterior cerebral branch of the basilar. It gives off the **deep cerebral artery** (A. cerebri profunda), which winds around the cerebral peduncle and is distributed chiefly to the mid-brain; it is often double. A smaller collateral branch is the **anterior chorioid artery** (A. chorioidea oralis), which passes along the optic tract and is distributed in the chorioid plexus of the lateral ventricle.

The **anterior cerebral artery** (A. cerebri oralis) unites with the corresponding branch of the opposite artery above the optic chiasma. From this junction proceeds the **artery of the corpus callosum** (A. corporis callosi), which turns around the genu of the corpus callosum, enters the great longitudinal fissure, divides into two branches, and is distributed to the medial aspect of the cerebral hemispheres. The anterior cerebral gives off the small internal ophthalmic artery (A. ophthalmica interna), which passes forward at first lateral to the optic nerve; then, crossing over the latter to its medial side, it joins a branch of the external ophthalmic. A small **anterior meningeal** branch (A. meningea oralis) of the anterior cerebral is distributed to the anterior part of the dura, and assists in forming a network in the ethmoidal fossa (Rete ethmoidale), anastomosing with the ethmoidal branch of the external ophthalmic artery and the artery of the corpus callosum.

The **middle cerebral artery** (A. cerebri media) passes outward in the fossa lateralis in front of the piriform lobe, reaches the lateral fissure, and divides into branches on the lateral surface of the hemisphere.

The **circulus arteriosus** (Fig. 559) is formed at the interpeduncular space of the base of the brain by the union of the anterior cerebral arteries in front, by the diverging posterior cerebral arteries behind, and is completed laterally by the junction of the latter with the posterior communicating arteries and by the internal carotid. It is irregularly polygonal in outline, and surrounds the optic chiasma and hypophysis cerebri.[1]

THE EXTERNAL CAROTID ARTERY (Figs. 561, 562)

This artery (A. carotis externa), by its size and direction, constitutes the continuation of the common carotid. It passes forward on the lateral wall of the pharynx at the lower border of the guttural pouch, covered by the mandibular gland and the occipito-mandibularis, digastricus and stylo-hyoideus muscles, and in relation to the parapharyngeal lymph glands. It then emerges between the stylo-hyoideus and the great cornu of the hyoid bone, ascends on the latter parallel with the posterior border of the lower jaw, and terminates about two inches (ca. 5 cm.) below the temporo-mandibular articulation by dividing into superficial temporal and internal maxillary branches. It is crossed deeply near its origin by the anterior laryngeal and pharyngeal branches of the vagus nerve. Just before its emergence its superficial face is crossed by the hypoglossal nerve, and the glosso-pharyngeal nerve passes over its medial surface at the ventral border of the great cornu. The chief collateral branches are the masseteric, external maxillary, and posterior auricular. It also furnishes variable branches to the mandibular and parotid glands, the guttural pouch, and the pharyngeal lymph glands, as well as twigs to some adjacent muscles.

1. The **masseteric artery** (A. masseterica) is given off from the external carotid at its emergence from beneath the stylo-hyoideus. It passes downward and slightly forward under cover of the parotid gland and over the tendon of insertion of the sterno-cephalicus to the posterior border of the mandible and appears on the masseter muscle, which it enters after a short course on its surface. It gives

[1] The cerebral arteries are very variable in arrangement, and the foregoing account is a brief statement of the more usual disposition of the larger vessels.

branches also to the medial pterygoid and occipito-mandibularis muscles and the parotid gland.

2. The **external maxillary artery** (A. maxillaris externa) arises from the external carotid on the deep surface of the posterior belly of the digastricus (Fig. 561). It runs downward and forward on the lateral wall of the pharynx across the deep face of the stylo-hyoideus toward the great cornu of the hyoid bone, accompanied by the glosso-pharyngeal nerve in front and the hypoglossal nerve behind. After giving off the lingual artery at the posterior border of the great cornu, it inclines more ventrally on the medial surface of the medial pterygoid muscle, crosses over the hyoglossus muscle, the hypoglossal nerve, the mandibular duct, and the intermediate tendon of the digastricus, and turns forward in the mandibular space. Here it lies on the lower part of the medial pterygoid muscle, and is related medially to the mandibular lymph glands, above to the anterior belly of the digastricus, and below to the homonymous vein. At the anterior border of the masseter it turns around the ventral border of the jaw and ascends on the face in front of that muscle. At the turn the artery is in front, the vein in the middle, and the parotid duct posterior. The artery is conveniently placed at its inflection for taking the pulse, since it is superficial and lies directly on the bone. Beyond this point it is commonly termed the **facial artery** (A. facialis). The artery and vein pass upward along the anterior border of the masseter, under cover of the facial cutaneous and the zygomaticus, and are crossed superficially by branches of the facial nerve and deeply by the parotid duct. The artery terminates over the levator labii superioris proprius by dividing into the dorsal nasal and the angular artery of the eye. The chief branches of the external maxillary are as follows:

(1) The **pharyngeal artery** (A. palatina ascendens) arises usually behind the stylo-pharyngeus, passes between that muscle and the great cornu, and runs forward on the lateral wall of the pharynx under the elastic pharyngeal fascia. It is distributed to the pharynx, soft palate, and tonsil.

(2) The **lingual artery** (A. lingualis) is a large branch which diverges from the parent trunk at an acute angle, runs along the ventral border of the great cornu of the hyoid bone, and dips under the hyoglossus muscle. It then passes across the kerato-hyoideus, turns inward under the intercornual joint of the hyoid bone, and runs forward in the tongue between the hyoglossus and genio-glossus. This part (A. profunda linguæ) is flexuous and is accompanied by branches of the hypoglossal and lingual nerves. It is the chief artery of the tongue, and anastomoses with the opposite artery and the sublingual.[1]

(3) The **sublingual artery** (A. sublingualis) is a smaller vessel which arises at the anterior extremity of the mandibular gland (Fig. 561). It passes forward on the anterior belly of the digastricus, between the ramus of the mandible and the mylo-hyoideus, perforates the latter, runs along the lower border of the sublingual gland, and ramifies in the mucous membrane of the anterior part of the floor of the mouth. It detaches branches to the muscles and skin in the mandibular space, the mandibular lymph glands, and the sublingual gland. It also gives off the small **submental artery** (A. submentalis) which runs forward superficially toward the lower lip, supplying twigs to the skin and the mylo-hyoideus.

In some cases the sublingual artery arises from the lingual and the submental from the external maxillary. Sometimes the sublingual remains on the superficial face of the mylo-hyoideus —thus resembling the submental of man—and the sublingual gland is supplied by a special branch of the lingual.

[1] In some cases the lingual trunk runs on the superficial face of the hyoglossus instead of passing beneath it; in such specimens a small branch extends forward a variable distance under the muscle.

A considerable branch may be given off in the mandibular space, which turns around the lower border of the jaw and enters the middle of the lower part of the masseter muscle. In some cases this artery is of large size and its pulsation can be felt. It is accompanied by a vein.

(4) The **inferior labial artery** (A. labialis inferior) arises from the external maxillary a little before it reaches the depressor labii inferioris (Fig. 560). It passes forward, dips under the depressor muscle, and continues to the lower lip. It supplies branches to the muscles and skin in this region, to the inferior buccal glands, the mucous membrane of the cheek, and the lower lip, anastomosing with the mental artery and the corresponding vessels of the opposite side. It detaches

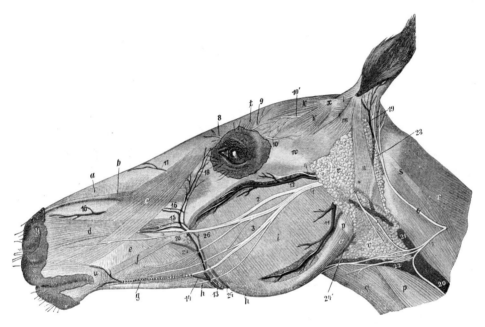

FIG. 560.—SUPERFICIAL DISSECTION OF HEAD OF HORSE. MOST OF THE CUTANEUS IS REMOVED.

a, Lateralis nasi; *b*, levator labii superioris proprius; *c*, levator naso-labialis; *d*, dilatator naris lateralis; *e*, buccinator; *f*, zygomaticus, posterior part of which is removed; *g*, depressor labii inferioris; *h*, stump of retractor anguli oris; *i*, masseter; *k, k*, scutularis; *l*, scutulo-auriculares superficiales; *m*, zygomatico-auricularis; *n*, parotido-auricularis; *o*, occipito-mandibularis; *p*, sterno-cephalicus; *p'*, tendon of *p*; *q*, omo-hyoideus; *r*, splenius; *s*, tendon of splenius and longissimus capitis; *t*, corrugator supercilii; *u*, orbicularis oris; *v*, parotid gland; *w*, zygomatic arch; *x*, scutiform cartilage; *y*, upper commissure of nostril; *1*, facial nerve; *2*, superior buccal nerve; *3*, inferior buccal nerve; *4*, transverse facial nerve; *5*, cervical branch of facial nerve; *6*, posterior auricular branch of second cervical nerve; *7*, cutaneous cervical branch of same; *8*, infratrochlear nerve; *9*, frontal nerve; *10*, lacrimal nerve; *10'*, end of auriculo-palpebral nerve; *11*, masseteric artery and vein; *12*, transverse facial artery and vein; *13*, facial nerve; *14*, inferior labial artery; *15*, superior labial artery; *16*, lateral nasal artery; *17*, dorsal nasal artery; *18*, angular artery of the eye; *19*, posterior auricular artery; *20, 21*, jugular vein; *22*, external maxillary vein; *23*, great auricular vein; *24*, parotid duct; *24'*, origin of same; *25*, superior buccal glands; *26*, facial vein. (After Ellenberger-Baum, Top. Anat. d. Pferdes.)

a branch (A. anguli oris) to the angle of the mouth, which anastomoses with the superior labial.

(5) The **superior labial artery** (A. labialis superior) arises from the facial in front of the facial crest (Fig. 560). It passes forward under the dilatator naris lateralis and levator nasolabialis to the upper lip, gives twigs to the upper part of the cheek and the lateral nasal region, and ramifies in the upper lip, anastomosing with the opposite artery and the palato-labial.

(6) The **lateral nasal artery** (A. lateralis nasi) arises usually a little above the preceding one, and runs forward parallel with it and under the levator nasolabialis to the nostril (Fig. 560). It supplies branches to the lateral nasal region and the nostril.

The vessel is often double. It may arise from the superior labial at the point of bifurcation of the facial or with the dorsal nasal from the infraorbital artery (as in the ox). In some cases it gives off a dorsal nasal branch.

(7) The **dorsal nasal artery** (A. dorsalis nasi) arises on the levator labii superioris proprius and passes forward under the levator nasolabialis to the dorsum nasi (Fig. 560).

(8) The **angular artery of the eye** (A. angularis oculi) runs toward the medial

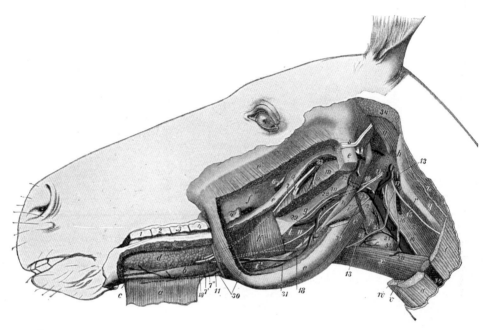

FIG. 561.—PAROTID, MASSETERIC, AND LINGUAL REGIONS OF HORSE; DEEP DISSECTION, THIRD LAYER.

a, Mylo-hyoideus, anterior part, reflected; *b*, genio-hyoideus; *c*, genio-glossus; *d*, sublingual gland; *e*, ramus of mandible, greater part removed; *e'*, stump of masseter; *f*, maxillary tuberosity; *g*, great cornu of hyoid bone; *h*, wing of atlas; *i*, intermediate tendon of digastricus; *i'*, anterior belly, *i''*, posterior belly, of digastricus; *k*, posterior part of mylohyoideus; *l*, hyo-glossus; *m*, pterygoideus medialis (cut); *n*, stylo-hyoideus; *o*, occipito-mandibularis; *p*, crico-pharyngeus; *q*, obliquus capitis ant.; *r*, tendon of longissimus atlantis; *s*, rectus cap. ventralis; *t*, brachiocephalicus (cut); *u*, sterno-cephalicus (cut); *v*, sterno-thyroideus (cut); *w*, sterno-hyoideus (cut); *x*, omo-hyoideus; *y*, obliquus cap. post.; *z*, splenius (cut); *1–4*, upper cheek teeth; *4'*, last cheek tooth; *5*, stump of facial nerve; *6*, stump of buccinator nerve; *7*, lingual nerve; *7'*, superficial branch, *7''*, deep branch of lingual nerve; *8*, stumps of mandibular alveolar vessels and nerve; *9*, mylo-hyoid nerve (cut); *10*, glosso-pharyngeal nerve; *11*, hypoglossal nerve; *12*, anterior laryngeal nerve; *13*, ventral branch of first cervical nerve; *14*, vagus and sympathetic; *15*, dorsal branch of spinal accessory nerve; *16*, ventral branch of same; *17*, ventral cerebral vein; *18*, mandibular duct; *19*, common carotid artery; *20*, parotid branch; *21*, thyro-laryngeal artery; *22*, pharyngeal artery; *23*, laryngeal artery; *24*, internal carotid artery; *25*, occipital artery; *26*, external carotid artery; *27*, *31*, external maxillary artery; *28*, pharyngeal artery; *29*, lingual artery; *30*, sublingual artery; *32*, external carotid artery after emergence; *33*, internal maxillary vein (origin); *34*, remnant of parotid gland; *35*, thyroid gland; *36*, jugular vein; *37*, parapharyngeal lymph glands. (After Ellenberger-Baum, Top. Anat. d. Pferdes.)

canthus of the eye, where it anastomoses with the orbital branch (Ramus malaris) of the infraorbital artery (Fig. 560).

In addition to the preceding, unnamed branches are supplied to the mandibular salivary gland and lymph glands. There is commonly a branch of considerable size which is given off as the external maxillary artery passes the anterior end of the mandibular gland; it runs upward and backward along the dorsal border of the gland, which it supplies.

3. The **posterior auricular artery** (A. auricularis posterior) arises at an acute angle from the external carotid just above the origin of the masseteric. It passes

upward under cover of the parotid gland, to which it gives branches, and divides into several branches which supply the skin and muscles of the external ear (Fig. 560). The **posterior branch** passes to the posterior part of the base of the ear, where it divides into two branches; of these, one (Ramus intermedius) passes up the convex surface of the external ear to the apex, while the other (Ramus medialis) winds around to the anterior (medial) border, and forms an arch with the inter-

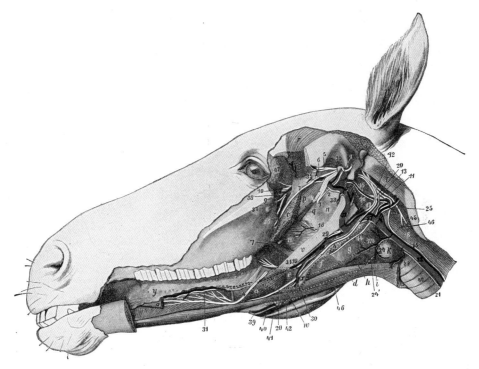

Fig. 562.—Deep Dissection of Head of Horse.

The left ramus of the mandible and structures connected with it have been removed. *a, a,* Stumps of styloglossus; *b,* genio-glossus; *c,* genio-hyoideus; *d,* omo-hyoideus; *e,* kerato-hyoideus; *f,* thyro-hyoideus; *g,* thyro-pharyngeus; *h,* crico-thyroideus; *i,* sterno-thyroideus; *k,* thyroid gland; *m,* crico-pharyngeus; *n,* palatinus and palato-pharyngeus; *o,* pterygoideus lateralis; *p,* tensor palati; *q,* levator palati; *r,* temporalis; *s,* rectus cap. ventralis major; *t,* obliquus cap. ant.; *u,* guttural pouch; *v,* great cornu of hyoid bone, extremity of which is removed and indicated by dotted line; *w,* position of small cornu, dotted line; *x,* thyroid cornu; *y,* tongue; *z,* anterior pillar of soft palate; *1,* superficial temporal nerve; *2,* chorda tympani; *3,* stump of inferior alveolar nerve; *4, 4,* lingual nerve, intermediate part removed; *5,* deep temporal nerve; *6,* masseteric nerve; *7,* buccinator nerve; *8,* great palatine nerve; *9,* infraorbital nerve; *10,* sphenopalatine and posterior nasal nerves; *11,* spinal accessory nerve; *12,* vagus; *13,* pharyngeal branch of vagus; *14,* anterior laryngeal nerve; *15,* vago-sympathetic trunk; *16,* sympathetic, with anterior cervical ganglion a little further back; *17,* glosso-pharyngeal nerve; *18,* pharyngeal and *19,* lingual, branches of glosso-pharyngeal; *20,* hypoglossal nerve; *21,* left recurrent nerve; *22,* common carotid artery; *23,* parotid branch; *24,* anterior thyroid or thyro-laryngeal artery; *24',* laryngeal artery; *25,* occipital artery; *26,* internal carotid artery; *27,* external carotid artery; *28, 30,* external maxillary artery; *29,* pharyngeal artery; *31,* lingual artery; *32,* external carotid artery; *33,* stump of mandibular alveolar artery; *34,* middle meningeal artery; *35,* deep temporal artery; *36,* buccinator artery; *37,* palatine artery; *38,* end of internal maxillary artery; *39,* right external maxillary artery; *40,* satellite vein of *39; 41,* right parotid duct; *42,* mandibular lymph glands; *43,* parapharyngeal lymph glands; *44,* trachea; *45,* wing of atlas; *46,* dotted line indicating outline of mandibular gland; *47,* lacrimal gland. (After Ellenberger-Baum, Top. Anat. d. Pferdes.)

mediate branch. The **lateral branch** (Ramus lateralis) passes up the posterior (lateral) border of the ear and forms an arch with the intermediate branch. The **deep branch** (A. auricularis profunda) enters the interval between the external acoustic process and mastoid process, and passes through an opening into the interior of the external ear and ramifies in the skin which lines it. It gives off the **stylomastoid artery,** which passes through the stylomastoid foramen into the tympanum, forms an arch around the membrana tympani, and supplies the middle ear and its muscles.

THE SUPERFICIAL TEMPORAL ARTERY

This artery (A. temporalis superficialis) is much the smaller of the two terminal branches of the external carotid, and is usually less than an inch (ca. 2 cm.) in length.

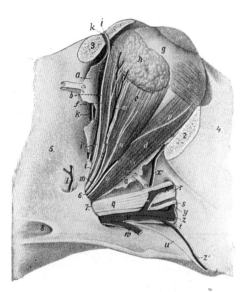

FIG. 563.—RIGHT EYE OF HORSE.

a, Remnants of periorbita; *b*, levator palpebræ superioris; *c*, obliquus oculi inferior; *d*, rectus oculi inferior; *e*, rectus oculi lateralis; *f*, rectus oculi superior; *g*, sclera; *g'*, cornea; *h*, lacrimal gland; *i*, frontal nerve; *i'*, trochlear nerve; *k*, supraorbital artery; *l*, branches of lacrimal nerve to gland; *m*, lacrimal artery; *n*, zygomatic nerve; *o*, branch of ophthalmic artery; *p*, branch of oculomotor nerve to obliquus oculi inferior; *q*, maxillary nerve; *r*, infraorbital nerve; *s*, posterior nasal nerve; *t*, great palatine nerve; *u*, small palatine nerve; *v*, internal maxillary artery; *w*, buccinator artery (cut); *x*, infraorbital artery; *x'*, malar artery; *y*, sphenopalatine artery; *z*, great palatine artery; *z'*, small palatine (or staphyline) artery; *1*, anterior deep temporal artery; *2*, stump of zygomatic arch (sawn off); *3*, stump of supraorbital process (sawn off); *4*, facial crest; *5*, temporal fossa; *6*, foramen orbitale; *7*, foramen rotundum and anterior end of alar canal; *8*, posterior opening of alar canal. (After Ellenberger, in Leisering's Atlas.)

It passes upward behind the posterior border of the ramus of the mandible, under cover of the parotid gland, and divides below the level of the condyle into the anterior auricular and transverse facial arteries. It is crossed superficially by the facial nerve.

The **anterior auricular artery** (A. auricularis anterior) ascends behind the temporo-mandibular articulation under cover of the parotid gland and reaches the temporalis muscle. It is crossed deeply at its origin by the superficial temporal nerve and is accompanied by a satellite vein and the auriculo-palpebral branch of the facial nerve. It is distributed to the skin and the temporal and anterior auricular muscles, and sends a branch through the conchal cartilage to the skin which lines it. Collateral twigs are detached to the parotid gland, and an anterior branch anastomoses with the supraorbital artery. A branch sometimes passes into the temporal canal and anastomoses with the posterior meningeal artery.

The **transverse facial artery** (A. transversa faciei) is larger than the preceding. It turns around the neck of the mandible and emerges from beneath the parotid gland (Fig. 560). It then passes forward a short distance on the masseter about half an inch below the zygomatic arch, and enters the muscle, in which it commonly divides into two chief branches. It is accompanied by a vein and a branch of the superficial temporal nerve. It supplies the masseter and the skin of this region, and anastomoses with the external maxillary and posterior deep temporal arteries.

THE INTERNAL MAXILLARY ARTERY (Figs. 562, 563, 564)

This artery (A. maxillaris interna) is much the larger of the two terminal branches of the external carotid. It begins at the medial side of the posterior border of the mandible, about two inches (ca. 5 cm.) below the articulation of the jaw, and ends in the anterior part of the pterygo-palatine fossa. On account of its complex course and the large number of branches given off it is convenient to divide it into three parts.

I. The **first part** is much the longest, forms a double curve, and is in great part in contact with the guttural pouch. It passes upward and forward on the medial surface of the mandible a distance of about an inch (ca. 2–3 cm.) and is related here to the vein, which is ventral. It then turns inward on the ventral surface of the lateral pterygoid muscle and the mandibular nerve, passes between that muscle and the tensor palati, and runs forward to enter the alar canal. This part gives off the following branches:

1. The **mandibular alveolar artery** (A. alveolaris mandibulæ) passes downward and forward with the homonymous vein and nerve, being at first between

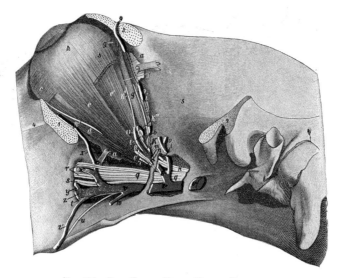

FIG. 564.—LEFT EYE OF HORSE, DEEPER DISSECTION.

The outer plate of bone has been removed behind the pterygoid crest to expose the vessels and nerves. *a, a,* Remnants of periorbita; *b, b,* stumps of rectus oculi superior; *c,* obliquus oculi inferior; *d,* rectus oculi inferior; *e,* rectus oculi lateralis; *e′,* retractor oculi; *f,* rectus oculi medialis; *g, g,* obliquus oculi superior; *h,* eyeball; *i,* trochlear nerve; *k,* ophthalmic nerve; *k′,* nasal nerve; *k″,* infratrochlear nerve; *k‴,* ethmoidal nerve; *l,* optic nerve; *m,* frontal nerve; *n,* lacrimal nerve; *o,* zygomatic nerve; *p,* nerve to obliquus inferior (from oculomotor); *q,* maxillary nerve; *r,* infraorbital nerve; *s,* sphenopalatine nerve; *t,* great palatine nerve; *u,* small palatine nerve; *v,* internal maxillary artery; *w,* buccinator artery (cut off); *x,* infraorbital artery; *x′,* malar artery; *y,* spheno-palatine artery; *z,* great palatine artery; *z′,* small palatine artery; *1, 2,* stumps of zygomatic arch; *3,* stump of supraorbital process; *4,* facial crest; *5,* temporal fossa; *6,* external ophthalmic artery; *7,* muscular branch of *6; 8,* lacrimal artery (cut); *9,* supraorbital artery; *10,* anterior deep temporal artery; *11,* ethmoidal artery. (After Ellenberger-Baum, Top. Anat. d. Pferdes.)

the lateral and medial pterygoid muscles, then between the latter and the ramus of the mandible. It enters the mandibular foramen, passes downward and forward in the mandibular canal, and terminates at the mental foramen by dividing into mental and incisor branches. The **mental branch** (A. mentalis) emerges through the mental foramen and anastomoses in the lower lip with the opposite artery and the inferior labial. The **incisor branch** (Ramus incisivus) continues forward in the bone, supplies twigs to the canine and incisor teeth, and anastomoses with its fellow of the opposite side. Collateral branches are detached to the pterygoid and mylohyoid muscles, and within the bone to the teeth, alveolar periosteum, the gums, and the spongy substance of the mandible.

2. The **pterygoid arteries,** two or three in number, are distributed to the pterygoid and tensor and levator palati muscles.

3. The **tympanic artery** is a very small vessel which passes along the Eustachian tube to the petro-tympanic fissure and enters the middle ear.

4. The **middle meningeal artery** (A. meningea media) arises beneath the buccinator nerve, where the internal maxillary turns forward. It passes backward across the temporal wing of the sphenoid to the antero-lateral part (foramen spinosum) of the foramen lacerum. Entering the cranium, it divides into branches which course in the grooves on the temporal and parietal bones and supply the dura mater. It anastomoses with the posterior meningeal.

The size of this artery is variable, and is in inverse ratio to that of the posterior meningeal.

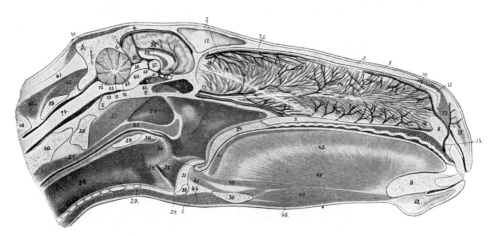

Fig. 565.—Sagittal Section of Head of Horse, Cut a Little to the Right of the Median Plane.

1, Skin; *2*, nasal bone; *3*, frontal bone; *4*, parietal bone; *4'*, tentorium osseum; *5*, occipital bone; *6*, sphenoid bone; *7*, hard palate; *8*, premaxilla; *9*, mandible; *10*, hyoid bone; *11*, septum between frontal sinuses; *12*, alar cartilage; *13*, transversus nasi; *14*, septum nasi with venous plexuses; *15*, palato-labial artery; *16, 16'*, upper and lower septal branches of *15*; *17*, septal branch of sphenopalatine artery and satellite vein; *18*, septal branch of ethmoidal artery; *19*, sphenoidal sinus; *20*, guttural pouch; *21*, pharynx; *22*, pharyngeal orifice of Eustachian tube; *23*, posterior naris; *24*, soft palate; *25*, palatinus muscle; *26*, pharyngeal muscles; *27*, œsophagus; *28*, dotted line indicating position of posterior pillar of soft palate; *29*, lamina, *29'*, arch of cricoid cartilage; *30*, arytenoideus transversus muscle; *31*, epiglottis; *32*, body of thyroid cartilage; *33*, vocal process and cord; *34*, arytenoid cartilage; *35*, lateral ventricle of larynx; *36*, trachea; *37*, ventral straight muscles of head; *38*, longus colli; *39*, atlas; *40*, axis; *41*, lig. nuchæ; *42*, dorsal spinal muscles; *43*, muscles of external ear; *44*, omo- and sterno-hyoideus; *45*, tongue; *46*, mylo-hyoideus; *47*, genio-hyoideus; *48*, genio-glossus; *49*, longitudinalis inferior; *50*, longitud. superior; *51*, hypo-epiglotticus; *52*, chin and mentalis muscle; *53*, venous plexus of hard palate; *54*, corpus callosum; *55*, septum pellucidum; *56*, fornix; *57*, thalamus; *58*, pineal body; *59*, corpora quadrigemina; *60*, cerebral peduncle; *61*, corpus mammillare; *62*, pituitary body; *63*, chiasma opticum; *64*, intercarotid artery; *65*, medulla oblongata; *66*, interventricular foramen; *67*, infundibulum; *68*, third ventricle; *69*, cerebral aqueduct; *70*, anterior medullary velum; *71*, fourth ventricle; *72*, posterior medullary velum; *73*, basilar artery; *74*, spinal cord; *75*, ethmoidal nerve; *76*, septal branch of posterior nasal nerve; *76'*, branch of same to vomero-nasal organ; *77*, olfactory nerve to vomero-nasal organ; *78*, nasal branches of palatine artery. (After Ellenberger, in Leisering's Atlas.)

5. The **posterior deep temporal artery** (A. temporalis profunda aboralis) arises from the internal maxillary just before the latter enters the alar canal. It passes upward and backward in the temporal fossa on the deep face of the temporalis muscle, in which it ramifies. It sends a branch outward to the masseter, and anastomoses with the superficial temporal and middle meningeal arteries.

In some cases the tympanic and middle meningeal arise from this artery.

II. The **second part** lies in the alar canal, and is about an inch (ca. 2–3 cm.) in length. It gives off two branches—the anterior deep temporal and the external ophthalmic.

1. The **anterior deep temporal artery** (A. temporalis profunda oralis) emerges from the canal through the small alar or temporal foramen, and ascends in the

anterior part of the temporal fossa on the deep face of the temporalis muscle, in which it is chiefly distributed. It gives twigs to the orbital fat and the skin of the frontal region.

2. The **external ophthalmic artery** (A. ophthalmica externa) emerges from the anterior opening of the alar canal, and enters the apex of the periorbita. Within this it forms a semicircular bend under the rectus oculi superior, and is continued by the ethmoidal artery. Its branches are as follows:

(*a*) The **supraorbital artery** (A. supraorbitalis) is a small vessel which often arises from the anterior deep temporal or the internal maxillary. It passes along the inner wall of the orbit in company with the nerve of the same name to the supra-orbital foramen, through which it emerges. It is distributed to the orbicularis oculi, the corrugator supercilii, and the skin of the supraorbital region.

(*b*) The **lacrimal artery** (A. lacrimalis) runs upward and forward within the periorbita along the lateral edge of the levator palpebræ superioris to the lacrimal gland, in which it is chiefly distributed. It also sends twigs to the upper eyelid.

(*c*) **Muscular branches** (Rami musculares) supply the orbital muscles, the periorbita, the third eyelid, and the conjunctiva.

(*d*) The **ciliary arteries** (Aa. ciliares), two sets of very slender branches, arise from the ophthalmic and from the muscular branches. The anterior ciliary arteries (Aa. ciliares anteriores) pierce the sclera in front of the equator and ramify chiefly in the ciliary body and the iris. The posterior ciliary arteries (Aa. ciliares posteriores) pierce the posterior part of the sclera; most of them ramify in the chorioid coat as the short ciliary arteries, but two of larger size, the long ciliary arteries, run forward, one on each side, between the sclera and chorioid to the periphery of the iris. Here they divide into branches which anastomose and form a circle (Circulus iridis major). From this secondary branches are detached which form a second circle around the pupil (Circulus iridis minor).

(*e*) The **central artery of the retina** (A. centralis retinæ) is a small vessel which arises from the ophthalmic or from a posterior ciliary artery. It pierces the optic nerve a short distance behind the sclera, and runs in its center to the lamina cribrosa, where it breaks up in thirty to forty fine branches. These appear in the fundus of the eye at the margin of the optic papilla and radiate in the posterior part of the retina.

(*f*) The **ethmoidal artery** (A. ethmoidalis) is the continuation of the ophthalmic. It enters the cranial cavity through the ethmoidal foramen, passes inward on the cribriform plate, and divides into meningeal and nasal branches. The former ramify in the anterior part of the dura mater and anastomose with branches of the artery of the corpus callosum. The nasal branch passes through the cribriform plate, gives branches to the mucous membrane of the lateral mass of the ethmoid and the adjacent part of the septum nasi, and runs forward on the dorsal turbinate.

III. The **third part** passes forward in the pterygo-palatine fossa, accompanied by branches of the maxillary nerve. On reaching the posterior palatine foramen it is continued by the greater palatine artery. Its branches are as follows:

1. The **buccinator artery** (A. buccinatoria) arises from the ventral aspect of the internal maxillary shortly after its emergence (Fig. 562). It turns around the maxillary tuberosity, accompanied by the buccinator nerve, and under the masseter muscle, enters the cheek, and runs forward in it. It supplies branches to the cheek, the superior buccal glands, and the masseter and pterygoid muscles. Near its origin it gives off a branch to the orbital fat behind the periorbita.

2. The **infraorbital artery** (A. infraorbitalis) arises from the upper aspect of the internal maxillary a little in front of the preceding vessel. It passes upward and forward to the maxillary foramen, runs in the infraorbital canal in company with the nerve of the same name, and is continued forward within the jaw to the incisor

teeth. It gives branches to the teeth and gums, and detaches a branch through the infraorbital foramen which anastomoses with the lateral nasal and superior labial.[1] About midway between its origin and the maxillary foramen it gives off the **malar branch** (Ramus malaris), which passes along the floor of the orbit to end in the lower lid and anastomose with the angularis oculi. It gives twigs to the inferior oblique muscle and the lacrimal sac.

3. The **lesser palatine artery** (A. palatina minor) is a small vessel which passes forward in the groove at the medial side of the maxillary tuberosity to the soft palate. In the groove it is accompanied by the nerve of the same name and the palatine vein.

4. The **sphenopalatine artery** (A. sphenopalatina) arises in the anterior part of the pterygo-palatine fossa, passes through the sphenopalatine foramen into the nasal cavity, and divides into two branches. The medial branch is distributed to the mucous membrane of the septum nasi; the lateral one goes to the ventral turbinate, the ventral meatus, the posterior nares, and the maxillary and frontal sinuses. It may arise from the infraorbital.

5. The **greater palatine artery** (A. palatina major) is the direct continuation of the internal maxillary. It passes through the palatine canal accompanied by the palatine nerve, and runs forward in the palatine groove, where it is joined by the vein. A little behind the plane of the corner incisor teeth it curves medially over a bar of cartilage to the foramen incisivum, where it unites with its fellow of the opposite side. The single artery thus formed (A. palato-labialis) passes up through the foramen and divides under the transversus nasi into two branches which ramify in the upper lip and anastomose with the lateral nasal and superior labial arteries. Other branches go to the anterior part of the septum nasi. Collateral branches go to the hard and soft palate and the gums, and others pass through the accessory palatine foramina to be distributed in the mucous membrane of the ventral part of the nasal cavity. Commonly two branches, right and left, are detached from the convexity of the arch formed by the union of the two arteries; these run forward in the anterior part of the hard palate.

ARTERIES OF THE THORACIC LIMB
THE BRACHIAL ARTERY

The **brachial artery,** after crossing the ventral border of the scalenus at the first rib, passes backward and downward across the origin of the coraco-brachialis and the insertion of the subscapularis muscle at the medial side of the shoulder joint.[2] At the posterior border of the subscapularis it gives off the subscapular artery, and turns distally on the medial surface of the arm. In its course in the arm it inclines a little forward, crosses the humerus very obliquely, and is continued by the median artery.

In the course over the chest-wall the artery is related medially to the ventral border of the serratus thoracis and the rectus thoracis. Opposite the ventral end of the first rib it is crossed medially by the median nerve and laterally by the musculo-cutaneous nerve; the two nerves usually unite below the artery, which is thus suspended in a sort of loop. In the arm it is related medially to the posterior deep pectoral muscle and is covered by the deep brachial fascia. Laterally it lies on the subscapularis, the brachialis, the insertion of the teres major and latissimus dorsi, and the medial head of the triceps. The coraco-brachialis muscle and the median

[1] The infraorbital artery is usually small at its emergence upon the face, but in some cases it is rather large and may partially replace the superior labial and lateral nasal arteries.

[2] The term axillary is often applied to the artery from the first rib to the point of origin of the subscapular artery, and the name brachial is given to the artery beyond this.

nerve lie along the front of the artery, which, however, overlaps the muscle distally. The vein crosses the medial face of the artery and runs down behind it, accompanied part way by the ulnar and radial nerves. The chief branches are as follows:

1. The **suprascapular artery** (A. thoraco-acromialis) is a small and somewhat flexuous vessel, which arises near the anterior border of the subscapularis and runs dorsally, to the furrow between that muscle and the supraspinatus. It gives branches to these muscles, the anterior deep pectoral, and the brachiocephalicus. A branch passes in front of the tendon of origin of the coraco-brachialis to the shoulder joint and the proximal end of the humerus.[1]

2. The **subscapular artery** (A. subscapularis) is a very large vessel which arises at the posterior border of the subscapularis muscle. It ascends in the interstice between that muscle and the teres major, on the medial surface of the long head of the triceps, turns around the posterior border of the scapula below the dorsal angle, and ends in the infraspinatus and deltoid. Besides collateral muscular branches (Rami musculares) to the subscapularis, teres major, triceps, and tensor fasciæ antibrachii, it gives off the following named branches:

(*a*) The **thoraco-dorsal** (A. thoracodorsalis) is usually given off about an inch from the origin of the subscapular, crosses the medial face of the teres major, and runs upward and backward on the latissimus dorsi. It gives branches to these muscles, the triceps, the abdominal cutaneous and the axillary lymph glands.

(*b*) The **posterior circumflex artery of the humerus** (A. circumflexa humeri posterior) arises a little above the preceding vessel, and passes outward behind the shoulder joint between the long and lateral heads of the triceps with the axillary nerve. It gives branches to these muscles, the joint capsule, and the muscles and skin of the lateral side of the shoulder, anastomosing with the anterior circumflex artery.

(*c*) The **circumflex artery of the scapula** (A. circumflexa scapulæ) arises about two or three inches (ca. 5–7.5 cm.) above the shoulder joint, passes forward to the posterior border of the scapula, and divides into two branches. The lateral one runs forward on the lateral surface of the scapula below the spine, and gives branches to the supraspinatus, infraspinatus, and teres minor. The medial branch passes forward in a similar fashion on the costal surface of the scapula and supplies branches to the subscapularis.

3. The **anterior circumflex artery of the humerus** (A. circumflexa humeri anterior)[2] arises usually at the anterior border of the teres major. It passes forward between the two parts of the coraco-brachialis or between the latter and the humerus. It gives branches to the coraco-brachialis and deep pectoral and ends in the upper part of the biceps and in the brachiocephalicus. It anastomoses with the posterior circumflex artery.

Not rarely it is replaced largely by an artery which arises from the brachial at the distal end of the coraco-brachialis, and ascends on the front of the humerus. In these cases a small branch for the coraco-brachialis is usually given off at the usual point of origin of the anterior circumflex.

4. The **deep brachial artery** (A. profunda brachii) is a large but short trunk which arises usually about the middle of the humerus. It passes backward to the interval between the tendon of the teres major and latissimus dorsi, and the long and medial heads of the triceps, where it divides into several branches which supply the triceps, tensor fasciæ antibrachii, anconeus, and brachialis. A branch runs in the musculo-spiral groove with the radial nerve to the front of the elbow joint and anastomoses with the anterior radial. A slender branch descends along the lateral

[1] This vessel may be double, or be represented by one or more branches of the inferior cervical artery.

[2] Also termed the prehumeral artery.

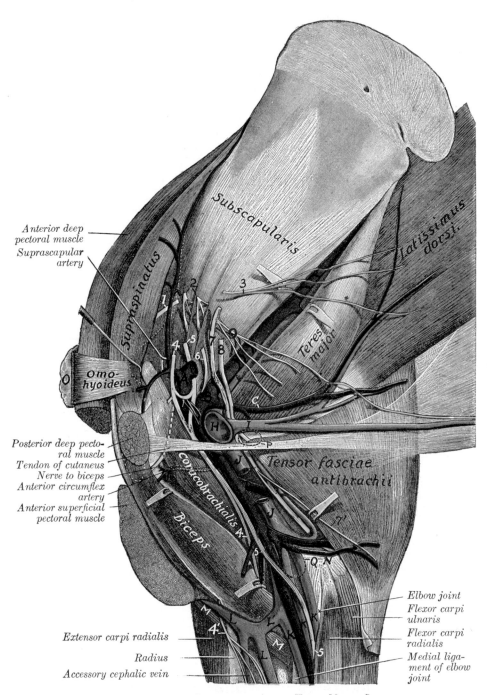

FIG. 566.—DISSECTION OF SHOULDER AND ARM OF HORSE; MEDIAL SURFACE.

A, Brachial artery, the stump of which has been turned backward; *B*, subscapular artery; *C*, thoraco-dorsal artery; *D*, deep brachial artery; *E*, ulnar artery; *F*, anterior radial artery; *G*, median artery; *H*, stump of brachial vein; *I*. external thoracic vein; *J*, brachial vein, part of which has been removed to expose deep brachial artery; *K*, *K*, *K*, median veins; *L*, cephalic vein; *L'*, medial cubital vein; *M*, brachialis muscle; *N*, medial epicondyle of humerus; *O*, prescapular lymph glands; *P*, indicating position of axillary lymph glands, should be dorsal to vein; *Q*, position of cubital lymph glands; *1*, suprascapular nerve; *2*, subscapular nerves; *3*, thoraco-dorsal nerve; *4*, musculo-cutaneous nerve; *4'*, cutaneous branch of median nerve; *5*, median nerve; *6*, axillary nerve; *7*, ulnar nerve; *7'*, cutaneous branch of ulnar nerve; *8*, radial nerve; *9*, thoracic nerves. The vein at the elbow which lies in front of the median artery should be shown crossing over the median nerve and the median and ulnar arteries, as in the next figure. The ulnar artery crosses the lateral face of the brachial vein or its radicles, not medially, as in the figure. (After Schmaltz, Atlas d. Anat. d. Pferdes.)

border of the extensor carpi and supplies cutaneous twigs. Anastomoses occur with the ulnar and recurrent interosseous arteries.

The point of origin is inconstant and it is not uncommon to find two arteries instead of one. Often a large branch for the posterior deep pectoral muscle is detached close to the origin or arises from the brachial directly.

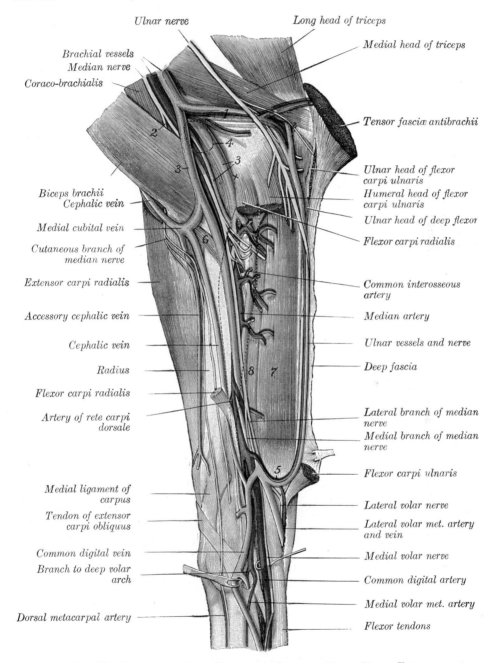

FIG. 567.—DISSECTION OF RIGHT FOREARM AND CARPUS OF HORSE; MEDIAL VIEW.

1, Ulnar vessels; 2, cutaneous branch of musculo-cutaneous nerve; 3, 3, satellite veins of median artery; 4, position of cubital lymph glands; 5, anastomosis of ulnar and lateral volar metacarpal arteries; 6, brachialis muscle; 7, superficial digital flexor; 8, deep digital flexor. Dotted lines indicate contour of flexor carpi radialis, most of which has been removed. (After Schmaltz, Atlas der Anatomie des Pferdes.)

5. **Muscular branches** (Rami musculares) are distributed to the teres major, deep pectoral, coraco-brachialis, and biceps. The largest and least variable of these supplies the distal part of the biceps.

6. The **ulnar artery** (A. collateralis ulnaris proximalis) arises at the distal end of the coraco-brachialis and passes downward and backward along the ventral edge of the medial head of the triceps under cover of the brachial vein and the tensor fasciæ antibrachii. It gives branches to these muscles, the posterior superficial pectoral, the cubital lymph glands, cutaneus, and skin. At the elbow it lies on the posterior part of the medial epicondyle, in relation in front to the ulnar nerve, and largely covered by the satellite vein; it then turns downward under the ulnar head of the flexor carpi ulnaris. It continues its descent with the vein and nerve under the deep fascia of the forearm between the ulnar and humeral heads of the deep flexor of the digit, and in the distal half of the region between the lateral and middle flexors of the carpus. It unites just above the carpus (under cover of the flexor carpi ulnaris) with the lateral volar metacarpal artery, with which it forms the **supracarpal arch.** It detaches small collaterals to the muscles along which it passes and terminal twigs to the lateral surface of the carpus.

7. The **nutrient artery of the humerus** (A. nutritia humeri) is a short vessel which enters the nutrient foramen of the humerus. It often arises from the ulnar.

8. The **anterior radial artery** (A. collateralis radialis distalis)[1] passes downward and a little outward on the anterior face of the humerus under cover of the biceps and brachialis to the front of the elbow joint, where it is in contact with the radial nerve. It then descends on the anterior surface of the radius, under cover of the common digital extensor, to the carpus, where it concurs in the formation of the rete carpi dorsale, anastomosing with the median and dorsal interosseous arteries. It supplies branches to the elbow joint, the biceps, brachialis, and the extensors of the carpus and digit. A cutaneous branch emerges between the distal end of the biceps and the brachialis.

THE MEDIAN ARTERY

The **median artery** (A. mediana)[2] is the direct continuation of the brachial. It descends, inclining slightly backward, at first on the medial surface of the humerus, and then over the capsule and medial ligament of the elbow joint, under cover of the posterior superficial pectoral muscle.[3] At the proximal third of the forearm it dips under the flexor carpi radialis and passes down the medial part of the posterior surface of the radius. In the distal part of the forearm it inclines backward and is separated from the radius by the reinforcing band (Caput tendineum) of the superficial flexor of the digit and is continued by the common digital or large metacarpal artery.

It is accompanied by the median nerve, which lies in front of the artery at its origin, then usually crosses over it obliquely at the elbow joint and becomes posterior. At the distal end of the arm the artery is crossed by the large anastomotic vein which connects the cephalic and brachial veins, and a radicle of the brachial vein lies behind and partly upon the artery; lower down there are usually two satellite veins, anterior and posterior. The chief collateral branches are as follows:

1. **Articular branches** are supplied to the elbow joint.

2. **Muscular branches** go to the flexors of the carpus and digit; the largest of these arise at the proximal third of the forearm.

3. The **common interosseous artery** (A. interossea communis) is a vessel of

---

[1] This vessel is apparently the A. transversa cubiti of comparative anatomy.

[2] Although the homology of some arteries in this region is still unsettled, it seems clear that this vessel should be termed the median artery.

[3] The pulse can be taken where the artery lies on the ligament, since the pectoral muscle is thin here.

considerable size which arises at the level of the interosseous space, through which it passes outward. Before entering the space it gives off a small branch, the **volar**

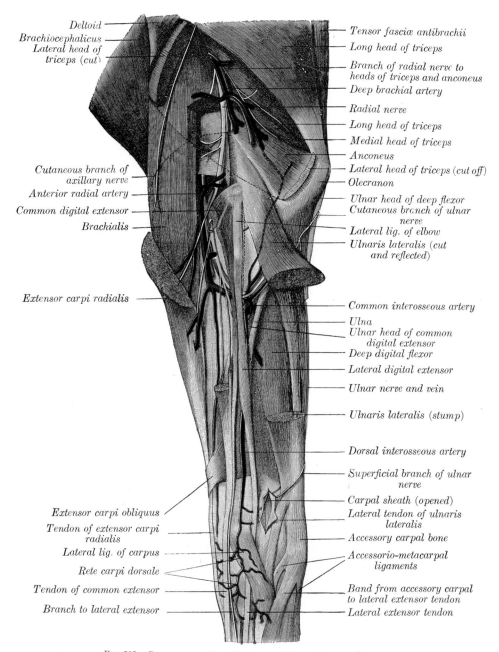

Deltoid

Brachiocephalicus

Lateral head of triceps (cut)

Cutaneous branch of axillary nerve

Anterior radial artery

Common digital extensor

Brachialis

Extensor carpi radialis

Extensor carpi obliquus

Tendon of extensor carpi radialis

Lateral lig. of carpus

Rete carpi dorsale

Tendon of common extensor

Branch to lateral extensor

Tensor fasciæ antibrachii

Long head of triceps

Branch of radial nerve to heads of triceps and anconeus

Deep brachial artery

Radial nerve

Long head of triceps

Medial head of triceps

Anconeus

Lateral head of triceps (cut off)

Olecranon

Ulnar head of deep flexor

Cutaneous branch of ulnar nerve

Lateral lig. of elbow

Ulnaris lateralis (cut and reflected)

Common interosseous artery

Ulna

Ulnar head of common digital extensor

Deep digital flexor

Lateral digital extensor

Ulnar nerve and vein

Ulnaris lateralis (stump)

Dorsal interosseous artery

Superficial branch of ulnar nerve

Carpal sheath (opened)

Lateral tendon of ulnaris lateralis

Accessory carpal bone

Accessorio-metacarpal ligaments

Band from accessory carpal to lateral extensor tendon

Lateral extensor tendon

FIG. 568.—DISSECTION OF LEFT FOREARM OF HORSE; LATERAL SURFACE.

The radial and ulnar heads of the anterior digital extensor are shown in front of the lateral extensor, but are not marked. The muscular branches of the radial nerve are shown, but not designated individually. Dotted lines indicate contour of parts of muscles which have been removed (lateral head of triceps, extensor carpi radialis, lateral flexor of carpus). (After Schmaltz, Atlas d. Anat d. Pferdes.)

interosseous artery (A. interossea volaris), which descends to the radial head of the deep flexor. In the space it supplies the nutrient arteries of the radius and ulna.

Emerging from the space it gives off branches to the ulnaris lateralis, and the small **recurrent interosseous artery** (A. interossea recurrens), which ascends on the lateral

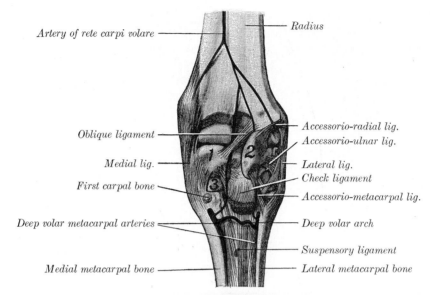

FIG. 569.—DEEP DISSECTION OF RIGHT CARPUS OF HORSE; POSTERIOR VIEW.

1, Radial carpal bone; *2*, accessory carpal bone; *3*, second carpal bone. (After Schmaltz, Atlas d. Anat. d. Pferdes.)

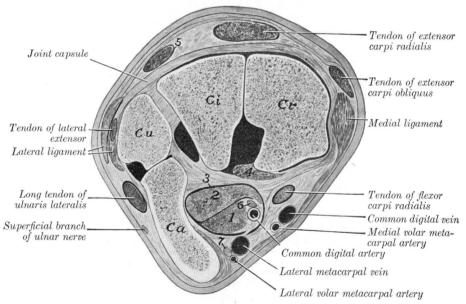

FIG. 570.—CROSS-SECTION OF PROXIMAL PART OF LEFT CARPUS OF HORSE.

Cr, Ci, Cu, Ca, radial, intermediate, ulnar, and accessory carpal bones; *1*, superficial flexor tendon; *2*, deep flexor tendon; *3* (on volar carpal ligament), carpal canal; *4*, oblique ligament from radius to radial carpal bone; *5*, tendon of common extensor; *6*, medial volar nerve; *7*, lateral volar nerve. Synovial cavities are black.

surface of the ulna and anastomoses with the deep brachial and ulnar arteries. Under cover of the common digital extensor it connects with the anterior radial artery and gives off the **dorsal interosseous artery** (Fig. 568). This vessel (A.

interossea dorsalis) descends between the common and lateral extensors of the digit and concurs with the anterior radial in forming a network on the dorsal surface of the carpus, the **rete carpi dorsale.** From the latter arise two small vessels, the **medial** and **lateral dorsal metacarpal arteries** (A. metacarpea dorsalis medialis, lateralis), which run distally in the grooves between the large and small metacarpal bones and anastomose with the volar metacarpal arteries.

4. The **artery of the rete carpi volare** (A. retis carpi volaris) is a small vessel which arises at the distal third of the forearm and descends on the radius to the posterior surface of the carpus, where it concurs with branches of the volar metacarpal arteries in forming the rete carpi volare.

5. The **lateral volar metacarpal artery** (A. metacarpea volaris lateralis) is a small vessel which arises just above the carpus and anastomoses under cover of the flexor carpi ulnaris with the ulnar artery, forming the **supracarpal arch.** From the arch the artery descends with the satellite vein and lateral volar nerve, inclines

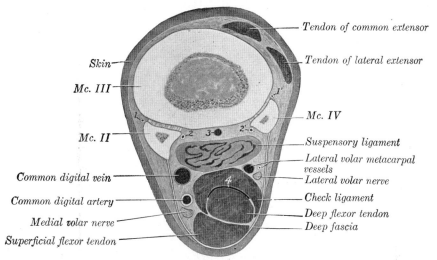

FIG. 571.—CROSS-SECTION OF RIGHT METACARPUS OF HORSE.
Section is cut a little above middle of region.

1, 1', Dorsal metacarpal arteries; 2, 2', deep volar metacarpal arteries; 3, deep volar metacarpal vein; 4, distal part of carpal sheath.

toward the posterior border of the accessory carpal bone, and arrives at the head of the lateral metacarpal bone. Here is it connected with the medial volar metacarpal artery, usually by two transverse branches, thus forming the **deep volar** or **subcarpal arch** (Arcus volaris profundus proximalis). One of these branches lies between the subcarpal check ligament and the suspensory ligament; the other (not always present) lies beneath the latter on the large metacarpal bone. A small branch descends to the fetlock with the lateral volar nerve. Below the arch the artery pursues a flexuous course downward on the volar face of the large metacarpal bone alongside of the lateral small metacarpal and under cover of the suspensory ligament. At the distal third of the metacarpus it commonly unites with the corresponding vessel of the other side to form a short trunk which passes backward through the angle of divergence of the branches of the suspensory ligament and joins the lateral digital or the common digital artery. This junction forms the **distal volar arch** (Arcus volaris distalis).

6. The **medial volar metacarpal artery** (A. metacarpea volaris medialis) is

given off from the median at an acute angle, usually a little above the lateral one or by a common trunk with it. It passes down the medial side of the carpus behind the tendon of the flexor carpi radialis and embedded in the posterior annular ligament. Arriving at the proximal end of the medial metacarpal bone it becomes more deeply placed and is connected with the lateral volar artery by one or two transverse branches, as stated above. It then pursues a flexuous course downward

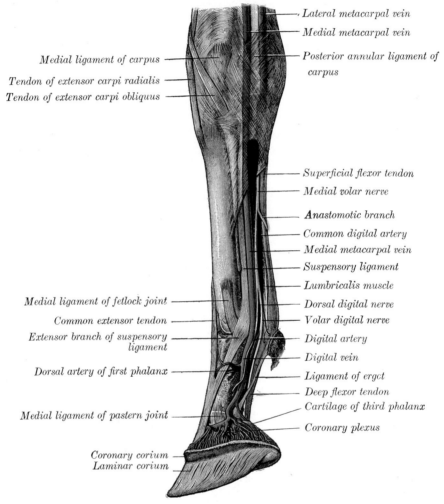

Lateral metacarpal vein

Medial metacarpal vein

Posterior annular ligament of carpus

Medial ligament of carpus

Tendon of extensor carpi radialis

Tendon of extensor carpi obliquus

Superficial flexor tendon

Medial volar nerve

Anastomotic branch

Common digital artery

Medial metacarpal vein

Suspensory ligament

Lumbricalis muscle

Medial ligament of fetlock joint

Common extensor tendon

Extensor branch of suspensory ligament

Dorsal artery of first phalanx

Dorsal digital nerve

Volar digital nerve

Digital artery

Digital vein

Ligament of ergot

Deep flexor tendon

Cartilage of third phalanx

Medial ligament of pastern joint

Coronary plexus

Coronary corium
Laminar corium

FIG. 572.—DISSECTION OF RIGHT CARPUS, METACARPUS, AND DIGIT OF HORSE; MEDIAL VIEW. (After Schmaltz, Atlas d. Anat. d. Pferdes.)

alongside of the medial small metacarpal bone, like the corresponding lateral artery, with which it commonly unites as described above. It is larger than the lateral artery, and supplies the nutrient artery to the large metacarpal bone.

The foregoing account describes the most common arrangement of the dorsal and volar metacarpal arteries. Variations in their origin and connections are common, but have no great surgical importance. Collateral branches are omitted for the same reason. In some cases the medial volar metacarpal is connected with the common digital artery a little below the carpus by a branch passing obliquely across the medial border of the deep flexor tendon; this forms a **super-ficial volar arch.**

THE COMMON DIGITAL ARTERY

The **common digital artery** (A. digitalis communis s. metacarpea volaris superficialis) is the direct continuation of the median. It descends in the carpal canal along the medial side of the flexor tendons in company with the medial volar nerve. Continuing down the limb it preserves this relation to the tendons to the distal fourth of the metacarpus, where it inclines toward the middle line of the limb behind the suspensory ligament and divides into the medial and lateral digital arteries (Fig. 241). In the metacarpus the artery is related to the vein in front and the nerve behind, and is covered by the fascia and skin. It furnishes collateral branches to the suspensory ligament, the flexor tendons, and the skin.

THE DIGITAL ARTERIES

The **digital arteries, medial** and **lateral** (A. digitalis volaris propria medialis, lateralis), are formed by the bifurcation of the common digital at the distal fourth of the metacarpus. They diverge, pass down over the abaxial surface of the corresponding sesamoid at the fetlock, and descend parallel with the borders of the deep flexor tendon to the volar grooves and foramina of the third phalanx. Entering the latter the two arteries unite in the semilunar canal and form the **terminal arch** (Arcus terminalis), from which numerous branches pass through the bone to the dorsal surface and ramify in the corium of the wall and sole of the hoof. A number of branches emerge through the foramina at the distal border, where they anastomose with each other in arciform fashion.

These branches were named by Spooner the inferior communicating arteries, and the anastomotic arch formed by them is termed the circumflex artery of the third phalanx (Chauveau) or the artery of the distal border of the third phalanx (Leisering).

Each artery is accompanied by a vein and by the digital nerves. Above the fetlock the artery is most deeply placed and is covered by the vein; the nerve is behind the vein. At the fetlock the artery has become superficial and is related to the vein in front and the posterior branch of the nerve behind. The anterior branch of the nerve crosses over the artery obliquely to the side of the first phalanx. The artery and nerves are crossed obliquely by a small band, the tendon or ligament of the ergot (*vide* digital fascia).

In addition to branches to the joints, tendons and synovial sheath, ergot, and skin, the digital arteries give off the following named branches:

1. The **artery of the first phalanx** (A. phalangis primæ) is a short trunk which arises at a right angle about the middle of the first phalanx, and divides into dorsal and volar branches. The **dorsal branch** (Ramus dorsalis) passes between the first phalanx and the extensor tendon and ramifies on the front of the digit, anastomosing with its fellow. The **volar branch** (Ramus volaris) dips in between the flexor tendons and the first phalanx and anastomoses with the opposite artery between the superficial and middle distal sesamoidean ligaments.

2. The **artery of the digital cushion** (A. pulvinus digitalis) arises at the proximal border of the cartilage of the third phalanx and passes backward and downward to ramify in the digital cushion and the corium of the heels and frog.

3. The **dorsal artery of the second phalanx** (Ramus dorsalis phalangis secundæ) arises a little above the level of the distal sesamoid bone, and passes forward under cover of the cartilage of the third phalanx and the extensor tendon to the front of the second phalanx, where it anastomoses with the opposite vessel. It gives

branches to the skin, the tendon, the coffin joint, and the coronary corium of the hoof.

4. The **volar artery of the second phalanx** (Ramus volaris phalangis secundæ) is smaller than the preceding, opposite to which it arises. It passes above the proximal border of the distal sesamoid and unites with the opposite artery (Fig. 241).

The arteries of the second phalanx form what is termed by Chauveau the **coronary circle.** The dorsal part of the circle gives off commonly an artery (A. coronalis phalangis tertiæ) near either side of the extensor tendon, which divides into two branches. The central branch unites with that of the opposite side, while the other joins a branch of the artery of the digital cushion. In this way is formed the **circumflex artery of the coronary corium,** an anastomotic arch which lies on the extensor tendon at the coronet. In some cases descending branches of the arteries of the first phalanx concur in the formation of the arch.

5. The **dorsal artery of the third phalanx** (A. dorsalis phalangis tertiæ) arises at the deep face of the angle of the third phalanx, passes through the notch or foramen there, and runs forward in the groove on the dorsal surface. It gives off ascending and descending branches, which ramify in the corium of the wall of the hoof, anastomosing above with the circumflex artery of the coronary cushion and distally with the circumflex artery of the third phalanx. Before passing through the wing it detaches a retrograde branch to the digital cushion, and after emerging, one which ramifies on the convex surface of the cartilage of the third phalanx.

BRANCHES OF THE THORACIC AORTA

In addition to the coronary arteries and the common brachiocephalic trunk (which have been described), the thoracic part of the aorta gives off branches to the thoracic walls and viscera and to the spinal cord and its membranes. The **visceral branches** (Rami viscerales) are the bronchial and œsophageal, which arise by a broncho-œsophageal trunk. The **parietal branches** (Rami parietales) are the intercostal and phrenic arteries.

1. The **broncho-œsophageal artery** (Truncus broncho-œsophageus) is a short, usually bulbous, trunk which arises at the sixth thoracic vertebra from the aorta or in common with the first aortic intercostal arteries. It descends (under cover of the vena azygos) over the right face of the aorta toward the bifurcation of the trachea and divides into bronchial and œsophageal branches. The **bronchial artery** (A. bronchialis) crosses the left face of the œsophagus to the bifurcation of the trachea, where it divides into right and left branches. Each enters the hilus of the corresponding lung above the bronchus, which it accompanies in its ramification. It supplies the lung tissue and also detaches twigs to the bronchial lymph glands and the mediastinum. The **œsophageal artery** (A. œsophagea) (Fig. 554) is a small vessel which passes backward dorsal to the œsophagus in the posterior mediastinum and anastomoses with the œsophageal branch of the gastric artery. It detaches twigs to the œsophagus and the mediastinal lymph glands and pleura, and gives off two branches which pass between the layers of the ligaments of the lungs and ramify in the subpleural tissue. Very commonly there is another artery which runs backward ventral to the œsophagus.[1]

2. The **intercostal arteries** (Aa. intercostales) (Figs. 553, 554) number eighteen pairs. The first arises from the deep cervical artery, the next three from the subcostal branch of the dorsal artery, and the remainder from the aorta. The **aortic intercostal arteries** arise from the dorsal face of the aorta in pairs close together; the fifth and sixth usually spring from a common stem. Each passes across the body of a vertebra to the corresponding intercostal space, detaches twigs to the vertebræ and the pleura, and divides into dorsal and ventral branches. The **dorsal**

---

[1] In some cases there is no broncho-œsophageal trunk, the bronchial and œsophageal arising separately. In other cases the second aortic intercostal arises in common with them also.

branch (Ramus dorsalis) gives off a spinal branch (Ramus spinalis) which passes through the intervertebral foramen, gives twigs to the membranes of the spinal cord, perforates the dura, and reinforces the ventral spinal artery. A muscular branch passes to the muscles and skin of the back. The **ventral branch** (Ramus ventralis) is much the larger. It descends, at first almost in the middle of the intercostal space between the intercostal muscles, then gains the posterior border of the rib, and is subpleural. Each is accompanied by a vein and nerve, the artery being in the middle and the vein in front. At the ventral part of the space it unites with a ventral intercostal branch of the internal thoracic or the musculo-phrenic artery. It supplies the intercostal muscles, the ribs and the pleura, and gives off perforating branches which pass out to the serratus ventralis, the abdominal muscles, and the skin.

3. The **phrenic arteries** (Aa. phrenicæ) are two or three small vessels which arise at the hiatus aorticus from the ventral aspect of the aorta, often by a common trunk. They supply the crura of the diaphragm. In some cases they arise in common with an intercostal artery.

BRANCHES OF THE ABDOMINAL AORTA

The collateral branches of the abdominal part of the aorta are distributed chiefly to the walls and contents of the abdominal cavity, but some branches are

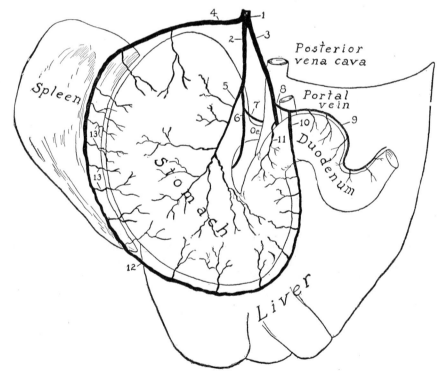

Fig. 573.—Plan of Branches of Cœliac Artery of Horse.

1, Cœliac artery; *2*, gastric artery; *3*, hepatic artery; *4*, splenic artery; *5*, posterior gastric artery; *6*, anterior gastric artery; *7*, œsophageal branch; *8*, gastro-duodenal artery; *9*, pancreatico-duodenal artery; *10*, right gastro-epiploic artery; *11*, pyloric artery; *12*, left gastro-epiploic artery; *13*, short gastric branches of splenic.

supplied to the spinal cord and its membranes, and others extend into the pelvis and to the scrotum. The **visceral branches** are the cœliac, anterior mesenteric, renal, posterior mesenteric, and internal spermatic or utero-ovarian. The **parietal branches** are the lumbar arteries.

I. The **cœliac artery** (A. cœliaca) is an unpaired vessel, usually half an inch or less (ca. 1 cm.) in length, which arises from the ventral aspect of the aorta at its emergence from the hiatus aorticus. It divides on the dorsal surface of the pancreas into three branches—the gastric, hepatic, and splenic.

1. The **gastric artery** (A. gastrica sinistra) passes downward and forward in the gastro-phrenic ligament, gives off œsophageal and pancreatic branches, and divides above and behind the cardia into anterior and posterior branches. The **anterior branch** (Ramus cranialis) crosses the lesser curvature just to the right of the cardia and ramifies on the parietal surface of the stomach. The branches pursue a flexuous course toward the greater curvature and anastomose with the short gastric arteries and the gastric branch of the hepatic artery. The **posterior branch** (Ramus caudalis) is distributed in a similar fashion on the visceral surface. The **œsophageal branch** (Ramus œsophageus) passes through the hiatus œsophageus into the thoracic cavity above the œsophagus and anastomoses with the œsophageal branch of the broncho-œsophageal artery.

The gastric artery often arises by a common trunk with the splenic. The two terminal branches may arise separately, or the anterior from the splenic and the posterior from the hepatic. The œsophageal branch often arises from the splenic or the posterior gastric.

2. The **hepatic artery** (A. hepatica) is larger than the gastric. It passes forward and to the right and ventrally on the dorsal surface of the pancreas, covered by the gastro-pancreatic fold, crosses obliquely under the vena cava, and reaches the medial border of the portal vein. It divides into three or four branches which enter the portal fissure of the liver and ramify within the gland with the portal vein and the hepatic duct. It gives off the following collateral branches: (1) **Pancreatic branches** (Aa. pancreaticæ) are given off as the artery crosses the pancreas, in which it is partly embedded. (2) The **pyloric artery** (A. gastrica dextra) arises above the first curve of the duodenum. It descends to the pylorus, sending branches to the pylorus and the first part of the duodenum, and anastomoses with the gastric and right gastro-epiploic arteries. It may arise from the gastro-duodenal. (3) The **gastro-duodenal artery** (A. gastroduodenalis) passes to the second curve of the duodenum and divides into the right gastro-epiploic and the pancreatico-duodenal. The **right gastro-epiploic artery** (A. gastroepiploica dextra) crosses over the posterior surface of the duodenum and enters the greater omentum, in which it runs to the left, parallel with the greater curvature of the stomach. It gives branches to the latter and to the omentum and forms an anastomotic arch with the left gastro-epiploic artery. The **pancreatico-duodenal artery** (A. pancreaticoduodenalis) divides into pancreatic and duodenal branches. The former (Ramus pancreaticus) supplies the middle part of the pancreas and is often replaced by a number of variable twigs. The duodenal branch (Ramus duodenalis) passes to the right along the lesser curvature of the duodenum and anastomoses with the first branch of the anterior mesenteric artery.

Variations in the branching of the hepatic artery are not uncommon. The pancreatico-duodenal may arise directly from the trunk, and there may be a common trunk for the pyloric and right gastro-epiploic which runs along the dorsal surface of the first curve of the duodenum to the pylorus; here it gives off the small pyloric branch and is continued across the parietal surface of the pylorus as the right gastro-epiploic, no gastro-duodenal trunk being present.

3. The **splenic artery** (A. lienalis) is the largest branch of the cœliac. It passes to the left (with the large satellite vein) on the left extremity of the pancreas and across the saccus cæcus of the stomach. Entering the suspensory ligament of the spleen, it runs in the hilus of the spleen to the apex, beyond which it is continued as the left gastro-epiploic. It gives off the following branches: (1) **Pancreatic branches** (Rami pancreatici), which supply the left extremity of the pancreas.

(2) **Splenic branches** (Rami lienales) which plunge into the substance of the spleen. (3) **Short gastric branches** (Aa. gastricæ breves), which pass in the gastro-splenic omentum to the greater curvature of the stomach, where they bifurcate and anastomose with the branches of the gastric arteries. (4) The **left gastro-epiploic**

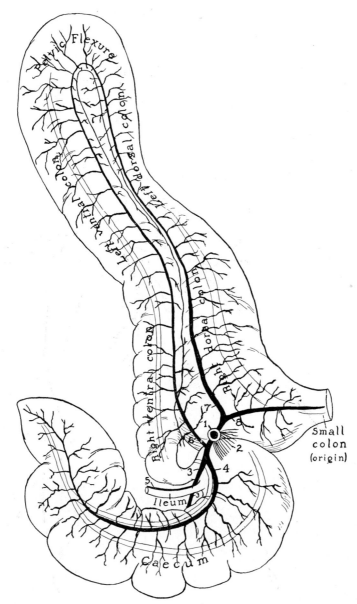

Fig. 574.—Plan of Chief Branches of Anterior Mesenteric Artery of Horse.

1, Stump of anterior mesenteric artery; *2*, stumps of arteries of small intestine; *3*, lateral cæcal artery; *4*, medial cæcal artery; *5*, ileal artery; *6*, ventral colic artery; *7*, dorsal colic artery; *8*, middle colic or first artery of small colon.

artery (A. gastroepiploica sinistra) is the continuation of the splenic artery. It passes to the right in the greater omentum, parallel with the greater curvature of the stomach, and anastomoses with the right gastro-epiploic. It gives off branches to the greater curvature of the stomach and twigs to the omentum.

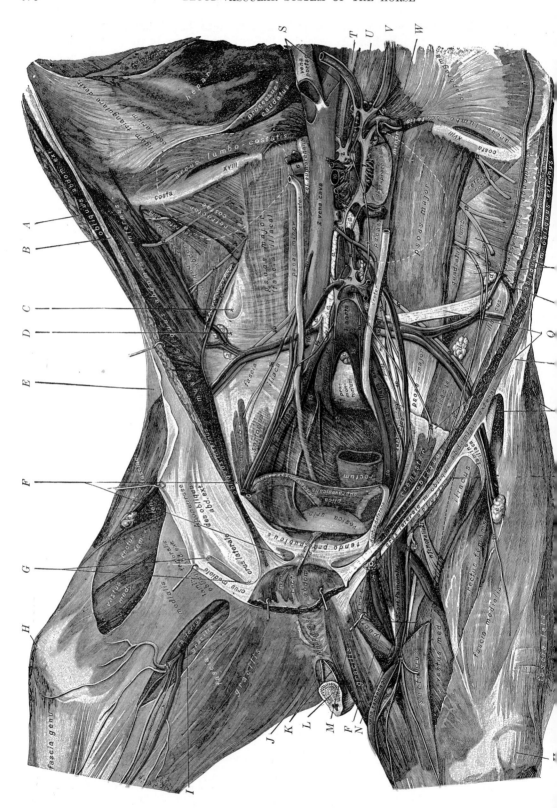

II. The **anterior mesenteric artery** (A. mesenterica cranialis) arises from the ventral face of the aorta at the first lumbar vertebra. It is a large unpaired trunk, about an inch (ca. 2–3 cm.) in length, which passes ventrally between the vena cava and the left adrenal into the root of the great mesentery, when it divides into three branches—left, right, and anterior.[1]

1. The **left branch** gives off at once about fifteen to twenty **arteries of the small intestine** (Aa. intestinales).[2] These come off close together and pass in divergent fashion between the layers of the great mesentery, each dividing into two branches which anastomose with adjacent branches to form a series of arches. In the anterior part of the series secondary arches are formed by the union of branches given off from the primary set of arches. From the convex side of these arches terminal branches pass to the wall of the small intestine, in which they ramify and form a vascular network. They are accompanied by satellite veins and by nerves and lymph vessels. The first artery anastomoses with the pancreatico-duodenal, and the last with the ileal branch of the great mesenteric artery. Branches are supplied to the mesenteric lymph glands.

2. The **right branch** (A. ileo-cæco-colica) might be regarded as the continuation of the trunk. It runs downward and a little forward and to the right, and gives off the ileal, the two cæcal, and the ventral colic arteries. (1) The **ileal** or ileo-cæcal artery (A. ilea) passes in retrograde fashion along the terminal part of the ileum and unites with the last branch of the left division. (2) The **lateral cæcal artery** (Ramus cæcalis lateralis) passes between the cæcum and the origin of the colon and runs on the lateral band of the cæcum to the apex, where it anastomoses with the medial artery. Besides numerous collaterals to the cæcum, it gives off the artery of the arch, which passes along the lesser curvature of the base of the cæcum and runs on the lateral face of the origin of the great colon. (3) The **medial cæcal artery** (Ramus cæcalis medialis) passes along the medial band to the apex of the cæcum, where it anastomoses with the lateral cæcal artery. (4) The **ventral colic**

[1] In the great majority of subjects this vessel and some of its branches are the seat of more or less extensive aneurysm, produced by the Sclerostoma. In the author's experience an entirely normal specimen is quite unlikely to be encountered except in young foals.

[2] The left branch is a descriptive convention rather than a reality, since the arteries of the small intestine spring from the mesenteric trunk either directly or by short common stems with an adjacent vessel.

artery (A. colica ventralis) runs along the dorso-medial bands of the opposed surfaces of the ventral parts of the great colon to the pelvic flexure, where it unites with the dorsal colic artery. It supplies the ventral parts of the great colon and sends a branch to the base of the cæcum.

3. The **anterior branch** divides after a very short course into the dorsal and middle colic arteries. (1) The **dorsal colic artery** (A. colica dorsalis) is a large vessel which passes along the dorsal parts of the great colon to the pelvic flexure, where it joins the ventral colic artery. (2) The **middle colic artery** or **first artery of the small colon** (A. colica media) is a much smaller vessel which passes to the origin of the small colon, enters the colic mesentery, and forms an arch by joining the first branch of the posterior mesenteric artery close to the lesser curvature of the bowel. It sends an anastomotic branch to the dorsal colic artery.

III. The **renal arteries** (Aa. renales), right and left, are relatively large vessels which arise from the aorta near the anterior mesenteric. The **right artery** is the longer of the two. It crosses over the dorsal surface of the vena cava to the right and forward. At the renal hilus it divides into several (five to eight) branches; some of these enter the gland at the hilus, while others pass to the ventral surface and enter there. The **left artery** is short and usually arises a little further back; it passes directly outward to the kidney and is then disposed like the right one. Small collateral branches are supplied to the ureters, the perirenal fat, the renal lymph glands, and the adrenals. The latter also receive small **adrenal arteries** directly from the aorta. The distribution within the kidney has been described.

Variations in the renal arteries are frequent. Two or more arteries may occur on one side or both. Accessory arteries are more common on the left side and usually enter the posterior part of the gland. They may arise from the aorta, the external iliac, or the circumflex iliac artery.

IV. The **posterior mesenteric artery** (A. mesenterica caudalis) is an unpaired vessel which arises from the ventral face of the aorta at the fourth lumbar vertebra, i. e., about five or six inches (ca. 12–15 cm.) behind the origin of the anterior mesenteric artery. It is much smaller than the latter and supplies the greater part of the small colon and rectum. It descends in the colic mesentery and, after a short course, divides into two branches. The **anterior branch** (A. colica sinistra) gives off three or four arteries which divide and form anastomotic arches close to the bowel. The first arch is formed by union with the middle colic branch of the anterior mesenteric. The **posterior branch** or **anterior hæmorrhoidal artery** (A. hæmorrhoidalis cranialis) passes backward in the upper part of the mesentery and the mesorectum and terminates near the anus by anastomosing with the internal pudic artery. Three or four of its anterior collateral branches form arches.

V. The **internal spermatic arteries** (Aa. spermaticæ internæ), right and left, are long slender arteries which arise from the aorta near the posterior mesenteric and supply the testicle and epididymis.[1] Each passes backward in a narrow fold of peritoneum (Plica vasculosa) to the internal inguinal ring and descends through the inguinal canal to the scrotum. In its course in the anterior border of the spermatic cord it forms numerous coils, surrounded by the pampiniform plexus of veins, and associated closely with the spermatic nerves and lymphatics and unstriped muscle-fibers. It passes between the epididymis and testicle, runs in flexuous fashion along the attached border of the latter, turns around the posterior pole, and runs forward on the free border to the anterior pole. The largest branches arise from its ventral part, pass tortuously up either side of the gland, embedded in the tunica albuginea, and give off fine branches to the gland substance. Small

---

[1] Variations in the origin of the internal spermatic artery are common. It may arise from the posterior mesenteric, or from the renal, or the two may arise by a short common trunk.

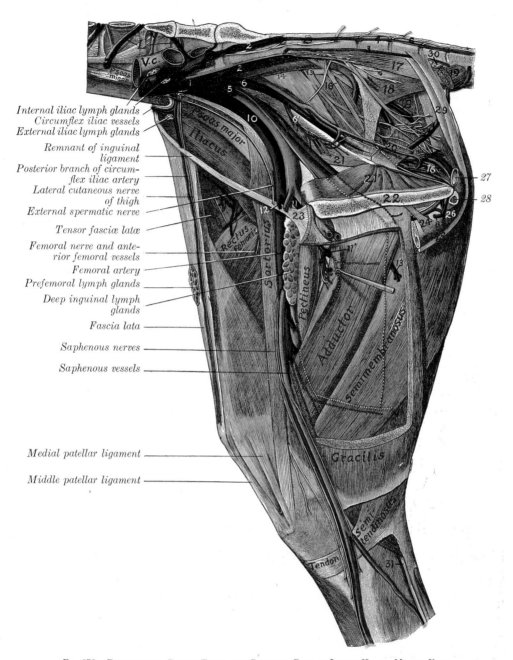

Internal iliac lymph glands
Circumflex iliac vessels
External iliac lymph glands

Remnant of inguinal
ligament
Posterior branch of circumflex iliac artery
Lateral cutaneous nerve
of thigh
External spermatic nerve

Tensor fasciæ latæ

Femoral nerve and ante-
rior femoral vessels
Femoral artery
Prefemoral lymph glands
Deep inguinal lymph
glands
Fascia lata

Saphenous nerves

Saphenous vessels

Medial patellar ligament

Middle patellar ligament

FIG. 576.—DISSECTION OF PELVIS, THIGH, AND PROXIMAL PART OF LEG OF HORSE; MEDIAL VIEW.

L, Lumbar vessels; V.c., posterior vena cava; A, aorta (termination); C, sympathetic trunk; 1, internal iliac artery; 2, lateral sacral artery; 3, middle coccygeal artery; 4, lateral coccygeal artery; 5, umbilical artery (cut off); 6, internal pudic artery; 6', vesico-prostatic artery; 7, obturator artery; 8, a. profunda penis (from left obturator); 9, posterior gluteal vessels; 10, external iliac artery; 11, 11', deep femoral artery; 12, prepubic artery; 13, branch of deep femoral artery; 14, great sciatic nerve; 15, posterior gluteal nerve; 16 (above), pudic nerve; 16 (below, near pelvic outlet), suburethral venous plexus; 17, sacro-coccygeus ventralis; 18, coccygeus; 19, recto-coccygeus; 20, retractor ani; 21, 21', two heads of obturator internus; 22, symphysis pelvis; 23, prepubic tendon; 24 suspensory ligament of penis; 25, retractor penis muscle; 26, bulbo-cavernosus muscle; 27, urethra (cross-section); 28, crus penis (cross-section); 29, suspensory ligaments of anus; 30, anal lymph glands; 31, tibial nerve. (After Schmaltz, Atlas d. Anat. d. Pferdes.)

collateral branches are detached to the ureter, the epididymis, and the spermatic cord.

V a. The **utero-ovarian arteries** in the female correspond to the preceding vessels, but are much larger and shorter. Each is placed in the anterior part of the broad ligament of the uterus and divides into ovarian and uterine branches. The **ovarian artery** (A. ovarica) pursues a flexuous course to the ovary, which it supplies. The **anterior uterine artery** (A. uterina cranialis) passes to the concave border of the cornu of the uterus, which it supplies, anastomosing with the middle uterine artery.

VI. The **lumbar arteries** (Aa. lumbales) are in series with the intercostal

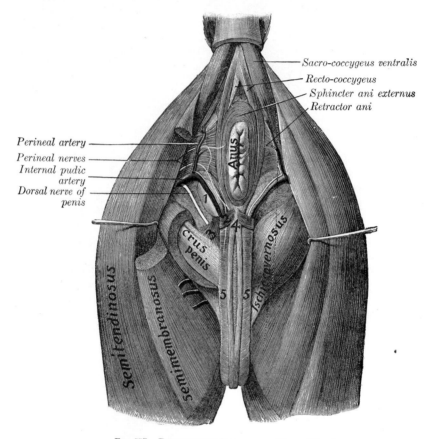

FIG. 577.—DISSECTION OF PERINEUM OF HORSE (MALE).

1, Bulbo-urethral gland; *2*, transversus perinei muscle (?); *3*, ischio-urethral muscle; *4*, retractor penis muscle; *5*, bulbo-cavernosus muscle. (After Schmaltz, Atlas d. Anat. d. Pferdes.)

arteries and have a similar origin and distribution. There are usually six pairs of lumbar arteries, of which five arise from the aorta and the sixth from the internal iliac or the lateral sacral at the junction of the last lumbar vertebra and the sacrum. Each passes across the body of a lumbar vertebra to the intertransverse space, gives branches to the sublumbar muscles, and divides into dorsal and ventral branches. The **dorsal branch** (Ramus dorsalis), the larger of the two, passes upward to ramify in the extensor muscles of the spine and the skin of the loins; it gives off a **spinal branch** (Ramus spinalis) which comports itself like the corresponding branch of an aortic intercostal artery. The **ventral branch** (Ramus ventralis) runs outward in the intertransverse space, passes between the transversus and obliquus internus abdominis, gives branches to these muscles, and ends in the obliquus externus, the cutaneus, and the skin of the flank.

THE INTERNAL ILIAC ARTERY

The **internal iliac** or **hypogastric arteries** (Aa. hypogastricæ) result from the bifurcation of the aorta under the fifth or sixth lumbar vertebra. They diverge at an angle of about 60 degrees, and each passes backward under the wing of the sacrum, then inclines downward on the pelvic surface of the shaft of the ilium, along the ventral border of the iliac head of the obturator internus, and divides a

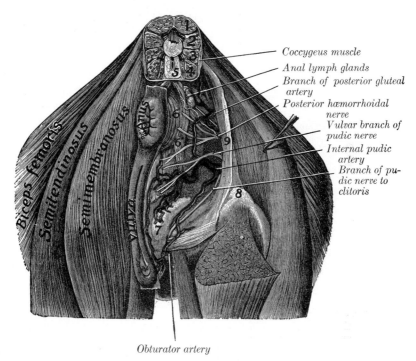

Coccygeus muscle
Anal lymph glands
Branch of posterior gluteal artery
Posterior hæmorrhoidal nerve
Vulvar branch of pudic nerve
Internal pudic artery
Branch of pudic nerve to clitoris

Obturator artery

Fig. 578.—Dissection of Perineum of Mare.

1, Sacro-coccygeus dorsalis; *2*, sacro-coccygeus lateralis; *3*, intertransversales; *4*, sacro-coccygeus ventralis; *5*, recto-coccygeus; *6*, sphincter ani externus; *6'*, branch connecting sphincter ani with constrictor vulvæ; *7*, vestibular bulb; *8*, tuber ischii; *9*, sacro-sciatic ligament. (After Schmaltz, Atlas d. Anat. d. Pferdes.)

little (ca. 2 cm.) above the psoas tubercle into iliaco-femoral and obturator arteries. The chief branches are as follows:

1. The last pair of **lumbar arteries** pass up through the foramina at the junction of the last lumbar vertebra and the sacrum and are distributed as already described.

2. The **internal pudic artery** (A. pudenda interna) arises near the origin of the internal iliac. It passes backward and somewhat downward, at first along the dorsal border of the iliac head of the obturator internus, then above the superior ischiatic spine on the deep surface of the sacro-sciatic ligament, perforates the latter and runs for a variable distance in its substance or on its lateral face. It then re-enters the pelvic cavity, passes backward on the retractor ani to the ischial arch, and divides into the perineal artery and the artery of the bulb in the male, perineal and artery of the clitoris in the female. It is accompanied posteriorly by the pudic nerve. Its chief branches are as follows:

(1) The **umbilical artery** is given off from the internal pudic about an inch (ca. 2–3 cm.) from the origin of that vessel. It is a very large artery in the fœtus, in which it curves downward and forward at the side of the bladder in the edge of the lateral umbilical fold of peritoneum, passes through the umbilical opening, becomes a component of the umbilical cord, and ramifies in the fœtal placenta. After birth it extends only to the vertex of the bladder and is much reduced. Its lumen is almost obliterated and its wall is very thick, giving the vessel a cord-like character, hence it is commonly termed the round ligament of the bladder.[1] It gives off small **vesical branches** (Aa. vesicales craniales) to the bladder, and twigs to the prostate and ductus deferens in the male. In the mare a small branch runs forward along the ureter into the broad ligament of the uterus.

(2) The **middle hæmorrhoidal artery** (A. hæmorrhoidalis media) in the male arises usually near the prostate and runs backward lateral to the rectum. It supplies branches to the rectum, bladder, urethra, and accessory genital glands. In the female the homologous vessel is much larger and gives off the **posterior uterine artery** (A. uterina caudalis). This runs forward on the side of the vagina, to which it gives branches, and ramifies on the body of the uterus, anastomosing with the anterior and middle uterine arteries. (In some cases this artery arises from the internal iliac or the umbilical.)

(3) The **perineal artery** (A. perinei) is relatively small in the male. It ascends at the side of the anus, which it supplies, and gives twigs to the bulbocavernosus muscle and the skin of the perineum. In the female it is large and is distributed to the anus and vulva, and gives a large branch to the vestibular bulb.

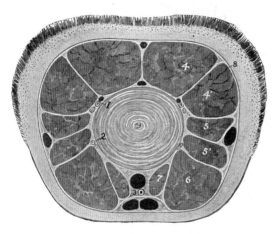

FIG. 579.—CROSS-SECTION OF TAIL OF HORSE.

1, Dorso-lateral coccygeal vessels and nerve; *2*, ventro-lateral coccygeal artery and nerve; *3*, middle coccygeal artery; *4*, sacro-coccygeus dorsalis; *4'*, sacro-coccygeus lateralis; *5, 5'*, intertransversales; *6*, sacro-coccygeus ventralis; *7*, recto-coccygeus; *8*, coccygeal fascia; *9*, fibro-cartilage between fourth and fifth coccygeal vertebræ. The veins are black.

(4) The **artery of the bulb** (A. bulbi urethræ) may be regarded as the direct continuation of the internal pudic in the male. It lies at the side of the urethra above the ischial arch, dips under the bulbo-cavernosus muscle, and ramifies in the corpus cavernosum urethræ. Before doing so it gives off a small branch which turns around the ischial arch to reach the dorsum penis, and anastomoses with the deep branch of the obturator.

(4 a) The **artery of the clitoris** (A. clitoridis) is the homologue in the female of the preceding vessel, but is much smaller. It passes to the ventral surface of the vulva with a branch of the pudic nerve, supplies the clitoris, and gives twigs to the vulva.

3. The **lateral sacral artery** (A. sacralis lateralis) arises at the lumbo-sacral articulation (Fig. 576). It passes backward under the wing of the sacrum, then along the pelvic surface of the bone below the ventral sacral foramina and the nerves emerging from them, and is continued by the lateral coccygeal artery. The branches are as follows:

(1) **Spinal branches** (Rami spinales) enter the vertebral canal through the

---

[1] The obliteration in the adult extends a variable distance from the vesical end toward the origin, but usually involves completely only a small part.

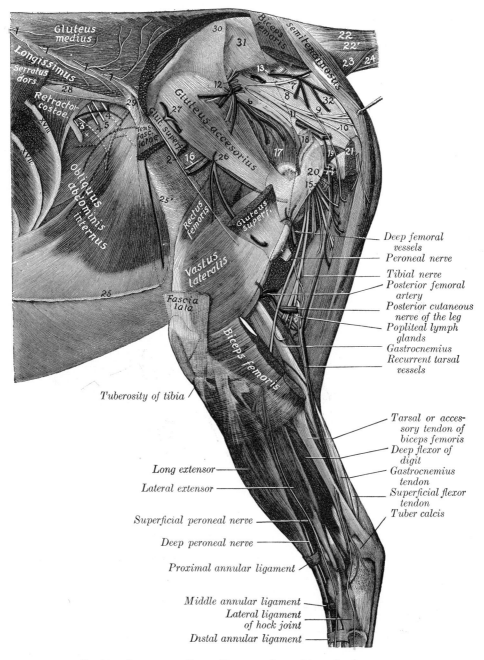

Fig. 580.—Dissection of Pelvis, Thigh, and Leg of Horse; Lateral View.

1, Dorsal branches of last thoracic and first three lumbar nerves; *2*, cutaneous branch of fourth lumbar nerve; *3*, ventral branches of last thoracic nerve; *4*, branches of ilio-hypogastric nerve; *5*, superficial branch of ilio-inguinal nerve; *6*, great sciatic nerve; *7, 8*, nerves to biceps femoris (from posterior gluteal nerve); *9*, nerve to semitendinosus (from same); *10*, posterior cutaneous nerve of thigh; *11*, pudic nerve; *12*, anterior gluteal vessels and nerves; *13*, posterior gluteal vessels; *14*, branches of obturator vessels; *15*, proximal muscular branches of great sciatic nerve to biceps femoris, semitendinosus, and semimembranosus; *16*, nerve to tensor fasciæ latæ (from anterior gluteal nerve); *17*, gluteus profundus; *18*, stump of gluteus medius; *19*, gemellus; *20*, stump of quadratus femoris; *21*, stump of biceps femoris; *22*, sacro-coccygeus dorsalis; *22'*, sacro-coccygeus lateralis; *23*, coccygeus; *24*, sacro-coccygeus ventralis; *25*, line of fusion of aponeuroses of internal and external oblique muscles of abdomen; *25'*, aponeurosis of external oblique muscle (lamina iliaca); *26*, branches of iliaco-femoral vessels; *27*, ilio-lumbar vessels; *28*, ilio-lumbar ligament or deep layer of lumbo-dorsal fascia; *29*, tuber coxæ; *30*, tuber sacrale; *31*, lateral sacro-iliac ligament; *32*, sacro-sciatic ligament. The ventral part of a nineteenth rib is shown in front of *3*.   (After Schmaltz, Atlas d. Anat. d. Pferdes.)

ventral sacral foramina. They give off branches to the spinal cord and its membranes, which reinforce the ventral spinal artery, and others which emerge through the dorsal sacral foramina and supply the muscles and skin of the croup.

(2) The **middle coccygeal artery** (A. coccygea) is an unpaired vessel which arises from the right or left lateral sacral or from a lateral coccygeal artery. It passes backward on the pelvic surface of the sacrum to the median line and continues in that position along the tail between the ventral muscles, supplying these and the skin (Fig. 579).

(3) The **posterior gluteal artery** (A. glutea caudalis) emerges through the upper part of the sacro-sciatic ligament and runs on the latter toward the tuber ischii, under cover of the biceps femoris (Fig. 580). It gives branches to that

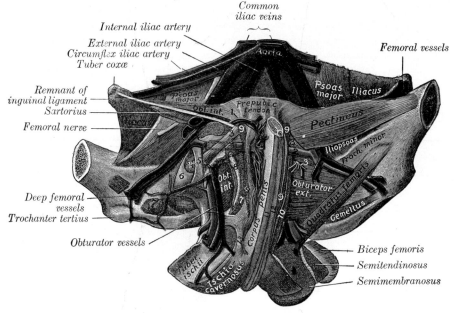

Fig. 581.—Deep Dissection of Ventral Wall of Pelvis of Horse (Male).

1, External pudic artery and small satellite vein; *2,* external pudic vein; *3,* accessory ligament; *3* (below *2*), obturator nerve; *4,* round ligament; *5,* transverse ligament; *6,* head of femur; *7,* obturator externus (stumps); *8,* medial margin of obturator foramen; *9,* origin of gracilis; *10,* origin of adductor; *11,* bulbocavernosus; *12,* retractor penis; *13,* suspensory ligament of penis. (After Schmaltz, Atlas d. Anat. d. Pferdes.)

muscle, the semitendinosus, semimembranosus, superficial gluteus, and coccygeus, and anastomoses with the obturator, deep femoral, and posterior femoral arteries.

(4) The **lateral coccygeal artery** (A. caudalis lateralis ventralis) continues the direction of the lateral sacral, but is much smaller than the preceding vessel. It passes back between the ventral and intertransversales muscles of the tail and divides into dorsal and ventral branches which supply the muscles and skin.

4. The **ilio-lumbar artery** (A. iliolumbalis) arises at a right angle from the internal iliac and runs outward behind the sacro-iliac joint, crossing the ventral surface of the ilium under cover of the iliacus muscle. It gives branches to the iliopsoas and longissimus, turns around the lateral border of the ilium a little behind the tuber coxæ, and ends in the gluteus medius and tensor fasciæ latæ (Fig. 530)

5. The **anterior gluteal artery** (A. glutea cranialis) is the largest branch of the internal iliac. It arises usually opposite to the preceding vessel, and passes outward

through the greater sciatic foramen, dividing into several branches as it emerges; these enter the gluteal muscles (Fig. 580).

6. The **iliaco-femoral** or **lateral circumflex artery of the thigh** (A. circumflexa lateralis) passes ventro-laterally between the shaft of the ilium and the gluteus medius dorsally and the iliacus muscle ventrally, and dips in between the rectus femoris and vastus lateralis. It is accompanied by two satellite veins. It gives collateral branches to the iliopsoas, the glutei, and the tensor fasciæ latæ, supplies the nutrient artery of the ilium, and terminates in the quadriceps femoris (Fig. 580).

7. The **obturator artery** (A. obturatoria), the medial terminal branch of the internal iliac, passes downward and backward on the pelvic surface of the shaft of the ilium, along the ventral border of the iliac head of the obturator internus, accompanied by the satellite vein and nerve, which lie ventral to the artery (Fig. 576). On reaching the obturator foramen it dips under the obturator internus and passes obliquely through the lateral part of the foramen. In this part of its course it gives off a vesical branch and twigs to the obturator internus and the hip joint. It emerges from the obturator foramen behind the obturator externus, passes between the quadratus femoris and the adductor, runs backward on the ventral face of the ischium, and, in the male, enters the crus penis, forming the **arteria profunda penis.** It anastomoses with the internal pudic, and usually with the external pudic by a branch, the **posterior dorsal artery of the penis** (A. dorsalis penis caudalis) which runs forward on the dorsum penis. Collateral branches go to the obturator, adductor, semimembranosus, biceps femoris, and semitendinosus muscles, and anastomoses are formed with the deep femoral and posterior femoral arteries. In the female the terminal part is small and enters the root of the clitoris.

ARTERIES OF THE PELVIC LIMB

The main arterial trunk of each pelvic limb descends to the proximal part of the posterior surface of the tibia, where it divides under cover of the popliteus muscle into the anterior and posterior tibial arteries. The different parts of the trunk receive names which correspond to the several regions through which it passes. In the abdomen it is termed the **external iliac artery,** in the proximal two-thirds of the thigh it is called the **femoral artery,** and distal to this it is termed the **popliteal artery.**

The External Iliac Artery (Figs. 575, 576)

The **external iliac artery** (A. iliaca externa) arises from the aorta under the fifth lumbar vertebra, and usually just in front of the origin of the internal iliac. It descends at the side of the pelvic inlet along the tendon of the psoas minor, crosses the insertion of that muscle, and reaches the level of the anterior border of the pubis, beyond which it is continued by the femoral artery. It is covered by the peritoneum and fascia, and is related behind to the corresponding vein. Its chief branches are as follows:

1. The **circumflex iliac artery** (A. circumflexa ilium profunda) arises from the external iliac at its origin or from the aorta directly. It passes across the iliac fascia toward the tuber coxæ, and divides into two branches at or near the lateral border of the psoas major. The artery lies between the fascia and the peritoneum and is accompanied by two veins. It furnishes small branches to the psoas muscles and the external iliac lymph glands. The **anterior branch** gives twigs to the iliacus and psoas muscles, and passes downward and forward in the flank on the transversus abdominis, along, or under cover of, the upper margin of the obliquus abdominis internus. It gives branches to these muscles, the obliquus abdominis externus, and the skin of the flank. The **posterior branch** perforates the abdominal wall close to the tuber coxæ, and runs downward on the medial face of the tensor

fasciæ latæ to the fold of the flank, supplying branches to that muscle, the cutaneous, the prefemoral lymph glands, and the skin.

2. The **external spermatic** or cremasteric **artery** (A. spermatica externa) is a very small vessel which arises in a variable manner. It springs most often from the external iliac near the origin of the latter, but may come from the circumflex iliac, the aorta between the external and internal iliac, or the latter vessel. It accompanies the cremaster muscle to the inguinal canal, supplies twigs to that muscle, the tunica vaginalis, and other constituents of the spermatic cord (Fig. 575).

2a. The **middle uterine artery** (A. uterina media) of the female is regarded as the homologue of the preceding vessel; it has a similar origin, but is a much larger artery. It enters the broad ligament of the uterus, in which it pursues a flexuous course to the posterior part of the horn of the uterus. Its branches are distributed to the uterus and anastomose with those of the other uterine arteries.

THE FEMORAL ARTERY (Figs. 575, 576)

The **femoral artery** is the main arterial trunk of the thigh. It begins at the level of the anterior border of the pubis, from which it is separated by the femoral

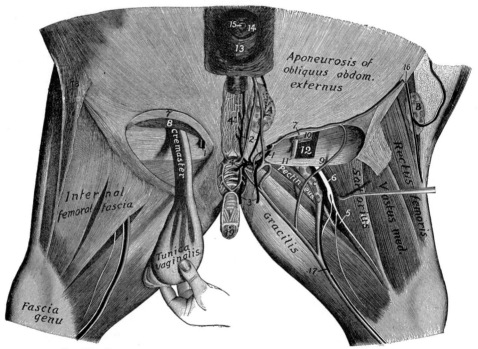

FIG. 582.—DISSECTION OF INGUINAL REGION AND MEDIAL SURFACE OF THIGH OF HORSE.

1, External pudic artery; *2,* anterior branches of *1;* *3,* posterior branches of *1;* *4,* transverse anastomosis between external pudic veins; *4',* venous plexus of dorsum penis; *5,* femoral artery; *6,* saphenous nerve; *7,* anterior border of external inguinal ring; *8,* obliquus abdominis internus; *9,* posterior border of external inguinal ring; *10,* tunica vaginalis; *11,* ductus deferens; *12,* cremaster muscle; *13,* prepuce; *14,* glans penis; *15,* external urethral orifice; *16,* posterior branches of circumflex iliac vessels; *17,* saphenous vessels; *18,* fold of flank; *19,* penis (cut); *A,* superficial inguinal lymph glands; *B,* prefemoral lymph glands; *C,* deep inguinal lymph glands. The testicle (on the right side) has been rotated somewhat to show the cremaster muscle. (After Schmaltz, Atlas d. Anat. d. Pferdes.)

vein. It descends almost vertically in the femoral canal behind the sartorius muscle, covered at first by the medial femoral fascia and lower down by the gracilis. After passing over the insertion of the pectineus, it perforates the adductor muscle, crosses in the vascular groove of the posterior surface of the femur, and is continued

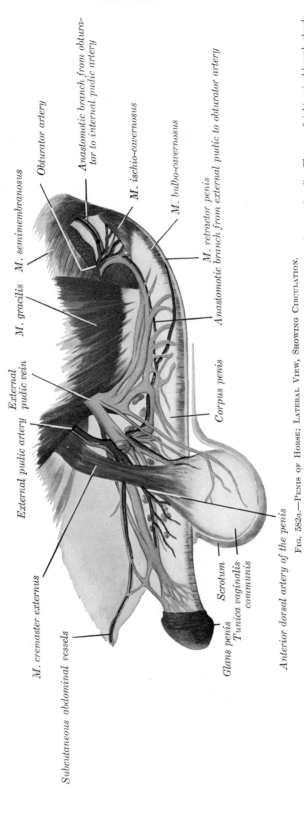

M. cremaster externus

External pudic artery *External pudic vein*

M. gracilis *M. semimembranosus*

Obturator artery

Anastomotic branch from obturator to internal pudic artery

M. ischio-cavernosus

M. bulbo-cavernosus

M. retractor penis

Anastomotic branch from external pudic to obturator artery

Corpus penis

Subcutaneous abdominal vessels

Glans penis *Scrotum*

Tunica vaginalis communis

Anterior dorsal artery of the penis

Fig. 582a.—Penis of Horse; Lateral View, Showing Circulation.

1, Dorsal artery of penis; *2*, branch of external pudic anastomosing with obturator artery; *3*, obturator, and *3′*, its branch connecting with internal pudic. The superficial inguinal lymph glands are shown in the meshes of the plexus dorsalis penis.

between the two heads of the gastrocnemius as the popliteal artery. It is related at its origin to the sartorius in front, the femoral vein behind (which separates it from the pectineus), and the iliacus laterally. Lower down it is related superficially to the deep inguinal lymph glands, and deeply to the vastus medialis, while the saphenous nerve is in front of it, and the vein passes to its lateral face. The chief branches are as follows:

1. The **prepubic artery** (Truncus pudendo-abdominalis) arises usually by a common trunk with the deep femoral, a little below the level of the pubis. It passes forward across the edge of the inguinal ligament, inclining ventro-medially, and then runs on the abdominal surface of the ligament to the medial part of the internal inguinal ring, where it divides into the posterior abdominal and external pudic arteries. (1) The **posterior abdominal artery** (A. abdominalis caudalis) (Fig. 370) passes along the lateral border of the rectus abdominis and anastomoses in the umbilical region with the anterior abdominal artery. It supplies branches chiefly to the rectus and obliquus internus muscles. (2) The **external pudic artery** (A. pudenda externa) descends on the inguinal ligament through the medial part of the inguinal canal, and emerges at the medial angle of the external ring. In the male it divides into the **subcutaneous abdominal artery** and the **anterior dorsal artery of the penis** (Fig. 582a). The former (A. abdominalis subcutanea) runs forward on the abdominal tunic a short distance from the linea alba, and gives branches to the superficial inguinal lymph glands, the sheath, and the scrotum. The latter (A. dorsalis penis cranialis) passes to the dorsum penis and ends at the glans as the arteria glandis. It gives off collateral branches (Rami profundi penis) to the corpus cavernosum, one of which usually passes backward and anastomoses with a branch of the obturator artery. Branches are also supplied to the superficial inguinal lymph glands, the prepuce, and the scrotum. In the female the **mammary artery** (A. mammaria) takes the place of the anterior dorsal artery of the penis; it enters the base of the mammary gland, in which it ramifies.

2. The **deep femoral artery** (A. profunda femoris) (Fig. 581) arises either by a common trunk with the prepubic or a little distal to it. The point of origin is usually at the level of the anterior border of the pubis, but may be an inch lower or higher. It passes backward and downward across the medial face of the femoral vein, then below the pubis in the space between the hip joint and the pectineus muscle. On reaching the obturator externus it inclines more ventrally and laterally, passes out between the posterior surface of the femur and the quadratus femoris, and ramifies in the biceps femoris and semitendinosus. It supplies large collateral branches to the medial femoral muscles and twigs to the deep inguinal lymph glands and the hip joint, and anastomoses with the obturator artery.[1]

3. The **anterior femoral artery** (A. femoris cranialis) (Fig. 575) arises a little distal to the preceding vessel, from the opposite side of the femoral trunk. It passes forward, outward, and a little downward across the deep face of the sartorius, dips in between the rectus femoris and vastus medialis, and ramifies in these muscles and the vastus intermedius. It is related laterally to the ilio-psoas and to the femoral nerve.

In some cases this artery is replaced by a large branch of the iliaco-femoral or external circumflex, which passes between the ilio-psoas and rectus femoris and enters the interstice between the latter muscle and the vastus medialis.

4. Innominate **muscular branches** (Rami musculares) of variable size and arrangement are given off to the muscles of this vicinity.

5. The **saphenous artery** (A. saphena) (Figs. 576, 582) is a small vessel which arises from the femoral about its middle, or from a muscular branch, and emerges between the sartorius and gracilis or through the latter to the medial surface of the

[1] In the revised nomenclature the term A. circumflexa femoris medialis is applied to the part which turns outward, while the part which runs backward is regarded as the continuing trunk.

thigh.   In company with the large saphenous vein and the saphenous nerve it descends superficially on the anterior part of the gracilis, continues on the deep fascia of the leg, and divides above the hock into two branches, which accompany the radicles of the vein.   It gives off cutaneous twigs and anastomoses with the recurrent tibial artery.

In some cases this anastomosis does not occur.   The artery may be larger and directly continuous with the medial tarsal artery.

6. The **articular branch** (A. genu suprema) is a slender artery which arises from the femoral just before it passes through the adductor.   It descends along the posterior border of the vastus medialis to the medial surface of the stifle joint, where it ramifies.

7. The **nutrient artery of the femur** (A. nutritia femoris) is given off at the middle of the femur and enters the nutrient foramen.

8. The **posterior femoral artery** (A. femoris caudalis) is a large vessel which arises from the posterior face of the femoral just before or as the trunk passes between the two heads of the gastrocnemius (Fig. 584).   It is very short and divides into two branches.[1]   The ascending branch passes upward and outward between the adductor (in front) and the semimembranosus (behind), and ramifies in the biceps femoris, vastus lateralis, adductor, and semitendinosus.   The descending branch passes downward and backward on the lateral head of the gastrocnemius, curves upward between the biceps femoris and semitendinosus (crossed by the tibial and peroneal nerves) and divides into branches to these muscles.   A branch descends between the heads of the gastrocnemius, gives branches to that muscle and the superficial digital flexor, and is continued by a slender artery which accompanies the tibial nerve and unites with the recurrent tibial artery.   A small branch often ascends alongside of the sciatic nerve, between the biceps and semitendinosus and anastomoses with a descending branch of the obturator artery.

This branch is frequently absent, but the large vein which accompanies it when present is constant and connects the obturator and posterior femoral veins.

THE POPLITEAL ARTERY

This artery (A. poplitea) is the direct continuation of the femoral.   It lies between the two heads of the gastrocnemius, at first on the posterior face of the femur, then on the femoro-tibial joint capsule.   It descends through the popliteal notch under cover of the popliteus, inclines outward, and divides near the proximal part of the interosseous space into anterior and posterior tibial arteries.   The satellite vein lies along its medial side at the stifle joint.   Collateral branches are supplied to the stifle joint and the gastrocnemius and popliteus.

One of the articular branches (A. genu media) runs directly forward, passes through the posterior part of the capsule of the femoro-tibial joint, and supplies the cruciate ligaments, synovial membrane, etc.   Another branch (A. genu lateralis distalis) passes outward under the lateral head of the gastrocnemius, and concurs with the articular branch of the femoral artery in forming a plexus on the stifle.

POSTERIOR TIBIAL ARTERY

The **posterior tibial artery** (A. tibialis posterior) is much the smaller of the two terminals of the popliteal.   It lies at first between the tibia and the popliteus, then between that muscle and the deep and medial heads of the deep digital flexor. Lower down it descends along the tendon of the flexor longus, becomes superficial in the distal third of the leg, and divides into lateral and medial tarsal branches.[2] The collateral branches include the **nutrient artery of the tibia** (A. nutritia tibiæ) and **muscular branches** (Rami musculares) to the muscles on the posterior surface of the tibia.

[1] The two branches may arise separately.

[2] Instead of dividing thus, the posterior tibial may be continued by the lateral tarsal.   The medial tarsal may be a continuation of the saphenous artery.

The **lateral tarsal artery** (A. tarsea lateralis) passes outward between the tibia and the deep flexor of the digit, and is distributed to the lateral surface of the hock.

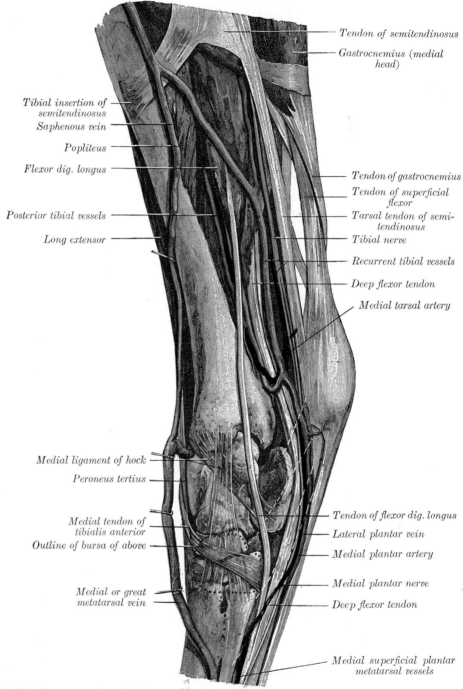

Tendon of semitendinosus

Gastrocnemius (medial head)

Tibial insertion of semitendinosus

Saphenous vein

Popliteus

Flexor dig. longus

Tendon of gastrocnemius

Tendon of superficial flexor

Posterior tibial vessels

Tarsal tendon of semi-tendinosus

Long extensor

Tibial nerve

Recurrent tibial vessels

Deep flexor tendon

Medial tarsal artery

Medial ligament of hock

Peroneus tertius

Medial tendon of tibialis anterior

Tendon of flexor dig. longus

Outline of bursa of above

Lateral plantar vein

Medial plantar artery

Medial or great metatarsal vein

Medial plantar nerve

Deep flexor tendon

Medial superficial plantar metatarsal vessels

Fig. 583.—Dissection of Right Leg and Hock of Horse; Medial View. (After Schmaltz, Atlas d. Anat. d. Pferdes.)

It gives off the small **recurrent tarsal artery** (A. tarsea recurrens), which ascends along the lateral margin of the gastrocnemius tendon with a satellite vein and nerve and anastomoses with a branch of the posterior femoral artery. In some cases an arch is formed by junction with the peroneal artery on the lateral surface of the deep flexor at the distal fourth of the leg.

The **medial tarsal artery** (A. tarsea medialis) usually forms a double curve in front of the tuber calcis, then descends on the deep flexor tendon with the plantar nerves, and divides into the two plantar arteries. From the second part of the curve there arises a small branch, the **recurrent tibial artery** (A. tibialis recurrens). This ascends along the medial border of the superficial digital flexor in company with a satellite vein and the tibial nerve, and anastomoses with a descending branch of the posterior femoral artery and with the saphenous artery.[1]

6. The **plantar arteries,** medial and lateral (A. plantaris medialis, lateralis), are the small terminals of the medial tarsal. They descend along the sides of the tarsal sheath of the deep flexor tendon with the plantar nerves to the proximal part of the metatarsus, where they unite with the perforating tarsal artery to form the **proximal plantar arch** (Arcus plantaris proximalis). Four **plantar metatarsal arteries** proceed from this arch. The two slender **superficial plantar metatarsal arteries** (A. metatarsea plantaris superficialis medialis, lateralis) may be regarded as the continuations of the plantar arteries; they descend on either side of the deep flexor tendon with the plantar nerves, and unite with the corresponding digital artery. The medial one is the smaller; it may give off or connect with the corresponding dorsal artery. The lateral, larger one usually unites with the lateral digital artery. Both may unite at the distal part of the metatarsus to form a short trunk which joins one of the digital arteries. They supply twigs to the flexor tendons and the skin. The two **deep plantar metatarsal arteries** (A. metatarsea plantaris profundus medialis, lateralis) descend on the plantar surface of the large metatarsal bone alongside of the corresponding small metatarsal bone and unite near the fetlock with the great metatarsal. The medial artery is the larger of the two and usually appears to be the continuation of the perforating tarsal. It supplies the nutrient artery of the large metatarsal bone. In other cases it is the direct continuation of the medial plantar artery, the lateral artery only uniting with the perforating tarsal. The connection of these vessels with the great metatarsal artery forms the **distal plantar arch** (Arcus plantaris distalis).

ANTERIOR TIBIAL ARTERY

The **anterior tibial artery** (A. tibialis anterior) is much the larger of the two terminal branches of the popliteal. It passes forward through the proximal part of the interosseous space and descends with two satellite veins on the lateral part of the front of the tibia, under cover of the tibialis anterior. At the distal part of the leg it deviates to the lateral border of the tendon of this muscle, passes on to the capsule of the hock joint, gives off the large perforating tarsal artery, and is continued as the great metatarsal artery.[2] It gives off **muscular branches** to the dorsolateral group of muscles of the leg and **articular branches** to the hock. The **peroneal artery** (A. peronea) is a variable vessel which descends along the fibula under cover of the lateral extensor; it gives off muscular branches and one which perforates the fascia and divides into ascending and descending cutaneous twigs.[3]

The **perforating tarsal artery** (A. tarsea perforans) arises under cover of the extensor digitalis brevis muscle. It passes backward through the vascular canal of the tarsus with a satellite vein and nerve and unites on the upper part of

---

[1] The artery may be double in part or throughout. It may join the popliteal artery. The S-shaped curve may be absent and the medial tarsal be the direct continuation of the recurrent tibial artery.

[2] The part of the arterial trunk which is on the dorsal surface of the tarsus may be distinguished by the term A. dorsalis pedis.

[3] In some cases the peroneal artery is larger than usual and forms an anastomotic arch with the lateral tarsal in the distal part of the leg.

the suspensory ligament with the plantar arteries (or only with the lateral plantar)
to form the **proximal plantar arch** (Arcus plantaris proximalis).

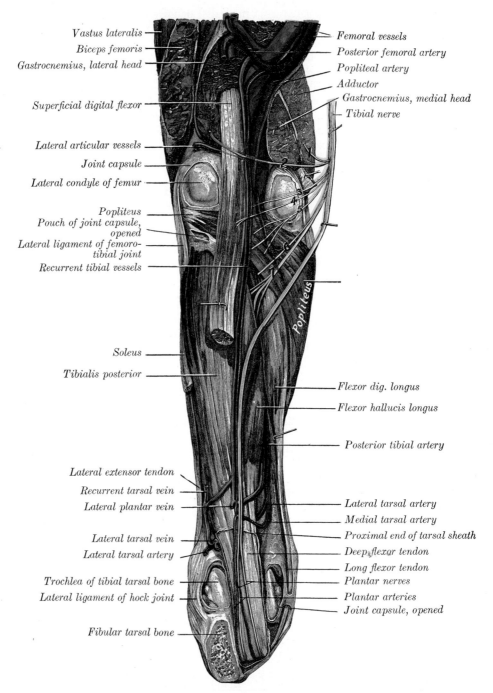

Vastus lateralis

Biceps femoris

Gastrocnemius, lateral head

Superficial digital flexor

Lateral articular vessels

Joint capsule

Lateral condyle of femur

Popliteus
Pouch of joint capsule,
opened
Lateral ligament of femoro-
tibial joint
Recurrent tibial vessels

Soleus

Tibialis posterior

Lateral extensor tendon

Recurrent tarsal vein

Lateral plantar vein

Lateral tarsal vein

Lateral tarsal artery

Trochlea of tibial tarsal bone

Lateral ligament of hock joint

Fibular tarsal bone

Femoral vessels

Posterior femoral artery

Popliteal artery

Adductor

Gastrocnemius, medial head

Tibial nerve

Popliteus

Flexor dig. longus

Flexor hallucis longus

Posterior tibial artery

Lateral tarsal artery

Medial tarsal artery

Proximal end of tarsal sheath

Deep flexor tendon

Long flexor tendon

Plantar nerves

Plantar arteries

Joint capsule, opened

Fig. 584.—Deep Dissection of Left Stifle, Leg, and Hock of Horse; Posterior View.

The hock is flexed at a right angle, and the tuber calcis is sawn off.   The tibial nerve is drawn aside to show its
muscular branches.   The capsules of the stifle and hock joints are partially removed.   Branches of tibial nerve: *1, 2,*
to gastrocnemius; *3, 4,* to superficial flexor; *5,* to popliteus; *6,* to flexor longus; *7,* to deep flexor. (After Schmaltz,
Atlas d. Anat. d. Pferdes.)

In well-injected specimens it is seen that there is a fine arterial network (Rete tarsi dorsale) on the dorsal surface of the hock, which is formed by twigs from the

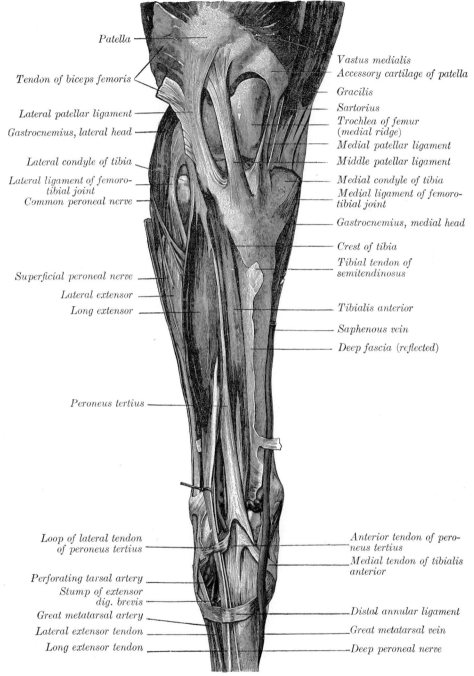

Patella

Tendon of biceps femoris

Lateral patellar ligament

Gastrocnemius, lateral head

Lateral condyle of tibia

Lateral ligament of femoro-tibial joint
Common peroneal nerve

Superficial peroneal nerve

Lateral extensor

Long extensor

Peroneus tertius

Loop of lateral tendon of peroneus tertius

Perforating tarsal artery
Stump of extensor dig. brevis
Great metatarsal artery
Lateral extensor tendon
Long extensor tendon

Vastus medialis
Accessory cartilage of patella

Gracilis

Sartorius
Trochlea of femur (medial ridge)
Medial patellar ligament
Middle patellar ligament

Medial condyle of tibia
Medial ligament of femoro-tibial joint

Gastrocnemius, medial head

Crest of tibia
Tibial tendon of semitendinosus

Tibialis anterior

Saphenous vein

Deep fascia (reflected)

Anterior tendon of peroneus tertius
Medial tendon of tibialis anterior

Distal annular ligament
Great metatarsal vein
Deep peroneal nerve

FIG. 585.—SUPERFICIAL DISSECTION OF RIGHT STIFLE, LEG, AND HOCK OF HORSE; FRONT VIEW. (After Schmaltz, Atlas d. Anat. d. Pferdes.)

anterior tibial and lateral tarsal arteries. From it proceed two very slender **dorsal metatarsal arteries** (A. metatarsea dorsalis medialis, lateralis). The medial one descends in the furrow between the medial small and large metatarsal bones, and anastomoses usually in the proximal part of the metatarsus with the medial superficial plantar metatarsal, uniting sometimes with the medial deep plantar metatarsal. The lateral vessel passes down under the periosteum on the dorsal face of the large metatarsal bone and becomes lost or joins the great metatarsal artery.

In rare cases the anterior tibial artery passes undivided through the tarsus, gives off the medial deep plantar metatarsal, and is continued as a very large medial superficial plantar metatarsal along the deep flexor tendon, thus resembling the arrangement in the forelimb.

In a few cases the perforating tarsal is a large vessel, directly continuing the anterior tibial, and is continued by a large medial deep plantar metatarsal. The great metatarsal is then small. Other variations are common.

THE GREAT METATARSAL ARTERY

This artery (A. metatarsea dorsalis lateralis) is the direct continuation of the anterior tibial. It descends, inclining outward, under cover of the extensor brevis and the tendon of the lateral extensor, at first on the joint capsule and then in the oblique vascular groove on the proximal part of the large metatarsal bone. It then descends superficially in the groove formed by the apposition of the large and lateral small metatarsal bones, passes medially between the two, and divides on the distal part of the plantar surface of the large metatarsal bone into the medial and lateral **digital arteries.** It is not usually accompanied by a vein. It is joined near its termination by two or more of the plantar arteries, and beyond this the term common digital artery (A. digitalis communis) may be applied to it. In the digital region the arterial arrangement is the same as in the thoracic limb; it is only necessary in reading the description to substitute the word "plantar" for "volar" (p. 671).

THE VEINS[1]

PULMONARY VEINS

The **pulmonary veins** (Vv. pulmonales), usually seven or eight in number, return the aërated blood from the lungs and open into the left atrium of the heart. They are destitute of valves. Their tributaries arise in the capillary plexuses in the lobules of the lungs, and unite to form larger and larger trunks which accompany the branches of the bronchi and pulmonary arteries. A very large vein is formed by the union at an acute angle of a trunk from each lung, where the latter are adherent to each other.

CARDIAC VEINS

The **coronary sinus** (Sinus coronarius) is a very short, bulbous trunk which receives most of the blood from the wall of the heart. It is situated just below the termination of the posterior vena cava, and is covered in part by a thin layer of atrial muscle fibers. It opens into the right atrium just below the posterior vena cava. It is formed by the union of two tributaries. The **great cardiac** or **left coronary vein** (V. cordis magna) ascends in the left longitudinal groove and turns backward in the coronary groove, in which it winds around the posterior border of the heart to the right side and joins the coronary sinus. The **middle cardiac** or **right coronary vein** (V. cordis media) ascends in the right longitudinal groove and joins the coronary sinus, or opens separately into the atrium just in front of the

---

[1] Most of the veins are depicted in the illustrations of the section on the arteries, to which reference is to be made. Many satellite veins which are homonymous with the arteries which they accompany, and present no important special features, are not described here.

orifice of the great cardiac vein, so that a common trunk (coronary sinus) does not then exist. Quite commonly two veins accompany the artery in the right groove and unite at the coronary groove. There is a crescentic fold (Valvula venæ cavæ caudalis) between the opening of the posterior vena cava and the coronary sinus. The **small cardiac veins** (Vv. cordis minores), three to five in number, are small vessels which return some blood from the right ventricle and atrium; they open into the latter near the coronary groove in spaces between the musculi pectinati.

THE ANTERIOR VENA CAVA (Fig. 554)

The **anterior vena cava** (V. cava cranialis) returns to the heart the blood from the head, neck, thoracic limbs, and the greater part of the thoracic wall. It is formed at the ventral part of the thoracic inlet by the confluence of the two jugular and two brachial veins. It passes backward in the anterior mediastinum, at first median and ventral to the common carotid trunk, then deviates to the right of the common brachiocephalic trunk, and opens into the right atrium opposite to the fourth rib. It is partly enclosed by the pericardium. The demarcation between vein and atrium is not very distinct. It contains no valves except at the mouths of its radicles. Its length is about five to six inches (ca. 12–15 cm.) and its caliber about two inches (ca. 5 cm.) in a subject of medium size. It is related, dorsally to the trachea, the right vagus and cardiac nerves, and anterior mediastinal lymph glands. Its right face is crossed by the right phrenic nerve, and on the left it is related to the brachiocephalic trunk and artery. The thoracic duct opens through the dorsal wall of the origin of the vena cava. It receives, in addition to small pericardial and mediastinal veins, the following tributaries:

1. The **internal thoracic vein** (V. thoracica interna) is a satellite of the artery of that name. It opens into the anterior vena cava at the first rib. The **ventral intercostal veins** (Vv. intercostales ventrales) open into the internal thoracic and musculo-phrenic veins.

2. The **vertebral vein** (V. vertebralis) corresponds to the homonymous artery. On the right side it terminates either in front of the deep cervical vein or by a short common trunk with it. On the left side it usually unites with the deep cervical and dorsal veins to form a common trunk.

3. The **deep cervical vein** (V. cervicalis profunda) corresponds to the artery. On the right side it passes downward and backward across the right face of the trachea and opens into the vena cava; it may form a common trunk with the dorsal or vertebral. On the left side there is usually a common trunk for all three. It receives the first intercostal vein.

4. The **dorsal vein** (V. costocervicalis) corresponds to the artery. On the right side it leaves the artery on entering the thorax, crosses the right face of the trachea, and opens into the vena cava behind the deep cervical or by a common trunk with it. On the left side it usually joins the deep cervical and vertebral to form a short common trunk which crosses the left face of the intrathoracic part of the brachial artery opposite the second rib and opens into the anterior vena cava. It receives the third, fourth, and fifth intercostal veins by means of the subcostal vein on the right side.

THE VENA AZYGOS

The **vena azygos** (Fig. 554) is an unpaired vessel which arises at the level of the first lumbar vertebra by radicles from the spinal and psoas muscles and the crura of the diaphragm. It passes forward along the right side of the bodies of the thoracic vertebræ, in contact usually with the thoracic duct, which separates the vein from the aorta. At the seventh vertebra it leaves the spine, curves downward and forward over the right side of the thoracic duct, trachea, and œsophagus, and opens into the right atrium opposite the fourth intercostal space. Its tributaries are:

1. The last fourteen **dorsal intercostal veins** (Vv. intercostales dorsales) of the right side go directly to the vena azygos; but on the left side a variable number (four to seven usually) at the end of the series go to the vena hemiazygos when that vessel is present.

2. The **vena hemiazygos** arises from a branch of the left first lumbar vein and twigs from the crura of the diaphragm. It passes forward through the hiatus aorticus and continues along the left dorsal face of the aorta, and about the middle of the back joins the vena azygos. It receives the last four to seven dorsal intercostal veins of the left side. It is inconstant and variable. In its absence its tributaries join the vena azygos.

3. The **œsophageal vein** (V. œsophagea), satellite of the œsophageal artery, joins the vena azygos as it inclines downward.

4. A **bronchial vein** (V. bronchialis) has been described as uniting with the preceding to form a short common trunk, or, according to Chauveau, it empties into the great coronary vein. The author is unable to find in the horse any distinct bronchial vein emerging at the root of the lung.[1]

VEINS OF THE HEAD AND NECK
JUGULAR VEINS

The **jugular veins** (Vv. jugulares), right and left (Fig. 556), arise behind the ramus of the mandible, about two and a half inches (ca. 6–7 cm.) below the temporo-mandibular articulation by the union of the superficial temporal and internal maxillary veins. Each passes downward and backward, at first embedded more or less in the parotid gland, and continues in the jugular furrow to the thoracic inlet, where it unites with its fellow and the two brachial veins to form the anterior vena cava. In the neck it is covered by the skin, fascia, and cutaneus muscle, and is superficial to the carotid artery, from which it is separated in the anterior half of the region by the omo-hyoideus muscle.[2] It contains valves at the mouths of its tributaries, and has several pairs of semilunar valves variably disposed along its course. Its tributaries are as follows:

1. The **internal maxillary vein** (V. maxillaris interna) is larger than the external maxillary. It may be considered to begin as the continuation backward of the buccinator vein where that vessel crosses the alveolar border of the mandible, about two inches (ca. 5 cm.) behind the last molar tooth. It runs backward on the medial surface of the ramus ventral to the lateral pterygoid muscle, and covered by the medial pterygoid muscle for a distance of about three inches (ca. 7–8 cm.), then inclines a little downward and runs ventral to the artery for about an inch (ca. 2–3 cm.). It crosses the lateral face of the artery at the posterior border of the jaw, and is joined by the superficial temporal vein to form the jugular. Its principal radicles are the following:

(1) The **dorsal lingual vein** (V. dorsalis linguæ) is not a satellite of any artery,

---

[1] In Chauveau-Arloing-Lesbre the statement is made that "the bronchial veins, which ramify on the bronchi like the arteries of which they are satellites, open into the great coronary vein very near its mouth, after having united to form a single vessel, which sometimes opens directly into the atrium." The arrangement is not illustrated. Ellenberger and Baum state that the bronchial and œsophageal veins open into the vena azygos separately or by a common trunk. Martin describes a short broncho-œsophageal trunk, but the vein which he figures as the bronchial does not come from the lungs, but is a small mediastinal vessel. The author finds such a vessel usually entering the terminal part of the œsophageal vein, but no distinct bronchial vein in the horse. The statement and figure in Bossi's recent work agree substantially with those of the German authors.

[2] There is usually only one jugular vein on each side in the horse, but in some cases there is an internal or deep jugular vein which accompanies the carotid artery and ends at the confluence of the external jugulars. M'Fadyean records a case in which the vein lay on the deep face of the omo-hyoideus with the carotid artery. This would appear to be an instance of remarkable development of the internal jugular in place of the usual external jugular vein.

but is in company with the lingual nerve. It receives tributaries from the tongue and soft palate.

(2) The mandibular or **inferior alveolar vein** (V. alveolaris mandibulæ) is a satellite of the corresponding artery (Fig. 648). It often unites with the preceding.

(3) The **middle meningeal vein** (V. meningea media) emerges through the foramen lacerum anterius.

(4) **Pterygoid veins** (Rami pterygoidei).

(5) The **posterior deep temporal vein** (V. temporalis profunda aboralis) is a

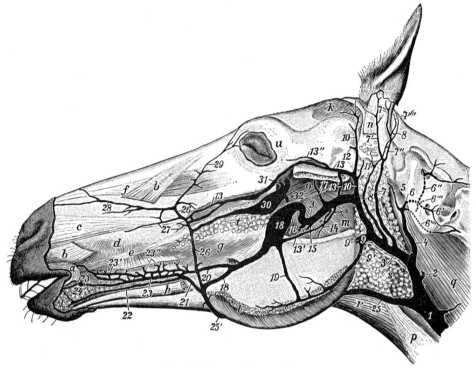

FIG. 586.—VEINS OF HEAD OF HORSE.

Parts of the superficial muscles and the ramus of the mandible, and all of the masseter muscle except its ventral margin, have been removed. Veins: *1, 3,* Jugular; *2,* thyroid; *3,* internal maxillary; *4,* cranio-occipital trunk; *5,* ventral cerebral; *6,* occipital; *6',* muscular branch of *6; 6'',* cerebrospinal branch of *6; 6''',* vein which emerges through foramen of lateral mass of atlas; *6'''',* vein which emerges through intervertebral foramen of axis; *7,* great auricular; *7'-7'''',* radicles of *7; 8,* posterior auricular; *9,* masseterico-pterygoid; *10,* superficial temporal; *11,* deep auricular; *12,* dorsal cerebral; *13,* transverse facial and *13',* anastomosis with buccinator; *13'',* palpebral radicle of *13; 14,* pterygoid; *15,* mandibular alveolar; *16,* dorsal lingual; *17,* deep temporal; *18,* buccinator; *19,* anastomosis between buccinator and masseteric; *20,* anastomosis between buccinator and common labial (*21*); *22, 23,* inferior and superior labial; *23', 23'',* buccal plexus; *24,* angular of mouth; *25, 25',* external maxillary; *26,* facial: *27,* lateral nasal; *28,* dorsal nasal; *29,* angular of eye; *30,* reflexa; *31,* trunk of infraorbital and sphenopalatine. Muscles, etc.: *a,* Orbicularis oris; *b,* levator nasolabialis; *c,* dilatator naris lateralis; *d,* buccalis; *e,* zygomaticus; *f,* levator labii superioris proprius; *g,* molaris and depressor labii inferioris; *i,* labial glands; *k,* m. temporalis; *l,* m. masseter; *m,* m. pterygoideus medialis; *n,* m. parotido-auricularis; *o,* m. pterygoideus lateralis; *p,* m. sterno-cephalicus; *q,* m. rectus capitis ventralis major; *r,* m. omo-hyoideus and sterno-hyoideus; *s,* parotid gland (dissected away from veins); *t,* dorsal buccal glands. (After Möckel.)

large vessel which receives tributaries from the temporalis muscle and emissaries from the temporal canal. It is connected with the dorsal cerebral vein and usually with the meningeal veins by its frontal branch. The latter drains chiefly the lacrimal gland and passes behind the supraorbital process.

2. The **superficial temporal vein** (V. temporalis superficialis) is the large satellite of the corresponding artery. It is formed by the confluence of the **anterior auricular** and **transverse facial veins**. The former is much larger than the cor-

responding artery. Its radicles come from the posterior part of the temporalis muscle and from the external ear. It receives the **dorsal cerebral vein** (V. cerebralis dorsalis), which is the emissary of the transverse sinus of the dura mater, and emerges from the temporal canal behind the postglenoid process. The **transverse facial vein** (V. transversa faciei) runs at first above the artery of like name, then plunges deeply into the masseter and unites in front with the facial vein. It is connected with the vena reflexa and with the posterior deep temporal vein by a branch which emerges from the temporal fossa through the mandibular notch.

3. The **masseteric vein** (V. masseterica) joins the jugular at the upper border of the sterno-cephalicus tendon. It is a short but large trunk which is formed by the confluence at the posterior border of the jaw of masseteric and pterygoid veins. The former is commonly connected by an anastomotic branch with the buccinator vein.

4. The **great auricular vein** (V. auricularis magna) is a satellite of the posterior auricular artery above, but joins the jugular a variable distance below and behind the point of origin of the artery.

5. The **occipital vein** (V. occipitalis) arises in the fossa atlantis by the union of two radicles. It passes downward and backward on the rectus capitis ventralis major and joins the jugular vein a variable distance in front of the termination of the external maxillary vein. The anterior radicle is the **ventral cerebral vein** (V. cerebralis ventralis). This is an emissary of the cavernous sinus of the dura mater; it emerges through the foramen lacerum posterius and is connected with a venous plexus in the infratemporal fossa. It receives the **condyloid vein** (V. condyloidea), which is an emissary of the basilar plexus and the petrosal sinus, and emerges through the hypoglossal foramen.[1] The posterior radicle is formed by the confluence of **muscular** and **cerebro-spinal branches.** The former (Ramus muscularis) comes through the foramen transversarium of the atlas from the muscles of the poll; it anastomoses with the vertebral and deep cervical veins. The latter (Ramus cerebrospinalis) receives emissary veins from the meningeal plexus in the atlas, which emerge through the intervertebral and alar foramina and the foramen of the lateral mass of the atlas.

6. The **external maxillary vein** (V. maxillaris externa) arises by radicles which correspond in general to the branches of the artery of like name. It passes down over the cheek along the anterior border of the masseter muscle behind the artery, crossing over the parotid duct, which lies behind the vein lower down. Thus on the ramus and as they turn around its ventral border the artery is in front, the vein in the middle, and the duct posterior. In the mandibular space the vein is ventral to the artery for some distance, then parts company with the artery, runs straight backward along the ventral border of the parotid gland, and opens into the jugular vein at the posterior angle of the gland.[2] The chief differences in the tributaries of the vein as compared with the branches of the corresponding artery are as follows:

The **labial veins** (Vv. labiales), superior and inferior, are in the substance of the orbicularis oris near the free edges of the lips. The upper one is the larger. They anastomose with the opposite veins. They and the **angular vein of the mouth** drain into a plexus in the submucous tissue of the cheek and the buccinator muscle. From this **buccal plexus** two veins emerge. The upper one passes back and joins the buccinator vein. The lower one, the **common labial vein** (V. labialis communis), receives a **submental vein** from the chin and joins the external maxillary vein.

Three veins connect with the external maxillary at the anterior border of the masseter.

---

[1] On account of the existence of these cranial affluents the term cranio-occipital has been proposed for the venous trunk.

[2] The venous angle formed by this junction indicates the position of the thyroid gland.

The upper one is the **transverse facial vein,** which unites close to the end of the facial crest.

A little lower is the large valveless **vena reflexa.** This passes back under the upper part of the masseter on the maxilla, turns around the tuber maxillare, perforates the periorbita, and joins the ophthalmic vein. It is relatively small at each end, but presents one or two large fusiform dilatations. Its posterior part is embedded in a mass of fat. It receives the following tributaries: (*a*) The **great palatine vein** (V. palatina major), separates from the palatine artery at the anterior palatine foramen, and passes in the groove between the tuber maxillare and the palate bone. The palatine veins form a very rich plexus of valveless vessels in the submucosa of the hard palate, which consists of several layers anteriorly. (*b*) The **sphenopalatine vein** (V. sphenopalatina) is the satellite of the artery; it forms a rich plexus of valveless vessels on the turbinate bones and the septum nasi. The venous plexuses are remarkably developed in certain parts of the nasal mucosa. On the septum a little below its middle and on the turbinates the veins are in several layers. The olfactory region does not share in this arrangement, and the veins here are small and join the ethmoidal vein. (*c*) The **infraorbital vein** (V. infraorbitalis) is also a satellite of the artery; it usually unites with the sphenopalatine to form a short common trunk. (*d*) The **ophthalmic vein** (V. ophthalmica) is a short trunk, which is connected in front with the vena reflexa and behind with the cavernous sinus through the foramen orbitale. It receives veins which correspond to the arterial branches.

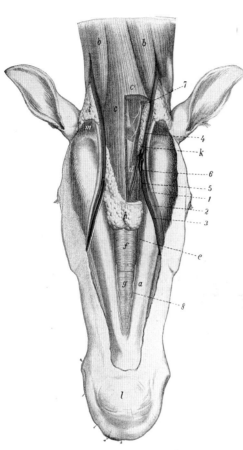

FIG. 587.—DISSECTION OF MANDIBULAR SPACE AND ADJACENT PART OF NECK OF HORSE.

a, Ramus of mandible; *b*, sterno-cephalicus muscle; *c, c'*, omo-hyoidei and sterno-hyoidei (portion removed on right side); *d*, hyoid bone; *e*, anterior belly of digastricus; *f, g*, mylo-hyoideus; *h*, mandibular lymph glands (portion removed on right side); *i*, parotid gland; *k*, mandibular salivary gland; *l*, chin; *m*, occipito-mandibularis; *1*, parotid duct; *2*, facial vein; *3*, facial artery; *4*, external maxillary vein; *5*, lingual vein; *6*, sublingual artery; *7*, ventral branch of first cervical nerve; *8*, mylo-hyoid nerve. (After Ellenberger, in Leisering's Atlas.)

The **buccinator vein** (V. buccinatoria) extends backward from the external maxillary along the ventral border of the depressor labii inferioris and buccinator under cover of the masseter, turns medially over the ramus of the mandible about two inches (ca. 5 cm.) behind the last molar tooth, and is continued as the internal maxillary vein. It has a large fusiform dilatation and is valveless. It receives a large vein from the buccal plexus, and is usually connected with the masseteric vein.

The **lingual vein** (V. lingualis) is formed at the side of the lingual process of the hyoid bone by the confluence of several veins which come from the substance of the tongue. One or two considerable radicles run partly in the substance of the hyo-glossus, and another in the genio-hyoideus. The vein is at first covered by the mylo-hyoideus, perforates that muscle, runs back along the omo-hyoideus in relation to the mandibular lymph glands, and joins the external maxillary near the posterior border of the jaw.

The **sublingual vein** (V. sublingualis) is smaller than the preceding. It receives veins from the skin and muscles of the mandibular space, the sublingual gland, and the gums. It opens into the external maxillary vein near the lingual or joins the latter.

7. The **thyroid vein** (V. thyreoidea) is a large vessel which joins the jugular near the external maxillary vein. It receives anterior thyroid, laryngeal, and pharyngeal radicles, and sometimes a posterior thyroid vein.

8. **Muscular, tracheal, œsophageal,** and **parotid** veins.

9. The **cephalic vein** (V. cephalica) enters the jugular near its termination. It will be described with the veins of the thoracic limb.

10. The **inferior cervical vein** (V. cervicalis ascendens) accompanies the ascending branch of the artery. It may open into the brachial vein.

The Sinuses of the Dura Mater

These (Sinus duræ matris) are blood-spaces between the meningeal and periosteal layers of the dura mater and are lined with endothelium. In many places

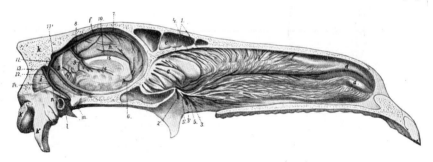

Fig. 588.—Median Section of Head of Horse, Upper Part, with Septum Nasi Removed.

a, Lateral mass of ethmoid bone; *b,* dorsal turbinate; *c,* ventral turbinate; *d, d′,* turbinate folds; *e,* frontal sinus; *f,* falx cerebri; *g,* tentorium cerebelli; *h,* medial surface of hemisphere; *i,* cerebellum; *k,* occipital bone; *k′,* occipital condyle; *k″,* paramastoid process; *l,* external acoustic meatus; *m,* temporal condyle; *n,* temporal canal; *1,* branches of ethmoidal artery; *2, 2′,* branches of sphenopalatine artery; *3, 3′,* branches of sphenopalatine vein; *4,* branches of ethmoidal nerve; *5, 5′,* branches of sphenopalatine nerve; *6,* artery of corpus callosum; *7,* dorsal longitudinal sinus; *8,* straight sinus; *9,* vena magna cerebri; *10,* ventral longitudinal sinus; *11, 11′,* transverse sinuses; *12,* dorsal petrosal sinus; *13,* occipital sinus; *14,* dorsal cerebral vein; *15,* corpus callosum; *16,* fornix. (After Ellenberger, in Leisering's Atlas.)

the lumen is crossed by fibrous strands. They receive the **cerebral veins** (Vv. cerebri), **meningeal veins** (Vv. meningeæ), **diploic veins** (Vv. diploicæ), and communicate with veins outside of the cranium; their connections with the latter are by means of **emissary veins** (Emissaria). They convey the blood directly or indirectly to the jugular veins. Some are paired, others unpaired. They may be divided into dorsal and basilar systems.

The **dorsal system** comprises the following:

The **dorsal longitudinal** or **sagittal sinus** (S. sagittalis dorsalis) is situated in the convex border of the falx cerebri along the internal parietal crest. It begins at the crista galli and ends near the tentorium osseum at the **confluence of the sinuses** (Confluens sinuum) formed by the junction with the straight sinus. It receives most of the ascending cerebral veins. Along each side are small pouches (Lacunæ laterales) into which the veins open. The lumen of the sinus is very irregular; it is traversed by fibrous bands and is partially divided by a longitudinal septum.

The **ventral longitudinal** or **sagittal sinus** (S. sagittalis ventralis) is much smaller than the dorsal sinus.[1] It runs backward on the corpus callosum in the concave edge of the falx cerebri, and joins the great cerebral vein to form the straight sinus. It receives veins from the medial surface of the cerebral hemispheres and from the corpus callosum.

The **straight sinus** (S. rectus) proceeds from the junction of the ventral longitudinal sinus with the great cerebral vein behind the corpus callosum. It ascends in the falx cerebri, inclining backward, and joins the dorsal longitudinal sinus at the confluens sinuum.

The **transverse sinuses** (Ss. transversi), right and left, proceed laterally from the confluens sinuum; they pass outward in the transverse grooves of the parietal bones, enter the temporal canals, and are continued by the dorsal cerebral veins to the superficial temporal veins. They receive the dorsal petrosal sinuses, veins from the posterior part of the cerebrum and from the corpora quadrigemina, and the posterior meningeal vein. The two sinuses are connected by the **sinus communicans,** which extends across the cranial vault in a channel at or in the base of the internal occipital protuberance.

The **dorsal petrosal sinuses** (Ss. petrosi dorsales) ascend in the tentorium cerebelli and join the transverse sinuses near the internal opening of the temporal canal. Each is the direct continuation of the vena rhinalis posterior and receives the vena basilaris cerebri. There is sometimes an accessory petrosal sinus alongside of the chief sinus, which is formed by the confluence of veins from the pons and medulla oblongata.

The **occipital sinuses** (Ss. occipitales) are situated in the dura mater on each side of the vermis cerebelli. They communicate in front with the sinus communicans, and one of them is continued posteriorly by the dorsal spinal vein. Each sinus is connected by a communicating branch with the transverse sinus and with the ventral petrosal sinus. The right and left sinuses are connected by anastomotic branches, so that the arrangement is more or less plexiform. They receive veins from the cerebellum, medulla oblongata, and diploë.

The **basilar system** consists of the following:

The **cavernous sinuses** (Ss. cavernosi) lie in the medial grooves of the root of the temporal wings of the sphenoid bone at either side of the pituitary fossa. The two are connected by a wide transverse branch, the **intercavernous sinus** (Sinus intercavernosus), behind and below the posterior part of the pituitary body.[2] Each is continuous in front with the ophthalmic vein and below with the ventral petrosal sinuses; it communicates also by small anastomotic veins with the basilar plexus. The third, sixth, and the ophthalmic and maxillary divisions of the fifth nerve lie along the lateral wall of the sinus. The internal carotid artery traverses the sinus and is connected with its fellow by a transverse branch which lies in the intercavernous sinus. An oval opening in the floor communicates with the ventral petrosal sinus and transmits the internal carotid artery.

The sinus is not subdivided by strands of fibrous tissue as in man, but a few delicate bands attach the artery to its wall.

The **ventral petrosal sinuses** (Ss. petrosi ventrales) lie along the borders of the basilar part of the occipital bone, enclosed in the thick dura which closes the foramen lacerum. The anterior part extends about half an inch (ca. 12 mm.) under the temporal wing of the sphenoid. Here communications exist with veins in the pterygopalatine fossa. The posterior end is bulbous and lies in the condy-

---

[1] It is also termed the vena corporis callosi major.

[2] A small anterior intercavernous sinus may connect the two cavernous sinuses in front of the pituitary gland. Mobilio states that he has seen the cavernous sinus having a blind anterior end, the ophthalmic vein passing laterally to the ventral petrosal sinus.

loid fossa; it communicates with the condyloid vein issuing from the hypoglossal foramen and is drained by the ventral cerebral vein; it also receives an emissary vein from the temporal canal. The sinus communicates with the cavernous sinus by an oval opening at the carotid notch which transmits the internal carotid artery; the latter forms the first bend of its **S**-shaped curve in the petrosal and the second in the cavernous sinus.

The **basilar plexus** (Plexus basilaris) is situated on the cerebral surface of the basilar part of the occipital bone, and is directly continuous behind with the venous plexus in the atlas. Its chief emissary is the condyloid vein, which brings it into communication with the ventral petrosal sinus. It is connected with the cavernous and intercavernous sinuses by small veins.

THE VEINS OF THE CRANIUM

The **cerebral veins** (Venæ cerebri) do not in general accompany the cerebral arteries. They have very thin walls, no muscular coat, and no valves. They are arranged in two sets, superficial or cortical and deep or central. The superficial veins are more numerous and larger than the arteries. They lie on the surface of the brain in the pia mater and the subarachnoid space.

The **ascending cerebral veins** drain most of the convex surface and the medial surface of the cerebral hemispheres. Most of them open into the dorsal longitudinal sinus, but some enter the confluens sinuum or the transverse sinuses. Near the termination they become bulbous, and open into the sinus obliquely and in such a manner as to tend to prevent reflux of blood into them.[1] The **descending cerebral veins** which come chiefly from the ventral part of the convex surface of the cerebrum open into the vena rhinalis posterior.

The **basal cerebral veins** converge to a large common trunk, the **vena rhinalis posterior;** this begins at the anterior end of the piriform lobe, runs backward in a groove on the latter, enters the tentorium cerebelli, and opens into the dorsal petrosal sinus.

The **deep cerebral veins** issue from the central or ganglionic parts of the brain at the transverse fissure. The principal ones come from the chorioid plexuses, the corpus striatum, and the septum pellucidum. These unite to form the **internal cerebral veins** (Vv. cerebri internæ), which run backward in the roof of the third ventricle and unite to form the **great cerebral vein** (V. cerebri magna). This passes upward and backward behind the splenium of the corpus callosum and is continued as the straight sinus to join the dorsal longitudinal sinus.

The **dorsal cerebellar veins** ramify on the upper surface of the cerebellum. They go chiefly to the occipital and dorsal petrosal sinuses. The **ventral cerebellar veins** are larger and go chiefly to the basilar plexus. The veins of the medulla and pons end chiefly in the basilar plexus and the occipital and dorsal (and accessory) petrosal sinuses.

The **meningeal veins** (Venæ meningeæ) arise in capillary plexuses in the superficial and deep faces of the dura mater. Some end in the sinuses of the dura, others accompany the meningeal arteries.

The **diploic veins** (Venæ diploicæ) are anastomosing channels in the spongy substance of the cranial bones. Their walls are thin, consisting in many places only of the endothelium, and they have no valves. Some open inward into venous sinuses, others into extracranial veins.

VERTEBRAL AND SPINAL VEINS

Two venous trunks, the **longitudinal vertebral sinuses** (Sinus vertebrales longitudinales), extend along the floor of the vertebral canal, one on either side of

---

[1] Most of these veins open into the sinus in the direction of the blood-stream in the sinus, but some of the posterior ones open about at a right angle, or even contrary to the direction of the current.

the dorsal longitudinal ligament. They are continuous in front with the basilar plexus. They lie in the grooves on the bodies of the vertebræ and are connected by a series of transverse anastomoses which pass between the central part of the bodies of the vertebræ and the dorsal longitudinal ligament or in channels in the bone. They receive veins from the spinal cord, the meninges, and the bodies of the vertebræ (Venæ basis vertebræ). Through the intervertebral foramina efferent vessels connect with the occipital, vertebral, intercostal, lumbar, and lateral sacral veins. The veins of the spinal cord are drained by dorsal and ventral longitudinal trunks. The ventral vein, which is the smaller, accompanies the ventral spinal artery.

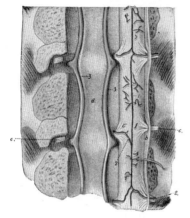

FIG. 589 —VERTEBRAL SINUSES OF HORSE.

The vertebral canal has been opened by sawing off the arches. The nerve-roots are cut on one side and the spinal cord turned over to right. *1*, Ventral spinal artery; *2*, reinforcing branches from vertebral, intercostal, or lumbar arteries (according to region); *3*, longitudinal vertebral sinuses; *a*, ventral surface of spinal cord; *b*, dura mater (cut); *c*, nerve-roots; *d*, dorsal longitudinal ligament. (After Ellenberger, in Leisering's Atlas.)

VEINS OF THE THORACIC LIMB

The **brachial vein** (V. brachialis) (Fig. 566) is the satellite of the extrathoracic part of the brachial artery. It arises at the medial side of the distal end of the shaft of the humerus and ascends in the arm behind the artery under cover of a layer of fascia and the posterior superficial pectoral muscle. At the shoulder it is ventral to the artery, crosses the anterior border of the first rib, and concurs with its fellow and the two jugulars in the formation of the anterior vena cava.[1] The roots of the vein are somewhat variable, but most often four veins in addition to a large oblique branch from the cephalic unite in its formation; two or three of these radicles are satellites of the median artery. Its tributaries correspond in general to the branches of the artery, but a few differences are worthy of notice. The **thoracodorsal vein** (V. thoracodorsalis) often joins the external thoracic or the deep brachial vein. The **external thoracic vein** (V. thoracica externa)[2] is a large vessel which arises in the ventral wall of the abdomen, passes forward (embedded partly in the cutaneous muscle) along the lateral border of the posterior deep pectoral muscle, and joins the brachial vein close to the subscapular or in common with it. It may receive a vein which is the satellite of the external thoracic artery.

The **cephalic vein** (V. cephalica) arises at the medial side of the carpus as the continuation of the medial metacarpal vein. It ascends on the deep fascia of the forearm at first in the furrow between the flexor carpi radialis and the radius. Toward the middle of the forearm it inclines gradually forward on the medial surface of the radius, accompanied by a branch of the musculo-cutaneous nerve, and arrives at the insertion of the biceps. Here it detaches the **large medial cubital vein** (V. mediana cubiti), which passes upward and backward over the medial insertion of the biceps and the median artery and median nerve, and joins the brachial vein. The vein to this point is often termed the internal subcutaneous vein of the forearm (V. cephalica antebrachii). It is continued (as the V. cephalica humeri) in the furrow between the brachiocephalicus and the anterior superficial pectoral muscle with a branch of the inferior cervical artery, crosses the deep face of the cervical cutaneous, and opens into the terminal part of the jugular or the brachial vein. It receives the **accessory cephalic vein** (V. cephalica accessoria), which arises from the carpal network, runs upward on the deep fascia along the

---

[1] Opposite the first rib the vein has a fibrous attachment (Lig. vena brachialis) to the sterno-thyro-hyoideus muscle which serves to prevent the collapse of the vein at this point.

[2] Often termed the spur vein.

medial border of the extensor carpi, and joins the cephalic vein at the proximal end of the forearm.

The deep veins of the forearm are variable. Commonly two **median veins**

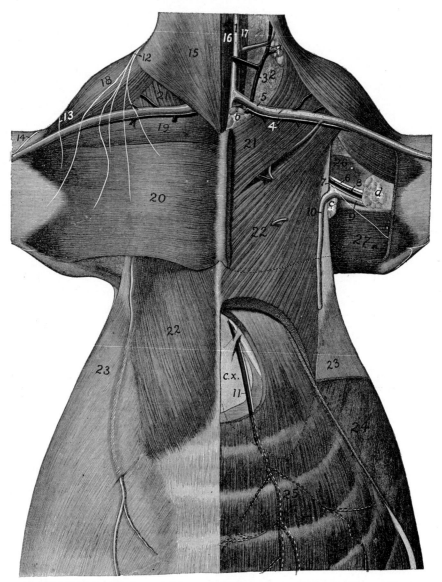

FIG. 590.—DISSECTION OF PECTORAL REGION AND ANTERIOR PART OF ABDOMINAL WALL OF HORSE.

1, Jugular vein; *2*, loose connective tissue of axillary space; *3*, ascending branch of inferior cervical artery; *4*, descending branch of same; *5*, cephalic vein; *6*, median nerve; *7*, ulnar nerve; *8*, brachial artery; *9*, brachial vein; *10*, external thoracic vein; *11*, anterior abdominal artery and vein; *12*, branches of sixth cervical nerve; *13*, cutaneous branch of axillary nerve; *14*, cutaneous branch of musculo-cutaneous nerve; *15*, cervical cutaneus; *16*, sterno-cephalicus; *17*, scalenus; *18*, brachiocephalicus; *19*, anterior superficial pectoral; *20*, posterior superficial pectoral; *21*, anterior deep pectoral; *22*, posterior deep pectoral; *23*, abdominal cutaneus; *24*, obliquus abdominis externus; *25*, rectus abdominis; *26*, coraco-brachialis; *27*, tensor fasciæ antibrachii; *a*, prescapular lymph glands; *b*, prepectoral lymph glands; *c*, axillary lymph glands; *d*, cubital lymph glands; *c. x.*, xiphoid cartilage. (After Schmaltz, Atlas d. Anat. d. Pferdes.)

(Venæ medianæ) accompany the artery of like name, one in front and one behind. A third vein arises by radicles emerging from the proximal part of the deep flexor;

it joins the posterior satellite of the median artery or forms one of the roots of the brachial vein. The **common interosseous vein** joins the posterior satellite. The **anterior radial vein** (V. collateralis radialis) is a satellite of the artery. The **ulnar vein** is usually double at its proximal part, and communicates with the deep brachial vein.

There are three chief **metacarpal veins.** The **medial metacarpal** or **common digital vein** (V. metacarpea volaris superficialis medialis) arises from the volar venous arch above the fetlock. It is the largest vein of the region and lies in front of the common digital artery. It separates from the artery at the proximal end of the metacarpus, passes upward on the medio-volar surface of the carpus, under cover of the superficial layer of the volar annular ligament, and is continued as the cephalic vein. It communicates at its proximal part with the origin of the median veins by a short but relatively large branch. The **lateral metacarpal vein** (V. metacarpea volaris superficialis lateralis) arises from the venous arch above the fetlock and passes upward behind the lateral border of the suspensory ligament in front of the lateral volar nerve and accompanied by a small artery. At the proximal end of the metacarpus it is connected with the deep metacarpal vein by two transverse anastomoses which pass across the suspensory ligament. It then ascends as a satellite of the lateral volar metacarpal artery and concurs in the origin of the ulnar and median veins. The **deep metacarpal vein** (V. metacarpea volaris profunda medialis) arises from the venous arch, passes forward between the two branches of the suspensory ligament, and ascends on the posterior surface of the large metacarpal bone. At the proximal end of the latter it communicates with the other metacarpal veins, ascends with the medial volar metacarpal artery, and concurs in forming the median veins; it often ends at the subcarpal arch instead. The **volar venous arch** (Arcus venosus volaris), from which the metacarpal veins arise, is situated above the sesamoids of the fetlock, between the suspensory ligament and the deep flexor tendon. It is formed by the junction of the two digital veins.

The **digital veins,** medial and lateral (V. digitalis medialis, lateralis), drain the venous plexuses of the foot. They arise at the proximal edge of the cartilages of the third phalanx and ascend in front of the corresponding arteries.

It is convenient to recognize the following venous plexuses of the foot (Plexus venosi ungulæ), which, however, communicate very freely:

1. The **coronary plexus** (Plexus coronarius ungulæ) encircles the upper part of the foot. It covers the terminal part of the extensor tendon, the cartilages of the third phalanx, and the bulbs of the digital cushion.

2. The **dorsal plexus** (Plexus dorsalis ungulæ) covers the dorsal surface of the third phalanx in the deep layer of the corium of the wall of the hoof. It forms the circumflex vein of the third phalanx, or vein of the distal border of the third phalanx, which corresponds to the artery of like name.

3. The **volar plexus** (Plexus volaris ungulæ) is in the deep layer of the corium of the sole of the hoof and on the deep surfaces of the cartilages of the third phalanx. It communicates around the distal border of the third phalanx with the dorsal plexus and through the cartilages with the coronary plexus.

The deep vein of the third phalanx accompanies the terminal part of the digital artery. It drains the **intraosseous plexus** (Plexus intraosseus ungulæ) contained in the third phalanx.

THE POSTERIOR VENA CAVA (Figs. 554, 575)

The **posterior vena cava** (V. cava caudalis) returns almost all of the blood from the abdomen, pelvis, and pelvic limbs. It is formed by the confluence of the right and left common iliac veins at the fifth lumbar vertebra, above the terminal part of the aorta, and chiefly to the right of the median plane.

The mode of origin is variable. In some cases there is a common trunk formed by the union of the two internal iliac veins so that the arrangement resembles the termination of the aorta. In other cases the internal iliac vein does not exist. Exceptionally there is a small middle sacral vein on the middle of the pelvic surface of the sacrum. It opens at the angle of divergence of the common iliac veins.

It passes forward on the ventral face of the psoas minor to the right of the abdominal aorta. At the last thoracic vertebra it separates from the aorta and runs forward between the right crus of the diaphragm and the pancreas till it reaches the liver. Here it inclines ventrally along the medial border of the right lobe and on the parietal surface of the liver, largely embedded in the gland substance, and passes through the foramen venæ cavæ of the diaphragm. It then runs forward and somewhat ventrally between the intermediate lobe and the main mass of the right lung at the upper margin of a special fold of the right pleura, accompanied by the right phrenic nerve, and opens into the posterior part of the right atrium opposite the fifth intercostal space. It receives the following tributaries:

1. The **phrenic veins** (Vv. phrenicæ), two or three in number, return the blood from the diaphragm. They are very large in comparison with the arteries, and join the vena cava at the foramen venæ cavæ.

2. The **lumbar veins** (Vv. lumbales) correspond to the arteries. Five pairs usually empty into the posterior vena cava. Sometimes the corresponding veins of opposite sides unite to form a common trunk. The first communicate with the vena azygos or hemiazygos, and the last usually enters the common iliac vein.

3. The **internal spermatic veins** (Vv. spermaticæ internæ) (Fig. 575) accompany the arteries of like name. In the spermatic cord they form a very rich network, the **pampiniform plexus** (Plexus pampiniformis) about the artery and nerves. Their termination is variable. The right one commonly joins the vena cava near the renal vein, often by a common trunk with the left one. Frequently the left vein joins the left renal, and sometimes the right one ends similarly.

3 a. The **utero-ovarian veins** are much larger than the preceding and are satellites of the arteries in the broad ligaments. The ovarian branch is plexiform near the ovary. The uterine branches form a rich plexus in the wall of the uterus. The trunk is very short and terminates like the corresponding vein of the male.

4. The **renal veins** (Vv. renales), satellites of the arteries, are of large caliber and thin walled. The right vein passes medially and backward on the ventral face of the kidney, between the artery in front and the ureter behind. It joins the vena cava above the right adrenal. The left vein is somewhat longer. It passes medially at first like the right one, then bends around the posterior end of the adrenal, crosses the origin of the renal artery, and opens into the vena cava a little further back than the right one. They receive veins from the adrenals, but some **adrenal veins** (Vv. adrenales) open directly into the vena cava.

5. The **hepatic veins** (Vv. hepaticæ) return the blood from the liver, and open into the vena cava as it lies in the groove in the liver. Three or four large veins open into the vena cava just before it leaves the liver, and numerous small ones discharge into its embedded part.

Of the foregoing, the phrenic and lumbar veins are termed **parietal radicles** (Radices parietales), and the remainder are **visceral radicles** (Radices viscerales).

THE PORTAL VEIN

The **portal vein** (V. portæ) is a large trunk which returns the blood carried to the viscera by the gastric, splenic, and mesenteric arteries; its average diameter is a little more than an inch (ca. 3 cm.). Its peripheral tributaries correspond closely with the branches of the arteries, but the trunks do so in part only. The vein is formed behind the pancreas and below the posterior vena cava by the confluence of the **anterior** and **posterior mesenteric** and **splenic veins**. It passes forward, traverses the posterior part of the pancreas very obliquely, inclines ventrally and a little to the right, and reaches the portal fissure of the liver. Here it divides into three branches which enter the liver and ramify in the substance of the gland like an artery, terminating in the lobular capillaries. From the lobules the blood passes into the hepatic veins and through these to the posterior vena cava. Thus the blood which is distributed to the stomach, nearly the entire intestinal tract, the pancreas, and the spleen, passes through two sets of capillaries prior to its return to the heart, viz., the capillaries of these viscera and of the liver.

1. The **anterior mesenteric vein** (V. mesenterica cranialis) is the largest of the portal radicles. It is situated to the right of the artery of like name, and its tributaries correspond in general to the branches of the artery. The dorsal colic vein usually unites with the ventral one at the pelvic flexure, thus forming a single trunk (V. colica dextra) which runs between the right parts of the colon. There is,

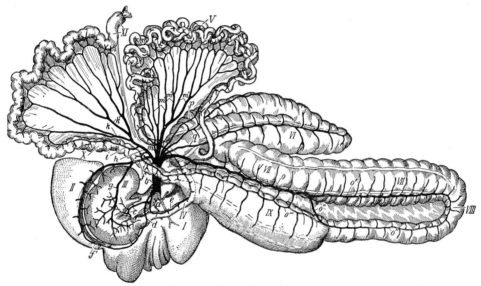

Fig. 591.—Portal Vein of Horse.

a, Intrahepatic part, b, extrahepatic part, of portal vein; c, anterior gastric vein; d, right gastro-epiploic vein; e, pancreatico-duodenal vein; f, splenic vein; f', left gastro-epiploic vein; g, posterior gastric vein; h, posterior mesenteric vein; i, middle colic vein; k, left colic vein; k', anterior hæmorrhoidal vein; m, jejunal trunk; m', jejunal veins; o, right colic vein; o', ventral colic vein; o'', dorsal colic vein; o''', small collateral vein connecting dorsal colic and posterior mesenteric veins; p, ileal vein; q, cæcal veins; I, liver; II, spleen; III, stomach; IV, duodenum; V, jejunum; VI, cæcum; VII, ventral parts of great colon; VIII, pelvic flexure; IX, dorsal parts of great colon; X, small colon; XI, rectum. (After Schmitz.)

however, a small vein on the right dorsal colon which is connected by numerous branches with the right colic vein; it joins the posterior mesenteric vein or its middle colic radicle. The veins of the small intestine (Vv. intestinales) unite to form a short trunk.

2. The **posterior mesenteric vein** (V. mesenterica caudalis) is the smallest of the radicles of the portal vein. It accompanies the artery in the colic mesentery, and its rectal branches (Vv. hæmorrhoidales craniales) anastomose with those of the internal pudic vein. It receives the middle colic vein from the initial part of the small colon and also the small vein of the right dorsal colon, as mentioned above.

3. The **splenic vein** (V. lienalis) is the very large satellite of the splenic artery. It is formed by the union of two radicles at the base of the spleen. On leaving the hilus of the spleen it passes medially between the anterior pole of the left kidney and the saccus cæcus of the stomach and above the left end of the pancreas, receives

commonly the **posterior gastric vein** (V. gastrica caudalis), and unites with the anterior mesenteric at the posterior border of the pancreas. Not uncommonly the splenic and posterior mesenteric veins form a short common trunk.

The collateral tributaries of the portal vein are as follows:

(1) **Pancreatic veins** (Rami pancreatici).

(2) The **gastro-duodenal vein** (V. gastroduodenalis), when present, corresponds mainly to the extrahepatic branches of the hepatic artery; but in most cases it does not exist, and the **right gastro-epiploic vein** (V. gastroepiploica dextra) and **pancreatico-duodenal vein** (V. pancreaticoduodenalis) open directly into the portal vein.

(3) The **anterior gastric vein** (V. gastrica cranialis) joins the portal vein at the portal fissure.

THE COMMON ILIAC VEINS (Fig. 581)

These (V. iliacæ communes) are two very large but short trunks, which result from the union of the internal and external iliac veins of each side at the sacro-iliac articulation. The left one is the longer, and crosses obliquely over the terminal part of the aorta. The chief tributaries of each are as follows:

1. The last **lumbar vein.**

2. The **circumflex iliac veins** (Vv. circumflexæ ilium profundæ) are the two satellites of the corresponding artery, on either side of which they are placed. They may open directly into the posterior vena cava or into the external iliac vein.

3. The **ilio-lumbar vein** (V. iliolumbalis) may open into the common iliac, the external iliac, or the internal iliac vein.

THE INTERNAL ILIAC VEINS

The **internal iliac** or **hypogastric veins** (Vv. iliacæ internæ s. hypogastricæ), right and left, are usually formed by the confluence of lateral sacral, gluteal, and internal pudic veins. The obturator vein may open into them also. They are short trunks, and are smaller than the external iliac veins. The tributaries correspond in general to the branches of the three arteries of like names. The internal pudic veins receive affluents from the anus and posterior part of the rectum; from the venous plexuses of the prepuce and penis in the male; and from those of the mammary gland, vulva, vagina, and vestibular bulb in the female. A large anastomotic branch connects the internal pudic and obturator veins at the lesser sciatic notch.

THE VEINS OF THE PELVIC LIMB

The **external iliac vein** (V. iliaca externa) (Figs. 576, 581) lies behind the corresponding artery at the brim of the pelvis. It is the upward continuation of the femoral vein, and unites at the sacro-iliac joint with the internal iliac to form the common iliac vein. Its tributaries are as follows:

1. The **obturator vein** (V. obturatoria) is a satellite of the artery, except in its terminal part; it usually opens into the external iliac at the insertion of the psoas minor. Its radicles anastomose with those of the internal and external pudic veins (Figs. 576, 658).

2. The **iliaco-femoral** or **lateral circumflex veins** (Vv. circumflexæ femoris laterales) are the two satellites of the homonymous artery. They open a little higher than the obturator.

The **femoral vein** (V. femoralis) (Figs. 575, 582) lies behind the artery in the proximal part of the thigh, lateral to it lower down. Its chief tributaries are:

1. A large but short trunk is formed by the union of the deep femoral and the external pudic vein. The **deep femoral vein** (V. profunda femoris) corresponds

otherwise to the artery. The **external pudic vein** (V. pudenda externa) arises chiefly from a rich plexus of large veins situated above and along the sides of the penis and prepuce in the male, the mammary glands in the female. It passes through a foramen in the anterior part of the tendon of origin of the gracilis and runs outward behind the pectineus to unite with the deep femoral vein. The right and left veins are connected by a large transverse anastomotic branch which lies in the subpubic groove, and each has a large connection with the obturator vein. Each receives the **posterior abdominal vein** (V. abdominalis caudalis), which accompanies the artery of like name. The **subcutaneous abdominal vein** (V. abdominalis subcutanea) arises in the skin and cutaneous muscle of the ventral abdominal wall, anastomoses with the internal and external thoracic and deep abdominal veins, and joins the external pudic or the posterior abdominal vein.

A small vein may accompany the external pudic artery in the inguinal canal.

2. The **anterior femoral vein** (V. femoris cranialis) accompanies the artery.

3. The **saphenous vein** (V. saphena) (Figs. 575, 576, 583) arises on the dorso-medial surface of the tarsus as the upward continuation of the medial metatarsal vein. Its course is distinctly visible. It ascends on the subcutaneous surface of the tibia and the popliteus muscle, enclosed between layers of the deep fascia, inclines a little backward to the proximal part of the leg, then deviates slightly forward, runs upward on the gracilis, passes between that muscle and the sartorius, and joins the femoral or the external pudic vein.[1] On the upper part of the capsule of the hock joint it forms an arch with the anterior tibial vein. The vein has numerous valves. The satellite artery is relatively small, and lies in front of the vein as far as the junction with the recurrent tibial vein, which it accompanies on the leg. It receives the **recurrent tibial vein** (V. recurrens tibialis) at the proximal fourth of the leg. This vessel arises at the distal third of the leg, where it forms an arch with the posterior tibial vein; here it is a satellite of the artery of like name. It ascends in the furrow in front of the gastrocnemius tendon, inclines forward at the proximal third of the leg, and joins the saphenous vein at an acute angle. It gives off a branch which ascends with the artery and joins the posterior femoral or the popliteal vein.[2] A smaller vein from the anterior face of the metatarsus joins the saphenous at the hock.

4. **Muscular branches** which correspond to the arteries.

5. The **posterior femoral vein** (V. femoris caudalis) accompanies the artery (Fig. 584). It receives the **recurrent tarsal vein** (V. tarsea recurrens), which arises at the lateral side of the hock, ascends on the deep fascia of the lateral surface of the leg in front of the tendo Achillis, passes between the biceps femoris and semitendinosus, and joins the posterior femoral vein. It is connected with the recurrent tibial vein by a large anastomotic branch which crosses in front of the tuber calcis. Usually a branch from it ascends along the great sciatic nerve and anastomoses with the obturator vein.

The **popliteal vein** (V. poplitea) lies along the medial side of the artery (Fig. 584). It is formed by the confluence of anterior and posterior tibial veins.

Two **anterior tibial veins** (Vv. tibiales anteriores) usually accompany the artery of like name; the lateral vein is much the larger (Fig. 659).[2] In other cases there is one

---

[1] The place and mode of termination are quite variable. It may disappear from the surface of the thigh at any point above the distal third. In some cases it passes through the anterior part of the gracilis instead of dipping in between that muscle and the sartorius, and more rarely it joins the external pudic vein at the origin of the gracilis.

[2] The arrangement here is subject to variation. Some authors regard the ascending branch of this description as the trunk, and the connection with the saphenous as an anastomotic branch. The latter is usually, so far as size is concerned, the trunk.

[3] The large size of this vein, the thinness of its wall, and the fact that it is separated only by a thin layer of muscle (lateral part of tibialis anterior) from the deep peroneal nerve should be noted with reference to section of that nerve. The vein is sometimes markedly varicose in the proximal part of the leg.

large vein in the proximal part of the leg, two lower down. They arise from a number of anastomosing radicles on the front of the capsule of the hock joint, chiefly as the continuation of the perforating tarsal vein. A large branch from the saphenous vein concurs in the formation of the somewhat plexiform arrangement on the flexion surface of the hock.

The **posterior tibial vein** (V. tibialis posterior) is commonly double (Fig. 583). It arises at the level of the tuber calcis, where it has a communication with the recurrent tibial vein. It is a satellite of the artery.

The **medial** or **great metatarsal vein** (V. metatarsea dorsalis medialis) (Figs. 583, 585) arises from the venous arch above the sesamoids at the fetlock, but is practically the upward continuation of the medial digital vein. It ascends along the medial border of the suspensory ligament, then in the groove on the proximal part of the large metatarsal bone to the capsule of the hock joint, and is continued by the saphenous vein. The small **middle dorsal metatarsal** vein (V. met. dorsalis media) joins this vein or the saphenous at the hock.

The **lateral metatarsal vein** (V. metatarsea dorsalis lateralis) is the very small satellite of the great metatarsal artery. It is inconstant, but may be double in the proximal part of the metatarsus.

The **medial plantar vein** (V. metatarsea plantaris superficialis medialis) is very small, and is not always present. It ascends along the medial border of the deep flexor tendon in front of the corresponding nerve. It is connected below with the medial digital vein, and above with the deep metatarsal or the lateral plantar vein.

The **lateral plantar vein** (V. metatarsea plantaris superficialis lateralis) arises from the venous arch above the fetlock, but appears to be the upward continuation of the lateral digital vein. It ascends along the lateral border of the deep flexor tendon in front of the plantar nerve, and is connected with the deep metatarsal vein at the proximal part of the metatarsus by a transverse branch. It then passes upward along the deep flexor tendon in relation to the plantar nerves and the medial tarsal artery, and is continued by the recurrent tibial vein.

The **deep metatarsal vein** (V. metatarsea plantaris profunda medialis) arises from the plantar venous arch, above the fetlock, passes forward between the branches of the suspensory ligament, and ascends on the posterior face of the large metatarsal bone. At the proximal end of the metatarsus it is connected with the lateral plantar vein by a transverse branch, thus forming the **deep plantar arch** (Arcus plantaris profundus). It then passes, as the **perforating tarsal vein** (V. tarsea perforans), through the vascular canal of the tarsus and forms the chief radicle of the anterior tibial vein.

The **distal plantar venous arch** (Arcus venosus plantaris distalis) and the digital veins are arranged like those of the thoracic limb.

LYMPHATIC SYSTEM OF THE HORSE

THE THORACIC DUCT (Figs. 553, 554)

The **thoracic duct** (Ductus thoracicus) is the chief collecting trunk of the lymphatic system. It begins as an elongated irregular dilatation, the **cisterna chyli,** which is situated between the right side of the aorta and the right crus of the diaphragm at the first and second lumbar vertebræ. The duct enters the thorax through the hiatus aorticus and runs forward on the right of the median plane, between the vena azygos and the aorta, covered by the pleura. At the sixth or seventh thoracic vertebra it inclines somewhat ventrally, crosses obliquely over the left face of the œsophagus, and passes forward on the left side of the trachea to the inlet of the thorax. The extrathoracic terminal part passes downward and forward a variable distance (3–4 cm.) on the deep face of the left scalenus muscle, bends inward and backward under the bicarotid trunk, and opens into the dorsal part of the origin of the anterior vena cava just behind the angle of junction of the jugular veins. The terminal bend is ampullate, and sometimes divides into two very short branches which open close together.

Since the duct develops from a plexus of ducts in the embryo, considerable variation from the more usual course occurs. There is often a left duct which arises at the cisterna or at a variable point from the right duct, runs across the left intercostal arteries parallel to the latter, and unites with it over the base of the heart or further forward. The two are connected by crossbranches. In some cases the left duct is the larger, and there may indeed be none on the right side. Other variations are common.

The chief tributaries of the thoracic duct are as follows:

1. The two **lumbar trunks** (Trunci lumbales) are formed by the confluence of the efferent ducts of the lumbar glands, and commonly unite with each other and with the posterior intestinal trunk before opening into the cistern.

2. The **intestinal trunks** (Trunci intestinales), two or three in number, receive the efferents of the lymph glands of the intestine, stomach, liver, and spleen.[1]

In its course through the thorax the thoracic duct receives efferents from the intercostal, mediastinal, and bronchial glands. At the thoracic inlet it is joined by ducts from the posterior cervical and right axillary glands, and by the left tracheal duct. The duct is provided with several pairs of valves; the best developed are at its termination.

THE RIGHT LYMPHATIC DUCT

This vessel (Ductus lymphaticus dexter)—when present—collects the lymph from the right side of the head, neck, and thorax, and from the right thoracic limb. It is commonly absent, being represented by a number of short ducts which terminate in the thoracic duct, the right jugulo-brachial junction, or the origin of the anterior vena cava. When present in its typical form, it results from the confluence of efferent ducts from the right axillary and posterior cervical lymph glands with the right tracheal duct. It lies on the deep face of the scalenus muscle, above the terminal part of the right jugular vein. It is more or less ampullate and usually opens into the anterior vena cava to the right of the thoracic duct. It may be connected with the latter by anastomoses or may join it.

The duct is very variable in form and in regard to its afferents. Often it is a very short, irregular, and bulbous trunk; in some cases it is about an inch and a half (ca. 3–4 cm.) in length and receives the tracheal duct at its terminal bend. The lymphatico-venous connections here have not yet been satisfactorily worked out by modern methods.

THE LYMPH GLANDS AND VESSELS OF THE HEAD AND NECK

1. The **mandibular lymph glands** (Lgg. mandibulares) (Figs. 265, 587) are arranged in two elongated groups in the mandibular space along each side of the omo-hyoid muscles. The two groups are in apposition in front of the insertion of these muscles, and diverge posteriorly in the form of a V, extending backward about four or five inches (ca. 10–12 cm.). They are covered by the skin and a thin layer of fascia and cutaneous muscle, and are therefore palpable. Anteriorly they are firmly attached to the mylo-hyoidei, but otherwise they are freely movable in the normal state. Each group is related laterally to the external maxillary artery and the anterior belly of the digastricus, ventrally to the external maxillary vein, and dorsally to the lingual and sublingual veins.

They receive afferent vessels from the lips, nostrils, nasal region, cheeks, the anterior part of the tongue, the jaws, the floor of the mouth, and the greater part of the hard palate and nasal cavity. The efferent vessels pass to the anterior cervical and pharyngeal glands.

[1] The lymph vessels of these organs appear to vary considerably in their mode of termination, and the arrangement needs further study. Some lymph vessels from the stomach, liver, and spleen open directly into the cistern.

Most of the superficial lymph vessels of the face converge to twelve to fifteen trunks which turn around the lower border of the jaw with and in front of the facial vessels. Those of the lips form plexuses at the commissures. The nasal mucous membrane is richly supplied with lymph vessels which accompany the veins; posteriorly they communicate with the subdural and subarachnoid spaces and send afferents to the pharyngeal and anterior cervical glands.

2. The **pharyngeal lymph glands** (Figs. 562, 706) usually comprise two groups. One lies on the upper part of the lateral surface of the pharynx, along the course of the external carotid artery. These glands are related laterally to the occipito-mandibularis and digastricus, and often to the mandibular gland also, above to the guttural pouch; they may properly be termed the **parapharyngeal lymph glands** (Lgg. parapharyngeæ). Other small glands are commonly found on the guttural pouch along the course of the internal carotid artery; they are best designated as the **suprapharyngeal lymph glands** (Lgg. suprapharyngeæ). They lie below the artery and are covered by the aponeurosis of the brachiocephalicus and the dorsal end of the mandibular salivary gland. In some cases a number of glands occur behind the mandibular articulation under cover of the parotid salivary gland and partly embedded in it. Other variations occur.

They receive afferent vessels from the cranium, the posterior part of the tongue, the soft palate, pharynx, guttural pouch, larynx, posterior part of the nasal cavity, and efferents from the mandibular glands.

3. The **anterior cervical lymph glands** (Lgg. cervicales craniales) (Fig. 646) are situated along the course of the common carotid artery, in the vicinity of the thyroid gland, under cover of the cervical angle of the parotid gland. Some occur between the thyroid and the mandibular salivary gland, others above and partly upon the thyroid. They are related deeply to the posterior part of the larynx, the trachea, the thyroid gland, the œsophagus and the recurrent nerve; below to the external maxillary vein and the lateral border of the omo-hyoideus.

These glands are variable. Often there are none in front of the thyroid and the group may extend back a considerable distance along the course of the carotid artery.

Their afferents are deep lymph vessels from the head, the pharynx, larynx, guttural pouch, and thyroid gland, and efferents from the mandibular and pharyngeal glands. Their efferent vessels go to the middle and posterior cervical glands.

4. The **middle cervical lymph glands** (Lgg. cervicales mediæ) form an inconstant group situated a little in front of the middle of the neck on the trachea below the carotid artery. The group is usually small, and in some cases is replaced by a number of glands occurring at intervals along the course of the carotid artery. In other subjects the group consists of several glands of considerable size. They are intercalated in the course of the tracheal lymph ducts.

5. The **posterior cervical lymph glands** (Lgg. cervicales caudales) form a large group below the trachea at the entrance to the thorax (Fig. 590). They occupy the interstices between the vessels and muscles and extend forward a variable distance on the ventral aspect of the trachea. Posteriorly they are continuous with the anterior mediastinal glands. They are covered by the cutaneus and sterno-cephalicus. Their afferent vessels come from the head, neck, thorax, and thoracic limb. They receive efferent ducts of the anterior and middle cervical, prescapular, and axillary glands. Their efferents go to the thoracic duct on the left, to the right lymphatic duct on the right, or open directly into the vena cava.

6. The **prescapular** or **superficial cervical lymph glands** (Lgg. præscapulares s. cervicales superficiales) lie on the anterior border of the anterior deep pectoral muscle, in relation to the omo-hyoideus medially and the brachiocephalicus laterally (Figs. 556, 566, 590). They are on the course of the ascending branch of the inferior cervical artery, and may form an elongated series which is continuous ventrally with the posterior cervical group. They receive afferents from the neck, breast, shoulder, and arm. Their efferents pass to the posterior cervical glands.

7. **Nuchal lymph glands** (Lgg. nuchalis profundus) lie on the course of the deep cervical vessel as it passes underneath the complexus. They receive afferents from the dorsal region of the neck and withers. Their efferents pass to the anterior mediastinal glands.

The **tracheal ducts,** right and left (Ductus trachealis dexter, sinister), are collecting trunks for the lymph of the head and neck. They lie on the trachea in relation to the carotid arteries. The right one goes to the posterior cervical glands or to the right lymphatic duct, the left one to the terminal part of the thoracic duct.

THE LYMPH GLANDS AND VESSELS OF THE THORAX

The **thoracic lymph glands** (Lgg. thoracales) are in general of small size, but are numerous. They comprise the following:

1. The **intercostal lymph glands** (Lgg. intercostales) are small and are situated at the sides of the bodies of the thoracic vertebræ, in series corresponding to the intercostal spaces; others are between the aorta and the vertebræ. They receive afferents from the vertebral canal, the spinal muscles, the diaphragm, intercostal muscles, and pleura. The efferent vessels go to the thoracic duct.[1]

2. The **anterior mediastinal lymph glands** (Lgg. mediastinales craniales) are numerous. Some are situated on the course of the brachial arteries and their branches; on the right side they are related deeply to the trachea, on the left to the œsophagus also. They are variable in size and disposition and are continuous in front with the posterior cervical glands. Other glands lie along the ventral face of the trachea on the anterior vena cava and the right atrium of the heart; these are continuous behind with the bronchial glands. A few glands usually occur along the dorsal surface of the trachea, and there is often one at the angle of divergence of the brachiocephalic trunk. The afferent vessels come chiefly from the pleura, the pericardium, the heart, the thymus or its remains, the trachea, the œsophagus, and the bronchial lymph glands. Their efferent vessels pass to the posterior cervical glands and the thoracic duct.

The glands along the ventral face of the trachea are frequently enlarged and commonly pigmented in dissecting-room subjects. The left recurrent nerve lies above them on the ventral face of the trachea.

3. The **bronchial lymph glands** (Lgg. bronchiales) are grouped around the terminal part of the trachea and the bronchi. On the right side there are commonly three or four glands (right bronchial). These lie upon the right bronchus, in relation medially to the œsophagus and in front to the vena azygos and right vagus nerve; they are in series with the anterior and posterior mediastinal glands. On the left side there are usually two glands (left bronchial). One of these is on the lateral surface of the left bronchus in the acute angle between the aortic arch and the pulmonary artery; it is related deeply to the left vagus and recurrent nerves. The other is on the medial surface of the bronchus in relation to the œsophagus dorsally. The middle bronchial gland fits into the angle of divergence of the bronchi. Small glands occur along the chief bronchi in the substance of the lungs (Lgg. pulmonales). They receive the deep and most of the superficial lymph vessels of the lungs, and the efferents from the posterior mediastinal glands. Their efferent vessels go to the thoracic duct and the anterior mediastinal glands. The deep lymph vessels of the lung arise in plexuses which surround the terminal bronchi and accompany the bronchi to the root of the lung. The superficial vessels form a rich network under the pleura; most of them pass to the bronchial glands, but some go to the posterior mediastinal glands.

The bronchial glands are commonly pigmented (except in young subjects) and are often enlarged and indurated.

4. The **posterior mediastinal lymph glands** (Lgg. mediastinales caudales) are

---

[1] These glands appear to be more numerous in the young subject than they are later in life.

usually small and are scattered along the posterior mediastinum chiefly above the œsophagus. They receive afferent vessels from the œsophagus, mediastinum, diaphragm, pleura, and liver. The efferents go to the bronchial and anterior mediastinal lymph glands, partly to the thoracic duct directly.

Sometimes one or two small glands are situated in the acute angle between the posterior vena cava and the diaphragm; and the occurrence is recorded of a gland between the apex of the pericardium and the sternal insertion of the diaphragm.

THE LYMPH GLANDS AND VESSELS OF THE ABDOMEN AND PELVIS

The **abdominal** and **pelvic lymph glands** (Lgg. abdominales et pelvinæ) consist of two main groups, parietal and visceral. The **parietal glands** lie in the subserous or subcutaneous tissue; they receive the lymph vessels from the abdominal and pelvic walls, from parts of the viscera, and from the proximal lymph glands of the pelvic limbs. The **visceral glands** lie on the walls of the viscera or in the peritoneal folds which connect the organs with the wall or with adjacent viscera. They receive all or most of the lymph vessels from the organs with which they are connected.

The **parietal glands** comprise the following:

1. The **lumbar lymph glands** (Lgg. lumbales) lie along the course of the abdominal aorta and posterior vena cava (Fig. 575). Some are placed along the ventral surface and sides of the vessels, others above. A few small glands may be found above the sublumbar muscles. The small nodes which are situated at the hilus of the kidneys are often termed the **renal lymph glands** (Lgg. renales). They receive afferent vessels from the lumbar wall of the abdomen and the paired viscera (kidneys, adrenals, genital organs), also the inguinal vessels and the efferents of the iliac glands. Their efferents go to the thoracic duct, constituting the lumbar trunks of origin of that vessel.

2. The **internal iliac lymph glands** (Lgg. iliacæ internæ) are grouped about the terminal part of the aorta and the origins of the iliac arteries (Fig. 575). Their afferent vessels come chiefly from the pelvis, pelvic viscera, and tail, and they receive efferent vessels of the external iliac and deep inguinal glands.

3. The **external iliac lymph glands** (Lgg. iliacæ externæ) form a group on either side on the iliac fascia, at the bifurcation of the circumflex iliac artery (Fig. 575). Their afferent vessels come from the flank and abdominal floor, the lateral surface of the thigh, and the prefemoral glands. The efferent vessels go to the lumbar and internal iliac glands.

4. The **sacral lymph glands** (Lgg. sacrales) are small nodes situated along the borders of the sacrum and on its pelvic surface. They receive afferents from the roof of the pelvis and from the tail, and their efferent vessels pass to the internal iliac glands.

5. The **superficial inguinal lymph glands** (Lgg. inguinales superficiales) lie on the abdominal tunic in front of the external inguinal ring (Fig. 582).[1] They form an elongated group along the course of the subcutaneous abdominal artery, on either side of the penis in the male, above the mammary glands in the female; in the latter they are often termed **mammary.** Their afferents come from the medial surface of the thigh, the abdominal floor, the sheath, penis, and scrotum in the male, and the mammary glands in the female. The efferent vessels ascend through the inguinal canal and go to the deep inguinal, internal iliac, and lumbar glands.

6. The **ischiatic lymph glands** (Lgg. ischiadicæ) are small nodes on the upper part of the sacro-sciatic ligament along the course of the posterior gluteal artery. They receive lymph from the adjacent parts and from the popliteal glands, and send efferents to the sacral and internal iliac glands.

[1] In rare cases two or three of these glands are found behind the ring.

The **visceral glands** include the following:

1. The **gastric lymph glands** (Lgg. gastricæ) are situated along the course of the gastric arteries. Several occur on the saccus cæcus ventral to the left part of the pancreas, and along the attachment of the gastro-phrenic ligament. A group lies at the lesser curvature a short distance below the cardia. There is another small group on the visceral surface where the posterior gastric artery divides into its primary branches. There are usually two or three small nodes on the ventral aspect of the pylorus. Other small glands are scattered along the course of the gastro-epiploic and short gastric arteries, in the great and gastro-splenic omenta. The efferent vessels pass largely to the cœliac radicle of the cisterna chyli, but along the left part of the great curvature they go to the splenic glands.

2. The **hepatic lymph glands** (Lgg. hepaticæ) lie along the portal vein and hepatic artery and in the lesser omentum. Their efferent vessels go to the cœliac radicle of the cisterna chyli.

Many of the lymph vessels from the parietal surface of the liver pass in the falciform and lateral ligaments to the diaphragm and join the lymphatics of the latter. Some pass through the diaphragm with the vena cava and go to the mediastinal glands.

The **pancreatic lymph vessels** follow the course of the blood-vessels which supply the gland; most of them go to the splenic and hepatic glands.

3. The **splenic lymph glands** (Lgg. lienales) lie along the course of the splenic blood-vessels in the hilus of the spleen and the gastro-splenic omentum. Their afferent vessels come from the subcapsular network of the spleen, from the greater curvature of the stomach, and from the left part of the pancreas. The efferents pass to the glands of the saccus cæcus of the stomach and to the cœliac radicle of the cisterna chyli.

4. The **mesenteric lymph glands** (Lgg. mesentericæ) are situated in the great mesentery, chiefly near its root. They are numerous and hence lie close together. They receive a very large number of afferent vessels (400 to 500) from the small intestine. They have several considerable efferents, which concur in the formation of the intestinal radicles of the cisterna chyli.

The lymph vessels of the intestine form three sets of capillary plexuses, viz., in the subserosa, submucosa, and mucosa. The lymph follicles, solitary and aggregate, lie in the zone of the plexus of the mucosa. The collecting vessels arise from the subserous plexus.

5. The **cæcal lymph glands** (Lgg. cæcales) are numerous and are distributed along the course of the cæcal blood-vessels. Their efferents enter into the formation of an intestinal radicle of the cisterna chyli.

6. The **colic lymph glands** (Lgg. colicæ) comprise those of the great colon and those of the small colon. The glands of the great colon are extremely numerous and are placed close together along the colic blood-vessels. Their efferent vessels are large and numerous. They converge to two large trunks which concur with those of the cæcum and small intestine to form an intestinal radicle of the cisterna chyli. The glands of the small colon are situated chiefly on the wall of the bowel along the attachment of the mesentery, but a few are between the layers of the latter along the course of the blood-vessels. The efferent vessels go to the lumbar glands and to the posterior intestinal radicle of the thoracic duct.

The intestinal radicles of the cisterna chyli are formed by the confluence of efferents from the intestinal lymph glands. The anterior trunk lies on the left side of the anterior mesenteric artery, passes between that vessel and the cœliac artery, turns sharply backward across the right renal vessels, and opens into the cisterna. It is formed by the union of the cœliac trunk with efferents from the glands of the small intestine, cæcum, and colon. It is about four inches (ca. 10 cm.) in length and is ampullate. The posterior trunk receives vessels from the small intestine and small colon. It usually opens into a trunk formed by the union of the right and left lumbar ducts. It is usually ampullate at its termination (Franck). The arrangement of these collecting trunks is, however, very variable.

The **rectal lymph glands** (Lgg. rectales) form a chain along the dorsal surface of the bowel. They receive afferent vessels from the rectum and anus, and their efferent vessels pass chiefly to the internal iliac glands.

7. The **anal lymph glands** (Lgg. anales) form a small group of three or four on either side, at the anterior border of the sphincter ani externus (Fig. 578). They receive afferents from the anus, perineum, and tail; their efferents go to the internal iliac glands.

THE LYMPH GLANDS AND VESSELS OF THE THORACIC LIMB

1. The **axillary lymph glands** (Lgg. axillares) (Fig. 590), some ten to twelve in number, are grouped on the medial face of the distal part of the teres major and the tendon of the latissimus dorsi at the angle of junction of the external thoracic and subscapular veins with the brachial (Fig. 566). Their afferents include most of the lymph vessels of the limb, which come directly or as efferents from the cubital glands. They receive also lymph vessels from the thoracic wall. The efferents accompany the brachial blood-vessels and end in the posterior cervical glands and the thoracic and right lymphatic ducts.

2. The **cubital lymph glands** (Lgg. cubitales), usually eight to ten in number, form a discoid oval group at the medial side of the distal part of the shaft of the humerus (Figs. 566, 590). They lie behind the biceps muscle on the brachial vessels and median nerve, and are covered by the deep fascia and the posterior superficial pectoral muscle. They receive as afferents most of the vessels from the limb below this point. Their efferents pass chiefly to the axillary glands, but in part to the prescapular glands also. In quite exceptional cases a lymph gland may be found on the brachial vessels about the middle of the arm.

A number of superficial lymph vessels ascend with or near the subcutaneous veins (cephalic and accessory cephalic), and join the prescapular and posterior cervical glands. Superficial vessels from the chest-wall and shoulder run across the latter to the prescapular glands. The superficial lymphatics of the pectoral region form a plexus which drains into the posterior cervical and prescapular glands by a number of vessels which accompany the cephalic vein. The deep lymph vessels of the pectoral region run with the external thoracic vein to the axillary glands.

Exceptionally there may be several small glands along the posterior branch of the dorsal artery under cover of the rhomboideus. In one case four glands were present over the deep cervical artery just after its emergence from beneath the multifidus muscle. In another case there were two glands on the volar surface of the radius at the level of the interosseous space and in relation to the interosseous vessels.

THE LYMPH GLANDS AND VESSELS OF THE PELVIC LIMB

1. The **prefemoral lymph glands** (Lgg. prefemorales) are situated above the fold of the flank on the anterior border of the tensor fasciæ latæ (Figs. 575, 576, 582). They lie on the course of the posterior branch of the circumflex iliac artery, and number usually about a dozen. They receive superficial lymph vessels from the hip, thigh, and flank. Their efferent vessels ascend with the posterior circumflex iliac vein, enter the abdomen near the tuber coxæ, and join the external iliac lymph glands.

2. The **deep inguinal lymph glands** (Lgg. inguinales profundæ) are situated in the proximal part of the femoral canal, between the pectineus and sartorius muscles (Figs. 576, 582). The group is elongated and is commonly four or five inches (ca. 10–12 cm.) in length. They cover the femoral vessels and are related superficially to the inguinal ligament. They receive nearly all of the lymph vessels of the limb below them. Their efferent vessels ascend to the internal iliac glands.

3. The **popliteal lymph glands** (Lgg. popliteæ), usually four to six in number,

lie behind the origin of the gastrocnemius and between the biceps femoris and semi-tendinosus at the division of the posterior femoral artery into its primary branches (Fig. 580). They receive the deep lymph vessels of the distal part of the limb. Their efferent vessels chiefly follow the course of the femoral vessels to the deep inguinal glands, but one or two ascend in company with a vein along the great sciatic nerve and may enter an ischiatic gland or accompany the internal pudic vein and join the internal iliac glands.

Several superficial lymph vessels ascend with or near the medial metatarsal and saphenous veins, enter the femoral canal, and end in the deep inguinal glands.

THE FŒTAL CIRCULATION

The blood of the fœtus is oxygenated, receives nutrient matter, and gives off waste matter by close contiguity with the maternal blood in the placenta. The chief differences in the blood-vascular system as compared with that which obtains after birth are correlated with this interchange.

The **umbilical arteries,** right and left, are large vessels which arise from the internal iliac arteries and pass downward and forward in the umbilical folds of peritoneum on either side of the bladder to the umbilicus. Here they are incorporated with the umbilical vein and the urachus in the umbilical cord, ramify in the allantois, and end as the capillaries of the fœtal placenta. They conduct the impure blood to the placenta. After birth these vessels retract with the bladder to the pelvic cavity; their lumen becomes greatly reduced and the wall thickened so that they are cord-like and are usually termed the round ligaments of the bladder.

The **umbilical vein** receives the oxygenated blood from the placenta. Its radicles converge to form in the horse a single large trunk which separates from the other constituents of the umbilical cord on entering the abdomen and passes forward along the abdominal floor in the free border of the falciform ligament of the liver. It enters the latter at the umbilical fissure and joins the portal vein, so that the blood conveyed by it passes through the capillaries of the liver before entering the posterior vena cava. The vein contains no valves.

In the ox and dog some of the blood in the umbilical vein is conveyed directly to the vena cava by the **ductus venosus.** This vessel is given off within the liver from a venous sinus formed by the confluence of the portal and umbilical veins and passes directly to the posterior vena cava.

The **foramen ovale** is an opening in the septum between the atria of the heart, by which the latter communicate with each other. It is guarded by a valve (Valvula foraminis ovalis) which prevents the blood from passing from the left atrium to the right. At birth the valve has the form of a fenestrated sac. After birth the foramen soon closes, but this part of the septum remains membranous, and there is a deep **fossa ovalis** in the right atrium which indicates the position of the former opening. In some cases a small part of the foramen persists in the adult without apparent disturbance of the circulation.

The **pulmonary circulation** is very limited in the fœtus, and most of the blood which enters the pulmonary artery passes through the **ductus arteriosus** to the aorta. This vessel is larger than the divisions of the pulmonary artery which go to the lungs, and joins the left side of the aortic arch. After birth the pulmonary circulation undergoes promptly an enormous increase and the ductus is rapidly transformed into a fibrous cord—the **ligamentum arteriosum.**

The only arterial blood in the fœtus is that carried by the umbilical vein. This blood is mixed in the liver with the venous blood of the portal vein, and after passing through the capillaries of the liver is carried by the hepatic veins to the posterior vena cava. The latter receives also the venous blood from the posterior part of the trunk and the pelvic limbs. It is generally stated that the blood carried into the right atrium by the posterior vena cava passes largely, if not entirely, through the foramen ovale into the left atrium, while the blood flowing into it through the anterior vena cava passes into the right ventricle. On this basis the blood received by the left atrium consists chiefly of mixed blood from the posterior vena cava, since the small amount of blood conveyed by the pulmonary veins is venous. This mixed blood passes into the left ventricle and is forced into the systemic arteries. The venous blood from the anterior part of the body and the thoracic limbs is conveyed by the anterior vena cava to the right atrium, passes into the right ventricle, and is forced into the pulmonary artery. A small amount is carried to the lungs, but the bulk of it passes by the ductus arteriosus into the aorta behind the point of origin of the brachiocephalic trunk, and is carried to the posterior part of the body, a large part passing by the umbilical arteries to the placenta.

THE BLOOD-VASCULAR SYSTEM OF THE OX

THE PERICARDIUM AND HEART

The **pericardium** is attached to the sternum between the facets for the sixth costal cartilages by two fibrous bands, the **sterno-pericardiac ligaments** (Ligg. sternopericardiaca); these ligaments, right and left, are embedded in the mass of fat about the apex of the pericardium on the floor of the thorax. On the left side the greater part of the pericardium is in contact with the chest wall as far back as the fourth intercostal space. On the right side the pericardium may be covered by the lung and have no contact with the lateral chest wall. But in most cases there is a triangular cardiac notch on the right lung opposite to the ventral part of the fourth rib and adjacent intercostal spaces.

The **heart** of the adult ox has an average weight of about five and a half pounds (ca. 2.5 kg.), or about 0.4 to 0.5 per cent. of the body-weight. Its length from base to apex is relatively longer than that of the horse, and the base is smaller in both its diameters. The ventricular part is more regularly conical and more pointed. A shallow **intermediate groove** (Sulcus intermedius) extends from the coronary groove down the left side of the posterior border, but does not reach the apex. The amount of fat in and near the grooves is much greater than in the horse. The proportions by weight on the left and right sides of the median plane is about 4 : 3. The base is opposite the chest wall from the second intercostal space or third rib to the fifth intercostal space or sixth rib. The apex is opposite to the sixth chondrosternal joint; it is median, and is about an inch (ca. 2.5 cm.) from the diaphragm. The long axis is less oblique than in the horse. The posterior border is opposite to the fifth intercostal space; it is practically vertical and is slightly concave. The left auricle is larger than the right.

The pulmonary orifice is chiefly opposite to the third intercostal space and fourth rib, about a handbreadth (ca. 10–12 cm.) above the sternal ends of the ribs. The aortic orifice is chiefly opposite to the fourth rib. The right atrio-ventricular orifice is opposite to the third intercostal space and fourth rib and space. The left atrio-ventricular orifice is chiefly opposite to the fourth intercostal space and fifth rib. The left longitudinal groove corresponds to the fourth rib. The right groove is chiefly posterior; it begins below the termination of the posterior vena cava. The intermediate groove begins below the posterior end of the left auricle, and in its descent inclines gradually toward the left side of the apex. There may be an accessory groove on the left side of the left ventricle.

The vena hemiazygos opens into the right atrium below the posterior vena cava. It receives at or near its termination the great cardiac vein, which is provided with a semilunar valve.

Two bones, the **ossa cordis,** develop in the aortic fibrous ring. The right one is in apposition with the atrio-ventricular rings, and is irregularly triangular in form. Its left face is concave and gives attachment to the right posterior cusp of the aortic valve. The right surface is convex from before backward. The base is dorsal. The posterior border bears two projections separated by a notch. It is usually a little more than an inch (ca. 4 cm.) in length. The left bone is smaller and is inconstant. Its concave right border gives attachment to the left posterior

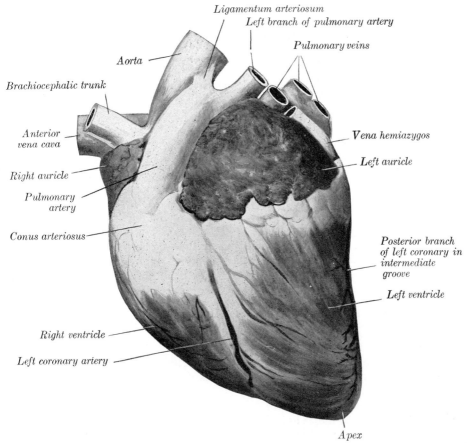

Fig. 592.—Heart of Ox; Left View.

cusp of the aortic valve. A large muscular moderator band in the right ventricle extends obliquely from the base of the anterior septal papillary muscle to the lower part of the anterior wall. Other trabeculæ extend up on the right to the attached edge of the tricuspid valve. In the left ventricle there are several branched moderator bands.

THE ARTERIES[1]

The great arterial trunks in the thorax resemble those of the horse in general disposition.

[1] Only the most important differential features of the arrangement of the vessels as compared with those of the horse will be considered.

The **left coronary artery** is much larger than the right one; it gives off a branch which descends in the longitudinal groove, another to the intermediate groove, and terminates by running downward in the right longitudinal groove. The **right coronary artery,** after emerging from the interval between the right auricle and the pulmonary artery, divides into branches which are distributed almost exclusively to the wall of the right ventricle.

The **brachiocephalic trunk** (anterior aorta) is usually four or five inches (ca. 10–12 cm.) in length.

The **brachial arteries** give off in the thorax the following branches:

1. A common trunk for the dorsal, deep cervical, and vertebral arteries.

(1) The **subcostal artery** commonly arises separately and runs forward along the sides of the bodies of the vertebra. It supplies the second to the fifth intercostal arteries.

(2) The **dorsal artery** is relatively small. It usually ascends in front of the first costo-vertebral joint, and is distributed as in the horse. It gives off the first intercostal artery.

(3) The **deep cervical artery** may arise from a common stem (Truncus vertebrocervicalis) with the vertebral, or may constitute a branch of that artery. It passes up between transverse processes of the first thoracic and last cervical vertebra, or between the sixth and seventh cervical, and is distributed as in the horse.

(4) The **vertebral artery** passes along the neck as in the horse to the intervertebral foramen between the second and third cervical vertebræ, gives off a muscular branch, and enters the vertebral canal (Fig. 594). It runs forward on the floor of the canal—connected with its fellow by two or three transverse anastomoses—and divides in the atlas into two branches. The smaller medial division (cerebrospinal artery) passes forward to the floor of the cranium and concurs with the condyloid artery and branches of the internal maxillary in the formation of a large **rete mirabile.** The large lateral branch emerges through the intervertebral foramen of the atlas and ramifies in the muscles of the neck in that region, and joins a branch of the occipital artery. It also sends a branch to the rete mirabile. The collateral branches detached to the cervical muscles are large and compensate for the small size of the deep cervical artery. The spinal branches pass through the intervertebral foramina, divide into anterior and posterior branches, and form two longitudinal trunks which are connected by cross-branches so as to form irregular polygonal figures.

2. The **internal thoracic artery** presents no remarkable features.

3. The **inferior cervical artery** corresponds usually to the ascending branch of that vessel in the horse.

4. The **external thoracic artery** is large and usually gives off a branch which is equivalent to the descending branch of the inferior cervical artery of the horse.

THE COMMON CAROTID ARTERY

The **carotid arteries** usually arise from a common trunk about two inches (ca. 5 cm.) in length, but in exceptional cases are given off separately from the brachiocephalic. Each pursues a course similar to that of the horse, and is accompanied by the small internal jugular vein, but is separated from the external jugular vein by the omo-hyoid and sterno-mastoid muscles. It divides at the digastricus into occipital, external maxillary, and external carotid arteries. The common carotid artery of the sheep differs somewhat from that of the ox, in that it divides into occipital, external carotid and lingual arteries. In addition to tracheal, œsophageal, and muscular branches, it gives off the thyroid, laryngeal and inferior parotid arteries. The **thyroid artery** (A. thyreoidea cranialis) bends around the anterior end of the thyroid gland, in which it ramifies. The accessory thyroid artery is usually absent. The **laryngeal artery** may arise with the thyroid.

1. The **occipital artery** is relatively small. It gives off the following:

(1) The **pharyngeal artery** (A. palatina ascendens) goes to the pharynx and soft palate; it may arise from the external carotid.

(2) **Muscular branches** go chiefly to the ventral straight muscles of the head and supply twigs to the atlanto-occipital joint.

(3) The **condyloid artery** passes into the cranium through the anterior foramen in the condyloid fossa, and joins the vertebral in the formation of the rete mirabile about the pituitary gland. Before entering the cranium it gives off a branch to the pharyngeal lymph glands and the **middle meningeal artery;** the latter passes

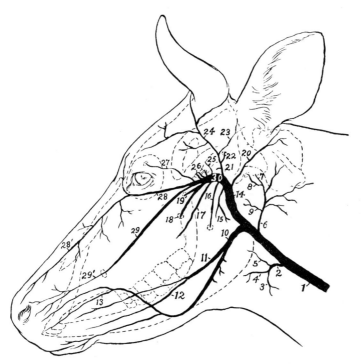

FIG. 593.—SCHEMA OF CHIEF ARTERIES OF HEAD OF COW.

1, Common carotid artery; *2*, thyro-laryngeal; *3*, thyroid; *4*, laryngeal; *5*, pharyngeal; *6*, occipital; *7*, condyloid; *8*, middle meningeal; *9*, pharyngeal; *10*, external maxillary; *11*, lingual; *12*, sublingual; *13*, superior labial; *14*, external carotid; *15*, masseteric; *16*, inferior alveolar; *17*, buccinator; *18*, great palatine; *19*, sphenopalatine; *20*, **pos**terior auricular; *21*, superficial temporal; *22*, posterior meningeal; *23*, anterior auricular; *24*, artery to corium of horn; *25*, deep temporal; *26*, arteries to rete mirabile; *27*, frontal; *28*, malar; *28'*, dorsal nasal continuation of malar; *29*, infraorbital; *29'*, lateral nasal continuation of *29*; *30*, internal maxillary.

through the foramen lacerum. Another branch enters the temporal canal and gives twigs to the temporalis muscle and the mucous membrane of the frontal sinus. A muscular branch joins the occipital as the latter emerges from the intervertebral foramen of the atlas. A diploic branch goes into the occipital condyle and squama, and emits twigs to the occipital muscles.

2. The **external maxillary artery** is smaller than that of the horse, but pursues a similar course.[1] It gives off branches severally to the parotid and mandibular glands. The **lingual artery** is large, and often arises separately from the common

[1] In the sheep the external maxillary artery is absent. The branches of the transverse facial, malar and superficial temporal arteries make up the chief arterial differences in the face. The superior and inferior labial arteries arise from the transverse facial artery which is a branch of the superficial temporal artery. The dorsal and lateral nasal arteries arise from the malar artery. In the goat the dorsal nasal artery arises from the superficial temporal artery.

carotid; it gives off a branch to the mandibular gland, and the **sublingual artery**. After turning around the jaw the facial gives off the labial arteries. The small **superficial inferior labial artery** runs forward along the ventral margin of the depressor labii inferioris; a somewhat larger **deep** artery lies on the deep face of the muscle. The **superior labial** is large; it passes forward ventral to the depressor labii superioris, and usually gives off a branch which runs forward almost parallel with the lateral nasal. The **angular artery** is very small or absent, and the **lateral** and **dorsal nasal arteries** are continuations of the infraorbital and malar, respectively.

3. The **external carotid artery** passes upward between the stylo-hyoideus and the great cornu of the hyoid bone, turns forward across the lateral face of the latter, and divides into superficial temporal and internal maxillary arteries. It gives off the following collateral branches:

(1) The **pharyngeal artery** may be a branch of the external carotid, but often arises from the occipital.

(2) The **posterior auricular artery,** which resembles that of the horse, sends a

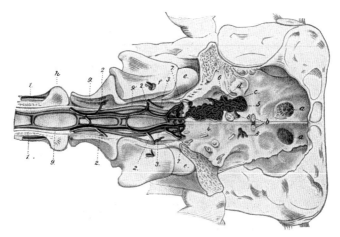

FIG. 594.—FLOOR OF CRANIUM AND ANTERIOR PART OF VERTEBRAL CANAL OF OX.

1, Vertebral artery; *2*, muscular branches of *1*; *3*, branches of *1* to the rete mirabile; *4, 5*, branches of internal maxillary artery to rete; *6*, branch of internal maxillary artery entering cranium through foramen ovale; *7*, condyloid artery; *8*, emergent artery from rete, distributed like internal carotid artery of horse; *9, 9′*, longitudinal vertebral sinuses; *a*, cribriform plate; *b*, optic formina; *c*, for. orbito-rotundum; *d*, foramen ovale; *e*, occipital condyle; *f, g, h*, first, second, and third cervical vertebræ. (After Leisering's Atlas.)

stylo-mastoid branch into the tympanum. It may arise from the superficial temporal.

(3) The **superior parotid artery** arises near the termination of the external carotid and enters the upper part of the parotid gland.

(4) The **masseteric artery** resembles that of the horse, but is smaller; it may arise from the internal maxillary artery.

The **superficial temporal artery** is large and presents the following special features: (1) The **transverse facial artery** passes into the central part of the masseter. (2) It gives off an **accessory meningeal artery** which enters the temporal canal, and ramifies in the dura mater, sending twigs to the external ear, the temporal muscle, and the frontal sinus. (3) It usually gives off the **anterior auricular artery.** (4) A large branch passes around the outer side of the base of the horn-core, supplies the corium of the horn, and anastomoses across the back of the frontal eminence with the artery of the opposite side. (5) Other branches go to the frontal muscles and skin and to the orbital fat, the lacrimal glands, and the eyelids.

The **internal maxillary artery** is entirely extraosseous, since the alar canal is absent. It passes forward along the side of the pharynx and the lateral pterygoid muscle and forms a double curve at the infratemporal fossa. It then runs forward to the pterygo-palatine fossa and divides into two terminal trunks; one of these divides into malar and infraorbital arteries, the other into sphenopalatine and greater palatine. It gives off branches to the pterygoid muscles, and the principal differential features in its branching are as follows:

(1) The **buccinator artery** arises from the first curve of the internal maxillary; it is relatively large, supplies the superior buccal glands, and divides into two branches. One of these enters the buccinator; the other, which is much larger, ramifies in the deep part of the masseter.

(2) The **anterior deep temporal artery** usually arises by a common trunk with the **middle meningeal artery**. The latter enters the cranial cavity through the foramen ovale and concurs in the formation of the rete mirabile cerebri.

(3) The **external ophthalmic artery** forms a **rete mirabile orbitæ** (Aa. retis mirabilis cerebri) within the periorbita. Its **frontal branch** enters the supraorbital canal and ramifies chiefly in the frontal sinus.

(4) Several branches which take the place of the internal carotid artery enter the cranial cavity through the foramen orbito-rotundum. They concur with branches of the occipital, vertebral, middle meningeal, and condyloid arteries in the formation of an extensive **rete mirabile cerebri** on the cranial floor around the sella turcica. From each side of the rete an artery arises which is distributed in general like the internal carotid and basilar arteries of the horse.[1]

(5) The **malar artery** is large; it emerges from the orbit near the medial angle and is continued as the **dorsal nasal,** giving off branches which take the place of the **angular artery** of the eye.

(6) The **infraorbital artery** is large and emerges from the infraorbital foramen to form the **lateral nasal artery.**

(7) The **greater palatine artery** passes through the palatine canal and along the palatine groove, enters the nasal cavity through the incisive fissure, and does not go to the upper lip. It forms a rete mirabile about the incisive canal and terminates in the mucous membrane of the anterior part of the nasal cavity.

ARTERIES OF THE THORACIC LIMB

The **brachial artery** pursues the same course in the arm as that of a horse. At the elbow it becomes the median.[2] The chief differential features in its branches are as follows:

1. The **subscapular artery** is almost as large as the continuation of the brachial. The **posterior circumflex artery** is large; it sends branches backward and downward into the triceps, taking the place in part of the deep brachial artery. The **thoraco-dorsal artery** supplies branches to the pectoral muscles and the triceps as well as the teres major and latissimus dorsi; it may arise directly from the brachial.

2. The smallness of the **deep brachial artery** is compensated, as noted above, by the large size of the posterior circumflex.

3. The **proximal collateral ulnar artery** is often double, and does not extend to the carpus. Its superficial descending branch goes to the superficial pectoral muscle and the skin, and its ascending branch is distributed chiefly to the medial head of the triceps and the anconeus.

(4) The (distal) **collateral radial artery,** which is given off at the elbow joint,

---

[1] The arteries which concur in the formation of the rete may be termed the arteriæ retis mirabilis cerebri.

[2] The homologies of the vessels of the lower parts of the limbs are still uncertain. The account given here is mainly based on the views of Sussdorf and Baum.

sends branches to the biceps, brachialis, and extensor muscles; it also supplies the nutrient artery of the humerus. It does not descend to the carpus.

The **median artery** descends along the medial part of the posterior surface of the radius and divides near the middle of the forearm into the radial and ulnar arteries. It gives off at the proximal third of the forearm the **common interosseous artery,** a large vessel which anastomoses with the deep brachial, passes through the proximal interosseous space, and descends as the **dorsal interosseous artery** in the groove between the radius and ulna, and concurs in the formation of the rete carpi

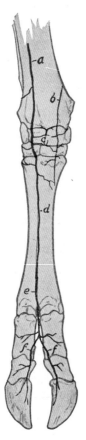

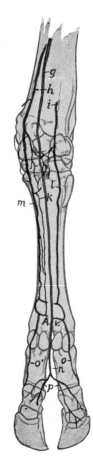

FIG. 595.—ARTERIES OF DISTAL PART OF RIGHT FORE LIMB OF OX; DORSAL VIEW.

a, Interosseous artery; b, dorsal branch of radial artery; c, rete carpi dorsale; d, dorsal metacarpal artery; e, dorsal common digital artery; f, f, dorsal proper digital arteries.

FIG. 596.—ARTERIES OF DISTAL PART OF RIGHT FORE LIMB OF OX; VOLAR VIEW.

g, Ulnar artery; h, radial artery; i, volar branch of common interosseous artery; k, l, m, deep volar metacarpal arteries; A.v., volar arches; n, volar common digital artery; o, o', p, volar proper digital arteries.

dorsale. At the distal end of the forearm it sends a branch through the distal interosseous space, which passes downward, assists in forming the rete carpi volare, and is continued in the metacarpus as the **lateral deep volar metacarpal artery.** This is a small vessel which passes down under the lateral border of the suspensory ligament and assists in forming the **deep volar arch near** the fetlock. The **recurrent interosseous** artery arises from the common interosseous and ascends to the lateral surface of the elbow. A large **muscular branch** arises from the median at the proximal end of the forearm; it is distributed chiefly to the flexor muscles.

The **radial artery** is the smaller of the two terminal branches of the median. It descends on the flexor carpi radialis, passes over the medio-volar surface of the carpus, and is continued as the medial deep volar metacarpal artery. At the distal end of the forearm and at the carpus it furnishes branches to the retia carpi. Another branch (A. met. perforans proximalis) runs outward between the suspensory ligament and the large metacarpal bone, passes through the proximal foramen of the bone, and unites with the dorsal metacarpal artery; before passing through the foramen it detaches the **middle deep volar metacarpal artery** (A. met. volaris prof. III.). This descends on the volar face of the metacarpal bone, receives an anastomotic branch from the medial deep artery, and concurs in the formation of the deep volar arch above the fetlock. The **medial deep volar metacarpal artery** (A. met. volaris prof. II.) descends along the medial part of the volar surface of the large metacarpal bone and is continued as the medial volar proper digital artery. At the distal part of the metacarpus it is connected by a transverse branch with the middle deep volar metacarpal artery, and similarly with the volar common digital, forming with the latter the superficial volar arch.

The **ulnar artery,** the larger of the two divisions of the median, descends under cover of the flexor carpi radialis without giving off any large branches in the forearm. It passes through the carpal canal and continues along the medial side of the deep flexor tendon as the **volar common digital artery** (A. met. volaris superficialis III.). At the distal third of the metacarpus this vessel is joined by a branch from the medial deep volar metacarpal artery, forming the superficial volar arch. Near this another branch of the common digital (or of the medial digital) passes around the lateral border of the flexor tendons to the posterior face of the metacarpal bone and concurs with the deep volar metacarpal arteries in the formation of the deep volar arch. A branch from the arch (A. met. perforans distalis) passes forward through the distal foramen of the metacarpal bone and joins the dorsal metacarpal artery which descends from the rete carpi dorsale in the dorsal metacarpal groove.

The **volar common digital artery** (A. metacarpea volaris superficialis III.) passes into the interdigital space and divides into two **volar proper digital arteries,** which descend along the interdigital surfaces of the chief digits and pass through the foramina at the proximal part of the interdigital surfaces of the third phalanges, enter the cavities in these bones, and ramify in a manner similar to the corresponding vessels in the horse. The volar common digital detaches a branch (A. interdigitalis perforans) which passes forward through the upper part of the interdigital space and anastomoses with the dorsal metacarpal artery.

The volar proper digital arteries (or the common digital) give off, in addition to other collaterals, branches which correspond to the arteries of the digital cushion of the horse. These pass to the bulbs of the claws and anastomose with each other and with the medial and lateral digital arteries, forming an arch from which numerous branches are distributed to the corium of the hoofs.

The **dorsal metacarpal artery** (A. met. dorsalis III.) is a small vessel which arises from the rete carpi dorsale, descends in the groove on the dorsal face of the metacarpal bone, and is joined by the distal perforating metacarpal artery from the deep volar arch to constitute the **dorsal common digital artery.** This vessel (A. digitalis communis dorsalis III.) divides into two **dorsal proper digital arteries.**

The **medial volar digital artery** (A. digiti III. medialis) is the continuation of the medial deep volar metacarpal artery. It descends on the medial side of the medial digit and terminates at the bulb of the claw by anastomosing with the corresponding volar proper digital artery. It gives off a branch to the rudimentary digit and forms a transverse anastomosis behind the first phalanx with the volar common digital or its medial division.

The **lateral volar digital artery** (A. digiti IV. lateralis) arises from the deep volar arch, passes down on the lateral side of the lateral digit, and is distributed like the medial one.

BRANCHES OF THE THORACIC AORTA

The **bronchial** and **œsophageal** arteries often arise separately.

There are thirteen pairs of **intercostal arteries.** The first comes from the dorsal, the next four from the subcostal, and the remainder from the aorta directly.

The two **phrenic arteries** are very variable in origin. They may come from the aorta, the cœliac, left ruminal, or an intercostal or lumbar artery.

BRANCHES OF THE ABDOMINAL AORTA

The **cœliac artery** is about four to five inches (ca. 10–12 cm.) in length. It passes ventrally and curves forward between the rumen and pancreas on the left and the right crus of the diaphragm and the posterior vena cava on the right. It gives off five chief branches.

1. The **hepatic artery** arises from the convex side of the curve of the cœliac artery as it crosses the posterior vena cava. It passes to the right and somewhat ventrally and forward above the portal vein to the portal fissure, and gives off the following branches:

(1) Pancreatic branches.

(2) Dorsal and ventral branches go to the corresponding lobes of the liver. The ventral branch is the larger; it gives off the right gastric artery, which runs in the lesser omentum to supply the origin of the duodenum and the pylorus, anastomosing with the dorsal branch of the omaso-abomasal artery.

(3) The cystic artery supplies the gall-bladder.

(4) The gastro-duodenal artery divides into right gastro-epiploic and pancreatico-duodenal branches. The right gastro-epiploic artery anastomoses with the left gastro-epiploic. The pancreatico-duodenal artery anastomoses with the first intestinal branch of the anterior mesenteric artery.

2. The **right ruminal artery** (A. ruminalis dextra) usually arises by a common trunk with the splenic. It forms a sharp curve and runs downward and backward on the right face of the dorsal sac of the rumen to the posterior transverse fissure, in which it turns around to the left and anastomoses with branches of the left ruminal artery. It gives off a pancreatic branch, dorsal and vental coronary arteries, branches to the great omentum, and ramifies on both surfaces of the rumen.

3. The **left ruminal artery** (A. ruminalis sinistra) descends on the anterior part of the right face of the rumen, enters the anterior furrow, in which it runs from right to left, and continues backward in the left longitudinal groove, anastomosing with branches of the right artery. It supplies chiefly the left face of the rumen, but not its posterior part. It usually gives off an inch or two (ca. 4 cm.) from its origin the **reticular artery** (A. reticularis); this rather small vessel passes forward on the dorsal curvature of the rumen and turns downward in the rumino-reticular groove, in the bottom of which it runs around ventrally to the right side. It gives off a branch which passes to the left of the cardia and along the lesser curvature of the reticulum to the neck of the omasum. The reticular branches anastomose with the omaso-abomasal and left ruminal arteries.

4. The **omaso-abomasal artery** (A. gastrica sinistra) appears as the continuation of the cœliac. It passes forward and downward to the greater curvature of the omasum, and divides after a course of four or five inches (ca. 10–12 cm.) into two branches. The **dorsal branch** curves sharply backward on the greater curvature of the omasum, continues along the lesser curvature of the abomasum, and anastomoses with the hepatic artery. It supplies branches to the omasum and to the

lesser curvature and pyloric part of the abomasum. The **ventral branch** (A. gastro-epiploica sinistra) runs forward and downward to the lesser curvature of the omasum, passes backward in the great omentum along the greater curvature of the abomasum, and anastomoses with the right gastro-epiploic. A considerable branch

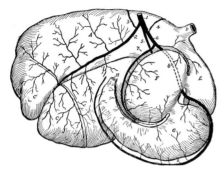 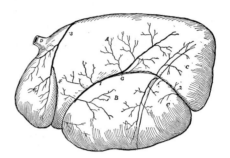

FIG. 597.—GASTRIC ARTERIES OF OX; RIGHT VIEW (PARTLY SCHEMATIC).

1, Cœliac; *2*, right ruminal; *3*, splenic; *4*, reticular; *5*, left ruminal; *6*, omaso-abomasal; *7*, dorsal branch of *6; 8*, ventral branch of *6* (= left gastro-epiploic); *A*, dorsal sac of rumen; *B*, ventral sac of rumen; *C, C*, posterior blind sacs; *D*, œsophagus; *E*, reticulum; *F*, omasum; *G*, abomasum; *H*, duodenum; *I*, right longitudinal furrow of rumen.

FIG. 598.—GASTRIC ARTERIES OF OX; LEFT VIEW (PARTLY SCHEMATIC).

1, Left ruminal artery; *2*, continuation of right ruminal artery; *3*, reticular artery, which disappears into rumino-reticular groove; *A*, dorsal sac of rumen; *B*, ventral sac of rumen; *C, C*, posterior blind sacs; *D*, œsophagus; *E*, reticulum; *F*, rumino-reticular groove; *G*, left longitudinal furrow of rumen.

from it curves around in front of the neck of the omasum to communicate with the reticular artery. Another branch runs back across the left side of the omaso-abomasal junction, and a third goes to the lesser curvature of the omasum.

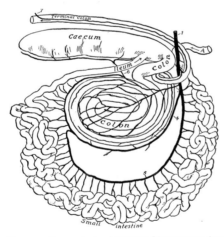

FIG. 599.—PLAN OF BRANCHES OF ANTERIOR MESENTERIC ARTERY OF OX.

1, Anterior mesenteric artery; *2*, middle colic artery; *3*, ileo-cæco-colic artery; *4*, ramus collateralis; *5*, continuation of anterior mesenteric artery, giving off branches to small intestine; *6*, cæcal artery; *7*, colic branch of posterior mesenteric artery; *A*, termination of duodenum.

5. The **splenic artery** usually arises by a common trunk with the right ruminal artery. It passes forward and to the left across the dorsal curvature of the rumen and enters the hilus of the spleen.

The **anterior mesenteric artery** arises from the aorta just behind the cœliac, and has about the same caliber as the latter. It has been observed arising as a branch of the cœliac, the caliber of the latter being correspondingly increased.

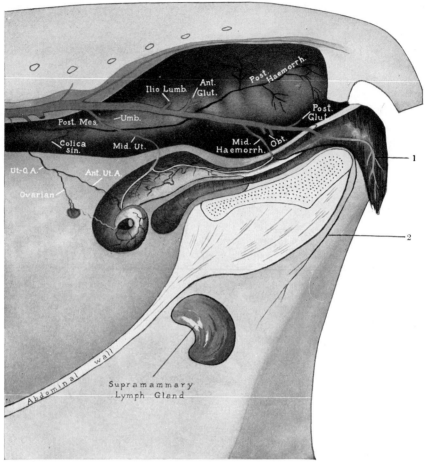

FIG. 600.—PELVIC ARTERIES OF THE COW.

Ant. Glut., Anterior gluteal; Ant. Ut. A., anterior uterine; Colica sin., left colic; Ilio lumb., ilio-lumbar; Mid. Haemorrh., middle hæmorrhoidal; Mid. Ut., middle uterine; Obt., obturator; Post. Glut., posterior gluteal; Post. Haemorrh., posterior hæmorrhoidal; Post. Mes., posterior mesenteric; Umb., umbilical; Ut. O. A., utero-ovarian; 1. artery of clitoris; 2, perineal.

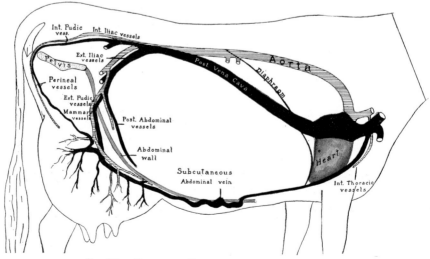

FIG. 600a.—DIAGRAM OF CIRCULATION OF UDDER OF THE COW.

It descends, inclining to the right and somewhat forward and passes between the pancreas and the posterior vena cava. It then inclines backward and crosses the colon as the latter emerges from the spiral mass to run backward. After detaching twigs to the pancreas it gives off in succession the following branches:

1. The **middle colic artery** (A. colica media) passes to the colon as it emerges from the spiral arrangement. This artery is comparable to the middle colic or artery of the small colon of the horse; it runs backward along the terminal part of the colon, which it supplies.

2. The **ileo-cæco-colic artery** ramifies on the right face of the spiral part of the colon. It gives off the ileo-cæcal artery, which divides into ileal and cæcal arteries.

3. The **ramus collateralis** runs in the mesentery in a curve along the ventral border of the coils of the colon. (This vessel is absent in the sheep.)

4. The continuing trunk (Truncus intestinalis) of the anterior mesenteric pursues a course in the mesentery corresponding to the series of mesenteric lymph glands and is connected with the ramus collateralis.

The two preceding vessels are essentially the arteries of the small intestine, which they supply with the exception of its initial and terminal parts. The ramus collateralis gives off no considerable branches in its course along the ventral border of the coils of the colon, but on curving upward along the latter it anastomoses with the continuing trunk of the anterior mesenteric artery and detaches numerous branches to the small intestine which form series of superposed anastomotic arches. It supplies, roughly speaking, about one-third of the small intestine and terminates by joining the ileal artery. The continuing trunk gives off numerous branches which also form arches and supply about the first two-thirds of the small intestine, exclusive of the small part supplied by branches of the cœliac artery. Both arteries give branches to the lymph glands.[1]

The **posterior mesenteric artery** arises from the aorta near its termination. It is small and supplies branches to the terminal part of the colon and to the rectum (A. colica sinistra; A. hæmorrhoidalis cranialis).

The **renal arteries** arise from the aorta close together. The right one passes outward and forward across the dorsal face of the posterior vena cava to the hilus of the kidney. The left one runs usually forward and ventrally, but necessarily varies in direction in conformity with the position of the kidney (q. v.).

The **spermatic arteries** resemble those of the horse.

The **utero-ovarian arteries** are small.

The five pairs of **lumbar arteries** derived from the aorta are distributed much as in the horse. The sixth usually comes from the internal iliac artery.

The **middle sacral artery** is a vessel about 5 mm. in diameter which continues the aorta. It arises from the dorsal face of the aorta at the angle of divergence of the internal iliacs, runs backward on the pelvic surface of the sacrum a little to the left of the median line, and is continued as the middle coccygeal artery. It gives off small collateral branches to the spinal cord and the muscles of the tail and the **lateral coccygeal arteries.** The latter may have a common trunk of origin, and each divides into dorsal and ventral branches. The **middle coccygeal artery** runs through the ventral (hæmal) arches of the coccygeal vertebræ. The coccygeal arteries are connected at rather regular intervals by segmented anastomoses.

The **internal iliac arteries** are much longer than in the horse. Each passes backward on the sacro-sciatic ligament and divides about the middle of the pelvic wall into posterior gluteal and internal pudic branches. The chief differences in its distribution are: (1) A large trunk gives origin to the umbilical and middle uterine arteries. The **umbilical artery** is usually largely obliterated, and its terminal branches receive their blood through anastomoses with the internal pudic. It

---

[1] It is difficult to make the arrangement of these vessels clear in a brief textual description, but a reference to the schematic figure will explain the main facts.

gives off near its origin two small-vessels, the ureteral artery (A. ureterica) and the deferential artery (A. deferentialis), which accompany the ureter and the ductus deferens respectively. The **middle uterine artery** (A. uterina media) arises by a common trunk with the umbilical artery and is very large. It descends on the lateral pelvic wall a short distance behind the external iliac and reaches the dorso-lateral surface of the uterus just in front of the body. It is distributed chiefly to the cornu of the uterus, and compensates for the small size of the utero-ovarian artery.[1] (2) The **ilio-lumbar artery** is relatively small and is distributed chiefly to the sublumbar muscles. It is sometimes replaced by branches of the circumflex iliac and gluteal arteries. (3) The **anterior gluteal artery** is commonly represented by several vessels. (4) The **obturator artery** is represented by several small branches supplying in part obturator and adductor muscles. (5) The **iliaco-femoral** and **lateral sacral arteries** are absent. The absence of the latter is compensated by the middle sacral and gluteal arteries. (6) The **posterior gluteal artery** is large. It emerges through the lesser sciatic notch and ramifies in the biceps femoris and adjacent muscles. (7) The **internal pudic artery** (A. urethro-genitalis) is the direct continuation of the internal iliac. It gives off branches to the rectum, bladder, urethra, and genital organs. In the male it supplies the accessory genital glands and divides into dorsal and deep arteries of the penis; the **a. dorsalis penis** runs along the dorsum penis to the glans and gives twigs to the prepuce; the **a. profunda penis** gives off a perineal branch and enters the corpus cavernosum penis. In the female it gives off the large **posterior uterine artery,** which supplies the posterior part of the uterus and gives branches to the vagina and bladder. It ends as the **a. clitoridis,** which supplies the clitoris and adjacent parts.

ARTERIES OF THE PELVIC LIMB

The **external iliac artery** has the same course as in the horse. The circumflex iliac artery is large. A branch from it emerges between the abdominal and lumbar muscles near the tuber coxæ and ramifies like the terminals of the ilio-lumbar artery of the horse.

The **femoral** and **popliteal arteries** pursue courses similar to those of the horse. The chief differences in their branches are as follows:

1. The **external pudic artery** is distributed chiefly to the scrotum in the male. In the cow it is usually termed the **mammary** and is very large, especially during lactation. Each divides at the base of the mammary gland into two branches which are distributed to the anterior and posterior parts ("quarters") of the gland. A small branch accompanies the subcutaneous abdominal vein to the xiphoid region.

2. The **deep femoral artery** gives off an **obturator branch** which passes up through the obturator foramen to supply the obturator internus and compensates otherwise for the absence of the obturator artery.

3. The **anterior femoral artery** is large. It often gives off the **external circumflex artery** of the thigh, which perforates the proximal end of the quadriceps, gives branches to that muscle, the iliacus, glutei, and tensor fasciæ latæ.

4. The **saphenous artery** is large. It descends in front of the homonymous vein over the medial surface of the leg, and divides near the hock into lateral and medial tarsal arteries. The **lateral tarsal artery** is small and is distributed on the outer part of the hock. The **medial tarsal artery** is the direct continuation of the saphenous. It descends along the medial border of the superficial flexor tendon and divides into medial and lateral plantar arteries. The **medial plantar**

---

[1] The middle uterine artery has recently become of special clinical interest in relation to the recognition of pregnancy. The artery of the gravid horn becomes enlarged and has a peculiar pulsation which can be recognized by palpation per rectum. As the period of gestation advances the artery changes its direction in conformity with the forward extension of the uterus.

artery descends along the medial side of the deep flexor tendon with the medial plantar nerve. It anastomoses at the proximal end of the metatarsus with the perforating tarsal artery, assisting in the formation of the **proximal plantar arch,** and continues distally as the a. met. plant. superfic. med. along the medial border of the deep flexor tendon. Near the fetlock it concurs with the perforating branch of the dorsal metatarsal artery and with a branch of the corresponding lateral artery in the formation of the **distal plantar arch.** Below this it is continued

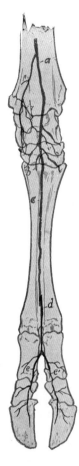

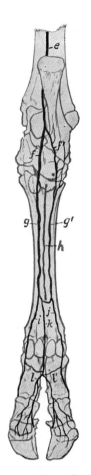

FIG. 601.—ARTERIES OF DISTAL PART OF RIGHT HIND LIMB OF OX; DORSAL VIEW.

a, Anterior tibial artery; *b,* proximal perforating metatarsal artery; *c,* dorsal metatarsal artery; *d,* dorsal common digital artery; *e, e',* dorsal proper digital arteries.

FIG. 602.—ARTERIES OF DISTAL PART OF RIGHT HIND LIMB OF OX; PLANTAR VIEW.

e, Saphenous artery; *f, f',* internal and external plantar arteries; *g, g',* medial and lateral superficial plantar metatarsal arteries; *h,* deep plantar metatarsal artery; *i, j,* medial and lateral plantar digital arteries, *k,* plantar common digital artery; *l, l',* medial and lateral plantar digital arteries.

as the **medial digital artery.** The **lateral plantar artery** is small.[1] It descends along the lateral border of the deep flexor tendon with the lateral plantar nerve, concurs with the perforating tarsal and medial plantar arteries in the formation of the proximal plantar arch, and gives branches to the rete tarsi dorsale. Continuing downward along the deep flexor tendon as the a. met. plant. superfic. lat., it assists in forming the distal plantar arch and becomes the **lateral digital artery.**

[1] This vessel may arise instead from the rete tarsi dorsale.

The **posterior tibial artery** is relatively small and is distributed chiefly to the muscles on the posterior surface of the tibia. Lower down it is replaced by the saphenous artery, as described above.

The **anterior tibial artery** has the same course as in the horse. It is continued down the groove on the front of the metatarsal bone as the dorsal metatarsal artery. At the tarsus branches are given off which concur with the lateral tarsal artery in the formation of the rete tarsi dorsale. The **perforating tarsal artery** passes back through the vascular canal and anastomoses with the plantar arteries, thus forming the proximal plantar arch. From this the small **deep plantar metatarsal artery** descends in the plantar groove of the large metatarsal bone to the distal plantar arch. The **dorsal metatarsal artery** (A. met. dorsalis) is the chief artery of the region and is accompanied by two veins. Near the distal end of the metatarsal bone it gives off the perforating metatarsal artery, which passes back through the distal metatarsal foramen and assists in forming the distal plantar arch.

The **dorsal common digital artery** is the direct continuation of the dorsal metatarsal. It divides into two branches which unite in the interdigital space with the corresponding branches of the plantar common digital to form the proper digital arteries.

The **plantar common digital artery** descends from the distal plantar arch, anastomoses in the interdigital space with the medial and lateral digitals, and divides into two branches which join those of the dorsal common digital artery as before mentioned.

The foregoing is a brief statement of the more common arrangement of the vessels in the distal part of the limb, but minor variations are very common.

THE VEINS [1]

The **vena hemiazygos** takes the place of the vena azygos. It lies along the left side of the aorta and the bodies of the thoracic vertebræ, turns down across the left face of the aorta and left pulmonary artery, runs back over the left auricle, beneath the pulmonary veins and usually joins the great cardiac vein, but may open into the right atrium. It receives the dorsal intercostal veins.

Two **jugular veins** often occur on either side. The **internal jugular vein** (V. jugularis interna) is a small vessel which accompanies the carotid artery. It arises by occipital laryngeal, and thyroid radicles, receives tracheal, œsophageal, and muscular branches, and joins the external jugular near its termination. Not uncommonly it is absent, but in some cases it appears, on the other hand, to be large enough to interfere with venesection practised on the external jugular. The **external jugular vein** (V. jugularis externa) is very large and corresponds to the jugular of the horse. It is separated from the carotid artery in the greater part of its course by the sterno-cephalicus and omo-hyoideus muscles.

The **ventral cerebral vein** usually joins the **internal maxillary vein.** The latter also receives the tributaries which in the horse go to the vena reflexa, this being absent in the ox.

The ventral longitudinal sinus is represented by a vein. There is an anterior intercavernous sinus. The transverse sinus is connected with the basilar plexus by a vein which traverses the condyloid canal. In the sheep there are two ventral occipital sinuses in place of the basilar plexus.

The **orbital veins** form a network between the periorbita and the muscles of the eyeball. This plexus communicates with the cavernous sinus and with the

---

[1] Most of the differences in the veins of the ox are correlated with those of the arteries of which they are satellites, and will not be described. The account here given consists chiefly of those differential features which could not be deduced from a knowledge of the arteries.

dorsal cerebral vein. It is also drained by the **frontal vein,** which runs in the supraorbital canal and groove and joins the **angular vein of the eye.** The latter is large (being visible under the skin in the sheep); it unites with the **dorsal nasal,** which is usually double, to form the **facial vein.** The latter curves downward and forward, and inclines backward in front of the facial tuberosity and follows the anterior and ventral borders of the masseter muscle, from which it is separated by the parotid duct; it joins the jugular vein at about a right angle ventral to the angle of the mandible and in relation to the ventral end of the parotid salivary gland. The **superior labial vein** usually joins the infraorbital.

The **sublingual vein** is very large.

The **veins of the thoracic limb** differ chiefly in the distal part; the special features are as follows:

The **dorsal digital veins** ascend on the front of the digits and are connected with the other digital veins by transverse branches. They unite near the fetlock to form the **dorsal metacarpal vein.** This runs upward on the dorsal face of the metacarpus and carpus, inclines to the medial surface of the radius, and joins the cephalic or the accessory cephalic vein.

The **volar digital veins** are larger than the dorsal veins. They lie on the interdigital surfaces of the digits and unite in the interdigital space to form a trunk which is a satellite of the volar common digital artery. This trunk, the **volar common digital vein,** which is often double, is connected distally by transverse branches with the lateral and medial digital veins to form the superficial volar arch; it is continued upward as the satellite of the ulnar artery.

The **medial** and **lateral digital veins** lie in front of the corresponding arteries. They are connected with the volar digital vein by a large branch which passes between the flexor tendons and the first phalanx. At the distal end of the metacarpus each inclines forward and anastomoses with the volar common digital vein to form the volar venous arch. The medial vein is continued as the medial volar metacarpal vein along the medial border of the suspensory ligament, and becomes a satellite of the radial artery in the forearm, while the lateral one is continued on the volar face of the metacarpal bone by the lateral volar metacarpal vein. The latter unites at the proximal part of the metacarpus with the middle volar metacarpal vein, and the trunk thus formed joins the medial vein to form the deep plantar arch. They unite below the carpus or join the volar common digital vein.

The digital veins arise from the venous plexuses of the corium of the hoof. They form by anastomotic branches a venous circle at the coronary border of the hoof, which may be termed the coronary circle. A vein which emerges from the foramen on the proximal part of the interdigital surface of the third phalanx is the principal radicle of the dorsal digital vein.

The **accessory cephalic vein** is the upward continuation of the dorsal metacarpal vein and is much larger than in the horse.

The **posterior vena cava** is partially embedded in the medial border of the liver. Its abdominal part has a thicker wall than in the horse. Its affluents correspond to the arteries of which they are satellites. The **renal veins** are large and thick-walled; they run obliquely forward and join the vena cava at an acute angle. The left one is much the longer.

Two **middle sacral veins** usually accompany the artery.

The **veins of the mammary glands** deserve special notice. They converge to a venous circle at the base of the udder, which is drained chiefly by two pairs of veins. The **subcutaneous abdominal vein** (anterior mammary or "milk" vein) is very large in animals of the dairy breeds, and its course along the ventral wall of the abdomen is easily followed. It is usually flexuous. It emerges at the anterior border of the udder about two or three inches (ca. 5–8 cm.) from the linea alba, runs forward (deviating a little outward), dips under the cutaneus, passes through a foramen in the abdominal wall about a handbreadth from the median plane, and joins the internal thoracic vein. The two veins are connected by a transverse anastomosis at the anterior border of the base of the udder, and each anastomoses behind with a branch of the external pudic vein. The **external pudic vein** (middle mammary vein) is also of considerable size. It ascends in the inguinal canal as a satellite of the artery and joins the external iliac vein. The right and left veins are connected at the posterior border of the base of the udder by a large transverse branch. From the latter arises the **perineal vein** (posterior mammary vein), which runs medially upward and backward to the perineum, turns around the ischial arch, and joins the internal pudic vein. Two veins may be present. In the male these veins are relatively small.

The deep veins of the thigh and leg resemble those of the horse, but there is no recurrent tibial vein.

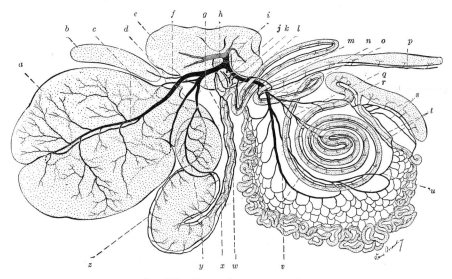

FIG. 602a.—PORTAL SYSTEM OF THE OX.

a, Rumen; *b*, spleen; *c*, right ruminal vein; *d*, left ruminal and reticular vein; *e*, liver; *f*, splenic vein; *g*, left and right gastric vein; *h*, gastro-splenic vein; *i*, mesenteric and portal veins; *j*, gastro-duodenal and anterior pancreatico-duodenal vein; *k*, large pancreatic vein; *l*, posterior pancreatico-duodenal vein; *m*, medial colic vein; *n*, ileo-cæco-colic vein; *o*, proper colic vein; *p*, left colic vein; *q*, colic trunk; *r*, ileo-cæcal vein; *s*, cæcal branch; *t*, ileal vein; *u*, ileal branch and intestinal trunk; *v*, intestinal trunk and collateral branch; *w*, right gastro-epiploic vein; *x*, right gastric vein; *y*, left gastric vein; *z*, left gastro-epiploic vein. (Martin, Anatomie d. Haustiere, III Band.)

The **saphenous vein** is much smaller than in the horse. It may be regarded chiefly as the upward continuation of the medial tarsal vein, which arises from the deep plantar arch.

The **recurrent tarsal vein** is large. It is the upward continuation of the dorsal metatarsal vein and anastomoses with the anterior tibial and saphenous veins. It arises on the lateral face of the hock, ascends at first in front of the tendo Achillis, then crosses the latter laterally, passes up between the biceps femoris and semitendinosus, and joins the posterior femoral vein.

There are three chief metatarsal veins. The large **dorsal metatarsal vein** arises at the distal part of the metatarsus by the union of the dorsal digital vein and a large branch from the venous arch above the sesamoids. It ascends superficially between the long and lateral extensor tendons and may be regarded as being continued in the leg by the recurrent tarsal vein; it also furnishes a large chief radicle of the anterior tibial vein. The **medial plantar metatarsal vein** arises from the venous arch above the fetlock, ascends between the medial border of the suspensory ligament and the plantar surface of the metatarsal bone; it is connected with the corresponding lateral vein at the proximal end of the metatarsus by a transverse anastomosis, thus forming the **deep plantar arch.** From this the **perforating tarsal vein** passes through the vascular canal of the metatarsus and centrotarsal (as the perforating tarsal) and joins the anterior tibial vein. The **lateral plantar metatarsal vein** pursues a similar course laterally, and is continued by the lateral tarsal vein, which joins the recurrent tarsal vein above the hock. It passes superficially over the lateral face of the hock and is continued by the recurrent tarsal vein.

The **digital veins** differ from those of the forelimb chiefly in that the dorsal common vein is large and the plantar absent or small.

The dorsal common digital vein arises at the distal part of the interdigital space by the union of branches coming from the venous plexuses of each digit. It deviates outward at the fetlock and joins the lateral digital vein to form the dorsal metatarsal vein. The medial digital vein ascends along the medial surface of the medial chief digit, turns laterally above the fetlock joint, and is connected with the corresponding lateral vein to form the plantar venous arch. From this the three chief metatarsal veins ascend and to it come small veins from the rudimentary digits.

The **portal vein** (Fig. 602a) is formed usually by the confluence of two radicles, gastric and mesenteric. It receives the gastro-duodenal vein and veins of the pancreas. The gastric vein is the largest affluent. It is formed by the junction of two trunks. One of these, the right ruminal vein, receives the splenic vein. The other is a short trunk which is formed by the confluence of the left ruminal and omaso-abomasal veins; it receives the reticular vein. The anterior mesenteric vein is formed by the confluence of three chief radicles which return the blood from the entire intestine, with the exception of part of the duodenum and rectum; from these the blood is conveyed by the gastro-duodenal and internal pudic veins. The portal tributaries are in general satellites of the corresponding arteries.

LYMPHATIC SYSTEM OF THE OX AND SHEEP

The **lymph glands** of the ox are in general less numerous but much larger than those of the horse; in some situations a single large gland occurs instead of a group of small ones, as found in the latter animal.

The **thoracic duct** arises from the cisterna chyli at the hiatus aorticus. In some cases it remains single, as is most common in the horse, pursues a similar course and opens into the origin of the anterior vena cava, or into the left common jugular vein. But in many cases the duct divides into two branches which lie on the right and left sides of the dorsal face of the aorta. The two ducts are united by anastomotic branches and are embedded in fat. They usually unite about the fifth thoracic vertebra. The terminal part is often ampullate, but the lymphatico-venous opening is small. When single, the duct is 6–10 mm. in diameter. The duct may receive efferent vessels from the intercostal, mediastinal, and bronchial lymph glands.

Many other variations have been described. In the anterior mediastinum there may be three or even four ducts (with connecting branches), which usually unite just before the lymphatico-venous opening, but may open separately.

The **cisterna chyli** lies in the hiatus aorticus, dorsal to the aorta and ventral to the last thoracic and first lumbar vertebræ. It receives the lumbar and intestinal lymph trunks. It is very variable in form and is commonly about three-fourths of an inch (1.5–2 cm.) wide.

The **intestinal trunk** (Truncus intestinalis) is formed at the ventral face of the posterior vena cava, just behind the dorsal border of the liver. It results from the union of the common efferent vessels of the gastric and intestinal lymph glands.

The trunk is a centimeter or less in diameter in the adult. It runs backward a short distance, bends sharply dorsally between the aorta and vena cava, and unites (usually) with the lumbar trunk to form the cisterna chyli.

The **lumbar trunk** (Truncus lumbalis) is formed in the sublumbar region by the confluence of efferent vessels from the iliac lymph glands. It concurs with the intestinal trunk in the formation of the cisterna chyli. It receives efferent vessels of the lumbar and renal lymph glands. The trunk is very variable in regard to its mode of formation and two may be present.

The **mandibular lymph glands** are usually two in number, one on each side. The gland is situated between the sterno-cephalicus muscle and the ventral part of the mandibular salivary gland, and is usually related dorsally to the external maxil-

Fig. 603.—Superficial Lymph Glands of Cow Projected on Surface of Body.

1, Mandibular; *2*, parotid; *3*, atlantal; *4*, parapharyngeal; *5*, anterior cervical: *6*, middle cervical; *7*, prescapular; *8*, prefemoral.   (With use of fig. in Ellenberger-Baum, Anat. f. Künstler.)

lary vein. The gland is oval and is commonly about an inch and a half (ca. 3–4 cm.) long and an inch (ca. 2–3 cm.) wide. In some cases a second, smaller gland is present. Its position is variable; it may be behind or dorso-medial to the large gland, or may be on the deep face of the ventral end of the mandibular salivary gland. Hæmal nodes often occur in this vicinity. The afferent vessels come from the muzzle, lips, cheeks, hard palate, the anterior part of the turbinates and septum nasi, the gums (in part), the sublingual and parotid glands; the tip of the tongue, the muscles of the head, except those of the eye, ear, tongue, and hyoid bone; the mandible, premaxilla, and nasal bone; the skin of the face in part. It also receives the efferent vessels of the pterygoid lymph gland when present. The efferent vessels, two to four in number, go to the atlantal gland.

The **parotid lymph gland** (Lg. parotidea)(Fig. 603a) lies on the posterior part of the masseter muscle and is partly covered by the dorsal end of the parotid salivary gland.[1] It is related deeply to the internal maxillary and superficial temp-

[1] In exceptional cases it is completely covered by the salivary gland.

oral vessels and the superficial temporal nerve. It is about three inches (ca. 6–8 cm.) long and about an inch (ca. 2–3 cm.) wide. In some cases there are instead two smaller glands. The afferent vessels come from the muzzle, lips, the gums (in part), the anterior part of the turbinates and septum nasi; the parotid salivary gland; most of the muscles of the head, including those of the eye and ear; the eyelids, lacrimal gland and external ear; the frontal, malar, nasal and premaxillary bones and the mandible; the skin of the head in great part. The efferent vessels, eight to twelve in number, go to the atlantal gland.

FIG. 603a.—HEAD OF OX, LATERAL VIEW, SHOWING LYMPHATICS, SUPERFICIAL MUSCLES AND MANDIBULAR JOINT.

Lymph Glands and Vessels.—*1*, Parotid; *2*, mandibular; *3, 4*, vessels from the conjunctiva of the lower and upper eye lids; *5*, vessels from the mandibular joint; *6, 6′*, vessels from the ear; *7*, vessels from the rotator muscles; *8*, vessels from omo-transversarius; *9*, vessels from the cleido-occipitalis; *10*, vessels from the omo-hyoideus; *11*, vessels from the obliquus capitis anterior; *12*, atlantal.

Muscles.—*a*, Levator nasolabialis; *b*, levator labii superioris proprius, dilator nares lateralis and depressor labii superioris; *c*, zygomaticus; *d*, malaris; *e*, buccinator; *f*, depressor labii inferioris; *g*, masseter; *h*, orbicularis oculi; *i*, frontalis; *k*, cleido-occipitalis; *m*, cleido-mastoideus; *n*, sterno-cephalicus; *o*, omohyoideus over sterno-hyoideus; *p*, parotido-auricularis; *q*, zygomatico-auricularis and scutulo-auricularis superficialis inferior; *r*, scutulo-auricularis superficialis superior; *s*, scutularis; *t*, external jugular; *u*, mandibular and *v*, parotid salivary glands. (Baum, D. Lymphgefässsystem d. Rindes.)

The **suprapharyngeal lymph glands** (Lgg. suprapharyngeæ) are usually two in number, right and left. They are situated about an inch apart, medial to the great cornu of the hyoid bone, and between the pharynx and the ventral straight muscles of the head (Fig. 386). They average about three inches (ca. 6–8 cm.) in length. In some cases an additional gland is present. The afferent vessels come from the tongue, the floor of the mouth, the hard palate, the soft palate, the gums (in part), the pharynx, the sublingual and mandibular salivary glands; the posterior part of the nasal cavity, the maxillary and palatine sinuses, and the larynx; and the rectus capitis ventralis major. The efferent vessels, four to eight in number, concur in forming the tracheal lymph duct.

A small **parapharyngeal lymph gland** is usually present on the lateral wall of the pharynx, under cover of the mandibular salivary gland or at its posterior border. It is ventral to the carotid artery and the atlantal gland. Its afferent and efferent vessels are similar to those of the atlantal gland.

The **atlantal lymph gland** is situated ventral to the wing of the atlas, on the cleido-mastoideus tendon, and partly under cover of the mandibular salivary gland. It is related ventrally to the carotid artery. It is usually discoid and an inch and a

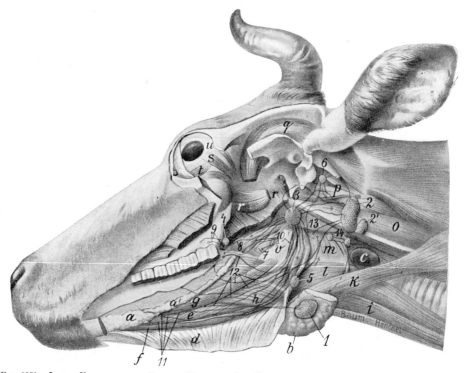

Fig. 603b.—Lymph Vessels of the Tongue, Hard and Soft Palate and Muscles and Adjacent Structures.

Lymph Glands.—*1*, Mandibular; *2, 2'*, atlantal; *3*, suprapharyngeal; *4*, pterygoid; *5*, anterior hyoid; *6*, posterior hyoid; *7*, vessels from the medial surface of the alveolar border of the mandible; *8*, vessels from the hard palate; *9*, vessels from the hard palate and gums of the upper jaw, a part going to the pterygoid and a part to the mandibular glands; *10*, vessels from the base of the tongue and palate; *11*, vessels from the point of the tongue; *12*, vessels from the body of the tongue; *13*, vessels from the mandibular foramen; *14*, anterior cervicals.

Muscles and Adjacent Structures.—*a, a'*, Sublingual salivary gland; *b*, anterior part of mandibular salivary gland; *c*, thyroid; *d*, mylo-hyoideus; *e*, genio-glossus; *f*, genio-hyoideus; *g*, stylo-glossus; *h*, hyo-glossus; *i*, sterno-hyoideus; *k*, omo-hyoideus; *l*, thyro-hyoideus; *m*, thyro- and crico-pharyngeus; *o*, rectus capitis ventralis major; *p*, rectus capitis ventralis minor and lateralis; *q*, temporalis; *r, r*, pterygoidei; *s*, rectus oculi lateralis; *t*, obliquus oculi ventralis; *u*, eye ball; *v*, great cornu of the hyoid bone. (Baum, D. Lymphgefässsystem d. Rindes.)

half to two inches (ca. 4–5 cm.) in length. One or more small lymph glands may occur near the large constant one, and small hæmal nodes are commonly present here. The afferent vessels come from the tongue, the salivary glands, the gums in part; the cervical part of the thymus; most of the hyoid and cervical muscles. It also receives vessels from the parotid, mandibular, and suprapharyngeal lymph glands. The efferent vessels, three to six in number, concur in forming the tracheal lymph duct.

The **pterygoid lymph gland** (Lg. pterygoidea), which is present in the majority of cases, is situated on the dorsal part of the lateral face of the pterygoid muscle, close to the maxillary tuberosity. It is usually about half an inch (ca. 1–1.5 cm.)

in length and width, but may be much smaller and escape observation. Its afferent vessels come from the hard palate and adjacent part of the gums. The efferent vessels, two or three in number, go to the mandibular lymph gland.

The **hyoid lymph glands** (Lgg. hyoideæ) occur in about 20 per cent. of cases. The anterior hyoid gland (Lg. hyoidea oralis) lies on the thyroid cornu of the hyoid bone, at the insertion of the stylo-hyoideus muscle. It is about half an inch (ca. 1–1.5 cm.) long. It receives afferent vessels from the tongue. The efferent vessels, two or three in number, go the to atlantal gland, and may go in part to the suprapharyngeal gland. The posterior hyoid gland (Lg. hyoidea aboralis) lies on the dorsal end of the great cornu of the hyoid bone or in the angle between the bone and the occipito-hyoideus muscle. It receives lymph vessels from the mandible which issue from the mandibular foramen. The efferent vessels go to the atlantal gland.

The **anterior cervical lymph glands** (Lgg. cervicales craniales) are situated on the anterior part of the trachea, along the course of the carotid artery. They are variable in number and size. Four or five may be present. They vary in length from about half an inch to two inches (ca. 1–2.5 cm.).

The **middle cervical lymph glands** (Lgg. cervicales mediæ) lie on each side of the trachea, in the middle third of the neck. They vary in position, number, and size. The series may extend to the anterior group, or may reach back almost to the posterior group. The number appears to vary from one to seven on either side. Their length ranges from about one-fourth inch to an inch or more (ca. 0.5–3 cm.). There are usually hæmal nodes near them.

The **posterior cervical lymph glands** (Lgg. cervicales caudales) are situated near the thoracic inlet. One of them lies dorsal to the manubrium sterni and the cervical muscles attached to it. It is usually about half an inch (ca. 1–1.5 cm.) long. Three or four others usually occur on either side. Of these, one is ventral to the brachial vein at the first rib, one or two lie on the brachial vessels here, and others are dorsal and ventral to the jugular vein. Hæmal nodes usually are present in the fat about this group.

The cervical lymph glands receive afferent vessels from the ventral muscles of the neck, the œsophagus, the larynx, the trachea, the thyroid gland, and the cervical part of the thymus. The anterior cervical glands receive efferent vessels of the atlantal gland. The efferent vessels go in general to the tracheal lymph ducts, but efferents from some of the posterior group may go to the terminal part of the thoracic duct or to the common jugular vein.

The **costo-cervical lymph gland** (Lg. costo-cervicalis)[1] is lateral to the trachea (right side) and œsophagus (left side) and dorsal to the carotid artery and the vago-sympathetic trunk. It is usually in front of the first rib, under cover of the scalenus muscle, but it may be partly medial to the first rib. Its length varies from half an inch to an inch or more (1.5–3 cm.). Its afferent vessels come from the muscles of the neck and shoulder, the costal pleura, the trachea, and the intercostal and anterior mediastinal glands. The efferent vessels on the right side usually go to the right tracheal duct or join the efferent vessel of the prescapular gland; on the left they go most often to the end of the thoracic duct, but are very variable.

The **tracheal lymph ducts** (Ductus tracheales), right and left, are formed essentially by the confluence of efferent vessels from the atlantal gland. They usually receive efferent vessels from the cervical, costo-cervical, and prescapular glands. The ducts pass along each side of the trachea and œsophagus; the right one usually opens into the right common jugular vein; the left one joins the terminal part of the thoracic duct or opens into the left common jugular vein.

These ducts are very variable in regard to formation, affluents, and termination. There may be an accessory tracheal duct, which receives part of the lymph vessels that otherwise go to

[1] This gland has been included in the posterior cervical group, but forms a connecting link, as it were, between the cervical and mediastinal glands. Baum has given it the above name and has shown that it receives lymph vessels from the pleura.

the chief duct; this accessory duct runs a variable distance along the neck practically parallel with the chief duct, and unites with the latter.

A short **right lymphatic duct** may be formed by the junction with the terminal part of the right tracheal duct of efferent vessels from the right cervical, costo-cervical, and prescapular lymph glands. It also usually receives an efferent vessel from the anterior sternal lymph gland.

The **prescapular** or **posterior superficial cervical lymph gland** (Lg. cervicalis superficialis caudalis) is situated at the anterior border of the supraspinatus, four

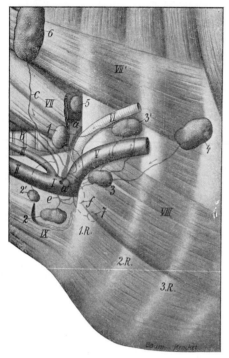

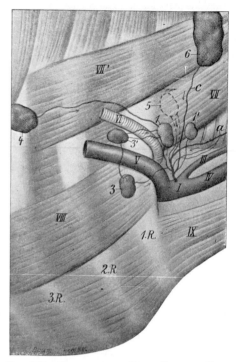

FIG. 603c.—TERMINATION OF THORACIC DUCT OF THE OX AND LEFT TRACHEAL DUCT; LEFT VIEW.

a, Thoracic duct; a', termination of a; b, left tracheal duct; c, efferents from posterior superficial cervical; e, communicating branch from right tracheal ducts; f, efferents from anterior mediastinal; 1, 2, 3, 3', posterior cervical; 4, axillary; 5, costo-cervical; 6, posterior superficial cervical; 7, lymph gland of the thoracic inlet. I, Common jugular; II, left external jugular; III, left internal jugular; V, right external jugular; V, left brachial vein; VI, left brachial artery; VII, VII', scalenus; VIII, rectus thoracis; IX, sternocephalicus; 1.R., 2.R., 3.R. = 1st, 2nd, 3rd ribs. (Baum, D. Lymphgefäss-system des Rindes.)

FIG. 603d.—TERMINATION OF RIGHT TRACHEAL DUCT; RIGHT VIEW.

a, Right tracheal duct; c, efferents from posterior superficial cervical; 1, 1', 3, 3', posterior cervical; 4, axillary; 5, costo-cervical; 6, posterior superficial cervical; I, common jugular; III, right internal jugular; IV, right external jugular; V, right brachial vein; VI, right brachial artery; VII, VII', scalenus; VIII, rectus thoracis; IX, sternocephalicus; 1.R., 2.R., 3.R., = 1st, 2nd, 3rd ribs. (Baum, D. Lymphgefässsystem d. Rindes.)

or five inches (ca. 10–12 cm.) above the level of the shoulder joint; it is covered by the omo-transversarius and brachiocephalicus muscle. It is elongated and is commonly three or four inches (ca. 7–10 cm.) long and an inch or more (ca. 3 cm.) in width. Its deep face has a long and distinct hilus. It receives afferents from the skin of the neck, shoulder, part of the ventral and lateral surfaces of the thorax, and the thoracic limb; from the muscles of the shoulder-girdle, and from the external scapular muscles; from the tendons of the muscles of the forearm and digit and the fascia of the forearm; from the joints of the carpus and digit. The efferent vessel descends over the scalenus muscle and opens on the right side into the end

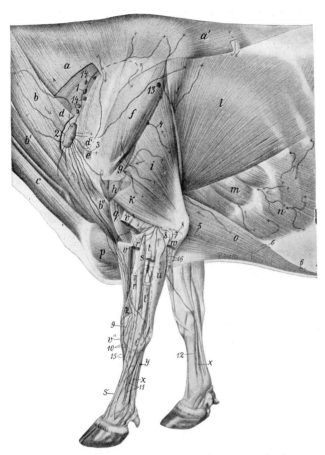

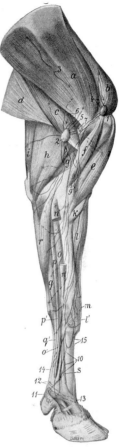

Fig. 603e.—Lymph Vessels of the Thoracic Limb of the Ox; Lateral View. Left Side.

a, a', trapezius; b, b', b'', brachiocephalicus; c, sternocephalicus; d, d', omotransversarius; e, supraspinatus; f, infraspinatus; g, teres minor; h, deltoideus; i, long head of triceps; k, lateral head; l, latissimus dorsi; m, serratus ventralis; n, obliquus abdominis externus; o, deep pectoral; p, superficial pectoral; q, brachialis; r, r, medial digital extensor; s, s', common digital extensor; t, t', t'', lateral digital extensor; u, ulnaris lateralis; v, v', v'', extensor carpi radialis; w, ulnar head of deep digital flexor; x, interosseus medius; y, flexor tendon; z, extensor carpi obliquus; 1, 2, posterior superficial cervical; 3, lymph vessel from the supraspinatus; 4, lymph vessels from long head; 5, lymph vessels from the deep pectoral to posterior cervical; 6, lymph vessels from deep pectoral to sternal glands; 7, lymph vessels from anconeus; 8, 8, lymph vessels from the lateral condyle and olecranon; 9, lymph vessels from the carpus; 10, 11, 12, lymph vessels from the metacarpus and interosseus medius; 13, infraspinatus lymph gland; 14, hæmal nodes; 15, 16, lymph vessels passing around the anterior and posterior borders of the limb. (Baum, D. Lymphgefässsystem d. Rindes.)

Fig. 603f.—Muscles and Lymphatics of the Thoracic Limb of the Ox; Medial View.

a, Subscapularis; b, supraspinatus; c, teres major; d, latissimus dorsi; e, biceps; f, coracobrachialis; g, medial head and h, long head of triceps; i, tensor fascia antibrachii; k, brachialis; l, l', extensor carpi radialis; m, tendon of extensor carpi obliquus; n, n', flexor carpi radialis with section removed; o, o', deep digital flexor; p, q, deep and superficial heads of superficial digital flexor; p', q', superficial digital flexor tendons; r, flexor carpi ulnaris; s, interosseus medius; 1, posterior cervical; 2, axillary; 3, vessel from the subscapularis to an intercostal; 4, 5, vessels from the infraspinatus; 6, vessels accompanying the subscapular blood vessels; 7, vessels from the flexor surface of shoulder joint; 8, vessels from the lateral to the medial side of triceps; 9, vessels from the flexor surface of elbow joint; 10, vessels arising on lateral surface of limb; 11, vessels from between branches of flexor tendons; 12, 13, vessels from the extensor tendons; 14, vessels from the flexor tendons; 15, vessels from lateral surface. (Baum, D. Lymphgefässsystem d. Rindes.)

of the right tracheal duct, on the left into the terminal part of the thoracic duct or the left tracheal duct.

In one case Baum found two efferent vessels on the right side: one opened into the end of the tracheal duct, the other went to a posterior cervical gland.

Two or more small nodes occur along the border of the supraspinatus, dorsal to the prescapular gland, and covered by the trapezius and omo-transversarius. These nodes, termed by Baum lymphoglandulæ cervicales nuchales, are in most cases dark red in color, and most of them are hæmal nodes. But some are lymph glands, since they receive afferent vessels from adjacent muscles and send efferent vessels to the prescapular lymph gland or to another gland of the group.

The **intercostal lymph glands** are situated in the dorsal ends of the intercostal spaces, on the course of the intercostal vessels, and embedded in fat. Most of them

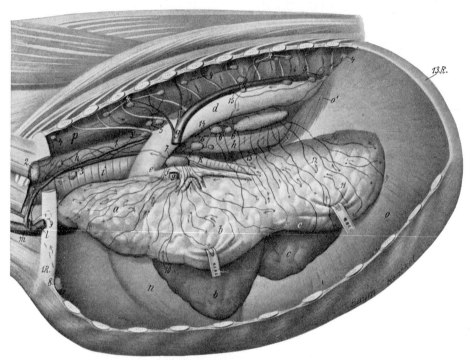

FIG. 603g.—THORAX OF OX, WALL REMOVED, SHOWING LYMPHATICS; LEFT SIDE.

a, Apical lobe; *b, b*, cardiac lobe; *c, c*, diaphragmatic lobe; *d*, aorta; *e*, ductus arteriosus; *f*, left pulmonary artery; *g, g*, vena hemiazygos; *h, h*, esophagus; *i*, trachea; *k*, left bronchus; *l*, brachial vein; *m*, external jugular vein; *n*, pericardium; *o, o'*, diaphragm; *p*, longus colli; *1.R.*, first rib; *13.R.*, thirteenth rib.

Lymph Glands.—1, Thoracic duct; *2*, costocervical; *3, 3'*, anterior mediastinal; *4, 4*, intercostal; *5, 5*, dorsal mediastinal; *6, 6', 6''*, posterior mediastinal; *7*, bronchial; *8*, anterior sternal; *9*, anterior mediastinal; *10*, lymph vessels from the costal surface of lung; *11*, subpleural lymph vessels passing deeply; *12*, deep vessels becoming subpleural; *13*, a vessel passing to the right side; *14*, efferent vessel of posterior mediastinal; *15*, efferent vessels passing to the right. (Baum, D. Lymphgefässsystem des Rindes.)

are small, but some may be nearly an inch (ca. 2 cm.) long. Not all of the spaces contain glands, and quite exceptionally two may occur in one space. Associated with them are hæmal nodes. The afferent vessels come chiefly from the intercostal and spinal muscles, the serrati, latissimus dorsi, trapezius, subscapularis, longus colli, obliquus abdominis externus; from the costal pleura and the peritoneum; from the thoracic vertebræ and the ribs. The efferent vessels go to the mediastinal lymph glands.

The **dorsal mediastinal lymph glands** (Lgg. mediastinales dorsales) are situated on each side of the thoracic aorta, in the fat which levels up the space between that vessel and the bodies of the vertebræ. On the right side they lie chiefly dorsal to the thoracic duct, and on the left side they are related to the vena hemiazygos. They are irregular in arrangement and their length varies from about half an inch to an inch and a half (ca. 1–3.5 cm.). They are in series with the anterior mediastinal glands.

Their afferent vessels come from the same parts as those of the intercostal glands; also from the diaphragm, the mediastinum, the pericardium, the ribs, and the intercostal lymph glands. The efferent vessels go chiefly to the thoracic duct or join the common efferent duct of the posterior mediastinal glands.

The **ventral mediastinal lymph glands** (Lgg. mediastinales ventrales) are situated on the transversus thoracis muscle. Several (2–5) occur constantly in the fat about the apex of the pericardium; they vary in length from about half an inch to an inch or more (ca. 1–3 cm.). In some cases other glands are present further forward. The afferent vessels come from the costal and mediastinal pleura, the diaphragm, the pericardium, and the ribs. The efferent vessels usually unite to form a trunk which goes to the anterior sternal lymph gland. Hæmal nodes may be present in this region.

The **anterior mediastinal lymph glands** (Lgg. mediastinales craniales) are situated in part at the thoracic inlet, in part along the œsophagus, trachea, anterior vena cava, and brachiocephalic trunk. The former group comprises two to four glands on either side, ventral to the trachea and œsophagus. Usually the largest of these, which may be an inch or more (ca. 2–3 cm.) in length, lies along the origin of the internal thoracic artery. The second group differs somewhat on the two sides. On the right side there is usually a large gland, which may be two or three inches (ca. 5–7 cm.) in length; it lies on the œsophagus and is crossed laterally by the dorsal vein. Behind this there are commonly two or three glands on the œsophagus or the longus colli, and in front two or three are placed similarly and on the trachea. On the left side a variable number (2–7) are situated on the œsophagus, trachea, brachiocephalic trunk, and anterior vena cava; glands may be between the vessels, or between the vessels and the trachea, and escape superficial examination. Hæmal nodes are often present in the vicinity of these glands. The afferent vessels come from the thoracic part of the œsophagus, trachea, and thymus; from the lungs, pericardium, heart, costal and mediastinal pleura; from the intercostal glands of the first four spaces and from the gland on the apical bronchus. In some cases these glands receive also efferent vessels from the anterior sternal, left bronchial, and other mediastinal glands. The efferent vessels for the most part go the thoracic duct, the right tracheal duct, and the costo-cervical glands.

The **posterior mediastinal lymph glands** (Lgg. mediastinales caudales) are situated along the œsophagus, from the aortic arch backward. The largest of these may be eight inches (ca. 20 cm.) or more in length; its anterior part is dorsal to the œsophagus, while posteriorly it lies in the angle between the aorta and the diaphragm (Fig. 389). But in some subjects there are two glands in place of this large one; in these cases the additional posterior one is usually the smaller. Several other glands of smaller size lie in front of the large one, in the angle between the aorta and the œsophagus. In front of these there are usually two or three on the right side on the aorta and the œsophagus.[1] The afferent vessels come from the œsophagus, the lungs, the pericardium, the mediastinum, the diaphragm, the peritoneum, the liver, and the spleen. The efferent vessels unite to form a common trunk which joins the thoracic duct.

The **diaphragmatic lymph glands** (Lgg. diaphragmaticæ) are small nodes which may be present at the foramen venæ cavæ and the termination of the phrenic nerves. The one most often present is at the acute angle between the vena cava and the diaphragm. The afferent vessels come from the diaphragm and mediastinum. The efferent vessels go to the posterior mediastinal glands.

[1] These are termed by Baum the middle mediastinal lymph glands.

The **bronchial lymph glands** (Lgg. bronchiales) are commonly three or four in number. The **left bronchial gland** (Lg. bifurcationis sinistra) lies in the angle between the aortic arch and the left division of the pulmonary artery (Fig. 389); it is crossed laterally by the vena hemiazygos. This gland is about an inch to an inch and a half (ca. 2.5–3.5 cm.) in length and an inch (ca. 2.5 cm) in width; it is often very irregular in shape. A **right bronchial gland** (Lg. bifurcationis dextra) is similarly situated on the right side in the majority of cases. It is smaller than the left gland and appears to be absent in about 25 per cent. of subjects; in some cases, on the other hand, two glands occur here. In about half of the cases a small **middle** or **dorsal bronchial gland** (Lg. bifurcationis dorsalis) is situated above the bifurcation of

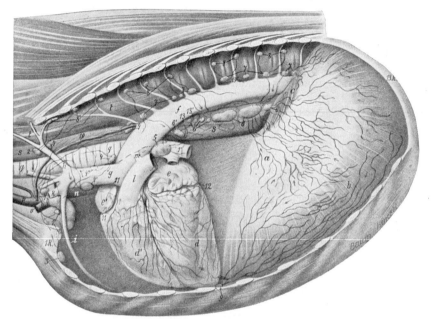

Fig. 603h.—Thorax of Ox, Showing Lymph Vessels of the Heart and Diaphragm; Left Side.

a, Tendinous center; b, costal part, and c, lumbar part of diaphragm; d, d', left and right ventricles, e, e', left and right auricles; f, aorta; g, brachiocephalic trunk; h, costocervical artery; i, internal thoracic artery; k, brachial artery; l, pulmonary artery; m, ligamentum arteriosum; n, anterior vena cava; o, brachial vein; p, external jugular vein; q, q', trachea; r, left bronchus; s, s, esophagus; t, t, longus colli; 1.R., first rib; 13.R., thirteenth rib.

Lymph Glands.—1, 1', Anterior mediastinal; 2, costocervical; 3, anterior sternal; 4, 4, 4', 4'', anterior mediastinal; 5, bronchial; 6, 6, 6', posterior mediastinal; 7, 7, 7, dorsal mediastinal; 8, 8, 8', intercostal; 9, ventral mediastinal; 10, thoracic duct; 11, 11, vessels from right coronary groove; 12, vessels from the right; 13, 13', 13'', vessels passing to the right. (Baum, Lymphgefässsystem des Rindes.)

the trachea. The **apical gland** (Lg. eparterialis) occurs at the origin of the bronchus of the apical lobe of the lung. Exceptionally a second small gland is present here. The afferent vessels of these glands come chiefly from the lungs and the pulmonary lymph glands, the thoracic part of the œsophagus, and the heart.[1] The efferent vessels of the left gland are quite variable. They may join the common efferent of the posterior mediastinal glands. Those of the right gland go to a middle mediastinal gland, those of the dorsal gland go to the right gland, and those of the apical gland go to anterior mediastinal glands.

The **pulmonary lymph glands** (Lgg. pulmonales) are inconstant and variable nodes which may be found on the chief bronchi in the lungs. They appear to be absent in one-third to one-half of the cases on one side or both. They vary in size

[1] Baum notes the curious fact that in many cases in which he injected the lymph vessels of the diaphragmatic lobes the vessels went around the dorsal gland without entering it.

from a fifth to half an inch or more (ca. 0.5–1.5 cm.) in length. The afferent vessels come from the lungs, and the efferent vessels go to the bronchial and posterior mediastinal glands.

It is worthy of note that in some cases lymph vessels of the left lung go to glands on the right (middle mediastinal glands), and lymph vessels of the right lung go to the left bronchial gland.

The **pericardiac lymph glands** (Lgg. pericardiacæ) are small and variable nodes which lie on the pericardium. The left gland is usually present and is situated at the space between the aortic arch and the vena hemiazygos. In some cases it may be unusually large—nearly three inches (ca. 7 cm.) in length—and extend back to

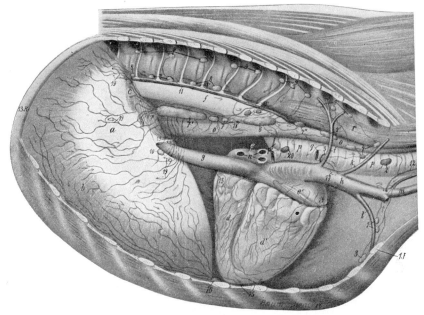

Fig. 603*i*.—Thorax of Ox, Showing Lymph Vessels of Heart and Diaphragm; Right Side. Arrows Show Direction of Lymph Flow.

a, Tendinous part; *b*, costal part; *c*, lumbar part of diaphragm; *d*, *d'*, left and right ventricles; *e*, *e'*, left and right auricles; *f*, aorta; *g*, posterior vena cava; *h*, anterior vena cava; *i*, vena azygos; *k*, costocervical vein; *l*, internal thoracic vein; *m*, external jugular; *n*, pulmonary veins; *o*, *o'*, œsophagus; *p*, *p*, trachea; *p'*, bronchi; *q*, apical bronchus; *r*, longus colli muscle; *1.R.*, first rib; *13.R.*, thirteenth rib.

Lymph Glands.—*1*, Anterior cervical; *2*, costocervical; *3*, anterior sternal; *4*, *4'*, *4''*, anterior mediastinal; *5*, bronchial; *6*, middle mediastinal; *7*, *7'*, posterior mediastinal; *8*, *8'*, dorsal mediastinal; *9*, *9'*, intercostal; *10*, diaphragmatic; *11*, thoracic duct; *12*, right tracheal duct; *13*, lymph vessel to the left coronary groove; *14*, lymph vessels passing to the left; *15*, lymph vessels passing to the left longitudinal groove; *16*, ventral mediastinal; *17*, anterior mediastinal; *18*, *18'*, lymph vessels coming from the left side; *19*, lymph vessels coming through the diaphragm from the liver; *20*, bronchial. (Baum, Lymphgefässsystem des Rindes.)

the left bronchial gland. Other small glands may be found in this vicinity or lower down. The right gland is only exceptionally present. It is situated just ventral to the termination of the posterior vena cava. The afferent vessels come from the pericardium, and the efferents go to the dorsal mediastinal glands (or their efferents) or to the left bronchial gland on the left side, to the apical bronchial gland or an anterior mediastinal gland on the right side.

The **sternal lymph glands** (Lgg. sternales) are situated along the course of the internal thoracic vessels. The largest, distinguished as the **anterior sternal gland** (Lg. sternalis cranialis), is embedded in the fat in front of the transversus thoracis. It is about half an inch to an inch (ca. 1.5–2.5 cm.) in length. The other glands are covered by the transversus thoracis, and vary in size, number, and arrangement.

There is not one at every interchondral space, and, on the other hand, two may occur at one space. The last of the series is often situated in the angle between the eighth and ninth costal cartilages and the sternum and may escape notice; it is constant. The afferent vessels come from the diaphragm, the intercostal, deep pectoral, serratus ventralis, rectus thoracis, and abdominal muscles; the costal and mediastinal pleura, the pericardium, the peritoneum; the liver; the ribs, costal cartilages, and sternum; the ventral mediastinal glands. The efferent vessels usually concur in forming one or two trunks which run forward along the internal thoracic vessels to the anterior gland. From the latter one or two efferents go to the anterior mediastinal glands or directly to the end of the right tracheal duct or the thoracic duct (on the left side).

The **axillary lymph gland** lies on the medial face of the distal part of the teres major on the course of the vein from the latissimus dorsi. It is oval in outline and is usually a little more than an inch (ca. 3 cm.) in length. Quite exceptionally two glands may be present. The afferent vessels come from most of the muscles of the shoulder and arm, the muscles of the forearm, the trapezius, latissimus dorsi, pectoralis profundus, and cutaneus; the fascia of the forearm; the shoulder, elbow, and carpal joints; the scapula, humerus, radius, ulna, and carpus; the infraspinatus gland. The efferent vessels (one to three) go to the posterior cervical glands.

The **infraspinatus lymph gland** (Lg. infraspinata) is a small node which is present in somewhat less than a fourth of the cases (Baum). It is situated at or near the posterior border of the infraspinatus, about on a level with the proximal end of the caput longum. It receives lymph vessels from the latissimus dorsi and sends an efferent vessel to the axillary gland.

The **rhomboid lymph gland** (Lg. rhomboidea) is small and only present in about 15 per cent. of subjects (Baum). It is situated under the rhomboideus cervicalis near its ventral border and the cervical angle of the scapula. It receives afferents from the rhomboideus, supra-spinatus, and serratus ventralis, and sends efferents to the costocervical gland.

The **lumbar lymph glands** (Lgg. lumbales) are situated along the abdominal aorta and the posterior vena cava, and in some of the spaces between the transverse processes.[1] Some of the glands are dorsal to the vessels. Hæmal nodes also occur in this region. The afferent vessels come from the spinal, sublumbar, abdominal, and serratus dorsalis muscles; the lumbo-dorsal fascia; the kidneys, adrenals, and the peritoneum; the lumbar vertebræ. The efferent vessels go to the lumbar trunk and the cisterna chyli.

The **renal lymph glands** (Lgg. renales) belong in reality to the preceding group, from which they are only conventionally distinguished. They are situated on the course of the renal vessels and vary in size and number. Their afferent vessels come from the kidneys and adrenals, and the efferent vessels go mainly to the cisterna chyli.

The **cœliac lymph glands** (Lgg. cœliacæ), two to five in number, are situated on and near the cœliac and anterior mesenteric arteries, and in relation to the left extremity of the pancreas, the dorsal curvature of the rumen, and the posterior vena cava. One is a large gland which lies on the cœliac artery and the origin of the chief branches of that vessel (Fig. 389). It is usually heart-shaped, marked by a deep notch, and is about two inches (ca. 5–6 cm.) long and an inch and a half (ca. 3–4 cm.) wide. The afferent vessels come from the spleen. The efferent vessels go to the common efferent vessel of the gastric lymph glands, or to the intestinal trunk, or to the cisterna chyli.

The **internal iliac lymph glands** are situated in relation to the terminal branches of the aorta and the radicles of the posterior vena cava. They number commonly six to eight and vary in length from half an inch to two inches (ca. 1–5 cm.). Their

---

[1] Baum distinguishes those about the vessels as lgg. lumbales aorticæ, and terms those in the intertransverse spaces lgg. lumbales propriæ, and regards them as corresponding to the dorsal mediastinal and intercostal glands respectively.

afferent vessels come chiefly from muscles of the sublumbar region, pelvis, tail, and thigh; from the genital organs; from the kidneys, bladder, and urethra. They also receive vessels which are efferents of the external iliac, sacral, ischiatic, deep inguinal, prefemoral, and coxal glands. Their efferent vessels go chiefly to the lumbar trunk.

The **deep inguinal lymph gland**[1] (Lg. inguinalis profunda) is situated ventral to the psoas minor, at the angle of divergence of the circumflex iliac from the external iliac artery. It is discoid and is commonly two to three inches (ca. 5–7.5 cm.) in length. A smaller gland may be present near the large one or at the origin of the prepubic artery. The afferent vessels come chiefly from the abdominal muscles; the pelvic limb; the urinary organs, the vesiculæ seminales, tunica vaginalis, cremaster muscle; and the superficial inguinal, external iliac, sacral, prefemoral, and popliteal glands. The efferent vessels go in part to the internal iliac glands, in part directly to the lumbar trunk.

The **external iliac lymph glands** (Lgg. iliacæ laterales) number one or two on each side, and are situated at the bifurcation of the circumflex iliac artery. In the majority of cases a single gland is found just in front of the origin of the anterior branch of the artery, but another may lie in the angle between the two branches. The more constant one is half an inch to an inch (ca. 1.25–2.5 cm.) in diameter. They may be absent on one side or (quite exceptionally) on both sides. The afferent vessels come from the abdominal muscles, the gluteus profundus, the tensor fasciæ latæ, the fascia lata; the peritoneum of the adjacent region; the pelvic bones. They also receive vessels from the prefemoral and coxal glands. The efferent vessels go in part to the lumbar trunk, in part to the internal iliac or deep inguinal glands.

The **epigastric lymph gland** (Lg. epigastrica) is small and inconstant. It is situated on the course of the posterior abdominal artery near the pubis. It receives afferent vessels from the adjacent part of the peritoneum and abdominal muscles, and sends an efferent vessel to the deep inguinal gland.

The **paralumbar lymph glands** (Lgg. paralumbales) are small and inconstant nodes, variable in number, which may be found under the skin of the upper part of the flank. Their afferent vessels come from the adjacent skin, and the efferents go in part to the prefemoral gland, in part to the deep inguinal gland. Hæmal nodes occur in this region.

The **superficial inguinal lymph glands** (Lgg. inguinales superficiales) differ in the two sexes. (1) In the bull they are situated below the prepubic tendon and in the narrow interfemoral space. They lie in the mass of fat about the neck of the scrotum and behind the spermatic cord, and are covered (in part) by the retractor of the prepuce. It is usual to find one or two on each side of the penis, but in exceptional cases one or two more may be present. A central one above the penis has been observed, and there may be one further back. The afferent vessels come from the external genital organs (except the testicles); also from the skin of the adjacent region, the medial and posterior surface of the thigh, and the medial surface of the leg. The efferent vessels ascend through the inguinal canal to the deep inguinal gland at the side of the pelvic inlet. (2) In the cow they are usually termed the **supramammary lymph glands** (Lgg. supramammaricæ), since they are situated above the posterior border of the base of the mammary glands.[2] Usually two are present on either side. The larger pair are close together dorsally and are sometimes united. The smaller glands are dorso-medial to or in front of the large ones. Exceptionally a third gland may be present or there may be only one on one

[1] This gland, designated by Chauveau-Lesbre as external iliac, is here named in accordance with the observations of Baum, who found that it derives its afferent vessels from substantially the same region as the deep inguinal glands of the horse.

[2] When enlarged, they can easily be felt, and when much enlarged, may produce a prominence.

side. The large glands are flattened and reniform in outline; they average about three inches (ca. 7–8 cm.) in height, and a little less in sagittal diameter. The hilus is anterior and is related to the mammary vessels. The smaller gland is rounded and thick, and is a fourth to half the size of the large one. The afferent vessels come from the udder, the external genital organs, and part of the skin of the thigh and leg. The efferent vessels converge to two or three large trunks which go to the deep inguinal glands at the side of the pelvic inlet.

The efferent vessels run forward on the base of the udder, then incline outward and pass through the aponeuroses of the oblique abdominal muscles at the lateral edge of the rectus abdominis, a handbreadth or more in front of the pubis. On reaching the femoral ring they follow the course of the external iliac vessels to the deep inguinal gland. When the **deep femoral gland** on the upper part of the quadriceps femoris is present on the course of the deep femoral artery, some efferents go to it. Efferents of one side may go to a supramammary or deep inguinal gland of the opposite side.

The **sacral lymph glands** (Lgg. sacrales) may be subdivided into two groups.[1]

(1) The **medial sacral lymph glands** (Lgg. sacrales mediales) are quite inconstant. When present, there is a gland on either side on the deep surface of the sacro-sciatic ligament, in the fat between the ligament and the rectum or the retractor ani. Its afferent vessels come from the pelvic urethra and urethral muscle, the root of the penis and its muscles, the prostate, the vagina and urethra, and the coccygeal muscles. The efferent vessels usually go to the internal iliac glands.

(2) The **lateral sacral lymph glands** (Lgg. sacrales laterales) comprise one or two inconstant nodes on the upper part of the outer surface of the sacro-sciatic ligament. One occurs in the majority of cases at the greater sciatic foramen; the other, which is further back, under the origin of the biceps femoris, is absent on one side or both in more than half the cases. Their afferent vessels come from the gluteus profundus, the lumbo-dorsal fascia, the pelvic bones, and the hip joint. The efferent vessels go to the internal iliac and deep inguinal glands.

The **ischiatic lymph glands** (Lgg. ischiadicæ) are one or two in number. The one which appears to be constant lies on the sacro-sciatic ligament, about an inch (ca. 2–3 cm.) above the lesser sciatic notch, and under cover of the biceps femoris. It is discoid and is an inch or more (ca. 2.5–3.5 cm) in diameter. A second gland occurs in the majority of cases at the medial side of the tuber ischii and the attachment of the sacro-sciatic ligament, covered only by the skin and subcutaneous fat.[2] The afferent vessels come from the rectum and anus; the vulva, the root of the penis, the prostate, the bulbo-urethral glands, the urethra and urethral muscle; the glutei, biceps femoris, semitendinosus, obturator internus, and gemellus, and the lumbodorsal fascia; the skin of the hip and tail; the hip joint. They also receive efferent vessels of the popliteal gland. The efferent vessels go to the internal iliac glands.

The **gastric lymph glands** (Lgg. gastricæ) are numerous, as might be expected, and are difficult to group satisfactorily. They comprise the following:

(1) The **atrial lymph glands** (Lgg. atriales) lie chiefly on the visceral surface of the atrium, just behind the cardia; commonly three or four are present. Their afferent vessels come from the atrium, from the adjacent part of the rumen and reticulum, and from the spleen. They receive efferent vessels of the right and anterior ruminal, reticular, omasal, and dorsal abomasal glands. Their efferent vessels commonly converge to a large trunk, the **common efferent vessel** (Vas efferens commune) of the gastric lymph glands. This runs upward and backward in relation to the cœliac artery and reaches the ventral face of the posterior vena

---

[1] Baum distinguishes three groups of sacral glands and terms the glands about the termination of the aorta and the origin of the vena cava as the lgg. sacrales hypogastricæ. These have been included in the internal iliac group of this description.

[2] This gland is termed by Baum the lg. tuberosa.

cava; here it unites with the common efferent vessels of the mesenteric glands to form the intestinal trunk.[1]

(2) The **right ruminal lymph glands** (Lgg. ruminales dextræ) (Fig. 603*j*) lie along the course of the right ruminal artery. Commonly four or five are present, and they are half an inch to an inch and a half (ca. 1–3.5 cm.) long. Their afferent vessels come chiefly from the rumen. They also receive efferent vessels of the other ruminal glands. The efferent vessels go from the anterior part of the series to the reticular glands and the common gastric efferent.

(3) The **left ruminal lymph glands** (Lgg. ruminales sinistræ) are inconstant. One or two may be present in the left groove of the rumen. Their afferent vessels

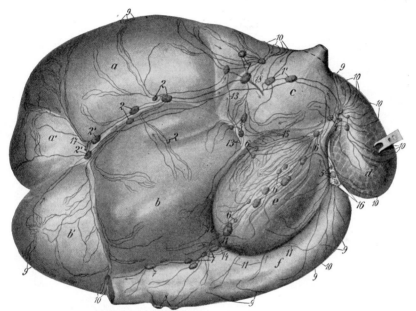

Fig. 603*j*.—Lymphatics of the Stomach of the Ox; Right View.

a, Dorsal sac of the rumen; *a'*, posterior dorsal blind sac; *b*, ventral sac; *b'*, posterior ventral blind sac; *c*, atrium ventriculi; *d*, reticulum; *e*, omasum; *f*, abomasum.

Lymph Glands.—*1, 1'*, Atrial; *2, 2'*, right ruminal; *3*, accessory right ruminal; *4*, reticular; *5*, reticulo-abomasal; *6*, omasal; *7*, dorsal abomasal; *8*, ventral abomasal; *9, 9*, vessels passing from right to left; *10, 10*, vessels passing from left to right; *11, 11*, vessels to the reticulo-abomasal; *12*, vessels to the anterior ruminal; *13*, efferent vessels to the anterior left ruminal; *14*, efferent vessels to the rumino-abomasal; *15*, vessels from the omasum to the reticulo-abomasal; *16*, efferent vessels to the rumino-abomasal; *17*, vessels from the left side; *18*, common efferent vessel from the gastric lymph glands. (Baum, D. Lymphgefässsystem d. Rindes.)

come from the rumen, and the efferent vessels go to the anterior or the right ruminal glands.

(4) The **anterior ruminal glands** (Lgg. ruminales craniales) are deeply situated in the anterior groove of the rumen. They average four or five in number and about half an inch (ca. 1.5 cm.) in length. They receive lymph vessels from the rumen and from the left ruminal glands, and their efferent vessels go to the right ruminal and atrial glands.

(5) The **reticular lymph glands** (Lgg. reticulares) are situated on the reticulum above and below its junction with the omasum. They receive afferent vessels chiefly from the reticulum and the adjacent parts of the omasum and abomasum. Their efferent vessels go chiefly to the atrial lymph glands.

(6) The **omasal lymph glands** (Lgg. omasicæ) lie on the omasum chiefly along

[1] Many variations occur in the arrangement of the efferent vessels. An efferent may go to a cœliac or mesenteric gland or to the intestinal trunk or cisterna chyli directly.

the course of the dorsal omasal vessels. Their afferent vessels come from the omasum, and the efferent vessels go chiefly to the atrial lymph glands.

(7) The **dorsal abomasal lymph glands** (Lgg. abomasicæ dorsales) form a series along the lesser curvature of the abomasum. They receive afferent vessels from the abomasum, duodenum, and ventral part of the omasum. The efferent vessels go chiefly in the lesser omentum to the hepatic lymph glands, but some from the anterior part of the series go to the omasal and reticular glands.

(8) The **ventral abomasal lymph glands** (Lgg. abomasicæ ventrales) comprise a few nodes in the fat along the greater curvature of the pyloric part of the abomasum or in the omentum an inch or two distant from the abomasum.[1] They

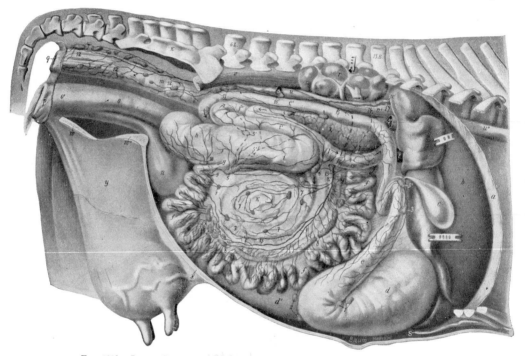

Fig. 603k.—Lymph Glands and Vessels in the Intestines of the Ox, Right View.

a, The diaphragm; b, liver; c, gall-bladder; d, abomasum; d', ventral sac of the rumen; e, e', the duodenum; f, f, f, jejunum; g, ileum; h, cæcum; i, i', i'', first portion of the colon; k, coils of the colon; k', termination of colon coils, l, first part of terminal loop of colon; m, rectum; n, bladder; o, vagina; o', vestibule of vagina; p, vulva; q, anus; r; right kidney; s, s', posterior vena cava; t, portal vein; u, u', u'', aorta; v, psoas; v', right crus of diaphragm; w, w', floor of pelvis; x, ventral abdominal wall; y, udder; z, pancreas; 13.B., thirteenth thoracic vertebra; 6.L., sixth lumbar vertebra; K, sacrum; S, xiphoid cartilage.

Lymph Glands.—1, Dorsal abomasal; 2, ventral abomasal; 3, 3', hepaticæ; 4, 4, 4, pancreatico-intestinal; 5, 5', 5,' 6, 6, 7, 7, 7, 7, 7, colic; 8, 8, 8, 8, 8, jejunal; 9, ileal; 10, cæcal; 11, internal iliac; 12, 12, 12, rectal; 13, 13, common efferents of the intestinal glands; 13', accessory to 13; 14, common efferent of gastric glands; 15, intestinal trunk; 16, lumbar trunk; 17, cisterna chyli. (Baum, D. Lymphgefässsystem d. Rindes.)

receive afferent vessels from the abomasum and the duodenum and their efferent vessels go to the hepatic lymph glands.

The **mesenteric lymph glands** (Lgg. mesentericæ) comprise a large number of nodes which receive lymph from the intestine. The following groups may be recognized, although the distinction is in part conventional.

(1) The **duodenal lymph glands** (Lgg. duodenales) are small nodes in the anterior part of the mesoduodenum. They receive afferent vessels from the duodenum and their efferent vessels go to the hepatic lymph glands.

(2) The **jejuno-ileal lymph glands** (Lgg. jejuno-ileales) lie in the part of the

---

[1] These glands are often difficult to find in the large mass of fat in which they are usually embedded; they are not always present.

mesentery to which the coils of the jejuno-ileum are attached. They vary in number from ten to fifty, and in length from about a quarter of an inch to four feet (ca. 0.5–120 cm.). As a rule, the long narrow glands are in the peripheral part of the mesentery, while numerous small nodes are scattered throughout the mesentery and extend centrally to the coils of the colon. Their afferent vessels come from the mesenteric part of the small intestine. The efferent vessels converge to form a large **common efferent vessel.** This receives efferent vessels of the cæcal and colic lymph glands, runs upward and forward on the right side of the spiral mass of the colon, and reaches the ventral face of the posterior vena cava just behind the anterior mesenteric artery; here it unites with the common efferent vessel of the gastric lymph glands to form the intestinal trunk.

(3) The **cæcal lymph glands** (Lgg. cæcales), usually not more than two or three in number, are situated along the attached surface of the cæcum. Their afferent

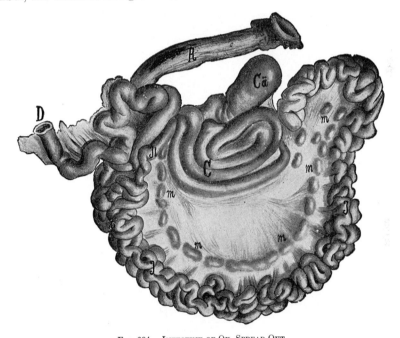

FIG. 604.—INTESTINE OF OX, SPREAD OUT.

Ca, Cæcum; C, colon; D, duodenum; Il, ileum; J, jejunum; R, rectum; m, mesenteric lymph glands. (After Edelmann.)

vessels come from the cæcum and ileum. The efferent vessels go to colic or ileal glands or to the common efferent vessel.

(4) The **colic lymph glands** (Lgg. colicæ) are situated in part superficially on the right side of the spiral mass of the colon, in part deeply between the coils. One or two are constantly present on the initial part of the colon, near the termination of the ileum. The afferent vessels come from the colon chiefly, but some of the glands receive vessels from the ileum and cæcum and their lymph glands. The efferent vessels go to the common intestinal efferent or to other colic glands.

(5) The **rectal lymph glands** (Lgg. rectales) are situated along the dorsal and lateral surfaces of the rectum. They receive afferent vessels from the rectum, anus, and terminal part of the colon. Most of the efferent vessels go to other glands of the group, but some unite to form one or two large trunks which end in the internal iliac lymph glands. There are many small hæmal nodes in relation to the rectal lymph glands.

(6) The **pancreatico-intestinal lymph glands** (Lgg. pancreatico-intestinales) lie on the ventral surface of the pancreas and along the right part of the latter in

relation to the duodenum. Some are at the pancreatic notch about the portal vein and its affluents, and others are covered by the adhesion of the colon to the gland. Their afferent vessels come from the pancreas, the duodenum, and the adjacent part of the colon. The efferent vessels go to the common intestinal efferent.

(7) The **hepatic lymph glands** (Lgg. hepaticæ) are situated in and ventral to the portal fissure. Most of them are grouped about the portal vein, the hepatic artery, and the bile duct, and are covered by the pancreas; but some are ventral

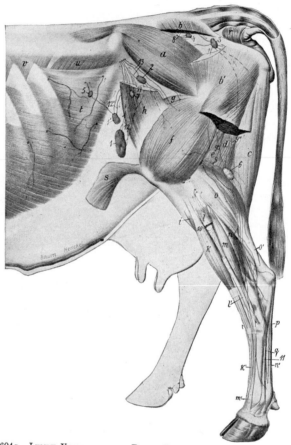

FIG. 604a.—LYMPH VESSELS OF THE PELVIC LIMB OF THE OX; LATERAL VIEW.

a, Gluteus medius; *b*, *b'*, biceps femoris; *c*, semitendinosus; *d*, semimembranosus; *e*, adductor; *f*, vastus lateralis; *g*, rectus femoris; *h*, tensor fasciæ latæ; *i*, tibialis anterior; *k*, peroneus tertius and common digital extensor; *k'*, tendon of the common digital extensor; *l*, *l'*, peroneus longus and tendon; *m*, *m'*, extensor digiti quarti and tendon; *n*, *n'*, deep digital flexor and tendon; *o*, *o'*, lateral head of gastrocnemius and tendon; *p*, superficial digital flexor; *q*, interosseus medius; *r*, coccygeus; *s*, cutaneous muscle in the fold of the flank; *t*, obliquus abdominis externus; *u*, obliquus abdominis internus; *v*, serratus dorsalis posterior.

Lymph Glands.—*1*, *1'*, Prefemoral; *2*, coxal; *3*, ischiatic; *4*, lateral sacral; *5*, paralumbar; *6*, popliteal; *7*, coxal; *8*, lymph vessels rising in the biceps femoris; *9*, *9'*, *9''*, efferents from popliteal; *10*, lymph vessels from tibialis anterior; *11*, lymph vessels from the medial side; *12*, *12'*, efferent vessels from prefemorals; *13*, efferent vessels from coxal; *14*, lymph vessels from the tensor fasciæ latæ. (Baum, Lymphgefässsystem des Rindes.)

to the pancreas. Their average number is ten to fifteen, but twenty or more have been counted. Their length varies from less than half an inch to three inches (ca. 1–7 cm.). They receive vessels from the liver, pancreas, and duodenum, and from the abomasal lymph glands. Their efferent vessels converge to a large trunk which passes along the portal vein and joins the common efferent vessel of the intestinal glands or that of the gastric glands.

The **prefemoral lymph gland** is situated on the aponeurosis of the obliquus abdominis externus, in contact with or close to the tensor fasciæ latæ and five or six inches (ca. 12–15 cm.) above the patella. It has an elongated elliptical outline and is flattened. Its average length is three or four inches (ca. 8–10 cm.), and its width about an inch (ca. 2.5 cm.) in the adult, but it may be considerably larger. In some cases a second small gland is present above or below the large one. It receives afferent vessels from the skin of the posterior part of the thorax, the abdomen, pelvis, thigh, and leg; also from the tensor fasciæ latæ and the prepuce. The efferent vessels ascend on the deep face of the tensor fasciæ latæ and end chiefly in the deep inguinal gland, but in some cases some go to the iliac glands.

One or two hæmal nodes are commonly found in relation to these glands.

The **popliteal lymph gland** (Lg. poplitea) is situated in a mass of fat on the gastrocnemius muscle, behind the tibial and peroneal nerves and between the biceps femoris and semitendinosus. Its average length is about an inch and a half (ca. 3–4 cm.) and its width about an inch (ca. 2–3 cm.). The gland receives afferent vessels from the lateral and posterior part of the leg and from the distal part of the limb; vessels from the biceps femoris and semitendinosus also go to it. The efferent vessels go chiefly to the deep inguinal gland, but some end in the ischiatic or internal iliac glands.

The **coxal lymph gland** (Lg. coxalis) is situated in front of the proximal part of the quadriceps femoris, under cover of the tensor fasciæ latæ. It is present in the majority of subjects on one side or both and may be an inch or more (ca. 2.5–3 cm.) in length. It receives vessels from the quadriceps femoris, tensor fasciæ latæ, fascia lata, and the prefemoral gland. The efferent vessels go to the iliac or the deep inguinal glands.

One or two lymph glands are commonly present on the superficial face of the tensor fasciæ latæ, an inch or two from the anterior border of the muscle and five or six inches from the tuber coxæ. They are often partially embedded in the muscle, and are usually small, but may be almost an inch (ca. 2 cm.) long. Hæmal nodes may be found here and in some cases appear to take the place of the lymph glands. The afferent vessels come from the skin of the hip and the efferent vessels go to the prefemoral or deep inguinal gland.

The **lymph glands of the sheep** resemble in general those of the ox, but a few special features may be noted. Hæmal nodes are numerous, especially along the course of the aorta; they are dark red or black and hence are easily seen, in spite of their small size, in the fat in which they are chiefly embedded.

The **mandibular lymph glands,** usually two on each side, are situated behind the angle of the jaw on the course of the external maxillary vein. The larger one is flattened and kidney-shaped and may be nearly an inch (ca. 2 cm.) long.

The **parotid lymph gland** lies on the posterior border of the masseter muscle, about midway between the mandibular joint and the angle of the jaw. It is related to and commonly partly covered by the anterior border of the parotid salivary gland. It is flattened and has a deep notch posteriorly. It is usually a little less than an inch (ca. 2 cm.) long.

The **suprapharyngeal lymph glands,** two in number, have an elongated oval outline. They are situated on the dorsal wall of the pharynx, a quarter of an inch or less (ca. 0.5 cm.) apart. They are related laterally to the dorsal end of the great cornu of the hyoid bone, and dorsally to the ventral straight muscles of the head. They are about an inch (ca. 2–3 cm.) long, and half as wide.

The **atlantal lymph gland** is related to the ventral part of the paramastoid process and is dorsal to the carotid artery. It is discoid, oval in outline, and about half an inch (ca. 1.5 cm.) long. Commonly there is a small node behind the atlantal gland and one or more hæmal nodes occur here.

The **sternal lymph gland**, which overlies the first segment of the sternum, is about the size of a hazel nut.

The **mesenteric lymph glands** consist chiefly of long narrow elongated masses instead of isolated small nodes.

The **prefemoral lymph gland** is in front of the anterior border of the tensor fasciæ latæ, about midway between the tuber coxæ and the patella. It is kidney-shaped and is a little more than an inch (ca. 3 cm.) long and nearly an inch (ca. 2 cm.) wide.

The **superficial inguinal** or **mammary lymph glands** are usually two in number on each side. The larger one is kidney-shaped; it may be an inch and a half (ca. 3.5 cm.) long and about half as wide. The smaller gland is oval and usually about half an inch (ca. 1 cm.) in length.

CIRCULATORY SYSTEM OF THE PIG

THE HEART

The **pericardium** is attached to the sternum from a point opposite to the third rib as far as the xiphoid cartilage, and also to the sternal part of the diaphragm.

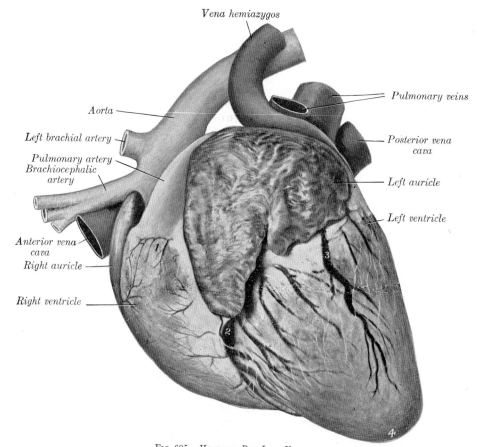

Fig. 605.—Heart of Pig; Left View.

1, Conus arteriosus; *2*, great cardiac vein in left longitudinal groove; *3*, cardiac vein in intermediate groove; *4*, apex.

It has extensive contact with the chest wall from the second intercostal space to the fifth rib.

The **heart** is small in proportion to the body-weight, especially in fat animals. Its weight in a large adult is usually less than a pound. It is broad, short, and blunt. When hardened *in situ* it is compressed dorso-ventrally. The ventral or sterno-costal surface (Facies sternocostalis) is only moderately convex; it overlies the sternum from the second sternebra to the anterior part of the last one. The left longitudinal groove is on its left part, and is almost parallel with the left border. The dorsal or diaphragmatic surface is more convex. The right longitudinal groove runs obliquely across this surface; it begins below the end of the posterior vena cava and extends to the left border. There is often an intermediate groove on the left border; it may extend to the apex, but it is frequently small and is sometimes

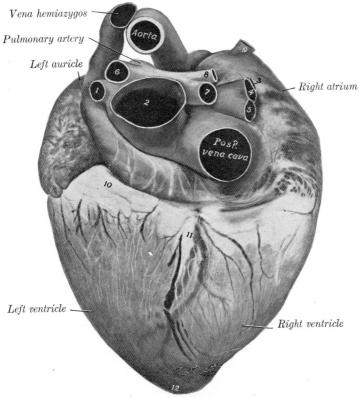

FIG. 606.—HEART OF PIG, DIAPHRAGMATIC SURFACE.

1–5, Pulmonary veins; *6*, left pulmonary artery; *7, 8*, branches of right pulmonary artery; *9*, vena azygos; *10*, fat in coronary groove; *11*, vessels and fat in right longitudinal groove; *12*, apex.

absent. The apex is blunt and is almost median; it overlies the anterior part of the last sternebra, and is about a quarter of an inch (ca. 5–6 mm.) from the sternal part of the diaphragm. When the ventricles are dilated, there is a notch at the apex (Incisura apicis cordis). The lower border of the left auricle is marked by several notches and is situated at a lower level than the right one.

In the right atrium the large orifice of the vena hemiazygos is seen below that of the posterior vena cava; the two are separated by a valvular fold with a concave free edge. The intervenous crest is broad and rounded, not prominent, as in the horse. The musculi pectinati radiate from a distinct crista terminalis and form a highly developed network in the auricle. The fossa ovalis is extensive. There is a large moderator band in the right ventricle.

The Arteries

The **pulmonary vessels** present no remarkable features.

The **aorta** resembles that of the horse and ox in its course and relations, but the arch is much more strongly curved. There is no common brachiocephalic trunk.

The **brachiocephalic artery** arises first from the aortic arch and passes forward below the trachea to the first rib. Here it gives off the **common carotid arteries,** separately or by a very short **bicarotid trunk,** and is continued around the first rib as the **right brachial artery.**

The **left brachial artery** arises from the aortic arch just above the brachiocephalic. It curves forward and downward and turns around the anterior border of the first rib.

The branches given off by the brachial arteries are as follows:

There is usually a common trunk for the dorsal, deep cervical, and vertebral arteries. This trunk or the dorsal artery gives off the **subcostal artery,** which supplies usually the third, fourth, and fifth intercostal arteries. The second intercostal artery arises separately. The **dorsal artery** emerges through the dorsal end of the second intercostal space and divides into dorsal and cervical branches; the dorsal branch passes upward and backward and ramifies in the deep muscles of the anterior part of the back; the cervical branch passes deeply to the atlantal region, where it anastomoses with the occipital artery. The **deep cervical artery** is a much smaller vessel, which emerges through the first intercostal space; it gives off the first intercostal artery, passes upward and forward deeply, and ramifies chiefly in the complexus and multifidus. The **vertebral artery** resembles that of the horse.

The **inferior cervical artery** is large; its ascending branch gives off the **posterior thyroid artery** and **parotid branches.**

The **internal** and **external thoracic arteries** give branches to the pectoral mammary glands; the external artery may be absent.

The **common carotid arteries** arise from the brachiocephalic close together or by a very short common trunk; they are accompanied by an internal jugular vein of considerable size, and their collaterals are similar to those of the horse. They terminate in occipital and internal and external carotid divisions.

The **occipital artery** resembles that of the horse.

The **internal carotid artery** usually arises by a common trunk with the occipital. After giving off a large meningeal branch which enters the cranium through the mastoid foramen, it passes through the foramen lacerum and forms with the opposite artery a rete mirabile which resembles that of the ox, but is smaller; it is not connected with the vertebral and condyloid arteries, but the meningeal branch just mentioned and the middle meningeal artery concur in its formation.

The **external carotid artery** has the same course and termination as in the horse. Its collateral branches present the following special features: (1) The **lingual artery** is relatively large and supplies the pharyngeal artery, the sublingual artery, muscular branches, and branches to the soft palate, mandibular gland, and larynx. (2) The **external maxillary artery** is represented by a small vessel which ends in the masseter muscle; it gives branches to the pterygoideus medialis, the parotid and mandibular glands, and the mandibular lymph glands, the masseter and the cutaneus. It does not extend upon the lateral surface of the face. (3) The **posterior auricular artery** is long and relatively large; it ascends along the anterior border of the paramastoid process and ramifies on the convex surface of the external ear. It gives off the posterior meningeal artery, which enters the cranial cavity through the mastoid foramen.

The **internal maxillary artery** pursues a flexuous course between the ramus of the mandible and the pterygoid muscles to the maxillary recess and divides into infraorbital and palatine branches. Its branches offer the following special features:

(1) The **inferior alveolar artery** is large; branches from it emerge through four or five mental foramina and take the place of the inferior labial. (2) The **middle meningeal artery** enters the cranial cavity through the foramen lacerum and concurs in the formation of the rete mirabile. (3) The **buccinator artery** is large and partly compensates for the lack of a facial artery. It ramifies in the cheek and its fine terminal branches extend to the lips. (4) The large **infraorbital artery** extends to the snout and replaces the superior labial largely and the lateral nasal in part. The malar branch compensates largely for the absence of the lateral and dorsal nasal arteries. (5) The **palatine artery** is small.

The **superficial temporal artery** ascends behind the temporo-mandibular articulation and ramifies in the temporalis muscle; it is small and may be absent. In the latter case the anterior auricular and transverse facial arteries arise separately from the external carotid artery, which is directly continued by the internal maxillary artery.

The **intercostal arteries** number usually fourteen or fifteen on either side; of these ten to twelve arise from the aorta, usually by short common trunks. Frequently an intercostal artery is given off from that of an adjacent space.

The **bronchial** and **œsophageal arteries** usually arise separately.

The **cœliac artery** is half an inch to an inch long. It supplies a branch to the left crus of the diaphragm, and divides into two primary branches, gastro-hepatic and splenic. The **gastro-hepatic artery** is the larger. It gives off pancreatic branches, the anterior gastric artery, branches to the lesser curvature of the stomach, pyloric, and gastro-duodenal arteries. The latter divides into pancreatico-duodenal and right gastro-epiploic. The anterior gastric usually supplies the œsophageal artery. The continuing trunk (A. hepatica propria) gives off a cystic branch and divides in the portal fissure into three or four branches which ramify in the liver. The **splenic artery** gives off the posterior gastric (usually), a branch to the stomach above the cardia (A. diverticuli), twigs to the pancreas, short gastric arteries to the left part of the great curvature, and splenic branches, and is continued as the left gastro-epiploic artery.

The posterior gastric may arise from the gastro-hepatic or in the angle of divergence of the two primary divisions of the cœliac. The œsophageal branch may come from the posterior gastric or the splenic. Other variations occur.

The **anterior mesenteric artery** arises an inch or more behind the cœliac and is long, like that of the ox. It gives twigs to the pancreas and is continued in the mesentery as the artery of the small intestine or **truncus intestinalis.** This gives off about a dozen branches which form a series of arches along the mesenteric lymph glands. From these is formed a rich network which gives off innumerable fine branches placed close together. The **ileo-cæco-colic artery** gives off **ileal** and **cæcal arteries,** and enters the axis of the spiral coil of the colon. Here it pursues a spiral course and gives off branches which form remarkable plexuses; from the latter numerous fine branches go to the centripetal coils. A short trunk gives origin to right and middle colic branches. The **right colic artery** is arranged like the colic branch of the ileo-cæco-colic artery, with which it anastomoses at the apex of the coil; it supplies the centrifugal parts of the coil. The **middle colic artery** goes to the colon as it emerges from the coil and anastomoses with the posterior mesenteric artery.

A **phrenico-abdominal artery** arises on either side a little in front of the renal arteries. It divides into branches which go to the costal part of the diaphragm and the abdominal muscles.

The **renal** and **spermatic arteries** present no special characters.

The **posterior mesenteric artery** arises near the termination of the aorta. It is small and is distributed like that of the ox.

Six pairs of **lumbar arteries** arise from the aorta.   The seventh comes from the middle sacral.

The terminal branches of the aorta resemble those of the ox.

The arteries of the shoulder, arm, and forearm resemble in general those of the ox.

The **brachial artery** is continued over the medial surface of the elbow by the **median artery.** The latter divides near the middle of the forearm into radial and ulnar arteries.

The **radial artery** is the smaller of the two terminal branches of the median. It descends along the medial border of the radius and divides at the proximal end

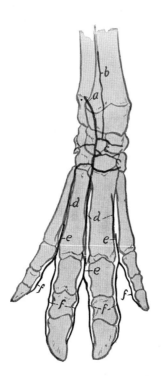

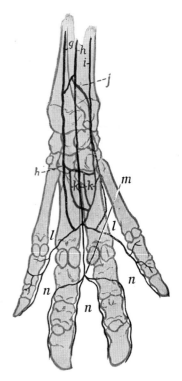

FIG. 607.—ARTERIES OF DISTAL PART OF RIGHT FORE LIMB OF PIG; DORSAL VIEW.

    a, Terminal part of volar interosseous artery; *b*, dorsal interosseous artery; *c*, rete carpi dorsale; *d*, dorsal metacarpal arteries; *e*, dorsal common digital arteries; *f*, dorsal proper digital arteries.

FIG. 608.—ARTERIES OF DISTAL PART OF RIGHT FORE LIMB OF PIG; VOLAR VIEW.

    g, Ulnar artery; *h*, superficial branch of radial artery; *i*, collateral ulnar artery; *j*, volar interosseous artery; *h*, deep branch of radial artery; *k*, deep volar metacarpal arteries; *l*, superficial volar metacarpal arteries; *m*, volar common digital artery; *n*, volar proper digital arteries.

of the metacarpus into two branches.   The superficial branch descends in the space between the second and third metacarpal bones and unites with the ulnar artery or with the lateral superficial volar metacarpal artery to form the superficial volar arch.   The deep branch joins the volar interosseous artery at the proximal end of the metacarpus to form the **deep volar arch.**   There is also a communicating branch between the radial and ulnar arteries at the carpus.

The **ulnar artery** descends along the medial side of the deep digital flexor and connects with the superficial branch of the radial artery to form the **superficial volar arch.**

The main facts as to the **metacarpal** and **digital arteries** are as follows: The rete carpi dorsale is formed essentially by the terminals of the interosseous artery of the forearm. It gives rise to three **dorsal metacarpal arteries,** which descend in the corresponding interosseous spaces and unite with branches of the volar meta-carpals to form three **common digital arteries.** Each of these divides into two **proper digital arteries,** which descend along the interdigital surfaces of the digits. From the superficial and deep volar arches described above there arise three **super-ficial** and three **deep volar metacarpal arteries.** The deep arteries unite near the distal end of the space between the principal metacarpal bones to form a stem which unites with the middle (third) superficial artery. The superficial arteries

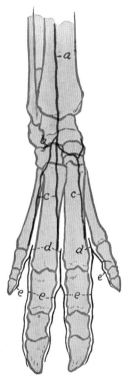

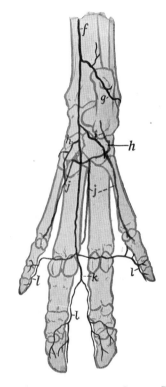

Fig. 609.—Arteries of Distal Part of Right Hind Limb of Pig; Dorsal View.

a, Anterior tibial artery, continued on tarsus as the dorsalis pedis; *b,* perforating tarsal artery; *c,* dorsal metatarsal arteries; *d,* common digital arteries; *e,* proper digital arteries.

Fig. 610.—Arteries of Distal Part of Right Hind Limb of Pig; Plantar View.

f, Saphenous artery, continued as medial tarsal artery; *g,* lateral tarsal artery; *h,* medial plantar artery, *h′,* lateral plantar artery; *i,* perforating tarsal artery; *j,* deep plantar metatarsal arteries; *k,* common digital artery; *l,* proper digital arteries.

unite to form an arch from which **proper digital arteries** are given off to the axial aspect of the small digits, and a common digital which supplies two **volar proper digital arteries** to each of the chief digits.

The arteries of the hip, thigh, and leg are arranged much as in the ox. A few special features may be noted.

The **ilio-lumbar artery** gives off a branch to the quadriceps femoris and lateral muscles of the thigh, and ramifies in the abdominal muscles. It may also supply the posterior abdominal artery, which otherwise arises from the deep femoral.

The **deep femoral artery** is given off above the level of the pubis. It is large and compensates for the absence of the obturator artery. The posterior abdominal and external pudic arteries may arise from it by a short common trunk or separately. The **external pudic** gives branches to the prepuce and preputial bursa but not to the penis. In the female it supplies the inguinal and abdominal mammary glands and anastomoses with the external thoracic artery. The **popliteal artery** gives off the peroneal.

The **femoral artery** gives off a short trunk which divides into anterior femoral and lateral circumflex arteries, the latter being much the larger.

The **saphenous artery** is large. It descends as in the ox on the medial surface of the leg and divides near the hock into lateral and medial tarsal arteries. The latter is the real continuation of the saphenous; it divides into medial and lateral plantar arteries, which concur with the perforating tarsal artery in forming the proximal plantar arch.

The **posterior tibial artery** is small, being replaced distally by the saphenous. It gives branches to the muscles on the posterior face of the tibia and supplies the nutrient artery of that bone.

The **anterior tibial artery** is continued as the dorsalis pedis on the dorsal surface of the tarsus. This gives off the **perforating tarsal artery,** which passes back through the vascular canal of the tarsus and unites with the plantar arteries to form the proximal plantar arch.

The **metatarsal** and **digital arteries** resemble in arrangement the corresponding vessels of the limb.

THE VEINS

The **veins** resemble in general those of the ox. Thus there is a hemiazygos vein and two jugular veins, the internal one being relatively larger than in the ox. A few differential features may be noted.

The **buccinator vein** resembles that of the horse, and unites with the **vena reflexa** to form a short common trunk which joins the external maxillary vein.

The **external maxillary vein** resembles in general that of the horse. The **dorsal nasal vein** is large, receives the veins from the snout, runs backward in the groove of the nasal bone, and joins the frontal vein; it is connected with its fellow by a transverse branch, and anastomoses freely with the malar and facial veins.

The veins of the distal parts of the limbs naturally present differences which are correlated with those of the arteries.

THE LYMPHATIC SYSTEM

The **thoracic duct** often divides near its termination into two branches which unite to form an ampulla. The latter suddenly contracts and opens into the terminal part of the left jugular vein. The lymph glands of animals in good condition are almost all embedded in fat. Many of them are dark red in color and may be mistaken for hæmal nodes, which do not appear to be present in the pig.

The **mandibular lymph glands** are situated in the space between the omohyoid and medial pterygoid muscles, in relation to the lower part of the anterior border of the mandibular salivary gland. There are commonly two on each side, one large, the other small.

The **parotid lymph glands** (Fig. 415) are reddish-brown in color. There are usually four of considerable size and several smaller ones on either side. One is situated at the upper part of the posterior border of the masseter, partly covered by the parotid salivary gland. A large subparotid gland lies below the base of the ear on the terminal part of the brachiocephalicus muscle. Ventral to this are two smaller glands, one above and one below the external maxillary vein.

The **suprapharyngeal lymph glands** (Fig. 416) are situated on the dorsal wall of the pharynx, dorsal to the external carotid artery and below and behind the paramastoid process. There are usually two of considerable size on either side.

They are related deeply to the rectus capitis ventralis major and are covered by the cleido-mastoideus.

The **middle cervical lymph glands** form a group on the brachiocephalicus on the course of the external jugular vein. Other small nodes are present in the fat around the trachea.

The **prescapular lymph glands** are situated at the anterior border of the anterior deep pectoral muscle, under cover of the trapezius and omo-transversarius.

The **posterior cervical lymph glands** are reddish in color and usually three in number. The largest is placed centrally under the trachea; the others are situated on the brachial vessels as they turn around the first rib.

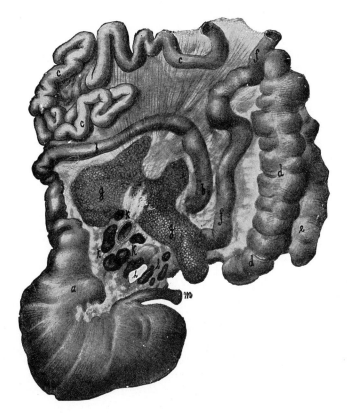

FIG. 611.—STOMACH AND PART OF INTESTINE OF PIG, SPREAD OUT.

a, Pyloric part of stomach: *b*, duodenum; *c*, jejunum; *d*, cæcum; *e*, *f*, colon; *g*, pancreas; *h*, epiploic foramen; *i*, portal vein; *k*, hepatic lymph glands; *l*, gastric lymph glands; *m*, œsophagus. (After Edelmann.)

The **axillary lymph glands** are usually absent, but very small nodes may be found near the insertion of the latissimus dorsi. Cubital glands are not present.

The **thoracic lymph glands** comprise the following:

(1) A **sternal lymph gland** of relatively large size lies on the first segment of the sternum. (2) The **mediastinal lymph glands** include: a number of small reddish nodes in the fat along the dorsal surface of the aorta; a gland on the left side of the trachea in front of the aortic arch; a gland on the aorta where it is crossed by the vena hemiazygos; two or three glands in the posterior mediastinum along the ventral surface of the aorta; several glands along the ventral surface of the trachea. (3) The **bronchial lymph glands** include one on the bifurcation of the trachea and another at the apical bronchus of the right lung.

The **lumbar lymph glands** are scattered along the abdominal aorta and the vena cava.   Those placed near the hilus of the kidney are often designated **renal.**

The **internal iliac lymph glands** are rounded and relatively large.   They comprise: (1) Three or four glands situated on and between the origin of the circumflex iliac and the external and internal iliac arteries; (2) a gland in the angle of divergence of the internal iliac arteries; (3) several glands along the course of the external iliac artery, the most ventral of which is usually the largest, and may be regarded as the **deep inguinal gland.**

The **external iliac lymph glands** are small, three or four in number, and lie in front of the circumflex iliac vessels.

The visceral lymph glands of the abdomen comprise the following:

1. The **gastric lymph glands** are situated on the lesser curvature of the stomach, covered by the pancreas *in situ.*   They are commonly five or six in number and are in series with the hepatic glands.

2. Several **hepatic lymph glands** (Fig. 429) are present about the portal vein at the portal fissure.   The largest ones are about an inch (ca. 2–3 cm.) long.

3. A long **splenic lymph gland** lies on the splenic vessels near the dorsal end of the spleen.

4. The **mesenteric lymph glands** are situated along the anastomotic arches formed by the vessels of the small intestine.

5. Several **cæcal lymph glands** are situated along the first part of the cæcal vessels.

6. Two series of **colic lymph glands** accompany the arteries of the spiral part of the colon, and are exposed by separating the coils of the bowel.   Small glands are placed in the colic mesentery and above the rectum.

7. The **anal lymph glands** are situated on either side on the retractor ani.

A small **ischiatic lymph gland** is usually present on the sacro-sciatic ligament near the lesser sciatic notch.

The **prefemoral lymph gland** is situated on the aponeurosis of the external oblique muscle at the anterior border of the tensor fasciæ latæ, and a little above the middle of the thigh.   It has an elongated oval outline, and in the adult may be about two inches (ca. 5 cm.) long, and nearly an inch (ca. 2 cm.) wide.   It is embedded in fat.

The **superficial inguinal lymph glands** form an extensive group, which may be five inches or more (ca. 10–12 cm.) in length.   The middle part of the group is at the external inguinal ring, and the series extends back on the upper part of the gracilis and forward and outward on the aponeurosis of the obliquus abdominis externus.   They number about a dozen; the largest are about an inch (ca. 2–3 cm.) long, and the others about the size of a pea.

The **popliteal lymph glands** are small normally and may escape notice.   They are more superficially placed than in the other animals, and are in part in contact with the skin.

A few small **tarsal glands** occur in front of the distal part of the tendo Achillis. The occurrence of a gland in the subcutaneous fat about a handbreadth above the tuber calcis has been noted by Hartenstein; it varies from the size of a pea to that of a hazel nut.

CIRCULATORY SYSTEM OF THE DOG

THE PERICARDIUM AND HEART

The **pericardium** is attached to the sternal part of the diaphragm by a fibrous band, the **pericardiaco-phrenic ligament** (Lig. pericardiaco-phrenicum). and is connected with the sternum only by the mediastinal pleura.

The area of contact of the pericardium with the chest wall is chiefly ventral, and is best seen with the subject on its back. In this position (after removal of the intercostal and rectus thoracis muscles), the area is seen to be almost triangular. The anterior border of the triangle (formed by the apical lobe of the right lung) is at the right fourth costal cartilage and extends across the median plane, ending at the third interchondral space near the costo-chondral junction. The right border extends from the sternal end of the fourth rib to the eighth chondro-sternal joint. The left border begins at the left end of the anterior border, crosses the fourth cartilage nearly an inch from its junction with the rib and the fifth and sixth chondro-costal junctions.

The **heart** differs greatly in form and position from that of the larger animals. In diastole it is ovoid and the apex is blunt and rounded. Its long axis is very oblique. Thus the base faces chiefly toward the thoracic inlet and is opposite to the ventral part of the third rib. The apex is on the left side at the sixth interchondral space or seventh costal cartilage, and in close relation to the sternal part of the diaphragm. The **sterno-costal surface** corresponds largely to the floor of the thorax from the fifth chondro-sternal joint backward. It is crossed obliquely

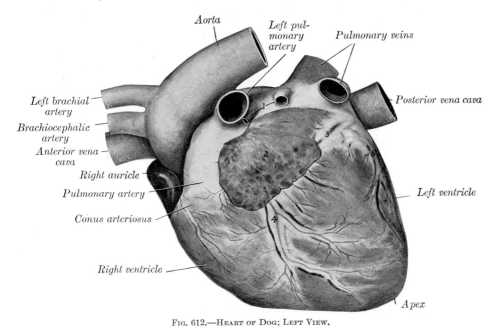

Fig. 612.—Heart of Dog; Left View.

1, Pulmonary veins; *2*, left auricle; *3*, vessels and fat in coronary groove; *4*, vessels and fat in left or ventral longitudinal groove; *5*, vessels and fat in intermediate groove.

by the left (or ventral) longitudinal groove, which begins behind the origin of the pulmonary artery, and joins the right (or dorsal) groove at the right border, thus forming a notch not far from the apex. The **diaphragmatic surface** is less extensive and less convex. On it is the right (or dorsal) longitudinal groove, which begins at the coronary groove just behind the termination of the posterior vena cava and joins the left (or ventral) groove to the right of the apex. There is frequently an intermediate groove between these on the left ventricle, which extends a variable distance toward the apex. The weight of the heart of a dog of medium size is five to six ounces, and is about 1 per cent. of the body weight.

The relative weight is subject to wide variation. It is large in hunting dogs and such as are trained for speed or worked. In fat dogs of sedentary habit it may be only about 0.5 per cent.

The opening of the pulmonary artery is at the fourth rib, and that of the aorta at the fifth rib. The fossa ovalis is very shallow and is bounded in front by the intervenous crest. The musculi pectinati form a rich network in the right auricle. The tricuspid valve has two chief cusps and three or four small ones. There are four musculi papillares in the right ventricle, all of which spring from the septal wall. They diminish in size from before backward, the anterior ones being long and cylindrical. Their bases are connected with the lateral wall by trabeculæ carneæ. Usually six pulmonary veins open into the left atrium. The bicuspid valve consists of two large cusps and four or five small ones. There are two musculi papillares in the left ventricle, both of which arise from the lateral wall; they are much larger than those of the right ventricle.

THE ARTERIES

The two **coronary arteries** usually spring separately from the origin of the aorta, but may arise by a common trunk. Each divides into circumflex and descending branches. The left artery is twice as large as the right one; it commonly gives off a branch of considerable size which runs in the intermediate groove.

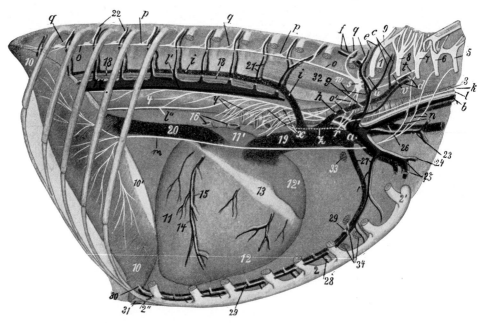

FIG. 613.—VESSELS, NERVES, ETC., OF THORAX OF DOG; RIGHT VIEW.

1, First rib (stump); *2*, sternum; *2'*, manubrium sterni; *2''*, xiphoid cartilage; *3*, trachea; *4*, œsophagus; *5–8*, ventral branches of fifth to eighth cervical nerves; *9*, ventral branch of first thoracic nerve; *10, 10'*, muscular and tendinous parts of diaphragm; *11, 11'*, left ventricle and atrium of heart; *12, 12'*, right ventricle and auricle of heart; *13*, coronary groove; *14*, right coronary artery; *15*, middle cardiac vein; *16*, pulmonary veins; *17*, aorta; *18*, thoracic duct; *19*, anterior vena cava; *20*, posterior vena cava; *21*, dorsal intercostal vessels; *22*, intercostal nerve; *23*, inferior cervical (or omo-cervical) artery; *24*, external thoracic artery; *25*, brachial vessels; *26*, common jugular vein; *27*, internal thoracic vessels; *28*, sternal branches of internal thoracic vessels; *29*, mediastinal arteries; *30*, musculo-phrenic artery; *31*, anterior abdominal artery; *32*, m. longus colli; *33*, anterior mediastinal lymph glands; *34*, sternal lymph glands; *a, a'*, right brachial artery and vein; *b*, common carotid artery; *c*, deep cervical vessels; *d*, vertebral vessels; *e*, dorsal vessels; *f*, subcostal vessels; *g, h*, dorso-cervical trunks; *i*, vena azygos; *k*, recurrent nerve; *l*, vago-sympathetic nerve; *l', l''*, dorsal and ventral branches of vagus; *m*, phrenic nerve; *n*, roots of phrenic nerve; *o*, thoracic trunk of sympathetic; *o'*, nerve loop formed around brachial artery by branches which connect posterior cervical and first thoracic ganglia of sympathetic (Ansa subclavia); *p*, thoracic ganglia of sympathetic; *q*, rami communicantes; *r*, posterior cervical ganglion; *s*, first thoracic ganglion; *t, u, v*, rami communicantes between *s* and seventh cervical, first thoracic, and eighth cervical nerves; *w*, cardiac branch of first thoracic ganglion; *x*, cardiac branches of posterior cervical ganglion; *y*, bronchial branches of vagus; *z*, depressor nerve. (After Bucher.)

The **aorta** runs at first almost straight forward and then turns backward, forming a very sharply curved arch. It gives off at its origin the two **coronary arteries.** From the convexity of the arch two large vessels arise. The first and larger of these is the **brachiocephalic artery;** this runs forward at first on the ventral surface of the œsophagus, then under the trachea. It gives off in succession the **left** and **right common carotid arteries,** and turns around the first rib as the **right brachial artery.** The **left brachial artery** passes forward on the left face of the œsophagus, forming a slight arch (concave ventrally), and turns around the first rib. The intrathoracic branches of the brachial arteries are as follows:

(1) The **vertebral artery** arises opposite the first intercostal space from the dorsal face of the parent trunk. It runs forward on the longus colli (crossing the trachea on the right side), and passes along the neck in typical fashion to the third cervical vertebra, where it divides into three branches. The largest of these supplies the muscles in this region, compensating for the absence of branches of the deep cervical artery. The second passes between the second and third cervical vertebræ into the vertebral canal and unites with the opposite artery and a branch of the occipital artery to form the basilar artery. The third branch is the small continua-

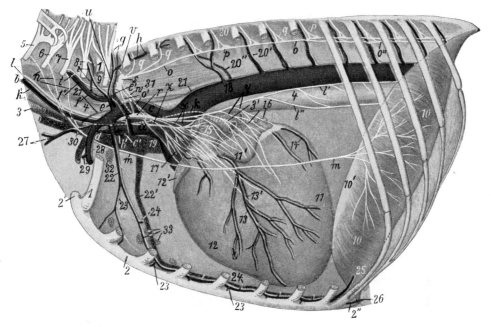

FIG. 614.—VESSELS, NERVES, ETC., OF THORAX OF DOG; LEFT VIEW.

1, First rib (stump); *2,* sternum; *2′,* manubrium sterni; *2″,* xiphoid cartilage; *3,* trachea; *3′,* bifurcation of trachea; *4,* œsophagus; *5–8,* ventral branches of fifth to eighth cervical nerves; *9,* ventral branch of first thoracic nerve; *10, 10′,* muscular and tendinous parts of diaphragm; *11, 11′,* left ventricle and auricle of heart; *12, 12′,* right ventricle and auricle of heart; *13, 13′,* left coronary artery (descending branch) and great cardiac vein; *14,* branch of left coronary artery in intermediate groove; *15,* pulmonary artery; *16,* pulmonary veins; *17, 18,* aorta; *19,* anterior vena cava; *20, 20′, 20″,* intercostal nerve, artery, and vein; *21,* thoracic duct; *22, 22′,* internal thoracic vessels; *23,* sternal branches of *22; 24,* mediastinal arteries; *25,* musculo-phrenic artery; *26,* anterior abdominal artery; *27,* inferior cervical (or omo-cervical) artery; *28,* brachial vessels; *29,* external thoracic artery; *30,* left common jugular vein; *31,* m. longus colli; *32,* anterior mediastinal lymph glands; *33,* sternal lymph glands; *a,* brachiocephalic artery; *b, b′,* common carotid arteries; *c, c′,* brachial arteries; *d,* left brachial vein; *e, e′,* dorso-cervical vessels; *f, f′,* vertebral vessels; *g,* dorsal vessels; *h,* subcostal vessels; *i,* deep cervical vessels; *k,* recurrent nerve; *l,* vago-sympathetic trunk; *l′, l″,* dorsal and ventral branches of vagus; *m,* phrenic nerve; *n,* roots of phrenic nerve from fifth to seventh cervical nerves; *o,* thoracic trunk of sympathetic; *o′,* ansa subclavia formed by branches connecting posterior cervical and first thoracic ganglia; *o″,* great splanchnic nerve; *p,* thoracic ganglia of sympathetic; *q,* rami communicantes; *r,* posterior cervical ganglion; *s,* first thoracic ganglion of sympathetic; *t, u, v,* rami communicantes connecting *s* with seventh and eighth cervical and first thoracic nerves; *w,* cardiac branch of first thoracic nerve; *x,* cardiac nerves from posterior cervical ganglion; *y,* bronchial branches of vagus; *z,* depressor nerve. (After Bucher.)

tion of the parent trunk; it passes to the wing of the atlas and anastomoses with the occipital artery.

(2), (3) The **dorsal** and **deep cervical arteries** arise by a common trunk close to the vertebral. The trunk crosses the lateral face of the latter, ascends on the longus colli, and divides into two branches. The anterior branch, the **deep cervical artery,** emerges medial to the upper end of the first rib and ramifies in the deep muscles of the neck. The **dorsal artery** gives off the **subcostal artery** (which supplies two or three intercostal arteries) and emerges through the dorsal end of the first intercostal space and ramifies in the spinal muscles.

(4) The **inferior cervical artery** arises at the first rib, and gives off the ascending cervical and transverse scapular arteries. The former runs on the deep face of the brachiocephalicus, in which it ramifies. The latter goes to the anterior border of the subscapularis, and its largest branch (equivalent to the prescapular of the horse) accompanies the suprascapular nerve.

(5) The **internal thoracic artery** is large and sends perforating branches to the pectoral mammary glands.

The axillary part of the brachial artery gives off the thoraco-acromial and external thoracic arteries.

The **thoraco-acromial artery** supplies branches to the deltoid and pectoral muscles.

The **external thoracic artery** passes backward under cover of the deep pectoral

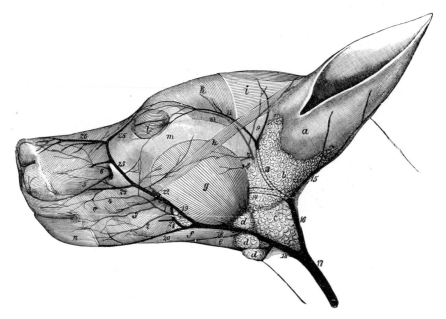

Fig. 615.—Superficial Vessels of Head of Dog.

1, Facial artery; *2*, inferior labial artery; *3*, artery of angle of mouth; *4*, superior labial artery; *5*, lateral nasal artery; *6*, dorsal nasal artery; *7*, superficial temporal artery; *8*, transverse facial artery; *9*, anterior auricular artery; *10*, zygomatico-orbital artery; *11*, satellite vein of *10*; *12*, ant. auricular vein; *13*, superficial temporal vein; *14*, internal maxillary vein; *15*, post. auricular vein; *16, 17*, external jugular vein; *18*, external maxillary vein; *19, 23*, facial vein; *20*, inf. labial vein; *21*, buccinator vein; *22*, vena reflexa; *24*, superior labial vein; *25*, vena angularis oculi; *26*, dorsal nasal vein; *a*, concha; *b*, parotid gland; *c*, mandibular gland; *d*, mandibular lymph glands; *e*, mylo-hyoideus; *f*, digastricus; *g*, masseter; *h*, zygomaticus; *i*, scutularis; *k*, temporalis; *l*, orbicularis oculi; *m*, zygomatic arch; *n*, retractor anguli oris; *o*, buccinator. (Ellenberger-Baum, Anat. d. Hundes.)

muscle and ends in the abdominal cutaneous muscle. It sends branches to the mammary glands.

The **common carotid arteries,** left and right, arise in that order from the brachiocephalic. In the neck the right one lies on the trachea, the left on the œsophagus. Collateral branches are the **posterior thyroid** (which may, however, arise from the right or left brachial or the inferior cervical), **pharyngeal, anterior thyroid, laryngeal, muscular, tracheal,** and **glandular** (to the mandibular gland). Each carotid divides under the wing of the atlas into occipital and internal and external carotid branches.

The **occipital artery** is small; it ascends behind the hypoglossal nerve to the paramastoid process, crossing laterally the internal carotid artery and vagus and cympathetic nerves. It curves over the paramastoid process and pursues a flexuous course on the nuchal surface of the occipital bone parallel with the nuchal crest, anastomoses with the opposite artery, and ramifies in the nuchal muscles. It gives collateral branches to the ventral straight muscles and to the pharynx. It also gives off the **condyloid** and **posterior meningeal arteries.** The latter passes through the mastoid foramen and ramifies in the dura mater. The **cerebrospinal artery** passes through the intervertebral foramen, and unites in the vertebral canal with its fellow and a branch from the vertebral artery to form the basilar artery. The **recurrent branch** anastomoses with the vertebral as in the horse.

The **internal carotid artery,** also small, arises just behind the occipito-mandibularis muscle; it passes to the foramen lacerum posterius, enters the carotid canal, and forms a bend before entering the cranial cavity through the carotid foramen. It forms a plexus which is connected by branches with the middle meningeal and external ophthalmic arteries. It then perforates the dura mater and enters into the formation of the circulus arteriosus, which is formed in a manner similar to that of the horse. The **anterior cerebral artery** gives off the **internal ophthalmic artery** which accompanies the optic nerve to the eyeball. The **middle cerebral artery** is large, and gives off the **chorioid artery.**

The **external carotid artery** is the direct continuation of the common carotid. It passes along the lateral wall of the pharynx, emerges from beneath the occipito-mandibularis, and divides behind the postglenoid process into superficial temporal and internal maxillary arteries. It gives off the following collateral branches: The large flexuous **lingual artery** passes to the side of the root of the tongue, runs forward under cover of the hyo-glossus, and continues to the tip of the tongue in company with a satellite vein and the hypoglossal nerve. It ramifies in the tongue and gives collateral branches to the pharynx and soft palate. The **external maxillary artery,** smaller than the lingual, passes along the upper border of the occipito-mandibularis, gives off the sublingual, gains the anterior border of the masseter, and divides into superior and inferior labial and the angularis oris. The last-named vessel passes forward on the cheek between the labials to the angle of the mouth. The **sublingual artery** passes along the upper border of the occipito-mandibularis, then between the mylo-hyoideus and the ramus of the mandible. The **great auricular artery** arises at the anterior border of the occipito-mandibularis, gives branches to the parotid and mandibular salivary glands and the adjacent muscles, and terminates in three auricular branches which ramify on the convex face of the concha. These branches anastomose with each other and the anterior auricular artery.

The **superficial temporal artery,** after giving off the **anterior auricular artery** and a small **transverse facial artery,** turns forward under the temporal fascia toward the eye, and divides into upper and lower branches which supply the frontal region and the eyelids. It also supplies branches to the parotid gland and the masseter and temporalis muscles.

The **internal maxillary artery** pursues a course similar to that of the horse, and ends in the pterygo-palatine fossa by dividing into the infraorbital artery and a common trunk for the greater palatine and sphenopalatine arteries. The mental branches of the **inferior alveolar artery** are of considerable size and are distributed in the lower lip and gums. Two or three **deep temporal arteries** are present; the anterior one may arise from the buccinator artery. The **middle meningeal artery** enters the cranium through the foramen ovale, ramifies in the dura mater, and sends a branch to the carotid plexus. The **external ophthalmic artery** is connected with the internal carotid by a large ramus anastomoticus which passes through the orbital foramen. The superficial branches of the **infraorbital artery** replace the dorsal and lateral nasal arteries, and compensate for the small size of the superior labial.

The **brachial artery** in its course in the arm presents no special features. At the elbow it passes between the biceps and the pronator teres, descends as the

median artery under the flexor carpi radialis about a third of the way down the forearm, and divides into radial and ulnar arteries. Among its collateral branches are the following: (1) The large **subscapular artery** passes up between the sub-

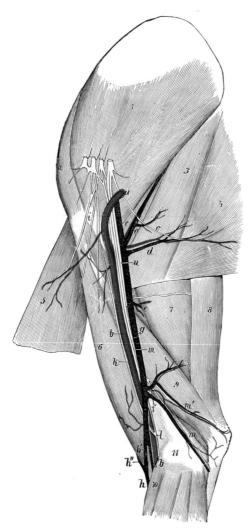

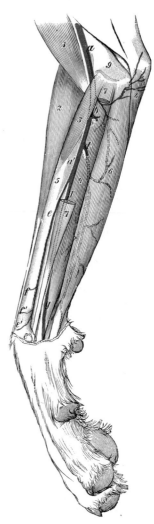

Fig. 616.—Vessels and Nerves of Medial Surface of Shoulder and Arm of Dog.

a, b, Brachial artery; c, subscapular vessels; d, thoraco-dorsal vessels; e, deep brachial vessels; f, proximal collateral ulna. vessels; g, brachial vein; h, h″, cephalic vein; h′, mediano-radial vein; i, anterior thoracic nerves; k, musculo-cutaneous nerve; l, median nerve; m, ulnar nerve; n, radial nerve; o, thoraco-dorsal nerve; 1, subscapularis muscle; 2, supraspinatus muscle; 3, teres major; 4, latissimus dorsi; 5, deep pectoral muscle; 6, biceps brachii; 7, long head of triceps; 8, tensor fasciæ antibrachii; 9, medial head of triceps; 10, pronator teres. (Ellenberger-Baum, Anat. d. Hundes.)

Fig. 617.—Arteries of Forearm of Dog; Medial View.

Arteries: a, Brachial; a′, median; c, common interosseous; d, volar antibrachial; e, radial; e′, e″, dorsal and volar branches of e; f, f′, cutaneous branches of e; g, ulnar. Muscles: 1, Biceps brachii; 2, extensor carpi radialis; 3, pronator teres; 4, deep digital flexor; 5, radius; 6, superficial digital flexor; 7, flexor carpi radialis; 8, flexor carpi ulnaris; 9, humerus. (Ellenberger-Baum, Anat. d. Hundes.)

scapularis and teres major, turns around the posterior angle of the scapula, and terminates in the supraspinatus, deltoid, trapezius, and brachiocephalicus. In about half the cases it gives off the **anterior circumflex,** which often arises with the

posterior circumflex. Its other branches resemble those of the horse. (2) The **anterior circumflex artery** in about half the cases arises from the brachial. (3) The **deep brachial artery** arises about a third of the way down the arm. (4) The **bicipital artery** (for the biceps) is given off at the distal third of the arm. (5) The **proximal collateral ulnar artery** arises almost opposite to the preceding vessel. It ramifies chiefly in the distal part of the triceps, and sends a superficial branch to the medial and posterior surfaces of the proximal part of the forearm. (6) The **proximal collateral radial artery** (not present in the horse) arises at the distal fourth of the arm, crosses over the terminal part of the biceps, descends on the extensor carpi radialis, and concurs with a branch of the volar interosseous artery in forming the rete carpi dorsale. It often supplies the bicipital artery. (7) The **distal collateral radial artery** is very small; it accompanies the deep branch of the radial nerve on the dorsal surface of the forearm and supplies branches to the elbow joint and the brachialis, supinator, and extensor muscles. (8) The **common interosseous artery** is given off from the median a little below the elbow. It supplies branches to the flexor muscles and gives off the **dorsal interosseous artery,** which passes through the interosseous space, gives branches to the extensor muscles, and by its terminal twigs concurs in the formation of the rete carpi dorsale. The direct continuation of the trunk is the **volar interosseous artery,** which descends along the interosseous space under cover of the pronator quadratus, gives off a branch to the rete carpi dorsale and the **fifth volar metacarpal artery,** and terminates by joining the volar branch of the radial artery to form the deep volar arch. (9) The **volar antibrachial artery** (Ramus volaris antibrachii) arises below the interosseous and descends at first under the flexor carpi radialis, then between the heads of the deep flexor, and divides into ascending and descending branches which ramify in the muscles mentioned.

The **radial artery,** the smaller terminal of the median, descends along the medial border of the radius, and divides near the carpus into dorsal and volar branches. The **dorsal branch** assists in forming the rete carpi dorsale. The larger **volar branch** descends behind the medial border of the carpus and joins the end of the volar interosseous in forming the **deep volar arch.** The arch extends across the interossei at the proximal part of the metacarpus. From this arch three **deep volar metacarpal arteries** descend in the second, third, and fourth intermetacarpal spaces and concur with the corresponding superficial volar and the dorsal metacarpal arteries to form the common digital arteries.

The **ulnar artery** is much the larger of the two terminal branches of the median. It descends with the median nerve along the medial border of the deep flexor of the digit, and sends a connecting branch to the radial above the carpus. It then inclines somewhat laterally and passes between the superficial and deep flexor tendons. Near the middle of the metacarpus it gives off the **first volar metacarpal artery** and divides into the **second, third,** and **fourth superficial volar metacarpal arteries.** The first volar artery unites with the corresponding dorsal artery to form the **first common digital artery,** which supplies proper digital arteries for the opposed surfaces of the first and second digits. The superficial volar arteries descend in the spaces between the other metacarpal bones, and unite near the metacarpo-phalangeal joints with the corresponding deep volar and dorsal metacarpal arteries to form three **common digital arteries.** Each of the latter divides after a short course into two **proper digital arteries,** which run along the opposed surfaces of the second to the fifth digits. The lateral digital artery of the fifth digit comes from the **superficial volar arch** formed by the union of a branch of the volar interosseous with the fourth superficial volar metacarpal artery.

The rete carpi dorsale gives off four **dorsal metacarpal arteries** which descend in the intermetacarpal spaces and unite near the metacarpo-phalangeal joints with the volar arteries to form the common digitals.

The **thoracic aorta** supplies the last nine or ten pairs of **intercostal arteries,** but no anterior phrenic arteries. It gives off two or more **œsophageal branches,** in addition to the **broncho-œsophageal,** which arises close to or with the sixth intercostal and ramifies in the usual manner.

The **abdominal aorta,** after giving off the external iliac arteries, continues about half an inch to an inch (ca. 1–3 cm.) under the last lumbar vertebra, gives off the internal iliac arteries, and is continued by the **middle sacral artery** (Fig. 624). This small vessel runs backward under the sacrum and coccygeal vertebræ and gives off branches in segmental fashion. Six pairs of **lumbar arteries** are given off from the aorta, the seventh coming from the internal iliac artery.

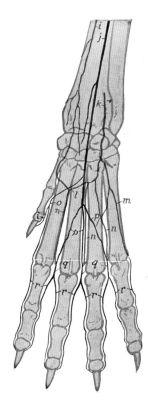

Fig. 618.—Arteries of Distal Part of Right Fore Limb of Dog, Dorsal View.

a, Branch of volar interosseous artery; *b,* proximal collateral radial artery (lateral branch); *c,* radial artery (dorsal branch); *d,* rete carpi dorsale; *e,* deep dorsal metacarpal arteries; *f,* superficial dorsal metacarpal arteries; *g,* common digital arteries; *h,* proper digital arteries.

Fig. 619.—Arteries of Distal Part of Right Fore Limb of Dog; Volar View.

i, Radial artery; *j,* ulnar artery; *k,* volar interosseous artery; *l,* deep volar arch; *m,* fifth volar metacarpal artery; *n,* deep volar metacarpal arteries; *p,* superficial volar metacarpal arteries; *o, q,* common digital arteries; *r,* proper digital arteries.

The **cœliac artery** gives off the hepatic artery and forms a short trunk from which the gastric and splenic arteries arise. The **hepatic artery,** after giving off several **proper hepatic arteries,** and the **right gastric artery,** which passes along the lesser curvature of the stomach and anastomoses with the left gastric artery, is continued by the **gastro-duodenal artery.** This divides near the pylorus into **right gastro-epiploic** and **pancreatico-duodenal arteries;** the former supplies branches to the pyloric part of the stomach and passes along the greater curvature of that viscus in the omentum and anastomoses with the left gastro-epiploic. The **left gastric artery** passes to the lesser curvature of the stomach and ramifies chiefly on the left part of the stomach, giving off a branch which anastomoses with the right gastric artery. The **splenic artery** gives off pancreatic branches, and reaches the ventral part of the spleen. It gives off the **left gastro-epiploic** and a **gastro-splenic** branch which passes to the dorsal end of the spleen, which it supplies, besides giving off twigs to the left extremity of the stomach.

The **anterior mesenteric artery** arises close behind the cœliac. It gives off a common trunk for two colic arteries and the ileo-cæco-colic: the **right colic artery,** a small vessel which goes to the right part of the colon, and the **middle colic artery,** much the largest of the colic vessels, which supplies the transverse colon and part of the left part of the colon. The ileo-cæco-colic gives off **ileal, cæcal,** and **colic** branches. Anastomoses are established between the colic arteries, and the ileal branch anastomoses with the last jejunal artery. The trunk is continued as the

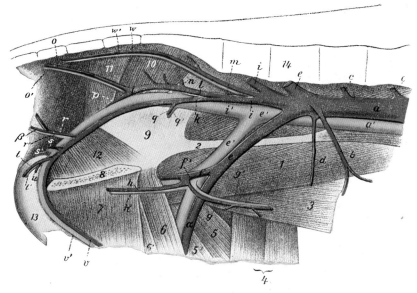

Fig. 620.—End Branches of Aorta and Radicles of Posterior Vena Cava of Dog.

a, Abdominal aorta; *b*, posterior mesenteric artery; *c*, lumbar arteries; *d*, circumflex iliac artery; *e*, external iliac artery; *f*, deep femoral artery; *g*, posterior abdominal artery; *h*, external pudic artery; *a*, femoral artery; *i, i*, internal iliac arteries; *k*, visceral branch of *i; l*, parietal branch of *i; m*, ilio-lumbar artery; *n*, anterior gluteal artery; *o*, lateral coccygeal artery; *p*, posterior gluteal artery; *q*, umbilical artery; *r*, middle hæmorrhoidal artery; *β*, posterior hæmorrhoidal artery; *s*, perineal artery; *t*, art. profunda penis; *n*, art. bulbi urethræ; *v*, art. dorsalis penis; *w*, middle sacral artery; *a'*, posterior vena cava; other veins are satellites of arteries and correspondingly named; *1*, ilio-psoas muscle; *2*, tendon of psoas minor; *3*, abdominal muscles; *4*, sartorius; *5*, rectus femoris; *5'*, vastus medialis; *6*, pectineus; *6'*, adductor; *7*, gracilis; *8*, symphysis pelvis; *9*, ilium; *10*, piriformis; *11*, gluteus superficialis; *12*, obturator internus; *13*, penis; *14*, lumbar vertebræ. (After Ellenberger, in Leisering's Atlas.)

artery of the small intestine, giving off fourteen to sixteen branches (Aa. jejunales), which form a series of anastomotic arches in the mesentery near the bowel.

Two **phrenico-abdominal arteries** (Aa. phrenicæ caudales) come off from the aorta behind the anterior mesenteric, and divide into phrenic and abdominal branches. Each phrenic artery diverges from its fellow in descending on the abdominal surface of the corresponding crus of the diaphragm to the sternal part. The medial branches anastomose with those of the opposite artery, the lateral branches with intercostal arteries chiefly. The abdominal arteries pass outward across the psoas muscles, give branches to the lumbar muscles, the renal fat and adrenals, and ramify in the oblique abdominal muscles.

The **renal** and **spermatic arteries** offer no special features.

The **utero-ovarian artery** divides near the ovary into three or four branches

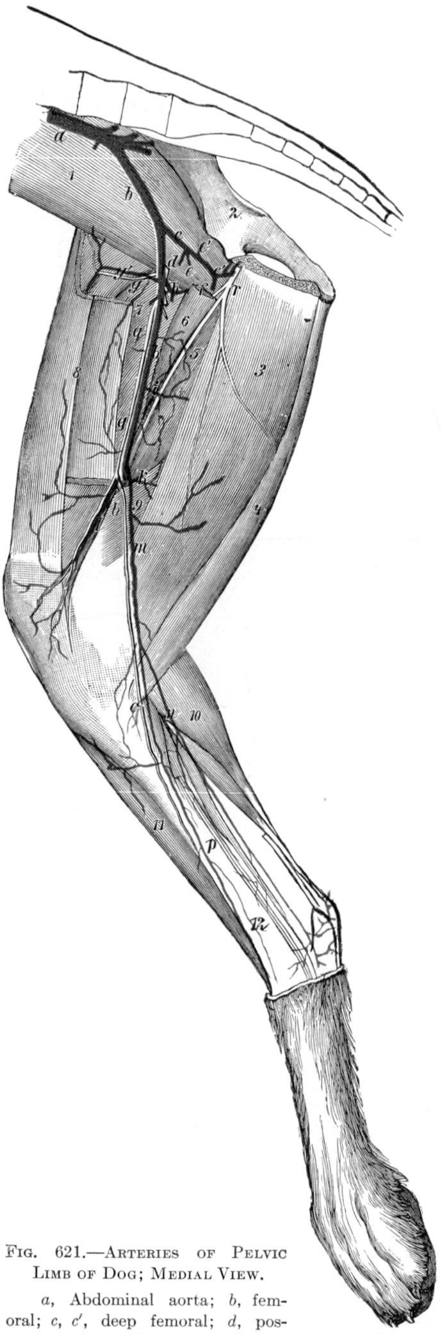

Fig. 621.—Arteries of Pelvic
Limb of Dog; Medial View.

a, Abdominal aorta; b, femoral; c, c', deep femoral; d, posterior abdominal; e, external pudic; f, medial circumflex; g, anterior femoral (accompanied by anterior branch of femoral nerve); h, lateral circumflex; i, k, muscular branches; l, articular branch; m, saphenous; n, o, plantar and dorsal branches of saphenous; q, saphenous nerve; r, obturator nerve; 1, iliopsoas; 2, ilium; 3, gracilis; 4, semitendinosus; 5, adductor magnus; 6, adductor longus; 7, quadriceps femoris; 8, sartorius; 9, semimembranosus; 10, gastrocnemius; 11, tibialis anterior; 12, tibia. (Ellenberger-Baum, Anat. d. Hundes.)

which supply the ovary and uterine tube and anterior part of the cornu of the uterus, anastomosing with the uterine artery.

The **posterior mesenteric artery** is small. It divides into two branches which supply the terminal part of the colon and the anterior part of the rectum; the former (A. colica sinistra) passes forward along the left part of the colon and anastomoses with the middle colic branch of the anterior mesenteric artery; the latter (A. hæmorrhoidalis cranialis) anastomoses with the middle hæmorrhoidal branch of the internal pudic artery.

The **circumflex iliac artery** usually arises from the terminal part of the aorta.

The **external iliac artery** usually gives off no collateral branches.

The **femoral artery** has the usual course in the femoral triangle and canal. The **deep femoral artery** gives off the **posterior abdominal** and **external pudic arteries** by a very short common trunk or separately. In the female the external pudic divides into anterior and posterior branches; the former runs forward, supplies branches to the superficial inguinal lymph glands, the mammary glands and skin, and anastomoses with the mammary branch of the internal thoracic artery; the posterior branch pursues a flexuous course between the thighs to the vulva, where its terminal branches anastomose with the internal pudic artery. In the male the artery crosses the medial side of the spermatic cord and runs forward to the umbilical region; it supplies the inguinal lymph glands, prepuce, and skin. The **anterior femoral artery** may arise by a short common trunk with the lateral circumflex. The former, accompanied by the anterior branch of the femoral nerve, dips in between the rectus femoris and vastus medialis. The **lateral circumflex artery** passes forward between the sartorius medially and the rectus femoris and tensor fasciæ latæ laterally and supplies branches to these muscles and the glutei. In addition to muscular branches of considerable size, an **articular branch** (A. genu suprema) arises a little below the middle of the thigh and runs down-

ward and forward to the medial face of the stifle joint. The **saphenous artery** is
large. It arises from the medial surface of the femoral a little below the middle of the
thigh, descends superficially to the proximal part of the leg, and divides into two
branches. The smaller **dorsal branch** (Ramus dorsalis) passes obliquely downward
and forward across the medial surface of the tibia to the flexion surface of the hock and
gives off the second, third, and fourth **superficial dorsal metatarsal arteries.** These
descend along the grooves between the metatarsal bones and each divides into two
proper digital arteries. The **plantar branch** (Ramus plantaris), which is much the

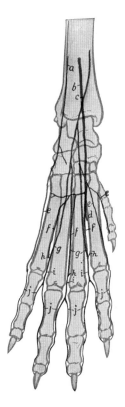 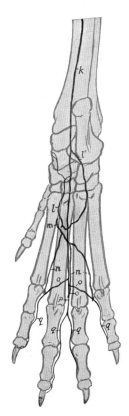

Fig. 622.—Arteries of Distal Part of Right Hind Limb of Dog; Dorsal View.

a, Lateral branch of anterior tibial artery; *b*, anterior tibial artery; *c*, saphenous artery (dorsal branch); *d*, perforating metatarsal artery; *e*, dorsal metatarsal arteries; *f*, deep dorsal metatarsal arteries; *g*, superficial dorsal metatarsal arteries; *h*, anastomoses between dorsal and plantar arteries; *i*, common digital arteries; *j*, proper digital arteries.

Fig. 623.—Arteries of Distal Part of Right Hind Limb of Dog; Plantar View.

k, Saphenous artery (plantar branch); *l, l'*, medial and lateral plantar arteries; *m*, perforating metatarsal artery; *n*, deep plantar metatarsal arteries; *o*, superficial plantar metatarsal arteries; *p*, common digital artery; *q*, proper digital arteries.

larger, descends on the medial face of the gastrocnemius and the long digital flexor.
It gives off the **lateral tarsal artery** to the lateral surface of the tarsus, and at the
plantar face of the tarsus detaches the **medial** and **lateral plantar arteries;** these
descend on either side of the deep flexor tendon and unite with the perforating
metatarsal artery to form the proximal plantar arch. The artery continues
down the middle of the plantar surface of the metatarsus and divides near the
metacarpo-phalangeal joints into three **superficial plantar metatarsal arteries**
(II, III, IV). These vessels unite with three **deep plantar metatarsal arteries,** which
descend from the proximal plantar arch and with branches from the dorsal meta-

tarsal arteries. From these anastomoses four **plantar digital arteries** result; of these, the central two have a common digital trunk.

The **popliteal** and **posterior femoral arteries** present nothing of special interest.

The **posterior tibial artery** is very small, being replaced largely by the saphenous. It supplies twigs to the flexor muscles at the proximal part of the leg.

The **anterior tibial artery** descends on the anterior face of the tibia and tarsus and is continued as the perforating metatarsal artery, which passes through the upper part of the space between the second and third metatarsal bones and concurs with the plantar arteries in the formation of the proximal plantar arch. Besides muscular and articular branches, the anterior tibial supplies the **fifth dorsal metatarsal artery** for the lateral side of the fifth digit. At the proximal part of the metatarsus it gives off three **deep dorsal metatarsal arteries** which descend in the intervals between the metatarsal bones and concur with the superficial dorsal metatarsal and the plantar arteries in the formation of the digital arteries. The latter resemble in general arrangement the corresponding arteries of the thoracic limb.

The **internal iliac artery** (Fig. 620) runs backward and a little outward across the ilio-psoas, and on reaching the ilium divides into parietal and visceral branches; it gives off the seventh lumbar artery. The **parietal branch** is the larger. It runs backward on the lateral wall of the pelvis, passes out through the lesser sciatic notch, and breaks up into branches which supply the muscles of this region; this terminal part may be regarded as the posterior gluteal artery. It gives off the following branches: (1) The **ilio-lumbar artery** passes outward between the ilio-psoas and the shaft of the ilium and ramifies in the gluteus medius, giving branches to the ilio-psoas and tensor fasciæ latæ; it may arise from the internal iliac. (2) The **anterior gluteal artery** passes out through the greater sciatic foramen and supplies branches to the glutei. (3) **Muscular branches** go to the obturator internus, coccygeus, and retractor ani. (4) The **superficial lateral coccygeal artery** (A. caudalis lateralis superficialis) passes back at first on the lateral face of the coccygeus and continues beneath the skin along the side of the tail. The **visceral branch** is equivalent to the **internal pudic artery;** it passes back below the parietal branch on the lateral face of the rectum, retractor ani, and coccygeus. Its chief collateral branches are: (1) The **umbilical artery,** which pursues a flexuous course and supplies twigs to the bladder, ureter, and ductus deferens. In the bitch it gives off a large **uterine artery** which ramifies chiefly in the body and neck of the uterus and the vagina and anastomoses with the utero-ovarian. (2) The **middle hæmorrhoidal artery** arises near the ischial arch, passes upward and forward on the lateral surface of the rectum, gains its dorsal surface, and anastomoses with the posterior mesenteric; it supplies the rectum and the anus, together with its muscles and glands. (3) A small **perineal artery** is detached to the perineum. In the male the trunk turns around the ischial arch as the **artery of the penis** (A. penis). This vessel, after giving off the **deep artery of the penis** (A. profunda penis), which supplies the **artery of the bulb** (A. bulbi urethræ) and enters the corpus cavernosum, is continued as the **dorsal artery of the penis** (A. dorsalis penis) along the dorsum penis. In the female the terminal branches of the trunk go to the vulva, vestibular bulb, and clitoris.

THE VEINS[1]

The arrangement of the veins is, of course, correlated in general with the arterial system, but a few special features are worthy of mention.

The **coronary sinus** is a large but short trunk formed by the confluence of the cardiac veins; it opens into the right atrium below the posterior vena cava. The

---

[1] Many of the veins are shown in the illustrations of the arteries.

great cardiac vein ascends in the left longitudinal groove of the heart to the coronary groove, in which it courses to the diaphragmatic surface. Here it is joined by one or two **lesser cardiac veins,** which are satellites of the right coronary artery, thus forming the coronary sinus. There is commonly a vein in the intermediate groove which joins the great cardiac vein.

The **anterior vena cava** (Figs. 613, 614) is formed by the junction of short right and left **brachiocephalic veins,** and each of the latter results from the confluence of **jugular** and **brachial veins.**

The **vena azygos** (Fig. 613) is continuous behind with the first lumbar vein; it resembles that of the horse, and receives at the ninth or tenth thoracic vertebra a **vena hemiazygos.**

Two **jugular veins** are present on each side. The **external jugular vein** is the chief vein of the neck; it is formed by the union of external and internal maxillary veins at the posterior border of the mandibular gland. The two external jugulars are commonly united by a transverse branch below the cricoid cartilage. Each passes along the neck on the sterno-cephalicus, covered only by the skin and cutaneous muscle, dips under the cleido-cervicalis, and joins the internal jugular. The **internal jugular vein** is the satellite of the common carotid artery. It results usually from the junction of laryngeal and thyroid veins, but in some cases it is formed by the confluence of the ventral cerebral and occipital veins.

The **external maxillary vein** arises on the lateral nasal region by the junction of the dorsal nasal vein with the angularis oculi. Near the infraorbital foramen it receives the lateral nasal vein, and a little lower the superior labial. In its course along the anterior border of the masseter it receives the vena reflexa, which arises in the pterygo-palatine fossa by the junction of infraorbital, sphenopalatine, and palatine radicles, together with a branch from the cavernous sinus. At the ventral border of the mandible it is joined by the inferior labial vein, which receives the buccinator vein. The lingual vein is connected with its fellow by a superficial transverse branch at the insertion of the sterno-hyoidei. The sublingual and submental veins terminate in a variable manner, but often form a common trunk which joins the lingual.

The **internal maxillary vein** arises from the pterygoid plexus, formed chiefly by dorsal lingual, inferior alveolar, deep temporal, pterygoid, and meningeal tributaries. It receives the dorsal cerebral, auricular, superficial temporal, transverse facial, and masseteric veins, and often a trunk formed by the union of the ventral cerebral and occipital veins.

The **brachial** and **radial veins** are satellites of the arteries.

The **ulnar vein** is usually double. It unites below the carpus with a branch of the interosseous vein to form the superficial venous arch.

The **cephalic vein** accompanies the ulnar artery in the forearm and joins the superficial venous arch below.

The **accessory cephalic vein** arises from the union of three dorsal metacarpal veins. It joins the cephalic vein about the middle of the forearm.

There are three short **volar metacarpal veins** which open into the superficial venous arch. They are formed above the metacarpo-phalangeal joints by the junction of the **volar digital veins,** of which there are two for each of the chief digits. The volar vein of the first digit joins the superficial venous arch.

Each of the chief digits has two **dorsal digital veins,** while the first digit has one.

The **portal vein** (Fig. 625) is formed by the union of a common intestinal or mesenteric vein with the gastro-splenic vein. It receives the gastro-duodenal vein. The intestinal trunk is formed in the mesentery by the confluence of veins from the jejunum; it receives an ileo-cæco-colic vein.

The **posterior vena cava,** its collateral affluents, and common iliac radicles present no special features of importance.

The **internal iliac vein** corresponds in regard to its tributaries with the branches of the artery, except that it is not divided into parietal and visceral branches.

The **external iliac, femoral,** and **popliteal veins** with their collateral tributaries are satellites of the arteries.

The **anterior tibial vein** is usually double, and the **posterior tibial vein** is very small.

The **saphenous vein** is the upward continuation of the medial plantar metatarsal vein. It communicates by a large branch with the dorsal metatarsal vein, and ascends the leg as a satellite of the saphenous artery and its plantar branch. The **recurrent tarsal vein** is larger. It is formed at the lower part of the leg by the union of dorsal metatarsal and lateral plantar metatarsal veins, crosses the lateral surface of the leg obliquely upward and backward, ascends behind the gastrocnemius, and joins the femoral vein.

The **metatarsal** and **digital veins** resemble in general the corresponding vessels of the forelimb.

THE LYMPHATIC SYSTEM

The **cisterna chyli** is relatively large and is fusiform; it is ventral to the last thoracic and first lumbar vertebræ and is related ventro-medially to the aorta, dorsally and laterally to the right crus of the diaphragm and the psoas minor. The **thoracic duct** passes forward to the right of the aorta and ventral to the vena azygos as far as the sixth thoracic vertebra; here it crosses to the left face of the œsophagus and runs forward, turns ventrally at the thoracic inlet, and opens into the left brachiocephalic or the common jugular vein. The duct may be single throughout, but often divides anteriorly into two branches, which may then unite and form a dilatation which receives the left tracheal duct and the vessels from the forelimb. Other variations occur and the primitive plexiform arrangement persists in varying degree. The **tracheal lymph ducts** accompany the internal jugular veins. The right duct opens into the right brachiocephalic vein.

The **mandibular lymph glands** (Fig. 615) are commonly two or three in number on each side, but as many as five have been observed. They are situated in the angle between the masseter and the mandibular salivary gland, above and below the external maxillary vein, and covered only by the skin and cutaneus muscle.

A small round **parotid lymph gland** is situated superficially between the upper part of the posterior border of the masseter and the parotid salivary gland or partly or completely under cover of the latter. Exceptionally two or three may be present.

The **suprapharyngeal lymph glands,** usually one on each side, lie dorsal to the pharynx, under cover of the sterno-mastoideus and the mandibular salivary gland. They are related deeply to the rectus capitis ventralis and the carotid artery, and the anterior end is just behind the occipito-mandibularis (Fig. 433). Each is about two inches (ca. 5 cm.) long in a good-sized dog. In a good many cases a second gland is present.

Anterior cervical lymph glands appear to be absent in the majority of subjects, but in other cases small nodes may be present in relation to the anterior end of the thyroid gland. It should be noted, however, that parathyroids may be mistaken for lymph nodes unless a microscopic examination is made. **Middle cervical lymph glands** are apparently not present, and the same is usually the case in regard to the **posterior cervical lymph glands;** but in some cases one or more of the latter occur on the ventral face of the trachea near the thoracic inlet.

The **prescapular** or **superficial cervical lymph glands** lie on the serratus ventralis, at the anterior border of the supraspinatus, embedded in a mass of fat. Usually two are present on each side, but there may be three or only one. They are oval and are about an inch long in a dog of medium size when two are present.

The **axillary lymph gland** lies in a mass of fat on the medial face of the distal part of the teres major. It is discoid and is about an inch (ca. 5 cm.) wide in a large dog. Exceptionally a second smaller gland is present.

The **cubital lymph gland** is usually absent. When present, it is situated on the medial face of the long head of the triceps or on the latissimus dorsi.

Intercostal lymph glands do not appear to be present.

Two **sternal lymph glands** (Fig. 613) are usually present, one on each side. They are situated on the course of the internal thoracic vessels, usually at the second sternebra. A third node may be present in front of the more constant one, and in some cases, on the other hand, the gland is absent on one side. In large dogs the gland may be nearly an inch long.

The **mediastinal lymph glands** are variable in number and arrangement. None have been found in the posterior mediastinum, and the following statement is to be understood merely as an account of what is most often found. Two or three glands usually occur on the ventral face of the trachea, œsophagus, and brachiocephalic artery to the left of the anterior vena cava; they are related ventrally to the thymus, when the latter is not too much reduced. Others may be found on the lateral face of the brachiocephalic artery. One or two glands are usually present between the trachea and the anterior vena near the thoracic inlet, and one or two are on the right side of the trachea, dorso-lateral to the right brachial artery. Another lies on the trachea at the crossing of the vena azygos over that tube.

The **bronchial lymph glands** are usually four in number. The largest one, the **middle bronchial gland** (Lg. bifurcationis) is situated in the angle of divergence of the chief bronchi, to which it is adapted, so that it is somewhat V-shaped. The **left bronchial gland** (Lg. bronchialis sinistra) lies on the left bronchus at its bifurcation and in the angle between the aortic arch and the left pulmonary artery.

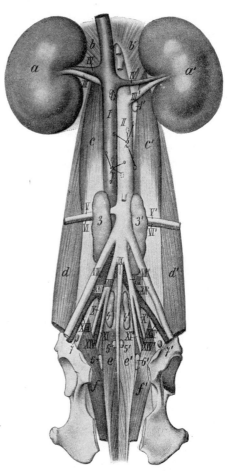

FIG. 624.—SUBLUMBAR AND PELVIC LYMPH GLANDS OF DOG.

1, 1', Renal lymph glands; 2, lumbar lymph glands; 3, 3', 4, 4', internal iliac lymph glands; 5, 5', medial sacral lymph glands; 6, 6', lateral sacral lymph glands; 7, 7', external iliac lymph glands; *a, a'*, kidneys; *b, b'*, crura of diaphragm; *c, c'*, psoas minor; *d, d'*, iliopsoas; *e, e'*, sacro-coccygeus ventralis; *f, f'*, coccygeus; *I*, posterior vena cava; *II*, abdominal aorta; *III, III'*, renal arteries; *IV, IV'*, renal veins; *V, V'*, *VI, VI'*, circumflex iliac vessels; *VII, VII'*, external iliac arteries; *VIII, VIII'*, internal iliac arteries; *IX*, middle sacral artery; *X, X'*, parietal branches of internal iliac arteries; *XI, XI'*, visceral branches of internal iliac arteries; *XII, XII'*, common iliac veins; *XIII, XIII'*, external iliac veins; *XIV, XIV'*, internal iliac veins. (After Merzdorf).

The smaller **right bronchial gland** (Lg. bronchialis dextra) lies on the right bronchus, lateral to the œsophagus; it is not always present. The **apical bronchial gland** (Lg. bronchialis apicalis) is anterior to the root of the apical bronchus, in relation in front to the vena azygos. These glands are commonly black, and the same is true of the gland on the right side of the trachea in relation to the vena azygos, indicating that all of these glands receive lymph from the lungs.

Minute **pulmonary lymph glands** occur in the lungs along the bronchial branches.

The **lumbar lymph glands** are situated in the sublumbar region around and between the aorta and posterior vena cava. Most of them are very small and are difficult to find in the fat in which they are usually embedded. Their number is very variable; as many as fifteen have been counted.

Usually two large **internal iliac lymph glands** are present. The right one lies along the posterior part of the posterior vena cava and the common iliac vein; the left one is similarly placed in relation to the aorta and left common iliac vein. They may be two inches or more (ca. 5–6 cm.) in length and nearly an inch (ca. 2 cm.) wide in large dogs. In some cases there is a third small gland anterior to the large one in relation to the origin of the circumflex iliac vessels. In most cases there is a gland on each side of the middle sacral artery, between that vessel and the internal iliac artery and its visceral branch. The gland may be absent on one side or there may be instead two or three glands.

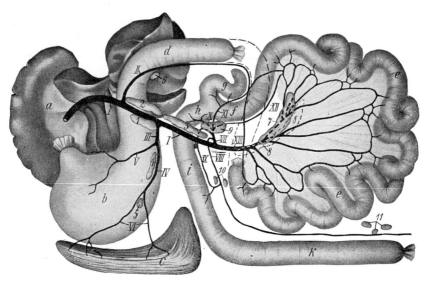

Fig. 625.—Lymph Glands of Abdominal Viscera of Dog.

1–6, Portal lymph glands; *7, 8*, mesenteric lymph glands; *9–11*, cæco-colic lymph glands; *a*, liver; *b*, stomach; *c*, spleen; *d*, duodenum (cut off and indicated by dotted line); *e*, jejunum; *f*, ileum; *g*, cæcum; *h, i, k*, right, transverse, and left parts of colon; *I*, portal vein; *II*, gastro-duodenal vein; *III*, gastro-splenic vein; *IV*, splenic vein; *V*, common gastric vein; *VI*, radicles of splenic vein; *VII*, ileo-cæco-colic vein; *VIII*, left colic vein; *IX*, middle colic vein; *X*, right colic vein; *XI*, cæcal vein; *XII*, ileal vein; *XIII*, jejunal venous trunk. (After Merzdorf.)

The **external iliac lymph glands** are situated on the ventral surface of the psoas minor, between the diverging external and internal iliac veins.[1] They are inconstant and variable. One may occur on each side or two on one side and none on the other.

The **sacral lymph glands** are situated along the roof of the pelvic cavity and may easily escape notice on account of the fat in which they are embedded. Their size, number, and arrangement are very variable. In the majority of subjects there are two or three glands on the anterior part of the sacro-coccygeus ventralis in relation to the middle coccygeal artery. In some cases one or two glands occur at the interspace between the sacro-coccygeus ventralis and the coccygeus. In other cases glands are present centrally or on one side only or appear to be absent.

The term **portal lymph glands** may be applied to those which occur along the course of the portal vein and some of its affluents. The larger and more constant of these are as follows: One lies to the left of the portal vein, on the origin of the

[1] It seems not unlikely that these glands correspond regionally to the deep inguinal glands of the horse.

duodenum and the duodenal angle (or head) of the pancreas. In most cases two glands occur on the right of the portal vein and further back along the mesenteric vein. Glands of variable size and number occur in the gastro-splenic part of the omentum along the splenic vein and its radicles.

The **mesenteric lymph glands** consist chiefly of two elongated nodes which extend from the root of the mesentery of the jejuno-ileum along the course of the artery of the small intestine and the corresponding vein.

The **colic lymph glands** comprise a variable number of nodes (5–8) in the meso-colon. One is at the origin of the ileo-cæco-colic vein; a second one may be found here. One or two may be found in the transverse mesocolon and others (2–5) occur at the terminal part of the colon.

The **renal lymph glands,** one on each side of the aorta, are in relation to the origin of the renal arteries; the right one is concealed by the vena cava.

The **superficial inguinal lymph glands** are embedded in the fat about the external inguinal ring in relation to the external pudic vessels. In the male they are related medially to the penis; in the female they are commonly termed **supra-mammary** on account of their relation to the base of the inguinal mammary glands. In the majority of cases two are present on each side, but there is often only one, and sometimes three occur on one side.

The **popliteal lymph gland** is situated in a mass of fat on the gastrocnemius at the level of the stifle joint. It is between the biceps femoris and semitendinosus, but is more superficial than in the other animals, and hence is commonly palpable. It is oval and in large dogs may be nearly two inches (ca. 4.5 cm.) long and more than an inch (ca. 3 cm.) wide.

NEUROLOGY

THE NERVOUS SYSTEM

The **nervous system** (Systema nervorum) is a complex mechanism by which the organism is brought into functional relation with its environment, and its various parts are coördinated. For purposes of gross description it is divided primarily into two parts, central and peripheral. The **central nervous system** (Systema nervorum centrale) comprises—(a) the **spinal cord** (Medulla spinalis), and (b) the **brain** (Encephalon). The **peripheral nervous system** (Systema nervorum periphericum) includes—(a) the **cranial** and **spinal nerves** with their **ganglia,** and (b) the **sympathetic nervous system.**

The division into central and peripheral parts is quite arbitrary, and is used simply as a matter of convenience of description. The fibers of which the nerves are composed either arise or end within the central system, and therefore constitute an integral part of the latter. The structural and functional unit of the nervous system is the **neurone,** which consists of the **cell-body,** usually termed the **nerve-cell** or **cyton,** and all its **processes.** The processes arise as outgrowths from the cell-body and conduct impulses to or from the cell; they vary greatly in length, some being less than a millimeter long, while others extend from a cell in the spinal cord to the distal end of a limb. A nerve is composed of such processes, usually enclosed in a protecting and insulating sheath, and united into bundles by areolar tissue. The neurones in the brain and spinal cord are embedded in a peculiar supporting tissue termed **neuroglia.** This consists of a very intricate feltwork of glia-fibers, many of which are connected with the small glia-cells or astrocytes. In addition the nervous tissue is invested closely by a vascular layer of connective tissue, the pia mater, from which ingrowths extend into the nervous substance proper.[1]

To the naked eye the central nervous system appears to be composed chiefly of two kinds of substance, white and gray. The **white substance** (Substantia alba) is dead white in color and is soft in the natural state. It consists largely of medullated nerve-fibers, packed closely together and arranged more or less clearly in large or small bundles or tracts (funiculi, fasciculi). The **gray substance** (Substantia grisea) is usually brownish-gray in color, often with a tinge of pink. It is softer than the white substance and much more vascular. It is composed chiefly of cell-bodies and non-medullated processes. In some situations it is modified to form the **gelatinous substance** (Substantia gelatinosa), which is pale yellowish-gray and jelly-like.

Ganglia are gray masses found on the dorsal roots of the spinal nerves and on the course of many nerves. They are commonly ovoid in form, but some are irregular in shape and branched. They vary greatly in size; some are microscopic, while others are several inches long. They are enclosed in a fibrous capsule. They are composed largely of the cell-bodies of neurones, but have connected with and passing through them nerve-fibers (processes) which extend peripherally and centrally. In origin and function the spinal ganglia belong properly to the central system, but it is customary to include them with the peripheral part in gross anatomical descriptions.

Nerves (Nervi) are conducting trunks composed of bundles of parallel nerve-fibers. They are enveloped in a fibro-elastic sheath, the epineurium, from which septa pass in between the bundles of fibers; it contains the blood- and lymph-vessels. Nerves are classified according to their central connections as **cranial** or **cerebral, spinal,** and **sympathetic.** The groups of cells of which the nerve-fibers are processes are termed the **nuclei of origin** (Nuclei originis) or **terminal nuclei** (Nuclei

---

[1] Limitations of space and the purpose of this work preclude consideration of the finer structure of the nervous system, for which ample literature is available.

terminales) of the nerves, according as the latter conduct impulses in a peripheral or central direction.[1] On the same basis the nerve-fibers are designated **efferent** and **afferent** respectively. A bundle of fibers which passes from one nerve-trunk to another is called an **anastomotic branch** (Ramus anastomoticus). In some situations the exchange of branches between adjacent nerves is so free as to constitute a **nerve-plexus** (Plexus nervorum). The term **ramus communicans** is properly restricted to branches which connect the ventral divisions of the spinal nerves with adjacent ganglia or nerves of the sympathetic system. The terminal twigs of the nerves are designated, according to their distribution, as **muscular branches** (Rami musculares), **cutaneous nerves** (Nervi cutanei), and **articular nerves** (Nervi articulares). The muscular branches are motor in function, the cutaneous and articular sensory, but all contain vasomotor fibers which control the caliber of the blood-vessels.

THE MENINGES

The central organs of the nervous system are enclosed in three meninges or membranes. From without inward these are: (1) the dura mater, (2) the arachnoidea, and (3) the pia mater.

THE DURA MATER

The **dura mater** is a dense, resistant membrane of white fibrous tissue; in the fresh state it is bluish-white in color. On account of the difference in its arrangement within the cranium from that in the spinal canal it is customary to describe it as consisting of two parts, cerebral and spinal; these portions are continuous with each other at the foramen magnum.

The **cerebral dura mater** (Dura mater encephali) is adherent to the interior of the cranium, and may be regarded as forming an internal periosteum for the bones here as well as being an envelope of the brain. Its outer surface is connected with the bony wall of the cranial cavity by numerous fine fibrous strands and by blood-vessels; hence it appears rough in many places when separated from the wall. The degree of adhesion varies greatly at different points. It is most firmly attached at the various projections, e. g., the petrosal, ethmoidal and internal parietal crests, and the internal occipital protuberance; also at the base and the foramen magnum. Before the sutures are closed the dura is connected with the sutural ligaments and through them is continuous with the external periosteum. The cranial nerves receive sheaths from the dura, which is thus continuous without the cranium with the epineurium and periosteum. Along the roof and sides (except as noted above) the adhesion is relatively slight, and lymph spaces are said to exist between the dura and the bone. The internal surface of the dura is smooth and glistening, since it is lined by endothelium and is moistened by a fluid resembling lymph; it forms the outer boundary of the subdural space. In accordance with its double function the dura is composed of two layers, which are, however, intimately adherent to each other in most places in the adult. The venous sinuses are channels between the two layers and are lined by endothelium. They have been described with the other vessels. Two folds or septa given off from the inner surface of the dura project into the cranial cavity between the gross subdivisions of the brain. These are: (1) the falx cerebri; (2) the tentorium cerebelli.

The **falx cerebri** is a sickle-shaped median partition which is situated in the longitudinal fissure between the cerebral hemispheres. It is attached dorsally to the internal parietal crest, in front to the ethmoidal crest, and behind to the internal occipital protuberance. Its dorsal border is convex and separates into two layers

---

[1] These cell-groups are the real origin or termination of a nerve. The term "apparent origin" is a convenient designation for the point at which a nerve is connected with the surface of the brain.

which enclose the dorsal longitudinal sinus. Its ventral border is concave and lies over the corpus callosum. The falx is thick above, but much thinner below, and is in some places cribriform.[1]

The **tentorium cerebelli** is a crescentic fold which occupies the transverse fissure between the cerebellum and the cerebral hemispheres. It is attached dorsally to the internal occipital protuberance and laterally to the petrosal crest. Its ventral border is thin, concave, and free; it forms an arch (Incisura tentorii) over the mid-brain.

The **diaphragm sellæ** is a thickening of the dura which roofs over the pituitary fossa; it covers the pituitary body and the cavernous and intercavernous sinuses. It is perforated centrally by an opening (Foramen diaphragmatis) for the infundibulum.

The falx cerebelli, a sickle-shaped fold which projects into the median notch between the cerebellar hemispheres in man, is not present in the domesticated animals. There is instead merely a slight thickening of the dura.

The **spinal dura mater** (Dura mater spinalis) forms a tube around the spinal cord from the foramen magnum to the second or third segment of the sacrum. It is separated from the periosteum of the spinal canal by a considerable **epidural space** (Cavum epidurale), which is occupied by fatty connective tissue and veins. It is held in position chiefly by the sheaths which it furnishes to the roots of the spinal nerves, and in its anterior part by two ligaments; the latter connect it with the ventral atlanto-occipital membrane and with the dens of the axis. It is large in proportion to its contents, but its diameter is not uniform. It is largest in the atlas, small in the thoracic region, and becomes very small in its terminal part, where it encloses the delicate filum terminale of the spinal cord.

The **subdural space** (Cavum subdurale) is the cavity between the inner surface of the dura mater and the arachnoidea. It is a mere capillary space which contains just sufficient fluid to moisten its surfaces; this fluid is usually regarded as lymph, which is replenished by filtration through the walls of the blood-vessels. The space is in communication with the lymph paths of the nerve sheaths.

The Arachnoidea

The **arachnoidea** is a very delicate and transparent membrane which is situated between the dura and pia mater. Its outer surface forms the inner wall of the subdural space and is covered by a layer of endothelium continuous with that of the opposed surface of the dura mater. Between it and the pia mater is the **subarachnoid space** (Cavum subarachnoideale), which contains the **cerebrospinal fluid.** An inner surface can scarcely be said to exist, since deeply the membrane becomes a reticulum of fine fibers which traverse the subarachnoid space and are attached to the pia mater. The arachnoidea furnishes sheaths to the cerebral nerves from their superficial origins to a variable but usually short distance beyond the emergence from the sac. In the case of the optic nerve this sheath extends to the eyeball.

The **cerebral arachnoidea** (Arachnoidea encephali), except in the case of the great longitudinal and transverse fissures, does not dip into the sulci on the surface of the brain. On the summits of the gyri it is so closely attached to the pia mater that the two form practically a single membrane. Its outer part bridges over the sulci, and here the subarachnoid space is partially divided up by the loose arachnoid tissue into intercommunicating cavities. In certain situations the arachnoidea is separated from the pia by spaces of considerable depth and extent. These enlargements of the subarachnoid space are termed **subarachnoid cisterns** (Cisternæ subarachnoidales). In them the subarachnoid tissue does not form a close network,

[1] In the horse the posterior part of the falx cerebri does not extend down to the corpus callosum, and the cerebral hemispheres are here in contact and adherent to each other over a small area. In the other animals the falx does not descend so far as in the horse.

but consists of a relatively small number of long, thread-like strands which traverse the cavity.

The chief cisternæ are: (1) the cisterna magna, which is at the angle formed between the posterior face of the cerebellum and the dorsal surface of the medulla oblongata. It communicates with the fourth ventricle through lateral openings in the latter, and behind with the wide subarachnoid space of the spinal cord; (2) the cisterna pontis, on the ventral surface of the pons; (3) the cisterna basalis, which lies at the base of the cerebrum and is divided by the optic chiasma into two parts (cisterna chiasmatis, cisterna interpeduncularis); (4) the cisterna fossæ lateralis, situated at the lower part of the lateral fissure and continuous with the cisterna basalis.

Along the dorsal border of the falx cerebri the arachnoidea bears bulbous excrescences, the **arachnoid granulations.** These are enclosed in thin evaginations of the dura mater and project into the dorsal longitudinal sinus or the parasinoidal sinuses along either side of it. In some cases they are sufficiently large to exert pressure on the bone and produce in it depressions of variable depth.

The **spinal arachnoidea** (Arachnoidea spinalis) is continuous with that of the brain at the foramen magnum. It forms a relatively wide tube around the spinal cord, so that the latter (enclosed in the pia) is surrounded by a very considerable quantity of cerebrospinal fluid. The spinal subarachnoid space is traversed by fewer trabeculæ than is the case in the cranium. It is partially subdivided by three imperfect septa. One of these, the septum dorsale, is median and dorsal. The other two, the ligamenta denticulata, are lateral and will be described with the pia mater.

PIA MATER

The **pia mater** is a delicate and very vascular membrane, which invests closely the surface of the brain and spinal cord and sends processes into their substance. It also furnishes sheaths to the nerves, which blend outside of the dural sac with the epineurium.

The **cerebral pia mater** (Pia mater encephali) follows accurately all the inequalities of the surface, dipping into all the fissures and sulci of the cerebrum, and into the larger fissures of the cerebellum. Its external surface, which forms the inner boundary of the subarachnoid space, is covered by a layer of endothelium. From its deep face numerous trabeculæ are given off which penetrate into the substance of the brain, forming a path for the blood-vessels, and concurring with the neuroglia in forming the supporting tissue of the nervous substance proper. The larger blood-vessels of the brain lie within the subarachnoid space, but the smaller vessels ramify in the pia, forming rich plexuses. The twigs which penetrate into the gray matter are enclosed in pial sheaths. They are end-arteries, *i. e.*, constitute the entire supply of the district which they enter and do not anastomose with adjacent vessels.

Important folds of the pia extend into two of the great fissures of the brain. One of these passes in at the transverse fissure between the cerebellum and the cerebral hemispheres, and is continued so as to overlie the third ventricle; it forms the **tela chorioidea** of that cavity. Another fold passes in at the fissure between the cerebellum and the medulla oblongata and forms the **tela chorioidea** of the fourth ventricle. They constitute paths for the deeper vessels and their edges contain vascular convolutions which are known as **chorioid plexuses.** They will receive further consideration more appropriately later.

The **spinal pia mater** (Pia mater spinalis) is thicker and denser than that of the brain. It has a strong outer layer of fibrous tissue, most of the fibers of which are longitudinal. The inner layer is vascular and adheres closely to the surface of the spinal cord, because numerous processes extend into the latter from it. It sends a fold into the median ventral fissure and also helps to form the median dorsal septum of the cord. Along the median ventral line it forms a band-like thickening, the linea splendens, along which the ventral spinal artery runs. On each side the pia mater gives off a strong longitudinal band, the **ligamentum denticulatum,** which is connected externally with the dura mater. The medial border extends in a line between the dorsal and ventral roots of the nerves. The lateral border is denticulated and to a large extent free. The denticulations are attached to the dura between the nerve-roots.

NERVOUS SYSTEM OF THE HORSE
THE SPINAL CORD

The **spinal cord** (Medulla spinalis) is the part of the central nervous system which is situated in the vertebral canal. It extends from the foramen magnum to about the middle of the sacrum. Its average length is about 77 inches (ca. 192.5 cm.), and its weight about 9½ ounces (ca. 270 grams).

It is approximately cylindrical, but more or less flattened dorso-ventrally. There is no natural line of demarcation between it and the medulla oblongata, but for descriptive purposes the division is usually assumed to be at the plane of the foramen magnum. Its posterior part tapers rapidly to a point, forming the **conus medullaris.** This is prolonged for a short distance by the slender **filum terminale.**

Forty-two pairs of spinal nerves are connected with the sides of the spinal cord. They are classified as eight cervical, eighteen thoracic, six lumbar, five sacral, and five coccygeal. According to the attachments of these series of nerves the spinal cord is divided into **cervical, thoracic, lumbar,** and **sacral** parts.[1]

In the embryo these divisions correspond primitively to the regions of the vertebral column, but later, through unequal growth of the cord and spine, the correspondence between the two is not at all exact in the anterior regions and is lost in the last two. The lumbar part of the cord in the horse ends at the junction of the fifth and sixth lumbar vertebræ, so that the roots of the last lumbar nerve must run backward the length of the last lumbar vertebra to reach the intervertebral foramen through which it emerges. The conus medullaris reaches only to the anterior part of the sacral canal, so that the roots of the sacral and coccygeal nerves extend backward in the spinal canal for a considerable distance, forming a leash of bundles, in the center of which lie the conus medullaris and the filum terminale. This arrangement is expressively designated the **cauda equina.**

Each pair of spinal nerves is attached by its root-fibers to a certain length of the cord, and the latter is, therefore, regarded as consisting of as many segments as there are pairs of nerves. It is to be noted, however, that there is no line of demarcation between the segments other than the intervals between the root-fibers of adjacent nerves.

The segments are of different lengths; the longest are the third to the sixth cervical, which measure 11, 10, 10, and 8.5 cm. respectively. The spinal nerves are in general designated according to the vertebræ behind which they emerge from the vertebral canal. In the neck, however, there are eight pairs of nerves and only seven vertebræ; here the first nerve emerges through the intervertebral foramen of the atlas and the eighth between the last cervical and the first thoracic vertebræ.

In the greater part of the thoracic region the spinal cord is fairly uniform in size, but there are two conspicuous enlargements which involve the segments with which the nerves of the limbs are connected. The **cervical enlargement** (Intumescentia cervicalis) begins gradually in the fifth cervical vertebra and subsides in

[1] In a horse about 16½ hands high these parts measured 65 cm. (ca. 26 in.), 86 cm. (ca. 34.4 in.), 27 cm. (ca. 10.8 in.), and 15 cm. (ca. 6 in.) respectively (Dexler).

the second thoracic. Its maximum transverse diameter is about an inch (ca. 25 mm.) and its dorso-ventral nearly half an inch (ca. 12 mm.). The **lumbar enlargement** (Intumescentia lumbalis) is situated in the fourth and fifth lumbar vertebræ.

It is a little narrower than the cervical enlargement, and its dorso-ventral diameter is also slightly smaller. Behind this the cord tapers rapidly to form the **conus medullaris.** The tip of the latter is continued by a delicate glistening strand, the **filum terminale,** which is composed largely of fibrous tissue continued from the pia mater, covered by arachnoid.

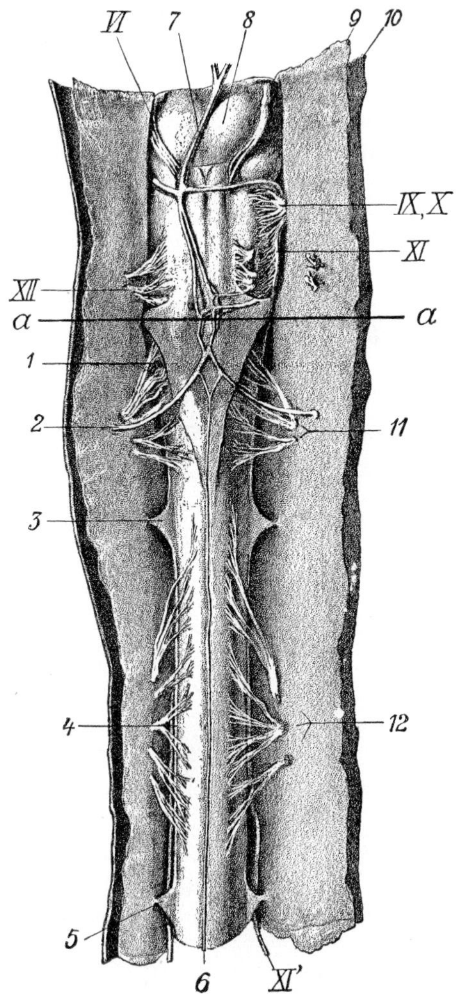

FIG. 626.—VENTRAL VIEW OF MEDULLA OBLONGATA AND FIRST AND SECOND SEGMENTS OF SPINAL CORD OF HORSE; THE MEMBRANES ARE CUT AND REFLECTED.

1, Lig. suspensorium arachnoideale; *2*, right cerebrospinal artery; *3, 5*, digitations of lig. denticulatum; *4*, free border of lig. denticulatum; *6*, middle spinal artery; *7*, basilar artery; *8*, pons; *9*, arachnoidea; *10*, dura mater; *11, 12*, ventral root-bundles of first and second segments of spinal cord; *VI*, N. abducens; *IX, X*, glosso-pharyngeus and vagus; *XI*, accessory, medullary part; *XI'*, accessory, spinal part; *a*, line between medulla oblongata and spinal cord. (Dexler, in Ellenberger-Baum, Anat. d. Haustiere.)

FIG. 627.—CAUDA EQUINA.

1, Dura and arachnoidea divided and reflected; *2*, spinal cord; *3*, nerve-roots. (From Leisering's Atlas, reduced.)

The surface of the spinal cord is divided into two similar halves by a **dorsal median groove** and a **ventral median fissure.** On either side of the former is the **dorso-lateral groove** (Sulcus dorsalis lateralis), at which the fibers of the dorsal nerve-roots enter the cord; it is faint except at the enlargements, and is represented by two grooves in the first cervical segment. The ventral root-fibers as they emerge from the cord do not form a continuous series, but arise from a zone (Area radicularis ventralis) 3 to 5 mm. in width, a little lateral to the ventral median fissure, and no groove is found here. In the greater part of the cervical region and the anterior part of the thoracic region there is a shallow **dorsal intermediate groove** (Sulcus intermedius dorsalis) a short distance lateral to the median groove. These grooves indicate the division of the white matter of the cord into columns to be described later.

Examination of cross-sections of the spinal cord shows that it is a bilaterally symmetrical structure, incompletely divided into right and left halves by a ventral fissure and a dorsal septum. The **ventral median fissure** (Fissura mediana ventralis) is narrow and penetrates nearly to the middle of the dorso-ventral diameter of the cord. It is occupied by a fold of pia mater. The **dorsal median septum** (Septum medianum dorsale) is a partition which descends from the dorsal median groove to about the middle of the cord. It apparently consists of condensed neuroglia with an admixture of pial tissue. The two halves of the cord are connected

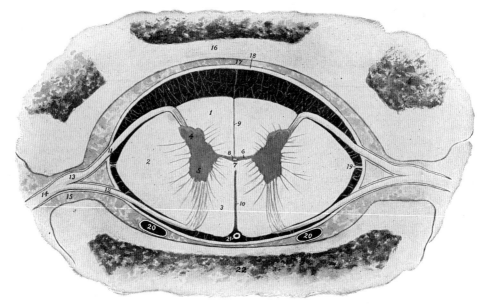

Fig. 628.—Cross-section of Spinal Cord *in situ*, Enlarged and in Part Schematic.

1, Dorsal column; *2*, lateral column; *3*, ventral column; *4*, dorsal horn; *5*, ventral horn; *6*, gray commissure; *7*, white commissure; *8*, central canal; *9*, dorsal septum; *10*, ventral fissure; *11*, dorsal nerve-root; *12*, ventral nerve-root; *13*, spinal ganglion; *14*, spinal nerve; *15*, intervertebral foramen; *16*, arch of vertebra; *17*, epidural space; *18*, dura mater (represented a little too thick); *19*, ligamentum denticulatum; *20, 20*, longitudinal venous sinuses; *21*, middle spinal artery; *22*, body of vertebra. The subdural and subarachnoid spaces (black) are traversed by delicate trabeculæ. The outer part of the arachnoid and the pia mater are not shown.

by commissures of gray and white substance. The **gray commissure** (Commissura grisea) is a transverse band of gray substance at the ventral end of the dorsal septum. It is traversed medially by the central canal of the cord. The **white commissure** (Commissura alba) is a bridge of white substance which connects the ventral columns of the cord over the dorsal end of the ventral median fissure, and constitutes a conducting path from one side to the other.

The **central canal** of the spinal cord (Canalis centralis medullæ spinalis), the spinal vestige of the lumen of the embryonal neural tube, is a minute passage which tunnels the gray commissure. It opens at its anterior end into the posterior part of the fourth ventricle of the brain, and its terminal part in the conus medullaris forms a slight dilatation, the ventriculus terminalis. It is lined by epithelium and is surrounded by a layer of modified neuroglia (Substantia grisea centralis).

The **gray substance** of the spinal cord as seen in cross-sections resembles roughly a capital **H,** the cross-bar of the letter being formed by the gray commissure. Each lateral part is considered as consisting of **dorsal** and **ventral gray columns** (Columna grisea dorsalis, ventralis), which appear in cross-section as the so-called **horns** (Cornu dorsale, ventrale). In the greater part of the cord the dorsal column or horn is elongated and narrow and tapers to a point which extends almost to the surface of the cord at the attachment of the dorsal root-fibers of the spinal nerves. Its apex or tip consists of gray substance which is lighter in color and less opaque than that of the rest of the horn, and is termed the **substantia gelatinosa.** The ventral column or horn is short, thick, and rounded, and is separated from the surface of the cord by a thick layer of white substance, through which the fibers of the ventral roots of the spinal nerves pass. From the middle of the cervical region to the lumbar region there is a medial projection of gray substance on the ventral part of the dorsal column; this is the **nucleus dorsalis.** In the anterior part of the cord there is an outward projection of the gray substance at the base of the ventral horn; this is termed the **lateral column** or **horn.** The demarcation between the gray and white substance is in many places indistinct; this is especially the case laterally, where processes of gray substance extend into the white substance, producing what is known as the **formatio reticularis.**

Cross-sections of the spinal cord present the following gross **regional characters**): (1) The cervical cord near the medulla is compressed dorso-ventrally. Its width is about 18 mm. and its greatest thickness about 8 mm. It has dorsally a deep median sulcus and a distinct dorso-lateral sulcus. Lateral grooves are also present. The dorsal cornua are strongly everted. Each has an expanded head, which comes very close to the surface of the cord, and has an extensive cap of substantia gelatinosa. The neck is distinct. The ventral cornua are short and blunt and diverge very little. The gray commissure is about in the middle of the section, and 2.5 mm. in length. According to Dexler, the column between the median and lateral grooves dorsally is the funiculus cuneatus, the funiculus gracilis being very small and not showing on the surface in this region. In the middle of the cervical region the diameters are about 16 mm. and 10 mm. respectively. The ventral surface is somewhat flattened. The dorsal cornua have pointed ends and turn decidedly outward. The ventral cornua are short and thick and are directed very slightly outward; their ends are about 4 mm. from the ventral surface. The gray commissure is just above the middle of the section and is about 2 mm. long. The cervical enlargement measures about 25 mm. transversely and 12 mm. vertically. The dorsal cornua are smaller than the ventral and have a large cap of substantia gelatinosa. The ventral cornua are short and thick, curve strongly outward, and are about 4 mm. from the ventral surface. Each bears a prominence on its medial side near the base. The gray commissure is considerably above the middle of the section and is about 4 mm. long. (2) In the middle of the thoracic region the cross-section is biconvex, the ventral surface being the more strongly curved. The transverse diameter is about 15 mm. and the dorso-ventral about 10 mm. The gray columns are close together, the gray commissure being only about 1 mm. in length, and lying considerably above the middle of the section. The dorsal cornua are short and have slightly enlarged ends. The ventral cornua have a uniform diameter, turn very little outward, and end about 3 mm. from the ventral surface. (3) The lumbar enlargement is much flattened, especially dorsally. The transverse diameter is about 22 mm. and the dorso-ventral 9 to 10 mm. The cornua are very large. The ventral cornua are thick and rounded and turn sharply outward; they end about 2 mm. from the ventral surface. The dorsal cornua are smaller and shorter and do not diverge so strongly. The gray commissure is about in the middle of the section and is about 3 mm. long. In the third lumbar vertebra the cord is about 3 mm. narrower and thicker, and both surfaces are about equally convex. The dorsal cornua are smaller, considerably everted, and constricted in the middle. The ventral cornua are very short and do not turn outward. (4) In the first sacral vertebra the cord is almost round and is 5 to 6 mm. in diameter; the cornua are relatively very large and the commissure has the form of a high intermediate mass.

The ventral horn contains large cells, the axones of which emerge as the fibers of the ventral nerve-roots (Fila radicularia). The axones of many cells cross to the opposite side in the white commissure and pass out in a ventral root of that side, or enter the white substance and pass forward and backward, associating various segments of the cord. Some pass to the ventral horn of the opposite side at the same or at different levels. Others pass to the periphery of the cord, join the cerebellospinal fasciculus, and extend to the cerebellum. Scattered through the gray substance are many smaller cells with axones which pursue a short course and serve to connect different parts of the gray substance.

The **white substance** of the spinal cord is divided into three pairs of **columns.** The **dorsal columns** (Funiculi dorsales) lie on either side of the dorsal median septum and extend outward to the dorso-lateral groove and the dorsal gray column.

The **ventral columns** (Funiculi ventrales) are situated on either side between the median fissure and the ventral gray columns. They are connected above the fissure by the white commissure. The **lateral columns** (Funiculi laterales) are lateral to the gray columns on either side; their limits are indicated superficially by the dorso-lateral groove and the emergence of the ventral root-fibers. The intermediate groove (where present) indicates a subdivision of the dorsal column into two fasciculi or tracts; the medial of these is the **fasciculus gracilis;** the lateral one is the **fasciculus cuneatus.**

The amounts of gray and white substance vary greatly in different parts of the cord both absolutely and relatively. In cross-section the absolute areas of both are greatest in the enlargements. The relative area of gray substance is smallest in the thoracic region (except at its anterior end), and increases from the lumbar enlargement backward.

Investigations have shown that in man the columns of white substance are subdivided into fasciculi or tracts, which constitute definite conducting paths of greater or less length. Our knowledge of the tracts in the domesticated animals is very limited, and it is quite unsafe to make inferences from the arrangement in man. As evidence of this it may be noted that the ventral cerebrospinal or direct pyramidal tract of man cannot be recognized as such.

The dorsal white columns consist essentially of two sets of axones. The afferent or sensory axones which come from the cells of the spinal ganglia enter as the dorsal roots of the spinal nerves and divide into two branches in the vicinity of the dorsal gray column. The anterior branches form the direct sensory path to the brain and extend in the fasciculus cuneatus and fasciculus gracilis or corresponding tracts to nuclei in the medulla oblongata. The posterior branches extend backward for varying distances and give off numerous collaterals to cells of the gray column, thus forming part of the mechanism for the mediation of reflex action. Some collaterals cross in the white commissure to the opposite side. Many of these fibers are collected in the comma-shaped tract between the fasciculus gracilis and cuneatus. The second set of axones arises from the smaller cells of the gray column. They enter the white substance, divide into anterior and posterior branches, forming the fasciculi proprii or ground bundles of the cord. Some branches cross to the opposite side. The function of this set of axones is chiefly to associate various levels of the cord.

The lateral columns contain some axones of the dorsal nerve-roots, which (in man) are grouped in the marginal tract of Lissauer, situated just dorsal to the apex of the dorsal horn. The cerebellospinal fasciculus (direct cerebellar tract of Flechsig) extends along the periphery of the lateral column. It contains the axones of the cells of the nucleus dorsalis (Clarke's column), which proceed to the medulla oblongata and enter the cerebellum by the restiform body. The rubrospinal tract (of Monakow) appears to take the place of the lateral cerebrospinal fasciculus or crossed pyramidal tract of man. It lies at the medial side of the cerebellospinal fasciculus. Its fibers arise in the nucleus ruber of the mid-brain, cross the median plane (decussation of Forel), and pass backward in the tegmentum and medulla oblongata to the lateral column of the cord. It is a path for motor impulses coming from the cerebral cortex and the cerebellum. The lateral fasciculus proprius or ground-bundle is deeply situated at the side of the gray columns. The bulk of its fibers are axones of cells of the dorsal column which divide into anterior and posterior branches. They are intersegmental paths which associate different levels of the gray substance of the cord. The significance of the remaining fibers is not yet known.

The ventral white columns do not contain a ventral cerebrospinal or direct pyramidal tract, as in man. There is a small tract (Fasciculus intracommissuralis ventralis) dorsal to the white commissure, which separates it from the rest of the ventral column. It extends to the middle of the thoracic region. It contists of intersegmental fibers, and contains in the anterior part of the cervical cord in the sheep and goat both crossed and direct pyramidal fibers. The descending cerebellospinal fasciculus extends from the cerebellum to the lumbar region. In the cervical region it occupies a semilunar area which reaches almost to the surface ventro-laterally. Scattered fibers belonging to it lie also in the medial part of the ventral column. Posteriorly it diminishes in size and comes to occupy a position next to the ventral median fissure, corresponding to the sulco-marginal fasciculus of man (Dexler).

THE BRAIN

The **brain** (encephalon) is the part of the central nervous system that is situated in the cranial cavity. It is the enlarged and highly modified cephalic part of the primitive neural tube. It conforms in great part in size and shape to the cavity in which it lies. Its average weight without the dura mater is about

23 ounces (ca. 650 gm.), and forms about $\frac{1}{7}$ of 1 per cent. of the body-weight in a subject of medium size.

It is desirable to examine the general external configuration of the brain before studying its various parts in detail.[1]

When divested of its membranes and vessels (Fig. 629), its ventral surface or base presents the median **brain stem** (Caudex encephali), which is continuous with the spinal cord without any natural line of demarcation; it divides in front into two branches, the cerebral peduncles, each of which disappears into the mass of the corresponding cerebral hemisphere. The brain stem consists of three parts. The **medulla oblongata** is the posterior part which extends forward as the direct continuation of the spinal cord. The **pons** is a transversely elongated mass which appears to turn up on either side into the cerebellum. The **cerebral peduncles** (Pedunculi cerebri) extend forward from the pons and diverge to plunge into the ventral part of the cerebral hemispheres. The area between them is the **interpeduncular fossa.** It is largely covered by the **hypophysis cerebri** or pituitary body, a yellowish-brown, discoid structure, which is connected with the base of the cerebrum by a delicate tube called the **infundibulum.**[2] On drawing the pituitary body gently aside, the infundibulum is seen to be attached to a slight gray eminence, the **tuber cinereum.** Behind this is the **mammillary body** (Corpus mammillare), a well-marked round prominence. The posterior part of the space is perforated by numerous openings for the passage of small arteries, and hence is termed the **substantia perforata posterior.** A large band of white matter, the **optic tract** (Tractus opticus), crosses the anterior end of the cerebral peduncle obliquely, and unites with the opposite tract to constitute the **optic chiasm** (Chiasma opticum), and form the anterior boundary of the interpeduncular fossa. Above and in front of the chiasm the hemispheres are separated by the median **longitudinal fissure.** In contact with the anterior extremity of each hemisphere is the **olfactory bulb** (Bulbus olfactorius), an oval enlargement which occupies the ethmoidal fossa of the cranium. This appears as a gray swelling on a wide flat band, the **olfactory tract** (Tractus olfactorius), which is continued behind by two divergent bands, the **olfactory striæ.** The **medial stria** (Stria medialis) disappears after a very short course on to the medial surface of the hemisphere. The **lateral stria** (Stria lateralis) is larger and longer; it runs backward, inclines at first outward and then curves medially and disappears on the concealed or tentorial surface of the hemispheres. It is separated from the lateral cerebral gyri by a distinct groove, the **sulcus rhinalis.** Along the medial side of the stria are two eminences. The anterior of these is the **trigonum olfactorium,** a gray elevation situated in the angle of divergence of the medial and lateral striæ. Behind this is a depression, the **fossa lateralis,** which is continued across the lateral stria and sharply limits the second and much larger eminence, the **piriform lobe.**

The superficial origins of most of the cranial nerves are visible on the base of the brain.

The **olfactory nerve-fibers** join the convex surface of the olfactory bulb and give it a shaggy appearance in specimens which have been removed intact—a difficult proceeding.

The **second** or **optic nerves** converge to the optic chiasm.

The **third** or **oculomotor nerve** arises from the medial part of the cerebral peduncle.

---

[1] The description given here is intended to present the chief facts in regard to the brain as they may be studied in the dissecting-room. The vessels and membranes, which must be examined first, have been described.

[2] Unless care is used in removing the brain, the infundibulum is likely to be torn and the hypophysis left in the cranium. In this case there is a small opening which communicates with the third ventricle.

The **fourth** or **trochlear nerve** may be seen emerging between the pons and the cerebral hemisphere, but its connection with the brain is not visible.

The **fifth** or **trigeminal nerve** is connected with the lateral part of the pons.

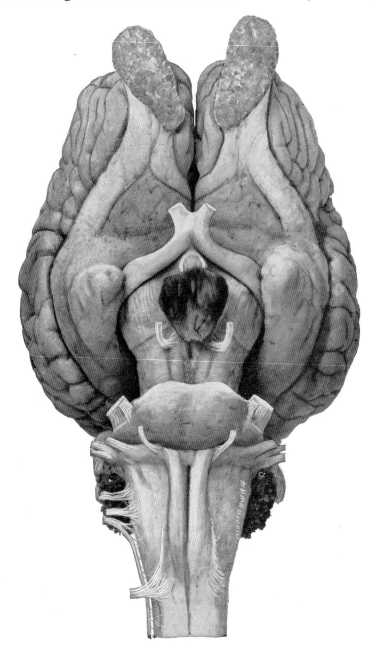

Fig. 629.—Base of Brain of Horse, About Natural Size.
Hardened *in situ.*

The **sixth** or **abducent nerve** arises just behind the pons and lateral to the pyramid of the medulla.

The **seventh** or **facial** and the **eighth** or **acoustic nerves** arise close together just behind the pons on the extremity of the corpus trapezoideum.

The **ninth** or **glosso-pharyngeal**, the **tenth** or **vagus**, and the **eleventh** or **spinal accessory nerves** are connected by a linear series of roots with the lateral aspect of the ventral surface of the medulla. The spinal part of the accessory nerve comes forward along the edge of the medulla to join its medullary root.

The **twelfth** or **hypoglossal nerve** arises from the posterior part of the medulla along the lateral edge of the pyramid.

The parts that are visible when the brain is viewed from above are the cerebral hemispheres, the cerebellum, and part of the medulla oblongata. The **cerebral hemispheres** (Hemisphæria cerebri) form an ovoid mass, and are separated from each other by the median **longitudinal fissure** (Fissura longitudinalis cerebri),

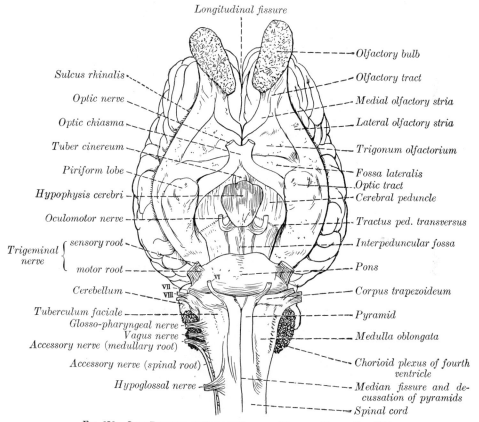

Longitudinal fissure

Sulcus rhinalis

Optic nerve

Optic chiasma

Tuber cinereum

Piriform lobe

Hypophysis cerebri

Oculomotor nerve

Trigeminal nerve { *sensory root* — *motor root* —

Cerebellum — VII VIII

Tuberculum faciale
Glosso-pharyngeal nerve
Vagus nerve
Accessory nerve (medullary root)

Accessory nerve (spinal root)

Hypoglossal nerve

VI

Olfactory bulb

Olfactory tract

Medial olfactory stria

Lateral olfactory stria

Trigonum olfactorium

Fossa lateralis
Optic tract
Cerebral peduncle

Tractus ped. transversus

Interpeduncular fossa

Pons

Corpus trapezoideum

Pyramid

Medulla oblongata

Chorioid plexus of fourth ventricle

Median fissure and decussation of pyramids
Spinal cord

Fig. 630.—Line Drawing of Base of Brain of Horse. (Key to Fig. 629.)
VI, Abducent nerve; *VII*, facial nerve; *VIII*, acoustic nerve.

in which the falx cerebri is situated. Their surfaces are marked by thick ridges, the **gyri cerebri,** separated by **sulci.** The upturned ends of the **olfactory bulbs** are seen in front of the frontal poles of the hemispheres. The occipital poles of the hemispheres overlie the anterior part of the cerebellum, from which they are separated by the **transverse fissure** (Fissura transversa cerebri) and the tentorium cerebelli contained in it. The **cerebellum** is a much smaller rounded mass which conceals the greater part of the medulla oblongata. Its surface is divided into a middle lobe, the **vermis cerebelli,** and two lateral **cerebellar hemispheres** (Hemisphæria cerebelli). It is marked by numerous gyri and narrow sulci which have in general a transverse direction. The posterior third of the **medulla oblongata** is not covered by the cerebellum.

The brain is developed from the expanded cephalic part of the neural tube of the embryo. The process comprises a series of thickenings, flexures, and unequal growth and expansion of various parts of the tube. In the higher animals the result is that [the tubular character of the brain is not very evident, since the lumen comes to consist of four irregular cavities, the cerebral ventricles, which are connected by narrow passages. The tube is first subdivided by two constrictions into three brain vesicles, termed respectively the hind-brain or rhombencephalon, the mid-brain or mesencephalon, and the fore-brain or prosencephalon. The hind-brain gives rise to three secondary segments and the fore-brain to two. The annexed table indicates the origin of the principal structures of the fully developed brain from the primitive vesicles. It has become customary to describe the brain with reference to its embryological relations.

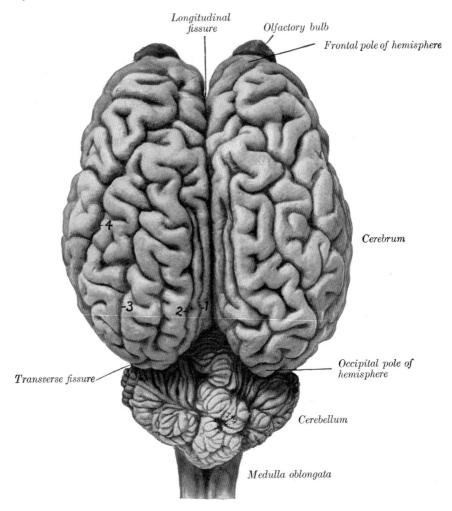

FIG. 631.—BRAIN OF HORSE; DORSAL VIEW, ABOUT ⅔ NATURAL SIZE. HARDENED *in situ.*

1, Entomarginal fissure; *2,* marginal fissure; *3,* ectomarginal fissure; *4,* suprasylvian fissure.

TABLE INDICATING THE DERIVATION OF THE PRINCIPAL PARTS OF THE BRAIN

PRIMARY SEGMENTS.	SECONDARY SEGMENTS.	DERIVATIVES.	CAVITIES.
Rhombencephalon (posterior vesicle)........	Myelencephalon	Medulla oblongata...........	Fourth ventricle
	Metencephalon	Pons........................ Cerebellum	
	Isthmus rhombencephali ..	Anterior cerebellar peduncles.. Anterior medullary velum	
Mesencephalon (middle vesicle).............	Mesencephalon	Corpora quadrigemina .... Cerebral peduncles	Cerebral aqueduct
Prosencephalon (anterior vesicle)........ ..	Diencephalon............	Optic thalami.............. Hypothalamic tegmenta...... Pineal body.................	Posterior part of third ventricle
	Telencephalon...........	Pituitary body .... Optic nerves and retinæ...... Cerebral hemispheres .... Olfactory tracts and bulb.....	Anterior part of third ventricle. Lateral ventricles and olfactory continuations.

THE RHOMBENCEPHALON
THE MEDULLA OBLONGATA

The **medulla oblongata** (Figs. 629, 632, 635) lies on the basilar part of the occipital bone. It is quadrilateral in outline, but much wider in front than behind, and compressed dorso-ventrally. Its length, measured from the root of the first cervical nerve to the pons, is about two inches (ca. 5 cm.).

Its **ventral surface** is convex in the transverse direction, and presents a **ventral median fissure** (Fissura mediana ventralis), which is continuous behind with the similar fissure of the spinal cord. The posterior part of the fissure is faintly marked, but in front it becomes deeper and ends in a small depression (Foramen cæcum) behind the central part of a transverse band, the **corpus trapezoideum.** On either side of the fissure is a rounded tract, the **pyramid** (Pyramis), which is bounded laterally by a faint groove (Sulcus intermedius ventralis). The pyramids join the pons in front; behind they become narrower and disappear into the substance of the medulla, in which their fibers intercross, forming the **decussation of the pyramids** (Decussatio pyramidum).[1] The superficial origin of the **abducent nerve** (N. abducens) is just lateral to the anterior end of the pyramid. The **corpus trapezoideum** is a transverse band which extends across the surface immediately behind the pons. It is crossed by the pyramids, which cut off a small central part. The lateral part extends out to the roots of the seventh and eighth nerves on either side. Behind the lateral part of the corpus trapezoideum there is a variably developed rounded eminence, the **tuberculum faciale.** The root-fibers of the **hypoglossal nerve** form an oblique linear series lateral to the posterior part of the pyramid.

The **dorsal surface** is largely concealed by the cerebellum and forms the greater part of the floor of the fourth ventricle. The **dorsal median fissure** (Fissura mediana dorsalis), the direct continuation of the corresponding groove of the spinal cord, extends forward to about the middle of the surface. Here the **restiform bodies,** which constitute the lips of the fissure, diverge to form the lateral boundaries of a triangular depression; this is the posterior part of the rhomboid fossa or floor of the fourth ventricle of the brain. The dorso-lateral groove winds outward and forward to the lateral aspect of the medulla, where it presents the roots of the **glosso-pharyngeal, vagus,** and **accessory nerves.** Lateral to it is a distinct oval eminence on the anterior part of the lateral column, termed the **tuberculum cinereum.** The central canal of the cord is continued in the posterior part of the medulla, inclines dorsally, and opens in the posterior angle of the fourth ventricle. Hence it is customary to distinguish a closed and an open part of the medulla. The dorsal aspect of the latter, which is concealed at present, will be considered later in the description of the fourth ventricle.

The lateral surface is narrow behind, wider and rounded in front. From it the root-fibers of the ninth, tenth, and eleventh cranial nerves arise in a linear series, and alongside of it the spinal part of the eleventh nerve passes forward to join the medullary root. Close inspection reveals the presence of striæ which curve ventrally and backward from the surface of the restiform body toward the hypoglossal root-fibers; these are the **external arcuate fibers** (Fibræ arcuatæ externæ). The recess between the lateral aspect of the medulla and the cerebellum is occupied by an irregular mass of villous projections of the pia mater, containing tufts of vessels; this is the **chorioid plexus of the fourth ventricle,** and is the lateral edge of the **tela chorioidea** of the ventricle. On raising the chorioid plexus, it is seen that the tela chorioidea is attached to the dorsal aspect of the medulla, and reinforces here the wall of the fourth ventricle; also that the restiform body ter-

---

[1] The decussation varies superficially in different specimens. In some there is a distinct superficial crossing of fibers so that the median fissure is practically effaced at this point.

minates in front by entering the base of the cerebellum, forming its posterior peduncle.

In the medulla the fiber tracts of the spinal cord either terminate in the nuclei of the gray matter or undergo changes in their relative position, and new tracts appear. The gray matter is highly modified and forms masses which have no homologues in the cord. The central canal of the closed part of the medulla is surrounded by a thicker layer of gray matter than is the case in the spinal cord. As the medulla opens out this gray matter is naturally spread in the floor of the fourth ventricle. The dorsal horns of gray matter become wide, spread apart, and are broken up to a great extent in the formatio reticularis. Two elongated masses of cells appear above the central gray matter; these are the **nucleus gracilis** and **nucleus cuneatus,** and in them the fasciculi of like name gradually end. In front of these are the **terminal nuclei** of the afferent or sensory cranial nerves and of the sensory portions of the mixed nerves. The ventral horns are succeeded by the **nuclei of origin** of the efferent or motor cranial nerves and the motor root-fibers of the mixed nerves. Of the twelve pairs of cranial nerves, the last eight are connected with nuclei in the medulla and pons. The **posterior olivary nucleus** (Nucleus olivaris caudalis) is a conspicuous gray mass which lies dorsal to the pyramid on each side. On cross-sections it appears

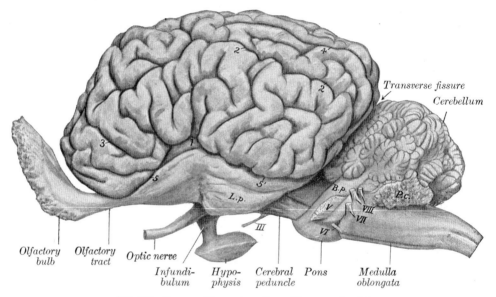

Fig. 632.—Brain of Horse; Left View; Hardened *in situ.*

1, Lateral fissure; *2,* suprasylvian fissure; *3,* presylvian fissure; *4,* ectomarginal fissure; *5, 5′,* sulcus rhinalis anterior et posterior; *L. p.,* piriform lobe; *B. p.,* middle peduncle of cerebellum (brachium pontis); *P. c.,* choroid plexus of fourth ventricle. Roman numerals indicate roots of cranial nerves.

as a wavy layer of gray matter which is folded on itself so as to enclose a mass of white matter. It is about 2 cm. long in the horse, but is smaller in circumference than in man and hence does not cause any very distinct external enlargement (olivary eminence), as in the latter. It is connected with the opposite side of the cerebellum by the cerebello-olivary fibers. At its medial side are two small accessory olivary nuclei. The **pyramidal tracts,** which are small in ungulates, send most of their fibers across to the opposite side in the posterior part of the medulla, forming the **pyramidal decussation.** Some fibers, however, continue in the ventral column of the same side of the cord, and others are connected with the nuclei of the motor nerve-roots. From the nucleus gracilis and nucleus cuneatus fibers arise which are traceable forward to the thalamus. These are the **internal arcuate fibers** (Fibræ arcuatæ internæ), which curve across the median plane ventral to the central gray matter and form with those of the opposite side the **decussation of the fillet** (Decussatio lemniscorum). Beyond the decussation the fibers form an important longitudinal tract which extends forward in the mid-brain. This is the **fillet** or **lemniscus,** the chief continuation of the sensory conducting path from the dorsal roots of the spinal nerves. The **external arcuate fibers** (Fibræ arcuatæ externæ), some of which were seen on the lateral aspect of the medulla, have a similar origin. Part of them (Fibræ dorsales) pass directly to the dorsal aspect of the restiform body of the same side; others (Fibræ ventrales) cross to the opposite side, descend close to the ventral fissure, and then curve upward and forward to the restiform body. The decussation of the arcuate fibers forms the distinct median **raphe** seen on cross-sections of the medulla anterior to the pyramidal decussation. The restiform body, situated dorso-laterally, contains, in addition to the arcuate fibers, the **cerebello-olivary fasciculus** before mentioned, and the **cerebellospinal fasciculus** or direct cerebellar tract. The **dorsal longitudinal fasciculus** corresponds to the ventral ground-bundle of the spinal cord, displaced dorsally by the decussation of the pyramids and fillet. In the posterior part of the medulla it is not marked off from the fillet, along the dorsal edge of which it lies. From the level of the hypoglossal nucleus forward it is distinct and can be traced as a conspicuous tract in the ventral margin of the gray matter of the floor of the fourth ventricle and of the central gray matter of the mid-brain. Ventral to the restiform body and related laterally to the external arcuate fibers there is a considerable bundle of longitudinal fibers, the **spinal root** (Tractus spinalis) **of the fifth nerve;** medial to it is the terminal nucleus of the sensory root of the nerve.

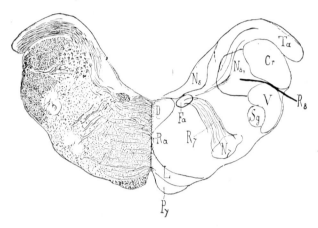

FIG. 633.—CROSS-SECTION OF MEDULLA OBLONGATA OF HORSE, PASSING THROUGH FACIAL NUCLEUS.

Cr, Corpus restiforme; D, dorsal longitudinal fasciculus; Fa, ascending part of facial nerve; L, fillet; $N7$, nucleus of facial nerve; $N8$, triangular nucleus of of vestibular root of eighth nerve; $N8'$, spinal root of eighth nerve; Py, pyramid; Ra, raphe; $R7$, radicular part of facial nerve; $R8$, vestibular root of eighth nerve; Sg, substantia gelatinosa; Ta, posterior end of tuberculum acusticum; V, spinal root of trigeminus. (Ellenberger-Baum, Anat. d. Haustiere.)

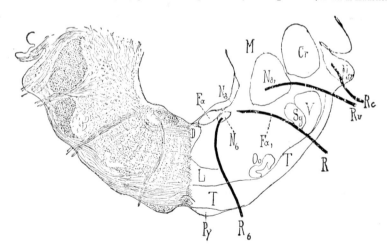

FIG. 634.—CROSS-SECTION OF MEDULLA OBLONGATA OF HORSE; SECTION PASSES THROUGH MIDDLE OF CORPUS TRAPEZOIDEUM.

Cr, Corpus restiforme; D, dorsal longitudinal bundle; Fa, ascending part of facial nerve; Fa', emergent or descending part of facial nerve; L, fillet; M, central white matter of cerebellum; $N6$, abducens nucleus; $N8$, triangular nucleus; $N8'$, nucleus of Deiters; $N8''$, tuberculum acusticum; Oo, anterior olive; Py, pyramid; $R6$, root of abducens nerve; $R7$, root of facial nerve; Rc, cochlear nerve; Rv, vestibular nerve; Sg, substantia gelatinosa; T, corpus trapezoideum; V, spinal root of trigeminus. (Ellenberger-Baum, Anat. d. Haustiere.)

THE PONS

The **pons** is that part of the brain stem which lies between the medulla and the cerebral peduncles; it is marked off from these ventrally by anterior and posterior grooves. Viewed ventrally, it is elongated transversely, convex in both directions, and presents a wide shallow median groove (Sulcus basilaris), which lodges the basilar artery. Laterally a large part of its mass curves dorsally and backward into the base of the cerebellum, forming the **middle cerebellar peduncle** (Brachium pontis). The superficial origin of the trigeminal (fifth) nerve is at the lateral limit of the ventral surface. Transverse striations indicate the course of superficial (ventral) fibers which connect the two sides of the cerebellum. The dorsal surface is blended on either side with the overlying anterior peduncles of the cerebellum; the central free portion forms the anterior part of the floor of the fourth ventricle, and will be considered in the account of that cavity.

On cross-section the pons is seen to be composed of dorsal and ventral parts. The **dorsal part** (Pars dorsalis pontis) consists superficially of a layer of gray matter covered by the ependyma of the fourth ventricle. Beneath this the median raphé of the medulla is continued into the pons, dividing it into similar halves. In the anterior part of the pons the fillet divides into a medial and a lateral part, the **medial** and **lateral fillets** (Lemniscus medialis, lateralis); the latter arches outward to reach the outer side of the anterior cerebellar peduncle. The **dorsal longitudinal fasciculus** becomes sharply defined into a round bundle which lies close to the raphé under the gray matter of the floor of the fourth ventricle. In cross-section the **formatio reticularis** forms a large area below the superficial gray matter and the longitudinal bundles. Dorso-laterally is the large rounded section of the **anterior cerebellar peduncle**. Lower down is a large bundle, the **sensory root of the fifth nerve**. In front of this is the **motor nucleus** of the same nerve, lateral to which is its **motor root**. The **basilar** or **ventral part** of the pons (Pars basilaris pontis) is composed of transverse and longitudinal fibers, and a large amount of gray matter which is broken up into small masses (Nuclei pontis) by the intersection of the fibers. The **transverse fibers** are gathered laterally into a compact mass which turns dorsally and backward and enters the central white matter of the cerebellum, forming the **middle cerebellar peduncle**. Centrally the fibers are arranged in bundles which intercross. The transverse fibers are chiefly of two kinds. Some arise from the Purkinje cells of the cerebellar cortex and pass either to the opposite side of the cerebellum or turn at the raphé and run forward and backward in the brain stem. Others are axones of cells of the nuclei pontis, and pass to the hemispheres of the cerebellum. The corpus trapezoideum is mainly the central continuation of the cochlear division of the acoustic nerve. Above it is the small **anterior olivary nucleus** (Nucleus olivaris nasalis). The longitudinal fibers of the ventral part of the pons consist chiefly of the **cerebrospinal** or **pyramidal fasciculi**. These come from the ventral part (basis) of the cerebral peduncles and are situated laterally, interspersed among the deep transverse fibers in the anterior part of the pons. Toward the posterior part the bundles incline toward the median plane and become collected into a compact mass which appears superficially at the posterior border. Many fibers come from the cerebral cortex and terminate in the nuclei of the gray matter of the pons; they may be designated **corticopontile fibers**.

THE CEREBELLUM

The **cerebellum** is situated in the posterior fossa of the cranium, and is separated from the cerebral hemispheres by the transverse fissure and the tentorium cerebelli which occupies it. It overlies the pons and the greater part of the medulla, from which it is separated by the fourth ventricle. Its average weight is about two ounces (ca. 60 gm.), or about 9 per cent. of the weight of the entire brain. Its shape is approximately globular but very irregular. It is somewhat compressed dorso-ventrally and its transverse diameter is the greatest.

The **anterior surface** faces dorsally and forward and is covered partially by the tentorium cerebelli. The **posterior surface** is almost vertical. The **ventral surface** or **base** lies over the fourth ventricle, and is connected by three pairs of peduncles with the medulla, pons, and mid-brain.

It is customary to recognize three gross divisions of the cerebellum, viz., the median vermis and two lateral hemispheres. The **vermis cerebelli** is curved in a circular manner so that its two extremities are close together, or even in contact on the ventral surface. The anterior extremity is termed the **lingula**; it lies between the cerebellar peduncles and gives attachment to the **anterior medullary velum** (Velum medullare orale), a thin lamina which forms the anterior part of the roof of the fourth ventricle. The posterior extremity, the **nodulus**, gives attachment to the **posterior medullary velum** (Velum medullare aborale), which covers the posterior recess of the fourth ventricle. The **hemispheres** (Hemisphæria cerebelli) are separated from the vermis by two deep paramedian fissures. They lie in the lateral depressions of the cerebellar compartment of the cranium.

In tracing the fissures from behind forward it will be noticed that they are nearly sagittal as far as the anterior surface, where they diverge widely, so that the vermis forms all of the fore part of the cerebellum.

The surface of the cerebellum is further cut up into numerous **gyri** (cerebelli) by narrow and relatively deep **sulci** (cerebelli), many of which approach a transverse direction. Certain of the sulci are more pronounced than the others, and by means of them it is possible to define groups of gyri. Such groups are termed **lobes,** and have received specific names, derived chiefly from the systematic descriptions of the human cerebellum.

The lobes of the vermis are readily distinguished on median section. Enumerated from the anterior to the posterior extremity they are: (1) lingula, (2) lobus centralis, (3) lobus ascendens, (4) lobus culminis, (5) lobus clivi, (6) tuber vermis, (7) pyramis, (8) uvula, (9) nodulus. Each hemisphere is cut into laterally by two sulci which mark off two sagittal discoid masses, termed by Ziehen tabulations. The lateral tabulation consists of four or five lobules, the lowest of which is regarded as the flocculus. The medial part of the hemisphere is divided into three or four lobes. Martin proposes the term tractus for the sagittal masses; on this basis the vermis would become the tractus medianus, and the others tractus laterales (primus, secundus, etc.).

The **cerebellar peduncles** (Pedunculi cerebelli), three on each side, join the central white substance of the cerebellum at the base. The **posterior peduncle** is the restiform body of the medulla, a large rounded tract derived from the lateral and ventral columns of the cord. Near the middle of the medulla it inclines outward, forms the lateral wall of the fourth ventricle, and ends by entering the central white substance of the cerebellum. The **middle peduncle** is formed, as previously seen, by the brachium pontis. The **anterior peduncle** (Brachium conjunctivum) passes forward on either side on the dorsal surface of the pons, forming the lateral boundary of the fore part of the fourth ventricle. They disappear under the corpora quadrigemina into the substance of the mid-brain. At the point of disappearance the **trochlear (fourth) nerve** emerges from the mid-brain. In some cases two or three bundles of fibers (Fila lateralia pontis) arise in the angle between the middle and anterior peduncle, curve obliquely forward and downward over the outer aspect of the latter, and spread out on the ventral face of the cerebeal peduncle just in front of the pons.

On sagittal section the cerebellum is seen to consist of a layer of gray **cortical substance** (Substantia corticalis) and the white **medullary substance.** The white substance consists of a large basal mass (Corpus medullare) which is joined by the peduncles and gives off primary **laminæ** (Laminæ medullares) to the lobules; from these secondary and tertiary laminæ arise, the latter entering the gyri. The arrangement on sagittal section is tree-like, hence the term **"arbor medullaris,"** which is applied to it. The central gray substance consists of groups of cells which form small **nuclei** embedded in the central white substance.

The principal connections established by the peduncular fibers of the cerebellum are as follows: The posterior peduncle (Corpus restiforme) is composed of afferent and efferent fibers which connect the cerebellum with the medulla and spinal cord. The **cerebello-spinal fasciculus** or **direct cerebellar tract,** which arises from the cells of the nucleus dorsalis (Clarke's column) of the cord, ends in the cortex of the vermis; many of its fibers cross to the opposite side. Numerous **arcuate fibers** from the nucleus gracilis and nucleus cuneatus of the same and opposite sides establish connections with cells of the cerebellar cortex. **Olivo-cerebellar** fibers (chiefly afferent) connect with the olivary nucleus of the same and of the opposite side of the medulla oblongata. The **nucleo-cerebellar fasciculus** comprises fibers derived from the nuclei of the fifth, eighth, and tenth cranial nerves (Edinger). The **descending cerebello-spinal fasciculus** consists of fibers which terminate in relation with cells of the ventral horns of the spinal cord. The chief facts concerning the middle peduncle have been mentioned in the description of the pons. The anterior peduncle is essentially an efferent tract, the fibers of which pass forward to the tegmentum of the cerebral peduncle, the hypothalamic region, and the thalamus. After the peduncles disappear under the corpora quadrigemina, they converge and many of their fibers intercross, forming the **decussation of the anterior peduncles.** A considerable number of fibers end in the nucleus ruber. Thence impulses are transmitted in two directions: first, by **thalamo-cortical fibers** to the cerebral cortex; second, by the **rubro-spinal tract** through the brain stem and lateral columns of the cord to the ventral horn cells. The ventro-lateral cerebellospinal fasciculus (Gowers' tract) is an ill-defined tract which connects the spinal cord with the cerebellum. Its fibers appear to be axones of cells of the dorsal columns of the cord; they pass in the lateral column of the cord, become scattered in passing through the reticular formation of the medulla and pons, and enter the cerebellum by way of the anterior medullary velum.

THE FOURTH VENTRICLE

The **fourth ventricle** (Ventriculus quartus) is the cavity of the rhombencephalon; it communicates with the central canal of the spinal cord behind and through

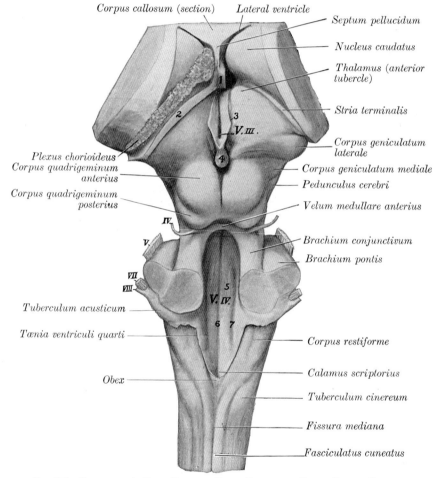

Fig. 635.—Dissection of Brain Stem and Basal Ganglia of Horse; Dorsal View.

1, Columns of fornix (section); *2*, remnant of hippocampus; *3*, tænia thalami; *4*, epiphysis cerebri or pineal body; *5*, eminentia medialis; *6*, sulcus medianus; *7*, sulcus limitans; *V.III.*, third ventricle; *V.IV.*, fourth ventricle. Stumps of cranial nerves are indicated by Roman numerals.

the cerebral aqueduct with the third ventricle in front. It is somewhat rhomboid in outline, elongated from before backward, and narrowest behind. It is lined completely by an epithelium (Ependyma) and contains a small amount of fluid.

The floor, the **fossa rhomboidea,** is formed by the medulla oblongata and pons and is marked by three longitudinal furrows which converge behind. It is widest and deepest a little in front of its middle. The posterior part narrows to a point at the opening of the central canal of the spinal cord, and on account of its appearance in man it has been termed the calamus scriptorius. The **median sulcus** (Sulcus medianus) extends the entire length of the floor and is deepest toward the ends. The **limiting sulci** (Sulci limitantes) begin on either side of the opening of the central canal and extend forward as the lateral limits of the rhomboid fossa. Just beyond the middle of the fossa they expand into a shallow depression, the **anterior fovea** (Fovea oralis). On either side of the median sulcus and margined laterally by the limiting sulcus is a slightly rounded column, the **eminentia medialis.** Opposite the fovea this presents an elongated prominence, the **colliculus facialis,** so named because it overlies the bend formed by the fibers of origin of the facial nerve. Lateral to the limiting sulcus is a long fusiform elevation, the **area acustica,** from which a band of fibers (Striæ acusticæ) winds over the anterior end of the restiform body to the superficial origin of the cochlear nerve.

The **lateral wall** is formed by the restiform body and the anterior peduncle of the cerebellum.

The roof **tegmen ventriculi quarti** is formed in its middle part by the vermis of the cerebellum, covered by the epithelium before mentioned. There is commonly a dorsal recess (Fastigium) between the extremities of the vermis. The anterior part of the roof is formed by a thin lamina of white substance, the **anterior medullary velum** (Velum medullare anterius), which extends backward from the corpora quadrigemina, and is attached on either side to the anterior peduncles of the cerebellum. Its anterior part is relatively thick and contains the decussation of the fibers of the trochlear nerves. Posteriorly it blends with the white substance of the cerebellum. A thin lamina of white substance, the **posterior medullary velum** (Velum medullare posterius), backed by pia mater, completes the roof posteriorly. After removal of the cerebellum the line of attachment (Tænia ventriculi quarti) to the medulla is seen; it begins ventrally over the opening of the central canal, runs forward on the inner face of the restiform body, and turns outward behind the brachium pontis. The thick part which stretches over the posterior angle of the ventricle is termed the **obex.** The posterior part of the ventricle forms three recesses, of which two are lateral and the third median and posterior. The **lateral recesses** (Recessus laterales) communicate with the subarachnoid space by **lateral apertures** (Aperturæ laterales). The layer of pia mater which actually forms the roof here is named the **tela chorioidea** of the fourth ventricle. It is triangular in outline and closely adherent to the velum. It forms three fringed masses which contain vascular convolutions and are designated the **median** and **lateral chorioid plexuses** of the fourth ventricle (Plexus chorioides ventriculi quarti). They appear to lie within the ventricle, but are really excluded from the cavity by the epithelial lining, which they invaginate.

THE MESENCEPHALON

The **mesencephalon** or **mid-brain** connects the rhombencephalon with the fore-brain. In the undissected brain it is covered dorsally by the cerebral hemispheres. It consists of a dorsal part, the corpora quadrigemina, and a larger ventral part, the cerebral peduncles, which are visible on the base of the brain. It is traversed longitudinally by a narrow canal, the cerebral aqueduct, which connects the fourth ventricle with the third (Fig. 639).

The **corpora quadrigemina**[1] are four rounded eminences which lie under the posterior part of the cerebral hemispheres. They consist of two pairs, separated

---

[1] In the revised nomenclature the term lamina quadrigemina is applied to the dorsal mass of the mid-brain, and the four eminences which it bears are the corpora quadrigemina.

by a transverse groove. The anterior pair (Colliculi nasales) are larger and much higher than the posterior pair. They are gray in color, almost hemispherical, and are separated by a narrow furrow which leads forward to the subpineal fovea. A wide groove intervenes between them and the optic thalami. The posterior pair (Colliculi caudales) are relatively small and are paler than the anterior pair. They are marked by a wide median depression, and are limited behind by a transverse furrow (Sulcus postquadrigeminus), at either side of which the **trochlear nerve** emerges. Laterally each is prolonged to the medial geniculate body by a band of white substance termed the **posterior peduncle** (Brachium aborale).[1]

The **cerebral peduncles** (Pedunculi cerebri) appear on the base of the brain as two large, rope-like stalks which emerge from the pons close together and diverge as they pass forward to enter the cerebrum (Fig. 629). At the point of disappearance the **optic tract** winds obliquely across the peduncle. About half an inch further back a small tract (Tractus peduncularis transversus) curves across the peduncles, and behind this, near the median line, is the superficial origin of the **oculomotor nerve.** The triangular depression between the diverging peduncles is the **interpeduncular fossa** (Fossa interpeduncularis). It is covered to a large extent by the **hypophysis cerebri,** a discoid brown mass which is connected with the base of the brain by a hollow stalk, the **infundibulum.** The posterior part of the fossa

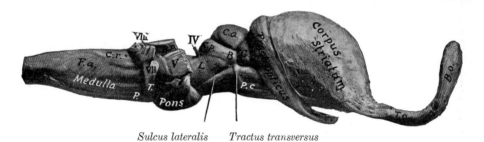

Sulcus lateralis   Tractus transversus

Fig. 636.—Brain Stem and Basal Ganglia of Horse; Right View.

F.a., External arcuate fibers; C.r., corpus restiforme; P, pyramid; T, corpus trapezoideum; B.p., middle peduncle of cerebellum; P.c., cerebral peduncle; L, trigonum lemnisci; C.a., corpus quad. ant.; C.p., corpus quad. post.; B, commissure of C.p.; G, corpus geniculatum mediale; T.o., olfactory peduncle; B.o., olfactory bulb.

is pierced by numerous minute openings which transmit blood-vessels, and is therefore termed the **substantia perforata posterior.** The objects here belong to the diencephalon, and will be described later. The lateral aspect of the peduncle is marked by a groove (Sulcus lateralis mesencephali) which indicates the division into a dorsal part, the **tegmentum,** and a ventral part, the **basis peduncli;** these are separated by a layer of dark gray matter, the **substantia nigra.** The triangular area (Trigonum lemnisci) above the lateral groove is faintly marked by fibers passing dorsally and backward to the anterior cerebellar peduncle; these belong to the fillet or lemniscus, an important tract that connects the thalamus and corpora quadrigemina with the sensory reception nuclei of the opposite side of the medulla.

The **mesencephalic canal** (Canalis mesencephali)[2] is the canal which extends through the mid-brain from the third to the fourth ventricle. It is largest beneath the posterior pair of corpora quadrigemina. It is surrounded by a layer of gray substance (Stratum griseum centrale), in the ventral part of which are the nuclei of origin

---

[1] In man a distinct superior brachium connects the superior pair with the lateral geniculate body, but in the domesticated animals the union with the optic thalamus is too direct to allow of any definite arm being recognized.

[2] Also termed the Aquæductus cerebri.

of the oculomotor and trochlear nerves, and laterally nuclei of the mesencephalic roots of the trigeminal nerves.

THE DIENCEPHALON

The **diencephalon** or **inter-brain** comprises the thalamus and a number of other structures grouped about the third ventricle, the cavity of this division of the brain.[1] To expose its dorsal aspect, the greater part of the cerebral hemispheres, the corpus callosum, the fornix, the hippocampus, and the tela chorioidea of the third ventricle must be removed (Fig. 635).

The **thalamus** is the principal body in this part of the brain. It is a large ovoid mass placed obliquely across the dorsal face of each cerebral peduncle, so that the long axes of the two thalami would meet in front about at a right angle. Medially they are fused to a large extent, and around the area of adhesion they are separated by a sagittal circular space, the third ventricle. The dorsal surface is convex, and is separated from the overlying hippocampus by the tela chorioidea. Laterally it is separated from the nucleus caudatus by an oblique groove in which there is a band of white matter termed the **stria terminalis.** When the tela chorioidea of the lateral ventricle has been detached from this band it leaves a torn edge, the tænia chorioidea. Medially it is bounded by a narrow white band, the **stria medullaris;** to this the tela chorioidea of the third ventricle is attached, and when the latter is removed in dissection, there remains a thin irregular edge termed the tænia thalami. The striæ unite posteriorly and blend with the stalk of the pineal body. Near this point they present a small enlargement caused by the nucleus habenulæ. Anteriorly there is a small eminence, the **anterior tubercle** of the thalamus (Tuberculum orale thalami). The posterior part of the thalamus has the form of a rounded ridge which is continuous laterally with the optic tract.[2] Behind the point of origin of the tract, in the angle between the thalamus and the cerebral peduncle, is the **medial geniculate body** (Corpus geniculatum mediale), a well-defined oval prominence.

The lateral surface is separated from the lenticular nucleus by the **internal capsule, an** important mass of white matter composed of fibers passing to and from the cerebral cortex. These fibers go to form a large part of the ventral portion (basis) of the cerebral peduncle. From the entire lateral surface of the thalamus fibers pass into the internal capsule and radiate to reach the cerebral cortex; similarly fibers coming from the cortex converge in the internal capsule to enter the thalamus. This arrangement is termed the thalamic radiation. Ventral to the thalamus proper is the **hypothalamic tegmental region.** This is the continuation of the tegmental part of the cerebral peduncle into the diencephalon. It contains the **red nucleus** (Nucleus ruber), an important ganglion on the course of the motor tracts. It receives numerous fibers from the cerebral cortex and the corpus striatum. From it fibers proceed to the thalamus and to the spinal cord; the fibers to the cord, which constitute the rubro-spinal tract (Tractus rubro-spinalis), cross to the opposite side and extend back in the tegmentum to the lateral columns of the cord. Lateral to the red nucleus a conspicuous lenticular area of dark gray matter is visible on cross-sections of the hypothalamic region; this is the **hypothalamic nucleus** (Nucleus hypothalamicus Luysi), which consists of pigmented nerve-cells scattered through a dense network of fine medullated fibers, and is richly supplied with capillary blood-vessels. The two nuclei are connected by a transverse commissure (Commissura hypothalamica), which crosses the floor of the third ventricle above the mammillary body.

The **epiphysis cerebri** or **pineal body** (Corpus pineale) is a small ovoid or fusiform red-brown mass situated in a deep central depression between the thalami and corpora quadrigemina. It is variable in size, but is commonly about 10 to 12 mm. long and 7 mm. wide. It is attached at the postero-superior quadrant of the third ventricle by a short stalk, in which is a small recess of that cavity. Its

---

[1] On a strictly embryological basis the optic part of the hypothalamus, comprising the anterior part of the third ventricle and the structures associated with it, belongs to the telencephalon, but will be considered here as a matter of convenience.

[2] This backward projection of the thalamus is equivalent to the pulvinar and lateral geniculate body of man, which are not superficially divided in the horse.

base blends in front with the junction of the striæ medullares of the thalamus. Immediately under the posterior part of the stalk is a short transverse band of white substance, the **posterior commissure of the cerebrum** (Commissura aboralis cerebri).

The epiphysis is enclosed in a fibrous capsule from which numerous trabeculæ pass inward, dividing the organ into spaces occupied by round epithelial cells of the same origin as the ependyma of the ventricle.

The **mammillary body** (Corpus mammillare) is a white, round elevation a little **larger** than a pea which projects ventrally at the anterior end of the median furrow of the interpeduncular fossa.   While it is a single body in external form in the horse,

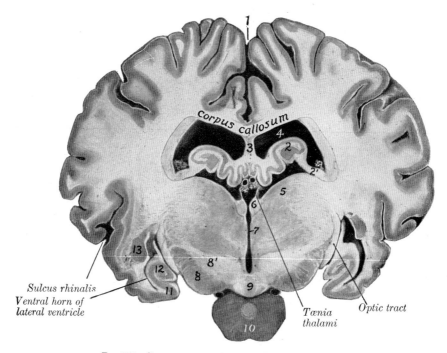

FIG. 637.—CROSS-SECTION OF BRAIN OF HORSE, NATURAL SIZE.

Section passes through posterior part of third ventricle and is viewed from behind. *1*, Longitudinal fissure; *2*, hippocampus; *2'*, fimbria; *3*, septum pellucidum; *4*, lateral ventricle; *5*, thalamus; *6*, habenula; *7*, third ventricle; *8*, cerebral peduncle; *8'*, hypothalmus; *9*, mammillary body; *10*, hypophysis or pituitary body; *11*, piriform lobe; *12*, ventral end of hippocampus; *13*, amygdaloid nucleus.   Between the upper parts of the tæniæ thalami is the chorioid plexus of the third ventricle, and above this are the internal cerebral veins.

sections show that it is double in structure and contains a nucleus of gray matter on either side (Fig. 637).

Three sets of fibers are connected with the mammillary body. The column of the fornix curves down in the lateral wall of the third ventricle to the body and many of the fornix fibers end in it. A bundle (Fasciculus thalamo-mammillaris) passes dorsally and backward from it into the anterior part of the thalamus, and a tract (Fasciculus pedunculo-mammillaris) extends back in the floor of the third ventricle to the tegmentum of the mid-brain.

The **hypophysis cerebri** or pituitary body was mentioned as covering part of the interpeduncular fossa. It is oval in outline, flattened dorso-ventrally, and nearly an inch (ca. 2 cm.) in width. It is attached by a delicate tubular stalk, the **infundibulum,** to the **tuber cinereum,** a small gray prominence situated between the optic chiasm in front and the mammillary body behind. A fibrous capsule, derived from the dura mater, encloses and is intimately adherent to it.

The body consists of two parts which can be distinguished on sections by their color (Fig. 639).   The glandular lobe is brown in color and forms the external and greater part of the body.

It is glandular in character and there is good ground for the view that it is an organ of internal secretion. Besides the chief cells, which stain lightly, it contains large, deeply staining chromophile cells. It arises as an outgrowth from the dorsal wall of the primitive mouth cavity. The cerebral lobe is pale and is connected with the infundibulum so as to form a rather flask-shaped arrangement. It is almost entirely enclosed by the glandular part. It arises as an outgrowth from the primitive diencephalon, but loses most of its earlier nervous character.

The optic chiasm and tracts form the anterior boundary of the interpeduncular fossa (Figs. 629, 636). The **optic chiasm** (Chiasma opticum) is formed by the convergence of the optic nerves and the crossing of the major part of the fibers of the nerve of one side to the tract of the opposite side. From the chiasm each **optic tract** (Tractus opticus) curves obliquely around the cerebral peduncle to the posterior part of the thalamus and the medial geniculate body; some fibers reach the anterior quadrigeminal body.

All the fibers in the chiasm are not derived from the optic nerves. The posterior part contains fibers which pass from one tract to the other and are connected with the medial geniculate bodies; this bundle is called the ventral commissure (Commissura ventralis). Above it is the dorsal commissure (Commissura dorsalis), the fibers of which enter the hypothalamic body.[1]

The **third ventricle** (Ventriculus tertius) is the narrow annular space between the thalami. It communicates by means of the cerebral aqueduct with the fourth ventricle behind, and in front it is continuous with the lateral ventricle on each side through the interventricular foramen. Its floor is formed by the structures of the interpeduncular fossa, and to a small extent by the tegmentum of the cerebral peduncles. The roof is formed in the strict sense only by the ependyma, above which is a fold of pia mater, termed the **tela chorioidea** of the third ventricle.[2] The roof is invaginated by the two delicate **chorioid plexuses** (Plexus chorioidei ventriculi tertii) which appear to lie within the ventricle, although they are excluded from the cavity by the epithelium. When the tela is removed, the delicate ependyma of the roof is torn away with it, leaving the line of attachment to the stria medullaris to constitute the **tænia thalami.** The anterior wall is formed by the **lamina terminalis,** a thin layer of gray matter which extends from the optic chiasm dorsally to the corpus callosum. A distinct rounded band of white matter extends across its posterior face, bulging into the ventricle. This is the **anterior commissure** (Commissura oralis) of the cerebrum; its fibers extend to the olfactory bulb and to the piriform lobe. A similar but more slender **posterior commissure** (Commissura aboralis) crosses the posterior wall above the entrance to the cerebral aqueduct; the connections of its fibers are not yet clearly known. The **interventricular foramen**[3] is situated on either side of the anterior part of the ventricle, and leads outward and slightly dorsally between the column of the fornix and the anterior tubercle of the thalamus (Fig. 639). The cavity presents three **recesses** or diverticula, of which two are ventral and the third is posterior. The **optic recess** (Recessus opticus) lies above the optic chiasm. Just behind it is the **infundibular recess** (Recessus infundibuli), which extends through the infundibulum to the pituitary body. The **epiphyseal recess** (Recessus pinealis) is in the stalk of the pineal body.

THE TELENCEPHALON

The **telencephalon** or **end-brain** comprises two principal parts, the cerebral hemispheres and the optic part of the hypothalamus. The latter has been considered as a matter of convenience in the description of the diencephalon.

THE CEREBRAL HEMISPHERES

The **cerebral hemispheres** (Hemisphæria) form the greater part of the fully developed brain. Viewed from above (Fig. 631) they form an ovoid mass, of which the broader end is posterior, and the greatest transverse diameter is a little behind the middle. The two hemispheres are separated by a deep median cleft, the **longitudinal fissure** of the cerebrum (Fissura longitudinalis cerebri), which is occupied by a sickle-shaped fold of dura mater, the falx cerebri. In front the separation is complete, and it appears to be behind also, but here the two hemispheres are attached to each other over a small area by the pia mater. When the hemispheres are gently drawn apart, it is seen that the fissure is interrupted in its middle part at a depth of a little more than an inch (ca. 3 cm.) by a white commissural mass, the **corpus callosum**; this connects the hemispheres for about half of their length. The **transverse fissure** (Fissura transversa cerebri) separates the hemispheres from the cerebellum, and contains the tentorium cerebelli.

The **convex** or **dorso-lateral surface** (Facies convexa cerebri) conforms closely to the cranial wall. The **medial surface** (Facies medialis cerebri) (Fig. 639) is flat and sagittal and bounds the longitudinal fissure; to a large extent it is in contact with the falx cerebri, but behind the great cerebral vein the two hemispheres are in contact and are attached to each other over a small area as noted above. In well-

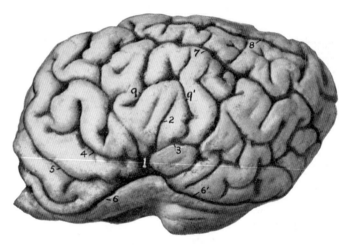

FIG. 638.—LEFT CEREBRAL HEMISPHERE OF HORSE; LATERAL VIEW. THE OLFACTORY BULB IS CUT OFF.

1, Lateral fissure (of Sylvius); *2, 3, 4*, middle, posterior, and anterior branches of *1*; *5*, presylvian fissure; *6, 6'*, sulcus rhinalis, anterior et posterior; *7*, suprasylvian fissure; *8*, ectomarginal fissure; *9, 9'*, ectosylvian fissure.

hardened specimens there is usually an impression for the vein in front of the area of adhesion. The **base** or **ventral surface** (Basis cerebri) (Fig. 629) is irregular. Its anterior two-thirds is adapted to the cerebral fossa of the cranial floor. Crossing this area in front of the optic tract is a depression, the **lateral fossa** (Fossa lateralis), which leads outward to the **lateral fissure** (Fissura lateralis), and lodges the middle cerebral artery. In front of the fossa there is a considerable rounded elevation known as the **trigonum olfactorium**. The trigonum and the medial part of the fossa are pierced by numerous openings for the passage of small blood-vessels and are equivalent to the substantia perforata anterior of man. Behind the lateral part of the fossa is the rounded anterior end of the **piriform lobe** (Lobus piriformis). Traced backward, the lobe curves dorso-medially over the optic tract and the thalamus to the tentorial aspect of the hemisphere; its continuation, the hippocampus, forms part of the floor of the lateral ventricle, and will be examined later.

The **tentorial surface** (Fig. 640) is flattened, faces medially and backward as well as ventrally, and rests largely on the tentorium cerebelli; on its anterior part there is a shallow depression adapted to the corpora quadrigemina and the pineal body.

The **frontal pole** or anterior extremity (exclusive of the olfactory bulb) is compressed laterally, and the **occipital pole** or posterior extremity forms a blunt point.

The hemisphere comprises: (1) The **pallium,** which consists of an outer layer of gray matter, the **cortex** (Substantia corticalis), covering a large mass of white matter (Centrum semiovale); (2) the **rhinencephalon** or olfactory portion of the brain; (3) the **corpus callosum** and **fornix,** the great commissural white masses; (4) the **lateral ventricle** and certain important structures associated therewith.

The **pallium** is thrown into numerous folds, the **gyri cerebri,** which are separated by **sulci** or **fissures** of varying depth. The general pattern of the gyri and sulci is similar in normal brains of the same species, but the details are very variable and are never alike on the two hemispheres of the same brain. In the horse the arrangement is complicated by the existence of numerous short accessory fissures which cut into the gyri at right angles and tend to confuse the observer. The principal fissures and sulci of the convex surface (Figs. 631, 632, 638) are as follows:[1]

1. The **lateral fissure** (Fissura lateralis Sylvii) ascends on the lateral surface of the hemisphere as the continuation of the fossa lateralis in front of the piriform lobe. After crossing the lateral olfactory stria it divides into three branches; of these one passes dorsally, one runs obliquely forward and dorsally, and the third is directed dorsally and backward. It contains the middle cerebral artery.

2. The **suprasylvian fissure** (F. suprasylvia) is long and divides a large part of the convex surface of the hemisphere into dorsal and lateral portions. It begins on the dorso-medial border near its anterior end, and, inclining gradually downward, passes back to end on reaching the tentorial surface. It is usually continuous medially with the transverse fissure and in front with the presylvian fissure.

3. The **presylvian fissure** (F. præsylvia) is on the anterior part of the hemisphere, passes forward and ventro-laterally almost to the frontal pole, and then inclines backward to end at the groove which marks the dorsal limit of the rhinencephalon (Sulcus rhinalis).

4. The **marginal fissure** (F. marginalis) extends along the dorso-medial border. It begins a little in front of the middle of the border and turns around the occipital pole to end on its tentorial aspect.

5. The **entomarginal fissure** (F. entomarginalis) lies medial to the dorso-medial border. It does not extend quite as far forward as the marginal fissure, from which it is separated by a narrow gyrus.

6. The **ectomarginal fissure** (F. ectomarginalis) lies about midway between the marginal fissure and the posterior part of the suprasylvian fissure.

7. The **sulcus rhinalis** is a very distinct furrow on the ventral part of the lateral surface which marks off the olfactory part of the brain (rhinencephalon) from the rest of the hemisphere. It is undulating and is highest where it is crossed by the lateral fissure.

Just above this point is a lobe which is homologous with the insula of man. When the overhanging gyri which partly conceal it—forming the operculum—are removed, there are disclosed several short, deeply placed gyri (Gyri breves).

On the medial surface (Fig. 639) the main fissures and sulci are as follows:

1. The **calloso-marginal fissure** (F. callosomarginalis) is extensive and well defined. It is approximately parallel to the dorso-medial border of the hemisphere, from which it is about half an inch distant. It begins in front a short distance below and in front of the genu of the corpus callosum, and forms a C-shaped curve, its posterior part extending on the tentorial surface to a point behind the depression

---

[1] The homologies and terminology of many fissures of the brain in the domesticated animals are still in a chaotic state. Only a few of the most important and constant ones are given here.

for the corpora quadrigemina. It separates the marginal gyri above from the gyrus fornicatus, which extends down to the corpus callosum.

2. The **transverse fissure** (F. transversa) begins a little behind the middle of the calloso-marginal fissure, passes obliquely dorsally and forward to the dorso-medial border—into which it cuts deeply—and usually joins the suprasylvian fissure.

3. The **sublimbic fissure** (F. sublimbica) curves over the gyrus fornicatus a short distance above the corpus callosum. Its middle part is commonly indistinct, and it is often divided into anterior and posterior parts.

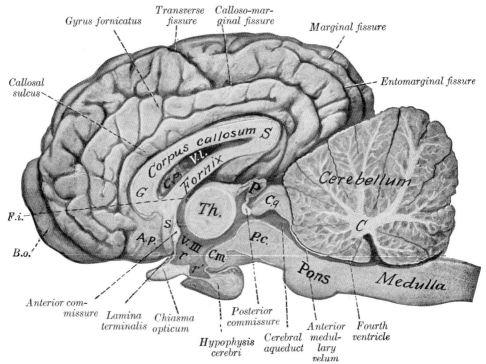

FIG. 639.—MEDIAN SECTION OF BRAIN OF HORSE.

The membranes and vessels are removed. *C*, Central white substance (corpus medullare) of cerebellum; *P.c.*, cerebral peduncle; *C.p.*, chorioid plexus of lateral ventricle (*V.l.*); *C.q.*, corpora quadrigemina; *P*, epiphysis or pineal body; *Th.*, thalamus; *V.III.*, third ventricle; *r*, optic recess; *r′*, infundibular recess; *C.m.*, mammillary body; *s*, subcallosal gyrus; *A.p.*, area parolfactoria; *G*, genu of corpus callosum; *S*, splenium of same; *F.i.*, interventricular foramen; *B.o.*, olfactory bulb. The cerebral lobe of the hypophysis cerebri is distinguished by its lighter color. The posterior medullary velum is not shown.

4. The **callosal sulcus** (Sulcus corporis callosi) separates the corpus callosum from the gyrus fornicatus.

The **hippocampus** is a gyrus which curves from the deep face of the piriform lobe around the thalamus and forms the posterior part of the floor of the lateral ventricle. It can be displayed by cutting away the brain stem up to the optic tract and the interventricular foramen. Viewed from below, the hippocampal gyrus is seen to form a semicircular curve from the apex of the piriform lobe to the angle of divergence of the crura of the fornix, *i. e.*, to a point under the central part of the corpus callosum. It is separated deeply by the hippocampal fissure from the **gyrus dentatus** (Fig. 640). Along the concave margin of the latter is a band of white matter, termed the **fimbria,** which is the prolongation of the greater part of the crus of the fornix into this region. The ventricular surface of the hippocampus (Fig. 642) is covered with a thin layer of white matter, the **alveus,** which is also derived from the crus of the fornix, and is therefore continuous with the fimbria. The two hippocampi are connected at their highest parts by transverse fibers which constitute the **hippocampal commissure.**

The interval between the hippocampus and fimbria on the one hand, and the brain stem on the other, is a lateral continuation of the transverse fissure of the brain, and is occupied by a fold of pia mater, the **tela chorioidea** of the third ventricle. This fold is triangular in outline and its apex reaches to the interventricular foramen. Its base is continuous at the transverse fissure with the pia which covers the surface of the brain. Its middle part lies over the epithelial roof of the third ventricle, as has been seen (Fig. 637). The lateral borders will be seen on the floor

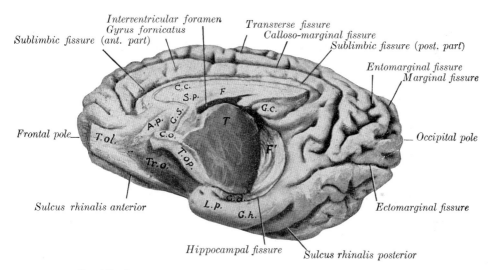

FIG. 640.—MEDIO-VENTRAL ASPECT OF RIGHT CEREBRAL HEMISPHERE OF HORSE.

The brain stem and olfactory bulb are cut off. *T.ol.,* Olfactory tract; *A.p.,* area parolfactoria; *Tr.o.,* trigonum olfactorium; *Tr.op.,* optic tract; *C.o.,* chiasma opticum; *G.s.,* subcallosal gyrus; *C.c.,* corpus callosum; *S.p.,* septum pellucidum; *F,* fornix; *F′,* fimbria; *G.c.,* callosal gyrus; *T,* cut surface of thalamus; *G.d.,* gyrus dentatus; *L.p.,* piriform lobe; *G.h.,* hippocampal gyrus.

of the lateral ventricles, where they form thick, rounded bands containing convolutions of blood-vessels, known as the **chorioid plexuses** of the lateral ventricles (Fig. 642).

When the tela is pulled out, one may easily get the impression that the lateral ventricle communicates with the exterior by means of the chorioid fissure. Such is not the case, since the chorioid plexus is covered by the epithelial lining of the ventricle, which has been torn away.

The **rhinencephalon** or olfactory part of the brain comprises the olfactory bulb, tract, and striæ, the trigonum olfactorium, the area parolfactoria, and the piriform lobe.[1]

The **olfactory bulb** (Bulbus olfactorius) is an oval enlargement which curves upward in front of the frontal pole of the hemisphere. Its convex superficial face fits into the ethmoidal fossa and receives numerous olfactory nerve-fibers through the cribriform plate; hence it is very difficult to remove the bulb intact. It contains a considerable cavity, the **ventricle of the olfactory bulb** (Ventriculus bulbi

[1] From the morphological point of view other structures should be included, but in descriptive anatomy it is usual to limit the application of the term to the parts enumerated above.

olfactorii) which is connected with the lateral ventricle by a small canal in the olfactory tract. The deep face is largely in contact with the frontal pole of the hemisphere and is connected with the olfactory tract.

The gray substance of the bulb is external and is thickest on the convex anterior surface. The posterior part consists to a large extent of fibers which are the axones of the mitral cells of the deep layer of the gray substance and go to form the tract and striæ.

The **olfactory tract** (Tractus olfactorius) is a very short but wide band of white substance which arises in the olfactory bulb and extends back to be continued by the olfactory striæ. It contains a canal which connects the ventricle of the bulb with the lateral ventricle.

The **olfactory striæ** (Striæ olfactorii) are two in number. The **lateral stria** (Stria lateralis) is much the largest and most distinct. It passes backward, upward, and outward, widens out and joins the piriform lobe. It is clearly defined dorsally by the sulcus rhinalis and is marked off from the trigonum olfactorium by the sulcus arcuatus. The **medial stria** (Stria medialis) is smaller, short, and not so

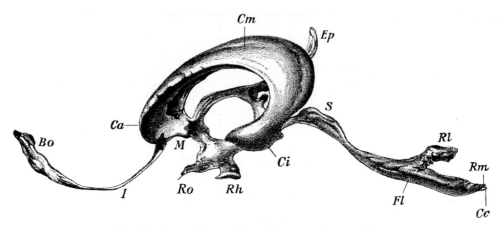

FIG. 641.—LATERAL VIEW OF CAST OF CAVITIES OF BRAIN OF HORSE.

Bo, Cavity of olfactory bulb, which communicates through the canal *I* with a lateral ventricle; *Ca*, anterior horn, *Cm*, body, *Ci*, ventral horn of lateral ventricle; *M*, interventricular foramen which connects lateral and third ventricles; *Ep*, suprapineal recess, below which is the small infrapineal recess (not visible); *Ro*, optic recess; *Rh*, infundibular and hypophyseal recess; *S*, aqueduct; *Fl*, ridge corresponding to sulcus limitans; *Rl*, lateral recess, *Rm*, posterior recess of fourth ventricle; *Cc*, beginning of central canal of spinal cord. (Dexler.)

well defined; it bends over to the parolfactory area on the medial face of the hemisphere below the genu of the corpus callosum.

The **trigonum olfactorium** is the prominent gray area situated in the angle of divergence of the medial and lateral olfactory striæ. It is bounded laterally by the lateral olfactory stria, from which it is defined by the sulcus arcuatus. It is continuous with the **area parolfactoria** on the medial surface; behind the latter a band descends from the rostrum of the corpus callosum and is continuous below with the anterior perforated substance; it is termed the **subcallosal gyrus** (Gyrus subcallosus).

The **piriform lobe** (Lobus piriformis) is the well-marked prominence on the base lateral to the optic tract and cerebral peduncle, from which it is separated by a deep fissure. Its nipple-like apex lies behind the fossa lateralis and covers the optic tract. The external surface is marked by one or two sulci (lobi piriformis). The lobe contains a cavity, the ventral horn of the lateral ventricle.

The fibers of the olfactory striæ go to the piriform lobe and hippocampus, the trigonum olfactorium, the area parolfactoria, the subcallosal gyrus, and part of the gyrus fornicatus. The central connections of the olfactory apparatus are complex and are not yet fully understood. The anterior cerebral commissure contains fibers which pass from the olfactory bulb of one side by way of the medial striæ to the bulb of the opposite side; also fibers which cross in it from the medial striæ of one side to the piriform lobe of the opposite side. Many fibers pass to the hippocampus by way of the septum pellucidum, fornix, and fimbria. Other fibers pass in the column of the fornix to the mammillary body and thence to the thalamus by the thalamo-mammillary bundle.

The **corpus callosum** is the great transverse commissure which connects the two cerebral hemispheres through about half of their length. On median section

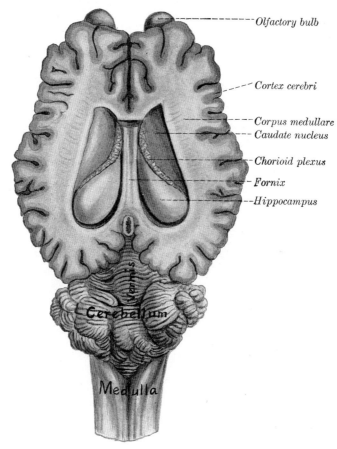

Olfactory bulb

Cortex cerebri

Corpus medullare
Caudate nucleus

Chorioid plexus

Fornix

Hippocampus

Vermis

Cerebellum

Medulla

FIG. 642.—BRAIN OF HORSE, WITH LATERAL VENTRICLES OPENED BY REMOVAL OF UPPER PART OF CEREBRAL HEMISPHERES AND MOST OF THE CORPUS CALLOSUM.

(Fig. 639) it is seen to be arched from before backward, white in color, and composed substantially of transverse fibers. The middle part or **truncus** (Truncus corporis callosi) slopes downward and forward and is thinner than the ends. The anterior thickened end, the **genu,** bends ventrally and backward and thins out to form the **rostrum;** the latter is continuous with the lamina terminalis. The posterior end, the **splenium,** also thick, lies at a considerably higher level than the genu. The **dorsal surface** is convex in its length, concave transversely; it forms the floor of the longitudinal fissure. It is covered by a thin layer of gray matter (Indusium griseum), in which are strands of longitudinal fibers (Striæ longitudinales); the latter are arranged in medial and lateral bundles (Stria medialis, striæ laterales). It is considered that these form an olfactory path. The **ventral surface** has the reverse configuration, and presents transverse ridges and grooves. It forms the roof of the lateral ventricles, and the septum pellucidum is attached to it medially. The fibers of the corpus callosum (with the exception of the longitudinal striæ) run transversely and spread out laterally in all directions in the central white substance of the hemispheres to the cortex, forming the **radiation of the corpus callosum** (Radiatio corporis callosi).

The **fornix** is a bilateral structure composed of white fibers which arch chiefly over the thalamus and the third ventricle. It is described as consisting of a body, two columns, and two crura. The **body** (Corpus fornicis) is formed by the fusion of the two arches of which the fornix is composed. It is triangular and overlies the anterior parts of the thalami and the third ventricle. The dorsal surface blends

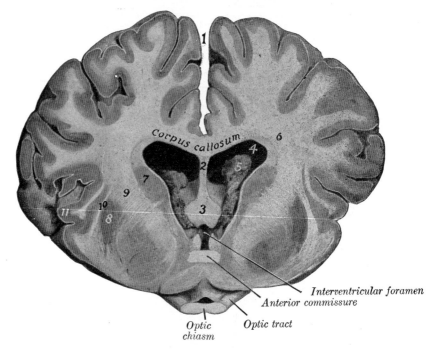

FIG. 643.—CROSS-SECTION OF BRAIN OF HORSE, ABOUT NATURAL SIZE.

Section passes through optic chiasm, and is viewed from in front. *1*, Longitudinal fissure; *2*, septum pellucidum; *3*, columns of fornix; *4*, lateral ventricle; *5*, chorioid plexus; *6*, corpus medullare (central white matter) of hemisphere; *7*, caudate nucleus; *8*, lenticular nucleus; *9*, internal capsule; *10*, external capsule; *11*, insula.

medially with the septum pellucidum, and on either side forms part of the floor of the lateral ventricle. The lateral border is related to the chorioid plexus of the lateral ventricle and forms the inner boundary of the interventricular foramen. The **columns** (Columnæ fornicis) (Fig. 643) are two slender round bundles which emerge from the body in front of the interventricular foramen and diverge slightly as they curve ventrally and backward to the mammillary body.

From the mammillary body the greater part of these fornix fibers are continued to the thalamus by the thalamo-mammillary fasciculus (or bundle of Vicq d'Azyr). Others pass to the cerebral peduncle. A portion of the fibers cross to the opposite thalamus and cerebral peduncle.

The **crura** (Crura fornicis) are much larger bands which diverge widely from the posterior angles of the body. Each curves outward and backward over the thalamus (from which it is separated by the tela chorioidea), and is chiefly continued as the **fimbria** along the concave border of the hippocampus. The crura give off fibers to form the alveus, a layer of white matter which covers the ventricular face of the hippocampi, and between them are transverse fibers which constitute the hippocampal commissure (Commissura hippocampi).

The **septum pellucidum** is the median partition between the two lateral ventricles. Its convex dorsal border blends with the corpus callosum and its concave ventral border joins the fornix. Its anterior part is received into the genu of the corpus callosum. Traced backward, it diminishes in height and the two edges meet at an acute angle at the splenium.

The septum consists of two layers (Laminæ septi pellucidi) which are in contact with each other. They consist of medullated nerve-fibers and gray matter. The latter exists in considerable amount in the thicker part of the septum adjacent to the columns of the fornix. Many of the fibers of the septum pass up through the corpus callosum to the gyrus fornicatus. Others are connected with the subcallosal gyrus and the parolfactory area.

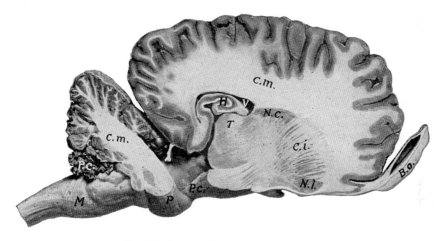

FIG. 644.—SAGITTAL SECTION OF BRAIN OF HORSE.

Section is cut about 1.5 cm. to the right of the median plane. *M*, Medulla oblongata; *P*, pons; *P.c.* (above *M*), chorioid plexus of fourth ventricle; *C.m.*, central white matter (corpus medullare) of cerebellum and of cerebrum; *P.c.* (in front of *P*), cerebral peduncle; *H*, hippocampus; *V*, lateral ventricle; *T*, thalamus; *N.c.*, caudate nucleus; *C.i.*, internal capsule; *N.l.*, lenticular nucleus; *B.o.*, olfactory bulb.

The **lateral ventricle** (Ventriculus lateralis cerebri) is the irregular cavity in the interior of each cerebral hemisphere.[1] Each communicates with the third ventricle through the **interventricular foramen** (Foramen interventriculare), and by a small canal with the cavity of the olfactory bulb. It is usual to describe the ventricle as consisting of three parts, viz., the central part or body, and anterior and ventral horns. The **central part** (Pars centralis) extends back to the splenium of the corpus callosum. It opens into the third ventricle through the interventricular foramen, which is situated between the fornix and the anterior part of the thalamus. The **anterior horn** (Cornu orale) is the part in front of the interventricular foramen; it communicates ventrally with the olfactory cavity. The **ventral horn** (Cornu ventrale) curves downward and forward into the piriform lobe. The roof of the ventricle is formed by the corpus callosum, and the medial wall is the septum pellucidum. After removal of the roof the floor is seen to be formed chiefly by two bodies.

[1] It is hardly possible to get an accurate idea of the shape of the ventricle except by studying a cast of it (Fig. 641). The size of the ventricles varies in different subjects, and it is common to find more or less disparity between the two ventricles of the same brain.

The anterior one is the **caudate nucleus** (Nucleus caudatus), a somewhat pear-shaped gray eminence, the long axis of which is directed obliquely upward, backward, and outward. Its anterior large end is termed the head (Caput nuclei caudati), and the posterior long tapering end the tail (Cauda nuclei caudati). The posterior body, the **hippocampus,** is white on its ventricular surface, which is strongly convex. It curves outward and backward and then turns ventrally and forward to join the piriform lobe. The two bodies are separated by an oblique groove which is occupied by the **chorioid plexus** of the lateral ventricle (Plexus chorioideus ventriculi lateralis). This is the thickened edge of a fold of pia mater, the tela chorioidea of the third ventricle, which lies between the hippocampus and the thalamus. It contains convolutions of small blood-vessels, and in old subjects there are often calcareous concretions in it. The plexuses of the two sides are continuous through the interventricular foramen. On drawing the chorioid plexus backward, a narrow white band, the **stria terminalis,** is seen along the margin of the caudate nucleus, where it bounds the intermediate groove. The plexus partially covers a wider white band which is blended with the white substance of the hippocampus; this is the **crus of the fornix** and its continuation, the **fimbria.**

The **corpus striatum**[2] is the great basal ganglion of the hemisphere. It is situated in front of the thalamus and the cerebral peduncle, and its anterior rounded end appears on the base of the hemisphere at the trigonum olfactorium. It is composed of two masses of gray matter, the caudate and lenticular nuclei, separated incompletely by tracts of white matter which are known collectively as the internal capsule. The **caudate nucleus** (Nucleus caudatus) is the dorso-medial and larger of the two gray masses; it was seen in the examination of the lateral ventricle. The **lenticular nucleus** (Nucleus lentiformis) lies ventro-laterally, over the trigonum olfactorium and the fossa lateralis. It is related externally to a layer of white matter termed the **external capsule** (Capsula externa), which separates it from a stratum of gray substance known as the **claustrum.** The two nuclei are fused in front, and further back they are connected by strands of gray matter which intersect the internal capsule.

The **amygdaloid nucleus** (Nucleus amygdalæ) (Fig. 637) is an ovoid mass of gray matter lateral to the ventral horn of the lateral ventricle and ventral to the posterior part of the lenticular nucleus. Some fibers of the stria terminalis are connected with it.

The **internal capsule** (Capsula interna) is a broad band of white matter situated between the thalamus and caudate nucleus medially and the lenticular nucleus laterally. A sagittal section through the brain (Fig. 644) shows that it is in great part directly continuous with the basis or ventral part of the cerebral peduncle. It contains most of the so-called **projection fibers** of the hemisphere, which connect the cerebral cortex with nuclei of other and more posterior parts of the brain. When the fibers of the internal capsule are traced forward it is evident that they spread out in all directions to reach the cerebral cortex. This arrangement, in which the fibers of the corpus callosum participate, is termed the **corona radiata.**

The internal capsule also contains fibers which connect the corpus striatum with the thalamus. These are termed the thalamo-striate and strio-thalamic fibers respectively, according to the direction in which they conduct impulses.

The fibers of the stria terminalis connect the amygdaloid nucleus with the septum pellucidum and trigonum olfactorium. It is therefore probably part of the complex connections between the primary and secondary olfactory centers.

Blood-vessels of the Brain.—The **arteries** of the brain are derived chiefly from the internal carotid and occipital arteries (pp. 651, 652). The basilar artery, formed by the union of the right and left cerebral branches of the occipital artery, enters the cranial cavity through the foramen magnum, and divides at the inter-peduncular fossa into the two posterior cerebral arteries. These concur with branches of the internal carotid arteries in forming the remarkable arterial circle on the base of the cerebrum. From these emanate basal arteries which supply in general the brain stem and basal ganglia, and cortical arteries which in general run superficially and supply the cortical substance and medullary white substance.

The **veins** enter the sinuses of the dura mater, and in the main are not satel-lites of the arteries. The sinuses communicate with the ophthalmic, dorsal and ventral cerebral, and spinal veins (pp. 700, 702).

THE CRANIAL NERVES

The **cranial** or **cerebral nerves** (Nn. cerebrales) (Figs. 629, 630) comprise twelve pairs which are designated from before backward numerically and by name. Their number, names, and functional characters are given in the subjoined table:

I.	Olfactory	Sensory (Smell)
II.	Optic	Sensory (Sight)
III.	Oculomotor	Motor
IV.	Trochlear	Motor
V.	Trigeminal	Mixed
VI.	Abducent	Motor
VII.	Facial	Mixed
VIII.	Acoustic	Sensory (Hearing and Equilibration)
IX.	Glosso-pharyngeal	Mixed
X.	Vagus	Mixed
XI.	Spinal accessory	Motor
XII.	Hypoglossal	Motor

THE OLFACTORY NERVE

The **olfactory nerve** (N. olfactorius) is peculiar in that its fibers are not aggre-gated to form a trunk, but are connected in small bundles with the olfactory bulb. They are non-medullated, and are the central processes of the olfactory cells which are situated in the olfactory region of the mucous membrane of the nasal cavity. This region is distinguished by its brown color and comprises the posterior part of the lateral mass of the ethmoid, a small adjacent area of the dorsal turbinate, and the corresponding surface of the septum nasi. The nerve-bundles are enclosed in sheaths derived from the membranes of the brain and pass through the foramina of the cribriform plate to join the convex surface of the olfactory bulb. Some fibers come from the vomero-nasal organ.

THE OPTIC NERVE

The **optic nerve** (N. opticus) is composed of fibers which are the central proc-esses of the ganglion cells of the retina. The fibers converge within the eyeball to the optic papilla, where they are collected into a round trunk, the optic nerve. The nerve thus formed pierces the chorioid and sclera, emerges from the posterior part of the eyeball, and passes backward and medially to the optic foramen. After traversing the latter it decussates with its fellow of the opposite side to form the optic chiasma. In the orbit the nerve is slightly flexuous and is embedded in the fat behind the eyeball and surrounded by the retractor oculi muscle. Its intraos-seous part is an inch or more (ca. 3 cm.) long. The sheath of the nerve is formed by prolongations of the membranes of the brain, and includes continuations of the subdural and subarachnoid spaces.

The greater part of the fibers of the optic nerve cross in the chiasma to the tract of the oppo-site side. In the tract the fibers proceed to (1) the medial geniculate body, (2) the posterior part of the thalamus, and (3) the anterior quadrigeminal body (indirectly). The fibers which go to the medial geniculate body appear to belong to Gudden's commissure and to be non-visual in function. The visual fibers, which come from the lateral part of the retina of the same side and the medial part of the retina of the opposite side, terminate about cells in the anterior quadrigeminal body and the part of the thalamus which corresponds to the pulvinar and lateral geniculate body of man. From the cells of the former fibers pass to the nuclei of the motor nerves of the eyeball, and complete the reflex arc. Fibers proceed from the cells of the thalamus to the visual area of the cortex in the occipital part of the hemisphere.

THE OCULOMOTOR NERVE

The **oculomotor nerve** (N. oculomotorius) arises by several radicles from the basal surface of the cerebral peduncle, a little lateral to the interpeduncular furrow.

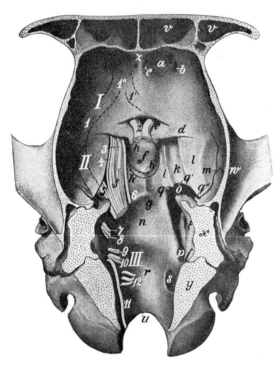

Fig. 645.—Floor of Cranial Cavity of Horse.

The roots of the cranial nerves are shown on the left side and are designated by number: *I*, Anterior cranial fossa; *II*, middle cranial fossa; *III*, posterior cranial fossa; *a*, ethmoidal fossa; *b*, ethmoidal foramen; *c*, foramen for nasal branch of ophthalmic artery; *d*, orbital wing of sphenoid bone; *e*, optic groove; *f*, hypophyseal fossa; *g*, spheno-occipital crest; *h*, *h'*, contour of hypophysis or pituitary body; *h"*, slight elevation representing dorsum sellæ; *i*, *k*, grooves for nerves and cavernous sinus; *l*, depression for piriform lobe of cerebrum; *m*, groove for middle meningeal artery; *n*, depression for pons; *o*, foramen lacerum anterius; *p*, foramen lacerum posterius; *q*, incisura carotica; *q'*, incisura ovalis; *q"*, incisura spinosa; *r*, depression for medulla oblongata; *s*, hypoglossal foramen; *t*, internal acoustic meatus; *u*, foramen magnum; *v*, frontal sinus; *w*, zygomatic process of temporal bone; *x*, section of petrous temporal; *y*, section of occipital bone; *z*, crista galli; 1, 1', 1", dotted lines indicating position of olfactory striæ and tract. (After Ellenberger-Baum, Top. Anat. d. Pferdes.)

It turns sharply outward and forward, crosses over the cavernous sinus, and continues above the maxillary nerve and in company with the ophthalmic nerve to the foramen orbitale. It emerges with the latter nerve and the abducens and divides at once into two branches. The **dorsal branch** is short and divides into two twigs which supply the rectus dorsalis and levator palpebræ superioris. The **ventral branch** (Figs. 563, 564) is much larger and longer. It supplies the motor fibers to the ciliary ganglion (which lies directly on this branch in the horse), short branches to the rectus medialis and rectus ventralis, and a long branch which passes forward on the latter to end in the ventral oblique muscle.

The deep origin of the fibers of the oculomotor nerve is in the oculomotor nucleus, situated in the gray matter of the floor of the cerebral aqueduct in the region of the anterior corpora quadrigemina.

THE TROCHLEAR NERVE

The **trochlear nerve** (N. trochlearis) is the smallest of the cranial nerves. It arises from the anterior cerebellar peduncle just behind the corpora quadrigemina, curves outward and forward, pierces the tentorium cerebelli, and passes forward along the lateral border of the maxillary nerve (Figs. 635, 636). It emerges from the cranium through a small foramen immediately above the foramen orbitale or through the latter and passes forward along the medial wall of the orbit to end in the posterior part of the dorsal oblique muscle of the eyeball (Fig. 564).

The fibers of the fourth nerve spring from a nucleus in the gray matter of the floor of the cerebral aqueduct behind the oculomotor nucleus. The fibers run backward in the tegmentum, then turn dorso-medially, and undergo total decussation with those of the opposite nerve in the anterior part of the anterior medullary velum. In addition to this peculiarity it is the only nerve which is connected with the dorsal aspect of the brain.

THE TRIGEMINAL NERVE

The **trigeminal nerve** (N. trigeminus) is the largest of the cranial series. It is connected with the lateral part of the pons by a large sensory root and a smaller motor root (Fig. 629).

The **sensory root** (Portio major) extends forward through a notch on the lower part of the petrosal crest and widens out to join the semilunar ganglion.

The **semilunar ganglion** (Ganglion semilunare) is a crescent-shaped mass of nerve-fibers and cells which overlies the antero-lateral part of the foramen lacerum basis cranii, and is partly embedded in the dense fibrous tissue which occupies the foramen except where vessels and nerves pass through. Its long axis, which is about an inch (2.5 cm.) in length, is directed forward and medially and its convex anterior face gives rise to the ophthalmic, the maxillary, and the sensory part of the mandibular division of the nerve. The surface of the ganglion is irregularly striated. It is connected by filaments with the adjacent carotid plexus of the sympathetic, and sends delicate twigs to the dura mater.

The fibers of the sensory root arise from the ganglion as axones of the ganglion cells, and the fibers of the nerves which extend peripherally from the ganglion are dendrites of the cells. The sensory root-fibers enter the tegmentum of the pons and divide into anterior and posterior branches, which terminate about the cells of the sensory nucleus of termination of the trigeminus. This nucleus extends from the pons to the sixth cervical segment of the spinal cord (Dexler). The posterior branches of the fibers are collected into a compact bundle, the spinal tract or root of the trigeminus, which lies lateral to the substantia gelatinosa in the medulla. The central connections of the sensory part of the trigeminus are very extensive. The most important paths are: (1) Axones of cells of the sensory nucleus and the substantia gelatinosa pass chiefly as arcuate fibers across the raphé to the thalamus, whence impulses are transmitted by thalamo-cortical fibers to the cerebral cortex. In ungulates a distinct tract extends from the anterior part of the sensory nucleus to the thalamus of the same side (Wallenberg). It is probable that collaterals of the arcuate fibers go to the motor nuclei of the fifth, seventh, ninth, and tenth cranial nerves. (2) Axones of cells of the sensory nucleus enter the posterior cerebellar peduncle of the same side and reach the cerebellar cortex. (3) Collaterals are distributed to the nuclei of origin of the hypoglossal and of the motor part of the trigeminal and facial nerves.

The **motor root** (Portio minor) extends forward beneath the sensory root and the semilunar ganglion and is incorporated with the mandibular division of the nerve. Its fibers arise chiefly from the so-called masticatory nucleus, which is situated in the pons near the inner face of the sensory nucleus; a few of these fibers come from the nucleus of the opposite side and cross in the raphé. Other fibers, which constitute the mesencephalic root, arise from cells in the outer part of the central gray matter of the mid-brain.

It is evident from the foregoing statements that the trigeminus has essentially the same arrangement as a typical spinal nerve. It divides into three branches.

I. The **ophthalmic nerve** (N. ophthalmicus) (Figs. 563, 564, 565) is purely sensory and is the smallest of the three branches of the trigeminus. It arises from the medial part of the front of the semilunar ganglion, passes forward along the outer side of the cavernous sinus, and is blended with the maxillary nerve for some distance. It enters the foramen orbitale with the third and sixth nerves and divides into three branches.

1. The **lacrimal nerve** (N. lacrimalis) runs forward on the rectus dorsalis and

the levator palpebræ superioris and ramifies chiefly in the lacrimal gland and the upper eyelid. A branch (Ramus zygomatico-temporalis) exchanges twigs with the zygomatic branch of the maxillary nerve, perforates the periorbita, and emerges from the orbital fossa behind the supraorbital process; it forms a plexus with branches of the auriculo-palpebral and frontal nerves, and ramifies in the skin of the temporal region.

2. The **frontal nerve** (N. frontalis), also termed the supraorbital, runs forward almost parallel with the dorsal oblique muscle, at first within, then outside of, the periorbita. It passes through the supraorbital foramen with the artery of like name and ramifies in the skin of the forehead and upper eyelid, forming a plexus with the lacrimal and auriculo-palpebral nerves. It divides into three branches.

3. The **naso-ciliary nerve** (N. nasociliaris), also termed the palpebro-nasal, runs forward and medially, passing under the rectus oculi dorsalis, and divides into two branches. Of these, the **ethmoidal nerve** (N. ethmoidalis) is the continuation of the parent trunk. It accompanies the ethmoidal artery through the foramen of like name into the cranial cavity and crosses the lower part of the ethmoidal fossa. Leaving the cranium through an opening in the cribriform plate close to the crista galli, it enters the nasal cavity and ramifies in the mucous membrane of the septum nasi and the dorsal turbinate. The **infra-trochlear nerve** (N. infratrochlearis) runs forward to the medial canthus and ramifies in the skin in this region; it detaches twigs to the conjunctiva and caruncula lacrimalis, and a long branch which supplies the third eyelid and the lacrimal ducts and sac. The naso-ciliary nerve furnishes the **sensory** or **long root** (Radix longa) of the ciliary ganglion.

The **ciliary ganglion** is placed on the ventral branch of the oculomotor nerve, close to its origin from the latter. It is usually not larger than a millet-seed, and is best found by following the nerve to the ventral oblique muscle back to its origin. The ganglion receives—(*a*) **sensory fibers** from the naso-ciliary nerve; (*b*) **motor fibers** from the oculomotor nerve; and (*c*) **sympathetic fibers** from the spheno-palatine plexus. It detaches filaments which unite with twigs from the ophthalmic and maxillary nerves and from the sphenopalatine ganglion to form the ciliary plexus. From the latter emanate five to eight delicate **short ciliary nerves** (Nn. ciliares breves), which pursue a somewhat flexuous course along the optic nerve, pierce the sclera near the entrance of that nerve, and run forward between the sclera and chorioidea to the circumference of the iris. Here the branches of adjacent nerves anastomose to form a circular plexus (Plexus gangliosus ciliaris), from which filaments go to the ciliary body, iris, and cornea.

The circular fibers of the iris and the ciliary muscle are innervated by fibers derived from the oculomotor nerve, the radial fibers of the iris by the sympathetic.

II. The **maxillary nerve** (N. maxillaris) is purely sensory and is much larger than the ophthalmic. It extends forward from the semilunar ganglion in the middle cranial fossa in the large groove on the root of the temporal wing of the sphenoid. It is related medially to the cavernous sinus and dorsally to the ophthalmic nerve, with which it is blended for some distance. It emerges through the foramen rotundum, passes forward in the pterygo-palatine fossa above the internal maxillary artery and embedded in fat, and is continued in the infraorbital canal as the infraorbital nerve (Fig. 564). Its branches are as follows:

1. The **zygomatic nerve** (N. zygomaticus), also termed the orbital branch, arises before the maxillary nerve reaches the pterygo-palatine fossa (Figs. 563, 564, 646). It pierces the periorbita and divides into two or three delicate branches which pass along the surface of the lateral straight muscle to the lateral canthus

and ramify chiefly in the lower lid and the adjacent skin. Anastomoses are formed with branches of the lacrimal nerve.

2. The **sphenopalatine nerve** (N. sphenopalatinus) (Fig. 646a) is given off in the pterygopalatine fossa from the ventral border of the maxillary nerve (Fig. 564). It is broad and flat and forms a plexus in which several small **sphenopalatine ganglia**

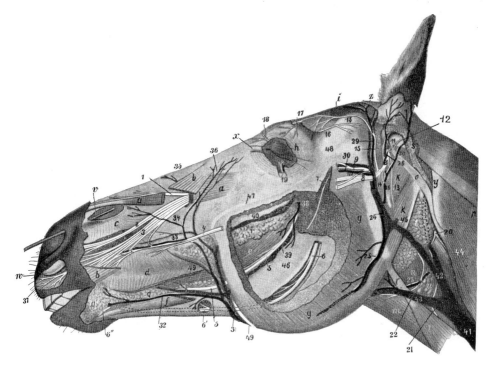

FIG. 646.—DISSECTION OF HEAD OF HORSE.

The masseter and superficial muscles and the parotid gland are in great part removed. *a, a,* Levator labii superioris proprius; *b, b,* levator nasolabialis; *c,* dilatator naris inferior; *d,* buccinator; *e,* common mass of buccinator and depressor labii inferioris; *f,* depressor labii inferioris; *g,* masseter; *h,* orbicularis oculi; *i,* temporalis; *k,* occipito-hyoideus; *k',* occipito-mandibularis; *l,* sterno-cephalicus; *l',* tendon of same; *m,* omo-hyoideus; *n,* crico-pharyngeus; *o,* mastoid tendon of brachiocephalicus; *p,* splenius; *q,* inferior buccal and labial glands; *r,* superior buccal glands; *s,* remnant of parotid gland; *t,* mandibular gland; *u,* anterior cervical lymph glands; *v,* probe passed into diverticulum nasi; *w,* cornu of alar cartilage; *x,* medial palpebral ligament; *y,* wing of atlas; *z,* scutiform cartilage of ear; *1,* external nasal nerve; *2,* anterior nasal nerve; *3,* superior labial nerve; *4,* anterior part of superior buccal nerve; *5,* buccinator nerve; *6, 6',* mandibular alveolar nerve; *6'',* mental nerve—continuation of *6; 7,* masseteric nerve; *8,* facial nerve (cut); *9,* superficial temporal nerve; *10,* anastomosis between *9* and *8; 11,* internal auricular nerve; *12,* posterior auricular nerve; *13,* digastric nerve; *14,* cervical branch of facial nerve (cut); *15,* auriculo-palpebral nerve; *16,* lacrimal nerve; *17,* frontal nerve; *18,* infratrochlear nerve; *19,* zygomatic nerve; *20,* spinal accessory nerve; *21,* ventral branch of spinal accessory nerve (to sterno-cephalicus); *22,* ventral end branch of first cervical nerve; *23,* thyro-laryngeal artery; *24,* internal maxillary artery; *25,* masseteric artery; *26,* great (posterior) auricular artery; *27,* external branch of *26; 28,* deep auricular artery; *29,* anterior auricular artery; *30,* transverse facial artery; *31,* facial artery; *32,* inferior labial artery; *33,* superior labial artery; *34,* lateral nasal artery; *35,* dorsal nasal artery; *36,* angular artery of eye; *37,* terminal branches of superior labial nerve; *38,* branch of buccinator artery; *39,* buccinator vein; *40,* vena reflexa; *42,* jugular vein; *43,* external maxillary vein; *44,* ventral cerebral vein; *45,* stump of great auricular vein; *46,* ramus of mandible; *47,* facial crest; *48,* zygomatic arch; *49,* parotid duct. (After Ellenberger-Baum, Top. Anat. d. Pferdes.)

are interposed. It divides into posterior nasal, and greater and lesser palatine nerves. (1) The **posterior nasal nerve** (N. nasalis aboralis) passes through the sphenopalatine foramen, in which it bears one or more minute ganglia, enters the nasal cavity, and divides into medial and lateral branches (Figs. 565, 588). The medial branch (N. septi narium) runs forward in the submucous tissue of the lower part of the septum nasi, gives twigs to the mucous membrane here and to the vomero-nasal organ, passes through the palatine fissure, and ramifies in the anterior part of the hard palate. The lateral branch (Ramus lateralis) ramifies in the mucous membrane of the ventral turbinate and the middle and ventral meatus nasi. (2) The **greater** or **anterior palatine nerve** (N. palatinus major s. oralis) (Figs. 563, 564) is the largest of the three branches. It runs forward in the palatine canal and groove and ramifies in the hard palate and gums. It also supplies twigs to the soft palate, and gives off branches which pass through the accessory palatine foramina to supply the mucous membrane of the ventral meatus.

The branches of the two nerves anastomose in the hard palate and form a plexus about the branches of the palatine arteries.

(3) The **lesser** or **posterior palatine nerve** (N. palatinus minor s. aboralis), also termed the staphyline, is much the smallest of the three branches (Figs. 563, 564). It passes downward and forward with the palatine vein in the groove at the medial side of the tuber maxillare and ramifies in the soft palate.

The sphenopalatine ganglia and plexus (Fig. 647) lie on the perpendicular part of the palatine bone and the pterygoid process, under cover of the maxillary nerve. The afferent fibers of the plexus and ganglia come chiefly from the branches of the sphenopalatine nerve and the nerve of the pterygoid canal. Interspersed in these are several minute ganglia and one or more larger ones. The **nerve of the pterygoid canal** (N. canalis pterygoidei) is formed by the union of sympathetic fibers with the superficial petrosal branch of the facial nerve. It passes forward at first between the Eustachian tube and the sphenoid bone, enters the canal between the pterygoid bone and process, and joins the posterior part of the plexus. It is probable that it furnishes the motor fibers to the levator palati and palatinus muscles. Efferent filaments go to the periorbita and the ophthalmic vessels, and others accompany the branches of the maxillary nerve, around which they have a plexiform arrangement:

3. The **infraorbital nerve** (N. infraorbitalis) is the continuation of the maxillary trunk. It traverses the infraorbital canal, emerges through the infraorbital foramen, and divides into nasal and superior labial branches. Along its course it gives off **maxillary alveolar** or **dental branches** (Rami alveolares maxillæ), which supply the teeth, alveolar periosteum, and gums.

Small **posterior alveolar branches** (Rami alveolares maxillæ aborales) are given off in the pterygo-palatine fossa, pass through small foramina in the tuber maxillare, and supply the posterior molar teeth and the maxillary sinus. The **middle alveolar branches** (Rami alveolares maxillæ medii) are given off in the infraorbital canal, and constitute the chief nerve-supply to the cheek teeth and the maxillary sinus. The **maxillary incisor branch** (Ramus alveolaris maxillæ incisivus) runs forward in the incisor canal and supplies branches to the canine and incisor teeth. The foregoing unite with each other to form the **maxillary dental plexus** (Plexus dentalis maxillæ) from which the dental and gingival branches are given off.

The **external nasal branches** (Rami nasales externi), two or three in number, accompany the levator labii superioris proprius and ramify in the dorsum nasi and the nasal diverticulum.

The large **anterior nasal branch** (Ramus nasalis oralis) gives branches to the upper lip and nostril, passes over the nasal process of the premaxilla under cover of the lateralis nasi, and ramifies in the mucous membrane of the nasal vestibule.

The **superior labial branch** (Ramus labialis dorsalis) is the largest of the terminals of the infraorbital nerve. It passes downward and forward under cover of the levator nasolabialis and, after supplying the skin of the anterior part of the cheek, forms a rich terminal ramification in the skin and mucous membrane of the upper lip. It anastomoses with the superior buccal branch of the facial nerve.

III. The **mandibular nerve** (N. mandibularis) is formed by the union of two roots; of these, the large sensory root comes from the semilunar ganglion, and the small motor root is the pars minor of the trigeminus. It emerges from the cranium through the oval notch of the foramen lacerum, and passes between the temporal wing of the sphenoid bone and the muscular process of the petrous temporal. It then runs forward, downward, and a little outward, between the ventral surface of

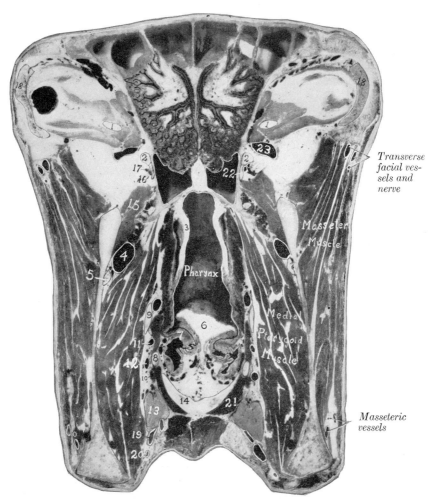

FIG. 646a.—CROSS SECTION OF HEAD OF HORSE.

The section passes through the head 1 cm. behind the lateral canthi, and is cut perpendicular to the dorsal surface of the head. *1, 1,* Optic nerves; *2,* infraorbital nerve; *3,* Eustachian tube, medial lamina; *4,* internal maxillary vein; *5,* mandibular nerve (lingual branch of mandibular nerve to right of *5*); *6,* epiglottis; *7,* soft palate (postvelar); *8,* thyroid cornu of hyoid bone (hypoglossal nerve to left of *8*); *9,* great cornu of hyoid bone (lingual branch of IX nerve below *9*); *10,* tendon of digastricus; *11,* lingual artery; *12,* external maxillary artery; *13,* anterior end of mandibular gland; *14,* body of thyroid cartilage; *15,* buccinator nerve (perforating origin of pterygoideus lateralis); *16,* internal maxillary artery; *17,* infraorbital artery; *18,* lacrimal gland; *19,* external maxillary vein (sublingual vein above and medial to *19*); *20,* parotid duct; *21,* thyro-hyoideus; *22,* sphenopalatine nerve; *23,* vena reflexa as it joins the ophthalmic vein; *24,* ramus of mandible.

the pterygoideus lateralis and the guttural pouch, and on reaching the lateral surface of the pterygoideus medialis, it divides into two terminal branches—the mandibular alveolar and lingual nerves. It gives off the following branches:

1. The **masseteric nerve** (N. massetericus) (Figs. 562, 646) passes outward through the mandibular notch across the anterior surface of the temporo-mandibular articulation, turns downward, and enters the deep face of the masseter muscle, in which it ramifies.

2. The **deep temporal nerves** (Nn. temporales profundi) (Fig. 562), two or three in number, arise from, or by a common trunk with, the masseteric. They supply the temporalis muscle.

3. The **buccinator nerve** (N. buccinatorius) passes downward and forward at first across the medial surface of the temporo-mandibular articulation, then through the anterior part of the lateral pterygoid muscle (Fig. 646a), then between the bucci-

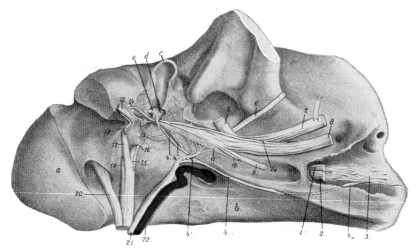

FIG. 647.—DEEP DISSECTION OF BASE OF CRANIUM, VIEWED FROM THE RIGHT AND BELOW.

The tympanic cavity is opened and the paramastoid process is sawn off. *a*, Occipital condyle; *b*, body of sphenoid; *c*, external acoustic meatus (part removed); *d*, malleus; *e*, incus; *1*, stump of ophthalmic nerve; *2*, stump of maxillary nerve; *3*, sphenopalatine plexus; *4*, nerve of pterygoid canal; *4'*, deep petrosal nerve; *4''*, branch to tympanic plexus; *4'''*, superficial petrosal nerve; *5*, superficial temporal nerve (cut off); *6*, masseteric nerve (cut off); *7*, mandibular nerve (raised); *8*, lingual nerve (cut off); *9*, pterygoid nerve (cut); *10*, nerve to tensor tympani; *11*, otic ganglion; *12*, facial nerve; *13*, stapedial nerve; *14*, chorda tympani; *15*, glosso-pharyngeal nerve (cut); *16*, tympanic nerve; *17*, vagus (cut off); *18*, auricular branch of vagus; *19*, spinal accessory nerve (cut off); *20*, hypoglossal nerve (cut off; *21*, sympathetic nerve (cut off); *22*, internal carotid artery. (After Ellenberger, in Leisering's Atlas.)

nator vein and the tuber maxillare (Fig. 646). It continues forward in the submucous tissue of the cheek along the ventral border of the depressor labii inferioris and divides into branches which ramify in the mucous membrane and glands of the lips in the vicinity of the commissure. It supplies small branches to the lateral pterygoid and temporal muscles and detaches numerous collateral twigs to the mucous membrane of the cheek and to the buccal glands. It also communicates with the inferior buccal branch of the facial nerve.

4. The **pterygoid nerve** (N. pterygoideus) arises in common with the preceding, passes downward and forward under cover of the parent trunk, and divides into branches which enter the posterior part of the pterygoideus medialis at the division between the two layers of the muscle (Fig. 647).

The **otic ganglion** (G. oticum) is situated on the mandibular near the origin of the buccinator nerve, and is related medially to the tensor palati and the Eustachian tube. It receives motor fibers from the pterygoid nerve and sensory fibers by the small superficial petrosal nerve from the tympanic plexus, through which communications are made with the facial and glosso-pharyngeal nerves. Sympathetic fibers are derived from the plexus on the internal maxillary artery. Efferent filaments go to the tensor palati, tensor tympani, and pterygoid muscles and to the Eustachian tube.

The ganglion is small and somewhat difficult to find, and in many cases it is replaced by a number of minute ganglia interspersed in a fine plexus.

5. The **superficial temporal nerve** (N. temporalis superficialis) (Figs. 562, 646, 647) runs outward across the pterygoideus lateralis, passes between the parotid gland and the neck of the ramus of the mandible, turns around the latter, and divides into two branches. The **transverse facial branch** (Ramus transversus faciei) accompanies the transverse facial vessels and ramifies in the skin of the cheek. The larger **ventral branch** unites with the ventral buccal division of the facial nerve. Before its division the nerve gives off twigs to the guttural pouch, the parotid gland, the external ear, and the skin of the external acoustic meatus and the mem-

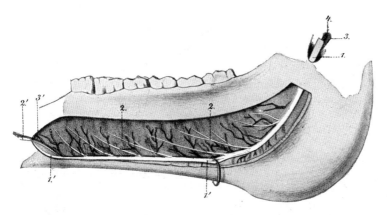

FIG. 648.—PART OF BRANCH OF LOWER JAW OF HORSE; MEDIAL VIEW.

The bone has been removed to show the vessels and nerves. *1, 1'*, Mandibular alveolar nerve; *2, 2*, branches to cheek teeth and gums; *2'*, branch to canine and incisor teeth; *3, 3'*, alveolar artery; *4*, satellite vein. (After Leisering's Atlas.)

brana tympani. Branches from it concur with filaments from the cervical branch of the facial nerve in the formation of the auricular plexus.

6. The **mandibular alveolar nerve** (N. alveolaris mandibulæ) (Figs. 561, 562, 646) arises with the lingual by a common trunk which passes forward at first on the lateral pterygoid muscle, then inclines ventrally between the medial pterygoid and the ramus of the mandible. The lingual and alveolar separate at an acute angle, and the latter enters the mandibular foramen and courses in the canal within the ramus (Fig. 648). Emerging at the mental foramen, it terminates by dividing into six to eight inferior labial and mental branches, which ramify in the lower lip and chin. Before entering the bone, the nerve detaches the **mylo-hyoid nerve** (N. mylohyoideus), which runs downward and forward between the ramus and the mylo-hyoid muscle; it supplies that muscle, the anterior belly of the digastricus, and the skin of the anterior part of the mandibular space. The dental and gingival branches detached from the nerve within the mandible are arranged like the corresponding nerves of the upper jaw.

7. The **lingual nerve** (N. lingualis) arises by a common trunk with the mandibular alveolar nerve (Figs. 561, 562). After separating from the latter it runs

downward and forward, lying at first between the ramus of the mandible and the medial pterygoid muscle, then on the medial face of the mylo-hyoid. On reaching the root of the tongue it divides into superficial and deep branches. The **superficial branch** (Ramus superficialis) runs forward on the stylo-glossus and accompanies the mandibular duct on the deep face of the sublingual gland. It supplies the mucous membrane of the tongue and the floor of the mouth. At the root of the tongue it gives off a recurrent branch to the isthmus faucium, which communicates with the lingual branch of the glosso-pharyngeal nerve. The larger **deep branch** (Ramus profundus) turns around the lower edge of the stylo-glossus and hyo-glossus, passes upward and forward between the latter muscle and the genio-glossus, and continues forward on the latter to the tip of the tongue. At the turn it gives off one or more ascending branches which ramify on the deep face of the hyo-glossus. It gives branches to the mucous membrane and the fungiform papillæ of the tongue, and anastomoses with branches of the hypoglossal nerve and with the superficial branch. Minute ganglia occur on the finer branches of the lingual nerve. The **chorda tympani** branch of the facial joins the lingual nerve at the origin of the latter and is incorporated with it in its distribution to the tongue.

THE ABDUCENT NERVE

The **abducent nerve** (N. abducens) emerges from the brain behind the pons and just lateral to the pyramid (Fig. 629). It passes forward across the pons, pierces the dura mater, and accompanies the oculomotor and ophthalmic nerves, below which it emerges through the foramen orbitale. In the orbit it divides into two very short branches which innervate the rectus lateralis and the retractor muscle of the eyeball. Within the cranium it receives filaments from the carotid plexus of the sympathetic.

The fibers of the abducent nerve are axones of the large multipolar cells of the abducent nucleus which is situated beneath the eminentia teres of the floor of the fourth ventricle. The nucleus lies within the loop formed by the fibers of origin of the facial nerve. It is connected with (a) the anterior olive; (b) the oculomotor nucleus of the opposite side; (c) the motor area of the cerebral cortex by means of the pyramidal tract of the opposite side.

THE FACIAL NERVE

The **facial nerve** (N. facialis) has its superficial origin at the lateral part of the corpus trapezoideum, immediately behind the pons (Fig. 629). It passes outward in front of the eighth nerve and enters the internal acoustic meatus. At the bottom of the meatus the two nerves part company, the facial coursing in the facial canal of the petrous temporal bone. The canal and nerve are at first directed outward between the vestibule and the cochlea, then curve backward and ventrally in the posterior wall of the tympanum to end at the stylo-mastoid foramen. The bend formed by the nerve is called the **knee** (Geniculum n. facialis), and bears at its highest point the round **geniculate ganglion** (G. geniculi).

The nerve consists of two parts, motor and sensory. The **motor part** constitutes the bulk of the nerve. Its deep origin is from the cells of the **facial nucleus**, which is situated in the medulla above the facial tubercle. On leaving the nucleus the root-fibers pass dorso-medially, incline forward close to the median plane, and then bend sharply downward to the point of emergence. The highest point of the bend is subjacent to the gray substance of the eminentia medialis in the floor of the fourth ventricle, and the abducent nucleus lies in the concavity of the curve. The small **sensory part** (N. intermedius) consists of axones of cells of the geniculate ganglion, which is interposed on the facial nerve as it bends downward in the facial canal. The fibers of this part, after entering the medulla, pass to the nucleus of termination which it shares with the ninth and tenth nerves. The peripheral fibers from the geniculate ganglion constitute the chorda tympani.

After its emergence through the stylo-mastoid foramen (Fig. 646) the nerve passes ventrally, forward, and outward on the guttural pouch under cover of the parotid gland, and passes between the origin of the superficial temporal and internal maxillary arteries medially and the superficial temporal vein laterally. It then crosses the posterior border of the ramus of the mandible ventral to the transverse facial artery and about an inch and a half (ca. 3.5–4 cm.) below the articulation of the jaw. It receives the ventral branch of the superficial temporal nerve, and emerges from beneath the parotid gland either before or after dividing into dorsal and ventral buccal branches. The following collateral branches are given off, the first five being detached within the facial canal, and the others between the stylo-mastoid foramen and the border of the jaw.

1. The **great superficial petrosal nerve** (N. petrosus superficialis major) arises from the geniculate ganglion.[1] It passes through the petrosal canal, contributing a filament to the tympanic plexus, receives the deep petrosal nerve from the carotid plexus of the sympathetic, emerges through the foramen lacerum, and is continued as the nerve of the pterygoid canal to the sphenopalatine plexus and ganglia (Fig. 647).

2. A delicate branch (R. anastomoticus cum plexu tympanico) emerges from the geniculate ganglion and unites with a filament issuing from the tympanic plexus to form the **small superficial petrosal nerve** (N. petrosus superficialis minor); this ends in the otic ganglion.

3. The **stapedial nerve** (N. stapedius) (Fig. 647) is a short filament detached from the facial nerve as it turns down in the facial canal. It innervates the stapedius muscle.

4. The **chorda tympani** (Fig. 647) is a small nerve which arises a little below the preceding and pursues a recurrent course in a small canal in the mastoid part of the temporal bone (Canaliculus chordæ tympani), to reach the tympanic cavity. It traverses the latter, passing between the handle of the malleus and the long branch of the incus. Emerging through the petrotympanic fissure, the nerve passes downward and forward on the guttural pouch, crosses beneath the internal maxillary artery, and joins the lingual nerve. It sends twigs to the mandibular and sublingual glands, and through its incorporation with the lingual nerve furnishes fibers to the mucous membrane of the anterior two-thirds of the tongue which are believed to mediate the sense of taste.

5. Anastomotic filaments unite with the auricular branch of the vagus near the stylomastoid foramen.

6. The **posterior auricular nerve** (N. auricularis aboralis) arises from the facial at its emergence from the facial canal (Fig. 646). It runs upward and backward with the posterior auricular artery under cover of the parotid gland, and supplies the posterior and dorsal auricular muscles and the skin of the convex surface of the external ear. It anastomoses with branches of the first and second cervical nerves.

7. The **internal auricular nerve** (N. auricularis internus) springs from the facial close to or in common with the preceding (Fig. 646). It ascends in the parotid gland just behind the styloid process of the conchal cartilage, passes through an opening in the cartilage, and ramifies in the skin of the concave surface of the ear.

8. The **digastric branch** (R. digastricus) (Fig. 646) arises from the facial below the auricular nerves and descends under cover of the parotid gland. Its branches innervate the posterior belly of the digastricus, the occipito-mandibularis, the stylo-hyoideus, and the occipito-hyoideus. At its origin it gives off a small branch which forms a loop around the great auricular artery or its posterior branch and rejoins the trunk.

9. The **auriculo-palpebral nerve** (N. auriculopalpebralis) (Fig. 646) arises

[1] Although this nerve springs directly from the ganglion, it contains motor as well as sensory fibers.

from the upper edge of the facial near the posterior border of the ramus. It ascends in the parotid gland behind the superficial temporal artery, and terminates in anterior auricular and temporal branches. The small **anterior auricular branches** form with the frontal and lacrimal branches of the trigeminus the **anterior auricular plexus.** They innervate the anterior auricular and parotido-auricularis muscles. The **temporal branch** runs forward and inward over the temporal muscle to the medial canthus of the eye, forms a plexus with the terminal branches of the ophthalmic nerve, and is distributed to the orbicularis oculi, corrugator supercilii, and levator nasolabialis.

10. The **cervical branch** (R. colli) (Fig. 560) is small; it arises from the ventral border of the facial opposite to the preceding nerve. It passes obliquely through the parotid gland, emerging under cover of the parotido-auricularis, passes downward and backward on or near the jugular vein, and anastomoses with the cutaneous branches of the cervical nerves. It gives branches to the parotido-auricularis and the cervical cutaneous muscle. In its course along the neck the nerve is reinforced by twigs from the cutaneous branches of the second to the sixth cervical nerves.

11. Small branches are detached to the guttural pouch and the parotid gland. The latter (Rami parotidei) concur with branches of the superficial temporal nerve in forming the **parotid plexus.**

12. The **dorsal buccal nerve** (N. buccalis dorsalis) passes forward on the upper part of the masseter, dips under the zygomaticus, and reaches the ventral border of the dilatator naris lateralis. It continues under cover of the last-named muscle and the levator nasolabialis in company with the superior labial artery and ramifies in the muscles of the upper lip and nostril. It gives collateral branches to the buccinator and anastomoses with the infraorbital and ventral buccal nerve.

13. The **ventral buccal nerve** (N. buccalis ventralis) crosses the masseter obliquely and continues forward along the depressor labii inferioris. It is connected by variable anastomotic branches with the dorsal nerve. It gives collateral branches to the cutaneus, buccinator, and depressor labii inferioris, and ramifies in the muscles of the lower lip.

The buccal nerves are subject to much variation in regard to their course, anastomoses, and relations to the sensory components derived from the superficial temporal nerve. Their distribution is constant. The point at which the branch of the superficial temporal nerve joins the facial is variable.

THE ACOUSTIC NERVE

The **acoustic nerve** (N. acusticus) is connected with the lateral aspect of the medulla just behind and lateral to the facial (Fig. 629). It has two roots, vestibular and cochlear (Radix vestibularis, cochlearis).

The acoustic nerve consists of two distinct parts which might well be regarded as separate nerves. The cochlear part mediates the sense of hearing, while the vestibular part is not auditory in function, but is concerned in the sense of the position of the body and the mechanism of equilibration (Sensus staticus).

The nerve passes outward to the internal acoustic meatus, which it enters behind the facial nerve. In the meatus it divides into two nerves, of which the upper is the vestibular and the lower is the cochlear nerve.

1. The **vestibular nerve** (N. vestibuli) is distributed to the utriculus, the sacculus, and to the ampullæ of the semicircular ducts of the internal ear. In the internal acoustic meatus the nerve is connected by filaments with the geniculate ganglion of the facial nerve. At the bottom of the meatus it bears the **vestibular ganglion** (G. vestibulare), from the cells of which the fibers of the nerve arise.

2. The **cochlear nerve** (N. cochleæ) detaches a filament to the sacculus, passes

through the lamina cribrosa to the labyrinth, and is distributed to the organ of Corti in the cochlea.

The fibers of the vestibular nerve arise from the vestibular ganglion as central processes (axones) of the bipolar cells of the ganglion. The peripheral processes (dendrites) of the cells form arborizations about the deep ends of the hair-cells of the maculæ and cristæ acusticæ of the utriculus, sacculus, and semicircular ducts. The fibers enter the medulla, pass between the restiform body and the spinal tract of the trigeminus, and spread out to end in the vestibular nucleus in the floor of the fourth ventricle. Among the central connections of the vestibular nerve are: (1) fibers which connect its nucleus with centers in the cerebellum (chiefly of the opposite side); (2) the vestibulo-spinal tract, which conveys impulses to the motor cells of the ventral columns of the spinal cord; (3) fibers which connect the nucleus with those of the abducent nerve of the same side, the third and fourth nerves, and the motor part of the trigeminus of both sides.

The fibers of the cochlear nerve are the central processes of the bipolar cells of the spiral ganglion of the cochlea. The peripheral processes of these cells end in relation to the hair-cells of the organ of Corti. Some of the nerve-fibers enter the ventral cochlear nucleus in the medulla close to the superficial origin of the nerve; others end in the dorsal nucleus of the tuberculum acusticum at the lateral angle of the floor of the fourth ventricle. From the ventral nucleus fibers pass in the corpus trapezoideum to the anterior olivary nucleus of the same and of the opposite side. Thence tracts pass to the nuclei of the motor nerves of the eye, and through the lateral fillet to the posterior quadrigeminal body and the medial geniculate body. The axones of the cells of the dorsal nucleus pass largely (as the striæ acusticæ) over the restiform body and across the floor of the fourth ventricle toward the median plane. They then turn ventrally, cross to the opposite side, and are continued by the lateral fillet. From the mid-brain a tract proceeds to the cortex of the temporal part of the cerebral hemisphere.

THE GLOSSO-PHARYNGEAL NERVE

The **glosso-pharyngeal nerve** (N. glossopharyngeus) is attached to the anterior part of the lateral aspect of the medulla by several filaments (Fig. 629). The root-bundles enter the furrow ventral to the restiform body; they are separated by a short interval from the origin of the facial nerve, but are not marked off behind from the roots of the vagus. The bundles converge laterally to form a nerve which perforates the dura mater and emerges through the foramen lacerum posterius just in front of the tenth nerve (Fig. 647). As it issues from the cranium the nerve bears an ovoid gray enlargement, the **ganglion petrosum**. It then curves downward and forward over the guttural pouch and behind the great cornu of the hyoid bone, crosses the deep face of the external carotid artery, and divides into pharyngeal and lingual branches (Fig. 562). The collateral branches are as follows:

1. The **tympanic nerve** (N. tympanicus) (Fig. 647) arises from the petrous ganglion and passes upward between the petrous and tympanic parts of the temporal bone to reach the cavity of the tympanum. Here it breaks up into branches to form, along with branches from the carotid plexus of the sympathetic, the **tympanic plexus**. From the plexus branches pass to the mucous membrane of the tympanum and the Eustachian tube. The continuation of the nerve issues from the plexus and unites with a filament from the geniculate ganglion of the facial to form the small superficial petrosal nerve; this runs forward and ends in the otic ganglion. Filaments also connect the petrous ganglion with the jugular ganglion of the vagus nerve and with the anterior cervical ganglion of the sympathetic.

2. A considerable branch runs backward on the guttural pouch, contributes filaments to the pharyngeal plexus, and concurs with twigs from the vagus and the sympathetic in forming the **carotid plexus** on the terminal part of the carotid artery and on its chief branches. In this plexus is the small **ganglion inter-caroticum**.

3. The very small nerve to the stylo-pharyngeus muscle (N. stylopharyngeus) arises from the dorsal border of the nerve.

The **pharyngeal branch** (R. pharyngeus) (Fig. 562) is the smaller of the two terminal branches. It runs forward across the deep face of the great cornu of the hyoid bone and concurs with the pharyngeal branches of the vagus and with sympathetic filaments in forming the pharyngeal plexus; from this branches pass to the muscles and mucous membrane of the pharynx.

The **lingual branch** (R. lingualis) is the continuation of the trunk (Fig. 562). It runs along the posterior border of the great cornu of the hyoid bone in front of the external maxillary artery, and dips under the hyo-glossus muscle. It gives collateral branches to the soft palate, isthmus faucium, and tonsil, and ends in the mucous membrane of the posterior part of the tongue, where it supplies gustatory fibers to the vallate papillæ. A considerable branch unites with a twig from the lingual nerve.

The glosso-pharyngeal is a mixed nerve, containing both motor and sensory fibers. The latter constitute the bulk of the nerve and include those which mediate the special sense of taste. They are processes of the cells of the petrous ganglion. The central processes of the ganglion cells enter the medulla, pass dorso-medially through the formatio reticularis, and end in the nucleus of termination in the floor of the fourth ventricle. The motor fibers arise from dorsal and ventral efferent nuclei in the medulla. The glosso-pharyngeal shares these nuclei with the vagus and has practically the same central connections as that nerve (q. v.).

THE VAGUS NERVE

The **vagus** (N. vagus)[1] is the longest and most widely distributed of the cranial nerves; it is also remarkable for the connections which it forms with adjacent nerves and with the sympathetic. It is attached to the lateral aspect of the medulla by several filaments which are in series with those of the ninth nerve in front and the eleventh nerve behind (Fig. 629). The bundles converge to form a trunk which passes outward, pierces the dura mater, and emerges from the cranium through the foramen lacerum posterius (Fig. 647). In the foramen the nerve bears on its lateral aspect the elongated flattened **jugular ganglion** (G. jugulare).

The ganglion communicates with—(a) the tympanic nerve, (b) The petrous ganglion of the glosso-pharyngeal nerve, (c) the spinal accessory, and (d) the hypoglossal. It also gives off the **auricular branch** (R. auricularis), which runs forward below the petrous ganglion and passes through a small canal in the petrous temporal bone to gain the facial canal. Here it gives filaments to the facial and emerges with that nerve through the stylo-mastoid foramen. It ascends behind the external acoustic meatus, dips under the deep auricular muscles, and passes through a foramen in the conchal cartilage to ramify in the integument which lines the meatus and the adjacent part of the ear. It may be noted that many fibers of the vagus pass over the medial face of the ganglion without entering it.

A **ganglion nodosum** in the form of a compact mass is not present in the horse. It appears to be represented by masses of ganglion cells in the nerve trunk which begin in front of the origin of the pharyngeal branch and continue a considerable distance behind the origin of the anterior laryngeal nerve.

Beyond the ganglion the vagus runs backward and downward with the spinal accessory in a fold of the guttural pouch (Fig. 562). Then the two nerves separate, allowing the hypoglossal to pass between them, and the vagus descends with the internal carotid artery and crosses the medial face of the origin of the occipital artery. Here it is joined by the cervical trunk of the sympathetic, and the two nerves continue along the dorsal aspect of the common carotid artery in a common sheath, forming thus a vago-sympathetic trunk (Fig. 558). At the root of the neck the vagus separates from the sympathetic, and from this point backward the relations of the right and left vagi differ somewhat and must be described separately.

The **right vagus nerve** (Fig. 554) enters the thorax in the angle of divergence of the right brachial artery and the truncus bicaroticus. It then passes backward and slightly upward, crossing obliquely the lateral surface of the brachiocephalic artery and the right face of the trachea. Reaching the dorsal surface of the latter near the bifurcation, it divides into dorsal and ventral branches.

[1] Also commonly termed the pneumogastric nerve.

The **left vagus nerve** (Fig. 553) enters the thorax on the lateral or the ventral face of the œsophagus, crosses obliquely under the left brachial artery, and passes back on the lateral surface of that vessel in company with a large cardiac nerve.[1] Separating from the latter, the vagus continues backward on the left face of the

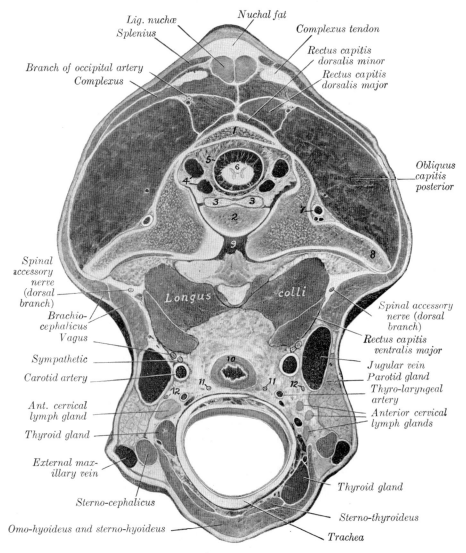

Lig. nuchœ
Splenius
Nuchal fat
Complexus tendon
Rectus capitis dorsalis minor
Rectus capitis dorsalis major
Branch of occipital artery
Complexus
Obliquus capitis posterior
Spinal accessory nerve (dorsal branch)
Brachio-cephalicus
Vagus
Sympathetic
Carotid artery
Ant. cervical lymph gland
Thyroid gland
External maxillary vein
Sterno-cephalicus
Omo-hyoideus and sterno-hyoideus
Longus
colli
Spinal accessory nerve (dorsal branch)
Rectus capitis ventralis major
Jugular vein
Parotid gland
Thyro-laryngeal artery
Anterior cervical lymph glands
Thyroid gland
Sterno-thyroideus
Trachea

FIG. 649.—CROSS-SECTION OF NECK OF HORSE, PASSING THROUGH POSTERIOR PART OF ATLAS.

The head and neck were extended. *1*, Dorsal arch of atlas; *2*, dens of axis; *3*, ligament of dens; *4*, vertebral sinuses; *5*, dura mater; *6*, spinal cord; *7*, vertebral artery; *8*, wing of atlas; *9*, atlanto-axial joint cavity; *10*, œsophagus; *11, 11*, recurrent nerves; *12, 12*, ventral branches of spinal accessory nerves. By an oversight the obliquus cap. post. (above wing of atlas) is unmarked; also the parotid gland between the jugular and external maxillary vein.

aorta, inclines to the upper surface of the left bronchus, and divides into dorsal and ventral branches.

The dorsal and ventral branches unite with the corresponding branches of the opposite nerve, thus forming **dorsal** and **ventral œsophageal trunks** (Truncus

[1] In some cases the left vagus passes back below the junction of the jugular veins and the termination of the left brachial vein. It then runs backward and somewhat dorsally across the left face of the anterior vena cava to reach its usual position.

œsophageus dorsalis, ventralis). These run backward in the posterior mediastinum, dorsal and ventral to the œsophagus respectively, and enter the abdominal cavity through the hiatus œsophageus; they supply branches to the œsophagus and anastomose with each other. The dorsal trunk receives the major part of its fibers from the right vagus. After entering the abdomen it passes to the left of the cardia, and divides into gastric and cœliac branches; the former gives branches to the visceral surface of the stomach, forming the posterior gastric plexus; the latter ends in the right cœliaco-mesenteric ganglion and the anterior interganglionic cord. The smaller ventral trunk passes to the lesser curvature of the stomach and ramifies on the parietal surface of the stomach; it forms here the anterior gastric plexus from which branches are supplied also to the first part of the duodenum and to the liver and pancreas.[1]

The collateral branches of the vagus are as follows:

1. The **pharyngeal branch** (R. pharyngeus) is given off in relation to the anterior cervical ganglion, turns around the internal carotid artery, and runs ventrally and forward on the guttural pouch to the dorsal wall of the pharynx (Fig. 562). Here its branches concur with the pharyngeal branch of the glosso-pharyngeal nerve and with filaments from the spinal accessory and the sympathetic in forming the **pharyngeal plexus.** This supplies the muscles of the pharynx and of the soft palate (except the tensor palati which is innervated by the mandibular nerve), filaments to the anterior cervical ganglion of the sympathetic, and a larger branch which passes along the side of the œsophagus and ramifies in its cervical part.

According to Ellenberger and Baum the pharyngeal plexus receives filaments also from the digastric, anterior laryngeal, hypoglossal, and first cervical nerves. The branches of the plexus form secondary intermuscular and submucous plexuses, in which there are numerous minute ganglia.

2. The **anterior** (or superior) **laryngeal nerve** (N. laryngeus cranialis) is larger than the preceding and arises a little behind it (Fig. 562). It crosses the deep face of the origin of the external carotid artery, runs downward and forward over the lateral wall of the pharynx behind the hypoglossal nerve, and passes through the foramen below the anterior cornu of the thyroid cartilage. Its terminal branches ramify in the mucous membrane of the larynx, the floor of the pharynx, and the entrance to the œsophagus; they anastomose with those of the recurrent. At its origin the nerve gives off its small **external branch** (R. externus); this descends to the crico-thyroid muscle, which it supplies, and sends filaments to the crico-pharyngeus also. It often arises from the vagus just below the anterior laryngeal and may come from the pharyngeal branch.

At the point of origin of the anterior laryngeal nerve there is a plexiform widening which is regarded by some authors as the homologue of the ganglion nodosum of man; it often contains minute ganglia. From it a filament arises which, after a short course, rejoins the vagus or enters the sympathetic trunk. Stimulation of its central end causes a reduction of the blood-pressure, and it is therefore termed the **depressor nerve** (N. depressor). On reaching the heart it passes between the aorta and the pulmonary artery and is distributed to the myocardium.

3. The **recurrent nerve** (N. recurrens), also termed the inferior or posterior laryngeal nerve, differs on the two sides in its point of origin and in the first part of its course. The **right nerve** (Fig. 554) is given off opposite the second rib, turns around the costo-cervical artery from without inward, runs forward on the right part of the ventral surface of the trachea, and ascends in the neck on the ventral face of the common carotid artery. The **left nerve** (Fig. 553) arises from the vagus where the latter begins to cross the aortic arch. It passes back over the ligamentum arteriosum, winds around the concavity of the aortic arch from without inward,

---

[1] It will be noted that the formation of the ventral œsophageal trunk usually occurs at the root of the lungs, while the union of the dorsal branches of the two vagi generally occurs nearer the hiatus œsophageus.

runs forward on the ventral part of the left face of the trachea, and continues in the neck in a position similar to the right nerve.

It is worthy of note that the left nerve passes beneath the bronchial lymph glands as it winds around the aorta; also that in the next part of its course it lies between the left surface of the trachea and the deep face of the aorta, and is then related to lymph glands which lie along the ventral aspect of the trachea. The left recurrent is often incorporated in part of its course in the anterior mediastinum with a deep cardiac nerve. Further, the left nerve lies at first ventral to, and then upon, the œsophagus in part of its course in the neck. The right recurrent is given off from, or in common with, a very large trunk which connects the vagus with the first thoracic ganglion of the sympathetic. The arrangement here is commonly more or less plexiform, and from it one or two cardiac nerves arise.

The terminal part of each nerve (Fig. 649) lies in the space between the trachea (ventrally) and the œsophagus (dorsally), losing contact with the carotid artery. It passes between the crico-arytenoideus dorsalis and the crico-pharyngeus, and enters the larynx at the medial side of the lamina of the thyroid cartilage. Before entering it gives branches to the crico-arytenoideus dorsalis and arytenoideus transversus, and afterward supplies the internal muscles of the larynx. It also communicates by delicate filaments with branches of the anterior laryngeal nerve. Collateral branches are given off to the cardiac plexus (Rami cardiaci), to the trachea (Rr. tracheales), to the œsophagus (Rr. œsophagei), and to the posterior cervical ganglion of the sympathetic. The recurrent nerves innervate all the intrinsic muscles of the larynx except the crico-thyroidei.

4. **Cardiac branches** (Rr. cardiaci), usually two or three in number, are given off from each vagus within the thorax (Figs. 553, 554). These concur with the cardiac branches of the sympathetic and recurrent nerves to form the cardiac plexus, which innervates the heart and great vessels.

5. Small **tracheal** and **œsophageal branches** (Rr. tracheales et œsophagei) are given off from both vagi in the thorax. These concur with branches from the recurrent nerves and the posterior cervical and anterior thoracic ganglia of the sympathetic in forming the **posterior tracheal** and **œsophageal plexuses,** from which twigs go to the trachea, œsophagus, heart, and large vessels.

6. **Bronchial branches** (Rr. bronchiales) are detached at the roots of the lungs and unite with sympathetic filaments in forming the **pulmonary plexuses.** From the latter numerous branches proceed in a plexiform manner along the bronchi and vessels into the substance of the lungs.

The vagus and glosso-pharyngeal nerves are so closely associated in origin and central connections that they may be described together in this respect.

The **sensory fibers** arise from the petrous and jugular ganglia, and their central parts enter the lateral aspect of the medulla and divide into anterior and posterior branches like the fibers of the dorsal roots of the spinal nerves. Most of the fibers end in arborizations about the cells of the vago-glosso-pharyngeal nucleus of termination, which consists of two parts. Of these, the **dorsal sensory nucleus** (Nucleus alæ cinereæ) is situated in the posterior part of the floor of the fourth ventricle and in the adjacent part of the closed portion of the medulla near the median plane. The other part is termed the **nucleus of the solitary tract,** and is so named because its cells are grouped about the bundle (Tractus solitarius) formed by the posterior divisions of the afferent nerve-fibers. It ends about the level of the pyramidal decussation. The secondary central connections are similar to those of the sensory part of the trigeminus.

The **motor fibers** (and those of the medullary part of the accessory) arise from the **dorsal motor nucleus** and the **ventral motor nucleus.** The cells of the former lie in groups along the ventro-medial side of the dorsal sensory nucleus. The latter, also termed the **nucleus ambiguus,** is situated more deeply in the lateral part of the formatio reticularis.

THE SPINAL ACCESSORY NERVE

The **spinal accessory nerve** (N. accessorius) is purely motor. It consists of two parts which differ in origin and function.

[1] The nerve lies here in relation to the anterior cervical lymph glands, and in some cases is in contact with the thyroid gland; commonly, however, the nerve is about a finger's breadth above the thyroid.

The **medullary part** arises from the lateral aspect of the medulla by several rootlets which are behind and in series with those of the vagus (Fig. 629). The **spinal part** arises from the cervical part of the spinal cord by a series of fasciculi which emerge between the dorsal and ventral roots. The bundles unite to form a trunk which is very small at its origin at the fifth segment of the cord, but increases in size when traced toward the brain, since it continually receives accessions of fibers. It passes through the foramen magnum and joins the medullary part.

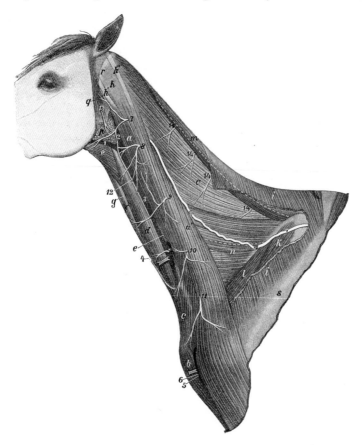

FIG. 650.—NECK OF HORSE, AFTER REMOVAL OF PART OF CUTANEUS AND TRAPEZIUS.

a, a′, Brachiocephalicus; *b,* anterior superficial pectoral muscle; *c,* cervical cutaneus; *d,* sterno-cephalicus; *e,* omo-hyoideus; *f,* sterno-thyro-hyoideus; *g,* trachea; *h, h′, h″,* tendons of splenius, brachiocephalicus, and longissimus atlantis; *i,* trapezius cervicalis; *k,* supraspinatus; *l,* anterior deep pectoral muscle; *m,* rhomboideus cervicalis; *n,* serratus cervicis; *o,* splenius, upper and lower borders of which are indicated by dotted lines; *p,* parotid gland; *q,* parotido-auricularis muscle; *r,* wing of atlas; *s,* spine of scapula; *1,* external maxillary vein; *2, 3,* jugular vein; *4,* carotid artery; *5,* descending branch of inferior cervical artery; *6,* cephalic vein; *7–11,* ventral branches of second to sixth cervical nerves; *12,* cutaneous branch of second cervical nerve; *13,* cervical branch of facial nerve; *14,* terminal branches of dorsal divisions of cervical nerves; *15,* dorsal branch of spinal accessory nerve. (After Ellenberger-Baum, Top. Anat. d. Pferdes.)

The trunk thus formed sends its medullary fibers to the vagus and glosso-pharyngeal nerves and emerges through the foramen lacerum posterius. It then runs backward and downward with the vagus in a fold of the guttural pouch, separates from that nerve, crosses the deep face of the mandibular gland and the occipital artery, and divides in the recessus atlantis into dorsal and ventral branches.

It is connected by anastomotic branches with the vagus and hypoglossal nerves and the anterior cervical ganglion of the sympathetic, and contributes a branch to the pharyngeal plexus.

The **dorsal branch** (R. dorsalis) (Figs. 558, 649, 650) receives a twig from the second and third cervical nerves and turns around the atlantal tendon of the splenius under cover of the brachiocephalicus. It then passes obliquely through the latter muscle and continues backward on the cervical part of the serratus, inclines upward across the anterior deep pectoral and the supraspinatus, and enters the deep face of the trapezius, in which it ramifies.

The **ventral branch** (R. ventralis) (Fig. 561) is smaller and much shorter. It passes downward and backward under cover of the cervical angle of the parotid gland and enters the deep face of the sterno-cephalicus muscle at the junction of the muscular substance with the tendon of insertion. It usually crosses over the carotid artery just behind the lateral lobe of the thyroid gland.

The fibers of the spinal part of the accessory arise from the ventro-lateral cells of the ventral gray column of the cord as far back as the fifth cervical segment. The fibers of the medullary part come chiefly from the nucleus ambiguus in common with the motor fibers of the vagus.

THE HYPOGLOSSAL NERVE

The **hypoglossal nerve** (N. hypoglossus) is purely motor; it innervates the muscles of the tongue and the genio-hyoideus (Fig. 562). Its root-fibers arise from the ventral face of the medulla in linear series about 3 to 4 mm. lateral to the posterior half of the pyramid (Fig. 629). The filaments converge to three or four bundles which perforate the dura mater and unite to form the trunk. The latter emerges through the hypoglossal foramen (Fig. 647) and runs downward and backward between the guttural pouch and the capsule of the atlanto-occipital articulation for a distance of a little less than an inch (ca. 2 cm.). It then passes between the vagus and accessory nerves, turns downward and forward, crosses the lateral face of the external carotid artery, and continues over the pharynx parallel with the great cornu of the hyoid bone and behind the external maxillary artery. It then crosses beneath the artery, runs forward on the lateral face of the hyo-glossus muscle, and divides into its terminal branches (Rami linguales). The smaller branch supplies the stylo-glossus, hyo-glossus, and lingualis. The larger branch passes upward and forward between the hyo-glossus and genio-glossus, ramifies on the latter, and supplies the remaining muscles and the genio-hyoideus. Anastomoses occur with branches of the lingual nerve.

In the first part of its course the nerve communicates with the anterior cervical ganglion and with the ventral branch of the first cervical nerve, and gives filaments to the pharyngeal branch of the vagus and the pharyngeal plexus.

The fibers of the nerve arise from the hypoglossal nucleus, an elongated group of large multi-polar cells situated chiefly under the posterior part of the floor of the fourth ventricle, close to the median plane. The two nuclei are connected by commissural fibers. The other central connections include: (*a*) communications by the medial longitudinal fasciculus with the nuclei of termination of other cranial nerves; (*b*) cortico-nuclear fibers which come from the cortex by way of the internal capsule and the pyramids and go largely to the nucleus of the opposite side; (*c*) fibers which join the dorsal longitudinal bundle of Schütz, a tract which underlies the floor of the fourth ventricle and is traceable forward below the cerebral aqueduct.

THE SPINAL NERVES

The **spinal nerves** (Nervi spinales) are arranged in pairs, of which there are usually forty-two in the horse. They are designated according to their relations to the vertebral column as **cervical** (8), **thoracic** (18), **lumbar** (6), **sacral** (5), and **coccygeal** (5). Each nerve is connected with the spinal cord by two roots, dorsal and ventral (Fig. 628).

The **dorsal root** (Radix dorsalis) is the larger of the two. Its fibers (Fila radicularia) spread out in fan shape and join the cord in a linear series along the dorso-lateral groove. The fibers converge laterally to form a compact bundle, on which there is a gray nodular enlargement, the **spinal ganglion** (Ganglion spinale). Beyond the ganglion the dorsal root joins the ventral root to constitute the nerve. The ganglia are external to the dura mater, and are situated in the intervertebral foramina, except in the case of the sacral and coccygeal nerves, the ganglia of which lie within the vertebral canal. Those of the coccygeal nerves are intradural.

The ganglia vary greatly in size; that of the first cervical nerve is scarcely as large as a hempseed, while that of the eighth cervical is about 2 cm. long and 1 cm. wide. On the large roots connected with the cervical and lumbar enlargement of the cord there are multiple ganglia of varying sizes interposed in the course of the root-bundles. The fibers of the dorsal roots arise from the cells of the spinal ganglia; connected with each ganglion cell there is a process which bifurcates, giving rise to a fiber which enters the spinal cord and another which passes into the nerve.

The **ventral root** (Radix ventralis) contains fewer fibers than the dorsal root, except in the case of the first cervical nerve. It arises from the ventral surface of the spinal cord (Fig. 626) by means of numerous small bundles of fibers which do not form a linear series, but emerge from the cord over an area three to five millimeters in width (ventral root zone). The fibers are processes of the large cells of the ventral gray columns of the spinal cord. There is no ganglion on the ventral root.

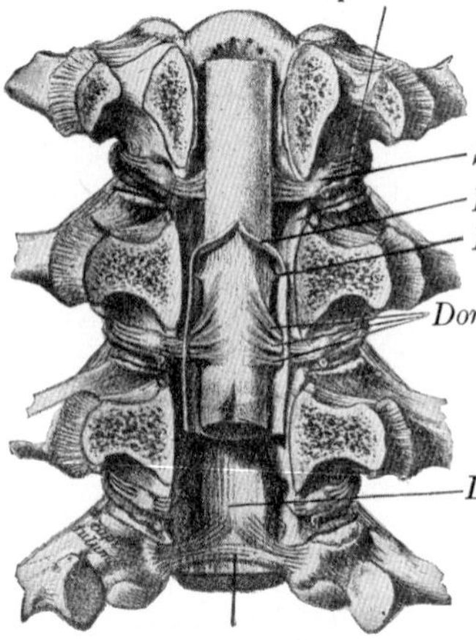

In the cervical, thoracic, and anterior lumbar regions the bundles of both roots pass through separate openings in linear series in the dura mater before uniting into a root proper. Further back the bundles of each root unite within the dura. In the anterior part of the cervical region and in the thoracic part of the cord there are intervals of varying length between adjacent roots, but in some places the fibers of adjacent roots overlap and an exchange of fibers may be observed. Many of the roots are directed almost straight outward or incline slightly backward, but the posterior lumbar, sacral, and coccygeal roots and nerves run backward to reach the foramina, through which they emerge. The distance thus to be traversed increases from before backward, so that these nerves form a tapering sheaf around the conus medullaris and filum terminale in the last lumbar vertebra and the sacrum, which is known as the cauda equina.

Spinal branch of intercostal artery

Spinal ganglion

Dura mater

Lig. denticulatum

Dorsal root bundles

Dorsal longitudinal ligament

Conjugal ligament

FIG. 651.—VERTEBRAL CANAL OPENED BY SAWING OFF THE ARCHES. (After Schmaltz, Atlas d. Anat. d. Pferdes.)

The **size** of the spinal nerves varies greatly. The largest are connected with the cervical and lumbar enlargements.

In, or immediately after its emergence from, the intervertebral foramen each spinal nerve gives off a small **meningeal branch** (Ramus meningeus). This is joined by a bundle of fibers from the ramus communicans and enters the vertebral canal, in which it is distributed. Each nerve then divides into two primary branches, dorsal and ventral (Ramus dorsalis, ventralis). The **dorsal branches** are smaller than the ventral, except in the cervical region. They are distributed chiefly to the muscles and skin of the dorsal part of the body. The **ventral branches** supply in general the muscles and skin of the ventral parts of the body, including the limbs. Each nerve or its ventral branch is connected with an adjacent ganglion of the sympathetic system by at least one small short branch known as a **ramus communicans**. Many nerves have two and some have three such rami. A nerve may be connected with two ganglia, and a ganglion may be connected with two nerves.

The dorsal root is sensory or afferent, *i. e.*, it conveys impulses to the central system; its fibers are axones of the cells of the spinal ganglion. The ventral root is motor or efferent, and conveys impulses toward the periphery; its fibers are axones of the large cells in the ventral gray columns of the spinal cord. The common trunk or nerve formed by the union of the two roots contains both kinds of fibers, as do also their primary divisions. In addition to these fibers, which are distributed to the skeletal muscles and the skin, the spinal nerves contain fibers derived from the sympathetic system through the rami communicantes; these go to the glands and unstriped muscle and are designated secretory and vasomotor fibers.

THE CERVICAL NERVES

The **cervical nerves** (Nervi cervicales) (Figs. 556, 558, 650, 655) number eight pairs. The first of these emerges through the intervertebral foramen of the atlas, the second through that of the axis, and the eighth between the last cervical and the first thoracic vertebra.

The **dorsal branches** are distributed to the dorso-lateral muscles and skin of the neck. They divide usually into lateral and medial branches. The medial branches (Rami mediales) run in general across the multifidus and the lamellar part of the ligamentum nuchæ to the skin of the dorsal border of the neck; they supply the deep lateral muscles and the skin. The lateral branches (Rami laterales) are chiefly muscular in their distribution. The dorsal branches of the third to the sixth nerves are connected by anastomotic branches to form the **dorsal cervical plexus.**

The **ventral branches** of the first four or five nerves are smaller than the dorsal ones. They increase in size from first to last. They supply in general the muscles and skin over the lateral and ventral aspect of the vertebræ, but the last three enter into the formation of the brachial plexus, and the two or three preceding the last give off the roots of the phrenic nerve. An irregular **ventral cervical plexus** is formed by anastomoses established between the ventral branches. The following special features may be noted:

The **first cervical nerve** emerges through the intervertebral foramen of the atlas. Its **dorsal branch** (N. occipitalis) passes dorso-laterally between the obliqui capitis and the recti capitis dorsales and supplies branches to these muscles, the scutularis and posterior auricular muscles, and the skin of the poll. The **ventral branch** descends through the alar foramen of the atlas, crosses over the ventral straight muscles and the carotid artery under cover of the parotid gland, and divides into two branches. The anterior branch enters the omo-hyoideus muscle. The posterior branch passes downward and backward under cover of that muscle, unites with a branch of the ventral division of the second cervical nerve, and continues its course on the ventro-lateral surface of the trachea to enter the sterno-thyro-hyoideus behind the intermediate tendon. In the recessus atlantis the ventral branch is connected by one or more twigs with the anterior cervical ganglion of the sympathetic, and a little lower with the hypoglossal nerve. It also sends branches to the ventral straight muscles of the head and the thyro-hyoideus. Below the atlas the ventral branch is crossed superficially by the spinal accessory nerve, the occipital artery, and the ventral cerebral vein.

The **second cervical nerve** is larger than the first. It emerges from the vertebral canal through the intervertebral foramen of the anterior part of the arch of the axis. Its **dorsal branch** ascends between the complexus and the ligamentum nuchæ and ramifies in the skin of the poll. The **ventral branch** gives off **muscular branches** to the rectus capitis ventralis major, and **anastomotic branches** to the spinal accessory and the ventral divisions of the first and third cervical nerves; one of these crosses over the carotid artery and concurs in the formation of the nerve to the sterno-thyro-hyoideus mentioned above. The ventral branch then becomes superficial by passing between the two parts of the brachiocephalicus, and divides into posterior auricular and cutaneous branches. The **posterior auricular nerve** passes upward and forward on the parotid gland parallel with the posterior border of the parotido-auricularis to ramify on the convex face of the external ear. The **cutaneous nerve of the neck** (N. cutaneus colli) crosses the brachiocephalicus muscle and turns backward along the course of the jugular vein. On the lower part of the parotid gland it is connected by a twig with the cervical cutaneous branch of the facial nerve. It gives off twigs to the subcutaneous muscles and the skin of the parotid and laryngeal regions, and a long branch which passes forward in the mandibular space.

The rami communicantes of the cervical nerves, except the first and last, unite to form a trunk (nervus transversarius) which accompanies the vertebral artery in the canalis transversarius to the posterior, or inferior, cervical ganglion which it joins.

The **third cervical nerve** leaves the vertebral canal through the foramen between the second and third cervical vertebræ. Its **dorsal branch** emerges between two bundles of the intertransversalis muscle, accompanied by a branch of the vertebral artery, turns dorsally on the multifidus, and divides into several branches which radiate on the deep face of the complexus. It gives branches to these muscles and to the skin, and a twig which joins the corresponding branch of the fourth nerve. The **ventral branch** emerges through the intertransversalis below the bundle above which the dorsal branch appears. It gives branches to the longissimus capitis et atlantis, rectus capitis ventralis major, longus colli, splenius, and brachiocephalicus. It also gives off a large cutaneous nerve which passes out between the two parts of the brachiocephalicus and divides into several divergent branches.

The **fourth** and **fifth cervical nerves** are distributed in general like the third. Their **dorsal branches** are united by anastomotic twigs with each other and with those of the third and sixth nerves to form the dorsal cervical plexus. The **ventral branch** of the fifth nerve often contributes a small twig to the phrenic nerve.

The **sixth cervical nerve** has a smaller **dorsal branch** than the fifth. Its **ventral branch** is larger and goes in part to the brachial plexus; it supplies twigs to the intertransversales, the longus colli, the brachiocephalicus, and the cervical parts of the serratus and rhomboideus, furnishes a root of the phrenic nerve, and gives off several considerable subcutaneous branches. One of the latter ramifies on the thick part of the cervical cutaneus, to which it gives branches; another and larger branch (N. supraclavicularis) sends twigs to the skin over the shoulder joint, and descends to the skin over the superficial pectoral muscles (Fig. 590).

The **seventh** and **eighth cervical nerves** have small **dorsal branches,** which ascend between the longissimus and multifidus, giving twigs to these muscles, the spinalis and semispinalis, the rhomboideus, and the skin. Their **ventral branches** are very large and go almost entirely to the brachial plexus; that of the seventh nerve contributes the posterior root of the phrenic nerve.

PHRENIC NERVE

The **phrenic nerve** (N. phrenicus) (Figs. 553, 554, 558), the motor nerve to the diaphragm, is formed by the union of two or three roots which run obliquely downward and backward over the superficial face of the scalenus muscle. The chief roots come from the ventral branches of the sixth and seventh cervical nerves. The root derived from the fifth nerve is small and inconstant. The root from the seventh cervical comes by way of the brachial plexus. The nerve crosses the ventral border of the scalenus a fingerbreadth in front of the first rib, passes through the angle of divergence of the inferior cervical and brachial arteries, and enters the thorax by passing between the latter vessel and the anterior vena cava. Beyond this the course of the nerve is not the same on both sides. The **right nerve** courses backward and somewhat downward over the right face of the anterior vena cava, crosses the pericardium, and continues along the posterior vena cava to the diaphragm. In the latter part of its course it is in a special fold given off from the plica venæ cavæ and inclines to the ventral face of the vein. The **left nerve,** in part with the vagus, runs its entire course in the mediastinum. In the anterior mediastinum it lies along the lateral face of the left brachial artery ventral to the left vagus and a cardiac nerve, and crosses over the dorso-cervical vein. It then parts company with the vagus, passes over the upper part of the pericardium, and runs backward in the posterior mediastinum to reach the tendinous center of the diaphragm considerably to the left of the median plane. Each nerve is usually connected near its origin with the first thoracic ganglion of the sympathetic by a ramus communicans, and each terminates by dividing into several branches which are distributed to the corresponding part of the diaphragm.

THE BRACHIAL PLEXUS

The **brachial plexus** (Plexus brachialis) (Figs. 558, 566) results from anastomoses established between the ventral branches of the last three cervical and first two thoracic nerves. It appears as a thick, wide band between the two parts of the scalenus muscle, and is covered by the anterior deep pectoral and subscapularis muscles. Each of the three chief roots, *i. e.*, those from the last two cervical and the first thoracic nerve, is connected with the sympathetic by a ramus communicans.

The root derived from the sixth cervical nerve is very small, while the ventral branches of the seventh and eighth cervical nerves go almost entirely to the plexus. The first thoracic nerve furnishes the largest root; its whole ventral branch goes to the plexus with the exception of its small first intercostal branch. The root from the second thoracic nerve is small, since most of its ventral branch goes to form the second intercostal nerve.

The **branches** emanating from the plexus go for the most part to the thoracic limb, but some are distributed on the chest-wall. The names of the branches, and their arrangement so far as they can be conveniently examined before removal of the forelimb, are as follows:[1]

1. The large **suprascapular nerve** (N. suprascapularis) arises from the anterior part of the plexus, passes ventro-laterally, and disappears between the supraspinatus and subscapularis muscles.

2. The much smaller **subscapular nerves** (Nn. subscapulares), usually two primary trunks, arise close behind the suprascapular, run backward a short distance, and divide into several branches which enter the subscapularis muscle below its middle. A branch may come from the axillary nerve.

3. The **anterior thoracic** or **pectoral nerves** (Nn. pectorales craniales), three or four in number, arise from the anterior part of the plexus and from the loop formed by the musculo-cutaneous and median nerves. One enters the anterior deep pectoral muscle. Another passes between the divisions of the deep pectoral to supply the superficial pectoral and brachiocephalicus, giving a twig usually to the posterior deep muscle. The latter receives one or two other nerves.

4. The **musculo-cutaneous nerve** (N. musculocutaneus) arises from the anterior part of the plexus behind the suprascapular and descends over the lateral face of the brachial artery, below which it is connected by a large but short branch with the median nerve, thus forming a loop in which the artery lies.[2] One or two branches to the pectoral muscles are given off from the nerve or the loop.

5. The **median nerve** (N. medianus) is usually the largest branch of the brachial plexus. It arises with the ulnar from the posterior part of the plexus and descends over the insertion of the scalenus, crosses the medial face of the brachial artery, and reaches the anterior border of that vessel. It is easily recognized by its large size and the loop which it forms with the musculo-cutaneous nerve.

[1] In order to examine the plexus and the origins of its chief branches conveniently and with as little disturbance of relation as possible, the subject should be suspended in imitation of the natural position and the forelimb abducted as much as is necessary. In doing this some disturbance of the position and relations of the nerves and vessels takes place. The brachial vessels are drawn away from the chest-wall so that their lateral surface now faces forward, and the nerves are similarly affected.

[2] The loop may be absent or double.

6. The **ulnar nerve** (N. ulnaris) arises with the median by a short common trunk. It descends behind the brachial artery and is accompanied a short distance by the radial nerve, from which it can be distinguished by its smaller size.

7. The **radial nerve** (N. radialis) arises from the posterior part of the plexus and is sometimes the largest branch. It descends with the ulnar nerve over the medial face of the origin of the subscapular artery and the lower part of the teres major and dips into the interstice between that muscle and the long and medial heads of the triceps.

8. The **axillary nerve** (N. axillaris) arises behind the musculo-cutaneous. It passes downward and backward on the medial face of the subscapularis and disappears between that muscle and the subscapular artery.

9. The **long thoracic nerve** (N. thoracalis longus) is wide and thin. It arises from the anterior end of the plexus, gives off (usually) three branches to the serratus ventralis at the junction of its cervical and thoracic parts, and passes backward across the surface of the serratus thoracis, to which it is distributed. The branches which enter the muscle are given off both upward and downward in fairly regular fashion.

10. The **thoraco-dorsal nerve** (N. thoracodorsalis) arises medial to the axillary and passes upward and backward across the subscapularis muscle to ramify in the latissimus dorsi.

11. The **external thoracic nerve** (N. thoracalis lateralis) arises by a common trunk with the ulnar. It passes backward and ventrally across the medial surface of the humeral tendon of the cutaneous muscle, and continues backward in company with the external thoracic vein. Its branches innervate the cutaneous muscle and the skin of the abdominal wall as far back as the flank. It gives collateral branches to the deep pectoral muscle and others which anastomose with perforating branches of intercostal nerves. A branch from it, accompanied by a large perforating intercostal branch, winds around the ventral border of the latissimus dorsi and ramifies in the cutaneous muscle and skin on the lateral surface of the shoulder and arm.

The term **posterior thoracic** or **pectoral nerves** (Nn. pectorales caudales) may be used to include 9, 10, and 11.

SUPRASCAPULAR NERVE

The **suprascapular nerve** (Fig. 566), short but large, is usually derived chiefly, if not exclusively, from the sixth and seventh cervical components of the brachial plexus. It passes between the supraspinatus and subscapularis muscles and turns around the distal fourth of the anterior border of the scapula ca. 7 cm. above the tuber scapulæ to reach the supraspinous fossa. It gives branches to the supraspinatus and continues backward and upward into the infraspinous fossa, and terminates in several branches which innervate the infraspinatus.

The direct relation of this nerve to the scapula renders it liable to injury, the result of which may be paralysis and atrophy of the muscles supplied by it. There is, however, a small tendinous band which extends over the nerve as it turns around the edge of the scapula.

MUSCULO-CUTANEOUS NERVE

The **musculo-cutaneous nerve** (Fig. 566) arises close behind the suprascapular, and is derived chiefly from the part of the brachial plexus which is supplied by the seventh and eighth cervical nerves. It descends across the lateral surface of the brachial artery, below which a great part of the nerve unites with the median to form the loop previously mentioned. It gives off a branch which enters the proximal part of the belly of the coraco-brachialis, passes downward and forward in company with the anterior circumflex vessels between the two parts of that muscle or between the muscle and the bone, and divides into branches which enter the biceps brachii. It contributes one of the nerves to the pectoral muscles. In some cases this nerve sends a branch to join the cutaneous branch of the median.

AXILLARY NERVE

The **axillary nerve** (Figs. 566, 652) derives its fibers chiefly from the eighth cervical root of the brachial plexus. It runs downward and backward across the distal part of the subscapularis, and, in company with the posterior circumflex artery, dips in between that muscle and the subscapular artery at the level of the shoulder joint. Continuing outward in the interval between the teres minor and the long and lateral heads of the triceps, it reaches the deep face of the deltoid and divides into several divergent branches. The **muscular branches** supply the teres major, capsularis, teres minor, deltoid, and brachiocephalicus. The **cutaneous branch** (N. cutaneus brachii lateralis) runs downward and a little forward across the lateral head of the triceps and ramifies on the fascia on the front of the forearm and on the superficial pectoral muscle.

RADIAL NERVE

The **radial nerve** (Figs. 566, 568, 652) is sometimes the largest branch of the brachial plexus. Its fibers are derived chiefly from the first thoracic root of the plexus. It passes downward and backward over the medial surface of the origin of the subscapular artery and the distal part of the teres major. In this part of its course it is related in front to the ulnar nerve, which separates it from the brachial vein.[1] It detaches a branch to the tensor fasciæ antibrachii, passes outward in the interval between the teres major and the long and medial heads of the triceps, and gains the musculo-spiral groove of the humerus. Accompanied by a branch of the deep brachial artery, it runs obliquely downward and outward in the groove, covered laterally by the lateral head of the triceps and the extensor carpi radialis, and reaches the flexion surface of the elbow joint. In this part of its course it gives off muscular branches to the three heads of the triceps and to the anconeus, and a **cutaneous nerve** (N. cutaneus antibrachii dorsalis); branches of the latter emerge below or through the lateral head of the triceps and ramify on the dorso-lateral surface of the forearm. At the elbow the nerve descends with the anterior radial vessels on the joint capsule, between the brachialis and extensor carpi radialis, and supplies branches to the extensor carpi and the common extensor of the digit and (inconstantly) to the brachialis. Below the elbow joint the nerve detaches a large branch which passes back between the lateral extensor and the radius to the ulnaris lateralis, and terminates by small branches which descend on the radius to enter the radial and ulnar heads of the common and lateral extensors of the digit, and the oblique extensor of the carpus. Thus the radial nerve innervates the extensors of the elbow, carpal, and digital joints, and supplies also the lateral flexor of the carpus.[2]

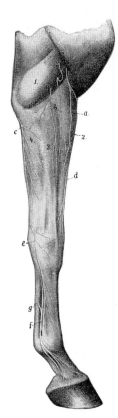

Fig. 652.—Cutaneous Nerves of Right Forelimb of Horse; Lateral Face.

a, Cutaneous branch of axillary nerve; *b*, cutaneous branches of radial nerve; *c*, posterior cutaneous branch of ulnar nerve; *d*, cutaneous branch of median nerve; *e*, superficial branch of ulnar nerve; *f*, lateral volar nerve; *g*, anastomotic branch connecting medial and lateral volar nerves; *1*, lateral head of triceps; *2*, extensor carpi radialis; *3*, common extensor; *4*, ulnaris lateralis. (After Ellenberger, in Leisering's Atlas.)

[1] The relative positions of the vessels and nerves here are variable; not rarely the ulnar nerve passes between the subscapular artery and vein, and in quite exceptional cases the radial nerve crosses the lateral face of the subscapular artery.

[2] Morphologically the last-named muscle belongs to the extensor group.

The **ulnar nerve** (Figs. 566, 567, 568, 652) arises with the median from the thoracic components of the brachial plexus. It descends between the brachial artery and vein, accompanied for a short distance by the radial nerve. It then crosses the vein and continues behind the latter along the anterior border of the tensor fasciæ antibrachii and dips under that muscle near the elbow. Here it is joined by the ulnar vessels and passes downward and backward over the medial epicondyle of the humerus. In the forearm it crosses obliquely the deep face of the ulnar head of the flexor carpi ulnaris and descends under the deep fascia with the

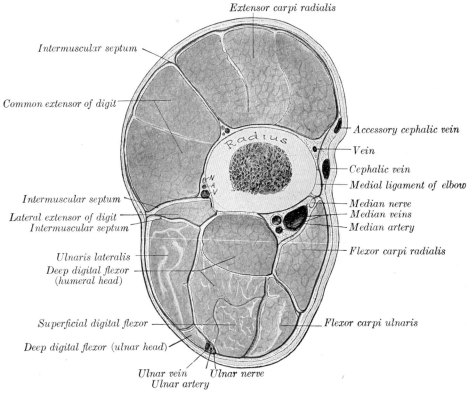

Fig. 653.—Cross-section of Forearm of Horse about Three Inches (ca. 7.5 cm.) below the Elbow Joint.

The deep fascia is designated by red line. *N, A, V,* Dorsal interosseous nerve and vessels.

vessels, at first on the ulnar head of the deep flexor, and then between the flexor carpi ulnaris and ulnaris lateralis. Near the level of the accessory carpal bone it divides into two terminal branches, superficial and deep. It gives off two principal collateral branches. The **cutaneous branch** (Ramus cutaneus volaris) is detached just before the nerve passes under the tensor fasciæ antibrachii; it runs downward and backward on that muscle under cover of the posterior superficial pectoral, becomes superficial below the elbow, and ramifies on the posterior surface and both sides of the forearm. The **muscular branches,** which are given off at the elbow, supply the superficial digital flexor, the ulnar head of the deep flexor, and the flexor carpi ulnaris. Of the two terminals, the **superficial branch** (Ramus superficialis) emerges between the tendons of insertion of the lateral and middle flexors of the carpus and ramifies on the dorso-lateral aspect of the carpus and metacarpus. The **deep branch** (Ramus profundus), after a very short course, unites under cover of the tendon of the flexor carpi ulnaris with the lateral branch of the median nerve to form the lateral volar nerve.

MEDIAN NERVE

The **median nerve** (Figs. 566, 567, 572, 652, 653) derives its fibers chiefly from the eighth cervical and first thoracic roots of the brachial plexus. It is usually the largest branch, and it accompanies the chief arterial trunks to the distal part of the limb. It descends over the medial face of the brachial artery, which it crosses obliquely, and continues down the arm in front of the artery. Near its origin it is

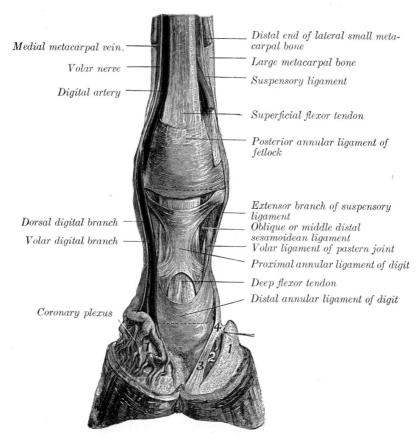

Medial metacarpal vein.

Volar nerve

Digital artery

Distal end of lateral small metacarpal bone

Large metacarpal bone

Suspensory ligament

Superficial flexor tendon

Posterior annular ligament of fetlock

Dorsal digital branch

Volar digital branch

Extensor branch of suspensory ligament
Oblique or middle distal sesamoidean ligament
Volar ligament of pastern joint
Proximal annular ligament of digit

Deep flexor tendon

Distal annular ligament of digit

Coronary plexus

FIG. 654.—DISSECTION OF DISTAL PART OF RIGHT FORE LIMB OF HORSE; VOLAR SURFACE.
1, Cartilage of third phalanx; *2, 3, 4,* ligaments from first phalanx to distal sesamoid, bulb of heel and cartilage of third phalanx. (After Schmaltz, Atlas d. Anat. d. Pferdes.)

joined by a large branch with the musculo-cutaneous nerve, thus forming a loop in which the artery appears to be suspended. Near the elbow it usually crosses obliquely over the median artery and lies behind it on the medial ligament. Below the joint it again crosses the artery and lies behind the radius and the lower part of the long medial ligament.

At the elbow the nerve is covered by the posterior superficial pectoral muscle and is crossed by the large oblique connection between the cephalic and brachial veins. The variable and often plexiform venous arrangement renders approach to the nerve here undesirable. It can be reached best by an incision just behind the lower part of the long medial ligament; here the nerve lies under the deep fascia in the furrow between the radius and the anterior border of the flexor carpi radialis, overlapped by the latter (Fig. 653). The nerve may retain its position in front of the artery at the elbow; in other cases it lies upon the artery, and rarely it crosses the deep face of the artery.

Passing beneath the flexor carpi radialis, the nerve continues downward in the forearm with the median vessels, and divides at a variable distance above the carpus into two branches; these are the medial volar nerve, and the lateral branch, which unites with the ulnar to form the corresponding lateral volar nerve.

At the proximal part of the forearm the nerve runs almost straight downward along the posterior border of the long medial ligament, while the artery here inclines somewhat backward. Thus the nerve is superficial to the artery for a short distance, then lies in front of the latter to about the middle of the region, where it inclines a little backward and arrives at the interval between the radial and ulnar flexors of the carpus. The division may occur about the middle of the region or even higher, but commonly takes place in the distal third or fourth.

The collateral branches are as follows:

1. The **musculo-cutaneous branch** is in reality the continuation of the nerve of that name. It is given off about the middle of the arm, passes beneath the lower part of the biceps, and divides into muscular and cutaneous branches. The **muscular branch** enters the brachialis. The **cutaneous branch** emerges between the brachiocephalicus and the biceps and divides into two branches; these descend on the fascia of the forearm with the cephalic vein and its accessory, and ramify on the front and medial face of the forearm, carpus, and metacarpus.

2. A **muscular branch** is given off at the proximal end of the radius. This inclines backward, passes under the flexor carpi radialis and divides into branches which enter that muscle and the humeral head of the deep digital flexor. In exceptional cases this branch descends for some distance (3–5 cm.) just behind the parent trunk before passing under cover of the flexor carpi.

3. The **interosseous nerve** gives off a small branch which descends to the radial head of the deep digital flexor, passes through the interosseous space and is distributed chiefly to the periosteum.

The **volar** or metacarpal **nerves,**[1] medial and lateral, are the continuations of the median and ulnar nerves in the distal part of the limb.

The **medial volar nerve** (N. volaris medialis) arises as the medial terminal branch of the median nerve at a variable distance above the carpus (Fig. 567). It descends in the carpal canal along the medial border of the superficial flexor tendon, and lies at first in front of the common digital artery (Fig. 570). It then passes behind the artery to the distal third of the metacarpus, where it lies behind the vein, as the artery here is deeper in position (Fig. 572). In addition to cutaneous twigs, the nerve gives off near the middle of the metacarpus a large **anastomotic branch** which winds obliquely over the flexor tendons and joins the lateral nerve below the middle of the metacarpus (Fig. 572). Near the fetlock the nerve divides into two digital branches.

1. The **dorsal** (or anterior) **digital branch** (Ramus dorsalis) descends at first between the digital artery and vein, then crosses over the vein and ramifies in the skin and the corium of the hoof on the dorsal face of the digit.

2. The **volar** (or posterior) **digital branch** (Ramus volaris) is the direct continuation of the trunk. It descends behind the digital artery, which it accompanies in its ramifications. A **middle digital branch** is sometimes described as descending behind the vein. In some cases this branch is distinct, but usually there is instead several small twigs derived from the volar branch, which cross very obliquely over the artery and anastomose in a variable manner with each other and with the dorsal branch.

The **lateral volar nerve** (N. volaris lateralis) is formed by the union of the lateral terminal branch of the median with the deep branch of the ulnar nerve (Fig. 567). It descends with the lateral volar metacarpal vessels in the texture of the posterior annular ligament of the carpus (Fig. 570). In the metacarpus it descends

---

[1] In some veterinary works these are frequently termed plantar nerves, which is an unfortunate misnomer.

along the lateral border of the deep flexor tendon behind the lateral metacarpal vein and is accompanied by the small branch of the lateral volar metacarpal artery. Toward the distal end of the metacarpus it is joined by the oblique branch from the medial nerve, and beyond this is arranged like the latter. Below the carpus it detaches a **deep branch** to the suspensory ligament and the interossei, and also supplies twigs to the skin.[1]

THE THORACIC NERVES

The **thoracic nerves** (Nn. thoracales) number eighteen on either side in the horse. They are designated numerically according to the vertebræ behind which they emerge. Most of them are arranged in a very similar manner and therefore do not require separate description. Each divides into a dorsal and a ventral branch, the latter being the larger.

The **dorsal branches** (Rami dorsales) emerge behind the levatores costarum and divide into medial and lateral branches. The medial branches ascend on the multifidus and supply the dorsal spinal muscles. The lateral branches run outward under the longissimus dorsi and emerge between that muscle and the longissimus costarum; after giving twigs to these muscles they pass through the latissimus dorsi and the lumbo-dorsal fascia and ramify as dorsal cutaneous nerves under the skin of the back (Fig. 655). In the region of the withers they give branches to the serratus dorsalis and rhomboideus, and their cutaneous terminals pass through these muscles and the dorso-scapular ligament to supply the skin over the ligamentum nuchæ and the trapezius muscle.

The **ventral branches** or **intercostal nerves** (Nn. intercostales) are much larger than the preceding, and are connected with the sympathetic by rami communicantes. The first goes almost entirely to the brachial plexus, but sends a small branch downward in the first intercostal space, which is expended in the muscle there without reaching the lower end of the space. The second ventral branch furnishes a considerable root to the brachial plexus, but its intercostal continuation is typical. The intercostal nerves (Fig. 273) descend in the intercostal spaces with the vessels of like name, at first between the intercostal muscles, but lower down they are chiefly subpleural. In the anterior spaces the artery lies along the posterior border of the rib, with the nerve in front of it; further back the nerve lies behind the border of the rib, with the artery in front of it. They supply the intercostal muscles, give off lateral perforating branches and terminate in the following manner: The second to the sixth inclusive emerge through the spaces between the costal cartilages and concur in supplying the pectoral muscles. The second to the eighth give branches to the transversus thoracis. The succeeding ones give branches to the diaphragm, pass between the transverse and internal oblique abdominal muscles, give twigs to these, and end in the rectus abdominis. There are three series of cutaneous nerves given off by the intercostal nerves. The dorsal series emerge through the latissimus dorsi and the lumbo-dorsal fascia parallel with the lateral border of the longissimus. The middle ones perforate the serratus ventralis, external intercostals, and external oblique. The ventral ones appear through the abdominal tunic. They supply the abdominal muscles, the cutaneus, and the skin. Some of the anterior ones anastomose with the posterior thoracic branches of the brachial plexus. The posterior three supply in part the skin of the flank. The ventral branch of the last thoracic nerve runs outward behind the last rib across the dorsal surface of the psoas major and divides into superficial and deep branches. The superficial branch passes over the superficial face of the transversus abdom-

---

[1] Anastomoses are established between the digital branches, and the areas innervated by them are not well defined, but really overlap each other. In certain diseased conditions, however, in which the lesions are confined to the volar structures, relief from pain may be afforded by section of the volar branches only.

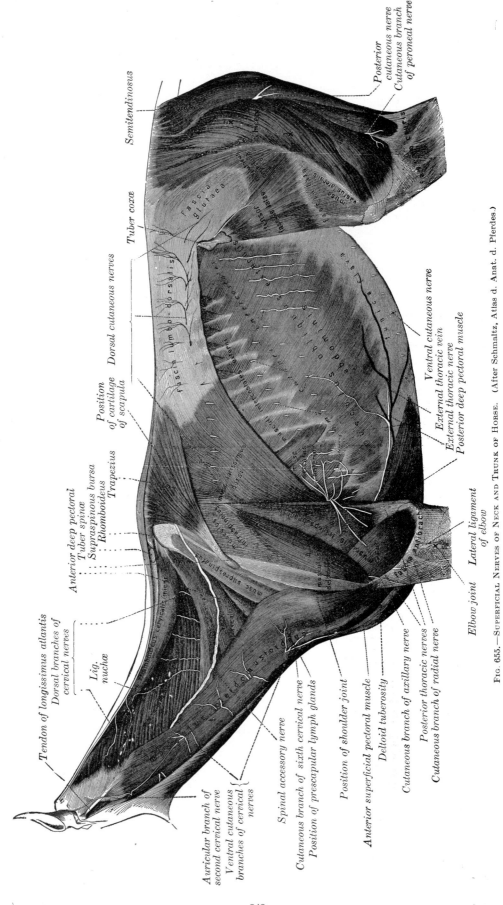

Tendon of longissimus atlantis
Dorsal branches of cervical nerves

Lig. nuchæ

Anterior deep pectoral
Tuber spinæ
Supraspinous bursa
Rhomboideus
Trapezius

Position of cartilage of scapula

Dorsal cutaneous nerves

Tuber coxæ

Semitendinosus

Posterior cutaneous nerve
Cutaneous branch of peroneal nerve

Ventral cutaneous nerve
External thoracic vein
External thoracic nerve
Posterior deep pectoral muscle

Lateral ligament of elbow

Elbow joint
Cutaneous branch of radial nerve
Cutaneous branch of axillary nerve
Posterior thoracic nerves
Deltoid tuberosity
Anterior superficial pectoral muscle
Position of shoulder joint
Position of prescapular lymph glands
Cutaneous branch of sixth cervical nerve
Spinal accessory nerve

Ventral cutaneous branches of cervical nerves
Auricular branch of second cervical nerve

Fig. 655.—Superficial Nerves of Neck and Trunk of Horse. (After Schmaltz, Atlas d. Anat. d. Pferdes.)

842

inis, perforates the obliquus externus, and ramifies under the skin of the flank (Fig. 657). The deep branch descends on the deep face of the internal oblique to the rectus abdominis, in which it ends.

THE LUMBAR NERVES

There are six pairs of **lumbar nerves** (Nn. lumbales) in the horse, the last of which emerge between the last lumbar vertebra and the sacrum. The anterior two or three are about the same size as the thoracic nerves, but the others are much larger. Their **dorsal branches** are small in comparison with the ventral ones. They are distributed to the muscles and skin of the loins and croup in a fashion similar to those of the thoracic nerves. The **ventral branches** are connected with the sympathetic by small rami communicantes, and give branches to the sublumbar muscles. Those of the first two nerves are arranged like the corresponding branch of the last thoracic nerve.

The ventral branch of the **first lumbar nerve** is termed the **ilio-hypogastric nerve** (N. iliohypogastricus). It passes outward between the quadratus lum-

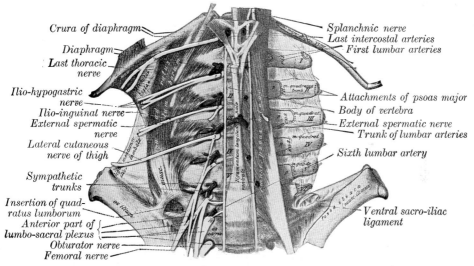

FIG. 656.—DEEP DISSECTION OF SUBLUMBAR REGION OF HORSE. (After Schmaltz.)

borum and the psoas major, and divides at the lateral border of the latter into a superficial and deep branch. The **superficial** or **cutaneous branch** passes over the dorsal edge of the internal oblique, descends between that muscle and the external oblique, perforates the latter, and runs downward and backward and ramifies under the skin of the posterior part of the flank and the lateral surface of the thigh. It gives branches to the transversus and obliquus abdominis externus. The **deep** (or **muscular**) **branch** is smaller; it runs downward and backward beneath the peritoneum to the lateral border of the rectus abdominis, gives branches to the internal oblique, and terminates in the rectus abdominis.

The ventral branch of the **second lumbar nerve** is usually connected by an anastomotic branch with that of the third nerve. It gives off a large branch to the psoas major and is continued as the **ilio-inguinal nerve** (N. ilioinguinalis). This divides like the ilio-hypogastric into superficial and deep branches. Its **superficial branch** perforates the external oblique muscle a little in front of the point of the hip, runs downward on the front of the thigh and the lateral surface of the stifle, and gives off cutaneous branches. The **deep branch** runs behind and parallel with that of the ilio-hypogastricus and detaches branches to the abdominal muscles. It joins a branch of the external spermatic nerve, and the trunk so formed descends the inguinal canal, to be distributed to the external genital organs and the surrounding skin in the inguinal region.

The ventral branch of the **third lumbar nerve** is connected by a small anastomotic branch with the second nerve and furnishes a root of the lumbo-sacral plexus. It gives off a branch to the psoas muscles, the external spermatic nerve, and is continued as the lateral cutaneous nerve. The **external spermatic nerve** (N. spermaticus externus) passes backward in the substance of the psoas minor and divides into two branches. One of these, the muscular branch, emerges in front of the circumflex iliac vessels and goes to the cremaster and internal oblique muscles. The other, the inguinal branch, emerges behind the vessels just mentioned. It then runs lateral to and parallel with the external iliac artery and descends in the medial part of the inguinal canal. It emerges at the external ring with the external pudic artery and ramifies in the external genital organs and the skin of the inguinal region. The **lateral cutaneous nerve of the thigh** (N. cutaneus femoris lateralis) runs backward in the substance of the psoas muscles and emerges at the lateral border of the psoas minor. It then passes outward and backward on the iliac fascia and accompanies the posterior branch of the circumflex iliac artery. With this vessel it perforates the abdominal wall by passing between the external oblique and the iliacus a short distance below the point of the hip, descends on the medial face of the tensor fasciæ latæ (near its anterior border), and ramifies subcutaneously in the region of the stifle.

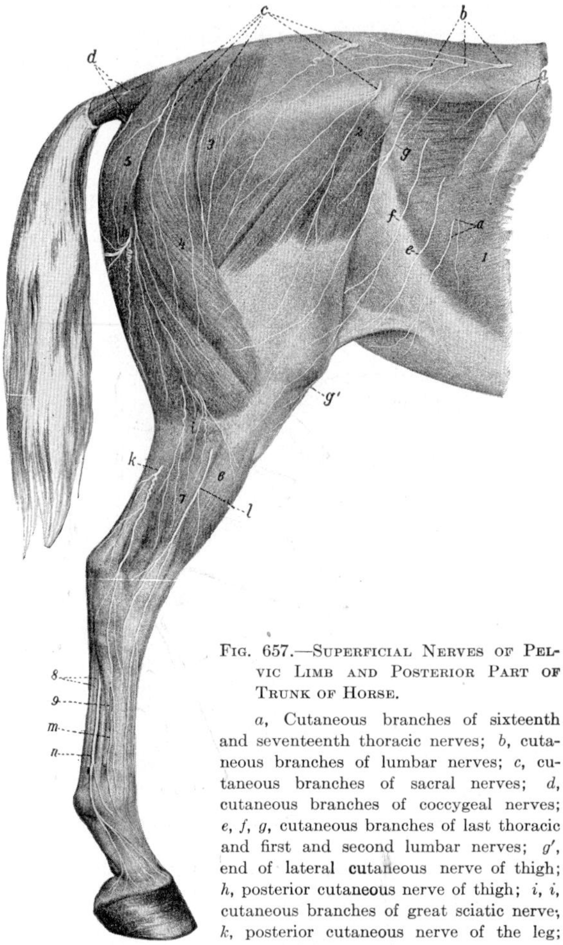

Fig. 657.—Superficial Nerves of Pelvic Limb and Posterior Part of Trunk of Horse.

a, Cutaneous branches of sixteenth and seventeenth thoracic nerves; b, cutaneous branches of lumbar nerves; c, cutaneous branches of sacral nerves; d, cutaneous branches of coccygeal nerves; e, f, g, cutaneous branches of last thoracic and first and second lumbar nerves; g', end of lateral cutaneous nerve of thigh; h, posterior cutaneous nerve of thigh; i, i, cutaneous branches of great sciatic nerve; k, posterior cutaneous nerve of the leg; l, superficial peroneal nerve; m, terminal part of deep peroneal nerve; n, lateral plantar nerve; 1, obliquus abdominis externus; 2, tensor fasciæ latæ; 3, gluteus superficialis; 4, biceps femoris; 5, semitendinosus; 6, common extensor; 7, lateral extensor; 8, flexor tendons; 9, great metatarsal artery. (After Ellenberger, in Leisering's Atlas.)

The origin and disposition of some of the foregoing nerves are variable. In some cases the ilio-inguinal nerve ends in the psoas major, and appears then to be absent. The mode of formation of the inguinal nerves is inconstant.

The ventral branches of the **fourth, fifth,** and **sixth lumbar** nerves concur in the formation of the lumbo-sacral plexus.

LUMBO-SACRAL PLEXUS

This plexus (Fig. 576) results substantially from the union of the ventral branches of the last three lumbar and the first two sacral nerves, but it derives a small root from the third lumbar nerve also. The anterior part of the plexus lies in front of the internal iliac artery, between the lumbar transverse processes and the psoas minor. It supplies branches to the ilio-psoas (designated by Girard the iliaco-muscular nerves). The posterior part lies partly upon and partly in the texture of the sacro-sciatic ligament. From the plexus are derived the nerves of the pelvic limb, which are now to be described.

FEMORAL NERVE

The **femoral nerve** (N. femoralis) is derived chiefly from the fourth and fifth lumbar nerves, but commonly, if not always, receives a fasciculus from the third nerve also and may receive one from the sixth (Fig. 656). It is the larger of the two nerves which are given off from the anterior part of the lumbo-sacral plexus. It runs ventrally and backward, at first between the psoas major and minor, then crosses the deep face of the tendon of insertion of the latter, and descends under cover of the sartorius over the terminal part of the ilio-psoas. It gives off the saphenous nerve, and divides into several terminal branches which dip into the interstice between the rectus femoris and the vastus medialis (Fig. 575). These branches are accompanied by the anterior femoral vessels and innervate the quadriceps femoris. A collateral branch is given off to the ilio-psoas.

The **saphenous nerve** (N. saphenus) (Figs. 575, 576, 582) is given off as the femoral crosses the terminal part of the ilio-psoas. It gives off a branch which enters the deep face of the sartorius, and descends with the femoral vessels in the femoral canal. About the middle of the thigh it divides into several branches which emerge from between the sartorius and gracilis, perforate the deep fascia, and ramify on the medial surface and the front of the limb as far downward as the hock. The longer posterior branches accompany the saphenous vessels, while the anterior branches deviate forward toward the stifle and the anterior surface of the leg.

OBTURATOR NERVE

The **obturator nerve** (N. obturatorius) is derived chiefly from the ventral branches of the fourth and fifth lumbar nerves, but may receive fibers from the third or the sixth (Fig. 656). It runs downward and backward, at first above and then upon the external iliac vein, inclines inward across the obturator vein, and passes through the anterior part of the obturator foramen (Fig. 576). It continues downward through the obturator externus, and divides into several branches which innervate the obturator externus, pectineus, adductor, and gracilis muscles (Fig. 581).

ANTERIOR GLUTEAL NERVE

The **anterior gluteal nerve** (N. glutæus cranialis) is derived chiefly from the last lumbar and first sacral nerves, but commonly has a fifth lumbar root. It divides into four or five branches which emerge through the greater sciatic foramen with the divisions of the anterior gluteal artery and supply the glutei, tensor fasciæ latæ, and capsularis (Fig. 658). The nerve to the tensor fasciæ latæ and the anterior part of the superficial gluteus passes between the deep part of the gluteus medius and the gluteus profundus, and is accompanied on the iliacus by branches of the lateral circumflex vessels.

POSTERIOR GLUTEAL NERVE

The **posterior gluteal nerve** (N. glutæus caudalis) is derived mainly from the sacral roots of the lumbo-sacral plexus (Figs. 576, 658). It divides into two trunks which emerge above the sciatic nerve. The dorsal nerve passes backward on the upper part of the sacro-sciatic ligament and divides into branches which enter the biceps femoris; it supplies a branch to the posterior part of the middle gluteus, and a nerve which turns around the posterior border of the latter and enters the posterior head of the superficial gluteus. The ventral nerve runs downward and backward on the sacro-sciatic ligament and divides into the **posterior cutaneous nerve of the thigh** (N. cutaneus femoris caudalis) and **muscular branches** which supply the semitendinosus. The former passes through the biceps femoris, emerges between that muscle and the semitendinosus at or a little below the level of the tuber ischii, and ramifies subcutaneously on the lateral and posterior surfaces of the hip and thigh (Fig. 657). The deep part of the nerve is connected by filaments with the pudic nerve.

SCIATIC NERVE

The **sciatic nerve** (N. ischiadicus) (Figs. 576, 580, 658), the largest in the body, is derived chiefly from the sixth lumbar and first sacral roots of the lumbo-

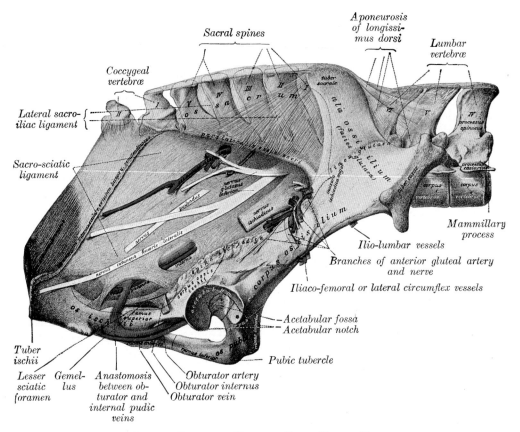

FIG. 658.—VESSELS AND NERVES ON PELVIC WALL OF HORSE.

Nervus ischiadicus = sciatic nerve; n. glut. inf. = posterior gluteal nerve; n. pudendus = pudic nerve. (After Schmaltz, Atlas d. Anat. d. Pferdes.)

sacral plexus, but usually has a fifth lumbar root and may receive a fasciculus from the second sacral nerve. It emerges through the greater sciatic foramen as a broad flat band which is blended at first with the posterior gluteal nerve and passes downward and backward on the lower part of the sacro-sciatic ligament and on the origin of the deep gluteus muscle. It turns downward in the hollow between the trochanter major and the tuber ischii over the gemellus, the tendon of the obturator internus, and the quadratus femoris. In its descent in the thigh it lies between the biceps femoris laterally and the adductor, semimembranosus, and semitendinosus medially, and is continued between the two heads of the gastrocnemius as the tibial nerve. Its chief branches are as follows:

1. In the pelvic part of its course the sciatic nerve supplies small **muscular branches** to the obturator internus, gemellus, and quadratus femoris; the branch to the obturator internus reaches the muscle by passing through the anterior end of the lesser sciatic foramen.

These very small nerves arise from the upper border or deep face of the sciatic, about half way between the two sciatic foramina. The nerve to the obturator internus lies along the dorsal margin of the sciatic and divides into branches for both heads of the muscle. The nerves to the gemellus and quadratus femoris commonly arise from the deep face of the sciatic by a common trunk which passes back between the latter and the sacro-sciatic ligament to the posterior border of the gluteus profundus, where it divides.

2. As the sciatic nerve turns down behind the hip joint it gives off a large **muscular branch** (Ramus muscularis proximalis), which divides to supply the semimembranosus and the short heads of the biceps femoris and semitendinosus.

3. The **posterior cutaneous nerve of the leg** or external saphenous nerve (N. cutaneus suræ caudalis) is detached from the sciatic about the middle of the thigh. It receives a fasciculus from the peroneal nerve and descends with the recurrent tarsal vein on the lateral face of the gastrocnemius to the distal third of the leg. Here it perforates the deep fascia and ramifies under the skin on the lateral surface of the tarsus and metatarsus (Fig. 657).

4. The **peroneal nerve** (N. peronæus) (Figs. 580, 585, 659) is a large trunk which arises from the sciatic nerve very shortly after the latter emerges from the pelvic cavity. It descends with the parent trunk to the origin of the gastrocnemius; here the peroneal nerve deviates outward and forward across the lateral face of the gastrocnemius under cover of the biceps femoris, and divides at the origin of the lateral extensor muscle into superficial and deep branches. The collateral branches include one to the biceps femoris, the reinforcing fasciculus detached about the middle of the thigh to the posterior cutaneous nerve, and, lower down, the **lateral cutaneous nerve of the leg** (Ramus cutaneus suræ lateralis). The latter emerges between the middle and posterior divisions of the biceps femoris at the level of the stifle joint and ramifies under the skin. The **superficial peroneal nerve** (N. peronæus superficialis) furnishes branches to the lateral extensor, and descends in the furrow between that muscle and the long extensor, perforates the deep fascia of the leg, and ramifies under the skin on the front and the lateral face of the tarsus and metatarsus. The **deep peroneal nerve** (N. peronæus profundus) is the direct continuation in point of size of the peroneal trunk. It dips in between the lateral and long extensors of the digit, gives branches to these muscles and the tibialis anterior, and descends in front of the intermuscular septum which separates the two muscles first named. It continues downward behind the tendon of the long extensor and divides on the front of the hock into medial and lateral branches. The **medial branch** (Ramus medialis) passes down under the skin on the anterior face of the metatarsus and supplies the cutaneous fibers of this region. The **lateral branch** (Ramus lateralis) furnishes a twig to the extensor brevis muscle and descends with the great metatarsal artery. It supplies the skin on the lateral face of the metatarsus and the fetlock.

In the greater part of its course in the leg the deep peroneal nerve is separated from the anterior tibial vessels by the tibialis anterior. It should be noted that the lateral one of the two veins which almost always accompany the artery here is usually very large, and the layer of muscle which intervenes between it and the nerve is often exceedingly thin. In the distal part of the leg the nerve is in direct contact with the vein, and on the front of the hock it lies behind the vessels. In very exceptional cases the nerve lies for a variable distance in the middle of the leg in the lateral part of the tibialis anterior.

TIBIAL NERVE

The **tibial nerve** (N. tibialis) is the direct continuation of the sciatic nerve (Figs. 576, 580, 583, 584, 659). It passes down between the two heads of the gastrocnemius, and accompanies the recurrent tibial vessels to the distal third of the leg, where it divides into the two plantar nerves. In the proximal third of the

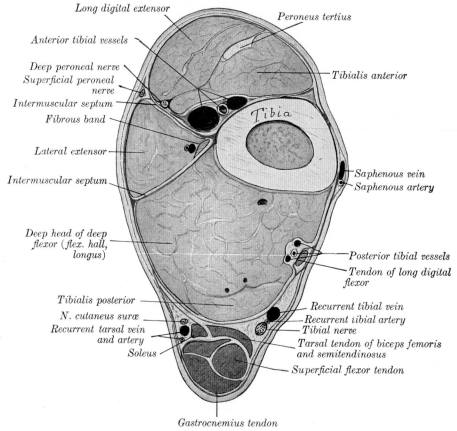

FIG. 659.—CROSS-SECTION OF DISTAL THIRD OF LEFT LEG OF HORSE.
The deep fascia is shown by red line.

leg it lies along the medial side of the superficial flexor under cover of the medial head of the gastrocnemius; lower down it is covered by the common deep fascia and is situated in the space between the deep flexor and the medial border of the tendo calcaneus (Achillis).

At the usual point of election for tibial neurectomy, *i. e.*, about a handbreadth above the level of the tuber calcis, the nerve lies in areolar tissue and fat in a fascial compartment formed by the special fascia of the deep flexor in front and by the common fascia and the tarsal tendon of the semitendinosus and biceps femoris behind and medially.

At its origin the tibial nerve gives off a **muscular branch** (Ramus muscularis distalis), the divisions of which pass between the two heads of the gastrocnemius and radiate to supply that muscle, the popliteus, the soleus, and the flexors of the digit. Small cutaneous twigs are also detached along the course of the nerve.

PLANTAR NERVES

The **plantar nerves,** medial and lateral (N. plantaris medialis, lateralis), result from the bifurcation of the tibial nerve in the distal part of the leg (Figs. 583, 584). They continue at first in the same direction and relations as the parent trunk, in direct apposition and enclosed in a common sheath. At the hock they diverge at a very acute angle and descend in the tarsal canal behind the deep flexor tendon in company with the plantar arteries. The **medial plantar nerve** supplies cutaneous nerves to the medial aspect of the tarsus and metatarsus, descends along the medial border of the flexor tendons behind the superficial plantar metatarsal vessels, and is otherwise arranged like the corresponding volar nerve of the forelimb. The **lateral plantar nerve** deviates outward between the two flexor tendons to reach their lateral border. It supplies a **deep branch** to the suspensory ligament, and in its further course resembles the corresponding nerve of the fore limb.

In so-called "tibial" neurectomy the operator really cuts the two plantar nerves which have not yet separated. The anastomotic branch between the two plantar nerves is smaller and more distal than that which connects the corresponding nerves of the fore limb, and is absent in 30 per cent. of the cases according to Rudert.

SACRAL NERVES

Five pairs of **sacral nerves** (Nn. sacrales) are present in the horse.

The small **dorsal branches** emerge through the dorsal sacral foramina and the space between the sacrum and the first coccygeal vertebra, and ramify in the muscles and skin of the sacral region and the adjacent part of the tail (Fig. 657). The fifth anastomoses with the dorsal branch of the first coccygeal nerve.

The **ventral branches** leave the vertebral canal through the ventral sacral foramina and the interval between the sacrum and first coccygeal vertebra. They are connected with the sympathetic by rami communicantes, and contribute branches to the pelvic plexus. The first and second are the largest, and unite with each other and with those of the last three lumbar nerves to form the lumbo-sacral plexus. The third and fourth are connected with each other, and the majority of their fibers go to form the pudic and posterior hæmorrhoidal nerves.

The **pudic nerve** (N. pudendus) (Figs. 576, 580, 658) passes downward and backward partly embedded in the sacro-sciatic ligament, then accompanies the internal pudic artery to the ischial arch, turns around the latter, parting company with the artery, and pursues a flexuous course along the dorsum penis as the **nervus dorsalis penis** and ramifies in the glans penis and the penile layer of the prepuce. Within the pelvis it anastomoses with the posterior hæmorrhoidal nerve, and gives branches to the bladder and urethra, the terminal part of the rectum, and the skin and muscles of the anus (Fig. 577). It also supplies the nerve to the ischio-cavernosus muscle and numerous branches to the corpus cavernosum of the penis and urethra. In the female it terminates in the clitoris and vulva (Fig. 578).

The **posterior hæmorrhoidal nerve** (N. hæmorrhoidalis caudalis) passes downward and backward above the pudic nerve, with which it anastomoses. It gives twigs to the terminal part of the rectum, the sphincter ani externus, and the surrounding skin (Fig. 577). In the female it supplies twigs to the vulva also (Fig. 578).

The ventral branch of the fifth nerve is small. It gives twigs to the sacrococcygeus ventralis lateralis and the skin of the root of the tail and joins the first coccygeal nerve.

COCCYGEAL NERVES

The **coccygeal nerves** (Nn. coccygei) commonly number five pairs. Their dorsal and ventral branches anastomose to form respectively two trunks on either side, which extend to the tip of the tail and supply its muscular and cutaneous nerves. The dorsal trunk runs with the dorso-lateral artery between the sacro-coccygeus dorsalis and intertransversales muscles (Fig. 579). The ventral trunk accompanies the ventro-lateral artery below the intertransversales.

THE SYMPATHETIC NERVOUS SYSTEM [1]

At present there seems to be confusion in the minds of some regarding the manner in which the sympathetic nervous system of the domestic animals can be applied to the autonomic nervous system as set up under the observations of J. N. Langley.

His division of the **autonomic nervous system** was based on the connection of the efferent part of the sympathetic system with the cerebrospinal system and on

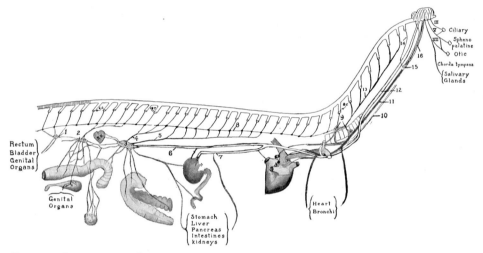

FIG. 659a.—DIAGRAM OF THE SYMPATHETIC NERVOUS SYSTEM OF THE HORSE. CRANIAL AND PELVIC PARTS MARKED BY TRANSVERSE LINES.

1, Pelvic plexus; 2, posterior mesenteric plexus; 3, cœliac plexus; 4, lesser splanchnic nerve; 5, greater splanchnic nerve; 6, dorsal branch of vagus nerve; 6 L, sixth lumbar spinal nerve; 7, ventral branch of vagus; 8, sympathetic trunk; 9, cervico-thoracic ganglion; 10, right recurrent nerve; 11, cervical trunk of sympathetic; 12, right vagus nerve: 13, nervus transversarius; 14, ramus communicans of first cervical spinal nerve; 15, anterior cervical ganglion; 16, branches to (15) from last four cranial nerves; III, V, VII, cranial nerves.

physiologic differences in the two parts of the autonomic system, which consists of the **craniosacral,** or parasympathetic system, and the **thoracolumbar,** or sympathetic system.

Under the veterinary anatomical arrangement the craniosacral portion would comprise the cephalic and pelvic parts and be classed as the parasympathetic system and the thoracolumbar portion would comprise the cervical, thoracic and lumbar parts and be classed as the sympathetic system.

The **sympathetic nervous system** (Systema nervorum sympathicum) is that part of the nervous system which serves (1) to transmit stimuli to the heart muscle, unstriped muscle, and glands; (2) to conduct impulses from the viscera to the cerebrospinal system.

[1] The special statements of this description refer to the system of the horse. A few important differential features will be mentioned in the account of the nervous system of the other animals.

Many of the fibers are derived from the cerebrospinal system and are rearranged and distributed in the sympathetic system. Numerous sympathetic fibers are contributed to the cerebrospinal nerves, through which they are distributed to the unstriped muscular tissue and glands, as vasomotor, pilomotor, and secretory nerves. The sympathetic, like the cerebrospinal system, consists of **neurones**, each of which comprises the cell-body, an axone, and numerous branched dendrites. The cell-bodies are aggregated into **ganglia**, some of which are large and more or less constant in position and form, while others are microscopic and are scattered in an irregular manner through the peripheral part of the system. Simple visceral reflexes may be mediated by sympathetic neurones alone.

In descriptive anatomy the sympathetic system is regarded as consisting of (1) a chain of **central ganglia** extending along each side of the vertebral column and connected by association fibers to form the **sympathetic trunk;** (2) **central branches** to and from the cerebrospinal nerves; (3) **peripheral branches,** which form **plexuses** (Plexus sympathici) with each other and the cerebrospinal nerves; (4) the **peripheral ganglia** which are interposed in the plexuses (Ganglia plexuum sympathicorum).

The **sympathetic trunk** (Truncus sympathicus) extends on either side from the base of the cranium to the tail. In it are interposed, at intervals of varying regularity, the **ganglia of the sympathetic trunk** (Ganglia trunci sympathici), These are connected with the cerebrospinal nerves by the central branches, the **rami communicantes.**

Two kinds of rami communicantes occur. Of these, one type consists largely of medullated fibers derived from the spinal nerves and ganglia; they have therefore a white appearance, and are termed **white rami.** They contain both efferent and afferent fibers. The **efferent splanchnic fibers** are derived from the ventral roots of the spinal nerves and terminate in great part about the cells of the nearest sympathetic ganglion; others end in more distant or in peripheral ganglia. The **afferent splanchnic fibers** are chiefly peripheral processes of the cells of the spinal ganglia, but some are sympathetic fibers which enter the spinal nerve-trunk and terminate about cells of the spinal ganglion. The **gray rami** consist mainly of non-medullated fibers derived from the sympathetic ganglia directly or through the trunk, which proceed centrally to the spinal nerves and are distributed along the somatic divisions of the latter to unstriped muscle and glands as **vasomotor, pilomotor,** and **secretory fibers.** Some go to the membranes of the spinal cord, and a few terminate about cells of the spinal ganglia as sensory sympathetic fibers.

Similar but more complex and irregular communications which exist between the sympathetic system and the cranial nerves—with the exception of the first and second—have been referred to in the accounts of the nerves.

It is convenient for descriptive purposes to divide the sympathetic system into cephalic, cervical, thoracic, abdominal, and pelvic parts.

1. The **cephalic part** (Pars cephalica systematis sympathici) comprises the **otic, sphenopalatine,** and **ciliary ganglia,** which may be regarded as homologues of the ganglia of the trunk of other regions. It also includes three plexuses formed by branches derived from the anterior cervical ganglion. The ganglion gives off two or three filaments which subdivide to form the **internal carotid plexus** (Plexus caroticus internus) around the artery of like name. The **cavernous plexus** (Plexus cavernosus) surrounds the artery within the cavernous sinus and communicates with that of the opposite side. The **external carotid plexus** (Plexus caroticus externus) is formed around the homonymous artery, and filaments from it go to the vessel and its branches and to the salivary glands.

2. The **cervical part** (Pars cervicalis s. sympathici) includes two ganglia and the trunk which connects them.

The **anterior** or **superior cervical ganglion** (G. cervicale craniale) lies on the guttural pouch below the occipito-atlantal articulation (Fig. 562). It is reddish-gray in color, fusiform, and about an inch (ca. 2–3 cm.) in length. It is connected by rami communicantes with the last four cranial and first cervical nerves, sends branches to form the plexuses mentioned above, and contributes to the pharyngeal plexus.

The **cervical trunk** of the sympathetic connects the anterior and posterior cervical ganglia. On leaving the former it is associated in a common sheath with the vagus along the dorsal face of the common carotid artery. At the root of the neck it separates from the vagus and joins the posterior cervical ganglion.

The **posterior** or **inferior cervical ganglion** (G. cervicale caudale) is situated under cover of the first rib and the insertion of the scalenus (Figs. 660, 661). On the right side it lies upon the longus colli and the trachea, on the left side upon the same muscle, trachea and the œsophagus. It is flattened, very irregular and variable in outline, and is blended more or less with the first thoracic ganglion,[1] so that the two may be considered together as the **ganglion stellatum.** This receives at its anterodorsal angle the **nervus transversarius,** which accompanies the vertebral artery in the canalis transversarius; it is a trunk formed by the rami communicantes

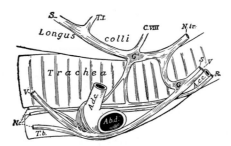

Fig. 660.—Right Cervico-thoracic Ganglion and Related Structures of Horse.

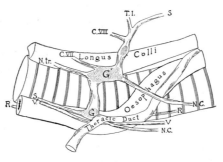

Fig. 661.—Left Cervico-thoracic Ganglion and Related Structures of Horse.

G, G', Ganglia; *S*, sympathetic trunk; *V*, vagus; *R*, recurrent nerve; *N.C.*, cardiac nerves; *C.VII., C.VIII, T.I.*, rami communicantes from last two cervical and first thoracic nerves; *N.tr.*, nervus transversarius; *T.b.*, brachio-cephalic trunk; *A.d.c.*, dorso-cervical artery; *A.b.d.*, right brachial artery; *A.c.c.*, common carotid artery.

of the cervical nerves except the first and last. Large rami connect with the last cervical and first and second thoracic nerves. Filaments also connect with the vagus. From the ventral part of the ganglion proceed the cardiac nerves now to be described.

The **cardiac nerves** (Nn. cardiaci) are formed by branches from the posterior

---

[1] In some cases there exists a more or less distinct middle cervical ganglion which receives the filaments from the vagus and is connected with the posterior cervical ganglion by a trunk. It occurs oftenest on the right side and gives off one or two cardiac nerves.

cervical and first thoracic ganglia, together with twigs from the sympathetic trunks and the vagi. They form the cardiac plexus (P. cardiacus) on the ventral face of the trachea by anastomoses with each other and with branches of the vagus and recurrent nerves. They are subject to considerable variation, but their general arrangement may be stated as follows:

(a) On the right side there are usually two cardiac nerves. Of these one passes back with the vagus in the angle between the right brachial artery and the bicarotid trunk, pierces the pericardium, crosses the aortic arch, and divides into branches which are mingled with those of the left nerves. The second crosses obliquely over the right face of the trachea and joins the vagus where the latter gives off the right recurrent nerve; a small plexus is formed here, from which two or three cardiac branches are detached. These pass back beneath the trachea and ramify on the atria and ventricles.

(b) On the left side there are commonly three cardiac nerves. One of these is distributed to the great vessels in the anterior mediastinum. The largest passes back at first with the vagus beneath the arch of the left brachial artery, inclines downward, perforates the pericardium, and divides into two branches. One branch passes beneath the bifurcation of the pulmonary artery and is distributed to the left atrium. The larger branch dips in between the aorta and the pulmonary artery, gives twigs to these vessels, and ramifies on the ventricles, especially along the course of the right coronary artery. The third nerve crosses the deep face of the left brachial artery, passes back below the trachea, and unites with filaments of a right cardiac nerve. It passes around the aorta and ramifies chiefly along the course of the left coronary artery on the left face of the ventricles.

3. The **thoracic part** (Pars thoracalis systematis sympathici) extends backward ventral to the costo-vertebral joints from the posterior cervical ganglion to the crura of the diaphragm, and passes between the latter and the psoas minor to be continued by the abdominal part.

The **trunk** is concealed in the first part of its course by the subcostal vessels and the lateral border of the longus colli, but further back it is visible under the pleura.

The **ganglia** are arranged segmentally at each intercostal space and partly on the heads of the ribs. They are flattened and are small and fusiform, with the exception of the first. This (G. thoracale primum) is extensive, irregularly quadrilateral in outline, and is united with the posterior cervical ganglion, as previously mentioned. The ganglia are connected with the thoracic nerves by white and gray rami communicantes. Distinct ganglia may be absent at two or three spaces succeeding the first, and here the trunk is thickened and contains ganglion cells.

The **visceral branches** comprise aortic, cardiac, pulmonary, and œsophageal branches, and the splanchnic nerves. The **aortic branches** ramify on the thoracic aorta, forming around that vessel the **thoracic aortic plexus** (P. aorticus thoracalis). The **cardiac branches** concur with those of the vagus in forming the **cardiac plexus** (P. cardiacus). From this branches go to form the **coronary plexuses** (P. coronarii) along the course of the vessels of like name. The **pulmonary branches** join with corresponding branches of the vagus and filaments from the cardiac plexus in forming the **pulmonary plexus** (P. pulmonalis) at the root of the lung. Branches of the plexus, on which are minute ganglia, ramify with the bronchi in the substance of the lung.[1] The **œsophageal branches** join with those of the vagus in the formation of the œsophageal plexus (P. œsophageus).

The **great splanchnic nerve** (N. splanchnicus major) arises by a series of roots derived from the sixth or seventh to the fourteenth or fifteenth thoracic ganglia

---

[1] The right and left plexuses communicate with each other, so that both lungs receive fibers from both vagi.

inclusive.   It extends along the bodies of the vertebræ medio-ventral to the thoracic trunk, then crosses the latter ventrally, passes back between the crus of the diaphragm and the lateral border of the psoas minor, and joins the cœliaco-mesenteric ganglion.   It is small at its origin, but becomes considerably larger than the sympathetic trunk.   Near its termination it may present a small **splanchnic ganglion,** from which and from the nerve filaments go to the aorta, the œsophagus, and the vertebræ.   The fibers of the nerve are derived chiefly from the spinal cord; hence its white appearance as compared with the sympathetic trunk.

The **small splanchnic nerve** (N. splanchnicus minor) is formed by roots derived from the last two or three thoracic ganglia.   It runs back with the great splanchnic nerve, but ends in the cœliac or in the renal and adrenal plexuses.

The splanchnic nerves are quite variable.   The greater splanchnic is often blended more or less with the sympathetic trunk and may be separate only in the posterior part of the thorax. The lesser splanchnic may be included in the greater, and thus appear to be absent.   Its roots communicate by filaments with the great splanchnic.

4. The **abdominal part** of the sympathetic trunk (Pars abdominalis systematis sympathici) lies along the medial border of the psoas minor, above the aorta on the left side and the posterior vena cava on the right (Fig. 656).   The trunk is smaller than the thoracic part, and presents usually six small fusiform **lumbar ganglia** (G. lumbalia), which are connected by rami communicantes with the ventral divisions of the lumbar nerves.   Visceral branches go to the aortic and pelvic plexuses and to the cœliaco-mesenteric ganglion.

5. The **pelvic** and **caudal part** of the sympathetic trunk (Pars pelvina et caudalis systematis sympathici) begins at the last lumbar ganglion and extends along the pelvic surface of the sacrum medial to the emergence of the ventral branches of the sacral nerves (Fig. 576).   At the third or fourth segment of the sacrum the trunk divides into medial and lateral branches.   The medial branch inclines to the median plane and unites with the opposite branch.   At the junction there is often found the small **coccygeal ganglion** (G. impar), which lies on the coccygeal artery at the joint between the first and second coccygeal vertebræ.   A filament from the ganglion accompanies the artery.   The lateral branch communicates with the last two sacral nerves and joins the ventral coccygeal nerves.   **Sacral ganglia** (G. sacralia) occur near each of the first three sacral foramina, and are connected by gray rami communicantes with the ventral branches of the sacral nerves.   The visceral branches are distributed through the pelvic plexus.   They supply motor fibers to the longitudinal, and inhibitory fibers to the circular, muscular coat of the rectum;   motor fibers to the bladder and uterus;   and the vaso-dilator fibers (Nn. erigentes) to the penis.

According to von Schumacher, minute segmental **coccygeal ganglia** occur along the caudal branches of the sympathetic trunk.   The lateral branch is regarded by van der Broek as an aggregate of rami communicantes.

THE ABDOMINAL AND PELVIC PLEXUSES

The chief plexuses which distribute nerves to the viscera and vessels of the abdominal and pelvic cavities are two in number, the cœliac and the pelvic.   From them fibers proceed to form numerous subsidiary plexuses which are named according to the organs which they supply or the vessels which they enlace.

The **cœliac plexus** (Plexus cœliacus) (Fig. 575) is situated on the dorsal wall of the abdominal cavity, in relation to the aorta and the origin of its chief visceral branches.   It is formed by the splanchnic nerves, branches of the vagi, and filaments from the anterior lumbar ganglia of the sympathetic.   It contains the cœliaco-mesenteric ganglia.   From the cœliac plexus and its ganglia subsidiary plexuses are continued upon the branches of the aorta.

The **cœliaco-mesenteric ganglia** (G. cœliaco-mesenterica) are two in number, right and left. They are situated on each side of the aorta, in relation to the origin of the cœliac and anterior mesenteric arteries. The right ganglion is concealed by the posterior vena cava; it is irregularly quadrilateral and is about two inches (4–6 cm.) in length. The left ganglion is largely covered by the left adrenal; it is narrower than the right one and is three or four inches (ca. 8–10 cm.) long. The two ganglia are united by irregular connecting branches in front of and behind the anterior mesenteric artery.[1] Each receives the great splanchnic nerve of its own side and branches from the dorsal œsophageal continuation of the vagus nerves. Branches from the ganglia and the cords which connect them pass back to the posterior mesenteric ganglion which is situated at the origin of the posterior mesenteric artery.

The following unpaired plexuses proceed from the cœliac plexus and cœliaco-mesenteric ganglia:

1. The **abdominal aortic plexus** (P. aorticus abdominalis) occurs along the abdominal aorta. It is connected with the renal plexuses and behind with the pelvic plexus. It receives filaments from some of the sympathetic lumbar ganglia.

2. The **gastric plexus** (P. gastricus) enlaces the gastric artery and divides like the artery into two parts, forming the anterior and posterior gastric plexuses. These receive branches of the vagus nerves.

3. The **hepatic plexus** (P. hepaticus) is formed by several nerves of considerable size which accompany the hepatic artery and the portal vein. It receives fibers from the left vagus, ramifies in the liver, and gives off branches which accompany the collateral branches of the hepatic artery and supply the areas in which these vessels are distributed.

4. The **splenic plexus** (P. lienalis) resembles the preceding in its arrangement. In addition to its terminal branches to the spleen it gives collateral twigs to the pancreas and the left part of the greater curvature of the stomach.

5. The **anterior mesenteric plexus** (P. mesentericus cranialis) is formed mainly by branches from the posterior part of the cœliaco-mesenteric ganglia; it is continuous with the cœliac plexus in front and the posterior mesenteric behind. It surrounds the anterior mesenteric trunk and its branches, and supplies the viscera to which these vessels are distributed.

The **posterior mesenteric ganglion** (G. mesentericum caudale) is unpaired; it is irregularly stellate, and is situated on the origin of the posterior mesenteric artery. It is connected with the cœliaco-mesenteric ganglia by anastomosing branches which concur in the formation of the aortic plexus. Two or more pairs of nerves proceed from it posteriorly. One of these, the **internal spermatic nerve** (N. spermaticus internus), accompanies the spermatic artery to the spermatic cord and testicle in the male; in the female it goes to the ovary, uterine tubes, and adjacent part of the uterine horn. These concur in the formation of the spermatic and utero-ovarian plexuses. The other branches from the ganglion pass back to the pelvis ventral to the great vessels and concur in the formation of the pelvic plexuses.

The **posterior mesenteric plexus** (P. mesentericus caudalis) accompanies the artery of like name in its distribution.

The secondary plexuses which accompany the branches of the mesenteric arteries give off branches which form two fine peripheral plexuses in the wall of the intestine. One of these, the **myenteric plexus** (P. myentericus), or plexus of Auerbach, lies between the layers of the muscular coat, and is provided with microscopic ganglia. The other is in the submucous tissue, and is therefore termed the **submucous plexus** (P. submucosus) or plexus of Meissner.

[1] A good preparation of the ganglia in the horse is often difficult to obtain on account of verminous aneurysm of the artery and the formation of a quantity of connective tissue about it.

The following paired plexuses are derived mainly from branches of the cœliac and aortic plexuses:

1. The **renal plexuses** (P. renales) proceed largely from the cœliaco-mesenteric ganglia, but receive fibers also from the small splanchnic nerves. They enlace the renal arteries and supply the kidneys. Minute renal ganglia occur on the course of the nerves along the renal vessels.

2. The **adrenal plexuses** (P. suprarenales) are formed by a relatively very large number of fine fibers derived in great part directly from the cœliaco-mesenteric ganglia. Numerous minute ganglia occur in their meshes.

3a. The **spermatic plexuses** (P. spermatici) proceed from the aortic plexus and branches from the posterior mesenteric ganglion. Each accompanies the corresponding (internal) spermatic artery to the testicle.

3b. The **utero-ovarian plexuses** (P. ovarici) are the homologues in the female of the preceding. They accompany the utero-ovarian arteries to the ovary and the cornua of the uterus.

The **pelvic plexuses** (P. hypogastrici) are the pelvic continuations of the aortic and posterior mesenteric plexuses. Two or more nerves proceed from the posterior mesenteric ganglion and enter the pelvic cavity ventral to the large vessels, anastomose with each other and with branches from the sacral nerves—especially the third and fourth—and ramify on the pelvic viscera. The peripheral plexuses derived therefrom are named according to the organs which they supply; the chief of these are the **hæmorrhoidal, vesical, utero-vaginal, prostatic, cavernous** (of the penis or clitoris) (P. hæmorrhoidalis, vesicalis, uterovaginalis, cavernosus penis s. clitoridis, etc.). Others enlace the arteries (P. iliacus, femoralis, etc.).

THE NERVOUS SYSTEM OF THE OX[1]

The **spinal cord** resembles that of the horse in conformation and structure. In cattle of medium size its length is about 165 to 170 cm. (ca. 65–67 inches), and its weight about 240 to 250 grams (ca. 8 ounces).

In a cow 140 cm. in height Dexler found the weight of the cord (including the intradural nerve-roots) to be 260 gm. and the length 162 cm. The lengths of the regions were: cervical 41 cm., thoracic 72 cm., lumbar 32 cm., sacral 7 cm.

The **brain** has an average weight of about 500 grams (ca. 16–17 ounces). Its differences in general form are correlated with those noted in the consideration of the cranial cavity.

The **medulla oblongata** is short, wide, and thick. Its ventral face is strongly convex. The pyramids are narrow, short, and close together in front. Near the decussation there is a well-defined oval prominence on either side which indicates the position of the posterior olive. The corpus trapezoideum is large; it has no central part between the pyramids. The external arcuate fibers are distinct. The restiform bodies are short and thick and diverge more strongly than in the horse. The floor of the fourth ventricle is only about two-thirds as long as in the horse. The area acustica is a well-marked oval prominence lateral to the middle part of the limiting sulcus. The tuberculum acusticum at the origin of the acoustic nerve is very large. The anterior fovea is distinct. The posterior recess of the fourth ventricle communicates through a median aperture (Apertura mediana) with the subarachnoid space.

[1] Only the most salient differences as compared with the horse will be mentioned.

The **pons** is smaller, both transversely and longitudinally, than that of the horse. It is strongly convex and has a distinct central depression.

The **cerebellum** is smaller and more angular in form than in the horse. The vermis is large and has a distinct depression on its anterior face for the posterior corpora quadrigemina. The hemispheres are relatively small and are not clearly divided into tabulations. The anterior peduncles are very short.

The **cerebral peduncles** are short. A small eminence in the interpeduncular

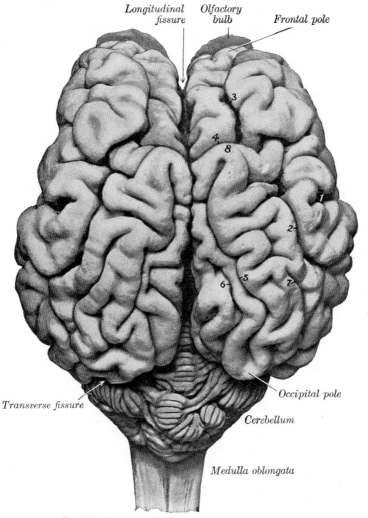

FIG. 662.—BRAIN OF OX; DORSAL VIEW; HARDENED *in situ.*
Fissures: *1*, Lateral; *2*, suprasylvian; *3*, coronal; *4*, transverse; *5*, marginal; *6*, entomarginal; *7*, ectomarginal. 8, Marginal or sagittal pole.

fossa is caused by the presence of the interpeduncular ganglion. The **medial geniculate body** is prominent. The **pineal body** is long and fusiform, and is often pigmented in spots. The third ventricle forms two considerable recesses in relation to the pineal body: one (R. pinealis) extends up into the body; the other (R. suprapinealis) is a long tubular prolongation in front of it.

The **optic tracts** cross the cerebral peduncles almost at a right angle.

The **hypophysis** is situated in a deep fossa and is surrounded by a plexus of vessels. It is much narrower and thicker than that of the horse. The **infundibulum** is relatively long and slopes downward and backward.

The **cerebral hemispheres** are shorter, higher, and relatively wider than in the horse. The frontal poles are small, the occipital, large. The length from pole to pole is about the same as the greatest transverse diameter of the two hemispheres.

Longitudinal fissure

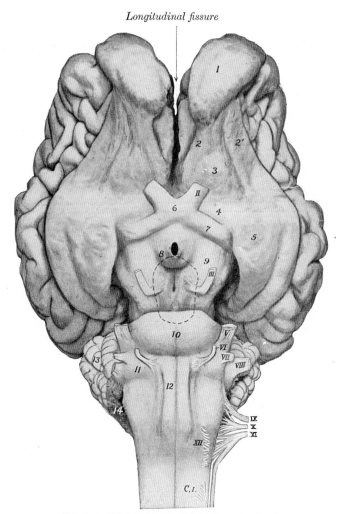

Fig. 663.—Base of Brain of Ox; Hardened *in situ*.

1, Olfactory bulb; *2*, *2'*, olfactory striæ; *3*, trigonum olfactorium; *4*, fossa lateralis; *5*, piriform lobe; *6*, optic chiasma; *7*, optic tract; *8*, tuber cinereum; *9*, cerebral peduncle; *10*, pons; *11*, corpus trapezoideum; *12*, pyramid; *13*, cerebellum; *14*, chorioid plexus of fourth ventricle; *C.I.*, first cervical nerve roots. The stumps of the cranial nerves are designated by Roman numerals. The hypophysis has been removed and its contour is indicated by dotted line. The central black area is the infundibular recess of the third ventricle opened up when the infundibulum is torn off.

Viewed from the side, the dorsal surface is strongly convex. The highest point of the dorso-medial border is a little in front of its middle and forms a marked prominence termed the **sagittal** or **marginal pole** (Polus sagittalis s. prominentia marginalis dorsalis). Anterior to this the border drops abruptly, being cut into by the deep transverse fissure. The arachnoid on the basal and anterior parts of the hemispheres is usually pigmented. The **corpus callosum** extends through a little more than a third of the length of the hemisphere. The pattern of the **fissures** and **gyri** of the pallium is somewhat simpler than in the horse.

1. The **lateral fissure** (of Sylvius) is very deep. Its middle branch extends almost vertically upward on the middle of the lateral surface of the hemisphere, and is separated by a gyrus of variable width from the suprasylvian fissure. The anterior branch runs forward about parallel with the sulcus rhinalis anterior, from which it is separated by the short gyri of the insula. The latter are covered to a small extent only by the overhanging gyri (operculum). The posterior branch may run back a distance of only about 1.5 cm. and end in T-shaped manner, or it may join the sulcus rhinalis posterior.

2. The **suprasylvian fissure** is deep and very distinct. It extends in an undulating manner from the lateral surface of the occipital pole to the lateral side of the sagittal pole. Here it may

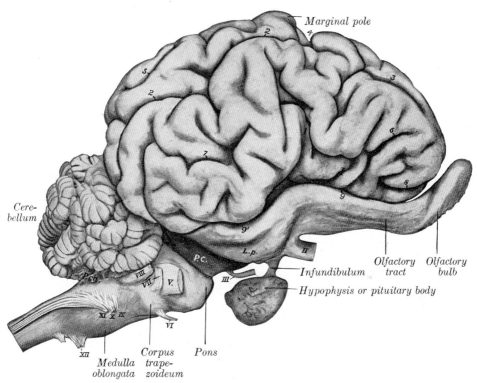

Fig. 664.—Brain of Ox; Right View; Hardened *in situ.*

Fissures: *1*, Lateral; *2, 2*, suprasylvian; *3*, coronal; *4*, transverse; *5*, ectomarginal; *6*, diagonal; *7*, posterior ectosylvian; *8*, presylvian; *9, 9'*, rhinal (anterior and posterior); *P.ch.*, chorioid plexus of fourth ventricle; *P.c.*, cerebral peduncle; *L.p.*, piriform lobe; *I*, insula. Stumps of cranial nerves are designated by Roman numerals.

be interrupted or may be continued by the **coronal fissure,** which descends to the frontal pole and divides into two short branches.

3. The **diagonal fissure** (S. diagonalis) begins in front of the stem of the lateral fissure and runs upward and forward. Its form is very variable.

4. The **transverse fissure** cuts obliquely into the dorsal border in front of the sagittal pole. It is short and deep and commonly communicates with the suprasylvian and coronal fissures, but may be separated from the former.

5. The **marginal fissure** is distinct. It extends from the sagittal pole to the occipital pole. It is flexuous and deviates outward somewhat in its posterior two-thirds.

6. The **entomarginal fissure** lies medial and parallel to the posterior part of the preceding.

7. The **ectomarginal fissure** is lateral and parallel to the marginal fissure. It does not extend so far in either direction as the latter, and is often more or less broken up by annectant gyri.

8. The **sulcus rhinalis** is more open than in the horse, since it is not overlapped by the gyri above it.

9. The **calloso-marginal fissure** is flexuous and not so regular as in the horse. It is often interrupted at or near the level of the genu of the corpus callosum, in which case the **genual fissure** continues it downward.

10. The **cruciate fissure** is faint and is confined to the medial surface. It lies about one centimeter in front of the transverse fissure, and commonly joins the calloso-marginal fissure below.

11. Short and variable fissures occur in front of and behind the middle branch of the lateral fissure (F. ectosylvia anterior, posterior).

The **olfactory bulb** is much smaller than in the horse. The lateral olfactory stria is large, the medial one small and not distinct.

The **cranial nerves** have in general the same superficial origin as in the horse. The more important differences in other respects are as follows:

The **oculomotor nerve** is larger than in the horse. It emerges with the fourth, sixth, ophthalmic and maxillary nerves through the foramen orbito-rotundum.

The **trigeminal nerve** presents the following differences in its distribution:

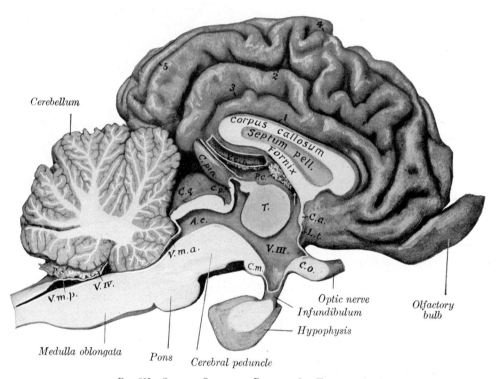

Fig. 665.—Sagittal Section of Brain of Ox; Hardened *in situ.*

V.IV. Fourth ventricle; *P.c.*, choroid plexuses; *V.m. a.*, anterior medullary velum; *V.m.p.*, posterior medullary velum; *A.c.*, cerebral aqueduct; *C.q.*, corpora quadrigemina; *C.p.*, posterior commissure; *C.pin.*, pineal body; *V.c.i.*, great cerebral vein; *T.*, thalamus; *V.III.*, third ventricle (arrow points to interventricular foramen); *C.a.*, anterior commissure; *L.t.*, lamina terminalis; *C.o.*, chiasma opticum. Fissures: *1*, Callosal; *2*, calloso-marginal; *3*, splenial; *4*, transverse; *5*, entomarginal.

The internal branch of the **lacrimal nerve** supplies twigs to the mucous membrane of the frontal sinus; the large outer branch, **N. cornualis** (Fig. 666), runs backward and supplies the corium of the horn. The **frontal nerve** emerges from the orbit below the supraorbital process. The **naso-ciliary nerve** is large and sends filaments to the ocular muscles. The **ciliary ganglion** is somewhat larger than in the horse, and is connected with the lower division of the oculomotor nerve by several short filaments. In consequence of the absence of the canine and upper incisor teeth the corresponding branch of the infraorbital nerve is naturally wanting. The **mandibular nerve** emerges through the foramen ovale. The **superficial temporal nerve** gives off a large branch which joins the superior buccal division of the facial on the masseter, about half-way between the zygomatic arch and the angle of the jaw. The **otic ganglion** is larger than in the horse. According to Moussu the buccinator nerve furnishes excitosecretory twigs to the parotid and inferior buccal glands.

The **facial nerve** divides into its two terminal branches before reaching the border of the jaw. The **superior buccal nerve** is the larger of the two; it crosses the masseter much lower than in the horse. The relatively small **inferior buccal nerve** runs beneath the parotid or in the gland substance parallel with the border of the lower jaw, crosses under the insertion of the sterno-cephalicus, and runs forward along the depressor labii inferioris. At the point where it crosses the facial

FIG. 666.—SUPERFICIAL NERVES OF HEAD OF OX.

Nerves: *a*, Facial; *a′, a″, a‴*, superior buccal and primary branches; *b*, deep auricular; *c*, posterior auricular; *d, d′, d″*, auriculo-palpebral and primary branches; *e*, parotid plexus; *f*, digastric; *g, g′*, inferior buccal; *g″*, anastomosis between *g* and *a′*; *h*, superficial temporal; *i, k, l*, branches of infraorbital; *m*, buccinator; *m′*, branch of *m* to zygomaticus and malaris muscles; *m″*, branch of *m* to parotid gland; *n*, branches of infratrochlear; *o*, frontal; *p*, cornual branch of lacrimal; *p′, p″*, lacrimal; *q*, dorsal branch of accessory; *r*, auricular branch of second cervical; *r′, r″*, branches of *r*; *s*, cutaneous branch of second cervical; *s′*, anastomotic branch connecting *s* and *t*; *t, t′, t″*, third cervical and branches; *u*, zygomatic. Muscles: *1*, Frontalis (part removed); *2*, levator nasolabialis (part removed); *3*, origin of levator labii superioris proprius; *4*, malaris; *5, 5′*, stumps of zygomaticus; *6*, buccinator; *7*, masseter; *8*, sterno-cephalicus; *10*, cleido-mastoideus; *11, 11′*, cleido-occipitalis; *12*, zygomatico-auricularis; *13*, fronto-scutularis; *14*, scuto-auricularis superficialis superior; *15*, scuto-auricularis superficialis accessorius; *16*, cervico-scutularis; *17, 17′*, stumps of parotido-auricularis. *18, 18′*, Remnants of parotid gland; *19, 19′*, mandibular gland; *9*, jugular vein; *30*, facial vein. (After Schachtschabel.)

vein and parotid duct it gives off an anastomotic branch to the superior nerve. The **auriculo-palpebral nerve** is large.

The **vagus** bears—in addition to the relatively large **jugular ganglion**—a **ganglion nodosum** at the point of origin of the anterior laryngeal nerve. The trunk is large. The **pharyngeal branch** is large and anastomoses with the anterior and external laryngeal nerves. The latter commonly arises directly from the trunk. The **dorsal œsophageal trunk** communicates with the splanchnic nerve, contributes twigs to the hepatic plexus, and ramifies chiefly on the right surface of the rumen and the adjacent surface of the abomasum. The **ventral œsophageal trunk** goes to the left surface of the rumen; it supplies branches to the hepatic plexus and to all the divisions of the stomach.

The **spinal accessory nerve** presents two special features. The part which joins the jugular ganglion bears a small ganglion. The ventral branch supplies both parts of the sterno-cephalicus.

The **hypoglossal nerve** is large. It is connected with the ventral division of the first cervical nerve by a branch of considerable size, and detaches a long branch which runs backward along the carotid artery.

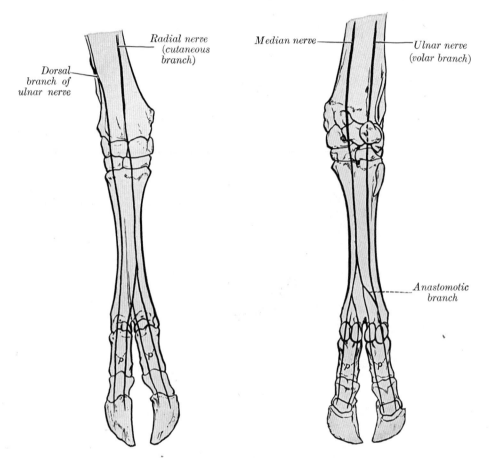

FIG. 667.—NERVES OF DISTAL PART OF RIGHT FORE-LIMB OF OX; DORSAL VIEW (SCHEMATIC).

p, Dorsal digital nerves.

FIG. 668.—NERVES OF DISTAL PART OF RIGHT FORE-LIMB OF OX; VOLAR VIEW (SCHEMATIC).

p, Volar digital nerves.

The **spinal nerves** resemble those of the horse in origin and general arrangement. The thoracic nerves number thirteen pairs. The more important differences in the limb-plexuses and their branches are as follows:

The **brachial plexus** is formed by the ventral branches of the last three cervical and first thoracic nerves; the second thoracic nerve usually furnishes no root, but the ventral branch of the sixth cervical goes almost entirely to the plexus after giving off the nerve to the rhomboideus and the serratus cervicis.

The differences in the nerves above the elbow are not of sufficient moment to receive notice in this brief account (the median and ulnar are in a common sheath), but below this point there are naturally important special features correlated chiefly with the arrangement of the digits.

The **radial nerve** is continued below the elbow by a large **cutaneous branch** (N. cutaneus antibrachii dorsalis) which emerges at the lower border of the lateral head of the triceps and descends on the dorsal aspect of the limb. It communicates above the carpus with the lateral cutaneous branch of the median nerve and terminates in three **dorsal digital nerves;** two of these descend along the axial or interdigital side of the dorsal surface of the chief digits, and the third along the medial (abaxial) side of the medial chief digit.

The **ulnar nerve** divides at a variable distance down the forearm into two branches. The **dorsal** (or superficial) **branch** emerges between the tendons of the ulnaris lateralis and flexor carpi ulnaris, and is continued as the **lateral dorsal digital nerve** on the lateral chief digit. The **volar** (or deep) **branch** descends along the superficial digital flexor, gives a branch to the suspensory ligament below the carpus, and unites with the lateral branch of the median nerve to form the **lateral volar digital nerve** (N. digitalis lateralis digiti IV).

The **median nerve** is much larger than the ulnar. It passes beneath the pronator teres, descends the forearm as in the horse, and divides in the distal part of the metacarpus into two branches. The **medial branch** gives twigs to the medial small digit and is continued on the medial side of the volar surface of the medial chief digit as the **medial volar digital nerve** (N. digitalis medialis digiti III); it also concurs with the lateral branch in forming the two digital nerves which descend along the interdigital aspect of the chief digits. The **lateral branch** is larger. It bifurcates, and one division unites with the twig from the medial branch to form a common digital trunk. From the latter two digital nerves proceed as mentioned above; these are the **lateral** and **medial volar digital nerves** of the medial and lateral chief digits respectively (N. digitalis volaris lateralis digiti III, medialis digiti IV). The other division unites with the volar branch of the ulnar nerve to form the **lateral volar digital nerve** of the lateral chief digit (N. digitalis lateralis digiti IV).

The **lumbo-sacral plexus** and its branches to the pelvis and thigh present no **very** striking special features.

The **superficial peroneal nerve** is much larger than in the horse. After crossing beneath the peroneus longus it passes down on the front of the tarsus and metatarsus and divides into three branches. The medial and lateral branches descend as the **medial** and **lateral dorsal digital nerves** on the chief digits. The larger middle branch joins a branch of the deep peroneal nerve in the interdigital space, and from this union proceed the **dorsal digital nerves** which descend on the opposed surfaces of the chief digits.

The **deep peroneal nerve** descends in the leg as in the horse, and continues down the dorsal groove of the metatarsus with the dorsal metatarsal artery. It gives collateral branches to the anterior muscles of the leg and to the extensor digitalis brevis. Its terminal branches concur with branches from the superficial peroneal nerve in the formation of the two axial **dorsal digital nerves** (N. dig. dors. lat. dig. III et dig. dors. med. dig. IV pedis), and with a branch of the medial plantar nerve in the formation of corresponding plantar digital nerves.

The **tibial nerve** divides at the back of the hock into medial and lateral plantar nerves. The **medial plantar nerve** descends between the superficial flexor tendon and the suspensory ligament and divides into two branches; the medial branch descends as the **medial plantar digital nerve** (N. dig. plant. med. dig. III) along the medial side of the flexor tendons of the medial chief digit; the lateral branch turns around the flexor tendons to reach the interdigital space, where it concurs with a branch of the deep peroneal nerve in the formation of two axial **plantar digital nerves** (N. dig. plant. lat. dig. III et dig. plant. med. dig. IV), which descend on the opposed surfaces of the chief digits. The **lateral plantar nerve** descends along the lateral border of the flexor tendons, gives a branch to the suspensory ligament and to the lateral small digit, and continues along the lateral face of the lateral digit as the **lateral plantar digital nerve** (N. dig. plant. lat. dig. IV).

The **sympathetic system** closely resembles that of the horse in its general arrangement, and only a few differential features will receive attention. The **anterior cervical ganglion** is closer to the cranial base and is thicker than in the horse; its branches to the carotid and cavernous plexuses are large, and no connection is formed with the spinal accessory nerve. The **cervical trunk** is smaller

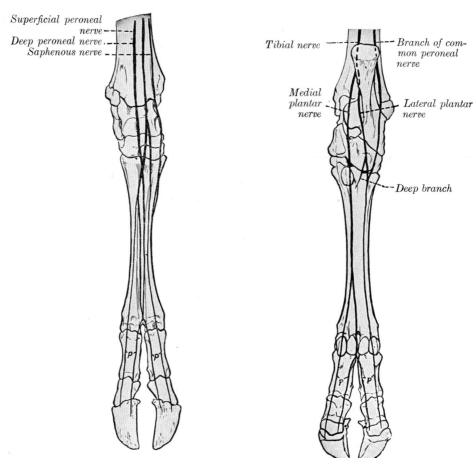

FIG. 669.—NERVES OF DISTAL PART OF RIGHT HIND LIMB OF OX; DORSAL VIEW (SCHEMATIC).

p, Dorsal digital nerves.

FIG. 670.—NERVES OF DISTAL PART OF RIGHT HIND LIMB OF OX; PLANTAR VIEW (SCHEMATIC).

p, Plantar digital nerves.

than in the horse, and arises by two or three bundles from the anterior cervical ganglion behind its middle. The **posterior cervical ganglion** is distinctly separable from the first thoracic; the latter is large. There are thirteen pairs of **thoracic ganglia**. The **great splanchnic nerve** begins at the fifth or sixth thoracic ganglion and receives branches from the succeeding ones; it is commonly difficult to distinguish clearly from the thoracic trunk. The **small splanchnic nerve** is represented apparently by filaments which go from the first lumbar ganglion to the adrenal plexus and the cœliac ganglion. The **cœliac ganglion** is rounded and lies on the cœliac artery. The **anterior mesenteric ganglion** is longer and is closely related to the anterior mesenteric artery. The two are connected by gangliated cords, and are similarly connected with the ganglia of the opposite side, so that the arrangement is plexiform. The **cœliac plexus** is more complex than that of the horse in correlation with the compound character of the stomach. The **posterior mesenteric ganglion** is small and is situated behind the artery of like name. It receives fibers from the last three or four lumbar ganglia and two fasciculi from the anterior mesenteric ganglia. The pelvic viscera receive branches from the posterior mesenteric ganglion and from the sacral ganglia; the latter number five pairs, and the right and left trunks are connected here by transverse anastomoses. The coccygeal trunks unite at a single fourth coccygeal ganglion, then separate, and reunite at the sixth coccygeal ganglion.

THE NERVOUS SYSTEM OF THE PIG

The **spinal cord** weighs about one and a half ounces (ca. 42 gm.). It is almost circular in cross-section, except at the enlargements, where it is somewhat flattened dorso-ventrally. The conus medullaris extends to the anterior part of the third sacral segment. The epidural space is occupied by a large quantity of fat.

The **brain** in adults of medium size weighs about four to four and a half ounces (ca. 125 gm.). When viewed from above, the **cerebrum** has an elongated oval form. The hemispheres are widest at the posterior third. The occipital pole is larger than the frontal pole. The **medulla oblongata** is relatively broad. The cuneate tubercle is very large and is limited laterally by a

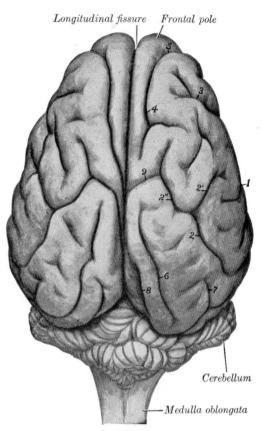

Longitudinal fissure   Frontal pole

Cerebellum

Medulla oblongata

FIG. 671.—BRAIN OF PIG; DORSAL VIEW; HARDENED *in situ.*

Fissures: *1*, Lateral, *2*, suprasylvian, with anterior (*2'*) and dorsal (*2''*) branches; *3*, diagonal; *4*, coronal; *5*, presylvian; *6*, marginal; *7*, ectomarginal; *8*, entomarginal; *9*, cruciate. Two different arrangements of the coronal and cruciate fissures are seen on the two sides.

groove. The corpus trapezoideum is very wide laterally. The **pons** is less prominent than in the ox. The **cerebellum** is very wide and short. Its anterior face is flattened and presents a depression for the corpora quadrigemina. The vermis is large. The hemispheres consist of a large medial part and a small lateral part. The **cerebral peduncles** are very short. The posterior corpora quadrigemina are wide apart, rounded, and relatively large. The medial geniculate body is prominent. The **cerebral hemispheres** are somewhat bean-shaped in lateral profile, the convex border being dorsal. The arrangement of the gyri and sulci is simpler than in the horse or ox.

The principal fissures are as follows:

1. The **lateral fissure** (of Sylvius) begins at the sulcus rhinalis and runs upward and somewhat backward on the depressed part of the lateral surface of the hemisphere: it appears

unbranched on superficial examination, but when the gyrus which almost completely conceals the insula is raised, an anterior branch is exposed which forms the dorsal boundary of the insula.

2. The **suprasylvian fissure** pursues a curved course approximately parallel with the dorso-medial border of the hemisphere. Its posterior end is separated by a short interval from the sulcus rhinalis posterior. From its highest point a branch proceeds obliquely upward and forward, crosses the dorso-medial border, and joins the cruciate fissure.

3. The **diagonal fissure** crosses the anterior part of the lateral surface. It is directed obliquely downward and backward.

4. The **coronal fissure** is constant and deep. It is directed upward and medially over the frontal pole, continues backward near the dorso-medial border, and often ends by passing obliquely over the border to the medial surface of the hemisphere. It is usually continuous in front with the presylvian fissure.

5. The **presylvian fissure** begins—apparently as a branch of the sulcus rhinalis anterior— about 2 cm. in front of the lateral fissure, and curves over the lateral aspect of the frontal pole.

6. The **marginal fissure** begins behind the cruciate fissure close to the dorso-medial border and extends in a gentle curve backward to the occipital pole.

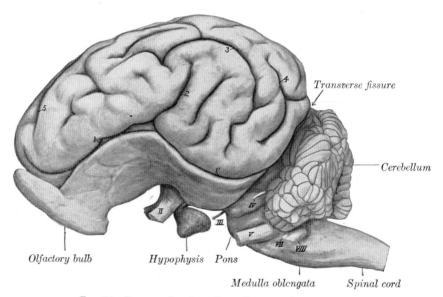

Fig. 672.—Brain of Pig; Left View; Hardened *in situ.*

Fissures: *1, 1',* Sulcus rhinalis; *2,* lateral; *3,* suprasylvian; *4,* ectomarginal; *5,* coronal. Stumps of cranial nerves indicated by Roman numerals.

7. The **ectomarginal fissure** lies above and nearly parallel to the posterior part of the suprasylvian fissure.

8. The **entomarginal fissure** lies along the posterior part of the dorso-medial border.

9. The **calloso-marginal fissure** consists of two separate parts. The more extensive posterior part is termed the **splenial fissure.** It extends from the tentorial aspect of the hemisphere in a direction parallel with the corpus callosum nearly to the middle of the medial surface; it is continued by the cruciate fissure and may be also connected with the coronal fissure by a branch which passes obliquely upward and forward. The anterior part, the **genual fissure,** lies about midway between the anterior part of the corpus callosum and the dorso-medial border.

10. The **cruciate fissure** runs obliquely upward and forward from the anterior end of the splenial fissure on the inner surface of the hemisphere, cuts obliquely into the dorso-medial margin about its middle, and usually joins the dorsal branch of the suprasylvian fissure.

11. The **sulcus rhinalis** extends in an undulating manner along the entire lower part of the lateral surface of the hemisphere and forms the upper limit of the rhinencephalon.

The **olfactory bulbs** are very large and the **tracts** extremely broad and short. The trigonum olfactorium is so prominent as to suggest the designation **tuberculum olfactorium.**

The **cranial nerves** present the following special features:

The **oculomotor, trochlear,** and **abducent nerves,** and the **ophthalmic** and **maxillary divisions** of the **fifth nerve** emerge together as in the ox.

The **lacrimal nerve** resembles that of the horse, the **frontal** that of the ox. The **naso-ciliary nerve** is relatively large and sends numerous filaments to the ocular muscles. The **maxillary nerve** has a very short course in the pterygo-palatine fossa. The **infraorbital nerve** is large in correlation with the development of the snout, which receives numerous branches. The **mandibular nerve** emerges through the foramen lacerum anterius. The **superficial temporal nerve** is small; according to Moussu it furnishes the excito-secretory fibers to the upper part of the parotid gland, while those going to the lower part are derived from the mylo-hyoid nerve.

The **inferior buccal nerve** passes downward and forward under cover of the parotid gland and accompanies the parotid duct, with which it turns around the lower border of the jaw in front of the masseter.

The **vagus** bears a **jugular ganglion** and a **ganglion nodosum**; the latter occurs

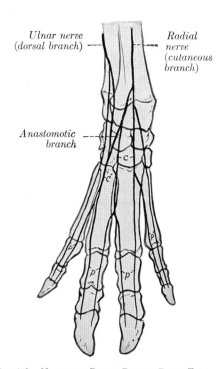

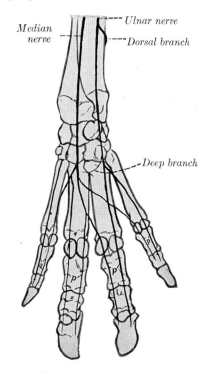

Fig. 673.—Nerves of Distal Part of Right Forelimb of Pig; Dorsal View (Schematic).

c, Dorsal common digital nerves; p, dorsal proper
digital nerves.

Fig. 674.—Nerves of Distal Part of Right Forelimb of Pig; Volar View (Schematic).

p, Volar proper digital nerves.

at the point of origin of the anterior laryngeal nerve, and may be as large as a small pea. Proximal to this the vagus is easily divided into two strands, one of which is the accessory component. The œsophageal trunks form a posterior œsophageal plexus, as in man, from which two nerves issue. The ventral nerve is small and ramifies on the parietal surface of the stomach. The dorsal nerve is much larger; it gives branches to the stomach, crosses the lesser curvature of that organ, and joins the cœliac plexus.

The **hypoglossal nerve** may present a small dorsal root, on which there is a minute hypoglossal ganglion.

The **spinal nerves** number on each side eight in the cervical region, fourteen (commonly) in the thoracic, seven in the lumbar, and four in the sacral. Some of the special features of the nerves of the limbs are as follows:

The **brachial plexus** is derived from the same nerves as in the ox, but the root furnished by the sixth cervical is relatively smaller. The plexus consists of two parts, the upper of which emerges above the scalenus, the lower between the two parts of that muscle. The more important differences in the nerves emanating from the plexus from the arrangement in the ox occur in the distal part of the limb. The cutaneous branch of the **radial nerve** divides at the carpus into branches which concur with the dorsal branch of the ulnar nerve in supplying the **dorsal digital nerves,** two for each digit. The **volar digital nerves,** also two for each digit, are formed by the terminal branches of the **median nerve** and the volar or deep branch of the **ulnar nerve.** The formation and arrangement of the digital nerves are indicated in the annexed schematic figures.

The **lumbo-sacral plexus** is derived from the ventral branches of the last three

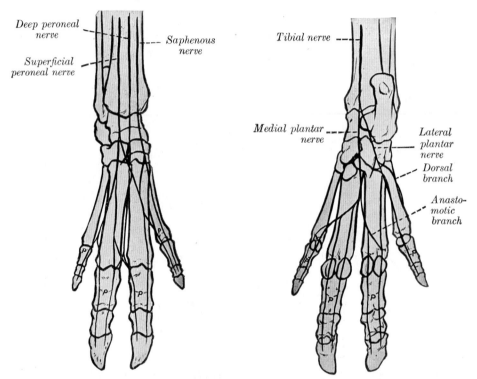

FIG. 675.—NERVES OF DISTAL PART OF RIGHT HIND LIMB OF PIG; DORSAL VIEW (SCHEMATIC).

p, Dorsal proper digital nerves.

FIG. 676.—NERVES OF DISTAL PART OF RIGHT HIND LIMB OF PIG; PLANTAR VIEW (SCHEMATIC).

p, Plantar proper digital nerves.

lumbar and first sacral nerves. The distribution of the branches of the plexus differs chiefly in the distal part of the limb. The **superficial peroneal nerve** is large and terminates by forming the greater part of the **dorsal digital nerves.** The latter, two for each digit, are also in part formed by the terminal branches of the **deep peroneal nerve.**

The **tibial nerve** divides at the tarsus into **medial** and **lateral plantar nerves.** The latter divide to form the **plantar digital nerves,** two for each digit. In addition, the lateral plantar nerve supplies a branch to the dorsal aspect of the lateral (fifth) digit. The arrangement of the digital nerves is indicated by the annexed schematic figures.

The **sympathetic system** of the pig has received very little attention from anatomists. The **anterior cervical ganglion** is long and fusiform. It gives off filaments which join the vagus near the ganglion nodosum.   The **cervical trunk** is short and relatively larger than in the ox; it is enclosed in a common sheath with the vagus in the neck and separates from that nerve to join the **middle cervical ganglion** at the thoracic inlet.

THE NERVOUS SYSTEM OF THE DOG

The **spinal cord** is almost circular in cross-section except at the well-marked cervical and lumbar enlargements, where it is compressed dorso-ventrally.   The conus medullaris lies over the junction of the sixth and seventh lumbar vertebræ. The length of the cord of a rather large dog was found to be about fifteen inches (ca. 38 cm.); of this, the cervical part was about four and a half inches (ca. 11 cm.), the thoracic a little less than seven inches (17.4 cm.), the lumbar a little less than three inches (ca. 7 cm.), and the sacro-coccygeal about an inch (ca. 2.6 cm.) (Flatau-Jacobson).

The **brain** weighs about two to two and a half ounces (ca. 60–70 gm.) in dogs of medium size, but there is, of course, a wide range of weight in the different breeds. Thus in small terriers the weight is about an ounce (ca. 30 gm.) or even less, while in very large dogs it may exceed five ounces (ca. 150 gm.).   It corresponds much more closely with the external form of the cranium in size and general form than in the animals previously described; this is specially true of the small breeds, in which the bony crests and frontal sinuses are little developed.

The **medulla oblongata** is broad and thick.   Its ventral surface is strongly convex from side to side.   The pyramids are large and prominent and are limited by a distinct median fissure and lateral grooves.   The median fissure ends at a small depression, the **foramen cæcum,** just behind the pons.   The olivary eminence is a well-defined oval elevation situated between the pyramid and the superficial origin of the hypoglossal nerve.   The external arcuate fibers form a wide band which crosses the lateral surface obliquely upward and forward, and obscures the facial tubercle and the groove which limits the restiform body laterally.   The cuneate tubercle is distinct.   The rhomboid fossa is deep and narrow.   The fourth ventricle communicates with the subarachnoid space on each side through a lateral aperture.

The **pons** is relatively small, and in correlation with this fact the **corpus trapezoideum** is very wide; it is divided by the pyramids into two lateral parts.   The **cerebellum** is very broad, but is low and also compressed from before backward. Rather more than half of it is overlapped by the cerebral hemispheres.   The anterior surface is accurately adapted to the concave tentorial surfaces of the hemispheres and to the posterior corpora quadrigemina and their commissure.   The posterior surface is almost vertical and is convex centrally and flattened laterally. The vermis is prominent and in general well defined, although it is connected in its middle part with the hemispheres.   The latter are three-sided and consist of four lobules.   The small lobule lateral to the origins of the facial and acoustic nerves is the flocculus.   Lateral to this, and separated from it by a deep fissure, is the paraflocculus; this is divided into dorsal and ventral parts by a sagittal fissure. The anterior peduncles are very short.

The **posterior corpora quadrigemina** are large, very wide apart, and prominent, and are connected by a curved commissure.   The **medial geniculate body** is large and distinct.   In the deep interpeduncular fossa are two small bands which indicate the course of the fasciculi retroflexi, tracts which connect the habenular and interpeduncular ganglia.   The **mammillary body** is double.   The **tuber cinereum** is relatively large.   The **hypophysis** or **pituitary body** is circular and rather small.

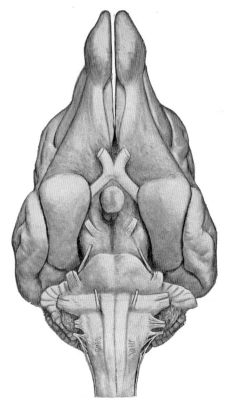

FIG. 677.—BASE OF BRAIN OF DOG; HARDENED *in situ.*

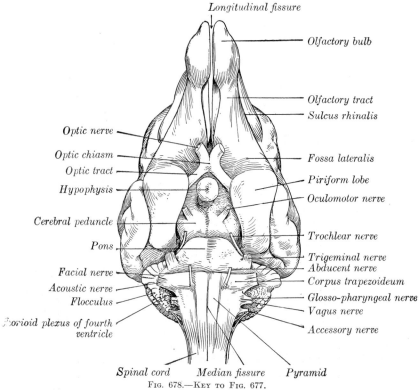

Longitudinal fissure

Olfactory bulb

Olfactory tract
Sulcus rhinalis

Optic nerve

Optic chiasm
Optic tract

Hypophysis

Fossa lateralis

Piriform lobe

Oculomotor nerve

Cerebral peduncle

Pons

Trochlear nerve

Trigeminal nerve
Abducent nerve

Facial nerve
Acoustic nerve
Flocculus

Corpus trapezoideum

Glosso-pharyngeal nerve
Vagus nerve

Chorioid plexus of fourth ventricle

Accessory nerve

Spinal cord   *Median fissure*   *Pyramid*

FIG. 678.—KEY TO FIG. 677.

Root bundles of hypoglossal nerve are shown lateral to pyramid in Fig. 677, but are not indicated in key figure.

The **cerebral hemispheres** are very broad behind and diminish in width anteriorly; there is a sudden narrowing at the frontal poles, which are flattened laterally. The tentorial surfaces are concave and form a deep cavity which receives the anterior part of the cerebellum. The arrangement of the fissures and gyri is simpler than in the animals previously examined.

The chief fissures are as follows:

1. The **lateral fissure** extends upward and backward from the sulcus rhinalis a little behind the middle of the lateral surface of the hemisphere.

2. The **ectosylvian fissure** has approximately the shape of an inverted **U**, and curves over the lateral fissure. It is regarded as consisting of three parts—anterior, middle, and posterior (F. ectosylvia anterior, media, posterior).

3. The **suprasylvian fissure** lies above and approximately concentric with the preceding. It also consists of three parts—anterior, middle, and posterior.

4. The **ectomarginal** or **collateral fissure** runs forward on the dorsal aspect of the hemisphere almost parallel with the dorso-medial border. A little in front of the middle of the surface it gives off a short **ansate fissure** (F. ansata) which runs obliquely medially and forward. It is usually continued anteriorly by the coronal fissure, and may be in continuity posteriorly with the **medilateral** (or post-lateral) **fissure.**

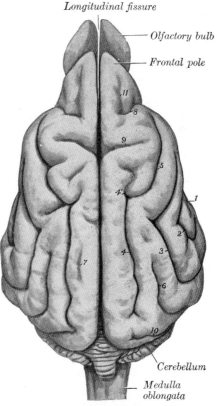

Longitudinal fissure

— *Olfactory bulb*

— *Frontal pole*

Cerebellum

— *Medulla oblongata*

FIG. 680.—BRAIN OF DOG; DORSAL VIEW.

Fissures: *1*, Lateral; *2*, ectosylvian; *3*, suprasylvian; *4*, ectomarginal (or collateral); *4'*, ansate; *5*, coronal; *6*, ectolateral; *7*, entomarginal; *8*, presylvian (or orbital); *9*, cruciate; *10*, medilateral (separated from entomarginal on right side, but connected with it on left hemisphere); *11*, f. proreæ.

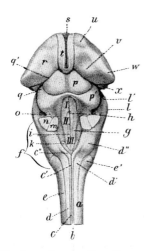

FIG. 679.—BRAIN STEM OF DOG; DORSAL VIEW.

a, Spinal cord; *b*, dorsal median groove; *c, c'*, funiculus gracilis; *c''*, clava; *d, d'*, funiculus cuneatus; *d''*, tuberculum cuneatum; *e*, funiculus lateralis: *e'*, tuberculum cinereum; *f*, medulla oblongata; *I, II, III*, foveæ of floor of fourth ventricle (fossa rhomboidea); *g*, limiting groove; *h*, median fissure; *i*, eminentia medialis; *k*, ala cinera; *l, l'*, pons; *m*, posterior peduncle, and *n*, middle peduncle, of cerebellum (cut); *o*, anterior peduncle of cerebellum; *p, p'*, corpora quadrigemina, anterior and posterior; *q, q'*, peduncles (brachia) of corpora quadrigemina; *r*, thalamus; *s*, massa intermedia; *t*, stria medullaris; *u*, anterior tubercle of thalamus; *v*, pulvinar; *w*, corpus geniculatum laterale; *x*, corpus geniculatum mediale. (After Ellenberger, in Leisering's Atlas.)

5. The **coronal fissure** is usually the continuation of the ectomarginal. It runs forward and downward, curving around the cruciate fissure, and ends behind the middle of the presylvian fissure.

6. The **ectolateral fissure** lies between the posterior part of the ectomarginal fissure and the suprasylvian fissure.

7. The **entomarginal fissure** lies between the anterior part of the ectomarginal fissure and the dorso-medial border. It is often indistinct and not rarely absent.

8. The **presylvian fissure**—sometimes termed the orbital—begins at the sulcus rhinalis, a little in front of its middle, and curves over the anterior third of the lateral surface of the hemisphere in front of the coronal fissure.

9. The **cruciate fissure** is the deepest and most characteristic. It cuts deeply into the anterior third of the dorso-medial border and runs almost straight outward. It is continuous on the medial surface of the hemisphere with the calloso-marginal or splenial fissure.

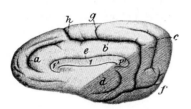

FIG. 681.—RIGHT CEREBRAL HEMISPHERE OF DOG; MEDIAL VIEW.

1, Corpus callosum; *1′*, genu; *1″*, splenium of corpus callosum; *a*, genual fissure; *b*, splenial fissure; *c*, suprasplenial fissure; *d*, hippocampal fissure; *e*, sulcus corporis callosi; *f*, postsplenial fissure; *g*, lesser cruciate fissure; *h*, cruciate fissure. (After Ellenberger, in Leisering's Atlas.)

10. The **sulcus rhinalis** is continued on the tentorial surface of the hemisphere by the occipito-temporal fissure. Anteriorly it is prolonged as the olfactory fissure, which is concealed by the olfactory bulb and tract..

11. The **calloso-marginal fissure** usually consists of two parts, splenial and genual. The **splenial fissure** is parallel with the splenium and middle part of the corpus callosum on the medial surface of the hemisphere. It is continuous in front with the cruciate fissure and runs forward and outward across the tentorial surface to join the occipito-temporal or calcarine fissure. It gives off from its highest part the short accessory cruciate fissure. The **genual fissure** is approximately parallel with the genu of the corpus callosum.

12. The **suprasplenial fissure** runs almost parallel with the posterior part of the calloso-marginal fissure on the inner and tentorial surfaces of the hemisphere.

13. The **occipito-temporal** or **calcarine fissure** is the continuation on the tentorial surface of the hemisphere of the splenial fissure.

14. The **hippocampal fissure** forms the medial boundary of the piriform lobe.

The **olfactory bulb** is large and is compressed laterally; its anterior end projects beyond the frontal pole of the hemisphere. The tract is short and is also flattened laterally. Both contain a narrow cavity which communicates with the lateral ventricle. The **piriform lobe** is large and rounded.

The **cranial nerves** present the following special features which are worthy of notice:

The **ophthalmic nerve** gives off frontal, long ciliary, ethmoidal, and infratrochlear branches. The **lacrimal nerve** arises from the ophthalmic at its origin;[1] its recurrent branch emerges at the orbital ligament and concurs with the zygomatic and frontal nerves in the formation of the anterior auricular plexus. The **frontal nerve** emerges from the orbit in front of the upper end of the orbital ligament, ramifies in the upper lid and the adjacent skin of the forehead, and sends branches backward to the anterior auricular plexus. The **long ciliary nerve** accompanies the optic nerve and divides into several branches which pierce the posterior part of the sclera. The **ethmoidal nerve** gives off internal nasal branches and ends in the muzzle. The **infratrochlear nerve** runs forward between the medial straight and the superior oblique muscles of the eye and ramifies on the face in the vicinity of the medial canthus.

The **maxillary nerve** emerges through the foramen rotundum and gives off five branches. The **lacrimal nerve** emerges from the orbit lateral to the frontal; its branches concur with the frontal and auriculo-palpebral nerves in the formation of the anterior auricular plexus. The **zygomatic nerve** emerges through an opening in the upper part of the orbital ligament and ramifies in the lower lid and on the adjacent surface of the face. The **infraorbital nerves,** two in number, divide within the infraorbital canal and after their emergence upon the face, thus forming seven or eight **external nasal** and **superior labial branches.** The **sphenopalatine nerve** gives off **lesser** and **greater palatine** and **posterior nasal nerves.**

The **mandibular nerve** passes out through the foramen ovale. The **superficial temporal nerve** divides into auricular, temporal, and malar branches; the last-named crosses the masseter and ramifies with the buccal nerves. The **mylo-hyoid nerve** is given off from the mandibular nerve almost immediately after the latter emerges from the cranium; it innervates the mylo-hyoideus and occipito-mandibularis and gives off a branch which turns around the lower jaw, joins the inferior

---

[1] The origin of the lacrimal nerve is such that Ellenberger-Baum and Martin describe it as a branch of the maxillary nerve.

buccal nerve, and ramifies on the lateral surface of the face.   The **inferior alveolar nerve** arises by a common trunk with the mylo-hyoid; it gives off dental branches and terminates in mental and inferior labial branches.   The **lingual nerve** supplies vaso-dilator and excito-secretory filaments to the mandibular and sublingual salivary glands; these fibers are derived from the chorda tympani.

The **facial nerve** divides near the posterior border of the jaw into four branches. The upper branch is the **auriculo-palpebral nerve,** which divides after a very short course into anterior auricular and zygomatic branches.   The latter curves upward and forward across the zygomatic arch toward the eye, and divides into branches which supply the eyelids and nasal region and concur with the frontal and lacrimal nerves in forming the anterior auricular plexus.   The **superior buccal nerve** accompanies the parotid duct across the masseter.   The **inferior buccal nerve** runs forward along the lower border of the masseter and the mandible.   The two nerves

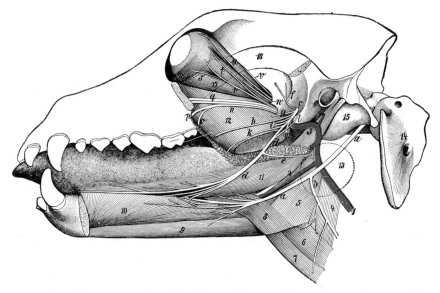

FIG. 682.—DEEP DISSECTION OF HEAD OF DOG, SHOWING ESPECIALLY TRIGEMINAL AND HYPOGLOSSAL NERVES.

a, Hypoglossal nerve; *b*, cervical branch of *a;* *c*, mandibular division of trigeminus; *d*, lingual nerve; *e*, nerve to mandibular gland; *f*, deep temporal nerve; *g*, pterygoid nerve; *h*, buccinator nerve (cut); *i*, inferior alveolar nerve; *k*, staphyline branch of lingual nerve; *l*, chorda tympani; *m*, mylo-hyoid nerve; *n*, sphenopalatine nerve; *o*, lesser palatine nerve; *p*, great palatine nerve; *q*, infraorbital nerve; *r*, n. subcutaneus malæ; *s*, branch of oculomotor nerve to inferior oblique muscle; *t*, lacrimal nerve; *u*, frontal nerve; *v*, trochlear nerve; *w*, abducens nerve; *1*, carotid artery; *2*, lingual artery; *3*, internal maxillary artery; *4*, m. thyro-pharyngeus; *5*, m. hyo-pharyngeus; *6*, m. thyro-hyoideus; *7*, m. sterno-hyoideus; *8*, m. hyo-glossus; *9*, m. genio-hyoideus; *10*, m. genio-glossus; *11*, m. stylo-glossus; *12*, m. pterygoideus medialis; *13*, outline of mandibular gland (dotted); *14*, atlas; *15*, bulla ossea; *16*, zygomatic arch (dotted); *17*, m. rectus oculi inferior; *18*, m. obliquus oculi inferior.   (Ellenberger-Baum, Anat. d. Hundes.)

ramify on the cheek and anastomose with each other and the infraorbital nerves to form a plexus from which branches go to the muscles of the lips and nostrils. The **cervical branch** runs downward and backward over the mandibular gland and ramifies in the cervical cutaneus muscle; it communicates with the inferior buccal nerve and sends twigs to the parotido-auricularis muscle and the mandibular space.

The **vagus** bears a **ganglion jugulare** and a **ganglion nodosum.**   The former is situated on the nerve just before the emergence of the latter from the cranium.   The latter is situated near the anterior cervical ganglion on the rectus capitis ventralis major and dorsal to the internal carotid artery; it is fusiform and may be about half an inch (ca. 1–1.5 cm.) long in a large dog.   In its course in the neck the nerve is enclosed with the sympathetic trunk in a common sheath and is related ventrally to the common carotid artery. The two nerves separate after entering the thorax (Figs. 613, 614). The right vagus crosses obliquely over the right face of the trachea and divides a short distance behind the bifurcation of the latter into dorsal and ventral branches. The left vagus crosses the lateral surface of the aortic arch and divides similarly. By the union of the dorsal and ventral divisions of the two nerves there are formed dorsal and ventral œsophageal trunks. The **dorsal trunk** concurs with branches of the cœliac plexus in forming the **posterior gastric plexus** on the visceral surface of the stomach. The **ventral trunk** ramifies on the parietal surface of the stomach, forming the **anterior gastric plexus,** from which a considerable branch passes along the lesser curvature to the pylorus. Some special features of the collateral branches are: Two pharyngeal branches are present. The **anterior pharyngeal branch** arises from the vagus above the ganglion nodosum. It passes under the deep face of the carotid artery and descends on the lateral surface of the pharynx to end in the crico-thyroid muscle. It furnishes a root of the inferior pharyngeal branch, and communicates with the pharyngeal branch of the ninth and with the

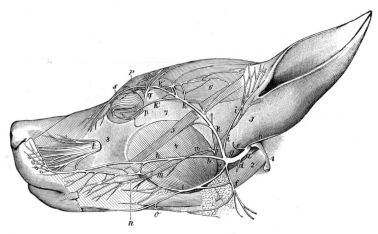

FIG. 683.—NERVES OF FACE OF DOG. PAROTID GLAND IS REMOVED.

Nerves: *a*, Facial; *b*, posterior auricular; *c*, internal auricular; *d*, digastric; *e*, inferior buccal; *f*, cervical branch of facial; *g*, auriculo-palpebral; *h*, superior buccal; *i*, temporal branch; *k, k′, k″*, zygomatic branch; *l*, auriculo-temporal; *m*, malar branch of *l; n*, buccinator; *o*, mylo-hyoid branch; *p*, subcutaneus malæ; *q*, lacrimal; *r*, frontal; *s*, infratrochlear; *t*, infraorbital. *1*, Paramastoid process; *2*, occipito-mandibularis; *3*, base of concha; *4*, masseter; *5*, zygomaticus; *6*, scutularis; *7*, zygomatic arch; *8*, maxilla. (Ellenberger-Baum, Anat. d. Hundes.)

anterior laryngeal and hypoglossal nerves. The **posterior pharyngeal branch** is formed by the union of roots derived from the anterior pharyngeal nerve and the ganglion nodosum, together with filaments from the anterior cervical ganglion. It crosses the side of the pharynx behind the anterior pharyngeal and ramifies on the posterior constrictor of the pharynx and the origin of the œsophagus. It contributes filaments to the pharyngeal plexus, communicates with the recurrent nerve, and supplies twigs to the thyroid gland. The **pharyngeal plexus** is formed on the lateral surface of the pharynx by branches of the pharyngeal nerves and the communications above described; branches from it innervate the muscles and mucous membrane of the pharynx. The **anterior laryngeal nerve** arises from the ganglion nodosum and descends over the side of the pharynx, crossing beneath the carotid artery and the anterior pharyngeal nerve. It passes through the thyroid notch and ramifies in the mucous membrane of the larynx. It communicates with the anterior cervical ganglion and the anterior pharyngeal branch of the vagus, and gives twigs to the hyo-pharyngeus muscle. Immediately after its entrance into the larynx it gives off a large branch which, besides uniting with the recurrent as in the other animals, has a peculiar arrangement. It runs back near the dorsal border of the thyroid cartilage, gives a branch to the crico-arytenoideus dorsalis as it passes over that muscle, and continues along the trachea medial to the recurrent nerve. At the thoracic inlet it communicates with the posterior cervical ganglion and continues backward to unite with the vagus at or near the point of origin of the recurrent nerve. Its collateral filaments supply the trachea and concur with the posterior pharyngeal branch in forming a plexus on the cervical part of the œsophagus which innervates that tube.[1] The **recurrent nerves** present no remarkable special features. The **depressor nerve** is a very delicate filament which arises usually from the anterior laryngeal nerve and is incorporated in the vago-sympathetic trunk to the thorax. Here the nerve separates from the ventral border of the vago-sympathetic trunk. The right nerve passes backward between the anterior vena cava and the trachea, inclines to the left, and reaches the medial surface of the aortic arch. The left nerve passes backward ventral to the vagus and across the lateral (left) face of the aortic arch. Both nerves give filaments to the cardiac nerves and to the aorta and pulmonary artery. Their terminal branches pass between these vessels and enter the wall of the heart. The **pulmonary** and **posterior œsophageal plexuses** are highly developed.

The **hypoglossal nerve** gives off a long branch (R. descendens) which runs downward and backward across the pharynx and larynx, communicates with the ventral branch of the first cervical nerve, and supplies the thyro-hyoid, sterno-hyoid, and sterno-thyroid muscles.

The **spinal nerves** number thirty-six or thirty-seven on either side, and comprise eight cervical, thirteen thoracic, seven lumbar, and five or six coccygeal.

The **brachial plexus** (Fig. 616) is derived from the ventral branches of the last four cervical and first thoracic nerves; the root supplied by the fifth cervical nerve is very small. The roots unite at the ventral border of the scalenus. The more important special features in the arrangement of the nerves which emanate from the plexus are as follows:

The **musculo-cutaneous nerve** passes between the coraco-brachialis and the brachial artery and descends in the arm in front of the artery. At the shoulder joint it gives off branches to the biceps and coraco-brachialis, and in the distal third of the arm is connected with the median nerve by an oblique branch. It terminates near the elbow by dividing into a branch for the brachialis and a small cutaneous nerve which passes down over the medial face of the elbow and, inclining a little forward, descends over the deep fascia of the forearm to the carpus.

The **radial nerve** descends behind the ulnar nerve, gives branches to the extensors of the elbow, dips in between the medial and the accessory heads of the triceps, winds around the arm, and divides between the brachialis and the lateral head of the triceps into two branches. The **deep branch** (R. profundus) supplies the extensor and supinator muscles on the forearm. The **superficial branch** (R. superficialis) emerges upon the flexor surface of the elbow and divides into two branches which terminate by supplying two **dorsal digital nerves** to each digit, except the fifth, which receives its lateral dorsal nerve from the ulnar. The medial branch descends along the medial side of the cephalic vein to the carpus, where it divides into dorsal nerves for the first digit and the medial side of the second. The lateral branch is much larger. It descends on the middle of the front of the forearm and supplies the remaining dorsal digital nerves except that to the lateral side of the fifth digit.

The **ulnar nerve** is as large as or larger than the median, with which it is united for some distance. At the distal third of the arm it separates from the median and passes over the medial epicondyle of the humerus. At the proximal part of

---

[1] Lesbre terms this the tracheo-œsophageal branch, and considers that it must be regarded as an accessory or internal recurrent nerve.

the forearm it gives off the **dorsal branch** (R. dorsalis), which supplies cutaneous twigs to the dorso-lateral surface of the distal part of the forearm and carpus and terminates as the **lateral dorsal digital nerve** of the fifth digit. Descending under cover of the flexor carpi ulnaris, the ulnar inclines medially under the tendon of insertion of that muscle and divides into superficial and deep branches. The **superficial branch** (R. superficialis) descends along the lateral border of the flexor tendons, gives off the **lateral volar digital nerve of the fifth digit** (N. dig. vol. lat. dig. V), and a branch (N. met. vol. IV) which descends in the space between the fourth and fifth metacarpal bones and unites with the deep branch. The **deep branch** (R. profundus) descends in the carpal canal and divides under the deep flexor

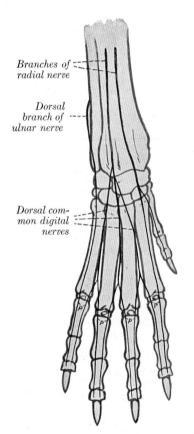

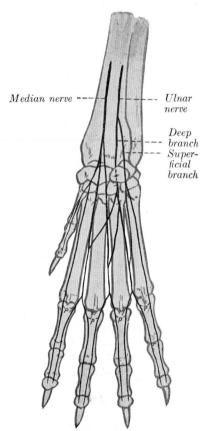

Branches of radial nerve

Dorsal branch of ulnar nerve

Dorsal common digital nerves

Median nerve

Ulnar nerve

Deep branch

Superficial branch

FIG. 684.—NERVES OF DISTAL PART OF RIGHT FORE-LIMB OF DOG; DORSAL VIEW (SCHEMATIC).

p, Dorsal proper digital nerves.

FIG. 685.—NERVES OF DISTAL PART OF RIGHT FORE-LIMB OF DOG; VOLAR VIEW (SCHEMATIC).

p, Volar proper digital nerves.

tendon into its terminal branches. The smaller of these supply the volar meta-carpal muscles. The larger terminals are the three **volar common digital nerves** (Nn. dig. col. comm. II, III, IV), which descend along the second, third, and fourth intermetacarpal spaces, subdivide, and concur with the volar metacarpal branches of the median nerve in forming the **volar proper digital nerves** (Nn. dig. vol. proprii).

The **median nerve** descends behind the brachial artery, passes over the medial epicondyle of the humerus, then under the pronator teres, and continues in the forearm under cover of the flexor carpi radialis. It gives branches below the elbow to the flexor and pronator muscles, and lower down a volar branch to the skin on the medial and volar aspect of the carpus, and terminates between the superficial and deep flexor tendons by dividing into three **volar metacarpal nerves** (N. met. vol.

I, II, III). These descend in the first, second, and third intermetacarpal spaces and unite with the volar common digital nerves in forming volar proper digital nerves. The arrangement of the digital nerves is indicated in the annexed schematic figures.

The **lumbo-sacral plexus** is formed from the ventral branches of the last five lumbar and first sacral nerves. The more important special facts in regard to the nerves of the pelvic limb are as follows:

The **saphenous nerve** (Fig. 621) is relatively large, and, in fact, might be considered as the continuation of the femoral nerve. It descends at first in front of the femoral artery, then passes over the lower part of the medial surface of the thigh with the saphenous artery, continues down the leg with the dorsal branch of

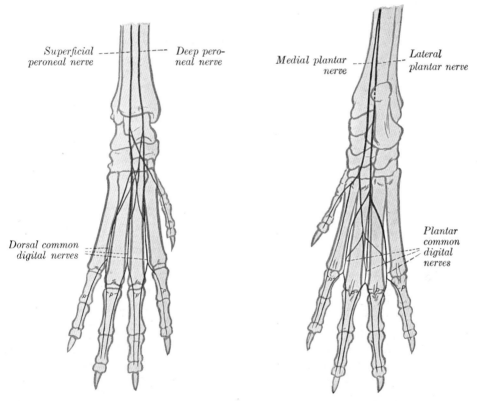

FIG. 686.—NERVES OF DISTAL PART OF RIGHT HIND LIMB OF DOG, DORSAL VIEW (SCHEMATIC).

p, Dorsal proper digital nerves.

FIG. 687.—NERVES OF DISTAL PART OF RIGHT HIND LIMB OF DOG, PLANTAR VIEW (SCHEMATIC).

p, Plantar proper digital nerves.

that vessel, and anastomoses with branches of the superficial peroneal nerve. It supplies cutaneous twigs from the stifle to the metatarsus.

The **common peroneal nerve** separates from the tibial above the origin of the gastrocnemius, runs downward and forward across the lateral head of that muscle, passes between the deep flexor of the digit and the peroneus longus, and divides into superficial and deep branches. The **superficial peroneal nerve** descends the leg along the peroneus tertius and longus, gives off a **dorsal branch** to the first digit (N. cutaneus dorsalis medialis), and divides at the proximal part of the metatarsus into three **dorsal common digital nerves** (Nn. dig. pedis dors. comm. II, III, IV). These descend with the superficial dorsal metatarsal arteries and concur with branches of the deep peroneal nerve in forming **dorsal proper digital nerves** (Nn. dig. ped. prop. dorsales). The **deep peroneal nerve** passes down the leg with the anterior tibial vessels.   It gives twigs to the hock joint and the extensor brevis muscle, and divides into three **dorsal metatarsal nerves** (Nn. met. dors. II, III, IV); these descend with the corresponding arteries along the intermetatarsal spaces and unite with the dorsal common digital nerves in supplying the dorsal proper digital nerves.

The **tibial nerve** divides at the tarsus into two plantar branches.   The **medial plantar nerve** descends along the medial border of the superficial flexor tendon and divides near the middle of the metatarsus into two branches.   Of these, the medial branch constitutes the **first plantar common digital nerve** (N. dig. comm. plant. I). The lateral branch descends on the superficial flexor tendon and divides into three **plantar metatarsal nerves** (Nn. met. plant. II, III, IV), which unite with the plantar common digital nerves.   The **lateral plantar nerve** passes down between the flexor tendons, sends twigs to the muscles on the plantar surface of the metatarsus, and divides into three **plantar common digital nerves** (Nn. dig. comm. plant. II, III, IV).   These descend with the deep plantar metatarsal arteries in the second, third, and fourth intermetatarsal spaces, receive the plantar metatarsal nerves, and divide into **plantar proper digital nerves,** which pass down the opposed surfaces of the second to the fifth digits.

The **sympathetic system** presents few special features worthy of mention. The **anterior cervical ganglion** is situated behind the bulla tympanica in close relation to the internal carotid artery and the ganglion nodosum of the vagus.   It is fusiform and is a little less than half an inch (ca. 1 cm.) long in a dog of medium size. It forms connections directly or through the carotid plexus with the last seven cranial and first cervical nerves.   The **cervical trunk** unites with the vagus so intimately as to form a vago-sympathetic trunk.   The **posterior cervical ganglion** is situated at the point where the sympathetic trunk separates from the vagus (Figs. 613, 614).   It is usually distinct from the first thoracic ganglion, which is stellate and lies on the longus colli opposite the first space.   The two are connected by filaments which cross each side of the brachial artery, forming the ansa subclavia.   Two or three **cardiac nerves** proceed from these ganglia on the left side; they pass to the lateral surface of the aortic arch, where they ramify and concur with the nerves of the right side in the formation of the cardiac plexus.   On the right side one or two cardiac nerves appear to come from the vagus and one from the first thoracic ganglion.   They ramify on the right side of the trachea and with those of the right side form the cardiac plexus at the base of the heart.   From the plexus branches go to the heart, pericardium, and pulmonary artery.   The **greater splanchnic nerve** separates from the posterior part of the thoracic trunk, most often from the twelfth ganglion.   It passes into the abdomen between the diaphragm and the psoas minor and joins a small adrenal ganglion close to the cœliac ganglion. The **lesser splanchnic nerve** arises from the last thoracic and first lumbar ganglia. It may be divided into two or three strands which go to the adrenal plexus.

The **cœliac** and **anterior mesenteric ganglia** are separate.   The former is elongated and lies along the posterior face of the origin of the cœliac artery.   The latter is smaller and rounded and is in contact with the origin of the anterior mesenteric artery.   On the left side the two ganglia are connected by a trunk which is ganglionic in character.   The **cœliac, anterior mesenteric,** and **subsidiary plexuses** enlace the corresponding arteries.   There is a small elongated **posterior mesenteric ganglion** in relation to the origin of the posterior mesenteric artery.   The **posterior mesenteric plexus** includes **left colic, anterior hæmorrhoidal,** and **spermatic plexuses.** The **lumbar trunk** is deeply placed at the medial side of the psoas minor.   It has seven ganglia, which are very small, with the exception of the last.   There is a well-developed aortic plexus.   The **sacral trunks** are close to the middle sacral artery and have each three ganglia when this part is fully developed.   The **caudal trunks** lie on each side of the coccygeal artery; the number and arrangement of the visible ganglia are variable.   The **pelvic plexus** is well developed and contains minute ganglia.

ÆSTHESIOLOGY

THE SENSE ORGANS AND COMMON INTEGUMENT

The **organs of the senses** (Organa sensuum) receive external stimuli and conduct impulses to the brain which result in sensations of sight, hearing, taste, smell, and touch. They consist essentially of specially differentiated cells (neuro-epithelium) and a conduction path which is simple in the more generalized sense organs, elaborate in those which are highly specialized—the eye and the ear.

THE SENSE ORGANS AND SKIN OF THE HORSE

THE EYE

The **eye** or **organ of vision** (Organon visus) in the broader sense of the term comprises the eyeball or globe of the eye, the optic nerve, and certain accessory organs associated therewith. The accessory organs (Organa oculi accessoria) are the orbital fasciæ and muscles, the eyelids and conjunctiva, and the lacrimal apparatus. These structures will be considered in the order in which they may be most conveniently examined, taking the horse as a type. The bony walls of the orbit have been described in connection with the skull; the periorbita, a fibrous membrane which encloses the eyeball together with its muscles, vessels, and nerves, may be appropriately included in the account of the fasciæ.

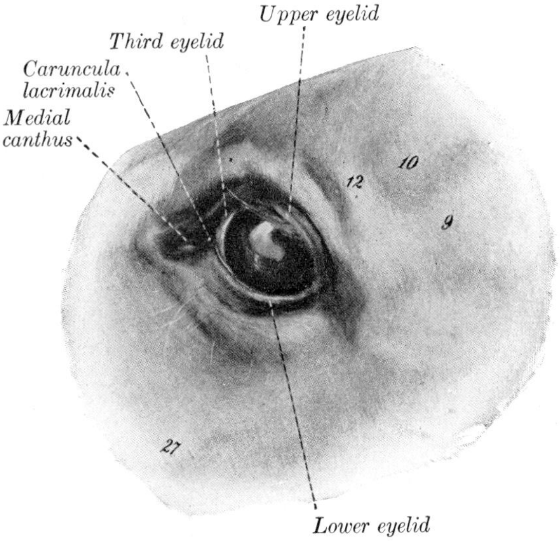

FIG. 688.—LEFT EYE OF HORSE.

9, Zygomatic arch; *10*, supraorbital depression; *12*, supraorbital process; *27*, facial crest. (After Ellenberger-Baum, Anat. für Künstler.)

THE EYELIDS AND CONJUNCTIVA

The **eyelids,** upper and lower (Palpebra superior et inferior), are movable folds of integument situated in front of the eyeball. When closed, they cover the entrance to the orbit and the anterior surface of the eyeball. The upper lid is much more extensive and more movable than the lower one, and its free edge is more concave. The interval between the lids is termed the **palpebral fissure** (Rima palpebrarum). When the eye is closed, it is an oblique slit about two inches (ca. 5 cm.) in length; when open, it is biconvex in outline. The ends of the fissure are the **angles** or canthi, and are distinguished as **medial** and **lateral** (Angulus oculi medialis, lateralis). The lateral angle is rounded when the eye is open, but the medial angle is narrowed and produced to form a ⊃-shaped bay or recess, termed the **lacrimal lake** (Lacus lacrimalis). In this there is a rounded pigmented prominence known as the **lacrimal caruncle** (Caruncula lacrimalis); it is about the size of a small pea, and is covered with modified skin, connected with that of the medial commissure, from which project a number of hairs provided with sebaceous glands. The lids unite on either side and form the **commissures,** medial and lateral (Commissura palpebrarum medialis, lateralis). The **anterior surface** of the lids (Facies anterior palpebrarum) is convex and is covered with very short hair. A considerable number of tactile hairs are scattered over the lower part of the lower lid, but on the upper lid they are very scanty. The infrapalpebral depression (Sulcus infrapalpebralis) indicates somewhat indistinctly the limit of the lower lid. The upper lid is marked by two furrows when raised. The **posterior surface** (Facies posterior palpebrarum) is adapted to the free surface of the eyeball and is covered by the palpebral conjunctiva. The free border of the lid is smooth and usually black. It has a well-defined posterior margin (Limbus palpebralis posterior), along which the ducts of the tarsal glands open. The anterior margin (Limbus palpebralis anterior) bears stiff hairs termed the **cilia** (eyelashes). On the upper lid the cilia are long and numerous except at its medial third, where they are very small or absent. On the lower lid the cilia are often scarcely distinguishable from the ordinary hairs; in other cases they may be clearly seen except near the lateral canthus, and are much finer and shorter than those of the upper lid. The edge of each lid is pierced near the medial angle by a minute, slit-like opening, the **punctum lacrimale,** which is the entrance to the lacrimal duct.

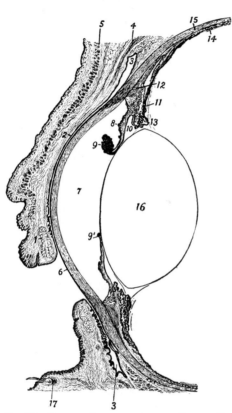

FIG. 689.—VERTICAL SECTION OF ANTERIOR PART OF EYE OF HORSE, WITH LIDS HALF CLOSED.

1, Tarsal gland of upper lid; *2,* palpebral conjunctiva; *3,* fornix conjunctivæ; *4,* levator palpebræ superioris; *5,* orbicularis oculi; *6,* cornea; *7,* anterior chamber; *8,* iris; *9, 9′,* granula iridis; *10,* posterior chamber; *11,* ciliary process; *12,* ciliary muscle; *13,* ciliary zone or suspensory lig. of lens; *14,* chorioid; *15,* sclera; *16,* lens; *17,* root of tactile hair. (After Bayer, Augenheilkunde.)

The **skin** of the eyelids is thin and freely movable, except near the free edge, where it is more firmly attached. The underlying subcutaneous tissue is destitute of fat. The **muscular layer** consists chiefly of the elliptical bundles of the orbicularis oculi, with which are associated fibers of the corrugator supercilii in the upper lid and the malaris in the lower lid. At the medial side there is a fibrous band, the **palpebral ligament,** which is attached to the lacrimal tubercle and furnishes origin to some fibers of the orbicularis. At the medial commissure a bundle detached from the orbicularis passes inward behind the lacrimal sac, and is known as the pars lacrimalis (or Horner's muscle). At the lateral side an indistinct palpebral raphé occurs where fibers of the orbicularis decussate. The **fibrous layer** is thicker and denser along the free edge of the lid, forming here the **tarsus.** The tarsus furnishes insertion to a layer of unstriped muscle known as the tarsal muscle. The **tarsal glands** (Glandulæ tarsales)[1] are partly embedded in the deep face of the tarsus, and are visible when the lid is everted if the conjunctiva is not too strongly pigmented. They are arranged in a linear series, close together, and with their long axes perpendicular to the free edge of each lid. In the upper lid they number forty-five to fifty; in the lower, thirty to thirty-five. Each consists of a tubular duct beset with numerous alveoli, in which a fatty substance, the **palpebral sebum,** is secreted. The **palpebral conjunctiva** lines the internal surface of the eyelids.

The **conjunctiva** is the mucous membrane which lines the lids as **palpebral conjunctiva** (C. palpebrarum), and is reflected upon the anterior part of the eyeball as **bulbar conjunctiva** (C. bulbi); the line of reflection is termed the **fornix conjunctivæ.** The palpebral part is closely adherent to the tarsus, but is loosely attached further back. It is papillated and is covered with stratified cylindrical epithelium in which many goblet-cells are present. In the fornix and its vicinity there are tubular glands. Near the medial angle there are numerous lymph nodules. The conjunctiva of the lateral part of the upper lid is pierced near the fornix by the orifices of the excretory ducts of the lacrimal gland—twelve to sixteen in number.

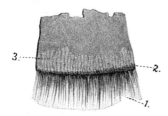

FIG. 690.—PIECE OF UPPER EYELID; INNER SURFACE.
1, Cilia; *2,* limbus palp. posterior; *3,* tarsal glands.
(After Ellenberger, in Leisering's Atlas.)

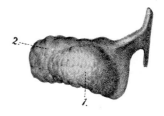

FIG. 691.—CARTILAGE OF THIRD EYELID OF HORSE;
CONVEX SURFACE.
1, Gland; *2,* fat surrounding deep part of cartilage.
(After Ellenberger, in Leisering's Atlas.)

The bulbar conjunctiva is loosely attached to the anterior part of the sclera and is pigmented in the vicinity of the corneo-scleral junction. On the cornea it is represented by a stratified epithelium. When the lids are in apposition, the conjunctiva (including the epithelium of the cornea) encloses a capillary space between the lids and the eyeball, and constitutes what is known as the **conjunctival sac.**

The **third eyelid** (Palpebra tertia) is situated at the medial angle of the eye. It consists of a semilunar fold of the conjunctiva, known as the **membrana nictitans,** which covers and partly encloses a curved plate of hyaline cartilage. Its marginal part is thin and usually more or less pigmented. The cartilage has an irregular triangular outline. The part of it which lies in the membrane is wide and thin. The deep part is narrower and thicker and is embedded in fat at the medial side of the eyeball. Numerous minute lymph nodules occur in the membrana nictitans, and the deep part of the cartilage is surrounded by a gland which resembles the lacrimal gland in structure (Glandula superficialis palpebræ tertiæ).

Ordinarily the third eyelid extends very little over the medial end of the cornea, but when the eyeball is strongly retracted, the membrana is protruded over it so as to measure about an inch (ca. 2–3 cm.) in its middle. This effect results from the pressure of the eyeball and its muscles on the fat which surrounds the deep part of the cartilage.

Vessels and Nerves.—The **arteries** which chiefly supply the eyelids and conjunctiva are branches of the ophthalmic and facial arteries, and the blood is drained away by corresponding veins. The **sensory nerves** are branches of the ophthalmic and maxillary divisions of the trigeminus. The **motor nerves** to the orbicularis oculi, corrugator supercilii, and malaris come from the facial nerve; the levator palpebræ superioris is innervated by the oculomotor nerve and the unstriped muscle of the lids by the sympathetic.

THE LACRIMAL APPARATUS

The **lacrimal apparatus** (Apparatus lacrimalis) comprises: (1) the lacrimal gland, which secretes the clear lacrimal fluid; (2) the excretory ducts of the gland; (3) the two lacrimal ducts or canaliculi, lacrimal sac, and naso-lacrimal duct, which receive the fluid and convey it to the nostril.

The **lacrimal gland** (Glandula lacrimalis) is situated between the supraorbital process and the dorso-lateral surface of the eyeball (Fig. 563). It is flattened, oval in outline, and measures about two inches (ca. 5 cm.) transversely and an inch or more (2.5–3 cm.) in the sagittal direction. Its superficial face is convex and is related to the concave lower surface of the supraorbital process. The deep face is concave in adaptation to the eyeball, from which it is separated by the periorbita. The **excretory ducts** (Ductuli excretorii) are very small and are twelve to sixteen in number; they open into the lateral part of the conjunctival sac along a line a little in front of the fornix conjunctivæ superior. In appearance and structure the gland resembles the parotid. It receives its blood-supply chiefly from the lacrimal artery. The sensory nerve is the lacrimal, and the secretory fibers are derived from the sympathetic.

The **puncta lacrimalia** are the entrances to the two lacrimal ducts. Each is a fine, slit-like opening (about 2 mm. long), situated close behind the free edge of the lid and about a third of an inch (ca. 8 mm.) from the medial canthus. The **lacrimal ducts** (Ductus lacrimales), upper and lower, begin at the puncta and converge at the medial commissure to open into the **lacrimal sac.** The latter (Saccus lacrimalis) may be regarded as the dilated origin of the naso-lacrimal duct. It occupies the funnel-like origin of the bony lacrimal canal, which is termed the fossa of the lacrimal sac, and leads to the **naso-lacrimal duct** (Ductus nasolacrimalis), which passes forward and a little downward along the outer wall of the frontal sinus and the nasal cavity and opens near the lower commissure of the nostril. Its length is about ten to twelve inches (ca. 25–30 cm.). In the first part of its course it is enclosed in the osseous lacrimal canal; further forward it lies in the lacrimal groove of the maxilla, covered at first by a plate of cartilage and then by the mucous membrane of the middle meatus (Figs. 55, 56, 57). The terminal part (Fig. 452) lies in the ventral turbinate fold and opens on the skin of the floor of the nostril near the transition to mucous membrane. In the mule it terminates on the lateral part of the floor or on the lateral wall of the nostril. Accessory openings may occur a little further back.

The first part of the duct, about 6 to 7 mm. in diameter, extends in a gentle curve, convex dorsally, from the medial commissure toward a point just above the level of the infraorbital foramen. The second part (isthmus) is narrower (ca. 3–4 mm.); it extends forward and a little ventrally about to a transverse plane through the first cheek tooth and lies in the groove above the ventral turbinate crest. Beyond this the duct inclines upward and widens very considerably, crosses the nasal process of the premaxilla obliquely, and contracts at its termination. The mucous membrane may present valvular folds, the most distinct of which is situated at the origin.

THE PERIORBITA

The **periorbita** is a conical fibrous membrane which encloses the eyeball with its muscles, vessels, nerves, etc. Its apex is attached around the optic and orbital foramina, and its base is in part attached to the bony rim of the orbit, in part continuous with the fibrous layer of the lids. Its medial part, which is in contact with the orbital wall, is thin; incorporated with it beneath the root of the supraorbital process is the bar of cartilage around which the superior oblique muscle is reflected. The lateral part is thicker, and is strengthened by an elastic band which is attached to the pterygoid crest and furnishes origin to the thin, unstriped orbital muscle. A quantity of fat (Corpus adiposum extraorbitale) lies about the periorbita, and within it is the intraorbital adipose tissue (Corpus adiposum intraorbitale) which fills the interstices between the eyeball, muscles, etc.

THE ORBITAL FASCIÆ AND OCULAR MUSCLES (Figs. 563, 564, 692)

The straight muscles of the eyeball and the oblique muscles in part are enclosed in fibrous sheaths (Fasciæ musculares), formed by superficial and deep layers of fascia, which are united by intermuscular septa in the interstices between the muscles. The **superficial fascia** is thin; it blends in front with the fibrous layer of the eyelids and is attached behind around the optic foramen. The **deep fascia** consists anteriorly of two layers, one of which is continuous with the fibrous tissue of the lids, while the other is attached at the corneo-scleral junction.

The posterior part of the eyeball is covered by the **fascia bulbi,** so that between them a lymph space (Spatium interfasciale) is enclosed which communicates with the subdural space along the course of the optic nerve.

The **levator palpebræ superioris** muscle[1] is a thin band about half an inch in width which lies above the rectus dorsalis. It is narrow at its origin above and behind the ethmoidal foramen and ends by an expanded tendon in the upper lid. Its action is to raise the upper lid.

The **muscles of the eyeball** (Mm. oculi) are seven in number—four straight, two oblique, and a retractor.

The straight muscles (Mm. recti) are designated according to their positions as **rectus dorsalis s. superior, rectus ventralis s. inferior, rectus medialis,** and **rectus lateralis.** They are all band-like, arise close together around the optic foramen, and diverge as they pass forward to the eyeball. On reaching the latter they end in thin tendons which are inserted into the sclera in front of the equator of the eyeball.

The **retractor oculi** almost entirely surrounds the optic nerve, and is incompletely divided into four parts which alternate with the recti. They arise around the optic foramen and are inserted into the sclera behind the recti.

The **obliquus dorsalis s. superior** is the longest and narrowest of the ocular muscles. It arises near the ethmoidal foramen and passes forward medial to the rectus medialis. Under the root of the supraorbital process it is reflected almost at a right angle around a cartilaginous pulley (trochlea), which is attached to the anterior part of the medial wall of the orbit, a bursa being interposed here. The muscle is then directed outward and somewhat forward, and ends in a thin tendon which passes between the rectus dorsalis and the eyeball, and is inserted into the sclera between the dorsal and lateral recti, about half an inch behind the margin of the cornea.

The **obliquus ventralis s. inferior** is wide and much shorter than the recti. It arises from the medial wall of the orbit in the small depression (Fossa muscularis) behind the lacrimal fossa. It curves around the rectus ventralis and is inserted into the sclera near and partly beneath the rectus lateralis.

Actions.—The dorsal and ventral recti rotate the eyeball about a transverse axis, moving the vertex of the cornea upward and downward respectively.[2] Simi-

---

[1] This belongs to the upper eyelid, but is described here on account of its position and the fact that in dissection it must be dealt with before the muscles of the eyeball.

[2] These terms are used with reference to the axis of the eyeball, not that of the head.

larly the medial and lateral recti rotate the eyeball about a vertical axis, turning the vertex of the cornea inward and outward respectively. The oblique muscles rotate the eyeball about a longitudinal axis; the dorsal oblique raises the lateral end of the pupil, while the ventral oblique lowers it. The retractor as a whole draws the eyeball backward, and its parts may separately reinforce the corresponding recti. Also the four recti acting together will retract the eyeball.

The actual movements of the eyeball are by no means so simple as might be inferred from the foregoing general statements. Practically all movements are produced by the coördinated actions of several muscles, involving combinations which are quite complex and difficult to analyze accurately. Further complication is caused by the fact that the recti are not inserted at equal

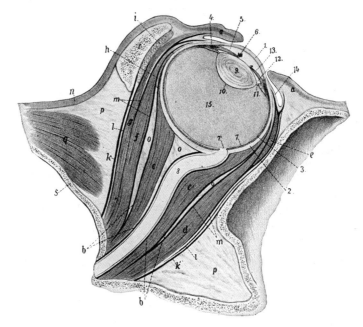

FIG. 692.—VERTICAL AXIAL SECTION OF ORBIT OF HORSE.

a, Eyelids; *b*, fascia bulbi; *c, c'*, retractor oculi; *d*, rectus ventralis; *e*, obliquus ventralis (in cross-section); *f*, rectus dorsalis; *g*, levator palpebræ superioris; *h*, obliquus dorsalis (in cross-section); *i*, lacrimal gland; *k, k'*, periorbita; *l*, superficial fascia; *m*, deep fascia; *n*, skin; *o*, retrobulbar fat; *p*, extraorbital fat; *q*, temporalis muscle; *r*, supraorbital process; *s*, cranial wall; *1*, cornea; *2*, sclera; *3*, chorioidea; *4*, ciliary muscle; *5*, iris; *6*, granula iridis; *7*, retina; *7'*, optic papilla; *8*, optic nerve; *9*, crystalline lens; *10*, capsule of lens; *11*, ciliary zone; *12*, posterior chamber; *13*, anterior chamber; *14*, conjunctiva bulbi; *15*, vitreous body. (After Ellenberger, in Leisering's Atlas.)

distances from the equator and the axes of rotation of the oblique muscles do not correspond to the longitudinal axis of the eyeball.

Nerve-supply.—The oculomotor nerve supplies the foregoing muscles, with the exception of the rectus lateralis and retractor, which are innervated by the abducens, and the obliquus dorsalis, which is supplied by the trochlearis.

THE EYEBALL

The **eyeball** (Bulbus oculi) is situated in the anterior part of the orbital cavity. It is protected in front by the eyelids and conjunctiva, and in its middle by the complete orbital ring, and is related behind to the fascia bulbi, fat, and ocular muscles.

It has the form approximately of an oblate spheroid, but is composed of the segments of two spheres of different sizes. The anterior transparent segment, which is formed by the cornea, has a radius of curvature of about 17 mm., and the posterior opaque, scleral segment one of about 25 mm. The anterior segment therefore projects more strongly, and the junction of the two segments is marked externally by a broad, shallow groove, the **sulcus scleræ**. The central points of the anterior and posterior curvatures of the eyeball are termed respectively the **anterior** and **posterior poles** (Polus anterior, posterior), and the line connecting the poles is the **external optic axis** (Axis oculi externa).[1] The angle of divergence of the optic axes is about 137 degrees. The **equator** (Æquator) is an imaginary line drawn around the eyeball midway between its poles, and **meridians** (Meridiani) are lines drawn around it through the poles.

The average transverse diameter of the eyeball is about 5 cm., the vertical about 4.5 cm., and the axial about 4.25 cm. The distance from the anterior pole to the point of entrance of the optic nerve is about 3 cm.

The eyeball consists of three concentric tunics or coats, within which three refractive media are enclosed.

THE FIBROUS TUNIC

The **fibrous tunic** (Tunica fibrosa oculi) is the external coat and is composed of an opaque posterior part, the sclera, and a transparent anterior part, the cornea.

1. The **sclera** is a dense fibrous membrane which forms about four-fifths of the fibrous tunic. Thickest in the vicinity of the posterior pole (ca. 2 mm.), it thins at the equator (ca. 0.4 mm.), and increases in thickness toward the junction with the cornea (ca. 1.3 mm.). It is in general white, but may have a bluish tinge in its thinnest parts. Its external surface furnishes insertion to the ocular muscles and is covered by the conjunctiva scleræ in its anterior part. The episcleral tissue, which is richly supplied with vessels and nerves, attaches the conjunctiva to the sclera; it is abundant and loosely meshed except at the junction with the cornea. The inner surface is attached to the chorioid coat by a layer of delicate, pigmented connective tissue, the **lamina fusca**. The anterior border, which is oval, the long axis

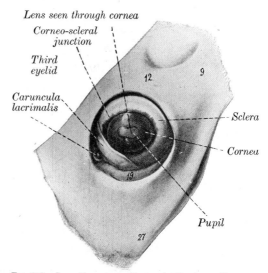

Lens seen through cornea
Corneo-scleral junction
Third eyelid
Caruncula lacrimalis
12   9
Sclera
Cornea
19
Pupil
27

FIG. 693.—LEFT EYEBALL OF HORSE, *in situ*, AFTER REMOVAL OF UPPER AND LOWER LIDS.

9, Zygomatic arch; *12*, supraorbital process; *19*, orbital fat; *27*, facial crest. (After Ellenberger-Baum, Anat. für Künstler.)

being transverse, is continuous with the cornea. The transition from the opaque scleral tissue to the transparent corneal substance occurs in such manner that the sclera appears to form a groove (Rima cornealis), into which the cornea fits somewhat as a watch-glass in the case. Near the corneo-scleral junction there is a circular venous plexus, the **plexus venosus scleræ**. The optic nerve passes through the posterior part of the sclera a little below and lateral to the posterior pole. The opening for the nerve is crossed by interlacing fibrous strands, forming the **lamina cribrosa scleræ**. The sclera consists of interlacing bundles of white fibrous tissue, associated with which there are a few elastic fibers. The

[1] The term internal optic axis (Axis oculi interna) is applied to a coincident line from the posterior surface of the cornea to the anterior surface of the retina.

bundles are arranged chiefly in meridional and equatorial layers. The very limited blood-supply is derived from the ciliary arteries, and the veins open into the venæ vorticosæ and ciliary veins. The lymphatics are represented by intercommunicating cell spaces. The nerves are derived from the ciliary nerves.

2. The **cornea** forms the anterior fifth of the fibrous tunic. It is transparent, colorless, and non-vascular. Viewed from in front it is oval in outline, the long axis being transverse and the broad end medial; it appears more nearly circular when viewed from behind. Its **anterior surface** (Facies anterior) is convex and is more strongly curved than the sclera; its central part is termed the **vertex corneæ.** The **posterior surface** (Facies posterior) is concave; it forms the anterior boundary of the anterior chamber, and is in contact with the aqueous humor. The margin (Limbus corneæ) joins the sclera; the latter overlaps the cornea more in front than behind, and more above and below than at the sides, thus explaining the apparent

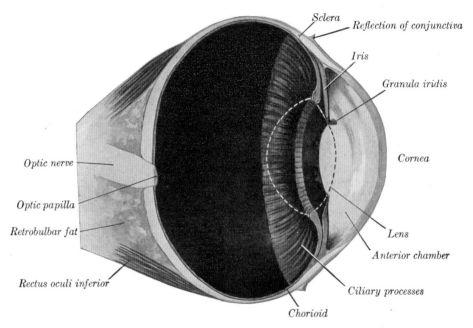

Fig. 694.—Vertical Section of Eyeball of Horse, about ⅔.
The contour of the crystalline lens is dotted.

difference in outline of the two surfaces. The cornea is thinnest at the vertex. The cornea consists, from before backward, of the following layers: (1) The **epithelium corneæ** is continuous with that of the conjunctiva scleræ, and is of the stratified squamous type. (2) The **lamina limitans** is merely a condensation of the next layer. (3) The **substantia propria** forms the bulk of the cornea and is composed of interlacing bundles of connective tissue, arranged in part in lamellæ disposed parallel with the surface. In the amorphous cement substance between the lamellæ are flattened connective-tissue cells, the corneal corpuscles. These have branching processes which unite with those of other cells, thus forming a protoplasmic network.[1] (4) The **lamina elastica** is a thin and prac-

---

[1] According to Piersol the system of spaces and canaliculi in the substantia propria is completely filled by the cells and their processes, upon which the nutrition of the cornea largely depends. The lamina elastica anterior, formerly described as a distinct layer between the corneal epithelium and the substantia propria, does not exist as such, but there is a condensation of the superficial part of the latter, which Rollett termed the anterior limiting layer; it is not elastic.

tically homogeneous membrane which is less intimately attached to the substantia propria than the anterior lamina. It is clear, glistening, and elastic. At the periphery the lamina divides into three sets of fibers. The anterior fibers join the sclera, the middle give attachment to the ciliary muscle, while the posterior pass into the iris and form the **ligamentum pectinatum iridis.** (5) The **endothelium** of the anterior chamber (Endothelium cameræ anterioris) consists of a layer of flattened polygonal cells, and is reflected on to the anterior surface of the iris. The cornea is non-vascular except at its periphery, where the terminal twigs of the vessels of the sclera and conjunctiva form loops. The **nerves** are derived from the ciliary nerves. They form a plexus around the periphery (Plexus annularis), from which fibers pass into the substantia propria, become non-medullated, and form the fundamental or stroma plexus. From this perforating branches go through the anterior limiting layer and form a subepithelial plexus, from which filaments pass between the epithelial cells. Other branches from the plexuses in the substantia propria end as fibrils which are in close relation with the corneal corpuscles.

THE VASCULAR TUNIC

The **vascular tunic** (Tunica vasculosa oculi) lies internal to the fibrous coat; it comprises three parts—the chorioid, the ciliary body, and the iris.

1. The **chorioid** (Chorioidea) is a thin membrane which lies between the sclera and retina. It is in general rather loosely attached to the sclera by the lamina fusca, but is intimately adherent at the point of entrance of the optic nerve and less closely in places where the ciliary vessels and nerves pass through. The inner surface is in contact with the layer of pigmented cells of the retina, which adhere so closely to the chorioid that they were formerly regarded as a part of the latter. The general color of the chorioid is dark brown, but an extensive semilunar area a little above the level of the optic papilla has a remarkable metallic luster, and is termed the **tapetum of the chorioid** (Tapetum chorioideæ). The appearance here varies in different individuals, but the prevailing colors in most cases are iridescent blue and green in various nuances shading into yellow. Posteriorly the chorioid is perforated by the optic nerve, and anteriorly it is continuous with the ciliary body.

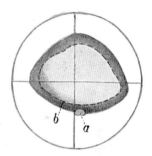

FIG. 695.—TAPETUM OF HORSE.

a, Optic papilla; *b*, lower border of tapetum. (After Ellenberger, in Leisering's Atlas.)

The chorioid consists of four layers, which from without inward are as follows: (1) The **lamina suprachorioidea** consists of interlacing fine lamellæ of fibrous tissue, each containing a network of elastic tissue. Among these are large, branched, pigmented, connective-tissue cells. The spaces between the lamellæ are lined with endothelium, and form a system of lymph-clefts which together form the perichorioid space (Spatium perichorioideale). (2) The **lamina vasculosa** is the outer part of the proper tissue of the chorioid. It contains the larger blood-vessels, which are supported by areolar tissue. (3) The **lamina choriocapillaris** consists of an extremely rich network of capillaries embedded in an almost homogeneous matrix. Between it and the lamina vasculosa is a layer of fibro-elastic tissue, the **tapetum fibrosum,** which causes the metallic luster mentioned above. (4) The **lamina basalis** is very thin and transparent. It is composed of an inner homogeneous part and an outer elastic part.

2. The **ciliary body** (Corpus ciliare), the middle part of the vascular coat, connects the chorioid with the periphery of the iris. In meridional section it has the form of a narrow triangle, the base of which is next to the iris. On its inner side are the ciliary processes and on its outer side is the ciliary muscle. It consists of three parts—the ciliary ring, ciliary processes, and ciliary muscle. The **ciliary**

ring (Orbiculus ciliaris) is the posterior zone, which is distinguished from the chorioid mainly by its greater thickness and the absence of the chorio-capillaris. Its inner face presents numerous fine meridional ridges, by the union of which the ciliary processes are formed. The **ciliary processes** (Processus ciliares), more than a hundred in number, form a circle of radial folds which surround the lens and furnish attachment to the zonula ciliaris (or suspensory ligament of the lens). They are small at their origin on the ciliary ring and become much thicker and higher toward their central ends. The width of the circle formed by them is narrower at the medial side than elsewhere. Their bases extend forward to the periphery of the iris, and their central ends are close to the margin of the lens. They bear numerous secondary folds (Plicæ ciliares). Their inner surface is covered by a continuation of the lamina basalis of the chorioid, on which there are two layers of epithelial cells which constitute the pars ciliaris retinæ. They consist of a rich network of tortuous vessels supported in pigmented connective tissue. The **ciliary muscle** (M. ciliaris) (Figs. 689, 692, 696) constitutes the outer part of the ciliary body, and lies between the sclera and the ciliary processes. It forms a circular band of unstriped muscle, the fibers of which are for the most part directed meridionally. They arise from the inner surface of the sclera and from the ligamentum pectinatum iridis close to the corneo-scleral junction, and run backward along the sclera to be inserted into the ciliary processes and ring. When the muscle contracts, it pulls the processes and ring forward, thus slackening the ciliary zone of the lens, and allowing the latter to become more convex. This is the mechanism of accommodation for near objects.

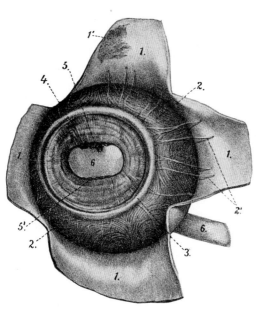

FIG. 696.—VASCULAR TUNIC OF EYEBALL OF HORSE; FRONT VIEW.

The cornea is removed and the sclera is reflected in flaps. *1*, Sclera; *1'*, lamina fusca; *2*, chorioidea; *2'*, ciliary veins; *3*, ciliary muscle; *4*, iris; *5, 5'*, granula iridis; *6*, pupil, through which the lens is visible. (After Ellenberger, in Leisering's Atlas.)

In man the muscle has the form of a prismatic ring which is triangular in meridional section, the base being directed toward the periphery of the iris. It consists chiefly of meridional fibers, but a ring of circular fibers forms the inner angle of its base. In the horse the muscle is much less developed, and has the form of a flat band; it does not contain distinctly circular fibers, but the arrangement is rendered more or less plexiform by the existence of oblique and equatorial fibers.

3. The **iris** (Figs. 689, 694, 696) is a muscular diaphragm placed in front of the lens, and is visible through the cornea. It is pierced centrally by an elliptical opening, the **pupil** (Pupilla), which varies in size during life and determines the amount of light admitted to act on the retina. In strong light the vertical diameter of the pupil is very short, but the opening is almost circular when the pupil is fully dilated. The **ciliary border** (Margo ciliaris) is continuous with the ciliary body and is connected with the corneo-scleral junction by strands of connective tissue which constitute the **ligamentum pectinatum iridis**. The bundles of the ligament interlace and enclose spaces (Spatia anguli iridis) which are lined with endothelium and communicate with the anterior chamber. The **pupillary border** (Margo

pupillaris) surrounds the pupil. Its upper part bears in its middle several black masses of variable size, termed the **granula iridis** or **corpora nigra**; similar, but much smaller, projections may be seen on the lower margin of the pupil. The **anterior surface** (Facies anterior) is usually dark brown in color; it presents fine folds (Plicæ iridis), some of which are concentric with the pupil, others radial; they fade out near the pupil. Some of these folds are permanent, while others are temporary, *i. e.*, produced by contraction of the iris. The smooth, narrow, central part is termed the annulus iridis minor, while the much broader plicated part is the annulus iridis major. The **posterior surface** (Facies posterior) is usually black; the color is caused by a layer of pigmented cells which is regarded as part of the retina. It presents numerous fine radial lines except at the pupillary margin. Its central part is in contact with the anterior surface of the lens, but peripherally the two are separated by a narrow space termed the posterior chamber. The iris consists chiefly of the **stroma iridis,** a delicate framework of connective tissue which supports numerous blood-vessels, and contains branched pigmented cells. The muscular tissue is unstriped and consists of a sphincter and a dilator of the pupil. The **sphincter pupillæ** lies in the posterior part around the pupil, with which the fibers are largely concentric. The **dilatator pupillæ** consists of fibers which radiate from the sphincter to the ciliary border. The anterior surface of the iris is covered by a continuation of the endothelium of the cornea. Beneath this is a condensation of the stroma, in which the cells are close together and are full of pigmented granules. In albinos the pigment is absent here, as elsewhere, and the iris is pink in color. There appear to be minute clefts here by which the lymph-spaces of the stroma communicate with the anterior chamber.

The **arteries** of the vascular tunic come from the ciliary branches of the ophthalmic artery. The arteries of the chorioidea are derived chiefly from the short posterior ciliary arteries. These (four to six in number) perforate the sclera around the posterior pole, run forward in the lamina vasculosa, and form the rich capillary network of the choriocapillaris. The two long ciliary arteries perforate the sclera obliquely near the optic nerve; they run forward in the lamina suprachorioidea in the horizontal meridian, one on the medial, the other on the lateral side of the eyeball. On reaching the ciliary body each divides into two diverging branches; the subdivisions of these unite with each other and with twigs of the anterior ciliary arteries, thus forming near the periphery of the iris the **circulus arteriosus major.** From this branches go to the ciliary muscle and processes and to the iris. The branches in the iris run toward the pupillary margin, and by anastomotic branches form an incomplete **circulus arteriosus minor.** The two anterior ciliary arteries, dorsal and ventral, form an episcleral plexus around the corneo-scleral junction, and give off branches which perforate the sclera. These supply twigs to the ciliary muscle and recurrent branches to the chorioid, and assist in forming the circulus arteriosus major. The blood is carried away from the vascular tunic chiefly by four or five venous trunks, the **venæ vorticosæ,** which are formed by the convergence in whorls of numerous veins from the chorioid, the ciliary body, and the iris. The venæ vorticosæ perforate the sclera about at the equator and join the veins of the ocular muscles.

The **nerves** come from the long and short ciliary nerves. They form a plexus in the lamina suprachorioidea, which contains ganglion cells, and sends numerous non-medullated fibers chiefly to the blood-vessels of the chorioid. At the ciliary muscle a second plexus (P. gangliosus ciliaris) is formed, which supplies the muscle and sends fibers to the iris. The sphincter pupillæ is supplied by fibers derived from the oculomotor nerve, while the dilatator pupillæ is innervated by the sympathetic.

THE RETINA

The **retina** or nervous tunic of the eyeball is a delicate membrane which extends from the entrance of the optic nerve to the margin of the pupil. It consists of three parts. The large posterior part, which alone contains the nervous elements, including the special neuro-epithelium and the optic nerve-fibers, is termed the **pars optica retinæ.** It extends forward to the ciliary body, where it terminates at an almost regular circular line called the **ora ciliaris retinæ.**[1] Here the retina rapidly loses its nervous elements, becomes much thinner, and is continued over the ciliary body and the posterior surface of the iris by two layers of epithelial cells as the **pars ciliaris retinæ;** the inner stratum is non-pigmented, while the outer layer is a direct continuation of the stratum pigmenti of the pars optica. The **pars iridica retinæ** is a layer of pigmented cells which covers the posterior surface of the iris. In the dead subject the pars optica is an opaque, gray, soft membrane which

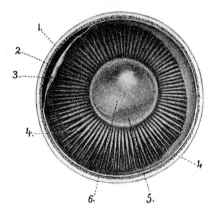

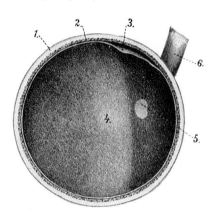

FIG. 697.—INNER SURFACE OF ANTERIOR PART OF EYEBALL OF HORSE (EQUATORIAL SECTION).

1, Sclera; 2, chorioidea; 3, retina (drawn away from chorioidea); 4, ciliary processes; 5, crystalline lens, through which the pupil (6) is seen. (After Ellenberger, in Leisering's Atlas.)

FIG. 698.—FUNDUS OCULI, SEEN ON EQUATORIAL SECTION OF EYEBALL OF HORSE.

1, Sclera; 2, chorioidea; 3, retina (loosened); 4, tapetum; 5, optic papilla; 6, optic nerve. (After Ellenberger, in Leisering's Atlas.)

can be stripped off the chorioid, leaving most of its outer pigmented layer on the latter. During life it is transparent, except as to its pigmented epithelium, and the reddish appearance of the fundus as viewed by the ophthalmoscope is caused by the blood in the network of the choriocapillaris. The entrance of the optic nerve forms a sharply defined, oval, light area, the **optic papilla** (Papilla nervi optici), situated about 15 mm. ventral to the horizontal meridian and 3 to 4 mm. lateral to the vertical meridian. The central part of the papilla is slightly depressed (Excavatio papillæ n. optici).

The transverse diameter of the papilla is about 6 to 7 mm., and the vertical about 4 to 5 mm. It is commonly situated a little below the margin of the tapetum, but the latter may extend down somewhat on either side of the papilla. The lower margin is often indented a little. In inspection of the fundus with the ophthalmoscope numerous fine branches of the arteria centralis retinæ are seen radiating from the periphery of the papilla.

The optic nerve fibers converge from all parts of the pars optica to the papilla, where they collect into bundles which traverse the lamina cribrosa of the chorioidea and sclera, and constitute the optic nerve. The **area centralis retinæ** is a round spot, 2 to 3 mm. in diameter, situated dorso-lateral to the optic papilla; it corre-

---

[1] In man the line is finely serrated and is termed the ora serrata.

sponds to the macula lutea of man, which is histologically more highly differentiated than the rest of the retina and is the area of most acute vision.

The **structure** of the retina is very complex. It consists of nervous elements which are supported in a peculiar sustentacular tissue, and are covered externally by a layer of pigmented epithelium (Stratum pigmenti retinæ). The nervous elements comprise a highly specialized neuro-epithelium, the rods and cones; ganglion-cells, the axones of which form the optic nerve; and intermediate neurones. Ten layers may be recognized in sections microscopically.[1]

The **arteries** of the retina are derived from the arteria centralis retinæ and anastomotic branches from the short ciliary arteries. The arteria centralis enters the optic nerve a short distance behind the eyeball and runs in the axis of the nerve. It divides two or three millimeters before reaching the papilla, and gives off thirty to forty branches which radiate in the posterior part of the retina and divide dichotomously into end-arteries in the layer of nerve fibers. The **veins** accompany the arteries except in the capillary plexuses; their walls consist merely of a layer of endothelial cells, around which are a lymph-channel and sheath.[2]

CHAMBERS OF THE EYE AND AQUEOUS HUMOR

The **anterior chamber** of the eye (Camera oculi anterior) is enclosed in front by the cornea and behind by the iris and lens (Figs. 689, 692, 694). It communicates through the pupil with the **posterior chamber** of the eye (Camera oculi posterior); this is a small annular space, triangular in cross-section, which is bounded in front by the iris, behind by the peripheral part of the lens and its ligaments, and externally by the ciliary processes. The chambers are filled by the **aqueous humor** (Humor aqueus), a clear fluid which consists of about 98 per cent. of water, with a little sodium chlorid and traces of albumin and extractives. It is carried off chiefly through the spaces in the zonula ciliaris (or suspensory ligament of the lens) into the plexus venosus scleræ.

REFRACTIVE MEDIA OF THE EYEBALL

The **vitreous body** (Corpus vitreum) is a semifluid, transparent substance situated between the crystalline lens and the retina. In front it presents a deep cavity, the **fossa hyaloidea,** which fits the posterior surface of the lens. It consists of a framework of delicate fibrils, the **vitreous stroma** (Stroma vitreum), the meshes of which are filled by the fluid **vitreous humor** (Humor vitreus). The surface is covered by a condensation of the stroma known as the **hyaloid membrane** (Membrana hyaloidea).

The **crystalline lens** (Lens crystallina) is a biconvex, transparent body which is situated in front of the vitreous body and in partial contact with the posterior surface of the iris. Its periphery, the **equator of the lens** (Æquator lentis), is almost circular and is closely surrounded by the ciliary processes. The **anterior surface** (Facies anterior) is convex; it is bathed by the aqueous humor and is in contact with the iris to an extent which varies with the state of the pupil. The **posterior surface** (Facies posterior) is much more strongly curved than the anterior. It rests in the fossa of the vitreous body (Fossa hyaloidea). The central points of the surfaces are the **anterior** and **posterior poles** (Polus anterior et posterior lentis). and the line which connects them is the **axis** of the lens (Axis lentis).

The transverse diameter of the lens is about 2 cm., the vertical diameter is slightly smaller, and the axis measures about 13 mm. The radius of curvature of the anterior surface is 13.5 mm.,

[1] For the minute structure of the retina reference must be made to histological works.

[2] Martin states that in the horse a capillary plexus does not exist, but that the arteries communicate with the veins by closely wound loops.

and of the posterior surface, 9.5 to 10 mm. But the curvatures of its surfaces—especially that of the anterior—vary during life according as the eye is accommodated for near or far vision.

The **zonula ciliaris** or suspensory ligament of the lens (Fig. 689) consists of delicate fibers (Fibræ zonulares) which pass in a meridional direction from the ciliary processes to the capsule of the equator of the lens. Many fibers cross each other, and the spaces between the fibers (Spatia zonularia) are filled with aqueous humor; they communicate with each other and with the posterior chamber.

The **substance** of the lens (Substantia lentis) is enclosed by a structureless, highly elastic membrane, the **capsule** of the lens (Capsula lentis), and consists of a softer **cortical substance** (Substantia corticalis), and a dense central part, the **nucleus** of the lens (Nucleus lentis). The capsule is thickest on the anterior surface, and here it is lined by a layer of flat polygonal cells, the **epithelium** of the lens (Epithelium lentis). The lens substance, when hardened, is seen to consist of concentric laminæ arranged somewhat like the layers of an onion, and united by an amorphous cement substance. The laminæ consists of **lens fibers** (Fibræ lentis), hexagonal in section, and of very different lengths. Faint lines radiate from the poles and indicate the edges of layers of cement substance which unite the groups of lens fibers. These lines, the **radii lentis,** are three in number in the fœtus and new-born, and form with each other angles of 120 degrees. On the anterior surface one is directed upward from the pole and the other two diverge downward; on the posterior surface one is directed downward and the others diverge upward. The developed lens has neither vessels nor nerves.

In the fœtus the lens is nearly globular, and is soft and pink in color. During part of fœtal life it is surrounded by a vascular network, the tunica vasculosa lentis. This is derived chiefly from a temporary vessel, the hyaloid artery, which is a continuation forward of the arteria centralis retinæ through the hyaloid canal that traverses the vitreous body. In old age the lens tends to lose its elasticity and transparency; it also becomes flatter and the nucleus especially grows denser.

THE EAR

The **ear** or **organ of hearing** (Organon auditus) consists of three natural divisions—external, middle, and internal.

THE EXTERNAL EAR

The **external ear** (Auris externa) comprises—(1) the **auricula,** a funnel-like organ which collects the sound waves, together with its muscles; and (2) the **external acoustic meatus,** which conveys these waves to the tympanic membrane, the partition which separates the canal from the cavity of the middle ear.

The **auricula** or pinna is attached by its base around the external acoustic process in such a manner as to be freely movable. In the following description it will be assumed that the opening is directed outward and that the long axis is practically vertical. It has two surfaces, two borders, a base, and an apex. The convex surface or dorsum (Dorsum auriculæ) faces medially and is widest in its middle part; its lower part is almost circular in curvature, while above it narrows and flattens. The concave surface (Scapha) is the reverse of the dorsum; it presents several ridges which subside toward the apex. The anterior border is sinuous; it is largely convex, but becomes concave near the apex. It divides below into two diverging parts (Crura helicis). The posterior border is convex. The apex is flattened, pointed, and curved a little forward. The base is strongly convex. It is attached to the external acoustic process of the petrous temporal bone, and around this there is a quantity of fat. The parotid gland overlaps it below and laterally. The structure of the external ear comprises a framework of cartilages (which are chiefly elastic), the integument, and a complicated arrangement of muscles.

The **conchal** or **auricular cartilage** (Cartilago auriculæ) determines the shape of the ear; its form can be made out in a general way without dissection, except below, where it is concealed by the muscles and the parotid gland. The basal part is coiled so as to form a tube, which encloses the cavity of the concha (Cavum conchæ). This part is funnel-shaped and curves outward and a little backward. Its medial surface is strongly convex, forming a prominence termed the **eminentia conchæ.** The lowest part of the medial margin bears a narrow, pointed prolongation, the **styloid process.** This process is about an inch long and projects downward over the annular cartilage; the guttural pouch is attached to its free end. Behind its base there is a foramen through which the auricular branch of the vagus passes.

The basal part of the posterior border is cut into by a notch, which separates two irregular quadrilateral plates. The upper plate (Tragus) is overlapped by the anterior border, and is separated from the adjacent part of the posterior border (Antitragus) by a notch (Incisura intertragica). The lower plate is curved to form a half ring and partly overlaps the anterior border and the annular cartilage. Behind the notch there is a foramen, which transmits the internal auricular artery and internal auricular branch of the facial nerve.

The **annular cartilage** (Cartilago annularis) is a quadrilateral plate, curved to form about three-fourths of a ring; its ends are a little less than half an inch (ca. 1 cm.) apart medially and are united by elastic tissue. It embraces the external acoustic process and forms with the lower part of the conchal cartilage the cartilaginous part of the external acoustic meatus.

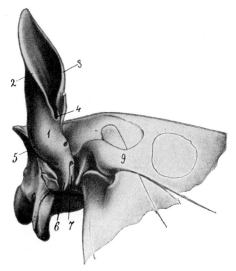

The **scutiform cartilage** (Cartilago scutiformis s. Scutulum) is an irregular quadrilateral plate which lies on the temporal muscle in front of the base of the conchal cartilage. Its superficial face is slightly convex from side to side and its deep face is correspondingly concave. The anterior end is thin and rounded; the posterior part or base is wider and thicker, and its medial angle is prolonged by a pointed process half an inch or more in length. The cartilage moves very freely over the underlying parts.

Fig. 699.—Conchal and Annular Cartilages of Ear of Horse, External View.

1, Base of concha; *2,* posterior border, *3,* anterior border of concha; *4,* intertragic notch; *5,* eminentia conchæ; *6,* styloid process; *7,* annular cartilage; *9,* zygomatic arch. (After Ellenberger-Baum, Anat. für Künstler.)

The **external acoustic meatus** leads from the cavum conchæ to the tympanic membrane. It does not continue the general direction of the cavity of the concha, but extends medially, downward, and slightly forward. It consists of a cartilaginous part (Meatus acusticus externus cartilagineus) which is formed by the lower part of the conchal cartilage and the annular cartilage, and an osseous part formed by the external acoustic process of the temporal bone. These are united by elastic membranes to form a complete tube. Its caliber diminishes medially, so that the lumen of the inner end is about half of that of the outer end.

The **skin** on the convex surface of the concha presents no special features; it is attached to the cartilage by a considerable amount of subcutaneous tissue except at the apex. The integument which lines the concave surface is intimately adherent to the cartilage and is relatively dark in color. There are three or four cutaneous ridges which run about parallel with the borders of the conchal cartilage, but do not extend to the apex or the cavum conchæ. The upper and marginal parts and the ridges are covered with long hairs, but the skin between the ridges and below is thin, covered sparsely with very fine hairs, and supplied with numerous sebaceous glands. In the external acoustic meatus the skin becomes thinner; in the cartilaginous part it is supplied with numerous large, coiled, **ceruminous glands** (Glandulæ ceruminosæ), and is sparsely covered with very fine hairs; in the osseous part the glands are small and few or absent and there are no hairs.

THE AURICULAR MUSCLES

The **auricular muscles** may be subdivided into two sets, viz., (a) extrinsic muscles, which arise on the head and adjacent part of the neck, and move the external ear as a whole, and (b) intrinsic muscles, which are confined to the auricula. In this connection the scutiform cartilage may be regarded as a sesamoid cartilage intercalated in the course of some of the muscles.

The **extrinsic muscles** are as follows:

1. The **scutularis** is a thin muscular sheet situated subcutaneously over the temporalis muscle. Its fibers arise from the zygomatic arch and the frontal and parietal crests, and converge to the scutiform cartilage. It consists of three parts:

(a) The **fronto-scutularis** comprises temporal and frontal parts, which arise from the zygomatic arch and the frontal crest, and are inserted into the lateral and anterior borders of the scutiform cartilage respectively.

(b) The **interscutularis** arises from the parietal crest, over which it is in part continuous with the muscle of the opposite side. Its fibers converge to the medial border of the scutiform cartilage.

(c) The **cervico-scutularis** is not well defined from the preceding muscle. It arises from the nuchal crest and is inserted into the medial border of the scutiform cartilage.

2. The **anterior auricular muscles** (Mm. auriculares orales) are four in number:

(a) The **zygomatico-auricularis** arises from the zygomatic arch and the parotid fascia, and is inserted into the outer face of the base of the conchal cartilage partly under, partly above, the insertion of the parotido-auricularis.

(b) The **scutulo-auricularis superficialis inferior** arises on the lateral part of the superficial face of the scutiform cartilage and ends on the base of the conchal cartilage with the preceding muscle.

(c) The **scutulo-auricularis superficialis medius** arises from the posterior part of the deep surface of the scutiform cartilage and is inserted into the dorsum of the conchal cartilage, close to the lower part of its anterior border, and above and behind the preceding muscle. It receives a slip from the cervico-scutularis.

(d) The **scutulo-auricularis superficialis superior** is a thin slip which is detached from the interscutularis over the medial border of the scutiform cartilage. It ends on the anterior aspect of the lower part of the dorsum of the conchal cartilage.

3. The **dorsal auricular muscles** (Mm. auriculares dorsales) are two in number.

(a) The **scutulo-auricularis superficialis accessorius** is a narrow band which is largely covered by the preceding muscle. It arises from the posterior prolongation and the adjacent part of the superficial face of the scutiform cartilage, and is inserted into the convex surface of the conchal cartilage medial to the preceding muscle, the two crossing each other at an acute angle.

(b) The **parieto-auricularis** is flat and triangular; it arises from the parietal crest under cover of the cervico-scutularis, runs outward and a little backward, and is inserted by a flat tendon into the lower part of the convex surface of the concha under cover of the cervico-auricularis superficialis.

4. The **posterior auricular muscles** (Mm. auriculares aborales) are three in number:

(*a*) The **cervico-auricularis superficialis** is a thin triangular sheet. It is wide at its origin from the nuchal crest and the adjacent part of the ligamentum nuchæ, and becomes narrower as it passes outward to be inserted into the medial side of the convex surface of the concha.

(*b*) The **cervico-auricularis profundus major** arises from the ligamentum nuchæ, partly beneath and partly behind the preceding muscle. It is directed outward and is inserted into the postero-lateral aspect of the base of the ear, partly under cover of the parotido-auricularis.

(*c*) The **cervico-auricularis profundus minor** arises under the preceding

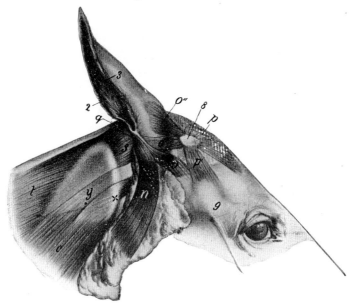

FIG. 700.—EXTERNAL EAR OF HORSE AND ITS MUSCLES; LATERAL VIEW.

The cervico-auricularis superficialis has been removed. *2*, Posterior border; *3*, anterior border of auricula; *8*, scutiform cartilage; *9*, zygomatic arch; *n*, parotido-auricularis; *o*, zygomatico-auricularis; *o′*, scutulo-auricularis superficialis inferior; *o″*, scutulo-auricularis superficialis medius et superior; *p*, interscutularis; *p′*, fronto-scutularis (pars temporalis); *q*, cervico-auricularis profundus major; *s*, anterior oblique muscle of head; *t*, splenius; *y*, tendon of brachiocephalicus; *x*, wing of atlas. (After Ellenberger-Baum, Anat. für Künstler.)

muscle and passes downward and outward to be inserted into the lowest part of the convex surface of the concha, partly under cover of the parotid gland.

5. The **parotido-auricularis** (s. M. auricularis inferior) is a ribbon-like muscle which lies on the parotid gland. It is thin and wide at its origin from the fascia on the lower part of the parotid gland, and becomes somewhat narrower and thicker as it ascends. It is inserted into the conchal cartilage just below the angle of junction of its borders.

6. The **deep auricular** or **rotator muscles** (Mm. auriculares profundi s. rotatores auriculæ), two in number, are situated under the scutiform cartilage and the base of the concha and cross each other.

(*a*) The **scutulo-auricularis profundus major** is the strongest of the auricular muscles. It is flat and is about an inch wide. It arises from the deep face of the scutiform cartilage and passes backward to end on and below the most prominent part of the base of the concha (eminentia conchæ).

(b) The **scutulo-auricularis profundus minor** lies between the base of the concha and the preceding muscle, and is best seen when the latter is cut and reflected. It is flat and about an inch in length.   It arises from the posterior part of the deep face of the scutiform cartilage and from the cervico-scutularis, and passes downward, backward, and outward to be inserted into the base of the concha under cover of the preceding muscle.

7. The **tragicus** is a very small muscle which arises from the temporal bone just behind the external acoustic process and from the annular cartilage; it passes

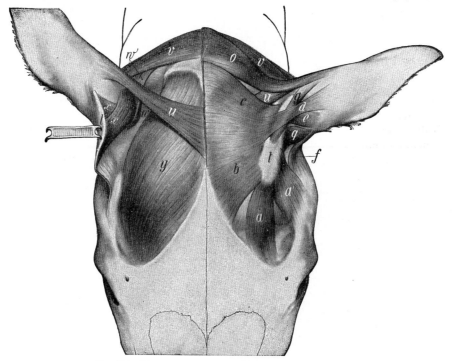

Fig. 701.—Muscles of External Ear of Horse; Dorsal View.

On the right side parts of the superficial muscles have been removed and the scutiform cartilage turned back to display the deeper muscles.   a, Frontal part; a′, temporal part of fronto-scutularis; b, interscutularis; c, cervico-scutularis; d, e, scutulo-auricularis superficialis superior and medius; f, zygomatico-auricularis; g, scutulo-auricularis superficialis accessorius; o, cervico-auricularis superficialis; q, scutulo-auricularis superficialis inferior; t, scutiform cartilage; u, parieto-auricularis; v, cervico-auricularis profundus major; w, cervico-auricularis prof. minor; x, x′, scutulo-auricularis prof. major et minor; y, temporalis.   (Ellenberger-Baum, Anat. d. Haustiere.)

upward to be inserted into the lower part of the anterior border of the conchal cartilage.

The **intrinsic muscles** are very small and of little importance.   They are as follows:

1. The **antitragicus** consists of a few bundles which are attached to the conchal cartilage behind the junction of its two borders, and are partially blended with the insertion of the parotido-auricularis.

2. The **helicis** is a small muscle attached in a position opposite to the preceding on the anterior border of the conchal cartilage; it extends also into the depression between the two divisions of the border.   It is in part continuous with the insertion of the parotido-auricularis.

3. The **verticalis auriculæ**[1] is a thin stratum of muscular and tendinous fibers which extends upward on the convex surface of the concha from the eminentia conchæ.

Actions.—The base of the concha is rounded and rests in a pad of fat (Corpus adiposum auriculæ), so that the movements of the external ear resemble those of a ball-and-socket joint. It is noticeable that movements about the longitudinal and transverse axes are accompanied by rotation. When the ear is vertical or drawn forward ("pricked up"), the opening is usually directed forward; conversely, when the ears are "laid back," the opening faces backward. These movements evidently result from the coördinated actions of several muscles which are very complex and cannot be discussed in detail here. The scutularis acting as a whole fixes the scutiform cartilage, so that the muscles which arise on the latter act efficiently on the concha. The anterior auricular muscles in general erect the ear and turn the opening forward. The interscutularis concurs in this action, causing adduction and a symmetrical position of the ears; it also acts directly on the conchal cartilage, since the scutulo-auricularis superficialis superior is in reality a conchal insertion of the interscutularis. The scutulo-auricularis superficialis accessorius draws the concha forward and turns the opening outward. The parieto-auricularis adducts the concha and inclines it forward. The cervico-auricularis superficialis is chiefly an adductor of the conchal cartilage, and directs the opening outward. The cervico-auricularis profundus major turns the opening outward and, acting with the parotido-auricularis, inclines the ear toward the poll. The cervico-auricularis profundus minor tends to direct the opening downward and outward. The parotido-auricularis draws the ear downward and backward, and acts with the cervico-auricularis profundus major in "laying back the ears." The scutulo-auricularis profundus major chiefly rotates the concha so that the opening is turned backward. The scutulo-auricularis profundus minor assists in rotating the ear so that the opening is directed forward. The tragicus shortens the external acoustic meatus. The actions of the intrinsic muscles are inappreciable.

Vessels and Nerves.—The **arteries** of the external ear are derived from the anterior auricular branch of the superficial temporal, the posterior or great auricular branch of the external carotid, and the anterior branch of the occipital artery. The **veins** go chiefly to the jugular and superficial temporal veins. The **nerves** to the muscles come from the auricular and auriculo-palpebral branches of the facial nerve and from the first and second cervical nerves. The sensory nerves are supplied by the superficial temporal branch of the mandibular nerve and the auricular branch of the vagus.

THE MIDDLE EAR

The **middle ear** (Auris media) comprises the tympanic cavity and its contents, the auditive or Eustachian tubes, and two remarkable diverticula of the latter, which are termed the guttural pouches.

The **tympanic cavity** (Cavum tympani) is a space in the tympanic and petrous parts of the temporal bone situated between the membrana tympani and the internal ear. It is an air-cavity, which is lined by mucous membrane, and communicates with the pharynx and the guttural pouches by the auditive or Eustachian tubes. It contains a chain of auditory ossicles by which the vibrations of the membrana tympani are transmitted to the internal ear.

The cavity consists of: (1) A main part or atrium, which lies immediately to the medial side of the membrana tympani; (2) the recessus epitympanicus, situated above the level of the membrane and containing the upper part of the malleus

---

[1] Ellenberger and Baum regard this as the homologue of the transversus and obliquus auriculæ of man.

and the greater part of the incus; (3) a relatively large ventral recess in the bulla tympanica.

The lateral, **membranous wall** (Paries membranacea) is formed largely by the thin **membrana tympani,** which closes the medial end of the external acoustic meatus, and thus forms the septum between the external and middle parts of the ear. The membrane is an oval disc, which slopes ventro-medially at an angle of about 30 degrees with the lower wall of the external acoustic meatus. The circumference is attached in a groove (Sulcus tympanicus) in the thin ring of bone (Annulus tympanicus) which almost completely surrounds it. The handle of the malleus (the outermost of the auditory ossicles) is attached to the inner surface of the membrane and draws the central part inward, producing a slight concavity of the outer surface. The periphery is thickened, forming the annulus fibrosus. The membrana tympani consists of three layers. The external **cutaneous layer** (Stratum cutaneum) is a prolongation of the lining of the external acoustic meatus. The

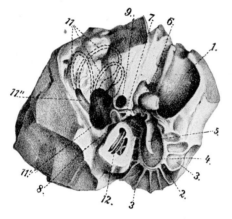

FIG. 702.—RIGHT PETROUS TEMPORAL BONE OF HORSE;
ANTERO-MEDIAL VIEW.

1, External acoustic meatus; *2*, annulus tympanicus; *3*, laminæ radiating from *2*; *4*, membrana tympani; *5*, malleus; *6*, incus; *7*, stapes; *8*, fenestra cochleæ (s. rotundum); *9*, facial canal; *11*, *11''*, semicircular canals; *11'*, vestibule; *12*, cochlea. (After Ellenberger, in Leisering's Atlas.)

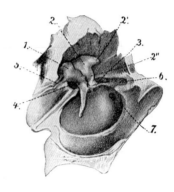

FIG. 703.—RIGHT AUDITORY OSSICLES AND MEMBRANA TYMPANI, ENLARGED AND VIEWED FROM INNER SIDE AND BELOW.

1, Malleus; *2*, incus; *2'*, *2''*, short and long processes of *2*; *3*, stapes; *4*, tensor tympani; *5*, ligament attaching long process of malleus; *6*, stapedius muscle; *7*, fenestra cochleæ (s. rotundum). (After Ellenberger, in Leisering's Atlas.)

middle **fibrous layer** or **membrana propria** includes two chief sets of fibers; the external layer (Stratum radiatum) consists of fibers which radiate from the handle of the malleus, while the internal layer (Stratum circulare) is composed of circular fibers which are best developed peripherally. There are also branched or dendritic fibers in part of the membrane. The internal **mucous layer** (Stratum mucosum) is a part of the general mucous membrane which lines the tympanic cavity.

The medial, **labyrinthine wall** of the tympanic cavity (Paries labyrinthica) separates it from the internal ear; it presents a number of special features. The **promontory** (Promontorium) is a distinct eminence near the center which corresponds to the first coil of the cochlea, and is marked by a faint groove for the superficial petrosal nerve. Above this is the **fenestra vestibuli,** a reniform opening which is closed by the foot-plate of the stapes and its annular ligament. The **fenestra cochleæ** is situated below and behind the preceding; it is an irregularly oval opening and is closed by a thin membrane (Membrana tympani secundaria), which separates the tympanic cavity from the scala tympani of the cochlea.

The anterior, **tubal wall** (Paries tubaria) is narrow, and is pierced by the slit-like tympanic opening of the auditive tube. Above this and incompletely separated from it by a thin plate of bone is the semicanal for the tensor tympani muscle.

The **tegmental wall** or **roof** (Paries tegmentalis) is crossed in its medial part by the facial nerve; here the facial canal is more or less deficient ventrally, and the nerve is covered by the mucous membrane of the tympanum.

The posterior, **mastoid wall** (Paries mastoidea) presents nothing of importance; a tympanic antrum and mastoid cells, such as are found behind the tympanic cavity proper in man and many animals, are not present in the horse.

The **tympanic wall** or **floor** (Paries tympanica) is concave and thin. It is crossed by delicate curved ridges, which radiate from the greater part of the annulus tympanicus.

The **auditory ossicles** (Ossicula auditus) form a chain which extends from the lateral to the medial wall of the cavity. They are named, from without inward, the **malleus**, the **incus**, the **os lenticulare**, and the **stapes**. The first is attached to the inner surface of the tympanic membrane and the last is fixed in the fenestra vestibuli.

The **malleus** or hammer, the largest of the ossicles, consists of a head, neck, handle, and two processes. The **head** (Capitulum mallei) is situated in the epi-

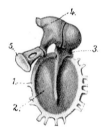

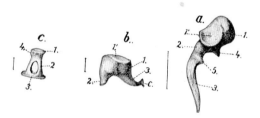

FIG. 704.—AUDITORY OSSICLES AND MEMBRANA TYMPANI; MEDIAL VIEW, ENLARGED.

1, Annulus tympanicus; *2*, membrana tympani; *3*, malleus; *4*, incus; *5*, stapes. (After Ellenberger, in Leisering's Atlas.)

FIG. 705.—RIGHT AUDITORY OSSICLES, ENLARGED AS INDICATED BY LINES GIVING THEIR ACTUAL LENGTH.

a, Malleus: *1*, head; *2*, neck; *3*, handle; *4*, long process; *5*, muscular process. **b,** Incus: *1*, body; *2*, short branch; *3*, long branch; *c*, os lenticulare. **c,** Stapes; *1*, head; *2*, crus; *3*, base; *4*, attachment of stapedius. (After Ellenberger, in Leisering's Atlas.)

tympanic recess. It is smooth and convex above and in front, and presents on its postero-medial aspect a concave facet for articulation with the body of the incus. The **neck** (Collum mallei) is the constricted part below the head; its medial surface is crossed by the chorda tympani nerve. The **handle** (Manubrium mallei) is directed downward, inward, and a little forward from the neck, and is attached along its entire length to the membrana tympani. On its medial surface, near the upper end, there is a slight projection to which the tendon of the tensor tympani muscle is attached. The **long process** (Processus longus) is a pointed spicule which projects forward from the neck toward the petro-tympanic fissure. The **short process** (Processus brevis) is a slight projection of the lateral side of the neck, and is attached to the upper part of the membrana tympani.

The **incus** or anvil is situated chiefly in the epitympanic recess. It may be said to resemble in miniature a human bicuspid tooth with two divergent roots, and consists of a body and two processes. The **body** (Corpus incudis) articulates with the head of the hammer. The **long process** (Crus longum) projects downward from the body and then curves inward; its extremity has attached to it a small nodule of bone, the **os lenticulare,** which articulates with the head of the stapes. The **short process** (Crus breve) projects chiefly backward, and is attached to the wall of the recess by a small ligament.

The **stapes** or stirrup consists of a head, two crura, and a base. The **head** (Capitulum stapedis) is directed outward and articulates with the os lenticulare. The **crura,** anterior and posterior (Crus anterius, posterius), are directed inward from the head, and join the ends of the base. The **base** or foot-plate (Basis stapedis) occupies the fenestra vestibuli, to which it is attached. The space between the crura and the base is closed by a membrane.

The **articulations** and **ligaments** of the auditory ossicles comprise: (1) A diarthrodial joint between the head of the malleus and the body of the incus (Articulatio incudomalleolaris), enclosed by a capsule. (2) An enarthrosis between the os lenticulare and the head of the stapes (Articulatio incudostapedia), also surrounded by a capsule. (3) The base of the stapes is attached to the margin of the fenestra vestibuli by a ring of elastic fibers (Lig. annulare baseos stapedis). (4) Small ligaments attach the head of the malleus and the short crus of the incus to the roof of the epitympanic recess. (5) The axial ligament (of Helmholtz) attaches the neck of the malleus to a small projection (Spina tympanica anterior) above and in front of the annulus tympanicus.

The **muscles** of the auditory ossicles are two in number, viz., the tensor tympani and the stapedius. The **tensor tympani** arises from the upper wall of the osseous Eustachian tube, and ends in a delicate tendon which bends outward and is inserted into the handle of the malleus near its upper end. When it contracts, it draws the handle of the malleus inward and tenses the membrana tympani; it probably also rotates the malleus around its long axis. It is innervated by the motor part of the trigeminus through the otic ganglion. The **stapedius** arises from a small prominence (Eminentia pyramidalis) of the posterior wall of the tympanum, runs forward on the facial nerve, and is inserted into the neck of the stapes. Its action is to draw the head of the stapes backward and rotate the anterior end of the base outward, thus tensing the annular ligament. It is innervated by the facial nerve.

The **tympanic mucous membrane** (Tunica mucosa tympanica) is continuous with that of the pharynx and the guttural pouch through the auditive or Eustachian tube. It is thin, closely united with the underlying periosteum, and is reflected over the ossicles, ligaments, and muscles, the chorda tympani, and the facial nerve in the open part of the facial canal. It contains minute lymph nodules and small mucous glands (Glandulæ tympanicæ). The epithelium is in general columnar ciliated, but over the membrana tympani, ossicles, and promontory it is flattened.

The **artery** of the tympanum is the stylo-mastoid, a small vessel which arises from the posterior auricular branch of the external carotid artery. It enters the tympanum through the stylo-mastoid foramen, and forms a circle around the tympanic membrane. The **nerves** of the mucous membrane come from the tympanic plexus.

The Auditive or Eustachian Tube

The **auditive** or **Eustachian tube** (Tuba auditiva) extends from the tympanic cavity to the pharynx; it transmits air to the former and equalizes the pressure on the two surfaces of the membrana tympani. It is directed forward, downward, and slightly inward, and is four to five inches (ca. 10 to 12 cm.) in length. Its posterior extremity lies at the medial side of the root of the muscular process of the petrous temporal, and communicates with the anterior part of the tympanic cavity by the small, slit-like **tympanic opening** (Ostium tympanicum tubæ auditivæ). For a distance of about a quarter of an inch (ca. 6–7 mm.) in front of this opening it is a complete tube, with a curved lumen which is little more than a capillary space. Further forward it has the form of a plate which widens anteriorly and is curved to enclose a narrow groove that opens ventrally into an extensive diverticulum termed the guttural pouch. The **pharyngeal opening** (Ostium pharyngeum tubæ audittivæ) is situated on the postero-superior part of the lateral wall of the pharynx, just below the level of the posterior nares (Fig. 349). It is a slit, about two inches (ca. 5 cm.) in length, which slopes downward and backward. It is bounded medially by the thin free edge of the tube, from the lower part of which a fold of mucous membrane (Plica salpingo-pharyngea) extends in the same direction on the lateral wall of the pharynx for a distance of a little more than an inch usually. The outer boundary of the opening is the lateral wall of the pharynx. The basis of the tube is a plate of fibro-cartilage (Cartilago tubæ auditivæ) which is firmly attached dorsally to the fibrous tissue which closes the foramen lacerum, the temporal wing of the sphenoid, and the pterygoid bone.[1] On cross-section the cartilage is seen to consist—except at its ends—of two laminæ which are continuous with each other above (Fig. 348). The medial lamina (Lamina medialis) gradually widens toward the pharyngeal end, where it forms a broad valvular flap; this is convex medially, and its thin anterior edge forms the basis of the inner margin of the pharyngeal opening. Behind this the lamina has a thick free edge which projects ventrally from the roof of the guttural pouch. The lateral lamina (Lamina lateralis) is narrow and thin, and is related laterally to the levator and tensor palati muscles, which are in part attached to it; it does not extend to the pharyngeal end of the tube. The mucous membrane of the tube is continuous behind with that of the tympanum and in front with that of the pharynx. On either side it is reflected to form a large diverticulum, the guttural pouch. It is covered with ciliated epithelium, and contains mucous glands and lymph nodules.

The pharyngeal opening appears to be closed ordinarily. Vermeulen states that it opens during deglutition, and that this action is apparently produced by the part of the palato-pharyngeus muscle which is attached to the flap-like expanded part of the tube.

THE GUTTURAL POUCHES

The **guttural pouches** (Sacci gutturales) (Figs. 349, 706), are large mucous sacs, each of which is a ventral diverticulum of the Eustachian tube (Diverticulum tubæ auditivæ); they are not present in the domesticated animals other than the equidæ. They are situated between the base of the cranium and the atlas dorsally and the pharynx ventrally. Medially they are in apposition in part, but are to some extent separated by the intervening ventral straight muscles of the head. The anterior end is a small cul-de-sac which lies below the body of the presphenoid, between the auditive tube and the median recess of the pharynx. The posterior end lies near or below the atlantal attachment of the longus colli. The pouch is related dorsally to the base of the cranium, the atlanto-occipital joint capsule, and the ventral straight muscles. Ventrally it lies on the pharynx and the origin of the œsophagus. Laterally the relations are numerous and complex. They comprise the pterygoid, levator palati, tensor palati, stylo-hyoideus, occipito-hyoideus, occipito-mandibularis, and digastricus muscles; the parotid and mandibular salivary glands; the external carotid, internal maxillary, and external maxillary arteries; the internal maxillary and jugular veins; the pharyngeal lymph glands; the glosso-pharyngeal, hypoglossal, and anterior laryngeal nerves. The vagus, accessory, and sympathetic nerves, the anterior cervical ganglion, the internal carotid artery, and the ventral cerebral vein are situated in a fold of the dorsal part of the pouch. The pouch is reflected around the dorsal border of the great cornu of the hyoid bone so as to clothe both surfaces of the dorsal part of the latter. It thus forms an outer compartment, which extends backward lateral to the great cornu and the occipito-hyoideus muscle; this compartment is related laterally to the parotid gland, the articulation of the jaw, the ascending part of the internal maxillary artery, the superficial temporal artery, and the facial nerve; dor-

---

[1] There is, strictly speaking, no osseous part of the tube such as occurs in man. In the horse the cartilage extends to the tympanic orifice.

sally it covers the mandibular nerve and its chief branches, and is attached to the styloid process of the conchal cartilage.

Each pouch communicates with the pharynx through the pharyngeal orifice of the Eustachian tube, and is in direct continuity with the mucous membrane of the latter. The average capacity of each pouch is about ten fluid ounces (ca. 300 c.c.); of this, the lateral compartment is about one-third. The pouch is a delicate

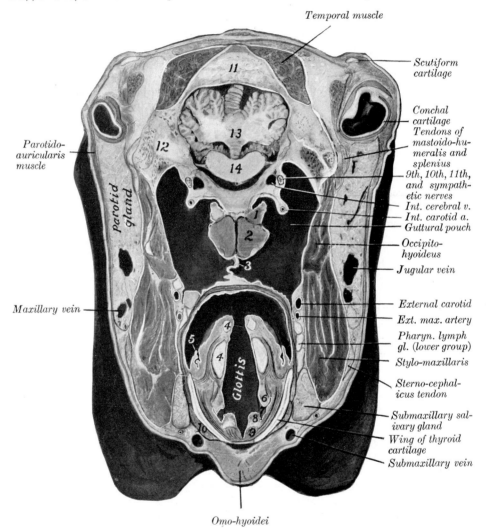

FIG. 706.—CROSS-SECTION OF HEAD OF HORSE.

The section passes through the base of the external ear and just behind the posterior border of the mandible. *1,* Rectus capitis ventralis minor; *2,* rectus capitis ventralis major; *3,* medial walls of guttural pouches in apposition; *4, 4,* arytenoid cartilage, upper piece being apex; *5,* posterior pillar of soft palate; *6,* false vocal cord; *7,* lateral ventricle of larynx; *8,* true vocal cord; *9,* vocal muscle; *10,* thyro-hyoideus muscle; *11,* supra-occipital; *12,* petrous temporal; *13,* cerebellum; *14,* medulla oblongata. The cavity in which the number *5* is placed is the pharynx.

mucous membrane which is in general rather loosely attached to the surrounding structures. It is lined with ciliated epithelium and is supplied with glands which are chiefly mucous in type. Numerous lymph nodules are present in the young subject.

It is worthy of note that the pharyngeal orifice of the Eustachian tube is at such a level as to provide (in the ordinary position of the head) only an overflow outlet for the escape of fluid which may accumulate in the pouch. The expanded part of the tube forms with the wall of the pharynx a sort of vestibule, at the posterior part of which is the opening of the guttural pouch.

This opening is only about an inch (ca. 2.5 cm.) long. The two pouches are often unequal in size, and variations in regard to the distance which they extend backward are not uncommon. In one case, for instance, a small aged horse, the right pouch extended along the œsophagus about five inches (ca. 12 cm.) behind the ventral tubercle of the atlas, and the left one a little more than two inches (ca. 6 cm.). No pathological changes were apparent, and the condition was not recognizable externally. Cases of extreme size—so-called tympanites— of the pouches occur, and are apparently congenital defects. In a case in a yearling colt, the head of which was 24 inches long, the left pouch extended about 12 inches (ca. 30 cm.) behind the tubercle of the atlas, and had a capacity of six quarts. The anterior end formed a cul-de-sac about two inches (ca. 5 cm.) long between the Eustachian tube and levator palati medially and the lateral pterygoid muscle laterally.

THE INTERNAL EAR

The **internal ear** (Auris interna) consists of two parts, viz.: (1) A complex membranous sac, which supports the auditory cells and the peripheral ramifications of the auditory nerve; (2) a series of cavities in the petrous temporal bone, which encloses the membranous part. The first is called the **membranous labyrinth,** and contains a fluid, the **endolymph.** The second is the **osseous labyrinth.** The two are separated by the **perilymphatic space,** which is occupied by a fluid termed the **perilymph.**

THE OSSEOUS LABYRINTH

The **osseous labyrinth** (Labyrinthus osseus) (Fig. 702) is excavated in the petrous temporal bone medial to the tympanic cavity. It consists of three divisions: (1) a middle part, the **vestibule;** (2) an anterior one, the **cochlea;** and (3) a posterior one, the **semicircular canals.**

1. The **vestibule** (Vestibulum) is the central part of the osseous labyrinth, and communicates in front with the cochlea, behind with the semicircular canals. It is a small, irregularly ovoid cavity, which is about 5 to 6 mm. in length. Its lateral wall separates it from the tympanic cavity, and in it is the **fenestra vestibuli,** which is occupied by the base of the stapes. The medial wall corresponds to the fundus of the internal acoustic meatus. It is crossed by an oblique ridge, the **crista vestibuli,** which separates two recesses. The anterior and smaller of these is the **recessus sphæricus,** which lodges the saccule of the membranous labyrinth. In its lower part there are about a dozen minute foramina which transmit filaments of the vestibular nerve to the saccule. The posterior and larger depression is the **recessus ellipticus,** which lodges the utricle of the membranous labyrinth. The crista vestibuli divides below into two divergent branches, which include between them the small **recessus cochlearis;** this is perforated by small foramina, through which nerve-bundles reach the ductus cochlearis. Similar foramina in the recessus ellipticus and the crista vestibuli transmit nerve filaments to the utricle and the ampullæ of the dorsal and lateral semicircular ducts. The anterior wall is pierced by an opening which leads into the scala vestibuli of the cochlea. The posterior part of the vestibule presents the four openings of the semicircular canals. The inner opening of the **aquæductus vestibuli** is a small slit behind the lower part of the crista vestibuli. The aquæductus passes backward in the petrous temporal bone, and opens on the medial surface of the latter near the middle of its posterior border; it contains the ductus endolymphaticus.

2. The **osseous semicircular canals** (Canales semicirculares ossei), three in number, are situated behind and above the vestibule. They are at right angles to each other, and are designated according to their positions as dorsal, posterior, and lateral. They communicate with the vestibule by four openings only, since the inner end of the dorsal and the upper end of the posterior canal unite to form a common canal (Crus commune), and the ampullate ends of the dorsal and lateral canals have a common orifice. Each canal forms about two-thirds of a circle, one end of which is enlarged and termed the **ampulla.** The **dorsal canal** (Canalis semicircularis dorsalis) is nearly vertical and is placed obliquely with regard to a

sagittal plane, so that its outer limb is further forward then than the inner one. The antero-lateral end is the ampulla and opens into the vestibule with that of the lateral canal. The opposite non-dilated end joins the adjacent end of the posterior canal to form the crus commune, which opens into the dorso-medial part of the vestibule. The **posterior canal** (Canalis semicircularis posterior) is also nearly vertical. Its ampulla is ventral, and opens into the vestibule directly, while the non-dilated end joins that of the dorsal canal. The **lateral canal** (Canalis semicircularis lateralis) is nearly horizontal. Its ampulla is external and opens into the vestibule with that of the dorsal canal.

3. The **cochlea** is the anterior part of the bony labyrinth. It has the form of a short blunt cone, the **base** of which (Basis cochleæ) corresponds to the anterior part of the fundus of the internal acoustic meatus, while the **apex** or **cupola** (Cupola) is directed outward, forward, and downward. It measures about 7 mm. across the base and about 4 mm. from base to apex. It consists of a **spiral canal** (Canalis spiralis cochleæ), which forms two and a half turns around a central column termed the **modiolus.** The modiolus diminishes rapidly in diameter from base to apex. Its base (Basis modioli) corresponds to the area cochleæ of the fundus of the internal acoustic meatus, and its apex extends nearly to the cupola. Projecting from the modiolus like the thread of a screw is a thin plate of bone, the **lamina spiralis ossea.** This begins between the two fenestræ and ends near the cupola as a hook-like process (Hamulus laminæ spiralis). The lamina extends about half-way to the periphery of the cochlea and partly divides the cavity into two passages; of these, the upper one is termed the **scala vestibuli,** and the lower the **scala tympani.** The membrana basilaris extends from the free margin of the lamina to the lateral wall of the cochlea and completes the septum between the two scalæ, but they communicate through the opening at the cupola (Helicotrema). The modiolus is traversed by an axial canal which transmits the nerves to the apical coil, and by a spiral canal (Canalis spiralis modioli), which follows the attached border of the lamina spiralis, and contains the spiral ganglion and vein. Close to the beginning of the scala tympani is the inner orifice of the **aquæductus cochleæ,** a small canal which opens behind the internal acoustic meatus, and establishes a communication between the scala tympani and the subarachnoid space.

The **internal acoustic meatus** has been described in part (*vide* Osteology). The fundus of the meatus is divided by a ridge (Crista transversa) into upper and lower parts. The anterior part of the upper depression (Area n. facialis) presents the internal opening of the facial canal; and the posterior part (Area vestibularis superior) is perforated by foramina for the passage of nerves to the utricle and the ampullæ of the dorsal and lateral semicircular ducts. The anterior part of the inferior depression (Area cochleæ) presents a central foramen and a spiral tract of minute foramina (Tractus spiralis foraminosus) for the passage of nerves to the cochlea. Behind these is an area of small openings which transmit nerves to the saccule (Area vestibularis inferior), and the foramen singulare for the passage of a nerve to the ampulla of the posterior semicircular duct.

The Membranous Labyrinth

The **membranous labyrinth** (Labyrinthus membranaceus) lies within, but does not fill, the osseous labyrinth. It is attached to the latter by delicate trabeculæ which traverse the perilymphatic space. It conforms more or less closely to the bony labyrinth, but consists of four divisions, since the vestibule contains two membranous sacs—the utricle and saccule.

1. The **utricle** (Utriculus), the larger of the two sacs, lies in the postero-superior part of the vestibule, largely in the recessus ellipticus. It receives the openings of the semicircular ducts, and the small **ductus utriculo-saccularis** leads from its lower part to the ductus endolymphaticus.

2. The **saccule** (Sacculus) is situated in the recessus sphæricus of the vestibule. From its lower part the **ductus reuniens** proceeds to open into the ductus cochlearis, a little in front of the blind end of the latter. A second narrow tube, the **ductus endolymphaticus,** passes from the posterior part of the saccule, and is joined by the ductus utriculo-saccularis; it then traverses the aquæductus vestibuli, and terminates under the dura mater on the posterior part of the medial surface of the petrous temporal bone in a dilated blind end, the saccus endolymphaticus.

3. The **semicircular ducts** (Ductus semicirculares)[1] correspond in general to the osseous canals already described, but it may be noted that while the ampullæ of the ducts nearly fill those of the osseous canals, the other parts of the ducts only occupy about one-fourth of the bony cavities.

4. The **cochlear duct** (Ductus cochlearis) is a spiral tube situated within the cochlea. It begins by a blind end (Cæcum vestibulare) in the cochlear recess of the vestibule, and ends by a second blind end (Cæcum cupulare), which is attached to the cupola of the cochlea. The vestibular part is connected with the saccule by the ductus reuniens. The duct is triangular in cross-section, and it is usual to regard it as having three walls. The vestibular wall or roof, which separates the cochlear duct from the scala vestibuli, is formed by the very delicate **membrana vestibularis** (of Reissner), which extends obliquely from the lamina spiralis ossea

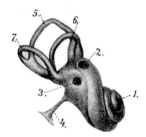

FIG. 707.—LEFT MEMBRANOUS LABYRINTH (ENLARGED).

1, Cochlea; *2*, fenestra vestibuli; *3*, fenestra cochleæ; *4*, ductus endolymphaticus; *5*, dorsal, *6*, lateral, *7*, ventral, duct. (After Ellenberger, in Leisering's Atlas.)

FIG. 708.—SCHEMATIC SECTIONAL VIEW OF LABYRINTH (ENLARGED).

1, 2, 3, Dorsal, lateral, and ventral ducts; *4,* utricle; *5,* saccule; *6,* cochlea; *7,* acoustic nerve. (After Ellenberger, in Leisering's Atlas.)

to the outer wall of the cochlea. The tympanic wall or floor intervenes between the cochlear duct and the scala tympani; it is formed by the periosteum of the marginal part of the lamina spiralis and the **membrana basilaris,** which stretches between the free edge of the lamina and the outer wall of the cochlea. The outer wall consists of the fibrous lining of the cochlea, which is greatly thickened to form the **ligamentum spirale cochleæ.**

Structure.—The membranous labyrinth consists in general of an outer thin fibrous layer, a middle transparent tunic, and an internal epithelium, composed of flattened cells. But in certain situations special and remarkable structures occur, among which are the following: (1) The **maculæ acusticæ** appear as small whitish thickenings of the inner walls of the saccule and utricle. The epithelium here consists of two kinds of cells, viz., supporting cells and hair cells. The latter are flask-shaped and are surrounded by the fusiform supporting cells. The free end of each hair cell bears a stiff, hair-like process composed of a bundle of cilia. Fibers of the saccular and utricular branches of the vestibular nerve form arborizations about the basal parts of the hair cells. Adherent to the surface of the maculæ are fine crystals of lime salts, embedded in a mucoid substance, and termed otoconia. (2) The **cristæ acusticæ** are linear thickenings of the wall of each ampulla of the semicircular ducts. Their structure is similar to that of the maculæ. (3) The **spiral organ** of Corti (Organon spirale) is an epithelial elevation which is situated upon the inner part of the membrana basilaris, and extends the entire length of the ductus cochlearis. It is very complicated in structure, but consists essentially of remarkable supporting cells and hair cells. Fibers of the cochlear nerve ramify about the basal parts of the hair cells.

Vessels and Nerves.—The **artery** of the internal ear is the internal auditory artery, a very small vessel which usually arises from the posterior cerebellar artery, and enters the internal acoustic meatus. The **veins** go to the ventral petrosal sinus. The **vestibular nerve** is distributed to the utricle, saccule, and semi-circular ducts, and mediates equilibration. The **cochlear nerve** gives a branch to the saccule and enters the central canal of the modiolus. Along its course it gives off fibers which radiate outward between the two plates of the lamina spiralis ossea, and ramify about the hair cells of the organ of Corti. The **ganglion spirale** is situated in the spiral canal of the modiolus near the fixed border of the lamina spiralis. The cochlear nerve mediates the sense of hearing.

THE COMMON INTEGUMENT

The **common integument** (Integumentum commune) is the protective covering of the body, and is continuous at the natural openings with the mucous membranes of the digestive, respiratory, and urogenital tracts. It consists of the **skin** (Cutis), together with certain appendages or modifications thereof, as hair, horn, feathers, etc. It contains peripheral ramifications of the sensory nerves, and is thus an important sense organ. It is the principal factor in the regulation of the temperature of the body, and by means of its glands it plays an important part in secretion and excretion. Some of its special horny modifications or appendages are used as organs of prehension or as weapons.

The **thickness** of the skin varies in the different species, on different parts of the body of the same animal, and also with the breed, sex, and age. The **color** also varies greatly, but this is masked in most places by the covering of hair or wool. The skin is in general highly elastic and resistant.

Permanent **folds** of the skin (Plicæ cutis) occur in certain situations, and in some places there are cutaneous **pouches** or **diverticula** (Sinus cutis).

The skin is attached to the underlying parts by the **subcutaneous tissue or subcutis** (Tela subcutanea). This consists of connective tissue containing elastic fibers and fat. When the fat forms a layer of considerable thickness it is termed the **panniculus adiposus.** Over a considerable part of the body the subcutis contains striped muscle, the **m. cutaneus;** in some regions the fibers of the muscle are inserted into the skin, and their contraction twitches the skin or produces temporary folds (it has been described in the myology). The amount of subcutaneous tissue varies widely; in some places it is abundant, so that the skin can be raised considerably; in other situations it is practically absent and the skin is closely adherent to the subjacent structures. **Subcutaneous bursæ** often develop over prominent parts of the skeleton where there is much pressure or friction, e. g., at the olecranon, tuber coxæ, tuber calcis.

Structure.—The skin consists of two distinct strata, viz., a superficial epithelial layer, the **epidermis,** and a deep connective-tissue layer, the **corium.** The **epidermis** is a non-vascular, stratified epithelium of varying thickness. It presents the openings of the cutaneous glands and the hair-follicles, and its deep surface is adapted to the corium.[1] It is divisible into a superficial, harder, drier part, the **stratum corneum,** and a deeper, softer, moister part, the **stratum germinativum.** The cells of the latter contain pigment, and by their proliferation compensate the loss by desquamation of the superficial part of the stratum corneum. In many places further subdivision into strata is evident on properly prepared cross-sections. The **corium** consists essentially of a feltwork of white and elastic fibers. It is well supplied with vessels and nerves, and contain the cutaneous glands, the hair-follicles, and unstriped muscle. The deeper part of the corium, the **tunica propria,** consists of a relatively loose network of coarse bundles of fibers, and in most places there is no clear line of demarcation between it and the subcutis. The superficial part, the **corpus papillare,** is of finer texture and is free from fat. Its superficial face is thickly beset with blunt conical prominences, the **papillæ,** which are received into corresponding depressions of the epidermis. They contain vascular loops and nerves, or, in certain situations, special nerve-endings.[2]

The **glands** of the skin (Glandulæ cutis) are chiefly of two kinds, sudoriferous and sebaceous. The **sudoriferous** or **sweat glands** (Glandulæ sudoriferæ) consist of a tube, the lower, secretory part of which is coiled in the deep part of the corium or in the subcutis to form a round or oval ball (Corpus glandulæ sudoriferæ). The excretory duct (Ductus sudoriferus) passes almost straight up through the corium, but pursues a more or less flexuous course through the epidermis, and opens into a hair-follicle or by a funnel-shaped pore (Porus sudoriferus) on the surface of the skin. The **sebaceous glands** (Glandulæ sebaceæ) are in great part associated with the hairs, into the follicles of which they open. Their size varies widely, and is in general in inverse ratio to that of the hair. The larger ones are easily seen with the naked eye, and appear as small, pale yellow or brownish bodies. In certain situations (e. g., the labia, vulvæ, anus, prepuce) they are independent of the hairs and are well developed. In form they may be branched alveolar, simple alveolar, or even tubular in type. They secrete a fatty substance, the **sebum cutaneum,** which serves as a protective against moisture, and may also (by its aromatic constituents) play an important part in the sexual life of animals.

The two kinds of glands described above are those which are most widely distributed, but many special types occur. Some of these are to be regarded as modified sweat glands, e. g., the naso-labial glands of the ox, the glands of the snout of the pig, and the glands of the digital cushion of the horse. Others, e. g., the tarsal glands of the eyelids, are modified sebaceous. Still others are not yet classified satisfactorily. Some of these special types have been referred to in previous chapters, and others will receive attention in the special descriptions which follow. The mammary glands are highly modified cutaneous glands, which are intimately associated in function with the genital organs, and have been described with the latter.

Vessels and Nerves.—The **arteries** of the skin enter from the subcutis, where they communicate freely. In the deeper part of the corium they form a plexus, and another network is formed under the papillæ. Small vessels from the deep plexus go to the fat and sweat glands, and the subpapillary plexus sends fine branches to the papillæ, hair-follicles, and sebaceous glands. The **veins** form two plexuses, one beneath the papillæ, and another at the junction of the corium and subcutis. The **lymph vessels** form subpapillary and subcutaneous plexuses.

The **nerves** vary widely in number in different parts of the skin. The terminal fibers either end free in the epidermis and in certain parts of the corium, or form special microscopic corpuscles of several kinds.

[1] To prevent a possible misapprehension, it may be stated that the epidermis primarily molds the corium, and that the glands and hair-follicles are invaginations of the epidermis.

[2] The papillæ are best developed where the epidermis is thick and hairs are small or absent. On thickly haired regions they are small or even absent. On certain parts of the body (anus, vulva, prepuce, scrotum, eyelids, etc.) the corium contains pigment in its connective-tissue cells.

THE APPENDAGES OF THE SKIN

The so-called appendages of the skin are modifications of the epidermis, and comprise the hairs, hoofs, claws, horns, etc.

The **hairs** (Pili) cover almost the entire surface of the body in the domesticated mammals, and some parts which appear at first sight to be bare are found on close inspection to be provided with sparse and very fine hair. The hairs are constantly being shed and replaced, but at certain periods in the horse, for example, they fall out in great numbers, constituting the shedding of the coat. It is customary to distinguish the ordinary hairs (the coat), which determine the color of the animal, from the special varieties found in certain places. Among the latter are the long

Fig. 709.—Lateral View of Horse to Show Hair-streams and Vortices. (After Ellenberger-Baum, Anat. für Künstler.)

tactile hairs (Pili tactiles) about the lips, nostrils, and eyes; the **eyelashes** or **cilia;** the **tragi** of the external ear; and the **vibrissæ** of the nostrils. Other special features will be noted in the discussion of the skin of the various species. The hairs are directed in such a way as to form more or less definite **hair-streams** (Flumina pilorum), and at certain points these converge to form **vortices** (Vortices pilorum).

The part of the hair above the surface of the skin is the **shaft** (Scapus pili), while the **root** (Radix pili) is embedded in a depression termed the **hair-follicle** (Folliculus pili). A vascular **papilla** (Papilla pili) projects up in the fundus of the follicle and is capped by the expanded end of the root, the **bulb** of the hair (Bulbus pili). The hair-follicles extend obliquely into the corium to a varying depth; in the case of the long tactile hairs they reach to the underlying muscle. Most of the follicles have attached to them small unstriped muscles known as the **arrectores pilorum;** these are attached to an acute angle to the under side of the deep part of the follicle, and their contraction causes erection of the hair and compression of the sebaceous glands, one or more of which open into the follicle.

The hairs are composed of epidermal cells, and consist from without inward of three parts. The **cuticle** is composed of horny, scale-like cells which overlap like slates on a roof. The **cortex** consists of horny fusiform cells which are packed close together and contain pigment. The **medulla** is the central core of softer, cubical or polyhedral cells; it contains some pigment and air-spaces.

The hair-follicles, being invaginations of the skin, are composed of a central epidermal part and a peripheral layer which corresponds in structure to the corium. The follicles of the tactile hairs have remarkably thick walls which contain blood-sinuses between their outer and inner layers; in ungulates the sinuses are crossed by trabeculæ and assume the character of cavernous or erectile tissue.

The **hoofs, claws, horns,** and other horny structures consist of closely packed epidermal cells which have undergone cornification. In structure they might be compared to hairs matted together by intervening epidermal cells. They cover a specialized corium from which the stratum germinativum derives its nutrition.

THE SKIN OF THE HORSE

The **thickness** of the skin of the horse varies from one to five millimeters in different regions, and is greatest at the attachment of the mane and on the dorsal surface of the tail.

The **glands** are numerous and are larger than those of the other domesticated animals. The sebaceous glands are specially developed on the lips, the prepuce, mammary glands, perineum, and labia of the vulva. The sweat glands are yellow or brown in color. They occur in almost all parts of the skin, but are largest and most numerous in that of the lateral wing of the nostril, the flank, mammary glands, and free part of the penis.

In addition to the ordinary and tactile **hairs** certain regions present coarse hairs of great length. The mane (Juba) springs from the dorsal border of the neck and the adjacent part of the withers; its anterior part, which covers the forehead to a variable extent, is termed the foretop (Cirrus capitis). The tail, with the exception of its ventral surface, bears very large and long hairs (Cirrus caudæ). The tuft of long hairs on the flexion surface of the fetlock (Cirrus pedis) gave rise to the popular name of this region.

The development of these special hairs varies widely, and is in general much greater in the draft breeds than in others. In Shire and Clydesdale horses, for instance, the hair on the posterior aspect of the metacarpus and metatarsus and fetlock is often so long and abundant as to account for the term "feather," which is commonly applied to it by horsemen.

Subcutaneous bursæ (Bursæ subcutaneæ) may be present at various prominent points, e. g., the olecranon, the tuber coxæ, the tuber calcis, the withers, etc. They are not present in the young subject and appear to be the result of traumatism.

THE HOOF

The **hoof** (Ungula) is the horny covering of the distal end of the digit. It is convenient to divide it for description into three parts, termed the wall, sole, and frog.

1. The **wall** (Paries ungulæ) is defined as the part of the hoof which is visible when the foot is placed on the ground.[1] It covers the front and sides of the foot, and is reflected posteriorly at an acute angle to form the bars. The latter (Pila ungulæ medialis, lateralis) appear on the ground surface of the hoof as convergent

---

[1] The term foot is used here in the popular sense, i. e., to designate the hoof and the structures enclosed within it.

ridges, which subside in front and are fused with the sole; they are united with each other by the frog. For topographic purposes the wall may be divided into an anterior part or " toe " (Paries ungulæ dorsalis), medial and lateral parts or " quarters " (Paries ungulæ medialis, lateralis), and the angles or " heels " (Anguli parietales). It presents two surfaces and two borders. The **external surface** is convex from side to side and slopes obliquely from edge to edge. In front the angle of inclination on the ground plane is about 50° for the forelimb, 55° for the hind limb; on the sides the angle gradually increases and is about 100° at the heels. The curve of the wall is wider on the lateral than on the medial side, and the slope of the medial quarter is steeper than that of the lateral one.[1] The surface is smooth and is crossed by more or less distinct ridges, which are parallel with the coronary border and indicate variations in the activity of the growth of the hoof. It is also marked by fine parallel striæ, which extend from border to border in an almost rectilinear manner and indicate the direction of the horn tubes.

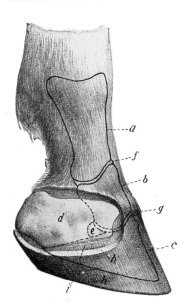

The **internal surface** is concave from side to side, and bears about six hundred thin **primary laminæ,** which extend from the coronary groove to the basal border of the wall. Each bears a hundred or more **secondary laminæ** on its surfaces, so that the arrangement is pennate on cross-section. The laminæ are continued on the inner surface of the bars, and dovetail with corresponding laminæ of the corium. The proximal **coronary border** (Margo coronarius) is thin. Its outer aspect is covered by a layer of soft, light-colored horn known as the **periople** (Limbus corneus); this appears as a ring-like prominence above and gradually fades out below; at the angle it forms a wide cap or bulb and blends centrally with the frog. The inner aspect of the border is excavated to form the **coronary groove** (Sulcus coronarius ungulæ), which contains the thick coronary corium. The groove narrows on the sides, and merges at the angles with the perioplic groove. It is perforated by innumerable small, funnel-like openings which are occupied by the papillæ of the coronary corium in the natural state. Above the thin border of the wall proper there is a small **perioplic groove** which contains the corium of the periople. At the heel this groove widens and is merged with the coronary groove.

FIG. 710.—DIGIT OF HORSE, SHOWING SURFACE RELATIONS OF BONES AND JOINTS. THE CARTILAGE IS LARGELY EXPOSED.

a, First phalanx; *b,* second phalanx; *c,* third phalanx; *d,* cartilage; *e,* distal sesamoid or navicular bone; *f,* pastern joint; *g,* coffin joint; *h',* cut edge of wall of hoof (*h*); *i,* laminar corium. (After Ellenberger, in Leisering's Atlas.)

The **basal or ground border** (Margo basilaris) of the unshod hoof comes in contact with the ground. Its thickness is greatest in front and decreases considerably from before backward on the sides, but there is a slight increase at the angles. Its inner face is united with the periphery of the sole by horn of lighter color and softer

---

[1] The slope of the wall varies considerably in apparently normal hoofs. Lungwitz found by careful measurements of 56 fore and 36 hind feet the following average angles:

	FORE FOOT	HIND FOOT
Toe	47.26°	54.1°
Medial angle	101.57°	96.5°
Lateral angle	101.37°	96.1°

The wall of the fore foot may even be more upright than that of the hind, and may have an angle of 60°. The **length** of the wall at the toe, quarters, and heels is in the ratio of about 3 : 2 : 1 in the fore foot and about 2 : 1½ : 1 in the hind hoof.

[2] The wide groove at the heels, however, contains chiefly the corium of the periople.

texture, which appears on the ground surface of the hoof as the so-called "white line" or **zona lamellata.**

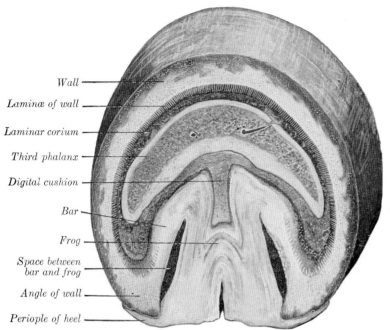

Wall
Laminæ of wall
Laminar corium
Third phalanx
Digital cushion
Bar
Frog
Space between bar and frog
Angle of wall
Periople of heel

FIG. 711.—CROSS-SECTION OF FOOT OF HORSE, CUT PARALLEL WITH THE CORONARY BORDER.
The wall appears much thicker at the angles than it actually is, because it is cut very obliquely.

In the case of unshod horses at liberty the wall is usually worn off to the level of the adjacent sole, but if the ground is too soft the wall is likely to become unduly long and split or break or undergo deformation. On very hard or rough ground, on the other hand, the wear may be in ex-

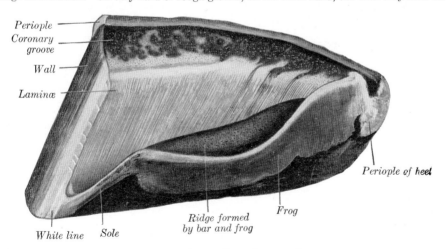

Periople
Coronary groove
Wall
Laminæ
Periople of heel
White line
Sole
Ridge formed by bar and frog
Frog

FIG. 712.—HALF OF HOOF OF HORSE; INTERNAL SURFACE.

cess of the growth. In the case of shod horses it is necessary to remove the excess of growth of the wall at each shoeing. The **thickness** of the wall at the toe, quarters, and heels is about in the ratio of 4 : 3 : 2 for the fore foot and about 3 : 2½ : 2 for the hind foot.

2. The **sole** (Solea ungulæ) constitutes the greater part of the ground sur-

face of the hoof. It is somewhat crescentic in outline, and presents two surfaces and two borders. The **internal surface** is convex, and slopes with a varying degree of obliquity downward to the convex border. It presents numerous small funnel-like openings which contain the papillæ of the sole corium in the natural state. The **external** or **ground surface** (Facies solearis) is the converse of the preceding. It is normally arched—and more strongly in the hind than in the fore foot—but the curvature is subject to wide variation; in heavy draft horses the sole is commonly less curved than in the lighter breeds and may even be flat. The surface is usually rough, since the horn exfoliates here in irregular flakes. The **convex border** (Margo parietalis) is joined to the wall by relatively soft horn, previously referred to as forming the "white line" on the ground surface of the hoof. The

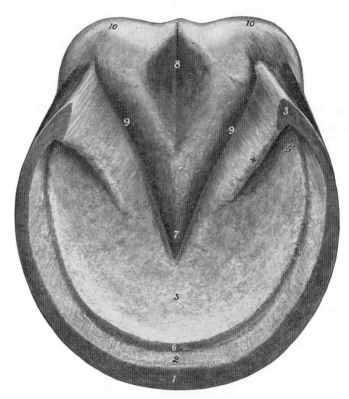

FIG. 713.—RIGHT FORE HOOF OF HORSE; GROUND SURFACE.

1, Basal or ground border of wall; *2*, laminæ of wall; *3*, angle of wall; *4*, bar; *5*, sole; *5′*, angle of sole; *6*, white line (junction of wall and sole); *7*, apex of frog; *8*, central sulcus of frog; *9, 9*, collateral sulci between frog and bars; *10, 10*, bulbs of hoof.

angle of junction is rounded internally and presents a number of low ridges and specially large openings for the papillæ of the corium. There is frequently a ridge of larger size at the toe. The **concave border** (Margo centralis) has the form of a deep angle which is occupied by the bars and the apex of the frog. It concurs in part with these in forming two pronounced ridges in the interior of the foot. The parts of the sole between the wall and bars are termed its **angles** (Anguli soleæ).

　　3. The **frog** (Cuneus ungulæ) is a wedge-shaped mass which occupies the angle bounded by the bars and sole, and extends considerably below these on the ground surface of the foot. It may be described as having four surfaces, a base, and an apex. The **internal surface** bears a central ridge, the **spine** or "frog-stay" (Spina cunei), which is high posteriorly and subsides abruptly in front. On either side of this there is a deep depression, which is bounded outwardly by the rounded

ridge formed by the junction of the frog with the bar and sole. This surface presents fine striæ and openings for the papillæ of the corium. The **external** or **ground surface** presents a **central sulcus** (Sulcus cunei centralis), which is bounded by two ridges, the crura (Crura cunei). The **medial** and **lateral surfaces** (Facies medialis et lateralis) are united at the upper part with the bars and sole, but are free below and form the central wall of the deep **collateral sulci** (Sulci cunei collaterales), which are bounded outwardly by the bars. The **base** (Basis cunei) is depressed centrally and prominent at the sides, where it unites with the angles of the wall; the junction here is covered by the expanded periople and constitutes the bulb of the hoof. A central projection points upward. The **apex** (Apex cunei) occupies the central angle of the concave border of the sole, and forms a blunt, round prominence a little in front of the middle of the ground surface of the hoof.

FIG. 714.—SECTION OF HOOF OF HORSE.

The section is cut just above the ridges of the frog and bars and parallel with the ground surface. *1*, Wall; *2*, sole; *3*, spine of frog or "frog-stay"; *4*, ridge formed by junction of frog and bar; *5*, central furrow over apex of frog; *6*, laminæ of wall; *7*, laminæ of bar.

Structure of the Hoof.—The hoof is composed of epithelial cells which are more or less completely keratinized except in its deepest part, the **stratum germinativum;** here the cells have not undergone cornification, and by their proliferation maintain the growth of the hoof. The cells are in part arranged to form **horn tubes** (Cylindri cornei) which are united by intertubular epithelium, and enclose medullary cells and air-spaces. The **wall** consists of three layers. The **external layer** comprises the periople and the stratum tectorium. The **periople** (Limbus corneæ ungulæ) is composed of soft, non-pigmented, tubular horn, and becomes white when the hoof is soaked in water. It is continuous with the epidermis of the skin above, and extends downward a variable distance. Usually it forms a distinct band somewhat less than an inch wide, except at the heels, where it is much wider, and caps the angle of inflection of the wall, forming the so-called bulb of the heel (Pulvinus corneus).

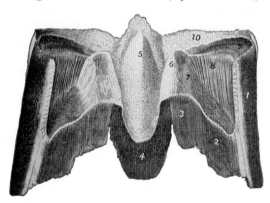

FIG. 715.—FRONTAL SECTION OF HOOF OF HORSE, POSTERIOR PART VIEWED FROM IN FRONT.

1, Wall; *2*, sole; *3*, bar; *4*, frog; *5*, central ridge of frog; *6*, lateral ridge formed by junction of frog and bar; *7*, laminæ of bar; *8*, laminæ of wall; *9*, coronary groove; *10*, periople of heel.

The **stratum tectorium** is a thin layer of horny scales which gives the outer surface of the wall below the periople its smooth, glossy appearance. The **middle layer**

(Stratum medium) forms the bulk of the wall, and is the densest part of the hoof. Its horn tubes run in a parallel direction from the coronary to the basal border. In dark hoofs it is pigmented except in its deep part. The **laminar layer** (Stratum lamellatum) is internal; it consists of the **horny laminæ** (Lamellæ corneæ), and is non-pigmented. The primary laminæ are narrow and thin at their origin at the lower margin of the coronary groove, but become wider and thicker distally. At the junction of the wall and sole they are united by interlaminar horn to form the white zone or line. Only the central part of the laminæ becomes fully keratinized. They are composed of non-tubular horn in the normal state.

The **sole** consists of tubular and intertubular horn. The tubes run parallel with those of the wall and vary much in size.

The **frog** is composed of relatively soft horn, which is much more elastic than that of the wall or sole, and is not fully keratinized. The horn tubes in it are slightly flexuous.

The hoof is non-vascular and receives its nutrition from the corium. It is also destitute of nerves.

THE CORIUM OF THE FOOT

The **corium** of the foot or **pododerm** (Corium ungulæ) is the specially modified and highly vascular part of the corium of the common integument which furnishes nutrition to the hoof. It is convenient to divide it into five parts which nourish corresponding parts of the hoof.[1]

1. The **perioplic corium** (Corium limitans) is a band 5 to 6 mm. in width which lies in the perioplic groove above the thin edge of the coronary border of the wall. It is continuous above with the corium of the skin, and is marked off by a groove from the coronary corium except at the angles; here it widens and blends with the corium of the frog. It bears very fine, short papillæ which curve downward and are received in depressions of the periople, to which it supplies nutrition.

2. The **coronary corium** (Corium coronarium) is the thick part of the corium which occupies the coronary groove, and furnishes nutrition to the bulk of the wall. It diminishes in width and thickness posteriorly, and along the upper border of the bar it is not clearly defined from the corium of the frog. The convex superficial surface is thickly covered with filiform papillæ 4 to 6 mm. in length, which are received into the funnel-like openings of the coronary groove. At the heels and along the bars the papillæ are arranged in rows, separated by fine furrows. The deep surface is attached to the extensor tendon and the cartilages of the third phalanx by an abundant subcutis which contains many elastic fibers and a rich venous plexus.

3. The **laminar corium** (Corium lamellatum) bears primary and secondary laminæ which are interleaved with the horny laminæ of the wall and bars in the natural state.[2] It is attached to the dorsal surface of the third phalanx by a modified periosteum (Stratum periosteale) which contains a close-meshed network of vessels, and to the lower part of the cartilages by a subcutis which contains a rich venous plexus. The laminæ are small at their origin above, become wider below, and end in several papillæ 4 to 5 mm. in length. They supply nutrition to the horny laminæ and to the interlaminar horn of the white line.

4. The **corium of the sole** (Corium soleare) corresponds to the horny sole, to which it supplies nutrition. It is often more or less pigmented and bears long papillæ, which are specially large along the convex border and at the angles.

[1] In some veterinary works the statement is made that the various parts of the corium "secrete" corresponding parts of the hoof. The statement is quite erroneous, as the relationship here, both anatomically and physiologically, is the same as in the case of the corium and epidermis of the skin. Hence the term "keratogenous membrane." The term **matrix** may be used to designate the stratum germinativum of the hoof, not the corium.

[2] The laminæ of the corium are commonly termed "sensitive" laminæ to distinguish them from the "horny" laminæ, which are, of course, insensitive.

Centrally it is continuous with the corium of the frog and bars. The deep surface is attached to the sole surface of the third phalanx by a modified and highly vascular periosteum.

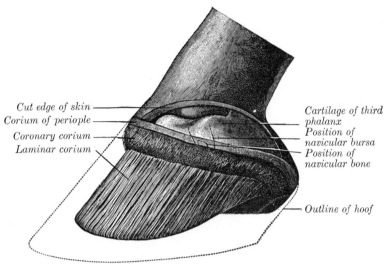

Cut edge of skin

Corium of periople

Coronary corium

Laminar corium

Cartilage of third phalanx

Position of navicular bursa

Position of navicular bone

Outline of hoof

FIG. 716.—LATERAL VIEW OF FOOT OF HORSE AFTER REMOVAL OF HOOF AND PART OF SKIN. (After Schmaltz, Atlas d. Anat. d. Pferdes.)

Dotted lines in front of navicular bone indicate position of coffin joint.

5. The **corium of the frog** (Corium cuneatum)—also called the sensitive frog—is moulded on the deep surface of the frog and bears small papillæ. Its deep face is

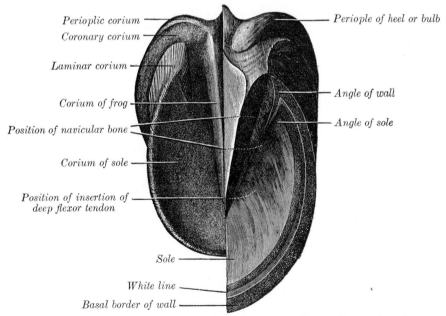

Perioplic corium

Coronary corium

Laminar corium

Corium of frog

Position of navicular bone

Corium of sole

Position of insertion of deep flexor tendon

Periople of heel or bulb

Angle of wall

Angle of sole

Sole

White line

Basal border of wall

FIG. 717.—GROUND SURFACE OF FOOT OF HORSE AFTER REMOVAL OF HALF OF HOOF TO SHOW CORIUM. (After Schmaltz, Atlas d. Anat. d. Pferdes.)

blended with the digital cushion. The germinal cells of the frog derive their nutrition from this part of the corium.

The **digital cushion** (Pulvinus digitalis) is a wedge-shaped mass which overlies the frog. It presents for description four surfaces, a base, and an apex.[1] Its **deep surface** faces upward and forward and is connected with the distal fibrous sheath of the deep flexor tendon. The **superficial surface,** covered by the corium of the frog, is moulded on the upper face of the frog. The **sides** are related chiefly to the cartilages of the third phalanx; distally the cushion is closely attached to the cartilages, but higher up a rich venous plexus intervenes. The **base,** situated posteriorly, is partly subcutaneous, and is divided by a central depression into two rounded prominences termed the bulbs of the cushion. The **apex** is adherent to the terminal part of the deep flexor tendon. The cushion is poorly supplied with vessels. It consists of a feltwork of white and elastic fibers, in the meshes of which are masses of fat and some islands of cartilage. The bulbs are soft and loose in texture and contain a relatively large amount of fat, but toward the apex the cushion

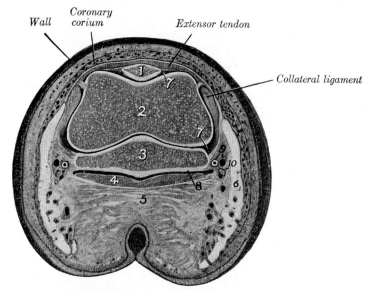

Fig. 718.—Section of Digit of Horse at Coronary Border of Hoof.

1, Extensor process of third phalanx; 2, distal end of second phalanx; 3, distal sesamoid or navicular bone; 4, deep flexor tendon; 5, digital cushion; 6, cartilage of third phalanx; 7, 7, cavity of coffin joint; 8, podotrochlear or navicular bursa; 9, digital vessels; 10, digital nerve.

becomes denser and more purely white fibrous tissue in structure. Branched **coil glands** occur chiefly in the part which overlies the central ridge of the frog. Their ducts pursue a slightly flexuous course through the corium and pass in a spiral manner through the frog. Their secretion contains fat.

Vessels and Nerves.—The corium is richly supplied with blood by the **digital arteries.** The **veins** are valveless, and form remarkable plexuses which communicate freely with each other and are drained by the **digital veins.** The **lymph vessels** form subpapillary plexuses in the corium of the sole and frog, and a wider-meshed plexus at the base of the digital cushion. A lymph vessel lies in the attached edge of each of the laminæ. The **nerves** are branches of the **digital nerves;** some fibers end in lamellar corpuscles and end-bulbs.

---

[1] The cushion is to be regarded as a special modification of the subcutaneous tissue, bearing on its superficial face the corium of the frog. It is an important factor in diminishing concussion.

THE ERGOT AND CHESTNUT

The **ergot** is a small mass of horn which is situated in the tuft of hair at the flexion surface of the fetlock. It is commonly regarded as the vestige of the second and fourth digits of extinct equidæ, since it is absent in cases in which these digits are developed. A small fibrous band, 3 to 5 mm. in width, extends downward and slightly forward from the fibrous basis of the ergot on each side, crosses over the digital vessels and nerves very obliquely, and blends below with the digital fascia and the digital cushion. It is known as the ligament or tendon of the ergot (Fig. 572).

The term **chestnut** is applied to the masses of horn which occur on the medial surface of the forearm, about a handbreadth above the carpus, and on the distal part of the medial face of the tarsus. They have an elongated oval form and are flattened. They are regarded usually as vestiges of the first digit. That of the hind limb is absent in the donkey and very small in the mule.

These horny excrescences are quite variable in form and size and are correlated with the fineness or coarseness of the integument in general. The supracarpal chestnut is usually about 1½ to 2½ inches long, oval in outline, the proximal end being pointed; it overlies the flexor carpi radialis at a quite variable distance above the carpus, and hence should not be used as a surgical landmark. The tarsal chestnut lies at a point behind the lower part of the medial ligament of the hock. When well developed it is about 2 to 2½ inches long, broad below and produced above to form a long pointed end, with a short blunt anterior process. They are composed of horn somewhat like that of the frog. Their morphological significance is undetermined.

ORGAN OF SMELL

The peripheral part of the olfactory apparatus or organ of smell (Organon olfactus) is that part of the nasal mucous membrane which was referred to in the description of the nasal cavity as the olfactory region; this (Regio olfactoria) is limited to the ethmoturbinates and the adjacent part of the dorsal turbinate and the septum nasi, in which the fibers of the olfactory nerve ramify. It is distinguished by its yellow-brown color, thickness, and softness. It contains characteristic tubular **olfactory glands,** which are lined by a single layer of pigmented cells, and a neuro-epithelium, the **olfactory cells,** the central processes of which extend as non-medullated fibers to the olfactory bulb.

The epithelium is non-ciliated and is covered by a structureless limiting layer. It consists essentially of three kinds of cells, supporting, basal, and olfactory. The supporting cells are of long columnar form above and contain pigment granules; below they taper and often branch, and their central processes unite with those of adjacent cells to form a protoplasmic network. The basal cells are branched and lie on a basement membrane. The olfactory cells are situated between the supporting cells; they have the form of long narrow rods, with an enlarged lower part which is occupied by the nucleus. The peripheral end pierces the limiting membrane and bears a tuft of fine, hair-like cilia (olfactory hairs). A central process extends from the nucleated pole of the cell to the olfactory bulb as a non-medullated olfactory nerve-fiber.

The **vomero-nasal organ** (Fig. 452) lies along each side of the anterior part of the lower border of the septum nasi. It communicates with the nasal cavity through the naso-palatine canal. It consists of a tube of hyaline cartilage lined with mucous membrane; a small part of the latter along the medial side is olfactory in character.

THE ORGAN OF TASTE

The peripheral part of the gustatory apparatus (Organon gustus) is formed by the microscopic **taste buds** (Calyculi gustatorii), which occur especially in the foliate, fungiform, and vallate papillæ, in the free edge and anterior pillars of the soft palate, and the oral surface of the epiglottis. The taste buds are ovoid masses, which occupy corresponding recesses in the ordinary epithelium; each presents a minute opening, the gustatory pore. The buds consist of fusiform supporting cells grouped around central **gustatory cells.** The latter are long and narrow; the peripheral end of each bears a small filament, the gustatory hair, which projects at the gustatory pore; the central end is produced to form a fine process which is often branched. The taste buds are innervated by fibers of the glosso-pharyngeal nerve and the lingual branch of the trigeminus.

THE SENSE ORGANS AND COMMON INTEGUMENT OF THE OX

THE EYE

The **eyelids** are thick, prominent, and less pliable than those of the horse. The lower lid bears a considerable number of cilia, which are, however, finer than those of the upper lid. The tarsal glands are more deeply embedded and therefore not so evident. The **conjunctiva** of the lower lid presents folds or ridges, and one or two prominences which contain numerous leukocytes; the conjunctival epithelium is transitional in type. The superficial part of the cartilage of the **third eyelid** is leaf or shovel-shaped and thicker than in the horse; the edge bears a narrower process, on which there is a transverse bar, giving the arrangement some resemblance to an anchor. The **gland** of the third eyelid is very large—an inch or more in length—and may be divided into two parts. The deep part is pink and consists of loose lobules, but the much larger superficial part is more compact. There are two large and several

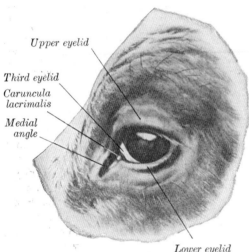

Fig. 719.—Eye of Ox. (After Ellenberger-Baum, Anat. für Künstler.)

smaller excretory ducts. The subconjunctival tissue of the third eyelid contains lymph nodules, which are specially numerous on the bulbar side.

The **lacrimal gland** is thick and distinctly lobulated. It is more or less clearly divided into a thick upper and a thinner lower part (Glandula lacrimalis dorsalis, ventralis). There are six to eight larger excretory ducts and several smaller ones. The **naso-lacrimal duct** is shorter than in the horse, and is almost straight. Its terminal part is enclosed between two plates of cartilage, and it opens near the nostril on the lateral wall of the vestibule of the nasal cavity; the orifice is placed on the medial side of the alar fold of the ventral turbinate, and is therefore not easily found.

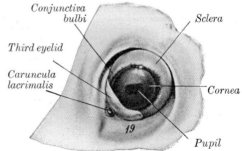

Fig. 720.—Left Eyeball of Ox *in situ.*

19, Orbital fat. (After Ellenberger-Baum, Anat. für Künstler.)

The **eyeball** resembles that of the horse in shape, but is considerably smaller.[1] The **sclera** is often more or less pigmented; where non-pigmented, it may have a bluish tinge. The point of entrance of the optic nerve is about 2 mm. lateral to the vertical meridian, and about 7 mm. below the horizontal meridian.[2] The **cornea** is thicker than that of the horse. The **tapetum** of the chorioid is extensive at the outer side, but is a narrow strip medially. It has a metallic luster, shading from a brilliant green to a deep blue; centrally it has a reddish sheen. The **iris is** usually very dark colored. The granula form a continuous series of small nodules along the upper margin of the pupil and are most prominent centrally; they are very small on the lower margin. The **optic papilla** is much smaller and is not so sharply defined on ophthalmoscopic examination as that of the horse. Several relatively large retinal arteries radiate from the center of the papilla to the periphery of the retina. They may be seen to wind spirally around the veins, which are very large. The **vitreous body** is less fluid than that of the horse.

The arteria centralis retinæ arises from a posterior ciliary artery and divides close to the optic papilla into three branches usually; the upper one is larger than the two lateral branches. The retina is more vascular than that of the horse; it has a round area centralis at the medial side, which is continued outward by a narrow strip of a similar histological structure.

THE EAR

The **external ear** is inclined outward. The middle part is much wider and less curved than in the horse. The apex is also wide and does not curve forward. The lower part of the anterior border is bent backward and bears long hairs. The posterior border is thin and is regularly convex, except below, where it is indented. The opening is wide and the concave surface presents four ridges; the convex surface presents corresponding depressions. The styloid process of the conchal cartilage is short and blunt. The edges of the annular cartilage are in contact at the medial side and the upper border is notched laterally. The scutiform cartilage is a very irregular quadrilateral plate; it is situated on the lateral aspect of the cranium, with its concave surface in contact with the fat and temporalis muscle. The osseous external acoustic meatus is directed practically straight inward; it is about twice as long as that of the horse, and tapers very gradually from without inward. The chief special characters of the **auricular muscles** are as follows: (1) The scutularis blends with the frontalis muscle. The interscutularis arises from the base of the processus cornus (or the corresponding area in polled cattle) and from the frontal crest. (2) The cervico-scutularis arises from the posterior surface of the cranium below the frontal eminence, and receives slips from the parieto-auricularis and cervico-auricularis superficialis. (3) The zygomatico-auricularis and scutulo-auricularis superficialis ventralis are fused. (4) The scutulo-auricularis superficialis dorsalis is distinct from the interscutularis; it arises from the superficial face of the scutiform cartilage. (5) The cervico-auricularis superficialis arises from the ligamentum nuchæ and ends on the convex surface of the conchal cartilage. (6) The parieto-auricularis arises from the nuchal surface of the frontal bone, the adjacent part of the parietal bone, and the ligamentum nuchæ; it is inserted below the preceding muscle. (7) The scutulo-auricularis superficialis accessorius arises from the superficial face of the scutiform cartilage and is inserted by a round tendon into the anterior part of the convex surface of the conchal cartilage. (8) The cervico-auricularis profundus minor consists of two fasciculi: the medial, narrow part is deep red in color, and arises from the fascia of the cervical muscles lateral to the occipital attachment of the ligament nuchæ; the lateral

[1] The average transverse diameter is about 42 mm., the vertical diameter, 41 mm., and the axis, 36 mm. The angle between the optic axes is about 119°.

[2] The thickness of the sclera is about 2 mm. at the posterior pole, 1 mm. at the equator, and 1.2 to 1.5 mm. near the cornea.

wider part is pale, and arises beneath the cervico-auricularis superficialis indirectly from the scutiform cartilage. The two unite and are inserted into the lower aspect of the base of the conchal cartilage. (9) The scutulo-auricularis profundus minor arises from the temporal crest above the external acoustic meatus and is inserted into the anterior part of the deep face of the scutiform cartilage.

The **cavum tympani** is small; it communicates ventrally with the air-cells of the bulla tympanica. The tympanic membrane is nearly circular and is not so oblique as in the horse. The auditory ossicles are smaller than those of the horse; the malleus is more curved, the body of the incus is longer, and there is a small prominence on the front of the head of the stapes for the attachment of the stapedius muscle.

The **auditive** or **Eustachian tube** is small and is only about two inches long. The pharyngeal opening is small and is situated on the side of the fornix of the pharynx close to the base of the cranium. There is no flap-like expansion of the cartilage, but the medial border of the orifice is formed by a fold of mucous membrane (Fig. 476).

The **internal ear** has essentially the same arrangement as in the horse.

FIG. 721.—HOOFS OF OX; VOLAR ASPECT. (After Ellenberger-Baum, Anat. für Künstler.)

COMMON INTEGUMENT

The thickness of the **skin** of the ox is greater than that of any of the other domesticated animals; in general it is about three or four millimeters, but at the root of the tail and the point of the hock it is about five millimeters and on the brisket six or seven millimeters. The variably developed prominence at the anterior part of the pectoral region known as the "brisket" consists of a fold of skin (Plica colli ventralis longitudinalis), which contains posteriorly a mass composed of coarse fibrous trabeculæ and fat.

The **cutaneous glands** are fewer and less developed than in the horse. Except about the natural openings, at the point of the hock, and the flexion surface of the fetlock, the **sweat glands** do not form a coil, but are enlarged at the deep end and are variably flexuous. The **sebaceous glands** are best developed about the natural openings and on the udder, but there are none on the teats. The **naso-labial glands** form a thick layer under the bare skin of the muzzle. They are compound tubular glands and are lined with cubical epithelium. The openings of their excretory ducts are easily seen.

The **hairs** are extremely variable in color and size in the different breeds and in different individuals. The hair of the frontal region is often curly, especially in the bull. There is no mane, and the long hairs of the tail occur only at the end, where they form the "brush" (Cirrus caudæ).

The **hoofs,** four in number on each limb, cover the ends of the digits. Those of the chief digits conform in a general way to the shape of the third phalanges, and each may be regarded as having three surfaces. The abaxial surface is convex from side to side, and is marked by ridges parallel with the coronary border. Its anterior part is concave from edge to edge, and the angle which it forms with the ground is about 30°. The interdigital surface is concave and grooved; it touches the opposite claw only at its ends. The basal or ground surface consists of two parts, viz., a slightly concave sole, which is pointed in front and widens behind, and a prominent bulb of soft thin horn, which is continuous above with the skin. The hoof may be regarded as consisting of three parts—periople, wall, and sole. The periople surrounds the coronary border in the form of a flat band, which is about half an inch wide, except at the heels, where it widens to cover the entire surface. The wall forms most of the abaxial part of the hoof and is reflected in front upon the interdigital surface. It thins out toward the bulb or heel, which appears, as stated above, to consist of the thin expansion of the periople. The sole occupies the angle of inflection of the wall; it is continuous without demarcation with the periople of the bulb. The periopic corium bears relatively long papillæ. The coronary corium is much less developed than in the horse and its papillæ are short. The laminæ are much narrower and are more numerous than in the horse; secondary laminæ are not present. The corium of the sole is not marked off behind from that of the periople; its papillæ are very small and close together. The corium of the bulbs

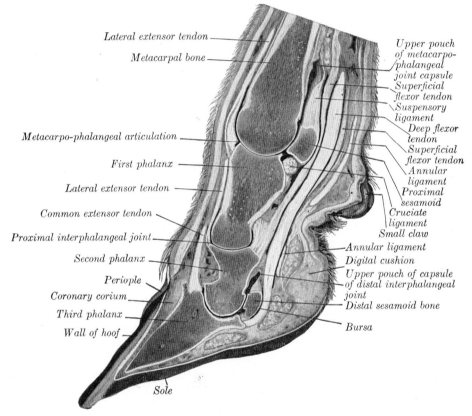

Fig. 722.—Sagittal Section of Distal Part of Forelimb of Ox.

is separated from the flexor tendon by a mass of elastic, fatty tissue, which is analogous with the digital cushion of the horse. The papillæ here are long and often compound.

The accessory digits bear short conical horn capsules which resemble in a general way those of the chief digits, and have a similar corium, which covers one or two nodular vestigial phalanges. From these a fibrous band descends obliquely on the volar aspect of each chief digit and is attached below to the distal phalanx and sesamoid bones, sending fibers also to the elastic pad of the heel.

The **horns** (Cornua) enclose the horn processes of the frontal bones (except in the polled breeds). They vary very greatly in size, form, and curvature. The root or base of the horn (Radix cornus) has a thin edge which is continuous with the ordinary epidermis. It is covered by a thin layer of soft horn similar to the periople of the hoof of the horse. Near the root of the horn it is encircled by variable rings. Toward the apex (Apex cornus) the thickness of the horn increases till it becomes practically a solid mass. The horn consists mainly of tubes which are very close together, except at the rings, where there is more intertubular horn. The corium of the horn (Corium cornus) is united to the horn process by periosteum which is traversed by numerous blood-vessels. The corium at the root of the horn is thick and bears long, slender papillæ; in the body of the horn it becomes thin and the papillæ are smaller, but increase in size apically. Rudimentary papillated laminæ also occur.

The **skin** of the **sheep** varies in thickness from 0.5 to 3 mm., but differs greatly in fineness and in other respects in various breeds. In Merinos large folds occur on the neck. Cutaneous pouches (Sinus cutis) are present in certain situations. The **infraorbital** or **lacrimal pouch** (Sinus cutaneus infraorbitalis) is an invagination about half an inch in depth, which is situated in front of the medial angle of the eye. It bears scattered fine hairs, into the follicles of which large compound sebaceous glands open; coil glands are also present. The secretion of the glands is fatty and forms a yellow, sticky covering on the skin when dry. The **inguinal** (or mammary) **pouch** (Sinus cutaneus inguinalis) is much more extensive, and is situated in the inguinal region in both sexes. The skin of the pouch bears scattered fine hairs and contains well-developed sebaceous glands and exceedingly large coil glands. An elastic lamina from the abdominal tunic is attached to the skin in the deepest portion of the pouch. The **interdigital pouch** (Sinus cutaneus interdigitalis) is a peculiar tubular invagination of the integument which opens at the anterior part of the interdigital cleft. On sagittal section it appears as a bent tube, an inch or more (ca. 2.5–3 cm.) in length, and about a fourth of an inch (ca. 6–7 mm.) in diameter. The pouch extends downward and backward, and then curves sharply upward between the distal ends of the first phalanges. Its deep blind end is somewhat ampullate. The subcutis forms a capsule around it. The skin of the pouch is thin and pale; it bears fine colorless hairs, the follicles of which receive the secretion of several sebaceous glands. The coil glands here are compound and very large; they open into the hair-follicles or directly into the pouch. The secretion of the glands is a colorless fatty substance. The skin is covered in great part by **wool** (Lana) which is similar in structure to hair, but is finer, curly, and usually contains no medullary cells. The follicles of the wool are curved, and are arranged more or less distinctly in groups of ten or a dozen, several of which open in common on the surface. A considerable part of the face and the limbs is covered with short, stiff hair, and long hairs occur more or less interspersed among the wool. The hoofs resemble those of the ox. The horns, when present, are more or less prismatic, distinctly ringed, and vary in length and curvature in different breeds. Their structure is similar to those of the ox.

The olfactory and gustatory organs resemble in general those of the horse.

THE SENSE ORGANS AND COMMON INTEGUMENT OF THE PIG

THE EYE

The posterior part of the orbital margin is formed chiefly by the orbital ligament, which extends from the extremely short supraorbital process to the small eminence at the junction of the malar and the zygomatic process of the temporal.

Cilia occur only on the upper eyelid. The medial angle is prolonged by a groove on the infraorbital region. The tarsal glands are very short and curved. The conjunctival epithelium is of the transitional type, with many goblet cells.

The deep part of the cartilage of the third eyelid is broad and spoon-like, the superficial part somewhat anchor-shaped. In addition to the gland which surrounds the deep part of the cartilage, there is a deeper one, often termed the gland of Harder (Glandula palpebræ tertiæ profunda), which is surrounded by a distinct capsule and a blood-sinus. This gland is brownish or yellowish-gray in color, elliptical in outline, and about an inch (2–3 cm.) in length. It is situated deeply below the attachment of the ventral oblique muscle.

The caruncula lacrimalis has the form of a ridge; it divides into two branches which join the skin at the medial commissure. It is red in color and contains numerous large coil glands.

The lacrimal gland is mucous in type. There is no lacrimal sac, and the two lacrimal ducts pass through separate openings at the infraorbital margin. The naso-lacrimal duct is usually short and opens into the ventral nasal meatus at the posterior end of the ventral turbinate.[1] The eyeball appears small, partly on account of the narrowness of the palpebral opening; it closely approaches the spherical form. The cornea, although in reality almost circular, appears oval when viewed from the front, the medial end being much the broader. The chorioid has no tapetum. The iris is usually dark grayish-brown or yellowish-brown, but sometimes has a blue tinge. The pupil is a transverse oval in ordinary light, but almost circular when dilated; granula are not present. The optic papilla is nearer the posterior pole than in the horse and ox, and has a distinct central artery and vein.

THE EAR

The external ear differs considerably in size, thickness, and position. It may be carried vertically, inclined inward, or hang downward. It is relatively wide and is little curved except at the base. The concave surface presents several cutaneous ridges which correspond approximately with the long axis of the ear. The anterior border of the concha is strongly recurved in its lower part, and divides into two branches, one of which passes almost horizontally backward in the cavum conchæ, while the other continues the general direction of the border. The posterior border is slightly concave above, strongly convex below, forming a prominence somewhat analogous to the lobule of the human ear. The osseous external acoustic meatus is very long and is directed ventro-medially. The tympanic membrane is almost circular. The tympanic cavity proper is small, but it is continuous with the numerous cells of the large bulla tympanica. The auditive or Eustachian tube is short; its pharyngeal opening is situated in the upper part of the wall of the pharynx, immediately behind the posterior nares. It is somewhat infundibular, and is bounded medially by a thick fold of mucous membrane (Torus tubarius).

THE SKIN AND APPENDAGES

The thickness of the skin in improved breeds is 1 to 2 mm., except in the adult boar the corium of the shoulder may become 3.5 to 4 mm. Fat usually accumulates in the subcutis and forms a distinct and often extremely thick panniculus adiposus over the greater part of the body. The sebaceous glands are in general small and much fewer than in the other animals. The sweat glands, on the other hand, are large, yellow or brownish in color, and are in many places visible to the naked eye. At the medial side of the carpus there are small cutaneous diverticula, the so-called **carpal glands,** into which numerous compound coil glands open. Large glands also occur in the skin of the digits and interdigital space. Compound tubular glands are

---

[1] The lower punctum lacrimale is frequently absent and the corresponding duct therefore blind. There is often a duct or its remnant which opens below the ventral turbinate fold, but is not connected behind with the functional duct.

present in the skin of the snout. Large sebaceous and sweat glands are found at the entrance to the preputial diverticulum. The hairs are sparsely scattered in improved breeds—indeed, in some cases the skin is almost bare. The long hairs or bristles (Setae) are arranged usually in groups of three. They are most developed on the neck and back. The bristles about the snout and the chin are sinus hairs.

The **hoofs** or **claws** and their corium resemble those of the ox, but the bulbs are more prominent and form a greater part of the ground surface; they are also better defined from the sole, which is small. The hoofs of the accessory digits are more developed and their parts better differentiated than those of the ox.

The olfactory region is extensive in correlation with the large size of the olfactory bulbs; the mucous membrane here is brown in color.

THE SENSE ORGANS AND COMMON INTEGUMENT OF THE DOG

THE EYE

The posterior margin of the orbit is formed by the orbital ligament, as in the pig. The orbital axes if produced backward would include an angle of about 79°, the optic axes an angle of about 92.5° (Koschel). The lower eyelid has no distinct cilia. The medial angle is wide, the lacus lacrimalis shallow, and the caruncula lacrimalis small and yellowish-brown. The conjunctival epithelium is cylindrical, with many goblet cells. The gland which surrounds the deep end of the cartilage of the third eyelid is large and pink; it is a mixed gland.

The lacrimal gland is flat and lies chiefly under the orbital ligament. It is pink in color and mixed in structure. The naso-lacrimal duct is variable in arrangement and may differ on the two sides. It may open into the ventral meatus immediately after its emergence from the osseous lacrimal canal; thence it continues forward and opens on the lateral wall of the nostril below the ventral turbinate fold.

The eyeball is almost spherical and is relatively large, especially in the small breeds. The sclera is thick in the ciliary region, where it contains a well-developed venous plexus; in the vicinity of the equator it is thin, and the chorioid shows through it. The cornea is almost circular. The chorioid is richly pigmented, and presents a well-defined **tapetum cellulosum;** this is somewhat triangular in outline and has a metallic luster. Its color is often golden green, shading to blue peripherally, but the blue tone may predominate, and in other cases it is mainly golden yellow or reddish-yellow. The appearance is due to several layers of peculiar flattened polygonal cells. The ciliary muscle is more developed than in the other species. The iris is commonly light or yellow brown, but not rarely has a blue tinge; the color often differs in the two eyes. The pupil is round; its edge is either smooth or bears minute round prominences. The retina presents a round area centralis lateral to the optic papilla. The latter is variable in outline; commonly it has the form of a triangle with the angles rounded off, but is often round or oval. Branches of the central vessels of the retina radiate from the middle of the papilla. The surfaces of the lens are not so strongly curved as in the other domestic animals, and there is little difference in the radius of curvature of the two surfaces.

THE EAR

The external ear differs greatly in size and form in the various breeds; in most it is relatively wide and thin and the greater part of it hangs down over the opening.

The anterior border has a prominence (Spina helicis) at its lower part, and below this it divides into two branches (Crura helicis). One of these continues down to a blunt point, while the other turns into the cavity of the concha. The posterior border forms a pouch below its middle, and is thick and rounded in its basal part. Here the conchal cartilage bears a pointed process (Processus uncinatus), which projects upward and backward. The outer wall of the cavum conchæ is supported by a quadrilateral plate (Tragus) above and a semi-annular cartilage below. The concave surface presents several cutaneous folds, and in the cavum conchæ there are ridges and irregular prominences. There are long hairs on the borders, apex, and the folds of the concave surface, but the skin of the cavum conchæ is bare. The annular cartilage is a complete ring. The osseous external acoustic meatus is wide and extremely short.

The auricular muscles are thin. The scutularis is extensive and is divisible into interscutularis and fronto-scutularis. It partly covers the occipitalis muscle, which is oval and unpaired and ends in the fascia of the frontal region. The scutulo-auriculares superficiales, ventralis et accessorius, and the cervico-scutularis are not differentiated as separate muscles. The cervico-auricularis superficialis and the parieto-auricularis both bifurcate and are inserted into the base of the concha and the scutiform cartilage. The parotido-auricularis is narrow and almost long enough to meet the opposite muscle. The tragicus consists of two parts; of these, the lateral one is long and arises fron the border of the mandible above the angular process. The helicis and the verticalis auriculæ are well developed.

The tympanic cavity is very roomy, extending ventrally into the large but simple cavity of the bulla tympanica. The tympanic membrane is extensive and oval. The promontory is very pronounced. The auditory ossicles are large. The auditive or Eustachian tube is short, and has a fibrous lateral lamina. Its pharyngeal opening is an oblique slit situated on the lateral wall of the naso-pharyngeal meatus, and is margined medially by a thick mucous fold. The cochlea has three and a half turns and is more sharply pointed than in the ungulates.

THE SKIN AND APPENDAGES

The skin varies greatly in thickness in different breeds. It is remarkably loose on the dorsal aspect of the neck and trunk, where it can be raised in extensive folds. The coat is also subject to extreme variation in length, thickness, color, etc. The hairs are arranged in groups of three to a large extent. The sebaceous glands are best developed in the short and rough haired breeds. They are largest and most numerous at the lips, anus, dorsal surface of the trunk, and sternal region. The sweat glands are relatively better developed in the long and fine haired breeds. The largest are found in the digital pads. Coil glands occur in the skin of the perineum and the paranal pouches. In the muzzle, glands are absent or very scanty.[1]

On the flexion surface of the carpus and digit there are hairless, cushion-like pads. The **carpal pad** (Torus carpalis) is situated medial and distal to the accessory carpal bone. The **metacarpal** and **metatarsal pads** (Torus metacarpalis, metatarsalis) are the largest and are situated behind the distal ends of the metacarpal or metatarsal bones and the greater part of the first phalanges. They are somewhat heart-shaped, with two unequal lateral lobes, and the apex distal. The metapodiophalangeal joints rest on them when the paw supports the weight. The **digital pads** (Toruli digitales) are oval and are much smaller; they similarly support the second digital joints. That of the first digit is small on the forelimb, and usually absent from the hind limb. Each receives two suspensory bands from the tubercles

[1] Trautmann has shown that the secretion which appears on the muzzle comes from the lateral nasal gland, which is well developed.

at the distal end of the corresponding second phalanx. The pads have a basis of fibro-elastic tissue and fat, which is intimately adherent to the skin and is connected by trabeculæ with the bones and tendons. The epidermis is thick and largely keratinized, and is studded with numerous rounded papillæ which are readily seen

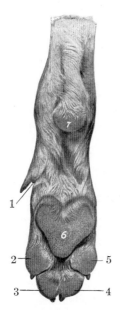
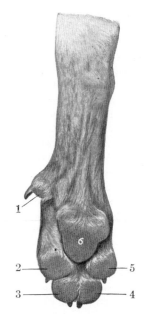

Fig. 723.—Pads of Right Fore Paw of Dog.   Fig. 724.—Pads of Right Hind Paw of Dog.
1–5, Digital pads; 6, 6, metacarpal and metatarsal pads; 7, carpal pad.

with the naked eye. The corium has large papillæ, and contains sweat glands and lamellar corpuscles.

The **claws** (Ungues) correspond in form to the ungual part of the distal phalanges, which they enclose. The horn of the claw consists of a body or wall and a sole. The former is strongly curved in both directions, and is compressed laterally.

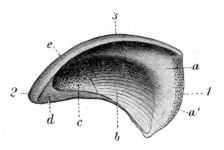

Fig. 725.—Half of Claw of Dog; Inner Surface.

a, a′, Coronary part; b, volar part of wall; c, sole; d, section of c; e, section of wall; 1, coronary border; 2, apex; 3, dorsal surface. (From Leisering's Atlas.)

Its coronary border fits into the depression under the bony collar or ungual crest of the third phalanx and is covered by skin. The lateral borders converge and enclose the sole anteriorly. The corium presents a coronary part which bears papillæ only near the coronary border. On the dorsal surface it is thickened to form a ridge, and the corresponding part of the horny covering is thick and maintains the pointed character of the claw. The corium of the sides of the wall bears small laminæ which converge to the corium of the sole. The latter is papillated. When the flexor muscles are inactive, the distal phalanges and the claws are maintained in dorsal flexion by two elastic ligaments. These arise from the tubercles at the proximal end of the second phalanx and converge to the dorsal aspect of the ungual crest of the third phalanx.

OLFACTORY AND GUSTATORY ORGANS

The **olfactory region** lies above the lamina transversa, which separates it from the naso-pharyngeal meatus. The mucous membrane is distinguished by its thickness and yellow color, and is very extensive. It covers about half of the large ethmoturbinates, and one-third to one-half of the septum nasi. The ethmoturbinate which projects into the frontal sinus and the adjacent inner wall of the sinus are olfactory in character. Olfactory nerve-fibers ramify in the vomero-nasal organ.

The gustatory apparatus presents no special features of importance.

THE CHICKEN

THE SKELETON OF THE CHICKEN

The skeleton may be divided into two parts, axial and appendicular.
The **axial skeleton** comprises the skull, vertebral column, ribs and sternum.

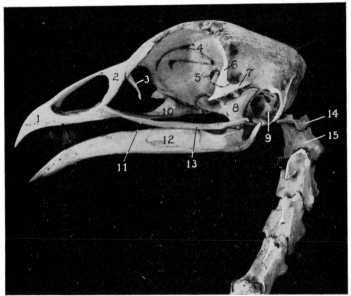

FIG. 726.—SKULL OF CHICKEN; LATERAL VIEW.

1, Premaxilla; *2*, nasal bone; *3*, lacrimal; *4*, olfactory foramen; *5*, optic foramen; *6*, supraorbital process of frontal; *7*, zygomatic process of temporal; *8*, quadrate; *9*, external acoustic meatus; *10*, palatine; *11*, maxilla; *12*, mandible; *13*, zygomatic; *14*, atlas; *15*, axis.

The **appendicular skeleton** includes the bones of the limbs which are so modified as to conform to their peculiar physiological requirements during locomotion.

THE AXIAL SKELETON

The **skull** of the chicken presents two large orbits, separated by a thin septum formed by the sphenoid and ethmoid bones. Behind the orbits is the rounded cranium whose cavity encloses the brain and its coverings.

The **cranial group** of bones are the same in name and number in the chicken as in the mammals, except for the interparietal bones which are absent in the chicken. The bones of the cranium lose their identity early after hatching as the sutures become ossified and the bones fuse together.

The occipital bone has a single condyle which is situated below the foramen magnum and articulates with the atlas and the odontoid process of the axis. The spaces of the spongy portions of the bones of the cranium contain air spaces connected with the Eustachian tube. The cranial wall is relatively thick, thus reducing the size of the cavity more than is actually expected when viewing the skull. A large tympanic cavity is a very outstanding feature. The cavity is the external acoustic meatus which is open into the middle ear in the macerated skull; but with the other tissues present the tympanic membrane separates them.

929

The two optic foramina are separated exteriorly by the interorbital septum while interiorly they are a single foramen. The foramina for the passage of olfactory nerves are on the dorsal part of the interorbital septum.

The **bones of the face** form a pointed cone and are made up of the same bones as in the domesticated mammals, except there is one more turbinate bone (three in all) in the chicken and a quadrate bone which articulates with the mandible below, and with the temporal, pterygoid and malar above.

The **maxillæ** are slender, rod-shaped bones, with a thin palatine process, which enter into the formation of the side of the face and also the hard palate. The palatine process does not meet its fellow, but joins the palatine and vomer bones posteriorly. The maxilla joins the premaxilla and nasal bone anteriorly and is continuous behind with the malar.

The **premaxillæ** which form the skeleton of the upper portion of the beak fuse before hatching to form a solid bone. They form the anterior boundary of the external openings to the nasal cavity. They present three pairs of processes; the palatine processes which meet the palatine bone, the maxillary processes which extend backwards to meet the maxilla and the nasal processes which extend dorsally and backwards along the median line and between the nasal bones, and meet the frontal bones.

The **nasal** bones are situated anterior to the frontal bones and form the greater part of the roof of the nasal cavity. The anterior extremity is notched to form the posterior boundary of the external openings of the nasal cavities. They join the nasal processes of the premaxillæ along the medial border and the anterior medial process extends along the dorsal boundary of the nasal opening while the anterior lateral process extends downward to meet the maxillæ. Posteriorly and laterally it joins the small lacrimal bone.

The **lacrimal** bones form part of the anterior margin of the orbit and join the frontal and nasal bones. They are very small bones ending in a pointed process ventrally.

The **palatine** bones form the lateral boundaries of the posterior opening of the nasal cavity and form part of the roof of the mouth. They articulate anteriorly with the maxillæ and premaxillæ and posteriorly with the pterygoid and sphenoid bones.

The **malar** or zygomatic bones are situated below the orbit and articulate anteriorly with the maxilla, and posteriorly with the quadrate bone. It is a slender, rod-shaped bone which is made up of two portions: the anterior part is termed the **jugal** bone while the posterior part is termed the **quadrato-jugal** bone.

The **pterygoid** bones form the posterior boundary of the posterior nares. They extend outward and backward from the sphenoid bone medially to the quadrate bone laterally. It is a comparatively strong, rod-like bone.

The **vomer** is median in position, being a part of the nasal septum, and articulates posteriorly with the sphenoid bone.

The **mandible** is the largest bone of the face. It articulates with the quadrate bone posteriorly where it presents a concave articular facet. Behind this facet the ventral border is carried backward and upward in a curved process. Each half of the mandible is made up of five parts: pars articularis bears the articular facet; pars supra-angularis which bears a small coronoid process; pars angularis, a slender strip of bone lying along the ventral border of the jaw; the splenial, lying along the medial surface of the mandible as a thin plate of bone, and the pars dentalis, which forms the anterior part of the jaw and fuses with its fellow of the opposite side.

The **quadrate** bones articulate with the pars articularis of the mandible below; above, it articulates with the temporal in front of the tympanic cavity; laterally, with the quadrato-jugal bone; medially, with the pterygoid bone. It gets its name from its irregular four sided outline. Its anterior medial angle is a muscular process which projects into the orbit. The presence of the quadrate bone, together with the mobility of the bones of the face, permits the extreme opening of the mouth.

The **turbinate** bones are three in number in each nasal cavity, anterior, middle and posterior. The middle one is the largest and the posterior one the smallest. The turbinates are attached to the lateral walls of the nasal cavity and greatly reduce the size of the cavity.

The **hyoid** bone is situated partly between the rami of the mandible and consists of seven bony segments: the entoglossal segment or lingual process is within the tongue, which it supports, and it articulates by a movable joint with the basi-hyal segment, or body, which is continued posteriorly by the uro-hyal segment, which rests upon the larynx; each lateral process consists of two bony segments, a basi-branchial segment joining the basi-hyal part anteriorly, and by cartilage to the cerato-branchial part posteriorly. The lateral processes extend posteriorly and upward around the occipital bone.

The Vertebral Column.—The **vertebral formula** for the chicken is $C_{14}T_7L\text{-}S_{14}Cy_6$.

The fourteen **cervical vertebræ** form the skeleton of the neck which is a long, double-curved structure.

The **atlas,** the first cervical vertebra, is a ring-like bone. Its anterior articular surface is deeply concave for articulation with the single occipital condyle. Posteriorly, there are three articular facets for articulation with the axis, one ventral median and two lateral.

The **axis,** the second cervical vertebra, articulates anteriorly with the atlas by three facets, and its odontoid process extends forward to articulate with the occipital condyle. There are two posterior articular processes which articulate with the anterior articular processes of the third cervical vertebra, also an articular surface on the posterior end of the body. It is provided with a dorsal and ventral spine.

The remaining cervical vertebræ consist of a rod-like body, an arch and the processes. The ends of the body articulate with adjacent vertebræ. The anterior surface is concave from side to side and convex dorso-ventrally. The posterior surface is less extensive and convex from side to side and concave dorso-ventrally. Most of the vertebræ present a ventral spinous process. The arch carries a small spinous process. There is an extensive intervertebral space, dorsally, between the arches which exposes the neural canal. These spaces are closed by intervertebral ligaments. There are two anterior and two posterior articular processes which articulate with those of adjacent vertebræ. The transverse processes are connected with the anterior articular processes. They are elongated slender processes projecting backward and are termed cervical ribs. A foramen transversarium pierces each transverse process which forms the canalis transversarius through which the vertebral vessels and nervus transversarius pass.

The seven **thoracic vertebræ** present well-developed dorsal spinous processes, and all except the last have a very prominent ventral spinous process. Each transverse process has a facet on its outer end for articulation with a rib. The second to the fifth vertebræ are fused together, including the dorsal and ventral spines and the transverse processes which are connected by bony plates. The first and sixth thoracic vertebræ are free and the seventh is fused to the lumbo-sacral mass of vertebræ.

The vertebræ of the **lumbo-sacral** region are fused into a bony mass consisting of sixteen vertebræ: the last thoracic, fourteen lumbo-sacral and the first coccygeal vertebræ.

The dorsal spinous processes are developed in the anterior portion and are fused together, but posteriorly they are absent. The segments are indicated mainly by the intervertebral foramina and transverse ridges ventrally, which mark the position of the transverse processes.

The six **coccygeal vertebræ** constitute the skeleton of the tail. The transverse processes are well developed and the dorsal spines are bifurcate. The first coccygeal vertebra is fused with the lumbo-sacral mass, while the last segment is a three sided pyramid, the **pygostyle.**

The coccygeal vertebræ are freely movable excepting the first.

The seven pairs of **ribs** make up the skeleton of the lateral wall of the thorax. The first two pairs of ribs (floating ribs) consist of one part each and do not reach the sternum. The remaining five pairs consist of two parts each and articulate with the vertebræ above and with the sternum below. The dorsal part is termed the

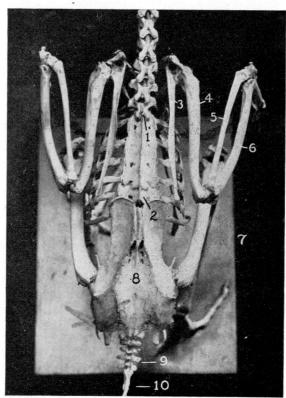

FIG. 727.—SKELETON OF CHICKEN; DORSAL VIEW.

1, First thoracic vertebra (placed on fused second, third, fourth and fifth thoracic vertebræ); *2,* (on ilium) sixth thoracic vertebra; *3,* scapula; *4,* humerus; *5,* radius; *6,* ulna; *7,* femur; *8,* lumbo-sacral vertebral mass; *9,* coccygeal vertebræ; *10,* pygostyle.

vertebral rib while the ventral part is bone and is termed the **sternal rib.** There are no costal cartilages in the chicken as there are in mammals. The vertebral ribs, excepting the first and last, bear on the middle of the posterior border a flattened uncinate process which overlaps the succeeding rib.

The **sternum,** or breast bone, is a very extensive bone which forms the floor of the thoracic cavity and the greater part of the abdominal cavity. It is a quadrilateral curved plate with processes attached to each angle and from the middle of the anterior and posterior borders. Its dorsal surface is concave and has several openings through which the air sacs communicate with the interior of the bone. The anterior medial projection, the **rostrum,** is pierced at its root by a foramen from which extend the articular surfaces for the coracoid bones. The **costal processes** extend forward and upward from the anterior angles. The plate-like **posterior-**

lateral process, extending from the posterior angles of the sternum, divides into two branches: the shorter **oblique process** becomes much wider at its free end and

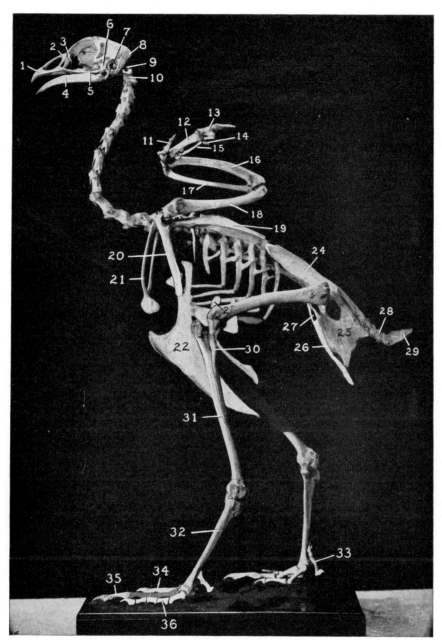

FIG. 728.—THE SKELETON OF THE CHICKEN.

1, Premaxilla; *2,* nasal bone; *3,* lacrimal; *4,* mandible; *5,* maxilla; *6,* quadrate bone; *7,* external acoustic meatus; *8,* occipital; *9,* atlas; *10,* axis; *11,* first digit (phalanges first and second); *12,* second metacarpal; *13,* second digit (phalanges first and second); *14,* third digit (first phalanx); *15,* third metacarpal; *16,* ulna; *17,* radius; *18,* humerus; *19,* scapula; *20,* coracoid; *21,* clavicle; *22,* sternum; *23,* (on femur) patella; *24,* ilium; *25,* ischium; *26,* pubis; *27,* obturator foramen; *28,* coccygeal vertebræ; *29,* pygostyle; *30,* fibula; *31,* tibia; *32,* metatarsus; *33, 34, 35, 36,* first, second, third and fourth toes.

overlaps the last two sternal ribs; the **posterior medial process,** the **metasternum,** is long and has a very prominent ventral ridge, the **sternal crest,** which is high in front and fades out posteriorly. The notches between the posterior processes of the sternum are filled in by a ligamentous membrane which forms a very extensive area for attachment of muscles. The lateral borders of the sternum present four or five depressions for attachments of the sternal ribs.

THE APPENDICULAR SKELETON

The **thoracic limb,** or **wing,** consists of the **shoulder girdle, arm, forearm** and **manus.** The manus is subdivided into **carpus, metacarpus** and **digits.**

The skeleton of the shoulder girdle consists of the scapula, coracoid and clavicle.

The **scapula,** or shoulder blade, lies on the dorsal wall of the thorax nearly parallel with the vertebræ and reaching almost to the ilium. It is a narrow, thin bone slightly thicker at its anterior or articular extremity where it forms part of the glenoid cavity for articulation with the humerus. Near the acromion process is located a pneumatic foramen. A process extends forward and medial to the shoulder joint which enters into the formation of the foramen triosseum.

The **coracoid** is the strongest bone of the shoulder girdle, directed downward, backward and inward, articulating with the clavicle, scapula and humerus at its upper extremity and with the sternum at its lower extremity. Its lower extremity presents a pneumatic foramen for communication with the clavicular air sac. The upper extremity unites with the scapula to form the glenoid cavity for articulation with the humerus. Medial to the joint it unites with the clavicle and scapula to form the foramen triosseum through which the tendon of major deep pectoral muscle passes.

The **clavicle** is a slender, curved, rod-like bone. It is enlarged somewhat at its dorsal extremity where it articulates with the scapula and coracoid. Ventrally it fuses with its fellow at an acute angle, forming a process which is connected to the sternum by a ligament. The united clavicles form the furcula, or wishbone, which forms a support for the shoulders, preventing them from coming too close together during flight.

The **humerus** is the bone of the arm. It is a curved, long bone carried nearly horizontal in position and parallel with the thoracic vertebræ except in flight. At its proximal extremity it articulates with the scapula and coracoid bones which form a shallow glenoid cavity. The head is an elongated convex articular surface. On the upper and lower sides of the extremity is a large tuberosity for attachment of muscles. Medial to the lower tuberosity is a large foramen through which the clavicular air sac communicates with the interior of the bone. The distal extremity bears two condyles for articulation with the radius and ulna, the condyle articulating with the ulna is the larger. On either side of the distal extremity is a prominent ridge for muscular attachment.

The **radius** is the smaller of the bones of the forearm. It, with the ulna, articulates with the humerus at its proximal extremity and distally the two bones articulate with the carpus. With the wing at rest the bones of the forearm almost parallel the humerus. The radius is cylindrical and is curved slightly with the concavity facing the ulna. The proximal extremity presents an articular border for articulation with the ulna and the articular area for the humerus is nearly circular in outline. The distal extremity articulates with the carpus and bears a small facet for articulation with the ulna.

The **ulna** is much larger than the radius and both bones extend the full length of the forearm. The ulna is curved with its concavity facing the radius, thus forming a very extensive interosseous space. The shaft decreases from proximal to distal end. The proximal extremity bears an articular cavity for articulating with the humerus; on the radial side there is a concave facet for the articulation of the head of the radius. It also bears a small extension process, the olecranon. The distal extremity is slightly enlarged and has two articular facets for articulating with the carpus, one for the radial carpal and one for the ulnar carpal bone.

The **carpus** of the chicken consists of two bones, the radial and ulnar, which represent the proximal row of mammals. The distal row is present in the embryo as cartilaginous bodies which fuse with the metacarpus.

The **metacarpus** of the chicken consists of three bony elements fused to form a single bone. The first metacarpal bone is a very small projection on the radial side of the metacarpus. The second and third metacarpals are much more extensive and are fused at their extremities enclosing a large interosseous space.

The **digits** are three in number; the first, second and third. The second digit is much the largest and it, with the first digit, contains two phalanges while the third has but one phalanx.

The **pelvic limb** consists of four chief segments, viz., **pelvic girdle, thigh, leg** and **pes**. The pes is subdivided into the **tarsus, metatarsus** and **digits**.

The **pelvic girdle** consists of the **os coxæ** which unites with the vertebræ dorsally, and does not meet its fellow ventrally as in mammals. The term "pelvic girdle" does not apply in birds so well as in mammals because there is no union ventrally.

The **os coxæ** consists of the **ilium, ischium** and **pubis**.

The **ilium** is the largest of the three bones and is fused in the adult chicken to the last thoracic vertebra and the lumbar and sacral vertebræ. The fusion includes the transverse and spinous processes of the lumbo-sacral mass. The medial border anteriorly is joined to the spinous processes which are present on this portion of the fused vertebræ. The ilium joins the ischium and pubis at the deep acetabulum, and behind the acetabulum it has a continuous junction with the ischium, except at the sciatic foramen. The gluteal surface is concave anteriorly to the acetabulum where the gluteal muscles are lodged. Posterior to this, the surface is convex. The pelvic surface forms a concavity which the kidneys occupy.

The **ischium** is triangular in outline and much smaller than the ilium. It joins the ilium anteriorly and along its dorsal border, except for the sciatic foramen. Ventrally it meets the pubis. These two bones form the obturator foramen, which is below and behind the acetabulum. The posterior border is free.

The **pubis** is a slender plate of bone lying along the ventral border of the ischium, but projecting beyond it posteriorly. It forms the ventral part of the acetabulum; behind this it concurs with the ischium in forming the obturator foramen. The bone is only attached to the ischium in part.

The **acetabulum** is a large, deep articular cavity which lodges the head of the femur. A large perforation passes through the wall of the cavity. Just above the rim of the cavity on the ilium is a facet for articulation with the trochanter of the femur.

The **femur** is the bone of the thigh extending downward and forward. Its proximal extremity articulates with the acetabulum and the distal extremity articulates with the tibia, fibula and patella. It is a strong, cylindrical, slightly curved bone, the head of which is well marked and joined to the shaft by a distinct neck. Lateral to the head is the trochanter for attachment of gluteal muscles. The nutrient foramen is placed on the posterior surface near the middle of the bone. The distal extremity presents a trochlea in front for articulation with the patella and two condyles behind for articulation with the tibia and fibula. The lateral condyle is marked by a groove for articulating with the fibula.

The **tibia** is the longer bone of the leg and it is directed downward and backward. It presents a shaft and two extremities. The **shaft** is much longer than the femur and nearly straight. The nutrient foramen is on the posterior surface near the junction of the proximal and middle thirds. On the lateral part of the upper third of the bone is a ridge for attachment of the fibula. The proximal extremity articulates with the femur above, and laterally is a surface for attachment of the fibula. Anteriorly there is a prominent crest, the tibial crest. The distal extremity presents two condyles for articulation with the metatarsus. The medial condyle is the larger. On either side of the distal extremity is a depression for attachment of the collateral ligaments of the joint.

The **fibula** is a much reduced long bone, situated lateral to the border of the tibia. The shaft is slender and terminates in a point one-half way down the tibia. The proximal extremity is enlarged and is flattened transversely. It articulates with the lateral condyles of the femur and tibia.

The **patella** or kneecap articulates with the trochlea on the anterior surface of the distal end of the femur.

The **tarsus** in the adult chicken does not consist of a group of small bones as in mammals. During fœtal life the tarsal bones do exist in the two rows. The proximal row fuses with the tibia and the distal row fuses with the metatarsus.

The **metatarsus** of the adult consists of one long bone built up by the fusion of the second, third and fourth metatarsal bones and the tarsal element united to its proximal extremity. It is directed downward and forward. In the male a curved, pointed projection lies on the medial side of the bone just above the junction of the middle and distal thirds, which serves as a support for the spur. The proximal extremity bears two concave areas for articulation with the tibia. The distal extremity bears three condyles, each of which articulates with a digit.

The **digits** of the chicken are four in number. The first consists of three phalanges and is attached to the medial side of the posterior surface of the distal extremity of the metatarsus by fibrous tissue. It is directed backwards. The second consists of three phalanges and projects forward. It articulates with the medial condyle of the distal end of the metatarsus. The third consists of four phalanges and is the middle one of the three which are directed forward. The fourth consists of five phalanges and is the lateral digit. It articulates with the outer condyle of the metatarsus. The distal phalanx of each digit is pointed and is covered by a horny claw which conforms to the shape of the phalanx it covers.

MYOLOGY

An extensive detailed description of the muscles will not be considered here. Many of the muscles of birds are modified, to meet the needs as to function in locomotion, so as to be greatly different from those of mammals.

The **diaphragm**, being quite rudimentary, does not form a partition between the thoracic and abdominal cavities but separates the lungs from the other viscera and is in contact with the ventral surface of the lungs. There are muscle bundles in the costal attachments.

The **muscles** of the thoracic limbs and thorax are developed for use in flight while the muscles of the pelvic limbs are developed for use in walking, scratching, sitting on a perch and other activities requiring their use. The muscles affecting the respiratory organs are arranged for breathing and for operating anterior and posterior larynges, and controlling the air sacs. This differs from those of the mammals.

THE DIGESTIVE SYSTEM

The digestive tract of the chicken is very different from that of the mammals.

The **mouth** of the chicken is characterized by the absence of lips and cheeks, and the jaws being covered by the beak, a dense, horny structure conforming to the shape of the jaw bones. **Teeth** are absent in the chicken.

The **tongue** is narrow and triangular in outline, the free portion is pointed. The structures of the tongue are supported by the entoglossal bone or lingual process of the hyoid bone. Very little muscle tissue exists in the tongue. The movements of the tongue are produced by the well developed hyoid muscles. It is covered by an epithelium which has a thick stratum corneum on the dorsum and tip. The root is crossed by a row of pointed, horny papillæ whose apices are directed backward.

The **hard palate** is narrow and triangular in outline conforming to the shape of the beak. In its anterior part is a median ridge, and posteriorly is a median slit which communicates with the nasal cavities. A lateral ridge, branching from each side of the median ridge, extends posteriorly the length of the palate. Behind the median ridge are five transverse rows of pointed, horny papillæ whose apices are directed backward. The posterior one of these rows and the transverse row of

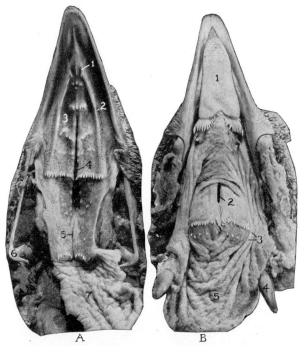

Fig. 729.—A, B, Roof and Floor of Mouth of Pharynx with First Portion of Œsophagus.

A. *1*, Opening of maxillary glands; *2*, openings of lateral palatine glands; *3*, openings of medial palatine glands; *4*, opening from nasal cavities; *5*, opening of Eustachian tubes; *6*, quadrate bone (slender zygomatic bone extending forward from it); *7*, œsophagus.

B. *1*, Tongue; *2*, aditus laryngis; *3*, transverse rows of papillæ between pharynx and œsophagus; *4*, process of hyoid bone; *5*, œsophagus.

papillæ on the root of the tongue is a convenient mark for determining the posterior limit of the mouth and the beginning of the pharynx.

The **maxillary glands** lie in the roof of the mouth and open anteriorly on either side of the median ridge. The **palatine glands** consist of two groups; viz., **lateral** and **medial palatine glands**. The former empty through a series of ducts just lateral to the lateral ridge of the palate, while the latter open by numerous ducts medial to the ridge and lateral to the median slit of the palate.

The **mandibular glands** which lie between the two halves of the mandible comprise several groups; their ducts open on the floor of the mouth by several very small orifices. A small round gland lying near the angle of the mouth is regarded by some as the homologue of the parotid gland of mammals.

The several glands of the mouth which lie in the submucous tissue produce a mucous secretion which does not contain a digestive ferment.

The Pharynx.—The roof of the pharynx presents a median slit which is the common opening of the Eustachian tubes; on each side of this opening, and anterior to it, are very small openings for the **sphenopterygoid glands;** behind the

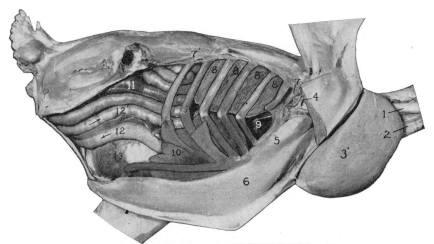

FIG. 730.—VISCERA OF CHICKEN; RIGHT VIEW.   UNCINATE PROCESSES ARE REMOVED FROM RIBS.

1, Œsophagus; *2,* trachea; *3,* crop; *4,* right brachial artery (placed on stump of superficial pectoral muscle); *5, 6,* pectoralis profundus minor and major muscles; *7, 7',* ribs first and last; *8, 8, 8, 8,* right lung; *9,* heart; *10,* liver; *11,* cæcum; *12, 12',* duodenum (pancreas between two parts of duodenum).

slit is a transverse row of conical papillæ which marks the beginning of the œsophagus. The floor is marked by a median fissure, which corresponds to the aditus laryngis of mammals, and is the opening into the anterior or cranial larynx. Be-

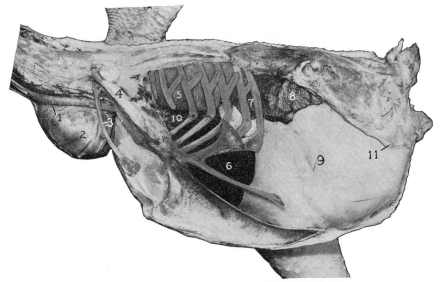

FIG. 731.—VISCERA OF HEN; SUPERFICIAL DISSECTION; LEFT VIEW.

1, Œsophagus; 2, crop; 3, clavicle; 4, coracoid bone; 5, lung; 6, liver; 7, ovary; 8, oviduct; 9, subperitoneal fat; 10. heart; 11, free end of pubic bone.

hind this are two transverse rows of papillæ, which, with the row on the roof, marks the beginning of the œsophagus. On each side of the laryngeal opening are several small openings of the **crico-arytenoid glands.**

The mucous membrane lining the mouth and pharynx is a stratified squamous epithelium.

The œsophagus is a muscular tube which extends from the pharynx to the proventriculus or glandular stomach; it is capable of great distention. In its first part it lies dorsal to the trachea, then inclines to the right, and at the entrance to the thorax is a large diverticulum, the **crop** (ingluvies) which is also to the right of the median plane. The inlet and outlet are on the medial side. Within the thorax the œsophagus is dorsal to the trachea. The mucous membrane is a stratified squamous epithelium. There are many mucous glands and lymph follicles present. The muscularis mucosæ is especially well developed with the fibers mostly longitudinal. The muscular coat is composed of two layers, an inner circular and an outer longitudinal layer. There is very little striped muscle in these layers of muscle in the chicken. Between the two layers of muscle the Auerbach's plexus of nerves is well developed.

The **stomach** consists of a glandular portion or **proventricularis** (pars glandularis) and the muscular portion or **gizzard** (pars muscularis). The proventricu-

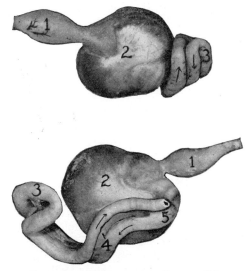

FIG. 732.—STOMACH, DUODENUM, AND PANCREAS OF CHICKEN; LEFT AND RIGHT VIEWS.
1, Glandular stomach; *2*, muscular stomach; *3*, duodenum (flexure); *4*, pancreas; *5*, pylorus.

laris is an elongated, fusiform, thick-walled, tubular organ, never greatly distended. It lies to the left of the median plane, related laterally and ventrally to the liver. The spleen is related to its posterior dorsal portion. Its lumen is continuous anteriorly with that of the œsophagus; posteriorly, it becomes quite constricted as it empties into the gizzard. The mucous membrane carries a simple columnar epithelium on the surface and many tubular glands developed within it which makes this layer of the wall quite thick. The tubular glands are grouped in such a manner that several empty into one common cavity. These cavities are small and each is on a small prominence.

The columnar cells lining the glands are arranged so that the one-third of the cell next to the basement membrane is in contact with adjacent cells and the remaining two-thirds is free.

Many lymph follicles are present. The muscularis mucosæ is well developed with its fibers arranged longitudinally. The muscle coat is composed of two layers, a thick inner circular and an outer longitudinal layer. The Auerbach's plexus is developed between the two outer muscle layers.

The **gizzard** is a dense, thickened, muscular disc with two small orifices, one opening into it from the proventricularis and the other out into the duodenum. The openings are close together on the anterior dorsal portion of the circumference. It is situated back of and partly between the two lobes of the liver. The mucous membrane, lining the gizzard, is thrown into ridges and is covered by a dense, horny substance which is quite probably secreted by the glands which lie beneath it. The muscular walls are very thick and heavy, with a tendinous center on each of the two surfaces. Three coats of muscle are distinguishable: a heavy, inner layer of oblique fibers, and a very thick, circulary layer with an outside thin layer of longitudinal fibers. The gizzard has a serous membrane (peritoneum) covering it.

The **small intestine** of the chicken consists of **duodenum, jejunum** and **ileum.** The **duodenum** leaves the gizzard, passes backward to the right, and forms a loop, the flexure lying in the posterior part of the abdominal cavity; it then continues forward past its origin to be continued by the remainder of the small intestine which is coiled between the abdominal air sacs. The two bile ducts and two pancreatic ducts empty near each other at the termination of the duodenum. The small intestines are lined with a simple columnar epithelium containing many goblet cells. Valvulæ conniventes are present in the duodenum. The villi are well developed, between which are well marked crypts of Lieberkühn. The glands of Lieberkühn empty into the bottom of these crypts, and are very short. No duodenal or Brunner's glands are present in the duodenum of the chicken. Lymphoid tissue is abundant in the form of nodules. The muscularis mucosæ is well developed and the fibers are mostly longitudinal. The inner circular layer of muscle is very well developed and the outer layer of longitudinal fibers is thin. There is an outer serous covering of peritoneum. There is no demarcation between jejunum and ileum which are attached to the roof of the abdomen by a well marked mesentery. They are lined with simple columnar epithelium containing many goblet cells, the villi are shorter, crypts of Lieberkühn are present and the lymphoid tissue is not so abundant.

The **large intestines** consist of the two **cæca** and the **colon.** The line of demarcation between the ileum and the colon is at the openings of the cæca. The **colon** is short and nearly straight, lying ventral to the vertebræ leading from the ileum to the cloaca. The colon is lined with a simple columnar epithelium. Short villi project into the lumen of the colon (in mammals villi are absent in the colon). The ducts of several tubular glands empty between adjacent villi. Many lymph nodules are present. The muscularis mucosæ is well developed. In the muscle coat the inner circular coat is well developed and the outer longitudinal layer is thin. An outer serous coat of peritoneum is present.

The **cæca** are two blind sacs about 7 inches long, and their lumen is slightly greater than that of the ileum. They empty into the intestines at the junction of the ileum and colon. They are lined with a simple columnar epithelium with many goblet cells. The surface is covered by villi similar to the colon, and glands empty between the villi. Lymphoid tissue is so abundant that it almost crowds out other glandular structures. The remaining portion of the wall is similar to the colon.

The **cloaca** is a tubular structure opening on the exterior, and is the common opening for the digestive, urinary and genital systems. It is divisible into three parts: **coprodeum,** into which the colon empties; the next portion, the **urodeum,** into which the ureters and genital ducts open; the last portion, the **proctodeum,** through which an opening leads from the dorsal wall to the **bursa of Fabricius,** a blind sac-like unpaired structure found best developed in chickens about four months of age. It has usually disappeared at one year of age.

The **liver** lies in the ventral part of the body cavity and its parietal surface is convex in adaptation to the ventral and lateral walls of the cavity, but is partly separated from the lateral walls by the abdominal and anterior thoracic air sacs.

The long axis of the liver is longitudinal. In front there is a deep cavity which corresponds to the pericardium and heart. The visceral surface is very irregular, but generally concave, and bears the hilus through which vessels and nerves enter, and bile ducts leave. It presents impressions produced by the muscular and gland-

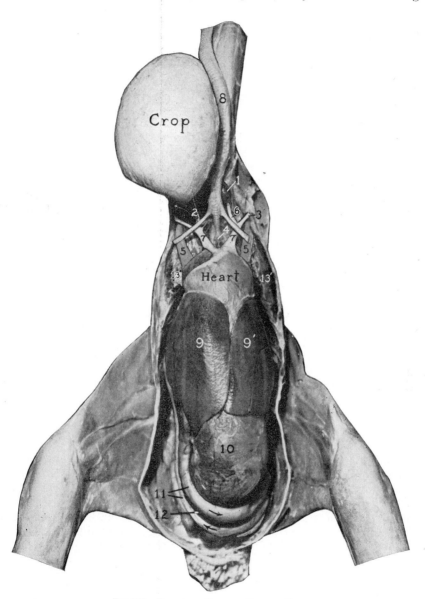

Fig. 733.—Viscera of Chicken; Ventral View.

1, Thyroid gland; *2*, sterno-trachealis dextra; *3*, A. brachialis sinistra; *4*, syrinx (larynx caudalis); *5*, cranial venæ cavæ; *6*, A. carotis communis sinistra; *7*, Aa. brachio-cephalicæ; *8*, trachea; *9, 9'*, right and left lobes of the liver; *10*, muscular stomach (gizzard); *11*, duodenum; *12*, pancreas; *13*, diaphragm.

ular portions of the stomach, while on the right there are impressions for the spleen and small intestines. The relatively large gallbladder is on the right posterior part of this surface. The gland is divided into two lobes, of which the right is usually the larger. The ductus hepatocysticus extends from the right lobe to the gallbladder, from which the ducts cysticus passes to the termination of the duodenum. Close to it is the opening of the hepato-enteric duct from the left lobe. The falciform ligament lies between the two lobes and is attached to the pericardium and ventral body wall.

The **pancreas** is a long, narrow lobulated gland which lies in the interval between the two parts of the duodenum. Two or three ducts open into the duodenum close to the hepatic ducts.

The **spleen** is a reddish-brown, rounded body situated dorsally and to the right of the junction of the glandular and muscular portions of the stomach. Its long diameter is about 2 cm.

THE RESPIRATORY ORGANS

The **nostrils** are two narrow, oval openings at the base of the upper part of the beak, their upper margin being a fold of integument.

The **nasal cavities** are very short and narrow and separated by a complete septum which is partly cartilaginous and partly bony. There are three rudimentary cartilaginous turbinates in each cavity. The cavities communicate with the mouth and pharynx by a long, slit-like opening. The very large naso-lacrimal canal opens into the nasal cavity on the lower part of the lateral wall below the middle turbinate bone, which places the opening just above the anterior part of the slit-like opening into the mouth.

The **anterior** or **cranial larynx** opens into the floor of the pharynx by a long, narrow aditus. The framework of the larynx consists of a **cricoid cartilage** composed of dorsal, ventral and lateral segments arranged to form a ring; the **arytenoid cartilage** composed of two small, three-sided rods which unite at a very acute angle in front, the ventral rod articulates with the cricoid and ossifies almost completely.

The **trachea** is a long tube, whose cartilaginous rings are complete. It connects the anterior and posterior larynges. The trachea is lined with a ciliated columnar epithelium which presents many small saccular glands.

The **posterior larynx** or **syrinx** (larynx caudalis) which is located at the terminal part of the trachea is also partly formed by the bronchi. Between the bronchial openings is a ridge (or carina) and on each side of this is an elastic membrane. These, together with two lateral folds, produce slit-like bronchial openings, comparable to the rima glottidis of the mammalian larynx.

The **lungs** are relatively small and occupy the most of the dorsal part of the thoracic cavity. The costal surface is convex and presents deep grooves in its upper part for the second to fifth ribs inclusive, which fade out ventrally. The ventral border is convex. The basal border parallels the sixth rib. The ventral surface is for the most part in contact with the diaphragm. The **stem-bronchus** enters the ventral surface of the lung in front of the middle; in the lung it forms a dilation, and continues to the posterior part of the lung where it opens into the abdominal air sac. Within the lung ten **secondary bronchi** are given off the stem-bronchus; some of them enter the cervical, clavicular and thoracic air sacs. **Tertiary bronchi** (para-bronchi) branch off from the secondary bronchi and the dorsal part of the stem-bronchus. These are very numerous and radiate toward the surface of the lung to end blindly. From them pass innumerable minute tubes, which are beset with dilations corresponding to the alveoli of the mammalian lung.

The **air sacs** are thin-walled sacs lined with a mucous membrane and covered with a serous membrane externally. They all form a means of communication between a bronchus and the interior of some of the pneumatic bones (except the thoracic). There are eleven air sacs in all, and named according to position as follows: cervical, clavicular, axillary, anterior thoracic, posterior thoracic, and abdominal (all are paired except the clavicular which is single).

The **thyroid** gland consists of two oval bodies situated at the root of the neck on each side of the trachea and œsophagus in relation to the common carotid artery, just anterior to the branching off of the brachial artery. They are deep red. The **parathyroids** lie posterior to, or may be in contact with the thyroid glands.

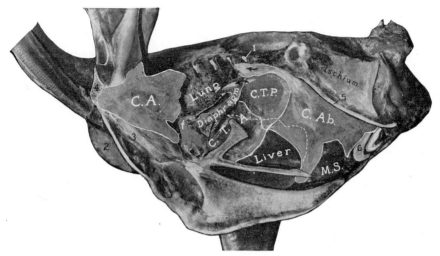

FIG. 734.—AIR SACS OF CHICKEN; LEFT VIEW.   SACS WERE INJECTED WITH GELATIN.

1, Rib 7; *2*, crop; *3*, coracoid; *4*, stump of pectoral muscle; *5*, pubis; *6*, duodenum; *C.A.*, axillary sac; *C.Ab.*, abdominal sac; *C.T.A.*, anterior thoracic sac; *C.T.P.*, posterior thoracic sac (arrows indicate entrance to lung for last three named sacs); *M.S.*, muscular stomach.

The **thymus** is present and fully developed in young chicks, and it has the form of a lobulated structure extending the length of the neck. It rapidly undergoes involution and may be entirely absent in the adult or old chickens.

THE URINARY ORGANS

The **kidneys** lie along each side of vertebral column from the vertebral end of the sixth rib to well back into the iliac fossa. They consist of three or four lobes each, are dark red in color and very friable.

The **ureters** arise on the anterior part of the ventral surface of the kidneys and parallel the long axis of the body posteriorly, to empty into the cloaca medial to the ductus deferens of the male or to the oviduct of the female.

The **adrenals** are small-sized bodies about the shape and size of a pea, and lie against the medial part of the anterior pole of the kidney.

THE MALE GENITAL ORGANS

The **testicles** lie ventral to the anterior lobes of the kidneys. The right one lies against the dorsal part of the right lobe of the liver. The left one is related to the glandular portion of the stomach and the intestine. They are bean shaped, pale yellowish color and vary in size in conformity with size of subject and the season. On the concave border (the hilus) of the testicle is a flattened projection, the rudimentary epididymis. From it the very flexuous ductus deferens arises to pass backward and open into the cloaca on the summit of a small papilla just lateral to the ureter.

THE FEMALE GENITAL ORGANS

The **ovaries** are two in number in the embryo, but the right one disappears soon. The left ovary is situated in the dorsal part of the abdominal cavity attached to the dorsal wall, and is chiefly opposite to the last two ribs and last intercostal space. It is in contact above and in front with the posterior end of the left lung; dorsally, with the anterior lobe of the kidney; ventrally, with the glandular stomach and spleen; and medially, with the posterior vena cava. In the active state it

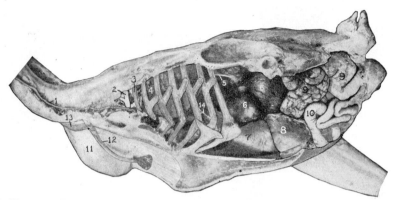

FIG. 735.—VISCERA OF LAYING HEN; LEFT VIEW. PART OF ISCHIUM AND PUBIS REMOVED TO SHOW OVIDUCT.

1, Left jugular vein; *2*, brachial plexus; *3*, first rib; *4*, lung; *5*, ligament of the ovary; *6, 6*, developing ova; *7*, liver; *8*, muscular stomach; *9, 9*, oviduct; *10*, duodenum; *11*, crop; *12*, clavicle; *13*, œsophagus; *14*, septum between anterior and posterior thoracic air sacs.

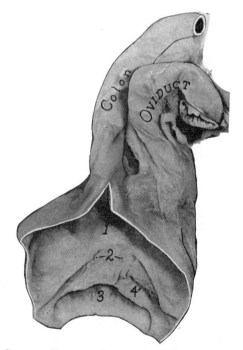

FIG. 736.—CLOACA OF HEN WITH A PORTION OF THE COLON AND OVIDUCT.

1, Coprodeum; 2, urodeum (with lines to urethral opening); 3, proctodeum; 4, outlet of oviduct.

has a very irregular racemose appearance which is due to presence of ova in the various stages of evolution.

The **oviduct** develops on the left side most commonly, but is present on both sides in the embryo; usually the right one soon disappears, but a functioning oviduct has been observed for both right and left sides. The oviduct varies in appearance according to its functional state. In the resting condition it is a very flexuous tube, which extends backwards against the dorsal part of the left body-wall in relation to the ilium and ischium, and empties into the cloaca lateral to the left ureter. Its anterior part, which corresponds to the uterine (or Fallopian) tube of the mammal, has a slit-like abdominal opening; this leads into the widely expanded **infundibulum,** which is succeeded by the **narrow isthmus.** This anterior part lies immediately below and behind the ovary. Behind this the oviduct immediately enlarges to form a wide, thick-walled tube which may be regarded as the homologue of the mammalian uterus. It is succeeded by a comparatively narrow portion which may be regarded as comparable to the vagina of the mammal. This opens into the cloaca by a dilatable slit lateral to the left ureteral opening. The oviduct is attached to the dorsal body-wall by a narrow fold of peritoneum. The wall of the tube consists of a serous coat of peritoneum, a muscular coat and a mucous membrane. The muscular coat consists of two layers, an outer layer of longitudinal and oblique fibers, and an inner circular layer. The two layers are not uniformly developed throughout the tube. The mucous membrane is the most important portion of the oviduct as its glands produce the albumen, shell-membrane and shell. The mucous membrane presents longitudinal folds which carry secondary folds on their sides. The folds are highest in the albumen-secreting portion of the tube; further back the folds are not so high and tend to be transverse or oblique. The free surface is covered by a simple columnar epithelium with ciliated and goblet cells about equal in numbers. The thickness of the membrane is due to the glands, which are long, branched, tubular structures closely packed together in the secreting portions of the tube.

The **ova,** when discharged from the ovary, consist of yolk only. Fertilization is believed to take place in the anterior part of the oviduct. In the middle part of the tube the albumen or "egg white" is produced and deposited around the yolk, the two being separated by a yolk-membrane, which is formed in the ovary before the yolk is discharged from the follicle. The shell is secreted by the posterior part of the oviduct shortly before the egg is laid. An air space is formed at the blunt end of the egg between the shell-membrane and shell.

THE CIRCULATORY SYSTEM

This system includes the pericardium, heart, arteries, veins, capillaries and lymphatics.

The **pericardium** is the fibro-serous envelope enclosing the heart, which helps furnish attachment for the heart, and to lubricate it. It is attached to the sternum, and the falciform ligament of the liver is attached to it from behind. The serous layer is reflected onto the heart at the base. Ventrally, the pericardium is related to the sternum; laterally, to the anterior thoracic air sac and liver; dorsally, to the trachea, œsophagus, and clavicular and thoracic air sacs.

The **heart** is the power apparatus for forcing the blood out to the lungs and the various tissues of the body through the efferent vessels, the arteries.

The heart of the chicken is enclosed by the pericardium and lies partly between the two lobes of the liver and partly anterior to them. It is conical in form with its apex directed backward and slightly to the left of the median plane. The exterior is marked to show the divisions into the four parts, right atrium and right ventricle, left atrium and left ventricle. The atria form the base, and the ventricles form the greater portion of the organ.

The **right atrium** receives the large veins, a posterior vena cava and two anterior venæ cavæ by which means the blood is returned to the heart from all parts of the body excepting the lungs.

The **atrio-ventricular** opening is a curved slit-like opening, with concavity medial; the valve guarding the opening is composed of one piece, a muscular fold attached to the lateral wall, the free edge projecting inward and downward, thus leaving the opening between the septal wall medially and the muscular fold laterally.

The **right ventricle** is thin-walled and does not reach the apex of the heart. The septum between the two ventricles bulges into the cavity of the right ventricle which gives it a crescentic outline on a transverse section of the heart. The pulmonary artery leaves the anterior part of the base and is guarded by the pulmonary valve composed of three semilunar cusps.

The **left atrium** receives the blood from the pulmonary veins. The septum between the two atria is thin and in its center has a very thin area, the fossa ovalis.

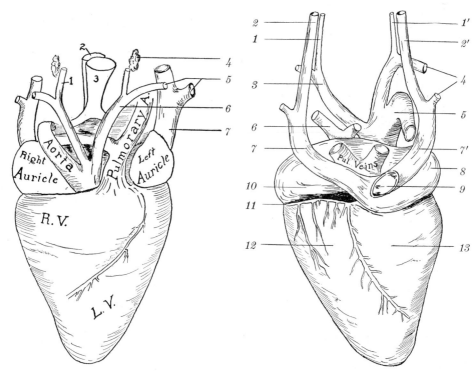

FIG. 737.—HEART OF CHICKEN; ANTERO-VENTRAL VIEW.

1, Right carotid artery; *2*, œsophagus; *3*, syrinx; *4*, thyroid; *5*, left brachial artery; *6*, left brachiocephalic artery; *7*, left anterior vena cava; *R.V.*, right ventricle; *L.V.*, left ventricle.

FIG. 738.—HEART OF CHICKEN. POSTERO-DORSAL VIEW.

1, 1', Left and right carotid arteries; *2, 2'*, left and right jugular veins; *3*, left brachiocephalic trunk; *4*, right brachial vessels; *5*, aorta; *6*, pulmonary arteries; *7, 7'*, left and right venæ cavæ; *8*, right atrium; *9*, posterior vena cava; *10*, left atrium; *11*, coronary groove; *12*, left ventricle; *13*, right ventricle; *Pul. Veins*, pulmonary veins.

The **atrio-ventricular** opening is circular in outline and is guarded by membranous valves.

The **left ventricle** is thick-walled and extends to the apex. The aorta leaves the base of the ventricle, and the orifice is guarded by the aortic valve composed of three semilunar cusps. **Chordæ tendineæ** extend from the edges of the membranous valves at the atrio-ventricular orifices to the **musculi papillares** on the ventricular wall.

The interior of the heart is lined by endothelium, which is continued throughout the vascular system.

The **arteries** are the efferent vessels in the circulatory apparatus.

The **pulmonary artery** is a short trunk arising from the right ventricle and soon branches to enter the lungs.

The **aorta** arises from the left ventricle. Its first branches are the right and left coronary arteries to the walls of the heart. The **brachiocephalic trunk** branches from the left side of the aorta close to the heart, and immediately divides into a **right** and **left brachiocephalic artery.** Each of these divides into a common carotid and brachial artery. The common carotid artery supplies the head and neck. The brachial artery supplies the thoracic limb and anterior and ventral thoracic region.

After giving off the brachiocephalic trunk the aorta curves around the right bronchus and reaches the vertebral column where it gives off intercostal and lumbar branches which are paired vessels. Visceral branches are given off to the organs of the abdomen and pelvis, and branches to the pelvic limb.

The **cœliac artery,** which is single, supplies branches to the glandular and muscular portions of the stomach, part of the small intestine, liver, pancreas and spleen.

The **anterior mesenteric artery,** also single, supplies the greater part of the small intestine.

The **renal arteries** are paired and enter the anterior lobe of the kidneys.

The **spermatic arteries** to the testicles, and the **ovarian arteries** are paired.

The **femoral** and **sciatic** arteries enter the pelvic limb. The sciatic also sends branches to the middle and posterior lobes of the kidneys. The femoral and sciatic arteries take the place of the external iliac artery of the mammal.

The **posterior mesenteric artery** is single and supplies the colon, cæca and cloaca.

The **internal iliac arteries** supply the pelvic wall and are small vessels.

The **middle sacral artery** is the termination of the aorta; it is a single trunk which supplies structures of the tail.

The **veins** are the afferent blood vessels returning the blood to the heart from the lungs and other tissues of the body.

The **pulmonary veins** return the blood from the lungs to the heart; they join and enter the left atrium by a common trunk.

The two **anterior venæ cavæ,** right and left, return the blood from the anterior part of the body, head and neck, and thoracic limb to the right atrium.

The short **posterior vena cava** is formed, by the union of the right and left common iliac veins, just medial to the anterior lobes of the kidneys; it carries the blood from the viscera and posterior part of the body and pelvic limb to the right atrium.

The **common iliac veins** are formed by the union of the external and internal iliac veins; the common iliac receives the renal vein. The internal iliacs are joined, by a communicating branch, medial to the posterior lobes of the kidneys.

The **coccygeo-mesenteric vein** arises from the communicating branch between the internal iliac veins and receives blood from the colon, cæca and cloaca, and passes forward to join the anterior mesenteric vein.

The **portal system** of the chicken consists of a right and left portion; the right portion is formed by the union of the anterior and posterior mesenteric veins, the latter connecting with the internal iliacs. Before entering the liver it divides, one branch going to the right lobe of the liver, and the other branch to the left lobe of the liver. The left lobe also receives the veins from the stomach, duodenum and pancreas.

The **hepatic veins,** one from each lobe of the liver, are very short, joining the posterior vena cava soon after leaving the liver, and this is very close to the heart.

The **capillaries** are the finest division of the blood vessels and their walls consist of little more than the endothelial lining.

The **lymphatics** of the chicken consist of lymph vessels and lymph glands. The lymph glands are very small and are in the form of lymph nodules, which are very numerous in the walls of the alimentary tract, and a few are found in the cervical region.

The **lymph vessels** from the abdomen and posterior part of the body come together to form a plexus about the cœliac artery; from this lymphatic plexus a right and a left thoracic duct leads forward to the jugular vein of its respective side. Before entering the jugular they receive the ducts from the head, neck, thoracic limbs and anterior part of the body.

THE NERVOUS SYSTEM

The nervous system of the chicken consists of the same essential structures as in mammals: the central nervous system (brain and spinal cord); the peripheral system (the spinal nerves and the sympathetic system).

The **brain** is composed of the cerebrum, cerebellum and medulla oblongata; all are within the cranial cavity. The **epiphysis cerebri** or **pineal body** (Corpus pineal), a small fusiform reddish brown mass, and the **hypophysis cerebri** or pituitary body, a small brown mass, are similarly situated to those of mammals. The **ventricles** of the brain are the same in the chicken and connected in a similar manner as in mammals. There are the twelve pairs of cranial nerves.

The **spinal cord** is the direct continuation of the medulla oblongata but it is much smaller. The central canal of the spinal cord is continuous with the fourth ventricle.

The **spinal nerves** are given off in the same manner, having two roots of origin from the spinal cord, the dorsal root possessing a spinal ganglion. The spinal nerves are connected to the vertebral chain of sympathetic ganglia by **rami communicantes.** There are fifteen cervical, seven thoracic, fourteen lumbo-sacral spinal nerves. The coccygeal spinal nerves are not developed as are the other spinal nerves, but the dorsal branches of a few exist.

The **brachial plexus** consists of parts of the ventral branches of the last two or three cervical and the first one or two thoracic nerves. It supplies the thoracic limb.

The **lumbo-sacral plexus** is divided into two parts: the anterior part is made up from the last two lumbar and a part of the first sacral; the posterior part is made up from a part of the first sacral and the three succeeding sacral nerves.

The **sympathetic system** consists of the two chains of vertebral ganglia. The ganglia are connected to each other, forming a trunk, and to the spinal nerves by rami communicantes. These chains of ganglia are connected with plexuses of the organs of the digestive, respiratory, circulatory and the uro-genital systems.

INDEX